THE

GREAT

SYNAXARISTES

OF THE

ORTHODOX

CHURCH

January

THE GREAT SYNAXARISTES OF THE ORTHODOX CHURCH

January

Translated from the Greek

Holy Apostles Convent
Buena Vista, Colorado

Dormition Skete
Buena Vista, Colorado

Printed in the United States of America

All Saints

Printed with the blessing of the Holy Synod of Bishops
of the Genuine Orthodox Church of America

Library of Congress Control Number: 2003111445
ISBN-13: 978-0-944359-23-5   ISBN-10: 0-944359-23-X

First Edition, December 2003
Second Edition, January 2007
Third Edition, December 2011
Fourth Edition, September 2020

© 2003 Holy Apostles Convent
Post Office Box 3118, Buena Vista, Colorado 81211

Iconography & Art Design: Courtesy of Dormition Skete, Buena Vista, CO 81211

TABLE OF CONTENTS FOR THE JANUARY SYNAXARISTES

January 1
CIRCUMCISION OF JESUS CHRIST 1
BASIL THE GREAT, ARCHBISHOP OF CAESAREA 9
Theodotos, Martyr 58
GREGORY, BISHOP OF NAZIANZOS 58
Theodosios, Hegumen of Trigleia in Bithynia 67
Peter of Tripoli, New-martyr 67

January 2
SILVESTER, POPE OF ROME 68
THEAGENES, BISHOP OF PARIUM, HIEROMARTYR 87
Theopemptos, reposed in peace 88
Theodote, Mother of Unmercenaries 88
Mark, Venerable Father 88
BASIL OF ANKYRA, MARTYR 88
Sergios, Martyr 89
Theopistos, Martyr 89
KOSMAS, PATRIARCH OF CONSTANTINOPLE, WONDER-WORKER . . 89
GEORGE (ZORZEES) OF GEORGIA, NEW-MARTYR 90

January 3
MALACHIAS (MALACHI), PROPHET 92
GORDIOS, MARTYR 104
Peter, Wonder-worker 107
3 Martyrs: a Mother and Her Two Children 107
GENEVIEVE OF PARIS, VENERABLE MOTHER 107

January 4
70, APOSTLES 113
ZOSIMOS AND ATHANASIOS OF CILICIA, MARTYRS 133
Theoktistos at Cucomo, Hegumen 133
APOLLINARIA, VENERABLE MOTHER 133
6 Martyrs 135
Efthymios the New, Ascetic 135
Chrysanthos and Ephemia, Martyrs 135
EFTHYMIOS, HEGUMEN OF VATOPEDI, AND 12 MONK-MARTYRS . 135
ONOUPHRIOS, HIERODEACON, NEW-MARTYR 136

January 5
THEOPEMPTOS AND THEONAS, MARTYRS 151
SYNCLETIKE OF ALEXANDRIA, VENERABLE MOTHER 155
GREGORY AT AKRITAS, VENERABLE FATHER 190
PHOSTERIOS, VENERABLE FATHER 191
Saïs, Martyr 193
Theoëidos, Martyr 193
Domnina, reposed in peace 193
ROMANOS OF KARPENESION, NEW-MARTYR 193

January 6

THEOPHANY, HOLY 197
Romanos, Hieromonk, New-martyr 211

January 7

JOHN, PROPHET, FORERUNNER, AND BAPTIST, SYNAXIS OF 212
JOHN, FORERUNNER, TRANSLATION OF THE RELIC OF HIS HAND . 223
JOHN, FORERUNNER, MIRACLE AT CHIOS 224
ATHANASIOS, NEW-MARTYR 227

January 8

DOMNICA OF CARTHAGE, VENERABLE MOTHER 229
GEORGE THE CHOZEVITE, VENERABLE FATHER 230
JULIAN, VASILISSA, KELSIOS, AND OTHER MARTYRS 236
2 Male Martyrs 239
1 Female Martyr 239
CARTERIOS OF CAESAREA, HIEROMARTYR 239
THEOPHILOS AND ELLADIOS, MARTYRS 240
AGATHON OF SKETIS, VENERABLE FATHER 240
KYROS (CYRUS), ARCHBISHOP OF CONSTANTINOPLE 242
ATTIKOS, PATRIARCH OF CONSTANTINOPLE 244
SAMAIAS (SHEMAIAH) THE ELAMITE, PROPHET 248

January 9

POLYEFKTOS AT MELITENE, MARTYR 250
EFSTRATIOS, WONDER-WORKER 255

January 10

GREGORY, BISHOP OF NYSSA 259
DOMETIANOS, BISHOP OF MELITENE 282
AMMONIOS, VENERABLE FATHER 283
MARCIAN, PRESBYTER AND OIKONOMOS 285

January 11

THEODOSIOS THE COENOBIARCH 295
THEODOSIOS OF PHILOTHEOU, BISHOP OF TREBIZOND 318
Angels, Synaxis of Myriads of 320
Stephen, Theodore, Agapios, Venerable Fathers 320
Maïros, Martyr 320
VITALIOS, VENERABLE FATHER 320

January 12

TATIANE OF ROME, DEACONESS, MARTYR 321
PETER THE AVESALAMITE, MARTYR 322
MERTIOS, SOLDIER, MARTYR 324
8 Martyrs of Nicaea 325
Efthasia, Martyr 325
Elias, Wonder-worker 325

January 13
HERMYLOS AND STRATONIKOS, MARTYRS. 326
IAKOVOS OF NISIBIS, ASCETIC 333
Athanasios, Martyr. 334
Pachomios and Papyrinos, Martyrs. 334
Consecration of the Monastery of Prophet Elias. 334
MAXIMOS, THE KAFSOKALYVES (HUT-BURNER). 335
HILARY, BISHOP OF POITIERS. 358
January 14
SINAI ABBAS, MARTYRS 376
RAITHU ABBAS, MARTYRS 378
SINAI AND RAITHU, NARRATIVE BY ABBA AMMONIOS. 380
THEODOULOS OF SINAI, VENERABLE FATHER 394
THEODOULOS, NARRATIVE BY SAINT NEILOS THE SINAITE 396
STEPHEN, BUILDER OF THE MONASTERY OF CHENOLAKKOS 403
Agnes, Martyr. 404
SAVA, ARCHBISHOP OF SERBIA, BUILDER OF HILANDAR 404
NINA, EQUAL-TO-THE APOSTLES, ENLIGHTENER OF GEORGIA. . . . 433
January 15
PAUL OF THEBES, VENERABLE FATHER 461
JOHN THE KALYVITE (HUT-DWELLER) 469
PANSOPHIOS, MARTYR. 485
6 Fathers, reposed in peace. 485
January 16
PETER, CHAINS OF THE APOSTLE 486
PEVSIPPOS, ELASIPPOS, MESIPPOS, AND NEONILLA, MARTYRS . . . 499
DANAKTOS (DANAX), READER, MARTYR 500
DAMASKENOS OF BULGARIA, HIEROMARTYR 500
January 17
ANTHONY THE GREAT, VENERABLE FATHER. 502
ANTHONY THE NEW, ASCETIC, WONDER-WORKER. 562
THEODOSIOS THE GREAT, EMPEROR 564
ACHILLAS (ACHILLES) OF SKETIS, ASCETIC 566
GEORGE OF IOANNINA, NEW-MARTYR. 567
January 18
ATHANASIOS AND KYRIL, SYNAXIS 576
ATHANASIOS THE GREAT, ARCHBISHOP OF ALEXANDRIA 577
THEODOULE OF ANAZARBOS, MARTYR 636
Evagrios, Makarios, Elladios, and Voëthos, Martyrs 638
Xene, Martyr. 638
Markianos of Cyprus, Venerable Father 638
January 19
MAKARIOS THE GREAT OF EGYPT, ASCETIC WRITER 639
MAKARIOS OF ALEXANDRIA, THE CITIZEN, PRIEST 648
EPHRASIA OF NIKOMEDIA, MARTYR. 660

Gregory the Theologian, Translation of Relics 661
Basil the Great, Miracle of 661
ARSENIOS, ARCHBISHOP OF KERKYRA, WONDER-WORKER 661
MELETIOS OF MOUNT GALESIOS, CONFESSOR 664
MARK EVGENIKOS, METROPOLITAN OF EPHESUS 679

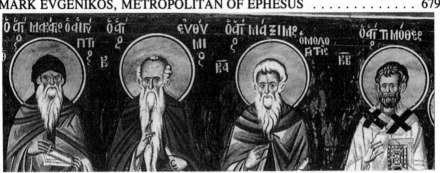

(L. to R): Saint Makarios of Egypt (January 19ᵗʰ); Saint Efthymios (January 20ᵗʰ); Saint Maximos (January 21ˢᵗ); Saint Timothy (January 22ⁿᵈ)

January 20
EFTHYMIOS THE GREAT, VENERABLE FATHER 779
BASSUS, EUSEBIUS, EUTYCHIUS, AND BASILIDES, MARTYRS 809
INNAS, PINNAS, AND RIMMAS, MARTYRS 811
Peter, Blessed 812
Thyrsos and Agnes, Martyrs 812
LEO THE GREAT, EMPEROR 812
Anna of Rome, Martyr 814
ZACHARIAS, NEW-MARTYR 814

January 21
MAXIMOS THE CONFESSOR, VENERABLE FATHER 819
NEOPHYTOS, MARTYR 866
ZOSIMUS, BISHOP OF SYRACUSE 874
EVGENIOS, VALERIAN, KANDIDOS, AND AQUILAS, MARTYRS 876
Irene, Church of Saint, Synaxis 879
AGNES OF ROME, MARTYR 879
4 Martyrs of Tyre 881
Neophytos of Vatopedi, Venerable Father 882
MAXIMOS THE GREEK 882

January 22
TIMOTHY, APOSTLE 897
ANASTASIOS THE PERSIAN, MARTYR 900
MANUEL, HIEROMARTYR, AND OTHER MARTYRS 912
JOSEPH THE SANCTIFIED OF CRETE, HIEROMONK 914

January 23

CLEMENT, HIEROMARTYR, AND AGATHANGELOS, MARTYR 920
EVSEVIOS OF TELEDA, ASCETIC 948
MAUSIMAS THE SYRIAN, ASCETIC 950
SALAMANES THE HESYCHAST, ASCETIC 952
2 Martyrs of Parion 953
PAULINUS, BISHOP OF NOLA 953
DIONYSIOS OF OLYMPOS, VENERABLE FATHER 967

January 24

XENE, DEACONESS, AND THOSE WITH HER 991
PAUL, PAFSIRIOS, AND THEODOTION, MARTYRS 998
BABYLAS OF SICILY, AND AGAPIOS AND TIMOTHY, MARTYRS . . . 999
MAKEDONIOS, ASCETIC 1000
ANASTASIOS THE PERSIAN, TRANSLATION OF RELICS 1003
Hermogenes and Mamas, Martyrs 1005
PHYLON, BISHOP OF KALPASIOS 1005
Philippikos, Presbyter 1005
Barsimas and His Two Brothers, Martyrs 1005
ZOSIMAS OF TYRE, ASCETIC 1006
John, Forerunner, nearby the Taurus 1007
NEOPHYTOS OF CYPRUS, THE ENCLOSED 1007

January 25

GREGORY THE THEOLOGIAN 1014
PUPLIOS OF ZEUGMA, ASCETIC 1046
MARIS THE CHANTER, ASCETIC 1048
APOLLOS OF HERMOPOLIS IN THE THEBAID, ASCETIC 1049
Medoule and Other Martyrs 1056
KASTINOS, BISHOP OF BYZANTION 1056
Demetrios, Skevophylax 1058
AFXENTIOS, NEW-MARTYR 1058

January 26

XENOPHON, MARY, AND SONS, VENERABLE FAMILY 1062
EARTHQUAKE AT CONSTANTINOPLE 1074
SYMEON THE ANCIENT, ASCETIC 1075
ANANIOS, PETER, AND SEVEN OTHER MARTYRS 1077
AMMONAS, VENERABLE FATHER 1077
Gabriel, Venerable Father 1079
2 Martyrs in Phrygia 1079
Clement of Mount Sagmation, Venerable Father 1079

January 27

JOHN CHRYSOSTOM, TRANSLATION OF RELICS 1080
Markiane, Empress, Philanthropist 1093
Klavdinos (Claudinus), Venerable Father 1093
PETER THE EGYPTIAN, ASCETIC 1093
DEMETRIOS OF GALATA, NEW-MARTYR 1094

January 28

EPHRAIM THE SYRIAN, VENERABLE FATHER, HYMNOGRAPHER . 1097
PALLADIOS, ASCETIC 1112
IAKOVOS, ASCETIC 1113
2 Female Martyrs 1121
Charis, Martyr 1121
ISAAC THE SYRIAN, BISHOP OF NINEVEH, ASCETIC WRITER 1122

Choir of the Venerable Fathers

January 29

IGNATIOS THE GOD-BEARER, TRANSLATION OF RELICS 1140
7 MARTYRS OF SAMOSATA: PHILOTHEOS AND OTHERS 1141
SILOUANOS, LUKE, MOKIOS, HIEROMARTYRS 1142
SARVELOS AND VEVAIA, MARTYRS 1143
BARSIMAIOS, BISHOP OF EDESSA, CONFESSOR 1144
APHRAATES, ASCETIC 1145
Akepsimas, Venerable Father 1147
DEMETRIOS, NEW-MARTYR 1147

January 30

3 HIERARCHS: SAINTS BASIL, GREGORY, AND JOHN 1158
HIPPOLYTUS, HIEROMARTYR, AND OTHER MARTYRS 1162
THEOPHILOS THE NEW, MARTYR 1164
HATZI THEODORE, NEW-MARTYR 1165

January 31

KYROS AND JOHN, UNMERCENARIES, AND WOMEN MARTYRS .. 1167
VICTORINOS, VICTOR, NIKEPHOROS, AND OTHER MARTYRS 1172
TRYPHAINA, MARTYR 1172
ELIAS ARDOUNES, NEW-MARTYR 1173

Bibliography 1179

Alphabetical Index 1191

Choir of the Hierarchs

**On the 1ˢᵗ of January, the holy Church commemorates
the CIRCUMCISION, according to the flesh,
of our Lord, God, and Savior JESUS CHRIST.**

The circumcision of our Lord Jesus Christ is commemorated today, brethren, which He condescended to receive in the flesh according to the commandment of the ancient law, "Ye shall be circumcised in the flesh of your foreskin, and it shall be a sign of a covenant between Me and you [Gen. 17:11]." Thus, we read in the Gospel according to Saint Luke: "And when eight days were fulfilled to circumcise the little Child, then His name was called Jesus, which He was called by the angel before He was to be conceived in the womb Lk. 2:21]."

The Circumcision

As a Hebrew mother, the Virgin-mother fulfilled all the requirements of the law. The first of these was circumcision of her Son, which represented voluntary submission to the conditions of the law, and acceptance of the obligations, but also the privileges, of the covenant between God and Abraham and his seed. The Child was then given the name Jesus (Jeshua or Jehoshua). Saint Kyril of Alexandria (378-444) adds, "On the eighth day, on which it was customary for the circumcision in the flesh to be performed, He received His name, even Jesus, which by interpretation signifies, the Salvation of the people. For so had God the Father willed."[1]

In the *Synaxarion* of the Feast, we read: "For what reason then did He (Jesus) will to be brought to this place by His Mother and Joseph, on the eighth day after His holy birth from the Virgin? Insofar as it was the custom of the Jews to be circumcised, He was circumcised. He accepted circumcision in the flesh in order to introduce the spiritual circumcision. If Christ our God had not taken on human flesh, then He could not have been circumcised. Therefore, none can say that He did not take on our flesh but only appeared to be born in the flesh." Thus, His circumcision would stop the mouths of the

---

[1] Saint Cyril of Alexandria, Hom. 3, *Commentary on the Gospel of Saint Luke*, Ch. 2, 56.

heretics who dared to say that He had not truly taken on flesh, but only in appearance (which is alleged by the God-fighters Mani and the Manichaeans). Secondly, the circumcision would bridle the mouths of Jews who accused the Lord not only of breaking the sabbath but also of transgressing the law. By His submission to circumcision, the Law-giver kept the law. We chant for this feast: "The Savior, condescending to mankind, accepted to be wrapped in swaddling clothes. Eight days old according to His Mother and without beginning according to His Father, He felt no loathing for the circumcision of the flesh."[2] There was also a mystical meaning in the number eight when circumcision was performed on the eighth day. At the consummation of the age, the eighth day, all sin and evil desire shall also be cut away. Moreover, since the circumcision was a symbol of cutting off the desires of the flesh, God wished to show to man that place where sin is activated and operates. For the seed of Abraham, it was not only as a symbol of their religion, but its deeper meaning was also the cutting away and deprivation of evil desires.

Saint John of Damascus (ca. 675-ca. 749) says: "Circumcision was given to Abraham before the law, after the blessings, after the promise, as a sign separating him and his offspring and his household from the Gentiles with whom he lived. By baptism we are circumcised from sin....After the Lord was baptized and the Holy Spirit had appeared to men, descending on Him like a dove, from that time the spiritual service and conduct of life and the kingdom of the heavens was preached." Saint Kyril of Jerusalem (ca. 318-386) says: "It was customary on the eighth day to celebrate the carnal circumcision. On the eighth day (Sunday) Christ rose from the dead, and wrought in us a spiritual circumcision, saying: 'Go therefore and make disciples of all the nations, baptizing them....'"[3] Saint Ambrose of Milan (ca. 339-397) says: "The cleansing from all guilt, that shall be at the time of the resurrection, was prefigured by the circumcision on the eighth day. This was because of the saying, 'Every male opening a womb shall be called holy to the Lord [Ex. 13:2, 12; Num. 8:16].' By the words of the law, the Child of the Virgin was promised. And He was holy....'That Holy One Who is born of thee shall be called Son of God [Lk. 1:35].' He alone of all that are born of woman is Holy: the Lord Jesus....He alone therefore opened the womb, for Himself."[4]

---

[2] January 1st, Vespers Sticheron, Mode Plagal Four. Unless otherwise specified, hymns in this section are taken from the feast on the 1st of January.
[3] Saint John of Damascus, *Exposition of the Orthodox Faith*, Bk. IV, Ch. XXV, NPNF (Nicene), 2nd Ser., Vol. IX: 97, 98. Saint Cyril of Jerusalem, "Hom. 17," Catena GP, cited in Toal's *The Sunday Sermons of the Great Fathers*, 3rd ed., I:187.
[4] Saint Ambrose of Milan, *P.L.* 60:1572.

In the Bible, we read that the procedure was done with either a sharp stone [Ex. 4:25] or a sharp knife [Josh. 5:2]. Blood must be shed in the operation, and the inner layer must be torn with the thumbnail. The bleeding would be stopped with wine. In biblical times, the procedure was done by either the father, the father-in-law (the mother's father), or by a circumciser (Mohel), who recited a special prayer and was unpaid for the service.[5] In Jesus' time, circumcision was usually performed by a priest.[6] The rite could be performed either in the house or in the synagogue. If the mother desired to be present during the ceremony, it had to be performed outside the temple, since she would not be allowed entry—even into the Court of Gentiles—until the period of her purification had expired [Lev. 12:2-5].[7]

According to the venerable monastic biographer and priest, Bede the Venerable (ca. 673-735): "On the same day of His circumcision He received His name....Abram, who first received the sacrament of circumcision, merited in the day of his circumcision, to be blessed in the enlargement of his name (Abraham) [Gen. 17:5]."[8]

In the Orthros canon of the feast, we hear: "Today are depicted the bright and all-shining nativity of Christ and the mystery of the regeneration to come. For the Savior is circumcised according to the decree of the law, not as God but as mortal man, as the Fulfiller of the law."[9] And, "Thou hast not thought it unworthy to put on the form of mortal man, but, as a babe, Thou

---

[5] Callinicos, *Our Lady the Theotokos*, 56.

[6] *The Great Synaxaristes* (in Greek, pp. 16, 17, note 1) then mentions that Ephraim the Syrian and Meletios of Athens (Vol. 1 of *The Ecclesiastical History*) say that the Lord was circumcised by Joseph, the putative father of Jesus, in the cave. Epiphanios comments concerning this that neither the evangelists have written anything, nor is it necessary that they should, since it has nothing to do with our salvation. Furthermore, Anastasios the Sinaite and other easterners claim that the Theotokos preserved what was circumcised as a sacred treasure. It remained incorrupt until the Lord's resurrection, when He took it to Himself again. In vain do some westerners claim to possess the circumcised flesh. One account maintained that it was kept at Cavillino, a city of Lower Burgundy (Fr. Bourgogne), in a certain church. The bishop of that place, one named Gaston, opened the reliquary supposedly containing the relic on the 19th day of April, in the year 1707, but he found nothing more than a little grain of sand and a tiny piece of gravel. In addition to this, Rome claimed to have the relic in the Church of Saint John of the Lateran, as footnoted by Calmette (Luke, ch. 2).

[7] See Josephus, *Contra Apionem* 2.133; *Kelim Tractate* of the *Mishnah*, i.8. Cited in Joachim Jeremias, *Jerusalem in the Time of Jesus* (Philadelphia: Fortress Press, 1969), p. 373.

[8] Saint Cyril of Jerusalem, cited in Toal, op. cit., p. 188.

[9] Orthros Canon, Ode Seven, Mode Two, by Stephen.

hast lawfully fulfilled the law."[10] For, "The eighth day, bearing a symbol of future things, has been made bright and sanctified by Thy voluntary impoverishment, O Christ; for on this day hast Thou been circumcised in the flesh according to the law."[11]

The Circumcision

The divine Apostle Paul writes: "When the fullness of the time came, God sent forth His Son, born of a woman, born under the law, in order that He might redeem those under the law, that we might receive what is our due, the adoption as sons [Gal. 4:4, 5]." In the hymns of the feast, we learn the following about the purpose of the Law-giver's condescension and fulfillment of the law: "In fulfilling the law, of Thine own will Thou didst receive circumcision in the flesh, that Thou mightest make the shadow cease and that Thou mightest roll away the veil of our passions."[12] This is because "The transcendent Logos was circumcised unto the ceasing of the law; and He gave us divine first fruits of grace and of life incorruptible."[13]

Circumcision prefigured holy Baptism. Now that the Mystery of Baptism had come, the old procedure, circumcision, was superfluous. Saint Athanasios (ca. 296-373), Patriarch of Alexandria, comments upon this, saying, "Circumcision expressed nothing more than the despoiling of the old man; by this, that part of the body was circumcised which served as the instrument of corporeal generation. This was then done in sign of the future Baptism in Christ. And so when that which was prefigured had come, the prefigurement became void; for all that was the old man is taken away by Baptism."[14]

Another Patriarch of Alexandria, Saint Kyril, writes that, after Christ's circumcision, "the rite was done away by the introduction of that which had been signified by it—Baptism; for which reason we are no longer circumcised. Circumcision seems to me to have effected three ends: First, it separated the posterity of Abraham by a sign and seal, and distinguished them

---

[10] Ibid., Ode Five.
[11] Ibid., Ode One.
[12] Dismissal Hymn, Mode One.
[13] Orthros Canon, Ode Three, Mode Two, by Stephen.
[14] Sermon *Omnia mihi tradita sunt.*

from the nations. Second, it prefigured in itself the grace and efficacy of holy Baptism (for as in ancient times, he who was circumcised was counted among the people of God). Thus, also he who is baptized, having formed in himself Christ the seal, is enrolled into God's adopted family. Third, it is the symbol of the faithful when established in grace, who cut away and mortify the tumultuous rising of carnal pleasures and passions by the sharp surgery of faith, and by ascetic labors; not cutting the body, but purifying the heart, and being circumcised in the spirit, and not in the letter."[15]

The passing away of the shadow of the law may be also heard in these hymns from Orthros: "By appearing, O Christ, Thou hast made the haughty behavior of the Jews with their sabbaths and circumcision to cease; and, by the Spirit, the spring of grace has shone."[16] And, "Since Christ has become a child and has been shown forth as the fulfillment of the law, the law has become of no effect; and He, by accepting circumcision, has set us loose from the curse of the law."[17] Our Lord submitted to this ritual, in order that He might introduce the spiritual circumcision made without hands. Saint Paul also says this: "For in Christ dwelleth all the fullness of the divinity bodily, and ye are made full in Him, Who is the head of all principality and authority, in Whom also ye were circumcised with a circumcision made without hands, in the putting off of the body of the sins of the flesh in the circumcision of the Christ, having been buried with Him in the Baptism, in which also ye were raised with Him through faith in the energy of God, Who raised Him from the dead [cf. Col. 2:9-12]."

At the end of this ritual it is not mentioned in the Scriptures if the holy Joseph took them back to Nazareth or if they tarried in Bethlehem. We read that they brought Jesus to Jerusalem [Lk. 2:22], that is, to the temple, on the fortieth day after the virginal birth, which is commemorated on the 2nd of February by the holy Church as the Feast of the Meeting in the Temple, when the Lord met the Elder Symeon and the Prophetess Anna [Lk. 2:22-38].

From the Old Testament, let us examine some of the mystical meanings and prefigurements of circumcision. In *The Epistle of Barnabas*, we read: "Abraham, the first who enjoined circumcision, looking forward in spirit to Jesus, purposed that rite, having received the mysteries of the three letters. For the Scripture saith, 'And Abraham circumcised ten and eight and three hundred men of his household.' What, then, was the knowledge given to him in this? Learn the eighteen first, and then the three hundred. The ten and the eight are thus denoted—ten by 'iota'(I) and eight by 'eeta' (H). You

---

[15] Saint Cyril of Alexandria, Hom. 3, *Commentary*, Ch. 2, 55, 57.
[16] Orthros Canon, Ode Six, Mode Two, by Stephen.
[17] Ibid.

have the initials of the name of Jesus. And because the Cross was to express the grace of our redemption by the letter 'taf' (T), he says, also, three hundred. He signifies, therefore, Jesus by two letters and the Cross by one. He knows this Who has put within us the engrafted gift of His doctrine."[18]

When Israel dwelt among the Egyptians, they kept the custom of circumcising their male infants. However, when they passed through the Red Sea and sojourned in the wilderness forty-two years, without mixing with other tribes, then they discontinued their habit of circumcising. Now when the time arose again for them to have contact with outside nations, the Lord commanded Jesus, the son of Navee, to make stone knives of sharp stone, and "circumcise the children of Israel the second time [Josh. 5:2]." He then circumcised the children of Israel, as many as were born in the way, at the Hill of Foreskins. The Lord then said, "'On this day I removed the reproach of Egypt from you'; and he called the name of that place Galgala [Jos. 5:9]."

Saint Justin Martyr (ca. 100-ca. 165) writes: "Jesus of Navee is said to have circumcised the people a second time with knives of stone (which was a sign of this circumcision with which Jesus Christ Himself has circumcised us from the idols made of stone and of other materials), and to have collected together those who were circumcised from the uncircumcision, that is, from the error of the world, in every place by the knives of stone, to wit, the words of our Lord Jesus Christ. For...Christ was proclaimed by the prophets in parables as a Stone and a Rock. Accordingly, the knives of stone we shall take to mean His words, by means of which so many who were in error have been circumcised from uncircumcision with the circumcision of the heart, with which God by Jesus commanded those from that time to be circumcised who derived their circumcision from Abraham, saying that Jesus would circumcise a second time with knives of stone those who entered into that holy land."[19]

Saint Gregory of Nyssa (ca. 335-ca. 395) adds, "When time had passed and the people had become more diligent in understanding the law's precepts, they understood and accepted the second circumcision instituted by Jesus of Navee [Jos. 5:2-9], for the stone knife cut away everything unclean."[20]

Blessed Jerome (ca. 342-420) comments: "As soon as Jesus of Navee reached the Jordan—the waters of marriage, which had ever flowed in the land—it dried up and stood in one heap; and the whole people, barefooted and

---

[18] *The Apostolic Fathers: The Epistle of Barnabas*, Ch. IX, Ante-Nicene Fathers, I:142, 143.

[19] Saint Justin, *Dialogue with Trypho*, Ch. CXIII, Ante-Nicene Fathers, I:255, 256.

[20] Saint Gregory of Nyssa, Hom. 6, *Song of Songs*.

on dry ground, crossed over, and came to Galgala, and were circumcised a second time. If we take this literally, it cannot possibly stand. For if we had two foreskins, or if another could grow after the first was cut off, there would be room for speaking of a second circumcision. But the meaning is that Jesus circumcised the people who had crossed the desert with the Gospel knife....Moreover the very foreskins were heaped together and buried, and covered with earth, and the fact that the reproach of Egypt was taken away, and the name of the place, Galgala, which is by interpretation, 'revelation,' show that while the people wandered in the desert uncircumcised their eyes were blinded. After this Gospel circumcision and consecration of twelve stones at the place of revelation, the passover was immediately celebrated, a lamb was slain for them, and they ate the food of the holy land. Jesus went forth, and was met by the chief commander (Josh. 5:14, Archangel Michael) of the host, sword in hand; that is, either to show that he was ready to fight for the circumcised people or to sever the tie of marriage."[21]

Elsewhere, Blessed Jerome wrote: "Moses died in the desert; Aaron died; Miriam died; and I hear now what is written in the prophet: 'I will cut off three shepherds in one month [Zach. 11:8].' They died, for they could not enter the promised land. They merely looked over toward the land of promise, but enter it they could not. The Jews beheld the promised land but could not enter it. They died in the desert, and their bodies lay in the wilderness. We, their children, under the leadership of Jesus, have come to the Jordan and have entered the promised land. We have come to Galgala and have been circumcised with a spiritual circumcision, and have been cleansed of the reproach of Egypt. Even now Jesus Himself, our Leader, holds the sword and always goes before us and fights for us and conquers our adversaries. And for seven days, we march around the city of Jericho, in other words, this world. We sound the priestly trumpets and march around Jericho, this world, and the walls fall, and we enter and consider ourselves victors. Next, we conquer the city of Ai; then we go to Jebus, to Azor, to other cities; we conquer the enemies that we were unable to vanquish under Moses.

"Jesus of Navee sent out two messengers on a secret mission to Jericho. Two messengers He sent: one to the circumcised; the other to the Gentiles, that is Peter and Paul. Jericho seeks to kill them; the harlot takes them in, meaning, of course, the Church gathered together of the Gentiles.

---

[21] Blessed Jerome, *Against Jovinianus-Book II, Nicene*, 2nd Ser., VI:361, 362.

She believes in Jesus; and those whom Jericho is determined to destroy, she protects in safety on her own roof."[22]

Now the Master Christ is also called the Rock. The Apostle Paul speaks of those who were under the cloud, passed through the sea, and had themselves baptized to Moses in the cloud and in the sea, saying that they "all ate the same spiritual food, and all drank the same spiritual drink; for they were drinking from a spiritual Rock that followed them, and the Rock was the Christ [1 Cor. 10:3, 4]." And that He is called a Knife, again the apostle says: "For the Logos of God is living and effective, and sharper than every two-edged sword, even going through as far as the dividing of both soul and spirit, and of both joints and marrows, and is a discerner of the ponderings and intents of the heart [Heb. 4:12]."

"'Behold, the days come,' saith the Lord, 'when I will visit upon all the circumcised their uncircumcision; on Egypt, and on Idumaea, and on Edom, and on the children of Ammon, and on the children of Moab, and on everyone that shaves his face round about, even them that dwell in the wilderness; for all the Gentiles are uncircumcised in flesh, and all the house of Israel are uncircumcised in their hearts [Jer. 9:25, 26].'" "Do you see," Saint Justin Martyr asks Trypho the Jew, "how God does not mean this circumcision which is given for a sign? For it is of no use to the Egyptians, or the sons of Moab, or the sons of Edom. But though a man be a Scythian or a Persian, if he has the knowledge of God and of His Christ, and keeps the everlasting decrees, he is circumcised with the good and useful circumcision, and is a friend of God, and God rejoices in his gifts and offerings."[23]

The first circumcision of the flesh would be made void, because the second circumcision of the Spirit was promised. "Circumcise yourselves to God, and circumcise your hardness of heart, ye men of Juda, and inhabitants of Jerusalem, lest My wrath go forth as fire, and burn, and there be none to quench it, because of the evil of your pursuits [Jer. 4:4]." "The circumcision of the body," says Saint John Chrysostom (ca. 347-407), "is no longer superior....Thus, Jeremias rightly brought forward, 'For ye shall circumcise the foreskins of your hearts [Jer. 4:4].'...Now if you must seek circumcision, Paul says that you will find it among us 'who worship God in spirit [Phil. 3:3],' that is, who worship spiritually."[24]

Saint Kyril of Jerusalem says, "By the likeness of our faith,...we become the adopted sons of Abraham; and consequent upon our faith, like him we receive the spiritual seal, being circumcised by the Holy Spirit

[22] Blessed Jerome, Hom. 18, *1-59 On The Psalms*, Vol. 1, FC, 48:137-139.
[23] Saint Justin, *Dialogue with Trypho*, Ch. XXVIII, Ante-Nicene, I:208.
[24] Saint John Chrysostom, Hom. X, *On Philippians*, Nicene, 1st Ser., XIII:230.

through the laver of Baptism, not in the foreskin of the body, but in the heart, according to the words of Jeremias [Jer. 4:4], and according to the apostle [Col. 2:11, 12]."[25]

On the 1st of January, the holy Church commemorates our holy father among the saints, BASIL the Great, Archbishop of Caesarea of Cappadocia.[26]

Basil the Great, our father among the saints, flourished during the years of Augustus Valens (r. 364-378). Basil was born circa 329 of wealthy and noble parents: Basil of Pontos and Emmelia of Caesarea in Cappadocia. A great personal friend of Saint Basil was Saint Gregory the Theologian (ca. 329/330-ca. 390), Patriarch of Constantinople (380). In a panegyric on Basil, Gregory mentions that despite the most frightful persecution of Maximinus, the paternal ancestors of Saint Basil exercised every form of piety during that period. Among the ranks of Basil's ancestors were they who wrestled with the persecution well-nigh to death, with only life enough left in them to survive their victory, and not pass away in the midst of the struggle, remaining to be trainers in

Saint Basil the Great

virtue, living witnesses, breathing trophies, silent exhortations.[27]

Saint Basil's father was conspicuous in the Church for probity and godliness. He married the orphaned gentlewoman Emmelia, whose father suffered impoverishment and even death for Christ's sake. Ten children were born in their happy union, five boys and five girls. The one surviving daughter was Makrina, the angel of the family. Of the five boys, one seems to have died in infancy. Basil was the eldest of the surviving sons; but he was

---

[25] Saint Cyril of Jerusalem, *Catechesis V, Vol. 1*, FC, 61:142, 143.

[26] This English version was taken from our publication, "The Life of Saint Basil the Great," in *The Lives of the Three Hierarchs*, 2nd edition, pp. 1-68.

[27] Saint Gregory Nazianzen (the Theologian). All quotations of Saint Gregory the Theologian are taken from his funeral orations: "The Panegyric on Saint Basil," *Orations*, Nicene, 2nd Ser., VII:395-422; and *Funeral Orations*, The Fathers of the Church, Volume 22.

not the only one who was blessed, for he had wondrous brethren and standard-bearers. Peter, the youngest of the brothers, became Archbishop of Sebasteia. Gregory, the third brother, became Metropolitan of Nyssa. Nafkratios became an ascetic, and he is commemorated by the holy Church on the 8th of June. Makrina was also sanctified, and she is commemorated by the holy Church on the 19th of July. Verily, the parents fulfilled the word of David who says, "The generation of the upright shall be blessed [Ps. 111:2]." Our Basil, however, surpassed his brethren in virtue and learning.

Saint Basil was close with his mother Emmelia; and later in life, he disclosed in a letter: "Now, for my sins, I have lost my mother, the only comfort I had in life. Do not smile, if, old as I am, I lament my orphanhood. Forgive me if I cannot endure separation from a soul, to compare with whom I see nothing in the future that lies before me."[28] He writes of his grandmother Makrina: "I was brought up by my grandmother, blessed woman....I mean the celebrated Makrina who taught me the words of the blessed Gregory; which, as far as memory had preserved down to her day, she cherished herself, while she fashioned and formed me, while yet a child, upon the doctrines of piety."[29] When assailed by the enemies of the Church, he declared, "The teaching about God, which I had received as a boy from my blessed mother and my grandmother Makrina, I have ever held with increased conviction. On my coming to ripe years of reason, I did not shift my opinion from one to another, but carried out the principles delivered to me by my parents. Just as the seed when it grows is first tiny and then gets bigger, but always preserves its identity, not changed in kind though gradually perfected in growth, so I reckon the same doctrine to have grown in my case through gradually advancing stages. What I hold now has not replaced what I held at the beginning."[30]

Saint Basil was growing up when the transferral of the chief seat of power in the empire went from Rome to Byzantium. He was born at a time when the Church had been recognized officially by the state for some sixteen years. The family estate, which was considerable, was located at Annesi, on the Iris River, amid lofty mountains. At Annesi, his mother erected a small church dedicated to the Forty Martyrs of Sebasteia, to which place their relics were translated.

From his childhood, the saint learned the sacred letters from his father Basil, who was a priest and teacher of the Christians. When he reached a

---

[28] Saint Basil, Letter xxx. All epistle quotations hereinafter are taken from Saint Basil, *Letters and Select Works*, Nicene, 2nd Ser. Volume VIII.
[29] Letter cciv.
[30] Letter ccxxiii.

suitable age, young Basil also desired to receive instruction in the learning of the Greeks at Athens. Certain people may speak against this study, because many philosophers became heretics, yet many saints and teachers of the Church were not worsened by their study. Secular learning is not the source for making one a heretic, but one's bad disposition. Learning is a tool for the service of mankind. A knife may be used to cut bread or slay someone, though it is a lifeless object, not being good or evil by nature. It is taken up for either service or slaughter by the user. The same may be said of learning, which was given by God for the service of mankind. If one uses it wickedly, God is blameless, even as the craftsman who fashioned the aforementioned knife. Saint Gregory the Theologian writes: "Many Christians, by an error of judgment, scorn external culture as treacherous and dangerous and as turning us away from God. The heavens, the earth, the air, and all such things are not to be condemned because some have wrongly interpreted them and venerate the creatures of God in place of God. On the contrary, we select from them what is useful both for life and enjoyment, and we avoid what is dangerous, not opposing creation to the Creator, as the foolish do, but acknowledging the Maker of the world from His works...."[31]

Saint Gregory, as a contemporary of Saint Basil at school in 351, writes: "As time went on, we avowed our mutual affection. Christian philosophy became the aim of our zeal. We were all in all to one another, house mates, messmates, soul mates, with one object in our lives, as our affection grew warmer and stronger."

At Saint Basil's repose, his friend wrote a funeral oration, saying: "He (Basil) was trained in general education, and practised in the worship of God, and, to speak concisely, led on by elementary instructions to his future perfection. For those who are successful in life or in letters only, while deficient in the other, seem to me to differ in nothing from one-eyed men....While those who attain eminence in both alike, and are ambidextrous, both possess perfection, and pass their life with the blessedness of heaven. This is what befell him, who had at home a model of virtue in well-doing, the very sight of which made him excellent from the first....

"He was an orator among orators, even before the chair of the rhetoricians, a philosopher among philosophers, even before the doctrines of philosophers: and what constitutes the highest tribute in the eyes of Christians, he was a priest even before the priesthood. So much deference was paid to him in every respect by all....

"What branch of learning did he not traverse—and that with unexampled success? He passed through all, as no one else passed through

---

[31] *The Great Synaxaristes of the Orthodox Church* (in Greek), January 1st, pp. 26, 27.

any one of them. He attained such eminence in each, as if it had been his sole study. The two great sources of power in the arts and sciences, ability and application, were in him equally combined....

"Who was like him in rhetoric, breathing forth the might of fire, though his character differed from that of the rhetoricians?...Who was like him in philosophy, that truly sublime science which soars aloft, whether one consider the practical or speculative side, or that which deals with logical demonstrations and oppositions and with controversies, namely, dialectic? In this he was so excellent that it would have been easier for those who disputed with him to extricate themselves from labyrinths than to escape the meshes of arguments he wove whenever he had need. As for astronomy, geometry, and mathematics, he was content with a knowledge sufficient to avoid being confused by those who were clever in these sciences. Anything beyond that he scorned as useless for those who wished to lead a pious life."

Saint Gregory the Theologian affirms that both he and his friend Basil only consorted with the most modest and peaceable of companions, avoiding the dissolute and quarrelsome. "Two ways were familiar to us: the first and most precious, led us to our sacred buildings and the masters there; the second and the one of less account, brought us to our secular teachers. Everything else—festivals, spectacles, assemblies, and banquets—we left to those who have a taste for such things."

Together with the holy young men, Basil and Gregory, the future apostate, Julian (332-363) was also attending school after the middle of the year 355 in Athens. Saint Basil attended the classes of Himerius, a pagan, and Prohaeresios, an Armenian Christian. Saint Gregory does report that the university town of the fourth century had its share of rough horse-play among the "undergraduates" affiliated with certain fraternities. These leagues usually consisted of boys from the same city or region. The rival fraternities looked out for every new pupil, with the aim of attaching him to the lectures or discussions of this or that teacher. Kinsmen were on the watch for kinsmen and acquaintances for acquaintances. The violence usually was good-natured which secured the incoming freshman. The matriculation consisted of conducting the freshman with a rowdy ceremonial procession through the marketplace to the entrance of the baths. They carried on wildly, and then refused him admission. Finally an entry was forced with mock fury, and the neophyte was made free of the mysteries of the baths and the lecture halls. Saint Gregory the Theologian, a student slightly senior to Basil, succeeding in sparing his new friend the ordeal of this grotesque initiation. Basil's dignity and sweetness of character successfully secured him immunity from rough usage without suffering in popularity.

Both young men studied under the sophist Libanios, and many other teachers from different places. The two Cappadocian classmates were noted among their contemporaries for their diligence, success in their studies, a stainless and devout life, and a close mutual affection. For all the time that Basil sojourned in Athens studying, he never ate meat, nor fish, nor used seasoning, nor did he drink wine. He sustained himself only with bread, water, and vegetables. As a result, his teacher, Evoulos, a sophist and the best of the philosophers in Athens, when he observed the saint's self-control and sober-mindedness, marvelled and was struck with astonishment. Afterward, Evoulos became a Christian through the advice of the holy Basil.

Therefore, in this manner he studied all the wisdom of the Greeks. Saint Basil reflects with regret that his youth was not entirely spiritual, as he gives us a sorrowful and bitter description of other experiences in his travels: "With the world's good things are mingled evil things, and the evil things distinctly have the upper hand. Once when I attended the spiritual assemblies I did with difficulty find one brother, who, so far as I could see, feared God, but he was a victim of the devil, and I heard from him amusing stories and tales made up to deceive those whom he met. After him I encountered many thieves, plunderers, and tyrants. I saw disgraceful drunkards; I saw the blood of the oppressed; I saw women's beauty, which tortured my chastity. From actual fornication I fled, but I defiled my virginity by the thoughts of my heart. I heard many discourses which were good for the soul, but I could not discover in the case of any one of the teachers that his life was worthy of his words. After this, again I heard a great number of plays, which were made attractive by wanton songs. Then I heard a lyre sweetly played, the applause of tumblers, the talk of clowns, all kinds of jests and follies, and all the noises of a crowd. I saw the tears of the robbed, the agony of the victims of tyranny, the shrieks of the tortured. I looked and lo, there was no spiritual assembly, but only a sea, wind-tossed and agitated, and trying to drown everyone at once under its waves....What good then do I get except the loss of my soul? For this reason I migrate to the hills like a bird. 'As a sparrow I was delivered out of the snare of the hunters [cf. Ps. 123:6].'"[32]

At the end of his studies, Basil was eager to return home. In 356, he left Athens and Gregory, who needed to stay a little while longer. Once in Caesarea, Basil was greeted as one of her most distinguished sons. A deputation from Neocaesarea invited him to take up educational work in the city, but he refused the position. Basil was already considering renouncing the world and devoting himself to Christ. Gregory, his younger brother, seems to remember his older brother with wry criticism, saying he was somewhat

---

[32] Letter xlii.

overconfident on account of his having completed a university career. "He was excessively puffed up by his rhetorical abilities."[33] However, on account of the influence and model of his older sister Makrina's asceticism, Basil finally resolved to devote himself to a life of self-denial. His brother Gregory notes in his hagiography of his sister that she was instrumental in persuading Basil to forsake the life of the rhetor and to pledge himself to a life of poverty and manual labor.

Pilgrimages

At length, Basil also wished to go to Jerusalem: first, indeed, in order to venerate the all-holy and life-bearing Sepulcher of Jesus Christ; and second, that he might be baptized in the Jordan River. This is because at that time, the Christians did not have the custom of infant baptisms, but waited until attaining thirty years of age. Both of Basil's much-desired aims took place.

Years later, in a letter, Basil reflected upon the time he spent in school, and his subsequent trip to the holy land. He wrote: "Much time had I spent in vanity, and had wasted nearly all my youth in the vain labor which I underwent in acquiring the wisdom made foolish by God. Then once upon a time, like a man roused from deep sleep, I turned my eyes to the marvellous light of the truth of the Gospel, and I perceived the uselessness of the wisdom of the rulers of this age, who are coming to nought [1 Cor. 2:6]. I wept many tears over my miserable life, and I prayed that guidance might be vouchsafed me to the doctrines of true religion. First of all I was minded to make some mending of my ways, long perverted as they were by my intimacy with wicked men. Then I read the Gospel, and I saw there that a great means of reaching perfection was the selling of one's goods, the sharing of them with the poor, the giving up of all care for this life, and the refusal to allow the soul to be turned by any sympathy to things of earth. And I prayed that I might find some one of the brethren who had chosen this way of life, that with him I might cross life's short and troubled strait.

"And many did I find in Alexandria, and many in the rest of Egypt, and others in Palestine, and in Coele Syria, and in Mesopotamia. I admired their continence in living and their endurance in toil. I was amazed at their persistence in prayer and at their triumphing over sleep. They were subdued by no natural necessity, ever keeping their souls' purpose high and free, in hunger, in thirst, in cold, in nakedness [cf. 2 Cor. 11:27]. They never yielded to the body; they were never willing to waste attention on it; always, as though living in a flesh that was not theirs, they showed in very deed what it is to sojourn for a while in this life [cf. Heb. 11:13], and what it is to have

---

[33] Saint Gregory of Nyssa, *Life of Saint Makrina*, 6.

one's citizenship and home in the heavens [cf. Phil. 3:20]. All this moved my admiration. I called these men's lives blessed, in that they did indeed show that they were 'always bearing about in the body the dying of the Lord Jesus [2 Cor. 4:10].' And I prayed that I, too, as far as in me lay, might imitate them."[34]

Leaving the holy city, he sojourned in Antioch where, at length, he was ordained to the diaconate by Patriarch Meletios of Antioch. It was then that they say he wrote the *Explanation of the Proverbs of Solomon*. But after he heard that his father had taken ill, he wished to transfer to his homeland, to Caesarea, in order to receive his parents' blessing.

Ordination

After Basil departed, an angel of the Lord appeared to Evsevios, the Metropolitan of Caesarea, saying, "The worthy successor of thy throne is coming this hour. Therefore send forth thy clergy and nobles to go and meet him at the gate of the city." Thereupon, after the clergy and the nobles went and saw the holy Basil coming, they marvelled and rejoiced. They were awed by the foresight of the angel, and rejoiced because they were counted worthy to obtain such a shepherd and renowned teacher, who possessed both virtue and a good report. The saint tarried there for some days and was ordained a presbyter. The ordination of Basil to the presbyterate was not wholly voluntary. He was forced against his inclinations to accept duties attending the dignity, for which he deemed himself unfit.

After being ordained to the priesthood in 364, Basil devoted his life to his ministry. He continued to emulate the lives of the monks he had visited in his earlier pilgrimages. Other monks had joined him, and he cared for them and imparted the word of God to them. Saint Basil easily attracted a large and loyal following. In his practical work in the diocese and in his writing, Basil also made himself quite useful to Evsevios, formerly a layman of rank and influence, who was elevated to the episcopate. At that time Julian and other objectors sought to have his appointment annulled, but they were unable to do so. At length, other bishops objected to the tumultuous nomination of Evsevios and were ready to consecrate Basil in his place, to the displeasure of Archbishop Evsevios. Astute and perceptive, Basil soon discerned this. Later he wrote: "To those who have chosen to live a holy life, the afflictions of this present world cannot come unforeseen."[35] Therefore, wishing neither to bring about another's fall nor to be the cause of a schism among the Orthodox clergy of Cappadocia, he removed himself. He refused personal elevation, which could lead to the detriment of the Church. He decided to go

---

[34] Letter ccxxiii.
[35] Letter xviii.

back home, to Pontos by the Iris River. Hence, Evsevios was left in place, and the character of Basil soared in the eyes of onlookers.

The Ascetic Life

Saint Basil asked, "What is more blessed than to imitate on earth the choir of angels?" He answered this ideal with his own actions. He distributed his property to the poor and retired to the wilderness of Pontos, in a glen not far from his old home and nearby his sister Makrina's convent. He once wrote: "Preparation of the heart is unlearning the prejudices of evil converse. It is the smoothing of the waxen tablet before attempting to write on it. Now solitude is of the greatest use for this purpose, inasmuch as it stills our passions and gives room for principle to cut them out of the soul. Quiet is the first step in our sanctification."[36]

Thus, he emulated the great ascetic feats of the fathers he met in Syria and Egypt. He abided in utter poverty, with only a single garment. He partook of only bread and water, which he supplemented with salt and roots from plants. This undermined his constitution considerably, leaving him weak and thin. It may even be said that his hard ascetic discipline at this point in his life contributed to the enfeeblement of his health and the shortening of his life. He never visited the baths while in his philosophical retreat, nor did he kindle a fire. At night, never by day, he wore a haircloth, lest he should appear ostentatious. He was a constant celibate. Being mindful of the Lord's words as to the adultery of an impure thought, he still accused himself of unchastity. As a magnet, he drew other men wishing to live the community life as monks.

In fact, Basil even drew his former schoolmate Gregory to Pontos, and wrote him a poetical account: "God has shown me a region which exactly suits my mode of life: it is, in truth, what in our happy jests we often wished. What imagination showed us in the distance, that I now see before me. A high mountain, covered with a thick forest, is watered toward the north by fresh perennial streams. At the foot of the mountain a wide plain spreads out, made fruitful by the vapors which moisten it. The surrounding forest, in which many varieties of trees crowd together, shuts me off like a strong castle. The wilderness is bounded by two deep ravines. On one side there is the stream, where it rushes, foaming down from the mountain, and forms a barrier hard to cross; on the other side there is a broad ridge which obstructs approach. My hut is so placed upon the summit that I overlook the broad plain, as well as the whole course of the Iris, which is more beautiful and copious than the Strymon near Amphipolis. The river of my wilderness, more rapid than any other that I know, breaks upon the wall of projecting rock, and rolls foaming into the abyss: to the mountain traveler, a charming, wonderful sight; to the

---

[36] Letter ii.

natives, profitable for its abundant fisheries. Shall I describe to thee the fertilizing vapors which rise from the moistened earth, the cool air which rises from the moving mirror of the water? Shall I tell of the lovely singing of the birds and the richness of blooming plants? What delights me above all is the silent repose of the place. It is only now and then visited by huntsmen; for my wilderness nourishes deer and herds of wild goats, not thy bears and thy wolves. How would I exchange such a place?"[37]

When Gregory came to the Pontic monastery, they restricted themselves to the study of sacred Scripture, to the exclusion of all secular literature. In 358, guided by the Holy Spirit, they formulated rules for their monastic community, which later served as a guide for the Orthodox coenobitic life. They cooperated together in creating a *Philokalia*, a collection of sayings on the nature of God, the understanding of Scripture, and free will. The anthology showed the harmony and usefulness for the intelligent Christian of the study of profane wisdom. Both young men also undertook all kinds of obediences in their outdoor refuge.

The seclusion did not come easy and unencumbered for Saint Basil. In a letter, he disclosed: "I have well forsaken my residence in the city as a source of a thousand evils, but I have not been able to forsake myself. I am like a man who, unaccustomed to the sea, becomes seasick, and gets out of the large ship, because it rocks more, into a small skiff, but still even there he keeps the dizziness and nausea. So is it with me, for while I carry about with me the passions which dwell in me, I am everywhere tormented with the same restlessness; so that I really do not get much help from this soli-tude....But we must strive after a quiet mind....The study of inspired Scripture is the chief way of finding our duty....Prayers, too, after reading, find the soul fresher and more vigorously stirred by love toward God. And that prayer is good which imprints a clear idea of God in the soul. And the indwelling of God is this: to hold God ever in memory....Thus we become God's temple, when the continuity of our recollection is not severed by earthly cares, when the mind is harassed by no sudden sensations, when the lover of God flees from all things and retreats to God, drawing away from all the passions that invite him to self-indulgence, and passes his time in the pursuits that lead to virtue."[38]

In a sequel to this letter, he admitted that seclusion from worldly affairs, celibacy, solitude, and perpetual study of holy Scriptures, and life

---

[37] Ep. xiv. See Philip Schaff, *History of the Christian Church*, Vol. III, p. 899.
[38] Ibid., Ep. ii, p. 900; Rousseau, p. 227; *Nicene & Post Nicene Fathers*, Letter ii, p. 111.

with godly men, prayer, and contemplation, with asceticism, are necessary for taming the passions and attaining peace of soul.

Saint Basil at a Synod Meeting

While Saint Basil was laboring in Pontos, the ecclesiastical world was in turmoil on account of the Arians. The Synod of Nicaea in 325 had condemned the errors of Arius. Efstathios was ousted from Antioch in 330 and Markellos from Ankyra in 336. But the Arians began reasserting themselves, and disputes in Antioch and Ankyra affected Basil. Markellos and his Sabellianism roused Basil's anxiety. Markellos' successor, Basil of Ankyra, whom Saint Athanasios later recognized as the leader of the Homoiousian party, held a vaguer theology. Emperor Constantius II (337-363) summoned a council, and deputations from each of the parties were dispatched to Constantinople. At the 341 Synod in Antioch, the gathering was dominated by the policies of the pro-Arian Evsevios of Nikomedia, who subscribed to the decisions of Nicaea. Also, Dianios, Bishop of Cappadocian Caesarea, was present. The Synod of Sardica, held in 343, rebuffed that meeting for the position of Saint Athanasios. The conflict escalated with Leontios, appointed to the see of Antioch in 344, who sympathized more with the Arians. Under this new climate, Aetios and his disciple Evnomios founded neo-Arianism, and Arianism was on the rise. The traditions of Evsevios of Nikomedia were asserted at the first council held in Sirmium (351). Aetios and Evnomios held to the notion that the Son was unlike (ἀνόμοιος) the Father, and they became known as Anomoeans. Basil of Ankyra and Efstathios of Sebasteia shunned such beliefs. They were attracted more to the beliefs declared at Nicaea, but they wished to keep some distance and called themselves the Homoiousians, because of their belief that the Son was of like essence (ὁμοιούσιος) to the Father. The more rigorous supporters of Nicaea, such as Saint Athanasios the Great, kept to the belief that the Son was of the same essence (ὁμοούσιος) as the Father; hence the name Homoousians. The complications that arose in the east from these distinctions were enormous. The Anomoeans were on one side and the Homoiousians on the other. A third, intermediate group arose, labeled the Homoeans, that were satisfied to say merely that the Son was like (ὅμοιος) the Father. Emperors Constantius and Valens favored this group, whose chief twin councils were held at Seleukeia and Ariminum (359). The Homoeans made preparations to gather in the capital toward the end of 359, where they hoped to be successful, especially after the death of Leontios in 357. Moreover, Bishop George of Laodikeia, originally a follower of Evsevios of Nikomedia, wrote to Macedonios of Constantinople and Basil of Ankyra, suggesting they counter the Anomoeans. Together they wished to persuade the emperor that the "like in essence" (ὁμοιούσιος) was equivalent to the term used by the Homoeans, "like the Father in all things" (ὅμοιος κατὰ πάντα). They were successful with Constantius, and Aetios and Evnomios were later exiled for a time.

The Deacon Basil attended some of the sessions in the capital. He accompanied to court Efstathios of Sebasteia, Basil of Ankyra, and Dianios of Caesarea. Although Saint Basil was highly esteemed everywhere, he was not a major player at this synod meeting, nor boldly championed their cause. His official position was a lowly one in that council. He stood aloof from their intrigues, and stood for the truth. He was in a good position to learn firsthand the intricacies of the conflict. Although he was in the company of the Homoiousians, he was not comfortable with their views, but it was the tradition at that time in the see of Ankyra. Nonetheless, he never intended to repudiate the definitions given at Nicaea. He insisted that the place to start was holy Scripture, with the baptismal formula given in Matthew 28:19, for formulating doctrine regarding the Trinity.

His brother Gregory notes that Basil was moved by love to undertake the cure of the Arian Evnomios. He had hoped to save Evnomios and restore him to the Church. Evnomios taught that God the Creator was ingenerate, but the Son was created and possessed a different essence and energy. The Logos-Christ was a created deity and never assumed human nature. The other party opposed the extreme Arianism of Evnomios. But at the same time, they did not team up with Saint Athanasios and the supporters of the Nicene Creed. They taught that the Son was of like essence with the Father, neither the same nor different from Him. Although Saint Basil was in association at first with the bishops of this party early on in life, he later left them and took up defending the Creed of Nicaea. In 360, when Dianios signed the Creed of Ariminum, brought to Caesarea by Bishop George of Laodikeia, Basil was so distressed that he shunned communion with his bishop. He left Caesarea and went to Nazianzos (Nazianzus) to seek consolation with his dear friend Gregory. He says his feelings toward Dianios as a person were always affectionate, and thus he was unwilling to anathematize him. Two years later, in 362, when Dianios was on his deathbed, he sent for Basil. Dianios insisted that he was always loyal to the doctrines promulgated at Nicaea. Basil believed him and communed again with his old bishop and friend.[39] In the intervening years Saint Basil used extreme caution when exercising terms. He expressed a willingness to accept the term ὅμοιος, but then qualified it saying it was to mean ὅμοιος κατ᾽ οὐσιαν, that is, "like in essence," and provided he was allowed to add yet another word, ἀπαραλλάκτως, "without

---

[39] Letter li.

variation."[40] When writing against Evnomios, he revealed his anxiety for the people, many who were simple-minded, who were unaware of the skillful use of words by the Arians to pervert the truth. He said, "I shall weep for the laity....The ears of the more simple-minded are being turned away; already they have become accustomed to the heretical impiety. The nurslings of the Church are being brought up in the doctrines of ungodliness....Baptisms are in the heretics' hands: attendance upon those who are departing this life, visits to the sick, the consolation of those who grieve, the assisting of those who are in distress, succor of all kinds, communion of the mysteries; all of these things, being performed by them, become a bond of agreement between them and the laity."[41]

In 364, Saint Basil sharpened his view when he wrote a reply to Evnomios' *Apology* wherein the latter affirmed that the Son is unlike the Father. Saint Basil argued that God is beyond knowing. He gave Scripture central attention, which underpinned his argument. He discoursed on those Scripture verses which the Arians misunderstood, such as the following: When we read on the subjection of the Son [1 Cor. 15:28], or that God granted Him a name above every name [Phil. 2:9], or that "I live because of the Father [Jn. 6:57]," His manhood is being spoken of; we understand this of the incarnation, and not the divinity. Again, he discusses "My Father is greater than I [Jn. 14:28]," explaining that the inferiority spoken of touches Jesus' manhood.

Episcopacy

However, since it was the will of God to place the lamp upon the lampstand, Archbishop Evsevios reposed in the Lord. The bishops of that province then gathered together. They canonically voted and ordained Basil as their hierarch and shepherd—and much more, a teacher of the world. In this capacity he had fifty country bishops (*chorepiscopoi*) under him. Meanwhile, Gregory's aged father, also named Gregory, who was Bishop of Nazianzos, called his son home to help battle the Arian heretics. Both men, beholding the great distress and turmoil besetting the beleaguered Church, answered her call, and emerged from seclusion. When Basil was elected to the archiepiscopal cathedra, he ordained his brother Peter to the priesthood and then Bishop of Sebasteia, that he might assist him in his labors against Arian madness. Basil was then saddened by the repose of his beloved mother, Emmelia, who was more than ninety years old.

But how might one narrate the virtues of the saint, the labors which he undertook, after he was vouchsafed the episcopacy? Even before his

---

[40] Philip Rousseau, *Basil of Caesarea*, Ch. IV.
[41] Ibid., p. 125.

elevation, he was indeed foremost in self-control and virtue. He tasted food only that he might keep his soul in his body, and partook of sleep only so far as not to confuse or ruin his mind from much wakefulness. Who might worthily praise his sober-mindedness, his abstinence from pleasures, his privation of the wants of the flesh? Saint Gregory describes his companion in the ascetical life thus: "He had a single coat and well-worn cloak. His bed was the bare ground. He kept vigils, and he went unwashed. Such were the forms of his luxury. He was content to live on mere necessities as long as he could, and the only luxury he knew was to prove himself free from luxury. He did have a care for the sick and the practise of medicine, our common intellectual avocation. For I must reckon myself his equal in distress, though his inferior in other respects." Elsewhere, he also mentions this occupation of the saint, saying, "Others have had their cooks, and splendid tables, and the devices and dainties of confectioners, and exquisite carriages, and soft, flowing robes. Basil's care was for the sick, and the relief of their wounds, and the imitation of Christ, by cleansing leprosy, not by a word, but in deed."

Who is able to search out his mellifluous teachings which took place every day? The saint's utterances and teachings, as the divine David says, "have gone forth into all the earth [cf. Ps. 18:4]," even as the teaching of the twelve apostles. On account of his preaching and the great grace which he was vouchsafed from God, even as the apostles, he ceased not working wonders daily. Throngs of working people came to hear him preach before they went to their daily labors. He was keen to protect the purity of ordination and the fitness of the candidates. He traveled great distances, and managed enormous charitable institutions. We know that his ongoing correspondence was involved, elaborate, and often showed his affectionate interest in the lives of his friends. He was active, and yet found the time to write eloquent and profound tracts and treatises that bespoke a daily and effective study of the sacred Scriptures.

However, there were many snares that surrounded his life, as he himself complains in a letter: "I was called to preside over the Church. Of the watchmen and spies, who were given me under the pretense of assistance and loving communion, I say nothing, lest I seem to injure my own cause by telling an incredible tale, or give believers an occasion for hating their fellows, if I am believed."[42]

If anyone desired to declare all the saint's accomplishments in detail, he would become as one who attempts to count the stars of the heaven or the sand of the sea. However, in order that those who love to hear this narration may not suffer loss, it is fitting that we set out in detail some of the accounts,

---

[42] Letter ccxxiii.

on the one hand to laud and praise the saint, and on the other, to the glory and offering of thanks to God Who is glorified in His saints. "Only out of my own love for the saint shall I (the hagiographer) recount those wonders of his which have been confirmed by trustworthy compilers and historians." Hearken and learn for what cause he wrote the divine Liturgy, which came to be named after the great Basil.

The Divine Liturgy

After the resurrection of Christ, the son of Joseph the Betrothed, Iakovos, who is called Adelphotheos or "Brother of God," became Bishop of Jerusalem. He wrote in the Hebrew tongue certain prayers and petitions to God, to be used whenever the priests were about to celebrate the divine Liturgy, which was handed down by our Lord Jesus Christ to the apostles during that night when He was about to be delivered up. Shortly thereafter those prayers and the rest of the service of the divine Liturgy were translated into Greek, as we have found it today, by Saint Klemes (Clement 88-97), the disciple of the holy Apostle Peter, who afterward became Bishop of Rome. He ordained as law that in this way the Christians are to perform the divine Liturgy.

In such a manner then the Christians conducted the Liturgy for about three hundred and fifty years. However, because the prayers were long and the service lengthy, the priests were negligent and did not liturgize. Saint Basil urged, "It is good and beneficial to communicate every day, and to partake of the holy body and blood of Christ....And who doubts that to share frequently in Life is the same thing as to have life abundantly? I, indeed, communicate four times a week, on the Lord's day, on Wednesday, on Friday, and on Saturday, and on other days if there is a commemoration of any saint."[43]

Nonetheless the Christians were feeling weighed down and began murmuring on account of the length of the service, and wished to go about their work in the world. The saint, observing this response of the people, was desirous to find a way to relieve their weariness. Consequent to this, he sought divine enlightenment by entreating the Lord to show him a sign that he might know whether his intention was God's will.

Thus he pondered and supplicated God for many days, with fasts and tears. "Then one night, the saint, as one pure and worthy, beheld a wondrous and paradoxical vision, which I (the hagiographer), as one unworthy and filled with every uncleanness, shudder to narrate, O blessed Christians." Well then, the Lord with His apostles appeared to come down to the saint. O Thy condescension, Lord Who loves mankind! And, according to hierarchical

---

[43] Letter xciii.

order, Christ celebrated the divine Liturgy with His apostles. Yet the Lord was not uttering those prayers which are written in the Liturgy of Saint Iakovos the Brother of the Lord, but an abridgement, which afterward Saint Basil placed in his Liturgy. After seeing this vision, the saint gave thanks to God Who had hearkened to his entreaty. Hence, he composed the shortened divine service, which has come down to us to this day, and which we know as the Liturgy of Saint Basil.

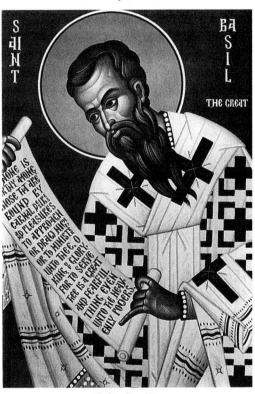

Saint Basil

After Christ and the apostles appeared to Saint Basil, he uttered the new prayers in the divine service. Evoulos and the clergy of higher rank then beheld a celestial light illuminating the sanctuary and Saint Basil. Certain radiant men clad in white shining garments surrounded the saint. All the clergy were astonished and fell prone to the floor, weeping and glorifying God.

About the same time the holy bishop commissioned a goldsmith to fashion a dove of pure gold, as an image of what took place at the Baptism of Christ, when John the Baptist bore witness, saying, "I have beheld the Spirit descending out of heaven as a dove, and He abode upon Him [Jn. 1:32]." He then suspended it above the holy table as a receptacle in which to store the Mysteries.

Whenever the saint served the divine Liturgy and elevated the holy gifts, that golden dove, which was suspended above the holy altar, shook thrice by the power of God. However, one day, when Saint Basil was serving, the usual sign of the movement of the dove did not take place. Saint Basil pondered why this should have happened now. Then he observed that one of the deacons, who was holding the fans (*ripidia*), was gazing earnestly at a woman standing in the church. The deacon was dismissed and given a penance. He was to pray and fast for seven days, and distribute alms to the poor. As a result of this incident, Saint Basil commanded that a veil be hung and a partition constructed before the sanctuary.

Today, the Liturgy of Saint Basil is celebrated by the Church only ten times a year: the five Sundays of the Great Fast, Great Thursday, Great Saturday, the eve of the Nativity of our Lord, the eve of the Theophany, and the feast day of the saint.

The Saint's Writings

Saint Basil the Great bequeathed to us many superb writings which may be arranged by categories: Liturgics, Dogmatic theology (*Against Evnomios, On the Holy Spirit, The Hexaemeron*), Exegetic (interpretations of the sacred Scriptures), Thirteen Homilies on the Psalms, Sermons for the various feasts of the martyrs, Instructions, Sermons on practical ethics, *The Moral Rules*, Asceticism (*The Long Rules, The Short Rules*, the basics of the coenobitic life, including enlistment in the sacred warfare, on renunciation of the world and spiritual perfection, and the virtues exhibited in the life of the solitary), Epistles (368 letters to diverse peoples on different subjects are extant), Canon of the Great Basil (contained in the Sixth Œcumenical Synod), and a *Philokalia* (compiled by Saints Basil and Gregory while they took up the ascetic life together in Pontos).

The Righteous Widow

Hearken to an account of our champion of widows. A certain widow was defrauded of money by the ruler of Caesarea. She betook herself to the saint, entreating him to intercede and write a letter to that nobleman that he might desist in troubling her. Consequently, the saint composed this letter: "This woman, who bears my epistle, has besought me to write to thee that thou troublest her no longer. She believes that thou lovest me and wouldest receive my word gladly. If, therefore, this is true, make it manifest to me in very deed." This is what the saint penned, and handed it over to the woman, who went and gave it to the noble. After he read it, he responded: "For the sake of thy love, father, I should like to be sympathetic to her, but I am unable, because she owes the principal tax." The saint wrote back: "If, indeed, as thou sayest, thou dost wish to be sympathetic to her, but thou art unable, it is well; but, if thou art able, and dost not wish, God shall also bring thee to the position of those who entreat, so that when thou art in need, thou shalt not be able to find sympathy."

These are the words of warning written by the saint; and, indeed, these words proved prophetic when they found their fulfillment in what took place. Not many days elapsed before the emperor became wroth with that very nobleman. Imperial officers were sent to arrest the nobleman, who was bound in chains and led about from city to city and land to land, that he might pay in full for the injustices he committed. Then that hapless man, perceiving the foresight of the holy Bishop Basil, implored him to entreat God that the emperor might be moved to feel pity for him. The saint, as one sympathetic and a true imitator of Christ, by his prayer only, made gentle the heart of the emperor. Then, after six days—from the time that the former nobleman besought the saint—an imperial letter arrived, granting him a reprieve from condemnation. Having received this unlooked-for deliverance, the nobleman quickly recognized from where such undeserved kindness and favor came. Indeed, he paid back twofold whatever he wronged the woman, and also offered thanks to the saint on account of his intercession.

Famine

There came to pass a great famine that befell the saint's diocese, so that many perished from the deprivation of food. What then did the holy man do to remedy this calamity? Seeing that the nobles and landed gentry of his diocese were greedily guarding their wheat in granaries, and not dispersing it to the poor, he was profoundly grieved by their harshness; for there is no greater inhumanity, at such a time of dearth, than for the rich to be unwilling to sell wheat. Indeed, by waiting to sell the wheat when demand for it was at its peak, they hoped for greater monetary gain. On this account the wise Solomon cautions: "May he that hoards corn leave it to the nation [Prov. 11:26]." These wretches do not know that as much as they oppress the poor in their putting off the sale of the stored wheat for a higher profit, so much more they multiply for themselves the displeasure of God. For is there anything worse than for them to hide or keep back the wheat, and to make money by aggravating the straits of the poor, and oppressing and starving the Christians? How could one name such persons as these Christians? What shall we call them? Shall we call them simply people, or say that they are more fierce than beasts? Nay, even the beasts, though they be wild, yet sense distress for their own species.

Such was the character of the nobles of Caesarea at that time. Therefore, every day the saint kept on teaching about almsgiving; he admonished them, he exhorted them, he put his words in writing. He brought to mind the hospitality of Abraham, the lodging of strangers by Lot, and how Joseph the all-comely, the wheat-giver, fed the Egyptians and others. Then especially these words were used by the saint as they are found in Scripture—which make for a sad epitaph for the rich man who did not have enough room where he could gather his fruit—"This will I do; I will take down my storehouses and I will build greater ones [Lk. 12:18]." As we know, dear Christians, God said to him, "Fool, this night they demand thy soul from thee; and what thou didst prepare, for whom shall it be [Lk. 12:20]?" This was one who treasured up for himself, and was not rich toward God. Thus the saint urged in his writings. With this manner of constraint he persuaded the wealthy to open the granaries. Then, as an imitator of the Master Christ Who washed the feet of His disciples, the holy Basil alone served in the apportionment of the wheat; he singlehandedly boiled the legumes, and solely distributed food to the poor. Now this he attended to for many days, until he took care of the hungry.

Saint Gregory the Theologian describes the scene, as follows: "Basil gathered together the victims of the famine with some who were but slightly recovering from it. He obtained contributions of all sorts of food which can relieve starvation. He set before men and women of every age, and even infants, basins of soup and such meat as was found preserved among us, on which the poor live. Then imitating the ministration of Christ, Who, girded with a towel, did not disdain to wash the disciples' feet, using for this purpose the aid of his own servants, and also of his fellow servants, he attended to the bodies and souls of those who needed it, combining personal respect with the supply of their necessity, and so giving them a double relief. Such was our young furnisher of corn, and second Joseph."

As one sympathetic and warm, he once wrote: "After men have fled for refuge to me, I should be ashamed not to be able to be of any use to them."[44] He was patient and long-suffering with the imperfections of his beloved flock, and once remarked, "I learned long ago the weakness of human nature, and its readiness to turn from one extreme to another; and so, be well assured, nothing connected with it can astonish me."[45] Yet "to be kind and gentle to the fallen is the mark of the man supereminent in greatness of soul, and in clemency."[46]

Emperor Julian

Our next account took place during the reign of the most defiled, abominable, and impious Emperor Julian, as he was advancing to parts of Persia, coming nearby the city of Caesarea. Now Saint Basil knew Julian from his own school days in Athens where they studied as contemporaries.

In a letter to Archbishop Basil, the anti-Christian Emperor Julian wrote: "While showing up to the present time the gentleness and benevolence which have been natural to me from my boyhood, I have reduced all who dwell beneath the sun to obedience. For lo! every tribe of barbarians to the shores of the ocean has come to lay its gifts before my feet....I must as soon as possible march to Persia and rout and make a tributary of that Shāpūr, descendant of Darius. I mean too to devastate the country of the Indians and the Saracens, until they all should acknowledge my superiority and become my tributaries. Thou, however, dost profess a wisdom, and beyond these things; thou dost call thyself clad with piety, but thy clothing is really

---

[44] Letter lxxii.
[45] Letter xxv.
[46] Letter cii.

impudence, and everywhere thou slanderest me as one unworthy of the imperial dignity. Dost thou not know that I am the grandson of the illustrious Constantius? I know this of thee, and yet I do not change the old feelings which I had toward thee, and thee unto me in the days when we were both young. But of my merciful will, I command that a thousand pounds of gold be sent to me from thee when I pass by Caesarea; for I am still on the march, and with all possible dispatch am hurrying to the Persian campaign. If thou wilt refuse, I am prepared to destroy Caesarea and to overthrow the buildings that have long adorned it. In their place I shall erect temples and statues, so as to induce all men to submit to the emperor of the Romans and not exalt themselves. Therefore I charge thee to send me without fail, by the hands of some trusty messenger, the stipulated gold, after duly counting and weighing it, and sealing it with thy ring. In this way I may show mercy to thee for thy errors.... I have learned to know, and to condemn, what once I read."[47]

Archbishop Basil replied in writing to Julian: "The heroic deeds of thy present splendor are small; and thy grand attack against me, or rather against thyself, is paltry. When I think of thee in purple, a crown on thy dishonored head, which, so long as true religion is absent, rather disgraces thine empire, I tremble. And thou thyself who hast risen to be so high and great, now that vile and honor-hating demons have brought thee to this pass, have begun not only to exalt thyself above all human nature, but even to lift thyself up against God, and insult His Church, Mother and nurse of all, by sending to me, most insignificant of men, orders to forward thee a thousand pounds of gold.

"I am not so much astonished at the weight of the gold, although it is very serious, but it has made me shed bitter tears over thy so rapid ruin. I bethink me how we have learned together the lessons of the best and holiest books. Each of us went through the sacred and God-inspired Scriptures. Then nothing was hid from thee. Nowadays thou hast become lost to proper feeling, beleaguered as thou art with pride. Your serene highness did not find out for the first time yesterday that I do not live in the midst of superabundant wealth. Today, highness, you have demanded of me a thousand pounds of gold. I hope your serenity will deign to spare me. My property amounts to so much that I really shall not have enough to eat as much as I should like today. Under my roof the art of cookery is dead. My servants' knife never touches blood. The most important viands, in which lies our abundance, are leaves of herbs with very coarse bread and sour wine, so that our senses are not dulled by gluttony, and do not indulge in excess....

---

[47] Letter xl. Julian to Basil.

"It is a serious thing for a private individual like myself to speak to an emperor; it will be more serious for thee to speak to God. No one will appear to mediate between God and man. What thou didst read thou didst not understand. If thou hadst understood, thou wouldest not have condemned."[48]

Esteeming his rank as emperor, the hierarch took along the people with him that they might anticipate Julian and meet him. Because they had no gift to present the imperial party, in accordance with the emperor's demand, three barley loaves were offered from those which the holy man ate at his table. The emperor accepted the gift, and repaid the kindness: he commanded his underlings to give grass from the pastureland. After the saint observed this display of contempt, he remarked to the emperor, "We indeed, O emperor, as thou didst request, offer thee from that which we eat; but thy kingly office requited us with a fitting gift from that which thou dost eat." Hearing this the emperor was very angered, and declared to the saint, "Receive now this gift: whenever I return from victory over the Persians, then I shall indeed burn down thy city, and take prisoner a foolish people that have been beguiled by thee, because they dishonor the gods to whom I pay homage; and thou also shalt receive fitting retribution!" After that tyrant against the Faith made his threats, he decamped for Persia. Saint Gregory the Theologian commented, "Julian deemed it a small matter to conquer the Persians, but one of the greatest importance to subject the Christians to his power."

After returning back into the city, the saint called to himself the crowd of people. At the time when he informed the people of the emperor's threats, he also counseled them, saying, "Cease grieving, my fellow Christians, and consider what money you need to live upon, but bring whatever other money you have that we might gather it up together in one place. Then, whenever we should hear that the emperor is returning, we shall cast heaps of money into the road, in order that after he should see the treasure, as the lover of money that he is, he shall be reconciled, and not commit that which he purposed to do." Thereupon, the Christians went their way and did as the saint directed. They brought forth immeasurable wealth, including gold, silver, and precious stones. Now the saint accepted what they brought forth from their stores, and put it in the care of the Church's keeper of the vessels (*skevophylax*). For safekeeping and so that they might account for the treasure until the emperor's return, each contribution was registered with the owner's name.

When the holy hierarch heard a rumor that the army was returning, he gathered together the multitude of Christians, with women and children, and commanded them that they should keep a fast of three days. Afterward, with the faithful, he ascended the summit of the mountain of Caesarea that is

---

[48] Letter xli.

named Didymon (Twin) because it has two peaks. On that mountain was also the Church of the Most Holy Theotokos. It was there that the Christians betook themselves, entreating and beseeching with a contrite heart the only compassionate God and His most pure Mother, that the will of the impious emperor might be changed. While the saint stood with the people in prayer, he was counted worthy of a vision. He beheld a multitude of the heavenly host encircling the mountain. In the midst of them, he beheld a certain Woman enthroned with great glory. She uttered to the angels standing by, "Call Mercurios to me, so that he might go and slay Julian, the enemy of my Son." It then was made manifest to Saint Basil that the Martyr Mercurios came. After he had taken up his weapons, he received his order from the Woman, who was the most holy Theotokos, and he quickly took leave. After the departure of the Martyr Mercurios, the Queen of the angels summoned Saint Basil and gave into his hands a book which had been written containing the creation of everything visible and invisible, and the fashioning of man by God. Indeed, at the beginning of the book the hierarch noticed an inscription, commanding: "Speak." At the end of the book, where it dealt with the making of man, he read, "The end." At this point in the vision, straightway, he awakened. "Now in order that none might have doubts about the meaning of the vision regarding the book, I (the hagiographer) shall explain it to you."

An eloquent interpretation, known as the *Hexaemeron*, has come down to us from Saint Basil, expounding in an interpretative manner the six days of creation, as it was formerly recorded by the God-seer Moses. Nine homilies were delivered by Saint Basil on the cosmogony of the opening chapters of Genesis. They were sermons during the Great Fast, delivered at both the morning and evening services. The saint speaks about the following: how God made the heaven and the earth; how the earth was invisible and unfinished; about the firmament; about the gathering together of the waters; the germination of the earth; the creation of luminous bodies; the creation of moving or creeping creatures; the creation of fowl and aquatic animals; and the creation of terrestrial animals. But when he was about to commence another homily on the sixth day and how God fashioned Adam and Eve, then it was in those days that the saint was translated into the heavens, leaving the work unfinished. Afterward his brother Gregory, who served as Archbishop of Nyssa, wrote about the making of man, and completed the book. The words, "Speak," and "The end," were prophetic for Saint Basil. It is true that, at the Theotokos' behest, the saint spoke in sermons about the creation. Then when he was about to begin speaking on the making of man, he was not vouchsafed to complete this labor, because it was the end of his earthly sojourn. But let us continue with our story.

After he beheld the vision, straightway, the saint descended with certain of the clergy into the city, where the Church of the holy Great-martyr Mercurios is situated. Within the church were to be found the precious relics of the martyr and his weapons, which were honored by the Christians. One hundred years had passed since the reigns of Decius, Gallus, Aemilianus, and Valerian, when the martyr lived and contested for Christ, by his martyrdom in Caesarea. Upon entering those sacred precincts, Saint Basil could find neither the relics nor the martyr's weapons. He questioned the *skevophylax* of the church to learn what happened to them. But he, not knowing the matter, solemnly replied that he knew nothing. The saint then came to know both that the vision was true, and that during that same night, the 26th of June, in the year 363, the ungodly emperor was slain. Immediately then, the holy man hastened up the mountain and exclaimed to the Christians, "Rejoice and be glad today, brethren! Our entreaty was heard, because a fitting punishment has befallen the profane emperor. Therefore, offering thanks to God, let us go into the city, that each might receive his money."

When the Christians heard this, they cried aloud with one voice, "We thought to give the money to the sacrilegious emperor in exchange for our lives. Now ought we not to offer that to the King of heaven and earth, Who granted us life?" Now the saint praised their eagerness. He determined, however, that each should receive one-third of whatever they originally contributed. The remainder was allocated for the building of poorhouses, hostelries, hospitals, old age homes, and orphanages.

Regarding the portion that was to be returned, Saint Basil arranged to have one-third of the treasure baked into large loaves of sweet bread, which were cut and shared among the populace. After centuries, pious Orthodox Christians maintain this custom on the 1st of January, eating freshly-baked Saint Basil's bread or Vasilopita, wherein a coin is placed. The head of each household slices the bread, dedicating the first piece to Christ, the second to the Theotokos, and so on to family and friends.

But let us return now to the fourth century. After the slaying of the profane emperor on the Persian frontier by Saint Mercurios, through the prayers of the saint, the God-fearing Jovian became emperor. Yet he reigned only for one year, and then reposed. The empty imperial throne then came to be occupied when Valentinian was proclaimed augustus by the generals and civil officials. He in turn elevated his brother Valens as co-ruler, who reigned from March 364 until August 378. This Valens was an Arian, who later began to persecute the Orthodox.

The Saint's Theology

Arianism continued its ravages and its battle against the term *homoousios* of the Nicaean Synod. The Arians tore the Church apart with factions. The enemies of true religion said the Son was not equal to the Father and was a pure creature. Others taught that Christ had a nature similar to that of the Father, though not the same. A third group denied the divinity of the Holy Spirit. Saint Basil's opinion was written in this memorandum to his brother Gregory: "Many persons fail to distinguish between what is common in the essence, and the meaning of the hypostases. What is to be common in the Holy Trinity refers to the essence insofar as relates to the infinite, the incomprehensible, the uncreate, the uncircumscribed, and other similar attributes. For the account of the uncreate and of the incomprehensible is one and the same in the case of the Father and of the Son and of the Holy Spirit. For One is not more incomprehensible and uncreate than Another. The hypostasis on the other hand is that which is spoken of in a special and peculiar manner as a distinctive sign. There is a certain Power subsisting ingenerate and unoriginate, Who is the Cause of the cause of all things. For the Son, by Whom are all things, and with Whom

Saint Basil

the Holy Spirit is inseparably conceived of, is of the Father. For it is not possible for anyone to conceive of the Son if he be not previously enlightened by the Spirit. Since then the Holy Spirit, from Whom all the supply of good things for creation has its source, is attached to the Son, and with Him is inseparably apprehended, and has His[49] being attached to the Father as Cause, from Whom also He proceeds, He has this note of His peculiar hypostatic nature, that He is known after the Son and together with the Son, and that He has His subsistence of the Father. The Son, Who declares the Spirit proceeding from the Father through Himself and with Himself, shining forth alone and by only-begetting from the unbegotten Light, so far as the peculiar notes are concerned, has nothing in common either with the Father or with the Spirit. He alone is known by the stated signs. But God, Who is over all, alone has, as one special mark of His own hypostasis, His being Father, and His deriving His hypostasis from no cause; and through this mark He is peculiarly known.

"Since then, as says the Lord in the Gospel, 'I am in the Father and the Father in Me [Jn. 14:11],' he that hath seen the Son sees the Father also. On this account Saint Paul says that the Only-begotten is 'the effulgence of the glory and impress of His hypostasis [Heb. 1:3],' that is, the express image of His Father. The Son is also called 'the image of the invisible God [Col. 1:15],' not because the image differs from the Archetype according to the definition of indivisibility and goodness, but that it may be shown that it is the same as the prototype, even though it be different. So he who has, as it were, mental apprehension of the form of the Son, prints the express image of the Father's hypostasis, beholding the latter in the former, not beholding in the reflection the unbegotten being of the Father (for thus there would be complete identity and no distinction), but gazing at the unbegotten beauty in the Begotten. For all things that are the Father's are beheld in the Son, and all things that are the Son's are the Father's; because the whole Son is in the Father and has all the Father in Himself. Thus the hypostasis of the Son becomes as it were form and face of the knowledge of the Father, and the hypostasis of the Father is known in the form of the Son, while the proper quality which is contemplated therein remains for the plain distinction of the hypostases."[50]

Emperor Valens

After a division of responsibilities between the reigning brothers, Valens retained the eastern part of their empire. He raised a great persecution against Orthodox Christians, especially in Caesarea. Now when Valens heard that the saint was preaching Christ openly, and boldly calling the emperor a heretic, he wished to enter into Caesarea. After he began his journey by road,

---

[49] It is to be noticed that Saint Basil uses the masculine and more personal form in apposition with the neuter *Pnevma*. There is scriptural authority for the masculine pronoun [Jn. 15:26; 16:13].

[50] Letter xxxviii. Elsewhere, he writes: "In the creation bethink thee first, I pray thee, of the original Cause of all things that are made, the Father; of the creative Cause, the Son; of the perfecting Cause, the Spirit." See *On the Spirit*, Ch. XVI(38).

the emperor sent on ahead Demosthenes, his chief cook (who was a great officer in Oriental courts). This officer was to make threats against the holy man. Now that impious soul was unable to change the judgment of the saint.

Since the chief cook could not persuade Saint Basil to accept the dogma of Arius, he returned utterly defeated to Valens. Undaunted, the emperor then dispatched a second grandee, the Praetorian Prefect Modestos, who was a great prince. He too was told to intimidate the hierarch with harsh punishments, if he should not consent to be of one mind with the emperor. But that irreverent one also was unable to convert the saint from true Orthodoxy. Saint Gregory the Theologian describes this creature of Valens as one behaving with "excessive arrogance, who strived by exceeding the letter of his instructions, so as to gratify his master in every particular, and thereby guarantee and preserve his own possession of power.

"Though he raged," continues Saint Gregory, "against the Church, and assumed a lion-like aspect, roaring like a lion, so that most men dared not approach him, yet our noble prelate was brought into or rather entered his court, as if bidden to a feast, instead of to a trial. He met the arrogance of the prefect with prudence. 'What is the meaning, Sir Basil,' said he, addressing him by name, and not as yet deigning to term him bishop, 'of thee daring, as no other dares, to resist and oppose so great a potentate?' Our noble champion answered, 'In what respect and in what does my rashness consist, for I have yet to learn?' The prefect said, 'In refusing to respect the religion of thy sovereign, when all others have yielded and submitted themselves.' The archbishop replied, 'Because this is not the will of my real Sovereign; nor can I, who am the creature of God, and bidden myself to be a god, submit to worship any creature.' The prefect said, 'And what do we seem to be to thee? Are we who give thee this injunction nothing at all? What dost thou say to this? Is it not a great thing to be ranged with us as thine associates?' Basil said, 'Thou art, I will not deny it, a prefect, and an illustrious one, yet not of more honor than God. And to be associated with thee is a great thing, certainly; for thou art thyself a creature of God. But so it is to be associated with any other of my fellow subjects. For faith, not personal importance, is the distinctive mark of Christianity.'

"The prefect became excited and arose from his seat, boiling with rage and making use of harsher language. 'What?' said he, 'hast thou no fear of my authority?' 'Fear of what?' said Basil, 'How could it affect me?' He exclaimed, 'Of what? Of any one of the resources of my power.' Basil replied, 'What are these? Pray, inform me.' 'Confiscation, banishment, torture, death.' The archbishop said, 'Hast thou no other threat? For none of these can reach me.' The prefect said, 'How indeed is that?' 'Because,' replied Basil, 'a man who has nothing is beyond the reach of confiscation;

unless thou shouldest demand my tattered rags and the few books, which are my only possessions. Banishment is impossible for me, who am confined by no limit of place, counting my own neither the land where I now dwell, nor all of that into which I may be hurled, or rather, counting it all God's, Whose guest and dependent I am. As for tortures, what hold can they have upon one whose body has ceased to be? Unless thou shouldest mean the first stroke, for this alone is in thy power. Death is my benefactor, for it will send me the sooner to God, for Whom I live, and exist, and have all but died, and to Whom I have long been hastening.'

"Amazed at this language, the prefect said, 'No one has ever yet spoken thus, and with such boldness, to Modestos.' 'Why, perhaps,' said Basil, 'thou hast not met with a bishop, or in his defense of such interests he would have used precisely the same language. For we are modest in general, and submissive to everyone, according to the precept of our law. We may not treat with haughtiness even any ordinary person, to say nothing of so great a potentate. But where the interests of God are at stake, we care for nothing else, and make these our sole object. Fire and sword and wild beasts, and rakes which tear the flesh, we revel in, and fear them not. Thou mayest further insult and threaten us, and do whatever thou wilt, to the full extent of thy power. The emperor himself may hear this—that neither by violence nor persuasion wilt thou bring us to make common cause with impiety, not even if thy threats should become still more terrible.'

"At the close of the colloquy, the prefect, having been convinced by the attitude of Basil that he was absolutely impervious to threats and influence, dismissed him from the court, his former threatening manner being replaced somewhat by respect and deference. He himself with all speed obtained an audience of the emperor, and said, 'We have been worsted, sire, by the prelate of this Church. He is superior to threats, invincible in argument, and uninfluenced by persuasion. We must make trial of some more feeble character, and in this case resort to open violence, or submit to the disregard of our threats.' Hereupon, the emperor, compelled by the praises of Basil to condemn his own conduct (for even an enemy can admire a man's excellence), would not allow violence to be used against him. And though he turned from threatening to admiration, yet like iron which is softened by fire but still remains iron, yet he would not enter into communion with Archbishop Basil, being prevented by shame from changing his course, but sought to justify his conduct by the most plausible excuse he could find, as the sequel shall show."

The prefect then turned to Valens, saying, "It is easier for one to soften iron than the opinion of Basil!" After considering all the discouraging reports from his officers, the emperor marvelled at the saint's courage of soul. Saint Basil displayed no personal haughtiness, but conducted himself courageously, revealing that sober manner which is exhibited by men who are fully conscious of the truth without regard for the consequences of their person.

Saint Basil once said, "So long then as the word of truth is on our side, never be in any wise distressed at the calumny of a lie. Let no imperial threats scare you; do not be grieved at the laughter and mockery of your intimates, nor at the condemnation of those who pretend to care for you, and who put forward, as their most attractive bait to deceive, a pretense of giving good advice. Against them let all sound reason do battle, invoking the championship and succor of our Lord Jesus Christ, the Teacher of true religion, for Whom to suffer is sweet, and to die gain [Phil. 1:21]."[51]

Now not much time had passed when the emperor wished to go into the church, so he might observe the hierarch and hear his teaching. Saint Gregory the Theologian describes the event for us: "The emperor entered the Church attended by the whole of his train. It was the Feast of the Theophany on the 6th of January, in the year 372. The church was crowded, and, by taking his place among the people, he made a profession of unity. The occurrence is not to be lightly passed over. Upon his entrance, he was struck by the thundering roll of the psalms, by the sea of heads of the congregation, and by the angelic rather than human order which pervaded the sanctuary and its precincts. Basil presided over his people, and stood as one appointed over them, as the Scripture says of Samuel [1 Kgs. (1 Sam.) 19:20], with body and eyes and mind undisturbed, as if nothing new had happened, but fixed upon God and the sanctuary, as if, so to say, he had been a statue, while his ministers stood around him in fear and reverence."

Valens listened quietly to the teaching of the saint, who stood erect with all decorum and modesty. The archbishop was now in the prime of life, though he bore the marks of premature age. He was upright in carriage, of a commanding stature, with a pensive countenance. He was thin, with brown hair and eyes. He had a long beard and was slightly bald, with bent brow, high cheekbones, hollow temples, and smooth skin. His every tone and gesture bespoke at once his noble birth and upbringing, his familiarity with the noblest of books and men, and the dignity of a mind focused and a heart of single purpose. Saint Basil taught as another apostle, so that his words pricked at Valens' heart and moved his soul. Valens was of swarthy complexion and had a disfigurement in one eye. He was of middle height and obese, but supported on his somewhat crooked legs a strong build. He faltered and was unready in conversation and in action.

---

[51] Letter xviii.

Saint Gregory continues his account, "At this sight—and it was indeed a sight unparalleled—the emperor was overcome by human weakness, and his eyes were affected with dimness and giddiness, and his mind with dread. This was yet unnoticed by most people. But when he had to offer the gifts at the Table of God, which he must needs do himself, since no one would as usual assist him, because it was uncertain whether Basil would admit him, his feelings were revealed. For Valens was staggering, and had not someone in the sanctuary reached out a hand to steady his tottering steps, he would have sunk to the ground in a lamentable fall....

"The emperor, in his quasi-communion with us, entered within the veil to see and to speak with Basil, as he had long desired to do. What else can I say but that the words of the archbishop were inspired words, which were heard by the courtiers and by us who had entered with them? This was the beginning and first establishment of the emperor's kindly feeling toward us; the impression produced by this reception put an end to the greater part of the persecution which assailed us like a river."

Now there was present the emperor's satellite Demosthenes, the chief of the imperial kitchen, a kind of Nabuzardan, also a chief cook in the days of Nebuchadnezzar [cf. 4 Kgs. (2 Kgs.) 25:8]. He impertinently intruded into the conversation between the archbishop and the emperor. He threatened the archbishop, and in rudely chiding the archbishop, the man who instructed the world, he made some blunder in speaking Greek. Basil smiled and said, "We see here an illiterate Demosthenes." The cook lost his temper and uttered threats. The archbishop said, "Thy business is to attend to the seasoning of soups; thou art not able to understand theology, because thine ears are stopped up." Unoffended in the least, but rather amused at the discomfiture of Demosthenes, the emperor gave Basil and the Church some fine land to endow their hospital.[52]

Having listened to the sound-minded words of the saint, the emperor departed peacefully. But after a certain number of days, there came to him those blaspheming hierarchs who championed the profane dogma of Arius. They succeeded in changing the emperor's understanding, and even prevailed upon him to agree to the exile of the saint. Thereupon, Valens determined to put in writing the decision of his banishment. The wicked had prevailed, and the decree for his banishment was signed, to the gloating satisfaction of those who furthered it. The night had come, the chariot was ready, the haters of the saint were exultant, and the pious were in despair, reports Saint Gregory. "We surrounded the zealous traveler, to whose honorable disgrace nothing was wanting."

---

[52] Theodoret, *The Ecclesiastical History*, Bk. 4, ch. xvi.

What, however, followed? Hearken to the boundless power of God, and in what manner He acted in that cheerless hour. When Valens put in writing the sentence of exile upon the saint, the hand of his son Galates became paralyzed. The lad took gravely ill, so that he was in danger of perishing. The horrified emperor, beholding this swift retribution, quickly perceived that it was not the Almighty's will to banish His hierarch.

Thus the treachery was undone by God. "For He," Saint Gregory reminds us, "Who smote the firstborn of Egypt [Ex. 12:29], for its harshness toward Israel, also struck the son of the emperor with disease. How great was the speed! There was the sentence of banishment, here the decree of sickness: the hand of the wicked scribe was restrained, and the saint was preserved, and the man of piety presented to us, by the fever which brought to reason the arrogance of the emperor. What could be more just or speedy than this?

"This was the series of events: the emperor's child was sick and in bodily pain. The father was suffering for it; for what else can the father do? On all sides he sought for aid in his distress; he summoned the best physicians; he betook himself to intercession with the greatest fervor, and flung himself upon the ground, as David of old [2 Kgs. (2 Sam.) 12:16]. But as no cure for the evil could be found anywhere, he applied to the faith of Basil, not personally summoning him, on account of his shame for his recent ill treatment of the holy man, but entrusting the mission to others of his nearest and dearest friends.

"On the archbishop's arrival, without the delay or reluctance which anyone else might have shown, at once the disease relaxed, and the father cherished better hopes. Now had not Valens blended salt water with the fresh, by trusting to the heterodox at the same time that he summoned Basil, the child would have recovered his health and been preserved for his father's arms. This indeed was the conviction of those who were present at the time, and shared in the distress, because a relapse and death followed. This was thought to have been brought about by the young prince's Arian baptism that very day.

"The same occurrence befell the prefect. He fell sick, and was in tears and pain. He sent for Basil, and entreated him, crying out, 'I own that thou wast in the right; only save me!' His request was granted, as he himself acknowledged, and convinced many who had known nothing of it; for he never ceased to wonder at and describe the powers of the prelate."

Observing these miraculous recoveries, the emperor marvelled at the virtue of the saint. Basil then returned to his archiepiscopal throne.

The Basiliad

For the benefit of the sick and poor, Saint Basil organized a hospital outside the gate of Caesarea, which especially treated lepers. Saint Basil treated them as brethren, and was not even afraid to kiss them! Saint Gregory the Theologian described it as almost a new city and worthy to be reckoned as one of the wonders of the world. It came to be called the Basiliad, and was famous even after the blessed founder's repose. It was actually a whole range of buildings for the care of the sick and the destitute, and for the distribution of surplus food to those in need. We are told that it took several years to develop fully. Care of the sick and the practise of medicine were the main activities.

In a consolatory epistle he counsels, "Afflictions are not sent by the Lord to the servants of God to no purpose, but as a test of the genuineness of our love to the divine Creator. Just as athletes win crowns by their struggles in the arena, so are Christians brought to perfection by the trial of their temptations, if only we learn to accept what is sent us by the Lord with becoming patience, with all thanksgiving. All things are ordained by the Lord's love. We must not accept anything that befalls us as grievous, even if, for the present, it affects our weakness. We are ignorant, peradventure, of the reasons why each thing that happens to us is sent to us as a blessing by the Lord; but we ought to be convinced that all that happens to us is for our good, either for the reward of our patience, or for the soul we have received, lest, by lingering too long in this life, it be filled with the wickedness to be found in this world....But if to them who love God, the sundering of the soul from these bodily fetters is the beginning of our real life, why do we grieve like them who have no hope [cf. 1 Thess. 4:13]? Be comforted then, and do not fall under your troubles, but show that you are superior to them and can rise above them."[53]

Thanks to Saint Basil's exhortations, a common treasury of the wealthy was organized, where superfluous riches were stored. Saint Basil himself greeted the sick like brothers, and was willing to dress their wounds. Since considerable financial investment was required, within the saint's correspondence, we find pleas for special tax concessions and exemptions for the clergy. He invited the officials to inspect the home for the poor, to ensure that it was exempt from the tax assessor. He reminded the Prefect Modestos that such a concession would "confer a great benefit even upon the public revenues."[54]

The Widow Vestiana

At that time, the new Prefect Evsevios, a colleague of the former Prefect Modestos and related to the emperor, attempted to constrain the young and beautiful Caesarean widow Vestiana, the daughter of former Senator

---

[53] Letter ci.
[54] Ep. 104, cited in Rousseau, pp. 142, 143.

Araxus, into a distasteful marriage with him. However, she in no wise accepted his proposal, since she desired to dedicate herself to the Bridegroom Christ as a nun. Unabashed, the blackguard, smitten with carnal love, sent his lackeys to bring her to him even by using force. However, she learned of the impending abduction and took refuge in the cathedral where the saint served. Seeking safety from the prefect's high-handed treatment, she resorted to a device no less prudent than daring. She entered the holy bema of the church. She took hold of the sacred Chalice, so that no one might drag her off.

Saint Gregory here comments, "She fled to the holy Table, and placed herself under the protection of God against outrage. What, in the name of the Trinity,...ought to have been done, not only by the great Basil who laid down the law for us all in such matters, but by anyone who, though far inferior to him, was a priest? Ought he not to have allowed her claim, to have taken charge of her, and cared for her? Ought he not to have raised his hand in defense of the kindness of God and the law, which gives honor to the altar? Ought he not to have been willing to do and suffer anything, rather than take part in any inhuman design against her, and outrage at once the holy Table and the Faith in which she had taken sanctuary? 'No!' said the baffled judge, 'all ought to yield to my authority, and the Christians should betray their own laws. The judge sought to seize the suppliant.' But Basil protected her with all his power."

It was not very long before the prefect heard that a woman had fled for refuge inside the cathedral. The prefect thought to use this as a pretext to bring an accusation against the man of God. The contemptible prefect dispatched his men to search the saint's bedchamber and even under his couch, supposing to find the woman hiding there. This was not their only order, for they were also to bring the hierarch bound to him, as soon as they found the woman in his cell. But Saint Basil had already secretly sent her to a convent, that of his venerable sister Makrina.

Saint Gregory comments here, "What! Search the house of a man so free from passion, whom the angels revere, at whom women do not venture even to look? Not content with this, Basil was summoned by the civil authority, and put on his defense; and that, in no gentle or kindly manner, but as if here were a convict. The judge was in his seat, full of wrath and arrogance. Basil remained standing, like my Jesus before the judgment seat of Pilate. His ragged omophorion was ordered to be torn away. 'I will also, if you wish it, strip off my coat,' said he. His fleshless form was threatened with blows, and he offered to submit to be torn with combs. He then said, 'By such laceration you will cure my liver, which, as you see, is wearing me away.'"

Now the Christians of the city learned of this plot. Both men and women perceived the outrage and the common danger of all—for each one considered this insolence a danger to himself. Thus the city became all on fire with rage, especially the men from the imperial small-arms factory and weaving-sheds. Each man was armed with the tool he was using, or with whatever else came to hand at the moment. Nor were the women weaponless when stirred by such an occasion. Their pins were their spears. All thought they would be sharing in an act of piety if they tore that impious judge into pieces, and that he would be most pious in their eyes who should be the first to lay hands on him who had dared this outrage.

What then was the conduct of this haughty and daring judge, whom the people were prepared to slay as a heretic and slanderer of the saint? He begged for mercy in a pitiable state of distress, cringing before them to an unparalleled extent, until the arrival of Basil, the bloodless martyr, who had won his crown without blows. The archbishop restrained the people by the force of his personal influence, and delivered the man who had insulted him and now sought his protection. "This," remarks Saint Gregory, "was the doing of the God of saints, Who works and changes all things for the best, Who resists the proud, but gives grace to the humble [cf. Jas. 4:6]." Therefore, ashamed of all that had transpired—but also because they feared the anger of the people—the assessor and magistrates left the saint in peace.

Division in the Province

Behold now what the enemy of truth, the devil, schemed upon surveying the Orthodox multiplying in the saint's diocese of Cappadocia. The Emperor Valens wished to divide this province into two parts, assigning a judge for each. One seat would be in Caesarea, and the other at Tyana. When all the bishops of Tyana learned of the emperor's plan, certain of them, who were Arian heretics and ofttimes contended with the saint, also wished to have a second see appointed at Tyana. The saint remained constant in his decision against dividing the diocese. The Arian bishops persisted in favor of this administrative mutilation, rationalizing that it was right to break up the diocese, so that the ecclesiastical boundaries might be the same as those created by the imperial design. The saint, however, kept on humbly saying to them that the Church has no obligation to follow the realm, but the ruler ought to follow the Church; and, furthermore, neither was it proper for the imitators of Christ to disunite the see.

Nonetheless, those bishops would not hearken to the saint's God-inspired and sound judgment. These bishops bore an old hostility toward the Orthodox hierarch and were only interested in realizing their own goals. Therefore, they ordained as Metropolitan of Tyana a certain Anthimos who upheld that ecclesiastical partitions ought to follow the civil ones, and that

Tyana now should enjoy the same metropolitan entitlements as those of Caesarea. "Synods were wrongfully gathered," says Saint Gregory, "by the new metropolitan, and revenues seized upon." Hence, those bad hierarchs not only acted uncanonically, but they practised other wicked deeds also. "Some of the presbyters of the churches refused obedience; others were won over. In consequence, the affairs of the churches fell into a sad state of dissension and division," reports Saint Gregory. In one instance, they targeted that area between neighboring Caesarea and Tyana. More particularly, they coveted the Church of Saint Orestes, which was situated at the foot of the Taurus Mountains. This church had sufficient income from the yield of its vineyards and fields, and other such things. All of these possessions, those covetous bishops seized from out of the authority of the saint. They were intending to cause him vexation.

The spurious metropolitan went so far on one occasion as to detain and harass Saint Basil. When the saint was journeying along his own road with servants and mules to collect the produce of the Monastery of Saint Orestes in Cappadocia Secunda, the property of his see, Anthimos and his retainers seized the archbishop's mules. With the help of a gang of brigands, he prevented Basil from proceeding further, though an unbefitting tussle took place between the domestics of the prelates. And what a specious pretext Anthimos proffered! "He pretended," says Saint Gregory, "concern for his spiritual children, and souls, and the doctrine of the Faith." These pleas masked his insatiable avarice. Anyone who displeased him, he labeled a heretic. "The holy man," describes Saint Gregory, "metropolitan as he was of the true Jerusalem above, was neither carried away with the failure of those who fell into error, nor allowed himself to overlook this conduct, nor did he desire any inadequate remedy for the evil. Let us see how great and wonderful it was, or, I should say, how worthy of his soul. He made of the dissension a cause of increase to the Church; and the disaster, under his most able management, resulted in the multiplication of the bishops of the country. From this ensued three most desirable consequences: a greater care for souls, the management by each city of its own affairs, and the cessation of the war in this quarter."

The saint's biographer then calls him an imitator of Christ Who uttered, "To the one who doth wish to go to law with thee and take thy tunic, yield to him thine outer garment also [Mt. 5:40]." Saint Basil, as one not loving scandals, made peace and held off in the Caesarea diocese, until God, having beheld the patience of His saint, should quickly visit with punishment Metropolitan Anthimos of Tyana. As a result of that fray, Saint Basil nominated his friend Gregory to undertake the episcopate of a townlet nearby the scene of the commotion. Saint Basil desired to strengthen his position there against Anthimos. He judged it wise to increase the number of suffragan bishops to compensate for losses and defections. It should be noted, however, that Saint Gregory was displeased with the appointment to such an obscure place as Sasima, and wished to resign the post. His father, Gregory, Bishop of Nazianzos, convinced him otherwise. Thus Basil won a suffragan, but it left Saint Gregory the Great with some hard feelings at that point in time. Saint Basil placed his younger brother, Gregory, as Bishop of Nyssa.

In an epistle to the senate of Tyana, he wrote: "Others may be great and powerful and self-confident, but I am nothing and worth nothing, and so I could never take upon myself so much as to think myself able to manage matters without support. I know perfectly well that I stand more in need of the succor of each of the brethren than one hand does of the other. Truly, from our own bodily constitution, the Lord has taught us the necessity of fellowship....I pray that I may for my remaining days remain in peace; in peace I ask that it may be my lot to fall asleep. For peace's sake there is no trouble that I will not undertake, no act, no word of humility, that I will shrink from; I will reckon no length of journey, I will undergo any inconvenience, if only I may be rewarded by being able to make peace. If I am followed by anyone in this direction, it is well, and my prayers are answered; but if the result is different I shall not recede from my determination. Everyone will receive the fruit of his own works in the day of retribution."[55]

So as not to make our account inordinately long, peace was gradually established, though relations between the two metropolitans were strained. That they achieved a workable coexistence is shown by an epistle, written in 372, to the bishops ministering in Italy and Gaul, which was signed by Saint Basil and Anthimos, together with Meletios of Antioch, Evsevios of Samosata, Gregory of Nazianzos (the elder), and others, condemning the infamous Arius, and the bad seeds that took root thereafter, and expressing their wish to restore the Creed drawn up by the holy Fathers at Nicaea.[56] Let us now end this anecdote here, and narrate other wonders of the saint. We beseech his love, blessed Christians, that we may hear this next one with faith and piety.

A Soul Renounces Christ

In Caesarea there was a prince named Proterios, who was both God-fearing and very rich. He had a fifteen-year-old daughter, his only child, who was beautiful in appearance. Well then, what did the crafty devil, the enemy of virginity, connive? He kindled a wicked lust in one of that prince's slaves, constraining that one to find any way to make the maiden his wife. Since he

---

[55] Letter xcvii.
[56] Letter xcii.

was unable to succeed in realizing his desire, he went to solicit a wizard of the idolaters, a minister of the devil, and said to him, "If thou shouldest turn around the heart of my master's daughter, so that she would be in love with me, and take me as her husband, I am willing to become thy slave, and whatsoever thou dost wish I shall give to thee." The magus then made this answer to the slave, "If thou wilt deny thy Christ in a document, I am willing to accomplish that which thou desirest." The lamentable slave answered, "I deny the Christ by both word and written record enough to bring my will to pass." The magus then said to him, "I intend to give thee a letter. At midnight thou art to go to the cemetery of the idol worshipers where, upon invoking the demons, thou shalt lift this letter into the air. Then the demons should come. They will take hold of thee, and conduct thee to their leader; and there shall come to pass that which thou dost yearn after." The magus went on writing: "Inasmuch as thou art my lord and master, it is fitting that I serve thy desire to turn about the Christians from the Faith of Christ, that they might believe in thee. For this reason, I am sending forth this youth, who is consumed by passionate love. I beseech thee to bring about his will that I too might enjoy splendor and dignity among the people, thereby causing them to hasten together to me."

After he wrote it, he handed it over to the beguiled youth. That wretched slave, according to the wizard's command, stood upon the tomb of one idolater at the appointed hour. He then called upon the demons, flinging the letter. Straightway, they appeared before him and said, "If thou wilt have what thou desirest take place, keep on following us." They conveyed him to that place where the profane devil was sitting upon a high seat, encircled by other demons. Having read the writing of the wizard, he said to the youth, "Believest thou in me?" That one answered, "Yea, I believe." Again the devil queried, "Dost thou deny the Christ?" The deluded youth responded, "Yea, I deny Him." The devil resumed speaking, saying, "An ungrateful lot are you Christians, because whenever a need should arise in your lives, then you come to me. Whenever it should come to pass that which you desire, you deny me and go to the Christ Who, since He loves mankind, receives you. But thou, deny in writing thy Faith and the Baptism, and write that thou shalt accept to be punished eternally with me in the day of judgment; and then I shall minister to thee."

Then that miserable and gullible young man, having been blinded by lust, gave the foul creature the document of his denial of the Faith, even as the demon sought. After committing this reckless act, he returned to his master's house. Forthwith, the devil dispatched his minions to lure the maiden, so that she might desire the youth. After a certain number of days, that maiden succumbed, and was compelled to cry out, "Either give me that slave as a husband, or else I wish to die!" Her parents, when they heard such desperate pleas, regularly and with increasing vehemence, and that she would hang herself, took advice from certain of their friends. They counseled it was better for what she longed for to take place, than for her to die wrongfully. With weeping and lamenting, the parents yielded, and the marriage was performed. Now after they were married, the young man never stepped into a church, neither would he receive the immaculate Mysteries, nor even make the sign of the Cross. This conduct was noticed by certain neighbors who said to his wife, "Know this well, that thy spouse is not a Christian." Therefore, one day, she said to her husband, "I have the ill-feeling that thou art not a Christian, since so many Sundays and feasts of the Lord have passed, and thou dost not go into the church—nay, not even to venerate the icons—nor dost thou make the sign of the Cross. I, however, thinking that thou wert a Christian, agreed to marry thee. If then thou wilt refuse to go to church with me, I want to be separated from thee."

Then that sufferer, not being able any longer to keep hidden what he committed, came out with it, saying to her, "I, in order to make thee love me, denied Christ in writing. I cannot, then, enter into a church of the Christians, nor may I receive Communion." When that unfortunate woman heard this doleful admission, she wept, wailed, and beat her breast because of the calamity which had befallen her. Therefore, she hastened to Saint Basil and related the matter to him. Then the saint called the young man and questioned him concerning the incident. He, with tears, confessed the whole truth. At that time the saint asked the young man, "Dost thou wish to repent?" He answered, "O holy master, I do wish it; but I am unable, because I denied my Faith in a document." The saint responded, "Hearken to whatever I should tell thee." Continuing, he declared, "Do thou not give a care on account of thy written confession; for repentance is yet powerful, even to render thy signature useless." The youth said, "My soul hangs on thy neck, holy master. Whatsoever thou shouldest command, I am willing to do." Then the saint enclosed the youth inside his own cell, and said to him, "Continue abiding here and praying and fasting for three days, and afterward I myself shall come to see thee."

Now the saint kept on praying and entreating, with fasting, for the sake of that man's salvation. After the third day, the holy hierarch came and asked him, "How art thou faring, my child?" The young man disclosed, "I find myself in great anguish, holy one of God, because I cannot endure the loud cries and thrashings of the devils, for they are holding my confession and warring against me, saying, "Regardless of how much thou toilest, thou shalt not be able to lighten the weight, since we hold the letter which is in thine own handwriting." The saint encouraged him, saying, "Cease fearing, child;

only keep on believing, and thou shalt be saved." After he pronounced these things, the saint also gave him bread and water; and again he immured him in the cell. After the passage of a certain number of days, again the saint went to him and asked him, "How is it with thee, child?" This time the youth answered, "Through thy holy prayers, well; because now I do not see the demons appearing before my eyes. I only hear their loud cries and threats from afar." And again, after the saint gave him food and prayed over him, he closed the door and departed.

When they completed forty days, again the saint went to him and inquired, "How art thou holding up, child?" That youth replied, "With thy prayer, very well, holy master. Now I do not even see the evil and ugly shadow of the demons, nor do I hear their cries. Above all, this night I beheld a vision that thou didst wrestle with the devil, and prevailed." Straightway, the holy man sent forth a message, ordering all the clergy and Christians to gather together into the Church. When all assembled, he appealed to them, "My beloved children, let us all give thanks unto the Lord, for the lost sheep is found. But it is fitting that we also should labor, for the love of Christ, and keep vigil during this night, that He might show mercy to the creation fashioned by His hands." Having, therefore, kept vigil with psalms and the shedding of hot tears, they were entreating God throughout the night. During the third hour of the day, the saint entered into the sanctuary to commence the divine Liturgy.

While he was performing the divine service, the demons audaciously entered that holy precinct, in order to seize the youth. That youth then, panicking with fear, dashed to Saint Basil, and took hold of him, imploring, "Have mercy on me, slave of God, have mercy on me, because the demons have come! They wish to snatch me away!" Bravely, Saint Basil said to the demons, "O shameless and defiled creatures, are you not satisfied with your own destruction, but have you come into the temple of God to carry off this man?" One of the demons gave answer to the hierarch's question, saying, "Thou didst wrong me, Basil. I did not go to him, but he, of his own will, came to me, and denied his Faith. Behold, the written record of his confession!" Undaunted, the saint replied, "Blessed be my God! These people are not willing to bring down their hands in prayer, unless thou shouldest give back the document." And having turned to the clergy, he bade them, "Raise up your hands to the heavens, and cry aloud with tears the 'Lord, have mercy.'" Standing before the people, the saint directed them also to repeat the same; and for a long time they supplicated, crying aloud, "Lord, have mercy." Behold, the document, bearing the youth's denial, was seen borne along in the air, until it came and lay in the saint's hands. After he received it, the holy hierarch offered up thanks to God. Saint Basil then asked the youth, "Dost thou recognize thy letter made with thine own hand?" He confirmed, "Yea, saint of God, this is it." The saint then shredded the document and went on celebrating the divine Liturgy. After this event, the holy man admonished him and anointed him with holy Chrism. He then handed him over to his wife. The couple returned to their house, glorifying and blessing the all-compassionate God.

A Righteous Couple

The saint wished at one time to go to a certain city of his diocese, which was ministered by the Priest Anastasios, a righteous and virtuous man. The priest was conspicuous for his self-control and fasting, which he kept exactly. He also had a wife whose name was Theognosia. In the eyes of the people she was his wife, but in reality he in no wise knew her carnally, living with her as a sister. The people of that city erroneously believed the couple's childlessness was due to her barrenness. Apart from this, the priest possessed another virtue: he kept a man who had a form of leprosy. No one was privy to the fact that the priest and his wife cared for the infirm man on their own property. Now when Saint Basil was moved to take this journey by road, Father Anastasios, filled with the Holy Spirit, remarked to his wife, "My sister, I intend to go to our field, since there is need. But today our master is coming. Now at that hour that I tell thee, thou shalt go forth and meet him with incense and lights." Hence, at the appointed time revealed by Father Anastasios, Theognosia made ready and went forth from the house. Indeed, as foreseen, the saint arrived. The archbishop exclaimed, "How is it with thee, Lady Theognosia?" Composing herself after being amazed that the hierarch knew to call her by name, she answered, "I am well, holy master." The saint took up the conversation, and inquired, "Lord Anastasios, the priest and thy brother, where is he?" She replied, "He is my husband, despota; and he has gone to the field to labor." The saint responded, "He has come. He is inside the house. Therefore, do not send men to fetch him."

Taking note of the hierarch's prophetic gifts, Theognosia fell at his feet and with tears petitioned, "Pray on behalf of me, the sinner, holy master, because I see in thee great and marvellous things!" And the hierarch then blessed her. As Saint Basil and Theognosia proceeded toward the house, the Priest Anastasios had anticipated their arrival, and went out of the door, so as to meet them. Saint Basil entered the priest's home and sat down. Not much time had passed when the hierarch asked, "Lord Anastasios, speak to us of thy virtue, to the benefit of the Christians who stand here." But Father Anastasios declared, "I am a sinful man, holy master. What kind of virtue dost thou seek from me?" The saint kept his eyes upon him, and the priest continued, "But this I say to thy prelacy. I have two plows. I, indeed, work with one, and the other my bondman. Now from the yield, we retain however much is sufficient for us to manage for the year; and the rest we give to the poor. I also have my spouse, and thy handmaid, who serves with me." The saint said at this point, "Say not thy wife, but call her thy sister, just as she actually is." He then resumed, saying, "Now disclose to me thine other virtues also." The Priest Anastasios then returned to his first position. "I do not even have one virtue, my master, and am desolate of every good work," said he. The saint then bade him, "Rise and come with me."

Thereupon the priest hearkened and followed, while the saint led him to a cell—the very chamber where Anastasios had cloistered the diseased man! Saint Basil then directed, "Open this door." The priest pleaded, "Do not enter, O saint of God, for the place is polluted." The saint assured him, "I also need this place." Since it was evident that the priest did not wish to open the door, lest his virtue should be made manifest, Saint Basil opened the door by his prayer alone. The saint entered therein; and turning to Anastasios, questioned him, "Why hast thou hidden this treasure from me?" The presbyter answered, "My master, I feared that if I had presented thee to him, perhaps the leper might have uttered an evil word against thee." The saint commented, "Well, father, thou didst struggle on account of his ill-temper for so many years, thus leave me also to serve him thus during this night." Therefore, the hierarch remained inside the sick room for that entire night, all the while offering fervent prayer to God. And—O the wonder!—in the morning, that man came forth from the chamber completely cured, without having even the least sign of the dreaded leprosy.

Unhappy Friendships

Saint Gregory the Theologian warned Saint Basil that his friendship with Efstathios of Sebasteia was the cause of suspicion of his friend Basil's Orthodoxy. The man was unworthy of Basil's friendship. In his earlier days of asceticism, the austerities of Efstathios overshadowed any doubts of his questionable theology. Basil even introduced him to his happy family gathering at Annesi. But Efstathios had a knack to appear to be all things to all men. Later Basil likened him to the leopard that cannot change its spots. At length it was well documented that he signed his name on almost every creed that went about for signature. It was a long time before Basil withdrew his trust and regard for the vacillating Efstathios. In the meantime, this friendship with Efstathios attached doubts to Basil's soundness in matters of the Faith. When Saint Basil visited Armenia in 373, a creed was drawn up, to be offered to Efstathios for his signature. It contained the Nicaean confession, with certain additions relating to the Macedonian controversy. Of course Efstathios signed with others. Later he tried to make light of his signature on that creed. Regarding it, he attempted to make peace with Basil but failed. As a result, Efstathios renounced communion with the saint, and even attacked Basil, circulating an old piece of correspondence between them, but only after having added certain appendages to Basil's letter. The expressions introduced were heretical, favoring the heretic Apollinarios. Demosthenes, the saint's old adversary at Caesarea, aided Efstathios in the fabrication. Saint Basil denounced the letter, but not everyone recognized the forgery as calumny. Among the most disappointed of Saint Basil's hopes was that those whom he expected to sympathize and support him failed to credit him with honor and right belief. In his later years, Efstathios became one of the ringleaders in Asia Minor furthering the Macedonian heresy.

Toward the latter years of Saint Basil's life, he was troubled by the hostile behavior of his old neighbors at Neocaesarea. The alienation was even more vexing because the bishop of that see, Atarbios, was distantly related to the holy man. At the root of the trouble was the suspicion that Atarbios was a Sabellian sympathizer. He had slandered Basil in the past and avoided meeting with him. He criticized Saint Basil for supposed innovations in the chanting in the Church of Caesarea and his promotion of the ascetic life. Saint Basil made every effort to win the Neocaesareans from their heretical tendencies. The clergy of Pisidia and Pontos, where Efstathios had been successful in alienating the district of Dazimon, were visited by Basil and won back to communion. Bishop Atarbios and his flock, on the other hand, refused Basil's kindly gestures and urgent appeals. Intractable to the point of paranoia toward the holy Basil, the Neocaesareans stirred themselves up into a frenzied panic once when the saint was visiting his youngest brother Peter at the old home at Annesi. They fled from Basil as though he were an invader. They charged him with seeking to win their favor for the sake of ambition, and accused him of entering their neighborhood uninvited.[57] Saint Basil was still anxious that Atarbios bring himself and the flock back to strict Orthodoxy, and wrote: "Unless we assume a labor on behalf of the churches equal to that which the enemies of sound doctrine have taken upon themselves for their ruin and total obliteration, nothing will prevent truth from being swept away to destruction by our enemies, and ourselves also from sharing in the condemnation...."[58]

Lasting Friendships

Saint Basil was close with the elderly Bishop Evsevios of Samosata, who was strongly opposed to Arianism, and a recipient of many of the saint's letters. In 374 he was exiled for his orthodoxy to Thrace, but later recalled by Emperor Gratian. In 380, he was slain when an Arian woman cast a brick at his head.

---

[57] Saint Basil, *Prolegomena*, Nicene, 2nd Ser., Logos Research Systems, Inc., 1997.
[58] Letter lxv; Rousseau, p. 272.

Another close friend of Saint Basil was Saint Amphilochios, Bishop of Iconium, and a cousin of Saint Gregory the Theologian. He fully defended the divinity of the Holy Spirit, as did Saint Basil, against the Macedonians. An Arian council was held at Ankyra which condemned the term *homoousion*. Charges were brought up against Saint Basil's brother, Bishop Gregory of Nyssa. At Kyzikos, a semi-Arian synod blasphemed the Holy Spirit. Saint Gregory of Nyssa was prevented by illness from appearing before the council at Ankyra, and Efstathios and Demosthenes, wishing to wound Basil through his brother, convened a council at Nyssa, where Saint Gregory of Nyssa was condemned in his absence, deposed, and thereafter banished. The Orthodox held their own synod. Bishop Amphilochios presided at Iconium, where his treatise on the Holy Spirit was upheld.[59]

Saint Ephraim the Syrian Visits

Late in Saint Basil's life, Saint Ephraim the Syrian was living a life of solitude in the wilderness. He is commemorated by the holy Church on the 28th of January. Having heard the good report of the wonders of Saint Basil, he supplicated God to reveal to him of what sort was the saint. Then Ephraim was vouchsafed to behold a pillar of fire, which was rising up unto the heaven; and he heard a voice saying, "Ephraim, Ephraim, even as this pillar of fire, so is the great Basil!" Then, without the least care, Ephraim took along with him an interpreter who knew both the Greek and Syriac tongues, and went to Caesarea. It was then the Feast of the Theophany. He entered the church and observed Saint Basil clothed in splendid and costly vestments, celebrating the sacred Liturgy with great boldness. Ephraim then reproached himself and said to his interpreter, "In vain have we labored, brother, because this man, though he is found in such glory, is not as I saw."

Though Saint Basil was rightly seen wearing splendid vestments when serving at the throne of the Lord of all, yet in his private life his apparel was simple and modest; and he once said, "I have nothing of my own, but depend upon the means of my friends and relatives."[60] In an epistle to solitaries, he writes: "Cheap things ought to be used for bodily necessity; and nothing ought to be spent beyond what is necessary, or for mere extravagance; this is a misuse of our property."[61]

Unnecessary abundance gives the appearance of covetousness, and covetousness is condemned as idolatry. The holy hierarch, having been informed in the Spirit of these words which were uttered by Saint Ephraim, called one of his deacons to him, and instructed him, "Go to the western door

---

[59] *Prolegomena*, op. cit.
[60] Letter xxxvi.
[61] Letter xxii.

of the church, and thou shalt see two monks standing there: the one is beardless, tall, and thin; and the other has a black beard. Address the beardless monk, saying, 'Thou art to come to the holy bema; for thy father, the archbishop, calls thee.'" Thereupon, the deacon went; and with force he managed to make his way through the multitude. He announced the words of Saint Basil to the righteous Ephraim who, through the interpreter, answered, "Thou art in error, brother, because we are strangers and unknown. How then does the archbishop know us?" Unable to answer, the deacon retreated to the archbishop. He related the words of Saint Ephraim to the sacred hierarch, who again sent him forth, instructing him, "Go and say, 'Lord Ephraim, come into the holy bema, because the archbishop calls thee.'" Therefore, the deacon went a second time. Greeting Ephraim with a prostration, he reported the message of the hierarch to the venerable monk. In turn, the righteous Ephraim made a prostration to the deacon, declaring, "Truly, the great Basil is a pillar of fire, but I beseech him that I may speak alone with him in the sacristy." When Saint Basil finished celebrating the divine Liturgy, he summoned Saint Ephraim. After he greeted him with a holy kiss, he conversed with the desert father on spiritual matters and divine purposes and design. He then encouraged Ephraim that if there were any hidden matter in his heart to tell him of it.

The righteous Ephraim spoke through the interpreter, saying, "I ask one favor of thy prelacy, slave of God." The saint interjected, "Whatever thou desirest, ask; for I am greatly obliged to thee on account of thy labor, which thou didst endeavor to undertake for the sake of my lowliness." Saint Ephraim continued, "I know, holy master, that if thou shouldest make supplication for something to God, He would bestow it. Well, I desire that thou shouldest supplicate that I might speak Greek, for I do not at all know this language of yours." The saint confessed, "Thy request, holy father and leader of the desert, is beyond my power. But inasmuch as thou dost ask this with faith, let us both entreat God, even as that One is able to make thy desire a reality; for even the Prophet David uttered, 'The will of them that fear Him shall He do, and their supplication shall He hear, and He shall save them [Ps. 144:20].'" After Saint Basil recited this, he stood together with Saint Ephraim for a long while in entreaty. And when they finished their prayer, the saint cried with a loud voice, "The grace of the Holy Spirit be with thee, and speak Greek!" Straightway, as the saint uttered this command—O the wonder!—Saint Ephraim opened his mouth, and was speaking Greek, even as Saint Basil and the Christians of that place. Afterward, they say that the holy hierarch ordained the venerable Ephraim to the diaconate, and his translator to the priesthood. Now Saint Ephraim remained with the saint for three days and greatly profited by his teaching. Afterward, he departed again for the wilderness, glorifying and blessing God. But let us recount another marvel of Saint Basil.

The Arian Madness and Seizure of the Cathedral

Saint Basil and monks under him were still harassed by the Arians. Archbishop Basil wrote to the monks: "In my judgment, the war that is waged against us by our fellow countrymen is the hardest to bear, because against open and declared enemies it is easy to defend ourselves, while now we are necessarily at the mercy of those who are associated with us, and are thus exposed to continual danger. This has been your case. Our fathers were persecuted, but by idolaters....The persecutors, who have lately appeared, hate us no less than they, but, to the deceiving of many, they put forward the name of Christ, that the persecuted may be robbed of all comfort from its confession, because the majority of the simpler folk, while admitting that we are being wronged, are unwilling to reckon our death for the truth's sake to be martyrdom. I am therefore persuaded that the reward in store for you from the righteous Judge is yet greater than that bestowed on those former martyrs. They indeed both had the public praise of men, and received the reward of God; to you, though your good deeds are not less, no honors are given by the people. It is only fair that the requital in store for you in the world to come should be far greater....I exhort you, therefore, not to faint in your afflictions, but to be revived by God's love, and to add daily to your zeal, knowing that in you ought to be preserved that remnant of true religion which the Lord will find when He comes on the earth....If traitors have arisen from among the very clergy themselves, let not this undermine your confidence in God. We are saved not by names, but by mind and purpose, and genuine love toward our Creator....Remember that it is not the multitude who are being saved, but the elect of God....If but one be saved, like Lot at Sodom, he ought to abide in right judgment, keeping his hope in Christ unshaken, for the Lord will not forsake His holy ones. Salute all the brethren in Christ from me. Pray earnestly for my miserable soul."[62]

During the time the Emperor Valens reigned in Constantinople, Arian-minded bishops and priests of the Nicaean diocese came to him, that he might vouchsafe to them the deliverance of the cathedral into their hands. They intended to conduct their services therein, after driving out the Orthodox hierarch. Valens was of one mind with them and agreed to the takeover. Straightway, after he sent forth soldiers, he drove out the archbishop of the Christians and determined that this holy temple should be occupied by Arians. The Orthodox Christians of Nicaea learned of this seizure and took recourse

---

[62] Letter cclvii.

in Saint Basil. They besought him to mediate on their behalf before the emperor and change his evil opinion.

To the holy bishops of the west, he explained the anguishing state of affairs wherein he found himself, especially because of the heresy of Arius: "Our distresses are notorious....The doctrines of the Fathers are despised; apostolic traditions are set at nought; the devices of innovators are in vogue in the Churches; now men are rather contrivers of cunning systems than theologians; the wisdom of this world wins the highest prizes and has rejected the glory of the Cross. Shepherds are banished, and in their places are introduced grievous wolves, harrying the flock of Christ....The elders lament when they compare the present with the past. The younger are yet more to be extended compassion, for they do not know of what they have been deprived."[63]

Therefore, the saint took up their cause and that of the Church, and repaired to the imperial city. When he visited with the emperor, he brought to his remembrance these words, "O emperor, the Prophet David saith, 'The king's honor loveth judgment [Ps. 98:3].' Why hast thy monarchy set at variance righteous judgment and cast out the Orthodox from the church given to them by their holy fathers, so as to deliver it up to the heretical Arians?" The emperor protested, "Again art thou turning out insults, Basil? It is not fitting for thee to utter such words." But the saint maintained, "On account of righteousness, it is fitting to die, O emperor." Then the emperor decided, "Go thyself alone to Nicaea, and judge with righteousness even the two factions. Behold, however, do not do whatever is the will of thy people." The saint stated, "Give to me the authority to judge, O emperor, and whenever thou shouldest hear that I acted unfairly on behalf of the Christians, slay me."

The saint, having received the authority from the emperor, went to Nicaea, where he called together all the Orthodox and the Arians. And he spoke to them these words, "Behold, I have come according to the command of the emperor. Well, then, this is what we shall do. Let us close the church, O you Orthodox and Arians. Afterward, the Arians shall offer up prayer first. And if the church should open, lay hold of it. But if it shall not open, then we shall offer prayer. And if through our own entreaty the church should open, then it remains to us. If on the other hand it should stay closed, it is yours." This judgment pleased all as righteous and blessed. Thereupon, both parties went to the doors of the church and affixed their own seals. After the church was secured, the Arians assembled; and for three days they chanted entreaties and petitions that the church might open to them. However, Christ did not hearken to the supplications of those who insult Him. The saint then said to

---

[63] Letter xc.

them, "And now let us offer up prayer." The saint then called to himself the Orthodox Christians, and with them they proceeded to the Church of Saint Diomedes the Great-martyr, which was nearby the cathedral. After he finished serving a vigil there, in the morning he went with the whole multitude to the doors of the cathedral, with the Arians following behind. Saint Basil made the sign of the Cross thrice with his hands over the doors, and exclaimed, "Blessed be the God of the Christians to the ages of ages!" Straightway—O the wonder!—the bars broke in pieces and the doors opened. The saint then entered the church with the whole multitude of Christians, and celebrated the divine Liturgy. Afterward, when he blessed the people, he delivered the church into the hands of the Orthodox Christians. The date was the 19th of January. Yet not only were the Orthodox Christians gladdened during that day on account of gaining back their church, but also many from among the Arians, after they beheld the miracle of the saint, returned to the Orthodox Faith and anathematized their heresy. Though there are many other wondrous occurrences to report, let this account have an end, so as to check it from being too lengthy. Let us close our narration by revealing those edifying events just prior to Saint Basil's blessed repose.

A Widow's Repentance

A certain widow, who had surpassed the other women of Caesarea with regard to her wealth and nobility, had come to enslave herself in gluttony and in profligacy, being enthralled in defiling carnal passions and squandering her fortune. At length, unsettled and shaking when she brought to mind everlasting torments, she resolved to go before the saint in order to confess the morass of her sins. But the enemy of the salvation of man, the devil, suggested to her thoughts of how intolerable her shame would be in confessing her deeds. Thus, he hindered her from coming to repentance by means of a thorough confession. Though the devil may have postponed her good intention, by the grace and mercy of God she did not abandon her decision to change her life. What then did she think to do? She wrote down upon a paper her every sin. At the end of her listing, she recorded one deadly sin; and then she sealed the letter appropriately. Then, while Saint Basil was on his way to church, she intercepted him and cast the sealed letter before his feet. With tears, she cried aloud, "Have mercy on me, O saint of God, who am the most sinful of all the people!" Standing still, the saint asked her the cause for such a flow of tears. She replied, "Holy master, I have written all my sins in this letter. I beseech thy holiness not to open it, but only through thy prayer thou mayest blot out my sins." The saint took the letter and looked up to heaven, praying thus, "It is Thy work, O Master and Lord, to forgive the sins of this Thy handmaid; for Thou, the only sinless One, art good and the lover of man, and didst bear the sins of the people."

After making this entreaty, the saint then entered the church and began to celebrate the divine Liturgy while holding the letter. After the dismissal, he summoned that woman who gave him the letter. "Hearken, woman, for no one is able to forgive sins, save God alone," the archbishop told her. "I did hear, holy master, and for this reason I besought thee to intercede with God for the forgiveness of my sins," said she. Then the woman broke the seal and unrolled the paper. And—O the wonder!—she found it unwritten upon, except for that last grievous sin she had penned. Seeing this one had remained, she became fainthearted and beat her breast with her hands. Falling at the feet of the saint, she held the letter and implored him, "Have mercy on me, O saint of the Most High God, even as my other sins were blotted out through thy holy prayers, in like manner entreat God to wipe out this lawless deed of mine." The saint, weeping, advised, "Arise, O woman, because I also am a sinful man, and I too have need of forgiveness. Go into the desert, and seek a certain great ascetic named Ephraim. When he offers up entreaty to God, He will blot out thy sin."

The woman, therefore, having received the blessing of the saint as a good fellow traveler, arrived in the desert and found the righteous Ephraim. Falling at his feet, she cast forth the paper and said, "The Archbishop of Caesarea, Basil the Great, sent me to thee, in order that after thou shouldest offer prayer to God that He might blot out my deadly sin. Therefore, do not esteem my request lightly, O holy father. Do thou entreat God to forgive also this lawless deed of mine." After he had given her a patient hearing, he counseled, "No, child, because that same one who besought God from Whom thou didst receive forgiveness of many sins is able to supplicate on thy behalf for even this one. Go, therefore, my child, and do not stop, to the end that thou mightest overtake him while he lives; otherwise by the time thou returnest, thou shouldest find him dead." As soon as she heard these words, she took her leave from him and sped off. But as she entered Caesarea, she met the precious relics of the saint being escorted by a multitude proceeding to the place of burial.

Straightway, the woman began to shout and cry out mournfully, "Woe is me, O slave of God! Didst thou send me out into the wilderness on this account, that thou mightest repose without annoyance from me? Thou didst send me forth to the righteous Ephraim; and behold, I returned unsuccessful. May God see this, and judge between me and thee; for even though thou wast able to have wrought the forgiveness of my transgression, thou didst send me off to another." After disclosing this, she cast the letter upon the bier of the saint and recounted her story before all the crowd. Now one of the clergy took up the letter, because he desired to know what was that great lawless deed, but he found the paper to be utterly blank. Then he cried out with a loud voice to the woman, announcing, "O woman, there is nothing written anywhere on the paper! Why art thou troubled? Dost thou not recognize the loving-kindness of God?" The woman laid hold of the letter; and acknowledging the compassion of God upon her, and the great help of the servant of God, she thanked Saint Basil and Saint Ephraim. Henceforth, she conducted the rest of her life in a prudent, chaste, and God-pleasing manner, until her repose in the Lord. However, it is fitting that we narrate one other extraordinary wonder, which took place at the end of the saint's earthly sojourn.

The Physician Joseph and the Repose of the Saint

There was in Caesarea a certain Jew by the name of Joseph. He was most excellent in the science of medicine and was quite wealthy. This physician studied the medical arts thoroughly and learned the prognostic techniques of Hippocrates. He could diagnose and determine, by the heartbeat and pulse alone, whether a patient might live or die. He was accurate to within three days. Saint Basil, foreknowing Joseph's subsequent repentance, loved him and ofttimes conversed with him about the Faith of the Christians. However, the Christians, observing that the saint spoke at length with the Jew regularly, were scandalized. But the saint, as we said, foreseeing that in the future he would become a Christian, ceased not instructing him to accept holy illumination in Baptism and to believe in the Christ. However, up until that time, Joseph remained unrepentant, and kept the sacrilegious religion of the Jewish elders. When it pleased God to turn him about, what did He manage by His providence?

Inasmuch as the saint foresaw the hour of his own death, he sent forth and called the Jew with the pretext that he required his medical assistance. When he arrived, Saint Basil asked, "What sayest thou, Joseph? When shall I die?" After checking the hierarch's heartbeat and pulse, he diagnosed that his patient had come to the end. "Today, master," he stated, "thou shalt die, by the setting of the sun." The saint asserted, "Thou dost not know." Joseph maintained, "Believe me, master. Today, two suns are about to set: thou, the brilliant lamp of Caesarea, and the perceptible sun." The saint then posed this question, "And if I do not die until midnight, what wilt thou do?" He answered, "It is not possible for this to happen. Only as long as thou hast voice, command whatever thou desirest for thy Church and thine own affairs, because thou shalt not last to the office of Vespers." The saint said, "But if I should live until the morning, what wouldest thou do?" The physician averred, "If thy holiness should live until tomorrow, may I die!" The saint exclaimed, "Well hast thou spoken. May thou diest to sin and live in Christ." The Jew conceded, "Thou knowest, O master, that I do desire to be baptized.

But it is not feasible that thy holiness shall live, because it is impossible for the nature of man to exceed the bounds of the laws of medical science."

After the Jew uttered this and other views, he also declared with an oath this serious wager: that if the holy hierarch should live until tomorrow, he would be baptized with all of his family. As the Jew departed, the saint besought God that he might live until tomorrow: first, in order that the aforementioned widow might meet his relics before interment; and second, that the Jew might be baptized. Now the all-good God hearkened to his soul-saving entreaties. Thus the saint sent for the doctor very early that next morning. He, in disbelief, came thinking to find the saint departed. But when he beheld the venerable Basil alive, he stood still in astonishment, and fell before the feet of the saint, proclaiming, "Great is the God of the Christians! There is no other God than He. I believe in Him. Bless me, holy master, to receive Baptism today." The saint then offered, "I wish to baptize thee and all thy family."

The Jew then approached the saint, taking his pulse and checking his heartbeat, and observed his veins were lifeless, and commented, "Thy powers, master, are waning, and thy constitution is completely without strength." He replied, "We have the Creator of nature Who is empowering us." Assuring him thus, the archbishop arose and walked to the holy church, where he baptized the physician and all of his family, giving Joseph the name of John. After he baptized him and communicated the immaculate Mysteries to him, the saint requested something to eat. He sat at table, and was teaching John and those Christians who were present. Then about the tenth hour of the day, the saint asked the physician, "When shall I die, Sir John?" And he answered, "Whenever thou wilt determine, holy master." As the physician answered, the saint surrendered his honorable soul, replete with light, into the hands of God. John then fell at his feet, weeping and wailing, "I believe, O slave of God, that if thou wert not willing, not even now wouldest thou have died." It was the 1st of January, in the year 379. His last words were, "Into Thy hands I will commit my spirit; Thou hast redeemed me, O Lord God of truth [Ps. 30:5]."

Since it was evening, the relics of the saint remained unburied. The next day the Christians gathered, the priests and all the lay people—crying and mourning at the calamity of being deprived of their archbishop, shepherd, and common father, the brilliant lamp of the habitable world—and buried his august relics in a notable place. Saint Gregory the Theologian, who was found at Arianzos at the time, learned of his friend's repose and wrote a funeral oration. Within a few days, he arrived and read it with tears at the tomb. Saint Basil, our holy father among the saints, was only forty-nine years old when he fell asleep in the Lord, after serving five years in the episcopal office.

Saint Basil's austere asceticism, his meager fare, his chronic liver ailment, and the burden of shepherding the flock, all contributed to his failing health. He wrote to his dear friend and disciple, Saint Amphilochios, who had sent him some food as a gift: "There is no munching for me at my time of life, for my teeth have long ago been worn away by time and bad health."[64] In 371, he wrote to his brother Gregory: "I might have prayed to have a heart of stone, so as neither to remember the past, nor to feel the present; so as to bear every blow, like cattle, with bowed head....I have entered on a life which is wearing out my strength, and is so far beyond my powers that it is injuring even my soul."[65] To another he wrote: "We should pray that our souls may be made insensible to the pain of our troubles, that we be not put under unendurable agony."[66] Yet it was he who said, "He who subjects himself to his neighbor in love can never be humiliated."[67]

Saint Basil had only a single worn-out garment, and ate almost nothing but bread, salt, and herbs. In 375, his health worsened, and he wrote: "I was so ill that I had lost all hope of life. It is impossible for me to enumerate all my painful symptoms, my weakness, the violence of my attacks of fever, and my bad health in general. One point only may be selected. I have now completed the time of my sojourn in this miserable and painful life."[68] He gave all glory to God, and confessed, "So far, I have sustained every assault unmoved. This has come about by the mercy of God, which supplies to me the aid of the Spirit and strengthens my weakness through Him."[69]

The Funeral Oration and the Saint's Relics

Saint Gregory lauds his friend in a funeral oration, saying, "After he (Basil) finished his course, and kept the Faith [cf. 2 Tim. 4:7], he longed to depart." He says that "Saint Basil, when he was almost dead, and breathless, and had lost the greater part of his powers, grew stronger in his last words, so as to depart with the utterances of piety on his lips. He gave religious instructions and injunctions for the benefit of those present. It was reported that he lay, drawing his last breath, and was awaited by the choir above, upon which he had long fixed his gaze. The whole city poured around him, unable to endure the loss of their shepherd. Their suffering drove them to distraction. All were eager, if it were possible, to add to the archbishop's life a portion

---

[64] Letter ccxxxii.
[65] Letter lviii.
[66] Letter xxxiv.
[67] Letter lxv.
[68] Letter cxcviii.
[69] Letter lxxix.

of their own. They were defeated, for he had to give proof that he too was mortal. When he spoke his very last words, 'Into Thy hands I will commit my spirit [Ps. 30:5],' he joyfully resigned his soul to the care of the angels who bore him aloft."

Saint Gregory continues, saying, "As the saint was being carried out, lifted high by the hands of holy men, all were eager, some to seize the hem of his garment, others only just to touch the shadow, or the bier which bore his holy relics, others to draw near to those carrying it, only to enjoy the sight, as if even this were beneficial." Squares, porticoes, houses of two and three stories were packed with people escorting him, preceding, following, accompanying, and treading upon one another: tens of thousands of every race and age, a sight unknown before that day. Psalmody was overborne by lamentation. "Our own people," he says, "vied with strangers, Jews, Greek pagans, and foreigners, and they with us, for a greater share in the benefit, by means of a more abundant lamentation. To close my story, the calamity ended in danger; many souls departed along with him, from the violence of the pushing and confusion, who have been thought happy in their end, departing together with him as 'funeral victims,' as perhaps some fervid orator might call them."

The saint's precious relics finally escaped from those who would seize him, and he was consigned to the tomb of his fathers, the high priest being added to the priests. "And now," adds Saint Gregory, "he is in the heavens, where, if I mistake not, he is offering sacrifices for us, and praying for the people; for though he has left us, he has not entirely left us....It seems to me also that widows should praise their protector, orphans their father, the poor their friend, strangers their host, brothers the man of brotherly love, the sick their physician—whatever be their sickness and the healing they need—the healthy the preserver of health, and all men him who made himself all things to all that he might gain the majority, if not all."

On the 1ˢᵗ of January, the holy Church commemorates the holy Martyr THEODOTOS, who was beheaded by the sword.

On the 1ˢᵗ of January, the holy Church commemorates Saint GREGORY, Bishop of Nazianzos.[70]

Gregory, the man of God, faithful servant and steward of the mysteries of God, was the father, according to the flesh, of Saint Gregory the Theologian. He reposed in his one hundredth year, and his wife, Saint Nonna,

[70] A complete service to Saint Gregory, Bishop of Nazianzos, was composed by Father Gerasimos Mikrayiannanites.

commemorated by the holy Church on the 5th of August, scion of an ancient Christian family, survived him. Saint Gregory the younger, not ashamed of the elder's origin, describes his father as springing from a stock unrenowned, an alien shoot, and not well suited for piety.[71] His son describes him thus: "My father was every inch a gentleman, simple in style, an example in his life, verily a second Patriarch Abraham. He did not just appear noble, as people nowadays; for he actually was. Once, indeed, he had gone astray; but then he had become a friend of Christ, then afterwards a presbyter, the best of all presbyters."[72]

The elder Gregory originally belonged to a sect called Hypsistarians which, according to Saint Gregory of Nyssa, acknowledged that there was a God Whom they termed the Highest or Almighty, but did not admit that He is Father.[73] The syncretistic sect, with its small membership mostly confined to Cappadocia, incorporated into their belief system both oriental and Jewish elements. Though they spurned idols, sacrifices, circumcision, and every outward form of worship, which they restricted to be an inferior and spiritual work, *Saint Gregory, Bishop of Nazianzos* they observed the Jewish sabbath and levitical prohibitions of certain foods. They also reverenced fire and lights. In 325, Gregory, at about forty-five years of age, by the grace and merciful kindness of God, was converted to Orthodoxy chiefly by the prayers, influence, and example of his devout Orthodox wife Nonna.

Saint Gregory the Theologian characterized his parents' marriage as the best. For the most excellent of men and of women were so united that their marriage was a union of virtue rather than of bodies. Indeed, though

---

[71] Saint Gregory Nazianzen (the Theologian), "Oration XVIII: On the Death of His Father," *Orations*, Nicene, 2nd Ser., VII:254-269. All subsequent extracts herein were revised and edited from this source.

[72] Saint Gregory, *A Poem Concerning His Own Life*, P.G. 37.1029-1166.

[73] Saint Gregory of Nyssa, *Against Eunomius*, Book II, §6, Nicene, 2nd Ser., Vol. V.

they excelled all others, yet one could not exceed the other; because in virtue they were equally matched. He says that "she was given by God to my father, and became not only his assistant, but even his leader, drawing him on by her influence in deed and word to the highest excellence; judging it best in all other respects to be overruled by her husband according to the law of marriage, but not being ashamed, in regard of piety, even to offer herself as his teacher. Admirable indeed as was this conduct of hers, it was still more admirable that he should readily acquiesce in it."

Saint Gregory said that when his mother was brought to live in his father's house, there was no spur to piety. On account of the excess of her faith, however, she could not bear to be unequally yoked. Although she endured it with fortitude, she could not brook being but half united to Christ, because of the estrangement of him who was a part of herself, and the failure to add to the bodily union a close connection in spirit. She fell down before God night and day, entreating for the salvation of her husband with many fasts and tears. All the while she was devoted to him and influenced him in many ways—by means of reproaches, admonitions, attentions, estrangements, and above all by her own character with its ardor for piety. Little by little, there was a gradual conviction of his reason. Then, at length, he was vouchsafed a vision. Gregory the elder thought that he was singing, as he had never done before, this verse from the Psalms of David: "I was glad because of them that said unto me, 'Let us go into the house of the Lord [Ps. 121:1].'" The psalm was a strange one to him, but along with the words the desire also arose. He disclosed to Nonna his dream. As soon as she heard it, she seized the opportunity, replying that the vision would bring the greatest pleasure, if it were accompanied by its fulfillment. Thus, she urged him forward towards salvation.

Now it happened at that time that a number of Orthodox bishops were hastening through Nazianzos onward to Nicaea to oppose the Arian madness at a synod meeting. Gregory the elder then made up his mind. He yielded to the calling of God and repaired to the heralds of truth. He confessed his desire for salvation before the bishops, especially Leontios, then metropolitan of the province. After a short space of time, Gregory approached the waters of regeneration. He drew near to the laver with warm desire and bright hope. It seemed that the whole of his past life had been a preparation for the enlightenment. As he ascended out of the waters, there flashed around him a light and a glory worthy of the disposition with which he approached the gift of faith. He who officiated at the Baptism also beheld this clearly. Others also who were present witnessed the divine and paradoxical manifestation. No one could hold back the mystery. The celebrant then publicly cried that he was anointing with the Spirit his very own successor to the episcopacy!

Gregory was entrusted with the priesthood, but only after a brief interval, in order to add to his own cleansing the skill and power to cleanse others. When he was entrusted with the dignity of the priesthood, the grace was the more glorified, being really the grace of God, and not of men. He received a woodland and rustic church, since its former pastor had reposed. He was consecrated Bishop of Nazianzos. The Romans called the place Diocaesarea, which would place it in the southwestern portion of the district called Cappadocia Secunda, a subdivision of the province, just northwest of Tyana.[74] Saint Gregory the elder was conspicuous as a competent administrator, a steadfast confessor of the Faith, a sympathetic shepherd, and loving father. In his life and ministry he was seconded by his wife and followed by his three children, Gregory (commemorated on the 25th of January), Gorgonia (commemorated on the 23rd of February), and Caesarios (commemorated on the 9th of March), whose names are in the collection of the saints. Saint Gregory strived without harshness to soften the habits of his new flock, both by words of pastoral knowledge, and by setting himself before them as an example of excellent conduct. Though a late student in such matters, by meditations on the divine words, he soon gathered so much wisdom, that he became a father and teacher of Orthodoxy. He acknowledged one God worshipped in Trinity, and Three, One in essence. He did not Sabellianize as to the One, or Arianize as to the Three, either by atheistically annihilating the divinity, or by tearing asunder each hypostasis (person) by distinctions of unequal greatness or nature.

Alas! however, all did not proceed in his churches without incident. By way of background, in 359 the Arian Emperor Constantius convened a counsel at Ariminum of four hundred western bishops. Some of the council members were duped or compelled by the imperial officers to put together a creed which recognized the deity of Jesus Christ but confessed Him to be "like" the Father. They omitted saying that He was "like" Him in all points. They also declined to use the word coessential (*homoousios*). Thus, though they condemned the Arian extremists, they favored the semi-Arians. Now in about 363, another council of one hundred fifty eastern bishops assembled under court influence at Seleukeia near Antioch. They accepted the Creed of Nicaea but promoted a similar formula as the Ariminum Council. Gregory the elder, due to his simplicity, was in some way influenced to add his signature to their compromising creed, though it was well known that he was a staunch supporter of Nicene Orthodoxy. Now his actions were misunderstood and criticized by a certain zealous faction in his churches, made up mostly of

----

[74] Tyana (Turkey) 37°48′N 34°36′E.

monks—but lay people also—of his diocese. They even rallied the support of other bishops and broke communion with Gregory the elder.

Gregory the younger quickly came to his father's aid, for he knew that the issue was the interpretation of certain terms in the document, which contained somewhat ambiguous language for his guileless father. Gregory the younger kept an all-night vigil with fasting and prayer, entreating the all-good God to bring unity and oneness of mind back to the flock. Little by little, confessing the true Faith with edifying words and examples, the son persuaded the father. The son prompted his father to ask pardon for his unintentional error and to make a public confession of Faith of his Orthodoxy. The elder Gregory sought forgiveness from God for his former error. He also taught the rest of the flock, leading them back to Orthodoxy. Only on account of Gregory the elder's reverence, which he inspired, and the purity of doctrine, the storm that rose in the Church was reduced to a breeze, and the opposing faction returned to him, and the schism was healed. Thus, he brought back the entire flock to the true Faith, and to peace and harmony. All the time, his son, Gregory, accompanied and ran beside him and contributed a very great share to the toil. He was his father's partner in piety and activity, aiding him in every effort on behalf of what is good.

Gregory the elder relieved poverty as liberally as he could, readily expending not only his superfluities but also his necessities. His magnanimity was accompanied by freedom from ambition. He exhibited genuine compassion for sinners. His dress had in it nothing remarkable. He avoided equally both magnificence and sordidness. He held in check the insatiability of the stomach, but without ostentation. However, what was most excellent and characteristic of him were his simplicity and freedom from guile and resentment. He never held a grudge against those who provoked him. He was absolutely uninfluenced by anger, although in spiritual things exceedingly overcome by zeal. There were times when his enemies threatened the wheel and scourge, even while those who could administer them stood near. The danger, however, ended in being pinched on the ear, patted on the face, or buffeted on the temple. His dress and sandals were dragged off. Then when someone defended the elder Gregory against an opponent by felling the scoundrel to the ground, the bishop directed his displeasure against his eager defender, as some kind of minister of evil, and not the assailant. He even made excuses for the man who had assailed him. Indeed, so remarkable was his gentleness!

Another wonder of the saint was that he suffered from sickness and bodily pain. Once, during Pascha, his whole frame was on fire with an excessive, burning fever. His strength failed, and he was unable to eat. Sleep departed from his eyes. He was in the greatest distress and agitated by palpitations. In his mouth, the palate, and the whole upper surface were so completely and painfully ulcerated that it was difficult and dangerous for him even to swallow water. Neither the skill of physicians, nor prayers—though most earnest as they were—of his friends, nor every possible attention could alleviate the disorder. While he was in this desperate condition, his breath was short and fast. In fact, he had no perception of things present but was entirely absent. His son Gregory explains that "we were in the temple, mingling supplications with the sacred rites, and betook ourselves to the great Physician Jesus, to the power of that paschal night, and to the last succor, with the intention, shall I say, of keeping a feast, or of mourning." All the people shed tears. Voices, cries, and hymns blended with the psalmody. Gregory the younger asks, "What was the response of Him Who is the God of that night and of the sick man? A shudder comes over me as I proceed with my story." The time of the awesome Mystery arrived, when silence is kept for the solemn rites. At first, Gregory the elder moved slightly, then more decidedly. Then in a feeble and indistinct voice he called by name one of the servants who was in attendance. He bade him come, and bring his clothes, and support him with his hand. The servant came in alarm and consternation, but was glad to wait upon him. Gregory leaned upon him as upon a staff. He then imitated Moses upon the mount. He arranged his feeble hands in prayer. Then on behalf of his people, he eagerly celebrated the Mysteries, in such few words as his strength allowed but with a most perfect intention. What a miracle! He was in the sanctuary without a sanctuary, sacrificing without an altar, a priest far from the sacred rites. Yet, all were present to him in the power of the Spirit. All was recognized by him, though it remained unseen to those present. Then after uttering the customary words of thanksgiving, he blessed the people and retired to his bed. After partaking of some food, he enjoyed a restful sleep. His health then gradually recovered, on the new day of the Feast of the Resurrection, the feast of feasts. He then entered the sacred temple and resumed his life which had been preserved, with the full complement of clergy, and offered the sacrifice of thanksgiving.

There is another story told by his son. The city of Caesarea was in an uproar about the election of a bishop, since their own bishop had departed. Rival parties of the candidates vied for the illustrious position of that see. Several bishops arrived to consecrate the bishop. At last the people came to an agreement, and with the aid of a band of soldiers quartered there, they took hold of their leading citizen as the candidate of their choice. Now he was a man of excellent life, yet he was not yet sealed with holy Baptism. They compelled him to enter the Church. They begged the bishops with entreaties, mingled with violence, to ordain their nominee. Though this was not the best order, the assembly was sincere and adamant. They declared their candidate to be illustrious and religious. The bishops yielded, and baptized him. They proclaimed him and enthroned him. Once it was over, those bishops were relieved to depart. Yet later, when the bishops assembled, they held that what had taken place was invalid, and the institution was void. They pleaded violence. But Gregory the elder was not carried away by this plan of theirs but remained unaffected. He believed that if any charge were brought against the new bishop, those who had elected him were also liable to a counter-charge.

Julian the emperor came and raged against the Orthodox. He was displeased with the election and threatened both the people and the city. The emperor was also angered and exasperated at the destruction of the Temple of Fortune. He considered all these things as an encroachment of his rights. The governor of the province also was eager to turn the occasion to his own interest. He was ill-disposed to the new bishop, mostly because they held different political views. Accordingly, he sent letters to summon the consecrating bishops to invalidate the election. He even threatened them, as if by command of the emperor himself. Gregory the elder responded to the epistle, writing: "Most excellent governor, we have one Censor of all our actions, and one King. He will view this present consecration, which we have legitimately performed according to His will. In regard to any other matter, thou mayest, if thou wilt, use violence with the greatest ease against us. But no one can prevent us from vindicating the legitimacy and justice of our action in this case; unless thou shouldest make a law on this point, thou hast no right to interfere in our affairs." Though the governor was annoyed for a while, the letter excited the admiration of the recipient. In addition, it stayed the action of the emperor and delivered the city from peril. Moreover, the consecrating bishops and the city were saved from disgrace. "This," notes Saint Gregory the Theologian with well-deserved pride for his father, "was the work of the occupant of an unimportant and suffragan see. Is not a presidency of this kind far preferable to a title derived from a superior see, and a power which is based upon action rather than upon name?"

When Gregory the elder was elderly and frail, he acknowledged that it was essential for him to secure a coadjutor in his pastoral duties. The people of Nazianzos, by popular demand, prevailed, and Gregory the elder ordained his son Gregory, in 361, during the nativity of our Lord, despite the son's protestations. He was a great boon to his father, as shown in the following example. A series of disasters had befallen the people of Nazianzos in 363. A deadly cattle plague, which had devastated their herds, had been followed by a prolonged drought. Recently ripened crops had been ruined by a storm of rain and hail. The people gathered together into the church. The gentle and compassionate soul of Saint Gregory the elder was so overwhelmed by his sense of these terrible calamities that he was unable to address them. He implored his son to enter the pulpit.

By 361, Julian the Apostate (332-363) had completely and openly broken communion with the Church. Gregory the elder's son, Caesarios, still held his position as a physician at Julian's court. The emperor harbored hopes of perverting Caesarios' Orthodox Faith. His attendance at court was a source of concern to both his father and brother, so that Gregory remonstrated with him in a loving letter. The pending danger feared by Caesarios' father and brother was kept from Nonna. Caesarios, however, soon made up his mind to resign and retire. Therefore, when Julian departed for his Persian campaign, Caesarios took the opportunity to withdraw from court. Now Julian had no intention of leaving the Orthodox to hold sway in Nazianzos. The governor of the province was sent with a formidable armed escort to demand possession of the Church. Gregory the elder, supported by his son and by the congregation, fearlessly rejected the imperial order. The governor quickly calculated that there was a powerful resistance, which necessitated his peaceful withdrawal. The governor never again took up that commission. Notwithstanding, both father and son collided with Julian while the latter passed through Cappadocia on his way to Persia. The holy Gregorys, father and son, together with the faithful, made a stout stand against imperial tyranny. By God's merciful and just providence, they averted a bloodbath, and Julian was diverted from assailing the Church in that province when he was slain in his expedition.

When the Bishop of Caesarea and Metropolitan of Cappadocia, Evsevios, reposed, the city was in an uproar. Saint Gregory the elder exerted his influence, together with his son, to secure the elevation of Saint Basil to this important see. Yet Saint Basil was a target of envy among the rival factions. But Saint Gregory the elder's sole aim was the advantage of the Church and the common salvation. The father and son addressed one letter to the people of Caesarea, and another to the provincial synod. Gregory the elder wrote, gave advice, and strived to unite the people and the clergy. Whether in the sanctuary or not, he gave his testimony, his decision, and his vote. At last, since it was needful that the consecration should be canonical, and there was lacking one of the proper number of bishops for the proclamation, Gregory the elder tore himself from his couch, exhausted and wasted as he was by advanced age and disease. He coped and manfully brought himself, or rather was borne, into the city, with his body scarcely breathing. He put aside his own personal safety and health, persuaded that, if anything should befall him, this devotion would be a noble winding-sheet. He went to the metropolis just in time. And God wrought wonderfully for him also. Gregory the elder received strength from his toil and new life from his zeal. He even

presided at the function, took his place, and enthroned Basil in 370. He then
looked to return home. Now his colleagues were annoyed both at the shame
of being overcome, and at the public influence of that great old man. In fact,
their annoyance was not hidden but was shown in their abuse of him. Yet
Gregory was superior to this, finding in modestly a most powerful ally. He
would not be vanquished by the tongue, but prevailed upon them by his
forbearance. Little by little, their irritation was exchanged for admiration.
They fell at his feet and begged his forgiveness, ashamed at their unbecoming
conduct and thoughts. The elder then returned home, no longer needing to be
borne about on a bier.

Later when Emperor Valens divided the civil province of Cappadocia
into two, a number of clergy also wished to divide the diocese, with one
metropolis at Caesarea and the other at Tyana. After Bishop Anthimos
claimed to be metropolitan of the new province, Saint Basil refused Anthimos'
title and claims. Saint Basil, wishing to strengthen his diocese, created new
bishoprics in the disputed province. In the remote village of Sasima, Basil
appointed his friend Gregory the younger, who was indignant to receive this
post. Nonetheless, Gregory yielded to the diligent requests of his father, and
submitted to Archbishop Basil. In the meantime, Anthimos stationed troops
at Sasima which prevented Gregory from entering peaceably into his see.
Therefore, at his father's behest, he remained in Nazianzos and continued his
services as coadjutor bishop. Eventually the contention regarding the
metropolitanate of Tyana was settled.

Saint Gregory also makes mention that his father left behind a temple,
which he reared for God and his flock. In fact, the people contributed little
to its construction, since the elder used his private means. The temple is
described as being graced with eight equilaterals, and is raised aloft by the
beauty of two stories of pillars and porticoes. It was surrounded by jutting
equiangular ambulatories of the most brilliant material, with a wide area in the
midst. Its doors and vestibules shed around it the luster of their gracefulness,
and offer from a distance their welcome to those approaching. The stonework
was perfectly fitted, both the marble in the bases and capitals which cover the
corners. There were various and multicolored friezes, projecting and inlaid,
from the foundation to the roof. Gregory the elder even provided a priest for
the sacred precinct at his own expense.

In 374, Gregory the elder reposed. His son was released from the
charge of his father's diocese. Saint Gregory the Theologian spoke a
panegyric at his father's funeral. Saint Gregory's flock was desolate and
downcast at the repose of their holy shepherd, despairing of ever obtaining
another wise pastor. Out of respect to his father, Gregory the younger
remained to administer the diocese for only a year, until the appointment of

another bishop could be secured. Albeit Saint Gregory of Nazianzos had been a wild olive tree that was grafted into a good olive tree, he became a mighty and celebrated champion of the Faith. He reposed in peace, in the fullness of days.

**On the 1ˢᵗ of January, the holy Church commemorates
our venerable Father THEODOSIOS,
Hegumen of Trigleia in Bithynia, who reposed in peace.**

**On the 1ˢᵗ of January, the holy Church commemorates
the holy New-martyr PETER of Tripoli of the Peloponnesos,
who suffered martyrdom by hanging
at Odemesion (Temisi) of Asia Minor (1776).**

Through the intercessions of Thy Saints,
O Christ God, have mercy on us. Amen.

Saint Basil the Great

On the 2nd of January, the holy Church commemorates
our holy father among the saints, SILVESTER, Pope of Rome.[1]

Saint Silvester

Silvester, our blessed father, was from the great city of Rome, conspicuous for its zeal and fame. His father was Rufinus, a Roman, and his mother was Justa, who was just in name and in deed. In his youth, Silvester became the disciple of a certain priest-monk, named Kyrion,[2] a God-loving and wise man, who was Orthodox in his beliefs. The blessed Silvester learned from him how to preserve correctly the doctrines of the Faith. Silvester also imitated the virtues of his teacher, advancing in piety and preaching the truth. Any danger that might ensue from these activities did not instill fear in the stout-hearted Silvester. Any hostile reaction on the part of the Greek pagans was a matter of complete indifference to him. He also occupied himself with offering abundant hospitality toward others, receiving many strangers and foreigners who came to his city.

On one occasion, among the foreigners he was attending, there was a priest-monk. His name was Father Timothy, recently come from Antioch, who was as another apostle preaching Christ in every quarter. The divine Silvester did not cower at the prospect of persecution, as his fellow Christians, so he received the Gospel preacher into his household. Silvester took him in with joy, generously offering hospitality for one year and three months. This gave Father Timothy the opportunity to proclaim the sacred Gospel to all of Rome, so that many converted to godliness. For this reason, the impious pagans imprisoned the priest-monk, punishing him for a long time with diverse tortures. Afterward, Father Timothy gained the crown of martyrdom when they severed his head. The divine Silvester witnessed his

---

[1] The Life of this saint was taken from *Neon Paradeison*, with the exception of the section regarding the Baptism of Constantine the Great. The text of a poem by John Zonaras to this saint is extant in the Athonite monasteries of the Great Lavra and Iveron, which begins, "The august and God-seeing apostles...." The Life of Saint Silvester is also found at the Great Lavra, which begins, "Eusebius Pamphili...."

[2] Kyrion, variously given as Quirinus or Cyrinus.

sufferings and martyrdom. When deep night fell, Silvester came and transferred the sacred relics to his own house, where they were interred. At length, a certain wealthy lady donated a huge sum to the holy Miltiades,[3] then archbishop, with which the Christians erected a church. The relics of Hieromartyr Timothy were then reverently and honorably placed therein, as was meet. A vigil was conducted that night with all the clergy and archbishop in attendance.

The prefect, Tarquin, learned of these events and ordered that Silvester be taken into custody and made to stand before him. Tarquin began his inquiry by threatening Silvester and saying, "Do thou either offer sacrifice to the gods, or I shall subject thee to bitter torments." The holy Silvester, foreseeing by the Holy Spirit the speedy death of the prefect, prophesied to him with those words from the Gospel: "'This night they demand thy soul from thee [Lk. 12:20]'; that is to say, this very night thou art about to give up the spirit that thou mightest receive thy recompense, for thou hast murdered the righteous unjustly." The prefect was maddened by this reply and ordered that Silvester be kept in prison and fettered with heavy chains. After this took place, Tarquin returned to his house. As he was sitting at table and eating a piece of fish, a bone became lodged in his throat. He could neither swallow it nor spit it out. Neither the physicians nor his frantic invocation of his gods were able to deliver him from choking. That bad man suffered miserably from dinner time until midnight, and then he gave up his soul, even as the holy man had predicted. The pious were relieved and gave thanks to God, but the impious were stricken with fear, in terror that they might similarly be punished. They removed Silvester from prison and fell before his feet, entreating him not to be angered with them for the dishonor they rendered him.

The blessed Silvester was exceedingly filled with God's grace, so that not only the pious but even the idolaters revered and loved him on account of his virtue. When Silvester became thirty years of age, Pope Miltiades ordained him to the office of Hierodeacon. The pope deemed his candidate humble, noble-minded, and adorned with heavenly ethics. Not only in his practises, but also in his contemplative style, Silvester was as an angel. All of his achievements were perfect. He shone forth as a flame in the darkness, turning many unbelievers to right belief. On account of his divine conduct of life, upon the repose of Saint Miltiades, the pious assembled and promoted Silvester as their candidate for Archbishop of Rome. All were concurring that Father Silvester was humble-minded, temperate, and moderate. Those who wished to press for their own candidate could only find one drawback for

---

[3] Miltiades or Melchiades, Pope of Rome (2nd of July, 310 until the 10th of June, 314).

electing Silvester to the dignity, and that was his young age. Silvester himself was also trying to shun the lofty office. Despite his strenuous opposition to the elevation, the will of the people prevailed, and he was elected. Thus, this light of his could not be hidden, even as a city situated on the top of a mountain cannot be hid. As a lamp, he was put upon the lampstand that he might give light to all those in the house [cf. Mt. 5:14, 15].

After Pope Silvester came to the throne of the chief of the apostles, Peter, he diligently and carefully applied himself to emulate that disciple's zeal and ardor, shepherding the rational sheep in the saving laws, that is, the commandments of the Lord, that he might keep the Church's true, upright, and holy doctrines. The holy Silvester, first among hierarchs, put in writing laws pertaining to the clergy in all ecclesiastic ranks. They were no longer to engage in secular businesses and material concerns. Their first occupation was prayer. He also enjoined no fasting on Saturday throughout the year, as commonly kept in the western countries. The only exception was that of Holy and Great Saturday, when our Lord kept the sabbath in the tomb. Now the pagan Romans at that time were assigning and calling the first day of the week as the day of the Sun, the second as the day of the Moon, the third as the day of Mars (Ares), the fourth as the day of Mercury (Hermes), the fifth as the day of Jupiter (Dios or Zeus), the sixth as the day of Venus (Aphrodite), and Saturday as the day of Saturn (Cronus). The pope loathed the deities who were being honored thus, so he named their Sunday as "the Lord's day" in honor of Jesus' resurrection.

There was in Rome at that time, beneath a hill, then known as the Tarpeian Rock, where they had built the Temple of Jupiter Capitolinus,[4] one very deep cave. It was the den of a huge and terrifying dragon. This creature was fed every month, when sorcerers and diviners brought both men and women as prey. They would pronounce demonic incantations before the cave. The serpent would then emerge from the cave, but never entirely exited. From its vile and malodorous breath alone, the air was being contaminated and causing death in the city. Mostly small children were affected by the creature's poisonous exhalations. During the term of Pope Silvester, the idolaters approached him and said, "Do thou enter into the cave and, by the power of thy God, make the dragon cease coming forth and destroying the people. Depend on it, we shall then believe that thy God is the Almighty." The saint was moved to compassion and gathered together all the faithful, both layfolk and those in holy orders. He announced the proposal of the pagans and then exhorted the flock, saying, "Let us keep a fast for three days, praying and entreating God to show forth His wonders that His most holy and

---

[4] This temple was build ca. 6th C. B.C., and rebuilt ca. 1st C. B.C.

saving name might be glorified." Then, on the third day, there appeared, while the hierarch slept, the holy Apostle Peter, who said to him, "Do thou take with thee Theodore and Dionysius, the priests, and also Honoratus and Romanus, the deacons, and liturgize at the entrance of the cave. After the divine mystagogy, take a strong chain and descend to the dragon's lair, until thou shouldest come to an iron door. Close it well and pass the chain through the iron rings. Bind the creature invoking the name of the Master Christ, uttering these words: 'This gate is not to be opened until the dreadful day of the judgment.'" The divine Silvester carried out the apostle's instructions. Thus, the city was delivered from that death-bearing creature. Moreover, those who previously worshipped the demons became initiates of the Holy Trinity. Many idolaters were baptized, both those who were involved in serving that monster and others who heard that the pope had emerged unharmed and put an end to the terror.

When Maxentius (306-312) assumed the imperial title and was proclaimed in 306 by the praetorian guard and the people of Rome, he avoided the title of augustus, but assumed it in 307. After he defeated Severus, Maxentius controlled Italy and Africa. His sister Fausta had married Constantine, but the alliance between the brothers-in-law broke down. At first Maxentius attempted to gain popular support with religious toleration. As time went on, Maxentius became more arbitrary and tyrannical. He commanded that all who were Christians were to deny their Christ and make offerings to the idols. If they refused, they would be subjected to diverse tortures. It was at that time that many Christians suffered martyrdom, but others fled and hid in the mountains from the tyrant's madness. Among the refugees were priests and other clergy who served the needs of the concealed Christians. It was also at that time that Silvester gave place to wrath. He departed and went into hiding, not because he was afraid of death, but rather that he might keep and preserve his flock. Domitus Alexander revolted and proclaimed himself augustus. Then in 310, Constantine I the Great annexed Spain. In 312, Constantine anticipated Licinius and invaded Italy. Maxentius was defeated and slain at the battle of the Milvian bridge over the river Tiber in Rome on the 28th day of October, in the year 312. Consequently, Constantine was sole emperor in the west and consolidated the position of Christianity. Hence it was at that time that the all-good and all-merciful God sent forth the great Constantine to deliver His flock. He came from the west with his army and vanquished the foe by the power of the Cross. This sign had been placed on his troops' shields and standards, before he went against Maxentius. The persecutor of the Christians was overcome when he fell into the Tiber and drowned.

The great Constantine (306-337) entered Rome, where he was proclaimed by the senate and army as autocrat. It was then that the God-promoted Emperor Constantine preached the life-creating Cross and had it displayed at the chief points of the city. Christians in prison were released, and exiles were recalled. A law was promulgated, declaring the Christians to be free to follow the worship of Christ. Further to this, he established other laws to the glory of God, thereby strengthening our holy and pious Faith. Blasphemy against Christ was prohibited. No one was permitted to harass a Christian. Those who troubled them were to be punished severely and have all their goods confiscated. These and many other laws were enacted to protect the Christians. With these laws in place, the concealed Christians began returning to the city. The clergy and the blessed Silvester came down from Mount Sirapte, having been invited by the emperor. Constantine requested this audience, because he had been vouchsafed a vision. The holy Apostles Peter and Paul bade him to call forth Hierarch Silvester.

The saint visited with the emperor and began teaching him the Mysteries of the Orthodox Faith of the Christ. The blessed Constantine readily believed all that the bishop imparted. He bowed his head and received the saint's blessing. Silvester uttered a prayer over Constantine, making him a catechumen. It was about that time that Constantine was being scourged by the disease of leprosy. Constantine wished to postpone Baptism, because he desired to receive the Mystery in the Jordan, where the Lord was baptized.[5]

---

[5] This is one account which is frequently found and said to be the earliest of the *Acts* of Silvester. Some of the many who repeat it are Ephraim, Kedrenos, and Zonaras. Malalas was familiar with the account in the 6th C. It is not known when the Latin *Acts* of Silvester, describing his miracles and the Baptism of Constantine, was translated into Greek. Theophanes the Confessor (d. 845) mentions the Baptism. George Hamartolos (mid-9th C.) used the *Acts*.

The following account is mainly from the Byzantine historian Michael Glycas [*Chronicle (Annals)*, ed. Bekker, (Bonn, 1836), pp. 461, 462; *P.G.* 158:1866]. "When Constantine was fighting against Maxentius, after he had seen the sign of the Cross, he was victorious....Since he was led away a second time into idolatry through his wife Fausta, he was divinely afflicted with leprosy. The pagan priests prescribed a bath in the blood of infants, and it was ordered; but when he heard the lamentations of the mothers, he said it was better to suffer than that so many infants should perish. Therefore the apostles, Peter and Paul as some say, appeared to him and told him Silvester would cure him, as he did. There are many varieties of the story and various details as to the Baptism, but in general the whole series of stories regarding his Baptism at Rome centers in this story, and gratitude for this cure is the supposed occasion of the famous Donation of Constantine."

This Donation of Constantine is a forgery that supposedly granted to the Pope

(continued...)

[5](...continued)
of Rome, Silvester, certain sweeping privileges in recognition of the miracle he had wrought for a grateful Constantine. The edict gives a long confession of Faith, followed by an account of the miracle and mention of the churches he has built. Then follow the grants to Silvester, sovereign pontiff and Pope of Rome, and all his successors until the end of the world—the Lateran palace, the diadem, several imperial insignia and privileges (*donatio*), as well as Rome, Italy, and the western regions. It is impossible here even to represent in outline the history of this extraordinary Latin fiction, composed not earlier than the latter part of the 8th C. During the middle ages, this fabrication was used for political and ecclesiastical ends. "Constantine the Great," Nicene, 2nd Ser., I:442.

The Great Synaxaristes (in Greek) maintains that, in accordance with historical sources and the universal glory of the Orthodox Church, Constantine the Great was not baptized in Rome by Saint Silvester, but in the suburbs of Nikomedia. This took place at the end of his earthly sojourn. Saint Silvester had catechized Constantine. Though the pope offered to baptize him in Rome, Constantine put off receiving divine illumination in Rome, preferring to be baptized in the Jordan as was Christ. This history regarding Constantine's Baptism has fomented great discord in historical accounts. Many stories have attached themselves to the name of Constantine. The one given above is such a specimen. Another history relates Constantine being baptized by the heretic Evsevios of Nikomedia. The Greek compilers, examining historical accounts, have proved this false. They maintain that he was baptized in a Nikomedian suburb by notable Orthodox hierarchs who had accompanied the emperor from Constantinople.

Meletios of Athens rejects the story that the Arian Evsevios officiated, but he admits that the holy Silvester catechized and baptized Constantine. He also concurs that, when the emperor emerged from the font, his health was restored [*Ecclesiastical History*, Vol. 1, p. 309]. Dositheos of Jerusalem [*Dodekavivlos*, p. 30] upholds that Constantine was baptized neither by Saint Silvester nor by Evsevios, but received the Mystery in a certain Nikomedian suburb, at the end of his life, with a company of Orthodox bishops present, who had accompanied him. Eusebius concurs with this in The Life of Constantine: "At first he experienced some slight bodily indisposition, which was soon followed by positive disease. In consequence of this he visited the hot baths of his own city; and thence proceeded to that which bore the name of his mother, Helenoupolis. Here he passed some time in the church of the martyrs, and offered up supplications and prayers to God. Being at length convinced that his life was drawing to a close, he felt the time was come at which he should seek purification from sins of his past career, firmly believing that whatever errors he had committed as a mortal man, his soul would be purified from them through the efficacy of the mystical words and the salutary waters of holy Baptism. Impressed with these thoughts, Constantine poured forth his supplications and confessions to God, kneeling on the pavement in the church itself, in which he also now for the first time received the imposition of hands with prayer. After this he proceeded as far as the suburbs of Nikomedia, and there,

(continued...)

The pious emperor ordered the building of a grand church to God the Savior. The design of the temple was drawn out in Constantine's own hand. Before all, he was first to begin the digging of the foundation. Thereupon, in but a few days, twelve thousand men were baptized—and that figure does not include the women and children. In every place and at all times, the idolaters were being catechized, which missionary work increased the ranks of the pious.

On one notable occasion, the emperor convened the senate and addressed them: "Be it known to you, dear friends, that the mind of the impure and profane is not able to receive soul-saving counsel. The mind of such wretched persons is enveloped in the darkness of ignorance. Those, however, who do succeed in opening the eyes of their minds, it is because they desire to understand the truth and put away the veneration of senseless and inanimate objects fashioned by the hands of man. Take, for example, my own actions, and how I came to believe with all my soul in the only true God. Let us only pay homage to Him, as the almighty and all-good One. Let us

---

[5](...continued)
having summoned the bishops to meet him, addressed them in the following words [Ch. LXI]: 'The time is arrived which I have long hoped for, with an earnest desire and prayer that I might obtain the salvation of God....I had thought to do this in the waters of the river Jordan, wherein our Savior, for our example, is recorded to have been baptized: but God, Who knows what is expedient for us, is pleased that I should receive this blessing here. Be it so, then, without delay....' After he had thus spoken, the prelates performed the sacred ceremonies in the usual manner, and, having given him the necessary instructions, made him a partaker of the mystic ordinance [Ch. LXII]." [Bk. IV, Nicene, I:555, 556.]
Theodoretos agrees that "the emperor was taken ill at Nikomedia, a city of Bithynia; and, knowing the uncertainty of human life, he received the holy rite of Baptism, which he had intended to have deferred until he could be baptized in the river Jordan." [*The Ecclesiastical History of Theodoret*, Bk. I, Ch. XXX, Nicene, 2nd Ser., III:63]. Sozomen records that Constantine "was indisposed and required to have recourse to bathing. He repaired for that purpose to Helenoupolis, a city of Bithynia. His malady, however, increased, and he went to Nikomedia, and was initiated into holy Baptism in one of the suburbs of that city." [*The Ecclesiastical History of Sozomen*, Bk. II, Ch. XXXIV, Nicene, 2nd Ser., II:282.] Socrates Scholasticus also writes: "The emperor, having just entered the sixty-fifth year of his age, was taken with a sickness; he therefore left Constantinople, and made a voyage to Helenoupolis, that he might try the effect of the medicinal hot springs, which are found in the vicinity of that city. Perceiving, however, that this illness increased, he deferred the use of the baths; and removing from Helenoupolis to Nikomedia, he took up his residence in the suburbs, and there received Christian Baptism." [*The Ecclesiastical History*, Bk. I, Ch. XXXIX, II:35.].

have done with making obeisance to soulless and insensate idols, which cannot bring us benefit. Indeed, much rather do they require help from us, to keep and maintain them, lest they should be broken or stolen. I do not desire to impose myself upon anyone against his will to embrace piety, but as a friend I should like to advise you for that which is to your advantage. Our God wishes for His creatures to turn to Him voluntarily. He compels no one. He desires that those who worship Him do so of their own free will with understanding and soundness."

After the godly Constantine spoke thus, they all cried out, "One is the true God, the Christ, Who delivered our emperor from disease." Constantine then ordered that they light the palace lamps. All in the city rejoiced and held a great festival. The graves of the saints were adorned. All those in iron fetters and imprisoned for the name of Jesus were set free, while more and more were returning from exile. Many good works to God's glory were in progress, which brought joy and stability to the Church of Christ. Now that the faithful were free to build and flourish, without the threat of atheistic tyrants and their persecutions, the Church increased as more united themselves to her and gave glory to the almighty God. The sole creature who remained embittered at the advancement of the Faith was the envious serpent of old, whose only joy, though malignant, is in doing evil. He could not endure the deadly wound he sustained from the Christians' victory. Hence, he was seeking a way that he might prevent the Church and godliness from thriving. He instigated some Jews to bring forward their case, so that piety might be strangled. Hearken to how the devil and his minions strove to hinder the spread of Orthodoxy and alter the emperor's course, even as the serpent once before had banished Adam from Paradise.

At that time, the mother of the emperor, Helen, not yet baptized, was in the Bithynian prefecture, where she was born.[6] Now certain Jews approached the augusta and said, "The emperor has done a good work by renouncing the idols. Nevertheless, he has fallen into another similar error, by venerating a condemned Man Whom our fathers crucified as a malefactor. Therefore, if thou lovest thy child, counsel him to render homage to the eternal God, that He might grant Constantine length of days and glorify him in the future everlasting life." These guileful words incited the augusta to report the words of the Jews to her son. She informed him in writing of this piece of intelligence, urging him to investigate their claims. She also told him that "I rejoice greatly and give glory to God that thou has been freed from the error of the idols."

---

[6] The Augusta Helen (Helena) was born circa 250 or 257, at Drepanon (later Helenoupolis).

The emperor received his mother's communication and responded: "Lady and my mother, rejoice in the Lord! He Who governs all of the universe and gives life and preserves us, in His œconomy has dispensed that I be made emperor. We therefore ought not to become ungrateful toward the Benefactor. Assemble the most learned of the teachers of the Jews and let them, before us, come and debate with the hierarchs of the Christ. Then shall the truth be known exactly, and we shall hasten to the Orthodox Faith. Fare thee well."

The emperor's pleasure was made known to the Jews. They selected twelve men, the chiefs of their Pharisees and most exceptional of their teachers. These Jews claimed not only knowledge of the prophets and traditions of their elders, but also of both the Greek and Latin languages and the philosophies of those peoples. Among the rabbis, there was Zambres, a wicked man. He was reputedly more erudite than the rest, and was a Kabbalist and magician. The Jewish contingent went to Rome with the augusta. They went before Constantine and asked that he choose twelve bishops of the Christians that they might have discussions with them, so that the truth should be made manifest. The blessed Silvester answered them and said, "We do not place our hope in the numbers of men, because the less human help one has, the more is he helped by divine power." The Jew Zambres then said to him, "If thou wilt appear to be a man of excellence and a good teacher, then do not quote from your Gospel or your books, but let the prophets be the texts used for testimony." Saint Silvester commented, "I also had this in mind, because when I prevail over you with the testimonies of your own teachers, then you shall no longer have any mouth by which to answer." The day of the debate was scheduled. The emperor, in the company of his senators, took his seat upon the throne. The augusta took her special place behind a curtain. One hundred and twenty Jews in all were present, while Pope Silvester entered with several bishops who had come from Rome, together with some followers.

Zambres then came forth and said, "The almighty God spoke these words: 'Behold, behold that I am He, and there is no God beside Me [Deut. 32:39].' If therefore God spoke this and He is the only God, why do you dare to name three? The One Whom you confess as Father, we do also. But then you confess the Son as second, Whom our fathers crucified. Then you speak of a third, the Holy Spirit, is this not so?" Saint Silvester replied, "We confess and revere one God Whom we declare to have a Logos or Word, even as spoken of by the prophet: 'By the Logos of the Lord were the heavens established, and all the might of them by the Spirit of His mouth [Ps. 32:6].' Elsewhere the prophet speaks of both the Son and Holy Spirit, uttering, 'Why have the heathen raged, and the peoples meditated empty things? The kings of the earth were aroused, and the rulers were assembled together, against the Lord, and against His Christ [Ps. 2:1, 2].' David speaks here not of one person but two, the Lord and His Christ. The same prophet then identifies Christ as the Son, when he wrote: 'The Lord said unto Me: "Thou art My Son, this day have I begotten Thee [Ps. 2:7]."' Thus, both the Begetter and the Begotten are spoken of here." The Jews then noted that David had spoken the words "this day." They declared, "Those words denote time. So then how can the Son be the eternal God?" The man of God Silvester answered, "The expression 'this day'

Saint Silvester

speaks not of the pre-eternal generation of the Son, but rather that generation which took place in time when the Logos became incarnate. The prophet understood this difference. In writing 'Thou art My Son,' he refers to the Only-begotten, begotten of the Father before all ages. This is followed by 'this day have I begotten Thee,' which bespeaks of the Only-begotten's incarnation of the Holy Spirit and the Virgin Mary. God the Father reveals His concurrence with the Son's taking on flesh. Even so, the words 'this day have I begotten Thee' pertain to the eternity of the divine generation, in which there is no past or future action, but always the present only. Indeed, no analogy can hold between divine generation or begetting and human generation or begetting. Divine generation does not imply any passion whatsoever. Man, having a transitive nature, begets passibly. God is not composed of parts. He is impassibly and indivisibly Father of the Son and Logos Who is the Father's Word and Wisdom. On the one hand, Scripture speaks of 'Son,' in order to declare the natural and true Offspring of His essence; but, on the other hand, that none may think of the Offspring in human terms, while signifying His essence, it also calls Him Word, Wisdom, and Radiance. For the Son's generation was impassible, and eternal, and worthy of God. The Logos is not a work or creation. As the Father always is, so what is proper to His essence must always be; and this is His Word and His Wisdom. The Begetter and the Begotten are coessential. There is no interval between them. The Son is co-beginningless with the Father.

"The Spirit is spoken of in numerous places. Do we not hear Him spoken of in these passages? 'Cast me not away from Thy presence, and take not Thy Holy Spirit from me [Ps. 50:11].' And, 'Thou wilt send forth Thy Spirit, and they shall be created [Ps. 103:32].' And, 'Whither shall I go from Thy Spirit [Ps. 138:6]?' So spoke David your king and prophet. What about your law-giver, Moses? Did he not write in Genesis: 'And God said, "Let Us make man according to Our image and similitude [Gen. 1:26]"?' God was not addressing the angels, for they do not possess His nature. David wrote: 'The Lord said unto My Lord: "Sit Thou at My right hand, until I make Thine enemies the footstool of Thy feet [Ps. 109:1]."' David calls the Christ 'Lord.' To which of the ministering spirits has God spoken thus? He spoke to His coessential Son, His express image." Zambres commented, "This belief of Father, Son, and Holy Spirit cannot be accepted by the mind of man." The hierarch answered, "The pagans are ignorant of Scriptures, but what excuse do you have? You claim to know the prophets; and without exception, they all prophesied of the Christ."

The emperor then interjected, "I am astonished that the Jews are being vanquished by so many testimonies from their Scriptures, and still they are contentious and filled with a spirit of contradiction." Constantine then turned to the Jews and said, "Behold, even through your own writings, I acknowledge that the evidence shines through that Father, Son, and Holy Spirit certainly exist. Therefore, there is no need to speak further regarding this matter; only if you have different evidence." The Jew Zambres then said, "In your Gospel it is written that 'Jesus kept on advancing in wisdom and stature [Lk. 2:52],' and that He was tempted by the devil. Afterward, a disciple delivered Jesus into the hands of men, so that He was bound, mocked, scourged, crucified, and died. If He therefore were God, how did He suffer?" Saint Silvester answered, "All of these events were preached by the prophets. Hearken then! Esaias spoke of the Christ's seedless conception when he uttered, 'Therefore the Lord Himself shall give you a sign: Behold, the Virgin shall conceive in the womb, and shall bring forth a Son, and thou shalt call His name Emmanuel [Is. 7:14].' As thou knowest, Emmanuel signifies 'God with us.'" The Jews shook their heads and said, "Nay, the Hebrew text speaks not of a virgin but a damsel, a young woman." The saint responded: "Well, what great thing or what sign should that have been? Why is it extraordinary that a young woman should conceive by a man and bring forth? Does this not occur to all women, bearing offspring? What sort of sign would that event be? Why do you contradict and say 'damsel' rather than 'virgin'? Even so, a virgin is called a damsel in holy Scripture. [cf. Deut. 22:27; 1 Kgs. (3 Kgs.) 1:4].[7] Furthermore, in other places the Scripture is

---

[7] Taking the issue up with the Jews, Blessed Jerome declares: "I know that the Jews are accustomed to meet us with the objection that in Hebrew the word *almah* does not mean a virgin, but 'a young woman.' And, to speak truth, a virgin is properly called *bethulah*, but a young woman, or a girl, is not *almah*, but *naarah*! What then is the meaning of *almah*? A hidden virgin, that is, not merely virgin, but a virgin and
(continued...)

wont to put the word 'youth,' for 'virginity'; and this with respect not to women only, but also to men. For it is said, 'young men and maidens, old men with younger ones [Ps. 148:12].' And again, speaking of the damsel who is attacked, it says, 'if the young woman (*neanis*) cry out [cf. Deut. 22:27],' meaning the virgin.

"Our version has not corrupted the text. In the first place, the Seventy translators are to be trusted above all the others. For the others may rightfully be suspected of enmity and tampering, since they made their versions after Christ's coming and continued in Judaism. But the Seventy, who took up this work a hundred years or more before the coming of Christ, are necessarily clear of any suspicion, not only on account of the date, but also their number and agreement."

The Jews then said, "But Mary bore Jesus, not Emmanuel. Jesus was not called Emmanuel by His disciples, friends, or enemies." The hierarch answered, "The name 'Emmanuel' was a kind of expression according to the issue of the event of His Incarnation that now 'God is with us.' You know that the prophets are wont to do this. Bring to mind Esaias who gave one of his sons a representative name which meant 'Spoil quickly, plunder speedily [Is. 8:3]', since the son was to be a type of Christ. His name describes the works of Christ. The name declares in a mysterious manner how the Lord would reign and spoil. The significance of the appellation relates to the issue of events. Again, this is customary in Scripture, to substitute the events that take place for names. Therefore, to say, 'They shall call Him "Emmanuel" [Mt. 1:23]' means nothing else than that they shall see God among men. Did not Baruch say, 'This is our God, and there shall none other be accounted of in comparison of Him. He hath found out all the way of knowledge, and hath given it unto Jacob His servant, and to Israel His beloved. Afterward did He show Himself upon earth, and conversed with men [Bar. 3:35-37]'?

"Thou speakest of Jesus being tempted by the devil. Hast thou never read of this prefigurement in Zacharias, who said, 'The Lord showed me Jesus the high priest standing before the angel of the Lord, and the devil stood on his right hand to resist him [Zach. 3:1]'? Jesus, the son of Josedec, spoken

---

[7](...continued)
something more, because not every virgin is hidden, shut off from the occasional sight of men. Then again, Rebecca, on account of her extreme purity, and because she as a type of the Church which she represented in her own virginity, is described in Genesis as *almah*, not *bethulah* [Gen. 24:43 sq.]....Where he speaks of the maiden coming forth to draw water, the Hebrew word is *almah*, that is, 'a virgin secluded,' and guarded by her parents with extreme care." *Letters and Select Works: Against Jovinianus.-Book I*, Nicene, 2nd Ser., VI:370.

of here, was a type of the Lord Jesus Who took up man's cause and condition, with the devil set at His right hand. Jesus, the son of Josedec, described as being clothed in filthy garments, was a type of the Lord Jesus Who had not committed any sin and yet bore our sins, on Whose right hand stood Satan to be His adversary [cf. Zach. 3:1, 4]. The Lord Jesus permitted Satan to stand at His right hand so that He could say, 'Begone, Satan [Mt. 4:10].' Consequently, the adversary was cast down from his place and departed. After the contest had been finished and victory had been won, it was said of Jesus, son of Josedec, 'Take away the filthy raiment from him,' and, 'Behold, I have taken away thine iniquities [Zach. 3:4(5)].'"

Saint Silvester then spoke of the Lord's Passion and resurrection. "Prophet David tells us that the Messiah would be delivered up by a disciple, saying, 'Yea, even the man of My peace in whom I hoped, who ate of My bread, hath magnified the lifting of heels against Me [Ps. 40:9].' Esaias informs us that the Messiah would be silent before His accusers: 'And He, because of His affliction, opens not His mouth; He was led as a sheep to the slaughter, and as a lamb before the shearer is dumb, so He opens not His mouth [Is. 53:7].' It was also prophesied that the Messiah would be smitten; so says Esaias: 'I gave My back to scourges, and My cheeks to blows; and I turned not away My face from the shame of spitting [Is. 50:6].' He was mocked, so says David: 'All that look upon Me have laughed Me to scorn; they have spoken with their lips and have wagged with their heads, saying, "He hoped in the Lord; let Him deliver Him, let Him save Him; for He desireth Him [Ps. 21:7, 8]."' This same prophet is clear regarding the Messiah's death by crucifixion: 'The congregation of evildoers hath surrounded Me; they have pierced My hands and My feet. They have numbered all My bones, and they themselves have looked and stared upon Me. They have parted My garments amongst themselves, and for My vesture have they cast lots [Ps. 21:16-18].' And, 'They gave Me gall for My food, and for My thirst they gave Me vinegar to drink [Ps. 68:21].' The Messiah also suffered with transgressors, as prophesied by Esaias: 'He was numbered among the transgressors; and He bore the sins of many, and was delivered because of their iniquities [Is. 53:12].' The same prophet tells us that 'He shall bear our sins....He was wounded on account of our sins, and was bruised because of our iniquities;...by His bruises we were healed....His life is taken away from the earth; because of the iniquities of my people He was led to death. And I will give the wicked for his burial, and the rich for his death [Is. 53:5, 6, 8, 9, 11].' But David also tells us that the Messiah was resurrected: 'For Thou wilt not abandon My soul in Hades, nor wilt Thou suffer Thy Holy One to see corruption [Ps. 15:10].'" These and many more things were explained by the hierarch, as he touched upon how the sun was darkened and the earth quaked, the tombs were opened and the dead came forth, and the veil of the temple was rent. Consequently, the Greek pagans who were present shouted aloud to Zambres, confessing, "Christ is the Son of God." Then they said to him, "Therefore, O Jew, unless thou art able to prove that the prophets did not utter these words, thou art vanquished as a liar and babbler. Moreover, if the words spoken by the prophets are true, which thou hast not denied, then thou oughtest to accept them as true, by confessing Christ as true God and Man. Indeed, if thou refusest to willingly accept the obvious, on account of stubbornness, then thou hast denied thine own religion by accusing thine own prophets of falsehood."

The Jews still would not quit, but resumed and asked, "Why should God take on flesh? Was there no other way to achieve man's salvation?" "With God," said Pope Silvester, "all things are possible. The Lord God 'formed man of the dust of the ground, and breathed into his nostrils the breath of life; and man became a living soul [Gen. 2:7].' The earth was then pure and virgin, not yet cursed in our labors [Gen. 3:17], not yet stained with Abel's blood and the killing of animals, and still unpolluted by decaying corpses and untainted by wicked deeds. As Adam came from uncorrupted earth, so Jesus was born seedlessly of the Ever-virgin. But Adam was a type of 'the coming One [Rom. 5:14].' Since 'by a man came death, also by a Man came a resurrection of the dead. For even as in Adam all die, so also in the Christ shall all be made alive [1 Cor. 15:21, 22].' So it has been written: 'The first man Adam became a living soul; the last Adam became a life-creating Spirit. But the spiritual was not first, but the animal, and afterward the spiritual. The first man is of earth, earthy; the second Man is the Lord from heaven [1 Cor. 15:45-47].' Thus all things are to be recapitulated in the Christ, both the things in the heavens and the things upon the earth [Eph. 1:10]. In becoming Man, Christ has brought about the communion of God and man. In Himself, He summed up and renewed all things and has procured for man a comprehensive salvation, that we might recover in Christ what in Adam we lost. I mean the image and similitude of God."

The emperor was happy and satisfied at this point. He deemed Silvester's words and reasoning most wise. Constantine then addressed the Jews: "You can gainsay him in nothing, since he has brought your own writings into evidence." The Jews then said to the bishop, "All those prophesies uttered by the prophets pertain to others, but you have falsely attributed them to the Christ." Saint Silvester then remarked, "Find for me another who was born of a virgin maiden, and who was crucified, and arose on the third day; only then shall I admit that these things were not spoken of regarding the Christ." These and many other things were uttered by Saint Silvester to Zambres and the rest of the Jews, so that much time passed. The emperor was then tired of the Jewish wrangling, because they kept making problems, casting forth useless arguments, and citing examples that came to nought. Constantine wished now to bring an end to the talks and assign the victory to Saint Silvester. However, lest the Jews should later complain, he asked them, "Have you anything else to say?" One of them, named Jubal, spoke up and said, "Silvester still has not answered our question. We asked him to tell us how Christ suffered if He is God. That alone demonstrates that Jesus was a man." After speaking thus, the Jew then turned to the hierarch and said, "It is impossible that thou shouldest demonstrate that in one person there exist two essences, so that one is capable of suffering insult and punishment, and the other does not partake of these things and abides unharmed." Saint Silvester replied, "And if I should demonstrate it, wilt thou confess before this whole company of nobles that thou art vanquished, or wilt thou contemplate sowing some other new tares?" Jubal then remained quiet. The emperor then said, "If he does not confess the victory, those standing here shall ascribe his nonacceptance as stubbornness."

Then Saint Silvester took up the emperor's purple cloak and said, "With this purple cloth, I shall overcome the adversary. Now this garment was formerly raw silk and white. Tyrian purple, a vat dye from certain shellfish from which the scarlet pigment is obtained, was used on this formerly unbleached cloth. Afterward, vigorous methods of dyeing are applied. The fibers may be in a loose form before spinning or partially or fully spun yarn. They are subjected to baths, rinses, paddles, rollers, drums, cages, spinning, and cutting, and whatever methods such skilled in this art employ, so that it might become worthy of the imperial wardrobe. Though the fibers and material undergo an extensive process, the wearer suffers nothing. In like manner was it so in the body of Christ; for only the flesh suffered. Again, let us use the example of the emperor's wool mantle. Colorant was used on the threads which were then twisted. What was twisted? The color that signifies the royal dignity or the wool that was wool before it was dyed purple? The wool stands for the man, the purple color for God. Though God was present in Christ's Passion, He was not subjected to suffering. As the dye, He did not partake of any outrage." "But wait," said one of the Jews, "was not the color twisted with the wool?" The saint then said, "If this example does not suffice, O Jew, hearken to a second and third, to the glory of the coessential Trinity. Let us picture a tree filled with the rays of the sun. Now let us imagine that someone has cut down that tree. Tell me, when the axe cleaved the tree, did the sun suffer anything? The tree sensed the axe, but the sunlight experienced no blow. The sun abides untouched and impassible." The Jew then said, "I beseech thee, tell me even a third example, that I might be better persuaded." Saint Silvester obliged him and said, "When iron, which is beaten with the hammer by the smith, is drawn from the fire, it is plainly evident that the fire endures no violence; only the iron is subjected to the pounding and cutting of those skilled in metal-working. In like manner, the divinity remained impassible, as it is immaterial, and only the flesh of the Christ suffered. He has two natures, one divine and one human, but in a single Person. Though He suffered in His human nature, yet not in His divinity. Now Christ was tempted in all respects according to our likeness, without sin [Heb. 4:15]. So says Esaias: 'He practised no iniquity, nor craft with His mouth [Is. 53:9].' But He suffered, leaving behind an example that we should follow in His footsteps [1 Pe. 2:21]."

All the bystanders, hearing these examples, acclaimed the most wise Silvester. At this juncture, the emperor ended the debate. The saint, however, did not wish this, for he had not yet discoursed with all twelve Jewish elders. One of them, Sileon, had not yet uttered a word. Lest there should be cause later for complaint, he said to Sileon, "Hast thou any questions?" He then said, "Justly hast thou discerned things. Tell us then if the prophets gave reasons for such outrages and so much suffering; that is, why should the Christ receive such a hideous and shameless death? Again, could not man be delivered by some other means?" To this question, the divine Silvester gave the proper answer. "Christ," said he, "suffered hunger that He might feed us. He thirsted in order to quench our dryness with a life-giving draft. He endured temptation to liberate us from temptation. He was taken captive to deliver us from capture by the demons. He was mocked to free us from the demons' mockery. He was bound in order to untie for us the knot of bondage and malediction. He was humiliated in order to exalt us. He was stripped of His garments to clothe us. He accepted the crown in order to give back to us the lost flowers of Paradise. He was hung upon the tree in order to condemn the evil desires that a tree had stirred. Even as Satan tricked the man in Paradise into eating from the tree, which ushered in our banishment, so with the Tree of the Cross Christ conquered the adversary and raised man, vouchsafing him again Paradise. Jesus was given gall and vinegar to drink in order to bring man into a land flowing with milk and honey. He took mortality upon Himself to confer immortality upon us. He was buried to bless the tombs of the saints. He rose to restore life to the dead. He ascended into the heavens to open heaven's gates. He is seated at God's right to hear and grant the prayers of the faithful.

"It was not possible that He should command an angel to take on flesh and free man, lest we should be obliged to the angelic nature, rather than to the Creator and Savior. The Son of God became Man, in order that He might again bestow that favor for which He created him, which was after His own image, endowed with intellect and free will, and after His own similitude, that is, perfect in all virtue as far as it was possible for man's nature.

"Jesus endured death voluntarily, thereby trampling upon Death against his will. In that very body by which Death had slain Jesus, Jesus bore away the victory over Death. Divinity, concealed in the manhood, fought against Death. Death slew the natural life, and the supernatural Life slew Death. When Jesus entered Sheol, clothed with the body of Adam, Death had no power over Him. Death swallowed Jesus, the Medicine of life, and discovered that the prey was God in the flesh and incorruptible. Thereupon, Death vomited forth the dead held captive. Jesus therefore despoiled Hades, plundering its storehouses and emptying its treasures. Thus, the Son of God, having assumed our nature and united it to Himself, conquered the devil who had the power of death."

Sileon remained voiceless, no longer able to resist. The spectators, hearing these things, marvelled, and applause rang out from all, including Constantine and the Jews. Zambres, being wicked and crafty, contrived a piece of knavery. Little did he know that such villainy would put him to shame and bring him into the very pit which he had prepared for the pope. Zambres thereupon addressed the emperor: "Sire, Silvester is loquacious and glib-tongued, by which he has bested us in the debate. He is plausible and beguiles the people with his ambiguous word games. He attempts to explain the divinity by human reasoning. Although he has exhausted all our arguments, we shall not abandon the traditions of our elders and worship the crucified One. Silvester talks much, but I am ready to show by deeds, which are more creditworthy than words, that there is nothing more powerful than the name of the almighty God, Whose name I know. Do thou command that they bring here a wild bull, and then you shall all know the power of my God, Whose name is so fearful that the hearing of it brings death. For this reason, when our forefathers wished to sacrifice great bulls, they would speak the divine name in the ear of the animal, and straightway it would expire. Let Silvester speak the name of his God in the ear of the bull, and if it should die, then the God Whom he reveres is the true One. If the beast remains alive, then I shall speak the name in the bull's ear; and if it should die, you will believe me." Saint Silvester, knowing this to be complete nonsense, then said to Zambres, "If verily none is able to bear hearing the name, how shalt thou hear it and not die?" Zambres replied, "Thou canst not know this mystery. Thou art the enemy of the Jews." The emperor then interposed and said, "If thou wilt not speak of the mystery to the bishop, then tell us: where and how didst thou learn this name? Perhaps thou didst read it in a book?" Zambres answered gravely, "The name may not be written on anything, lest the writer and what he has written upon should suffer destruction." Constantine demanded impatiently, "This does not explain how the name was revealed to thee, if it cannot be spoken or written." Zambres then disclosed, "I fasted for seven days, entreating the Lord to manifest His name. Then I beheld a silver basin filled with water. An invisible finger traced the letters of the name over the waters. Only after exerting myself and with much toil was I able to comprehend it." The holy and discerning Silvester understood this to be a demonic manifestation, and repeated his earlier question, "When thou speakest that name, it is evident that thou hearest it at the same time. Therefore, how didst thou survive it?" Zambres answered him contemptuously, saying, "I have already answered thee. Thou art the enemy of the Jews and unfit to know our secrets. I therefore shall whisper the name into the bull's ear. When the beast expires, thou shalt know my religion to be the true one." The holy hierarch responded with much gravity, saying, "My God does not bestow death, but rather life and blessedness." Zambres retorted, "Enough talk; there are deeds yet to do."

Then the divine Silvester besought the emperor and all the senate to dispatch men to lead forth the most wild bull that they could find. The beast was found, and even thirty men restraining it with ropes could hardly manage it. Since Zambres initiated the challenge, he went forth first to the bull, which suddenly calmed at his approach. Zambres spoke some secret words of sorcery into the creature's ears. Forthwith, the bull fell down to the ground and died. The Jews exulted, as they shouted and laughed scornfully at the holy man, who spoke boldly, saying, "He pronounced not the name of God, but of the foulest of demons." The bishop then mounted a high place and commanded all to remain silent, for he wished for them to hear every word of his address. The crowd hushed, and he spoke with a great voice and said, "I proclaim the Master Christ Who granted light to the blind, cleansed lepers, raised up paralytics, resurrected the dead, and healed every illness. It is therefore clear that Zambres did not speak the name of God, but that of the devil, who gives death, as he is a murderer and manslayer; but to raise up from the dead, this the devil can in no wise do. Therefore, O Zambres, if thou dost wish for us to believe thee, raise up from the dead the bull which thou hast slain; then all of us shall believe in thy God." Zambres then rent his garment and shouted aloud, saying, "O emperor, many years to thee! Dost thou see how I have overcome with my deeds, but how he persists in confusing us with his sophistries and nonsense?"

The emperor patiently heard Zambres, but said to the bishop: "Well didst thou speak, O Silvester, that the merciful God grants life to all and not destruction." The bishop then asked the Jews, "Is it not written that the Lord said: 'I kill, and I will make to live: I will smite, and I will heal; and there is none who shall deliver out of My hands [Deut. 32:39]'?" The Jews answered,

"So spoke the Lord." The bishop continued and said, "If Zambres has slain the bull by the name of God, then let him restore it to life." Constantine then said to the Jew, "Well then, either raise up the bull that we might believe in thee, or thou shalt be put to death as a deceiver and wizard, lest thou shouldest draw the people into perdition." But Zambres quickly interjected, "This thing thou askest, O emperor, no man can do. Once more Silvester uses words instead of deeds." Zambres then looked upon the bishop and said, "Let Silvester raise the bull in the name of this Jesus." The holy bishop then said, "But if I should raise up the bull, invoking the life-giving and saving name of the Master Christ, then what wilt thou do?" Zambres replied, "Thou dost boast, Silvester. The bull is dead. Even if thou shouldest fly in the heavens, thou couldest not raise the creature." Constantine became angry and said, "I marvel, O Zambres, at thy shamelessness. Was it not thee who said that we should have done with words and let only deeds be given as proof? And now that the bishop gives his word that he shall raise the bull, thou sayest, how is it possible? If the bishop's word comes to pass in very deed, and he raises the animal, wilt thou and the rest of the Jews here come to believe in the Christ?" The Jews, believing that it could not possibly happen, promised with an oath that if Silvester should raise up the bull from the dead, then they would become Christians on the spot.

Then Saint Silvester, bowing his knees to the ground, raised up his hands and eyes heavenward. With tears, he offered up words of secret entreaty to the Lord. He then rose up and spoke with a great voice so that all might hear: "O Master, Lord Jesus Christ, Son of God, I entreat and supplicate Thy goodness, to raise up this animal, which Zambres slew by invoking the name of the devil, so that all the people shall come to know Thy great power and believe in Thine all-holy name." After he uttered these words, he cried out to the beast, saying, "In the name of the Master Jesus Christ, Who was born of the Virgin Mary and was crucified by Pontius Pilate, rise up and be thou tame from henceforth." The bull then—O the wonder!—rose up and calmly approached the saint, who removed the ropes from its horns. The bishop then said to the bull, "Go to thy place gently and dare never again to injure anyone. No one shall injure thee nor slay thee. Thou shalt live out thine appointed time and end with a natural death." The Jews with Zambres, witnessing such an extraordinary marvel, fell to their knees before the saint, imploring him to pardon their former impiety. In like manner, the godly emperor venerated the saint and acclaimed him. The empress and the nobles then sought holy Baptism from the bishop. The blessed Silvester catechized them, including the Jews and idolaters, commanding them to fast a certain number of days, as they shed tears and performed works of mercy and charity. Saint Silvester then baptized them in the name of the Father and of the Son and of the Holy Spirit, the true God, to Whom is due all glory, honor, and veneration, to the ages of the ages. Amen.

Now Saint Silvester was an ardent zealot for right belief. He dispatched two legates, Vitus and Vincentius, to attend the First Œcumenical Synod, convened during the reign of Constantine the Great (325) in Nicaea of Bithynia. The western bishop, Hosius of Cordova, presided. This synod condemned the heresy of Arius. Saint Silvester reposed in Rome in the year 335. During his pontificate, Constantine had given him the palace of the Lateran, where he set up his cathedra, the official chair or throne of a bishop, and established the Lateran basilica as the cathedral church of Rome. He also built the first churches of Saint Peter on the Vatican, Holy Cross in the Sessorian palace, and Saint Laurence outside the Walls.[8] Saint Silvester also built a church at the cemetery of Priscilla on the Salarian way, where he was himself buried. In 761, his relics were translated by Pope Paul I (757-767) to Saint Silvester *in Capite* at Rome. He was the first pope of Rome after the Church emerged from the catacombs.[9]

On the 2nd of January, the holy Church commemorates the holy Hieromartyr THEAGENES.[10]

Theagenes, the holy hieromartyr, was bishop of a city called Parium,[11] which had been built by people of the same name. It was located between Kyzikos and Lampsakos on the Hellespont.[12] During the reign and persecution of Licinius (320), Theagenes was informed against to the tribune Zelikinthios. Since it was a state crime to be a Christian, the bishop was brought in for questioning. Theagenes confessed Christ as true God, for

---

[8] On the left side of the Esquiline Hill is the Church of S. Martino ai Monti, the site of an oratory built by Pope Silvester, which Pope Symmachus (498-514) transformed into a basilica in honor of Saint Martin of Tours. It was rebuilt in the 9th C. and again in the 17th C. See Freeman-Grenville's *The Beauty of Rome*, p. 77.

[9] *Butler's Lives of the Saints*, December 31st, IV:644.

[10] The *Synaxaristes* of Maximos records the saint's name as Theogenes.

[11] Parium (Parion, Kemer) 40°25'N 27°04'E.

[12] The northwest corner of the peninsula had been in former times a land of many cities. Ancient Ilium (Ilion), from which the district took its name, had been eclipsed by Alexandria Troas, Lampsakos, Parium, and Assos, facing the island of Lesbos on the south coast. On the north shore of the Propontis (Marmara) was Kyzikos, the capital of the Hellespont province, which had thirty cities assigned to it. In the 7th C. the civil province disappeared, but the ecclesiastical diocese survived, with Kyzikos as metropolis and suffragan bishops including Abydos, Germe, Ilion, Lampsakos, and Troas. S. Lloyds, *Ancient Turkey*, p. 152; *The Oxford Dictionary of Byzantium*, s.v. "Hellespont."

which the pagans thrashed him with wood. Afterward, they bound the holy bishop and cast him into the depths of the sea. Thus, Saint Theagenes completed the course of martyrdom, for which he received the amaranthine crown from the Lord.

**On the 2nd of January, the holy Church commemorates
Saint THEOPEMPTOS, who reposed in peace.**

**On the 2nd of January, the holy Church commemorates
the holy THEODOTE, mother of the first pair of
holy Unmercenaries Kosmas and Damian,
who reposed in peace.[13]**

**On the 2nd of January, the holy Church commemorates
the Venerable MARK, who reposed in peace.**

**On the 2nd of January, the holy Church commemorates
the holy Martyr BASIL of Ankyra.[14]**

Basil, the holy martyr, lived during the time of Julian the Apostate (361). He hailed from the city of Ankyra,[15] the civil and ecclesiastical metropolis of Galatia, on the main highway across Anatolia. In the fourth century, Ankyra was still dominated by a cultivated pagan landowning aristocracy. Since Basil believed in the Christ, he was arrested by the pagans and presented to Governor Satorninos. Basil boldly confessed Christ before him, for which he was suspended and made to suffer scrapings and carvings of his flesh. After undergoing these tortures at Ankyra, Basil was conveyed to Constantinople, where he was subjected to further destruction of his flesh and stretching inflicted by the rack. As a result of these punishments, the joints of the ever-memorable one's hands and shoulders were dislocated. The executioners proceeded to flay his skin in strips, which fell from his body. The cruel tormenters then fired iron instruments, with which they pierced his flesh. All of these intolerable tortures the brave Basil bore manfully, for God rendered succor and help to the stout-hearted spirit of His martyr. Basil was

---

[13] Saints Kosmas and Damian are commemorated by the holy Church on the 1st of November.

[14] The compilers of *The Great Synaxaristes* (in Greek) and other *Synaxaristae* are clear on the point that the Saint Basil whom we commemorate today is not to be confused with the hieromartyr of the same name and city commemorated by the holy Church on the 22nd of March.

[15] Ankyra (Turkey, near Ankara) 39°55'N 32°50'E.

then cast into a fiery furnace, from which he was miraculously preserved unharmed through prayer. After these barbarous punishments, he was referred to Caesarea, where he was condemned by the ruler to fight with wild animals. The martyr uttered a prayer that he might end his struggle there and suffer the attack of a lioness, for which he won a true crown. Afterward, his sacred relics were meticulously collected. Certain kinfolk and others of the same stock wrapped Basil's martyric relics with myrrh and linen cloths. With fitting honor, Saint Basil was interred in a distinguished place. Later, a sacred church was built to commemorate his holy name.

On the 2nd of January, the holy Church commemorates the holy Martyr SERGIOS, who was slain by the sword.

On the 2nd of January, the holy Church commemorates the holy Martyr THEOPISTOS, who was stoned to death.

On the 2nd of January, the holy Church commemorates our holy father among the saints, KOSMAS the Wonder-worker, Archbishop of Constantinople.

Kosmas I, the holy patriarch, ascended the throne of Constantinople (1075-1081). Before his elevation, he had come from Jerusalem to take up the monastic struggle near the palace of Vlachernai, where the basilica of the most famous shrine to the Theotokos was located in the northwest corner of the capital. When Patriarch John VIII Xiphilinos reposed in August of 1075, the Monk Kosmas was elected, though he was nearly ninety years of age. Michael VII Doukas (1071-1078) was then reigning. It was a time when Anatolia was being beset by Turks, the Seljuk menace kept increasing around the capital, and rebels were devastating Asian and Balkan provinces. One of the rebels, Nikephoros III Botaneiates (1078-1081), with Turkish troops, defeated Michael's troops near Nicaea. Michael abdicated and entered a monastery, but later became Metropolitan of Ephesus. In the meantime, Nikephoros entered the capital in April of 1078 and received the imperial insignia. He was crowned that July by Patriarch Kosmas. Then, in 1179, the elderly Nikephoros (b. ca. 1001) married the distinguished beauty Maria of Alania (Georgia, b. 1050), his predecessor's wife. When Maria's first husband had fallen from power, she fled with her son, Constantine Doukas, to the Petrion Monastery. Then, in order to protect her son's position, she agreed to marry the aged Nikephoros.

Now Kosmas was adorned with many virtues, for which he was much beloved, especially by the emperor. Nevertheless, due to his advanced years, Saint Kosmas was becoming increasingly fragile and found he could not serve the Church with the energy required. He resigned on the 8th day of May, in the year 1081. He was succeeded by Efstratios Gardias (1081-1084). The holy Kosmas then returned to a monastery, where he reposed in deep old age. He was interred at the Monastery of the Savior in Chora, situated in the northwest section of the capital. He is remembered as a wonder-worker.

**On the 2nd of January, the holy Church commemorates
the holy New-martyr GEORGE or ZORZEES the Geourtze
(the Georgian), who suffered martyrdom by hanging at Mytilene.**[16]

George or Zorzees, the holy new-martyr, was a youth when he was sold as a slave by a certain Hagarene. His master converted him to Islam and raised George as a Turk. Later, when George's master died, he continued as a Moslem for seventy years. He never married throughout that period. George led a peaceful life, working in a certain shop and selling various items, knowing no other language except that of the Moslems. In spite of his advanced age, one day, the blessed one left his workshop and appeared before the judge of that territory and took off his turban, giving it to the judge and saying, "I was born a Christian, and I will die a Christian. My name is Zorzees; and with the name Zorzees shall I die." The judge, observing the change in him and his age and white beard, said to him, "Hey, Saleh, what has happened to thee? Hast thou taken leave of thy senses, brother?" Zorzees answered, "A Christian, a Christian, as a Christian I wish to die." The judge repeated, "Why art thou doing this?" Zorzees replied, "Because I am a Christian." Then the judge enclosed him in a chamber, but without bonds, in the hope that Saleh would come to his senses.

The following day they brought forth Zorzees for further examination, but again he confessed the Orthodox Faith. Then they threatened to put him to death. Now the martyr was a man of few words. His only reply was that he was a Christian. On the third day, the judge questioned him again. Seeing that he was adamant toward the Christian Faith, the judge turned him

---

[16] The Life of New-martyr George or Zorzees was originally taken from the *Neon Martyrologion* of Nikodemos the Hagiorite.

　　Georgia was called Geourgtzistan by the Turks during the Turkish occupation, while the Georgians called themselves Geourtzides. In antiquity, Georgia was called Iberia and its inhabitants Iberians. Georgia lies in southwestern Russia between the Black and Caspian Seas, with the Great Caucasus Mountain range to the north. To the southeast, it is adjoined by Azerbaidzhan, and to the south by Armenia and Turkey. The capital of Georgia is Tiflis (Tbilisi). In the middle ages, it was closely connected with Byzantium. The Georgians have their own language, which belongs to the southern Caucasian, or Kartvelian group, but Greek was known and spoken until as late as 1936.

over to the executioners. They led him away to the place of execution. On the way they lashed him mercilessly, but he endured everything quietly and with strength. Finally they arrived near a shop, finding the place ideal for hanging. The executioners put the noose around Zorzees' neck and urged him to confess Islam; but the martyr held his hand to his mouth, lest he should speak. Since they deemed his refusal to speak as defiance, they flogged him more. They paraded him about the marketplace, ridiculing him so as to intensify his torment.

At last, they brought Zorzees to a place called Parma Kale. They kept piercing him with their knives, attempting to compel him to declare himself one of them. Since he refused, they showed the martyr one of their fingers, saying to him, "Hold up one of thy fingers in this fashion, acknowledging that God is One." But the blessed one clasped his hands together, so that no one could open them. He also did not wish to look upon them, so he turned his eyes toward the wall. Following this, the executioners administered many blows with rods and punched him with their fists. They also kept raising him up and letting him down, hoping that he would change his mind. Finally, seeing that he was undaunted and that nothing swayed him from the love of Christ, they decided to hang him. Thus the Martyr Zorzees received the crown of martyrdom in the year 1770.

Through the intercessions of Thy Saints,
O Christ God, have mercy on us. Amen.

On the 3rd of January, the holy Church commemorates the holy Prophet MALACHIAS (MALACHI).

Malachias (Malachi), the divine prophet, of the tribe of Levi in the territory of the tribe of Zabulon, was born in Sopha (Sophero, Supha) after the return of the captives from Babylon (538 B.C.). He was chronologically the last of the Minor Prophets. After him there was no prophet in Israel until the coming of the Forerunner, Saint John the Baptist. When Malachias was a very young man he took up the life of virtue and excellence. He received the name Malachias, meaning "angel" (Heb. *mal'āk*) for two reasons: firstly, for his goodly appearance and splendid conduct of life; and secondly, whatever he uttered in prophecy, straightway, that very day, an angel of God appeared and reiterated the prophet's words. However, only those counted worthy were able to see the angel; but all, even the unworthy, were able to hear the voice of the angel's testimony. The angel was the prophet's companion, with whom he often spoke as a man speaks to a friend. The prophet is described as having an oval-shaped face, and hair that appeared as if twisted up and untrimmed which crowned his broad and large head. While still a young man, he was added to his fathers in his own field.[1]

Background

Vexing dilemmas confronted Prophet Malachias: a priesthood that was slovenly in its performance of the ritual [Mal. 1:6-2:9], negligent payment of requisite tithes and offerings [Mal. 3:7-12], intermarriage with heathen wives [Mal. 2:10-16], a loss of domestic commitment to their Hebrew wives [Mal. 2:16] (in itself a sign of a slackening devotion to God which was sapping their family life), and financial abuses [Mal. 3:5-10]. It is assumed that our prophet was in Juda or, more particularly, Jerusalem, at the time of the writing [cf. Mal. 2:11]. Most of the people addressed by the prophet were either the former exiles or the exiles' children who had poor spiritual vision and lived a weak religious life. They murmured against God and began to foster doubts as to the righteousness of the divine administration. They yearned for judgment to fall upon the nations, without considering that judgment would begin at the house of God [Amos 3:2; 1 Pe. 4:17]. Therefore, they grew weary waiting for the messianic promises, and their disappointment led to indifference. Their outlook was made manifest when rituals became empty for them by an unholy performance of the service.

Prophet Malachias, Chapter 1

The prophet begins his book, saying, "The burden of the word of the Lord to Israel by the hand of His messenger. Lay it, I pray you, to heart [Mal. 1:1]." Saint John Chrysostom (ca. 347-407) defines for us the word

---

[1] *The Great Synaxaristes of the Orthodox Church*, 6th ed., Vol. 1, p. 78.

"messenger," saying, "A messenger's business is this, to convey from one to another only what is told him. For which cause also the priest is called a 'messenger [cf. Mal. 2:7],' because he speaks not his own words, but those of Him Who sent him."[2]

In his prophecy, the people are advised of the honor due God: "'A son honors his father, and a servant his lord: if then I am Father, where is Mine honor? And if I am Lord, where is My fear?' saith the Lord almighty [Mal. 1:6]." Saint Kyril of Alexandria (378-444) says, "For either we ought to fear the Lord of all as a master, or to honor Him at least as a father—a thing which is far greater and better than the former; for love casteth out fear."[3]

The Lord speaks of His altar receiving polluted bread: "Wherein have ye polluted it [Mal. 1:7]?" Saint Gregory the Theologian (ca. 329/330- ca. 390) writes: "Malachias brings bitter charges against the priests and reproaches them with despising the name of the Lord [Mal. 1:6]. He explains wherein they did this: they offered polluted bread upon the altar and meat that was not of the firstfruits, which they surely would not have offered to one of their governors, lest they should receive dishonor for themselves. Yet they offered such as these to fulfill a vow to the King of the universe, to wit, the lame and the sick, and the deformed, which are utterly profane and loathsome [Mal. 1:13]."[4]

Prophet Malachias

After their captivity in Babylon, the Jews did rebuild their temple and restored the place where they were allowed to observe all these rituals according to the law. But now the power of Christ, the power which founded the Church, has also destroyed their restored temple. Their prophets foretold this and showed that God would reject Judaism and introduce a new way of worship; the ancient sacrifice would be made void, and a new one celebrated.

---

[2] Saint John Chrysostom, Homily V, *Acts*, Nicene, 1st Ser., XI:344.

[3] Saint Kyril of Alexandria, Homily 42, Ch. 8, *Commentary on the Gospel of Saint Luke*, p. 183.

[4] Saint Gregory the Theologian, *Oration in Defence of His Flight to Pontus*, Nicene, 2nd Ser., VII:218.

"Scripture," says Saint John Chrysostom, "did not pass over in silence the rejection of the Jews. Notice how Malachias foretold this, too: '"Even among you the doors shall be shut, and one will not kindle the fire of Mine altar for nought. I have no pleasure in you," saith the Lord almighty, "and I will not accept a sacrifice at your hands [Mal. 1:10]."' He also foretold who would now pay God worship. 'For from the rising of the sun even to the going down thereof My name hath been glorified among the nations. And in every place incense is offered to My name, and a pure offering; for My name is great among the nations [Mal. 1:11].' Do you see how He made clear the nobility of the worship, how He showed that the new worship had a special honor and differed from the old? Worship will not be confined to a place or a way of sacrifice, nor will it consist in savor or smoke or omens; it will now be a different ritual."[5]

Saint John Chrysostom informs us that "Moses had forbidden the Jews to bring their sacrifice to any place other than that which the Lord God would choose; and then He confined their sacrifices to one particular place. If Malachias said that sacrifices were going to be offered everywhere and that it would be a pure offering, he was contradicting and opposing what Moses had said. But there is no contradiction or quarrel. For Moses spoke about one kind of sacrifice, and Malachias later predicted another....Paul contrasted the old law and the new law of grace, and said that the old law had been glorified but is now without glory, because of the surpassing glory of the new law [cf. 2 Cor. 3:10]. I, too, would make so bold as to say in this case that, if the new sacrifice should be compared to the old, only this new sacrifice would properly be called pure. For it is not offered by smoke and fat, nor by blood and the price of ransom, but by the grace of the Spirit."[6]

Saint John of Damascus affirms (ca. 675-ca. 749): "Surely this is that pure and bloodless Sacrifice which the Lord through the prophet said is offered to Him from the rising to the setting of the sun [Mal. 1:11]."[7]

Saint Justin Martyr (ca. 100-ca. 165) adds that "Malachias is speaking of those Gentiles who in every place offer sacrifices to Him, that is, the bread of the Eucharist, and also the cup of the Eucharist, affirming both that we glorify His name, and that the Jews profane it."[8]

Saint Irenaeos (ca. 130-ca. 200), Bishop of Lyons, writes: "These words indicate in the plainest manner that the former people (the Jews) shall indeed cease to make offerings to God, but that in every place sacrifice shall

---

[5] Saint John Chrysostom, *Demonstration Against the Pagans*, FC, 73:176, 215, 259.
[6] Saint John Chrysostom, *Discourse V Against Judaizing Christians*, FC, 68:141-143.
[7] Saint John of Damascus, *Exposition*, Bk. IV, Ch. XIII, Nicene, 2nd Ser., IX:84.
[8] Saint Justin, *Dialogue with Trypho*, Ante-Nicene, I:215.

be offered to Him, and that a pure one; and His name is glorified among the nations. But what other name is there which is glorified among the nations than that of our Lord, by Whom the Father is glorified, and man also? And because it is the name of His own Son, Who was made Man by Him, He calls it His own....Now John, in the Apocalypse, declares that the 'incense' is 'the prayers of the saints [cf. Rev. 5:8].'"[9]

Saint Athanasios the Great (ca. 296-373) says that "the shadow hath received its fulfillment, and the types have been accomplished....As it is in the historical account, in no other place might the feast of the passover be kept, save only in Jerusalem; yet when the things pertaining to that time were fulfilled, and those which belonged to shadows had passed away, and the preaching of the Gospel was about to extend everywhere,...they asked the Savior, 'Where dost Thou want us to prepare [cf. Mt. 26:17]?' The Savior also, since He was changing the typical for the spiritual, promised them that they should no longer eat the flesh of the lamb, by His own saying, 'Take, eat; this is My body....Drink of it, all of you; for this is My blood [Mt. 26:26-28].' When we are thus nourished by these things, we also, my beloved, shall truly keep the feast of the Passover."[10]

Saint Theodore the Stoudite (759-826) praises the Theotokos here, writing: "Rejoice, altar of purification for all mortal creatures, through which the Lord's name is glorified among the nations from the rising of the sun to its setting, and where a sacrifice is offered to His name in every place, according to the holy Malachias!"[11]

Prophet Malachias, Chapter 2

Speaking of the sacerdotal office, Saint Cyprian of Carthage (d. 258) writes: "A heavier labor is incumbent on the priests in asserting and maintaining the majesty of God, that we seem not to neglect anything in this respect, when God admonishes us thus. Is honor then given to God when the majesty and decree of God are so contemned, that when He declares that He is indignant and angry with those who sacrifice, and when He threatens everlasting penalties and perpetual punishments, it is proposed by the sacrilegious and said, 'Let not the wrath of God be considered, let not the judgment of the Lord be feared, let not any knock at the Church of Christ'? But repentance is done away with, and no confession of sin is made; the bishops are despised and trodden underfoot. Deceitful words are proclaimed by the

---

[9] Saint Irenaeus, *Against Heresies*, Bk. IV, Ch. XVII, Ante-Nicene, I:484.
[10] Saint Athanasios, "Letter IV, Pascha, dated 332," Nicene, 2nd Ser., IV:517.
[11] Saint Theodore Stoudite, "Encomium on the Dormition of Our Holy Lady, the Mother of God," *On the Dormition of Mary*, p. 254.

presbyters."[12] He charges elsewhere, "Can it be satisfactory in the day of judgment for a priest of God, who maintains, approves, and acquiesces in the baptism of blasphemers, when the Lord threatens and says, 'And now, O priests, this commandment is to you. If ye will not hearken, and if ye will not lay it to heart, to give glory to My name, then I will send forth the curse upon you, and I will bring a curse upon your blessing [Mal. 2:1, 2].' Does he give glory to God, who communicates with the baptism of Marcion? Does he give glory to God, who judges that remission of sins is granted among those who blaspheme against God? Does he give glory to God, who affirms that sons are born to God without, of an adulterer and a harlot? Does he give glory to God, who does not hold the unity and truth that arise from the divine law, but maintains heresies against the Church? Does he give glory to God, who, a friend of heretics and an enemy to Christians, thinks that the priests of God, who support the truth of Christ and the unity of the Church, are to be excommunicated?...

"But if there be among us, most beloved brother, the fear of God,...let us keep what God has entrusted to us with faithful valor. Nor ought custom, which had crept in among some, to prevent the truth from prevailing and conquering; for custom without truth is the antiquity of error. On which account, let us forsake the error and follow the truth....But it happens, by a love of presumption and of obstinacy, that one would rather maintain his own evil and false position than agree in the right and true which belongs to another. Looking forward to which the blessed Apostle Paul writes to Timothy, and warns him that 'a bishop must not be litigious, nor contentious, but gentle, and apt to teach [cf. 1 Tim. 3:3, 4].' Now he is teachable who is meek and gentle to the patience of learning. For it behooves a bishop not only to teach, but also to learn; because he also teaches better who daily increases and advances by learning better....

"If the priests of God wish to keep the divine precepts, but have in any respect wavered or vacillated from truth, we should return to our Lord and to the evangelical and apostolic tradition....For it has been delivered to us that there is one God, and one Christ, and one hope, and one Faith, and one Church, and one Baptism ordained only in the one Church, from which unity whosoever will depart must needs be found with heretics; and while he upholds them against the Church, he impugns the sacrament against divine tradition."[13]

"For the priest's lips should keep knowledge, and they should seek the law at his mouth: for he is the messenger (angel) of the Lord almighty [Mal. 2:7]." Saint Dionysios the Areopagite (1st C.) answers the following question:

---

[12] Saint Cyprian of Carthage, "Epistle LIV, to Cornelius," Ante-Nicene, V:344.
[13] Ibid., "Epistle LXXIII to Pompey," Ante-Nicene, V:388, 389.

Why are human hierarchs called angels? "I see nothing wrong in the fact that the word of God calls even our hierarch an 'angel,' for...like the angels, he is, to the extent of which he is capable, a messenger, and he is raised up to imitate, so far as a man may, the angelic powers to bring revelation."[14] Elsewhere, he advises, "The divine hierarch makes known the judgment of God....The hierarch, insofar as he interprets the justice of God, would take care to seek nothing which conflicted at all with God's wishes and with what He has promised to grant....If he does otherwise, he would be acting on his own initiative within the hierarchy and not under the guidance of the One Who is the source of every rite. Besides, his unrighteous prayer would be rejected....Thus the hierarch, being a man of God, asks only for what is suitable to the divine promises, for what pleases God, and for what God will freely give."[15] In an epistle, Saint Dionysios affirms that "the priests come next after the hierarchs as messengers and interpreters of the divine judgments."[16]

Saint Aphrahat (early 4th century) writes: "The angels who are the priests, of whose mouth the law is inquired, when they transgress the law, shall be judged at the last by the apostles [1 Cor. 6:3], and the priests who observe the law."[17]

The people did things which God hated, and covered with tears the altar of the Lord, Who asks, "Is it meet for Me to have respect to your sacrifice, or to receive anything from your hands as welcome [Mal. 2:13]?" Saint Basil the Great (ca. 330-379) explains: "If you give alms to the poor after you have despoiled them of their goods, it were better for you neither to have taken nor given. Why do you defile the wealth that is rightfully yours by adding unjust gains to it? Why do you make the gift from injustice?...Be merciful to the one whom you have wronged....God will have no part in avarice, nor will the Lord be a comrade to thieves and robbers. He has not left us the poor to feed because He is unable to do this, but He asks from us, for our own good, the fruit of justice and mercy. Mercy does not spring from injustice, nor blessing from a curse, nor benefits from tears. Alms given out of unjust gain attest to the vainglory and aspiration of the giver for the praises of men, not the praise which is from God....You are not entitled to offer gifts to God if you offend your brother."[18]

---

[14] Saint Dionysius, "The Celestial Hierarchy," Ch. 12, *The Complete Works*, pp. 175, 176.

[15] Ibid., III, 7, pp. 255, 256.

[16] Ibid., "Epistle 8," p. 272.

[17] Saint Aphrahat, *Demonstration XXII*, § 16, Nicene, 2nd Ser., XIII:407, 408.

[18] Saint Basil, *Ascetical Works: On Mercy and Justice*, FC, 3rd ed., IX:509.

Saint John Chrysostom also warns against alms which had their source from covetousness and injustice. "These giving of alms are judaical, or rather they are satanical. For there are those now who by violence take countless things belonging to others. And they think that an excuse is made for all if they cast in some ten or a hundred gold pieces, touching whom also the prophet says, 'Ye covered My altar with tears [Mal. 2:13].' Christ is not willing to be fed by covetousness, He accepts not this food. Why dost thou insult thy Lord, offering Him unclean things? It is better to leave men to pine with hunger, than to feed them from these sources."[19]

Prophet Malachias, Chapter 3

This chapter foretells the coming of the Forerunner John. "Behold, I send forth My messenger, and he shall survey the way before My face. And the Lord, Whom ye seek, shall suddenly come into His temple, even the Angel of the covenant, whom ye take pleasure in; behold, He is coming [Mal. 3:1]."

Saint Ephraim the Syrian (ca. 306-383) asks, "What then was this greatness by which John surpassed all those born of woman? Was it not what the prophet said, 'Behold, I am sending My angel before you [cf. Mal. 3:1; Mt. 11:10]'? He was not called angel by name only, but also because of his manner of life. If you examine carefully, his honor was not inferior to that of the angels; for he disdained all worldly things, and was attentive to those of heaven. If you say that one of the twelve prophets was called 'My angel' (Malachias), well, he was only named thus by his parents, just as all other names are usually given. The name given by one's parents is one thing, but the honor given by God as a reward for one's actions is quite another. If you say he was named 'My angel' by supernal dispensation, we will not dispute this; but the Lord bore witness to John, 'There is none among those born of women greater than he [cf. Mt. 11:11; Lk. 7:28].'"[20]

Saint Kyril of Jerusalem (ca. 315-386) writes: "The Lord heard the prayer of the prophets. The Father disregarded not the perishing of our race; He sent forth His Son, the Lord from heaven, as Healer. And one of the prophets says, 'The Lord, Whom ye seek, shall suddenly come [Mal. 3:1].' Whither? 'The Lord shall come to His own temple [cf. Mal. 3:1].'"[21] Continuing, he says, "Now by the temple he here means the body, holy of a truth and undefiled, which was born of the holy Virgin by the Holy Spirit in the power of the Father....And he styles Him the 'Messenger (Angel) of the covenant,' because He makes known and ministers unto us the good will of

---

[19] Saint John Chrysostom, Homily LXXXV, *Matthew*, Nicene, 1st Ser., X:509.

[20] *Saint Ephrem's Commentary on Tatian's Diatessaron*, p. 157.

[21] Saint Kyril of Jerusalem, "Lecture XII," *Catechetical Lectures*, Nicene, 2nd Ser., VII:74.

the Father. For He has Himself said to us, 'All things which I heard from My Father I made known to you [Jn. 15:15].'"[22]

The immutability of God is proclaimed by the prophet, "For I am the Lord your God, and I am not changed [Mal. 3:6]." Saint Athanasios asks, "How is He subject to change and variation Who says, by Himself, 'I am in the Father and the Father is in Me [Jn. 14:10],' and 'I and the Father are one [Jn. 10:30],' and by the prophet, 'Behold Me, for I am, and I change not [cf. Mal. 3:6]'? For although one may refer this expression to the Father, yet it may now be more aptly spoken of the Logos, namely, that though He has been made Man, He has not changed. But as the apostle has said, 'Jesus Christ, the same yesterday and today and to the ages [Heb. 13:8].' And who can have persuaded them (Arius and his fellows) to say that He was made for us, whereas Paul writes: 'For it was becoming to Him, because of Whom are all things and by means of Whom are all things [Heb. 2:10]'?"[23]

Elsewhere, Saint Athanasios comments, "The nature of all things originate and created is alterable and changeable, yet excepting the Son from these, it shows us thereby that He is in no wise a thing originate. Nay, it teaches that He changes everything else, and is Himself not changed. For, 'Thou art the same, and Thy years shall not fail [Ps. 101:27; Heb. 1:12]'; and with reason: for things originate, being from nothing, and not being before their origination, because, in truth, they came to be after not being, have a nature which is changeable; but the Son, being from the Father, and proper to His essence, is unchangeable and unalterable as the Father Himself. For it is sinful to say that from that essence which is unalterable was begotten an alterable Logos and a changeable Wisdom."[24]

Saint Hilary of Poitiers (ca. 315-358) says, "No one who is endued with reason can impute to God a soul; though it is written in many places that the soul of God hates sabbaths and new moons, and also that It delights in certain things. But this is merely a conventional expression to be understood in the same way as when God is spoken of as possessing body, with hands, eyes, fingers, arms, and heart. As the Lord said, 'A spirit hath not flesh and bones [Lk. 24:39].' He then Who is, and changes not [Mal. 3:6], cannot have limbs and parts of a tangible body. He is a simple and blessed nature, a single, complete, all-embracing Whole. God is therefore not quickened into life, like bodies, by the action of an indwelling soul, but is Himself His own life."[25]

---

[22] Saint Kyril, Homily 94, Ch. 12, *Commentary*, op. cit., p. 378.
[23] Saint Athanasios, *Deposition of Arius*, Nicene, 2nd Ser., IV:70.
[24] Saint Athanasios, *Discourse I Against the Arians*, Nicene, 2nd Ser., IV:327.
[25] Saint Hilary of Poitiers, *On the Trinity*, Bk. X(58), Nicene, 2nd Ser., IX:198.

"How then," asks Saint Hilary, "does He then lay down His soul, or take it up again? What is the meaning of this command He received? God could not lay it down, that is, die, or take it up again, that is, come to life. But neither did the body receive the command to take it up again; it could not do so of itself, for He said of the temple of His body, 'Destroy this temple, and in three days I will raise it [Jn. 2:19].' Thus it is God Who raises up the temple of His body. And Who lays down His soul to take it again? The body does not take it up again of itself: it is raised up by God. That which is raised up again must have been dead, and that which is living does not lay down its soul. God then was neither dead nor buried: and yet He said, 'For in putting this perfumed ointment upon My body, she did it for My burial [Mt. 26:12].' In that it was poured upon His body it was done for His burial: but the 'His' is not the same as 'Him.' It is quite another use of the pronoun when we say, 'It was done for the burial of Him,' and when we say, 'His body was anointed'; nor is the sense the same in 'His body was buried,' and 'He was buried.'"[26]

Saint Ambrose of Milan (ca. 339-397) writes that Christ "was in the womb, was born, was nursed, was placed in the crib,...that you might believe that it was God Who renewed nature, and it was man who was born of man according to nature. For not, as some have concluded, was the very nature of the Word changed, which is always unchangeable....You have learned that He offered the sacrifice from our nature. For what was the cause of the incarnation except that flesh which had sinned might be redeemed through itself? Therefore, that which had sinned was redeemed....The nature of the Word was not turned into the nature of the flesh, because divinity immune from sin was not obliged to offer Itself for sin which it had not committed. Christ offered in Himself that which He put on, and He put on what He did not have before. He did not, then, put on the divinity of His own divinity, in which was the fullness of eternal divinity, but He assumed flesh that He might put off the covering of the flesh, and might both crucify in Himself the spoils of the devil and erect the trophies of peace."[27]

Prophet Malachias, Chapter 4

There are two comings: The one in which Christ became a man subject to stripes and knowing what it is to bear infirmity [Is. 53:3]; "but at the second," says Saint Irenaeos, "He will come on the clouds [Dan. 7:13], bringing on the day which burns as an oven [Mal. 4:1], and smiting the earth with the word of His mouth [Is. 11:4], and slaying the impious with the breath of His lips, and having a fan in His hands, and cleansing His floor, and

---

[26] Ibid., Bk. X(59, 60), pp. 198, 199.
[27] Saint Ambrose, *The Sacrament of the Incarnation of Our Lord*, FC, 44:240.

gathering the wheat indeed into His barn, but burning the chaff with unquench-able fire [cf. Mt. 3:12; Lk. 3:17]."[28] The prophet describes this: "'Behold, a day cometh burning as an oven, and it shall consume them; and all those of another descent (ἀλλογενεῖς), and all that do lawlessness (ἄνομα) shall be stubble. And the day that is coming shall set them on fire,' saith the Lord almighty, 'and there shall not be left of them root or branch [Mal. 4:1].'"

Saint Cyprian remarks, "The Lord prophesies that those of another descent or race shall be burnt up and consumed; that is, aliens from the divine race, and the profane, those who are not spiritually born anew, nor made children of God. For only those can escape who have been born anew and signed with the sign of Christ....And this sign pertains to the Passion and blood of Christ; and whosoever is found in this sign is kept safe and unharmed...."[29]

"But to you that fear My name shall the Sun of righteousness arise, and healing shall be in His wings; and ye shall be in His wings [Mal. 4:2]." Saint Hippolytos (ca. 170-ca. 236) comments on the Apocalypse where the woman shall be given "two wings of the eagle, the great one, in order that she may fly into the wilderness, into her place, there where she is being nourished for a time and times and half a time, from the face of the serpent [Rev. 12:14]," and says this refers to the one thousand two hundred and sixty days (the half of the week), during which time the tyrant is to reign and persecute the Church. "She flees from city to city, and seeks concealment in the wilderness among the mountains, possessed of no other defense than the two wings of the great eagle, that is to say, the Faith of Jesus Christ, Who, in stretching forth His holy hands on the holy Tree, unfolded two wings, the right and the left, and called to Him all who believed upon Him, and covered them as a hen her chickens."[30]

Saint Ephraim says, "Our Lord is the Sun of righteousness, for He gave health of body and healing of soul to humanity."[31]

Saint Kyril of Jerusalem says, "Christ is the Sun of righteousness setting out from heaven, circumscribed by His visible nature, and returning unto Himself—being on every side equal to Himself and alike; and not only this, but also as giving life to all the circle of the virtues, gently commingled and intermixed with each other, according to the law of love and order....But he that persecutes the Light that shines in darkness cannot overtake Him."[32]

---

[28] Saint Irenaeus, *Against Heresies*, Bk. IV, Ch. XXXIII, Ante-Nicene, I: 506.

[29] Saint Cyprian, *Treatise V*, Ante-Nicene, V:464.

[30] Saint Hippolytos, *Treatise on Christ and Antichrist*, Ante-Nicene, V:217.

[31] Saint Ephraim, *Commentary*, pp. 124, 125.

[32] Saint Kyril of Jerusalem, *The Second Oration on Easter*, Nicene, 2nd Ser., VII:428.

Blessed Jerome (ca. 342-420) speaking of the Lord's day and Sunday, writes: "The Lord's day, the day of the resurrection, the day of Christians, is our day. It is called the Lord's day because on this day the Lord ascended to the Father as Victor; but when the heathens call it the day of the sun, we are most happy to acknowledge their title, for today has risen 'the Sun of justice with its healing wings [cf. Mal 4:2].' Does the sun really have wings?...We say, whoever has been under the wings of this Sun Who has said in the Gospel, 'How often would I have gathered together thy children, in the way a hen gathereth together her chicks under her wings, and ye would not [Mt. 23:37],' shall be safe from the devil-hawk, safe under the great wings of that mighty eagle [cf. Ez. 17:3, 7], and all the wounds of his sins shall be healed."[33]

Saint Bede the Venerable (ca. 673-735) comments, "It was His rays which the blessed Virgin received when she conceived the Lord. But that same Sun, that is, the divinity of our Redeemer, cloaked itself with the covering of human nature as with a shade, and by such means a virgin's womb was able to bear Him. Thus the power of the Most High overshadowed her at the time when the divine might of Christ filled her with His presence, and, in order that His substance could be received by her, He veiled Himself with our weakness."[34]

Saint Symeon the New Theologian (949-1022) discourses: "From the beginning God created two worlds, the visible and the invisible....And in accordance with these two worlds there are two suns shining: one can be seen with the senses, the other comprehended. What our sun is for this visible and sensory world, God is for the invisible and intelligible world. He is called the Sun of righteousness, and so He is [Mal. 4:2]....On the one hand, sensory things are illuminated by the sensible sun; and, on the other hand, intelligible reality is illumined by the intelligible sun. But there is no full union or understanding or communion between the two, either from the intelligible to the sensible, or from the sensible world to the intelligible [cf. Lk. 16:26]....The sensible sun rises to shine on the world of sense and all it contains....But then it goes down and again leaves in darkness the place where once it shone. The intelligible sun shines eternally,...complete in all complete reality....It is separate and distinct from its creatures, yet not separated from them. It is complete in all places, yet nowhere, and complete in all visible creatures yet

---

[33] Blessed Jerome, *Homily 94, on Easter Sunday*, FC, 57:253.
[34] Saint Bede, *Homilies on the Gospels, Bk. II*, p. 25.

completely outside them. It is complete in the visible and complete in the invisible."[35]

Saint Hippolytos mentions here that "it is a matter of course that His forerunners must appear first, as He says by Malachias and the angel, 'I will send to you Elias the Thesbite (Tishbite), before the great and glorious day of the Lord cometh, who shall turn again the heart of the father to the son, and the heart of a man to his neighbor, lest I come and smite the earth grievously [Mal. 4:5, 6].' These then shall come and proclaim the manifestation of Christ that is to be from heaven; and they shall also perform signs and wonders, in order that men may be put to shame and turned to repentance on account of their surpassing wickedness and impiety [cf. Rev. 11:3]."[36]

Saint Justin says to Trypho the Jew, "Our Lord in His teaching proclaimed...that Elias would also come. And we know that this shall take place when our Lord Jesus Christ will be about to come in glory from heaven. Just as the Spirit of God that was in Elias, was in the person of John—a prophet of your nation—after whom no other prophet appeared among you,...in like manner, while Moses was still among men, God took of the spirit which was in Moses and put it on Jesus of Navee,[37] even so God was able to cause the spirit of Elias to come upon John."[38]

The holy Church chants on the day of the prophet's commemoration: "Illumined by the divine Spirit, thou didst proclaim the awesome day of the coming of Christ, the calling of the nations, and the ending of the force of the law."[39]

Saint John Chrysostom reminds us that "the Scriptures speak of two advents of Christ, both this that is past, and that which is to come....And the prophets too mention both; of the one, however, that is, of the second, they say Elias will be the forerunner. For of the first, John was forerunner, whom Christ called also Elias, not because he was Elias, but because he was fulfilling the ministry of that prophet. For as the one shall be forerunner of the second advent, so was the other of the first. But the scribes, confusing these things and perverting the people, made mention of that other only to the people, the second advent, and said, 'If this man is the Christ, Elias ought to have come beforehand.' Therefore the disciples too speak as follows: 'How

---

[35] Saint Symeon the New Theologian, *The Practical and Theological Chapters and The Three Theological Discourses*, 2.22-2.25, pp. 69-71.

[36] Saint Hippolytos, "Treatise on Christ and Antichrist," Ante-Nicene, V:213, 214.

[37] Cf. Num. 11:17; Num. 27:18; Deut. 34:9.

[38] Saint Justin, *Dialogue with Trypho*, Ch. 49, Ante-Nicene, I:219.

[39] Prophet Malachias, January 3rd, Orthros Canon, conflation of Odes 5 and 6, Mode Plagal Four.

then say the scribes, "Elias must first come?"...Therefore also the Pharisees sent unto John, and asked him, "Art thou Elias [Jn. 1:21]?"' They make no mention anywhere of the former advent.

"What then is the solution which Christ alleged? 'Elias indeed cometh then, before My second coming; and now too is Elias come'; so calling John. In this sense Elias is come: but if thou wouldest seek the Tishbite, he is coming [cf. Mt. 17:11, 12; Mk. 9:12, 13]. Seest thou the accuracy of prophetical language? Now, because Christ called John, Elias, by reason of their community of office, lest thou shouldest suppose this to be the meaning of the prophet too in this place, He added his country also, saying, 'the Thesbite [Mal. 4:5]'; whereas John was not a Thesbite....To show therefore that the Thesbite comes before that other advent, which hath the judgment, He said this....'And he shall restore all things [cf. Mt. 17:11; Mk. 9:12]'; that is, shall correct the unbelief of the Jews that are then in being. Hence the extreme accuracy of the expression: the Lord said not that He would restore (ἀποκαταστήσει) the heart of the son to the father, but 'of the father to the son [Mal. 4:6; cf. Lk. 1:17].' For the Jews being fathers of the apostles, the meaning is that He will restore to the doctrines of their sons, that is, of the apostles, the hearts of the fathers, that is, the Jewish people's mind."[40]

Saint John of Damascus speaks on the book of Revelation and the end times, saying, "Enoch and Elias the Tishbite shall be sent and shall turn the hearts of the fathers to the children, that is, the Synagogue to our Lord Jesus Christ and the preaching of the apostles: and they (the two prophets) shall be destroyed by him (Antichrist). And the Lord shall come out of heaven, just as the holy apostles beheld Him going into heaven, perfect God and perfect Man, with glory and power, and will destroy the man of lawlessness, the son of the perdition, by the breath of His mouth [cf. 2 Thess. 2:3, 8]. Let no one, therefore, look for the Lord to come from earth, but out of heaven, as He Himself has made sure."[41]

On the 3rd of January, the holy Church commemorates the holy Martyr GORDIOS.[42]

Gordios, the holy martyr, was a native of Caesarea. In 314, he was degraded from his rank of centurion, when Licinius (308-324) removed Christians from the army. He could no longer bear to view the audacity and

---

[40] Saint John Chrysostom, Homily LVII, *Matthew*, Nicene, 1st Ser., X:352, 353.
[41] Saint John of Damascus, *Exposition*, Bk. IV, Ch. XXVI, Nicene, 2nd Ser., IX:99.
[42] Saint Basil the Great wrote of Saint Gordios in his panegyrical Homily XVIII, which begins, "It is a law of nature...[*P.G.* 31:489-507]."See also Saint Basil, *Prolegomena*, Nicene, 2nd Ser., VIII:lxx.

outrages that the Greek pagans perpetrated upon the Christians. He could no longer endure to hear the blasphemies they hurled at Jesus Christ. He was resolved to take himself away from the city, preferring to dwell in the mountains with wild beasts and irrational animals. Upon retiring into the wilderness, he led the life of an anchorite.

The ever-memorable one was filled with love and desire for Christ. Empowered by God, he was endowed with courage to take action against the error of the Greek pagans, for "the righteous is confident as a lion [Prov. 28:1]." One day there was a great festival at Caesarea in honor of Mars. There were to be races in the theater, and thither the whole population trooped, so that not a Jew, not a heathen, was wanting. No small company of Christians also had joined the crowd, men of careless life, sitting in the assembly of folly, and not shunning the counsel of the evildoers, to see the speed of the horses and the skill of the charioteers. Masters had given their slaves a holiday. Even boys ran from their schools to the show. There was a multitude of common women of the lower ranks. The stadium was packed, and everyone was gazing intently on the races.

Then that noble man, great of heart and of courage, came down from the uplands into the theater. He took no thought of the mob. He did not heed how many hostile hands he might meet. In a moment the whole theater turned to stare at the extraordinary sight. The man looked wild and savage. From his long sojourn in the mountains, his head was squalid, his beard long, his dress filthy. His body was like a skeleton. He carried a stick and a bag. Yet there was a certain grace about him, shining from the unseen all around him. He cried out the words of Prophet Esaias: "I became manifest to them that asked not for Me; I was found of them that sought Me not: I said, 'Behold, I am here,' to a nation, who called not on My name [Is. 65:1; Rom. 10:20, 21].'" He was recognized. A great shout arose. Those who shared his Faith clapped for joy, but the enemies of the truth urged the magistrate to put in force the penalty he had incurred, which condemned him beforehand to die. Then a universal shouting arose all round. Nobody looked at either the horses or the charioteers. The exhibition of the chariots was mere idle noise. Every eye was wholly occupied with focusing on Gordios, and every ear was engaged on hearing only his words. Then a confused murmur, running like a wind through all the theater, sounded above the din of the course. Heralds were told to proclaim silence. The pipes were hushed, and all the band stopped in a moment. Gordios was being listened to; Gordios was the center of all eyes, and in a moment he was dragged before the magistrate who presided over the games.

With a mild and gentle voice, the magistrate asked him his name, and whence he came. He told him his country, his family, the rank he had held, the reason for his flight, and his return. "Here I am," he cried, "ready to testify by creed to the contempt in which I hold your orders, and my faith in the God in Whom I have trusted. For I have heard that you are inferior to few in cruelty. This is why I have chosen this time in order to carry out my wishes." With these words he kindled the wrath of the governor like a fire, and roused all his fury against himself. The order was given: "Call the lictors. Where are the plates of lead? Where are the scourges? Let him be stretched upon a wheel. Let him be wrenched upon the rack. Let the instruments of torture be brought in. Make ready the beasts, the fire, the sword, the cross. What a good thing for the villain that he can die only once!" "Nay," replied Gordios. "What a bad thing for me that I cannot die for Christ again and again!"

The Martyrdom of Saint Gordios

All the town crowded to the spot where the martyrdom was to be consummated. The spiritually resourceful Gordios uttered his last words. "Death is the common lot of man. As we must all die, let us through death win life. Make the necessary voluntary. Exchange the earthly for the heavenly." The martyr then urged them not to tarry. He then raised his eyes heavenward and chanted, "The Lord is a helper to me, and I will not fear what man shall do to me [Ps. 117:6]." And, "Even though I should walk in the midst of the shadow of death, yet I will not be afraid of evils; for Thou art with me [Ps. 22:4]." He also chanted many other verses which he knew. Anxious to receive his reward and be with the Master Christ, he chided the pagans for delaying in putting him to the test. The magistrate, however, attempted to entice Gordios with the promise of a promotion to a high rank and the endowment of properties and titles. Gordios made light of his offers and smiled, saying, "Whatever thou shouldest promise, it would not be superior to the kingdom of the heavens." The magistrate then passed the death sentence.

Gordios' friends gathered about him and embraced him. They attempted to soften his resolve. They counseled him to save himself by denying Christ in word only, and keeping to his own beliefs privately, saying, "God cares only what is in thy heart, while talk is of no account." Gordios remonstrated with them, saying, "Why do you ask me to exchange a few days longer here on earth for everlasting life? Words are of great account. 'For with the heart one believeth unto righteousness, and with the mouth one confesseth unto salvation [Rom. 10:10].' Has not the Lord said, 'Everyone therefore who shall confess in Me before men, I also will confess in him before My Father Who is in the heavens. But whosoever shall deny Me before men, him will I also deny before My Father Who is in the heavens [Mt. 10:32, 33]'? Ask me not to renounce my Lord Whom I have worshipped since childhood. 'The one who findeth his life shall lose it; and the one who loseth his life on account of Him shall find it [cf. Mt. 10:39].'"

The martyr then made the sign of the Cross over himself. The whole city followed him to the execution site. Next he stepped forward for the fatal blow, without changing color or losing his cheerful mien. It seemed as though he were not going to meet an executioner, but to yield himself into the hands of angels. The executioner raised the sword and severed his honorable head. Thus, Saint Gordios received the crown of martyrdom.

**On the 3rd of January, the holy Church commemorates
our venerable Father PETER, the bearer of miracles and signs,
of the Coenobium of Saint Zacharias at Atroa, Bithynia.**

**On the 3rd of January, the holy Church commemorates
the holy THREE MARTYRS, a MOTHER and her TWO CHILDREN,
who were slain in the fire.**

**On the 3rd of January, the holy Church commemorates
our venerable Mother GENEVIÈVE of Paris.**[43]

Geneviève, our holy mother, was born (ca. 422) at Nanterre, a small village four miles from Paris, near Mont Valérien. The remembrance of the Feast of the Nativity of Christ was ever alive among the people of Nanterre who kept their sheep in the surrounding hills and on the slopes of the mount. If the gentle wooded hills of the Seine in the environs of Paris bore slight resemblance to the stark, rock-strewn slopes and jagged crests of the hills of Judaea, where those simple shepherds were glorified with the divine vision a mere five hundred years earlier, nevertheless, in the days of Saint Geneviève's youth the same spirit of simple faith prevailed among the shepherds of Gaul.

---

[43] This Life has been reprinted in *The Great Synaxaristes* (in English), courtesy of the editor of the bi-monthly periodical, *Orthodox Life*, published by Holy Trinity Monastery, Jordanville, NY. See "Saint Geneviève of Paris," *Orthodox Life*, Volume 22, Number 6, November-December 1972:6-11.

Geneviève was of wealthy parents, but, as was the custom of the time, she nevertheless shepherded her father's flock in the pasture of Valérien. Nourished from the cradle with the Gospel message and with the pious example of her parents' life, the scenes from the life of the Savior and the iconography of the parables so vivid in the life around her, Geneviève grew in stature not only physically but spiritually as well. God, Who knows all things from eternity, beheld the heart of this gentle maiden. Seeing in it the flame of love for the Creator and an undefeatable faith, He bestowed upon her special gifts of divine grace.

Saint Geneviève

When Germain (Germanus, ca. 378-448), the renowned and holy Bishop of Auxerre, was on his way to Britain to preach the Savior's Gospel against the Pelagian heresy,[44] which threatened the salvation of many, he, together with his companion Saint Lupus of Troyes, chanced to stop over at Nanterre. As the bishop drew near the town, the people, as sheep at the approach of their good shepherd, flocked to meet him. Among those who went were Severus and Gerontia with their daughter Geneviève. As in an enactment of the entry of Christ into Jerusalem (for the bishop is an icon of Christ), the people accompanied their shepherd to the village church. As he paused and turned to bless the faithful, the eyes of the aged saint fell upon the child Geneviève. "He called to himself the little child, and set her in their midst [cf. Mt. 18:2]." He then asked her name. Someone standing next to the lass replied, "Geneviève." The venerable old bishop kissed her. The parents of the child then drew near. Saint Germain, perceiving who they were, turned to them and inquired, "Is this your child?" "Yes," they replied. He said, "Blessed are you in having so blessed a child! She will be great before God; and because of her, many shall turn from evil and follow after good and shall obtain salvation from Christ the Lord."

---

[44] Pelagianism: A heretical teaching, originating with the British Monk Pelagius (5th C.), who held that man can take the initial and fundamental steps toward salvation by his own efforts, without divine grace. *The Oxford Dictionary of the Christian Church*, s.v. "Pelagianism."

Turning to the maiden he said, "Geneviève, my daughter. Tell me, dost thou desire to dedicate thyself pure and undefiled to Christ, as His bride?" With a radiant smile, the blessed one replied, "Holy master, thou hast spoken exactly the desire of my heart. I pray that God will grant it to me." "Be assured, my daughter, that He will. Be courageous, and what thou dost believe in thy heart and confess with thy lips, so also conduct thy life and perform thy works. And God will add to thy comeliness both virtue and fortitude." Then, in the image of the entrance of the all-holy Theotokos into the temple,[45] the holy archpastor took Geneviève by the hand and led her into the church for the service of the Ninth Hour and Vespers. Throughout the service the bishop placed his hand on the child's head. At the close of the evening, after the night's hymns had been chanted, the bishop gave the child over to her father, instructing him to bring her into his presence very early in the morning. At the break of dawn, Severus hastened to obey the holy bishop, and appeared before him with his daughter.

"Rejoice, my daughter Geneviève!" the bishop greeted her. "Dost thou recall thy vow of yesterday, to keep thy body pure and undefiled?" "I remember, holy master, that I promised thee and God to preserve the chastity of my mind and my body until the end of my life." Then Saint Germain gave her a little brass medallion, with a cross engraved on it, saying, "Bore a hole in this and wear it round about thy neck, in remembrance of thy promise made before me. And do not let any other ornaments, neither gold, nor silver, nor stone, adorn thy neck or fingers." Then, taking leave of the people of Nanterre and bestowing upon them his episcopal blessing, the holy bishop set out again on his journey.

At the age of fifteen, Geneviève was taken to Paris to be consecrated to the monastic life.[46] With her went two other virgins, and though she was the youngest of the three, the bishop, inspired by the Holy Spirit, placed her first, saying that heaven had already consecrated her. Not long after Geneviève entered the monastic life, her parents reposed, and she began to live in a community in Paris. Her sanctity soon became known throughout the city. By means of a strict life and constant struggles, she began more and more to acquire the Holy Spirit. She received from God the gifts of clairvoyance and

---

[45] The Feast of the Entrance of the Virgin Mary into the Temple is commemorated by the holy Church on the 21st of November.

[46] Butler comments when Geneviève asked to go to church, her mother struck her on the face. In punishment, the mother lost her eyesight. She recovered it two months later, by washing her eyes with water, which Geneviève fetched from the well and over which she had made the sign of the Cross. The people of Nanterre considered that well blessed by the saint. *Butler's Lives of the Saints*, January 3rd, I:28.

wonderworking. Nevertheless, by the time Saint Germain passed through Paris, returning to Auxerre from Britain, the maliciousness of the evil one had stirred envious persons to slander the morals of the blessed Geneviève. This was an attempt to poison the mind of the holy bishop against her. Saint Germain responded to these slanders by receiving Saint Geneviève publicly with great warmth and visible reverence. Gradually the people of Paris and the entire region began to venerate the consecrated virgin as a chosen vessel of God. Her prayers were sought by the sick and afflicted. Those with troubles came for her advice on various matters. Her prophetic words were heeded without question by the sincere faithful.

It was not long before the storm broke out once more against the sacred virgin, so that her detractors, instigated by the evil one, wished to drown her. A report had come of the Mongolian march and the invasion of Attila the Hun with his army (451). Therefore, the Parisians prepared to abandon their city. That her influence was tremendous in Paris is obvious from the fact that she was able to dissuade the Parisians from fleeing their city when the hordes of Huns approached. The devil, not wishing to see the mercy and power of God manifested in His saint, stirred up a mob of citizens, weak in faith. The various leaders of this mob began shouting that Geneviève was a false prophetess. They claimed that she was leading the people to a horrible death by dissuading them from escaping with their possessions to a safer place. The rabble, headstrong and cruel, searched out the saint to stone her and drown her in the Seine. At this very time, her ancient benefactor and spiritual father, Saint Germain, lay dying in Auxerre. Suddenly he raised himself up on his bed, called his archdeacon to him and said, "Take a basket of antidoron[47] and go quickly to Paris. Find my daughter Geneviève and give her the holy bread as a token of my love and esteem. But see that thou goest quickly." The archdeacon arrived at the most critical moment for the besieged nun. He knew the prophecies concerning the blessed one. He began to push through the crowd with the antidoron sent by the holy bishop, reminding them of the great esteem and veneration the Saint held for Geneviève. On the force of this sudden show of support from Bishop Germain, who was already revered as a saint of God, the crowd repented and dispersed. Thus was the saying of the apostle fulfilled: "Not all have the faith. But faithful is the Lord, Who shall establish you and guard you from the evil one [2 Thess. 3:2, 3]." Geneviève thereupon assembled her sisterhood, and together they fasted and prayed fervently to God to deliver the city from the barbarians. The Lord heeded the prayers of His servant Geneviève, and spared Paris. Suddenly, and

---

[47] Antidoron (lit. "instead of the gift") is the bread that is blessed but not consecrated and is distributed to the faithful at the end of the divine Liturgy.

for no apparent reason, the Huns turned away from the city and went in an opposite direction.

The Franks had gained possession of the better part of Gaul, and Childeric (d. 481 or 482), their king, had taken Paris. On that occasion, Paris had been blockaded by the Franks, and the district suffered greatly from famine, since the crops had been destroyed and the countryside laid waste. Saint Geneviève, seeing the suffering of the people, led a group of boats to Arcis-sur-Aube and, by the grace of God, managed to return with sufficient grain to feed Paris.

Now Childeric, though a pagan, had great respect and awe for Saint Geneviève. It is said that he was unable to refuse her any request which she made in behalf of others. Geneviève was especially compassionate toward prisoners. She would constantly intercede to save them from death. On one occasion, Childeric was about to execute a large number of war prisoners some distance outside the city. In order to be left in peace to carry out this sorry deed, the king ordered that the city gate be closed, barred, and sealed, lest Saint Geneviève should follow him and obtain pardon for the condemned ones. But when the saint heard that the blood of so many men was to be shed, she fell into a fit of compassion and love. She rushed along the street to the gate, followed by a crowd of curious citizens. Seeing the gate locked and sealed, the holy one raised her hands up to God, signed the gate with the sign of the all-honorable Cross and laid her hand upon it. And what fear and wonder passed through the crowd, for the gate began to swing open as if moved by the hands of invisible angels [cf. Acts 12:10]. The saint wasted not a second, but pursued the king with tears. Overtaking him, she threw herself on the ground before him and would not be comforted, until she had obtained mercy for the hapless prisoners. And the victorious warrior-king, helpless as a child before the sacred entreaties of God's saint, pardoned and released the entire company of captives. All Paris marvelled and wondered: if her intercessions before this sanguinary and pagan king are so powerful, then how much more so must they be before the King of mercy, Who is ever ready to bestow His compassion upon mankind? On another occasion, King Clovis (ca. 466-511), who embraced the Faith in 496, listened with deference to the holy nun. More than once he granted liberty to captives at her request.

Saint Geneviève nourished herself on a small piece of barley bread and a few beans stewed in oil; but when she was fifty the bishop commanded her to eat fish and drink some milk also. In her later years, the grace of God was especially manifested in the saint. Feeling a great reverence for Saint Denys (Dionysios the Areopagite [Acts 17:34]), the blessed one was filled with ardor to build a church in his honor. She commissioned several priests to undertake the work. They replied that they felt unable to fulfill this task because, among other reasons, there were no means of firing the lime. To this Saint Geneviève calmly replied, "Go and cross over the city bridge; then return and tell me what you heard there." The priests went immediately, and after they had crossed over the bridge, they heard two swineherds conversing. "I was chasing one of my pigs the other day," said the first, "and he led me into the forest to a large limekiln." "What a coincidence," replied the second, "I found a tree in the forest uprooted by the wind, and under its roots there was an old kiln." On hearing this the priests returned with fear, praising God, and told the saint what they had heard. The holy one, lifting her hands heavenward, said, "Blessed be the Lord Who sends His help in time for every need!" She set a certain Father Jean (John) over the project and urged the citizens to assist. The saint also encouraged the workmen until the Church of Saint Denys was built and finished.

Saint Geneviève always considered the Saturday all-night vigil service to be especially important. "It is a likeness of how our whole lives should be," she would say. "We must keep vigil in prayer and fasting, so that the Lord will find us thus when He comes. And the Lord comes to us especially in the holy Eucharist in the Liturgy." It happened that one stormy night, as it drew near to Sunday morning and the saint set out with her sisterhood to the Church of Saint Denys, the lantern which was carried before her was extinguished by a sudden strong gust of wind. The sisters became frightened at the pitch darkness, the howling storm, and the rain. The road was so winding and muddy that without a light they could not find their way. Then Saint Geneviève took the lantern and signed it with the Cross; immediately the candle in the lantern burst into a bright flame. Holding it before herself, she went forth and entered the church.

The holy one undertook several pilgrimages to the cave at Tours of Saint Martin, in the company of her sisterhood. Saint Geneviève reposed at the age of eighty-nine in 512. Her relics were laid to rest first at the Church of Saint Denys. Her relics were then transferred to the Church of Saint Étienne (Saint Stephen)-du-Mont in Paris. The greater part of her relics, however, were destroyed or pillaged by a mob during the French Revolution (1787-1799). They had been publicly burnt at the Place de Grève in 1793, and cast into the Seine. It is, however, reported that a large relic had been kept at Verneuil, Oise, in the eighteenth century, and is still extant. The reliquary itself was later recovered and rests in the Church of Saint Étienne. Many miracles have been attributed to the patroness of Paris, but she was especially famed for her cures of fevers and epidemics.

Through the intercessions of Thy Saints,
O Christ God, have mercy on us. Amen.

**On the 4ᵗʰ of January, the holy Church commemorates
the holy and glorious APOSTLES OF THE SEVENTY.**

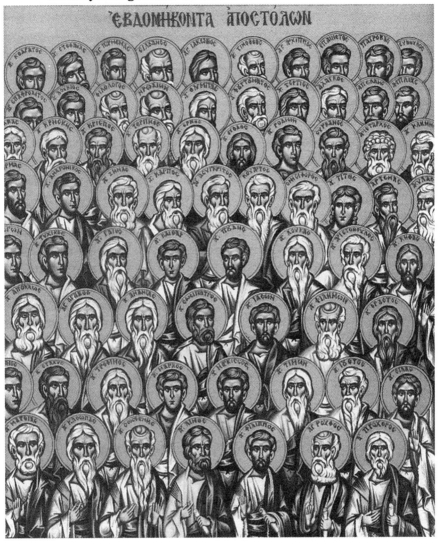

Apostles of the Seventy

Seventy disciples and apostles were appointed by our Lord Jesus Christ. These beacons illumined the world with the radiance of piety, casting out the darkness of impiety. They were sent forth, even as the Twelve, with authority to bind and to loose, to uproot impiety, and plant the knowledge of God. The power of their divinely wise words put to shame the pagan rhetoricians and their deceptive ancient impostures. They enlightened the

Jews, illuminating them regarding the fulfillment of the Scriptures in Christ. Their words were confirmed in faraway lands by both signs and wonders.

Now the number seventy has spiritual significance in the Old and New Testaments. After the exodus of the children of Israel from Egypt and their entry into the wilderness, "they departed from before Iroth, and crossed the middle of the sea into the wilderness; and they went a journey of three days through the wilderness, and encamped in Picriae (Heb. Marah; lit. Bitternesses) [Num. 33:8]." The bitter waters were made sweet by wood [Ex. 15:23-25]. Then "they departed from Picriae, and came to Aelim; and in Aelim were twelve fountains of water, and seventy palm trees, and they encamped there by the water [Num. 33:9]." This event foretold the twelve Apostles and the Seventy who are watered by the streams of grace. They were commissioned to spread the Gospel and the message of the Cross of Christ [1 Cor. 1:17]. Blessed Jerome comments that "as wood sweetens Marah (Merrha), so that seventy palm trees are watered by its streams, so the Cross makes the waters of the law life-giving to the Seventy who are Christ's apostles."[1] Saint Gregory of Nyssa (ca. 335-ca. 395) also observes that "the Israelites came upon twelve bountiful springs that were shaded by a grove of date palms. There were seventy date palms which, even though few in number, made a great impression on those who saw them, because of their exceptional height and beauty."[2]

We also read that the Lord spoke to Moses, saying, "Gather Me seventy men from the elders of Israel, whom thou thyself knowest that they are the elders of the people, and their scribes; and thou shalt bring them to the tabernacle of witness, and they shall stand there with thee [Num. 11:16]." And, "The Lord came down in a cloud, and spoke to him, and took of the Spirit that was upon him, and put it upon the seventy men that were elders; and when the Spirit rested upon them, they prophesied...[Num. 11:25]."

The number seventy also came to be the symbol of perfection and multitude, for seven is deemed perfect and ten is the sign of quantity. The prophets understood the number to signify the completion or fulfillment of the Lord's will. Prophet Jeremias wrote: "For thus said the Lord, 'When seventy years shall be on the point of being accomplished at Babylon, I will visit you, and will confirm My words to you, to bring back your people to this place [Jer. 36(29):10].'" And, "I Daniel understood by books the number of the years which was the word of the Lord to the Prophet Jeremias, even seventy years for the accomplishment of the desolation of Jerusalem [Dan. 9:2]." And, "Seventy weeks have been determined upon thy people, and upon the

---

[1] Blessed Jerome, "Letter LXIX, to Oceanus," ¶ 6, Nicene, 2nd Ser., VI:145.
[2] Saint Gregory of Nyssa, *The Life of Moses*, Bk. I, ¶ 34.

holy city, for sin to be ended, and to seal up transgressions, and to blot out the iniquities, and to make atonement for iniquities, and to bring in everlasting righteousness, and to seal the vision and the prophet, and to anoint the Most Holy [Dan. 9:24]."

When Peter asked Jesus, "How often shall my brother sin against me, and I forgive him? Until seven times?" Our Lord answered, "I say not to thee, 'until seven times,' but, 'until seventy times seven [Mt. 18:21, 22].'" Saint John Chrysostom comments: "What then saith Christ, the good God, Who is loving toward man? 'Until seventy times seven.' Thus, He sets not a number here, but what is infinite and perpetual and forever. For even as ten thousand times signifies often, so here too. For by saying, 'The barren hath borne seven [1 Kgs. (1 Sam.) 2:5],' the Scripture means many. So that He hath not limited the forgiveness by a number, but hath declared that it is to be perpetual and forever."[3] Thus, by all this, we understand by analogy that the Seventy whom we commemorate today were a type of the multitude to be sent forth through the generations to bring the Gospel message.

The Gospel Reading Commentary

Saint Luke the evangelist tell us that Christ "sent them forth two by two before His face into every city and place where He Himself was about to go. Therefore He was saying to them, 'The harvest indeed is great, but the workers are few. Entreat therefore the Lord of the harvest that He would send out workers into His harvest. Go; behold, I send you forth as lambs in the midst of wolves. Cease carrying a purse, neither a leathern pouch, nor sandals; and do not begin to greet anyone along the way. And into whatsoever house ye enter, first say, "Peace be to this house." And if, indeed, there be there a son of peace, your peace shall come to rest upon it; but if not so, it shall return to you. And in that very house keep on remaining, eating and drinking the things given by them, for the worker is worthy of his hire. Do not have the habit of moving from house to house. And into whatsoever city ye enter, and they receive you, go on eating the things which are set before you; and keep on curing the sick in it, and saying to them, "The kingdom of God hath drawn near to you." But into whatsoever city ye enter, and they receive you not, go out into its broad streets, and say, "Even the dust of your city, which cleaveth to us, we wipe off ourselves against you; but know this, that the kingdom of God hath drawn near to you." But I say to you that it shall be more tolerable in that day for Sodom than for that city. Woe to thee, Chorazin! Woe to thee, Bethsaida! For if the works of power which took place in you took place in Tyre and Sidon, they would have repented long

---

[3] Saint John Chrysostom, Homily LXI, *Gospel of Saint Matthew*, Nicene, 1st Ser., X:375, 376.

ago, sitting in sackcloth and ashes. But it shall be more tolerable for Tyre and Sidon in the judgment than for you. And thou, Capernaum, which hath been lifted high unto the heaven, shall be brought down as far as Hades. The one who heareth you heareth Me, and the one who rejecteth you rejecteth Me, and the one who rejecteth Me rejecteth the One Who sent Me forth [Lk. 10:1-16].'

"And the seventy returned with joy, saying, 'Lord, even the demons are being made subject to us in Thy name.' And He said to them, 'I was beholding Satan as lightning having fallen out of the heaven. Behold, I give you the authority to tread upon serpents and scorpions, and upon all the power of the enemy; and nothing in anywise shall injure you. However cease rejoicing in this, that the spirits are being made subject to you; but be rejoicing that your names were written in the heavens.' In the same hour Jesus rejoiced in the Spirit, and said, 'I give thanks to Thee, O Father, Lord of the heaven and of the earth, that Thou didst hide these things from the wise and intelligent, and didst reveal them to babes. Yea, Father, for thus it was well-pleasing before Thee.' And having turned to the disciples, He said, 'All things were delivered to Me by My Father. And no one doth fully know Who the Son is, except the Father, and Who the Father is, except the Son, and he to whomsoever the Son is willing to reveal Him.' And He turned around to the disciples, and said privately, 'Blessed are the eyes which see what ye see. For I say to you, that many prophets and kings wished to see what ye see, but saw not, and to hear what ye hear, but heard not [Lk. 10:17-24].'"

Saint Kyril comments on the pericope: "How can a sheep prevail against a wolf [Lk. 10:3]? How can one so peaceful vanquish the savageness of beasts of prey? 'Yes,' He says, 'for they all have Me as their Shepherd—small and great, people and princes, teachers and taught. I will be with you and aid you, and deliver you from all evil. I will tame the savage beasts, I will change wolves into sheep. I will make the persecutors become the helpers of the persecuted....For I will make and unmake all things, and there is nothing that can resist My will.'"[4]

Saint Gregory the Great, speaking of the character of the preacher, writes: "Such confidence in God should the preacher have that, although he does not provide for the necessities of this life, nevertheless he is persuaded that he will never lack them....Now these words can be understood metaphorically: they can signify that money, which is usually carried in a purse,

---

[4] Saint Cyril of Alexandria, Homily 61, *Commentary on the Gospel of Saint Luke*, Ch. 10, 264.

represents hidden wisdom. Then he who has wisdom of speech, but neglects to use it for the benefit of others, carried it, as it were, tied up in a purse."[5]

Saint Gregory the Great, commenting on this Gospel reading, says, "If anyone wishes to take up these words figuratively, we ask, do not the sandals [Lk. 10:4] signify the example of dead works? It is not fitting that he who undertakes the task of preaching should burden himself with worldly affairs, lest, engrossed in such matters, he forget the business of eternal life. He must not consider the example of others' foolish conduct, thinking to improve his own words with such lifeless leather. There are many who try to defend their own wicked deeds by comparing them to the wickedness of others. As they have seen others do, they consider that they have a right to do also: is not this to act as if they sought to cover their feet with the skins of dead animals?"[6] Saint Ambrose adds that "Jesus wishes nothing mortal to be on us."[7] Saint Kyril points out: "Let no one say that the object of His teaching was to make the holy apostles refuse the use of ordinary articles of equipment. For what good, or what harm, would it do them to have sandals or to go without them? But what He does wish them to learn by this command, and to endeavor to practise, is certainly this, that they must lay all thought of their sustenance upon Him....For it was fitting that those who were adorned with apostolic honors should have a mind free from covetousness and altogether adverse from receiving gifts, and content with what God provides....Thus He clearly teaches them to abandon all carnal wealth."[8]

Saint Kyril asks: "What, therefore, does Christ teach by saying not to greet anyone along the way [Lk. 10:4]? He does not enjoin them to be rude, nor command them to lay stress upon not making salutations; such conduct He rather teaches them to avoid. But, it is not a thing unbefitting to suppose that, when the disciples were traveling about among the cities and villages to instruct people everywhere in the sacred doctrines, they might wish to do this, perhaps, not with haste, but, so to speak, in a loitering manner, making deviations from the road and permitting themselves to pay visits, because they wished to see someone or other as being an acquaintance or friend, and so might waste time prodigally in unnecessary matters when it was the fitting time for preaching. With great industry, therefore, says He, be zealous in delivering your sacred message; grant not to friendship an

---

[5] Saint Gregory the Great, Homily XVII, *The Harvest is Great*, Parables of the Gospel, 81; *P.L.* 76 (col. 1139).

[6] Ibid., p. 80.

[7] Saint Ambrose, *Exposition of the Holy Gospel According to Saint Luke*, Bk. VII, § 57.

[8] Saint Cyril, Homily 62, *Commentary*, Ch. 10, 267.

unprofitable delay, but let that which is well pleasing to God be preferred by you to all other things; and so practising an irresistible and unhampered diligence, hold fast to your apostolic cares."[9]

Saint Gregory the Great: "He who salutes another along the way, wishing him good health merely because he is on a journey and not through any real concern for the other's health, is compared to one who preaches salvation to his hearers, not out of love for his everlasting home but from desire for a reward he wins for himself, desiring their salvation because of the circumstances, but not through any good will."[10]

Saint Ambrose concludes: "When divine commands are given, human obligations are surrendered for a while. Even honorable acts are prohibited, lest the grace of ceremony deceive and hinder the ministry of the task."[11]

They are told that in whatsoever house they should enter, first say, 'Peace be to this house [Lk. 10:5].'" Saint Kyril however advises us, saying: "He further commanded them 'never to give that which is holy to the dogs,' nor again 'to cast pearls before the swine [cf. Mt. 7:6],' by bestowing upon unbelievers their society in lodging with them; they were rather to grant it to such as were worthy of having it deigned them, by being sons of peace, and yielding obedience to their message. For it would have been a most disgraceful act for them to wish to be intimate with any who were resisting Christ's glory, and guilty of the charge of ungodliness. For according to Saint Paul, 'What portion hath a believer with an unbeliever [2 Cor. 6:15]?'"[12]

Christ told the Seventy upon their return to cease rejoicing that the spirits were made subject to them, but to rejoice that their names were written in the heavens. Saint Kyril asks: "'How then didst Thou command them not to rejoice in the honor and glory which Thou didst Thyself bestow?' What can we say to this? I answer that Christ raises them to something greater, and commands them to account it their glory that their names were written in heaven....But besides, to rejoice solely in the fact that they were able to work miracles and crush the heads of demons was likely to produce in them possibly the desire also of vainglory—and the neighbor, so to speak, and kinsfellow of this passion constantly is pride. Therefore, though we receive some gift from Christ not unworthy of admiration, we must not think too highly of it, but rather make the hope prepared for us our cause of rejoicing, and that our names are written in the companies of the saints, by Christ's gift,

---

[9] Ibid., 268.
[10] Ibid.
[11] Saint Ambrose, *Exposition*, Bk. VII, § 63.
[12] Saint Cyril, *Commentary*, op. cit., 269.

the Savior of us all."[13] And, "Let us, therefore, examine the words, and especially what is meant by the expression, that Jesus 'rejoiced in the Spirit [Lk. 10:21],'...that is, in the works and miracles wrought by means of the Holy Spirit."[14]

Roster of the Seventy

Eusebius comments, "The names of the apostles of our Savior are known to everyone from the Gospels. But there exists no catalogue of the Seventy disciples."[15] Saint Hippolytos compiled a register,[16] as well as Saint Dorotheos, Bishop of Tyre, the hieromartyr. Some of those listed lapsed from the Faith (Nicholas, Phygellos, Hermogenes, and Demas) and others filled their places. Other lists contain duplications or evince uncertainties. We have followed the schedule of names given by the Greek compilers of *The Great Synaxaristes*, who have presented the names alphabetically. By way of disclaimer, the listing given herein is by no means exhaustive or closed.

1. **Achaikos (Achaicus)**, together with Stephanas and Fortunatos, was the bearer of Saint Paul's First Epistle to the Corinthians. The Apostle Paul rejoiced at their coming, and said to the Corinthians "that which ye lacked, these supplied. For they refreshed my spirit and yours. Therefore be acknowledging such ones as these [1 Cor. 16:17, 18]." For the sake of the Gospel, Achaikos suffered with hunger and thirst. He is also commemorated on the 15th of June. He is depicted as an old man with a long beard.[17]

2. **Agavos (Agabus)** is mentioned by the Evangelist Luke in Acts. He was filled with the gift of prophecy, so that when he came down from Jerusalem to Antioch, he rose up and signified by the Spirit that there was about to be a great famine over all the inhabited world, which also came to pass in the time of Claudius Caesar [Acts 11:27, 28]. At another time, when he came down from Judaea, he also took up the belt of Paul and bound his own hands and feet, and said, "Thus saith the Holy Spirit, 'Thus shall the Jews bind in Jerusalem the man whose belt this is, and shall deliver him up into the hands of the Gentiles.'" But Saint Paul would not be dissuaded from going up to Jerusalem [Acts 21:10-14]. The holy Apostle Agavos preached the Gospel in many lands. He is also commemorated on the 8th of April. He is depicted as an old man with a beard divided into two points.

---

[13] Saint Cyril, Homily 64, *Commentary*, Ch. 10, 275, 276.
[14] Ibid., Homily 65, Ch. 10, 277.
[15] Eusebius, *The Church History*, Bk. I, Ch. XII.
[16] Saint Hippolytos, *Appendix: On the Seventy Apostles*, Ante-Nicene, V:255, 256.
[17] The depictions of the saints are cited as noted in *The Painter's Manual of Dionysius of Fourna*, pp. 53, 54.

3. **Amplias** was ordained by the Apostle Andrew as Bishop of Odyssopolis, where he suffered martyrdom. He is greeted by Saint Paul as "my beloved in the Lord [Rom. 16:8]." He is also commemorated on the 31st of October. He is depicted as a young man with an incipient beard.

4. **Ananias** hailed from Damascus [Acts 9:10]. He baptized the Apostle Paul, three years after the Lord's ascension. He became Bishop of Damascus. He suffered martyrdom. He is also commemorated on the 1st of October. He is depicted as an old man with a long beard.

5. **Andronikos (Andronicus)**, a soaring eagle, sped throughout the inhabited world, accompanied by the faithful and exceedingly marvellous Junia, proclaiming in every quarter the name of the Christ. They are spoken of by the Apostle Paul: "Greet Andronikos and Junia, my kinfolk and my fellow prisoners, who are notable among the apostles, and who have been in Christ before me [Rom. 16:7]." Andronikos converted many to the knowledge of God. He reposed in peace. He is not on all lists, but Saint Demetri of Rostov lists him as Bishop of Pannonia. Andronikos and Junia are commemorated on the 17th of May. Saint Andronikos is also commemorated on the 30th of July. He is depicted as a young man, beardless by nature.

6. **Apelles** is he of whom the divine Paul says, "Greet Apelles, the approved in Christ [Rom. 16:10]." He became Bishop of Smyrna. He worked reverently for Christ and was translated to the Lord. He is also commemorated on the 10th of September. He is depicted as a young man with a short beard.

7. **Apelles**, another of the same name, became Bishop of Herakleia. He led men to the Christ and received a blessed end. He is also commemorated on the 31st of October.

8. **Apollos** was an Alexandrine Jew "mighty in the Scriptures [Acts 18:24]." He was further catechized by Aquila and Priscilla [Acts 18:26]. He is mentioned by the Apostle Paul as a "minister [1 Cor. 3:5]." He became Bishop of Caesarea. He is also commemorated on the 8th of December. He is depicted as an old man with a wide beard.

9. **Aquila** was a Jew of Pontos (Pontus) [Acts 18:2; Rom. 16:3]. With his wife Priscilla, he followed the Apostle Paul, with whom they endured hardships and perils together [Acts 18:1]. He ended his earthly sojourn in martyrdom, when unbelievers apprehended him and severed his head. He is commemorated with Saint Priscilla on the 13th of February and individually on the 14th of July.

10. **Archippos** became a disciple of the Apostle Paul. Saint Paul sent a message to him, saying: "Be taking heed to the ministry which thou didst receive in the Lord, that thou be fulfilling it [Col. 4:17]." He was addressed by Saint Paul as his "fellow soldier [Phile. 1:2]." According to Saint Demetri

of Rostov, he succeeded Epaphras as Bishop of Colossae, where he suffered martyrdom. Saint Hippolytos identifies him as Bishop of Andriace. He is also commemorated on the 22nd of November and the 19th of February.

11. **Aristarchos** was as another John the Baptist, according to his diet, partaking of the same fare, that is, locusts and wild honey. The locusts are a kind of herb, which is also melagra; others say it is a type of fruit growing on the upper branches of trees, especially hard-shelled fruits. He also wore a leathern belt [Mt. 3:4; Mk. 1:6]. He was caught in the riot at Ephesus [Acts 19:29] and was called by Saint Paul his "fellow prisoner [Col. 4:10]" and "fellow worker [Phile. 1:24]." He became Bishop of Apameia, Syria. He brought all the unbelievers to the knowledge of God. He was beheaded by Nero. He is also commemorated on the 27th of September and the 14th of April. He is depicted as an old man with curly hair.

12. **Aristoboulos** followed the Apostle Paul, who greeted his household [Rom. 16:10]. He became Bishop of Britain. He is also commemorated on the 31st of October and the 15th of March. He is depicted as an old man.

13. **Artemas** [Tit. 3:12] was the Apostle Paul's companion, whom the latter proposed sending to Titus at Crete. He became Bishop of Lystra. He is also commemorated on the 31st of October. He is depicted as a young man with a pointed beard.

14. **Asynkritos (Asyncritus)** [Rom. 16:14], a preacher of the Gospel in different places of the world, turned many to piety. He was tortured by the Jews and Greeks, suffering martyrdom. Saint Hippolytos identifies him as Bishop of Hyrcania in Asia Minor. He is also commemorated on the 8th of April. He is depicted as an old man with a beard divided into three points.

15. **Barnabas** or Joses was a scion of the tribe of Levi [Acts 4:36] and a Cypriot by birth. His name stands first on the list of prophets and teachers of the Church at Antioch [Acts 13:1]. Luke speaks of him as "a good man and full of the Holy Spirit and of faith [Acts 11:24]." When Saul (Saint Paul) returned to Jerusalem after his conversion, Barnabas took him and introduced him to the apostles [Acts 9:27]. Both labored for a whole year at Antioch [Acts 11:25, 26]. The two were then sent to Jerusalem with the contributions that the Church at Antioch had donated to the poorer brethren of Judaea [Acts 11:28-30]. They were appointed as missionaries to the heathen world, and in this capacity visited Cyprus and some of the principal cities of Asia Minor [Acts 13:14]. Afterward, they went to Jerusalem and consulted regarding the relation of Gentiles to the Church [Acts 15:2; Gal. 2:1]. As they were about to set forth on a second missionary journey, a dispute arose between Paul and Barnabas regarding John Mark. The dispute ended by Paul and Barnabas taking separate routes. Paul took Silas as his

companion, and journeyed through Syria and Cilicia; while Barnabas took his kinsman John Mark, and visited Cyprus [Acts 15:36-41]. Thus, he preached the Gospel in Jerusalem, Asia Minor, Rome, Alexandria, and Cyprus, where he was stoned by the Jews and Greeks. Afterward, he was delivered to the flames. He is also commemorated on the 11th of June. His personal appearance is supposed to have been dignified and commanding [Acts 14:11, 12]. He is depicted as a grey-haired man with a long beard.

16. **Caesar** [Phil. 4:22] became Bishop of Koroneia, Greece.[18] Saint Hippolytos identifies him as Bishop of Dyrrachium. He is also commemorated on the 8th of December. He is depicted as a young man, beardless.

17. **Clement (Clemes)** is mentioned by Saint Paul in the Philippian Epistle: "Keep on assisting those women who struggled together with me in the Gospel, and Clement also, and the rest of my fellow workers, whose names are in the book of life [Phil. 4:3]." He became Bishop of Sardis. He is also commemorated on the 10th of September. He is depicted as an old man with a short beard.

18. **Crescens (Kreeskees)** was one of the Apostle Paul's companions who had gone to Galatia [2 Tim. 4:10], where he preached the Gospel. He became Bishop of Chalcedon (or more correctly, Carchedon), in upper Spain by the border of Gaul. He is also commemorated on the 30th of July. He is depicted as an old man with a pointed beard.

19. **Epaenetos** became Bishop of Carthage. Saint Paul greets him as "my beloved, who is the firstfruits of Achaia for Christ [Rom. 16:5]." He is also commemorated on the 30th of July. He is depicted as a young man with a beard divided into three points.

20. **Epaphroditos** brought the Philippian contribution to Paul [Phil. 4:18], who wrote to the Philippians and called him "brother and my fellow worker and fellow soldier, but your apostle, and minister of my need [Phil. 2:25]." He became Bishop of Kolophon. He is also commemorated on the 8th of December. He is depicted as a young man.

21. **Erastos** became *œconomos*, a city administrator [Rom. 16:23]. He spent time in Macedonia [Acts 19:22] and Corinth [2 Tim. 4:20]. He also was steward in the Church at Jerusalem. Afterward he became Bishop of Neados or Paneados (Caesarea of Philippi), and then reposed in peace. He is also commemorated on the 10th of November. He is depicted as a young man with a brown, rush-like beard.

---

[18] Some believe that the Caesar mentioned by Saint Paul refers to the emperor. Saint Joseph the Hymnographer, however, identifies an Apostle Caesar as one of the Seventy in the divine office for this day [Orthros Canon, Ode Five, Mode Four].

22. **Evodos** became Bishop of Antioch. He is also commemorated on the 7th of September. He is depicted as a young man with an incipient beard.

23. **Evoulos** [2 Tim. 4:21]. He is also commemorated on the 28th of February.

24. **Fortunatos** [1 Cor. 16:17, 18] was a disciple of the Apostle Paul. Together with Stephanas and Achaikos, he was an ambassador of the Corinthian church, whose presence at Ephesus refreshed the spirit of the Apostle Paul. He preached the Gospel and suffered martyrdom and beheading, being slain by the sword. He is also commemorated on the 15th of June. He is depicted as an old man with a rounded beard.

25. **Gaios (Gaius)** [Rom. 16:23] became Bishop of Ephesus after Saint Timothy. He is also commemorated on the 5th of November. He is depicted as an old man with a long and pointed beard.

26. **Hermas** [Rom. 16:14] became Bishop of Philippi. He is also commemorated on the 5th of November. He is depicted as a young man with an incipient beard.

27. **Herodion** or **Rodion**, Paul's kinsman [Rom. 16:11], followed the holy apostles in preaching. Afterward he became Bishop of Patras. He followed the Apostle Peter to Rome, where he suffered beheading under Nero (A.D. 54).[19] He is also commemorated on the 10th of November and the 28th of March.

28. **Iakovos (James)**, the brother of the Lord and son of Joseph the Betrothed [Mt. 13:55], became the first Bishop of Jerusalem [Acts 15:13; 21:18]. He was cast down from the temple parapet, stoned, and then struck with a fuller's club, by which he was slain. He is also commemorated on the 23rd of October. He is depicted as an old man with a long beard.

29. **Jason** was a Thessalonian who received Apostles Paul and Silas [Acts 17:5 ff.]. The mob, in consequence of Jason's welcome of the apostles, attacked his house and dragged him before the rulers of the city. Jason had to pay bail before he was let go. Later, Paul sent Jason's salutations from Corinth [Rom. 16:21]. Jason became Bishop of Tarsus of Cilicia. Afterward, he journeyed with Apostle Sosipater to the west, coming to Kerkyra (Corfu). He taught the holy Gospel and underwent many sufferings. He was translated to

---

[19] Dionysios of Fourna deemed Herodion and Rodion to be two different men. Herodion is depicted as an old man but Rodion as a young man. The Orthros Canon for today also mentioned both saints in separate hymns at today's divine office. Saint Herodion is listed in Ode Four, Mode Four, by Saint Joseph, and the Orthros Oikos, while Saint Rodion is chanted to during Vespers, at the Sticheron, and Orthros Canon, Mode Four.

the Lord in deep old age. He is also commemorated on the 29th of April. He is depicted as a young man with an incipient beard.

30. **Justos (Justus)**, who was also known as Jesus [Col. 4:11], Joseph called Barsavas, and Joses [cf. Mt. 13:55; Mk. 6:3], was the brother of the Lord, who placed after Matthias in the casting of the lot [Acts 1:23]. Saint Paul also sends along the greetings of Jesus-Justos, writing: "Aristarchos, my fellow prisoner, greeteth you, and Mark,...and Jesus, the one who is called Justos, who are of the circumcision. These are the only fellow workers for the kingdom of God who became a consolation to me [Col. 4:10, 11]." He became Bishop of Eleftheroupolis (Arabic, Bekt Gebrin), and many were drawn to the Faith of the Christ. He is also commemorated on the 30th of October. He is depicted as an old man with a pointed beard.

31. **Karpos (Carpus)** [2 Tim. 4:13] ministered to the Apostle Paul, who left his cloak, books, and parchments with Karpos at Troas. Afterward, he became Bishop of Thracian Beroe or Verea (Beroe-Stara Zagora), Thrace. He is also commemorated on the 26th of May. He is depicted as an old man with a beard divided into two points.

32. **Kephas (Cephas)** is not to be confused with the Apostle Peter [Jn. 1:42]. This Kephas became Bishop of Iconium. He is also commemorated on the 8th of December. He is depicted as a young man with an incipient beard.

33. **Linus (Linos)** [2 Tim. 4:21] became Bishop of Rome after the Apostle Peter. He is also commemorated on the 5th of November. He is depicted as a young man with a rounded beard.

34. **Luke (Lucius)** became Bishop of Laodikeia in Syria. He is also commemorated on the 10th of September.

35. **Mark** who was also called **John** [Acts 12:12]. He is not the evangelist. He was ordained by the apostles as Bishop of Byblos, where he distinguished himself as one approved in laboring for the Gospel. His shadow also cured sicknesses. He is also commemorated on the 27th of September.

36. **Mark** here is also not the evangelist. He was the kinsman of Barnabas [Col. 4:10]. He is mentioned by Saint Paul when he writes to Saint Timothy: "Take Mark and bring him with thee, for he is useful to me for ministering [2 Tim. 4:11]." He became Bishop of Apollonias and destroyed the ancestral imposture of idol worship. He is also commemorated on the 30th of October. He is depicted as a young man, beardless.

37. **Narcissos (Narcissus)** and his household were at Rome. Saint Paul sent greetings to those of the household of Narcissus, who were "in the Lord [Rom. 16:11]." The Apostle Andrew ordained him as Bishop of Athens. He suffered martyrdom for the Gospel. He is also commemorated on the 31st of October. He is depicted as a young man with an incipient beard.

38. **Nikanor (Nicanor)** was one of the seven deacons [Acts 6:5]. A great persecution had risen against the Jerusalem Church [Acts 8:1]. He suffered martyrdom on the same day the Protomartyr Stephen was stoned, though he is not commemorated the same day. He is also commemorated on the 28th of July. He is depicted as a young man with an incipient beard.

39. **Nymphas** became a disciple of the Apostle Paul. It is written of him: "Greet the brethren in Laodikeia (Laodicea), and Nymphas, and the church in his house [Col. 4:15]." He is also commemorated on the 28th of February.

40. **Olympas** [Rom. 16:15] followed the Apostle Peter and was beheaded in Rome under Nero. He is also commemorated on the 10th of November. He is depicted as an old man.

41. **Onesimos** became a disciple of the Apostle Paul. He had been the runaway slave of Philemon of Colosse, whom the Apostle Paul calls "the faithful and beloved brother, who is one of you [Col. 4:9]." Saint Paul wrote an epistle to Philemon on Onesimos' behalf, of whom he says: "I begot Onesimos in my bonds [Phile. 1:10]." According to apostolic tradition, he was emancipated by Philemon. He suffered martyrdom at Puteoli (near Naples), where they shattered his bones. He is also commemorated on the 22nd of November and the 15th of February.

42. **Onesiphoros** was a disciple of the Apostle Paul, who writes: "May the Lord grant mercy to the house of Onesiphoros, for many times he refreshed me, and was not ashamed of my chain; but having been in Rome, he sought me out most diligently and found me—may the Lord grant him to find mercy from the Lord in that day—and in how many things he ministered in Ephesus thou knowest better than I need say [2 Tim. 1:16-18]." And elsewhere he writes: "Greet Prisca and Aquila, and the house of Onesiphoros [2 Tim. 4:19]." He was Bishop of Kolophon, which is northwest of Ephesus and thirty-five kilometers south of Smyrna. Saint Hippolytos lists him as Bishop of Korone. He is also commemorated on the 7th of September. He is depicted as an old man.

43. **Parmenas** was one of the seven deacons [Acts 6:5]. He eagerly performed his ministry. According to Saint Hippolytos, Parmenas became Bishop of Soli (Soloi, Cyprus). He fell ill and reposed, surrendering his soul into the hands of God before the apostles who mourned his passing and interred him honorably. He is also commemorated on the 28th of July. He is depicted as a young man.

44. **Patrobas** [Rom. 16:14] became Bishop of Puteoli (Pozzuoli), Italy. He is also commemorated on the 5th of November. He is depicted as a young man with a brown, rush-like beard.

45. **Philemon** was a disciple of the Apostle Paul who ordained him as the first Bishop of Gaza. In the Apostle Paul's Epistle to Philemon, regarding Onesimos, he is addressed as "the beloved and our fellow worker." The purpose of writing an epistle to him was on behalf of Onesimos, who had deserted his master Philemon. Paul humbly and courteously requests Philemon to receive Onesimos no longer as a slave, but as a brother beloved [Phile. 1:16]. Paul promises to repay Philemon if Onesimos had wronged him in anything or owed him, though he adds, "not that I may mention that to me thou owest even thyself [Phile. 1:19]." Philemon graciously granted what Paul requested. In the year 64, the Apostle Philemon was at Colossae, where he preached the word of truth, together with Archippos and Apfia. While serving in a house-church, they were arrested and suffered martyrdom. He is also commemorated on the 22nd of November. He is depicted as an old man with a smoke-like beard.

46. **Philip** was one of the seven deacons [Acts 6:5]. He was called the evangelist and had four daughters who prophesied [Acts 21:8, 9]. He preached the Gospel and wrought cures of all kinds in Samaria, where he labored successfully [Acts 8:5-13]. He baptized Simon, previously a magician, who hypocritically believed [Acts 8:13]. Philip was snatched by a divine angel and brought into the path of Candace's eunuch. He catechized and baptized the eunuch [Acts 8:27-39], who became the first apostle to Ethiopia and later suffered martyrdom. Philip was next found at Azotus, whence he went forth in his evangelistic work till he came to Caesarea. He is not mentioned again for about twenty years, when he is still found at Caesarea [Acts 21:8], as Paul and his companions were on the way to Jerusalem. Saint Demetri of Rostov cites him as Bishop of Tralles. He is also commemorated on the 11th of October. He is depicted as a young man with an incipient beard.

47. **Philologos**, saluted by Paul in an epistle [Rom. 16:15], was ordained by the Apostle Andrew as Bishop of Sinope, a major port of Pontos on the Black Sea. He is also commemorated on the 5th of November. He is depicted as a grey-haired man with a short beard.

48. **Phlegon**, saluted by Paul in an epistle [Rom. 16:14], preached in many different places of the world and suffered martyrdom. He became Bishop of Marathon, Thrace. He is also commemorated on the 8th of April. He is depicted as a young man, beardless.

49. **Prochoros** was one of the seven deacons [Acts 6:5]. He later followed the Evangelist John, enduring together with him many afflictions and hardships. He also took down the dictation of the evangelist. After the translation of the Evangelist John, Prochoros became Bishop of Nikomedia. He is also commemorated on the 28th of July. He is depicted as a grey-haired man with a short beard divided into two points.

50. **Pudens** [2 Tim. 4:21] followed the Apostle Paul. He was beheaded under Nero. He is also commemorated on the 14th of April. He is depicted as a young man with an incipient beard.

51. **Quadratus (Kodratos)** was a disciple of Jesus Christ. He became Bishop of Athens, where he converted many to the Faith of the Christ. After he was persecuted and driven out of Athens, he went to Magnesia where he taught until A. D. 117, when he received a martyric end in deep old age. He is also commemorated on the 21st of September.

52. **Quartus (Kouartos)** is mentioned in one of Paul's epistles when he sends Quartus' greetings [Rom. 16:23]. He became Bishop of Beirut. He underwent many troubles and persecutions, but reposed in peace. He is also commemorated on the 10th of November. He is depicted as a grey-haired man with a long beard.

53. **Rufus** is named by the Apostle Paul as "the chosen in the Lord [Rom. 16:13]." He became Bishop of Thebes, Greece. He is also commemorated on the 8th of April. He is depicted as a grey-haired man with a wide beard.

54. **Silas**, described as one of the "leading men among the brethren [Acts 15:22]," suffered toils and troubles with the Apostle Paul in his evangelic labors. He was a Roman citizen [Acts 16:37] and delegated by the Jerusalem Synod to accompany Paul and Barnabas with the decree for Antioch. Then he returned to Jerusalem [Acts 15:33], for "it seemed good to Silas to abide there [Acts 15:34]." He revisited Antioch, where he was chosen by Paul to be his companion on his second missionary tour [Acts 15:40-17:14]. We remember also Silas' public witness for Christ against the girl with the spirit of Python, his scourging for His name's sake, and the hymns chanted in the prison to God, and the jailer's conversion [Acts 16:19 ff.]. We are also mindful of his struggles during the uproar in Thessalonike [Acts 17:1-9] and how he left by night with Paul and went to Verea [Acts 17:10], where Silas stayed behind with Timothy, when Paul went on to Athens, but was charged to join him there with all speed [Acts 17:15]. Silas and Timothy leave Macedonia, and then we find him with Paul at Corinth [Acts 18:5]. Silas became Bishop of Corinth. He is also commemorated on the 30th of July. He is depicted as a young man with an incipient beard.

55. **Silouanos (Silvanus)** preached with Paul and Timothy [2 Cor. 1:19]. In both epistles to the Thessalonians, Saint Paul commences: "Paul, and Silouanos, and Timothy, to the Church of the Thessalonians...." Saint Peter calls him "the faithful brother [1 Pe. 5:12]." He became Bishop of Thessalonike. He is also commemorated on the 30th of July. He is depicted as an old man, bald, with a short beard.

56. **Simon**, also known as **Symeon** and **Cleopas**,[20] a kinsman of the Lord. He became the second Bishop of Jerusalem and lived to be one hundred and twenty years of age. In A.D. 52, he was administered poison by Dometian but suffered no ill effects. In A.D. 98, he was crucified under Trajan. He is also commemorated on the 27th of April, and is mentioned in a list of apostles on the 30th of June. He is depicted as a man of extreme age.

57. **Stachys** [Rom. 16:9], who was called "my beloved" by Paul, was the first Bishop of Byzantion, at the southern mouth of the Bosporos. He was ordained by the Apostle Andrew. He built a church in Argyroupolis, which lies near Constantinople, where he was teaching the multitude that had gathered. He covered considerable distance in his preaching for sixteen years, until he reposed in the Lord. He is also commemorated on the 31st of October. He is depicted as a young man with a pointed beard.

58. **Stephanas** [1 Cor. 16:17, 18] was a disciple of the Apostle Paul. He is also commemorated on the 15th of July.

59. **Stephen**, the First-martyr and archdeacon, was a "man full of faith and of the Holy Spirit [Acts 6:5]." He was stoned to death by the Jews because he preached the Christ. He is also commemorated on the 27th of December. He is depicted as a beardless young deacon.

60. **Sosipater**, a kinsman of Paul [Rom. 16:21], hailed from Achaia. He became a disciple of the Apostle Paul, who ordained him as Bishop of Iconium. Afterward, Sosipater journeyed with Jason to western parts. They came to Kerkyra (Corfu), where they taught the Faith of Jesus Christ. They suffered many tribulations and were translated to the Lord in deep old age. He is also commemorated on the 10th of November and the 29th of July. He is depicted as a young man with a rounded beard.

61. **Sosthenes** and **Crispos (Crispus)** are given as one and the same person in *The Great Synaxaristes* (in Greek). Saint John Chrysostom comments, "This same Crispos, whom Paul mentions in his epistle to the Corinthians [1 Cor. 1:14], I take to be called Sosthenes—evidently a believer,

---

[20] Cleopas, in *The Great Synaxaristes* (in Greek), is identified with Simon, a son of Joseph the Betrothed and his first wife Salome. Eusebius [*The Church History*, Bk. III, Ch. XI(1)], Nikephoros Kallistos Xanthopoulos, and George Kedrinos concur with the early historian Hegesippos that Cleopas was in fact the younger brother of Joseph the Betrothed. Cleopas and his wife Mary had a son named Simon, who was one of the Seventy, whom we commemorate today. The weight of this historical evidence can be neither ignored nor disproved. Thus, these historians conjecture that another Simon was listed among our Lord's brothers Iakovos, Joses, and Jude [cf. Mt. 13:55; Mk. 6:3], who was neither one of the Twelve nor one of the Seventy, but he was among those who had fallen asleep in the Lord before the apostles were scattered abroad after the stoning of Protomartyr Stephen.

insomuch that he is beaten, and is always present with Paul."[21] Other sources (Saint Demetri of Rostov and Dionysios of Fourna) list the two names as separate apostles.[22] In the divine office for these Seventy, Saint Joseph the Hymnographer only lists the Apostle Sosthenes in his hymns.

A. Crispos, a Corinthian synagogue ruler, who "believed in the Lord with his whole house [Acts 18:17], is mentioned by Saint Paul: "I thank God that I baptized none of you, except Crispos and Gaios, lest any should say that in mine own name I baptized. And I baptized also the household of Stephanas [1 Cor. 1:14-16]." Crispos became Bishop of Aegina.

B. Sosthenes, a Corinthian synagogue ruler after Crispos, was beaten before the tribunal [Acts 18:8]. Saint Paul converted him, and mentions him in his epistle: "Paul, a called apostle of Jesus Christ by the will of God, and Sosthenes our brother, to the Church of God which is in Corinth...[1 Cor. 1:1, 2]." He became Bishop of Kolophon (modern-day Sigatzik, Turkey). He is also commemorated on the 8th of December. He is depicted as an old man, bald, with a long beard.

62. **Tertios**, the Apostle Paul's amanuensis in writing the Epistle to the Romans [Rom. 16:22] from Corinth, inserted his greetings in the midst of those of Paul. He became Bishop of Iconium after Sosipater. He is also commemorated on the 30th of October.

63. **Timon** was one of the seven deacons [Acts 6:5]. He became Bishop of Bostra, Arabia. He suffered martyrdom when the pagan Greeks gave him a thrashing and cast him into the fire. He is also commemorated on the 28th of July. He is depicted as a grey-haired man with a brown, rush-like beard.

64. **Timothy** hailed from Lystra of Lykaonia. He was one of Paul's converts, whom Paul calls "my genuine child in the faith [1 Tim. 1:2]" and "my beloved child [2 Tim. 1]." His father was a heathen Greek [Acts 16:1, 3] and his mother Evnike was a Jewess. Both his mother and grandmother Lois [2 Tim. 1:5] had converted to Christianity. Timothy had not been circumcised in infancy, though from early childhood he had known the sacred writings [2 Tim. 3:15]. He became a co-worker with Saint Paul. In order to conciliate the Jewish Christians who would otherwise have caused trouble, which would have weakened Timothy's position and his work as a preacher of the Gospel, Paul took Timothy and circumcised him [Acts 16:3]. He was ordained by Paul who wrote: "Do not neglect the gift of grace in thee, which was given thee by prophecy with laying on of the hands of the presbytery [1

---

[21] Saint John Chrysostom, Homily XXXIX, *The Acts of the Apostles*, Nicene, 1st Ser., XI:241.
[22] See, Durkit's *The Lives of the Seventy Apostles*, pp. 40, 47.

Tim. 4:14]," and "I remind thee to rekindle the gracious gift of God which is in thee by the laying on of my hands [2 Tim. 1:6]." He accompanied the Apostle Paul through Phrygia, Galatia, and Mysia; also to Troas and Philippi and Verea [Acts 17:14]. Thence he followed Paul to Athens and was sent by him with Silas on a mission to Thessalonike [Acts 17:15; 1Thess. 3:2]. He then went with Paul to Corinth [1Thess. 1:1; 2Thess. 1:1]. Years later he is found with the apostle at Ephesus [Acts 19:22], whence he is sent on a mission into Macedonia. He accompanied Paul afterward into Asia [Acts 20:4], where he spent some time with him. While Paul was a prisoner at Rome, Timothy joined him [Phil. 1:1] and suffered imprisonment [Heb. 13:23]. During Paul's second imprisonment, he wrote to Timothy, asking him to rejoin him [2 Tim. 4:13]. Saint John the Theologian consecrated him Bishop of Ephesus. He suffered martyrdom. He is also commemorated on the 22nd of January.

65. **Titus**, a Greek [Gal. 2:3], hailed from Crete. At twenty years of age he left his island and went to Jerusalem, where he became acquainted with Jesus Christ. Titus was present at the Lord's Passion and the Feasts of the Ascension and Pentecost. At the latter feast he was among the one hundred and twenty disciples of the Lord [Acts 1:15]. Afterward, he was ordained by the chief apostles and sent forth with Paul in order to proclaim the Gospel. Saint Paul addresses him in his epistle, writing: "To Titus, my genuine child according to the common faith [Tit. 1:4]." He was with the Apostles Paul and Barnabas at Antioch. He also accompanied them to the synod at Jerusalem [Gal. 2:1; cf. Acts 15:2], though his name nowhere occurs in the Acts of the Apostles. He was chiefly engaged in ministering to Gentiles; for Paul sternly refused to have him circumcised. He was with the Apostles Paul and Timothy at Ephesus, whence he was sent by Paul to Corinth for the purpose of getting the contributions of the church there in behalf of the poor saints at Jerusalem [2 Cor. 8:6; 12:18]. He rejoined the apostle when he was in Macedonia, and cheered him with the tidings he brought from Corinth [2 Cor. 7:6 ff.]. When consecrated a bishop, he was engaged in the organization of the church in Crete, where the apostle had left him for this purpose that he might "ordain presbyters in every city [Tit. 1:5]." In the last notice of Saint Titus, we find him with Paul during his imprisonment at Rome, whence he was sent into Dalmatia. He went about many lands and lived to the age of ninety-four, when he reposed in the Lord. He is also commemorated on the 25th of August. He is depicted as a young man, beardless.

66. **Trophimos**, an Ephesian [Acts 21:29], followed the Apostle Paul in Asia, accompanying him during a part of his third missionary journey [Acts 20:4]. He was with Paul in Jerusalem. There, the Jews raised a tumult, supposing Paul had introduced Trophimos, a Gentile convert, into the temple;

this resulted in Paul's imprisonment. We also know that Saint Paul left Saint Trophimos sick at Miletus, just before his own second Roman imprisonment [2 Tim. 4:20]. Trophimos was beheaded under Nero. He is also commemorated on the 14th of April. He is depicted as a grey-haired man with a long beard.

67. **Tychikos (Tychicus)**, an Asiatic Christian, is mentioned five times in the New Testament [Acts 20:4; Eph. 6:21; Col. 4:7; 2 Tim. 4:12; and Tit. 3:12]. He is spoken of as the Apostle Paul's companion and fellow laborer in the Gospel [Acts 20:4]. He accompanied him in part on his return journey from the third missionary circuit. While Trophimos and Paul went to Jerusalem [Acts 21:29], Tychikos stayed behind in Asia. He was with Saint Paul again during his first Roman imprisonment [Col. 4:7, 8]. In Saint Paul's second Roman imprisonment, Paul says he has sent Tychikos to Ephesus [2 Tim. 4:12]. Saint Hippolytos identifies him as Bishop of Chalcedon, while Blessed Theophylact lists him as Bishop of Caesarea. He is also commemorated on the 8th of December. He is depicted as a young man with an incipient beard.

68. **Urbanos (Urban)** was called "our fellow worker [Rom. 16:9]" by Saint Paul. He was ordained by the Apostle Andrew as Bishop of Macedonia, where he preached to the Greek pagans. He suffered martyrdom after being tortured in manifold ways. He is also commemorated on the 31st of October. He is depicted as a young man with a long beard.

69. **Zacchaeos** [Lk. 19:2] was he who climbed a sycamore tree that he might better see the Lord. He is also commemorated on the 20th of April, and he is remembered on the first Sunday before the commencement of the *Triodion*. He accompanied the Apostle Peter after our Lord's ascension. He became Bishop of Caesarea, Palestine.

70. **Zenas** [Tit. 3:13] had been experienced in the law of the Hebrews. He became Bishop of Diospolis. He is also commemorated on the 27th of September. He is depicted as a grey-haired man with a rounded beard.

+ + +

The names of the Seventy given above are by no means final. In the midst of the Seventy, there are also other well known personages which we shall mention herein, since they are commemorated together with the Twelve, even as Matthias [Acts 1:23, 26] who was also one of the Seventy. He is mentioned in the divine office for this day by Saint Joseph the Hymnographer.[23]

---

[23] January 4th, Orthros Canon, Ode Nine, Mode Four, by Saint Joseph, and the Oikos after the Sixth Ode of the Canon.

Also numbered with the Seventy are the divine apostles and Evangelists Luke and Mark, given in Saint Hippolytos's list and sung to in today's divine office. They are not mentioned with the Seventy, since they are commemorated with the Twelve on the 30th of June. The Apostle Luke is especially commemorated on the 18th of October, as well as the Apostle Mark on the 25th of April.

Others also are commemorated who were deemed among the ranks of the Seventy, including, but not limited to, Saint Hermes, who is to be distinguished from Saint Hermas [Rom. 16:14], whom Saint Hippolytos identifies as Bishop of Dalmatia. Saint Joseph the Hymnographer in today's service also cites the two saints separately.[24]

The Apostle Thaddaeos, though not given in the listing of *The Great Synaxaristes* (in Greek), is mentioned in today's divine office by Saint Joseph the Hymnographer. Saint Hippolytos includes him in his list, as well as Saint Demetri of Rostov. He is not to be confused with Thaddaeos or Jude of the Twelve [Mt. 10:3; Mk. 3:18]. He is known to have baptized Abgar, prince of Edessa. He is also commemorated on the 21st of August.

Saint Epaphras is mentioned by Saint Demetri of Rostov, but the saint's name is not included in today's divine office. In the Apostle Paul's Epistle to the Colossians, Epaphras is called by him "our beloved fellow slave, who is a faithful minister of the Christ on your behalf [Col. 1:7]" and "my fellow captive in Christ Jesus [Phile. 1:23]." Epaphras also sends his greetings to the Colossians [4:12]. He is listed as Bishop of Colossae, who also had the care of the churches at Laodikeia and Hierapolis.

Due to deficiencies and duplications in the lists, it is not within the scope of this work to investigate them thoroughly. Other apostles of that period, deserving of mention herein, include the Apostles Antipas (11th of April), Cornelius (13th of September), Gamaliel (2nd of August), Hierotheos (4th of October), Ignatios (20th of December and the 29th of January), Joseph of Arimathea (Third Sunday After Pascha), Lazarus (17th of October), Longinos (16th of October), Nikodemos (Third Sunday After Pascha), and Polycarp (23rd of February).

We ask the prayers of this holy synaxis of fathers who feared neither hardships, nor persecutions, nor tyrants, that they might confess the holy Faith to the nations. Let us therefore correct our lives, brethren, and emulate them, to the glory of God Who is wondrous in His saints. Amen.

---

[24] Saint Hermas is mentioned in a hymn of the Vespers Sticheron, Mode Four. Saint Hermes is cited in today's Orthros Canon, Ode Four, Mode Four, by Saint Joseph.

On the 4ᵗʰ of January, the holy Church commemorates the holy Martyrs ZOSIMOS the Monk and ATHANASIOS the court clerk.

Zosimos, the holy martyr, was from Cilicia. He dwelt in the wilderness amid wild beasts. He came to be apprehended by the ruling pagan of those parts, Dometian. Zosimos was tortured and made to endure burning of his ears with red-hot irons. Afterward, they cast him within a cauldron of boiling water. Since he emerged unscathed from these punishments, the exe-

Saint Zosimos Suspended.
Saints Zosimos and Athanasios Enter a Rock.

cutioners suspended him upside down. In the theater, a lion was set loose to pounce on the martyr, but the creature was a recently captured animal friend from the wilderness. The lion not only did not harm Zosimos, but also spoke in a human voice concerning the divinity of Christ. One of the pagan officials, Athanasios the court clerk (Lat. *commentariénsis*), converted to Christianity. He received the release of the saint from the tyrant, and the two men retreated together into the wilderness. Zosimos spent time catechizing Athanasios and then baptized him. It was then that they beheld a rock rent asunder in a mysterious manner. The two holy men entered the rock where they surrendered their souls into the hands of God.

On the 4ᵗʰ of January, the holy Church commemorates THEOKTISTOS the Hegumen at Cucomo of Sicily, who reposed in peace.

On the 4ᵗʰ of January, the holy Church commemorates our venerable Mother APOLLINARIA of senatorial rank.

Apollinaria, our ever-memorable mother, lived during the time of Emperor Leo the Great (457-474), who was also known as "the Butcher." She was the daughter of Anthemius, who was appointed imperial procurator of Rome. With regard to her beauty and understanding, she surpassed most women of that time. From her youth, she desired to preserve her virginity. She besought God day and night that she might achieve her aim and remain a virgin until death. To further this cause, she implored her parents to allow her to make a pilgrimage to Jerusalem. Upon receiving their permission, the blessed maiden took along her menservants and maidservants, as well as gold, silver, and costly materials. When the holy Apollinaria entered Jerusalem, she distributed all her goods and money to the poor. She then venerated the shrines of the holy land and freed all her servants. She only retained one old manservant and one eunuch. Together they left for Alexandria. As they came to a plain, they thought to rest in that place from the toils of their journey.

When the old man and the eunuch fell asleep, the thrice-blessed virgin, forsaking everything, fled secretly. She took refuge in a nearby forest, which she inhabited for many years. She suffered multitudinous bites from mosquitoes, which had infested that place. Consequently, her soft skin became as hard as a tortoiseshell. At length, she took herself away to Sketis (Wadi el-Natrun), west of the Nile Delta, where many venerable fathers were struggling in ascetic contests. She feigned being a eunuch and called herself Father Dorotheos. The venerable Makarios of Sketis accepted her and assigned her a cell. She remained immured therein and offered up prayer at all times.

In the meantime, her father, Anthemius, had another daughter, Apollinaria's sister, living at home, who was afflicted by an unclean demon. At his wit's end, the desperate Anthemius decided to send his daughter to the fathers of Sketis that they might heal her of that insidious demonic possession. The fathers in turn entrusted the demonized young woman to Father Dorotheos the eunuch. Apollinaria recognized her sister but did not reveal her own true identity. The sister therefore remained with Father Dorotheos for a few days and was delivered from the demon that troubled her. Thereupon, the young woman was returned by the fathers to the arms of her father.

Not much time passed before that young woman began to show that she was with child. Anthemius suspected Abba Dorotheos of seducing his daughter and sent officers to apprehend the monk. They left immediately and sped off to the Egyptian desert to bring back the monk to the procurator. Apollinaria went back peaceably with the officers and was presented to Anthemius. He in no wise recognized the ascetical monk before him to be Apollonaria, his long-lost daughter. When the charges were laid upon Abba Dorotheos, it was then that she divulged, by giving signs and offering disclosures known only to the family, that she was his flesh and blood and the daughter who disappeared so many years ago. Anthemius was astonished and in awe. He understood then that his youngest daughter had not been molested by Father Dorotheos but actually delivered from demonic possession by her very own older sister.

Apollinaria then tarried a few days with her parents and then returned to her cell. Now none of the fathers at Sketis were apprised of the events that had transpired in Rome or came to the knowledge of her true gender. Upon her repose, it was then that the monks understood that Father Dorotheos was a woman. All were beside themselves at this revelation and were moved to give thanks to God.

On the 4th of January, the holy Church commemorates
the holy SIX MARTYRS who suffered martyrically
but reposed in peace.[25]

On the 4th of January, the holy Church commemorates
our venerable Father EFTHYMIOS the New,
who struggled in asceticism and was laid to rest
in the sanctuary of Saint Mokios in Constantinople.

On the 4th of January, the holy Church commemorates
the holy Martyrs CHRYSANTHOS and EPHEMIA,
near the Church of Saint Akakios in Constantinople.

On the 4th of January, the holy Church commemorates
our venerable Father EFTHYMIOS
the Hegumen of the Athonite Monastery of Vatopedi,
who censured the Latin-minded
Emperor Michael and Patriarch Vekkos,
and who was drowned in the sea;
as well as the holy TWELVE MONKS of Vatopedi, who censured
the Latinizers and were hanged after torture on a hilltop.[26]

Efthymios, the venerable martyr, and those holy fathers with him, flourished in 1280 when the Latin-minded Emperor Michael VIII Palaiologos (r. 1259-1282) and Patriarch John XI Vekkos (1275-1282) dispatched troops and surrounded the Holy Mountain Athos. The purpose of their mission was

---

[25] *The Great Synaxaristes* (in Greek) suggests that these six living martyrs could be identical with the six fathers who are commemorated on the 15th of January, since the two lines of verse given in their notices of the *Menaion* are the same for both sets of saints. "Six luminous souls shone forth from the smelting pot of life and now stand on the same threshold as the six-winged minds of the seraphim."

[26] A fuller account of the venerable martyrs and confessors of Mount Athos who suffered at the hands of the Latinizers may be found in *The Great Synaxaristes*, on the 22nd of September, when the holy Church commemorates the martyrs of Zographou, and also on the 5th of December, for the commemoration of the venerable monks and confessors of Athos.

to enjoin the monks to follow them on their erroneous path of union with the papacy.

Saint Efthymios

Since the holy Athonite fathers refused such a union, many were made to suffer hardships and atrocities which led to their martyric deaths. When the soldiers came to Vatopedi, one of the larger monasteries atop a green slope built above a small inlet on the northeast side of the peninsula, the fathers rejected union with Rome. Some resisted, but many fled for refuge elsewhere. Those who were captured included the holy Prohegumen Efthymios and twelve other monks. After the tyrants subjected them to diverse torments, the Unionists sought vengeance against the monks who defied them, by hanging them. They could not be persuaded to embrace strange and unorthodox doctrines, which were unacceptable to the Orthodox Church.

When the Latinizers began their hostilities at the Lavra, some of the monks, terrified at being condemned to death, accepted the Unionists. They handed over to them many holy vessels, including chalices, Gospels, censers, and other such sacred articles of the monastery. Thus the monastery was looted, and those monks agreed to commune with the Latin-minded. At their repose, their miserable bodies remained as solid as wood and blackened all over, emitting a foul smell, so that they could not be buried in the cemetery of the brethren, but instead were placed in an underground cave, which needed to be fenced off. Thus, they died as foreigners and strangers to the holy Orthodox Church and her right-believing doctrines.

On the 4th of January, the holy Church commemorates
the venerable New-martyr ONOUPHRIOS the Bulgarian,
Hierodeacon of Hilandar, who suffered at Chios (1818).[27]

Onouphrios, the venerable new-martyr of Christ, lived in these latter times. He has inspired all pious Christians with his wondrous courage. In every time and place there have been such holy martyrs, worthy of admiration, who demonstrated courage, munificence, and perseverance. The fiery and incomparable love for Christ of these latter day new-martyrs, we deem extraordinary and special. Why is this so? In these last times, on account of our own knaveries, malice, wickedness, and cowardice, the words of David

---

[27] The Life of Saint Onouphrios was authored by the ever-memorable Monk Onouphrios of the Athonite Monastery of Iveron.

have overtaken us: "A righteous man there is no more; for truths have diminished from the sons of men. Vain things hath each man spoken to his neighbor; deceitful lips are in his heart, and in his heart hath he spoken evil [Ps. 11:1, 2]." Piety and godliness have been defaced and are in peril of being extinguished from the earth, for which reason the Prophet Michaeas (Micah) also mourned: "Alas for me!...Alas my soul! For the godly is perished from the earth. And there is none among men that orders his way aright. They all quarrel even to blood. They grievously afflict, each one his neighbor. They prepare their hands for mischief, the prince asks a reward, and the judge speaks flattering words; it is the desire of their soul [Mic. 7:1-3]."

There is a perverse universal indifference and disdain for things divine, so that every lawlessness is fulfilled in the earth. The people are intoxicated with licentiousness and bent on unbridled entertainments and amusements. Ecclesiastical traditions are shamelessly and recklessly set aside. Insults, outrages, and blasphemies against the Most High are perpetrated in every quarter, even as the divine Paul once prophesied to Timothy: "But know thou this, that in the last days difficult times shall set in; for men shall be lovers of self, lovers of money, boasters, proud, blasphemers, disobedient to parents, unthankful, unholy, without natural affection, implacable, slanderers, incontinent, savage, not lovers of the good, traitors, reckless, puffed up, lovers of pleasure rather than lovers of God, having a form of piety, but denying the power of it. Turn thyself away from these. For of these are those who creep into the houses and take captive little women who have been heaped up with sins, being led away by various desires, always learning and never able to come to a full knowledge of the truth [2 Tim. 3:1-7]." In these difficult and hard times, the all-famed new-martyrs, worthy of memory, withstood the most profane and Christ-hating tyrants. They appeared before them with unshakeable resolve and most marvellous valor. Some contested for Christ that they might preserve and keep Christ's Faith and love, while others, for various other reasons, confessed the all holy and venerable name of Jesus, not altering their love in the least. There were also others who struggled and suffered, lest their previous example of impiety should become a stumbling block. Therefore, they confessed well the divine Faith, which they formerly denied. Now such cases happened even in ancient times.

Nevertheless, the difference between the new-martyrs and those of old is significant. In earlier times, there was "so great a cloud of witnesses [Heb. 12:1]" around the faithful that they were zealous to exchange this present life for the everlasting one. Men, women, and children, the aged and the very young, rich and poor, learned and uneducated, clergy and layfolk, all despised the shame and endured their cross. But now, where are such models of piety? Can they be found? Alas! Where now is the zeal, the emulation? Even as it is written: "When the Son of Man cometh, shall He find the faith on the earth [Lk. 18:8]?" Christ tells us that "because lawlessness shall have been multiplied, the love of the multitude shall grow cold [Mt. 24:12]." The Apostle Paul also warns, "Now the Spirit speaketh expressly that in latter times some shall apostatize from the faith, giving heed to deceiving spirits and teachings of demons, speaking lies in hypocrisy, having been branded as to their own conscience [1 Tim. 4:1, 2]." Therefore, when we find in these latter times zealous faith and love of Christ, and one willing to courageously present oneself on behalf of Christ and suffer death, is this not truly wonderful and worthy of tens of thousands of praises?

Such a one in truth was the noble and heaven-minded Onouphrios. On account of one word, which he uttered thoughtlessly in his early childhood, he was not gladdened or satisfied that he had expiated his sin before God when he forsook the world and became a monk. He took up his cross and followed Christ with sufferings, pangs, and afflictions in the monastic state, adding obedience, cutting off his own will, ever-flowing tears, appointed fasts, countless prostrations, and all-night vigils standing. His soul was aflame, his heart was smitten and consumed with Christ's love. O good purpose! O marvellous disposition! Immaterial fire, which Christ placed on earth in the heart of man and which incited a willing Onouphrios, set him in motion for giving witness of Christ and suffering martyrdom. Inviting himself, he stood before the antichrist tyrants. His mind guarded by divine grace, his mouth filled with words of wisdom which Christ promised to His divine martyrs, Onouphrios boldly and openly proclaimed Christ the God of the universe. He censured them fearlessly for their antichrist error and deceit. Therefore, instead of ink, he used his own blood to admit and certify in writing his sacred confession of the Faith and his ever-memorable death on behalf of the Christ [Mt. 10:19], for Whom he demonstrated his love in a wonderful manner.

"I," writes the author, "O pious lovers of the martyrs, have come not only to narrate the martyric end of this gloriously triumphant martyr, but also his early life and ascetical conduct as a monk, so that you might perceive that our Onouphrios did not rush forward on impulse to be slaughtered for Christ, but rather he approached rationally and with discernment, together with the blessings and counsels of spiritual fathers and godly teachers. Those who were vouchsafed to be witnesses of his martyrdom marvelled and wondered exceedingly. It is meet therefore that I should begin my narration at this point."

The divine Onouphrios, the offspring of Christian parents, hailed from great Tŭrnovo,[28] and more particularly from the village of Kabrova. His father was Detzio but was later renamed Daniel when he received the monastic Schema. His mother was called Anna. They were people of means and consequence in their village. When they gave birth to a son, our Onouphrios, he was named Matthew in holy Baptism. When the lad reached school age, he was enrolled and began his studies, learning Bulgarian letters. When he reached eight or nine years of age, it came to pass that his parents scolded and spanked him for some misdemeanor. Matthew, both saddened and angered, then blurted out some words before the Turks, who happened to be present, saying, "I wish to become a Turk!" Now even though his parents were startled at this foolhardy outcry, they somehow managed to gloss over the incident; but this did not prevent the Moslems from attempting to snatch the boy for circumcision and make him as one of the Turks.

In some unspecified manner the problem was dealt with, and Matthew remained a Christian, continuing his life as before, neither being enjoined to confess the antichrist religion of Islam nor being put under the knife in circumcision. "Regarding this terrible mischief," comments the author, "I cannot imagine how the parents contended with the Moslems, nor do I know how they corrected so young a child." In any event, when Matthew came to an age of true understanding and discernment of how things were in this world, he decided to depart his homeland and enter the Holy Mountain of Athos. He repaired to Hilandar, the Serbian monastery on the northeast side of the peninsula, which is the most northerly of the Athonite monasteries. When Matthew came to the monastery, the decline of it already had begun in the seventeenth century. The influx of Serbs diminished, so that by the end of the eighteenth century, the monastery was inhabited largely by Bulgarian monks.[29]

Matthew spent considerable time at Hilandar and was counted worthy to be ordained to the office of Hierodeacon. "I think," says the author, "that either Matthew did not mention the childhood incident, or his spiritual father

---

[28] Tŭrnovo is a city on the river Jantra in northern Bulgaria. By the 6th C., it was a modest Byzantine city. When Peter and Asen began their revolt against Byzantine rule in 1185, Tŭrnovo became the capital of the Second Bulgarian Empire, seat of the exarch, and from 1235 seat of the Patriarch of Bulgaria. In July of 1393, the Ottomans captured and burned the city, deporting many of its natives to Asia Minor. In the early 14th C., it had been a center of trade, industry, literature, and scholarship; but after its capture, many Bulgarian scholars found refuge in Russia. *The Oxford Dictionary of Byzantium*, s.v. "Tŭrnovo."

[29] Among them was the great writer Paisios, who is famous for his *History of the Bulgarian People*, and other notable works. Sotiris Kadas, *Mount Athos*, p. 56.

did not deem mere words spoken by a child—those few spoken carelessly by a child in a tantrum—as an impediment to ordination, because Matthew was not circumcised." Matthew was also renamed in the tonsure, so that he became Father Manasses.

According to the holy fathers, as a man advances in virtue, so much more does he become humble. Even the tiniest of sins he deems great, and he believes that they require repentance. Consequently, the blessed Manasses, as he made progress in virtue, examined his entire previous life with his deeds. He gave considerable thought to the boyhood incident that caused him a profound fall, for by a word he denied the Christ. He knew he had fallen and lapsed on account of childish thoughtlessness and foolishness. Together with his remorse, he also kept recapitulating in his mind the martyrdom of Saint Barlaam of Antioch, commemorated by the holy Church on the 19th of November, who was led to an altar of the idols and ordered to stretch out his right hand, on which they placed lit coals with incense. Christ's champion, undaunted, without his hand flinching, proved to be stronger than bronze or iron. The embers penetrated the flesh and, of their own accord, fell to the earth. Thus Barlaam chose to burn his hand rather than offer incense and homage to the demons—even if only in appearance. Father Manasses also kept ruminating on the Master Christ's words: "Everyone therefore who shall confess in Me before men, I also will confess in him before My Father Who is in the heavens. But whosoever shall deny Me before men, him will I also deny before My Father Who is in the heavens [Mt. 10:32, 33]." These words and past memories became fixed in Father Manasses' mind, so that he was continually pondering on them and filled with fear. "Peradventure the fruits of repentance that I have offered," he asked himself, "are inadequate for that denial uttered in my childhood? Then the Christ shall deny me before His Father in the heavens."

He thereupon struggled to expiate that sin before God that he might be granted pardon for his renunciation. His thoughts and remembrances continued to weigh heavily upon him, giving him no peace. What began as fear, later grew into a passion and desire for martyrdom. His sole aim became to confess Jesus Christ before men and to receive a martyric death. As the days passed, so did his zeal heighten. He, however, understood man's proclivities and weaknesses. He maintained a reverential fear not to do anything rash. He entreated the Savior, asking, "Is this Thy will? Is it good and God-pleasing?" He needed to be firm in his mind that God's grace would be with him and empower him, that he might make a perfect confession of God, the Creator of heaven and earth, before the enemies of His Faith. This is what Father Manasses yearned to attain; this is what he was always envisioning in his mind. But since, in accordance with the words of Solomon,

"The thoughts of mortal men are miserable, and our devices are but uncertain [Wis. 9:14]," Father Manasses prudently thought to reveal his intentions. He sought spiritual counsel, which he received. He was told to contemplate well what awaited him and not to rush forward heedlessly to such a fearful and dreadful contest. The man of God hearkened to that advice and continued his ascetical struggles. Then news reached him that the venerable New-martyr Ignatios, commemorated by the holy Church on the 8th of October, had completed his course of martyrdom. Father Manasses then became more inflamed in his heart, so that his desire increased, even as report of the venerable New-martyr Efthymios, commemorated by the holy Church on the 22nd of March, kindled an intense yearning in him to witness for Christ. But after he heard of the martyric end of Saint Akakios,[30] the flame of his love for Christ and longing for a martyric death, confessing His name, he could no longer suppress his ardor or endure putting off for another instant a martyric course for himself.

From beginning to end, the blessed Manasses demonstrated great thought, purpose, sense, and judgment. He therefore wished to inform and take counsel with others regarding his goal. He went to the sacred Skete of the Honorable Forerunner, where he visited with the most reverent and experienced spiritual father in such matters. Father Manasses unveiled his entire intention before this spiritual trainer who had already anointed athletes for the spiritual wrestling match. He was Father Nikephoros, the elder and trainer, who managed the three previous new-martyrs, Efthymios, Ignatios, and Akakios. Father Manasses fervently begged Father Nikephoros to receive him into his hut that he might prepare and instruct him, even as he had done with the other three. Father Nikephoros replied, "I do accept thee. However, in the first place, I must tell thee not to inform anyone outside of this arrangement. In the second place, there are stern proofs and preparations needed to be undergone by thee, as though thou wert experiencing the tortures of martyrdom. Now if thou wilt consent and bear with these tests, then indeed I receive thee." The blessed contestant answered happily, saying, "I consent, gladly." Then Father Manasses took his leave. He went and distributed all his money to the poor. He even went to his father's monastery, for Detzio had become Father Daniel, and left sufficient money for him to support and nourish himself. Afterward, Father Manasses feigned that he was going on a

---

[30] The martyrdoms of New-martyrs Ignatios, Efthymios, and Akakios were written by the Monk Onouphrios of Iveron, who also recorded the Life of Saint Onouphrios. These three other new-martyrs are commemorated together on the 1st of May. The holy relics of these three are stored in the Iveron Skete of Saint Nicholas, within the church of the same name.

pilgrimage to the holy places of Jerusalem. In this manner, the brethren, and even his own father, gave him leave. Father Manasses then secretly went to the holy and spiritual Father Nikephoros. In accordance with the agreement they reached, Elder Nikephoros placed Father Manasses in a hut, secluded and separate from himself. He gave Manasses commands regarding how to conduct his life and engage in struggles, praying alone to God. The elder then assigned one of the brethren to care for the needs and maintenance of Father Manasses. This brother was also further instructed not to engage in any conversation with Father Manasses, who was no longer to have any further association with anyone.

"At this point, I beseech the listeners," says the author, "that they give fitting attention to what shall be said." The truth is that only with the proper heed to such narrations can one reap benefits. The blessed Manasses was enclosed in that training camp and began his spiritual contests. In the beginning he passed forty days in fasting. Thereafter, on some occasions he would fast three days and on other occasions two days. He consumed thirty drams of bread and partook of a little water. During the entire period of this trial, he would eat cooked food only on Saturday and Sunday, but never to satiety. He usually made four thousand prostrations daily, or at least three thousand five hundred. The number of Jesus Prayers made on his prayer rope cannot be counted. His inward attention was unremitting, in both his mind and what he uttered. Mourning, contrition, and compunction ever filled his heart. His eyes were as two springs, producing an ever-flowing stream of tears. He kept vigil at every hour. He only took some bodily consolation with his small fare of dry food with no oil. After the passage of four months, he had only consumed a little over five pounds of raisins.[31] During the forty-day fast, he would at times keep a three-day fast or a two-day fast, partaking of nothing. He therefore mortified his flesh and diminished his bodily powers to such an extent that he was no longer able to execute the bodily toils of his prayer rule. Father Manasses' prolonged fasts were then moderated by his spiritual elder, to whom the athlete of Christ was always obedient.

Since Father Manasses was tried as gold in a furnace for that four-month period, the flame of the love of the Christ and the desire for martyrdom were mightily kindled in him. He also at that time received the Great Schema of the monastics. Father Manasses was renamed Father Onouphrios, his final name in which he contested to the end. Afterward, with the counsel, judgment, and blessing of his spiritual Elder Nikephoros and the brothers of that holy synodia, it was decided that the time had come for Father Onou-

---

[31] One oke or oka, a unit of measure in Greece, Turkey, and Egypt, is approximately 2.8 pounds.

phrios to enter the stadium of martyrdom. Now since it is written in the Scriptures that "two are better than one, seeing they have a good reward for their labor [Eccl. 4:9]," the discerning spiritual father gave Father Onouphrios one of his disciples. This was Father Gregory, a Peloponnesian, and he was to escort the contestant, working with him and helping him. He was experienced, sagacious, and venerable. He had also previously accompanied the three other righteous martyrs to Constantinople, namely, Efthymios, Ignatios, and Akakios.

Father Onouphrios thereupon took letters of recommendation from the august personages of the Holy Mountain, after making a round of visits and being examined. Fathers Onouphrios and Gregory then took ship and were bound for the island of Chios. They remained where the letters had advised them. In that place, they found all that they required and desired, and gave glory to the Lord and magnified His divine providence. They tarried there seven days in solitude, quiet, prayer, fasting, and tears. They partook of, and received great delight in, the immaculate Mysteries. It was Saturday when they arrived, and they were waiting for that coming Friday, that day in the week when the saving Passion of the Christ occurred. It was planned that Father Onouphrios should at that time present himself before the judgment hall of the impious. Once there, he would profess the good confession on that particular day that he might become a communicant of the Master's Passion. It is not outside the scope of this work to relate to the lovers of martyrs the impression of those at Chios who received the two Athonites just prior to the contest: "Father Onouphrios arrived on the 25th of December, a Saturday, with the most reverend Elder Gregory, who presented letters and also gave verbal explanations regarding their mission. Onouphrios remained silent and did not so much as lift up his head to look anyone in the face, and wept unceasingly. Toward those Christians whom he encountered, he would beseech their forgiveness and request their cooperation by offering prayers and entreaties on his behalf. He was wont to say, 'I am the most sinful of all men and unworthy to be named among the Christians.'"

During the whole time of those seven days and nights that they spent at Chios, they remained immured in a separate dwelling place, where they engaged in continual prayer, prostrations, and use of the prayer rope. We read, however, that such toils and weariness that come from these exertions are deemed relaxation and recreation to the new-martyrs. Only on one evening did these fathers partake of a little food, but no oil, meat, or dairy, and no wine or strong drink. One night, after the blessed contestant toiled greatly, he sat down and was overtaken by a light sleep. Straightway, he was vouchsafed a vision. Even as one beholds in the holy icons many saints in their ranks, in like manner two choirs of saints appeared and stood before

Father Onouphrios. One choir was comprised of priests and hierarchs, and the other of soldiers. They declared to Father Onouphrios: "Come, because the King seeks thee." Standing in awe of them, with fear and trepidation, he said, "Why should the King ask for me? What man am I? How should I be vouchsafed to stand in the presence of the King? I beseech you, leave me be." "Nay," they answered. "It is necessary that thou shouldest be presented, only do not tarry." In his vision, Father Onouphrios went with those two sacred choirs. They escorted him to a bright and joyous place, which was broad. He beheld the King sitting on the throne, and all making obeisance to Him. The King then turned to those standing and uttered, "This place is prepared." Then they showed Father Onouphrios a place more brilliant.

After beholding such things, the saint then awoke and rejoiced. He gave thanks to Christ the King and offered up supplications and entreaties to Saint Basil the Great, since it was the night of that saint's commemoration, the 1st of January. He asked that Saint Basil mediate on his behalf before God and prepare him to communicate the immaculate Mysteries in the Liturgy. It then seemed to the blessed Onouphrios that he sensed divine energy and spiritual warmth in his heart. The following night, however, he was filled with fear and trembling; for he perceived the departure of grace. He spoke to the Elder Gregory regarding this, saying, "Father, the fire has extinguished and burns not in my heart. O, to what have I, the miserable one, come?" Gregory answered him, "Thou dost ask what hast thou suffered? Thou hast become proud. For this cause the grace of God has departed from thee. Dost thou wish to become the plaything of the demons and grieve the holy angels and shame men? Woe to me, the wretched one! All my toils and labors, and the good hopes of the brethren, what a pity! Instead of hearing thee called a new-martyr, they shall hear that thou hast denied Christ for a second time! Why dost thou not come to thyself, O hapless one?"

"Here I," the biographer, "leave each listener to ruminate upon with what kind of disposition the martyr responded to this jarring rebuke and to what depth of humility he was plunged." He dropped down at the feet of the elder, weeping inconsolably. He then stood in prayer, shedding many tears, until he sensed that usual warmth which did not cease. The elder himself did not leave off praying, until the martyr, in a humble voice, said to him: "Father, blessed be God, I am well now." Thereupon, in the morning, the elder commanded him to make a prostration before those present and to kiss their feet, seeking their prayers and blessings with humble-mindedness. As we said earlier, Gregory, as one most experienced, was a trainer of other venerable new-martyrs. He employed strictness and careful training fit for the purpose. He instructed using these methods that he might protect his pupil from any and all thoughts of vainglory and pride, thereby bringing him to the heights of humility.

There was in that neighborhood a church, which was adorned with many icons all around the walls. Among those depicted were new-martyrs. Father Onouphrios that day was enclosed alone within that sacred precinct. Before each icon, he prayed the Jesus Prayer with his prayer rope, making bows and prostrations. His heart became excessively inflamed and filled with contrition, so that, at times, he let out mournful and plaintive shouts. At that hour, Father Gregory heard his laments but did not hinder him. He perceived that Father Onouphrios was in an ecstasy and inspired by God. Later, however, the elder resumed his former sternness and said to Father Onouphrios, "Hearken to the Lord Who said, 'Let not thy left hand know what thy right hand is doing [Mt. 6:3].' Why dost thou, O vainglorious and proud one, cry out in thy prayer? Is it not certainly nothing else other than that thou mightest be praised for how easily thou hast come to compunction? Thou hast therefore once more lost thy labor, O wretched one, being deceived by the spirit of pride!" Then the genuine imitator of the humility of the meek Christ stood, looking down and with tears streaming from his eyes, and said in a humble voice, "I have sinned, father; forgive me and entreat God that He deliver me from the snares of the devil."

Thus, by these contests and struggles, the elder brought to nought the machinations of the devil. Indeed, even before the martyric contest, Father Onouphrios arrived at the full measure of sanctity. What happened thenceforth? As we know, the Lord celebrated the Mystical Supper on Thursday and communicated His holy disciples, saying, "Take, eat; this is My body." And He took the cup, and gave thanks, and gave it to them, saying, "Drink of it, all of you; for this is My blood, that of the new covenant, which is being poured out for many for remission of sins [Mt. 26:26-28]." Saint Paul writes that our Lord said, "'This cup is the new covenant in My blood; be doing this, as often as ye may drink it, in remembrance of Me.' For as often as ye may eat this bread and drink this cup, ye proclaim the Lord's death until He should come [1 Cor. 11:25, 26]." Afterward, our Lord surrendered Himself to the voluntary Passion. In like manner, the imitator of the Passion, Onouphrios, on that Thursday evening, prepared himself in advance. He prayed all that night that he might be delivered up to death on behalf of Christ, that he might offer Him his soul and body in sacrifice. Afterward, the Elder Gregory first shaved Father Onouphrios' beard and all the hairs of his head. Next, the elder took holy oil from all the oil lamps of the holy icons of that church. He proceeded to anoint with oil, making the sign of the Cross, all of Father Onouphrios' bodily members, even as when the newly baptized receive holy Chrism. Then together Father Onouphrios and the elder passed the night in prayer. After the office of Orthros, Father Onouphrios venerated and kissed the holy relics of many saints, among which were those of the new-martyrs. Father Onouphrios then asked the parish priest if he would make the sign of the Cross over him with all the relics of the saints. Next, Christ's athlete venerated and kissed the holy icons. He then communicated the Mysteries, which had been prepared at the Presanctified Liturgy. He then clad himself in Hagarene attire and went forth into the darkness with a guide; for it was not possible then to go about Chios without being directed. They traversed some roads, and then the sun began rising in the east. The son of light, Onouphrios, walked that path toward the city, and no one knew what he was about to do.

On his way, he came to a place called Vounaki, where he encountered a Christian baker readying his furnace. Since Onouphrios was feeling cold, he entered the shop that he might warm himself. In the course of conversation, Onouphrios revealed his intention to the baker. The Christian then gave him directions on how to find the court, where he might present himself to the Muslims. Onouphrios left and then purchased a pair of red shoes. In that shop, the emir or governor himself was the Hagarene merchant. The emir observed Onouphrios' clothing, for he was wearing a green turban on his head. The emir began conversing with him in a cordial manner, as though they had a previous acquaintance. Onouphrios then put on his new shoes and left that place. Another Hagarene was also present and made this comment in Turkish to the emir: "That fellow seems to me to be masquerading in an assumed dress and is not one of our own." The emir, an Islamic zealot, said to him, "Hush! What a pity! What a pity! May God not consume thee! Didst thou not see his green turban?" In the meantime, Onouphrios returned to the baker. That good Christian man, whom he found preparing and selling pastries, cakes, and breads, left off his business and escorted Onouphrios to the Church of Saint Matrona of Chios. On the way, Onouphrios was giving alms.

Upon arriving, Onouphrios requested permission from the sacristan that he might enter the attached infirmary. Permission was granted, and Onouphrios distributed alms in that place. He then went forth and found the Church of the Theotokos Keharitomene. He made a donation, and then a Supplicatory Canon was chanted. Afterward, he venerated and kissed the holy icons. He then departed and went toward the *mahkeme*, the Court of Justice, at the center of the city, where he asked, "I need to see the *cadi* (judge)." The name of the judge was Mouxurbasees. When Onouphrios located the judge, the latter inquired, "What is thy business with me?" Christ's witness answered, "I wish to take an action against someone." Mouxurbasees then asked, "Dost thou have a *fetfan*, a written decision by an official? Because first thou must obtain this document and then bring a suit." Now all of this intercourse took place by divine œconomy, so that the martyr's confession should shine forth brilliantly before many of the ungodly. It was therefore the Lord's good pleasure that Onouphrios' first attempt abort. Since Onouphrios did not succeed in his aim, he returned to the baker at his shop. Onouphrios then took up his cross into his right hand. He then leaned on his forehead and cried for a considerable time. The Christian baker joined him, and they wept together. The baker, clearly sympathetic to Onouphrios' cause, then counseled him, "Go again to the *mahkeme*. Do not speak a work to any of the clerks or officers at the court, but go straight to the same *cadi*, lift the curtain to his chamber, and present thyself."

Onouphrios hearkened to the baker's advice. As though guided to that very place and moment, he drew back the curtain and entered the judge's chambers. He found at that very hour that all the aghas, or men in authority, were present, both Ottoman military and civil officials. Onouphrios then made an open address: "I, fifteen years ago, sustained a wound in such a place as this; and, from that time until now, I have been going about to many and diverse places that I might treat the wound, but healing was not possible. The physicians told me that if I should return to the place where I suffered the wound, then healing would follow. For this cause, I have come here that I might be cured." The judge asked, "What kind of wound didst thou receive and what seekest thou from us?" The martyr replied, "My wound is this. When I was a small child, out of ignorance, I denied the Christian Faith and confessed your own religion. However, I in no wise offered worship, but rather continued to live as a Christian, because I grew up in a Christian land. But when I came of age and understood the evil which I had committed, that is, renouncing my holy Faith, I deemed that incident to be a deadly wound to my soul. I besought my Christ and God, my Creator and Fashioner, to pardon this transgression of mine. But my thoughts would never leave me in peace and quiet. I kept considering the magnitude of the sin which I committed, renouncing my true Faith and confessing your false one. But now, I boldly and openly confess before all of you that I am a Christian and deny and anathematize your belief." Forthwith, Onouphrios took the green turban which he was wearing, and with much disdain cast it before them.

Beholding such daring, the Muslims remained speechless. Then the emir, anxious for the honor of his religion, before he spoke to any of his coreligionists, asked the martyr, "What art thou doing, man? Thou hast taken and placed on thy head that holy article." The martyr, hearing that the emir described the turban as holy, took the opportunity to show his contempt for the object. He began speaking many things against Mohammad. (Afterward the judge told a Christian who was a close acquaintance that "the words that

Onouphrios uttered against Mohammad, no mouth could repeat and no ear could stand hearing for any length of time.") The assembly of aghas then lifted up their voices, crying out, "This man ought not to draw breath for much longer!" Straightway, they commanded the officers to arrest Onouphrios and place him in prison. His feet were secured in the stocks, whereupon the tension was set to stretch him to the second notch. Afterward, they took him outside the judgment hall, where he was slapped and cudgeled. He was also made to undergo other extreme punishments. A police officer then arrived with four bailiffs. They took hold of Onouphrios and brought him to another prison and placed him in wooden stocks. The blessed one sat in them and continued in prayer. Then a Hagarene man came and reviled the martyr, but Onouphrios was not made to suffer any further torments. Some Christians, also held as prisoners, questioned him: "What is thy name and thy homeland?" The martyr answered, "I am from great Tŭrnovo, and my name is Matthew." He gave his baptismal name rather than his monastic name, lest knowledge that he was a monk should implicate his monastery. He also did not wish to divulge the reason for his being in Chios. Now it was Friday, and the aghas went to the temple. When they emerged, they fell into a discussion with one another regarding the prisoner. They decided to ask the opinion of a pasha who was in exile. As a result, it was unanimously agreed that the prisoner receive the death sentence.

They acted immediately and determined that he be brought out of the prison. With a few words they examined him. Since, however, their opinion was unchanged, they decreed his beheading and determined that his body was to be cast into the sea. They also stated that the ground upon which the execution would take place and soak up his blood, was to be removed and cast into the sea, lest any Christian should be allowed to take keepsakes from the body. Thus it was decided, and they removed Onouphrios from the courthouse. The martyr, thinking that the place where they were about to sever his head was near at hand, wished to kneel. But the executioners took him further away, about a stone's throw. They then told him he could bend his knees in that place. But now he wished to go further still, to the place where the Muslims had previously beheaded the holy New-martyr Mark, commemorated by the holy Church on the 5th day of June, in the year 1801. They obliged the prisoner, and he knelt on the spot where Saint Mark had been executed. Forthwith, the cook of that prison unsheathed his knife and struck the martyr in the neck. His blade entered in about the depth of three fingers. The martyr bent his head, and then fell down without the least agitation to any of his bodily members. The cook stood next to the martyr and administered a second and third blow to his neck, which finally resulted in the martyr's death. All of these events took place within five hours. A great crowd of Christians hastened and assembled to that site, including, men, women, and children. Even though Father Onouphrios was unknown to the inhabitants of that city, they deemed him a holy martyr in the strictest sense.

Saint Onouphrios finished his sacred contests of martyrdom on the 4th day of January, in the year 1818. It was a Friday, at the ninth hour. He was thirty-two years of age.[32] All were marvelling at the martyr's disposition, courage, and manliness. It had been reported that his countenance, which before his contests had the pallor of death, afterward received radiance and grace. The Christian spectators received great joy through him, as they gave thanks and blessed God for the splendid victory of Onouphrios. Each one attempted to take some part of his martyric relics, whether his blood, or hair, or clothing, even as they had previously done with the Martyrs Mark and Angelis. The latter New-martyr Angelis suffered martyrdom in Chios on the 3rd day of December, in the year 1813. Now before his body emptied its blood on the ground, the unbelievers lifted up his sacred relics and cast them into the sea, at which juncture the Christians were downcast with sorrow. Since it was the decision of the tyrants, the executioners quickly put the sacred relics in a large straw basket, lest the earth around the beheading should receive any other drops of blood. The basket was then placed within a barrel, a kind of large funerary urn. The accursed ones then dug up the ground that was splattered with blood and filled two straw baskets. Then all the remains were conveyed to a fishing boat. Not one Christian man was selected to help in transporting or lifting the containers with the sacred relics. Only Turkish porters were called to do the work. Meanwhile, the teacher of Islamic error cried out in his fanaticism with much indignation, "Guard the remains, keep watch over them, lest the Christians should snatch something from you! The decedent, by Allah's concession, wished to die as a Christian." So carefully and diligently did the abominable ones carry out his order that not only were no relics secured by the Christians, but even the boat was washed down, lest the Christians should come and venerate the place where his sacred relics lay.

---

[32] The saint earlier declared to the aghas that he had sustained a wound fifteen years ago. Here, the author gives the martyr's age at the time of his death as thirty-two. We also know that little Matthew spoke those careless words when he was eight years of age. Therefore, his death, fifteen years later, would have taken place when he was twenty-three years of age. This is unlikely, since the required age for the diaconate is twenty-five, to which dignity he had already attained some years earlier. Therefore, when he says that he was wounded fifteen years earlier, he is probably calculating from the time that he entered the monastic life, that is, from seventeen years of age, at which time he was deeply wounded when he came to fully understand the enormity of his rashness on that unhappy day in his childhood.

At this point, we have finished narrating the martyrdom of Hiero-deacon Onouphrios. What became of his sacred relics and at which place they were submerged, we do not know. We only glorify the holy God Who was glorified in this venerable martyr, the friend of God, and honor Saint Onouphrios yearly on his feast day. He is our ever ready intercessor.

This, O pious brethren and Christ-lovers, is the ascetical life of the holy and venerable Martyr Onouphrios. This was his evangelic mode of life. This was his martyrdom in behalf of his witness for Christ. This was his blessed and glorified end. From his adolescent years, as you have heard, he gave himself over to virtuous struggles. With much exactness, he kept the rules of the monastic profession. The fear of the Lord, which is the beginning of wisdom, caused him to ascend to divine love; that love brought him to perfection and a martyric death for Christ. And death exalted him to heavenly glory—the splendid, magnificent, and lofty glory.

Then let us magnify, let us offer encomiums, and let us genuinely glorify the venerable Martyr Onouphrios, that we may become martyrs by disposition and receive the same rewards from Christ God, to Whom is due glory and dominion, honor and homage, together with the unoriginate Father, and the all-holy and life-creating, co-beginningless and coeternal Spirit, now and ever and unto the ages of the ages. Amen.

Through the intercessions of Thy Saints,
O Christ God, have mercy on us. Amen.

**On the 5th of January, the holy Church commemorates
the holy Hieromartyr THEOPEMPTOS and the Martyr THEONAS.**

Theopemptos and Theonas, the holy martyrs, lived during the time of Emperor Diocletian (284-305). In the year 290, when Diocletian called for the persecution of the Christians, Theopemptos was Bishop of Nikomedia (now Izmit). This saint was the first martyr to confess the Christ and receive martyrdom, after he was arrested by Diocletian in the Bithynian suburbs of Nikomedia. The bishop was made to stand before Diocletian, whom he censured for his deceit and error of idol-madness. Diocletian then

Saint Theopemptos

showed his displeasure, banished his cold civility, and bellowed, "Give homage to Apollo! I did not bring thee here to have a discussion." The hierarch replied in the words of the psalmist, "Those that worship graven things and boast themselves in their idols shall be put to shame. But our God is in the heaven and in the earth. The idols of the nations are silver and gold, the works of the hands of men: A mouth have they, but they shall not talk; eyes have they, and they shall not see; ears have they, and they shall not hear; noses have they, and they shall not be made to smell; hands have they, and they shall not feel; feet have they, and they shall not walk; they shall not give utterance in their throat [Ps. 113:11-15]." Diocletian was losing patience and threatened the holy man with terrifying tortures. Not intimidated in the least, Theopemptos answered calmly, "Our Lord Christ has told us not to fear those who kill the body, but are not able to kill the soul. Much rather, we fear the one God Who is able to send away both our souls and bodies into Gehenna [cf. Mt. 10:28]."

Exasperated, Diocletian then put his words into effect. The holy hierarch was to be cast into a lit furnace, which was being stoked all that morning. At noon, the hierarch said to the officers who were preparing the furnace, "Take your ease now, for I am ready to be sacrificed. My God is able to save me, according to His marvellous works, from the fiery furnace. But if not, be it known to all, that I shall not worship the image of Apollo or those of any other demons." The saint then made ready to enter the flames and said, "Prove me, O Lord, and try me; prove by fire my reins and my heart [Ps. 25:2]." He made the sign of the Cross and uttered those words of the holy Three Children: "O Lord, give glory to Thy name. Let them be confounded in all their power and might. Let their strength be broken. Let them know that Thou art Lord, the only God [cf. 3 Children, 19-21]." The saint then leaned back and reclined in the midst of the burning furnace.

Diocletian departed, as well as the soldiers, after they closed the furnace door. All assumed that the bishop would be immolated in minutes.

But wait! At midnight, Bishop Theopemptos emerged unscathed from the furnace. No one prevented him from entering Diocletian's palace and very bedchamber, for the doors opened of themselves to the holy man. He found Diocletian sleeping on his bed, so he awakened him. "Behold, O emperor, I live! The slave of Jesus Christ stands before thee. No harm has come to me in the furnace all these hours. Neither my hair has been singed, nor has my garb been scorched." Diocletian observed him and could not speak a word. He was fixed in astonishment, wondering if what he beheld was an apparition. The emperor was unable to take any action from his terror. The bishop then departed and returned to the furnace. When Diocletian finally came to himself, he interrogated his officers: "After the Christian bishop entered the flames, did anyone open the furnace door and release him?" The soldiers, filled with fear at the possible implications of that question, answered, "Nay, sire, all was done as thou didst command." Diocletian, with the wildest anxiety, ordered his men to follow him to the furnace. As they approached, the sound of chanting could be heard from within the furnace. The bishop was in the midst of the roaring flames, singing, "O ye children of men, bless ye the Lord. Praise and exalt Him above all forever. O all ye that worship the Lord, bless the God of gods, praise Him and give Him thanks, for His mercy endureth forever [3 Child. 59, 67]." The bishop then addressed the emperor and his men: "My God has delivered me out of the midst of the furnace and the roaring flames." Diocletian, seeing that the fire had no power over the bishop, was amazed, even as Nebuchadnezzar and his court in centuries past [Dan. 3:27]. But unlike that king who blessed the God of the Prophet Daniel and the holy Three Children, Diocletian scowled and remarked, "This is the work of sorcery. I have heard that the Christians employ the magical arts when they invoke their Christ's name; thus, they are able to overturn the order of nature." But Diocletian, wishing to test the fire that he might trust his senses, cast in a dog, which perished immediately. Diocletian's anger then waxed even hotter, as he threatened Theopemptos with frightening punishments and mutilations. The bishop was then thrown into prison until a public trial could be arranged.

The man of God was left without any food or water for twenty and two days, but was sustained in a mysterious and miraculous manner by Christ. After the passage of that time, Diocletian went with his guards to ascertain whether the bishop had died of hunger and thirst. When the cell door was opened, they were astounded to find the holy Theopemptos not only alive but also in good health. Diocletian tore at his clothing and cried out, saying again, "This is nought but the work of sorcery!" Theopemptos then asked the emperor, "How long wilt thou refuse to acknowledge the true God of the universe Who has wrought all these signs and wonders?" Unable to bear the public reproach for his wilful blindness, Diocletian ordered his executioners to pluck out the saint's right eye. This was done, and the sadistic executioners planted the orb in the bishop's palm as a keepsake. Theopemptos was then returned to his cell. The saint in no wise despaired, but offered up earnest prayer. In that doleful prison, light suddenly shone in the darkness, and the saint's eye was miraculously restored to its socket. No trace of the hideous disfigurement was evident. Therefore, when Theopemptos was brought before Diocletian for further examination, the emperor was angered and bewildered upon seeing the prisoner without any trauma to the eye. "By the great Apollo," he shouted aloud, "I am resolved to find a wizard who shall overcome thy magic!" Theopemptos was then returned to the prison. In the meantime, Diocletian dispatched letters throughout his kingdom, commanding that a wizard capable of overcoming Christian sorcery be brought to the emperor at Nikomedia. If the wizard should succeed, he would acquire for himself costly gifts and be accorded high honor from the emperor himself.

The sorcerer Theonas answered the emperor's call to challenge the Christian bishop. Confident in his powers, Theonas assured the emperor of his ability to revoke any Christian spell or charm. As he vaunted his abilities before Diocletian, the emperor was filled with malignant joy at the prospect of bringing down the Christian bishop and making him appear ridiculous. Before he proceeded, however, Diocletian wished to put Theonas to the test, lest the wizard's words should be merely those of a braggart. "Do thou perform something here that we may be assured of thy powers." Theonas then said, "Bring forth a bull, a wild one, sire, and I shall slay it with but a word." The beast was brought forward by men who handled it with ropes. Theonas approached and whispered some words into the creature's ear. The bull immediately was sundered and died. Diocletian and those present were considerably impressed by this display. Diocletian then summoned the prisoner Theopemptos that he might humiliate him before the entire company.

Diocletian announced the contest before all. Theonas, prepared to withstand the man of God, said to the bishop, "I shall put thee to the test twice. If thou shouldest remain unscathed, then I myself will believe in thy Christ." Theonas then prepared two poisonous pastries, over which he pronounced some satanic words. They were then offered to the bishop. Upon his making the sign of the Cross and putting the deadly cake to his mouth, it became as sweet and innocuous as honey. This unexpected outcome made a deep impression upon Theonas, who could not conceal his surprise. But he collected himself quickly and prepared for the second test. This time he concocted a deadly drink. He also invoked the devils to empower the drink with death. Theopemptos made the sign of the Cross over that toxic draft and swallowed it. All expected him to collapse and die. When no such effect was forthcoming, it was Theonas who fell at the bishop's feet, exclaiming, "Christ is the true God!" Theonas then said to Diocletian, "The gods are impotent. I confess the crucified Jesus as God." Diocletian was disgusted with this turn of events and sent both Theopemptos and Theonas away, back to the prison.

Saint Theonas

Bishop Theopemptos then catechized Theonas, baptizing and naming him Synesios. His new name bespoke one filled with understanding. When Theopemptos was brought forth for further examination, Diocletian did not relax his attempts to convert the bishop. Diocletian, finally perceiving that he was hard aground and had not the smallest hope of changing the martyr's resolve, ordered the tortures to commence. A heavy pillar, carried only with difficulty by eight mighty soldiers, was placed on the bishop's abdomen. As soon as it touched the bishop's martyric body, it miraculously was hurled some twenty feet away. Diocletian then bade his men to suspend the bishop upside down, with a heavy stone tied to his neck. The holy martyr remained in that position until the third hour, when the tyrant ordered him cut down. This was not out of pity, but so that the falling stone should either break the bishop's neck or strike his head. Nevertheless, this device was thwarted by God, Who instead had His servant fall from that height and land on the ground in an upright position with that heavy stone cast off. The tyrant wearied at being vanquished in every contest, so he ordered the bishop's beheading. Upon hearing his sentence, the bishop was filled with joy and thanksgiving, as he gave thanks to God Who had vouchsafed him much longed-for martyrdom. Not wasting any time, the wearied emperor had the execution carried out immediately.

Theonas was then brought forth, who had turned witness for Jesus Christ. Diocletian nevertheless attempted to coax and threaten him by turns, but every inducement proved useless. Theonas spurned all the earthly things offered by Diocletian. It was then ordered that Theonas be cast into a pit, which was dug deep for the purpose of burying him alive. The executioners filled in the pit and placed much dirt over the martyr's head. The ground was then tamped down, to assure Theonas' suffocation.

Thus, the holy Martyrs Theopemptos and Theonas, after having set at nought the savagery of the tyrant and all ungodly worship, triumphantly confessed Christ as Lord and surrendered their souls into the hands of God, before Whose throne they now stand with the angels.

**On the 5th of January, the holy Church commemorates
our venerable Mother SYNCLETIKE of Alexandria.**[1]

Syncletike, our blessed mother, was born in Alexandria of Egypt, ca. A.D. 400. Her parents hailed from Macedonia, but when they heard of the reputation of the God-loving city of Alexandria, they decided to emigrate. In Alexandria, they found the pure Faith and true love, which caused them to prefer living abroad to remaining at home. Syncletike's family was distinguished and among the fortunate, possessing all those things that people of this world seek after. However, even as a young girl in her parents' arms, the young maiden placed all her desire and love in God. She gave no care to bodily concerns and preserved herself from the unruly surges of nature. Syncletike's great personal beauty, distinguished family, and large inheritance incited many young suitors to

Saint Syncletike

seek her hand in marriage. In the midst of all these wooers, her parents encouraged her to enter into wedlock, especially since she would inherit their estate.

---

[1] This extraordinary account with sayings of Saint Syncletike was written in Greek by Saint Athanasios the Great of Alexandria (296-373). It has been suggested that the virgin Syncletike was responsible for aiding Saint Athanasios when he hid in a well or cistern for six years. The manuscript of her biography was revised by Nikodemos the Hagiorite (d. 1809) and placed into the *Neon Eklogion* (Venice, 1803). The text was later revised and incorporated into *The Great Synaxaristes* (in Greek). A divine office to Saint Syncletike was composed by the hymnographer Father Gerasimos Mikrayian-nanites, and published by Father Augustine Kantiotos with the publishers of the Philoptochou Brotherhood (Φιλοπτώχου᾽ Αδελφότητος ἡ᾽ Αγάπη, 1959).

Now Syncletike was both wise and noble of conduct, yet she refused to be persuaded by her parents on the issue of marriage. She had already bestowed her heart and mind solely upon the heavenly Bridegroom, Christ, and not upon an earthly one. No ornaments, gold-embroidered dresses, or worldly goods could turn her gaze from Christ. Neither could the supplications of relatives soften her resolve or diminish the desire of her soul. Setting her sights and her thoughts solely upon the desired One, Christ, she closed her senses to bodily pleasures and conversed with her noetic Bridegroom. If, in the midst of company, worldly conversations arose, she would dismiss them or avoid them; then she went to recollect her thoughts. If a conversation arose that was spiritually uplifting, she would open wide her ears to receive it into her soul. Syncletike regarded herself as her most dangerous enemy, so she decided early on to subdue her flesh by fasts and other mortifications. The young maiden loved to keep fasts, believing that it was not only conducive to physical health, but that it also was the foundation and preservation of all the virtues, in which she had no peer.

There are some people who eat simply for pleasure, and thus their flesh becomes soft and corpulent. Syncletike, on the other hand, never allowed more than what was needful, which was more than she desired. When she did partake of nourishment, it was with much distaste and all absence of pleasure. As a result, her complexion had become sallow and her figure quite thin. Although her flesh was weakened, her spirit gained strength. She was able to say with the Apostle Paul, "Even if our outward man is being utterly destroyed, yet the inward man is being renewed day by day [2 Cor. 4:16]." Now all these struggles were done in secret without anyone's knowledge.

Syncletike is Tonsured

Upon the repose of her parents, Syncletike was left as sole heiress to their estate. Her two brothers had died before her parents; her blind sister was committed entirely to her guardianship. The holy maiden, after distributing her fortune among the poor and destitute, retired with her blind sister to a disused sepulcher chamber on the estate of a relative. This was outside of Alexandria in a place called Eroön. In this place, Syncletike sent for a priest and was tonsured a nun. With the four snips of her hair, she was delivered from the concerns of this world. After she was made a nun, with utter humility, she remarked, "I have been vouchsafed a great gift. What worthy gift can I, who have nothing, render unto Him Who granted me to become a nun? If people spend all their wealth for a temporary gift or rank of this world, how much more am I obliged who have been vouchsafed this great grace of becoming a nun? Indeed, all my wealth and even my body belongs to the Master Christ, the Lord of the earth and all its fullness." Thereupon, she clothed herself with humility and retired.

Before Syncletike became a nun, we know that she struggled in asceticism while living in her parents' home. Together with distributing all her worldly possessions among the poor, she put away wrath and remembering past injuries, and rejected any feelings of envy and vainglory. Thus, she established her soul on the sure Cornerstone, Christ [Eph. 2:20]. Syncletike was like that wise man, spoken of by Christ, who heard Jesus' sayings, performed them, and built his house founded upon a rock [Mt. 7:24]. Therefore, with the holy Tonsure, she quickly advanced in the virtues. If one enters upon the divine mystery of the monastic state without any exercise of forethought about its destination, she is unlikely to finish the course successfully. Indeed, if she chooses to take a certain path, she must ascertain what provisions she will need for the road. In like manner, the blessed maiden first prepared herself with the well-known exercises of asceticism. Then, dauntless, she took the road that leads to heaven. From the outset, Syncletike, possessing a devoted and fervent spirit, surpassed even those nuns with many years in the ascetic life. We cannot describe all the facets of her life with any accuracy, because of the young nun's self-imposed strict retirement. She desired to keep her life and works hidden from all eyes, lest she should receive any fame or praise. In fact, she thought more of concealing her good works than embarking on new feats. Thus, she has deprived us of the knowledge of her conduct of life. Divine grace and Scripture instructed her not merely to avoid human glory, but also not to let thy "left hand know what thy right hand is doing [Mt. 6:3]."

The Struggles of the Saint

From her first years as a young nun until she reached middle age, Syncletike avoided speaking with men and even women, lest they should laud her on account of her excessive asceticism. She feared this would create stumbling blocks in her quest for virtue and silence. She mortified all movements of the flesh, lest they should hurl her down. For as the gardener prunes away branches and removes fruit, thus she cut off from her thoughts the thorns of the passions, by means of fasting and prayer. If she noted that any passion gained admittance, she would exact various penalties, often painful, upon herself, so that she might subdue her flesh. For example, she would afflict herself with hunger and, at other times, with thirst.

Whenever she had any type of spiritual warfare from the devil, she would resort to prayer and invoke the Master Christ for help. It was insufficient solely by asceticism to stave off the devil who, walking about like a roaring lion, seeks whom he may devour [1 Pet. 5:8]. Then, straightway, by her prayer to the Lord, the adversary fled. There were occasions, however, when the Lord would permit the enemy to war with His handmaiden, so she might increase the virtue of her soul by further training and practise. Far from being perturbed, Syncletike looked upon these as opportunities for an increase of grace. Her only aim was to win a victory over the enemy. By curbing her already meager fare, she deadened the passions, and even restrained lawful satisfactions and desires. She would eat bread made with bran, yet, ofttimes, she would not drink any water. For weapons, so she might prevail in battle, she wore the breastplate of prayer and the helmet of faith, joined with hope, love, and compassion.

On those occasions when she overcame the enemy of our salvation, she relaxed her rule of severe asceticism, so as not to weaken unduly her bodily members. For if a warrior has an unstrung bow in battle, how can he hope for victory? Yet, some, with immoderate and unreasonable fasting, have actually made themselves accessories with the enemy in vanquishing themselves. When the seaman encounters a tempest, what does he do? He abstains while he spends all his time battling mighty swells; but when the peril has passed, he then attends to his bodily needs. Nevertheless, although calm seas might presently prevail, he is not asleep and heedless; he is watchful and mindful of possible future tempests; for he knows that though the high waves and winds have subsided, still the sea and the air are ever present.

In like manner, the holy Syncletike would not destroy her bodily members, for she did everything with discernment. Thus, in warfare, she would have recourse to prayer; and when peace was granted, she would relent. Yet, even during times of tranquility, we must pray unceasingly; for just as the sea is unpredictable, so temptations may rise up unexpectedly. Our saint understood well the high seas of this present life and foresaw the agitations of the evil spirits. Therefore, she exercised care to guide on course the ship of her soul. Her rudder was devotion to God, which would direct her to the harbor of salvation and, thus, moor her ship with the sure anchor of faith.

The life of the holy woman was apostolic in that she joined faith and poverty, and shone forth in love and humility. As it is written in the Psalter, she would "tread upon the asp and basilisk [Ps. 90:13]" and upon all the power of the enemy. Thus, she would hear from our Savior, "Well done, O good and faithful slave! Over a little thou wast faithful, I will appoint thee over much [Mt. 25:21]." In other words, "Since thou hast overcome the carnal warfare of the flesh and the world, thou shalt attain victory over the bodiless and evil host by My help and protection. Moreover, since thou hast vanquished the powers of the devils, draw nigh to the good powers of the angelic host."

In the foregoing manner, the blessed woman conducted her struggle for virtue. With the passage of time, she blossomed forth in the virtues. Moreover, the wonderful fragrance of her contest was perceived by many; for thus saith the Lord, "For nothing is secret which shall not become manifest [Lk. 8:17]." The Lord, in a manner known only to Him, knows how to bring to fruition the achievements of those whom He loves.

A Convent is Founded

By God's enlightenment and for the amendment of other women, other nuns resorted to the holy Syncletike for counsel. Upon receiving enormous spiritual benefit from her holy conversations, these women hastened often to her. On one occasion, the blessed one was asked to explain to them how they might find salvation. Syncletike then sighed heavily and, shedding many tears, remained silent. Her humility made her unwilling to take upon herself the task of instructing others. Nevertheless, the sisters coerced her to speak about the great things of God, for only to catch a glimpse of the holy woman sparked enthusiasm and wonder in the beholder. Syncletike, however, only said, "Do not compel me, O laborers, for I am poor." Yet they constrained her with even more vehemence, and said, "Thus saith the Lord, 'Freely ye received, freely give [Mt. 10:8]'and 'take heed lest thou shouldest be condemned as the servant who hid his talent [Mt. 25:24-30].'" The saint then said, "Why, O sisters, do you suppose that I, a sinner, have anything worthwhile to say? We have, as our common Teacher, the Lord and the sacred Writ." The sisters replied, "We also know that our Lord is the Teacher, and, moreover, we do hearken to holy Scriptures. Yet thou, with thine earnest and zealous vigilance, hast advanced and become proficient in the virtues. Hence, those nuns who have succeeded in obtaining those good things should counsel the novices!" Then, charity prevailing, Syncletike took courage and spoke.

The Sayings of Saint Syncletike

On Love

"My children, all of us know how to be saved; however, due to our negligence, we lose our salvation. First, we must preserve what was revealed by the grace of God: Thou shalt love the Lord thy God with all thy soul, and thy neighbor as thyself [Lk. 10:27]. These two commandments are the summit of the law, and upon them rests all the fullness of grace. These words are few, but great and continuous is their power, because all that is good and beneficial to the soul hangs on these two commands. According to the testimony of the divine Paul, 'the end of the commandment is love [1 Tim. 1:5].' Whatever useful words have been spoken, according to the grace of the Holy Spirit, they commence with love and they conclude with love. Therefore, salvation is this two-fold love. I must, however, add what each of us should know. We must always desire to possess love, which is the greatest virtue of all."

Saint Syncletike

On Monasticism

The nuns were awed at her words. The saint continued, "Do you not know the parable of the sower, as told by the Lord, that a crop was yielded in some places a hundredfold, in another sixty, and another thirty [Mt. 13:8; Mk. 4:8]? The crop that increased and produced a hundredfold is our rank, the monastics. The crop of sixty is the rank of those who gain the mastery over themselves and exercise self-control and do not marry. Those of the rank of thirty-fold have been united in wedlock, but live wisely and prudently.

"Now it is good that one who is ranked among the thirty ascend to those of the sixty and from sixty to the fold of a hundred; for it is beneficial and favorable to advance from what is small to what is greater. On the other hand, to descend from what is greater to what is lesser is perilous. One who turns her back even once to what is worse, will be unable to remain steadfast in what is little, but dangles over the pit of destruction. Many who are weak-minded, though they promised to preserve their virginity, make excuses with the devil. They utter (or should I say, they speak with the devil) that it is better to marry and live soberly; thus, they rank themselves among the thirty-fold. They also add that those righteous ones of the Old Testament did not cast off the procreation of children, but desired it. However, when they utter such things, they must know that this pretext is from the devil. For one who plunges from what is high to what is low is led astray by the deceiver. It is much like the soldier who deserts his position within a superior army and enlists in a lesser one. This soldier will not be granted a pardon, but will be punished. In like manner will it be for one who forsakes the rank of the virgins for a lower rank, even if among the temperate. In this regard, we must rise to what is higher; for the apostle exhorts: 'Forgetting the things which are behind, and stretching forth to those things which are before, I pursue toward the mark for the prize of the high calling of God in Christ Jesus [Phil. 3:13].'

"Therefore, we who are ranked among the hundred must be always on guard and circumspect. However, when we have done all that is commanded of us, we must say, 'We are unprofitable slaves, for we have done

that which we were bound to do [Lk. 17:10].' Since we have preferred to
undertake a vow of virginity, we must keep watch and ward to maintain a
sound mind, prudence, temperance, and self-control.

On the Behavior of Monastics

"You know that, in the world, many women, married and unmarried,
conduct their lives wisely and in moderation. However, there are those who
are imprudent, ignorant, and act rashly. These latter women defile their
bodily senses. For instance, they look upon unseemly things, listen to foul
stories, and laugh inordinately. We, the monastics, are enjoined to multiply
the virtues. We are to depart from such undisciplined living and turn our eyes
away from vain sights. Thus saith the Scripture: 'Let thine eyes look straight
on [Prov. 4:25].' We must also restrain, as with a horse's bit, our mouth.
This organ is to be used for divine hymns and to glorify God, not to speak
shamefully and impudently. Further, it is not enough to refrain from speaking
evil, but we also must not hearken to them that speak thus.

"The foregoing is not possible to keep if we often leave our cells; for
when we do so, the thieving demons and passions steal in, even if we do not
want them to gain entry. How is it possible not to dirty a home with outside
smoke if the windows and doors are left open? Therefore we are directed not
to go into the cities and commercial festivals. If we believe that it is grievous
and incorrect to behold the nakedness of our siblings and parents [Lev.
18:6-18], how much more disorderly and harmful to the soul is it to observe,
in the streets and the marketplace, people inappropriately dressed, and
speaking provocative and shameless words? Know for a surety that when such
sights and sounds enter our soul, they bring harmful and disgraceful
imaginings. However, let it be known that even inside our cells, we must not
be inattentive but mindful and carefully collect our thoughts. Thus saith the
Lord, 'Be watching [Mt. 24:42].' The more that you seek discretion and
virginity, so much more will the acrid smoke of fierce thoughts attempt to
divert you. As it is written in the Book of Ecclesiastes: 'In the abundance of
wisdom is the abundance of knowledge; and he that increases knowledge will
increase sorrow [Eccl. 1:18].' In like manner, those contenders that succeed
in wrestling matches will find, as they advance, that their opponents will also
become more powerful.

On True Virginity

"Endeavor to surmise how far thou art from true virginity, and thou
wilt not be lax in thy combat with the enemy. Even if thou dost not physically
commit fornication, yet the devil will seek to apprehend thee by the senses.
Indeed, this may take place though thou hast not departed from thy cell or
heard anything lewd. The enemy will strive to have thee do something
unbecoming within the imaginings that he will conjure, whether thou

shouldest be awake or asleep. This is because the vile one dwells within the heart. He will attempt to bewitch those with permissive minds, through the memory of handsome faces and former conversations, so as to excite and impassion the chaste. Therefore, we must disregard the fantasies created by the evil one. As it is written in Ecclesiastes: 'If the spirit of the ruler rise up against thee, leave not thy place; for soothing will put an end to great offenses [10:4]'; that is, 'If the spirit or the operation of the devil rises up in thy mind, do not give place in thy heart, but cast him out.' Thus, do not submit and go down together with Satan. If a virgin but only condescends to indecent thoughts, she is to be compared to a harlot in the world.

"Therefore the conflict with the demon of fornication is great and dreadful. This is the chief evil of the enemy, by which he attempts to manipulate and ruin our souls. This also arose as an enigma to righteous Job, who said that all the power of the enemy is in the navel; that is 'Behold now, his strength is in his loins, and his force is in the navel of his belly [Job 40:11].' Thus with many and varied machinations, the devil provokes the lovers of Christ to commit fornication and idolatry. Many have turned back from the love of Christ because of the craftiness of the treacherous one. Those virgins who have refused marriage and every worldly illusion, he scornfully laughs at them and hurls them down headlong into unchastity, by means of sisterly love toward men. Likewise, monks who have forsaken every indecency and unchaste creature, he leads astray by means of pious dialogue with women. This is the occupation of the deceiver, to creep in and to feign the divine and the spiritual, so he can secretly sow his own works. Hence, the top of the grain may appear as a wheat kernel, but the stem is an ambush. Concerning insidious appearances, the Lord says that they will come to you as devils 'in sheep's clothing, but within they are rapacious wolves [Mt. 7:15].'

"Consequently, what must we do against the schemes of the devils in order to be saved? We must 'become wise as the serpents and guileless as the doves [Mt. 10:16].' We must endeavor to anticipate the snares sent against us by the devil. When Christ instructs us to become as 'wise as the serpents,' He means that we must be on guard to suspect the deceiving children of the evil one. The expression, 'guileless as the doves,' refers to the guilelessness and purity of the dove—and such should be our works. Therefore, every good work expels the bad, since it is unwilling to be tainted. Now how are we to avoid what we do not know? We cannot forecast the future, but we can be watchful and wary of the wiles of the evil one, and thus safeguard ourselves from many disasters. Listen to the divine Apostle Peter: 'Be sober, watch; because your adversary, the devil, as a roaring lion, walketh about, seeking whom he might devour [1 Pet. 5:8].' Also the Prophet Abbakoum said, 'He hath made his portion fat, and his meats choice [Hab. 1:16].' Understand this: we must always be alert and wakeful, because our enemy certainly is always on the rise to start a conflict, either by outside means or by suggestive thoughts. The challenge may come by day or night, in a clandestine and unsuspecting manner.

"What do we need in this battle? It is plain that we require ascetic toil and pure prayer. These two works are the customary and basic remedies used against harmful thoughts. There are, however, other devices that can be employed in carnal warfare. Whenever a shameful thought intrudes, we must counter it with another thought. If the enemy introduces a handsome face in a fantasy to us, we must oppose it with an upright thought. Thus, in our mind, gouge out the eyes of that face, strip off the flesh from his cheeks, and slice his lips. When you do this, such a face will then remain a skeleton, repulsive and frightening. With such a system let us handle seductive thoughts that they may be rejected. We would never desire to embrace what is a mixture of blood and phlegm. Hence, with such a method, you will drive out indecent images of iniquity. It will be like a stake with which you may be able to pin down the demon of fornication. Reckon in your mind that the entire body of him whom you love is gushing forth with putrefaction and foul-smelling matter, predetermined for decay and death. This, most certainly, will cast out of our hearts the unclean desire. Nonetheless, the most excellent weapon used in warfare of the flesh is the blunting of the assault of our bellies. By this, we shall overcome the destructive passions which derive their vigor from the belly." With such wise and soul-saving words, the blessed Syncletike edified the sisterhood.

On Poverty and Riches

Then one of the nuns asked the righteous woman if poverty were the perfect good. She answered, "There are many things that are good for the strong and the brave. Those that endure poverty shall undergo bodily suffering, yet the soul is at leisure. Similarly, when beautiful and new dresses are trodden underfoot and rent, they may later be used to clean and brighten objects. In like manner, a stouthearted soul, when it is in straits and afflictions with voluntary poverty, will be rendered stronger and more steadfast. On the other hand, for those that are weak-minded and easily disheartened, they only become more feeble and faltering. She who is discomfited by a slight privation will not bear the good that comes from penury. This may be compared to torn and old dresses which cannot withstand washing, for they will shred and perish. Now the end of the tattered garment and the durable garment is not the same, as the end is not the same for the vacillating soul and the faithful soul. The durable fabric may be used to clean and restore objects, but the tattered fabric will shred. Hence, poverty is a precious treasure for the courageous soul. Poverty may be used as a bit and bridle to curb one from sinning. Those who wish to avoid sin must first exert themselves in fasting, lying on the ground, and other hardships of the body. After this, they can gain through impoverishing themselves. She who without exercise and practise casts away her money, for the most part will come to regret this action. This is because riches are the components of a life of rest and ease. Thus, she who does not take the proper prerequisites will be like one who squanders her goods without careful deliberation, only to repent of her rashness.

"Once thou hast cast out gluttony and pleasant foods and the rest of the comforts and refreshments of the body, then thou shalt easily put away earthly goods and money. Therefore, when the Lord spoke to the rich man, He did not straightway command him to give away his riches. The Lord first related to the rich man the commandments that one should keep: Do not commit adultery, murder, or theft. Neither shalt thou defraud or bear false witness. Keep honoring thy father and mother. The rich man answered the Teacher, saying that he observed all these commands even from his youth. Then the Lord Jesus, beholding him, loved him, and said, 'One thing thou lackest: if thou art willing to be perfect, go thy way and sell as much as thou hast and give to the poor, and thou shalt have treasure in heaven; and come, take up the cross, and keep on following Me [Mk. 10:21].' Now, if the rich man, in fact, had not observed the commandments as he claimed from his youth, then surely the Lord would not have encouraged him to become poor; because how could he have come to perfection without having first taken hold of the other things mentioned by Jesus?

"Good, therefore, is poverty for them that labor in the life of austerity; they will easily take possession of those good things. These people cast off all that is superfluous and place their mind and all their hope solely on God, chanting the words of the Psalm, 'The eyes of all look to Thee with hope, and Thou gavest them their food in due season [Ps. 144:16].' There is also another benefit to be derived from poverty: Those that do not have their mind attached to earthly things may contemplate those heavenly good things, so they might say with David, 'I became as a beast before Thee, and I am ever with Thee [Ps. 72:21].' For beasts of burden that labor for men suffice with only their own food and do not seek anything else. It is the same for those in privation; they seek only their daily food, and disdain money as nought and useless. Those in poverty remain steadfast in faith. Therefore, the Lord said to them, 'Cease being anxious for your soul, what ye shall eat and what ye shall drink; nor for your body, what ye shall put on. The soul is more than food and the body is more than raiment, is it not? Look at the birds of the heaven, for they sow not, neither do they reap, nor do they gather into storehouses; and yet your heavenly Father feedeth them. Ye much more excel them, do ye not [Mt. 6:25, 26]?' Now they know that it is God Who said this; thus, with boldness they cry out, 'I believed, therefore, I spoke [Ps. 115:1].'

"The devil is most often routed by them in privation. This is because it is not possible to wound them in anything, since greater torment and temptation follow those people who are despoiled of their abundance. Now for them that have nothing, what kind of affliction can befall them? Nothing obviously. What evil then does the enemy endeavor to bring upon them? To burn their fields? They do not have any. To lay waste their livestock? But where are their farm animals? To ruin their property? Yet they have put all things aside. Thus, poverty is one of the harshest punishments to inflict upon the devil; and yet its value to our precious and deathless soul is worth an inestimable treasure.

"As much as poverty is a great and wonderful virtue, so is avarice a great evil and depravity; as the blessed Paul said, 'The love of money is a root of all evils, by which some, reaching out for themselves, were led astray from the faith and pierced themselves with many griefs [1 Tim. 6:10].' From the desire for wealth have come false witnesses, thefts, seizures, envious covetousness, rapine, murders, hatred of one's kinfolk, wars, idolatries, and other wrongs of the same nature, including hypocrisy, flattery, and deceitfulness. The cause of all these deeds is avarice. Not only does the Lord chastise the lovers of money, but they also bring a sorry plight upon themselves by their discontent with the amount of money that they do possess. They take upon themselves endless concerns to protect and care for their wealth. Thus, this self-inflicted wound is incurable. Symptoms of this sickness begin when the person who has nothing desires a little of something. When she has obtained that little thing, she desires even more. So when she has acquired a hundred, she yearns for a thousand; and upon gaining a thousand, she seeks to take hold of an unlimited amount. As you may perceive, there is no end to this desire, though the seekers grasp what they desire; and if they fail, they lament their poverty. You must also know that avarice always has in its company the element of envy. Envy consumes those that lack something. They are jealous of another who has what they covet. They will injure others to seize what they want, much like young serpents leaving the wombs of their mothers. Even those who have possessions are still susceptible to envy and will afflict their neighbors.

"Great will be the reward of the monastics if we undergo commensurate labors as those in the world who struggle to procure vain profits. If we were to endure similar pains as the worldlings, we would attain to the heavenly kingdom, which is that pure treasure that cannot be gained by fraud. Indeed, those of the world are willing to suffer shipwreck, encounter pirates, confront thieves in the wilderness, and endure tempests. After attempting all, daring all, and hazarding all, they achieve their goal; they claim they are poor, so as not to arouse jealousy. We, the monastics, however, in no way expose ourselves to such perils that we might gain the true and heavenly reward.

On Acquiring the Virtues

"When we acquire some minuscule virtue, straightway, we magnify ourselves. Furthermore, we hope to make this virtue known among the people. Ofttimes, we not only mention that virtue we have achieved, but we even add others to it which we do not possess. Then, instantly, the enemy steals even what little we enjoyed. Now those of the world and the avaricious, when they have come into some great thing, desire even more; and that which they already possess they count as nought. Therefore, their desire swells to obtain what they lack, and, moreover, they attempt by every means to deny before others how much they actually possess. On the other hand, we, the monastics, do everything to the contrary. Although we are serving so great a Master, for so immense a good, yet we fear and falter at every contradiction. We possess no good thing, nor do we desire to gain what is good. We are destitute of the virtues, and yet we boast that we are wealthy in them. It is good, therefore, that one who succeeds in good works should not reveal them to others; otherwise, such a one shall suffer great loss. Then she shall be bereft of the good which she believed herself to possess.

"Therefore, we must conceal, as much as we can, our virtues. Those that wish to reveal their virtues to others must also reveal their vices and passions to them. But, on the contrary, they conceal their vices, so as not to suffer condemnation by these same people. It would have been better if they concealed their virtues, so as not to be estranged from God. Those that are truly virtuous do the reverse. They hide their good works but declare unto people even their small sins and omissions, so they may cast off the praise of people. A treasure is secure as long as it remains hidden. Yet, once it is discovered and laid open publicly, it is plundered. It is the same with virtue. It is secure as long as it is undisclosed; but if rashly exposed, it often evaporates as smoke. As wax melts before fire, so praise weakens the pitch of the soul; whereas, reproach and maltreatment strengthen the soul and engender greater virtue. Thus saith the Lord: 'Be rejoicing and be exceedingly glad whenever they reproach you and persecute you, and say every evil word against you falsely on account of Me [cf. Mt. 5:11, 12].' Listen to what David says: 'In mine affliction, Thou hast enlarged me [Ps. 4:1]' and 'my soul hath awaited reproach and misery [Ps. 68:24].' There are a myriad of examples to be found in the sacred Scriptures.

On Sorrow

"Some sorrows are beneficial, while others are injurious. A good sorrow is when we grieve for our sins and for the unknown ones of our neighbors. Another goodly sorrow is when we groan, until we should reach the perfect virtue. These are the pure and expiating afflictions. There are some sorrows, however, that are detrimental and emanate from the devil; for he instigates sorrow of soul. However, it is a sorrow that is devoid of understanding and without reason, which some call despondency and apathy. This demon must be cast out by prayer and psalmody.

"We, the nuns, therefore, who have good concerns and sorrows should not conclude that people in the world do not have cares and sorrows. The Prophet Esaias says, 'The whole head is pained, and the whole heart sad [Is. 1:5].' By these words, the Holy Spirit reveals the monastic life and the secular life. The verse 'the whole head is pained' reveals the monastic life; for as the head is the governing member of the human body, thus the monastic life is superior to the secular. The eye of wisdom (that is of the distinguishing or clear-sighted soul) is to be found in the head. As saith Solomon, 'The wise man's eyes are in his head; but the fool walks in darkness [Eccl. 2:14].' The pains referred to are those required to achieve virtue. The pain of the heart illustrates the changeability and grief found in the lives of people living in the world, where both anger and envy dwell. For this reason, if they are not glorified by others, they are saddened. If they covet, they wear themselves away. If they are poor, they are indignant. If they are rich, they are carried away by fallacious reasoning and high-mindedness. They cannot find rest in slumber, because they are anxious to protect their wealth.

"Let the nuns not be deceived in presuming those of the world are exempt from cares and pains. If we compare ourselves with them, their labors are greater; and much more do women in the world endure profound sufferings. This is because with great pangs and peril to their lives do they bring forth a child. Thereafter, with much travail, they rear their offspring. When the children become ill, they ache along with them. In addition to this, there are many other griefs, to which they find no end. They oft have children who are accursed, possessed of evil and perverse ideas and dispositions. These children tempt their parents in multifaceted ways, and often slay them with treachery. Since we already are aware of these happenings, let us not be duped into imagining their lives are spent in ease and comfort, as those that are single. Their lives are filled with much distress on account of their children. Even if a woman is barren, she still bears the reproach of family disgrace and withers away. I am telling you these things to counter the machinations of the enemy. However, what I told you is appropriate to nuns, and not to women living in the world. Much as those in the animal kingdom do not have one food, so this discourse is not suited to all people. As the Lord saith, 'No one putteth new wine into old wineskins [Mk. 2:22].'

"For in different ways should one speak to those that are perfect and have attained to divine vision and contemplation, and to those that are struggling with the active life of virtues, and to those that dwell in the world. The same is found in the wild kingdom: some creatures abide on land, others in the water, and still others in the air. It is the same with people. Some soar to the heights as the winged birds, others are somewhere in the middle, while others wallow in sin.

On Spiritual Warfare

"We, the nuns, however, should be as eagles and climb to the heights, and trample upon lions and dragons, and have authority over these mighty ones. Now we can achieve this if we dedicate all our mind and thought to Christ our Savior. We also must expect that the higher we ascend, so much more does the devil aim to entangle us in flight. Now this should not puzzle you. For the devils bear malice for them in the world in their pursuit for the shabby and worthless things of the world, and will not let them unearth treasures hidden beneath the earth. Therefore, why should we count it contrary to expectation if they envy us who work with zeal to attain those heavenly good things?

"For this, we should arm ourselves in every way against the demons, because they contend with us outwardly through the material world and inwardly with thoughts. Just as a ship can suffer shipwreck either from the fury of the waves or from the breaking of the hull; likewise when we sin with either outward means or inner thoughts, we can crash or capsize. Therefore, we must always guard our inner thoughts against assault from the demons. We must be vigilant in banishing external shameless thoughts that defile us, for frequently these skirmishes take place. Ofttimes, when a ship is in the midst of a tempest, the seamen call out for help to nearby vessels, and thus are rescued. At other times, when the sea is calm and the men are at rest, the vessel experiences a fissure from within, thereby submerging and drowning many. Therefore, we must keep our minds attentive to inner thoughts. The enemy desires to hurl down headlong the abode of our souls. He may do this by razing it to the foundation or by destroying the roof, so that it collapses. He may also gain access by one of the windows. Upon entering, he shall bind the mistress of the house, so he might take command of everything in the house. The foundation of the spiritual house is good works; the roof is faith, the windows are the senses, and the occupant is each of us who must battle the enemy.

"Wherefore, one who desires salvation must have many eyes, because in this present life it is not prudent to be carefree. Thus saith the Scriptures:

'The one who thinketh he standeth, let him take heed lest he should fall [1 Cor. 10:12].' The uncertain sea that we sail upon is the sea of this present life. Some parts of the sea have rocks or sea monsters, while other areas lie undisturbed. It appears that nuns voyage upon the quiet and tranquil waters of life, whereas those of the world pass through perilous waters. Furthermore, nuns voyage by day and are guided by the noetic 'Sun of righteousness [Mal. 4:2],' Christ; whereas, those of the world travel the unknown by night. Having to confront unknown shadows and hazardous spots, those that are wakeful will often cry out unto God that He might save the vessel of their soul. On the other hand, nuns, making their journey across certain waters, may suffer capsizing. This overturn or shipwreck is due to negligence when we let the rudder of righteousness slip out of our hands.

"Therefore, whoever stands must take care not to fall, because the one who has fallen has one thought: how to get up. The one who stands, must take care not to fall, because there are various ways to go down. Though one who has fallen is in need of arising, yet, in that lying position, one shall not sustain very severe injury. However, one who stands, must not condemn the one who has fallen. She must fear, lest she should suffer a fatal tumble into a precipice where she would be crushed in the lowest abyss. Once there, it may happen that no one will hear the cries for help, since the one who has plummeted to the depths is down too deep. Listen to David: 'Let not the tempest of water overwhelm me, nor let the deep swallow me up, nor let the pit shut its mouth upon me [Ps. 68:19].' Now look: the one who fell previous to the one that fell into the pit, yet abides. Therefore, watch that thou dost not fall into the pit, to become the prey of wild beasts. Be sure, that the one who had fallen did not secure the door of the house. Therefore, thou who dost stand, do not doze, but always chant these words: 'Look upon me, hear me, O Lord my God; enlighten my eyes, lest at any time I sleep unto death [Ps. 12:3].' Let us be vigilant at all times, because the noetic lion, as it roars, threatens to pounce upon thee.

"These words benefit those that stand, lest they should succumb to high-mindedness. These words are also appropriate to those who have fallen. They can make a complete turnabout, with sighs from the depths of their souls for their salvation and by not entertaining those passions which they once hosted. This is also a further reminder to those that stand, to be circumspect, for a double fear is upon them: that they not allow collaboration with any former vice and, if the season of faintheartedness should overcome them—a most inviting time for the enemy to challenge us—that they not beguile themselves with conceit. Our enemy, the devil, hissing behind us, espies when one is timid or indolent. He also targets as his victims the diligent who hasten to asceticism. He then subtly slithers into our souls, nestled in prideful thoughts and, in such a manner, causes that sister to plunge to the depths. This weapon of pride, wielded by the enemy against us, is the perfection and highest form of wickedness. On account of this, the devil was cast down from the heavens [Is. 14:12]. In like manner, he strives to bring down with himself those strugglers in the virtues. All experienced warriors, when they have depleted their stockpile of arrows, observing that the enemy has the advantage, produce a greater weapon when they unsheathe their swords. Likewise the devil, having expended his weapons on the first offensive, then maneuvers into position his most powerful weapon—pride. However, his tactics of ambush against raw recruits will include gluttony, fondness of pleasure, and fornication. The next stage of the offensive is to attack with avarice, greed, arrogance, and the like.

On Pride

"When the soul has overcome the passions and is mistress over her belly and other pleasures associated with it, including contempt of money, then that knave, the devil, who has been devastated of all his weapons, secretly plants pride in that soul. He lifts her thoughts up about herself, so she considers herself superior to her sisters. Truly, grave and ruinous is the venom of pride by which the enemy waters the soul. Many, brilliant in the virtues, have been eclipsed by this vice, and are straightway cast into darkness. Why has this happened? This is because pride fatally introduces unreal thoughts about oneself. This person believes that she has come to the comprehension of matters that others have not yet begun to understand. She believes that she has surpassed others in keeping fasts and in other virtues. However, before pride can creep in, the enemy will cause his victims to forget their own sins, so they might imagine themselves to have far excelled their peers. Also, by snatching away the remembrance of their own shortcomings and faults, the enemy hopes to prevent them from calling out with David, 'Against Thee only have I sinned,...have mercy on me [Ps. 50:4, 1].' Nor will Lucifer give them leave to utter, 'I will give Thee thanks, O Lord, with my whole heart [Ps. 110:1]'; for the enemy prefers us to say in our hearts, 'I will go up to the heaven, I will set my throne above the stars of heaven [Is. 14:13].' Thus, proud people fancy they possess some authority and are entitled to the first seats in teaching or in gifts of healing. Those misled by the deceiver in this manner seduce and carry themselves away, because they have sustained a wound hard to heal.

"Therefore, whenever thou hast thoughts of pride, thou must meditate always on the divine words of David: 'I am a worm, and not a man [Ps. 21:6]'; and the words of Abraham: 'I am earth and ashes [Gen. 18:27]'; and also, Esaias: 'All our righteousness is as a filthy rag [Is. 64:6].' If high-minded thoughts of her ascetical feats persist, that anchoritess should betake herself to a coenobium and force herself to partake of food twice daily. After being disciplined, she is to be reproached by her companions for not performing one good thing, though she be assigned to every obedience. She must also hearken to the lives of the renowned saints. On certain days, her fellow ascetics should also increase their austerities, so that the proud nun may see that her sisters' great virtues excel her own; and, thus, this may lead her to humility. The cause of pride is disobedience. Hence, the remedy to this malady is obedience. Listen to the Prophet Samuel: 'Obedience is better than a good sacrifice [1 Kgs. (1 Sam.) 15:22].' Therefore, the abbess must break vainglory at the proper time.

"If a nun is careless and indolent, hesitates, and is slow to advance in virtue, the abbess should encourage and praise her labors openly. If the troubled nun then makes even the slightest improvement, the abbess must exhibit her approval and commend her. However, she should deprecate the greater mistakes. As we said earlier, the devil will often make light of our faults so he might puff up the strugglers for the virtues with pride. However, in some cases, with young people or beginners in the contest, the devil will present their faults before them. He does this so he may cast them into dejection or a feeling of hopelessness. The latter group will then say there is neither forgiveness for their fornications nor salvation for their greed. Toward them, the abbess must offer comfort and consolation, for the enemy troubles them on many sides. The abbess may bring forward the example of Rahab, the harlot, who was saved due to her faith [Heb. 11:31], or Saul the persecutor who became Paul the elect vessel [1 Cor. 15:9-10]. Then there is Matthew the tax collector who went on to become an evangelist [Mt. 9:9], or the thief and murderer who first entered Paradise [Lk. 23:43]. Therefore, my sisters, ponder upon these models and do not despair of thy soul.

"The cure for those souls swollen with pride is to declare to them: 'Why art thou proud, O miserable soul? Is it because thou dost not eat meat or thou dost not even glance at fish? Is it because thou dost not drink wine or perhaps thou dost not take oil? Art thou proud because thou dost fast till nightfall or even for two and three days? Perhaps it is because thou hast refrained from bathing?' Indeed, there are many passionate people who do not bathe at all. Perhaps thou art proud because thou hast only a hair shirt for thy bed? There are others who lie on the bare earth. Thou doest nothing that is remarkable, for there are others who stay upon rocks so as to find no comfort. There are some who suspend themselves with ropes all night that they might find no rest. Even if thou doest all these mortifications and dost reach the pinnacle of ascetic feats, do not entertain high thoughts about thyself, for even the demons can surpass thee. Remember, they neither eat, drink, sleep, nor marry, but traverse waterless wastes. Even if thou wert to take up thy dwelling in some cave, do not imagine that this is anything grand.

"Accordingly, with opposing thoughts, we may counter the vices of depression and pride. Take the example of fire. When a mighty wind blows, fire spreads and destroys what is in its path. It is the same with virtue, which can be destroyed by swelling pride when we take upon ourselves unrestrained asceticism. Conversely, where there is no wind, a fire will be extinguished. Again, it is the same with virtue. If we do not 'fan' the virtues by the Holy Spirit, but stifle them by our negligence and inactivity, they will suffocate and die. Another example is a sharp cutting knife which is easily blunted by stone. The same may be said for sharp asceticism, which is readily dulled by pride. Therefore, a person must defend the soul from every position. Consequently, the soul that is consumed by flammable pride, when considering her own asceticism, must be brought down and humbled by the grace of God. In a timely manner, she must curtail that which is excessive and unbounded, thus strengthening the root of virtue that she may branch forth fruit more abundantly. On the other hand, the soul that contends with depression and has fallen under the weight of her many sins, must compel herself to dwell on those thoughts which we mentioned earlier, so she may ascend and hope in the mercy of the man-loving God.

On Humility

"For further illustration, let us examine how the experienced farmer will water more often the plant that is weak and small. He exercises greater care toward that plant, so that it might improve. If he observes that the plant has put forth shoots prematurely, he will prune it to prevent further withering. The same case exists when a physician will encourage certain patients to increase their intake of food and to exercise more; whereas to others, the physician will order a fast. This same type of care is to be used by physicians of souls. It is plain that humility is the summit of the virtues, and difficult for one to obtain. For, if we do not spurn every glory, we shall not gain the great treasure of humility. The devil may imitate all the other virtues, but the greatness of the virtue of humility he can in no wise know. The Apostle Peter understood the soundness and full value of humility and commanded us to 'gird ourselves with humility [cf. 1 Pet. 5:5].' Though thou mightest fast, be merciful, teach, preserve thy virginity or remain continent, thou must always be adorned with humility which, as a sturdy wall, defends the other virtues.

"Hast thou not heard the hymn of the Three Children which they chanted in the Babylonian furnace? In the flames they did not mention before God the virtues of continence, virginity or poverty, but uttered, 'in a contrite soul and in a spirit of humility may we be accepted [3 Child. 15].' As it is impossible to build a ship without nails, it is impossible to be saved without humility. To show us that humility is good and soul-saving, the Lord clothed Himself with this virtue when He became incarnate. Thereupon, He said, 'Learn from Me, for I am meek and humble in heart [Mt. 11:29].' Ponder upon Who it was that uttered these words, and become a perfect pupil and emulator of His humility. Let humility be for thee the beginning and the end of good things. If thou wouldest but examine the word 'humble-minded (ταπεινοφροσύνη),' it means 'lowly in mind'; hence, it does not mean to appear outwardly lowly. For if the soul is not proud, neither is the body. However, dost thou claim to keep all the commandments? Our Lord knows it, and He commands us to say, 'We are unprofitable slaves, for we have done that which we were bound to do [Lk. 17:10].'

"Humility is cultivated with reproaches, insults, and wounds. This includes when thou art called senseless and mad, or thou art needy and demeaned, or sickly and incapable, unproductive in thy work, illogical in thy reasoning, contemptible in dress, and weak of body. These slurs are the sinews and strength of humility. Our Lord heard and bore the same charges, such as when some Jews accused the Master of being demonized or a Samaritan [Jn. 8:48]. Since He took on the form of a servant and was slapped, mocked, and received blows, therefore, we, too, must emulate the efficacious humility of the Lord. There are, however, some who wish to construe our humble raiment as our way to receive glory among people. Though some may accuse us of this, we must not immediately spew forth venom as do serpents. We must humbly endure and reap fruits from our accuser's efforts."

On the Angelic Schema

The nuns received sublime joy hearkening to the words of the holy Syncletike. Never quenching their thirst in partaking of her words, they waited to hear more. Tirelessly, the blessed woman taught them, saying, "A fierce struggle have they that come to God in the monastic Schema, for at its very commencement, they will struggle in many labors; yet, they will also receive inexpressible joy."

On Love

Saint Syncletike also counseled: "In order for us, the monastics, to kindle the divine fire in ourselves, we must first weep. Thus saith the Lord, 'I came to cast fire upon the earth [Lk. 12:49].' However, the fainthearted are tried by smoke. Since they never kindled a fire, they are lacking in patience and long-suffering. As a result, their love for God is weak. Therefore, it is a great treasure to love God. Listen to the Apostle Paul, who says, 'If I speak with the tongues of men and of angels, but I have not love, I have become as sounding brass or a clanging cymbal [1 Cor. 13:1].'

On Anger

"If love is a great good, conversely, anger is a great evil. This is because anger darkens the soul, makes it savage, and misleads us with fallacious reasoning. Therefore, our Lord, Who ever makes provision for our salvation, left no part of the soul unprotected and unguarded. When the enemy attacks with fornication, the Lord has armed us with self-control. If the enemy attacks us with pride, humility is not far. If the enemy suggests hatred, we may find love close by. Though the enemy wages war by strategically moving many weapons against us, our Lord, for the sake of our salvation, fences us about with greater weapons to ensure our victory. As I said earlier, anger is one of the greatest evils; for it does not work the righteousness of God. The Apostle Paul identifies anger as a 'work of the flesh,' and they that have it 'shall not inherit the kingdom of God [Gal. 5:21].' Thus, all anger must be put away [Eph. 4:26; Col. 3:8]. Anger must be appropriately governed and may be used at the proper time. Again, hear the apostle: 'Be ye angry, and sin not [Eph. 4:26].' Anger is effective for us when we use it against the demons, but it is not productive when we sin and wield it against others. If we cannot put anger away, then we must continually repent of it.

Remembrance of Wrongs

"Anger is a much smaller sin when compared to the remembrance of past injuries. To bear malice is the gravest of all sins. Anger, like smoke, for a while will perplex and cloud the soul; but holding a grudge is to be compared to a hammered stake in the soul that renders it more brutal than a beast. When a mad dog is about to attack someone, it is possible to cajole the animal with some food. Thus distracted, the animal forgets its fierceness and becomes tame. On the other hand, one that is mastered by and bent on revenge cannot be persuaded by pleas or with the passage of time. This spiritual sickness is the worst impiety and lawlessness. Listen to the words of our Savior Christ: 'If, then, thou offerest thy gift on the altar, and there rememberest that thy brother hath something against thee, leave there thy gift before the altar, and go thy way. First be reconciled to thy brother, and then come and offer thy gift [Mt. 5:23, 24].' Hearken to the words of the Apostle Paul: 'Let not the sun set upon your provocation [Eph. 4:26].'

"Therefore it is good never to be angry. To remember wrongs for a twenty-four-hour day is not permitted by the divine Paul. Hence, do not let the sun, which rules by day, abate till thy wrath against anyone has subsided. Why, O nun, dost thou wait until thy declining years to promote friendship with her whom thou hast confounded or frustrated? Dost thou not bring to mind the words of the Lord that 'sufficient to the day is the evil of it [Mt. 6:34]'? Therefore, why should we allow the day to pass wrangling with one another? Why dost thou hate the one that saddens thee? She is not the one that has wronged thee, but the devil. Therefore, abhor not thy weak sister, but the weakness suffered by thy sister. The Psalmist David speaks to thee, saying, 'Why dost thou boast in evil, O mighty one, and in iniquity all the day long? Thy tongue hath devised unrighteousness [Ps. 51:1, 2].' All thy life hast thou been lawless, because thou hast disobeyed the law of God. He commands thee, by the mouth of the divine Paul, not to let the sun go down on thy provocation. Why dost thou not cease thy slander and violence? For this art thou justifiably chastised by God. Listen again to David speaking through the inspiration of the Holy Spirit: 'Therefore, may God destroy thee forever, may He pluck thee up and utterly remove thee from thy dwelling, and thy root from the land of the living [Ps. 51:5].' Dost thou heed what was just recited? Know that these are the fruits and rewards of remembering wrongs.

"We must, therefore, take precautions to avoid remembering wrongs, because, through it, many other evils are introduced. I speak of envy, grief, babbling, and other evils—though they may seem small—which bring death. Ofttimes, such grievous sins as fornication, murder, and greed are healed by the saving remedy of repentance, but the remembrance of wrongs undermines spiritual health.

On Talkativeness

"Pride, bearing grudges, and loquacity, though they appear insignificant, destroy the soul as a needle in the most hazardous part of the soul. They devastate the soul with large wounds, due to our negligence. Most consider talkativeness and the like as just tiny sins; therefore, they do not attempt to correct themselves. Hence, little by little, they are consumed by them. Truly, garrulousness is a grave and contemptible sin. It is as nourishment and recreation for some people. You, however, must not engage in vain conversations or listen to them. Do not hearken to strange sins, but keep thy soul simple and pure. If thou dost admit the filthy uncleanness of chatter, thou shalt conduct foul thoughts into thy soul. These thoughts shall incline thee to loathe those who speak or those with whom thou art speaking. Then when thou hast utterly defiled thy hearing with their evil speaking and loquacity, thou wilt not pass through unscathed. Indeed, thou wilt view all people as such.

"It is the same with the eye. When the sight continually beholds only one color and is completely absorbed by it, other colors become difficult to discern; for the observer sees all things tinged with that color. We must, therefore, put a watch on our tongue and ears. We must not weary anyone with our talking. Furthermore, we should not listen sympathetically to those who are given to talk. Let us ever have in our mind the words of the Prophet David: 'Him that privily talked against his neighbor did I drive away from me [Ps. 100:5]'; and, again, 'That my mouth might not speak of the works of men [Ps. 16:4].' We also must not believe the words of one that speaks against others, nor should we judge them that utter such things. We must do and say as commanded by the sacred Scriptures: 'I was dumb and opened not my mouth [Ps. 38:12].'

On Gloating

"We must not rejoice at the calamities of others, though they be great sinners. We should not behave as those without understanding who, when they see a sinner, thrash and imprison such a one, and recite the worldly proverb, 'Whoever makes a bad bed, then badly shall that one sleep.' Though thou, as a nun, hast put thy life in order in accordance with thy vows, art thou confident that thou wilt find rest all thy life? Then how canst thou reconcile the words of holy Scripture: 'Vanity is in all: One event happens to the righteous and to the wicked; to the good and to the bad; both to the pure and to the impure; both to him that sacrifices and to him that sacrifices not. As is the good, so is the sinner: as is the swearer, even so is he that fears an oath [Eccl. 9:2]'; and 'the wise man's eyes are in his head; but the fool walks in darkness: and I perceived, even I, that one event shall happen to them all [Eccl. 2:14].' All the earthborn travel on the same path, though they have different conducts of life. None are exempt from encountering misfortune. How then dost thou rejoice in the calamities of others?

On Loving Enemies

"We must not hate our enemy. The Lord Himself says, 'For if ye love those who love you, what reward are ye having? Even the tax collectors are doing the same, are they not? And if ye greet your brethren only, what extraordinary thing are ye doing? Even the tax collectors are so doing, are they not [Mt. 5:46, 47]?' Therefore, our Savior says, 'Keep on loving your enemies, blessing those who curse you, doing well to those who hate you, and keep on praying for those who despitefully use you and are persecuting you [Mt. 5:44].' This divine teaching demands much labor to wipe out former evil practises, such as, 'Thou shalt love thy neighbor and hate thine enemy [Mt. 5:43].' The kingdom of the heavens is not taken by the negligent and the carefree, but by the prudent and diligent.

On Those Who are Wayward

"Just as we are not to hate our enemies, likewise we should not avoid and hold in contempt the careless and reluctant. Some, however, will put forward the following verse of the Prophet: 'With the perverse Thou shalt turn aside (διαστρέψεις) [Ps. 17:26].' They strongly contend that they bypass such people, so as not to be sinners too. However, they do the opposite of what was written by the prophet through the inspiration of the Holy Spirit. The verse does not tell us to be perverse with the perverse, but to remedy their perversity; for the verb (διαστρέφω) means to turn to a different way. Hence this verse declares unto us that we should draw the froward to us that we might turn them aside to a different way, that is, to bring them from the evil to the good.

On People

"People may be found in three types of categories. The first group is involved in the utmost of evil; the second group is midway, inclining to both good and evil; and the third group is exalted in virtue. Those numbered in this last group are not only those who are vigorous and confirmed in what is good, but also those who always seek to be guided to the good. When evildoers join with those worse than themselves, their wickedness is increased. The middle group strives to avoid evildoers, fearing their company may corrupt them, since they themselves are not yet firmly established in what is good. The conduct of the third group exhibits steadfastness, prudence, and courage in all that is good. They may associate with the evildoers for their salvation.

"Ofttimes, those of the third group receive reproaches when others see them associating with the wicked and negligent. Nevertheless, to them, the condemnations of others are regarded as commendations. Undaunted, they fearlessly complete their holy struggle for the salvation of their brother or sister. They bring to mind the words of the Lord, 'Blessed are ye whenever they reproach you and persecute you, and say every evil word against you falsely on account of Me. Be rejoicing and be exceedingly glad, for your reward is great in the heavens [Mt. 5:11, 12].' Indeed, this is truly the work of the Master Christ Who also ate with publicans and sinners. These activities much more show love for one's brother or sister than just a general philanthropy, because we show that we love others more than ourselves. For example, when neighbors behold the house of another neighbor engulfed in flames, they leave their own homes and hasten to rescue their neighbor who is in trouble. It is the same with this third group. Beholding their brothers or sisters sinning, they make light of the reproaches and accusations of others. They endure all that they might deliver others from peril.

"When the middle group beholds one burning from sin, they wish to get clear of such a one. They dread the idea of also being consumed by the flame of sin. The first group, as evil neighbors, when they behold one engulfed in the fire of sin, kindle even a greater inferno. Instead of throwing water on the flames of sin to extinguish them, they cast in, as wood, their own wickedness, so that the sinner might be entirely consumed by sin. The compassionate third group, counting their own affairs as subordinate, consider only the sinner's salvation. They are a model of true and guileless love.

"As the vices follow one another, that is, avarice is followed by envy, deceit, perjury, anger, and bearing grudges, so love is followed by the virtues of meekness, long-suffering, forbearance, and the perfect goodness of poverty. There exists no way to acquire perfect love other than to first take on poverty; for our God has commanded us to love all people and not only one. Therefore, we have an obligation not to look askance at those in need, but to assist them. If we do not give to all, but just to a few, our love is secretly defrauded and lessened, because we do not love all. However, to serve and offer assistance to everyone is impossible for the individual; for this is the work of God only.

On Almsgiving

"Though one has nothing, she must struggle to give alms. This command is directed only to those of the world and not to monastics. For the command of God to give alms is not so much that we might guide and minister to the poor, but that we might gain their love and practise mercy. For just as God oversees the wealthy, He oversees the poor. Some may say, 'Therefore, it is commanded that alms should be given from what is in abundance.' May it never be so! Almsgiving is the beginning of love to those who would acquire it. As circumcision of the foreskin was the paradigm of the circumcision of the passions of the heart [Rom. 2:29; Col. 2:11], thus, almsgiving is the established teacher of love. However, to those who, by the grace of God, give love, to them is the abundance of mercy.

"I say these things not to criticize almsgiving, but to show the greater purity of poverty. Therefore, the lesser good is almsgiving; so let us not have it become an obstacle to the greater good of poverty, which is love. Thou, O nun, in a short time or with little effort, hast achieved the lesser good by distributing thy goods among the poor. Now strive to accomplish the greatest virtue, which is love. Of thine own free will, thou didst utter: 'Behold, we left all and followed Thee [Mk. 10:28; Lk. 18:28].' By uttering these words, thou hast been vouchsafed to be imitators of the glorious Apostles Peter and John, who were one in faith, and said, 'Silver and gold have I none [Acts 3:6].'

"The giving of alms for those living in the world is neither a simple matter nor to be done haphazardly. Listen to David who says, 'As for the oil of the sinner, let it not anoint my head [Ps. 140:6].' Therefore, the one who renders works of mercy should have the mentality of Abraham who fulfilled them in a pure manner. When the righteous Abraham offered hospitality and set a table [Gen. 18:1-8], he also set in his mind to share with his servants what he gained by hospitality. Truly, the one who offers hospitality, after the custom of Abraham, receives the compensation of almsgiving, though that individual is numbered among those of the second rank.[2]

Monastics and Lay People

"When the Lord made the world He placed two ranks of beings to dwell therein: those who wisely conduct their lives within the boundaries of marriage and childbearing, and those who enter pure into life and are commanded to remain virgin, so as to be equal to the angels. To the married, He gave laws, instructions, and vengeance against unrighteousness. However, to virgins, He says, 'Vengeance is mine, I shall repay [Deut. 32:35; Rom. 12:19].' To the married He says, 'Work the earth [Gen. 3:24],' but to the monastics He says, 'Do not become anxious for the morrow [Mt. 6:34].' Moreover, to the married He gave laws, but to nuns and monks He revealed His commandments through grace.

"The Cross for us is the trophy of victory; for our calling and our vows are none other than forsaking this life and remembering death. Just as the dead do not produce movement in their corpses, we, too, must not invigorate our bodies. For whatever we perform in our carnal bodies, we did as ignorant children. Therefore the Apostle Paul says, 'The world hath been crucified to me, and I to the world [Gal. 6:14]'; that is, 'to me the world is dead, and I too am dead to the world.' We live with our soul only, and with this we must reveal the virtues and mercy; for, as the Lord says, 'Blessed are the merciful: for they shall find mercy [Mt. 5:7].' She who merely desires the beauty of someone, though she does not act to fulfill the desire, yet, secretly, she commits the sin in her soul. Similarly, those who have mercy and sorrow for others in their souls, practise charity, because they fulfilled the deed in their minds, though they had no silver.

"We are honored with a greater position than those of the world. Just as a lord or lady in the world has servants for various ministrations, that is, some to manage their property, while others work their grounds, they keep in the house those that are superior. It is the same with the Lord of all: Those that are married, He appoints to live in the world; yet those that excel, possessing pure and good intentions, He places before Him to serve. Those of the latter group are strangers to all that is of the earth; for they have been vouchsafed to eat at the Master's table. They do not take care for raiment, for they are clothed with Christ. Nevertheless, the Lord is Master of both these positions. As He has provided that wheat yields both chaff and kernel, so has He provided offspring among those of the world and the monastics. Both are needed, for just as leaves protect and benefit the fruit, so the fruit sows and

---

[2] The two ranks that the saint refers to in this instance are the unmarried and the married.

reproduces. As it is not possible for fodder to flower, likewise it is not possible to produce any heavenly fruit if we have the glory of the world. Similarly, if leaves do not fall and the stalks do not wither, then the gleaner cannot produce a harvest. It is the same with us. If we do not discard worldly fantasies as foliage and do not mortify our flesh as a stalk, then we cannot raise our thoughts to God. Moreover, it is impossible to bear seed, that is, the word of salvation.

On Teaching

"It is dangerous to be a teacher of beginners in the active virtues. If the teacher's house is unsound, upon inviting others inside, all shall surely be injured by the collapse of the house. Such who teach, without having first built their own house on a sound foundation, have not previously learned the active virtues. Thus, they bring ruin upon themselves and their disciples. Though false teachers appear to inspire others with their words of salvation, by their bad works they actually bring about more harm. Teaching is very much like drawing, which is accomplished by colors that eventually fade. An image loses its properties and is eradicated with the passage of time, the dew of rain, and the elements blown by the wind. On the other hand, teaching coupled with works may not be erased for centuries. This is because one who practises what is taught has fixed a permanent stamp on the soul. Teachers that emulate the virtues of Christ inscribe durable and lasting impressions upon their listeners and pupils. Therefore, we should cleanse not only the outward appearance of the soul, but we also should beautify it entirely. Indeed, we should be diligent in purifying the soul from its inner depths.

On Cleansing the Passions

"We have cut the hairs of our head in the holy Tonsure; let us also remove the lice and worms that infest our heads. If we allow them to remain on our scalps, they will prick us even more. The hairs that we have shorn bespeak the cutting away of the worldly life, that is, honor, glory, wealth, splendid dresses, bathing, and good food. Though we have cast off all these things, let us throw off the soul-corrupting worms, that is, talkativeness, avariciousness, lying, swearing, and whatever other passions we detect in our souls. These parasitical passions did not appear since they were covered by hair, that is, the material things of the world. However, now that we have been denuded of worldly things, all the passions appear clearly. Therefore, the smallest sin is manifest to the monastic, just as in a clean house the smallest vermin are noticed by all.

"Those who live in the world lurk about in the hidden holes of great and unclean caves with poisonous snakes. However, these caves and snakes are concealed, that is, cloaked with many worldly trappings. Hence, we must clean the house of our souls and give strict attention that no soul-damaging vermin creep inside. What is meant by 'vermin' is passion hidden in the recesses of our souls. We must also perpetually burn incense over our hearts, that is, offer up the divine incense of prayer. As the most pungent incense repels poisonous creatures, so our prayer, coupled with fasting, dispels pernicious thoughts.

On Thoughts

"Nuns must stand on guard as thoughts enter. For example, there was a certain virtuous monk who, while sitting in his cell, was guarding his thoughts. He reckoned which came first and which came second, and how long each thought remained. The following day, he was again watchful to determine which came first. In this manner, he understood exactly, by the grace of God, not only his own patience and strength, but the mastery of the enemy. Let us follow his example.

On Despair

"When those engaged in worldly business make a daily accounting, they rejoice upon making a profit, but sorrow when they tally losses. How much more shall we remain alert who are engaged in transacting the true treasure? How much more should we desire to gain those good things? If, through stealth, we suffer even a petty theft from the enemy, we should grieve and judge ourselves; but never should we succumb to despair and throw everything down on account of the fault that caused us to stumble. Keep in mind the ninety-nine sheep [Mt. 18:12; Lk. 15:4]! Seek the one that is gone astray. Do not fear for the one loss when thou didst deviate from the Master God. Take heed lest the blood-sucking devil should capture all thine actions and thou dost sink into despair. Therefore, do not desert thy post because of one loss. Our Master is good, and well does David write: 'By the Lord are the steps of a man rightly directed, and His way shall he greatly desire. When he falleth he shall not be utterly cast down; for the Lord upholdeth his hand [Ps. 36:23, 24].'

On Life

"Whatever we transact or gain in this world, deem it insignificant when compared with the everlasting riches of the future life. We may parallel life in this world with being in the womb. When we were in our mother's womb, where our lives and movements were much different, we were deprived of the sun, of any other light, and of all those things of the world. Similarly, now that we are living in this world, we do not have access to many of the good things in the kingdom of the heavens. Therefore, as we enjoy the things of the world, likewise let us love to find rest in those heavenly good things. As we behold material light in this world, likewise, let us desire to behold the noetic Sun of righteousness. Let us ponder upon the upper Jerusalem as our own country and mother; and let us call God our Father. Let us live here prudently and wisely that we may attain eternal life.

"Look at the example of infants in the wombs of their mothers. When they come to full term, delivery follows. From their formerly tiny being, sustained with little nourishment, they become greater and comelier. This example may be likened to the righteous who have departed this life and enter the heavenly and superior life; for, as it is written, they shall go 'from strength to strength [Ps. 83:7].' However, for sinners who have surrendered to the darkness of the world, there is the darkness of Hades. They are to be compared to the infants that miscarry in the wombs of their mothers. Similarly, sinners of the earth, floundering in the multitude of sins, descend into the darkness of the nether world upon death.

"In this present life, we may be born three times. First, when we are delivered from our mother's womb; thus coming from earth we again go to earth. The other two births cause us to ascend from earth to heaven. The one, wrought by divine grace, comes to us through holy Baptism, which is true rebirth and regeneration. The third birth, wherein we now find ourselves, takes place through repentance, which is achieved by means of tears and good struggles.

On Spiritual Brides

"We who are brought near to the true Bridegroom Christ are obliged to adorn ourselves with better fineries. When brides of the world are about to take a mortal husband, they give serious attention to bathing and anointing themselves with myrrh. Then they adorn themselves with various dresses and accessories, so they might appear desirable to their husbands. Now how much more should we adorn ourselves who are betrothed to the heavenly Bridegroom? How much more should we wash away the uncleanness of our sins by ascetic labors, and beautify ourselves with spiritual garments? Brides in the world also decorate themselves with earthly flowers, but let our souls radiate with the brightness of virtues. Upon our heads let us place the thrice-plaited crown of faith, hope, and love, instead of a crown of precious stones. Let us embellish our necks with humble-mindedness as with a highly-valued scarf. In the place of a sash, let us gird ourselves with temperance and discretion, and don the dress of poverty. At our table, let us offer imperishable foods, consisting of prayers and chanting. Furthermore, the Apostle John commands, 'Let us not be loving in word, neither in tongue, but in deed and in truth [1 Jn. 3:18].' Therefore, let us not only control our tongue, but let us also preserve in our minds those virtues which our calling doth profess; for, ofttimes, we guard the tongue, but the heart and mind contemplate other things.

"We who have contracted a heavenly marriage must make provision not to be wanting in oil lamps, that is, the virtues; for then we shall be worthy of His wrath and utterly cast out if we do not perform what we promised. Now what are those promises? They consist of furnishing less for the flesh and supplying more for the needs of our souls. It is to the soul that we should give drink. You know it is impossible to bring up simultaneously two full buckets of water from a well. The reason is that the force or weight applied to the rope around the pulley will cause one bucket to move upward and the other downward in the shaft of the well. Thus, only one bucket at a time may be filled with water. It is the same with us when we apply all our power exclusively to the needs of the soul. The soul then fills up with virtues and moves upward toward the much desired heights. At the same time, through asceticism, our bodies remain light and easy to bear, and do not weigh down the soul toward earthly things. The Apostle Paul himself bore witness to this when he said, 'Even if our outward man is being utterly destroyed, yet the inward man is being renewed day by day [2 Cor. 4:16].'

On the Coenobitic Life

"If thou shouldest find thyself in a coenobium, do not go to another place. Thou shalt sustain great harm. As when winged creatures molt their feathers after breeding, so it is with the nun or the monk that moves about from place to place; his or her faith becomes frigid and withers. However, the coenobitic life is not suited for everyone. Each must examine herself in this matter as to which will be more spiritually profitable: the community life or to abide alone. Study the plant world and thou shalt observe that some bloom in a moist environment, while others thrive in drier conditions. It is the same with people: some flourish in mountains, others in the desert. The monk or nun should dwell in that place which is to his or her benefit. There are some who dwell in the middle, that is, in cities, and find salvation, because they abide virtuously as though they were in the wilderness. It is possible for a mindful monastic to dwell among many and yet abide alone. Similarly, the lax monastic, dwelling alone, may abide with many in mind and thought. We, the monastics, must govern our souls with judgment and wisdom. If we dwell in a coenobium, let us not seek our own will. Let us be subject to our spiritual mother, the abbess. We have surrendered ourselves to living in exile. We have left the borders of worldly things and matters. Therefore, let us not seek after them again. In the world, we had glory and honor; but here, let us stand in need of bread. In the world, those that commit offenses are cast into prison against their will. However, let us voluntarily confine ourselves on account of our sins, so we may be released from future condemnation.

On Food

"Be not deceived by the heavily laden table of the wealthy, nor the pleasure derived from various foods. Those that esteem the art of cooking and the concocting of desirable and delicious foods are fooled. However, do thou defeat these dainties and the pleasure derived from fancy foods by fasting and the partaking of inexpensive and simple fare. This is what Solomon says: 'A full soul scorns honeycombs; but to a hungry soul even bitter things appear sweet [Prov. 27:7].' Therefore, neither satiate thyself by simple fare nor with bread, and then thou wilt not even desire wine.

Three Evils

"There are three chief and foremost evils of the enemy, through which every other evil may trace its origin: desire, pleasure, and sorrow. One induces and follows the other. To overcome pleasure is possible. To defeat desire is impossible. The reason for this is that pleasure comes about by means of the flesh, whereas desire emanates from the soul. Sorrow, however, derives its source from both desire and pleasure. If thou wilt not stimulate desire in thyself, pleasure and sorrow can be cast out. If thou wilt allow desire to emerge, this will usher in pleasure which will be followed by sorrow. Heed, therefore, the Scripture verse, 'Give the water no passage [Wisdom of Sirach 25:25].' If you permit entry, then desire, pleasure, and sorrow will never permit the soul to recover sobriety.

The Attacks of the Enemy

"Many are the goads of the devil. If he is unable to injure one through poverty, he will venture to destroy that one with wealth. If he cannot damage one with dishonor and reproach, he will seek to wound that one by honors and popular repute. If one defeats him through good health, the deceiver endeavors to harm that one through sickness. When the enemy is unable to thwart us through joy, he undertakes to afflict us with sorrows and involuntary pains. According to divine permission [Job 1:12], the evil one strives to wound us through grave illnesses. Thus, he endeavors to render our soul mean and little, thereby confounding and making turbid our love toward God. Therefore, O beloved ones, let us withstand bodily maltreatment, the heat of the day, and unquenchable thirst, since, as sinners, we suffer these things. Only bring to thy mind the damnation, the inextinguishable fire, and the punishments of Hades. Then thou shalt not fall fainthearted in these present troubles, which we are made to endure. Much rather, be glad in the visitation of the Lord, to Whom Thou shalt render thanksgiving, and offer these words of praise with David: 'With chastisement hath the Lord chastened me, but He hath not given me over unto death [Ps. 117:18].' By means of illness and weakness, we may purge the pollution of our sins, just as smelting iron from its ores in a charcoal forge fire causes the gangue or cinder to run out from the bottom of the fire or hearth. If thou, being righteous, shouldest suffer illness, know that thou shalt advance from the lesser to even greater good things. If thou art gold, thou shalt become more brilliant in the furnace of affliction. If thy flesh has been handed over to a minister of Satan, thou hast been vouchsafed to be as the Apostle Paul [2 Cor. 12:7], which is an occasion to rejoice. If thou art tormented by the scorching sun or shivering from the cold, stand thy ground in the face of battle, until thou art refreshed and find consolation. As it is written in the divine Scriptures: 'We went through fire and water, and Thou didst bring us out into refreshment [Ps. 65:12].' Hast thou withstood the first? Then also stand fast in the second. If thou art poor and burdened with toils and sufferings, utter with the prophet: 'I am poor and needy and in sorrows [cf. Ps. 68:29; 69:6].' By these three things thou shalt come to perfection; for, as it is written in the psalms: 'In mine affliction Thou hast enlarged me [Ps. 4:1].' Hence, with these words let us strive in the remainder of the contest, because our contentious opponent is before us.

On Sickness

"Let us not sorrow because of bodily weakness, when we are unable to keep vigilance in prayer or to chant mellifluously. Though standing, fasting, lying on the ground, and every other bodily hardship are done to counter shameful desires and pleasures, yet weakness and sickness may also deaden these things. The effort of fasting and other austerities are supplemental. What do we mean by supplemental? The ruinous passions are stifled somewhat by extreme illness and weakness, yet they are stimulated by strength and good health. Sickness is the greatest asceticism. It is a time when we must exercise patience and offer up thanksgiving and glory to God. If we are deprived of the light of our eyes, let us not appear downtrodden, because we have lost those organs that incite unrestrained desires; much rather, let us behold with the noetic eyes of the soul the glory of the Lord. If we have become deaf, let us give thanks, because we have muted all vain talking. If our hands suffer from paralysis, let us raise the inward hands of our soul, ready to strike the enemy. If disease has riddled our entire body, yet the health of the soul is greatly increased.

On Asceticism

"If we find ourselves in a coenobium, let us prefer obedience before asceticism, because asceticism often will be the agent of pride, whereas obedience guides us to humble-mindedness. Excessive asceticism can be from the enemy, for whoever listens to that deceiver is led to extreme immoderation. How shall we distinguish divine and majestic asceticism from that which is tyrannical and demonic? It is manifest that we should recognize moderation. Let all the season of thy life be one of fasting. Do not fast four or five days and then dine sumptuously; immoderation is destructive. Do not deploy all thy weapons in one engagement, so that in the time of war thou art found unequipped and easily routed by the enemy. Our suit of armor is the body; the soldier is the soul. Unfailingly, recruit both body and soul for the battle. Fast if thou art young and healthy, for old age may bring feebleness and infirmity.

Therefore, as much as thou art able, gather up food, so thou mightest find it when thou art weak or ill. Fast sensibly and carefully, so the enemy, by thine indiscretion, doth not secretly take possession of thine endeavor and the reward of fasting. This discernment, I believe, is also mentioned by the Lord, Who asks, 'Whose image and inscription is on the coin?' In other words, we should recognize those things that belong to God [Mt. 22:17-22]. This is because there are counterfeit coins; though they are gold, yet their inscription and stamp are a forgery. Now what I mean by gold is fasting, continence, and mercy. However, the pagan Greeks and heretics take these virtues and affix their own seals. We must be wary and bypass these frauds, so as not to be duped by them. Therefore, with exactness and genuineness, let us take up the Lord's Cross which is inscribed with the divine virtues of correct Faith and reverent deeds.

"If thou wilt fast, do not make excuses to break it off, saying that thou wilt become sick and weak. It is those who do not fast that succumb to sickness and weakness. Hast thou commenced well? Do not abandon thy work when the devil places stumbling blocks in thy way. Be patient, and thou shalt nullify the work of the enemy. Look at them that are about to commence a voyage. When they find an advantageous wind, they spread the sails. When they encounter contrary winds, they do not immediately lower the sails, but wait a short while. It should be the same for a monastic. When, after faring well, we are overcome by a threefold wave of the passions, instead of a sail, let us raise up before us the Cross and fearlessly continue our passage through life."

These were some of the words of our spiritual mother; much rather, these were the works of the all-virtuous Syncletike. Indeed, there are many other great labors and words which were known and taught by her, to the benefit of all who heard her. However, it is not possible for the tongue of man to relate their magnitude.

The Trials of the Saint

The hater of all that is good, the devil, could not bear to behold all the good things that were wrought by Syncletike. The enemy was consumed with how he might cloud her radiant light and gain the advantage over her. The devil sought, according to divine permission, to contend with the brave virgin in a final contest.

Damage to the Lungs

With relentless malice, the devil fought against the athlete of Christ. He did not strike a blow to her outward members, but to her inward parts, causing an exceedingly deep pain. Her suffering could not be soothed by human means. The first members to be infected were her life-supporting lungs. Shortly thereafter, incited by more treachery, the bloodthirsty murderer brought about a slow and insidious sickness that left her at the threshold of death. The chronic disease lingered for a very long time, creating many more complications. As her lungs deteriorated with the formation of lesions and pus, her spittle contained blood. She also suffered from an interminable fever, which debilitated her body, rendering it as beeswax.

The holy woman was eighty years old when the evil one brought this sickness upon her, as he had done in the past to the righteous Job [2:7]. Desiring to inflict more suffering upon her, he smote the virgin's consecrated body with many painful internal ulcers, which she suffered for three and one-half years. "It is my opinion," says the hagiographer of this present life, "not even the martyrs of Christ endured the hardships that the ever-memorable Syncletike suffered. They were attacked from without, that is, by fire and sword, which I think were more tolerable than the torments of the venerable virgin." It was as though her inner parts were in a slow-burning fiery furnace. This is, in fact, a truly grave and savage punishment. Even those in authority, when they desire to administer harsh torture upon one, burn the prisoner with a small fire; then, little by little, they let it consume the victim. In like manner, day and night, did the enemy rage hotly to burn her organs.

During this calamity, the spirit of the saint neither fell nor grew fainthearted. On the contrary, she battled the enemy by continuing her soul-saving teachings, which were of special benefit for those that were also suffering physical ailments. In fact, her discourses rescued many from the jaws of the lion. There were certain ones whom she preserved unscathed, by revealing to them the snares of the devil, thus delivering them from potential sin. The wondrous woman of God exhorted them, saying, "We should never be carefree about our souls that are dedicated to God. While those nonchalant souls are lying content, the enemy grinds his teeth waiting for the appropriate time of day to strike. Then he launches an assault against them, often overcoming them by the very thing in which the carefree person has been negligent.

"It is not possible for those who do much evil not to have a spark of some good. Conversely, one will always find something that is bad in those who are good. It often happens that one is laden with every shameful passion, yet they are merciful. The latter is also true of those who are talkative or avaricious. We must not be careless or indulgent with our own shortcomings, considering that they cannot ultimately cause any damage; for a little falling water over a long period will eventually wear away the stone. Great and good things come to people by divine grace. The appearance of lesser passions within us should teach us to struggle with them. When we come to reject the lesser passions, then the grace of God overcomes the greater ones. This is because our Lord, as our genuine Father, extends His hand to His spiritual children when they first learn to walk, to prevent their stumbling and to rescue them from falling into dangers. However, He leaves us in small dangers to walk with our own feet, thereby showing that we possess free will. Now one who is overcome by the lesser, how shall that one be preserved against the greater?"

Saint Syncletike

Damage to the Vocal Cords

The hater-of-good, observing that the holy Syncletike courageously contended against him, was discomfited. He then considered that his reign of tyranny was brought to nought by the saint. Unrelenting, he plotted another evil against her. He brought damage to her vocal cords, to prevent any utterance from her. He perpetrated this with the hope that those nuns who came to see the venerable woman would be spiritually starved of the word of God. Though the nuns were deprived of hearing the words of the saint, nevertheless, they received greater benefit through the chief of the senses, the eyes. Solely by beholding the athlete of God, wounded from the contest, they were immeasurably strengthened in the struggle for virtue. The bodily wounds of the saint healed their wounded souls. To all that observed the blessed one's greatness of soul and patience, she stood as a guard and remedy for their ailing souls. In this manner, the holy Syncletike laid blows upon the enemy.

Damage to the Mouth

Among her many medical complications, the saint had one large tooth that caused pain. A hideous gum disease resulted from that tooth, which eventually fell out. The decay, rapidly spreading to her jawbone within two months, emitted an extremely offensive odor. The odor was repugnant to the sisterhood and to those nuns that ministered to the needs of the saint. Unable to endure the odor, in order to draw near to her, they would burn incense to help mask it; and then they quickly would withdraw. The blessed Syncletike clearly beheld the enemy that was warring against her; hence, she would permit no human assistance. On account of their own human frailty, the nuns besought her to at least anoint the diseased areas with myrrh, but she refused. To be the recipient of human help, she considered a detraction from her glorious contest against the enemy.

At one point, the nuns summoned a physician with the hope that he might persuade her to receive medical attention. The saint would not acquiesce, and said, "What phenomenon do you behold and do not wonder at that which is hidden? What explanation do you give this condition and do not see who has instigated it?" The physician candidly answered, "We seek neither to heal thee nor to console thee, but to honor thee with funeral rites, as is the custom. Due to the weakness of the nuns that minister unto thee, I wish to minister to that part of thy body which is dysfunctional from sepsis, so the nuns do not get sick. I will do that which is done upon the dead, that is, wash the putrid areas with wine, and then cover them with aloe mixed with myrrh and myrtle-juice." The venerable one listened to him and received his advice, only because she pitied those nuns who ministered unto her. The physician shuddered when he observed her insufferable sicknesses. He then understood the patience of the saint and perceived that the devil was beaten and proved inferior by her. Though the vile one, as a predatory beast, sought to rend asunder his prey through cancer and by laying a blow to that speech organ, which proved to be a spring of soul-saving and sweet words, instead he became her spoil. He was caught on the very hook with which he angled for the saint. He presumed that she was just a weak woman, not realizing her courageous character. The blind one beheld her withered body but could not perceive her dauntless resolve. The saint then continued to struggle in this contest for three additional months. Her debilitated body was kept alive only by divine power. She could then not sleep due to her many pains. She was unable to partake of nourishment, due to the excessive and ill-smelling putrefaction.

The Vision and Repose of the Saint

At eighty-four years old, toward the finish line of her contest, the holy contestant beheld a vision. She saw angels and virgin saints, radiant with divine light, in a place in Paradise. After beholding such things, she revealed them to the nuns who were with her. She advised them to bear bravely temporal afflictions and not to become fainthearted. The holy woman then foretold that her soul would separate from her body in three days. She predicted not only the day, but even contemplated the very hour of her departure into eternity. When the appointed day and hour arrived, enveloped by a heavenly light and overjoyed by consoling visions, the blessed Syncletike was transported to the Lord. She received from Him the prize and reward of her contest for the kingdom of the heavens. May we also be vouchsafed these heavenly good things. Amen.

On the 5ᵗʰ of January, the holy Church commemorates our venerable Father GREGORY at Akritas.

Gregory, our venerable father, hailed from the famous island of Crete. He was the son of the most pious Theophanes and Juliane. After Gregory had spent sufficient time in his studies, his parents bade him tend the flock of sheep. Inflamed by divine zeal and love, he departed his homeland and went to Seleukeia (Seleucia).[3] The ever-memorable one dwelt there for a little time, subsisting on the barest amount of bread and water. When he reached the age of twenty-six, the iconomach, Emperor Leo IV the Khazar (775-780), died of fever, after persecuting the defenders of the icons. Orthodoxy then triumphed with the devoted iconophile Irene as regent for Constantine VI. The venerable Gregory then made a pilgrimage to Jerusalem, for he conceived a desire to venerate the holy places and shrines. While he sojourned there for some twelve years, he endured much harassment and unpleasantness from the Hagarenes and Jews. After that passage of time, the holy man traveled to Rome, where he received the Angelic Schema of the monastics. He mortified his body and gained the mastery over it by exercising self-control and temperance.

Now when the co-emperor, Stavrakios (811), was gravely wounded during his father Nikephoros I's fatal confrontation with the Bulgarian khan Krum (ca. 802-814), he abdicated and died the following year. Michael I Rangabe, a high-ranking palace dignitary (*kouropalates*), who was married to Stavrakios' sister Prokopia, became emperor (811-813). Nikephoros, Patriarch of Constantinople (806-815), made Michael vow in writing that he would uphold Orthodoxy. This patriarch was urged by the imperium to correspond with Pope Leo III (795-816), who had crowned Charlemagne, which coronation resulted in a rival empire in the west. Envoys were sent in 812, and a new treaty was issued jointly by Charlemagne and Pope Leo. The patriarch then dispatched to the pope in Rome his apocrisiary, the righteous Confessor Michael of Synnada.[4] While at Rome, the holy Michael met with

---

[3] Seleukeia (mod. Silifke) is a coastal city of Isauria, a mountainous district in southern Asia Minor. Seleukeia was an ecclesiastical metropolis and a busy port.

[4] Saint Michael of Synnada, the Confessor, commemorated by the holy Church on the 23ʳᵈ of May, was *apokrisiarios* or apocrisiary (Lat. *responsalis*). This was the office of a representative or messenger of a bishop to higher authorities, or, in the case of Saint Michael, the patriarch to the pope. Justinian I had established this institution in

(continued...)

our venerable Father Gregory. He invited him to return to Constantinople with him. Father Gregory agreed and was brought to a monastery on Cape Akritas, which lies near Bithynian Chalcedon across the Bosporos, where he was numbered with the brotherhood.

The venerable man went about barefoot, clad in only one shirt-garment. His bedding consisted of one straw mat. He ate and drank only once every two or three days, partaking then of only the smallest amount of bread and water. He confined himself within a very deep pit, where he lamented, as a new Jeremias,[5] the destruction and tumult that struck the Church of Christ, regarding the displacement of the holy icons. Afterward, when he came forth from the pit, he immured himself in the narrowest of cells, covering himself with a leather undershirt. In the monastery garden, he found a large cask filled with water. He removed his undershirt at night and entered the cask of water, where he would read aloud the

Saint Gregory

entire Psalter. Upon completing the psalms, he would come out of that barrel. The blessed man practised this for the remainder of his days, together with similar contests, until he surrendered his soul into the hands of God.

On the 5th of January, the holy Church commemorates our venerable Father PHOSTERIOS.

Phosterios, our father among the saints, rose to fame in the east. In his lifetime, however, he had visited the west. He had ascended a serene mountain and, as if he were bodiless, prayed to God and imposed a harsh rule upon himself. He fasted, kept vigil, and went through every kind of privation. Owing to this, he became a true light—synonymous with his name—shining forth to everyone. He maintained the purity of both soul and body undefiled, in the image of God, and became a dwelling place of the Holy Spirit. In

---

[4](...continued)
order to prevent the prolonged absence of bishops from their flocks.
[5] Prophet Jeremias was cast into the house of Jonathan, which contained a pit (λάκκος) that was used as a dungeon [Jer. 44(37):16; 45(38):10, 13]. The well-known Lamentations of Jeremias were composed when Israel was taken captive and Jerusalem made desolate.

addition to this, he was granted the gift to perform miracles, curing every malady, whether chronic or otherwise, for those who came with faith.

Furthermore, it is said that he received bread from heaven, as did Prophet Elias by a raven. However, to the great Phosterios, it was sent by an angel, though, by divine œconomy, he did not gaze upon him. The angel brought bread daily and would lay it on a certain spot, unseen by the saint. If it happened that the holy one was visited by one, two, or even three of the brethren, the number of loaves left in that same spot would always be equal to the number of visitors. Who has ever heard of such a miracle? Indeed, this occurs seldom and to very few saints. However, blessed Phosterios was not vouchsafed this gift to the end of his days, as divine providence deemed otherwise. As long as he lived alone and prayed to God, an angel brought him bread. Yet, when he began a monastery and, with the help of God, gathered many monks, he no longer received bread in this manner, but supported himself and the brethren with the work of his own hands.

This discontinuance of ready sustenance had not occurred because God was unable to provide for the monks or because He turned away from the prayer of His slave. God forbid! For did not the same Lord nourish in the wilderness so many tens of thousands of Hebrews, and mostly ungrateful ones? The truth is that Father Phosterios did not pray for that food which is perishable, because he was mindful of Christ's words: "Be seeking first the kingdom of God and His righteousness, and all these things shall be added to you [Mt. 6:33]." When the holy man was in solitude, without human consolation and assistance, God provided what was needful. When others came and wished to share the life in Christ with the holy man and engage in God-pleasing ascesis, it was the Lord's will that Phosterios set an example. For this cause, Phosterios was laboring with his own hands, indicating to his disciples that they should shun idleness and not eat their bread at the expense of others. Much rather, it was more blessed to work and toil, and also give to others who were in need. God commanded His servant Phosterios that he ought not to receive the necessities of life from anyone, but to labor with his hands, thus teaching his disciples not only with words but also with deeds. Hence, he became a model and outline of piety to them that they should accept God's will for their lives, which was a conduct and discipline of sacred prayer and work.

Now also about that time, a heresy broke out, and a great number of fathers convened to form a synod. Phosterios was also invited to this synod. He did not tarry, but was present and played an important role, which brought his name consequence. Many heretics who attended were convinced by his words and returned to Orthodoxy. Indeed, a great number of them were influenced to the extent that they became monks. In short, numerous miracles were performed by him, not only when he lived, but even after his repose which occurred on the 5th of January.

**On the 5th of January, the holy Church commemorates
the holy Martyr SAÏS, who was cast into the sea.**

**On the 5th of January, the holy Church commemorates
the holy Martyr THEOËIDOS,
who was trampled underfoot by executioners.**

**On the 5th of January, the holy Church commemorates
DOMNINA, who reposed in peace.[6]**

**On the 5th of January, the holy Church commemorates
the holy New-martyr ROMANOS of Karpenesion, Monk of Athos,
who was slain by the sword at Constantinople (1694).**

Romanos, the blessed holy new-martyr, was born at Karpenesion and was the son of pious though illiterate parents. He, too, remained uneducated and knew nothing other than that he was a Christian. One day he overheard some people as they spoke concerning the Holy Sepulcher of our Lord. Consequently, he was inspired by this and traveled to Jerusalem, where he worshiped at the life-giving Tomb and all the holy places. He also went to the Monastery of Saint Savvas, where he heard from the fathers concerning the martyrdoms of the saints and how they endured manifold tortures for the name of Christ with the hope of achieving future rewards. Naturally, he inquired about the future rewards, and learning what they were, he himself became desirous to attain them through martyrdom.

When he returned to Jerusalem, he made his intentions known to the patriarch who, at that time, dissuaded him from seeking martyrdom. "The outcome is uncertain, child," said the patriarch, "and it might provoke a calamity upon the Holy Sepulcher." The saint, however, desired martyrdom with all his soul and was unable to extinguish the flame that burned in his heart. After he departed thither, he went to Thessalonike. Once there, he appeared before the judge, confessing with boldness that Christ was God and the Creator and Savior of mankind. He declared that the religion of the Hagarenes was false, a farce, and full of ludicrous myths. He proclaimed their prophet to be a deceiver and an enemy of the true God and Lord Jesus. When the judge heard this, he ordered that Romanos be flogged mercilessly. The Muslims broke a number of his ribs, tore at his sides with horseshoes,

---

[6] In some older *Synaxaristae* Saint Domnina's name is given as Domna.

and applied various other devices that they might force him to deny Christ. But because he would not yield in any way and remained firm in the Faith, the judge decided to have him put to death by the sword. However, at that time, the captain of the frigates of Thessalonike was present. He demanded that they turn the Christian over to him, so that he might put him to use as an oarsman. He explained saying, "This form of punishment in the frigates shall be an even worse condemnation than death by the sword; for he shall suffer for the rest of his life." These words pleased all the Muslims present. Therefore, Romanos was turned over to him. After the captain had the hair and beard of Romanos shaven clean, he placed him as an oarsman on his ship.

Saint Romanos

After a short lapse of time, some Christians who were friends of the captain convinced him to free Romanos, by giving him a certain sum of money. Upon securing his release, those Christians sent Romanos to Mount Athos. When he arrived there, he stayed with Saint Akakios, who had retired at Kafsokalyvia. Romanos struggled there with him in a superhuman way, but his thoughts would afford him no rest. He was as a stranger to this life. He cared for neither food nor drink, but only contemplated martyrdom. It was revealed to Saint Akakios that it was the will of God that Romanos should finish his course of martyrdom for Christ. Then Romanos was attired with the holy Schema of the monks on Pentecost Sunday. Strengthened by the prayers of the saint and the holy fathers of that place, he departed again for Jerusalem, wishing to go to the Holy Sepulcher in monastic garb in order to achieve that which he desired. But when he received word that should he appear there, either as a monk or a layman, the Holy Sepulcher would be in great jeopardy at the hands of the Hagarenes, Father Romanos turned to Constantinople, where he presented himself in the following manner.

The saint found a small dog, which he tied to his belt. He walked about with it in the marketplace. When the Turks saw the monk, they asked him why he walked the dog in that odd fashion. And he said to them, "So that I may feed it, as we Christians feed all you Hagarenes." They immediately found his insult offensive in the extreme. Utterly enraged, they attacked him as wild beasts, striking and pushing him, until they brought him to the vizier who questioned him. After he heard the same things from the saint, he turned him over to the tormentors. They were advised to administer torture until he should recant his Christian Faith. Then they seized the martyr and threw him into a dry well, where they usually disposed of murderers. The blessed one endured there for forty days without eating. Afterward, they lifted him out and tortured him mercilessly in many other ways. But since they could not convert him, they returned him to the vizier, who ordered that Father Romanos should be put to death by the sword. As they led him to the place of execution, wherever Father Romanos observed a Christian, he greeted him and ran eagerly, as if he were going to a wedding and not to the slaughter. At that time, he was also seen by a certain Christian, a nobleman, who keenly perceived the joyous state of the martyr. He was perplexed at the monk's reaction to such a violent death. He then learned that Father Romanos was hastening to die for Christ. Thereupon, the nobleman ran behind the martyr to see his end. Shortly afterward, they passed by a minaret, occupied then by the hodja, a teacher of the Koran, who was delivering his call to prayer at noon, according to Islamic custom. The martyr saw him and spat in his face. The executioners thereupon cut off his tongue, which he himself extended gladly; and again, with joyous gestures, he greeted all those Christians that he met as the blood ran from his mouth. When they arrived at the place of execution, Father Romanos, noetically and with gestures, gave thanks to God. He thereupon received the crown of martyrdom in 1694. Indeed, his blessed soul ascended with great glory into the heavens in order to rejoice with the choirs of the martyrs.

Concerning his relics when he was beheaded, his head fell with much deliberateness to the east, as if it were living. For this reason, the Hagarenes were envious. They consequently began beating and driving away the multitude of Christians who had assembled. The holy relics were honored from above by divine grace. A heavenly light shone forth where the relics were kept, for three whole nights. All saw this phenomenon and wondered. Now the Christians rejoiced and glorified God, but the Hagarenes were put to shame. At that time, there came into port an English ship, whose captain, for five hundred piasters, obtained the holy relics and carried them to England.

The aforesaid nobleman, who was following the martyrdom, observed that the Hagarenes were forcibly driving out the Christians. He gave one Turkish child five piasters. The child took it and dipped a napkin into the blood of the martyr and brought it to him. Afterward, however, the child told another Hagarene. Therefore, they sent back the child with the demand for five more piasters from the Christian. Since the Christian did not wish to meet the money demand, he was betrayed to the vizier; and so the Muslims were resolved to put to death the nobleman also. Nevertheless, since he was a personal friend of the sultan, that connection spared him from death. Instead, they cast him into a bleak dungeon, where he languished for six months. Every evening he saw a ray of light which brightened his prison cell. The supernatural light emanated from the site where the martyr had been beheaded. This consoled him; otherwise, "I should have perished from my extreme hardships," said he. Later, four thousand piasters were given toward his release from prison, and he and his brother sold all of their belongings. The brothers then went on pilgrimage to venerate the holy places in Jerusalem and Mount Sinai. Afterward, they sailed to Mount Athos and became monks, changing their names at the tonsure. The elder one, Agapios, completed his life in a God-pleasing manner in the monastery of Docheiariou, to which he donated the napkin with the blood of the martyr. The other ended his days at the monastery of Koutloumousiou.

Thus was the excellent end of the blessed Romanos, who received the crown of martyrdom, to the glory of Christ our God, to Whom is due glory and power to the ages of the ages. Amen.

Through the intercessions of Thy Saints,
O Christ God, have mercy on us. Amen.

On the 6ᵗʰ of January, the holy Church commemorates
the HOLY THEOPHANY
of our Lord and God and Savior Jesus Christ.[1]

The Feast of the Theophany or Epiphany, which we celebrate today, took place when our Lord Jesus Christ had lived thirty years from the time He

---

[1] The great Feast of Theophany (*Theophaneia*), meaning "manifestation of God," is also known as the Epiphany (*Epiphaneia*), meaning "manifestation from above." The divine office for this feast celebrates the Baptism of Christ in the Jordan, thus sanctifying both man and the waters, and His manifestation as Christ and the manifestation of God in Trinity. Epiphany is the oldest feast of our Lord next to Pascha, and has always been celebrated on the 6ᵗʰ of January. The first mention of the feast is found in Clement of Alexandria (ca. 150-ca. 215). Originally, Epiphany commemorated not only the Baptism of Christ but also His nativity. However, the day on which Christ was born, He was not manifested to all; when He was baptized, He was made manifest to all; and so says Saint John Chrysostom [Homily XXIV on the Baptism of Christ]. During the early centuries, this day of our Lord's theophany, together with Pascha and Pentecost, and later the Feast of the Nativity, were the solemn occasions of Christian initiation through Baptism. The remnant of this practise is observed in the chanting of this hymn during the divine Liturgy: "As many as were baptized into Christ, ye put on Christ [Gal. 3:27]. Alleluia." It was not until the fourth century that the Feast of the Nativity of our Lord Jesus was commemorated as a separate feast. As a historical note, according to the old Egyptian calendar, the 6ᵗʰ of January was the day of the winter solstice, at which time the benighted pagans celebrated the conquest of winter darkness by the sun god. Later, the new Roman calendar placed the winter solstice on the 25ᵗʰ of December, at which time the polytheistic Romans glorified their deified emperor. Therefore, at the time the idolaters were commemorating the conquest of winter darkness by their sun god or deifying their emperor, the Christians were celebrating the manifestation of Jesus Christ, true God and true Man, Who conquered the darkness of ignorance and sin, leading our race to worship of the Creator rather than the creature. The establishing of the Feast of the Nativity did not diminish the Feast of the Theophany, which is celebrated from the 2ⁿᵈ of January to the 14ᵗʰ of January, with the 6ᵗʰ of January being the principal day of this feast. The four days preceding it constitute the forefeast (*proeortia*), and the eight days after it constitute the afterfeast or postfeast (*metheortia*). The Service of the Great Sanctification of the Waters (*Megas Agiasmos*) is a conspicuous feature of this feast day, which is observed twice, on the eve and on the day of the Feast of Theophany. The hymns of this divine office emphasize that Christ was not baptized in order to be sanctified, but to grant sanctification to us and the waters. In the west, Epiphany was observed in Rome. At first the commemoration of the Feasts of the Nativity and Baptism of Christ were together, but it gradually came to be associated with the visit of the Magi. Evidence of this is found in the sermons of Pope Leo I (440-461). At length, the western Epiphany was fixed as the twelfth day of Nativity, that is, the 6ᵗʰ of January.

The Baptism

took flesh and became Man. Our Lord's descent into the Jordan and His holy Baptism were a patent manifestation of His incarnation. We therefore cry aloud with the Psalmist David, "Blessed is He Who cometh in the name of the Lord....God is the Lord, and hath appeared unto us [Ps. 117:26, 27]." This theophany is fulfilled in the prophecy of Prophet Baruch: "This is our God, and there shall none other be accounted of in comparison of Him....Afterward did He show Himself upon earth, and conversed with men [Bar. 3:35-37]." Thus, we chant, "Divinity was seen with flesh by those of the earth [cf. Bar. 3:37]."[2] "For the grace of God which bringeth salvation appeared to all men [Tit. 2:11]." Saint Hippolytos (ca. 170-ca. 236) comments that "Christ came down as the rain [Hos. 6:4], and was known as a spring [Jn. 4:14], and diffused Himself as a river [Jn. 7:38], and was baptized in the Jordan [Mt. 3:13]."[3]

At our Lord's Baptism, the heavens were opened. Prophet-King David prophesied, "Great was the resounding sound of the waters, the clouds gave forth a voice [Ps. 76:16]." "Wherefore," asks Saint John Chrysostom (ca. 347-407), "were the heavens opened? To inform thee that at thy Baptism this also is done: God is calling thee to thy country on high, and persuading thee to have nothing to do with earth. And if you see it not, yet never doubt it....Though no visible signs take place, nevertheless, we receive the things that were once made manifest (at our Lord's Baptism)....This is also to teach thee that upon thee no less at thy Baptism the Spirit comes."[4]

Saint John of Damascus (ca. 675-ca. 749) at this feast chants, "The Father, in a voice full of joy, made manifest His Beloved Whom He had

---

[2] January 5th, Orthros Aposticha, Mode Two.
[3] Saint Hippolytus, *The Discourse on the Holy Theophany*, Ante-Nicene, V:234, 235.
[4] Saint Chrysostom, Homily XII, *On Saint Matthew*, Nicene, 1st Ser., X:77.

begotten from the womb [Ps. 109:3]. 'Verily,' said He, 'He is begotten of Me, and of the same essence as Myself: bearing light, He has come forth from mankind, My living Logos, in divine providence made a mortal man.'"[5]

In the Old Testament, the Lord carried back the sea with a strong wind, and the water was divided for Moses [Ex. 14:21]. In the time of Jesus of Navee, when the priests bore the ark of the covenant, as soon as they entered a part of the Jordan River during that season when its banks overflowed, the water that came down from above stopped and stood in one solid heap [Josh. 3:15,16]. Prophet Elias took his mantle and wrapped it together, and smote the water, and it was divided on this side and on that, and both he and Elisaios went over on dry ground [4 Kgs. (2 Kgs.) 2:8]. After the translation of Prophet Elias, Prophet Elisaios stood upon the brink of the Jordan, and smote the waters, and they were divided hither and thither, and he went over [4 Kgs. (2 Kgs.) 2:13, 14].

Also at our Lord's Baptism the streams of Jordan were turned back, as Prophet-King David prophesied: "The waters saw Thee, O God, the waters saw Thee, and feared; and the depths were troubled [Ps. 76:15]. The sea beheld and fled, Jordan turned back [Ps. 113:3]. At the presence of the Lord the earth was shaken, at the presence of the God of Jacob [Ps. 113:7]."

At the Lity service of the feast, we chant, "How could Jordan, that stood in awe of Jesus the son of Navee, not be afraid before the Maker of him?" Saint John of Damascus confirms that "when Jordan parted in two for the people of Israel, it prefigured the Lord Who would bear the creation down into the stream, bringing it to a better and changeless path."[6] When the waters parted and became a dry path for Elisaios, this formed a true figure of the Baptism, "whereby we pass over the changeful course of life."[7] Jordan is personified when it is asked during the Theophany Hours, "Why dost thou turn back thy streams, O Jordan? Why dost thou not proceed upon thy natural course? 'I cannot bear,' said he, 'the Fire that consumes me. I am filled with wonder and with dread before His extreme condescension. For I am not used to washing the clean: I have not learnt to bathe the sinless, but to purge filthy vessels. Christ Who is baptized in me, teaches me to burn the thorns of sin.'"[8]

The Prophet David announced in the Spirit that "of the torrent of Thy delight shalt Thou give them to drink [Ps. 35:8(9)]." At the Theophany this Torrent is identified. "The Torrent of delight is baptized in the stream: He

---

[5] January 6th, Orthros Canon, Ode Six, Mode Two.
[6] January 6th, Orthros Canon, Ode Seven, Mode Two.
[7] January 5th, Dismissal Hymn of the Forefeast, Mode Four.
[8] January 6th, Extract, Sixth Hour, Mode Plagal One.

dries up the fount of evil and pours forth divine remission."[9] And, "The Master, as the Torrent of Thy delight, cometh forth to be baptized in the streams of the river; for He desired giving me to drink and cleansing me with the flowing spring water."[10] Prophet Michaeas also wrote: "He will return and have mercy upon us; He will sink our iniquities, and they shall be cast into the depths of the sea, even all our sins [Mic. 7:19]."

Saint Kosmas (7th C.) affirms that at our Lord's Baptism in the Jordan He did "break the heads of the dragons upon the water [Ps. 73:13]."[11] The Monk John, at this feast's divine office, also mentions that at Christ's descent into the waters, "He gave light to all things and crushed the heads of the dragons."[12] Blessed Jerome (ca. 342-420) writes: "Pharaoh and his host, loathe to allow God's people to leave Egypt, were overwhelmed in the Red Sea, figuring thereby our Baptism. His destruction is described in the book of Psalms [73:14, 15]."[13] Saint John of Damascus chants for the Feast of the Theophany, "From the ancient snares have we all been set loose, and the jaws of the devouring lions have been broken,"[14] as prophesied by David: "God will shatter their teeth in their mouth; the molars of the lions did the Lord crush together [Ps. 57:6]."

Prefigurations of Baptism in the Old Testament

Blessed Jerome says that "over the waters, the Spirit of God bore Himself along [cf. Gen. 1:2], and produced from them the infant world, a type of the Christian child that is drawn from the laver of Baptism."[15] He also observes, "When the world falls into sin, nothing but a flood of waters can cleanse it again. But as soon as the foul bird of wickedness is driven away, the dove of the Holy Spirit comes to Noah [Gen. 8:8, 11], as it came afterward to Christ in the Jordan [Mt. 3:16], carrying in its beak a branch betokening restoration and light, and bringing tidings of peace to the whole world."[16]

Saint Gregory of Nyssa: "Jacob, hastening to seek a bride, met Rachel unexpectedly at the well. Now a great stone lay upon the well, which a multitude of shepherds were wont to roll away when they came together; and then they gave water to themselves and to their flocks. But Jacob alone rolls away the stone, and waters the flocks of his spouse [Gen. 29:10]. The

---

[9] January 5th, Vespers Aposticha, Mode Plagal Two.
[10] January 5th, extract of Orthros Sessional Hymn, Mode One.
[11] January 6th, Orthros Canon, Ode One, Mode Two.
[12] January 6th, Vespers, Mode Two.
[13] Blessed Jerome, "Letter LXIX," Nicene, 2nd Ser., VI:145.
[14] January 6th, Orthros Canon, Ode Three, Mode Two.
[15] Blessed Jerome, "Letter LXIX," loc. cit.
[16] Ibid.

thing is, I think, a dark saying, a shadow of what should come. For what is the stone that is laid but Christ Himself?...And none rolled away the stone save Israel, who is 'mind seeing God.' But he both draws up the water and gives drink to the sheep of Rachel; that is, he reveals the hidden mystery, and gives living water to the flock of the Church....Add to this the history of Jacob's three rods. For from the time they were laid by the well, Laban the polytheist thenceforth became poor, and Jacob became rich and wealthy in herds [cf. Gen. 30:37-43]. Now let Laban be interpreted of the devil, and Jacob of Christ. For, after the institution of Baptism, Christ took away all the flock of Satan and Himself grew rich."[17]

In the exodus, Saint Ambrose (ca. 339-397) tells us, "Holy Baptism was prefigured in that passage of the Hebrews, wherein the Egyptian perished and the Hebrew escaped. For what else are we daily taught in this sacrament, but that guilt is swallowed up and error done away, but that virtue and innocence remain unharmed?"[18]

In the life of Prophet Elisaios he healed the barren waters with salt [4 Kgs. (2 Kgs.) 2:19-22], "which prefigured the fruitfulness that the august Font should bring forth mystically."[19] Also he "sweetened the waters by means of salt, manifestly proclaiming the grace of Baptism."[20] Saint Kosmas says, "Jordan received into its deep bosom a sharp axe, and then was forced by a stick of wood to give it back again [4 Kgs. (2 Kgs.) 6:1-7], thus betokening the cutting of error by the Cross and Baptism."[21] At the prophet's behest, the Syrian leper Naaman washed seven times in the Jordan, and was cleansed [4 Kgs. (2 Kgs.) 5:14].

Saint Kyril of Jerusalem (ca. 349-386), speaking of the true circumcision mentioned by Prophet Jeremias, says, "By the likeness of our faith,...we become the adopted sons of Abraham; and consequent upon our faith, like him, we receive the spiritual seal, being circumcised by the Holy Spirit through the laver of Baptism, not in the foreskin of the body, but in the heart, according to the words of Jeremias: 'Circumcise yourselves to God, and circumcise your hardness of heart [Jer. 4:4],' and according to the apostle: 'In Christ, Jesus the Lord, also ye were circumcised with a circumcision made without hands, in the putting off of the body of the sins of the flesh in the circumcision of the Christ, having been buried with Him in the

---

[17] Saint Gregory of Nyssa, *On the Baptism of Christ*, Nicene, 2nd Ser., V:521, 522.
[18] Saint Ambrose, *On the Mysteries*, Ch. III, Nicene, 2nd Ser., X:318.
[19] January 5th, extract of Orthros Canon, Ode Seven, Mode One.
[20] June 14th, Orthros Ikos.
[21] September 14th, Exaltation of the Cross, Orthros Canon, Ode Four, Mode Plagal Four.

Baptism, in which also ye were raised with Him through faith in the energy of God, Who raised Him from the dead [cf. Col. 2:11, 12].'"[22]

Saint Basil the Great (ca. 330-379) interprets the triple immersion of the baptismal rite by the three days of Christ's burial in accordance with the sign of Jonas.[23] Saint John of Damascus regards the Prophet Jonas' three nights in the belly of the sea monster and his coming forth again as a manifestation beforehand of our being saved through the washing of regeneration [Titus 3:5] and our deliverance from the dragon that slays mankind.[24]

Saint Gregory of Nyssa (ca. 335-ca. 395) remarks that "most manifestly does Zacharias prophesy of the high priest Joshua (Jesus) [Zach. 3:4], a type of Christ, who was clothed with the filthy garment (to wit, the flesh of a servant, even ours); and stripping him of his ill-favored raiment, adorns him with clean and fair apparel. He teaches us by the figurative illustration that, verily, in the Baptism of Jesus, we, putting off our sins like some poor and patched garment, are clothed in the holy and most fair garment of regeneration."[25]

The Purpose of the Theophany and Baptism

Saint Kosmas, Bishop of Maiuma, tells us that "our Lord, Who clothed material flesh with the immaterial fire of His divinity, formed Adam anew, who fell into corruption, in the streams of the Jordan."[26] David prophesied, "Draw nigh unto Him and be enlightened, and your faces shall in no wise be ashamed. This poor man cried out, and the Lord heard him, and He saved him out of all his afflictions [Ps. 33:5, 6]." Saint Kosmas the Melodist chants, "Fallen Adam, the poor man, cried and the Lord heard him: He has come and in the streams of Jordan He has made him new again, who was sunk in corruption."[27]

Speaking eloquently upon Christian Baptism, Saint Justin Martyr (ca. 100-ca. 165) says, "As for this rite, we have learned from the apostles this reason. Since at our birth we were born without our own knowledge or choice, by our parents coming together, and were brought up in bad habits and wicked training, in order that we may not remain the children of necessity and of ignorance, but may become the children of choice and knowledge, and obtain in the water the remission of sins formerly committed, there is

---

[22] Saint Cyril of Jerusalem, *Catechesis V*, FC, 61:142, 143.
[23] Saint Basil, *On the Spirit*, Nicene, 2nd Ser., VIII:14, 32.
[24] January 6th, Theophany, Orthros Canon, Ode Six, Mode Two.
[25] Saint Gregory of Nyssa, *On the Baptism of Christ*, Nicene, 2nd Ser., V:522, 523.
[26] January 6th, Orthros Canon, Ode One, Mode Two.
[27] January 6th, Orthros Canon, Ode Nine, Mode Two.

pronounced over him who chooses to be born again, and has repented of his sins, the name of God the Father and Lord of the universe....And this washing is called Illumination, because they...are illuminated in their understandings. And in the name of Jesus Christ, Who was crucified under Pontius Pilate, and in the name of the Holy Spirit, Who through the prophets foretold all things about Jesus, he who is illuminated is washed."[28]

The Baptism

Holy Bishop Hippolytos of Rome asks, "Do you see, beloved, how the Prophet Esaias [Is. 1:16, 18] spake beforetime of the purifying power of Baptism? For he who comes down in faith to the laver of regeneration, renounces the devil, joins himself to Christ, denies the enemy, makes the confession that Christ is God, and puts off the bondage and puts on the adoption, comes up from the Baptism brilliant as the sun. Such a one, flashing forth the beams of righteousness, most importantly of all, returns a son of God and joint-heir with Christ."[29]

Saint Athanasios (ca. 296-373) says, "Christ divinized that which He put on, and gave it graciously to the race of man."[30] When we read, "And on behalf of them I sanctify Myself, that they also may be sanctified in truth [Jn. 17:19]," and "Now God anointed Him with the Holy Spirit [cf. Acts 10:38]," He Who sanctifies Himself is the Lord of sanctification. "If then, for our sake, He sanctifies Himself, and does this when He is become Man, it is very plain that the Spirit's descent on Him in the Jordan was a descent upon us, because of His bearing our body. For when the Lord, as Man, was washed in Jordan, it was we who were washed in Him

---

[28] Saint Justin Martyr, *First Apology of Justin*, LXI, Ante-Nicene, I:183.

[29] Saint Hippolytus, *Discourse of the Holy Theophany*, Ante-Nicene, V:237.

[30] Saint Athanasius, *Four Discourses Against the Arians: Discourse I*, Chapter XI(42), Nicene, 2nd Ser., IV:330.

and by Him. And when He received the Spirit, it was we who by Him were made recipients of the Spirit."[31]

"Moreover," says Saint Kyril of Jerusalem (ca. 315-386), "Jesus sanctified Baptism when He Himself was baptized. If the Son of God was baptized, can anyone who scorns Baptism pretend to piety? Not that He was baptized to receive the remission of sin—for He was without sin—but being sinless, He was nevertheless baptized, that He might impart grace and dignity to those who receive the Mystery."[32]

Saint Gregory of Nyssa explains the words of Esaias: "'Be glad, O thirsty wilderness: let the desert rejoice and blossom as a lily: and the desolate places of Jordan shall blossom and shall rejoice [Is. 35:1, 2].' It is clear that it is not to places without soul or sense that he proclaims the good tidings of joy: but he speaks by the figure of the desert, of the soul that is parched and unadorned, even as David also, when he says, 'My soul is unto Thee as a thirsty land [cf. Ps. 142:6],' and, 'My soul is athirst for the mighty, for the living God [cf. Ps. 41:2].' So again the Lord says in the Gospel, 'If anyone thirst, let him come to Me and drink [Jn. 7:37]'; and to the woman of Samaria, 'Everyone who drinketh of this water shall thirst again; but whosoever drinketh of the water which I shall give him in no wise shall ever thirst [Jn. 4:13,14].'"[33]

Saint Leo the Great (461), Pope of Rome, writes of our rebirth: "The Word became flesh by exaltation of the flesh, not by failure of the Godhead (Divinity) that so tempered its divine power and goodness as to exalt our nature by taking it, and not to lose His own by imparting it....For the earth of human flesh, which in the first transgressor was cursed, in this Offspring of the blessed Virgin only produced a seed that was blessed and free from the fault of its stock. And each one is a partaker of this spiritual origin in regeneration; and to everyone, when he is reborn, the water of Baptism is like the Virgin's womb; for the same Holy Spirit fills the font, Who filled the Virgin."[34]

Saint John Chrysostom tells of the prodigious renewal in the baptismal font: "All the fabric of our nature is framed above, of the Holy Spirit and water. The water is employed, being made the birth to him who is born. What

---

[31] Ibid., *Discourse I*, Chapter XII(47), IV:334.

[32] Saint Cyril of Jerusalem, *Catechesis*, FC, 61:115.

[33] Saint Gregory of Nyssa, *On the Baptism of Christ*, Nicene, V:523.

[34] Saint Leo, *Sermon XXIV, On the Feast of the Nativity, IV,* § 3, Nicene, 2nd Ser., XII:135.

the womb is to the embryo, the water is to the believer; for in the water he is fashioned and formed."[35]

Saint Ephraim the Syrian (ca. 306-383) writes: "Within the womb is the conception of all men; but here, out of the water, is the birth whereof the spiritual are worthy."[36]

Thus, the fruits of Baptism are manifold, according to both the prophets and the holy fathers. Saint Kyril of Jerusalem writes: "Great is the prize set before you in Baptism: ransom for captives, remission of sins, death of sin, a new spiritual birth, a shining garment, a holy seal inviolable, a heaven-bound chariot, delights of Paradise, a passport to the kingdom, the grace of the adoption of sons."[37]

The Baptism of John

Saint Chrysostom says that the Baptism of Christ "partook of the old, and it partook also of the new. To be baptized by the prophet marked the old, but the coming down of the Spirit foreshadowed the new....He hath joined the old covenant with the new, God's nature with man's, the things that are His with ours. Therefore the birth was twofold, both made like unto us, and also surpassing ours. For to be born of a woman indeed was our lot, but to be begotten not of blood, nor of the will of the flesh, nor of the will of man [cf. Jn. 1:13], but of the Holy Spirit, was to proclaim beforehand the birth surpassing us, the birth to come, which He was about freely to give us of the Spirit."[38]

Saint Chrysostom remarks upon the Baptist's response to those sent by the Pharisees who asked: "'Art thou Elias?...Who art thou?...What sayest Thou about Thyself [Jn. 1:21, 22]?' The holy Baptist answered, 'I am a voice crying in the wilderness, "Make straight the way of the Lord," even as the Prophet Esaias said [Is. 40:3; Jn. 1:23]'; and, 'I baptize in water; but there standeth One in your midst Whom ye know not. He it is, the One Who cometh after me, Who hath come to be before me, of Whom I am not worthy that I should loose the strap of His sandal [Jn. 1:26, 27].' John informed them who he was, and spoke of the nature of his own baptism, that it was but a slight and mean thing, nothing more than some water, and told of the superiority of the Baptism given by Christ."[39]

Saint Gregory the Great (ca. 540-604): "It is apparent to all who read, that John not only preached a baptism of repentance [Mk. 1:4; Lk. 3:3], but

---

[35] Saint Chrysostom, Homily XXVI, *On Saint John*, Nicene, 1ˢᵗ Ser., XIV:90.

[36] Saint Ephraim, *Hymns for the Feast of the Epiphany*, Nicene, 2ⁿᵈ Ser., XIII:277.

[37] Saint Cyril of Jerusalem, "Procatechesis," *Catechesis, Vol. 1*, FC, 61:82.

[38] Saint Chrysostom, Homily II, *On Saint Matthew*, Nicene, X:9, 10.

[39] Saint Chrysostom, Homily XVI, *On Saint John*, Nicene, XIV:56, 57.

likewise that he bestowed it on some; yet he was not able to bestow a Baptism for the remission of sins. Forgiveness of sins is bestowed upon us only by the Baptism of Christ. John was proclaiming a Baptism of repentance which would take away sins, but which he himself could not confer. As he preceded the incarnate Word of the Father by the word of his own preaching, so he preceded the Baptism of repentance, by which sins are taken away. And as in his preaching he went before the living presence of the Redeemer, so going before Him also in baptizing, his preaching of baptism was a foreshadowing of the Truth."[40]

Saint Ambrose: "John is the Forerunner of Christ, the law is the forerunner of the Church, and penitence that of grace."[41]

Blessed Jerome says, "Those who have received only John's baptism and have no knowledge of the Holy Spirit are baptized again, lest any should suppose that water unsanctified thereby could suffice for the salvation of either Jew or Gentile." If they who received the baptism of the Forerunner need holy Baptism, how much more those who are baptized outside of the Church?

Infant Baptism

Saint Kyril of Alexandria comments on the Gospel of Luke, writing: "The mothers, desiring His blessing, brought the babes, begging for their infants the touch of His holy hand [cf. Lk. 18:15-17]. I do not think that anyone will dispute that the passage means that parents desired Christ to bless their little children or infants. Now, here, although the infants plainly could neither bring themselves to Christ nor confess faith in His ability to sanctify them with His blessing, yet Christ not only blessed and sanctified them, but He even forbade anyone to hinder infants from being brought to be blessed and sanctified. If Christ considered the state of an infant no impediment to receiving His sanctifying blessing, why would He consider the infantile state a hindrance to Baptism?"[42]

Saint Dionysios the Areopagite (1st C.) responds to someone who was dubious about the worth of infant Baptism and the qualifications of the candidate's sponsor, writes: "But let me set down what our blessed teachers, in their knowledge of the earliest tradition, have passed down to us. What they say is this, and it is true. Children raised up in accordance with holy precepts will acquire the habits of holiness. They will avoid all the errors and

---

[40] Saint Gregory the Great, Homily 6, On the Mystical Church, *Forty Gospel Homilies*, Homily 6, 36, 37; Homily 20, *P.L.* 76 (col. 1160-1161).

[41] Saint Ambrose, *Exposition of the Holy Gospel According to Saint Luke*, Bk. II, § 68.

[42] Saint Kyril of Alexandria, *Commentary on the Gospel of Saint Luke*, Ch. 18, Homily 121, pp. 483-485.

all the temptations of an unholy life. Understanding the truth of this, our divine guides, the apostles, decided it was a good thing to admit children to holy Baptism, though on condition that the parents of the child would entrust him to some good teacher who is himself initiated in the divine things and who could provide religious teaching as the child's spiritual father and as the sponsor of salvation. Anyone thus committed to raise the child up along the way of a holy life is asked by the hierarch to agree to the ritual renunciations and to speak the words of promise. Those who scoff at this are quite wrong in thinking that the one is initiated into the divine mysteries instead of the other, for he does not say, 'I am making the renunciations and the promises for the child,' but 'the child himself is assigned and enrolled.' In effect what is said is this: 'I promise that when this child can understand sacred truth, I shall educate him and shall raise him up by my teaching in such a way that he will renounce all the temptations of the devil, that he will bind himself to the sacred promises and will bring them to fruit.' So I do not think there is anything ridiculous if the child is brought up with a godly upbringing, provided of course that there is a holy guide and sponsor to form holy habits in him and to guard him against the temptations of the devil. When the hierarch admits the child to a share in the holy Mysteries, it is so that the child may derive nourishment from this: so that he may spend his entire life in the unceasing contemplation of the divine things; that he may progress in his communion with them; that he may therefore acquire a holy and enduring way of life; and that he may be brought up in sanctity by the guidance of a holy sponsor who himself lives in conformity with God."[43]

Saint Irenaeos of Lyons (ca. 130-ca. 200) concurs and writes: "The Son of God came to save all persons by means of Himself—all, I say, who through Him are born again to God—infants, children, boys, youths, and old men."[44] Saint Hippolytos of Rome also says, "Baptize first the children; and if they can speak for themselves, let them do so. Otherwise, let their parents or other relatives speak for them."[45]

Saint Gregory the Theologian (ca. 388) urges parents and guardians to baptize their children, saying, "Give your child the Trinity, that great and noble Protector....Do you have an infant child? Allow sin no opportunity; rather, let the infant be sanctified from childhood. From his most tender age

---

[43] Saint Dionysios the Areopagite, disciple of Saint Paul and first Bishop of Athens (A.D. 95), made this written response in the 7th chapter of his epistle, entitled "On the Ecclesiastical Hierarchy," to Saint Timothy, disciple of Saint Paul and first Bishop of Ephesus, who had the question posed to him.

[44] Saint Irenaeos, *Against All Heresies*, Bk. 2, 22:4.

[45] Saint Hippolytos, *The Apostolic Tradition*, 21.

let him be consecrated by the Spirit. Do you fear the seal of baptism because of the weakness of nature? O, what a pusillanimous mother and of how little faith! But some will say, 'What do you have to say about those, being children, who are unaware of what is taking place and the grace inherent in the sacrament? Shall we baptize them too?' Certainly, especially if there is any pressing danger. Better that they be sanctified unaware, than that they depart unsealed and uninitiated."[46]

Saint John Chrysostom also lauds this practise of infant Baptism, preaching: "Blessed be God, Who alone does wonderful things! You have seen how numerous are the gifts of Baptism. Although many men think that the only gift it confers is remission of sins, we have counted its honors to the number of ten. It is on this account that we baptize even infants...that they too may be given the further gifts of sanctification, justice, filial adoption, and inheritance, that they may be brothers and members of Christ, and become dwelling places of the Holy Spirit."[47]

Councils and synods are also in favor of this usage. The Synod of Carthage (ca. 418/419) recognizes the regeneration of infants. It speaks on infant Baptism for the remission of sins in reference to the words of Saint Paul, "Therefore, even as through one man sin entered into the world, and death through sin, and thus death passed to all men, on account of which all have sinned [Canon 121]." In the year 816, at the Council of Celchyth (Canterbury, England), it was decreed: "Let ministers take notice that when they administer the holy Baptism, that they do not pour the holy water upon the heads of the infants, but that they be always immersed in the font; as the Son of God has in His own person given an example to every believer, when He was thrice immersed into the waters of the Jordan. In this manner it ought to be observed [Canon 6]."

Is There Holy Baptism Outside of the Church?

Prophet Jeremias wrote: "Why do they that grieve me prevail against me? My wound is severe; whence shall I be healed? It is indeed become to me as deceitful water, that has no faithfulness (as to healing) [Jer. 15:18]." Saint Cyprian (d. 258) asks, "What is this deceitful and faithless water? Certainly that which falsely assumes the resemblance of Baptism, and frustrates the grace of faith by a shadowy pretense. But if, according to a perverted faith, one could be baptized without (outside of Orthodoxy) and obtain remission of sins, according to the same faith he could also attain the Holy Spirit; and there is no need that hands should be laid on him when he comes, that he might

---

[46] Saint Gregory the Theologian, *Oration On Holy Baptism*, 40:17.
[47] Saint John Chrysostom, "Homily Addressed to Neophytes," *Baptismal Instructions: Third Instruction*, ¶ 6, Ancient Christian Writers, 31:57.

obtain the Holy Spirit and be sealed. Either he could obtain both privileges without by his faith, or he who has been without has received neither."[48] In an epistle to the bishops, Saint Cyprian states, "For certain no one can be baptized abroad outside the Church, since there is one Baptism appointed in the holy Church. And it is written: 'They have hewn out for themselves broken cisterns, which will not be able to hold water [Jer. 2:13].' And again, sacred Scripture warns, and says, 'Do thou abstain from strange water, and drink not of a strange fountain [Prov. 9:18].' It is required, then, that the water should first be cleansed and sanctified by the priest (bishop), that it may wash away by Baptism the sins of the one who is baptized; because the

The Baptism

Lord says by Prophet Ezekiel: 'I will sprinkle clean water upon you, and ye shall be purged from all your uncleannesses and from all your idols, and I will cleanse you. And I will give you a new heart, and will put a new spirit in you [Ez. 36:25, 26].' But how can he cleanse and sanctify the water who is himself unclean, and in whom the Holy Spirit is not? The Lord says, 'Whatsoever the unclean man shall touch shall be unclean, and the soul that touches it shall be unclean till evening [Num. 19:22].' Or how can he who baptizes give to another remission of sins, who himself, being outside the Church, cannot put away his own sins?[49]

"Furthermore, one is not born by the imposition of hands when he receives the Holy Spirit, but in Baptism, that so, being already born, he may receive the Holy Spirit, even as it happened in the first Adam. For first God formed him, and then breathed into his nostrils the breath of life. For the

---

[48] Saint Cyprian, "Epistle LXXII," Ante-Nicene Fathers, V:381.

[49] Saint Cyprian, "Epistle LXIX," Ante-Nicene, V:375, 376; and, "Letter 70," FC, 51:259.

Spirit cannot be received, unless he who receives should first have an existence. As the birth of Christians is in Baptism, while the generation and sanctification of Baptism are with the Spouse of Christ alone, Who is able spiritually to conceive and to bear sons to God, where and of whom and to whom is he born, who is not a son of the Church, so that he should have God as his Father, before he has had the Church for his Mother?"[50]

Saint Athanasios warns, "There are many other heresies too, which use the words only, but not in a right sense,...nor with sound Faith, and in consequence the water which they administer is unprofitable, as deficient in piety; so that he who is sprinkled by them is rather polluted by the irreligious than redeemed."[51] Saint Ambrose concurs, "The baptism of unbelievers does not heal, does not cleanse, but pollutes."[52]

Baptism must also be performed in the proper manner by the priest. Canon 50 of the holy apostles requires triple immersion as the proper form of Baptism. This is the tradition that has been handed down to us. Saint Basil says, "Whether a man has departed this life without Baptism, or has received a baptism lacking in some of the requirements of the tradition, his loss is equal."[53]

Canon 46 of the holy apostles clearly states: "We order any bishop, or presbyter, that has accepted any heretics' baptism or sacrifice, to be deposed; for 'what consonance hath Christ with Belial? Or what portion hath a believer with an unbeliever [2 Cor. 6:15]?'" The early document of *The Didache* cautions, "Let no one eat and drink of your Eucharist, but those baptized in the name of the Lord."[54] Saint Hippolytos also cautions, "Let all take care that no unbaptized person taste of the Eucharist...."[55]

"But," hypothesizes Saint Cyprian, "what if someone should say, 'What then shall become of those who in past times, coming from heresy to the Church, were received without Baptism?' The Lord is able by His mercy to give indulgence, and not to separate from the gifts of His Church those who by simplicity were admitted into the Church, and in the Church have fallen asleep. Nevertheless, it does not follow that, because there was error at one time, there must always be error; since it is more fitting for wise and God-fearing men gladly and without delay to obey the truth when laid open

---

[50] Saint Cyprian, "Epistle LXXIII," Ante-Nicene, V:387.

[51] Saint Athanasius, *Four Discourses Against the Arians: Discourse II*, Ch. XVIII(43), Nicene, IV:371.

[52] Saint Ambrose, *The Mysteries*, Ch. 3(23), FC, 44:13.

[53] Saint Basil, *On the Spirit*, Ch. X(26), Nicene, 2nd Ser., VIII:17.

[54] *The Didache, Teaching of the Twelve Apostles*, Ancient Christian Writers, p. 20.

[55] *Treatise on the Apostolic Tradition*, G. Dix, ed., Morehouse Pub., p. 59.

and perceived, than pertinaciously and obstinately to struggle against brethren and fellow-priests on behalf of heretics."[56]

Saint John Chrysostom leaves this warning to the bishops: "I do not think there are many bishops that shall be saved, but many more that perish....Do you not see what a number of qualifications a bishop must have? [cf. 1 Tim. 3:2-9; Tit. 1:7-9]. What troubles and pains does this require! And when others do wrong, he bears all the blame. To pass over everything else: if one soul departs unbaptized, does not this subvert all his own prospect of salvation? The loss of one soul carries with it a penalty, which no language can represent."[57]

On the 6th of January, the holy Church commemorates the holy New-martyr ROMANOS, Hieromonk of Lakedaimon, of the village of Diminitzes, who was slain by the sword at Constantinople (1695).

Through the intercessions of Thy Saints,
O Christ God, have mercy on us. Amen.

---

[56] Saint Cyprian, "Epistle LXX," Ante-Nicene, V:385.
[57] Saint Chrysostom, Homily III, *On Acts*, Nicene, 1st Ser., XI:23.

On the 7th of January, the holy Church commemorates the Synaxis of the honorable Prophet, Forerunner, and Baptist JOHN.

Saint John the Forerunner

John, the glorious prophet, Forerunner, and Baptist, is commemorated today by the holy Church. The word synaxis signifies a gathering or assembling. In this case, today's synaxis is an assembly of the congregation for public worship, with a vigil and Eucharist, and instruction regarding the feast day of Saint John, following the major Feast of the Theophany, in which he materially participated.

Saint John the Baptist's Life and Ministry

Saint Ephraim the Syrian (ca. 306-383) says that "the daughter (Elisabeth) of Aaron the priest gave birth to the voice in the desert [Is. 40:3; Mt. 3:3], and the daughter (Mary) of King David to the Logos of the heavenly King."[1] The hymnographers of the Church proclaim John as that "voice." Hear Elisabeth speaking to the Virgin Mary: "Whence is this to me, that the Mother of my Lord should come to me [Lk. 1:43]?" "Thou dost carry the King and I the soldier; thou the Law-giver and I the enactor of the law; thou the Logos, and I the voice proclaiming the kingdom of heaven [Is. 40:3]."[2] Saint Kyril of Jerusalem (ca. 349-386) observes: "John (the Baptist) alone, while carried in the womb, leaped for joy [Lk. 1:44]; and though he saw not with the eyes of the flesh, he knew his Master by the Spirit. For since the grace of Baptism was great, it required greatness in its founder also."[3] Saint Ephraim writes:

---

[1] *Saint Ephrem's Commentary on Tatian's Diatessaron*, Journal of Semitic Studies Supp. 2, 58.

[2] June 24th, Nativity of Saint John the Baptist, Vespers Theotokion, Mode Plagal Four.

[3] Saint Cyril of Jerusalem, *Catechetical Lectures: Lecture III*, Nicene, 2nd Ser., VII:16.

"He who was to baptize with water would proclaim Him Who would baptize in fire and in the Holy Spirit [cf. Mt. 3:11]."[4]

Saint Kosmas the Melodist (7th C.), referring to the prophecy of Esaias, chants: "He whom Thou hast called, O Lord, 'The voice of one crying in the wilderness,' heard Thy voice when Thou hast thundered upon many waters, bearing witness to Thy Son."[5] Prophet Esaias also said, "Be glad, thou thirsty desert: let the wilderness exult, and flower as the lily. And the desert places of Jordan shall blossom and rejoice [Is. 35:1, 2]." And, "The voice of one crying in the wilderness, 'Prepare ye the way of the Lord, make straight the paths of our God.'...And the glory of the Lord shall appear, and all flesh shall see the salvation of God, for the Lord hath spoken it [Is. 40:4, 5]."

Saint Kyril of Alexandria (378-444) says, "The blessed Esaias knew the work of the Forerunner in proclaiming Christ, and styled John His minister and servant, and said that he was a lamp advancing before

Saint John the Forerunner

the true Light, the morning star heralding the Sun. He foreshadowed the coming of the day that was about to shed its rays upon us; and that he was a voice, not a word, forerunning Jesus, as the voice does the word."[6]

Saint John Chrysostom (ca. 347-407) writes of the Forerunner's life and ministry: "Conceive, for example, how great a thing it was to see a man after thirty years coming down from the wilderness, being the son of a chief priest [Lk. 3:2], who had never known the common wants of men, and was

---

[4] *Saint Ephrem's Commentary on Tatian's Diatessaron*, loc. cit.
[5] January 6th, Theophany, Orthros Canon, Ode Four, Mode Two.
[6] Saint Cyril of Alexandria, Homily 6, *Commentary on the Gospel of Saint Luke*, Ch. 3, p. 69.

on every account venerable, and had Esaias with him....For so great was the earnestness of the prophets touching these things, that not their own Lord only, but him also who was to minister unto Him, they proclaimed a long time beforehand. And they not only mentioned him, but the place too in which he was to abide, and the manner of the doctrine which he had to teach when he came, and the good effect that was produced by him."[7]

Saint John the Forerunner

Saint Kyril of Alexandria also praises him, saying, "The blessed Baptist was entirely devoted to piety unto Christ; nor was there in him the slightest regard either for fleshly lusts or for the things of this world. Having altogether abandoned, therefore, the vain and unprofitable distractions of this world, he labored at that one and very urgent task of blamelessly fulfilling the ministry entrusted to him."[8]

Saint John Chrysostom speaks of the Baptist's single-mindedness: "See, at least, how both the prophet and the Baptist go upon the same ideas, although not upon the same words. Thus the prophet saith that he shall come, saying, 'Prepare ye the way of the Lord, make straight the paths of our God [Is. 40:3].' And he himself when he was come said, 'Produce therefore fruits worthy of repentance [Mt. 3:8],' which corresponds with, 'Prepare ye the way of the Lord.' Seest thou that both by the words of the prophet, and by his own preaching, this one thing is manifested alone: that he came making a way and preparing beforehand, not bestowing the gift, which was the remission, but ordering in good time the souls of such as should receive the God of all?"[9]

His humility is lauded by Saint Chrysostom: "The character and heavenly wisdom of the witness showed that his testimony proceeded not from

[7] Saint John Chrysostom, Homily XVI, *On Saint John*, Nicene, 1st Ser., XIV:56, 57.
[8] Saint Cyril of Alexandria, Homily 39, *Commentary*, p. 166.
[9] Saint John Chrysostom, Homily X, *On Saint Matthew*, Nicene, 1st Ser., X: 63.

flattery, but from truth; which is plain also from this, that no man prefers his neighbor to himself, nor, when he may lawfully give honor to himself, will yield it up to another, especially when it is so great as that of which we speak."[10]

The Festal Reading from the Gospel According to the Evangelist Luke

"The word of God came to be upon John, the son of Zacharias, in the wilderness [Lk. 3:2]." Blessed Theophylact (765-840) explains: "By 'the word,' he means the Holy Spirit or the command of God. The word of God, literally, 'came to be' or 'arose' upon John. This is in order that you may learn he did not call himself to bear witness concerning Christ, but rather was moved by the Holy Spirit."[11] Saint Ambrose, Bishop of Milan (374-397), adds that "Saint Luke fittingly says that the word of the Lord came to be upon John, so that the Church will not begin from a man, but from the Word."[12]

The Prophet Esaias wrote: "The voice of one crying in the wilderness, 'Prepare the way of the Lord; be making His paths straight [Lk. 3:3-6; cf. Is. 40:4, 5]. Every ravine shall be filled full, and every mountain and hill shall be made low. And the crooked ways shall be made a straight path, and the rough into smooth ways. And all flesh shall see the salvation of God.'" Saint Chrysostom comments: "Do you see how the prophet anticipated all by his words—the concourse of the people, the change of things for the better, the easiness of that which was preached?...He is signifying the exaltation of the lowly, the humbling of the self-willed, the difficulty of the law changed into easiness of faith. For it is no longer sweat and pains, but grace and forgiveness of sins, affording great facility of salvation....Now not only Jews and proselytes shall see the salvation of God, but all. The crooked things signify our whole corrupt life;...as many as were previously perverted, afterward they walked in the right way."[13] Saint Gregory the Great (ca. 590-604) explains this passage, saying, "What is here meant by ravines unless the humble, and by the hills and mountains but the proud?...The Gentiles shall receive the fullness of grace, and the Jewish race by reason of its error of pride which has caused it to swell, shall be brought low. Every ravine shall be filled, because the hearts of the humble will be replenished, by the teachings of sacred truth, with the gift of the virtues....Now crooked ways become straight when the hearts of sinners, twisted by evil, conform to the way of righteousness. And rough ways are changed to smooth when cruel and

---

[10] Saint Chrysostom, Homily XVI, *On Saint John*, Nicene, loc. cit.

[11] Blessed Theophylact, *P.G.* 123:292C (col. 736).

[12] Saint Ambrose, *Exposition of the Holy Gospel According to Saint Luke*, Bk. II, § 67.

[13] Saint Chrysostom, Homily 10, *Commentary on Saint Matthew the Evangelist*, *P.G.* 57:143 (col. 187).

wrathful men turn to the mildness of clemency, through the infusion of heavenly grace. Now what does this mean, that 'all flesh shall see the salvation of God'? We know that in this life not every man sees the salvation of God, which is Christ. So in his prophetic vision the prophet speaks of the day of the last judgment."[14]

Saint John said, "Produce fruits worthy of repentance [Lk. 3:8]." According to Saint Kyril, "The fruit of repentance is, in the highest degree, faith in Christ; and next to it, the evangelic mode of life, and in general terms the works of righteousness in contradistinction to sin, which the penitent must bring forth as fruits worthy of repentance."[15] The Baptist then says, "Think not to say within yourselves, 'We have Abraham for a father'; for I say to you that God is able from these stones to raise up children to Abraham [Lk. 3:8]." Saint Kyril observes that John "skillfully humbles their foolish pride. For of what benefit is nobility of birth, if men practise not the like earnest deeds, nor imitate the virtue of their ancestors? The relationship God requires is one in character and manners; so that it is a vain thing to boast of holy and good parents, while we fall short of their virtue."[16] With reference to the "stones," Saint Ambrose tells us that "although God can change and transform diverse natures, yet, because a mystery is of more benefit to me than a miracle, I should acknowledge in the (words of) Christ's Forerunner nothing greater than the building of the growing Church, which is constructed not of stony rocks, but of living stones [1 Pe. 2:4, 5], through the conversion of our spirits that rise into a habitation of God and pediment of the temple [Eph. 2:21, 22]....Therefore, faith is prophesied to be imparted to the stony hearts of the Gentiles."[17] Saint Gregory the Great agrees and writes: "The Gentiles, who worshipped stones, are properly signified by that name."[18]

The Forerunner then pronounced: "Even now the axe is laid at the root of the trees. Therefore every tree which produceth not good fruit is being cut out and cast into the fire [Lk. 3:9]." Saint Gregory the Great comments that "the tree is the entire human race. Our Redeemer is as it were an axe, made from haft of wood and steel, which is wielded by His humanity, but cuts by the power of His divinity. Even now it is laid at the root of the trees, because though He delays through patience, yet already He had declared that which the axe shall do. For everyone who has scorned to lay by the fruits of

---

[14] Saint Gregory the Great, Homily 6, On the Mystical Church, *Forty Gospel Homilies*, 37-40.

[15] Saint Cyril of Alexandria, Homily 7, *Commentary*, Ch. 3, p. 71.

[16] Ibid.

[17] Saint Ambrose, *Exposition*, Ibid., Bk. II, § 75.

[18] Saint Gregory the Great, Homily 6, *Forty Gospel Homilies*, 41.

good works has speedily found prepared for him the fiery consummation of Gehenna. Note that the axe is laid at the root, not at the branches. The unfruitful tree is cut out, thus destroying both offspring and parent, so that nothing remains from which an evil shoot may rise."[19]

The Baptist John answered those who asked whether or not he was the Christ, saying, "I indeed baptize you in water, but the One mightier than I cometh, of Whom I am not fit to loose the strap of His sandals. He shall baptize you in the Holy Spirit and in fire [Lk. 3:16]." Saint Kyril comments: "To be able to impart the Spirit to men suits not anyone whatsoever of things created, but, together with God's other attributes, is the distinct property of almighty God alone."[20] Saint Ambrose explains: "Since man is of two natures, namely, he subsists from a soul and a body, the visible is hallowed by the visible things, the invisible by an invisible mystery; for the body is washed in water, but blemishes of the soul are cleansed in the Spirit."[21]

What is the mystical significance of the sandal, when the Baptist says, "I am not fit to loose the strap of His sandals [Lk. 3:16]"? Blessed Jerome (ca. 342-420) says: "This seems to be an expression of humility, as though he were saying, 'I am not worthy to be His servant,' but, in these very simple words, there is evidence of another mystery, which is what we read in the Old Testament [Deut. 25:7-10; Ruth 4:7]."[22]

Saint Ambrose: "By law, when a man died, the marriage bond with his wife was passed on to his brother, or to another man that was next of kin, in order that the seed of the brother or next of kin might renew the life of the house. This is what happened in the case of Ruth who first loosed the shoe from the foot of him whose wife she ought, by the law, to have become [Deut. 25:5-10; Ruth 4:5-7]. The story is simple, but it is a foreshadowing of One Who was to arise from Jewry—whence Christ was, after the flesh—Who should, with the seed of heavenly teaching, revive the seed of His dead kinsman, that is to say, the people, and to Whom the precepts of the law, in their spiritual significance, assigned the sandal of marriage, for the espousals of the Church. Moses was not the Bridegroom [Ex. 3:5]...nor Jesus of Navee [Josh. 5:16(15)]....None other is the Bridegroom but Christ alone, of Whom the Evangelist John spoke [Jn. 3:29]. They, therefore, loose their shoes, but His shoe cannot be loosed, even as John the Baptist said, 'I am not worthy that

---

[19] Saint Gregory the Great, Homily 6, On the Mystical Church, § 10, *P.G.* 76 (cols. 1159-1170), in Toal, *Sunday Sermons*, I:92, 93.
[20] Saint Cyril of Alexandria, Homily 11, *Commentary*, Ch. 3, p. 79.
[21] Saint Ambrose, *Exposition*, Bk. II, § 79.
[22] Blessed Jerome, Homily 75(1), *Homilies 60-96, Vol. 2*, FC, 57:127.

I should loose the strap of His sandal [Jn. 1:27].'"[23] Saint Ambrose also explains that "Thus Christ alone is the Bridegroom to Whom the Church, His bride, comes from the nations, and gives herself in wedlock. Aforetime she was poor and starving, but now she is rich with Christ's harvest....But He also does not begrudge the Synagogue the sheaves of His harvest. Would that she had not of her own will shut herself out! She had sheaves that she might herself have gathered, but, her people, being dead, she, like one bereaved by the death of her son, began to gather sheaves, whereby she might live, by the hand of the Church, even as it is written: "The ones coming shall come with great joy, taking up their sheaves [Ps. 125:8].'"[24]

Saint Bede (ca. 673-735) admonishes us that "if we are attentive to the mystical meaning, this is clearly a reference to a decree of the law, for one who did not wish himself to receive a wife due to him, by the rule of next of kin, but wished instead to permit another to receive her, was ordered to give his sandal, undone from his foot, to the one who would receive her, as a sign of his permission in this regard [Deut. 25:5-9; Ruth 4:7]. And because the people believed, as a result of his virtues, that John was the Christ, they surely believed that he was the Bridegroom of the Church [Eph. 5:21-32]. But in order to show who he was, John himself said, 'The one who hath the bride is the bridegroom, but the friend of the bridegroom, who standeth and heareth him, rejoiceth with joy because of the bridegroom's voice [Jn. 3:29].' And so he did not allow them to believe that he was the Bridegroom, lest he should lose the Bridegroom's friendship, which is the meaning of his bearing witness that it was not befitting that he should undo Christ's sandals."[25]

Saint John then tells the people that the Christ has the winnowing fan "in His hand, and He will thoroughly purge His threshing floor, and will gather the wheat into His storehouse, but the chaff He will burn completely with fire unquenchable [Lk. 3:17]." Saint Ambrose explains: "Through the sign of the fan the Lord is said to have the right to distinguish merits, inasmuch as when the grain is winnowed on the threshing floor, the full are separated from the empty, the fruitful from the worthless, as if by a weighing of a blowing breeze. So through this comparison, the Lord is manifest, because on the day of judgment, He separates the merits and fruits of solid virtue from the unfruitful shallowness of worthless ostentation and inadequate deeds."[26]

Thus, Saint John "exhorted many and different things, he was preaching the good tidings to the people [Lk. 3:18]." Saint Bede observes,

---

[23] Saint Ambrose, *Of the Christian Faith*, Bk. III, § 71, Nicene, 2nd Ser., X:253.
[24] Ibid., Bk. III, §§ 70, 72, 73.
[25] Saint Bede, Homily 1.1, In Advent, *Homilies on the Gospels*, Book One, p. 6.
[26] Saint Ambrose, *Exposition*, Bk. II, § 82.

"Who could more fittingly prophesy the transference of the priesthood of the law and its replacement by the priesthood instituted in the Gospel than the son of a high priest under the law? Even though it would seem that John could have been a high priest according to the law, by reason of the inward and unchanging teaching of the truth, he preferred being a herald of the new priesthood rather than continuing as a successor and heir of the old."[27]

The Festal Readings from the Gospels
According to the Evangelists Matthew and Mark

John was clothed with camel hairs, and he wore a leathern belt about his loins [Mt. 3:4; Mk. 1:6]. The Venerable Bede remarks, "As regards the literal meaning, this shows the poor quality of the garments and means of sustenance to one who was a solitary and a herald of repentance; but, figuratively speaking, repentance and continence, which he carried out himself and also instructed others in, are represented by camel's hair, out of which sackcloth is made. A leather girdle, which is taken from a living thing that has died, expresses the fact that he had put to death his earthly members."[28] Saint Chrysostom tells us: "For this reason his outer garment was of hair, in order that by his form he might instruct the people to leave human things, and to have nothing in common with the earth, but to hasten back to their earlier nobility, wherein Adam was before he wanted garments and coverings. Thus that dress bore the tokens of a kingdom and repentance."[29]

As to his food, he ate locusts and wild honey [Mt. 3:4; Mk. 1:6]. Blessed Theophylact comments that "some say that the locusts are a kind of herb, which is also melagra; but others say it is a type of fruit growing on the upper branches of trees, especially hard-shelled fruits which were wild fruits."[30] Saint Bede writes: "By the locusts, which fly briskly up but quickly settle back to earth, and the wild honey, which he was eating as well, are suggested the brevity as well as the sweetness of his preaching; for, when he was preaching, the people willingly listened to him; and by coming so quickly to the Lord, he put an end to his own preaching and baptism."[31] Saint Ambrose says: "In the locusts we fittingly denote the Gentile people, who by no practise of labor, no fruit of their work, without dignity, without voice, produce the sound of complaint and ignore the word of life. So this people is the food of the prophets, for the more numerous a people is assembled, the

---

[27] Saint Bede, Homily II.19, Vigil of the Nativity of John the Baptist, *Homilies on the Gospels*, Book Two, p. 189.
[28] Saint Bede, Homily I.1, In Advent, *Homilies on the Gospels*, Book One, 4.
[29] Saint Chrysostom, Homily 10, *On Saint Matthew*, P.G. 57:144 (col. 188).
[30] Blessed Theophylact, *P.G.* 123:16BC (col. 172).
[31] Saint Bede, Homily I.1, In Advent, *Homilies on the Gospels*, Bk. I, 5.

more abundant the use of the prophet's mouth. Furthermore, the grace of the Church is prefigured in the wild honey, discovered not among the offspring of the Jewish people in the apiary of the law, but scattered by the error of the Gentiles in the plains and leaves of the forest, as it is written: 'We have found it in the plains of the wood [Ps. 131(132):6].' And he indeed ate wild honey, preaching that the peoples would be filled with the honey from the rock, as it is written: 'He satisfied them with honey out of the rock [Ps. 80(81): 15(16)].'"[32]

The Baptist John was proclaiming a baptism of repentance toward remission of sins. "And all the land of Judaea, and of Jerusalem, were going out to him; and all were being baptized in the Jordan River by him, confessing their sins [Mk. 1:4, 5]." Blessed Theophylact comments: "John preached the baptism of repentance which led toward the remission of sins....The Forerunner proclaimed the baptism of repentance so that those who repent and receive Christ would have the forgiveness of sins."[33] And elsewhere, "John's baptism gave neither spiritual grace nor the forgiveness of sin, but Christ will forgive you and give you the Spirit abundantly."[34]

Saint Gregory the Theologian, Archbishop of Constantinople (380), explains further, saying, "Let us here treat briefly of the different kinds of baptism. Moses baptized, but in water, in the cloud and in the sea; but this he did figuratively. John also baptized, not indeed in the rite of the Jews, not solely in water, but also toward remission of sins; yet not in an entirely spiritual manner, for he had not added, 'in the Spirit.' Jesus baptized, but in the Spirit; and this is perfection. There is also a fourth baptism, which is wrought by martyrdom and blood....There is yet a fifth, but more laborious, by tears."[35]

Saint John says that Christ "shall baptize you in the Holy Spirit and in fire [Mt. 3:11]." Saint Chrysostom comments: "'He shall baptize you in the Holy Spirit'; and by this metaphor he declares the abundance of the grace. For he said not, 'He shall give you the Holy Spirit,' but 'He shall baptize you in the Holy Spirit.' And by the additional mention of the fire, he again indicates the exceedingly strong and roving quality of the grace."[36]

The Festal Reading from the Gospel According to the Evangelist John

In the Gospel Reading for this day, Saint John records that John saw Jesus coming to him, and said, "Behold the Lamb of God Who taketh away

---

[32] Saint Ambrose, *Exposition*, Bk. II, §§ 71, 72.

[33] Blessed Theophylact, *Commentary on Saint Mark*, P.G. 123:175BC (col. 496).

[34] Idem, *Comm. on St. Matthew*, P.G. 123:18D (col. 176).

[35] Saint Gregory the Theologian, *Oration 39*, in Toal, *Sunday Sermons*, Vol. I:74, 75.

[36] Saint Chrysostom, Homily 11, *On Saint Matthew*, P.G. 57:154 (col. 197).

the sin of the world. This is He concerning Whom I said, 'After me cometh a Man Who hath come to be before me, for He was before me.' And I knew Him not; but that He should be made manifest to Israel, therefore I came baptizing in the water [Jn. 1:29-31]." Saint Chrysostom comments: "The Baptist is saying, 'My coming has no further object than to proclaim the common Benefactor of the inhabited world, and to afford the baptism of water. But this One cleanses all mankind and bestows the energy of the Spirit. 'He hath come to be before me,' that is, 'He is shown to be more brilliant than I, for "He was before Me [Jn. 1:15]."'"[37]

The Forerunner Declaring the Christ

Saint Chrysostom notes that the Baptist John "repeatedly says, 'I knew Him not.' On what account and wherefore? They were kinsmen according to the flesh....And that he may not seem to bestow glory upon Him because of the relationship, he continually says, 'I knew Him not [Jn. 1:31, 33].'"[38]

---

[37] Saint Chrysostom, Homily 17, *On Saint John*, *P.G.* 59:97 (col. 109).
[38] Ibid., Homily 17, *On Saint John*, *P.G.* 59:99 (col. 110).

The Spirit Descending as a Dove

John bore witness, saying, "I have beheld the Spirit descending out of heaven as a dove, and He abode upon Him. And I knew Him not, but the One Who sent me to baptize in water, that One said to me, 'Upon whomsoever thou shalt see the Spirit descending and abiding on Him, this is the One Who baptizeth in the Holy Spirit. And I have seen and have borne witness that this is the Son of God [Jn. 1:32-34].'"

Saint Matthew also writes: "And He saw the Spirit of God descending like a dove, and coming upon Him [Mt. 3:16]." It is not certain whether "He saw" refers to Christ or John. Saint John Cassian (ca. 360-435) comments: "Who saw? Christ indeed."[39] Saint Chrysostom: "The dove appears...that it might point out to them that were present, and to John, the Son of God."[40]

Saint Ambrose comments: "It was not a dove that descended, but the Holy Spirit 'as a dove [Mt. 3:16; Mk. 1:10].' Luke, however, added that 'the Holy Spirit descended in a bodily shape as a dove upon Him [Lk. 3:22].' You must not think that this was an incarnation, but an appearance. He, then, brought the appearance before him, that by means of the appearance he might believe who did not see the Spirit, and that by the appearance He might manifest that He had a share of the one honor in authority, the one operation in the mystery, the one gift in the bath, together with the Father and the Son....And he said fittingly, 'He abode on Him,' because the Spirit inspired a saying or acted upon the prophets as often as He would, but abode always in Christ. Nor, again, let it move you that he said 'upon Him,' for he was speaking of the Son of Man, because He was baptized as the Son of Man. For the Spirit is not upon Christ, according to the Godhead (Divinity), but in Christ; for, as the Father is in the Son, and the Son in the Father, so the Spirit of God and the Spirit of Christ is both in the Father and in the Son, for He is the Spirit of His mouth....He is, then, not over Christ according to the Godhead of Christ, for the Trinity is not over Itself, but over all things: It is not over Itself but in Itself."[41]

Saint Gregory the Great: "We must ask why the Spirit appeared over our Redeemer, the Mediator between God and men, like a dove? The Only-begotten is the Judge of the human race. Who could bear His righteousness if before He gathered us in through His gentleness He had willed to examine our sins through His righteous fervor? Having become Man, He showed Himself mild to us, willing rather to gather us than to smite us. He willed first

---

[39] Saint John Cassian, *The Seven Books of John Cassian on the Incarnation of the Lord, Against Nestorius*, Bk. III, Ch. XVI, Nicene, 2nd Ser., XI:572.

[40] Saint John Chrysostom, Homily 12, *On Saint Matthew*, *P.G.* 57:163 (col. 205).

[41] Saint Ambrose, *Of the Holy Spirit*, Bk. III, Ch. I, ¶¶ 3-6, Nicene, 2nd Ser., X:136.

to correct us gently....Thus, the Spirit appeared over Him like a dove, since He was not coming to smite our sins now in His fervor, but to continue to put up with them in His gentleness."[42]

Saint Athanasios, Archbishop of Alexandria (328), observes that "the Spirit's descent on Him in the Jordan was a descent upon us, because of His bearing our body. For when the Lord, as Man, was washed in the Jordan, it was we who were washed in Him and by Him. And when He received the Spirit, it was we who by Him were made recipients of the Spirit."[43]

On the 7th of January, the holy Church commemorates the translation of the most honored hand of the FORERUNNER JOHN to Constantinople.

Today we celebrate the Synaxis of the glorious Prophet and Forerunner, John the Baptist, for he ministered in the mystery of the Lord's Baptism, and this feast has been observed by our forefathers. Now in conjunction with this holy day, there is also numbered another feast of the Forerunner. It is mentioned here, not only because his marvellous and preternatural gifts should not remain hidden, but also because the translation of his sacred right hand had coincided with the eve of the holy Theophany. Therefore, we shall narrate herein in what manner the sacred relic reached Constantinople.

It is recorded that, in the city of Sebasteia, the sacred relic of the honorable Forerunner was buried. The Evangelist Luke visited that site, taking the right hand of the prophet, and bringing it to his home in Antioch, where it wrought numerous miracles, one of which is the following. In the outskirts of Antioch, there lurked a dragon, which the idolaters had deified, and honored annually with human sacrifices. One year, by chance, the lot fell to a certain Christian to offer his daughter to the dragon. It would be a fearful sight to behold as that creature emerged from its cave, opening its mouth, and crushing and devouring the sacrificial victim in its jaws.

The father of the maiden besought God and the divine Baptist with tears and sighs to liberate his country from this dreadful scourge. As he entreated God, he conceived the following plan (for he who is in dire need, easily finds a means out of his crisis). He asked permission to venerate the sacred hand of the Baptist. Now while he kissed it, he bit off the thumb with his teeth. After accomplishing this, he exited the temple stealthily. When the

---

[42] Saint Gregory the Great, Homily 30, *Forty Gospel Homilies*, 240-243; cf. Homily 30, *P.L.* 76 (col. 1220).

[43] Saint Athanasius, *Four Discourses Against the Arians*, Discourse I, Ch. XII(47), Nicene, 2nd Ser., IV:333.

day of his daughter's sacrifice arrived, a great multitude assembled. The father went with his daughter, and together they drew nigh before the dragon. When the dragon opened its jaws to devour his only daughter, the father pitched the sacred thumb of the Forerunner into its mouth. Lo, the miracle! The dragon fell dead on the spot. After this, the father took his daughter and returned to his house, joyfully proclaiming the miracle to everyone. The multitudes, witnessing this marvel, were astonished. They exceedingly praised the God of the Christians and the divine Baptist. In thanksgiving, they erected a splendid and spacious church to the Forerunner.

Concerning the holy and sacred hand of the Baptist, it is said that, during the day of the Exaltation of the Holy Cross, commemorated by the holy Church on the 14th of September, the hand would rise at times, flexing or clenching its fingers. By these intermittent signs, the Baptist indicated either future happiness or misfortune. For this reason, many sovereigns desired to possess this priceless treasure, especially the emperors of the Macedonian Dynasty, Constantine VII Porphyrogennetos (b. 905; r. 945-959) and his son and co-emperor (945), Romanos II (b. 939; r. 959-963). When they governed the empire of the Romans, they set after this prize, by having the sacred hand procured through a deacon named Job. According to Christian tradition, on the eve of the holy Theophany, the waters are sanctified. Hence, the God-loving Emperor Constantine venerated the hand with great respect and treasured it in his royal palace. The Synaxis of Saint John took place in the Phorakion. Presently, one relic of his hand is at the Athonite Monastery of Dionysiou, which is dedicated to Saint John the Baptist and celebrates his nativity on the 24th of June. Another relic of his forearm is in a glass display case at the Seraglio (Topkapi Saray), which had been the palace of the Ottoman sultans in Constantinople.[44]

On the 7th of January, the holy Church commemorates the miraculous event of the FORERUNNER JOHN in Chios.[45]

John, the honored Forerunner of Christ, performs many miracles from time to time, one of which is the following. In 1740, the great Forerunner and wondrous right hand of God wrought a superb and wonderful

---

[44] Saint John was exceedingly venerated at Constantinople, where he had thirty-six churches and monasteries dedicated to his memory, of which the most famous was the Stoudios; others were Lips, the Prodromos in Petra, and in Sphorakion, etc. The Monastery of Phoverou on the Asiatic shore of the Bosporos was also dedicated to the Forerunner. *The Oxford Dictionary of Byzantium*, s.v. "John the Baptist."

[45] The narration of this miracle was authored by the ever-memorable and holy teacher Athanasios of Paros, which text was taken from the *Neon Leimonarion*.

miracle, which is commemorated and heralded everywhere, as it was recorded with the utmost exultation by those who were eyewitnesses and participated in the events of that time.

On the outskirts of the city in the vicinity known as Atzike, a short distance from the countryside, there was a church dedicated to the honored and glorious Prophet John the Forerunner and Baptist. In the surrounding area, there were many minarets of the Moslems, near which there was no mosque. By necessity, the Moslems were made to travel to the countryside, where there were mosques, in order to say their prayers. In Islam, one is compelled to fulfill this, especially at the times of Ramazan and Bairam. This presented a hardship to them, especially during the winter, when the weather was very cold and the rains heavy.

Therefore, what did these wicked neighbors of the divine Baptist scheme in their minds? The foolish ones plotted to take the holy church by force, for the purpose of converting it into their own sacrilegious mosque. These were not common or insignificant citizens belonging to the lower class. They were among the foremost of the Ottoman citizenry, better known as aghas (military and civil officers) and beys (district governors), totaling seven in number. They slyly determined that the lawless deed, which they were about to perpetrate, should not be executed arbitrarily. In order to have the seizure appear legitimate, they sought imperial support by decree.

They sent letters to the Kapitan-Pasha and to other prominent Chiotes who were members of the royal court, in order to obtain with their cooperation the desired firman (mandate, order, or license) to suit their insidious purpose. However, two of the aforementioned seven beys did not concur with the method. They even attempted to dissuade their coreligionists, admonishing them, "Do not commit such an act. You might suffer ridicule in the end." Furthermore, they refused to sign the letters, which the others drafted, but their objections went unheeded. The letters were sent by sea with a trusted messenger. It seemed as if these accursed ones would have succeeded in their impious endeavor had not God intervened from on high; for He is the Helper of the helpless and of victims of injustice. Moreover, He is the Protector of our holy Faith, Who foiled the desecrators' godless scheme in the following paradoxical manner. (Therefore, I pray thee, brethren, give proper attention.)

It was the evening of the 7th of January, which is the Synaxis of the great Forerunner and the feast day of the aforesaid church which was under attack. When this Christian holy day coincided with a religious holiday of the Turks, the above-mentioned beys rode to the countryside on horseback, in order to observe the festival according to their custom. That very night, there was a frightening earthquake. This caused great panic in the church of the divine Baptist, so that the priest, sacristans, and congregation were utterly

terrified; for it seemed to them that the roof of the church would surely collapse. With these fearful signs, the great Forerunner demonstrated that he
would zealously guard his sacred church from defilement on that night of his
hallowed feast. As the beys returned from the country, six of them stopped
at the tower, the one near the bridge, where they conducted all their meetings.
This time, however, it was the seventh dignitary who did not share in their
opinion. He continued on his way, even though the others pressed him to ride
along with them. Though not persuaded, he yet answered them, "I will go to
my house, leave my horse, and return."

The tower was three stories high. The severe winter cold forced them
to stay on the first floor, which was the warmest. In the company of those six
dignitaries was the other one who objected to the original plans of the five to
confiscate the church. They sat proudly and joyfully inside the tower as they
boasted about what they had done. One of them dared to brag in a haughty
tone that he would climb to the top of the church and deliver the impious
sermon of their religion. At that moment, before the first objector came
back—behold, thy supreme and mighty power, O Forerunner!—the three
floors suddenly collapsed and fell on top of the five audacious ones, crushing
them to death. They all descended into Hades alive, perishing on account of
their iniquities, while no one else was harmed in that building. (According to
Islamic custom, the women's quarters were kept separate.) It is obvious,
therefore, that the collapse of that building was the work of divine wrath in
that only the men's side collapsed and not the women's (which was filled with
innocent women and children). More paradoxical than this (apparently the
work of divine wrath), two great slabs of stone fell edgewise, joining to form
a vault. Beneath these, the one who had been opposed to the impious plan of
the others was preserved unscathed. When rescue efforts began to recover the
bodies, that man shouted from beneath the rubble that he was still alive. He
was rescued and found to have suffered no harm, not even the slightest
damage to his clothing.

What evidence is greater than this? The divine Forerunner sent the
five impious ones to their destruction, while the innocent Turk, who took his
horse home, lived for thirty more years. The other Turk, whose name was
Toptzibasis, was also spared. He was found safe in the tower and lived to a
venerable age. Toptzibasis was hailed by all that he had escaped miraculously.
As for the other villainous ones, divine justice dealt with them. The godless
letters were lost at sea, and the messenger was drowned. Thus, the divine
Forerunner completed his work. It would have been an easy task for the
enemies of the Faith to distort the truth, for they could have said that he was
drowned by the Christians. To this end, divine providence plunged the entire
ship to the bottom of the sea with its crew, extinguishing the hopes of the

godless ones. The following day, news reached the countryside concerning the fate of those grossly irreverent ones, thereby causing two emotions to emerge. Among the infidels there could be found great mourning, lamentation, and sorrow, mixed with intense shame and humiliation; while amidst the Christians the contrary truly existed—happiness, joy, and exultation.

The result of all this was that the words of the Psalter came to pass: "For wrath is in His anger, but in His will there is life; at evening shall weeping find lodging, but in the morning rejoicing [Ps. 29:5]." The designs of the infidels were evident, as they revealed their plan with haughtiness; but the divine Forerunner frustrated and thwarted them, since it was impossible to prevent the schemes of the lawless ones by human means. Divine wrath was so pronounced that to this very day the tower remains desolate with only four walls standing in testimony to the Scriptural verse: "The Lord scattereth the plans of the heathens [Ps. 32:10]." Likewise, the Davidic prophecy, or imprecation, was made manifest: "Let their habitation be made desolate, and in their tents let there be none to dwell [Ps. 68:30]." For the pious Christians this was a pleasant and welcome sight; yet, at the same time, mourning and everlasting shame befell the unbelievers. There are additional indications which attest to the truth of this splendid miracle. Nevertheless, we do not wish to exceed our bounds. Hence, after confining our account to the details already mentioned, which have been proven irrefutable, we bring this account to a close, glorifying the Worker of wonders, Jesus Christ, and His great Forerunner and Baptist John, to the ages of the ages. Amen.

On the 7th of January, the holy Church commemorates the holy New-martyr ATHANASIOS of Attaleia, who suffered martyrdom in Smyrna (1700).[46]

The holy New-martyr Athanasios was born in Attaleia.[47] While he was in Smyrna on the Aegean coast of Asia Minor, he encountered the Ottomans. They were constantly harassing him, while jeering and laughing at the Faith of the Christians. But the blessed one, even though an illiterate, always answered them with logic and wisdom. He often rendered them speechless, as they were unable to refute what Athanasios asserted. They

---

[46] The account of the martyrdom of New-martyr Athanasios was taken from Nikodemos the Hagiorite's *Neon Martyrologion*, 3rd ed. (p. 109), and incorporated into *The Great Synaxaristes* (in Greek).

[47] Attaleia (mod. Antalya) had been a city and bishopric of Pamphylia of southern Asia Minor, and then capital of the Kibyrrhaiotai theme. It had formerly been a main base of both the Byzantine navy and the imperial post. It was taken by the Italian Aldobrandini family circa 1204 and by the Seljuks in 1207. *Oxford*, s.v. "Attaleia."

were ashamed of the frivolous doctrines of their faith; and so they conspired to slander and trap him.

On a certain day—"I know not how," says the author—Athanasios shouted aloud the *lai-lala* in their own tongue. Now in Islam, this declaration constitutes a doxology to their Allah and is sometimes considered as their creed. Immediately, the Muslims surrounded him. They seized him and led him before the judge, charging him with accepting their religion publicly. Athanasios in turn replied that the words which he uttered were not a confession of faith, but in and of itself it was only a doxology of God—and it is permissible for all to recite it. But his accusers insisted that he had accepted Mohammedanism and disavowed Christ. Objecting to this, the blessed one said they spoke falsely and that he would rather receive ten thousand deaths than renounce the Orthodox Faith. They imprisoned him, bringing him up for repeated interrogations and floggings, further threatening him with other gruesome tortures. They also attempted to sway him by flattery and promises of gifts. Nevertheless, the contestant of Christ considered all these as child's play.

Finally the judge recognized that Athanasios' beliefs were steadfast and immovable, and handed down the decision of death. The blessed martyr was beheaded, receiving the crown of martyrdom in the year 1700. His sacred relics were discarded carelessly and exposed for three days beside a lair of wild dogs, yet none of these dogs approached the martyr. At the same time, on the evening of one of those days, two condemned Ottomans were also beheaded. Since there was insufficient time to bury their corpses, they were abandoned till the morning. The dogs, nonetheless, tore the Ottoman corpses apart and devoured them. The Turks later rationalized that the dogs consumed the bodies of the Turks because they were sweet and savory, while the flesh of the Christian was spurned. After three days, the Christians received the judge's permission to gather up the relics of Saint Athanasios, which they interred with honor in the Church of Saint Paraskeve.

Through the intercessions of Thy Saints,
O Christ God, have mercy on us. Amen.

**On the 8th of January, the holy Church commemorates
our venerable Mother
DOMNICA of Carthage.**

Domnica, namesake of the Lord, was born in 384 at Carthage of Africa,[1] during the reign of Emperor Theodosios I the Great (379-395). After completing her education, she traveled to Constantinople in the company of four other maidens. At that time, Domnica was ignorant of God, but was enlightened to the knowledge of true Faith in Christ while in the capital of Byzantium. Inspired by the Holy Spirit, Patriarch Nectarios of Constantinople (381-397) vouchsafed Domnica and her companions the holy Mystery of Baptism.

After the divine initiation, all five young ladies answered the blessed call to become nuns. The sanctified virgin Domnica struggled courageously in holy asceticism, wherein she reached the heights. It pleased God to grant longevity to Domnica, who never once vacillated in her God-fearing zeal. During her monastic life, she soared above the snares of the flesh and became the shepherdess of a flock of sacred souls.

Our holy mother, during her long life, was granted divine grace by God that she might perform miracles for those who took recourse in her. One

Saint Domnica

such wonder included rescuing sailors, tempest-tossed at sea, by transforming the storm into calm. God also bestowed the gift of clairvoyance upon the goodly maiden. A divine voice spoke mysteries, so that she knew many events beforehand, including the death of the emperor. She also knew precisely the day of her own repose. This radiant virgin reposed in the Lord in about the year 474.

---

[1] Carthage is situated on a peninsula in the Gulf of Tunis opposite western Sicily. It was ideally located to dominate the western Mediterranean, both commercially and politically. By 258, the administrative ability of Saint Cyprian, Bishop of Carthage, transformed the see into the ecclesiastical capital of Africa outside Egypt. Several important synods, under Saint Cyprian in 251, 252, 254, 255, and 256, met in Carthage where, early in the fourth century, began the schism of the Donatists, which rent the African Church for over a century.

On the 8th of January, the holy Church commemorates our venerable Father GEORGE the Chozevite.[2]

Saint George

George the Chozevite, out holy father, was born in a village on the island of Cyprus. His parents lived piously, and their substance was moderate. He had an elder brother named Herakleides who, while his parents were still alive, went to the holy city of Christ our God, to worship at the holy places. After his descent to the Jordan River, Herakleides visited and worshipped at the Lavra at Kalamon. It was there that Herakleides became a monk. Meanwhile, the commendable George remained alone with his parents and was reared in every form of piety and respect.

Not long afterward, his parents reposed, and the youth was orphaned. His uncle took him, along with the possessions that George had inherited. Since the uncle had an only daughter, he planned to have them marry. The youth, however, abhorred secular concerns and did not wish to be married, so he fled to another uncle who was the hegumen of a monastery. The holy George, as his brother Herakleides, desired to live a monastic life. Now when the uncle who controlled the articles of his inheritance learned that George was there, he went and argued with the hegumen, his own brother, demanding that their young nephew be returned to him. The hegumen replied, "I did not entice our nephew to come here; therefore, neither will I drive him away. He is of age; let him choose what is most profitable to him!" When the young George learned that his two uncles quarreled over him, he abandoned everything and left Cyprus. After he reached the holy city of Jerusalem and worshipped at the holy places of Christ our God, he descended to the area

---

[2] The wonderful account of Saint George the Chozevite, in its entirety, was written in Greek by his student Anthony, in about A.D. 600, or a few years after the destruction of Palestine by the Persians. Until recently the text was completely unknown, as it was discovered in a manuscript of the 10th C. at the Coeslinian Library in Paris (No. 303), from which it was published in 1888 by the Bollandists (*Analecta Bollandiana*, Vol. VII). It was reprinted by Cleopas Koikylides, Archdeacon of the Patriarchate of Jerusalem, in 1901. Recently, in 1962, it was published by the Chozevites, Abbot Amphilochios and the Monk Paul, at the Hagioritic Library of Soterios Schoinas in Volos.

about the Jordan River. After praying there, he joined Herakleides at the Lavra of Kalamon. When his brother saw that George was just a beardless adolescent, he did not think it wise to keep him in the lavra, in accordance with the rules of the holy fathers. Therefore, he led his brother to the Monastery of the Holy Mother of God, named Chozeva. There, Herakleides entrusted George to the hegumen and then returned to his cell.

The hegumen, after he observed the youth's fervor and monastic piety, tonsured him a monk. Shortly thereafter, he garbed him with the holy Schema. Then he summoned an elderly monk, one proficient in austerity, who held the office of gardener, and assigned George to assist him. The elder was a native of Mesopotamia and was extremely harsh. One day, he sent the young monk to the winter torrent to fetch water, which proved inaccessible. Father George, moreover, had gotten tangled up in the reeds and was unable to draw any water; therefore, he returned with nothing. The elder ordered him to take off his outer garment and to garb himself with only his rason. He was then dispatched to bring back water. Now since Father George was late in returning, the elder hid his garment and went directly to the communal meal or trapeza. When the young monk returned and found neither the elder nor his garment, he went to the monastery without his outer garment or cassock. After he knocked at the door, the caretaker opened up. When he saw Father George improperly clad and nearly naked, he asked, "What has happened to thee, father?" George explained what occurred. Then the caretaker brought him a garment and admitted him into the monastery.

As his elder was returning from trapeza, he met George by the tombs of five holy fathers who were laid to rest in that place. He looked upon George with anger and scorn. Then he raised his hand and struck the young monk across the face, demanding, "Why wast thou late?" At once, the old man's whole arm shriveled from top to bottom! Then he fell down before the youth, imploring and saying to him, "My child, do not expose me, nor ridicule nor deride me. But forgive me, and plead on my behalf before the Lord that I may be cured." The youth replied with humility and meekness, "Go, father, and make a prostration before the tombs of the saints; and they shall heal thee." But the elder persisted, begging him, saying, "It is thee whom I have sinned against. Do thou beseech God on my behalf." Then the righteous George took him by the hand, and together they went to the sepulcher of the saints, and bowed down. As they prayed, the elder was immediately healed. Henceforth, the elder became meek, submissive, and very respectful. Soon, the entire brotherhood learned of this incident. Everyone was overwhelmed by the extraordinary miracle and glorified God, especially as it had been wrought by a youth and a beginner. Father George, for his part, was frightened by the bait of vainglory. He thereupon secretly left the monastery and descended to the lavra, the one near his brother, with whom he lodged in the so-called "Old Church." Their manner of life in this place was as follows. Never did they partake of food which was cooked on the fire, except when they were visited by others. The doorman of the tower was ordered to keep the leftover food from one Sunday to the next. By this, the brothers sustained themselves. The basin used for food was never washed, nor was it emptied. It abounded with worms, so that the stench it emitted was sensed from afar. They never tasted wine. These things were sufficient to them.

There was once a farmer from Jericho, who was dearly loved by the brothers. He had an only child, an infant, that—alas!—died. Thereupon, the father placed the dead infant into a basket. On top, he placed a few fruits, which he had grown, and then covered them with vine leaves. He then took the basket and went to the lavra. Once there, he knocked on the door to the cells. Abba George came out and let him in. After the farmer entered, he made a prostration to the monastery elder and then placed the basket in front of the brethren, requesting that they bless the fruit of his field. He then took their leave. The brothers took the fruits from the basket, only to find the dead infant. When Abba Herakleides beheld the dead infant, he was shaken and said to his brother, "Call the man back, for temptation has visited us sinners today." Then Father George, who at that time was forty years of age or more, bowed before Abba Herakleides and said, "Do not distress thyself, father, neither be thou angered. Instead, let us beseech the all-merciful and benevolent God with faith. If He should overlook our sins and resurrect the child, then the father would receive the babe alive, even according to his faith, and depart strengthened in God. If His divine grace will not grant this request, then we shall call the father and say, 'We are sinful men and have not obtained such heights, nor do we have such boldness before God.'" The elder was persuaded. Thus, they stood in prayer, shedding tears and offering contrite hearts. The all-merciful God and Lover of man does the will of those who fear Him. He hearkened to their supplications and resurrected the child. Then they called the child's father and said to him, "Behold, thy son lives by the mercy of God. Do not tell anyone of this, lest thou shouldest bring upon us toil, trouble, and affliction." The farmer received his son and departed, blessing and glorifying the benevolent, merciful, and life-giving God.

Thus, they went through their lives in piety and devotion. No one ever saw them quarrel or in a disagreement, for the elder brother had much respect and meekness, and Abba George was obedient and humble. At age seventy or more, Abba Herakleides completed his present life as a man full of goodness and faith, adorned with all the virtues and famed throughout the Jordan Valley as a virgin, a man of stillness, and merciful. He had no possessions and was continent above everyone else. Throughout his life, he followed the diet that we mentioned before, eating only every two or three days, or even only once a week. He attained such virtue with that regimen so that if the occasion called for a common meal with the fathers and they urged him to attend, he yielded to their will. But if he did not mix his own food with what was served, he did not eat. He always fell ill on account of his austerity. He also possessed the mother of the virtues, humility. This is why he never wished to stand in the choir of the holy fathers in church while chanting, judging himself unworthy to stand among them. He always stood in a corner of the church, wearing an old rason and a mantle over his head, and recited the Psalms from the beginning of the service, with many tears and without speaking to anyone at all. Therefore, the fame of the miracles Christ wrought through him went abroad. After Abba Herakleides shined thus with a pious and God-pleasing life, he finished his course in a good old age and was buried there, in the tombs of the holy fathers. And now, with the choirs of the saints, he intercedes unceasingly with boldness before God on our behalf and for all the world.

Thus, afterward, Abba George was alone in the cell. He grieved and lamented the death of his brother. Nevertheless, he courageously continued his way of life and austerity, being beloved by all. Many times he served the fathers with peace and devotion, as he had received the dignity of the diaconate, wherein he served with fear and contrition. He strengthened everyone, liturgizing and assisting them.

One day, a necessity arose, and Father George had to leave the monastery. When he opened the door, he saw a lion sitting in the entrance-way. Now, because he had no fear in his heart, he pushed the beast with his foot in order to gain access, so that he could continue with his obedience. The lion growled slightly and shook its tail, not wishing to leave. Then Abba George pushed him two or three times with his foot, so as to make room; but because the beast would not obey, he said to it, "Well then, because thou dost not have obedience, as it is written in holy Scriptures, 'The Lord hath broken the great teeth of the lions [Ps. 57:6].' Blessed be the Lord. Therefore, open thy mouth, and we shall see." The lion then reluctantly opened its mouth, allowing Father George to look inside as he wished. The saint put his hand into the beast's mouth. After he touched his teeth, he said: "As one touches a stake imbedded in a wall, thus are the teeth of a lion." Then the lion arose and left, and the saint departed and went about his chores.

At that time, the hegumen of the lavra reposed, and his death resulted in great dissension and internal discord. In attempting to select a new abbot, the monks divided into two factions. So, they began to break the rules of the lavra and the customs of their fathers. For this, the elder was grieved and distressed. He besought God to reveal to him where he might go. Suddenly, he beheld a vision of two tall and luminous mountains. One was much taller and brighter than the other. Now the one who showed him this vision, said to him, "Where dost thou wish to ascend and dwell?" And the elder requested the taller of the two mountains. Then the one that appeared to the blessed one said, "Ascend therefore to the monastery in which thou wast tonsured a monk, and dwell in the Cells." As soon as George reached this place, he besought to be accepted by the hegumen of the monastery, Leontios, a very kind man, who was merciful and a friend of the poor. He had achieved such virtue through almsgiving that, after his repose, one of the elders saw the holy Leontios standing completely enveloped in fire before the altar.

The elder, upon seeing his disciple, was most gladdened in spirit. He immediately assigned Father George a cell. So he ascended and dwelt in the cells at Chozeva. No one knew how he fared or conducted himself in his cell, except that he had neither wine, nor oil, nor bread, nor garments, other than a short rason that he wore in church. He made the rounds of all the refuse containers, collected rags and, after he sewed them together, made his garment; from this same material, he made his mattress. He also begged the kitchen cellarers to keep the leftovers from the trapeza of the fathers, from one Sunday to the next, including those of the visitors, whether they were vegetables, legumes, or shellfish. Afterward, he took these and ground them with a stone mortar and made spheres, which he dried up in the sun. After he soaked them in water, he ate them, once every two or three days, if he ate at all in his cell. On every Saturday evening, the cell dwellers had the custom of going to the coenobium and participating in the vigil service, divine Liturgy, and the trapeza of the fathers of the monastery. "After the incursion of the Persians, we," writes the author of this present life, Anthony, "and a few brethren, climbed up to the monastery; and, believe me, O reverend fathers and brethren, when we entered his cell and found the leftover spheres, then were we amazed as to how he used them."

When the Persians reached Damascus, a great panic occurred in that land. One day, the blessed one sat on a rock, warming himself in the sun, since he had become very thin from excessive abstinence. As one who had become completely inflamed by spiritual love for the fulfillment of the divine will, he supplicated the man-loving God with continuous tears to take pity upon His people. Abba George then heard a voice, "Go down to Jericho and see the works of the people." Then he arose; and, since certain brothers of the coenobium were also descending to Jericho, he went with them. When they arrived just before the city's gardens, suddenly he heard in the air a great commotion of people who fought among themselves. They dealt blows to each other and yelled aloud, as in a battle. So he raised his eyes upward and saw the air filled with Indians, clashing against each other as in fray. Thereupon the earth shook and trembled beneath their feet.

Then the brethren said to the saint, "Come, father, so we may enter into the city. Why dost thou stand fixed in one place so long, gazing into the air?" The holy George replied in affliction and tears, "Let us leave, O brethren, and go back. Do you not see and feel the earth shaking?" As he said these things, behold, suddenly exiting from the city, there came forth armed young men. Some were on horseback, and others were foot soldiers who were holding swords and spears in their hands, hastening hither and thither. The brethren now understood what the elder had meant regarding the tremor of the earth. They returned to the monastery in great fear, since he related to them the vision he had seen take place in the air. After the elder went up to his cell, he wept and lamented, because of the irreverence and perversity of the people, or rather on account of their ignorance and impiety. The following day, he came out of his cell and sat on a rock warming himself in the sun. He always conducted himself in this manner, due to his bodily weakness. He consequently supplicated and besought God, saying, "Master, God and Lord, Who willest that all be saved and come to the knowledge of the truth, raise Thy rod and punish this people, for they walk not according to knowledge." Suddenly, he saw a rod of fire in the air, which extended from the holy city to Bostra. The saint knew that the people would be gravely punished; and, thence, he cried and wailed.

When the Persian assault reached and surrounded the holy city, the brethren of the coenobium and the cell dwellers departed. Some fled into Arabia with the hegumen, whereas others entered into the caves or hid in the thickets of reeds. With them was the blessed Elder George, whom the brethren had to constrain to come out and conceal himself with them. The Saracens diligently searched the wadi and interrogated the mountaineers concerning the monks' property. After they found the elder and many other fathers, they transferred them to another wadi. Among them was the elderly Stephen the Syrian, who was one hundred years old or more. He was a holy and famed father whom they murdered in that place, but the others were carried away into captivity. When they saw Saint George to be poor, very thin, and venerable, they revered his state; and, being incited by God, they gave him a straw bag filled with bread and a vessel of water, and released him, saying, "Go wheresoever thou dost wish to save thyself!" Therefore, by night, he descended to the Jordan. He tarried there, until the Persians should pass by Jericho, fleeing into Damascus, having with them captives from the holy city. Thereupon, Abba George entered the holy city, where he remained until he should go again to Chozeva. He did not go to his cell any longer, but rather he chose to stay inside the monastery, where he was daily teaching the brethren and working a great number of miracles.

However, since he too was a man and desired to go to the much-desired Lord, he succumbed to an illness which resulted in his repose. During the evening, when the blessed one reposed, in order to show the confidence with which he departed to the Lord, by God's œconomy, a crowd of strangers arrived at the monastery. "They had exceedingly diverted me," remarked Anthony, his disciple, "from my duties. Now certain of the brethren, who sat near the elder, came and told me, 'The elder is asking for thee, saying, "Where is Anthony? Call him for me, because now I am about to repose."' I was distressed by the message, because I wished to accomplish both tasks at the same time, that is, complete my duties to the guests and hasten to the elder. The elder, through the Spirit, understood my dilemma and sent word to me, saying, 'Do not be grieved or agitated, my child, but complete thy ministering; I will wait until thou shouldest come.' When the strangers finally arose from the table, others arrived. They tarried till midnight, but the elder waited. So after I finished my serving and was relieved of the visitors, I went down to him. When the holy man beheld me, he embraced and kissed me. He then gave me his blessing. I then observed that he turned to the east and uttered, 'Come forth, my soul, now in Christ, come forth!' After he repeated this three times, he surrendered his spirit to the Lord, with Whose help he strove and accomplished a life worthy of praise and above reproach. Thus, he was translated to the Lord, as one would take a footstep, very peacefully and serenely. It is evident that he commended his spirit into the hands of God, as it is written: 'The souls of the righteous are in the hand of God, and there shall no torment touch them [Wisdom of Solomon 3:1].' And, again, 'Precious in the sight of the Lord is the death of His saints [Ps. 115:15].' When I realized that he had delivered up his spirit, I fell on his breast, lamenting and crying for being deprived of such a holy father. After they buried him to the sound of psalms, hymns, and spiritual odes, they laid him to rest in the tombs of the holy fathers. Now he is found among the choirs of the saints and intercedes with them on our behalf and for all the world."

On the 8th of January, the holy Church commemorates
the holy Martyrs JULIAN and VASILISSA,
and those with them, KELSIOS and ANTHONY.[3]

---

[3] Together with Saint Julian, commemorated by the holy Church also on the 21st day of June, were fellow martyrs Anthony the priest, Anastasios (who was raised from the dead), Kelsios and his mother, twenty prison guards, and seven brothers.

Saint Julian

Julian, the holy martyr, lived during the reign of Emperor Valerius Diocletian (284-305), when Marcian was governor (290). He hailed from Antinoöpolis of Egypt. He had been lawfully wed to Vasilissa. They agreed, however, to live together in temperance and virginity. Eventually, they gave their goods to the poor, and Vasilissa was tonsured a nun in a convent. Julian then also decided to become a monk in a monastery where, later, he was elevated to the abbacy over twelve thousand monks.

In 303, a great persecution broke out. Diocletian issued an edict at Nikomedia on the 23rd of February, decreeing the demolition of churches and the burning of Christian books. The many unholy incidents that followed as a result of this led to further edicts. The next two edicts were directed solely against the clergy. The punishment meted out for resistance was imprisonment, torture and, in some cases, death. By the year 304, a fourth edict extended these grim penalties upon the laity as well. The persecution was to adorn the Church in the purple robe of martyrdom.

Our holy Mother Vasilissa, during this perilous time, was made abbess over one thousand nuns. As a true and caring spiritual mother, she besought God that none of her spiritual daughters might suffer torture or humiliation by Diocletian's men. In the event that it was God's will that she or any of the nuns suffer this cross, she prayed that none might recant the Faith. The tender-loving Lord hearkened to the prayer of the holy virgin and—lo, the wonder!—during the next six months, one by one, every nun in the convent fell asleep in the Lord, leaving Abbess Vasilissa alone.

Saint Vasilissa

Before her own blessed repose, Vasilissa was vouchsafed a vision of her synodia (monastic community) in the life beyond the grave. She beheld all her nuns enveloped in radiant light, rejoicing as angels of the Lord. When they addressed Vasilissa, they begged their spiritual mother to join them speedily. Vasilissa, after she had endured severe persecutions, reposed in peace.[4]

---

[4] See the 9th of January in the *Acta Sanctorum* (64 vols., Antwerp, 1643), which records that Saint Vasilissa reposed in peace.

In the meanwhile, Father Julian had been arrested and brought before Governor Marcian. Christ's confessor, Julian, refused to deny the Faith and ridiculed the idols, leaving Marcian beside himself with anger. Therefore, straightway, the vile governor commanded some of his men to put to the flames Julian's monastery and all those who dwelt therein. Now many honorable bishops and the lower ranks of clergy had taken refuge in this monastery; thus they all received the crown of martyrdom, when their lives were snuffed out. The holy Julian was then tortured by being stretched out on the ground and beaten. Afterward, they bound up his limbs with iron chains and broke his bones. At that time, there was a man who was blind in one eye. When he beheld the fearful torments of Christ's athlete, he confessed Christ and was healed by Julian. Forthwith, that newly-enlightened man was also beheaded and received the laurel of martyrdom.

Saint Kelsios

Now Governor Marcian had a son, the soldier, Kelsios. When Kelsios, together with twenty of his men, witnessed Julian resurrecting one named Anastasios from the dead, they too confessed Christ. Marcian was soon informed of his son's conversion and ordered that Kelsios be the first cast into prison. Kelsios, together with seven of his brothers, who also came to believe in Christ, were then cast into a cauldron of boiling water. After the brothers were cast in, the Priest Anthony, together with the recently-resurrected Anastasios, were made to enter the boiling cauldron. Behold the miracle! All ten, by the grace of our Lord Christ, were preserved. At this juncture, many idolaters came to believe in Christ, including Kelsios' mother, who was the governor's wife. All were then made to stand before the tribunal of Governor Marcian. Then, while all prayed—O, the wonder!—the idols of the temple collapsed, and the temple was swallowed up by the earth. Thereupon, the idolaters collected linen cords and soaked them with oil. They took them and bound the saint's hands and feet, then set them on fire. Again, by divine grace, the holy martyrs remained unscathed and not in the least singed. The idolaters, taking hold of Julian and Kelsios, began flaying the skin from their heads. The Priest Anthony had both his eyes plucked out with iron hooks. The mother of Kelsios was hanged, but she did not die. They then cast her to the wild beasts as prey, but she remained unharmed. Finally, they resolved to behead her; and, thus, the ever-memorable woman received many crowns of martyrdom. After all these holy martyrs completed their contest, they were interred, nearby the church erected at Phoros, where they remain at the time of this writing.

On the 8th of January, the holy Church commemorates
the TWO MALE Martyrs,
who believed in Christ through Saint Julian
and were slain by the sword.

On the 8th of January, the holy Church commemorates
the ONE FEMALE Martyr, the wife of the governor,
who believed in Christ through Saint Julian
and was slain by the sword.

On the 8th of January, the holy Church commemorates
the holy Hieromartyr CARTERIOS of Caesarea of Cappadocia.

Carterios, the holy martyr, lived at the time of Emperor Diocletian, and when Urbanus was governor of Caesarea in Cappadocia in 298. He was a priest and teacher of the Christians. The saint had erected a small church, where he assembled a number of Christians and taught them to honor Christ as the true God and to acknowledge no other gods beside Him. In consequence, he was slandered to the governor and had to go into hiding. But the Lord appeared to him and said, "O Carterios, go thou and appear before them that seek thee, and I shall be with thee; for thou must suffer greatly for My name, and many will come to believe through thee and be saved!"

The holy one was overjoyed at this announcement and gave thanks to God. He then presented himself before the authorities. At first, they confined him to jail, but later they took him to the governor's residence, where he was ordered to sacrifice to the god Serapis. Thereupon, he toppled the idol by his prayer. As a result he was flogged by sixteen soldiers with bullwhips.

He then was stretched out on a rack, and with razors they sheared off the nails of his hands and feet, and raked his entire body with steel claws. Yet, with the aid of an angel of God, he rose above this trial and was restored to health. Again, by the order of the governor, they pierced his ankles with a steel wire and set a glowing hot steel plowshare on his chest. They then forced him to sit on a fiery stool and afterward locked him in jail again. At night, the Lord appeared to Carterios, releasing him from the bonds and restoring his health. The Lord then led out His priest from that jail through the gate. Many of the idolaters, witnessing Carterios emerging whole and sound, hastened to him and were baptized and delivered from their infirmities. For this, the holy Carterios was apprehended and tortured again. This time, they suspended great rocks from both his hands and feet, lashing him with bullwhips about the abdomen. Next they scorched him with lighted torches, while they poured sulfur and molten tar on him. Then they poured molten

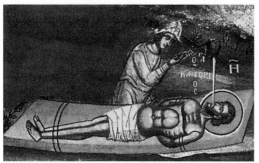

The Martyrdom of Saint Carterios

lead into his mouth. Finally, they cast him into a fire, but he remained unharmed, as he chanted hymns and gave thanks unto God. Now a certain Jew, standing nearby, seized a spear and, out of malice, pierced Carterios' side. At first water copiously flowed therefrom, and put out the fire; then blood issued forth. Thereafter, Carterios, the courageous struggler, surrendered his soul into the hands of God and received from Him the laurel of victory.

On the 8th of January, the holy Church commemorates the holy Martyrs THEOPHILOS the Deacon and ELLADIOS the Layman.

Theophilos and Elladios, the holy martyrs, were from Libya in northeast Africa. They were arrested on the charge of being confessors of Jesus Christ. They were hauled before the proconsul and governor of Libya. Since the two witnesses for Christ stood steadfast in their Faith, the executioners chastised them by scraping and flaying their flesh. Afterward, with their hands and feet bound, they were made to undergo the application of fire over the broad of their backs. Their flesh also endured the piercing of sharp bricks, fashioned into spear points. After these relentless torments had taken place over many hours without respite, the holy victors surrendered their souls into the hands of God and ascended into the heavens.

On the 8th of January, the holy Church commemorates the venerable AGATHON, who reposed in peace.[5]

Agathon, our venerable father, entered the desert of Sketis,[6] circa 364. He was a man of profound spiritual discernment and judgment, so that

---

[5] Many of Abba Agathon's words and practises may be found in *Evergetinos* (in Greek) and in E.A. Wallis Budge's *The Paradise of the Fathers* (in English), Volume 2, passim.

[6] Sketis or Scetis, a monastic settlement in the Wadi el-Natrun, is west of the Nile Delta. "The natural approach to Scetis is not from Nitria, forty miles away across the desert to the north (though naturally monks often traveled this way between the two centers), but from the nearest point on the Canopic branch of the Nile at Terenuthis, little more than twenty miles away." See D. J. Chitty's *The Desert a City*, p. 12.

even as a young man he was deemed an elder among the fathers. His deeds and words are found in many of the sayings of the desert fathers and elders (*Gerontikon*). He was conspicuous for his patient endurance, which was put to the test by certain brethren who heard it said that Abba Agathon exercised great care, lest his mind should become disturbed by anything. They came to him and tested him, asking, "Art thou Agathon, the whoremonger and boaster?" The holy man replied, "Yes, I am." They continued their questioning: "Art thou the same one who talks nonsense and is a slanderer?" He answered, "Yes, I am the one." Again they put forth another inquiry, asking, "Art thou Agathon, the heretic?" This time he answered, "I am not a heretic." They then besought him, saying, "Why didst thou bear with our other insults, but this last one thou didst not endure?" The elder replied, "The others I received as profitable to my soul, but to be a heretic is separation from God; and this I do not accept." Upon hearing his response, they were astonished at his discernment and went away spiritually edified.

On another occasion, Abba Agathon went into the city to sell his handiwork. A stranger was lying ill in the marketplace, with none to care for him. The elder decided to remain and assist him. Agathon went and hired a room nearby and continued toiling with his hands that he might meet the rent and procure whatever the sick man needed. After six months of care, the sick man recovered, and Abba Agathon returned to his cell at Sketis.

At another time, when the disciples of Abba Agathon were building a cell, the elder remained with them four months. Then with the passage of the first Sunday, the elder observed something about the arrangement which ill afforded him spiritual benefit. He then turned and addressed his disciples, saying: "Arise, let us go from here." The brethren were troubled at his sudden discomfiture and asked, "If it had been in thy mind that we should depart this place, then why wouldest thou allow us to undergo all this toil? Will not our actions be a stumbling block to others who shall say, 'Behold, how they have left, not being able to abide in any place'?" The elder saw their distress, written broad across their faces, and said, "Though some should become offended in us, others would be edified and say, 'See how these men departed for the sake of God and considered everything as nought.'" The elder then said, "However, should any of you wish to accompany me, come; for I shall certainly go from this place." The brethren then prostrated themselves before him, beseeching him to take them along with him.

Another situation occurred while Abba Agathon was traveling in the company of some young disciples. On the road, one of them discovered a small bag and said to the elder, "Abba, shall I take up the little bag?" The elder gazed upon the young man with wonder, saying, "My son, didst thou place it there?" The young man answered, "Well, no." Agathon then said, "If thou didst not place it there, why shouldest thou desire to take it?"

A brother being troubled by the spirit of fornication came to Abba Agathon and revealed his thoughts. The elder said, "Go and cast thy frailty before God, and thou shalt find relief." The abba was wont to say, "I have never laid down to sleep and kept anger in my heart; nor have I ever nourished a thought of enmity against another. Indeed, I have never allowed any man to lie down and sleep, harboring any anger against me." He would also say, "Whenever I saw any deed or something which I thought to judge or condemn, I would say to myself, 'Do not commit the thing thyself,' and thus I quieted my mind and held my peace."

Once Abba Abraham came to Abba Agathon, seeking his counsel and saying, "The devils war against me, father. Why is that?" The elder replied, "So the devils war against thee. But they do not war against us so fiercely as do we ourselves by means of our own desires, though they do make war against us in proportion as do our desires. Our desires have become our devils, and they enjoin us to fulfill them. Now if thou wouldest see against whom the devils have made war, it is against Moses and those who resemble him."

As the time of his earthly sojourn drew to an end, he spent three days gazing straight ahead with wide-open eyes. His disciples asked him to explain why he seemed transfixed. The elder answered, "I am before the judgment seat of God." The fathers, startled by this response, were curious to learn more and asked, "Art thou frightened, abba?" He answered, "Up until now I have tried to keep Christ's commandments, but how should I know whether I have been God-pleasing?" They answered, "But thy godly works, shall they not give thee confidence?" He replied, "What confidence? The judgment of men is one thing and that of God another." Though they pressed to ask him more, he replied meekly, "If you please, converse with me no longer. The time has drawn nigh." He then bade them farewell and departed filled with joy.

On the 8th of January, the holy Church commemorates our holy father among the saints, KYROS (CYRUS), Archbishop of Constantinople, and the Synaxis of the august Monastery of Chora and the Great Church on Sunday.

Kyros (Cyrus), our holy father among the saints, flourished at the end of the seventh century and the beginning of the eighth century. Before ascending the patriarchal throne of Constantinople (706-712), he was a monk on a tiny island in the vicinity of Amastris, a city on the Black Sea coast of

Anatolia. He struggled in asceticism for a considerable number of years when, in 695, he encountered Justinian II. This exiled emperor (685-695 and 705-711), the son of Constantine V and Anastasia, had held the scepter of the empire from his father's death. He had convoked an Orthodox synod in 686-687, which upheld the rejection of Monotheletism. When his former general Leontios seized the throne, accusing him of heavy taxation and excesses, he mutilated Justinian by cutting his nose. Therefore, Justinian was then nicknamed "cut-nose" (*rhinotmetos*) and wore a gold prosthetic. He had been exiled to Cherson on the Crimean peninsula which, at that time, was suffering decline and desertion. Justinian, while banished, thought to visit the local monastery. He went and there met Father Kyros. The holy monk prophesied to the emperor that he would once again take possession of the throne of Byzantium, and that very soon.

Justinian took to heart the monk's words and treasured them. Justinian then sought help from the Khazar khagan (khan). He married the khagan's sister in 703, and she took the name Theodora. In 705, Justinian regained his throne with help from Tervel, the Bulgar khan, who raised a combined force of Bulgars and Slavs. Tervel marched with Justinian against Tiberios II, who had overthrown Leontios. After Justinian retook the capital, he paraded Leontios through the city and beheaded him in the Hippodrome.

Now Justinian remembered Father Kyros and his prophecy. He then had Patriarch Kallinikos I (694-706), a good and holy man—commemorated by the holy Church on the 23rd of August—removed from office. Father Kyros was then made to ascend the patriarchal throne and proved to be most competent and Orthodox. During his term, Justinian campaigned against Cherson in order to halt Khazar advances in the Crimea. The fleet performed mutiny and proclaimed Philippikos (Philippicus) Bardanes (711-713) as emperor. The latter, a supporter of Monotheletism and ardent revivalist of Christological disputes, compelled Justinian to flee his capital again for Asia Minor. Justinian was decapitated by Elias, his former retainer and governor at Cherson, who joined with Philippikos. Justinian's body was cast into the sea, but the head was returned to the capital, where it later was exhibited in both Rome and Ravenna. Philippikos deposed Patriarch Kyros, appointed John VI (712-715), and convened a council to overturn and anathematize the Third Synod of Constantinople.

The holy Kyros had been conspicuous in his efforts to prevent the revival of the theological movement known as Monotheletism ("one will") for which, previously, Patriarch Sergios I (610-638) coined the phrase "a single will in Christ." The major opponent to this heresy of course had been the far-famed Saint Maximos the Confessor (580-662), who suffered exile together with his supporter Pope Martin I (649-653). The Synod of Constantinople

(680) condemned Monotheletism and its adherents. Philippikos, on his own authority, declared Monotheletism to be the only Orthodox doctrine. His opposition to the Sixth Œcumenical Synod incited Rome's displeasure and antagonism. Philippikos addressed an edict to Pope Constantine (708-715), enjoining all to profess Monotheletism and to honor the memory of Sergios and those with him who had been condemned earlier by the synod. Thus a terrible estrangement occurred between the heretic emperor and the pope as the defender of Orthodoxy. Philippikos was eventually deposed and blinded. Though he had wished to revive the heresy, it yet eventually disappeared after his demise. The holy Kyros meanwhile had been sent to the Constantinopolitan Monastery of Chora, where he lived in a righteous and holy manner, until he was translated to the Lord.

On the 8ᵗʰ of January, the holy Church commemorates Saint ATTIKOS, Patriarch of Constantinople, who reposed in peace.[7]

Attikos (Atticus), our holy father among the saints, was born in Sebasteia of Armenia on the Halys. He took the monastic habit at an early age, but the monks who taught him were caught up in the heretical philosophy of Macedonius (Makedonios), former Archbishop of Constantinople (d. ca. 362). After the latter's deposition, disputes arose about the divinity of the Holy Spirit, so that from the end of the fourth century the sect came to be known as the Pnevmatomachoi or fighters against the Spirit. These heretics denied the full divinity of the Holy Spirit, considering Him a created being and a gift of God but not God Himself. This resulted in their condemnation by Pope Damasus in 374. The great Cappadocian fathers also attacked their teaching; and, in 381, at the first synod at Constantinople, it was anathematized. Now Attikos recanted their teaching when he came into the capital.

Sozomen comments: "Attikos had been instructed from his youth in the principles of monastic philosophy by monks of the Macedonian heresy. These monks, who then enjoyed a very high reputation at Sebasteia for philosophy, were of the discipline of Efstathios (Eustathius), their bishop and

---

[7] The Life of Saint Attikos is spread across various sources. The principal authorities include Socrates and Sozomen in their *Ecclesiastical Histories*, and Palladius, *Dialogus de Vita S. Johannis Chrysostomi*, ix-xi. The unhappy account of Saint Attikos' participation in the Synod of the Oak is found in *The Great Synaxaristes*, under the Life of Saint John Chrysostom, who is commemorated by the holy Church on the 13ᵗʰ of November.

leader of the monks. When Attikos attained the age of manhood, he embraced the tenets of the catholic Church."[8]

Saint Attikos

Attikos became a priest at the Great Church (Hagia Sophia). He unfortunately came to be Saint John Chrysostom's major accuser at the Synod of the Oak (403). After Saint John's patriarchate (398-404), Arsakios (404-405) was elected, but he did not long survive his accession to the bishopric. Consequently, many aspired to the vacant see. At length, during the sixth consulate of Arkadios and the first of Provos (406), the devout Attikos was promoted to the episcopate. He was known to have followed an ascetic life from an early age. He had a moderate share of learning and possessed a large amount of natural prudence. During his term, Saint John died in exile at Comana on the Black Sea. Not long after his blessed repose, the Emperor Arkadios also died (408). The emperor left behind an eight-year-old son Theodosios (408-450) and his teen-aged virgin sister, the ardently religious Pulcheria, who assumed power. Attikos was on good terms with the court, and especially with the dedicated Pulcheria and her younger sisters who lived as nuns in the palace. The holy patriarch dedicated a now-lost tract to all the royal sisters, entitled *On Faith and Virginity*.

"When Theodosios the emperor was in the eighth year of his age," reports Socrates Scholasticus, "Attikos was in the third year of his presidency over the church. Under Attikos' episcopate, his piety and discretion brought the churches to a very flourishing condition. For he not only united those of 'the household of faith [Gal. 6:10],' but also by his prudence called forth the admiration of the heretics, whom indeed he by no means desired to harass. But if sometimes he was obliged to impress them with the fear of himself, he soon afterward showed himself mild and clement toward them. But indeed he did not neglect his studies; for he assiduously labored in perusing the writings of the ancients, and often spent whole nights in the task. Thus, he could not be confused by the reasonings of the philosophers and the fallacious subtleties of the sophists. Besides this, he was affable and entertaining in conversation, and ever ready to sympathize with the afflicted. In a short word, to sum up his excellences in the apostle's saying: 'To the weak I became as weak, that I might gain the weak. To all these I have become all things, that by all means

---

[8] Sozomen, *The Ecclesiastical History*, Bk. VIII, Ch. XXVII, Nicene, 2nd Ser., II:417.

I might save some [1 Cor. 9:22].' Formerly, while a presbyter, he had been accustomed, after composing his sermons, to commit them to memory, and then recite them in the church. (For he had an extraordinary memory.) But by diligent application, he acquired confidence and made his instruction extemporaneous and eloquent. His discourses, however, were not such as to be received with much applause by his auditors, nor to deserve to be committed to writing. Let these particulars respecting his talents, erudition, and manners suffice."[9]

Sozomen reports that "Attikos possessed more by nature than by learning, and became a participant in affairs, and was as skillful in carrying on intrigues as in evading the machinations of others. He was of a very engaging disposition, and was beloved by many. The discourses which he delivered in the church did not rise above mediocrity; and although not totally devoid of erudition, they were not accounted by his auditors of sufficient value to be preserved in writing. Being intent, if an opportunity offered itself anywhere, he exercised himself in the most approved Greek authors; but lest, in conversation about these writers, he should appear unlettered, he frequently concealed what he did know. It is said that he manifested much zeal in behalf of those who entertained the same sentiments as himself, and that he rendered himself formidable to the heterodox. When he wished, he could easily throw them into alarm; but he at once transformed himself and would appear meek. Such is the information which those who knew the man have furnished."[10] His writings were mostly directed against heresy: Nestorianism, Pelagianism, and Messalianism.

During his term of office there was no lack of miracles and healings, as reported by Socrates. Now on one occasion there was a certain Jew, a paralytic, who had been confined to his bed for many years. Neither any kind of medical skill nor the prayers of his Jewish brethren had availed anything. At length, he had recourse to Christian Baptism, trusting in it as the only true remedy to be used. When Attikos was informed of his wishes, he instructed him in the first principles of Christian truth. After the patriarch preached to him to hope in Jesus Christ, he directed that the catechumen be brought in his bed to the font. The paralytic Jew indeed received Baptism with a sincere faith. As soon as he was taken out of the baptismal font, he found himself perfectly cured of his disease, and continued to enjoy sound health afterward. The fame of this miraculous occurrence caused many heathens to believe and be baptized. Though it is said that the Jews zealously 'ask for a sign [1 Cor.

---

[9] Socrates, *The Ecclesiastical History*, Bk. VII, Ch. II, Nicene, 2nd Ser., II:154.
[10] Sozomen, loc. cit.

1:22],' not even the signs which actually took place induced them to embrace the Faith.[11]

The Great Church, in 404, during the time of Saint John Chrysostom, had been burned down on the night of his unjust exile. It had been rebuilt again as a basilica by Theodosios and completed in 415. At that time, Patriarch Attikos officiated at the consecration. Theodosios also bestowed a personal privilege upon Attikos, prohibiting the election of a bishop in the neighboring area of the capital without notifying the Archbishop of Constantinople. He also obtained a rescript from the emperor, which put the whole of Illyria and the "Provinicia Orientalis" under his authority. He thus enlarged his see, though these extended rights were later lost.

Now there had been a renewal of hostilities between the Romans and Persians after the death of Yazdgird I (399-420) of the Sasanian dynasty. Though the latter in no way molested the Christians in his dominions, when he died, his son Bahrām (420-438) succeeded and hearkened to the Magi in his kingdom. Rigorous persecution followed with hideous punishments and tortures, Persian-style. The Christians therefore, on account of such unspeakable oppression, were obliged to desert their country and seek refuge among the Rhomaioi (Byzantines), lest they should be utterly extirpated. Attikos received these fugitives with great benignity and did his utmost to help them in whatsoever way possible. Accordingly, he made the Emperor Theodosios acquainted with the facts.[12]

In 421, Theodosios took an Athenian wife who had been the daughter of a pagan philosopher. Attikos baptized her, a little while previous to her marriage with the emperor on the 7th of June, and then gave her the Christian name of Evdokia (Eudocia), instead of her pagan one of Athenaïs.

In the meantime, Attikos caused the affairs of the Church to flourish in an extraordinary manner. He administered all affairs prudently, inciting the people to virtue by his instruction. Perceiving that the Church was on the point of being divided—inasmuch as the Johannites, those who had sided with Saint John Chrysostom, assembled themselves apart—he ordered that mention of John should be made in the Church prayers, as was customarily done with other deceased bishops. Attikos believed that many then would be induced to return to the Church. Though Saint Chrysostom's name was admitted to the diptychs, this annoyed Saint Kyril of Alexandria, which account is better reserved for the days of his commemoration, the 9th of June and the 18th of January.

Now Attikos was so generous that he not only provided for the poor of his own parishes, but also transmitted contributions to supply the wants and

---

[11] Socrates, op. cit., Bk. VII, Ch. IV, Nicene, 2nd Ser., II:155.

[12] Ibid., Bk. VII, Ch. XVIII, II:161, 162.

promote the comfort of the indigent in the neighboring cities. On one occasion alone, he had sent to Kalliopios, a presbyter of the church at Nicaea, three hundred pieces of gold that he might feed the hungry and give to those too proud to beg.[13] The saint was also wont to abolish superstitions among the people.

Now when his end drew nigh, Attikos had a presentiment of his own repose. He remarked to Kalliopios, the same presbyter at Nicaea with whom he had been visiting: "Hasten to Constantinople before autumn, if thou dost wish to see me again alive; for if thou shouldest delay beyond that time, thou shalt not find me surviving." Nor did he err in this prediction.[14] He reposed in 425. Upon his decease, there arose a strong contest about the election of a successor, some proposing one person, and some another; but the general desire of the people was that the bishopric should be conferred on Sisinios (426-427). All of the laity were warmly attached to the man because he was famous for his piety, and especially because he was diligent in the care of the poor even beyond his jurisdiction. He is commemorated by the holy Church on the 11th of October. Meletios also notes that Pope Celestine I (422), in an epistle to Attikos, called the archbishop "teacher of the catholic (universal) Faith."[15]

Prophet Samaias

On the 8th of January, the holy Church commemorates the holy Prophet SAMAIAS the Elamite.

Samaias (Shemaiah), the holy prophet, whose name signifies "God hears," lived during the reign of Roboam (Rehoboam, 931-914 B.C.), son of Solomon and king of the southern kingdom of Juda. God had commissioned this prophet to charge the king and his one hundred and eighty thousand warriors of Juda not to fight against their brethren of Israel, the northern kingdom of ten tribes under Jeroboam I (931-910 B.C.), but to return every man to his house, instead of striving to regain northern

---

[13] Ibid., Bk. VII, Ch. XXV, II:166.

[14] Socrates describes the day of his repose as follows: "He died on the 10th of October, in the 21st year of his episcopate, under the eleventh consulate of Theodosios, and the first of Valentinian Caesar. The Emperor Theodosius indeed, being then on his way from Thessalonike, did not reach Constantinople in time for his funeral, for Attikos had been consigned to the grave one day before the emperor's arrival." Ibid., Bk. VII, Ch. XXV, II:167. Meletios (vol. 2, p. 5) concurs with Socrates' date.

[15] Ibid.

Israel. "And the word of the Lord came to Samaias the man of God, saying, 'Speak to Roboam the son of Solomon, king of Juda, and to all the house of Juda and Benjamin, and to the remnant of the people, saying, "Thus saith the Lord, 'Ye shall not go up, neither shall ye fight with your brethren the sons of Israel: return each man to his own home; for this thing is from Me.'"" They hearkened to the word of the Lord, and they ceased from going up, according to the word of the Lord [3 Kgs. (1 Kgs.) 12:22-24; cf. 2 Chr. 11:2]."

Samaias also prophesied of the invasion (ca. 925 B.C.) of Juda by Sousakim (Shishak): "It came to pass when the kingdom of Roboam was established, and when he had grown strong, that he forsook the commandments of the Lord, and all Israel with him. And it came to pass in the fifth year of the reign of Roboam, Sousakim king of Egypt came up against Jerusalem, because they had sinned against the Lord....And Samaias the prophet came to Roboam, and to the princes of Juda that were gathered to Jerusalem for fear of Sousakim, and said to them, 'Thus said the Lord, "Ye have left Me, and I will leave you in the hand of Sousakim."' And the elders of Israel and the king were ashamed, and said, 'The Lord is righteous.' And when the Lord saw that they repented, then came the word of the Lord to Samaias, saying, 'They have repented; I will not destroy them, but I will set them in safety for a little while, and My wrath shall not be poured out on Jerusalem. Nevertheless they shall be servants, and know My service, and the service of the kings of the earth.' So Sousakim king of Egypt went up against Jerusalem, and took the treasures that were in the house of the Lord, and the treasures that were in the king's house: he took all; and he took the golden shields which Solomon had made....And Sousakim set over Roboam captains of footmen, as keepers of the gate of the king....Then the anger of the Lord turned from him, and did not destroy him utterly; for there were good things in Juda....Roboam reigned seventeen years...and had done evil, for he directed not his heart to seek the Lord. And the acts of Roboam, the first and the last, behold, are they not written in the book of Samaias the prophet, and Addo the seer, with his achievements [2 Chr. 12:1-15]."[16] This book is not extant.

Through the intercessions of Thy Saints,
O Christ God, have mercy on us. Amen.

---

[16] Historians are divided regarding the invasion of Shishak (Sheshonq I). A relief in the temple of Amun at Karnak lists the captive cities, which do not include Jerusalem, but does list the northern kingdom, Israel, at Megiddo, where a fragment of a stela of Sheshonq I provides evidence for the capture of that city. Some have suggested that Rehoboam raided the temple and palace treasuries in order to pay tribute and avert the threat. See J. Rogerson's *Chronicle of the Old Testament Kings*, pp. 95, 126.

On the 9th of January, the holy Church commemorates the holy Martyr POLYEFKTOS at Melitene.[1]

Saint Polyefktos

Polyefktos, the martyr, lived during the reigns of Emperors Decius (249-251) and Valerian (253-259). He was a soldier according to profession and was stationed in the city of Melitene of Armenia.[2] He has the distinction of being the first martyr of that city.[3] He had a beloved comrade-in-arms, Nearchos. The two men were bound together in deep friendship, so that they were thought to be related by blood. Now Nearchos was a Christian, faithful and exact in his belief. Polyefktos, a man of character, lived as though he were a Christian, adorned with deeds of righteousness. But he was still unillumined with the full truth and kept to the religion of the pagan Greeks. When the two soldiers were together, their conversations were not ill-chosen. Nearchos was wont to read the Gospels and Epistles to Polyefktos, who listened carefully, and slowly the words captivated him. Nearchos also explained many elements of the Christian Faith and clearly demonstrated the futility of idol worship and how it debased men, made in the image of God.

Valerian, as Decius before him, was a notorious persecutor of Christians. Decius, however, had legislated only against those who refused to take the pagan oath of allegiance. Valerian, by contrast, aimed his twin edicts (257, 258) specifically against Christians. This included not only those of the Church hierarchy but also senators and military officers. They were to be eradicated from the upper echelons of Roman society, as Valerian blamed them for the wars, famines, and plagues which afflicted his empire.

---

[1] The Life of this saint was recorded in Greek by Saint Symeon the Metaphrastes [*P. G.* 114:417-429]. The manuscript is extant in the Athonite monasteries of Iveron and in other places. The text was rendered in simpler Greek by Prohegumen Kyril of the Peloponnesos, and is extant at the Athonite Great Lavra. A divine office was composed by the hymnographer Father Gerasimos Mikrayiannanites.

[2] The Roman legionary base was the core of this extensive city of Melitene (modern Malatya, 38°22′N 38°18′E). Circa 400, the city became the civil and ecclesiastical metropolis of Armenia.

[3] A church is known to have been dedicated to him at Melitene before 377.

Therefore, when the heralds proclaimed these edicts in every quarter of the realm, those who refused worship to the idols were sentenced to torture and death. Nearchos prepared himself that he might confess the Christ faithfully, for he in no wise would offer homage to wooden and stone images. He was however grieved for the condition of his bosom friend, Polyefktos, and sighed from the depths of his heart. Now Polyefktos noticed his friend's anxiety, reddened eyes, and tears which could not be concealed. He thought that perhaps he had said or done something to distress Nearchos; and so he inquired. Weeping and sighing heavily, Nearchos opened his heart, aflame with love, to his friend, saying, "I am in dire straits regarding our future separation, my beloved comrade. I have been thinking of our sympathy and compassion for each other, and how it shall soon come to an end." These words deeply wounded the heart of Polyefktos, who managed to say, "What are these things that shall part us? Tell me, Nearchos! Why art thou speaking these words as one without hope? And how shall such a separation come to pass, when death in no wise threatens us?" Nearchos replied, "The imperial edict, by necessity, shall divide us. I shall become subject to execution, but thou shalt go on thy way, I fear, to a bleak lot."

Polyefktos now understood what was troubling his friend and perceived the peril. His mind was then filled with divine remembrances of their discussions and readings. God had shown His mercy and grace upon Polyefktos, though he had not yet perceived how. Looking upon his trusted friend, Polyefktos said, "Nothing shall separate us. I shall tell thee of a dream of mine, which I had only a couple of days ago. Indeed, I beheld the Christ Whom thou dost revere. He came toward me and garbed me with a costly garment of mother-of-pearl, which was fastened on the shoulder with a gold brooch. After that, He presented me with a winged horse." Nearchos, enlightened by God, understood by this vision what the future held for his friend. Greatly heartened that his beloved Polyefktos would not perish with the pagans, he disclosed, "That beautiful robe indicates that thou shalt put off the old man and put on the new. Thou shalt change from that which is inferior to what is superior, and exchange thine earthly soldiering for the heavenly and divine enlistment. Thou shalt be numbered with the ranks of the martyrs. As for the winged horse, this signifies that thou shalt speedily mount on high to the heavens." Nearchos then looked intently upon his friend and asked, "The Christ, dost thou know Him, O Polyefktos, verily as true God?" Polyefktos, filled with good cheer, replied, "When did it appear that I was ignorant of Him? Or when didst thou ever speak of Him, and my soul trembled not? Or when wouldest thou read to me, and I marvelled not at the words? I would call upon Him, even though I was not yet called a Christian, but I was disposed to be one. When I came to myself, I daily considered forsaking the ignominy of idol worship. I truly wished to exchange man-made philosophies for true and heavenly piety, and submit myself wholly to the Master Christ. Therefore, my good friend, what shall we do? Has it not been made manifest to us that we ought to bestir ourselves and confess Christ?" Nearchos was of course gladdened by these words, but gnawing at him was his concern that Polyefktos might falter at the prospect of leaving behind his children orphaned, his wife widowed, and his considerable possessions to another. Rather than bringing up these issues directly, Nearchos then said, "As for myself, Polyefktos, neither wealth, nor glory, nor military rank, nor wish for distinction, nor anything else of this world is preferred to the life in Christ." The divine Polyefktos, making trial of these declarations, asked, "What art thou saying? Wouldest thou not reach for greater dignity and rank?" Nearchos, not wishing to prove his friend, answered him with all his heart, saying, "It appears to me, Polyefktos, that thou art yet ignorant of the true dignity in Christ, the glory from Him, and the blessedness which never ends." The goodly Polyefktos, stopping a moment for recollection, then said in a pleasant manner to his friend, "Thou dost suspect me to be ignorant of the glory in Christ and that blessedness with Him. But even as I revealed to thee earlier: Christ appeared to me and garbed me in a heavenly mantle. But I do have one question. Without the initiation ceremony and the Mysteries of Christ, can one become His warrior?" Nearchos' heart was filled with warmth for his friend, and he straightway put to rest Polyefktos' concerns and said, "My most beloved friend, do not have any doubt or hesitation about this. It is written that 'God is able from these stones to raise up children to Abraham [Mt. 3:9].' What are these stones other than those without hope or from the nations, whom He is able to save and enroll them as soldiers of Christ? The heavenly gate is opened to all those seeking Him. The entry is shut to none. Whether one began laboring in His vineyard at the first, or third, or sixth, or ninth hours, or even at the end, the reward, everlasting life, is the same." Polyefktos, who had a natural ardor of mind, was heartened by his friend's explanation and declared to him, "I do remember that thou didst read to me that account. When it came time to pay the laborers their hire, both those who came first and those who came last, all received a denarius apiece. Those who had worked but one hour were made equal to those who had borne the burden of the day and the heat. Christ was pleased to give to the last as He had given to the first [Mt. 20:8-16]." Nearchos then said, "Marvellous is thy judgment. Furthermore, there are many other such examples to be found. Bring to mind the thief who, after committing tens of thousands of crimes, was crucified with Christ. In but a short space of time and with a concise phrase, he found a huge recompense. He was conducted first into Paradise, even before those who offered much toil and perspiration. But thou must also know that martyrdom substitutes for Baptism and ushers in immediate enrollment in the heavenly ranks."

After Polyefktos heard these words, his soul straightway soared on wings of divine love. He conceived the desire to witness for Christ. He felt sure of the Master's love for men and said to his friend, "Behold, Nearchos, I have seen in my mind's eye those heavenly good things. Christ stood before my very eyes with a countenance gleaming with light. I renounce therefore the idols and forsake all the things of this world. I profess to be Christ's soldier. This very hour I am going to read the imperial decree." He took leave of his friend and went to the marketplace where the edict had been posted. After he read it aloud to those in the market, he spat upon the decree and tore it to pieces in the presence of many. At that same moment, statues for the idol-mad were being transported to their temple. As the porters crossed the square, Polyefktos let out a mighty laugh. He then contrived a plan, inspired by God: He feigned to approach the idols, as though he were about to venerate them. As he drew close, he quickly took action and cast the twelve idols to the ground. They fell and smashed into debris and dust. After this damage took place, Felix, who was Polyefktos' father-in-law, came forward. He was a high-ranking official, charged with implementing the imperial decree and persecuting the Christians. Upon observing his son-in-law's attack on the idols, he thought him cavalier and bold as brass. He fell into despair, uttering, "Alas! I have suddenly lost my son. He shall find mercy with neither the gods nor men, now that he has dared to shatter to pieces our deities." Polyefktos, however, rejoiced and said, "I have now censured the impotence of the idols, the works of men's hands. If thou hast others, bring them forth that Christ's slave may spit upon them." Felix was in a state of violent emotion and found it heartrending to make a decision. The open display in the square provided incontrovertible proof for the state. Pointing to the damage, Felix nodded significantly at his son-in-law. With as much humanity as he could muster, Felix said, "I wish to give thee a little time to consider what thou art doing, Polyefktos. But know that I cannot get around the imperial decrees after this public exhibition. Therefore, return to thy home and see thy wife." Christ's warrior answered, "Who is my wife? And who are my children? Why should I now return to the concerns of men, when my mind is filled with only those heavenly and imperishable good things? If thy daughter, on the one hand, should cherish what I have done, blessed is her judgment; on the other hand, if she should not heed my admonition, then she shall perish badly with your gods."

Felix shed tears. He felt fainthearted and spiritless, yet he was blinded by his devotion to the idols. Benighted in mind and darkened in spirit, he exclaimed, "Alas! O Polyefktos, the Christ has deceived thee by magic arts."

Polyefktos answered valiantly and with prudence, saying, "I was neither bewitched nor subjected to charms. Know this, father-in-law, I shall not flee from those sacred martyric contests on behalf of Christ Who has called me to the full knowledge of the truth. He has led me by the hand from darkness to light, from error to truth. He has vouchsafed me to be numbered in the ranks of His soldiers." After Polyefktos expressed his convictions with much resoluteness, Felix's partiality caused him to wilfully misunderstand. The officers arrested the martyr and beat him on his mouth. Undaunted, Polyefktos valiantly bore the wounds they inflicted. He concentrated on the sufferings of Christ, in Whom he took refuge, and rejoiced at having a share in them. Thus, the holy man underwent ill-treatment at their hands.

Then the evil one devised a temptation for the martyr. It was a heavy scene as Polyefktos was undergoing torments, in the midst of the weeping and lamenting of his father-in-law and wife, Paulina, who were before him. The noble soldier, not ignorant of the crafty one's malice to break his resolve, raised his mind above all earthly concerns. Since they carried on excessively, the martyr reproved Felix, who was a mixture of servility to the emperors and self-importance, saying, "O profane one and initiate of the secrets of the idols, think not that this lowly trick of copious tears shed by thee and my wife shall cause me to recant my profession of Christ. Put that thought clean out of thy head. Would to God that you were weeping and wailing for yourselves! If you adhere to idol-madness, the everlasting fire shall be your reward." Paulina then cried out, "What has befallen thee, O Polyefktos? How wast thou deceived into destroying our twelve gods?" At these words, the holy one laughed and remarked, "Where is the difficulty? I have vanquished thy twelve gods. Thus, I invite thee to consider: what is there to be found in them? Now look to the God of all. I pray thee earnestly that thou wilt be guided by me. Come with me, Paulina, and know the true God Who only is worthy of worship. Make haste to exchange this transitory life for the everlasting one." Now there were many spectators present who were unbelievers. They hearkened to the martyr's words and came to embrace the Faith of Christ. Not much time passed before the pagan judges assembled that they might try the martyr. They employed promises, then threats, but the martyr stood firm. He would remain steadfast, cost him what it might. Hence, neither his wife's desire, nor love for his children, nor aspiration for rank and dignities, nor his possessions and estates sufficed to keep him back. He was empowered by the Holy Spirit and endued with grace. He had now found riches which could not be stolen and dignity which would abide and would not fall away. After they abandoned all hope of converting Polyefktos, he was sentenced to death by the sword.

The saint was marched to the execution site. No gloomy or lowering look filled his face, but rather a joyful countenance was seen by all. Instead of looking as if under affliction, he appeared filled with gladness and good cheer. A radiant youth was accompanying him. No one but the martyr beheld the angelic being, who was conversing and encouraging the saint to forget all earthly cares. As the saint proceeded on the path to martyrdom, in the midst of the crowd that had gathered, he caught sight of his beloved friend and cried out in a clear voice, "O Nearchos, farewell, and remember the pact between us!" Polyefktos then bent his head beneath the sword and by means of his blood received sacred and divine Baptism and the seal in Christ. For his sufferings and confession, he received an imperishable crown from Christ, for Whom he sacrificed everything. He set at nought the demented tyrants and their edicts and crushed the machinations of the demons. As the armies of angels danced for joy, the Christians were diligent about collecting his relics and buried him honorably after four days. It should also be mentioned that Nearchos drew near to his martyred friend, dipped a linen cloth into his blood, and took the precious relic, the following year, to the city of Chananeoto, deeming it a weapon of salvation and blessed inheritance that fell to his lot. O valiant warrior of Christ, Polyefktos, intercede for those who honor thy memory!

**On the 9th of January,
the holy Church commemorates
our venerable Father
EFSTRATIOS the Wonder-worker.**

Efstratios, our venerable father, came from a place called Tarsios, of the Optimatoi theme of northwestern Asia Minor. Tarsios was classified as a village and subdivision of the village-city of Vitiane. Efstratios was the offspring of godly parents, George and Megethous. They were moderately comfortable and self-sufficient with good things. The year was 808. Efstratios was reared well by his parents. When he reached twenty years of age, he was mastered by divine love. He was di-

Saint Efstratios

vinely inspired to leave his parents and take refuge at Bithynian Mount Olympos, the holy mountain and monastic center located southeast of Prusa.

He applied at the Monastery of Agavros,[4] where two luminaries of asceticism, Basil and Gregory, shone forth radiantly. They were Efstratios' uncles from his mother's side of the family. The nephew was received by the uncles, but only after they tested him. They warned Efstratios that the monastic life required vigilance and humility. The warfare against desires, self-will, and the demons was continuous. Efstratios made a prostration before the holy fathers and said, "I know that I am not worthy of the angelic life. But I believe I am called of God Who had long ago put this inclination in my heart and the willingness to forsake my home and parents." Since Christ in no wise casts out those who come to Him, the fathers accepted him. Efstratios became a monk, being tonsured by his uncles.

After Father Efstratios attained to that which he desired, he served all the brethren with a ready heart and humble mind. His mind was never occupied with the things of this present age. His discipline of non-acquisition was so complete that he only possessed a hair shirt and a coverlet made from sheep's wool which served as his bedding. It was said by the brethren that when Efstratios became a monk, he would never lie down or sleep horizontally or rest flat on his left side. These practises in his sleeping habits were exercised for seventy-five years. At length, he was also ordained to the priesthood. He was very much beloved and respected by the brotherhood. When the two previous abbots of the monastery reposed, that is, the Abbots Gregory and Efstathios, the saint's uncle and cousin respectively, the great Efstratios was elected by the brotherhood. He, however, accepted the office only after much exertion and supplication from the brotherhood.

Now at that time, the beastly-named Leo V was emperor (813-820). He was known as "the Armenian," since his father, the *patrikios* Bardas, was of Armenian descent. Leo restored Iconoclasm, deposed Patriarch Nikephoros I (806-815), and convoked a local council in the capital (815) that rejected the Synod in Trullo. How he became emperor was due to some questionable maneuvering on his part. The general, Leo, and his Anatolikon troops were the first to retreat at the battle of Versinikia, which led to the defeat of the

---

[4] Agavros (Agauros) had four or five dependencies (*metochia*). The famous monasteries of Olympos included Atroa, Medikion, Pelekete, Chenolakkos, Heliou Bomon, Sakkoudion, and the lavra of Symboloi. The monks of Olympos were renowned for their iconophile activities against Iconoclasm. Many signatories of the Second Synod of Nicaea (787) were the abbots (*hegumenoi*) of this region, so that their communities suffered abominably under Leo V's persecution. The monastics were compelled to disperse, though temporarily. Also, at that time, the isolation of the monasteries of Olympos exposed them as the target of Arab raids. *The Oxford Dictionary of Byzantium*, s.v. "Olympos, Mount."

Byzantines by the Bulgarians and the end of the rule of Emperor Michael I Rangabe (811-813), resulting in the latter's abdication in favor of Leo. Afterward, Michael's sons were castrated. The former emperor became a monk at Prote, one of the Princes' Islands, taking the name Athanasios. One of his sons, Niketas, later became the holy Patriarch Ignatios of Constantinople.[5] As emperor, the wretched Leo rehabilitated the local Council of Hieria in Chalcedon, which condemned the sacred icons.[6] The emperor cruelly persecuted those who defied him, so that many iconodules fled their homes and monastics departed their monasteries.

Father Efstratios encountered Saint Ioannikios the Great, commemorated by the holy Church on the 4th of November, who counseled him to depart. Father Efstratios therefore took to the outdoor life, abiding in mountains and wildernesses, living at times in the caves of Olympos. He then went to the capital, where he was arrested with other iconophiles and suffered ill-treatment. Now the odious emperor had justifiable fears for his throne. While Leo was attending a service in Hagia Sophia, he was murdered in front of the altar by the followers of his old comrade-in-arms, Michael II the Amorian (820-829). Thereupon, Emperor Michael was crowned by Patriarch Theodotos. Though the emperor supported Iconoclasm and prohibited public discussions of the issue, he restored the iconophiles, yet not the deposed Patriarch Nikephoros. Michael's son, Theophilos, reigned, as did Iconoclasm, from 829 to 842. He prohibited any aid to those who venerated icons, exiling many and being ever ready to maim and mutilate. It is unclear how much time Father Efstratios spent in prison for confessing the veneration of icons. When he and others were delivered from bonds, Father Efstratios returned to Bithynia. The churches and monasteries, however, did not fully recover until the death of Emperor Theophilos in 842. He left behind his widow, the devout iconodule Empress Theodora (842-856), the regent of their three-year-old son Michael III. She ushered in the restoration of the icons in March of 843, known as the Triumph of Orthodoxy, and approved the elevation of Patriarch Ignatios (847-858 and 867-877). Thereupon, the venerable and God-bearing fathers, who had scattered that they might worship in peace and freedom, returned to their monasteries. Father Efstratios also went back to Agavros and collected his beloved community.

---

[5] Meletios' *Ecclesiastical History*, Vol. 2, p. 258.

[6] At Hieria, Emperor Constantine V (741-775) and three hundred and thirty-eight bishops argued that an icon of Christ either depicted His humanity alone, or both His humanity and divinity. They believed that the only true image of Christ was the Eucharist. Their Christological argument was condemned as heretical by Nicaea II (787), under the patronage of Empress Irene and the presidency of Patriarch Tarasios.

Thenceforth, during the day, he could be seen toiling alongside the brothers in their bodily labors. The saint's nights were passed in vigils and prostrations. Furthermore, when the brotherhood was conducting the canonical services and chanting the hymns of the Church, the ever-memorable one would enter into the holy sanctuary and stand from the beginning of the service to the very end, reciting to himself "Lord have mercy."

Now many wonderworkings were performed by the saint in his lifetime, which it is not possible in this writing to record, since they were without number. We wish to disclose here that those deeds wrought by the grace of God working in him were not limited to healing the sick, raising the dead, and halting fires. These manifold miracles were a most true sign of how the saint was pleasing to God. He was also conspicuous for his generosity to the poor and needy. Since Agavros had a number of monastic dependencies, he was wont to visit the brotherhoods that he might offer them spiritual counsels and exhortations. It was not unusual for him to find on the road a beggar, to whom he would remove and offer his coat, or a soldier in need of a horse, to whom he would give away the animal he was riding. When an impoverished farmer came to the monastery, the saint made a present to him of the brotherhood's ox. Upon returning from the capital and an audience with the emperor, Saint Efstratios distributed all of the imperial donation to the poor he encountered. Then on one occasion, God dispensed that he encounter a man on the verge of suicide. Even as he was about to take his life with a rope, Father Efstratios intervened and took hold of that self-destroying hand and placed it upon his own neck. Our holy father then spoke lovingly to the distraught man, saying, "Child, may thy sins be upon me, for which I shall answer on the day of judgment. I only ask that thou wouldest cast away this noose and despair not in God's mercy and providence." Heartened by the venerable elder's words, he desisted from hanging himself.

When the time arrived to depart to the Lord, he invited all his monastic disciples and addressed them, saying, "Brothers and fathers, the time of my life is coming to an end. Therefore, my children most beloved, preserve the sacred trust of the holy Schema. You know that these present things are transitory and vain, and that the future things are everlasting and imperishable. Thus, be mindful and diligent, my children, that you may be accounted worthy of a portion among those being saved." He then uttered a prayer and made the sign of the Cross over the disciples. Father Efstratios then raised his eyes heavenward and uttered, "Into Thy hands, O Lord, I surrender my spirit." Straightway, he slept that restful sleep, having lived for ninety-five years.

Through the intercessions of Thy Saints,
O Christ God, have mercy on us. Amen.

On the 10th of January, the holy Church commemorates our holy father among the saints, GREGORY of Nyssa.[1]

Gregory, Bishop of Nyssa (372),[2] is to be praised for the holiness of his conduct of life, his theological knowledge, and his zealous promotion of the Orthodox Faith embodied in the Nicene clauses. He is believed to have been born at Caesarea, the capital of Cappadocia, ca. 335 or 336. The family of Saint Gregory was wealthy, distinguished, and conspicuously Orthodox. He was the younger brother of Saint Basil the Great (ca. 330-379). Our saint made no account of his honorable descent. He left blood lines, wealth, and splendor to the friends of this world. He believed that the Christian's lineage was his affinity with the divine.

Saint Gregory

During the persecution of Diocletian (284-305), Saint Gregory's grandparents departed with their family. Searching for safety in the mountains of Pontos, they underwent rigorous vicissitudes and deprivation. His maternal grandfather, whose name has not been left to us, lost all his worldly possessions, and even his life. A few years later, the family returned to Caesarea. The saint's father, Basil (who gave his name to his eldest son), was a recognized and notable rhetorician. He died at a relatively young age, after fathering a family of ten children, five boys and five girls. The children were reared by their paternal grandmother Makrina and their mother, the beauteous Emmelia. Both of these estimable ladies were celebrated for their strict traditional Orthodoxy. The ten

---

[1] Saint Gregory the Theologian praises Saint Gregory of Nyssa, writing, "A faithful friend is not to be exchanged...." It is noted in the Sixth Act of the Seventh Œcumenical Synod that he is named the divine Gregory of Nyssa. He is also called "Father of the Fathers," and the "Luminary of Nyssa" [Nicaean Synod II, Act VI; Nikephoros Kallistos, *Ecclesiastical History*, xi.19]. The saint's Treatises are to be found in Migne's *Patrologia Graeca* 44-46. For English translations of Treatises, see Saint Gregory of Nyssa, *Select Works, Letters, Dogmatic Treatises*, Nicene, 2nd Ser., Volume 5, translated by William Moore, M.A. and Henry Austin Wilson, M.A. of Oxford. See also Harvard Professor Verner Zenger's translations.

[2] Nyssa (37°52′N 28°10′E) is a city in northwest Cappadocia, south of the Halys, near the village of Harmandali.

children, in order of their birth, are as follows: Makrina, a son that died in infancy, Basil, Nafkratios, Gregory, four daughters whose names are unknown to us, and lastly, Peter. Makrina shared in the upbringing of her younger siblings. There was not one brother or sister who did not owe to the elder sister their settlement in the Faith and constancy of pious conduct. Later, with her mother Emmelia, Makrina established a convent on the family estate in Pontos, at a place called Annesi, on the banks of the Iris River. As a result of her gentle but firm persuasion, Saint Basil renounced secular pursuits, and took up a life of more rigorous asceticism with his school friend Saint Gregory (the Theologian). Nafkratios entered his father's profession but reposed early. Saint Peter eventually became the Bishop of Sebasteia.

Saint Gregory, the third surviving son, was not of a strong constitution. He received his first instruction in grammar and rhetoric from his father. Gregory's father reposed when he was twelve years old. He continued to study at home. He acknowledged that his brother Basil, his senior by at least five or six years, later undertook his education. Saint Basil had been at Athens, and shared his learning from the Greeks with his younger brother. Saint Gregory, in his work *The Life of Moses*, commented: "Many bring to the Church of God their profane learning as a kind of gift. Such a man was the great Basil, who acquired the 'Egyptian wealth' in every respect during his youth, and dedicated his wealth to God for the adornment of the Church, the true tabernacle."[3] Regarding his religious training, the credit lies with his mother and sister, for whom he had the tenderest regard. There is every reason to believe that Makrina the grandmother lived well into Gregory's early boyhood.

Unlike his brother Basil, Gregory did not have the broadening experience that travel often offers. He was diffident and retiring, and preferred to remain at home. He did not choose a profession as did his brothers, but continued living on his share of the paternal property. With a self-appointed discipline, he managed to educate himself quite well. Yet he defers to his brother Basil, and praises him in a letter, remarking, "I found no rich nourishment in the precepts of my teachers, inasmuch as I enjoyed my brother's society only for a short time, and got only just enough polish from his divine tongue to be able to discern the ignorance of those who are uninitiated in oratory."[4] Some believe Gregory's writings characteristically share with those of Basil's a wide acquaintance with ordinary human life, and one who is thoroughly conversant with human nature.

---

[3] Saint Gregory of Nyssa, *The Life of Moses*, Bk. II, ¶ 116, p. 81.
[4] Saint Gregory of Nyssa, "Epistle X, To Libanius," Nicene, 2nd Ser., V:533.

He is described as resembling his brother Saint Basil in appearance, that is, dark-haired, handsome, slender, and tall—with the difference that his hair was grayer. Gregory was also perceived by others as somewhat less graceful and clever than his older brother.

He did not enjoy the benefit of infant Baptism, and remained for many years unbaptized, according to the custom of the time. It is unclear whether he delayed it himself, or it was delayed for him. Later in life (376), he wrote *On the Baptism of Christ*, saying, "We baptize in the name of the Father (He is the primal Cause of all things) and of the Son (He is the Maker of the creation) and of the Holy Spirit (He is the Power perfecting all)."[5] He describes Christ as "the Repairer of evil doing. He assumes manhood in its fullness, and saves man, and become the type and figure of us all, to sanctify the first fruits in every action."[6] He informs us that "after the dignity of adoption the devil plots more vehemently against us, pining away with envious glance. When he beholds the beauty of the newly born man, earnestly tending toward that heavenly city, from which he fell, he raises up against us fiery temptations, seeking earnestly to despoil us of our second adornment, as he did our former array."[7]

The Vision of the Forty Martyrs

Gregory was first moved to make a public avowal and receive holy Baptism due to an extraordinary vision in which he was made to take part. While his mother Emmelia was at her sacred retreat at Annesi, she implored her son to attend a service commemorating the holy Forty Martyrs. At his mother's behest he went, though reluctantly; for he had been studying in Caesarea, and felt incommoded that he should have to leave his studies at such an inconvenient time. The journey to the retreat proved tiring to him, and the length of time for the divine office was protracted. The vigil was already well into the night, and Gregory found himself physically unable to remain on his feet. He withdrew to the garden, where he was overtaken by sleep. He beheld a vision of the very forty martyrs. They reproved him for his lack of zeal, and started to strike him with rods. Only through the efforts of one of the warrior martyrs did he escape the thrashing.

Straightway, Gregory was roused from his slumber. Filled with remorse at his past laxity, he was resolved to change his ways. He begged God and the martyrs for mercy and forgiveness. Still struck with the effect the vision laid upon his tender conscience, he was inspired to accept the rank of Reader in the Church. This acceptance meant a public profession of the Faith.

---

[5] Saint Gregory of Nyssa, *On the Baptism of Christ*, Nicene, 2nd Ser., V:520.
[6] Ibid., *On the Baptism of Christ*, V:519.
[7] Ibid., V:524.

Saint Gregory assumed the duties of that position for a short time, but could not dedicate himself exclusively to it. He then turned to the profession of a rhetorician or advocate. His retirement from his duties as a Reader led to a reprimand from his elder brother Basil and his good friend Gregory (the Theologian).

Saint Gregory the Theologian chided him in a letter, which moved the young man to remorse. He frankly told him, "Why shouldest thou not hear from me what all men are saying in whispers? They do not approve thine inglorious glory...and thy gradual descent to the lower life, and thine ambition....For what has happened to thee, O wisest of men? And for what do thou condemnest thyself, that thou hast cast away the sacred and delightful books which thou wast reading to the people...and applied thyself to bitter ones, and preferred to be called a Professor of Rhetoric rather than of Christianity?...Though it is full late, become sober again, and come to thyself once more, and make thine apology to the faithful, and to God, and to His altars and Mysteries, from which thou hast taken thyself away....What of the offense given to others by thy present employment?...For a man lives not for himself alone but also for his neighbor....I shall be grieved—to speak gently—if thou dost not see what is right, nor follow the advice of others....Forgive that my friendship for thee makes me grieve."[8]

Saint Theosevia

There is a strong possibility that Saint Gregory had taken to wife Theosevia, who later became a deaconess of the Church of Nyssa. In a letter upon her repose from Saint Gregory the Theologian to Saint Gregory of Nyssa, she is expressly called his sister. Yet in the same letter he calls Theosevia "consort" or "yokefellow (*syzygon*)," saying she is "the glory of the Church, the adornment of Christ, the helper of our generation, the hope of woman, the most beautiful and glorious among all the beauty of the brethren, truly sacred, the yokefellow of a priest, and of equal honor and worthy of the great Mysteries."[9] The Theologian also describes her as having tasted the joys of life, yet escaped its sorrows through the shortness of her life. He tells Gregory that "before she had to wear mourning for you, she was honored by thee with that fair funeral honor which is due to such as she."[10]

Saint Gregory of Nyssa composed a treatise *On Virginity*, and writes: "I should have undertaken this labor with the greatest readiness, if I could

---

[8] Saint Gregory (the Theologian), "Epistles 1, To Saint Gregory of Nyssa," Nicene, 2nd Ser., VII:459.

[9] Ibid., "Epistle CXCVII, A Letter of Condolence on the Death of Theosevia," Nicene, VII:462.

[10] Ibid.

have hope of sharing, according to the Scripture, in the fruits of the plow and threshing-floor....As it is, this my knowledge of the beauty of virginity is in some sort vain and useless to me;...happy are they who have still the power of choosing the better way, and have not debarred themselves from it by the engagements of the secular life, as we have, whom a gulf now divides from glorious virginity. No one can climb up to that who has once planted his foot upon the secular life. We are but spectators of others' blessings and witnesses to the happiness of another class."[11] Of course, Saint Gregory may also be speaking of a higher virginity, that of the soul. The essence of spiritual virginity was not embodied in sensual abstinence, but in the purity of one's whole life. These two passages, namely the Theologian's letter of condolence and Gregory's admission in his treatise, have given rise to the tradition that he and Theosevia were husband and wife.

Saint Gregory makes mention of the value of virginity, saying that it enables us "to look with a free and devoted gaze upon heavenly delights. The soul will turn itself from earth. It will not even partake of the recognized indulgences of the secular life. It will transfer all its powers of affection from material objects to the intellectual contemplation of immaterial beauty. Virginity of the body is devised to further such a disposition of the soul. It aims at creating in it a complete forgetfulness of natural emotions; it would prevent the necessity of ever descending to the call of fleshly needs."[12]

Asceticism

Gregory's sister Makrina, after much prayer and persuasion, prevailed upon Gregory to leave his secular concerns and the law court, and devote himself entirely to asceticism. Gregory removed himself to his brother's retreat in Pontos, which was in the same neighborhood as the convent of his mother and sister. Gregory stayed in that monastic foundation for several years, hallowing his time with the study of sacred Scriptures and holy writings. He also studied the works of Origen, as did his brother and Saint Gregory the Theologian, who also was a sometime member of the monastic community.

In 365, elder brother Basil was called from his monastic retreat to act as coadjutor to Evsevios, Metropolitan of Caesarea in Cappadocia, that he might assist him in the Church battle against the heretical Arians. Five years later, after the repose of Evsevios, Basil was acclaimed by popular choice to the bishopric. His election was not without opposition. With the help of Saint Gregory the Theologian and the latter's father, Saint Gregory of Nazianzos, he succeeded to that see. Arians and other contenders against the Faith and

---

[11] Saint Gregory of Nyssa, *On Virginity*, Ch. III, Nicene, 2nd Ser., V:345.

[12] Ibid., *On Virginity*, Ch. V, V:351.

unity in Cappadocia were at odds with the great Basil. The holy man decided the best way to uphold the Faith in his troubled diocese was to surround himself with bishops confessing true Orthodox Faith. In 372, he enjoined his reluctant brother Gregory to shepherd the flock at Nyssa, a small town in western Cappadocia. Saint Gregory had his own ideas about the true priesthood, and those who presume upon it. Later in life, in his work, the *Life of Moses*, he observes, "If you should now see someone purifying himself to some degree of the disease of pleasure, and with great zeal considering himself above others, as he thrusts himself into the priesthood, realize that this man whom you see is someone who is falling to earth by his lofty arrogance. For in what follows, the law teaches that the priesthood is something divine and not human."[13]

Evsevios, Bishop of Samosata, was amazed that Basil chose such a little-known bishopric for Gregory. Saint Basil answered Evsevios in a letter, stating: "I, too, was anxious that our brother Gregory should have the government of a church commensurate with his abilities; and that would have been the whole Church under the sun gathered into one place. But, as this is impossible, let him be a bishop, not deriving dignity from his see, but conferring dignity on his see by himself. For it is the part of a really great man not only to be sufficient for great things, but by his own influence to make small things great."[14]

It was with similar sentiments that Basil placed his close friend Gregory the Theologian in the tiny hamlet and marshes of Sasima. This Gregory also took exception to the nomination.

Family Troubles

With the election of Saint Basil to the bishopric, there was universal rejoicing in the Orthodox world that Caesarea was ruled by so splendid a prelate; and congratulations were even forthcoming from Saint Athanasios the Great of Alexandria. The Arian-minded Emperor Valens (364-378), however, was resolved to make trouble for the faithful in Basil's diocese. The bishops of the province who had been narrowly outvoted, and who refused to take part in Basil's consecration, forsook communion with the new archbishop. Even Saint Basil remarked that the Cappadocian character was hard to move.[15] The suffragans' lack of feeling for Church unity disquieted the new archbishop. Now Basil and Gregory had an uncle, also named Gregory, who

---

[13] Saint Gregory of Nyssa, *The Life of Moses*, ¶ 283, pp. 126, 127.
[14] Saint Basil, "Epistle XCVIII, To Eusebius, Bishop of Samosata," Nicene, 2nd Ser., VIII:182.
[15] Ibid., "Epistle XLVIII, To Eusebius, Bishop of Samosata," Nicene, 2nd Ser., VIII:153.

was a bishop that sided with the disaffected bishops. Saint Gregory tried to reconcile his brother and uncle, but was unsuccessful. Thus, in his guilelessness, he thought to reunite them by using less than scrupulous means.

Our well-meaning Gregory made a clumsy attempt at a forgery in the name of his uncle. The counterfeit was found out when the uncle repudiated the letter. Saint Basil wrote his brother Gregory in a letter: "How am I to dispute with thee in writing? How can I lay hold of thee satisfactorily, with all thy simplicity?...Thou didst forge one letter, and brought it to me as though it came from our right reverend uncle, the bishop, trying to deceive me; I have no idea why. I received it as a letter written by the bishop, and delivered by thee. Why should I not? I was delighted; I showed it to many of my friends; I thanked God. The forgery was found out, on the bishop's repudiating it in person. I was thoroughly ashamed, covered as I was with the disgrace of cunning trickery and lies; I prayed that the earth might open for me. Then they gave me a second letter, as sent by the bishop himself by the hands of thy servant....Even this second had not really been sent by the bishop....Now Adamantios has come bringing me a third..How ought I to receive a letter carried by thee or thine? I might have prayed to have a heart of stone....But what am I to think, now that, after my first and second experience, I can admit nothing without positive proof? Thus I write attacking thy simplicity, which I see plainly to be neither what generally becomes a Christian man, nor appropriate to the present emergency. I write that, at least for the future, thou mayest take care of thyself and spare me. I must speak to thee with all freedom, and I tell thee that thou art an unworthy minister of things so great. However, whoever be the writer of the letter, I have answered as is fit....If the right reverend bishops are really willing to meet me, let them make known to me a place and time, and let them invite me by their own men. I do not refuse to meet my own uncle, but I shall not do so unless the invitation reaches me in due and proper form."[16]

Initially Gregory's letters only widened the breach between uncle and nephew. But Saint Basil took up his pen and wrote a polite, warm, and conciliatory letter to his uncle. In a second letter to his uncle, he mentions his brother Gregory, saying, "I received my brother on his coming to visit me with the same feelings, and have lost none of my affection. God forbid that I should ever so feel as to forget the ties of nature and be at war with those who are near and dear to me. I have found his presence a comfort in my bodily sickness and the other troubles of my soul; and I have been especially delighted at the letter, which he has brought me from your excellency. For a long time I have been hoping that it would come, for only this reason, that I

---

[16] Saint Basil, "Epistle LVIII, To Gregory, my brother," Nicene, VIII:159.

need not add to my life any doleful episode of quarrel between kith and kin, sure to give pleasure to foes and sorrow to friends, and to be displeasing to God, Who laid down perfect love as the distinctive characteristic of His disciples....If thy reverence really does not disdain to come down to my lowliness and to have speech with me, whether thou shouldest wish the interview to take place in the presence of others or in private, I shall make no objection."[17] At length a reconciliation was brought about.

The Bishopric of Nyssa

Saint Gregory was still to experience his older brother's reproof and advice, as he was yet unseasoned in the ways of ecclesiastical politics. In his enthusiasm for the unity of the Faith and love toward his brother, Gregory was moved by zeal to help uphold Archbishop Basil's honor and esteem. He keenly felt that it was important to assist his brother's objectives for the strengthening of the Church and true Orthodoxy. Thus Gregory thought his idea would be well received by his brother, if he were to encourage the convening of synods. Yet Saint Basil perceived that such assemblies, under the then present unsettled situation in the Church, would not enhance the prospects for unity. He understood that what his inexperienced brother hoped to achieve should openly place him as a pawn before unscrupulous men who were not inclined to serve the Church, but instead their own wishes. Therefore, he deterred his brother from calling such synods.

On another occasion, Saint Gregory wished to accompany a commission to Rome. The purpose of their mission was to invite Pope Damasus (366-384) and the western bishops to help mediate the turmoil in the Antiochian see, as a consequence of a disputed election to the see. Basil himself had already experienced the effects of the unsatisfactory intervention of Rome, which, he believed, lacked the sensitivity and capacity for sharing in the interests of those in the east. Moreover, he in no way wanted to assist Rome in her assertions of supremacy, nor give her the opportunity of making inroads into the Eastern Church, and thus curtail the latter's autonomy. Therefore he denied such application to himself and his brother.

Saint Gregory was celebrated for his gentle spirit. He was better suited to a life of monasticism and study. His diocese was troubled with controversy and hostility from the Arian and Sabellian heretics. Antagonisms did not end with his pen, or with his writings on the Trinity and incarnation. Problems in his diocese were intensified also on account of the imperial patronage for the heretics—the throne was occupied by Valens (364-378), whose twisted mind was bent on the uprooting of Nicene Orthodoxy. To this end did Valens appoint his evil minion Demosthenes, a former clerk of the

---

[17] Ibid., "Epistle LX, To Gregory, his uncle," Nicene, VIII:161.

imperial kitchen, as viceroy of the civil diocese of Pontos. Thereby, Saint Gregory was to taste his unsavory arts, and suffered many persecutions as Bishop of Nyssa. Demosthenes already had made a quarrel with the great Basil, and persecuted Saint Gregory in many irksome ways.

Exile

Now certain Arian bishops trumped up an accusation against Gregory, charging him with uncanonical irregularity in his ordination. He was summoned by them to appear and make his defense at a synod meeting in Ankyra. The emperor's officer and chief cook, Demosthenes, added the false charge of embezzlement of Church monies. Some time in A.D. 375, in order to ensure his appearance, the Arians dispatched soldiers to fetch him. Having a delicate constitution, and burdened with much disquiet of mind, Gregory found the hardships of the journey nearly insupportable. The conduct of those escorting him was abominable. In fact, he contracted a fever which prevented his attendance.

Saint Basil hastened to his brother's side by convening a synod meeting of true Orthodox bishops in Cappadocia. They composed a polite letter, which they all signed, apologizing for Gregory's unavoidable absence from the synod meeting in Ankyra, on account of an attack of pleurisy. They succeeded in disproving the falsehood of the charge of embezzlement. Concurrently, Saint Basil also communicated by letter to one named Astorgos who had considerable influence at court, asking if he might intercede and spare his brother Gregory the embarrassment of being brought before a secular court. The communication did not secure the desired end. Demosthenes managed to have another synod meeting convened at Nyssa, where Gregory was summoned to answer the same charges. This time, Saint Gregory refused to attend. The false council, deeming him intractable, charged him with unwillingness to submit to authority, and deposed him in his absence. Emperor Valens also interfered, and in 376 he decreed banishment for Gregory. The saint repaired to Seleukeia.

During his exile, Saint Gregory was in ill humor—almost a kind of melancholy—at the ostensible victory of the heretics. Though he was in exile, the malice and persecution of the heretics followed him there. He suffered from a lack of physical comforts and necessities and was incommoded often by having to change his lodging place. During his time away, however, moving about from place to place, he consoled the Orthodox wherever he met them. He also maintained his warm friendship with Saint Gregory, who was himself an excellent and faithful correspondent. The latter attempted to raise the spirits of the dejected and isolated hierarch, and he wrote: "Do not let your troubles distress you inordinately. For the less we grieve over things, the less grievous they become....The heretics shall be overcome both by the truth and by the times, and all the more so the more we commit the whole matter to God."[18] As the Theologian wrote this note, sometime in 378, Valens was killed, and the new emperor in the west, Gratian (367-383), was prepared to restore exiled bishops to their lawful sees. He encouraged Gregory of Nyssa, consoling him with these words: "Although I am at home, my love is expatriated with thee, for affection makes us have all things in common. Trusting in the mercy of God, and in thy prayers, I have great hopes that all will turn out according to thy mind, and that the hurricane will be turned into a gentle breeze, and that God will give thee this reward for thine Orthodoxy....May God grant thee health and good spirits in all circumstances—thou who art the common prop of the whole Church."[19] Shortly thereafter, Gratian, a disciple and friend of Saint Ambrose (374-397), decided Bishop Gregory of Nyssa ought to be rightfully restored to his episcopal throne. To the utter gladness of the Orthodox faithful of his diocese, the sentence of banishment was revoked.

He returned in triumph to his people. In a letter which is believed to have been written on his return from exile, he describes that much longed-for day of his return. "Suddenly the clouds gathered thick, and there was a change from a clear sky to deep gloom. A chilly breeze blew through the clouds, bringing a drizzle. It ushered in a damp feeling. Rain such as had never yet been known threatened us. On the left there were continuous claps of thunder, and keen flashes of lightning alternated with the thunder. On each side we were shrouded in clouds. Already a heavy cloud hung over our heads, caught by a strong wind and big with rain. Yet, we, like the Israelites of old in their miraculous passage of the Red Sea, surrounded on all sides by rain, arrived dry at Vestena. When we had already found shelter there, and our mules were rested, then the signal for the downpour was given by God to the air. When we had spent some three or four hours there, and had rested enough, again God stayed the downpour, and our conveyance moved along more briskly than before, as the wheel easily slid though the mud just moist and on the surface.

"Now the road from the point to our little town is all along the riverside, going downstream with the water, and there is a continuous string of villages along the banks, all nearby the road, and with short distances between them. Therefrom, an unbroken line of the inhabitants came out to meet us. Some escorted us, mingling their abundant tears with joy. Now there was a little drizzle, but it was not unpleasant. There was enough just to moisten the air. Then, a little way before we reached home, the cloud that

---

[18] Saint Gregory the Theologian, "Epistle LXXII," Nicene, VII:460.
[19] Ibid., "Epistle LXXIV," Nicene, loc. cit.

overhung us was condensed into a more violent shower. Our entrance was then very quiet, and no one was aware of our coming beforehand. As we entered inside our portico, as the sound of our carriage wheels along the dry hard ground was heard, the people turned up! I know not whence or how. They flocked around us so closely that it was not easy to step down from our conveyance, for there was not a foot of clear space. With difficulty then we persuaded them to permit us to descend, and to let our mules pass. We were crushed on every side by folks crowding all around us, so much so that their excessive kindness nearly made us faint.

"When we were inside the portico, we caught sight of a stream of fire flowing into the church. There was a choir of virgins carrying their wax torches in their hands. They were marching in file along the entrance of the church, kindling the whole into the splendor of a blaze. When I was within the church, I rejoiced and wept with my people. I experienced both emotions from witnessing both in the multitude."[20]

The Repose of Saint Gregory's Siblings

Saint Gregory's joy was soon mingled with mourning when his elder brother, whom he loved and owed very much, reposed at about fifty years of age in 379, worn down by his inimitable labors and harsh asceticism. Saint Gregory the Theologian wrote to Saint Gregory of Nyssa a letter of condolence, saying, "I think though thou hast many friends and will receive many words of condolence, yet thou wilt not derive comfort so much from any as from thyself and thy memory of him; for you two were a pattern to all of philosophy, a kind of spiritual standard, both of discipline in prosperity, and of endurance in adversity; for philosophy bears prosperity with moderation and adversity with dignity. This is what I have to say to your excellency. But for myself who write thus, what time or what words shall comfort me, except thy company and conversation, which our blessed one hath left me in place of all, that seeing his character in thee, as in a bright and shining mirror, I may think myself to possess him also!"[21]

In the same year, during the month of July, after an eight-year absence, Gregory went to visit his sister Makrina at her convent. He had been hindered from seeing her, due to his troubles with the Arians. After walking a considerable distance on the road, he was about a day's journey from his sister. He beheld a vision which forebode unhappiness in the future. He remembers the event and says, "I was holding in my hands the relics of martyrs. Such a brilliant light emanated therefrom, that my eyes were dazzled by the brilliance." He says he beheld the dream three times that night. As he

---

[20] Saint Gregory of Nyssa, "Letter III, To Ablabius," Nicene, V:529, 530.

[21] Saint Gregory the Theologian, "Epistle LXXVI," Nicene, VII:461.

approached the convent, he learned that his sister had been taken ill. After he entered the convent with his sister's nuns, he went into the church and made the customary prayer and blessing. He then went to visit his sister, who was lying not on a bed or cushion, but on the floor. She was in an exceedingly feeble state, but managed to raise herself to greet her brother, and spoke with cheerful words. Gregory's heart was heavy, contemplating the pending grief. They spent a good deal of time together, reminiscing and speaking of godly matters. Saint Makrina supplied her brother with arguments for the resurrection of the dead. She remonstrated with him for his disconsolate attitude toward her departure. She bade him not to sorrow as those without hope.

Saint Gregory says, "I then began to tell of my own toils by which I was tried. First, there was the persecution against Orthodoxy by the Arian Emperor Valens. At length, I then said, 'Later, due to the confusion and turmoil in the churches of Christ, which summoned us to struggles and pains....' Then the great lady stopped me, and said, 'Wilt thou not cease from appearing ungrateful for the good which God has granted thee? Wilt thou never correct thine ingratitude? Wilt thou not set aright thy judgment? Dost thou not compare the good of thy parents with thine own? Yea, many esteemed our father for his learning, and among rhetors he was considered first; yet his fame did not spread beyond our homeland. Yet thou hast become renowned in cities and among peoples and nations. The churches of Christ send thee and invite thee to aid and set them aright. Dost thou not give attention to this grace? Dost thou not know the cause of these blessings? Thank God Who, by the prayers of our parents, hast raised thee up to this lofty height; because thou, by thyself, dost not have any strength.'"[22] Saint Gregory was not offended at his sister's reproof, but only wished the day were longer, so that they might continue conversing.

The following day, the 19th of July, Saint Makrina reposed peacefully. Saint Gregory became unnerved from the sorrow at beholding her precious relics and the mourning of the virgins. Saint Gregory felt his sister would have preferred orderliness and discipline among the sisterhood, so he instructed the nuns to calm themselves and take up psalmody. After her body was arranged, Saint Gregory was bequeathed his sister's ring, which contained a relic of the true Cross. He then conducted an all-night vigil, dividing the congregation by placing the women together with the virgins and nuns, and the men with the ranks of the monks. "I then made two groups," he says, "into two choirs that they might chant harmoniously and in an orderly fashion." Amid the press of the crowd, after daybreak, the bishop of that place came with an entire complement. Gregory was urged to be a

---

[22] See *Vita Makrina*, *P.G.* 46:981B.

pallbearer until they reached the grave. When they arrived at the Church of the Holy Martyrs at Annesi, where Gregory's parents and his brother Nafkratios had been laid to rest, Saint Makrina was also interred with her mother. As a result of his visit and his sister's deathbed discourse with him, Gregory composed his famous work, *On the Soul and the Resurrection*.

The Champion of the Orthodox Faith

With the repose of the glorious Basil, Saint Gregory was called to fill the vacancy. He rose in preeminence and exerted a powerful influence as the chief defender of the Nicene Creed, but was still harassed by the heretics. Neighboring Galatians were attempting to foster their own brand of heresy in Saint Gregory's diocese. On the other hand, the people of Ibera in Pontos wished by popular feeling to have him as their own bishop. However, their desire never came to fruition.

Saint Gregory, as his brother Basil's worthy pupil, completed his brother's description of the six days of creation, the *Hexaemeron*, and wrote *On the Making of Man*. In the latter, he explains the reason why man appeared last, after the creation. "It was not to be looked for that the ruler should appear before the subjects of his rule. When his dominion was prepared, the next step was that the king should be manifested."[23] He says that man is "a two-fold organization: blending the divine with the earthly, and properly disposed to each enjoyment, enjoying God by means of his more divine nature, and the good things of earth by the sense that is akin to them."[24] He writes that the body denotes the nutritive part, the soul denotes the sensitive, and the spirit the intellectual. Speaking of the three divisions of dispositions, he calls one "carnal," which is busied with the belly and the pleasures connected with it; another "natural," which holds a middle position with regard to virtue and vice, rising above the one, but without pure participation in the other; and another "spiritual," which perceives the perfection of godly life.[25]

Saint Gregory notes that the kinship of passions which appear alike in ourselves and in the brutes, such as anger or cowardice and like affections, entered man's composition by reason of the animal mode of generation. "Since God saw beforehand by His all-seeing power the failure of their will to keep a direct course to what is good, and its constant declension from the angelic life,...He formed for our nature that contrivance for increase which befits those who had fallen into sin, implanting in mankind, instead of the angelic majesty of nature, that animal and irrational mode by which they now

---

[23] Saint Gregory of Nyssa, *On the Making of Man*, § II, ¶ 1, Nicene, 2nd Ser., V:390.

[24] Ibid., *On the Making of Man*, § II, ¶ 2, loc. cit.

[25] Ibid., § VIII, ¶ 6, Nicene, V:394.

succeed one another. David, pitying the misery of man who, being in honor, understands not, says he is compared to the beasts that have no understanding and is made like unto them [cf. Ps. 48:12]. For truly he was made like the beasts, who received in his nature the present mode of transient generation, on account of his inclination to material things."[26]

He affirms the doctrine that the cause of the existence of the soul and body is one and the same. "We are to suppose that the beginning of his existence is one, common to both parts,...neither the soul before the body, nor the contrary, that man may not be at strife against himself, by being divided by the difference in point of time";[27] and that "the energies of the soul also grow with the subject in a manner similar to the formation and perfection of the body."[28]

Saint Gregory was now a celebrated teacher in the Orthodox world. He was one of the prelates at the Synod of Antioch in 379, which was convened in order that the schisms in that see might be made to cease. At that synod meeting, it was decided that Saint Gregory was to visit the Churches of Arabia and Babylon; for they had fallen into an embarrassingly low and reprehensible state. They were plagued with two radical and polarized sects: the Antidikomarianites who refused to venerate the Theotokos, and the Kollyridians who worshipped the Theotokos as a goddess. The acclaim of Gregory had reached the ears of Emperor Theodosios (392-395), and he provided carriages for the holy hierarch to visit these sects. The saint went and found them in a condition worthy of a torrent of tears. The saint, by the grace of God made every effort to complete his mission successfully. Although he was elected to bring regularity and the true Faith, he admitted that it was beyond his competence to usher in sweeping reforms.

In 380, he wrote *On the Holy Trinity*, and of the divinity of the Holy Spirit, saying, "It is said, 'The angels continually behold the face of My Father Who is in the heavens [cf. Mt. 18:10],' and it is not possible to behold the hypostasis (person) of the Father otherwise than by fixing the sight upon it through His image; and the image of the person of the Father is the Only-begotten, and to Him again no man can draw near whose mind has not been illumined by the Holy Spirit. What else is shown from this but that the Holy Spirit is not separated from any operation which is wrought by the Father and the Son?"[29]

---

[26] Ibid., § XVII, ¶¶ 1-5, Nicene, V:406, 407.
[27] Ibid., § XXIX, ¶ 1, Nicene, V:420, 421.
[28] Ibid., § XXIX, ¶ 6, Nicene, V:421.
[29] Saint Gregory of Nyssa, *On the Holy Trinity*, Nicene, 2nd Ser., V:329.

The Holy Land

Saint Gregory also visited Jerusalem and the holy places. From his observations, the inns and hostelries of the cities of the east presented examples of license and of indifference to vice. At Jerusalem, he met three devout and respectable ladies: Efstathia, Ambrosia, and Vasilissa. He was disappointed with what he had seen in the holy land, and writes them: "I was saddened in my journey back to my native land, estimating now the truth of the Lord's words, that 'the whole world lieth in the evil one [1 Jn. 5:19],' so that no single part of the inhabited earth is without its share of degeneracy. For if the spot itself that has received the footprints of the very Life is not clear of the wicked thorns, what are we to think of other places where communion with the Blessing has been inculcated by hearing and preaching alone?"[30] Once a Cappadocian abbot asked his advice about making a pilgrimage with his monks to Jerusalem. Saint Gregory remarked, "Change of place brings us no nearer to God, but where thou art, God can come to thee, if only the inn of thy soul is ready."

While Saint Gregory was abroad, the Arians entered by stealth into his dioceses. Upon his return, the holy man had to exercise a good deal of formidable effort to repair whatever the Arians ruined. He also took part in the election of bishops for the sees of Ebora (Ibora in Armenia Minor) and Sebasteia. The faithful of those dioceses applied to him when their Orthodox bishops had fallen asleep in the Lord. They were apprehensive, fearing that their bishops' successors might be heretics.

The Second Œcumenical Synod

In 381, a second œcumenical synodal meeting was convened in Constantinople. It was primarily to be held against Makedonios (Macedonius), who declared that the Holy Spirit was a thing constructed or created by the Son. Also, it was convened against Apollinarios, and the Evnomians, Evdoxians, Sabellians, Markellians, and Photinians. Among the one hundred and fifty bishops summoned by Emperor Theodosios, Saint Gregory was also invited with other bishops—Nectarios of Constantinople, Timothy of Alexandria, Meletios of Antioch, Kyril of Jerusalem, and Gregory the Theologian. There was no bishop from the west attending, nor did Pope Damasus come in person or send a legate. The Western Church later agreed and acceded to the things decreed at the synod meeting. Saint Gregory carried the sheets that he had thus far collected as an installment of his treatise against the Evnomian heresy. Evnomios had written a pamphlet as a reply to Saint Basil's refutations. Hence, Saint Gregory composed a defense on behalf of his

---

[30] Saint Gregory of Nyssa, "Epistle XVII, To Eustathia, Ambrosia, and Basilissa," Nicene, V:542.

blessed brother Basil, on the issues of the Holy Trinity and the incarnation. He first had a hearing of what he had written with Saint Gregory the Theologian and Blessed Jerome, and others. His treatise comprised twelve books. He opens by saying, "We have been unjustly provoked to make this answer, being stung by Evnomios' accusation of our brother."[31] He describes Evnomios and his master in heresy as "two men thirsting for notoriety and publicity. They mar the living building of the Church, with the slow canker of their teaching."[32] Evnomios charged the great Basil with not defending his Faith at the time of the trials. His charge of cowardice is baseless, for Saint Basil displayed the highest courage before the emperor and his lord-lieutenants. Evnomios' dogmatic theology of the Trinity, according to Saint Gregory, declares "there is the supreme and absolute Being, and another Being existing by reason of the First—but after It, though before all others; and there is a third Being, not ranking with either of These, but inferior to the One, as to Its cause, to the Other, as to the energy which produced It."[33] Thus Evnomios believed that the Son is alien in nature, unlike in being to the Father and quite devoid of His essential character. They deny His grand, sublime, ineffable generation from the Father, and would prove that He owes His existence to a creation.

Saint Gregory attacks Evnomios' depraved doctrines and blasphemy on the non-existence of the Lord before creation, and responds: "This is the sum of our Faith, that the Son is from all eternity, being glorified by the Father."[34] He is antecedent to times, the words "before" and "after" having no place as applied to Him.[35] Speaking of human nature, he writes: "Christ took to Himself humanity in completeness, and mingled His life-giving power with our mortal and perishable nature, and changed, by the combination with Himself, our deadness to living grace and power."[36] And, "The divine nature is always one and the same, and with the same mode of existence, while the flesh in itself is that which reason and sense apprehend concerning it, but when mixed with the divine no longer remains in its own limitations and properties, but is taken up to that which is overwhelming and transcendent."[37] For, "The divinity 'empties' Itself that It may come within the capacity of the human nature, and the nature is renewed by becoming divine through its

---

[31] Saint Gregory of Nyssa, *Against Eunomius*, Bk. I, § 2, Nicene, 2nd Ser., V:36.
[32] Ibid., *Against Eunomius*, Bk. I, § 6, Nicene, V:41.
[33] Ibid., Bk. I, § 13, Nicene, V:50.
[34] Ibid., Bk. II, § 11, Nicene, V:120.
[35] Ibid., Bk. IX, § 2, Nicene, V:214.
[36] Ibid., Bk. V, § 4, Nicene, V:179.
[37] Ibid., Bk. V, § 5, Nicene, V:180.

commixture with the divine."[38] He tells us that "the Son, as God, is certainly impassible and incapable of corruption; and whatever suffering is asserted concerning Him in the Gospel, He assuredly wrought by means of His human nature which admitted such suffering."[39] Christ "was born among us for the cure of the disease of sin. The aim of the dispensation of the incarnation was not that the Son should be subject to suffering, but that He should be manifested as a Lover of man."[40] The Holy Spirit, in delivering to us divine mysteries, conveys instruction on those matters which transcend language. In speaking of the Only-begotten, the Son of God, and His close relationship of nature with the Father, Saint Gregory comments, "Because human poverty is incapable of the truths that are too high for speech or thought, the Spirit uses our language and calls Him by the name of Son. Hereby in the word Son is declared concerning the Only-begotten the close and true character of His manifestation from the Father."[41] Now the Son is conceived to be of the Father and also with Him. "There is no intermediate interval existing between the Father and that Son Who is of Him."[42] The difference of "begotten" and "unbegotten" is apart from the essence, and does not affect It.[43] As spokesman for the Nicaean party he concluded, saying that "our salvation would not have been wrought, had not the good will of the Father proceeded to actual operation for us through His own power. And we have learned from Scripture that the Son is the power of the Father [cf. 1 Cor. 1:24]."[44]

Saint Gregory delivered the inaugural address at the synod. The first president of the Second Œcumenical Synod was Meletios of Antioch. He reposed at Constantinople, and Saint Gregory gave the funeral oration to his beloved friend, saying, "For him, indeed, better it was by his departure hence to be with Christ, but it was a grievous thing for us to be severed from his fatherly guidance....Where is that sweet serenity of his eyes? Where that bright smile upon his lips?"[45]

Before the closing of the synod, by a decree of the emperor, issued at Herakleia, Saint Gregory was nominated as one of the bishops who were to be esteemed as chief authorities on the Orthodox Faith. Helladios, Archbishop of Caesarea, was to be his colleague in his province. The primacy

---

[38] Ibid., Bk. V, § 5, Nicene, V:181.
[39] Ibid., Bk. VI, § 1, Nicene, V:183.
[40] Ibid., Bk. VI, § 3, Nicene, V:186.
[41] Ibid., Bk. VIII, § 4, Nicene, V:205.
[42] Ibid., loc. cit.
[43] Ibid., Bk. X, § 3, Nicene, V:223.
[44] Ibid., Bk. XII, § 3, Nicene, V:245.
[45] Ibid., *Funeral Oration on Meletius*, Nicene, 2nd Ser., V:514.

of Rome and Alexandria was being replaced by Constantinople, with this Canon (III): "Let the Bishop of Constantinople have the priorities of honor after the Bishop of Rome, *because of its being New Rome.*"

At this œcumenical synod, Saint Gregory also upheld his friend Saint Gregory the Theologian's rights, as archpastor of Constantinople. Also, through the God-inspired endeavors of Saint Gregory of Nyssa, the Symbol of the Faith (Creed) was enlarged by the addition of the article concerning the Holy Spirit, and four other clauses were also added to the Creed. The additional clause "of Whose kingdom there shall be no end" was supplied, due to the heresy of Apollinarios the millenarian. Article 8, in reference to the Holy Spirit, was also provided: "...the Holy Spirit, the Lord, the Giver of Life, Who proceeds from the Father, Who with the Father and the Son is equally worshipped and glorified, Who spoke by the prophets." In his treatise

Saint Gregory

On The Holy Spirit, written against the followers of Makedonios, he affirms that "we confess that the Holy Spirit is of the same rank as the Father and the Son, that, while not to be confounded with the Father in being never originated, nor with the Son in being the Only-begotten."[46]

Helladios

Much to Gregory's regret, profound ill will began to fester in the heart and mind of Archbishop Helladios of Caesarea against Gregory. Saint Gregory was distressed about the unfriendly feeling displayed by Helladios. He took up his pen, ca. 393, and wrote to Flavian, Archbishop of Antioch (384-403). Saint Gregory informed Flavian that it was others that informed him that Helladios was disgruntled with him. At first he did not believe it, but the report was corroborated on many sides. Saint Gregory then describes a pitiful incident.

He was serving in Sebasteia at the memorial for his brother Peter and the holy martyrs. When he finished his visit, as he was journeying, one of Helladios' relations took the trouble to meet Gregory, declaring that Helladios was ill. The holy man wrote: "I left my carriage at the spot where this news arrested me. I went on horseback for the rest of the journey, which took us over a road that was like a precipice and well-nigh impassable with its rocky

---

[46] Ibid., *On the Holy Spirit*, Nicene, V:315.

ascents. The journey was painful—now on foot, now mounted....We finally arrived at Andumocina; for that was the name of the place where Helladios, with two other bishops, was holding his conference....Slowly, and on foot, my company and I passed over the intervening ground, and we arrived at the chapel, just as Helladios retired to his residence. A messenger was dispatched to inform him of our arrival. Shortly thereafter, Helladios' deacon met us; and we requested him to inform Helladios at once, so that we might spend as much time as possible with him, and so have an opportunity of leaving nothing in the misunderstanding between us unhealed." Saint Gregory then said that he remained sitting, in the open air, waiting for an invitation to enter indoors. Saint Gregory says he then became "a gazing stock to all the visitors at the conference." A long time passed. Drowsiness set in upon Gregory, and languor was intensified by the excessive heat of the day. "People kept staring at me, pointing me out to others." He was made to wait until noon.[47]

"Heartily did I repent of this visit, and that I had brought upon myself this piece of discourtesy." At last they were admitted to the altar. Saint Gregory entered with his deacon, who had to support his exhausted frame. "I addressed him," says Gregory, "and stood for a moment, expecting from him an invitation to be seated." Nothing of the kind was forthcoming from Helladios, so Gregory turned toward one of the distant seats, and rested himself upon it. "I was still expecting Helladios to utter something that was friendly; or at least give a nod of recognition. But my hopes were doomed to complete disappointment." A long interval ensued. Saint Gregory says, "So struck was I with this reception, in which he did not deign to accord me the merest utterance even of those chance salutations by which you discharge the courtesies of a chance meeting—'Welcome,' for instance, or 'Where dost thou come from?' or 'To what am I indebted for this pleasure?' or 'On what important business art thou here?'" Gregory then reflected upon the treasuries of social courtesies we have inherited from our fathers. "Why, indeed, should I speak at all of that affectionate disposition of our fathers toward each other?" Saint Gregory then clearly witnessed Helladios' conceit and overweening pride. He said to Flavian, "I had no means whereby to advise myself to keep quiet; for my heart within me was swelling with indignation at the absurdity of the whole proceeding, and was rejecting all the reasons for enduring it."[48]

Then the saint broke the silence, and uttered, "Is it, then, that some of the things required for your personal comfort are being hindered by our presence, and is it time that we withdrew?" Helladios declared that he had no

---

[47] Ibid., "Letter XVIII, To Flavian," Nicene, V:545.
[48] Ibid., V:546.

bodily needs. Saint Gregory then spoke some words calculated to heal his ill-feeling. Helladios then declared that the anger he felt toward Gregory was owing to many injuries done him. Saint Gregory replied, "Lies possess an immense power to deceive; but in the divine judgment there will be no place for the misunderstandings thus arising. In my relations toward yourself, my conscience is bold enough to prompt me to hope that I may obtain forgiveness for all my other sins, but that, if I have acted in any way to harm you, this may remain forever unforgiven." Helladios was indignant at his words. It was then after six o'clock. It was evident that Helladios considered it a sin and a pollution to have Saint Gregory and those with him at his board, even after all that fatigue which they underwent on the journey, and the excessive heat out of doors while they baked in the sun at Helladios' gates. The holy man was sent off, in a state of great fatigue, across the same distance and difficult and dangerous route. Saint Gregory scarcely reached his traveling party at sunset, after suffering a storm which drenched him to the skin. He declared to Flavian: "Something, therefore, I think, must be done on our part, in order that Helladios may improve upon himself, and may be taught that he is human, and has no authority to insult and to disgrace those who possess the same beliefs and the same rank as himself." What trial, what proofs, what canons, what legitimate episcopal decision did Helladios bring forward to justify his abominable behavior? None.[49]

Saint Gregory set forth that they both were of the priestly dignity, and there was no advantage in education, or birth, or lineage, or theology. "These things," he says to Flavian, "will be found either equal, or at all events not inferior in me." Saint Gregory then suggested that the cause of Helladios' resentment might be the revenues, that is, the funds of his diocese. He said to Flavian, "I would rather not be obliged to speak of this in his case. Suffice it to say that our own was so much at the beginning, and is so much now." He then ended his communication, saying, "I deem it right that this malady of puffed-up pride is not left without a cure....The manner of effecting the cure, we leave to God."[50]

Archbishop Helladios had a difficult character. His resentment was implacable. He had also made trouble for Saint Gregory the Theologian when he contested the validity of the election of Evlasios to the Bishopric of Nazianzos, on account of party zeal. It has not been left to us what precisely were the grounds of Helladios' ill will toward Saint Gregory of Nyssa. The holy Gregory was saddened by this incident which ushered in such an indelicacy of feeling on the part of Helladios; especially when Gregory

---

[49] Ibid., V:547.
[50] Ibid., V:548.

brought to mind the affectionate disposition of the fathers of old toward one another; for they wished no advantage over one another, but thought to exceed each other only in humility.

In Constantinople

Saint Gregory was present at the synod meeting in 383, where he gave a discourse on the divinity of both the Son and the Holy Spirit. Now Saint Gregory's estimable abilities as an orator received the general approbation of the imperial court. In 383, he delivered the funeral oration on behalf of Empress Flaccilla (Plakilla). Two years later, he was selected to deliver the funeral oration in honor of the infant Princess Pulcheria. In his homily *On Infants' Early Deaths*[51] he urges that God's omnipotence is to be recognized in every direction. God's dispensations have no element of chance or confusion.

Very little is known of the saint's latter years. He felt that those who attempted to lead the flock astray were men who deceived themselves, being swayed by one mental impulse or another. He said they openly idolized their own imaginations. Therefore, in 384, he wrote an *Answer to Evnomios' Second Book*, saying: "God is not an expression, neither has He His essence in voice or utterance. But God is of Himself what also He is believed to be, but He is named, by those who call upon Him, not what He is essentially (for the nature of Him Who alone is, is unspeakable), but He receives His appellations from what are believed to be His operations in regard to our life."[52] Saint Gregory also answered Evnomios regarding Christ, saying, "We maintain that our Lord, the image of the invisible God, is immediately and inseparably one with the Father in every movement of His will. He needs not, therefore, to know the Father's will by word, being Himself the Logos of the Father, in the highest acceptation of the term."[53] Regarding the Holy Spirit, he says, "Neither does the Holy Spirit require instruction by speech; for being God, as saith the apostle, He searcheth all things, even the deep things of God [1 Cor. 2:10]."[54]

His highly acclaimed treatise on *The Life of Moses* and the *Homilies on the Song of Songs* are assigned somewhere between 385 and 392. In 385, he wrote *The Great Catechism*, wherein he states that man was created not in view of any necessity, but from superabounding love, that there might exist a being who should participate in the divine perfections. Moreover, God did

---

[51] See Saint Gregory of Nyssa, *On Infants' Early Deaths*, Nicene, 2nd Ser., V:372-381.

[52] Saint Gregory of Nyssa, *Answer to Eunomius' Second Book*, Nicene, 2nd Ser., V:265.

[53] Ibid., *Answer to Eunomius' Second Book*, Nicene, V:272.

[54] Ibid.

not, on account of His foreknowledge of the evil that would result from man's creation, leave man uncreated; for it was better to bring back sinners to grace by the way of repentance and physical suffering than not to create man at all. "For needful it was that neither His light should be unseen, nor His glory without witness, nor His goodness unenjoyed, nor that any other quality observed in the divine nature should in any case lie idle, with none to share it or enjoy it."[55] In 394, a synod was called by the prefect of the east, Rufinus, under the presidency of Nectarios, which is the last record we have of the saint, where the claims of the see of Bostra in Arabia had to be settled. In the roll of the last synod, his name was placed between those of the Metropolitans of Caesarea and Iconium.

The Saint's Repose

It is believed that he reposed in peace at about sixty or sixty-five years of age, ca. 394 or 395, leaving us with the glorious memory of his life, work, and writings which won him a high reputation. He contributed materially to the Church when he wrote important dogmatic works on the Trinity, the incarnation, the redemption, and the mysteries of holy Baptism and the Eucharist. Within the wealth of his intellectual life, it must be acknowledged that there were some inconsistencies in his writings, especially regarding the origin and destiny of the soul and the restoration of things. In any case, this was not a significant part of his writings. He was a foremost adherent and defender of the Nicene Faith. He was a man of profound thoughts. His defense of the mystery of the Trinity and the incarnation, and the distinction between essence and hypostasis, was of lasting service to the Church. He was known as an advocate of apophaticism, and said, "This is the seeing that consists in not seeing, because that which is sought transcends all knowledge, being separated on all sides by incomprehensibility, as by a kind of darkness. Wherefore, John the sublime, who penetrated into the luminous darkness, says, 'No one hath seen God at any time [Jn. 1:18],' thus asserting that knowledge of the divine essence is unattainable, not only by men, but also by every intelligent creature."[56] And "What does it mean that Moses entered the darkness, and then saw God in it?...As the mind progresses and, through an ever greater and more perfect diligence, comes to apprehend reality, as it approaches more nearly to contemplation, it sees more clearly what of the divine nature is uncontemplated."[57]

He struggled on behalf of Orthodoxy against the heretics who attempted to penetrate his flock. He assigned the will as the source of evil,

---

[55] Saint Gregory of Nyssa, *The Great Catechism*, Ch. V, Nicene, 2nd Ser., V:478.
[56] Saint Gregory of Nyssa, *The Life of Moses*, ¶ 163, p. 95.
[57] Ibid., ¶ 162, pp. 94, 95.

and considered the gift of free will as the most precious of blessings. To this end, he wrote in *The Life of Moses* about the Egyptian Pharaoh's heart and free will, remarking, "God gives up to dishonorable passions the one who gives himself up to them. It lies within each person's power to make this choice. God gives up to passion him whom He does not protect, because He is not acknowledged by him. But his failure to acknowledge God becomes the reason why he is being pulled down into the passionate and dishonorable life. The Egyptian tyrant is hardened by God not because the divine will places the resistance in the soul of Pharaoh, but because the free will, through its inclination to evil, does not receive the word which softens resistance."[58] Thus, "each man makes his own plagues."[59]

Although Saint Gregory endured many disappointments and vexations, he was consoled by this fact, and he declared it in a letter, that "I am rich in friendships."[60] In his writing, *The Life of Moses*, he leaves us with two thoughts: "The vision of God is never to be satisfied in the desire to see Him. But one must always, by looking at what he can see, rekindle his desire to see more."[61] And this is true perfection: "Not to avoid a wicked life, because like slaves we servilely fear punishment, nor to do good because we hope for rewards, as if cashing in on the virtuous life by some business-like and contractual arrangement. On the contrary, disregarding all those things for which we hope and which have been reserved by promise, we regard falling from God's friendship as the only thing dreadful, and we consider becoming God's friend as the only thing worthy of honor and desire. This, as I have said, is the perfection of life."[62]

As a theologian, he defended Orthodoxy with brilliant refutations against the heretics. Thus, we see that the prophecy of Saint Basil the Great was surely fulfilled in him, that Saint Gregory would be the one to bring honor to Nyssa, and not the city to the man.

After the catastrophe which took place in Asia Minor during the 1920s, the precious relics of his sacred skull were removed. Together with the relics of the Great-martyr Theodore and the holy New-hieromartyr George of Neapolis, Saint Gregory's relics were translated to the Church of Saint Efstathios in Perissos, Attike, located in the outskirts of Athens.

---

[58] Ibid., ¶¶ 74-76, pp. 71, 72.
[59] Ibid., ¶ 86, p. 74.
[60] Saint Gregory of Nyssa, "Letter V, A Testimonial," Nicene, 2nd Ser., V:530.
[61] Saint Gregory of Nyssa, *The Life of Moses*, ¶ 239, p. 116.
[62] Ibid., *The Life of Moses*, ¶ 320, p. 137.

On the 10th of January, the holy Church commemorates
our venerable Father DOMETIANOS, Bishop of Melitene.

Saint Dometianos

Dometianos (Dometian), our venerable father, was born in 550. He lived during the reigns of Emperors Justin II (566-578) and Maurice (578-602). Since Dometianos' parents, Theodore and Evdokia, were affluent, they were able to afford an excellent education for their son. His curriculum included both secular subjects and the study of the divine writings and Scriptures. He spent a few years as a married man until the repose of his wife. He thereafter devoted himself to true philosophy and the study of God's word. At length, he was ordained to the priesthood and then elevated to the episcopacy. In the year 580, at thirty years of age, he was consecrated for the Church of Melitene.[63] This saint combined civic virtue, political prudence, and ascetical conduct, which resulted in the salvation of many, not only the Christians of his diocese but also the Greek pagans in many places. Moreover, his skill and discretion resulted in peace and safety to many of the empire's subjects. Bishop Dometian spent 582 to 585 and 591 to 598 mostly in Constantinople as Maurice's advisor. He was not only cousin to the emperor, but was also the guardian to Maurice's children. Pope Gregory I (590-604) addressed several epistles to the saint. The emperor and his wife Constantina placed large contributions in the hands of Bishop Dometianos, who then would speedily set off building churches and hospices for the poor of his diocese.

Bishop Dometianos played the key role in the empire's Persian policy. Chosroes II (590-628) of Sasanian Iran had come to power after putting down the rebellion of Bahrām Chōbīn, a high Persian dignitary, against Chosroes' father, Hurmazd IV (579-590). Bahrām had revolted after he defeated the Turks who had invaded Iran.

---

[63] Melitene (mod. Malatya, 38°22′N 38°18′E) was a city of eastern Cappadocia at the head of routes leading from Asia Minor to Mesopotamia. Circa 400, it became the civil and ecclesiastical metropolis of Armenia II. In 575, Melitene was captured and burned by Chosroes I (531-579). The Arabs attacked in 635 and took the city in 656. *Oxford*, s.v. "Melitene."

In 591, when Chosroes fled to Byzantine territory, it was Bishop Dometianos who befriended him. That same year, both Maurice and Dometianos restored Chosroes to his throne. Chosroes was then a vassal of Maurice and paid tribute. The holy man, as Chosroes' confidant, had accompanied him on his expedition to Iran. The saint took this opportunity to preach the word of truth in Persia. Both bishop and diplomat, the godly Dometianos also negotiated the treaty with Chosroes. Byzantine generals Komentiolos and John Mystakon were dispatched to support Chosroes. The treaty provided the Byzantine empire with Dara and Martyropolis. Chosroes remained friendly with the bishop, so that rumors circulated that Chosroes had even converted to Christianity. Bishop Dometianos was also instrumental in determining the religious policy, which was anti-Monophysite, in the eastern regions.

The saint reposed in 602 at Constantinople. Emperor Maurice and the entire Church offered their veneration and respects to the holy bishop's relics. Saint Dometianos was escorted to Melitene, his homeland, in the midst of a procession chanting hymns and bearing lamps. The ever-memorable Dometianos wrought many miracles both during this present life and after his repose. His memory was celebrated in the Great Church, Hagia Sophia, in the capital.

The revolt of Phokas (602-610), led to the overthrow of Maurice and his execution with that of his male relatives. Chosroes rose up to avenge the murdered Maurice, and used the occasion to invade Byzantine territory. Chosroes' generals, Shahrbarāz and Shāhīn, were successful. They occupied Egypt and captured Jerusalem and the Cross of the Lord. But in 626, Emperor Herakleios (610-641) won a decisive victory near Nineveh and recaptured Jerusalem and restored the precious Cross.

On the 10th of January, the holy Church commemorates
our venerable Father AMMONIOS, who reposed in peace.

Ammonios, our venerable father, was the name of at least three holy men. It is unclear which one of three Egyptian fathers is commemorated today. There is one Father Ammonios, mentioned in the *Lausiac History*,[64] who had been a disciple of Abba Pambo (d. 393). This Ammonios had three brothers (Dioscoros, Evsevios, and Efthymios), also referred to as the "Tall Brothers," whose history is spoken of in the Life of Saint John Chrysostom, who is commemorated by the holy Church on the 13th of November. He also had two sisters, who were disciples of the Elder Pambo. When these siblings

---

[64] The account of this Saint Ammonios is given in E.A. Wallace Budge's *The Paradise of the Fathers*, I:105, 106.

attained to perfection in both word and deed, they left the desert and founded monasteries, one for men and one for women, which lay apart at a sufficient distance. Father Ammonios was a man who did not care to engage in conversation; but because of his reserve, the people of the city wished to have him for their bishop. They approached Archbishop Timothy of Alexandria (381-385) and requested that Abba Ammonios be appointed their chief shepherd. Archbishop Timothy was amenable to their proposition and sent a large party to escort the candidate to the cathedral. Now when Abba Ammonios caught sight of their approach, he attempted to escape but was unable to hide. He tried to dissuade them from elevating him to such a dignity, but he was unable to alter the course which they had selected for him. When he perceived that there was no turning them away, he took up a razor and cut off his left ear, even at the root. He then said, "I am indeed persuaded that now I cannot become a bishop." The party departed and returned to Timothy, recounting all that had taken place. The archbishop commented, "Even if his nose were split and he had fine qualities, I would consecrate him." The people went out again to fetch Ammonios. They entreated him but to no avail. They then thought to lay hold of him by force. When he saw them close in upon him, he declared, "If you do not depart from me, I shall also slit my tongue." Since they had no reason to doubt that he would make good on such a threat, they departed.

Now this same Abba Ammonios said elsewhere, "Whensoever a carnal thought should enter my thoughts, I never spare my flesh. I would heat a peace of iron in the fire and then lay it upon my members, so that I was always wounded." The holy man also had the custom never to eat food cooked by fire. God endowed him with the gift of reciting the books of the Old and New Testament. The elder was a clairvoyant and a great comfort to the brethren. An experienced monk of the desert, Father Evagrios, used to say, "I never beheld any man who had attained more closely unto impassibility than Abba Ammonios."

Another Egyptian ascetic of the same name was a disciple of Saint Anthony the Great, who is mentioned in the Life of Hieromartyr Milos, commemorated by the holy Church on the 10th of November.

There is also another Ammonios of Sketis, who was conspicuous for his love toward all. He was in possession of a number of small, beautiful houses with a nearby well. When men came to him who wished to live the eremitical life, he would offer them hospitality within his chambers, while he himself departed and summoned the brotherhood. He directed one to fetch water, another to carry bricks, and so on, until they constructed a new dwelling place for the latest hermit, who was left behind in Father Ammonios' chambers. The new cell would be fitted up in one day's time with everyone working. Thereafter, the new resident would take up occupancy at eventide, being given bread, food, and whatever else he needed. Now the new occupants were not told that their benefactor was Father Ammonios, for he preferred to remain anonymous.[65]

On the 10th of January, the holy Church commemorates our venerable Father MARCIAN, Presbyter and Oikonomos of the Great Church.[66]

Marcian (Markianos), our venerable father, flourished during the reign of the emperor having the same name, Marcian (450-457), and Empress Pulcheria (d. 453). Marcian's parents hailed from Rome. They were the scions of distinguished lines, celebrated for their exceedingly brilliant rank and wealth, though their wealth was more so to be reckoned according to their rich piety. After Marcian learned his first letters, his parents decided to leave Rome and dwell at Constantinople. Marcian was put to school and educated. He excelled not so much in secular studies as in those disciplines of greater magnitude and perfection. He thereupon became known by name to all and much talked of in diverse quarters. The patriarch also observed the virtue of the young man and was inspired to ordain him to the rank of presbyter. Afterward, he appointed him as *oikonomos* (steward) of the Great Church (Hagia Sophia);[67] not that Marcian sought this dignity, but it was decided by vote that he should have the office on account of his divine conduct of life.

---

[65] *The Paradise of the Fathers*, I:378.

[66] The Life of this saint was recorded in Greek by Saint Symeon the Metaphrastes [*P.G.* 114:429-456]. The text is extant in the Athonite monasteries of the Great Lavra, Iveron, and in other places. The text was rendered in simpler Greek by Agapios the Cretan, who published it in his *Neon Paradeison*.

[67] "The *oikonomos* was usually a priest, responsible for managing the property, income, and expenditure of a see or religious foundation. The Synod of Chalcedon (451) required every bishop to appoint an *oikonomos* from his clergy and not to administer the affairs of his see in person (Canon 26). Under Justinian I (527-565), the Great Church of Constantinople was served by nine *oikonomoi*, each with a subordinate staff. This eventually evolved into a single patriarchal *oikonomos* of the 9th C. and later. By the 10th C., the appointment came under imperial control. At that time, the epithet *megas* was attached to the title, so that Byzantine lists of patriarchal offices always name the *megas oikonomos* as the patriarch's highest-ranking subordinate, though after 1204, the office declined. *Oikonomoi* were attached to large public churches of Constantinople such as Saint Mokios. The institution was also widespread among imperial foundations." In other instances, "the *oikonomos* of a monastic foundation was usually a senior monk or nun, responsible for the management of its properties, especially agricultural estates and the maintenance of monastic buildings." *Oxford*, s.v. "Oikonomos."

Saint Marcian

Now all these incidents described above took place much later; so let us recount what occurred earlier. While Marcian was a young man, he received the priestly rank (453) from Patriarch Anatolios (449-458). His parents reposed at that time, leaving Father Marcian as sole inheritor of their wealth, which was a considerable fortune. He, however, did not spend it on bodily enjoyments and pastimes, bur rather as being one truly wise and a lover of God, he made the poor and needy his joint heirs. He therefore distributed the estate liberally. He proved to be their benefactor and abundant supplier of the needy in their physical necessities, by feeding the hungry and clothing the naked. As for himself, the prudent one profited his own soul even more by enriching it with treasures in the heavens. He loathed the will of the flesh and physical pleasures. His only passion was reading the sacred Scriptures. By these activities, he significantly benefitted and procured for himself all the virtues. He especially excelled in warring mightily against sating the stomach and indulging in wandering eyes and unlicensed vision. He understood that, through these two means, young men are most likely to suffer injury or loss. He never partook of rich foods and delectable dishes, nor did he gaze into the faces of beautiful women, fair of form. He spent most of the night in prayer. Now Father Marcian had extreme devotion and piety toward the holy martyrs, and was responsible for the adorning of many of their temples. Whatever was required in the church building, he applied himself to it tirelessly. One project in particular, to which he devoted much time and attention, was the building of a magnificent church to Saint Anastasia.

Now he had learned that a certain woman, who went by the name Niko, had been widowed. She had a grand and notable house in the city, which property he was interested in obtaining for the newly proposed church. When he came to view the house with her, and he saw that it was suitable and handsome, he came to terms with the widow and gave her two thousand florins for its purchase. But the envious hater of men put a stumbling block in the way of this deal that it might not proceed, lest that marvellous structure should be converted into a church. The devil suggested to the mind of the seller that she was losing an exquisite house, which had a renowned and august history, as it had been built by the great Constantine, and was tax exempt. Mulling over these thoughts, this fickle woman not only was saddened, but even allowed herself to be vanquished. She was determined to return the money to the buyer. Father Marcian did not wish to exercise his legal right to take possession, so he accepted the returned money. He cherished the hope that God would provide another opportunity and appropriate property according to His will. Thus this transaction was allowed to take this unexpected turn according to divine providence.

One day, as Father Marcian was conversing with the patriarch, he learned that there was an ancient church in a place called the Portico of Domninos. The patriarch advised him to renew that temple and make the martyrium exceedingly comely. Father Marcian complied. As a result he spent an incalculable sum which included the cost of marble, columns, arches, and iconography. Many other beautiful and splendid furnishings and vessels were obtained, so that the congregation stood and marvelled at such solemn grandeur.[68]

With the completion of such a beautiful and splendid church, the patriarch with his clergy, together with the imperial couple, Leo I and Verina, were invited to celebrate its consecration. It was the 22nd of December—the same day as the commemoration of the holy Great-martyr Anastasia, the deliverer from potions—when nearly the entire city was preparing to be in attendance. As the clergy readied themselves for the divine service according to Church tradition, Father Marcian was approaching the church. It was then that some beggar in dire need drew nigh and asked, "Give alms for the Lord's sake." The righteous man, being a man of profound sympathy and compassion, was caught at that moment without his purse. Though the beggar's desire was to receive money, Father Marcian found it repugnant to send away empty-handed the man who requested his help. Father Marcian then took the beggar by the hand, and they went to a corner that was hidden from public view. Father Marcian then proceeded to remove his garment and give it to the beggar, lest he should grieve his Lord in the person of the beggar. Thus, Father Marcian was left with merely his undershirt, for it was not his habit to wear two garments, but only one garment. That a man in his position should

---

[68] Circa 457-458, when Leo was emperor and Anatolios (449-458) was Bishop of Constantinople, the relics of Saint Anastasia (d. 304) were brought from Sirmium (Yugoslavia) and deposited in her church. This event demonstrated the influence of Aspar, Ardabourios, and the Goths, for they had paid for the reconstruction of the church under Saint Marcian, who arranged for the Scriptures to be read in Gothic on festal days. See C. Mango & R. Scott, eds., *The Chronicle of Theophanes Confessor*, pp. 170, 171.

have only one garment to his name was extraordinary, but he ever trod the path following the evangelic command: "Be giving to him who asketh of thee, and turn not thyself away from him who doth wish to borrow from thee [Mt. 5:42]." Father Marcian then wrapped himself with his vestment, a large phelonion, since he was to concelebrate with the other clergy that day. He then left and entered the church and the holy altar.

As the saint was liturgizing, his phelonion, on a number of occasions, was being pulled and drawn. He in turn kept gathering it together, lest any of the other priests should catch sight of his nakedness. The hierarch and the rest of the clergy could not help but notice an extraordinary and awesome wonder. They observed Father Marcian clad in what was suitable for the imperial wardrobe. They saw him arrayed in a splendid garment of inwoven gold that shone forth as lightning. When it came time to extend his hand and communicate the faithful, that divine fabric appeared more brilliant, so that none could miss its radiance. Now at this sight, the other priests bore him ill-will and discredited him as extravagant before Patriarch Gennadios I (458-471).

At the completion of the divine service, the patriarch summoned Father Marcian, who appeared with his phelonion draped about him. He surprised the holy priest when he reprimanded him for donning imperial dress that was evidently costly and bright. Father Marcian then prostrated himself before the patriarch's feet, weeping and saying, "There is some mistake, despota; it is an illusion, for I am undressed." Father Marcian then arose and drew back his vestment. The patriarch was stunned to see his priest clothed in but his undergarments. The patriarch then asked for him to explain his lack of any raiment. Since Father Marcian could no longer hide his charitable act, he disclosed how he came to lose his attire. The other clergy also learned of this account, which raised Father Marcian not only in their estimation but also in the eyes of everyone else. It was evident to all that Father Marcian's act of giving his own raiment to the beggar had been recompensed by the Lord Himself Who covered His priest's nakedness with fitting royal garb. Now at that time there were many adhering to the heresy of Arius. Upon hearing of this miracle and benefaction, together with the mellifluous words of Father Marcian, many Arians returned to Orthodoxy.

On another occasion, a fire broke out in the north quarter of the city and enveloped it in flames. The conflagration spread until it reached the sea to the south. A roaring inferno surrounded the temple of the saint, that is, the Church of Saint Anastasia. The man of God, Marcian, not in the least intimidated, but maintaining a pure faith and guileless in God, took up the holy Gospel into his arms and ascended to the roof of the church. He stood in the midst of the flames, uttering these words: "O Christ, the God of our fathers, Who preserved safe and sound the Three Children in the Babylonian furnace, do Thou keep this house unharmed, which we built with much toil, labor, and desire. And let not the fire destroy it, lest the Arians should reproach us. But do Thou perform a miracle even now, worthy of Thy magnanimity and goodness, to the glory of Thy name, and for the sake of us, Thy Orthodox slaves, who have Thee as our boast and joy." He spoke this entreaty as a torrent of tears flowed from his eyes. All those below who witnessed him standing and praying on the roof then beheld a great wonder. They observed that from behind the flames, which were round about the church, there was a sudden rushing energy that quenched and turned back the vehemence of the fire. It seemed to eyewitnesses that a mightier power, an invincible one, was driving away the fire. Hence the sacred precinct of the martyr's church was left unscathed, even as the Three Children survived the furnace.

This wonderful miracle took place not only at this church, but also in many other instances, both during the lifetime of Saint Marcian and after his repose when he was invoked by those faithful who took recourse in him. We also wish to mention that, inside the narthex of this church, there was an icon of the Theotokos, above the beautiful gate, which wrought boundless miracles for the sick, demon-possessed, bedridden, and those afflicted by other kinds of pain and suffering.

Let us now leave off narrating such miracles and mention just this one wrought by the saint in his lifetime, that we might concisely prove the point of his sanctity. On one festive holy day, when the Church of Saint Anastasia was crowded with men and women, a pregnant woman fell from one of the arches on the left side, the north side, of the church. It was surmised that either she leaned over the balcony too far or demonic complicity caused her to lose her footing and fall. She fell from that considerable height to the marble floor below and immediately expired. Thereupon, in the midst of that feast, there was great wailing and mourning. But hearken now how the saint turned the flock's lamentation into rejoicing. He lifted up his hands in prayer and urged the congregation to do so in like manner, that they might all together offer up common entreaty to the God of the universe. Forthwith—O the extraordinary wonder!—the pregnant woman was resurrected, and the unborn babe leaped in her womb.

Let us now recount other events which took place in the saint's life. There was the Church of Saint Irene, which had been a Christian church even before Constantine I enlarged it and gave it the name of Eirene (Peace). Before the inauguration of Hagia Sophia (Holy Wisdom), in 360, Saint Irene had served as the cathedral of the capital. By the fifth century, the two churches were contained within the same precinct, served by the same clergy, and regarded as forming the patriarchate's complex.[69] Originally, this church was not very large; neither was it beautiful nor well adorned, as we see it today. The all-good God, however, revealed His will to Patriarch Gennadios, saying, "Pull down the existing temple that thy successor might build anew after thy translation from this life." Gennadios therefore executed the divine command. Later, when Gennadios reposed, Marcian heard of this divine revelation. Now with regard to the new construction, either God put it in the mind of the *oikonomos* of the Great Church, or Father Marcian may have been vouchsafed a divine vision. Thereupon, Father Marcian took along with him certain individuals, and they went secretly by night to the old church. They offered up prayer to God with much piety, saying, "O God of hosts, Who dashed to the ground the altars of the idols, Thou hast delivered us from their profane deception and commanded us to build churches to Thee. As Thou didst then, do Thou also now look down upon this site and sanctify it. Empower us to build a house to Thee, which Thou didst command." After supplicating in this manner, Father Marcian fell asleep, according to God's œconomy. The Lord Himself then appeared to him in a vision and revealed the site and dimensions. After this, Father Marcian heard a divine voice, saying, "Marcian, all is possible to those who believe."

The saint then rose up with a sense of both fear and joy. He related his vision to the archbishop, who gave him whatever authority was needed to build the church in accordance with the divine pattern shown to him in the vision, even as the Lord once showed Moses in the mount [Ex. 25:9, 40]. The plan and work involved much toil and outlay, especially preparing the foundation toward the sea. Afterward, columns and marble added to the expenses. The roof was covered with lead, even as it appears to this day. All who beheld the holy structure were filled with awe, admiring the firm and well-placed walls and the beautiful ground floor. There was general approbation for the Church's arrangement and adornments.

We must mention, however, that this grand undertaking and its accomplishment did not go unnoticed by the devil, and incited his malice toward the project. When two pillars were being set before the altar, the devil sat upon one of the pillars. It was the larger of the two pillars which was intended to be placed on the north side. This pillar, however, became so heavy that the builders and craftsmen together could not lift it. It would not stir from its place. It ignored all natural laws and remained indifferent to the application of force with wood and ropes. The saint alone then began offering up fervent prayer to the Lord. He then made the sign of the Cross over the

---

[69] See *Oxford*, s.v. "Church of Saint Irene."

pillar, rebuking the demon and saying, "O enemy and adversary of that which is good, do thou desist and hinder not what is to become to the glory of God." After he uttered these words of reproof, the saint also helped with the lifting of the pillar. Though he was elderly and his physical powers were diminished, he placed his hands on the pillar with the workers. Forthwith, the marble pillar moved with great ease and was lifted into its appointed place. In order that this miracle might not be forgotten with the passage of time, but that it might ever remain in the memory of men, God permitted that the pillar should lean slightly. It remains so to this day, though every effort was made to set aright the angle.

The two churches mentioned herein were not the only achievements of the blessed Marcian. He was also responsible for the building of the Church of Saint Isidore and the translation of that saint's relics. Many people marvelled at the saint's dedication and reverence for the churches, which entailed no small expenditure. He would answer them and say, "Brothers, if I had a daughter to marry, would I not adorn her with the most beautiful of jewels that I was able to provide? How much more then should we array the Church, the Bride of Christ, for whom the Master has shed His blood?" The great Marcian endeavored earnestly to honor the saints, so that he never grieved or bemoaned any expense. He also built churches in other places, including Saint Theodore at Tainaro and Saint Stratonikos at Rhegium.

Despite all the disbursements made by the saint on behalf of the churches, he was not negligent in distributing alms to the poor, among whom he offered abundant help. On account of his profound empathy, he would go about in the evening throughout the city byways. In his rounds, he found that those who were formerly wealthy, but had fallen on hard times and destitution, were needing alms. During daylight hours, these men and women were ashamed to be seen. It should also be mentioned here that the saint's philanthropy was not only toward the living but also toward the dead. If someone died penniless and needy, without any to attend to burial preparations, Father Marcian undertook that ministration and saw to it that all was done properly. He deemed these opportunities, that is, showing charity to the dead, for which there is no hope of return from the recipient, a great and precious treasure. He would wash and dress the decedent and then speak to him, as though he were yet alive, saying, "Rise, brother, let us exchange the last kiss according to custom." Straightway—O the unspeakable wonder!— the corpse obeyed and would rise. After the newly reposed kissed the saint, he would fall asleep again in death, as before.

These superhuman feats of the saint were recognized by others. Indeed, Father Marcian was wont to visit at night a certain servant of a banker who used to exchange his florins for coins. This happened many times in the same night, as the saint was in need of coins as he distributed alms. Father Marcian wished to remain anonymous during these bank transactions, so he would cover his face. Now the banker did not know that it was the patriarchal *oikonomos* before him, and he would use unfair balances in weighing the gold. Consequently, the banker held back a tidy sum. The saint knew that he was being cheated, but being a meek man, he said nothing. He merely feigned that he did not know that he was being shortchanged. As these interchanges happened quite frequently, the banker became inquisitive and began wondering about his night visitor's identity. He took it upon himself one night to have one of his faithful menservants secretly follow him and discover his home. The saint went out, not realizing that he was being watched. In the meantime, the saint went about his customary charities. When he encountered a dead man in the street, he was seen to go to the retailers and purchase what was needed for burial. He was also observed to wash and dress the decedent. He was then detected not only speaking to the dead but also being kissed by the corpse when it came to life. When the young manservant beheld all these events, he was in terror. He returned to his master, disclosing all he had seen that night. The banker, hearing this report from his trustworthy servant, was moved to fear God. He then gathered up the money of which he had earlier defrauded the saint, and hastened to return it. He found Father Marcian and received his forgiveness.

The thrice-blessed one not only was possessed of these virtues, but also often went into the midst of harlots, in imitation of our Master Christ Who befriended such women.[70] Father Marcian offered them generous alms for their necessities, lest they continue to prostitute themselves on account of poverty. During every feast day, he assembled many such women whom he previously would tell to exercise continence for a number of days. He then would have them bathe from the pollution of the flesh. Afterward, the loving *oikonomos* brought them into church and spoke to them so sincerely of the punishments of everlasting perdition, that they came to repentance for their iniquities. Now many of these women even became nuns. Thus, in a wondrous manner, they came to full spiritual health, to the glory of the Lord. Father Marcian even then undertook their needs and expenses in the convent, so that they should not have the concern of providing for themselves. Thus they could spend their time weeping for their sins and thereby finish their lives in a God-pleasing manner.

The goodly Marcian therefore dispensed alms not only by giving money, goods, and other types of wealth, but also did not hesitate to donate the only garment on his own back, though he did not retain another change

---

[70] Cf. Mt. 21:31, 32; Mt. 11:19; Lk. 7:34.

of clothing in his wardrobe. On one occasion, Father Marcian was returning to his rooms after celebrating the feast of a saint, as he was wont to go and participate in the chanting. He was caught in a heavy downpour and became drenched. When he entered his chamber, he thereupon lit a fire that he might dry his rason (cassock). After he removed his garment and placed it near the fire, it was just then that the patriarch sent a message that he was to come, since he needed him. Now the messengers stood and knocked at the door for a considerable time, but Father Marcian was too embarrassed to open to them, as he was naked. He therefore finally called out to them, asking, "What do you want?" They answered, to which he replied, "I shall be coming out in a little while." Now one of the messengers peeked in through an opening and observed that the *oikonomos* was undressed and his dripping garment was set before the fire. He told the others and they all left together to report it to the patriarch, who was not completely ignorant of his steward's practises. He addressed the messengers, saying, "Father Marcian is not anxious for his body or raiment or what he shall put on. He knows that the 'soul is more than food and the body is more than raiment [Mt. 6:25, 28].' As we read in the Epistle: 'For we brought nothing into the world, and it is manifest that neither are we able to carry anything out; but having sustenance and coverings, we shall be satisfied with these [1 Tim. 6:8].' Thus, what more can I say?" He then smiled and said, "This is how our *oikonomos* conducts his life."

The account up to this point has briefly put forward some of the virtues and deeds of this great man of God. He not only was revered by the common folk, but also had the genuine esteem of hierarchs and senators, and the emperor himself. Moreover, he also had the respect of the powers behind Germanic soldiery in the capital, which dominated the eastern court after the death of Emperor Marcian, since they secured the elevation of Leo I. We speak now of the former consul and military commander Aspar and his father Ardabourios. Though they were Arian heretics, they yet venerated the patriarchal steward, before whom they would never dare gaze directly into his eyes. These Goths also sent contributions and gifts for the building up of the Church of Saint Anastasia, including costly gold and silver vessels. Consequently, Father Marcian had Orthodox books translated into their mother tongue and presented to them that they might read them and become pious Orthodox Christians.

Not only the Byzantines held the saint in awe, but even as far west as his former homeland had his good fame spread. Many from abroad flocked to Constantinople and sojourned there that they might behold the holy man. Some sought to receive healing for their souls, and others cures for their bodies. Indeed, many sick folk received their much-desired health by means of his acceptable intercessions before God. Let us recount one such miracle performed on behalf of a fellow countrywoman, and then we shall conclude our narration. There was a woman from Rome who was seriously ill. She was diseased with an issue of blood, from which she had already suffered many years. She had spent an incalculable amount on physicians and medicines, but enjoyed no remedy or relief from the hemorrhaging. After she heard of the signs and wonderworkings of the venerable Marcian at Constantinople, she decided to go to that capital, having as her companions piety and faith. As soon as she entered the city, she went to find Father Marcian. Upon locating him, she went and prostrated herself before him, recounting her lamentable and incurable case. Straightway, as Father Marcian uttered a prayer on her behalf, the flow of blood stopped, the disease fled, and the woman was left healthy. She returned to Rome rejoicing.

These and many other good works were performed by the saint during his God-pleasing life. At last, he knew his earthly sojourn was soon to end. He was in the midst of the project for the Church of Saint Irene, which had not yet been consecrated. Therefore, prior to his repose, he uttered these words of prayer to the Lord as he was about to be translated: "Into Thy holy hands, O Master, I leave this soul which Thou hast made, and the church which I have been constructing with Thy counsel and design." Saint Marcian then reposed on the 10th day of January, in the year 471. The entire city gathered together for his funeral, with the patriarch and his presbyters officiating. The emperor also with his senators attended. The assembly was solemn as they interred our holy father with honor, as was meet. Empress Verina (d. ca. 484), wife of Leo, undertook the supervision of the Church of Saint Irene and saw that it was completed. She spared no expense to beautify the church and had the roof sheathed in gold. The consecration took place in the second year on the 20th day of January.

This then is the account of the divinely blessed Marcian and his wonderworkings by which the Lord glorified him, according to the God-given promise, "I shall glorify those who glorify Me." By the intercessions of Saint Marcian, may we also be vouchsafed everlasting blessedness in Christ our Lord and God, to the ages of the ages. Amen.

Through the intercessions of Thy Saints,
O Christ God, have mercy on us. Amen.

**On the 11th of January, the holy Church commemorates
our venerable and God-bearing Father
THEODOSIOS the Coenobiarch.**[1]

Theodosios, our holy and God-bearing father, who is known also as "the Coenobiarch,"[2] lived at the time of Leo the Great (r. 457-474) and reached the era of Emperor Anastasios Dikoros (r. 491-518) and Justin I (518-527). He came from Mogarissos, a village in Cappadocia, the great Saint Basil's province. In that humble and obscure hamlet, the sublime and wondrous Theodosios was born of parents, Proheresios and Evlogia, who were God-loving and pious. Later, Evlogia became a nun at the hands of her son, who became her spiritual father. Therefore, just as she gave him being in the flesh, he was the cause of her spiritual well-being and rebirth.

Saint Theodosios

As he grew, the blessed Theodosios increased in physical and spiritual stature. He led a remark-able life even from his youth, thus showing what he would later be-come. He never indulged in any physical pleasure, nor did he have any improper desire. He had no love for wealth or money or any material thing, but wished only to see the holy land. This divine aspiration was so

---

[1] The Life of this saint was recorded in Greek by Saint Symeon the Metaphrastes, whose manuscript begins, "The sweetest spring...[*P.G.* 114: 469-554]." The text is extant in the Athonite monasteries of the Great Lavra, Iveron, and in other places. The text was rendered in simpler Greek and published in the *Neon Paradeison*. The work of Constantine Koukey, *Saint Theodosios the Coenobiarch*, Kymis: Transfiguration Monastery, 1983, was incorporated herein. Father Gerasimos Mikrayiannanites has composed a Supplicatory Canon to the saint.

[2] The coenobium or "common life" housed a community of monks or nuns, emphasizing a communal mode of life.

deeply rooted in his heart that he rarely thought of anything else or entertained any other thoughts. He was an excellent student of holy Scripture. He
once read in Genesis that God ordered Abraham to abandon his parents,
friends, relatives, and everything else for the love of Him, if he wished to
inherit everlasting blessedness [Gen. 12:1]. Theodosios then nurtured a deep
desire in his heart to tread the narrow road, so as to find that blessedness in
the age to come.

Therefore, he besought the Lord to guide him to his salvation. He
ventured to go to Jerusalem at the time when Emperor Marcian (450-457)
ruled and the holy Fourth Œcumenical Synod at Chalcedon (451) was about
to convene against Nestorios and all the other heretics.

Saint Symeon the Stylite

When the goodly-minded Theodosios arrived in Antioch, he went to
venerate Saint Symeon the Stylite, commemorated by the holy Church on the
1st of September, to receive his blessing and to seek his advice concerning
salvation. As he approached the stylite, and before he could greet him, the
holy Symeon exclaimed from atop the pillar, "Welcome, Theodosios, O man
of God!" The latter was amazed by this and, without thinking about it, fell to
the ground and reverenced the saint with all humility. He attempted to answer
him, but, after a short while, Symeon invited him up. Theodosios arose and
went toward him smiling. Then he climbed up the pillar, and Symeon greeted
and embraced Theodosios with a holy kiss. The youth thought it was very
significant to be able to embrace the venerable body of the stylite. He then
received his kiss as a divine seal that strengthened him along the road toward
virtue. The great Symeon then prophesied all that Theodosios would
accomplish later, that is, how he would become a leader over so many
coenobia; how he would rescue many souls from the jaws of the devil; and
many other things that would happen to him. Elated in soul, and thereby
encouraged by the prayers and blessing of the venerable Symeon, Theodosios
hastened to Jerusalem. At that time Juvenal was patriarch (ca. 422-458).

Jerusalem

After Theodosios worshipped at the holy places, he thought about
how to begin his exercises in divine philosophy; that is, whether to start with
the eremitical life or to create a synodia first.[3] He thereupon reflected within
himself thus: "If the soldiers of the earthly king dare not march into battle
unless they have been previously trained by able generals in the arts of war,
how can I, who am inexperienced, attempt to contend against the bodiless and
cunning demons? Therefore, I should search out spiritual fathers and remain

---

[3] A synodia is a group of monks living under the tutelage of an elder or spiritual
father.

under them for a long time to achieve mastery, and then I will dwell in the desert."

Abbot Longinos

He weighed these considerations most wisely, as he was prudent by nature, knowing that if one does not train under an artisan and teacher, one shall never become expert. Therefore, he approached a certain blessed father, named Longinos, who was the most virtuous and experienced elder at that time. He stayed with him for a long period, keeping the same regimen and abiding in safety with him in a small abode near the Tower of David. In that place, he admirably gathered the sweet honey of virtue. Theodosios thereafter was ably trained to be discerning by this astute teacher; and, furthermore, he hearkened to his elder in all matters, so as not to do his own will.

At that time, there was a certain woman named Ikelia who was very pious and respected by all. She was wealthy materially, but more so in the virtues. She happened to marry a man much older than herself, and, on account of her godly life, he quickly became a deacon. Now there was a certain *kathisma*[4] or cell on the road to Bethlehem. Close by to this *kathisma*, Ikelia refurbished the church and dedicated it to the Theotokos. This holy woman also rendered many valuable services to the Elder Longinos, and she requested that Theodosios settle in that place. Longinos hearkened to Ikelia's request and agreed to it, without his disciple's knowledge; for the blessed Theodosios would have preferred to remain with his elder than relocate. This is because Theodosios was very pleased to abide in obedience to another's commands, rather than to give orders to others. Nevertheless, Theodosios obeyed and took his departure to the *kathisma*. After he had stayed there a short while, his fame spread everywhere, inasmuch as virtue manifests the man, just as a lighted candle reveals the one who carries it. The result of his stay there was that he was visited by many pilgrims who distracted and deprived him of his beloved solitude. Therefore, he ascended to the peak of the mountain and lived in a cave. This is where his holy relics lie today.

There is also a tradition from the ancient fathers that, in that hallowed cave, the three blessed Magi spent the night after they had worshiped the Lord, and that an angel was sent there and ordered them to return to their own country by another road, which they did, leaving the unscrupulous Herod to strive against God foolishly and in vain.

---

[4] The word *kathisma* (lit. "sitting, seat") has a number of meanings in Byzantine studies. In this instance it is a generic term for a small monastic habitation, housing only a few monks and dependent on a larger monastery. *The Oxford Dictionary of Byzantium*, s.v. "Kathisma."

The Cave

The saint fled to this cave that he might better dedicate himself to God. The main reason he did this, however, was to escape being in authority over others, as this is burdensome and even dangerous. Many of the fathers in that area attempted to place him in that position because Theodosios was so far ahead of all others in virtue. However, he preferred to live in solitude that he might multiply the fruits of his labors for virtue. Nevertheless, this move to the cave was not his own will, but God's. As the saint lived in such a sacred abode, he took the divine Apostle John as his example. It was here that Theodosios laid down the foundation of all the blessed virtues, the principal one being love, and especially to love the Lord with all the powers of his soul and with all his heart and will, disdaining all earthly things and desiring only Him as the Provider of life and as the universal Savior.

Therefore, as one expert in music, the divine Theodosios also harmoniously set the energies of his soul in motion, like a musical instrument, with proper timing and melody. He controlled his body with much wisdom and prudence, doing all things that are fitting and having only one goal in mind, that is, to do nought that was displeasing to God. Thus, he displayed courage and fearlessness in the perils he underwent for God. He would never succumb to threats or yield to flattery when that which was demanded of him was not the will of God. With divinely endowed grace and wisdom from the almighty God, he discerned the thoughts of his heart by examining and proving them with exactness. Theodosios knew the wiles of the ruler of this world, that he might steal "from the right"; that is, on account of his excessive asceticism, the enemy might plunge him into pride and conceit. He was ever vigilant, prayed at all times, and shed torrents of tears. He had suspended a rope that it might prop him up, in case sleep should overtake him, and thus he would stand through the night in prayer. Moreover, he was humble in spirit, meek, and possessed all the other virtues. He was most austere and unbending in the temperance of the flesh; never did he satisfy his hunger, but ate only enough so that he should not fall ill from excessive fasting. Again, his little nourishment did not consist of rich food, but only of dates, carob, wild vegetables, and legumes soaked in water. When he could not procure these things, because the land was arid and unproductive, he soaked the tender hearts of palms and ate them only from excessive need; thus, he survived as well as he could. He never tasted bread for thirty whole years. And just as he deprived his body, so much more did he nourish the soul day and night by meditating on the laws of God. Therefore, as a tree planted by the rivers of water, he harvested his fruit in due season—sweetly and abundantly. Now not only in his youth did he inure himself to such hardships, but also in his old age he adhered to abstinence and rejoiced in labors and pains, as others rejoice in the pleasures of the body.

Because of these virtues and attributes, he shone from afar and appeared as a city that is built on top of a mountain. Therefore, many thronged to Theodosios in order to partake of the honey of his virtue and to make progress. They preferred to live the hard life of the desert rather than to inhabit splendid cities and to enjoy themselves with the king himself. But at first, he would not receive them, so as not to disrupt his silence. Therefore, after much persuasion and even force, they built cells near to his. They enjoined upon Theodosios that he should not think only of his own benefit, but also care for the spiritual problems of those about him. Thereupon, observing their great zeal and good intention, he accepted them, realizing that great is the perdition of him that neglects to love his neighbor and loves him not as himself. At that time, about six or seven disciples gathered around him.

The Monk Basil

He exhorted them all with beneficial words and examples to live in a God-pleasing way, that is, having the remembrance of death as the true philosophy, for it can induce one to live in virtue. Consequently, he ordered his disciples to build a cemetery, so that each one of them might behold his future grave and thus prepare himself beforehand accordingly. After they had completed it, the saint, knowing the future by divine grace, turned to his disciples and, in a jesting tone, said, "Behold, the tomb is ready, but which one of you shall be buried first?" Although he spoke in a teasing manner among them, he impressed upon them its seriousness; for he knew the proper time and place to be austere and when to be joyous and playful in moderation, that he might ease their distress. Now there was among them a virtuous and obedient priest-monk named Basil. He was very zealous and emulated and resembled Theodosios in all things, even as a child in relation to his father. For wax does not receive the impress of signet-rings as much as Basil bore the distinctive marks of Theodosios. He spoke first and answered, "I, my teacher, will inaugurate it, by the prayer of thy holiness." This is because Basil thought that death was a boon and would bring great gain. And after he had said this, he bowed low in respect and, begging Theodosios to permit him to enter, he asked his blessing. And so it happened. Without any apparent fever, illness, or injury to his mind or other members whatsoever, Basil surrendered his blessed soul to God. He entered the tomb and became as one that slept a light and healthful sleep. Indeed, his end was the reward of a virtuous life and of one eager to be translated to that blessedness, to behold the face of the Lord.

Theodosios ordered them to perform the customary memorial service and liturgies for the third, ninth, and fortieth day, and thus they did. Behold how one miracle followed another! During the period of those forty days, when they came together to celebrate the service of Vespers, in the midst of their holy synodia, the divine Basil was seen. He was heard chanting together with the great Theodosios. However, not all saw and heard this event. One who did was Aetios, who followed very carefully in the footsteps and life of his teacher, for he wished to emulate him in every possible way. Now this Aetios was unable to see Basil, but he certainly heard him chanting. He turned to Theodosios and asked him if he also heard Basil chanting, and Theodosios said to him, "Not only did I hear him, but I also saw him; and tonight thou shalt behold him too, as thou desirest." That night when they gathered in church to celebrate the divine Liturgy, Basil again stood among the brethren while they chanted. Then Theodosios, who clearly saw Basil, uttered a prayer on behalf of Aetios, saying, "Open, O Lord, his eyes that he might behold the great mystery of Thy wondrous works!" Straightway, the spiritual eyes of Aetios were opened, and he saw Basil clearly. He ran eagerly to embrace Basil, but the latter vanished. Basil was then heard saying to the brethren, "Be saving yourselves, O fathers and brethren. You shall see me here no longer!" Thus, our Savior says in the Gospel: "The one who believeth in Me, though he die, he shall live; and everyone who liveth and believeth in Me, in no wise shall ever die [Jn. 11:25, 26]." This is the first token of Saint Theodosios' saintliness. But listen to another account.

God Sends Bread

One year, on Holy Saturday, the eve of the resurrection of our Lord, the fathers had no victuals with which to celebrate the holy Pascha. They were twelve in number and distraught, not for their lack of material food, but because they had no bread with which to celebrate the Liturgy and receive the divine Mysteries. Moreover, they had no oil and nothing else edible. The saint observed their sullen expressions and knew that they murmured in their hearts against him, so he said to them, "Prepare the holy Table and be not grieved, for the One Who fed the multitudes in the wilderness and satisfied the hunger of so many thousands with five loaves of bread shall also send help to us, unworthy though we be." Thus he spoke, and his word became deed; for as God sent a ram to Abraham to sacrifice [Gen. 22:13], thus at this time He sent a man to the monastery with two mules laden with bread, wine, and other necessities. Furthermore, he even had bread (that is, prosphora) for the divine service. The latter appeared to them to be a gift of God; it was like rain from heaven, as was manna in olden times. The fathers, overjoyed at Christ's providential care, glorified the merciful God Who did not abandon them. Indeed, until the holy Feast of the Pentecost, Christ nourished them spiritually and physically to their plenitude. Thus, little by little, the disciples perceived the holiness of their teacher.

The Fruit of Faith and Hope

But let us relate another account. At that time, there lived a wealthy man, who was merciful and sent alms to all the hermits, so that they might entreat the Lord on behalf of his soul. He knew that this was a blessed and good work, that by distributing his material wealth he might gain the salvation of his soul. Therefore, both he and those with him, who obeyed the commandments and will of God, continued this practise of sending alms to the hermits who had left the world that they might come closer to God. However, he never sent alms to Saint Theodosios or his disciples, probably because it escaped him or because it was the will of God to test His servant. Therefore, Theodosios' disciples would approach and pester him to have a word with this wealthy man that they might enjoy some of his almsgiving, since they had only a few carobs to eat and soon would be left with nothing. The holy man told them not to despair, but to hope in God; for He Who nourished the ravens [Lk. 12:24] would also assist them as before.

Shortly after he said this, they noticed a man on the road with an animal. He was attempting to guide the beast in a direction away from the monastery. But when the beast spotted the monastery, it refused to proceed. Even though its master struck the creature, it stood still as a rock. The man perceived that it was not the will of God that he should go where he had planned. So he exchanged roles with the beast and allowed the animal to lead in whichever direction it chose. The beast of burden went to the Monastery of Saint Theodosios. When the man saw that they had nothing to eat there, he was astonished at the mercy and mysterious providence of God, discerning that the disobedience of the pack animal was the will of God, that His good servants might have provisions in order to serve Him better. Henceforward, he brought them a double portion of all those provisions vital to their survival. From this event, Theodosios' disciples no longer troubled him over this matter, but instead attempted to emulate him in his steadfast faith and hope in God.

The Building of the Monastery

The number of brethren increased day by day. Many came to live with him, because he was as a fountain of virtue. He attracted virtue-loving souls, among whom were many wealthy and prominent people. Their number outgrew what the cave could accommodate. Therefore, some of his disciples approached him and importuned him to build a monastery that they might expand. Then the saint pondered what he should do, whether to retire alone elsewhere or to bear the responsibility of so many brethren. He then remembered the words of Saint Symeon and entreated the Lord to enlighten him to do what was to their interest, for his heart was more inclined to dwell alone, yet he thought of the brethren. So he took a censer and put incense on

Saint Theodosios the Coenobiarch

unlit coals. Then he walked about the desert, uttering only one prayer on his lips to God, as follows: "My Lord and God, Thou art the One Who performed such great wonders for Israel and appointed Moses with so many signs to undertake the guardianship of the people, such as when his staff changed to a serpent, or his hand became leprous and was miraculously healed, or the water became blood and then reverted to its original nature. Thou art the One Who, for Gideon's sake, gave him a sign of future victory by dropping dew on the fleece of wool and drought on all the ground; and then that night Thou didst cause the fleece to be dry when the ground all around was bedewed [Judg. 6:36-40]. Thou art the One Who also hearkened to Ezekias (Hezekiah) who, when sick, turned to the wall, and prayed to Thee, and Thou didst add fifteen years to his life [4 Kgs. (2 Kgs.) 20:2]; and also Thou didst grant the prayer of Thy Prophet Elias, sending fire from heaven to consume the sacrifice and the altar and the dust, licking up the water in the trench, so that the people that had forgotten Thee and acted impiously might return to Thee, the true God [3 Kgs. (1 Kgs.) 18:17-40]. Hearken, O God, Who art the same now as then, to Thy servant, O almighty Lord, and show us a sign to indicate where we should build a church and monastery to Thy glory, to dwell in it and to praise Thee!" As he uttered this, he held the unlit censer, and the brethren followed him. And just as the saint advised them, they were resolved to erect the monastery on that spot where the coals would ignite. They walked for a long time, bypassing even those spots that might have been suitable, until they reached the Desert of Coutila and then the Lake of Asphalt, but the coals did not ignite. Then the saint decided to turn back, surmising that it was not the will of God.

As they passed by a deserted cave—behold, who can extol Thy might, O immortal King?—smoke rose up from the coals, and also a wonderful and ineffable fragrance. The monastics were overjoyed at this and immediately laid the foundations, to the glory of God. They built a holy tabernacle and "arsenal" for virtues, that is, a lofty and magnificent church and a spacious monastery with cells. An infirmary was built, including accommodations for visitors, and every other convenience, so that not only monks would have comfort, but also the pilgrims who came to worship devoutly, as the blessed Theodosios was most compassionate. He not only guided people spiritually, but he also labored for their physical needs. One source, we are told, says that Theodosios was especially famous for three things: exact asceticism with true faith throughout life, glad hospitality without distinction of persons, and concentration almost without ceasing in the divine office.[5] Thereupon, great numbers frequented that monastery. These included the poor and needy, and those who languished from other causes. The sympathetic saint attended to everyone and no one left there unaided. All were greeted with great joy and much love, for he was the eye of the blind, the vesture of the naked, the shelter of the destitute, the physician of the sick, and the servant of all who suffered in body and soul and from mental diseases. He tended to their bodily sores and wounds, cleaning and dressing them. He would comfort them and encourage them to have patience in their misfortunes, so as to achieve the kingdom to come.

Certain monks, who were negligent, grumbled against the visitors. They not only refused to serve them, but they would not even lay eyes on them; for these ill-disposed monks were proud and fainthearted. They never considered that they too were human and of the same fiber. Yet the righteous one, who was possessed of a noble and great spirit, served all generously, assisted by the more devout monks. Therefore, no one was left there unattended due to his poverty or indigence. Indeed, the more needy and insignificant one was, the more so did Theodosios minister to such a one. In fact, a day did not pass by when they did not receive a hundred or more visitors in the monastery. There were many witnesses to the activities of Theodosios within the monastery and how he endured all things with the sick. For this reason, one would be correct to describe his monastery as a harbor and general clinic, an open house and refuge for the hungry and cold, the infirm, pilgrims, and strangers. His humility and simplicity in dealing with the weaknesses and frailties of his fellow man caused him never to cast anyone

---

[5] Chitty, *The Desert a City*, p. 109.

out of the monastery, nor did he overlook or ignore anyone, nor did he judge that anyone was unworthy of being shown understanding. The last trait is something which even some fathers after the flesh have difficulty displaying—that is, unconditional affection—toward their own children. Indeed, the more the monastery tended to the poor and destitute, the more the generous Benefactor bestowed upon them in return, and they never lacked any of their necessities, as one shall discover herein.

He Has Filled the Hungry with Good Things

Once a great famine visited that area, when God chastised the people for their sins. On Palm Sunday, the feast day of the Lord's entry into Jerusalem, the impoverished swarmed the monastery. They used the feast as a pretext, for a great multitude had assembled more from hunger than for the holy day. The stewards, observing such a multitude, despaired, fearing that the bread would not suffice, and distributed much less than usual. As the saint saw this unfamiliar conduct, he reproached their weak faith and ordered them to open the doors so that everyone could enter the refectory. Next he set all the food before them, saying to the visitors, "Brethren, all of you, eat to the glory of God and satisfy your hunger!" While the poor were generously fed, God filled the storeroom with more bread than ever before. For the God of wonders multiplied the few provisions which they had, so that the visitors ate to their contentment, even as once did the five thousand with the five loaves. Thereafter, the servants went to the storeroom to examine if there were any loaves left for the monks, and, seeing that it was full, they were truly amazed. So they blessed the saint whom they earlier had criticized and murmured against. Thus the benevolent God rewarded Theodosios plentifully for his good intention, making him famous and respected everywhere, as God honors all those who honor Him with their acts.

On another occasion, there was a celebration of the Theotokos, and a great crowd gathered to attend the service and to receive alms, as usual. So many people had congregated that the monks were at a loss how to serve them, not having food to accommodate even one-third of the pilgrims. But the right hand of God, which nourishes the world, generously increased the bread so miraculously that they all ate to satiety. So many baskets of bread were left over that they took them to their homes, and many more were left at the monastery, so that what remained sufficed for days.

The Saint Continues to Build

Our venerable father, who had great love and compassion toward his neighbor, genuine and unconditional, then had a desire to construct all edifices that were necessary for the monastery. Therefore, he built three great structures: one to accommodate monastics, who came thither from other monasteries (for visiting and veneration), and two buildings for the laymen, one for the noblemen and the noteworthy, and the other for the poor and humble folk who had need of help from others. However, he also built a rest home in a more remote place for the elderly monks that were sick, so that they would find rest from the long labors of asceticism.

More Church Buildings

The saint also built four churches within the monastery complex. The main church, where Greek was chanted, was where he and most of the brethren worshipped. Two other churches were built for the Armenians and the Bessi (Thracians). Yet a fourth, which was set apart, was built for those who were troubled by the snares of the demons. The monks would pray seven times daily. However, whenever the divine Liturgy was to be performed, each would remain in his respective church until after the reading of the Gospel, when all (except the demonized) would assemble in the big church, where Greek was used, so that they might all commune the sacred Mysteries together. Saint Theodosios also appointed who would begin to chant or lead the choir and who would read while the others sat.

The Shepherd and His Flock

Is it possible to describe the virtues of this God-loving shepherd and the attainments of his sacred flock? He reared seven hundred and ninety-three monks and brought them to God, as they lived a God-pleasing life. Some ended their days in the desert; others became bishops and abbots, and not because they sought the honor, as certain foolish ones do today, who give silver to become abbots in wealthy monasteries, but because people elected them against their own will, knowing that they were capable of guiding souls and leading them to life everlasting. Some of his disciples absolutely refused to go into the world, and they struggled in the desert for many years—eighty or more. With the passage of time, they accumulated spiritual wealth, and through them the blessed one was acclaimed and became famous everywhere, so that not one area remained that was not uplifted spiritually by the wonderful Theodosios.

His fame spread throughout the world, and great numbers flocked to him, soldiers and wealthy nobles, who renounced glory and honor as if they were a dream, and became his disciples, preferring obscurity and lowliness, for the sake of the life to come. Many learned and erudite men left their studies, the cities and the esteem of human wisdom, preferring to become fools for Christ and disciples of the great Theodosios, in order to be taught by him another type of wisdom which transcends nature. Consequently, the astute shepherd directed and guided many with much discretion, rendering the yoke lighter for the infirm ones and, for the sturdy ones, imposing an austere rule. He trained everyone not with a rod, but with words seasoned with salt. He counseled them, calling upon the words of the Prophet Jeremias that, though the Lord visited Jerusalem with punishments, He would never be far from them; for He chastened every son out of His compassion and not out of the fruit of wrath, that they might be instructed and edified. He reminded them that it was worse to have never suffered here in this life with sickness or tribulation, so that we might cleanse our sins with many afflictions, than to undergo everlasting torments for not having corrected ourselves here. Therefore, he told them to accept joyfully such visitations and to offer God thanksgiving, for He Who chastens us can also heal us. He was so wise and knowledgeable that he knew the movements of the mind and benefitted the brethren as well as himself; for whosoever benefits his neighbor, leading his soul to salvation, benefits himself even more.

More Concerning the Saint

Saint Theodosios was so deeply smitten with the sweet arrow of love and held so fast in love's fetters that he practised in actual deed the highest of God's commandments: "Thou shalt love the Lord thy God with all thy heart, and with all thy soul, and with all thy strength, and with all thy mind [Lk. 10:27]." This can be achieved by no other means than to concentrate all the natural powers of the soul in single desire for the Creator alone. Such also was the work of Theodosios' mind. When he offered consolation, he inspired awe. When reprimanding someone, he was always kind and sweet. Who else, as he did, could converse with many and appear quite at their service, yet at the same time collect his senses and marshal them back within him? Who, as he did, could enjoy, in a crowd or in the midst of tumult, the same inner peace as others who live in solitude in the wilderness? Theodosios the Great, by collecting the senses and turning them within, became pierced by love for the Creator.

Among his many excellent attributes, the saint loved to read. Books never left his hands, neither when he was ill nor in his old age, but he read day and night in order to receive benefit from the sacred words. In truth, he was worthy of admiration, for even though he never studied rhetoric, he was endowed to speak well by the grace of the Holy Spirit, and not by human wisdom, so that he surpassed even trained orators. He possessed an excellent memory and recited excerpts from Saint Basil, whom he emulated closely, and strived to adorn his soul with his ways, and his tongue with his words. He memorized parts of Saint Basil's writings that would stimulate even the supine. From these, we shall recite a few lines: "I beseech thee, O brethren, for the love of our Lord Jesus Christ, Who was crucified for our sins, let us attend to our souls. Let us repent for our transgressions, now that we have available time, so that we may not weep to no avail when condemned. Our Lord assists those who return from their evil ways now. Later, as the righteous Judge, He shall examine their thoughts, deeds, and words. Then each one of us shall receive according to his deeds—some to blessed life everlasting, and others, unending perdition." With these words, the saint guided his reason-endowed sheep and urged them to be ever alert.

Confrontation with the Emperor

As we said, the venerable one was meek, humble, and serene, but when the integrity of the Faith was at stake, he showed himself adamant and ready for dispute. According to the holy Scriptures, he was like a consuming fire and a blade mowing down the weeds of evil. To this end he clashed with the iniquitous Emperor Anastasios, the relentless enemy of the Fourth Œcumenical Synod, who was a follower of the heresies of Eftyches, Dioscoros, and Severos, who taught that Christ had one nature. In various ways had this sovereign cajoled certain fathers into supporting the heresy, while others he persecuted openly. He attempted to entice the wise Theodosios with money, by sending a donation of thirty liters (approximately two thousand one hundred gold coins). In order to conceal the fact that he sent the donation as a snare, and aware that the holy man might reject it, he disguised the hook with bait. He bade Theodosios to accept it and spend it on the poor and needy. The saint accepted the gold, that a scandal might not arise, but despised its real intent and countered it with sound arguments and remarks. Thus, the emperor was vanquished as a stag is by a lion, as we shall see further.

A short while after he had donated the gold, he sent emissaries to our Saint Theodosios, asking him to subscribe to the aforementioned heresy. The latter gathered together all the fathers of the desert and, with their common consent, made the following reply to him: "Since thou hast given us two choices—either to live in shame and without freedom by complying with the opinion of the Akephaloi[6] or to suffer a violent yet honorable death, in the event that we remain steadfast to the correct dogmas of the holy fathers—know this: we prefer death. And not only will we not deviate from the Faith, but also we condemn all those whom thou hast induced to share thine opinions. And if thou ever ordainest any of the Akephaloi, we shall not accept

---

[6] Akephaloi were heretics of Monophysite derivation that were adamant in their support of the term "one nature of Christ." They broke away from the heretic and Monophysite Bishop of Alexandria, Peter Mongos (477-490), who, in 482, accepted the *Henotikon*, a compromise conceived by heretics and adopted by Emperor Zeno (474-491) for the purpose of settling the differences between Orthodox and Monophysite. It was signed by the Monophysite Patriarchs Akakios of Constantinople (472-489), Peter Mongos of Alexandria, Peter the Fuller of Antioch (d. 488), and Martyrios of Jerusalem (478-486). The Monophysites that did not accept it were left without bishops, and thus they were called Akephaloi ("headless"), in that they were without leaders. *The Great Synaxaristes* (in Greek), p. 232.

the ordination as valid. We shall never abandon Orthodoxy in the slightest; whether the holy land is set ablaze or whether we suffer all else, we shall never conform, even if thou wert to shed all our blood. We shall ever abide by the Four Œcumenical Synods: At the First Synod, when three hundred and eighteen fathers assembled at Nicaea, they condemned Arius as one who declared that the essence of the Son is alien to that of the Father; the Second Synod was convoked against Makedonios, who blasphemed against the Holy Spirit; the Third Synod at Ephesus pronounced against Nestorios, who uttered many foul and sordid things against the œconomy of Christ; and the Fourth Synod at Chalcedon, consisting of six hundred and thirty fathers who, in compliance with the other synods, upheld the apostolic Faith and excommunicated Eftyches and Nestorios, ousting them from the Church. It branded them as outcasts and their beliefs as alien to the Church of Christ. Therefore, understand this quite well, because we shall never betray the Orthodox Faith, nor shall we deny those decisions of the holy fathers, though we were to receive ten thousand deaths. Nay! Those founders were martyrs who endured many trials on account of correct doctrine, which shall always remain firm and unwavering. Therefore, as these doctrines were standards to them, they are for us also. May the peace of God, which is above every intellect, guide and preserve your majesty!"

The emperor received this epistle and, respecting the saint as a man of God, sent him a reply, speciously declaring that he was not at fault, but that wicked hierarchs and clerics, who wished to appear wise, brewed scandals. This and similar other writings of the emperor to the saint ensued, but he ceased his attempts to pressure Theodosios into following the heresy. Not long after, the emperor changed his mind, and again the vain one sent letters against piety. Yet, the brave zealot of the true Faith, Saint Theodosios, would not accede to the resolutions in the letters, but, as a lion, opposed those sent to him; he ascended the ambo in the presence of a multitude of people and in a loud voice declared, "Whosoever is against the holy Four Œcumenical Synods, and refuses to honor them as the four Gospels, let him be anathema!"

The Saint's Zeal

This was how Saint Theodosios confessed the Faith. Moreover, he hastened as an angel to the neighboring countryside and cities, being followed as a general by many monastics. He strengthened the faithful and spoke to the indolent, the careless, and whomsoever had doubts regarding the Orthodox Faith. He exhorted them to show readiness. He encouraged them not to fear the threatening tyrant and, if the need arose, to be ready to die for the Faith. The blessed one taught them to know that the Son and Logos of God is co-eternal God and man, in one hypostasis or person, having both the divine and the human nature. He brought forth as a witness the holy Fourth Œcumenical Synod, which refuted the following two heresies explicitly: that of the impious and mindless Nestorios, who divided the one Christ into two Sons and two hypostases; and that of Eftyches, Dioscoros, and Severos, who confused into one nature the divinity and manhood of Christ. Indeed, Nestorios believed Christ has two natures and two hypostases; and that there are even two Sons, one born from the Father and another from the holy Virgin. Again, Eftyches, Dioscoros, and Severos, of like mind, perhaps wished to war against Nestorios' erroneous division, but the foolish ones fell once more into another senseless heresy, saying that Christ has one nature, confusing His human nature with the divine nature, and thereby concluding that the divinity suffered. For if Christ had one nature, as they prattle, then the divinity knew death.

However, let us close their vile mouths, because the holy Fourth Œcumenical Synod made it a matter of dogma to honor two natures, divine and human, in one hypostasis immiscible, one Son immutable and undivided from the Father before all ages according to divinity; and, afterward, born of the holy Virgin, above the law of nature, according to humanity, yet co-essential with the Father. With this and other similar teachings, the sagacious Theodosios boldly taught the flock. Thereupon, the emperor was enraged and unjustly exiled him. But God, the just Judge, cut short the life of this mad emperor; hence, the saint returned to his monastery, and the persecution and scandals against the Church were stilled. The heterodox hierarchs who wrought wickedness were deposed from their sees, and the pious regained their sees as in former times. Many of them lauded Theodosios for the way in which he confessed the Faith and would not sanction the emperor's commands. Archbishops Agapetos (535-536) of Rome and Ephraim of Antioch (526-546), in particular, sent letters of praise and greatly acclaimed him.

The Woman with Cancer

Now let us also relate a miracle. One day, all the distinguished elders of the desert and foremost monks met with the clergy, as was the custom from time immemorial, for the Feast of the Exaltation of the Precious Cross. Just as they all sat, a certain woman entered, who had a grave and incurable illness that the physicians call cancer, but the common folk name "the devourer," which consumes the flesh of the afflicted one and is incurable by human means. She approached one of the spiritual fathers, Isidore, the hegumen of the Souka Lavra. He noticed the apparent pain that she was in and the tears in her eyes. She then asked him, "Might there might be within this holy assembly the wondrous Theodosios?" When Isidore learned from her the reason for her coming, he indicated Theodosios by pointing with his finger; for he knew that the saint possessed the powerful medicine of divine grace. The infirm one then hastened as a thirsty hart to the fountain of water. With pure faith, she bared her breast, and with extreme solemnity and calmness, took the koukoulion (cowl) of the saint (in imitation of the woman with the issue of blood mentioned in the Gospel),[7] and straightway, as it touched her chest—O the sublime therapy!—the pain vanished as darkness flees when light comes, and as grass is consumed by the fire. The saint then turned to her and said with humility, "Be of good cheer, O daughter, my Master Christ has told me that thy faith has saved thee!" The blessed Isidore, who had seen her before and was grieved in his soul for her, then saw that her chest had not even a tiny trace of this intractable disease. He trembled and declared the miracle in every place. In this manner the Lord reveals virtue, no matter how much the virtuous attempt to conceal it, and He proclaims and acclaims them everywhere.

From One Grain of Wheat

It was at this time, July of 518, that the swift stroke of death cut down the tyrannical autocrat Anastasios. Then the military commander Justin I (518-527) was proclaimed emperor by the army and factions. He was responsible for the break with his predecessor's Monophysite policy, accepted the Chalcedonian course, and put an end to the Akakian schism. The fathers that were exiled and persecuted for true Orthodoxy finally returned to their monasteries.

However, let us here continue recounting the saint's wondrous works, for it would be a serious sin to remain silent concerning them. On one occasion, he went to Bethlehem for the purpose of venerating the holy shrine there. He returned tired from the journey, so he stayed at the cell of a certain virtuous man, named Markianos, who was replete with spiritual gifts. They embraced each other with a holy kiss and conversed on many edifying matters. They sat down at the table and spread it with spiritual discourses to the satisfaction of their souls. Afterward, when the hour to sup arrived, the excellent Markianos was grieved because he had neither bread nor wheat in his cell, but only a few lentils, which he had his disciples prepare in order to treat Theodosios. Therefore, they served lentils but without bread. Now the blessed Theodosios was aware of the evident poverty of his host, who did not even have bread, so he had his acolyte bring from their rations what he carried for his travel. Thus, in this instance, the guest from abroad offered rather than the host. Hence they ate. Then Markianos said to Theodosios with a cheerful countenance, "Do not reproach me, fathers, that I did not generously offer appropriate hospitality, for I have absolutely no wheat, and

---

[7] Cf. Mt. 9:20; Mk. 5:27; Lk. 8:44.

for this reason, I made no bread." Yet, when the marvellous and great Theodosios glanced at Markianos' face, he saw a grain of wheat (I, the biographer, know not how this happened) resting upon his beard. He took it and joyfully exclaimed, "Behold, wheat! Why didst thou say thou hadst none?" Then Markianos took it with respect and faith from the right hand of the saint and dropped the one grain of wheat into the storeroom, believing

that, without toil and trouble, he would obtain an abundant yield through the blessing of the saint; and so it would come to pass as he believed.

The following day, as they opened the door of the storeroom—O Thy mysterious marvels, O Master!—they found it filled up to the top. His companions were astonished when they beheld its volume. He dispatched a disciple immediately to fetch the saint to see this strange sight. When he arrived and opened the door slightly and with great difficulty, the blessed grain spilled out. This miracle is not inferior to the one that Christ performed when He multiplied the loaves and satisfied the people in the wilderness. But this came about by one grace and energy, inasmuch as there it was

Saint Theodosios

wrought by the Master's power and the apostles served as ministers; and here, the Lord again performed it invisibly by means of His servant, whom He glorified for his good intention. But hearken to another miracle.

The Miracle in the Deep Well

There was a wealthy woman from Alexandria, who was pious and of irreproachable character. She took great care that her life was God-pleasing and in accordance with the divine will. She had an only beloved son who would accompany her on the frequent visits she paid to the monastery, where she would lean her child against Theodosios' feet. One day, her son, while playing with other children, either from carelessness or demonic complicity, fell into a deep well. The bystanders lowered down volunteers with ropes to pull the boy up in order to bury him, for no one really believed they would find him alive and well. They arrived near the bottom and saw the child sitting—O the wonder!—upon the water, as if something solid were holding him up, not allowing him to get wet at all. Beholding this awesome wonder, they were astonished, for it was God Who caused this miracle to come about. When they hoisted him up, and his mother saw that he was still alive—let everyone share the relief that she experienced, for all had assumed the lad had drowned—they asked him to describe how it happened that he did not sink into the deep waters. He replied that an elderly monk helped him and would not allow him to sink. Furthermore, he described the monk's garments with all the characteristics of the holy Theodosios. The spectators discerned from the given description that verily it was Saint Theodosios.

Then his God-loving mother, in order not to appear ungrateful for this benefit, went with the child to the monastery of the saint, to render thanks to the blessed man properly. Forthwith, the child, upon seeing the saint from afar, shouted, exclaiming to his mother, "He is the one who held me, and I did not drown!" Then the woman fell at the feet of the venerable elder and tenderly kissed them with fervent tears and thanksgiving, naming the saint the salvation of her life and the cause of her joy; for if the child had not been drawn up alive, she would have died an untimely death from grief. She made the miraculous episode known to all, just as we have written it.

A Child is Granted

Another woman, year after year, had experienced complications during her pregnancies, resulting in the death of each successive unborn child in her womb, which also endangered her own life. This occurred frequently, and the grieving woman was given potions to abort each dead child from her womb. At that time, she had heard of the wondrous works of the blessed one and hastened to him, entreating him ardently with tears to help her to find a cure for such a serious condition. She said to the saint, "Command me to name my first live child after thee; only by this will I hope to find my cure!" The saint acquiesced, and, after he had given her his blessing, she departed. Hence, when her time came to bring forth, she gave birth with no complications. The child was then baptized with the name Theodosios. After weaning him, she brought him to the monastery, so that the one who by prayer blessed his safe delivery into this life might also instruct and direct him to eternal life.

In like manner, another woman, who had difficulty during her confinement—just as the aforementioned—the saint delivered from danger by his prayer, and she brought forth spontaneously. She also named her firstborn Theodosios, in imitation of the other woman. She dedicated her son to the monastery of the blessed one, and many years later he became an excellent steward of the saint's monastery. Wondrous are the things we have mentioned, but even stranger are those we have omitted!

Locusts and Other Insects

During one season, a great horde of locusts and other insects descended upon the farmlands, destroying all crops and vegetation. At that time, the saint was elderly and, being unable to walk, had to be assisted by two priest-monks, who propped him up from under his shoulders. Therefore, he would move about with extreme difficulty, trusting God to have compassion on his labor and to hearken to his prayer. Upon arriving at the place which suffered these woes and losses, he first made a supplicatory prayer to God. Next he took one of the locusts and one of the other insects into the palm of his hand. He then spoke in a calm voice to the insects, as if they were reason-endowed creatures, saying, "Your common Lord orders you not to injure the poor by devouring their provisions." Thus spoke the saint—O wonderful narration!—and the entire swarm of locusts and insects ceased to cause any destruction. They did not migrate from place to place but remained on the property where they were. Nor did they touch the sprouts or vegetable plants—as if they had a sort of kinship with them—but they sustained themselves on thorns and thistles.

Again, at a different place and time, the same devastation occurred, when an army of locusts appeared and destroyed the entire wheat crop. The saint filled a vessel of oil and made a prayer of blessing over it and sent it by reverent and God-loving men to the aforementioned land. Straightway, all the locusts disappeared.

The Monastery in Need

At another time, the monastery did not have any money to purchase garments. The steward complained to the saint that the brethren were troubling him over their nakedness. The saint answered, "Be not concerned, for tomorrow the Lord will send us aid." Indeed, the word he pronounced became reality. The next day, a certain man came and brought alms of one hundred gold pieces, all of which they spent for clothing.

Severian Adherents

On one occasion, the saint went to the coenobium at Bostra, to observe how the monastics were faring and to visit his virtuous friend Julian, who was the elected abbot. While there, a woman, well known for her perversity, began to scream at Theodosios, calling him deluded and making other similar vile remarks. The saint, before our eyes (says the author), rebuked her for the immoderate use of her tongue. Indeed, this shameless woman, who dared to deride him, later on gave up her soul by a painful death.

Also, near Bostra was another monastery, where the inhabitants were adherents to the Severian heresy. They harbored an intense hatred for the blessed one. Therefore, upon descrying Saint Theodosios from afar, they struck the semantron to assemble the monastics. Then they began reviling and mocking him. Therefore, the saint justifiably rebuked that monastery and warned them that not one stone should remain. In a few days, the Hagarenes raided by night this heretical monastery. They burned it to the ground, after seizing the monks' possessions and taking the remaining wretches as slaves. The rebuke of the saint had overtaken them. Verily, some narratives are for instruction and correction, and some we relate for the sake of spiritual benefit, and others are to delight the listener.

Kerykos the Commander

A commander in chief of the Byzantine army, Kerykos, a nobleman from the east, was valorous and daring in battle. He was about to embark on a campaign against the Persians. Therefore, being a devout man, he stopped in the holy land to worship, so that the Lord might help him. He heard of the fame of Theodosios and went to honor him and to ask his blessing. The venerable elder instructed him not to place his hope in his sword and bow and arrows, according to the divine David [cf. Ps. 43:6], but in divine power. This brought contrition to the heart of Kerykos, and he requested of Theodosios his hair shirt that he might wear it on the outside, as a protection and safeguard, instead of a breastplate in battle. The saint, upon perceiving his piety, handed it over to him. Kerykos then garbed himself with the robe made of hair as armor. He then marched off to Persia, performing magnificent feats and exploits, and returned in honor and triumph. Not wishing to appear ungrateful for the benefaction, he went to visit the blessed man again and said, "Thanks to thy sanctity, most holy father, thou wast the cause of my victory. For when I donned thy hair shirt, as armor, and we were in battle formation, a great darkness overshadowed the land. We furthermore were unable to discern the enemy from ourselves, but I beheld only thy saintliness, and it guided me to a particular position, where I overpowered my adversaries, until I completely put them to flight!"

Other Miracles of the Saint

Not only was this Kerykos wondrously aided by the saint, but numerous others also were delivered from various dangers. Indeed, many on stormy seas, although their ships were ready to capsize, called upon Theodosios for help, and the turbulence of the winds subsided, and they were rescued. Others on dry land were preserved from wild beasts and were saved from being torn to pieces. Endangered individuals, either awake or asleep, were succored in a marvellous manner. Furthermore, not only men but sometimes even the unreasoning animals were aided, as Theodosios was benevolent.

A Man and His Donkey

At one time, a poor man went with his donkey on an errand. On the road, he was attacked by a ferocious lion. The man ran as quickly as he could, and the donkey likewise fled in another direction to escape the jaws of death. Then the lion left the man and pursued the donkey with great speed to devour him. The poor man, being in such dire straits, remembered the holy Theodosios and called upon his name to be delivered. Forthwith, the moment he pronounced the name of the saint, the vehemence of the lion ceased. Hence, the wild beast left them both unharmed and departed.

The Saint's Clairvoyance

The wise Theodosios could see clearly into the future, as he was clairvoyant. One particular day, he ordered the sounding of the bell before the usual hour. The brethren gathered and asked him what was happening and why he ordered it to be rung before the appointed hour, since it was two o'clock in the morning. Sighing deeply and weeping, he answered, "Fathers, let us make a prayer before the Lord, for I see the wrath of God coming speedily from the east!" Inasmuch as the others saw nothing threatening them, they were not disturbed about the imminent calamity, neither did they care. On the sixth day, a message arrived, that a tumultuous earthquake had shaken Antioch; then the brethren remembered the prediction and were amazed. However, in everything, Theodosios was most humble and did not fancy himself anything extraordinary.

Two Brothers

Once he noticed that two brothers were fighting and striking one another. He ordered them to cease their strife, according to the Master's command. When he saw that they were overcome by anger and had no intention of complying, Theodosios fell at their feet and supplicated as a shepherd to his sheep, a father to his children, a teacher to his pupils, a physician to the sick in order to heal their wounds; yet they still would not listen. Therefore, in order to prevail upon them, with extreme humility, he put his holy head to the earth and would not raise it from the ground until their hatred softened in their hearts. He thereafter made them give each other a kiss of peace, and in the end they departed friends.

The Saint Falls Ill

Verily, these and numerous other things did the divine Theodosios accomplish. Then the time approached for him to depart to his desired dwelling place. He found himself stricken by a grave illness of such severity that for one year he lay in grievous pain. The skin on his flanks and loins was ulcerated, due to weakness and constant reclining, and eventually eroded to the bone. Notwithstanding, the ever-memorable one neither murmured nor exhibited a despondent attitude, nor did he grumble bitterly, but rather he glorified the Lord with greatness of soul. One elder observed his intense pain and said to him, "Father, make an entreaty before the Lord, that He deliver thee from this oppressive sickness." The saint, looking at him askance, remarked: "Do not speak unbecoming words, for the same thought has many times entered my mind. But knowing that it was demonic, I expelled it as injurious to my soul. For I have enjoyed many good things in my life, and my name was acclaimed and spread abroad. So now I gladly suffer slightly in order to find consolation in the next life, lest I should hear the same dreadful judgment as the rich man, 'Be mindful that thou didst have rendered to thee thy good things in thy life, and Lazarus likewise the bad things; but now, here, he is being comforted and thou art suffering pain [Lk. 16:25].'"

Therefore, he spent the entire duration of that illness in thanksgiving, glorifying the Lord. He prayed every hour, even in the depths of affliction. Chanting was never absent from his lips. He also prophesied to the brethren many things, which all came to pass. When he recognized that the end was near, he assembled his spiritual children; and they bewailed the loss of their father. He comforted them and instructed them to have patience to the end, in whatever temptation should befall them. He exhorted them to be in subjection to their leader, whoever might come to govern them. He also disclosed many other indispensable directions, especially the following: "If you see that after my repose the flock increases and the monks multiply with the passage of time, have good hope that the rest of what I told you shall be accomplished."

Thus it all came to pass. Not only when he was alive did the monastery thrive, but also after he reposed, the coenobium continued as before, keeping unadulterated the order and traditions that he had given them, which they preserved inviolate. Therefore, many blessed elders under his tutelage performed diverse miracles. However, let us return to the subject matter.

Translation to the Lord

When the saint was aware that after three days he would be translated to the Lord, he called three hierarchs to himself. They came, and he greeted them with a kiss. He also took forgiveness from them. They wept at his departure, believing that his death was a great loss to them. He again rejoiced, reminding them that he was going to his desired Christ, in order to consort with the angels eternally. After this, he raised his hands slightly and uttered a secret prayer to the Lord. Next he folded his hands over his chest in the sign of the Cross (which is fearful to the demons) and surrendered his magnanimous soul into the blameless hands of the all-good God, having attained one hundred five years of age. Moreover, God honored also His servant to the end by this great miracle.

After the Saint's Repose

Stephen, a man from Alexandria, had been possessed by a demon for a considerable length of time. He had gone to the saint, while the holy man was still among the living, to seek deliverance, but he was never healed. However, whenever he approached where the saint was abed, his soul was calm, and he was not troubled by the demon. Stephen knew that, without the benefit of the holy man's prayer, he had hope in no other. Therefore, he would not depart from the monastery but remained there until the saint's repose. Now when Stephen beheld the dormition of the saint, he wept bitterly over his bier, pulling his hair and striking his face upon the earth. He appealed to the holy man, lamenting, "Woe is me; today I have lost my hope, my refuge, and help, for in thee was I encouraged, O holy one! Deliver me, wretch that I am, from the evil demon. For, at this time, I, the fainthearted one, am completely hopeless. It would be better if I fell into the fire or the sea, or even to be buried along with thee, than to be tormented by this merciless tyrant." This in addition to many other things he bewailed, as he kissed the saint and shed a river of tears. Then the demon cast him to the ground to demonstrate that he was leaving against his own will, being driven out by divine power. Hence, Stephen was greatly disturbed when the thrice-accursed one exited, but then he was left healthy and glorified the Lord.

The Saint's Funeral

In this manner was Theodosios wondrous and awesome to all, not only when he was alive but even after his death. He subdued the world, heaven, man, the sea, and the demons. For he would command the beasts of the earth, and they did not cause him harm. He would charge the sky that it not rain; or the wind that it carry away the locust; or the sea that it become calm; or the demons that they flee from people, as they did in terror. Thereupon his fame had spread far and wide. Huge crowds of the faithful hastened when the great Theodosios departed to the Lord. These included layfolk, priests, and bishops. The multitudes that converged pushed against each other that they might bestow a kiss upon his sacred relics. Archbishop Peter (524-552), who was then Patriarch of Jerusalem, with other respected hierarchs, could only by force persuade the crowd to clear the way, that they might bury the saint. This is because everyone had a longing to kiss even his rason (cassock), if possible, or his hair, or anything, just to take his blessing. After many hours, Theodosios, the most precious treasure, worthy of the heavens, was concealed in the earth. They executed everything as was appointed by the order of our Church, and departed, glorifying the Father, the Son, and the Holy Spirit, the One Divinity, to Whom is due power, honor, and worship, always: now and ever and to the ages of the ages. Amen.

Saint Theodosios

**On the 11th of January,
the holy Church commemorates
Saint THEODOSIOS of the
Athonite Monastery of Philotheou
and Bishop of Trebizond.[8]**

Theodosios, our holy father, was born in the early fourteenth century, in the village of Korēssos, in the vicinity of Kastoria. His parents were farming people who were neither rich nor poor but were self-supporting. They were also reverent and virtuous. Theodosios had a younger brother, named Dionysios, who is commemorated by the holy Church on the 25th of June, from which this Life has been extracted. The brothers bore a strong resemblance to each other. They also were similar in virtue of soul, character, and attitude. When Theodosios reached eighteen years of age, he wished to go to Constantinople, where he hoped to meet virtuous men and benefit from their words. Therefore, Theodosios left his homeland, parents, and little brother.

When Theodosios entered the capital, he stayed at the patriarchate, wherein virtuous and marvellous monks excelled in chanting and asceticism. From such teachers, Theodosios received great benefit and learned letters sufficiently well that, in a short time, he surpassed all others. Thereupon, he learned all of the divine Scriptures and dogmas, because his mind was apt, and he comprehended the lessons easily. Therefore, he was sought after and well regarded, due to his noble countenance, modesty, cheerful disposition, reasonable and sweet speech, and remarkable virtue. In fact, even the patriarch of that time took note of him and loved the young man. Beholding the great virtues within Theodosios, he ordained him as a deacon, and later to the office of presbyter. As Theodosios received the dignity of the priesthood, he increased his struggles in the virtues. Father Theodosios advanced in each virtue and made great strides forward, going from "strength to strength [Ps. 83:7]."

Desiring to go to a place that was calm and untroubled, Father Theodosios left the city and went to the Holy Mountain of Athos. He offered up prayers and worship at all the hermitages and monasteries. Yet, it was at the

---

[8] The Life of this saint was translated from the Greek of *The Great Synaxaristes*, primarily from the 25th of June—the commemoration day of his brother, Saint Dionysios, builder of the Athonite Monastery of Dionysiou, dedicated to the holy Forerunner (1370-1374). Other information was also borrowed from *The Holy Monastery of Philotheou* (Holy Mountain Athos: Philotheou Monastery, 1990), p. 19.

Monastery of Philotheou that he decided to live in prayer and obedience. Indeed, the virtuous fathers at that monastery were true to the name of their monastery, Philotheou, that is, "lovers of God." The ever-memorable one, in emulating them and partaking in their zeal, in a short time, outshone all. Father Theodosios became a type and rule of the monastic conduct and order. He appeared as a living icon, adorned with every virtue in the midst of that synodia and assembly. As in the words of the Prophet David, he "was as a fruitful olive tree in the house of the Lord [Ps. 51:8]."

After the passage of a certain number of years, the hegumen of Philotheou reposed. All the brethren besought Theodosios to accept the abbacy of the monastery, since he excelled and was experienced. At first, though he was unwilling, so as not to appear disobedient, he took on the care and concerns of all. Taking the burden upon his shoulders, he shepherded, resolutely and with considerable diligence, in life-giving pastures, according to the divine commandments. Thereupon, his fame passed around to nearly every land, and many came to Philotheou to receive spiritual benefit. Eventually, his brother Dionysios also came and was tonsured a monk.

Then on one occasion, since the Feast of the Annunciation was fast approaching, Father Theodosios went down to the shore with others to catch fish for the festal trapeza. As they were fishing by night, Hagarenes captured them, and brought the monks to Prusa to sell them. There were certain Christians in that city who bought the captives and set them free to go wherever they wished. Though the others chose to return to the monastery, Theodosios went to Constantinople. Patriarch Philotheos (1364-1376) saw him and, together with many others, rejoiced exceedingly at his presence, which bespoke a genuine slave of God. Therefore, they appointed him abbot of a certain monastery.

In a little while, the Metropolitan of Trebizond (Pontos) reposed during the time of the Trapezuntine Emperor Alexios III Komnenos (1349-1390). The emperor instructed the patriarch to find a worthy holy man and ordain him as metropolitan. Then the patriarch and the clergy, in concord, preferred the holy Theodosios, who not only was pure and holy of soul, but also evinced reverence in his physical aspect. He was lofty in deed and humble-minded. His beard reached to his waist. His sweet conversation drew many to him, as a magnet attracts iron. He was educated in the highest levels of Church canons, laws, and decrees. Why be verbose? The God-inspired man was worthy of the office. Therefore, the patriarch, with all the clergy present, ordained him, though Theodosios did not desire the dignity. Therefore, in 1368/1369, those who were sent from Trebizond returned rejoicing. The most pious Emperor Alexios, with all his senators, received Metropolitan Theodosios gladly, as one sent from God. Consequently, they offered up thanks to God for granting them such a marvellous shepherd; and thus, they submitted to all his commands.

When Dionysios learned of his brother's elevation to the episcopacy, he rejoiced wholeheartedly. Thereupon, he decided to go and take pleasure in his company, hoping to have him as a mediator before the emperor, so the latter might donate money for expenses required for building. The brothers met again and rejoiced. Theodosios was gladdened by his brother's desire to build a monastery. He promised to help, as much as possible, in the construction. Straightway, the two brothers went together to Emperor Alexios Komnenos and his wife, Theodora Kantakuzene. They gave a generous grant and ensured the future of the monastery through a chrysobull, published in September of 1374. Thus, as a builder of the Athonite Monastery of Dionysiou, the Trapezuntine emperor financed the construction of its principal buildings. Nothing further is known of the holy Theodosios. He reposed in peace, having lived a God-pleasing life, receiving a double crown for his labors as a hierarch and ascetic.

On the 11th of January, the holy Church commemorates the Synaxis of MYRIADS OF ANGELS, which is celebrated within the Martyrium of Saint Anastasia at the Portico of Domnikos.[9]

On the 11th of January, the holy Church commemorates Saint STEPHEN at Plakidian, Saint THEODORE, and Saint AGAPIOS the Archimandrite.

On the 11th of January, the holy Church commemorates the holy Martyr MAÏROS, who reposed under torture.

On the 11th of January, the holy Church commemorates the venerable VITALIOS, who reposed in peace.[10]

Through the intercessions of Thy Saints,
O Christ God, have mercy on us. Amen.

---

[9] "I," says Nikodemos the Hagiorite, "have written 'myriads of angels,' that is, without number. I quote here Saint Dionysios the Areopagite, who says, 'I think we also ought to reflect on the tradition in Scripture that the angels number a thousand times a thousand and ten thousand times ten thousand [Dan. 7:10; Rev. 5:11]. These numbers, enormous to us, square and multiply themselves and thereby indicate clearly that the ranks of the heavenly beings are innumerable. So numerous are the blessed armies of transcendent intelligent beings that they surpass the fragile and limited realm of our physical numbers.'" See *The Celestial Hierarchy*, Ch. 14, p. 181.

[10] The inspiring account of Saint Vitalios is given within the Life of Saint John the Merciful, commemorated by the holy Church on the 12th of November, which is found in our November volume of *The Great Synaxaristes* (pp. 410-412).

On the 12th of January, the holy Church commemorates
the holy Martyr TATIANE,
Deaconess of Rome.

Tatiane, the holy martyr, lived during the reign of Emperor Alexander Severus (222-235), and hailed from Old Rome. Her father, thrice made consul, though wealthy and widely known, was also a deacon of the Church. Enlightened by the light of the Holy Spirit, Saint Tatiane spurned perishable riches. She spent her childhood years in the catacombs of Rome, where the Christians secretly gathered, and was made a deaconess. The maiden quelled the passions of the flesh and desired to consecrate herself to her Bridegroom Christ through afflictions and martyrdom.

Saint Tatiane

Since the maiden Tatiane professed and preached Christ, she was arrested in the catacombs and made to stand before the emperor. Hoping to publicly discredit this deaconess of the Church, the emperor escorted her to the temple of the idols, so she might make a sacrifice. Tatiane, instead, continued to pray, and said, "There is none more holy than Thou, O Lord!" Then, by virtue of her prayers that rose mightily to God, she brought the idols crashing down. Maddened at the damage and the disgrace, the emperor had her facial skin flayed and her eyelids torn away with iron hooks. Angels, however, were sent by God to assist Tatiane. Her eight executioners, seeing four angels about the martyr, were then suddenly blinded by a heavenly light. All eight soldiers, refusing to further punish the maiden, confessed Christ. Thereupon, they were immediately tortured and slain by other soldiers.

Though many marvelled at the maiden's patient endurance, to shame her, the emperor ordered her hair shaved. Tatiane then withstood the brutal removal of her breasts. Afterward, Christ's athlete was cast into the flames. In no wise fearing the flames, Tatiane trampled the fire underfoot. When she was drawn out of the fire, she was tossed to wild beasts. Nevertheless, the animals left off their inherent ferocity and fawned about her. Thus, neither fire, sword, wounds, starvation, nor brutal torture quenched her love for Christ Who bestowed His grace upon her.

Her members were then severed, broken, and mutilated when she was suspended aloft. Shedding her blood profusely, she resolutely announced, "I know none other God than Christ!" After she was cast into prison, the angels of heaven appeared to her and glorified her as a ewe-lamb and incorrupt bride

of their Master. God's ministers then took away her pain and disfigurement. Made radiant with divine light, Tatiane rendered glory to God with her incorporeal visitors. Since the grace of God restored her unscathed, the cruel emperor, perceiving that all his punishments were for nought, ordered her head struck off. Undaunted, the holy maiden was ready to offer herself to Christ as an unblemished sacrifice when she cried aloud, "Loving Thee, O Savior, I am brought to the slaughter!" At her execution, the holy Tatiane, as she desired, fulfilled His sufferings in her flesh, and received the unfading crown of martyrdom.

The Martyrdom of Saint Tatiane

On the 12th of January, the holy Church commemorates the holy Martyr PETER the Avesalamite.[1]

Peter, the glorious martyr, was brave and strong, not so much in body as in soul and in the Faith. He was a native of Aeneas, near Eleftheropolis

---

[1] This saint's Life resembles that of Saint Peter the Avselamos, commemorated by the holy Church on the 14th of October, which martyrdom *The Great Synaxaristes* (in Greek) places during the time of Diocletian (292). Some believe that today's Saint Peter the Avesalamite is to be identified with October's Saint Peter Avselamos. Eusebius in his *Martyrs of Palestine*, Ch. X, Nicene, 2nd Ser., I:351, places the day of his commemoration as the 11th of January. He describes Peter as an ascetic, also called Apselamus (Absalom in the Syriac), from the village of Aeneas. Both Eusebius and *The Great Synaxaristes* (in Greek) record that he ended his life on a funeral pyre, which Eusebius places in Caesarea. See ancient icon, dating from 1318, shown herein of Saint Peter, found in the narthex of the Yugoslavian Church of Saint George, Staro Nagoricino. In Bishop Nikolai Velimirović's *The Prologue from Ochrid* (Part One, January 12th, p. 51), he lists the cause of death to be crucifixion, as does Butler in *The Lives of the Saints* (January 3rd, Saint Peter Balsam, pp. 26-28). Alban Butler records that Saint Peter was apprehended at Avlona (Aulana) in the persecution of Maximinus (308-314) and brought before Severus, the governor of the province, and gives the date of 311 for his martyrdom.

(Bethozabris), some forty miles southwest of Jerusalem. Though in the bloom of youth, he was living the life of an ascetic when he was called upon to profess Christ boldly. However, the ruler of that city could not soften Peter's firm piety either by flattery or by dreadful threats. Though the judge and others around him ofttimes besought Peter to have compassion on himself, he gave noble proof of his Faith and disregarded them all. Therefore, after terrible tortures, the judge commended the young martyr to the flames of a funeral pyre. When he heard his sentence, Peter exclaimed, "My one desire is to die for my God!" The victorious contestant in piety then received the crown of martyrdom.

Butler gives the following narrative of the saint's published acts. Governor Severus began interrogating Peter and said, "Of what family and country art thou?" Peter answered, "I am a Christian." Severus asked, "What is thine employment?" Peter answered, "What employment can I have more honorable, or what better thing can I do in the world, than to live as a Christian?" Severus gave no consequence to these words and continued, "Dost thou know the imperial edicts?" Peter replied, "I know the laws of God, the Sovereign of the universe." Severus discounted these words also and declared, "Thou shalt quickly know that there is an edict of the most clement emperors, commanding all to sacrifice to the gods, or be put to death." Peter remarked, "Thou wilt also know one day that there is a law of the eternal King, proclaiming that everyone shall perish who offers sacrifice to devils. Whom dost thou counsel me to obey? And which, thinkest thou, ought I to choose—to die by thy sword, or to be condemned to everlasting misery by the sentence of the great King, the true God?" Severus answered, "Since thou didst ask my advice, here it is. Thou oughtest to obey the edict and sacrifice to the gods." Peter said, "I can never be prevailed upon to sacrifice to gods of wood and stone, even as those which thou dost worship." Severus said, "I would have thee know that it is within my power to avenge these affronts by putting thee to death." Peter said, "I had no intention of affronting thee. I only expressed what is written in the divine law." Severus said, "Have compassion on thyself, and sacrifice." Peter said, "If I am truly compassionate to myself, I ought not to sacrifice." Severus said, "I want to be lenient; I therefore still allow thee time to reflect, that thou mayest save thy life." Peter replied, "This delay will be to no purpose, for I shall not alter my mind. Do now what thou wilt be obliged to do soon, and complete the work which the devil, thy father, has begun; for I will never do what Jesus Christ forbids me."

Severus, on hearing these words, ordered him to be stretched upon the rack, and whilst he was suspended said to him scoffingly, "What sayest thou now, Peter? Dost thou begin to know what the rack is? Art thou willing to offer sacrifice?" Peter answered, "Tear me with hooks, and talk not of my sacrificing to thy devils. I have already told thee that I will sacrifice only to that God for Whom I suffer." Hereupon the governor commanded his tortures

to be redoubled. The martyr, far from giving any form of complaint, sang with alacrity those verses of the prophet-king: "One thing have I asked of the Lord, this will I seek after: that I may dwell in the house of the Lord all the days of my life [Ps. 26:4]. I will take the cup of salvation, and I will call upon the name of the Lord [Ps. 115:4]." The spectators, seeing the martyr's blood run down in streams, cried out to him, "Obey the emperors! Sacrifice, and rescue thyself from these torments!" Peter replied, "Dost thou call these torments? I feel no pain. But this I know, that, if I be not faithful to my God, I must expect real pain, such as cannot be conceived." The judge also said, "Sacrifice, Peter, or thou wilt repent of it." Peter said, "Neither will I sacrifice, nor shall I repent of it." Severus said, "I am on the point of pronouncing sentence." Peter said, "It is what I most earnestly desire." Severus then dictated the sentence in this manner: "It is our order that Peter, for having refused to obey the

The Martyrdom of Saint Peter edict of the invincible emperors, and obstinately defending the law of a crucified Man, be put to death." Thereupon, the brave contestant of piety received the crown of martyrdom when he reposed amidst flames.[2]

On the 12th of January, the holy Church commemorates the holy Martyr MERTIOS.

Mertios, the holy martyr, was a soldier in the Mauritanian battalion during the reign of Diocletian (284-305). In the year 298, it was reported to his superiors that he was a Christian. He was arrested and brought before the emperor, who attempted to force Mertios to offer sacrifice to the idols. Since he stood firm and unpersuaded, they stripped him of his belt which was a symbol of his military rank. Afterward, he was subjected to a cruel beating

---

[2] Butler, loc. cit., records that the saint was nailed to a cross, finishing triumphantly at Aulana. The date given in the acts is the 11th of January, but he is honored in the Roman martyrology on the 3rd of January.

as they thrashed his flesh with staves. The holy man demonstrated valor and constancy of purpose during such harsh torture. Not the slightest noise escaped from his mouth. His noble conduct astonished the tyrant so that he was beside himself with awe. Since for many hours he was made to un-

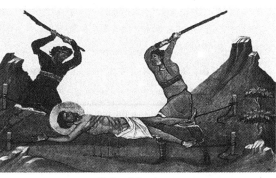

Saint Mertios

dergo blows from those wood rods, there was not one place on his martyric body that was left unwounded. The tyrant then commanded them to take the prisoner and cast him into prison. After the passage of eight days, a heavy discharge of pus exuded from the saint's wounds, which also emitted a foul odor. The strength of the brave athlete of Christ flagged utterly, from both pain and infected tissue. He surrendered his precious and honorable soul into the hands of God, from Whom he received the crown of martyrdom.

On the 12th of January, the holy Church commemorates
the holy EIGHT MARTYRS of Nicaea, who were slain by the sword.

On the 12th of January, the holy Church commemorates
the holy Martyr EFTHASIA, who was beheaded by the sword.

On the 12th of January, the holy Church commemorates
our venerable Father ELIAS the Wonder-worker.[3]

Through the intercessions of Thy Saints,
O Christ God, have mercy on us. Amen.

---

[3] Saint Elias the Wonder-worker lived during the 4th C. in the Thebaid. He is well known for his ever-memorable apothegm: "There are three things which I fear: when my soul is about to leave the body; when I shall be made to stand before God; and when the decision regarding me is issued."

**On the 13th of January, the holy Church commemorates
the holy Martyrs HERMYLOS and STRATONIKOS.**[1]

Hermylos and Stratonikos, the holy martyrs, flourished during the reign of the impious Licinius (308-324), the guileful emperor who was devoted to sacrificing to the idols.[2] He punished the Christians mercilessly with the application of various torments, that they might be coerced into denying piety or suffer a harsh death. Those who would act as informants and point out a Christian were handsomely rewarded. Consequently, all the Greek pagans sought to discover Christians and inform against them, so that they might appear distinguished and useful to the emperor and reverent toward the idols.

On one occasion, as the profane Licinius was sitting upon his throne, one soldier came forth and said to the emperor, "Sire, I know a man who holds the rank of deacon among the Christians. His name is Hermylos, and he mocks the gods of thy realm." Licinius bade the soldier to bring Hermylos

---

[1] The Lives of these saints were recorded in Greek by Saint Symeon the Metaphrastes, whose manuscript begins, "Licinius the impious was reigning...[*P.G.* 114:553-566]." The text is extant in the Athonite monasteries of the Great Lavra, Iveron, and in other places. The simplified text was published in *Neon Paradeison*.

[2] Imperator Licinius held the Balkans and the east, while Imperator Constantine (307-337) held the western provinces including Italy and North Africa. There was an uneasy truce between the two rulers, which was flimsily held together when Licinius married Constantia, Constantine's half-sister. At the Battle of Cibalae, in October of 316, Constantine defeated Licinius' larger army. Licinius fled east to Serdica, where he proclaimed Valens to be commander of the Danube frontier forces. Valens fought Constantine, and both Valens and Licinius were forced to come to terms. Valens was executed, and Licinius was compelled to cede most of the Balkan provinces to Constantine. A treaty between them was confirmed in 317. Over the next six years, Licinius remained tolerant of Christianity but maintained close association with pagan writers and philosophers. Constantine became a champion of Christians, so that Licinius came to suspect that the Christians were in Constantine's service. He took action against the Christians, which provided Constantine with the just cause needed for a final war with Licinius. Licinius in the meantime dismissed Christians from the imperial bureaucracy and the army. When he suspected bishops of disloyalty, he had them executed and their churches destroyed. In 324, Constantine gathered a great army and fleet and attacked Licinius. In July of 324, Constantine won a decisive victory at Hadrianopolis. Licinius fled and appointed a co-ruler, Martius Martinianus, to help him. Constantine then brought his army across the Bosporos and defeated Licinius at Chrysopolis in September of 324. Licinius and Martinianus surrendered. Licinius was exiled to Thessalonike, where in the spring of 325 he was hanged with his son and heir. Scarre's *Chronicle of the Roman Emperors*, pp. 214, 215.

forthwith to the theater. That soldier took fellow men in arms and went to arrest Hermylos. They found the deacon in a state of prayer. Eager to carry out their orders, they announced the royal directive. Straightway, Deacon Hermylos readily complied and followed them peaceably, with no sign of a sad countenance. Much rather, he rejoiced that he was about to suffer torture for the sake of the Christ. Therefore, he presented himself gladly in the theater. The emperor interrogated him, "Art thou a Christian?" Hermylos answered, "Not only with a loud and clear voice do I confess that I am a Christian, but also with a firm judgment and set purpose; for I am dedicated to the one God and have become His deacon; that is, I serve Him and minister at His altar." Licinius then asked, "Well then, minister to the gods that I might honor thee as is meet." The deacon replied,

Saint Hermylos

"Art thou deaf or dost thou feign that thou art an imbecile or mindless? I have told thee that I am a deacon of the invisible God, and tellest thou me to render worship to stones and wood, deaf and inanimate idols, works of the hands of men? Whosoever has discernment would scorn such a suggestion. Those objects which thou, as one in error and foolish, dost venerate and to which thou dost bid me to offer homage should excite laughter in anyone with discrimination."

The tyrant was angered by this reproof. He ordered his minions to strike the deacon on his jaw and cheeks with brass instruments. As this punishment was being administered, the royal herald cried in a loud voice, "Keep thy tongue, O Hermylos, and honor the autocrat. Sacrifice to the gods that thou mightest flee the punishments to come." The martyr endured the blows and wounds, and even rejoiced. As one triumphant, he reproached the tyrant and said, "I, on the one hand, receive these small and temporal wounds, but thou, on the other hand, shalt inherit everlasting punishment, because thou hast forsaken the One Who fashioned thee; and instead, thou offerest obeisance to deaf and dumb figures and statues. The worst of it is that thou wouldest begrudge others of their salvation in thine attempts to cast them into destruction." After Hermylos was subjected for a long while to their blows, the indignation of the tyrant subsided. He then ordered that Hermylos be incarcerated for three days. "Perhaps," said the emperor, "he shall come to some remorse."

As the deacon was taken away, he began chanting, "The Lord is a helper to me, and I will not be afraid of what man shall do to me [Ps. 117:6]. In God I have set my hope; I will not fear what flesh shall do to me [Ps. 55:3]." When he was brought to the prison, he began saying, "O Thou Who sittest on the cherubim, manifest Thyself [Ps. 79:2],...and come to save us [Ps. 79:3]." The martyr endured that doleful prison nobly for the Lord's sake; and the man-loving God was not negligent in sending forth help from on high. He endowed His martyr with greater courage and fortitude, by sending His angel, who spoke these words of consolation: "Take courage and in no wise fear, O Hermylos. Do thou struggle and cower not, that thou mightest receive from the heavens that most radiant crown of martyrdom." In this manner therefore did the Lord arm His slave, giving him deliverance and power against the tyrant.

After the third day, as Licinius sat on the judgment seat, the martyr was brought forward. Licinius addressed the deacon and said, "Hast thou sobered somewhat, O Hermylos? Wilt thou render homage to the gods that thou mightest be delivered from perils, or dost thou, as one filled with pride, still keep to thine initial stubbornness?" The holy man answered, "Since I have told thee from the very beginning my opinion, why dost thou labor to put me to the test again? Why wilt thou waste thy time in fruitless questioning? I only revere the God of heaven, for Whom I shall become a sacrifice, and I await His mighty help." The tyrant then replied, "Now I shall see if He, Whom Thou dost venerate in the heavens, is powerful, and whether or not He shall help thee." Immediately, Licinius charged six of his strong men to stretch the martyr on the ground and give him a pitiless beating with rods. Those murderous men thrashed Hermylos with extreme harshness and cruelty, obediently discharging the miserable will of their corrupt emperor. As this punishment was being dispensed, the martyr kept praying to heaven. As he manfully endured their chastisements, he was saying, "O Lord, my God, Thou wast scourged by Pilate for my salvation. Do Thou empower me who am suffering for Thy love's sake, and do Thou vouchsafe me to become a sharer in Thy Passion and Thy splendor."

After the martyr made this declaration, a voice was heard: "Amen. So be it, Hermylos. After three days, thou shalt be delivered from sorrows, and thou shalt come to Me that I might render a rich recompense to thee for thy pains." This voice gave courage and confidence to the saint, so that he became even more strengthened and vigorous. The soldiers, hearing the voice, became terrified and fell prone to the ground, trembling. In like manner, the emperor and his retinue became timid and cowardly. Nevertheless, benighted by impiety and godlessness, Licinius was not able to come to an understanding of the truth. He therefore chose to return the martyr to his prison cell.

Now the warden of the prison was a friend of the prisoner. His name was Stratonikos. He was a crypto-Christian. Out of fear, he dared not reveal himself, but he was sympathetic toward the saint and helped him secretly. Hermylos was heartened by this act of charity and chanted in Stratonikos' hearing: "The Lord is my light and my saviour; whom then shall I fear? The Lord is the defender of my life; of whom then shall I be afraid [Ps. 26:1]?" He then continued the melody with the remainder of that psalm. When he came to the final verse, there shone forth a wondrous light from on high, which reassured the one who was chanting. He was given further assurance when he heard a voice, even as he had earlier, saying, "Fear not; for the third day thou shalt go forth to the heavens."

Saint Stratonikos

The following day, as the tyrant sat upon the throne, the martyr was brought to him. Licinius addressed him and said: "How does the dark dungeon suit thee? Hast thou had a change of mind? Wilt thou do that which is to thine advantage, or dost thou still require coercive measures?" Hermylos gave his answer with sweetness and joy, saying, "I beheld that dark dwelling place become filled with immeasurable light, which ushered in tremendous joy for me, filling my soul with delight and ineffable good cheer with the hope of enjoying life everlasting. However, I wonder about thee and why the darkness of thy soul refuses to be dispelled, lest thou shouldest comprehend the truth." The tyrant raised his voice, saying, "Hast thou learned nothing good? Dost thou know only to insult, a result of thine unbridled tongue and arrogant soul that knows no restraint? I tell thee, make obeisance to the gods, or I shall give thee what thou dost deserve, O shameless one!" The saint replied, "I have given answer to thee, O emperor. Therefore do that which thou dost intend." Licinius was vexed at these words and commanded his executioners to stretch out on the ground Hermylos on his back. The men were charged with bringing down blows on the deacon's naked abdomen with rods tipped with iron shaped as a triangle. This particular torture was cruel and painful, for the tips of the triangles were as sharp knives which sundered the flesh. They continued to rain down blows upon him without showing the least pity. Hermylos had no other consolation than to recite the sweetest name of Christ. He kept uttering, "O Lord, make all haste to help me," and other such phrases. God indeed hearkened speedily and stood by him invisibly and relieved his pain. The Lord then announced to him the end of it. The tyrant, as many times as he looked upon the martyr, observed that Hermylos persevered under torture. This caused Licinius' anger to wax hotter. Being unable to contain his rage, he contrived to heighten the horrible torment. That monster ordered that the executioners flay and scrape the flesh of the martyr's belly with the claws of an eagle. They were to continue this procedure until his entrails should be exposed. But even this heinous act was endured by the saint, as he prayed these words: "My heart and my flesh have rejoiced in the living God [Ps. 83:2]." And, "As with marrow and fatness, let my soul be filled; and with lips of rejoicing shall my mouth praise Thee [Ps. 62:5]."

The goodly Stratonikos stood close and witnessed the proceedings. His heart was convulsed, both at the sight of his friend suffering such atrocities and at being unable to offer any help. All he could do was weep. Now some of the other soldiers who were standing by had observed Stratonikos' tears and the empathy expressed on his face. They surmised that Stratonikos must be a Christian, so they informed against him to the tyrant. Licinius summoned Stratonikos and asked, "Art thou a friend of Hermylos, and dost thou hold to his opinion and religion?" Stratonikos adjudged that the opportune moment had arrived for him to make a confession of the Faith. He thereupon professed to Christian piety, censured the tyrant fearlessly, and contemptuously mocked the idols. Licinius wasted no time in directing his other men to strip Stratonikos and lay open his flesh with staves. Stratonikos, as he was being scourged and wounded mercilessly, kept looking toward his friend the deacon. He then said to him, "O Hermylos, entreat thou the Christ that I be granted help, and that I might overcome the tyrant and receive the crown of the contest." After he spoke these words to the deacon, he then rebuked Licinius, saying, "By employing violence and coercion: is that how thou dost gain converts? Wilt thou cause men to fall down and worship thy blind gods, thereby abandoning the true God Who in the future shall judge all the world and punish all those who transgressed and set up their own gods in His place?" The tyrant mindlessly ignored these words which set him at nought, but he noticed that the martyr's body was as one wound. He then ordered that Stratonikos be jailed until the following day. It was the tyrant's hope that Stratonikos might have a change of heart and come to venerate the idols, if he were left to himself and the gnawing pain of his traumatized flesh.

Both Hermylos and Stratonikos were then placed together in the prison, where they prayed together and said, "O Lord: 'Remember not our iniquities of old; let Thy compassions quickly go before us, O Lord, for we are become exceedingly poor [Ps. 78:8]. Help us, O God our Savior, for the sake of the glory of Thy name; O Lord, deliver us and be gracious unto our sins for Thy name's sake [Ps. 78:9].'" Then a divine voice was heard that said: "You have finished the course, you have kept the Faith. Henceforth there is laid up for you the crown of righteousness [cf. 2 Tim. 4:7, 8]."

When dawn broke the following day, Hermylos was again brought forward for examination. The tyrant again inquired: "Wilt thou sacrifice to the idols?" The holy deacon repeated what he said earlier, and then remarked, "Burn, punish, cut, do whatever thou wilt, for I do not fear those who slay the body and are unable to injure the soul in the least, but rather render it benefit." The emperor then ordered his men to suspend the martyr from a wooden pole and to flay his flesh. As the deacon endured the slicing and cutting of his body, he kept constant in prayer, invoking God for help. God indeed hearkened, and a voice was heard from on high, saying, "Cease being afraid. I am thy God; and I am He Who helps thee." Licinius was thrown into confusion and fear when he heard the voice. Thereupon, the saint was taken down from the wood. Licinius then pronounced another sentence. Hermylos was to be cast into the river Istros (Danube). He chose this manner of death, lest the Christians should retain any relics.

With regard to Stratonikos, Licinius was still attempting to persuade him to return to the impiety of idol-madness and said, "At least offer sacrifice to the gods, so that thou mayest not suffer as thy friend." Stratonikos answered, "If he would die for the sake of Christ, how could I be so wretched and mindless as to perform thy word?" The tyrant retorted, "Dost thou therefore wish to die together with Hermylos?" The holy Stratonikos answered, "Yes, that is the truth, for even as friends share in happiness and rejoicing, so they ought to share in afflictions and troubles; for indeed nothing is more honorable or sweeter than to receive death for the sake of our Christ." The emperor then deemed this soldier's case to be hopeless, for he perceived he would never change Stratonikos' mind.

Saints Hermylos and Stratonikos

Licinius therefore handed down the decision to put to death the two Christians together. They were to suffer the same death in the waters of that great river. Thus as they shared death together, so they would enjoy in Paradise the same crowns and common rejoicing. While Hermylos and Stratonikos were led to death, they were saying, "Glory to God in the highest, and on earth peace, good will among men [Lk. 2:14]." Both were filled with gladness, as though they were invited to experience some great advantage or enjoyment. When they arrived at the riverbank, the prisoners were placed inside one large straw basket and submerged. The Istros welcomed their holy bodies as a sanctification of the waters. Afterward, the mighty river delivered them up on dry land, not enduring to hide in its depths such a precious treasure. But these things were commanded and dispensed by the all-good God, lest the Christians should be deprived of such an excellent catch. Therefore, after the third day, certain God-loving men discovered the martyric relics and took them up reverently. The saints were buried to the accompaniment of sacred hymns and funeral prayers. Thus all was done for the

Saints Hermylos and Stratonikos

martyrs as prescribed by the rites of the Church. The martyrs were buried together at a distance of eighteen stadia (slightly over two miles) outside of Singidunum (Belgrade) at the confluence of the Sava and Danube Rivers. Thus, after they confessed Christ together, and also contested, suffered prison, and a watery death in common, they shared the same grave and then a common crown and glory in the heavens, through the grace of our Lord Jesus Christ, to Whom is due glory, dominion, honor, and homage, together with the Father and the Holy Spirit, now and ever and to the ages of the ages. Amen.

On the 13th of January, the holy Church commemorates
our venerable Father IAKOVOS of Nisibis.[3]

Iakovos (James), our holy father, lived at the time of Constantine the
Great, in the year 318. He was born and raised in the great city of Nisibis,
which was formerly called Antioch Mygdonios, which is found in the region
of Mesopotamia. By nature, he always loved the solitary and quiet life.
Consequently, he ascended to the peaks of the surrounding mountains; there,
the blessed one persevered courageously against the elements of nature. He
endured the burning summer heat and the winter cold, living on wild herbs
and drinking very little water. Thus, while he was mortifying his body with
the strictest form of abstinence, his soul was continually being nourished and
vivified with spiritual food, that is, with divine prayer and the reading of the
holy Scriptures.

By the strength of these godly virtues, he was vouchsafed God's favor
and boldness. He was endued with divine power, through the grace of the Holy
Spirit, to perform miracles and foresee the future. On one occasion, as he was
passing by a certain area, he observed some women near a fountain of water.
As they were making shameless gestures, he was suddenly inspired to curse
that spring and it dried up. Then when he spoke against those sorry creatures,
their black hair turned to white. Only in response to the entreaties of the
Christians of that locality did he restore the water to its source, but the hair
color of the women he would not bless to become black again. This was not
hardness on his part, to which Theodoretos attests and writes: "Furthermore,
the holy one did in fact search for these women, to cure them and to make their
hair black again; but because they did not come to be healed, he did not heal
them. He left their hair white, for their prudence and correction. For they were
washing garments with their legs, and they had their clothes rolled up and their
heads uncovered, without any shame, when they beheld the saint."

Once the holy one observed a certain Persian judge who had rendered
an unjust verdict, and he cursed the rock which was nearby him, and—O the
wonder!—the rock burst asunder into innumerable fragments. When the judge
saw this strange miracle (Theodoretos adds), he reconsidered the judgment,
and instead of the former unjust decision, he made a righteous one. Apparently, the inanimate and senseless rock was cursed by the saint's word, that
through the suffering of creation rational man would become wise and be set
aright.

At another time, the blessed one went into a village, and behold, there
came certain paupers, who desired to receive alms from the saint. One of

---

[3] The Life of this saint was written by Theodoretos, in Volume One of his *Philotheos*
or *Religious History*, and was included in the present *Synaxaristes* in an abridged form.

them pretended that he was dead, and the others mockingly entreated Saint Iakovos to donate the expenses for the burial of the deceased. The blessed one, on the one hand, begged forgiveness for the sins of him who was feigning death, and, on the other hand, he caused his soul to depart from his body; and verily he reposed. But afterward, the holy Iakovos revived him again at the entreaties of the others in his group.

This godly Iakovos, because of his many virtues, became bishop of his own place of Nisibis. He was present in Nicaea at the convocation of the First Œcumenical Synod, at which the impious Arius was anathematized. Now while Arius earnestly sought to be received again into the Church and guilefully concelebrate the Liturgy, this Iakovos, together with the other fathers, by their prayers, brought swift judgment from God. Arius' death came about when all his entrails spilled out, at a time when he was responding to a call of nature.

When Shāpūr II, king of the Persians, laid siege to Nisibis (338) with his armies, he utilized many stratagems in his attempt to capture the city. But the divine Iakovos appeared to them alone, and put the Persians to flight. The holy man had besought God to send upon them a cloud of tiny gnats and mosquitoes. The Lord dispatched this army of insects, which swarmed about the horses and elephants of the Persians, and bit them all. The animals broke their harnesses and escaped. When the king beheld this strange occurrence, not knowing what to do, he retreated to Persia without having succeeded in his purpose. After all these brilliant wonderworkings, the divine Iakovos reposed in the Lord, full of days, in a blessed state.

**On the 13th of January, the holy Church commemorates
the holy Martyr ATHANASIOS,
who was slain when beaten with rods.**

**On the 13th of January, the holy Church commemorates
the holy Martyrs PACHOMIOS and PAPYRINOS,
who were cast into a river.**

**On the 13th of January, the holy Church commemorates
the Consecration of the Monastery of Prophet ELIAS,
which is also known as Deep Mountain Spring
(Vatheos Ryakos).**[4]

---

[4] Vatheos Ryakos is located at Trigleia of Moudanion, a village-town of Asia Minor toward the Propontis.

**On the 13ᵗʰ of January, the holy Church commemorates
our venerable Father MAXIMOS the Kafsokalyves (Hut-burner)
of Mount Athos, who reposed in peace.⁵**

Saint Maximos the Hut-burner

Maximos, our venerable father, was from Lampsakos.⁶ He was the scion of godly and virtuous parents who had been childless. They had always prayed to God fervently and with tears that He might grant them a child. Now God hearkened to their supplication and granted them this blessed Maximos, who had been named Manuel in holy Baptism. They received him as a gift of God, which he was in very truth. They raised him with much love and care, as they taught him the divine writings.

When the child reached a mature age, they brought him to the Church of the Theotokos, at which time he was dedicated to God. While Manuel remained in the temple of the all-holy Theotokos, he chanted melodiously and with divine love, supplicating her at all times with much compunction for his salvation. In truth, he was as another young Samuel, advancing in both stature and grace. He was lauded and beloved by all. From the beginning he did not exhibit a childish mentality but a mature mind. Now the youth was wont to visit certain holy elders that he might listen to their soul-saving exhortations. They sojourned in quietude in the vicinity of that church. Since he kept company with them, he showed a proper feeling toward his elders and served them whenever he had opportu-

---

⁵ The Life of this saint was recorded in Greek by Prohegumen Theophanes Peritheorios of the Athonite Monastery of Vatopedi. The text was rendered in simpler Greek by Nikodemos the Hagiorite and set down by him in the *Neon Eklogion* (Venice, 1803). Four different vitae of Saint Maximos were composed during the century after his repose; the most detailed is that which is presented herein. Another account was written by the Monk Niphon. The idiorrhythmic Athonite Skete of Kafsokalyvia, founded in the 18ᵗʰ C., is named after the saint. It is situated beyond Eremos in the direction of the Great Lavra, on cliffs above the sea, and consists of some forty *kalyves* (huts). A divine office for this saint's feast day was composed of old but was reworked by the hymnographer Father Gerasimos Mikrayiannanites.

⁶ Lampsakos (40°22′N 26°42′E) was an ancient city on the eastern shore of the Hellespont facing Kallipolis.

nity, for he was yet in obedience to his parents. But in these frequent spiritual visits to the elders, their godly examples inflamed in him a desire to lead a God-pleasing life. Therefore, that divine yearning, which was kindling in his heart, incited him to forsake the world. He conceived the desire to put on the garb of the holy Schema of the monastics and live the hesychastic life. For this reason, he would ofttimes remove his worldly attire and dress the poor. As a result, the blessed youth endured the cold, undressed and trembling. He was also generous in giving bread to the indigent and hungry. In order to hide this virtue, he feigned before his parents and others that he was feeble-minded. Thus he became a kind of fool for Christ's sake. However, this feigned simplicity did not mislead or deceive his parents, who perceived his goodness and excellent deeds. His parents, as do many others, nonetheless appeared to have forgotten that they had dedicated their son to God, and they began making plans for him to marry. They were preparing to bind him to attachments of this world, that they might have him before them and rejoice as long as they were in this life.

The good-intentioned Manuel, being nourished by divine thoughts in his mind, was seventeen years of age when he left his parents, homeland, and the world. He repaired to Mount Ganos,[7] the holy mountain of Thrace, where he was garbed with the monastic Schema and given the name Maximos. He was placed under obedience to a proven and effective elder, Father Mark, that he might be instructed in the monastic conduct of life. It was soon discovered, however, that Father Maximos was already taught and accustomed to the monastic life. He appeared to those elders advanced and apt for any task or endeavor, whether it was fasting, or keeping vigil, or prayer, or sleeping on the ground, or any hardship. He showed fitting disdain for all vanities, even his own body. Though he was universally loved by the brethren, he yet had to bear with the reproach and insults of his elder. This occurred despite Maximos' excessive austerities, which he undertook without an intermission. After the passage of considerable time, the Elder Mark was translated to the everlasting abodes, having shone radiantly in virtue throughout all of Thrace and Macedonia.

The divine Maximos departed from that place and passed through Macedonia and all the surrounding countryside. He was seeking another

---

[7] Mount Ganos, on the western shore of the Sea of Marmara, is about fifteen kilometers southwest of Rhaidestos and near the small town of Ganos (mod. Gaziköy). By the 10th and 11th C., Mount Ganos was the site of a federation of monastic communities. These monasteries suffered destruction during the onslaughts of the Bulgarians (1199), the Crusaders (1203), and the Catalan Company (early 14th C.). *The Oxford Dictionary of Byzantium*, s.v. "Ganos, Mount."

virtuous spiritual father, as his first one; and God indeed fulfilled his desire. Father Maximos went to Mount Papikion (Papekion), where he found holy men similar to the anchorites of old. Some of them dwelt on the mountains, and others took shelter in the caves. These were wilderness places, wherein the inhabitants had nothing other than their old cassocks which they were wearing. Father Maximos associated with them for a long time and took upon himself to emulate and acquire their superhuman virtues, even as wax conforms to the imprint of the seal. Afterward, Father Maximos went to Constantinople, where he beheld that city's most exquisite churches. He venerated the relics of the saints which were treasured in those holy precincts. He also hastened to make a pilgrimage to Vlachernai, that is, to the Church of the Most Holy Theotokos, which is called Odegitria, that he might witness greater miracles, which were taking place within that temple. Having been a spectator of the greatest wonderworkings, by which he was left awestruck, he collected his thoughts. He reviewed all that he had seen and heard, pondering upon what great glory the Theotokos possesses in the heavens. Contemplating this sublime subject, he stood there utterly beside himself, in an ecstatic state. As he kept vigil in that church, he was seen to be without shoes and monastic head covering. His only raiment was one ancient hair shirt. From that ecstatic contemplation, he appeared to observers to be a fool, which was the image he invented for himself, that he might imitate the great Andrew, Fool for Christ's sake, who is commemorated by the holy Church on the 28th of May. Therefore, since he was not truly known, he was conjectured by many to be also a fool for Christ.

The emperor, Andronikos II Palaiologos (1282-1328), learned of the holy man and invited him to the palace. Father Maximos complied with the royal invitation. Andronikos opened the conversation in the midst of his court, where many were in attendance. The divine Maximos responded to the emperor's queries. At times he recited the words of Gregory the Theologian, with which he was well acquainted and which he often recounted, and at other times he spoke about other writings. His speech excited wonder in the rhetoricians who were in attendance. Though they generally admired his familiarity with the sacred writings, yet since Father Maximos was not taught letters, there were times in his speech that words were used incorrectly according to the rules of grammar. The great *logothete*, a high official in the civil administration, Kaniklios,[8] was present and commented, "The voice is

---

[8] It is curious how this functionary, named Kaniklios, bore a name synonymous with the post of the emperor's private secretary, known as *kanikleios*, though the same term in Latin (*canicula*) signifies dog-star or backbiter. It is not without precedence that he

(continued...)

Jacob's voice, but the hands are the hands of Esau [Gen. 27:22]." The venerable Maximos heard this remark and departed forthwith from the court, calling them vain-minded and senseless. He never again entered the palace. Now the patriarch at that time was Saint Athanasios (1289-1293 and 1303-1309), commemorated by the holy Church on the 28th of October, who was a fellow veteran of Mount Ganos. He often went to hear the most sweet words of Father Maximos, naming him a new Chrysostom. The patriarch perceived the saint's virtue and tried very much to place Father Maximos in one of the coenobia that had risen up in Constantinople. Father Maximos, however, did not wish to depart from the Vlachernai Church of the Theotokos, where he stayed in the vestibule, hungry and thirsty. He spent his time keeping vigil and standing, and always sighing and weeping. He struggled in this manner throughout the nights, but during the day he feigned foolishness and simplicity, so that he appeared to be a fool for Christ's sake. Though in reality he was a wise elder, he nevertheless assumed this guise, lest he should please men and scatter the fruit of virtue to the wind.

After he had spent adequate time in the capital, he went to Thessalonike that he might venerate the Great-martyr Demetrios the Myrrh-gusher. After he fulfilled this pious desire, he went directly to the Holy Mountain. He went about and venerated the shrines and relics at the sacred monasteries. He then came to the Lavra of Saint Athanasios, founded in 963. It was the earliest and largest foundation on Athos, built on a rocky outcrop where the peninsula ends. Its foundation marked the change from the individual ascetic life to organized monasticism on Athos. It was in that place where Maximos read the life and struggles of Saint Athanasios (d. ca. 1001), the founder of the Great Lavra, as well as the life of Saint Peter the Athonite.[9] Maximos marvelled at both the solitude and the inner silence kept by Peter and the coenobitic life observed by Athanasios. He meditated upon the readiness, eagerness, and diligence which each possessed, and how both kept the commandments of God. He then conceived the desire to remain in that place that he might emulate one of these two conducts of life. The God-bearing Maximos first deemed it prudent to consult with the venerable and righteous fathers who struggled in asceticism in that very place. He asked them which of the two modes of life he ought first to pursue. They counseled him to first remain in obedience to an elder that he might be exercised and disciplined, as was fitting, so that he might achieve to blessed obedience and learn to cut off

---

[8](...continued)
could have held both posts. See *Oxford*, s.v. "Kanikleios."
[9] The holy Church commemorates Saint Athanasios on the 5th of July, and Saint Peter on the 12th of June.

his own will and desires. Then, after having laid that good foundation upon the rock of the Christ—that is, divine humility, which is the beginning and root of all the virtues—he could then go on his own and struggle in hesychasm.

The venerable man, hearing these things, submitted to the hegumen and dwelt with the other brethren. First he was put to the test in performing lowly and menial ministrations, which is customary monastic practise. Afterward, he was assigned to chant in the church choir, to the glory of God; for he had learned the music of the sacred chant when he was young. As the blessed one chanted hymns of praise to God, he elevated his understanding. He shed many tears of compunction, which also occurred to him while reflecting upon the sacred readings. He was completely beside himself in a state of ecstasy, marvelling at God's boundless love of man. For the Lord granted us this grace that by the Holy Spirit we may apprehend these things while still in the body. Thereupon, his heart was all ablaze with divine fire, which inflamed his inward parts by divine grace dwelling within him. Even though he was in the midst of many, he yet found stillness and peace, as though he were in the wilderness, and was never hindered from noetic or interior prayer; that is, "Lord Jesus Christ, Son of God, have mercy on me." He occupied himself with the Jesus Prayer unceasingly, so that it moved always inside of his heart and mind. This is indeed rare and difficult to accomplish, but since childhood the blessed one had enjoyed the gift of prayer, by means of his virtue and the piety with which he cherished the most holy Theotokos.

Thus, while under obedience in the monastery, the blessed man undertook all commands readily. He also conducted his life with similar austerity as he had earlier when he was in the Vlachernai Church. He did not have his own cell inside the lavra. He possessed nothing whatsoever that might afford some bodily comfort. Out of necessity he ate, but only partook of what was offered in the trapeza (refectory); and even then he exercised self-control, subsisting on only what was needed to support life. For his dwelling place, he occupied one of the stalls (*stasidia*) in the church narthex, where he struggled with all-night standing and keeping vigil, according to his custom. At length, even as Mount Sinai called Moses, Carmel Elias, and the wilderness John the Baptist, in like manner the venerable Maximos was called to the summit of Athos, the blossom of the Holy Mountain, that the righteous one might flower atop that summit and bring forth the fruits of the Holy Spirit. Then, on the Sunday of the Holy Fathers, that is the Sunday before the Thursday of the divine Feast of the Ascension of the Lord, the Lady Theotokos appeared to him, bearing in her arms the Lord and saying, "Follow thou me, most trusted Maximos, and ascend Athos that thou mayest receive the grace of the Holy Spirit, even as thou desirest." Now the holy elder beheld this divine vision twice and thrice. He therefore left the Great Lavra; and, inside of seven days, he ascended the summit. It was the Saturday before the Feast of Pentecost. He passed the entire night in vigil. Also present were other monks who, after the celebration of the divine Liturgy, departed.

The divine Maximos abided there for three days and nights, praying unceasingly to God and the Theotokos. But who is able to recount the temptations perpetrated against the holy man by the enemy? For it seemed that thunder and lightning occurred, which shook the great Mount Athos, so that rocks broke and mountains were sundered and hills fell away. Now all of these happenings by night were false, an illusion of the demons, that they might instill terror in Maximos. During the day, there could be heard wild and fierce voices. Great was the confusion and agitation, as though a multitude of unsightly men were approaching, as they ascended to the summit from every direction. They appeared to be armed with slings and poles that they might drive Father Maximos down from that height. This was also demonstrated to be an apparition; for the divine Maximos, possessed of the grace of the Holy Spirit, felt no fear in the least. He neither prepared to encounter them nor planned an escape. He solely concerned himself with noetic prayer, supplicating God and the Theotokos, his protectress, who sponsored him.

Then the Theotokos appeared to him in celestial glory, as a queen, surrounded by a host of noble youths. Again she was holding in her hands Jesus, her Son, the Creator of all. The holy man beheld lightning-like divine light, which shone forth and illuminated the area round about. He straightway resorted to prayer, lest he should be misled by demonic deceit. He perceived that this was a divine vision, which truly manifested the Theotokos. He offered up a doxology and pious exclamations with inexpressible joy, saying also, "Rejoice, thou who hast been shown grace, the Lord is with thee!" Next he prostrated himself to the Lord and the Lady Theotokos. Then, as he received the blessing of the Lord and was filled with joy, he heard these words from the all-holy one, Panagia: "Receive thou grace against the demons, O august one who bears away the prize, and dwell at the foot of Mount Athos; for this is the will of my Son that thou mightest mount to the height of virtue and become a teacher and guide to many for their salvation." After this, she gave him heavenly bread for the nourishment and refreshment of his constitution, since he had been fasting all those days. Straightway, as he received the bread and placed it in his mouth, a divine light surrounded him from above. He heard an angelic hymn; and thereupon the Theotokos ascended into the heavens. The magnitude of that radiance and fragrance was such that the effect abided at the summit of the mountain. The saint was in a state of ecstasy and had no wish to descend, lest he should be deprived of that scent and brilliance. However, after three days he began to go down, according to the command of the Theotokos. He entered into a church, dedicated to the Panagia, where he tarried for some days. He then climbed again to the summit and venerated that place where the Theotokos stood in glory. With tears, he implored the return of her divine appearance. He was vouchsafed to behold a divine light and sense a fragrance, with which he could not satiate himself, even as at the other time, but he was filled entirely with joy and ineffable good cheer. These happenings occurred twice and thrice during the time he ascended to the summit.

Father Maximos came down from the peak and went to Carmel, to the church dedicated to Prophet Elias. He found within a monastic elder, to whom he revealed all that he had seen and heard at the top of the mountain. The old man, hearing him recount the vision, thought that the divine Maximos was deceived and misled. He thought that Maximos had fallen victim to the spectacle of a demonic fantasy. He called Father Maximos "the deluded one," and "the splendor and guide of the deceived." Henceforth, most of the brethren were saying that Father Maximos was in prelest.[10] They turned from him that they might drive him off, lest he should draw near to anyone. Now he who was far from benighted, but rather was a luminary, accepted their ostracism with exceeding joy, preferring to be called deluded than a saint. This general rejection and ill-judgment of himself suited him fine, for he was always feigning to be wandering and having a scattered mind that he might seem a simpleton and fool. Thus he would use this misjudgment to his profit, to vanquish pride, falling prey to pleasing men, and being wise in his own conceit. He could thereby cultivate the fruits of humble-mindedness, which preserves in man the grace of the Holy Spirit. That he might succeed in his aim, he chose not to dwell in one place, as the other fathers; but as a vagabond, he would go from place to place. Wheresoever he went, he constructed a tiny hut from grass. The dimensions were just enough to shelter his body during manifold contests. Then, after a short spell, he would burn down the hut and move on and start over somewhere else. So superhuman were his indigence and lack of acquisition that he had nothing to call his own—neither a two-pronged fork, nor hoe, nor shovel, nor bag, nor a small stool, nor table, nor earthen pot. He had no provisions, that is, neither flour, nor oil, nor wine, nor wheat, nor bread, nor anything necessary to support human life. But as one immaterial, he passed his life in desolate and

---

[10] Prelest, a technical term in ascetic theology, is a translation of the Greek πλανή, which literally means "wandering" or "going astray." Prelest is a state of beguilement and illusion, accepting a delusion as reality.

untraversed places. For this reason they were calling him not only the deluded one, but also the hut-burner. These other Athonites neither perceived the indwelling divine grace, which gave him hope and sheltered him, nor were aware of his unceasing mental prayer, which gave him relief.

Saint Maximos

No one could possibly represent, as is fitting, what he endured. He bore with hunger and thirst, since he had no supplies. He was naked in the midst of the cold and ice of winter, barefoot and without a second garment. He was exposed without a covering under the unrelenting rays of the scorching summer sun. There were some instances, when compelled by the force of nature, when he would have recourse to some brother, that he might console the flesh a little, and receive bread and salt, and perhaps a little wine, that is, if he found any. In very deed, on account of his mode of life, the Athonites spoke of him and recited those words of Christ in the Gospel which read: "Look at the birds of the heaven, for they sow not, neither do they reap, nor do they gather into storehouses; and yet your heavenly Father feedeth them [Mt. 6:26]." They spoke this way of him, because the saint was as a bird of the sky; or is it better to say that he was as an incorporeal who inhabited that wilderness? Verily, the ever-memorable one "crucified the flesh," even as the divine Paul says, "with the passions and the lusts [Gal. 5:24]."

Who would not marvel at such an angelic conduct of life? Who would not be astonished at hearing of such superhuman and supernatural contests? We speak here of his patient endurance, all-night standing, continual flow of tears, unceasing prayer, solitude, and isolation. We should also mention that these were accompanied by his repentance, meekness, and humility. Thus he became a dwelling place of the Holy Spirit. He was as Peter and Athanasios the Athonites; for he struggled, with all his power, in their modes of life that he might emulate the two masters of monasticism. He was also in zeal as another Paul of Thebes and Anthony the Great, having arrived at their heights of excellence. For this cause, his mind, even as the minds of those great fathers, seized by contemplation, beheld divine visions and the revelation of mysteries. How did these things ever become manifest to others? Now Father Maximos was not always hidden. At length, but gradually, he became known when he conversed with other holy elders and great ascetics. Though they marvelled and respected the divine Maximos on account of his tremendous labors, yet the evil suspicion persisted that he was in prelest. But as time passed and their acquaintance of him improved, they perceived by divine grace that he was a habitation of the Spirit. Thus it was no longer rumored that Maximos was deluded; much rather, he was esteemed as the honorable Maximos, the exceedingly bright light.

At that time, there came to the Holy Mountain the venerable Gregory the Sinaite, who is commemorated by the holy Church on the 6th of April. After he had made a tour of Mount Athos, he went to the Skete of Magoula. He proved to be the spiritual elder for whom all the fathers, especially the hesychasts, of the Mountain were longing to visit, because he was a marvellous teacher of quietude and noetic prayer. He knew very well the machinations and cunning artifices of the demons. It is rare and difficult to find such grace, knowledge, and experience in one man. The hermits and hesychasts were hastening to be instructed by him in the mysteries of interior prayer and to learn what might be the unerring signs of grace and those of the enemy. Now some who had come to Father Gregory happened to mention the venerable Maximos. They related his superhuman conduct of life and his behavior of foolishness, which they suspected to be misleading. The divine Gregory both wondered and marvelled at these descriptions of Maximos. He desired to behold the man and converse with him. The holy Gregory therefore dispatched some of his disciples to invite the sacred Maximos for a visit, that he might enjoy his company. Those who were sent on this obedience did not find Father Maximos in his hut. For two days they wandered about in search of him, but they could not discover his whereabouts. The difficulty was increased because it was winter, when Father Maximos was wont to spend time in the caves and the forests. The monks, on account of the season, began to overexert themselves and became exhausted. They decided to go to the Kellion of Saint Mamas,[11] where they might refresh themselves a little. They went there; and, as soon as they arrived, the divine Maximos, for whom they

---

[11] Kellion (cell) is an interchangeable term for various kinds of monastic settings, whether a cell in a coenobium, housing one or two monks, or a cell at a lavra, or a cell of a hermit. On Mount Athos, it was considered a small monastery. *Oxford*, s.v. "Kellion."

had been searching so long, greeted them all by name, though there had been no prior acquaintance. He also spoke before they uttered a word, indicating that the counsel of the venerable Gregory was to leave the Holy Mountain. Father Maximos not only foretold that the holy Gregory would go to the frontier, to Paroria (on the border, present day Thrace), but also spoke of other events. The disciples of Father Gregory hearkened to all that was spoken to them by Father Maximos and then delivered their Elder Gregory's message. Father Maximos immediately left with those disciples to see the righteous Gregory. As he went, he started chanting the psalm which begins with these words: "I have lifted up mine eyes to the mountains, from whence cometh my help [Ps. 120:1]."

Just as they approached the kellion of the holy Gregory, the divine Maximos spoke to the disciples, saying, "The elder is taking his rest now, since he has toiled much in prayer. Therefore you also should take a little rest, as will I, until I should see the elder." Upon uttering these words, he turned about and went inside the forest, praying and chanting these words with tears: "My steps do Thou direct according to Thy saying, and let no iniquity have dominion over me [Ps. 118:133]." After he finished that psalm, the divine Gregory called him, and he quickly went. After they greeted and kissed one another, Father Gregory dismissed the others that he might converse privately with the God-bearing Maximos. He wished to learn from Father Maximos himself concerning those reports circulating about him. When Father Gregory began questioning him regarding his method of prayer, Father Maximos replied, "Forgive me, father, I am deceived." Father Gregory said, "Leave off those things now, and tell me, for the Lord's sake, thy virtue, that I might be enlightened. Make this exception, so that we might be edified and build up virtue and be of service to one another, because I am not as the others who lay snares for a neighbor by their words; nay, much rather, I love my neighbor as myself. Therefore, tell me, for the Lord's sake, what is thy virtue?"

Then the divine Maximos revealed to him whatsoever had happened to him from his youth; that is, he spoke of his early zeal inspired by God, his renunciation of the world, his submission, his feigned foolishness for Christ's sake, and his ascetical struggles. He spoke of the awesome vision of the Theotokos and the light which had enveloped him and had surrounded him on other occasions. He also mentioned his manifold trials and the temptations of the demons. The divine Gregory then interrupted his narration and said, "Tell me, if thou wilt, dost thou hold to mental prayer, most honorable Father?" Father Maximos smiled a little and said, "I do not wish to hide from thee, my father, the miracle of the Theotokos, which happened to me. I, from my youth, possessed much faith in my Lady Theotokos. I would supplicate her with tears that she might grant to me the grace of noetic prayer. Then, on one of those days, she passed over to her church, where I was accustomed to attending and fervently implored her with boundless warmth of heart. In that sacred place, where I would kiss with much desire her holy icon, I straightway sensed in my breast and in my heart a warmth and flame coming from the holy icon. I was not burned, but rather bedewed and sweetened. Great compunction was brought into my soul. From that time, father, my heart began to speak from within the prayer; and my mind was sweetened in the remembrance of my Jesus and my Theotokos. Consequently, both heart and mind are ever together with the remembrance of them; so that, my father, forgive me, the prayer never leaves my heart."

The divine Gregory then said to the venerable Maximos, "Tell me, O saint, when thou art reciting the prayer, 'Lord Jesus Christ,' and the rest, has there followed at any time a divine transformation or ecstasy or other fruit of the Holy Spirit?" The sacred Maximos replied, "O father, for this cause I passed over to the wilderness district and am always desiring silence and solitude, that I may better enjoy the fruit of prayer, which is one excessive love for God and a captivity of the mind toward the Lord." Saint Gregory then remarked, "I beseech thee, father, dost thou possess these things of which thou speakest?" Then the divine Maximos smiled again and said, "Give me something to eat, and do not try to examine my wandering." Saint Gregory then remarked, "Would to God that I too had the same wandering as thyself, O saint! However, I beseech thee to tell me that when thy mind is seized by contemplation, dost thou see with noetic eyes? And also, tell me if it is possible then for the mind, together with the heart, to mention the prayer?"

The divine Maximos, filled with the Holy Spirit, answered and said, "No, it is not able, my father." Father Maximos spoke to Father Gregory in connection with mental prayer and the accompanying mystical state: "When the grace of the Holy Spirit enters one at the time of prayer, then the prayer ceases, since the mind is entirely dominated by the Holy Spirit and cannot energize its powers. It is still and not laboring, subordinating itself to the Holy Spirit. It is directed as the Holy Spirit wills, either to the realm of the immaterial divine light, or to some other ineffable contemplation, or ofttimes to divine converse. And in short, even as the Holy Spirit wills, in that manner He consoles and comforts His slaves, granting grace even as is meet for each one. This state to which I am referring is that which had been attained to by the prophets and apostles who were accounted worthy to behold such contemplations, though the people would mock them as ones deceived or in error or intoxicated. For instance: Prophet Esaias 'saw the Lord sitting on a high and exalted throne,...and seraphs stood round about Him [Is. 6:1, 2].'

Then there was the Protomartyr Stephen who 'gazed intently into the heaven, and saw the glory of God, and Jesus standing on the right of God; and he said, "Behold, I see the heavens having been opened and the Son of Man standing on the right of God [Acts 7:55, 56]."' In such a manner, even now, the slaves of God are vouchsafed to behold diverse divine visions. But some people in no wise will believe that these visions are true. They deem such persons who do see such things as being in prelest. I therefore marvel much at this and wonder how these people proceed. As ones blind in the soul, they do not believe the unfeigned promise of the Lord Who spoke by the mouth of the Prophet Joel: '"And it shall be in the last days," saith God, "I will pour out of My Spirit upon all flesh; and your sons and your daughters shall prophesy, and your young men shall see visions, and your old men shall dream dreams [cf. Joel 2:28]; and even upon My bondmen and upon My bondwomen in those days I will pour out of My Spirit [Joel 2:29]," and they shall prophesy [Acts 2:17, 18].' This grace has the Lord granted us, and He bestows it even now, and wishes to be giving it until the consummation. This is in accordance with His promise to all His faithful slaves.

"Therefore, when this grace of the Holy Spirit comes to one, it does not reveal to him the customary things, nor those things of this world which are apprehended by the senses, but it shows him those which he has never seen before nor imagined. And then the mind of that man is taught by the Holy Spirit mysteries—lofty, hidden, and unknown—which, according to the divine Paul, are those which 'eye hath not seen, and ear hath not heard, and neither hath it entered into the heart of man the things which God prepared for those who love Him [1 Cor. 2:9]'; that is, such things cannot be seen by the bodily eye nor can the mind of man ever reckon them on his own. That thou mayest understand my meaning, holy father, how our mind beholds such things which the eye has not seen, consider what I shall say to thee: wax, when it is far from the fire, is firm and can be grasped. When, however, it is put in the fire, it bursts into flame, emits light, and begins melting. It is surrounded by light and becomes light. Thus it is made perfect or completed in fire, and it is not possible that it should not become loose from itself and come to flow. In like manner, the mind of man, when it is alone, without mixture with God, by whatsoever powers it may possess, it forms its own notions. Yet whenever the fire of the divinity and the Holy Spirit should approach it, then it is completely dominated by that divine light and becomes all light. And there, in the flame of the Holy Spirit, it is lit, kindled, and consumed by divine perceptions, so that it is not possible, in the midst of the fire of the divinity, for the mind to form its own notions and take thought of those things which it wills."

Then the divine Gregory said to the blessed Maximos, "And where there is error, my hut-burner, with what signs ought one to compare?" The great Maximos answered, "The signs of error are another matter with regard to those of grace. Whenever the evil spirit of error should approach one, that spirit confuses the mind and makes him savage. It hardens and darkens the heart. It brings cowardice, fear, and pride. It makes wild the eyes, agitates the mind, and causes all the body to shiver. It displays to the eyes of the imagination, not a light radiant and pure, but red. It makes the mind beside itself, demonizing it. It incites one with his mouth to utter both unseemly and blasphemous words. Whosoever sees the spirit of error is ofttimes in a passion and full of anger. Humility he in no wise knows, neither true mourning nor tears, but he is always vaunting his accomplishments and extolling himself, without constraint and the fear of God. Thus he finds himself filled with the passions; and, in the end, he loses his reason altogether and goes quite mad, thereby perishing. From such error and deception, may the Lord deliver us through thy prayers!

"The signs of grace, however, are as follows. When the grace of the Holy Spirit comes and overshadows one, it collects for itself the mind and causes it to be attentive and humble. It brings about in one the remembrance of death and one's sins, and the future judgment and everlasting punishment. It makes the soul easily come to compunction that it might weep and mourn. It produces eyes full of tears in the sober-minded. As much as it draws near to a man, such a one perceives calm in his soul. He receives consolation by means of our Lord Jesus Christ's boundless love for man and His holy Passion. This acts as an agent to the mind, conferring upon it lofty and true contemplation. First, he meditates upon the incomprehensible power of God, regarding how He created all things from out of nothing. Second, he meditates upon God's infinite power, by which He holds together and governs all things in His providence. Third, he meditates upon the incomprehensibility of the Holy Trinity, the unsearchable and inscrutable gulf of the divine essence, and the rest. Then, when the mind of man is seized by that divine light and is illumined with the divine illumination of knowledge, his heart becomes serene, still, and meek, gushing forth the fruits of the Holy Spirit—that is, joy, peace, long-suffering, kindness, sympathy, love, humility, and the rest [Gal. 5:22]; thus, the soul of such a one partakes of one inexpressible joy. This is why I have sought the wilderness; and this is why I have always longed for quietness, in order to enjoy more the fruits of prayer."

Saint Gregory, hearing these experiences described, was beside himself and marvelled. He called Saint Maximos an earthly angel and not a man. He then fervently besought him, saying, "Cease, I beseech thee, from the custom of setting fire to thy cell, and concentrate thyself in one place. Abide therein, even as the wise Isaac the Syrian says, that thou mightest yield more fruit and benefit others—as one experienced in virtue, asceticism, and mental prayer—because thou hast arrived at old age, and death is often coming before one's time. For this cause, hide not thy talent—that is, the grace which thou hast received and the seed of thy divine teaching— but share it with the people of God, by means of a stationary residence, before the end should arrive. Thus thou shalt receive in the heavens an even greater reward for benefitting others. Consider how the Lord bestowed the grace of the Holy Spirit upon the apostles. It was not so that they might sojourn in the mountains, but among men, benighted sinners, that they too might become holy and partakers of that grace by means of their sanctity. On this account the Lord said to them, 'Let your light shine before men [Mt. 5:16],' and not before rocks. Therefore, let thy light shine before men that they might see your good works and glorify your Father Who is in the heavens. Leave off pretending to be a fool, for thou hast become a scandal and stumbling block to those who do not know thine accomplishments. I therefore implore thee to hearken to my counsel and do as I have bidden thee. I speak as a best friend and brother; for 'a brother helped by a brother is as a strong and high city [Prov. 18:19].'"

The other great elders learned of these counsels of Father Gregory to Father Maximos. They concurred with his advice and took up the cause in persuading Father Maximos to remain in one place. Thereupon, the divine Maximos showed himself compliant and obeyed the consensus of the fathers. He found a cave which was close by, some three miles from Kyr Esaias. He put up a fence round about the cave, about six feet in height by six feet in length. He erected it without stones or wood or boards or nails, but with branches and grass, according to his custom of building, so that it might appear that he constructed a kellion and that he took up dwelling therein. Although he no longer took to burning, still he passed the rest of his life with his usual nonacquisitiveness. His poverty was such that he neither possessed a needle nor had a slice of bread. As though he were one of the bodiless host, he resumed his superhuman ascetical contests. Afterward he dug a grave for himself, situated near to his cave. He visited it daily, during the hour of Orthros, where he would weep and chant funeral hymns—mostly Exaposteilaria[12] in the Third Mode, after the hymn, "As God Thou hast adorned the heaven with stars..."—specially composed by himself.

---

[12] Exaposteilaria are hymns that come at the end of the Orthros Canon, following the small ektenia.

The demons, however, continued their warfare with the saint on a daily basis, contriving to drive him forth from the place. Instead, the venerable elder chased them away by interior prayer, so that they vanished as smoke. His prayer, an invincible divine power, overshadowing and guarding him, appeared—to those worthy of such contemplation—as a kind of fire which burned his enemies. Thereupon, by his word only, Father Maximos cured many. He cast out demons from the demon-possessed, who were then able to depart in peace. He was wont to command the brethren to avoid remembrance of slights, wrongdoing, taking oaths, drunkenness, fornication, and eating meat. He bade them to offer alms, according to their strength, and cleanse themselves from every sin by means of repentance. In this manner, they would be prepared beforehand to partake of the immaculate Mysteries on major feast days, receiving healing of soul and body continually. At this juncture, in order to render praise to the saint, we shall narrate one of his many miracles to give assurance of the truth of the others.

A certain monk, named Mercurios, was urged by the venerable Maximos to cast a demon out of one demonized. Mercurios, obedient to the elder, cast out the unclean spirit in the presence of Maximos, invoking the name of Jesus Christ. In this paradoxical and mysterious manner, the demonized man was delivered.

On another occasion, one in obedience to an elder was suffering badly from a demon. In the middle of the road, the venerable Maximos commanded the disciple to preserve perfect obedience to his elder. He was also instructed to avoid cheese, wine, and that which defiles, and be healed in the name of Jesus Christ. And—O the wonder!—he straightway, with that word was cured.

One day, some monks from the Lavra came to see the venerable Maximos that they might receive spiritual benefit. In their company they had a learned secular man, named Gregory Akindynos.[13] Akindynos was his adopted name, which in the Greek language signifies "free from danger." As soon as Father Maximos gazed upon that man, he began to drive that man far from him. Without ever having laid eyes on him before or suffering an

---

[13] Gregory Akindynos (1300-1348) was involved in the controversy over Palamism, that is, the inaccessible and unknowable essence of God and His uncreated energies, taught by Saint Gregory Palamas, Archbishop of Thessalonike (1347-1359). Akindynos questioned the orthodoxy of Palamite doctrine on divine grace; as a result he supported Barlaam of Calabria. During the reign of John VI Kantakouzenos (Cantacuzene, 1347-1354), Akindynos was excommunicated at the Synod of 1347 and died in exile. Also, anti-Palamite Patriarch John XIV Kalekas (1334-1347) was deposed by a synod convoked by Empress Anna of Savoy, before Kantakouzenos entered the city. Kalekas also died in exile. See the Life of Saint Gregory Palamas, commemorated the 14th of November.

introduction, he began saying, "Thou art he who mightily endangers others, O faithless one!" The venerable man came down heavily upon Akindynos, naming him "bad danger" and "demonized," and "a servant of Antichrist, having communion with every heresy." Father Maximos, not only in this instance but also in dealing with other such heretics, cast them out and boldly anathematized them. Again some other monks came to the venerable elder. The moment he laid his eyes upon them, he began shouting at them, "Drive out the Messalian!"[14] He then named the monk among them who was a Messalian, and continued, saying to the rest, "And then come to me." Those monks were terrified at these words, for they knew not that one of them was a Messalian. However, as obedient ones, dutifully they cast off the deceived one from their company and then went to the holy man.

A certain monk, having some business to transact, wished to travel by ship from Constantinople to Thessalonike. The venerable Maximos would not permit or bless the voyage, predicting that the vessel would be imperilled at sea. Indeed, after three days, that ship sank to the bottom of the sea with all passengers lost.

On another occasion, a ship entered the harbor of the Great Lavra. The men on board went to see the holy man. Among them was one who was demonized, being possessed by the demon of ravenous hunger. The sufferer was eating at all hours of the day, enough food for five men, but was never sated. Those who brought him cast him before the feet of the holy man. Both they and the sufferer were beseeching Father Maximos that he be delivered from that demon. The saint, taking a biscuit, gave it to the sufferer and said, "In the name of our Lord Jesus Christ, eat so much and be filled and at peace." Thenceforth, he was delivered from the demon of insatiability. He never ate more than what was equal to that biscuit. That same man came to

---

[14] Messalians (also termed Euchitai or Efchitai) believed that a demon is encamped in each man's soul. This demon cannot be expelled by either holy Baptism or the other Mysteries, other than the "baptism of fire." The instrument of purification was prayer, through which man can attain to freedom from the passions and to the descent of the Holy Spirit. This sect was criticized by Saints Ephraim the Syrian, Epiphanios, Amphilochios, and John of Damascus. *Oxford*, s.v. "Messalianism." The Messalians equated the divine light with the divine essence. These heretics thought that the vision of God was simply a matter of the spiritual ability of the believer, and that sanctification was a work of a man's efforts, unaided by grace or perhaps with grace playing a little part. Saint Gregory Palamas warned against this error of the Messalians, who believed that the grace of divinization is a natural state, the activity and manifestation of a natural power. If divinization depended on our natural powers, the divinized man would necessarily be God by nature. See *The Triads: The Uncreated Glory*, III.i.26, p. 82. The Efchites (Euchites) were condemned at the Synod of Ephesus (431).

renounce the world and was tonsured a monk. He remained close to the saint, being guided by him, so that he advanced by divine grace in virtue and became one well tested and approved in the monastic life.

There was another monk, named Barlaam, who was in obedience to a certain elder. The venerable Maximos reproached Barlaam for his harshness and disobedience which he showed to his elder, saying to him, "On account of these transgressions, thou shalt receive a bad end, dying by either cold or ice." Thus it came to pass that the word of the venerable saint was fulfilled.

There was another monk, Father Athanasios, whom Father Maximos predicted was about to be put to death by Ishmaelites. This prophecy was also fulfilled. The saint was so enriched with the grace of the Holy Spirit, that what was at a distance he beheld as one near, and what was unseen and in the future, he foreknew and foretold as though he were present.

The saint also foreknew the coming of the emperors and said, "The emperors of the Rhomaioi wish to come to me that they may hear prophecies and receive prognostications of future happenings, not that they might benefit spiritually." Indeed, it was not long before there came to the Holy Mountain, in 1351, both Emperors John VI Kantakouzenos and John V Palaiologos (1341-1391). The venerable Maximos predicted all that would befall them and exhorted them to endure all the coming sorrowful events. After he advised them with soul-saving teachings and instructions suitable for kings, he dismissed them in peace. But then he went on before them and addressed Kantakouzenos, saying, "Behold, an abbot in a monastery." He then said to Palaiologos, "Hold fast, intemperate one, and be not deceived; for though thou dost wish to rule long, yet thou shalt be insignificant, and thy reign shall bring thee many tumults." After these forecasts, he said to them, "Hail, and go in peace." After the passage of a little time, Father Maximos sent to Constantinople a parcel to Kantakouzenos containing a biscuit, one onion, and one garlic. He also sent along a message with these words: "In the future, when thou shalt become a monk, thou shalt be eating such food." Thus it came to pass in but a short time. Palaiologos approached the Genoese, the old enemies of Kantakouzenos. After making promises to the Genoese, the conspirators forced their way into the capital. Kantakouzenos was enjoined to abdicate in November of 1354 and enter a monastery. He became the Monk Ioasaph at the Monastery of Mangana in the capital, exchanging the royal purple for the humble black cassock of the monk. He no longer occupied himself with politics. He lived nearly another thirty years, which time he spent writing his famous history and theological works in defense of hesychast doctrine. Thus once, as he was sitting in the monastery refectory and eating a biscuit, he brought to mind the prophecy of the venerable Maximos and marvelled. In like wise, Palaiologos remembered and wondered at the predictions of Father Maximos, for they all came to pass. His reign included a series of rebellions and a civil war. In an attempt to gain western assistance against the Turks, in December of 1355, Palaiologos sent a letter to Avignon, requesting help from Pope Innocent VI (1352-1362) in the form of galleys, transport vessels, and soldiers. In return, he promised to convert his subjects to the pope's religion within six months. He even said he would send his son to the papal court to be educated by the pope; and should he not fulfill these promises, he would prepare to abdicate. Though the pope did not give credence to these extravagant promises, he nonetheless dispatched his legate to the capital. Union was at a standstill for years. Palaiologos then traveled to Hungary (1366) and Rome (1369), where he declared his personal conversion to Catholicism. In the meantime, he had crushing debts and was troubled by the rebellions of his son Andronikos IV and his grandson John VII.

Patriarch Kallistos of Constantinople (1350-1353; 1355-1363), commemorated by the holy Church on the 20th of June, had been a former Athonite and disciple of Saint Gregory of Sinai. He had been a hieromonk at Magoula and hegumen at the Athonite monastery of Iveron. Under Kantakouzenos, he had been elected patriarch and presided over the local Synod of Constantinople (1351), which upheld again the doctrine of Saint Gregory Palamas. On one occasion, in the company of his clergy, he was going to Serbia, for the union and peace of the Church, and was passing through the Holy Mountain. On that pastoral visit, he also went to the hut of Saint Maximos that he might see him. The venerable Maximos went out first to overtake him and receive his blessing. After Father Maximos kissed and greeted him, he said in a pleasant and graceful manner to those present, "This elder has lost his eldress," and similar other comments. Afterward, since he had conversed for a considerable time, he went ahead of the party as they were leaving, chanting the burial hymn in Mode Plagal Two, "Blessed are the blameless in the way, who walk in the law of the Lord [Ps. 118:1]," and the rest of the psalm. By this action and sounding the funeral dirge, Father Maximos foretold both the patriarch's repose and burial, which also came about. In but a short time, they all died in that foreign land. Some say the cause of death was the result of poisoning; others comment that the patriarch had fallen gravely ill. They were interred in the cathedral of the Serbians. Thus the prophecy of the venerable Maximos was fulfilled.

On one occasion, a certain ascetic, named Methodios, went to the venerable elder and saw the divine light all around Father Maximos. He dared not draw near until Father Maximos gave the command to approach.

On another occasion an extraordinary scene was witnessed, wherein heavenly bread was received by the holy elder. It was wintertime when the nurse at the infirmary of Great Lavra, Father Gregory, together with his brother, went to visit the elder. On account of the heavy snowfall, not only was the ground completely covered, but also the path made for men to tread upon could no longer be discerned. Therefore, those fathers needed to make a new path to the elder's hut. Now they were carrying both bread and wine, and other necessary items for the elder's consolation. As they entered the hut, they observed a warm and fresh loaf, very pure, which emitted a marvellous fragrance. Those fathers then became curious to see if there were any sign of fire in that hut. Not finding any such thing, they were beside themselves at this phenomenon, marvelling at the heavenly bread and its scent. They fell at the elder's feet, seeking a portion of that bread which they perceived to be celestial. The saint had compassion upon them. He cut the loaf in two and gave them half, admonishing them, "Take, eat, and be mindful not to speak to anyone of this as long as I live." The elder then offered them sweet drinking water. Father Gregory and his brother kept the elder's command, speaking nothing of what they experienced, until his blessed repose. Some of the brethren say that the water, which the elder drank himself and offered to others, was seawater that the elder blessed and made sweet.

On yet another occasion, when it was dry and the season of fruit gathering, two monks went to see the venerable old man. After they conversed, Father Maximos took one biscuit and gave it to them, saying, "Make haste and go to the monastery of Dorotheos, lest you suffer perils on the road from the winter." They marvelled at what he said, for it was not wintertime; neither was it cold nor cloudy. But before they left for the monastery of Dorotheos, a dramatic change occurred in the sky. A fierce wind arose, followed by many volleys of thunder and lightning. Such hail and rain fell that all creation was agitated, resulting in no harvest, since the un-picked crop from the vineyards disappeared. The two monks, beholding such an alteration in the weather, cried out, "Lord have mercy!" Afterward they kept proclaiming to all the prophecy of the righteous elder.

There once came to the venerable elder a dignitary from Constantino-ple, holding the office of *grammatikos*, which at that time was a scribe or secretary. As soon as Father Maximos gazed upon him, he knew the visitor's evil thoughts which he had been entertaining. The elder began to say to him, "Where hast thou seen the struggles and wrestlings of the saints, and the grace granted them by God, that thou shouldest utter blasphemies against them? Why dost thou maintain that the saints contested slightly? Why hast thou contended that they who record their lives do them the favor of falsely inflating their achievements? Furthermore, thou dost have the notion that their miracles are fables. Cease such satanic thoughts, lest thou shouldest move the wrath of God to cast a bolt of lightning thy way and consume thee. Know this:

the saints, since they have entirely dedicated themselves to God, submit all their thoughts and labors to God Who works mightily through them who have proven to be proved God-pleasing. And who, tell me, is able to describe the entire life of every saint, even as it was? Who can know every detail? Their writing is select and limited from the myriads of events which testify of the saints. And know this also: that the grace of the Holy Spirit, which is bestowed upon the saints, is not only that which appears, but also is rich and incomprehensible, transcending every mind and thought. If thou wilt truly be wise, forsake the silly talk of the wise and learned of the world, that thou mayest know God by means of the true knowledge and spiritual quiet. Thus spoke David regarding the wisdom brought to infants [Ps. 18:7] and that of the world being swallowed up [Ps. 106:27]. Only then canst thou become His initiate and habitation, as much as thou art able; and then thou shalt know the grace of the Holy Spirit and the divine things and incomprehensible wonders of God. In this manner, thou shalt wonder and judge thyself, as thou reflectest upon how benighted thou wast previously. For without the light, the darkness is not manifest. Come to the light of quiet and prayer, and the previous darkness shall flee from thee. And then thou shalt really behold the spiritual free gift of grace and the power of the saints; and then thou shalt have desire to enjoy it." The *grammatikos*, hearing such a revelation of his secret thoughts, panicked and became afraid. Nevertheless, he was much benefitted and corrected this blasphemous thinking on his part, so that he afterward edified and made right the thinking of others with the saint's teaching.

"I should also like to recount," says the author of this account, "as God is my witness, that which I beheld with my own eyes and have no wish to conceal. For the saint knows that I know what I saw with him. One day, with another brother, I departed from the Athonite Monastery of Vatopedi. I then went to the saint's hut. Not finding him there, I was saddened. I looked round about, in the hope of beholding him whom I desired to gaze upon. I then mounted up to higher ground, behind his hut, that I might better see the road of Kyr Esaias, the saint's neighbor. I did catch sight of Father Maximos in the basin of Agelario, at a distance of some two miles, in a rocky place difficult to traverse. And—behold the marvel!—I saw the saint borne aloft, high above the ground, as a winged eagle. He flew over the forest and the great rocks, coming toward me. I was in terror and cried out, 'Great art Thou, O Lord!' From fear, I pulled back a little. Then, in the twinkling of an eye, he was before me, chanting. Now what he was chanting I took no thought of, on account of the miracle, but I did fall before his feet. He then welcomed me and asked how long I had been in this spot. He then took me by the hand, and we entered his cell. After he counseled me, he said, 'Take heed that thou speakest to no one regarding that which thou hast seen, until

I am no longer in this present life. And know this: thou shalt become an abbot and then Metropolitan of Ohrid. And in the future thou shalt suffer much. However, do thou endure, imitating the crucified Lord on the Cross; for He desires to become a helper in temptations, which shall take place in the witness of thy contest.' All that the saint prophesied in my regard came to pass.

"But there was something else which I had seen, and about which I do not wish to remain silent. A monk of Lavra, named Iakovos, came to ask of the saint a letter of introduction. The point of this request was that he might go all about and collect money for the deliverance of his brother. The saint abided patiently till Iakovos finished speaking, and then he spoke with much sternness, saying, 'Go and remove thy sixty over the fire, that is, the gold florins concealed in the tower wall; and give those for the ransom of thy brother. Be thou not grasping and false, lest thou shouldest be enslaved again.' When Iakovos heard his secret revealed, he confessed to the truth of the charge. After he had asked forgiveness for what he had dared, he went to carry out Father Maximos' command.

"At another time, a certain secular came to the venerable elder and was weeping and saying, 'Help me, O saint of God, for a priest has excommunicated me and then died; and now I, the hapless one, know not what to do.' The saint said, 'Go to the Metropolitan of Verea, who was the archbishop who appointed that deceased priest, that thou mayest receive forgiveness according to the laws.' Thus it took place as the saint bade him. But also, at that very same hour, Father Maximos addressed a certain monk who was present, though unknown to him, and said, 'Do thou also go to the Priest John that thou mayest receive forgiveness before thou diest; for thou hast been excommunicated from that time when thou didst insult and slap him.' That monk marvelled how the saint recounted his transgression. He then accompanied that secular man to Verea and also received pardon.

"Now on another occasion the Bishop of Trajanoupolis, a city of Thrace by the river Evros, came with his deacon to see the saint. The bishop wished to try the saint and determine if Father Maximos were truly a clairvoyant. On the road, the deacon and bishop exchanged raiment. When they came to the elder's hut, the archbishop, in the deacon's guise, entered first and addressed the elder, saying, 'Give the blessing, father. The archbishop is without and would enter herein.' The saint then replied, 'Thou art the archbishop, and do thou bless me. And do not be telling me of thy fraud, for I was above the pit wherein you worked out this theft.' And saying this, he made a prostration and was blessed by the archbishop. He then kissed him; and the bishop, stunned, greatly marvelled.

"This was also spoken of the saint by the God-bearing and righteous Niphon the Athonite. 'There was a small cave above Father Maximos' hut. Now one day Maximos entered the cave and slept. When he arose from his sleep, he sat up in the cave. He then observed before him a bedecked woman. Knowing the crafty ploys of the evil demon, he thrice made the sign of the honorable Cross and the apparition vanished.'

"Now Abba Niphon was also saying this about Father Maximos: 'On one Monday, there came a certain monk who sat opposite my cell. I had not seen him before,' said Niphon, 'but his appearance was withered from much abstinence. On Tuesday, in the morning, he came to see me and spoke of edifying matters. Now there was no bread for either of us—not that he cared—that I might invite him. He then went out and sat above my hut until Thursday morning, when he once more visited and counseled me. He afterward went out and sat in the same place until Saturday morning. I then also left the hut for bodily refreshment, and from then I no longer saw him.'" Abba Niphon had learned later that the ascetic he had seen was Father Maximos.

After fourteen years had transpired that the venerable Maximos sojourned in the cave where he had his hut, nearby Panagia, he then moved closer to the Great Lavra that he might hear the spiritual instruments, that is, the bells. He put together a small hut, where he remained until the end of his life. Now there are many other narrations about the divine Maximos, regarding his clairvoyance, great wonderworkings, and godly-wise teachings. With these spiritual gifts, he spiritually led and guided seculars and monastics and every condition of man. It is, however, impossible to record the multitude of his achievements. What we have written is only a cup's worth from the waters of the sea. But again, what little is presented herein is sufficient for the Christians to recognize that not only in ancient times has God glorified His saints, but even now, as in every time, those who glorify Him with good works He has glorified with signs and wonders, which are an earnest of that immaterial glory that they shall enjoy in the kingdom of the heavens. Therefore, we have hastened by many things and have come to the most august end of the saint's earthly sojourn.

There was a monk, named Nikodemos, who went to the venerable elder that he might partake of spiritual benefit. The saint said to him, "Brother Nikodemos, I shortly am about to die." Following this statement, he revealed to that brother the day of his falling asleep. The elder then pronounced the names of each who would be in attendance. When the predicted day arrived, the venerable Maximos fell asleep in the Lord at the age of ninety-five. It was the 13th of January. He was buried in the very tomb which he himself had dug near to his hut. His interment took place with only those in attendance whom he had foretold would be present. He did not want his funeral to be an open event with a crowd of people. He also had given a previous command to those who would bury him that they not transfer his relics to another place, but that they should leave him whole and concealed inside the tomb, lest the people should come to honor him.

When the news of his repose was learned, all the fathers of the Mountain were greatly sorrowed and wept over their orphanhood; for now they would be deprived of his teachings, as he had been wise in the things of God and the monastic state. He had been deemed by all to be a radiant luminary for his brave feats and divine spiritual gifts. Yearly his memory was commemorated, even as is meet for the saints. Thus he was glorified by men on earth, and on high, in the heavens, his cleansed and holy soul was received by the Holy Trinity. He now dwells in the tabernacles of the saints, amid the inexpressible and incomprehensible light of the divinity, standing before Christ Whom he desired from his youth, rejoicing with the angels and the saints from the ages, who intercede unceasingly on our behalf.

In order to make manifest that the grace of the Holy Spirit abides inseparably in his divine relics, thereafter there was no lack of miracles. There was a monk, Dionysios Kontostephanos, who had been suffering from head pains for many days. He approached the tomb of the venerable Maximos and besought him with faith and tears to grant him his health. Father Dionysios then slumbered a little and when he rose up—O the wonder!—he found that he was healthy and gave thanks to the saint. He took up in his hands a little dirt from the saint's tomb, which showed itself to be as myrrh, filling his senses with an indescribable scent.

"Still even I," the author, "who had previously seen the saint's flight through the air, had become very ill and was near death. With tears, I had invoked the saint, and he appeared to me in a vision and healed me. I rose up, glorifying God and the saint, for as one dead had I been raised."

There was a certain virtuous priest-monk, named Niphon, who, with another ascetic, came to the saint's tomb. They dug and then took a little portion of the sacred relics. Such a fragrance emanated from the sacred relic that they could not endure the overpowering scent. They then thought to sponge down the portion which they had taken up. With faith and piety, they took that sponge and anointed their senses, that is, their eyes and ears. Afterward, they returned the relic to its place that they might keep the saint's command; for he charged that he should remain whole and inviolate. Those fathers then only took up the dirt which they had excavated. They gave glory to God and then kept returning to the tomb daily, that they might partake of that fragrance which wafted forth. This same custom was also observed by all those who lived in the neighborhood of the tomb, that they might enjoy that scent, to the glory of Christ our God, to Whom is due all glory, honor, and veneration, together with His unoriginate Father and His life-creating Holy Spirit, now and ever, and unto the ages of the ages. Amen.

**On the 13th of January, the holy Church commemorates
our holy Father HILARY, Bishop of Poitiers.**

Hilary (Hilarius), our holy father, is believed to have been born at the start of the fourth century (ca. 315). He was born and reposed in Poitiers in

Saint Hilary

Aquitaine, France.[15] He came from a distinguished and illustrious family. Though the saint's writings do not explicitly settle the question of whether he was from a pagan family, the better opinion seems to be that he had been a pagan. He also married and had one daughter, Abra. In his writings, Hilary is silent about himself. He is rarely mentioned by contemporaries. Ancient historians knew little beyond what could be gleaned from his writings.

Hilary received an education in philosophy and classics. Birth in the Gallic provinces at that time brought with it no sense of provincial inferiority. Society was thoroughly Roman. Education and literature were more vigorous than in other parts of the west. The citizens of Gaul and of Northern Italy were more in the center of this world's life than the native of Rome. Hilary came from a province of decisive importance, both for its position and wealth. Amid such a prosperous and highly civilized society, the best education was available. From the Roman poet Ausonius (ca. 310-ca. 395), a native of Bordeaux, who had established a school of rhetoric, we know how complete was the provision for teaching not only in Bordeaux but elsewhere in Gaul. Greek was taught habitually as well as Latin. Not since the days of Hadrian (117-138) had educated society throughout the empire been so bilingual. To Hilary, Greek was certainly familiar from his youth; for the

---

[15] Poitiers (46°35′N 0°20′E).

Latin-speaking west still turned for its culture and philosophy to the literature of Greece. Hilary's earlier thoughts were molded by Neoplatonism. So complete was his literary and technical knowledge of Latin that Blessed Jerome called Hilary "the Rhone of Latin eloquence."[16]

Before his conversion to Christianity, he had acquired literary skill and philosophical training. He had been drawn toward the Christian Faith by a yearning for the truth which he could not find in philosophy. His conviction that Christ and His Church were the truth was made firm by private study and meditation upon the sacred Scriptures, not by consulting with Christian teachers. Upon reading the Bible, he quickly uncovered the absurdity of a plurality of gods. He converted from Neoplatonism to Christianity. This renunciation of polytheism took place while he was still a young man. He speaks of it in his work *On the Trinity*,[17] writing on what impressed him most: that is, those sublime words spoken to Moses. "I chanced," he writes, "upon the books which, according to the tradition of the Hebrew Faith, were written by Moses and the prophets. I found these words in the texts, spoken by God the Creator testifying of Himself: 'I Am that I Am [Ex. 3:14]'; and again, 'He Who is hath sent me unto you.' I confess that I was amazed to find in them an indication concerning God so exact that it expressed in the terms best adapted to human understanding an unattainable insight into the mystery of the divine nature. For no property of God which the mind can grasp is more characteristic of Him than existence, since existence, in the absolute sense, cannot be predicated of that which shall come to an end, or of that which has had a beginning....Whatsoever is divine can neither be originated nor destroyed. Therefore, since God's eternity is inseparable from Himself, it was worthy of Him to reveal this one thing, that He is, as the assurance of His absolute eternity."[18] He was filled with joy when he learned that the Word of God became Man. He accepted whole-heartedly the doctrine of the Holy Trinity and received holy Baptism. He also exhorted the pagans to abandon their delusion. Again, it is uncertain whether or not his family was Christian, but the majority of opinion is that he had been a pagan. This is assumed from a description of the manner of his conversion in the opening chapters of his work *On the Trinity*. In addition, the fact that he was not baptized until he was

---

[16] See "Introduction: The Life and Writings" (pp. ii, iii), Saint Hilary of Poitiers, *Select Works*, Nicene, 2nd Ser., Volume IX. For Blessed Jerome, see *Comm. in Gall.* ii. *pref.*

[17] *On the Trinity* or *Against the Arians*, *Patrology*, Vol. 4, ed. DiBernardino with intro. by Quasten, §§ 38-42; Clavis Patrum Latinorum (Steenbrugge, 1995), 433; Corpus Christianorum, Series Latina (Turnhout), 62 and 62A, ed. P. Smuthers.

[18] Saint Hilary, *On the Trinity*, Bk. I, § 5, Nicene, 2nd Ser., 9:41.

an adult advances this view. He converted his wife and daughter. Later, when he took orders, his wife agreed to love him as a spiritual daughter. His daughter Abra chose to unite herself to Christ rather than an earthly bridegroom.

It was by popular acclaim that he was elected Bishop of Poitiers (Pictavium)[19] in 350 or 353. It is unknown whether he was raised directly from lay life to the episcopate. He attempted all that was in his power to avoid the elevation to that episcopal chair. But on the contrary, his humility only stirred the flock to make him their choice. Western bishops were isolated from one another. They were not able to exercise any sustained surveillance over each other's orthodoxy, which exercise was a regular happenstance in Church life of the east. The west often presumed the orthodoxy of its bishops. But at the time of Bishop Hilary's consecration, two great sees, in immediate relation to his, those of Arles and Milan, were possessed by the Arians.

Hilary's major literary activity would be connected with the Arian controversy. He would take up the defense of the Trinity, as the doctrine had been declared previously at Nicaea (325) against the Arians. At that time, Emperor Constantius II (b. 317-361; Caesar from 324 and augustus from 337), who was influenced by moderate Arianism, resisted the urging of his royal brothers who wished to recall the Archbishop of Alexandria, Athanasios the Great (ca. 296-373, patriarch from 328).

Constantius was resolved to force his religious opinions upon the bishops of the west. He summoned the prelates of western Europe to councils at Arles and Milan in 355. In Milan he required that all bishops put their signature to the condemnation of Saint Athanasios, the standard and rule of Nicene Orthodoxy. Athanasios was the flesh and blood symbol of the Nicene Synod and its definition of the Logos (*Verbum*) as "coessential with the Father." With very few exceptions, the bishops at both these councils yielded to Constantius' demands. Those who refused to repudiate Athanasios could expect banishment, among whom were Eusebius of Vercelli (Vercella),[20] Lucifer of Cagliari (Caralis) in Sardinia, and Dionysius of Milan. Hilary separated himself from the three Arian bishops of the West: Ursacius, Valens, and Saturninus.

---

[19] Pictava was a city of the Pictones (or Pictavi), who are mentioned by Caesar, *Bell. Gall.* iii II. Their territory corresponded to the modern diocese of Poitiers.

[20] Bishop Eusebius of Vercelli (Piedmont), a Sardinian by birth, reposed in 371. His family had suffered persecution. He endured the trials of exile—first to Palestine, then to Cappadocia, then to Egypt. With the death of Constantius, he was allowed to return to his see.

In *The Ecclesiastical History* by Sozomen (early fifth-century Church historian), we read about the Council of Milan (355): "The emperor was extremely urgent to convene a council in Milan, yet few of the eastern bishops repaired thither; some, it appears, excused themselves from attendance under the plea of illness; others, on account of the length and difficulties of the journey. There were, however, upwards of three hundred of the western bishops at the council. The eastern bishops insisted that Athanasios should be condemned to banishment and expelled from Alexandria; and the others, either from fear, fraud, or ignorance, assented to the measure. The only bishops who protested against this decision were: Dionysius, Bishop of Alba, the metropolis of Italy; Eusebius, Bishop of Vercelli in Liguria; Paulinus, Bishop of Treves; Rhodanus;[21] and Lucifer. They declared that Athanasios ought not to be condemned on such slight pretexts; and that the evil would not cease with his condemnation; but that those who supported orthodox doctrines concerning the Godhead (divinity) would be forthwith subjected to a plot. They represented that the whole measure was a scheme concerted by the emperor and the Arians with a view to the suppression of the Nicene Faith. Their boldness was punished by an edict of immediate banishment, and Hilary was exiled with them. The result plainly showed for what purpose the Council of Milan had been convened. The councils, which were held afterward at Ariminum and Seleukeia (Seleucia), were evidently designed to change the doctrines established by the Nicaean Synod."[22]

Our Hilary does not seem to have been present at either Arles or Milan, but had been summoned to a meeting at Béziers. At the Council of Biterrae, in the year 356, Hilary opposed the activities of the pro-Arians in Gaul. With his absolute refusal to condemn the great Athanasios, whom he never met face to face, and his unshakeable defense of Orthodoxy, he was condemned at that council. The event is spoken of by Sulpitius Severus (ca. 360-ca. 420) in his work *The Sacred History*: "Accordingly, when our friends did not accept of the judgment which they had pronounced in regard to Athanasios, an edict was issued by the emperor to the effect that those who did not subscribe to the condemnation of Athanasios should be sent into banishment. But, at that time, councils of bishops were held by our friends at Arles and Biterrae, towns situated in Gaul. They requested that before any were compelled to subscribe against Athanasios, they should rather enter on a discussion as to the true Faith." But the Arians did not wish to have a

---

[21] The monk, historian, and translator Rufinus (ca. 345-410) and the historian and hagiographer Sulpicius Severus call him Rhodanius. Rhodanius was Bishop of Toulouse.

[22] Sozomen's *Ecclesiastical History*, Bk. III, Ch. XV, Nicene, 2nd Ser., II:295.

discussion respecting the Faith. They only wished to secure by force the condemnation of Athanasios. Owing to this conflict of parties, Bishop Paulinus was driven into banishment. In the meantime, an assembly was held at Milan. The emperor was present. The same controversy was there continued without any relaxation of its bitterness. Then Eusebius, Bishop of the Vercelli, and Lucifer, Bishop of Cagliari, were exiled. Dionysius, however, priest of Milan, subscribed to the condemnation of Athanasios, on the condition that there should be an investigation among the bishops as to the true Faith. But Valens and Ursacius, with the rest of that party, through fear of the people, who maintained the true Faith with extraordinary enthusiasm, did not venture to set forth in public their monstrous doctrines, but assembled within the palace. From that place, and under the name of the emperor, they issued a letter full of all sorts of wickedness....Well, when the letter was read in the church, the people expressed their aversion to it. And Dionysius, because he did not concur with them, was banished from the city, while Auxentius was immediately chosen as bishop in his place. Liberius, too, bishop of the city of Rome (352-366), and Hilary, Bishop of Poitiers, were driven into exile. Rhodanius, also, Bishop of Toulouse (who, being by nature of a sorer disposition, had resisted the Arians, not so much from his own powers as from his fellowship with Hilary) was involved in the same punishment. All these persons, however, were prepared to suspend Athanasios from communion, only in order that an inquiry might be instituted among the bishops as to the true Faith. But it seemed best to the Arians to withdraw the most celebrated men from the controversy. Accordingly, those whom we have mentioned above were driven into exile, forty-five years ago, when Arbitio and Lollianus were consuls. Liberius, however, was, a little afterward, restored to the city, in consequence of the disturbances at Rome. But it is well known that the persons exiled were celebrated by the admiration of the whole world, and that abundant supplies of money were collected to meet their wants, while they were visited by deputies of the catholic people from almost all the provinces."[23]

Thereupon, the emperor sent an order to his commander in Gaul, Julian (b. 332-363), later known as the Apostate, to enforce Hilary's banishment into Phrygia, a mountainous region and rough country of Asia Minor, between the Aegean plains and the central plateau. Hilary went into exile about the middle of the year 356. Hilary said to the emperor, "Thou mayest easily exile bishops, but canst thou exile the truth?" Hilary went forth as one would take a pleasure trip. He reckoned as nothing every hardship,

---

[23] Sulpitius Severus, *The Sacred History*, Bk. II, Ch. XXXIX, Nicene, 2nd Ser., XI:115, 116.

danger, or enemy. There were no means at hand by which Bishop Hilary could influence his widespread flock of his large diocese. Thus, he was prevented from fomenting any strong public opinion against the emperor or exciting devotion to himself. Thus, Hilary could be deported into exile at the emperor's will with little commotion.

Nevertheless, it would be in Phrygia that Hilary came to learn Greek well and to study the works of the Greek fathers. He already had an adequate knowledge of the Greek language and a strong sympathy for it, together with a familiarity of Greek modes of thought. Consequently, at Phrygia, in his work, entitled *On the Councils* or *De Synodis*, also known as *The Faith of the Easterns*,[24] he worked to reunite the common front of the Nicene anti-Arians of the west and the anti-Nicenes of the east. He wrote: "Though long ago was I regenerated in Baptism, and for some time a bishop, I never heard of the Nicene Creed until I was going into exile; but the Gospels and Epistles suggested to me the meaning of *homoousion* (ὁμοούσιον) and *homoiousion* (ὁμοιούσιον).[25] Our desire is sacred. Let us not condemn the fathers, let us not encourage heretics, lest while we drive one heresy away, we should nurture another. After the Council of Nicaea our fathers interpreted the due meaning of *homoousion* with scrupulous care. The books are extant; the facts are fresh in men's minds. If anything has to be added to the interpretation, let us consult together. Between us we can thoroughly establish the Faith, so that what has been well settled need not be disturbed, and what has been misunderstood may be removed."[26] Hilary, while among the Greeks, also came into contact with those from the Homoiousians,[27] anti-Arians, and anti-

---

[24] *On the Councils*, Clavis Patrum Latinorum, 434, 468f., 818; *Patrology*, Vol. 4, §§ 42, 43.

[25] Homoousios, literally "coessential," is a term needed to understand the relationship among the Persons (Hypostases) of the Trinity. The term *homoousios* was under attack during the 4th C. The semi-Arians wished to replace it with *homoios* ("similar") as representing a looser relationship. It was the interpretation of the Cappadocian fathers which produced the canonical formula "one *ousia* (essence), three hypostases." The word essence is often transcribed as "substance" by westerners. *Oxford*, s.v. "Homoousios."

[26] Saint Hilary, *On the Councils*, § 91, Nicene, 2nd Ser., IX:28, 29. See also *P.L.* 10:471-475, wherein Saint Hilary gives an account of the schemes of the Arians and semi-Arians, and the various formulas of faith which they had drawn up.

[27] The Homoiousians, often called semi-Arians, refused the term *homoousios*, but said they believed in the perfect divinity of Christ and the similarity of Christ's divine nature to that of the Father. Though their beliefs may be traced back to Origen, they came into being as a party circa 356 in an attempt to find a compromise between

(continued...)

Nicenes. He had formed his own convictions before he heard the words *homoousion* or *homoiousion*, or read the Nicene Creed. He now obtained first-hand testimony about the controversies regarding the divinity of Christ that had been raging in the Eastern Church since the days of Paul of Samosata, a third-century heretical bishop of Antioch. He became thoroughly acquainted with the heresy of Arius and the answers given by Orthodox apologists. Hilary also actively participated in encouraging prelates to resist the Arian tendencies found among so many other bishops and the imperial court.

In 357, Hilary's enemies, Ursacius and Valens, at the Council of Sirmium, published a creed which was plainly Arian. The forces of conservatism were powerful, so that the unscrupulous Ursacius and Valens thought nothing of signing a conservative creed. Liberius was exiled for two years, according to Saint Athanasios' record, but was returned to Rome by Constantius on account of acts of sedition perpetrated by the disgruntled flock. See the date of his commemoration (27th of August), refuting the claims that this pope lapsed. Hilary was left to deal with the conservatives and their leader Basil of Ankyra, a moderate Arian, with whom he had some dialogue and communication. Basil had been deposed by the Council of Sardica (343), but reinstated by Constantius (ca. 348). He participated in the Arianizing Councils of Sirmium (351), of Ankyra (358), and Seleukeia (359). He criticized extreme Arian doctrines, which led his opponents to remove him from his see (360) and banish him to Illyria, where he died.

Constantius attempted to restore unity to the Church by interfering in her affairs. He convoked councils held in Ariminium and Seleukeia in 359-360. He assembled the Arians at Seleukeia of Isauria for the purpose of undermining the decrees of the Nicene Synod. Constantius would force the prelates to declare that the Logos was "like the Father in all things." This formula not only repudiated Nicaea, but would eventually lead to a denial of Christ's divinity. The Seleukeian Council, which met in September of 359, was one in which the emperor hoped for a final settlement. He wished the council to be as large as possible. He instructed the governors of provinces to collect bishops and send them, at the public expense, to Seleukeia. In that council, which numbered about one hundred and sixty prelates, the Semiarians were in a majority of three to one. Those who would not compromise, namely, the Nicenes of Egypt and the stubborn Arians, did not number more than a quarter of the whole. Hilary came and was welcomed.

---

[27](...continued)
Orthodoxy and Arianism. They are to be distinguished from the Homoians, who maintained closer ties to strict Arians. *Oxford*, s.v. "Homoiousians."

Sulpitius Severus tells us of this council, saying that "in the meantime, in the east, after the example of the west, the emperor ordered almost all the bishops to assemble at Seleukeia, a town of Isauria. At that time, Hilary, who was now spending the fourth year of his exile in Phrygia, was compelled to be present among the other bishops, the means of a public conveyance being furnished to him by the lieutenant and governor. As, however, the emperor had given no special orders regarding him, the judges, simply following the general order by which they were commanded to gather all bishops to the council, sent him also among the rest who were willing to go. This was done, as I imagine, by the special ordination of God, in order that a man who was most deeply instructed in divine things, might be present when a discussion was to be carried on respecting the Faith. He, on arriving at Seleukeia, was received with great favor, and drew the minds and affections of all toward himself. His first inquiry was as to the real belief of the Gauls, because at that time the Arians had spread evil reports regarding us, and we were held suspected by the easterns as having embraced the belief of Sabellius, to the effect that the unity of the one God was simply distinguished by a threefold name. But after Hilary had set forth his Faith in harmony with those conclusions which had been reached by the fathers at Nicaea, he bore his testimony in favor of the westerns. Thus the minds of all having been satisfied, he was admitted to communion; and being also received into alliance, was added to the council. They then proceeded to actual work, and the originators of the wicked heresy being discovered, were separated from the body of the Church. In that number were George of Alexandria, Akakios, Evdoxios, Vranios, Leontios, Theodosios, Evagrios, and Theodoulos. But when the synod was over, an embassy was appointed to go to the emperor and acquaint him with what had been done. Those who had been condemned also went to the prince, relying upon the power of their confederates, and a common cause with the monarch."[28]

Though Saint Hilary was invited thither by the semi-Arians, thinking he could be useful to their party in putting down decisively the doctrine of Arius; instead Hilary upheld the decrees of Nicaea and the doctrine of the Trinity. The Homoousion party remained firm. Constantius thereupon persecuted the Orthodox. While in exile, Hilary was permitted freedom of movement. He was not severely restricted. He was permitted to write to his flock in Poitiers and the bishops in Gaul. Hilary's diocese did not forget their bishop. Sulpicius Severus says that he and the others of the little band of exiles, who had suffered at Arles, Milan, and Béziers, were the heroes of the

---

[28] Sulpitius Severus, *The Sacred History*, Bk. II, Ch. XLII, Nicene, 2nd Ser., XI:115, 116.

day in their homeland.[29] The correspondence which Saint Hilary preserved patently demonstrates how difficult it must have been for the laity to determine who was, and who was not, a heretic, when all parties used the same scriptural terms commending themselves and condemning their opponents.[30]

Saint Hilary's writings were significant in the development of Latin theology. He wrote *On the Trinity* or *De Trinitate*, which comprises of twelve books. The first three books were written before 356, the last nine were probably done in exile in Phrygia (356-360). It is the first extended study on this doctrine in the Latin tongue.

Saint Hilary opens his sixth book on the Trinity, writing: "It is with a full knowledge of the dangers and passions of the time that I have ventured to attack this wild and godless heresy, which asserts that the Son of God is a creature. Multitudes of churches, in almost every province of the Roman Empire, have already caught the plague of this deadly doctrine; error, persistently inculcated and falsely claiming to be the truth, has become ingrained in minds which vainly imagine that they are loyal to the Faith. I know how hardly the will is moved to a thorough recantation, when zeal for a mistaken cause is encouraged by the sense of numbers and confirmed by the sanction of general approval. A multitude under delusion can only be approached with difficulty and danger. When the crowd has gone astray, even though it should know that it is in the wrong, it is ashamed to return. It claims consideration for its numbers, and has the assurance to command that its folly shall be accounted wisdom. It assumes that its size is evidence of the correctness of its opinions; and thus a falsehood which has found general credence is boldly asserted to have established its truth."[31] Though we do not know if anyone requested that Saint Hilary write this treatise, yet, on account of his office of Bishop, he felt the necessity to preach the Gospel in order to counter the wide extension of Arianism. Piety was necessary in a bishop, but he also needed knowledge and dialectical skill in the face of such heresies. Undaunted in his love for souls, he went forth to combat heresy. He desired to expose the Arians' perverse use of Scripture in unscriptural senses and their fraudulent imitation of the Faith.[32]

In the saint's tenth book of his treatise on the Trinity, he comments: "It is manifest that there is nothing which men have ever said which is not liable to opposition. Where the will dissents the mind also dissents: under the

---

[29] Sulpitus Severus, *Chron.* ii. 39. Ed. Helm, 240c; trans. Donalson, 48.

[30] Saint Hilary, *Fragments* xiii-xv.

[31] Saint Hilary, *On the Trinity*, Bk. VI(1), Nicene, IX:98.

[32] Ibid., Bk. VII(1), Nicene, IX:118.

bias of opposing judgment it joins battle, and denies the assertions to which it objects. Though every word we say be incontrovertible if gauged by the standard of truth, yet so long as men think or feel differently, the truth is always exposed to the cavils of opponents, because they attack, under the delusion of error or prejudice, the truth they misunderstand or dislike. For decisions once formed cling with excessive obstinacy: and the passion of controversy cannot be driven from the course it has taken, when the will is not subject to the reason. Inquiry after truth gives way to the search for proofs of what we wish to believe; desire is paramount over truth....From these defects of partisan spirit arise all controversies between opposing theories. Then follows an obstinate battle between truth asserting itself, and prejudice defending itself: truth maintains its ground and prejudice resists....

"Not unmindful of this sin of wilfulness, the apostle, writing to Timothy, after many injunctions to bear witness to the Faith and to preach the word, adds, 'For there will be a time when they will not uphold sound teaching, but according to their own desires, they who have an itching ear will heap up to themselves teachers; and indeed they shall turn away their ear from the truth, and shall be turned aside over to fables [2 Tim. 4:3, 4].'...They will heap up teachers for their lusts, that is, construct schemes of doctrine to suit their own desires, not wishing to be taught, but getting together teachers who will tell them what they wish: that the crowd of teachers whom they have ferreted out and gathered together, may satisfy them with the doctrines of their own tumultuous desires. And if these madmen in their godless folly do not know with what spirit they reject the sound, and yearn after the corrupt doctrine, let them hear the words of the same apostle to the same Timothy, that the Spirit speaks expressly, that in latter times some shall apostatize from the Faith, 'giving heed to deceiving spirits and teachings of demons, speaking lies in hypocrisy [cf. 1 Tim. 4:1, 2].' What advancement of doctrine is it to discover what one fancies, and not what one ought to learn? Or what piety in doctrine is it not to desire what one ought to learn, but to heap up doctrine after our desires? But this is what the prompting of seducing spirits supply. They confirm the falsehoods of pretended godliness, for a canting hypocrisy always succeeds to defection from the Faith....

"We have clearly fallen on the evil times prophesied by the apostle; for nowadays teachers are sought after who preach not God but a creature. And men are more zealous for what they themselves desire, than for what the sound Faith teaches....

"But though many may heap up teachers according to their desires, and banish sound doctrine, yet from the company of the saints the preaching of truth can never be exiled. From our exile we shall speak by these our writings, and the word of God which cannot be bound [2 Tim. 2:9] will run unhindered, warning us of this time which the apostle prophesied. For when men show themselves impatient of the true message, and heap up teachers according to their own human desires, we can no longer be in doubt about the times, but know that, while the preachers of sound doctrine are banished, truth is banished too. We do not complain of the times: we rejoice rather, that iniquity has revealed itself in this our exile, when, unable to endure the truth, it banishes the preachers of sound doctrine, that it may heap up for itself teachers after its own desires. We glory in our exile, and rejoice in the Lord that in our person the apostle's prophecy should be fulfilled."[33]

In the eleventh book of the treatise, Saint Hilary maintains that the Faith is one, even as God is One. But the faiths of heretics are many. "The apostle," he writes, "in his letter to the Ephesians, reviewing in its manifold aspects the full and perfect mystery of the Gospel, mingles with other instructions in the knowledge of God the following: 'There is one body, and one Spirit, even as ye also were called in one hope of your calling; one Lord, one faith, one baptism; one God and Father of all, Who is over all, and through all, and in you all [Eph. 4:4-6].' He does not leave us in the vague and misleading paths of an indefinite teaching, or abandon us to the shifting fancies of imagination, but limits the unimpeded license of intellect and desire by the appointment of restraining barriers. He gives us no opportunity to be wise beyond what he preached, but defines in exact and precise language the Faith fixed for all time, that there may be no excuse for instability of belief.

" But how can it be any longer one faith, if it does not steadfastly and sincerely confess one Lord and one God the Father?...How can the faith be one, when its preachers are so at variance?...And yet, who will deny that whatever is not the one faith, is not faith at all? For in the one faith there is one Lord Christ, and God the Father is one. But the one Lord Jesus Christ is not one in the truth of the confession, as well as in name, unless He is Son, unless He is God, unless He is unchangeable, unless His Sonship and His Godhead (divinity) have been eternally present in Him. He who preaches Christ other than He is, that is, other than Son and God, preaches another christ. Nor is he in the one faith of the one baptism, for in the teaching of the apostle the one faith is the faith of that one baptism, in which the one Lord is Christ, the Son of God Who is also God."[34]

Thus, through these twelve books on the Holy Trinity, Saint Hilary made known the mystery and true teaching of the Church to those of western Europe. He exposed the hypocrisy and audacity of the heretics who appealed to Scripture only to justify their prejudices and false doctrines. They

---

[33] Ibid., Bk. X(1-4), Nicene, IX:182, 183.
[34] Ibid., Bk. XI(1, 2), Nicene, IX:203.

pretended to be concerned with keeping the oneness of God, while they denied the divinity of Christ the Logos. Saint Hilary earnestly hoped that those who had succumbed to the Arianizers, through ignorance, might return to the knowledge of the truth and the true Church. Though the name of Arius only appears twice in *De Trinitate*, he designates the Arians as "the new apostolate of Antichrist." The central idea of all twelve books is the being or essence of God. The hypostasis of the Holy Spirit is not given equal treatment in this treatise as one might expect, given the title *On the Trinity*. This is because Saint Hilary was concerned, as were the Ariomaniacs, with the relationship between the Father and the Son. Hilary also refutes Sabellius so that he might combat the Arians more decisively. The saint also alternates his usage of a direct translation from the Septuagint, for the Old Testament, and a Latin version, for the New Testament, which is no longer extant in its entirety.

The man of God was mindful of the awesome task of writing on the Trinity, and so he begged God for enlightenment, saying, "The errors of heretics and blasphemers force us to deal with unlawful matters, to scale perilous heights, to speak unutterable words, to trespass on forbidden ground. Faith ought in silence to fulfill the commandments, worshipping the Father, reverencing with Him the Son, abounding in the Holy Spirit, but we must strain the poor resources of our language to express thoughts too great for words. The error of others compels us to err in daring to embody in human terms truths which ought to be hidden in the silent veneration of the heart. For there have risen many who have given to the plain words of holy Writ some arbitrary interpretation of their own, instead of its true and only sense; and this in defiance of the clear meaning of words. Heresy lies in the sense assigned, not in the word written; the guilt is that of the expositor, not of the text."[35]

Now the holy Hilary also had the added difficulty, which he fully realized, that while the subject had been treated for so many years by the best minds in the Eastern Church, no Latin writer had written such a systematic treatise before him. He was not able to borrow from the Cappadocian fathers, since at the time of his exile, Saint Gregory the Theologian, the eldest of the three great writers—the other two being Basil the Great and Gregory of Nyssa—was not more than twenty-five years of age. Hilary, therefore, pioneered and coined many new words that he might express his thoughts accurately. "Among the neologisms attributed to him are *abscissio*,

---

[35] Ibid., Bk. II(1, 2), Nicene, IX:52.

incarnatio, *innascibilitas*, *ininitiabilis*, *supercreo*, *circuminsession*,[36] and *consubsisto*. He also gave new meanings to words already in current use, as *sacramentum*, *dispentio*, and *substitutio*....The saint devoted particular care to the composition of this work and even prayed that he might receive the 'nobility of diction' befitting so exalted a subject. Everywhere he gives evidence of the careful training that he had received in Latin rhetoric."[37] Thus, Saint Hilary was the first to bring westward the vast theological riches of the Orient. His work on the triune God would become one of the foundation stones upon which other writers would build.

In the same year, 359, Hilary also prepared and attended the Council of Rimini, where he defended right belief, though Emperor Constantius forced some Orthodox bishops to subscribe to an Arian creed. The last two months of 359 revealed that disputes concerning the Faith continued. The emperor remained fixed in his resolve to usher in a compromise which could embrace all those who were not extremists and assiduous Arians. The Homoian leaders supported him without any scruples. Hilary had been led to believe that the emperor had been on the side of Basil of Ankyra and his friends. Hilary, a man of courage, made three respectful petitions to the emperor.[38] Hilary, at length, withdrew to Constantinople. In sending Hilary to Asia Minor, Constantius had injured his own cause, because the confessor Hilary, with no restriction on his movements, so long as he kept within the allotted bounds, spread and confirmed the Faith.

Hilary, in his work, entitled *De Synodis*, wrote not only for all the Gallic provinces and of Britain, but also addressed the anti-Arians in the east. Part I examines the formulae of faith published from 341 to 357, condemning what was openly Arian. In Part II, Hilary compares the terms *homoousios* and *homoiousios*. He shows how both terms are capable of orthodox and heterodox interpretations. Hilary sincerely tries to minimize doctrinal differences between east and west in order to promote understanding. His work as a whole demonstrates perfect knowledge of the complex reality of the east and a rare capacity to see the question in its essential lines, without being led astray by the various adjuncts and by marginal aspects. This is something almost unique for a westerner. He is the one Latin father whose thought is closest to that of the Greek fathers.

Hilary was by nature the gentlest of men, full of courtesy and cordiality to all. Yet he perceived that such conduct was proving ineffectual.

---

[36] *Circuminsession = perichoresis.*
[37] See "Introduction" (pp. xiii, xiv), Saint Hilary of Poitiers, *The Trinity*, translated by Stephen McKenna, C.SS.R, Fathers of the Church Series, Vol. 25.
[38] Sulpitius Severus, *Chron.* ii. 45.

He employed the strongest language possible against Constantius. The so-called *Liber I ad Constantium* consists of two texts. There was a letter sent by the western bishops of the Council of Sardica (343), asking Constantius to stop persecuting the supporters of the Nicene Creed. Hilary therefore entreated Constantius to restore peace to the Church. The other text is a narrative recording the irregularities of the Council of Milan, written before his exile (356). The *Liber II ad Constantium*, written in 359 at Constantinople, requests that the emperor consent to a debate between Hilary and the Arian Saturninus of Arles. This same Saturninus had been the originator of Hilary's banishment. Hilary also asked the emperor not to approve the vague formula of Rimini.[39] Hilary entreated the emperor to allow him to expound the Faith. His exposition would be scriptural, using the words of Christ. He asks audience rather for the emperor's sake and the Churches of God than for himself. Seeing the uselessness of his attempts and Constantius' resoluteness to support the pro-Arians, Hilary wrote a violent libellus, *Liber contra Constantium*,[40] after the emperor's death. Hilary considered Constantius worse than Nero, Decius, and Maximian. Hilary believes this to be true since Constantius is not an open enemy of the Church, as those former persecutors, but a furtive oppressor.

Sulpitius Severus continues the history here, commenting: "Thus, then, the Arians, with their affairs in a very flourishing condition, and everything turning out according to their wishes, went in a body to Constantinople to the emperor. There they found the deputies from the Council of Seleukeia, and compelled them by an exercise of the royal power to follow the example of the westerns, and accept that heretical confession of faith. Those who refused were tortured with painful imprisonment and hunger, so that at length they yielded up their consciences captive. But many who resisted more courageously, being deprived of their bishoprics, were driven into exile, while others substituted in their place. Thus, the best priests were either terrified by threats, or driven into exile; all gave way before the unfaithfulness of a few. Hilary was there at the time, having followed the deputies from Seleukeia; and as no certain orders had been given regarding him, he was waiting on the will of the emperor to see whether perchance he should be ordered to return into banishment. When he perceived the extreme danger into

---

[39] The formula of Rimini was so vague that it was capable of an interpretation consonant with Arian doctrine. For this reason the council was held throughout Christendom as a victory for the Arians who later appealed to this council as the solemn conciliar sanction of their doctrine. *Encyclopedia of the Early Church*, s.v. "Rimini, Council of."

[40] *Against Constantius*, Clavis Patrum Latinorum, 461; *Patrology*, Vol. 4, § 44.

which the Faith had been brought, inasmuch as the westerns had been beguiled, and the easterns were being overcome by means of wickedness, he, in three papers publicly presented, begged an audience of the emperor, in order that he might debate on points of Faith in the presence of his adversaries. But the Arians opposed that to the utmost extent of their ability. Finally, Hilary was ordered to return to Gaul, as being a sower[41] of discord, and a troubler of the east, while the sentence of exile against him remained uncanceled."[42]

Since Hilary was considered a troublemaker, he was sent back to Gaul without having his banishment annulled. The Arians had pressed the emperor to allow Hilary to return home that they might be rid of the man who never ceased to disturb the peace of the east. They wanted to avoid any further confrontations with Hilary, especially a much-dreaded public debate between Hilary and Saturninus. Hilary, therefore, was allowed back to Gaul, though not restored to his bishopric.

Sulpitius Severus remarks that when Hilary "wandered over almost the whole earth, which was infected with the evil of unfaithfulness, his mind was full of doubt and deeply agitated with the mighty burden of cares which pressed upon it. Perceiving that it seemed good to many not to enter into communion with those who had acknowledged the Council of Ariminum, he thought the best thing he could do was to bring back all to repentance and reformation. In frequent councils within Gaul, and while almost all the bishops publicly owned the error that had been committed, he condemned the proceedings at Ariminum, and framed anew the Faith of the churches after its pristine form. Saturninus, however, Bishop of Arles, who was, in truth, a very bad man, of an evil and corrupt character, resisted these sound measures. He was, in fact, a man who, besides the infamy of being a heretic, was convicted of many unspeakable crimes, and cast out of the Church. Thus, having lost its leader, the strength of the party opposed to Hilary was broken. Paternus also of Petrocorii, equally infatuated, and not shrinking from openly professing unfaithfulness, was expelled from the priesthood: pardon was extended to the others. This fact is admitted by all, that our regions of Gaul were set free from the guilt of heresy through the kind efforts of Hilary alone. But Lucifer of Cagliari, who was then at Antioch, held a very different opinion. For he condemned those who assembled at Ariminum to such an extent, that he even separated himself from the communion of those who had received them as friends, after they had made satisfaction or exhibited

---

[41] Sower (Lat. *seminarium*), literally seed-plot.
[42] Sulpitius Severus, *The Sacred History*, Bk. II, Ch. XLV, Nicene, XI:118.

penitence. Whether this resolution of his was right or wrong, I will not take upon myself to say. Paulinus and Rhodanius died in Phrygia."[43]

Hilary returned through Illyricum and Italy, preaching the true Faith. He was received triumphantly by his flock at Poitiers in 361. His old disciple, Saint Martin of Tours, commemorated on the 12th of November, soon thereafter joined him. Upon Hilary's return, he labored diligently on behalf of the Trinity, first in Gaul, then in Italy, from which he was finally ordered back to Gaul. In *The Ecclesiastical History* by Socrates Scholasticus (ca. 380-450), a Greek Church historian, it is written concerning the saint: "Hilary, Bishop of Poitiers, a city of Aquitania Secunda,...confirmed the bishops of Italy and Gaul in the doctrines of the Orthodox Faith; for he first had returned from exile to these countries....Hilary, being a very eloquent man, maintained with great power the doctrine of the *homoousion* in books which he wrote in Latin. In these he gave sufficient support to the doctrine and unanswerably confuted the Arian tenets."[44]

In Sozomen's *Ecclesiastical History*, the following accolade is written of Hilary and Eusebius of Vercelli: "In Italy and its territories, Eusebius and Hilary were conspicuous for the strength of their discourses as they used their native tongue. Their treatises, which concerned the Faith and addressed the heterodox, it is generally said, were approvingly circulated."[45]

The death of Constantius at Cilicia in November of 361 and the short reign of Julian the Apostate (361-June of 363) brought about temporary relief for the Church. As we said earlier, when Hilary returned home, his activities were not confined to his own diocese. He went about Gaul and Italy preaching and binding up the wounds of the people brought about by the heretical beliefs of Constantius. In general, Bishop Hilary was successful. One measure, however, which he failed to achieve was the removal of the Arian bishop at Milan. In Hilary's writing of *Contra Auxentium*,[46] he addressed catholic bishops and gave them an account of his unsuccessful attempt with Eusebius of Vercelli to expel the Arian usurper of the see of Milan, Auxentius, in the year 364. The *Fragmenta ex opere historico* contains documents relating to the Arian controversy.[47] Hilary went to Milan with Eusebius. A public disputation

---

[43] Sulpitius Severus, *The Sacred History*, Bk., Ch. XLV, Nicene, XI:118, 119.

[44] Socrates' *Ecclesiastical History*, Bk. III, Ch. X, Nicene, 2nd Ser., II:84.

[45] Sozomen's *Ecclesiastical History*, Bk. III, Ch. XV, Nicene, II:295.

[46] *Against Auxentius*, Clavis Patrum Latinorum, 462; *Patrology*, Vol. 4, §§ 44, 45.

[47] *Fragmenta historica*, a collection of documents, was first published in 1598 [*P.L.* 10] and republished by Feder in 1916 (CSEL 65), under the title *Collectanea antiariana Parisina*. Part I of Hilary's commentary, which also contains *Liber I ad*

(continued...)

ensued, whereupon Auxentius conceded that Christ is true God, of the same substance and divinity with the Father.[48] Auxentius then insisted that he had never known Arius. Of course, Hilary saw through Auxentius' hypocrisy, for the latter had imposed on Emperor Valentinian I (364-375) that he was orthodox in belief. Hilary bade the people to shun Auxentius as an angel of Satan, an enemy of Christ, a deceiver, and a blasphemer. The bishop's last words were: "Let Auxentius assemble against me what councils he will. Let him proclaim me, as he has often done already, a heretic by public advertisement. Let him direct, as he will, the wrath of the mighty against me. Yet being an Arian, he shall be nothing less than a devil in my eyes. Never will I desire peace except with them who, following the doctrine of our fathers at Nicaea, shall make the Arians anathema and proclaim the true divinity of Christ."[49] Thereafter, the heretics managed to drive the man of God from their city. He returned to Poitiers and continued to guide the flock.

A synod in Gaul was convened at the insistence of Hilary. The decrees of Rimini were condemned. Saturninus, a stubborn Arian, was excommunicated and deposed. Stumbling blocks and scandals were removed. Discipline, peace, and the true Faith were restored. The death of Constantius in 361 put an end to persecutions by the Arians. Later, the western bishops in the Roman Council of 369 formally annulled the proceedings of Rimini, and so deprived Auxentius of his position. Since Emperor Valentinian refused to give support to their sentence, Auxentius remained Bishop of Milan until his death in 374.

The saint's exegetical activity began before his exile with the *Commentary on Matthew* or *Tractatus super Matthaeum*.[50] He favors the allegorical method which brings out the spiritual meaning behind the literal

---

[47](...continued)
Constantium, brings together documents relating to the Council of Sardica and the following years. Part II consists of documents relating to the Council of Rimini, with letters of Pope Liberius added. Part III comprises documents from 359 to 366. *Encyclopedia of the Early Church*, s.v. "Hilary of Poitiers."

[48] With regard to language usage when expressing the divine substance, the word "essence" is not used by Saint Hilary. "'Substance' and 'nature' are freely used as synonyms. The word 'essence' occurs in *De Synodis*, § 69, but there the saint is writing as an advocate in defense of language used by others, not as the exponent of his own thoughts." See "Introduction: The Theology of Saint Hilary" (p. lxii), Saint Hilary of Poitiers, *Select Works*.

[49] "Introduction: The Life and Writings" (p. liii), Saint Hilary, *Select Works*.

[50] *Commentaries on Matthew*, Clavis Patrum Latinorum, 430; *Patrology*, Vol. 4, §§ 47, 48.

one. His *Commentary on the Psalms* or *Tractatus super Psalmos*,[51] containing the interpretation of over fifty psalms, may have been more extensive. We do not know if he had a complete commentary on the Psalter. The psalms prefigure Christ's earthly life, from birth to resurrection, ascension and exaltation. The same hermeneutical criterion of interpreting the Old Testament in terms of Christ and the Church is applied in the short *De mysteriis*, which interprets well-known episodes from Genesis and Exodus, using an Alexandrian technique. In that same manuscript there are three hymns of Saint Hilary. They were composed on different subjects (*Ante saecula* on the Trinity, *Fefellit saevam* on Baptism, and *Adae carnis* on Christology. The strophes are composed of various lyrical meters (asclepiadeic, glyconeic, iambic, trochaic). The form is intricate, according to the classicizing canons of Latin poetry at the time. Hilary wrote these first Latin hymns as an instrument of doctrinal familiarization for his congregation. These hymns, though incomplete, make Hilary the first known hymnodist at that time in the Western Church.[52]

He was called the "Athanasios of the West."[53] He preached, wrote, and suffered banishment in defense of Jesus' divinity. As a result of his four-year exile in Asia Minor, he was able to acquaint the Latin west with the theological treasures of the Greek fathers.

Blessed Jerome dates Saint Hilary's repose in the year 367, on the 13th of January, but neither the year nor the day of the month can be determined with certainty.[54] Sulpitius Severus adds that Saint Hilary died in his native country in the sixth year after his return.[55]

A radiant light filled the chamber in which he was found before his departure. At the moment of his repose, the light waned and vanished. Blessed Jerome styles Saint Hilary "a most eloquent man, and the trumpet of the Latins against the Arians." Elsewhere, he writes: "In Saint Cyprian and Saint Hilary, God had transplanted two fair cedars out of the world into His Church."

Through the intercessions of Thy Saints,
O Christ God, have mercy on us. Amen.

---

[51] *Commentaries on the Psalms*, Clavis Patrum Latinorum, 208, 428, 592. For *Tractates* on Psalm 63 and on Psalm 132, see Patrologiae Latinae Supplementum, 1:241-246.

[52] *Encyclopedia of the Early Church*, s.v. "Hilary of Poitiers." See also *A Book of Hymns*, Clavis Patrum Latinorum, 463, 464; *Patrology*, Vol. 4, §§ 50, 51.

[53] *Encyclopedia of Early Christianity*, s.v. "Hilary of Poitiers."

[54] The Roman Martyrology names his feast on the 14th of January. Butler's *Lives of the Saints*.

[55] Sulpitius Severus, *The Sacred History*, Bk. II, Ch. XLV, Nicene, XI:119.

On the 14th of January, the holy Church commemorates
the venerable fathers and holy THIRTY-EIGHT MARTYRS,
together with other ABBAS,[1] who were massacred at Mount Sinai.[2]

The abbas at Mount Sinai, who were living in the caves and grottos surrounding the holy mountain, by the middle of the fourth century, numbered in the thousands. These venerable fathers loved the ascetic life of the desert. Among them was our venerable Father Neilos, the former prefect of Constantinople, who is commemorated by the holy Church on the 12th of November. Since his office brought too many distractions upon him for a spiritual life, he persuaded his spouse to quit Constantinople and retreat with him to the monasteries of Egypt, to which she agreed. On their arrival there, they separated the children: Neilos took their son, Theodoulos; and his wife took their daughter. Both mother and daughter retired to one of the convents there, while Neilos and Theodoulos went to Sinai and dwelt with the fathers. The year was then A.D. 390. Neilos, who was mighty in his words by the grace of the Holy Spirit, recorded many beautiful and beneficial writings, which have incited people toward the excellence of ascetical conduct.[3] He also wrote of the captivity and murder of those holy fathers, because of the inroads of the barbarians, known as Blemmyans, who lived like wild animals in the desert between Egypt and the Red Sea. They slew the ascetics pitilessly and stole their meager provisions.

---

[1] The names of two of the surviving eyewitnesses were Abba Esaias and Abba Savvas.

[2] The carnage committed by the pagan barbarians occurred during different epochs. Some historians date one of the massacres during the time of Diocletian (288), while others place the event toward the end of the 4th C. Our venerable Father Neilos, an ascetic of Sinai, who lived during the reign of Theodosios the Great (379-395), wrote down this important account in Greek, wherein he also describes the lives of some of the righteous fathers of the desert. The text of Saint Neilos' account is extant in the Athonite monasteries of the Great Lavra, Iveron, and in other places. Another work concerning these abbas was penned by Ammonios, a monk of Egypt, whose manuscript begins, "It happened once that I was sitting in my humble cell...." It is extant in the Athonite monasteries of the Great Lavra and Iveron. The text was rendered in simpler Greek by Agapios the Cretan, who published it in his *Neon Paradeison*, which is presented herein. The longer account given by the venerable Neilos, including the capture of his son, Theodoulos, who is commemorated by the holy Church this day, is also given in part herein under Saint Theodoulos.

With regard to the destruction at Sinai, which took place under Diocletian's reign, nothing further is known. The narratives of our venerable Fathers Neilos and Ammonios, describing massacres which took place at different places and times, are brought together today that the martyred fathers of Sinai and Raithu might have a common feast day.

[3] Saint Neilos the Sinaite, *P.G.* 79.

The Holy Fathers of Sinai

Many years earlier, when Diocletian reigned (288) and Peter was Patriarch of Alexandria (ca. 300),[4] there were righteous fathers living in silence and prayer about Mount Sinai. At that time, the Saracens came and sojourned in those parts. When their tribal leader died, in their anger they

---

[4] The Archbishop of Alexandria, the Hieromartyr Peter is commemorated by the holy Church on the 24th of November.

murdered many of the ascetics. Those who managed to escape took refuge in the stronghold and tower which was situated there. The Saracens then converged on the tower. By divine providence, Mount Sinai smoked and appeared to be all afire, with flames blazing high into the heavens. The Saracens beheld this phenomenon and were stricken with terror and cast into confusion. The fathers prostrated themselves and invoked God's help. Thereupon, the barbarians cast down their weapons and fled, leaving the fathers filled with gratitude and praise for God.

Now the barbarians had slain thirty-eight fathers who sustained multitudinous wounds to their bodies. Some had their heads cut off, others had skin hanging from members, and others were sawn apart in the middle. From this martyric company, two saints survived, named Savvas and Esaias, who buried the slain and afterward related the event.

On the 14th of January, the holy Church commemorates the venerable fathers and holy THIRTY-THREE MARTYRS, together with other ABBAS, who were massacred at Raithu.[5]

The abbas, living as anchorites of the desert of Raithu, were two days' journey from Sinai in that previously famed place where the congregation of the children of Israel "came to Aelim, where there were twelve fountains of water, and seventy stems of palm trees; and they encamped there by the waters [Ex. 15:27]." Raithu, as a monastic settlement, was situated in the southwestern part of the Sinai peninsula. The Blemmyes were a tribe that inhabited the eastern desert between the Nile and Red Sea in Upper Egypt. They have been described as half-naked warriors, all of equal rank, riding swift horses and camels. In 297, Diocletian ended the raids of the Blemmyes in Egypt by assigning them the territory south of the First Cataract and by fortifying the island of Philae. The desert fathers were living in peace until three hundred Blemmyes assailed the Church at Raithu. They traversed the sea from Ethiopia on large wooden rafts. When they came ashore, they found boats, which they set upon and commandeered for themselves. They put out to sea and came to Pharan, which is located in Petra Arabia near the Arabian Gulf. The Pharanites saw this and mobilized for war. They were vanquished, however, and suffered the loss of forty-seven people. The Blemmyes then took captive the women and children of Pharan. The barbarians then moved against the venerable fathers at the fortified place, which contained the church. The fathers closed the door but awaited death. The infidels stormed and penetrated the complex and began searching for money. Paul, the abbot

---

[5] The names of some of those who were martyred include Paul the superior, and Abbas Psoes of the Thebaid, Jeremias, Adam, and Domnus of Rome.

of Raithu, incited his monks, saying, "O athletes of God, do not regret this good conflict. Let not your souls be fainthearted. Do nothing unworthy of your monastic Schema, but be clothed with strength, joy, and courage, that you may endure with a pure heart and receive God's everlasting kingdom." The barbarians, not finding any money, put to death all those righteous hermits, numbering thirty-three. Abba Paul encouraged his disciples to forsake this transitory life which they had renounced when coming into the desert and receiving the tonsure. As Abba Paul completed his stirring exhortation, the Blemmyes burst into the church. They seized Father Jeremias, dragged him to the courtyard, disrobed him, and shot him full of arrows. The madmen then asked for money, but the abba kept telling them that each one's wealth was solely his monastic garb. The disbelieving and angered barbarians then raised their swords and split open Abba Paul's skull.

The pagans then rushed into the church and slew the fathers, save for a fifteen-year-old monk. The young man took hold of a tribesman's sword and struck another barbarian's shoulder. His fellows then raised their swords and cut to pieces the youth, whose last dying words were of thanksgiving to God Who permitted him to die with his brothers. One monk, however, did escape the sword and recounted the massacre.

The tribesmen then moved out and went toward where their boat was lying anchored. They took with them the captive women, children, and whomsoever else they had seized. As they drew near to the shore, they observed that their boat was gone. A Christian had severed the cable on the barbarians' transport boat, causing it to founder on the rocks. In their rage, the tribesmen fell on their captives and slaughtered them. Then when armed Christians arrived, they slew every man of the barbarians.

The august Saint Helen, mother of Saint Constantine the Great, was concerned for the welfare of the monks who were harassed and raided by the nomads. Consequently, in 325, she financed the construction of a huge tower of refuge for the monastics. They resumed their attacks in 373, which created multitudes of refugees in Egypt around Tabennesis.[6] Those fathers who survived the raids or escaped then dispersed into Palestine and Egypt. In 536,

---

[6] The Blemmyes were perhaps a tribe of Libyan Berber origins. An uprising of the Blemmyes was quelled circa 452, when Maximos, the military commander of the Thebaid, defeated them and negotiated a one-hundred-year peace treaty. In the 5th C. they had an alliance with the Noubadees (Nobatae), a neighboring tribe, but were conquered by them. In the 6th C. Christianity began to enter into their pagan society. Justinian I destroyed their sanctuaries at Philae, which were dedicated to Isis, Osiris, and Priapus. They possessed several emerald mines, from which they were selling to the Axumites in Nubia. *The Oxford Dictionary of Byzantium*, s.v. "Blemmyes."

Emperor Justinian built a monastic haven with massive fortifications by the holy Bush, at the foot of Mount Sinai, in the thirtieth year of his reign (556-557), it is said, when Doulas was hegumen and Theodore his prior.[7] This became known as the Monastery of Saint Katherine.

A Narrative of Abba Ammonios
of the Murderous Destruction of the
Venerable Fathers at Mount Sinai and Raithu.

It happened once that I, Ammonios, was sitting in my humble cell, which was situated near to Alexandria, in a place called Canopus, when the thought came to me that I might go to those parts of Palestine for two reasons. First, I was not able to look upon the afflictions, diverse trials, and perils which the Christians were undergoing from the unbelievers and lawless tyrants. I found particularly grievous those tribulations that befell Peter, our archbishop, who must flee and hide in place after place. There is no abatement to his trials, so that he is prevented from openly shepherding his rational sheep. As though he were some thief and criminal, do the lawless officials hunt him. Second, I have had an incomparable desire to venerate the precious and august holy places of Jerusalem, especially the site of the life-giving resurrection of our Lord Jesus. I also long to see the other solemn places of the holy land, upon which Christ trod with His immaculate and inviolate feet, performing those great miracles and wonders as the almighty One. I believe also that most of the saints of our Church—or at least it appears so from their hagiographies—had the same yearning; that is, to go and venerate the holy places in Jerusalem for a greater recompense.

Even as I had desired, so it came about. I arrived in the holy land and made pilgrimages all around that I might see and venerate the shrines. Afterward, I longed to go to that holy mount, which is called Sinai. I also wished to traverse that wilderness and pay homage there also, as it is a site worthy of reverence. I commenced my pilgrimage on the road and found other Christ-loving souls who were also going to Mount Sinai. We walked together for eighteen days. With divine help, we arrived at that sacred mount. I offered up my prayers and venerated the holy sites. I also wished to enjoy the spiritual counsels of the venerable fathers. I went from cell to cell, that I might receive spiritual profit from each one. Those wondrous and righteous fathers, with their great virtues and practises, are good and worthy models for all, because such as they pass their lives with much understanding and discernment, regarding their food and conduct.

---

[7] D. Chitty, *The Desert A City*, p. 169.

These righteous ones have searched the desert that they might find some places where there might be a little food to sustain them. They especially sought to discover where water might be had, since this was indispensable for their survival. I observed that some made huts and others concealed themselves in the caves. Most of them have a regimen that consists of vegetables and herbs that grow in the wild. They also nourish themselves with grass roots and fruits that grow on the upper branches of trees, especially hard-shelled fruits. They have no wish to waste their time with the care and treatment of the body. They deemed more essential and useful those labors which nourish the soul, rather than spending time preparing broiled fish, cooked vegetables, or other such foods for the flesh. Those among them who had the strength and knowledge undertook cultivation. Utilizing a hoe, they would sow a little wheat or a few vegetables. All of them observed abstinence. Never did anyone sate himself or overeat. They ate only that they might not die or injure themselves from excessive fasting. Now there were some who only partook of food every Sunday. There were others who ate twice weekly, and others every two days but only once. Simply put, each proceeded according to his own strength or as God provided. In that place, Caesar's coin was not to be found. No one sought money, since they neither bought nor sold. Whatever one required, another would eagerly give it to him, with all his soul and genuine love.

Again, whosoever was lacking in bread or vegetables or fruit, someone who had these things would give them, thereby showing rich love even in small things. These men led a life that was truly superhuman and angelic. Rivalry or envy or bearing a grudge in no wise could be found among them. There was no maligning and disparaging between the greatest and the least. No one lifted himself up with the thought of being the most virtuous. Much rather, one was of the opinion that he was the lowliest, for such a one acknowledged that it was God Who granted the power and grace for each to accomplish any good thing. The lowest or least among them would reproach himself that he was unable to attain to the level of the first. All diligently applied themselves to excel in virtue and outdo one another in humility and obedience. After all, for this reason they left and renounced the world. This is why they came to dwell in the desert and desolate places that they might know God, through His energies, without distraction. As the divine Peter wrote: "His divine power hath freely given to us all the things for life and piety, through the full knowledge of Him Who called us by glory and virtue, by which He hath freely given to us the very great and precious promises, that through these ye might become partakers of the divine nature, having escaped the corruption which is in the world by desire [2 Pe. 1:3, 4]." Their only desire was to please God and have union with Him. For those who are men-pleasers and reach for the praise of men that they might be glorified by men, "Verily," said the Lord, "they have received their reward [Mt. 6:2]."

These venerable men had their huts and hermitages far from one another, approximately twenty stadia (2.3 miles). This was so that each might have quiet and solitude, lest they should mingle and confound one another. Every Sunday they would assemble in the Church and communicate the divine Mysteries. They partook of a communal meal together in the trapeza (refectory). One of the abbas, the most learned among them, would deliver edifying instructions, concerning how they should beware of the craftiness of the demons and guard against soul-injuring debates and dialogues. (For all those who reside in the desert seek to put a bit and bridle on the senses. They must be watchful and vigilant with regard to their tongues, ears, and eyes, that they in no wise converse or gaze upon soul-destroying sights. The godly strugglers need to exercise great heed, lest they should suffer loss from the warfare of wandering thoughts or remembrances.) Thus, the learned were to exhort and edify the unlearned, lest they should be vanquished by the demons. Special attention was to be given in maintaining continence and self-control, especially among the younger men who, after they sated their bellies, might easily fall into fornication. They were to be particularly on guard against pride, which is the worst iniquity. With these and other beneficial words, the more wise among the elders edified the fathers, leading them up to a mode of life that was equal to that of the angels.

Verily, wondrous was their manner of life. Though their countenances might be pale from extreme abstinence, yet their appearance was venerable, so that they radiated light as earthly angels. They did not eat the usual foods; no oil or wine at all. No choice foods were included in their fare, except for some dates and fruits. Their superior, however, kept a little bread in his kellion,[8] both for the divine Liturgy and that he might treat strangers—that is, should any pilgrims come—to something to eat in that wasteland.

The Attack of the Saracens at Sinai

Now after I had spent a few days among them, there suddenly arrived a multitude of bloodthirsty Saracens. The chieftain of those unholy barbarians had just died. They vented their rage upon the weaponless and unarmed fathers. They slew both those in their hermitages and as many as they could find in the neighborhood of the main church. Many managed to come inside the walls, where they took refuge in the tower with the superior, Father Doulas. As his name bespoke in the Greek tongue, he was a slave of God. He was a man like no one else in his degree of forbearance, long-suffering, and

---

[8] This kellion is either a small religious house or a monastic cell.

extraordinary meekness. He was also called Father Moses by many on account of these traits, for which the prophet also was renowned and spoken of: "Moses was very meek beyond all the men that were upon the earth [Num. 12:3]." The barbarians put to death as many reverend fathers as they found in Thramven, Choreb, Kodar, and other places which lie nearby.

Afterward, they came toward us, when we were at the mount. In just a short while they would have slain us, if it had not been that a great and wondrous sign took place. The man-loving God helped all of those who, with all their minds, called upon His name. He commanded and there appeared a towering flame upon the summit of holy Sinai, so that the entire mount smoked. The fire seemed to reach to heaven itself. All of us were terror-stricken and fell to the ground, supplicating the Lord to aid us. The barbarians also witnessed this spectacular and mysterious sight. Immediately they fled, abandoning in their haste both camels and weapons. Those

The Massacre of the Abbas of Sinai

among us who witnessed their abrupt flight kept glorifying the all-good God and giving thanks for His compassion. We descended from the tower in a state of astonishment. We then diligently went to attend to those who were brutally slaughtered.

The Thirty-Eight Martyrs at Sinai with Abbas Esaias and Savvas

We counted eight and thirty slain fathers. Their wounds were diverse on their bodies. We did not witness the actual mutilations and murders, so the exact cause of each father's death we did not learn. The righteous fathers whom we found in Thramven numbered twelve, while the rest came from different places and cells. We did find two who were still breathing, Fathers Esaias and Savvas. We buried the massacred ascetics with laments and wailing that cannot be described. Their violent deaths were harsh, cruel, and merciless. Beholding those reverent, august, and sweet fathers with bodily members strewn about the ground ushered in incalculable sorrow and tears. The injuries, cuts, and blows inflicted upon them varied with each one. One had his severed head hanging on his chest, another had his head slumped on his back, attached only by a few strips of skins. The body of one was sundered in half. Another was lying on the ground without hands and feet, while another had his abdomen rent apart with his inward parts strewn about. The dismemberments and mutilations of the others were diverse. Why speak at length of these gory findings? No matter how extensively or how exactly we report the findings, can it approach to what we had seen?

The Massacre of the Abbas of Sinai

As we interred those holy and martyric bodies, we also attended to the two wounded fathers. On the second day at evening, Father Esaias reposed. With regard to Father Savvas, we cherished hopes for his survival, as his wounds were not life-threatening. On the one hand, he gave thanks to God for the afflictions that He had permitted; but on the other hand, he was saddened that he was not accounted worthy to receive the crown with the others. Therefore he was weeping and saying, "Woe is me, the sinner and unworthy one, that I was not vouchsafed to be in the choir of those august martyrs of everlasting blessedness. I only came into the harbor of Thy kingdom, O Lord, but as one undeserving I entered not. Nonetheless, I entreat Thee, O Almighty, Who didst send forth Thine only-begotten Son for our salvation, do not separate me from those holy fathers who have gone on ahead. As Thou only art good and the Lover of man, allow me to complete their number, thus making Thy slaves total forty. Yea, O Lord Jesus Christ, in Thy good pleasure, do Thou bring to pass this request; for Thou knowest that I have followed Thee from my mother's womb and that I have very much desired Thee, though I be a sinner and unclean." After offering up such a prayer, the blessed Savvas surrendered his holy soul on the fourth day after the murderous destruction of his fellow ascetics.

The Martyrs of Raithu

While this took place and our eyes were wells of tears and our souls were yet filled with grief for the fathers who were dispatched so heinously, there came to us an Ishmaelite. He informed us that all the ascetics, those who dwelt in the inner desert, which is called Raithu, had died. Raithu is a distance of approximately two days from Mount Sinai, and in those parts that lie by the Red Sea, where it is spoken of in Scripture that there were twelve wells of water and seventy palm trees [Ex. 15:27], which multiplied with the passage of time. We questioned him regarding how many of those holy fathers suffered martyrdom and in what manner were they executed. He told us that he did know any particulars, only that it was reported in every quarter that the fathers were slaughtered. After a few days, a monk from Raithu came to Mount Sinai that he might stay with us. It was he who told us everything exactly concerning the report of the killing of those venerable fathers. He was familiar with how each one conducted his life and with what kind of virtues each father was adorned. He also knew the manner of each one's cruel death. Thus, we put to him many queries.

He spoke to us of his fellow ascetics and his own harrowing escape, saying: "I, honorable fathers, have put in only twenty years at Raithu. The others, however, had been there for forty, fifty, and sixty years. I should explain that Raithu is entirely level, and the plain extends well to the south. As for its breadth, it is broad and flat for twelve miles. Toward the east it is bounded by a wall of mountains, which have rendered the whole place difficult to traverse for those unfamiliar with the terrain. Above the sea there is one mountain, where there gush forth twelve fountains that water a multitude of palm trees. To that mountain, many anchorites went to dwell in the caves and holes of the earth. This also was spoken of by the heaven-treading apostle who says that 'they were made to wander in deserts, and in mountains, and in caves, and in the holes of the earth [Heb. 11:38].' The fathers gathered in the main church, not at the one atop the mountain, but the one close by. They may have been men by nature, but their virtues rendered them equal to the angels, since the conduct of those thrice-blessed souls emulated the angels. They disdained their bodies as though they belonged to others, and only diligently lavished care upon the soul. They were not endowed with one virtue only, but each was well-adorned and graced with all of them. Even if I should wish to narrate their struggles and trials, I would not be able on account of their magnitude. I shall only recount one or two that you might learn that as it was with those, so it was with all of them, to a man."

Abba Moses and Ovedianos

"There was Moses who was from Pharan. He became a monk at a very young age. Nearby the main church he struggled in one cave for seventy-three years. In truth he was as a second Prophet Elias, for whatsoever he sought from God he received. He also was endowed with the gift to work wonders. Consequently, many sick folk and demonized were healed. Moreover, all the people of the Hagarenes, those who dwell in those borders of the Ishmaelites and in Pharan, the thrice-blessed one converted to Christianity. These people, upon witnessing the signs and wonders which he wrought, came to believe in the Christ and were baptized. This venerable Moses never tasted bread from the day he became a monk. He partook of only a few dates, and the least amount of water was his drink. He loved silence more than anyone else. He welcomed all with a cheerful countenance and gave a fitting response to every question, so that all received spiritual benefit. After Vespers, he was constant in prayer, glorifying the Lord, and would not sleep until he finished the office of Orthros. During the entire Great Fast before Pascha, he did not come forth from the door of his cell until Great Thursday. Within that cell he had nothing more than twelve dates and a little pitcher of water, which things, many times, were found again intact.

"During the Great Fast, the chieftain of the Ishmaelites, a demonized man, named Ovedianos, was brought from Pharan to the holy man for healing, as he was known to have easily cast out other demons. When Ovedianos was still about six hundred feet from the elder's cell, the demon agitated him mightily so that he began shouting, 'O the violence! Not even for a short spell was I able to hinder that bad old man from his prayer rule!' Having said this, that man-hating demon came forth and departed from Ovedianos. Since he was now delivered of that demon, the Ishmaelite believed in the Christ and was baptized with others. I know of many other such incidents, but I shall remain silent; for now is not the time for verbosity.

Abba Psoes

"I should mention here that one father, named Psoes, who came from those parts of the Thebaid, became the disciple of the blessed Moses. He abided in a cell above that of his elder. He so emulated his teacher that he received all of his virtues, even as wax fully takes the imprint of the seal. With him I, the unworthy one, spent considerable time. But at length I was unable to endure the extreme harshness of his mode of life; and so I left. This wondrous ascetic was among those slaughtered by the barbarians. I do not have the time to recount before you the virtues of all those righteous fathers. I shall only speak briefly of the work of one holy man, for it would be a sin to keep silent regarding such a fearful and extraordinary sight.

Abbas Joseph and Gelasios

"This particular father was named Joseph, who hailed from Ailesios. He dwelt two miles from the spring in the plain. He was a saintly man of profound discernment, perfect in everything, and replete with divine grace. He had spent thirty years in a cell that he built when he became a monk. His disciple inhabited another kellion near to his. Now another brother had come to consult with Abba Joseph. He knocked at the door of the cell, but no answer was forthcoming. He then stooped and peered in through a tiny opening. He observed Abba Joseph praying. From the abba's head to his feet he was as a flame of fire. The visiting brother remained still, filled with fear and trembling. He then fell to the ground, where he lay motionless for one hour, as though paralyzed. When he came to himself, he rose up and sat before the door. The saint meanwhile was still occupied in contemplation and in a state of ecstasy, unaware of the brother outside his door. After the passage of five hours, the saint appeared as he always had to that brother. Abba Joseph then opened the door to his cell and found that brother still sitting outside. He asked, 'When didst thou come?' He answered, 'Though I have been here a long while, yet I chose not to keep knocking. I did not wish to disturb thee.' The holy man comprehended then that his visitor had seen and knew what had transpired, but he said nothing about that matter. He invited the brother inside and only answered those questions for which that brother came to consult with him. After he had answered him fully, hearing him convey his thoughts, he then bade him farewell. Abba Joseph then wasted no time in departing from his cell wherein he had passed decades. He did this because he wished to flee the praise of men and transitory glory. After this incident occurred, his distraught disciple, called Gelasios, went about seeking his elder. He diligently investigated diverse places and could not find him. He therefore took up his abode in Abba Joseph's former cell. One day, after six years had passed, he heard a knock at the door. He opened it and found his abba standing before him. Father Gelasios at first thought it might be an apparition fabricated by a demon. In order to verify in truth if what he beheld was an illusion, he addressed his abba, saying, 'Recite the prayer'; that is, the Jesus Prayer, 'Lord Jesus Christ, Son of God, have mercy on me.' For this was common practise among monastics when visiting one another. After Abba Joseph made the sign of the Cross and uttered that prayer, Father Gelasios then received him inside gladly.

"They greeted and embraced one another. Abba Joseph then said, 'Thou didst well, my child, that thou didst ask to have the prayer pronounced

by me, for many are the snares of the demon.' The venerable Gelasios
replied, 'Why didst thou leave me as an orphan, honorable father, rendering
me incomparable affliction?' The abba answered, 'The reason why I was not
made manifest is known to the Lord; however, neither was I missing from
this place even to this day, nor was I ever absent one Sunday from Church
where I communicated the divine Mysteries.' Gelasios wondered and marvelled at this response, thinking to himself, 'But how did the elder come and
go, remaining invisible? For it is certain that no one among us has seen him
all these years.' That disciple then said aloud, 'And why now hast thou
appeared before thy slave?' Abba Joseph answered, 'Since today, child, I
shall be departing from my body and going to my Master, I came that I might
leave thee my relics to bury, even as thou hast wished.' The disciple learned
much from that last encounter. The elder spoke to him, concerning the soul
and everlasting blessedness, and then surrendered his soul to God. Gelasios
then gathered together all the ascetics. They bore Abba Joseph to the main
church, chanting hymns and burning incense. Abba Joseph's face was radiant
as the sun. He was then interred by the venerable fathers. Now I should very
much have liked to speak of other narrations, but because I see that you long
to hear more of the martyric end of those fathers, I shall cut short my account
here, and ask your pardon. But at least you have formed an idea of the
sanctity and virtue of these wondrous fathers. Each one of those fathers
bravely underwent every hardship of the desert and ill-treatment to the body,
that he might devote himself to being the Lord's slave by continual entreaty
with the prayer of Jesus. Forty-three was the number of these thrice-blessed
fathers who struggled with excessive ascetical contests, winning trophies by
their wrestlings against the demons, as known only of God, the Knower of
secrets, Who richly requites each contestant for his inspired contest. This
therefore was their manner of life.

The Attack of the Blemmyes at Raithu

"One day it happened that three Ethiopian men came and said to us,
'The Blemmyes have come and have put up in one port. Take heed, lest you
should be ill-used by them.' We therefore placed men to keep watch toward
the sea. During the second night, the watch espied an approaching boat. The
lay people who inhabited Pharan and Raithu made ready for war. Their
women, children, and camels were left in one place. As for us, we entered
into the church, entreating God that He might grant that which would be most
beneficial to our souls. The barbarians arrived in the harbor, nearby the
mountain, where they camped that night. In the morning they had their
seamen, all of whom were Christians, disembark from the boat. They bound
their hands and feet, lest they should escape with the boat. The vessel was
then patrolled by one of their own tribesmen. The barbarians next ascended

to the fountains of the waters. They found the Christians and engaged in fighting. Our Christian men, who numbered two hundred strong, were overcome by the three hundred barbarians who were experienced in warfare. The tribesmen slew one hundred and forty-seven of our men, while the others fled; some hid in the mountain, while others fled to the palm trees. The barbarians then captured the women and children, whom they left beside the fountains. They then advanced toward us, running as savage animals, thinking that they were about to uncover wealth without measure among us. They surrounded the church, screaming and shouting wildly in a disorderly manner. We from within could hear their terrifying voices and stood there quaking. Our hands and eyes were lifted toward God, as we offered up prayer with much affliction and lamentation. The reaction among the fathers was diverse. Some were fearful, others stood rejoicing, while others wept and trembled. But all of us were crying out, 'Lord have mercy!'

Abba Paul

"Our superior, who was among us, Abba Paul, stood in the middle of the church. He then addressed us with a joyful and gladsome countenance, saying, 'You know well, my holy fathers, that for the love of the Christ we left the world, the corruptible and vain one, and came to this harsh and difficult-to-traverse desert, that we might take up the sweet and light yoke, in the company of hunger and thirst and other straits, disdaining all the bodily wants, so as to be vouchsafed His kingdom. Therefore, if it be His determination that we should now be delivered from toils, troubles, and the vanity of this life, that we might come to everlasting rest, then we ought not to grieve or be downcast at all. Indeed, much rather let us rejoice and be glad, since there is nothing sweeter or more desirable than to behold His divine and most beautiful countenance. You remember that many times, whenever we heard the life of a righteous one or martyr, how we were desiring to become partakers with them in tribulation and in heavenly glory. Behold then, the hour has come according to our desire that we might be glorified together with the saints unto the ages. Therefore, let not one among you cower. But for the Lord's sake, let us manfully endure death. The punishments are as a twinkling of the eye, which shall pass in a moment. The recompense and enjoyment, however, is always and to the ages. There shall be rejoicing and everlasting good cheer, together with the holy martyrs, in the heavenly kingdom.' The response given by those present was as that of one mouth: 'Yea, honorable father, even as thou hast marked out our course, thus shall we proceed. With rejoicing we shall drink the saving cup of martyrdom, giving thanks to the Lord.'

"Therefore, that most holy Father Paul turned toward the east, and spoke to another father, of the same name, and prayed thus: 'O Lord Jesus

Christ our God, the only good and almighty One, the hope and help of us all, do not overlook Thy slaves. Thou knowest our poverty and infirmity. Do Thou help us at this hour of danger, and receive our souls as a sweet savor and God-pleasing sacrifice. For to Thee only is due honor and glory, now and ever and unto the ages of the ages.' Then the others pronounced the 'Amen.' A voice was then heard from the holy altar saying, 'Come to Me, all ye who labor and are burdened, and I will give you rest [Mt. 11:28].' Upon hearing this response, they all trembled. Their hearts and knees were paralyzed, for, as the Lord said, 'The spirit indeed is willing, but the flesh is weak [Mt. 26:41].' Having lost hope of this life, they turned their faces to the heavenly one.

Abba Jeremias

"The barbarians, meanwhile, not having anyone oppose them, placed long wooden poles against the walls and climbed up. They entered the enclosure and opened the doors. They all hastened as wild beasts, waving in their hands naked swords. The first among us whom they took hold of was Monk Jeremias. The barbarians had an interpreter with them, and he said, 'Show us your superior!' That ever-memorable abba was not in the least timid or cowardly. He answered courageously, 'Neither am I afraid, nor shall I show you him whom you seek.' Those unholy ones marvelled at the venerable man's boldness and courage that he in no wise showed fear or cringed. They began insulting him and further outraged him by placing him naked in the middle of the court and shooting him so full of arrows that there was not one portion of his body that remained sound. Thus, Abba Jeremias contested well. That blessed man struggled manfully against the devil. He was the first among them to receive the crown, thus becoming the holy beginning of the sacrifice, the firstfruits, and good example.

Abba Paul's Martyrdom

"The most holy Paul then exited the temple and approached those murderous fiends, saying, 'I am he whom you seek.' They took hold of him and demanded, 'Tell us the truth. Where hast thou hidden the money?' Abba Paul replied with his customary meekness, 'Believe me, children, for I have obtained nothing throughout my life, except for this old hair shirt and rason (cassock) which you see I am wearing on my back.' The barbarians then picked up rocks and struck Abba Paul on his neck as they punctured and inflicted wounds to his jaw and cheeks, saying, 'Bring to us here the money.' After they tortured him for a long while, they struck a blow to his head with a knife. They cleaved that sacred skull in two, so that both halves of his cranium fell to each shoulder. It was then that the righteous and venerable martyr fell dead, after first enduring many torments.

"I, the wretched one, beholding the bitter and savage death of our superior, Father Paul, was shaking from fear. I kept looking about for a place to hide and flee the danger. I then went toward one corner, where there were date palm branches in a heap. I raised them and hid underneath them, lest the barbarians should find and slay me. I could not be sure that I had escaped death, because I did not know whether any of them noticed me. I remember that I thought that if they should discover me, death would swiftly follow. But, as it was, I went unnoticed by them; and thus, I warded off those torments. The barbarians then left the two dead fathers, and lunged forward as ravenous wolves into the church.

The Martyrdom of the Abbas of Raithu

"Once inside, those wild wolves, those unholy barbarians, murdered the holy ones who were then promoted to those holy things. Some of the fathers suffered the removal of their heads; some received blows to their abdomens, which caused their inward parts to spill forth; some were mowed down and severed in twain; and still others were tortured in other diverse ways."

The Martyrdom of Father Adam

Now that brother who witnessed these macabre and grisly manslaughters was weeping violently. But he was not the only one sighing heavily. We also, the brethren, who were hanging on his every word, shed copious tears. Having collected himself somewhat, he continued and said, "How can I recount, my brothers and fathers, all that I saw with my own eyes? I should tell thee of one young monk. His name was Adam. He was a kinsman of one of the elders, Abba Sergios, who had raised him from infancy. As the lad grew, he was taught and trained with exactness everything that pertained to the holy Schema. Now the barbarians took one look at his comely face and saw that he was young. He was grabbed by one hand and dragged outside. The ever-memorable Adam, seeing that he was not vouchsafed to be counted among the other venerable fathers, but that he was being taken by the impious barbarians so as to live among them as their fellow, what did he do? That most pious one indeed wept bitterly and cried out with a loud voice. But afterward, seeing that those tears benefitted him nothing, he courageously ran forth with the mind of a valiant soldier. He drew one of the barbarian's swords and delivered a blow to the shoulder of another. He did this that he might provoke them and they would put him to death. What that most wise one contrived became reality. As untamed animals, the barbarians were extremely vexed. They gnashed their teeth and cut Father Adam into pieces. As they were putting him to death, he was chanting these words joyously: 'Blessed be God, for He has not left us for the hands of sinful men.' After he had spoken these words, the thrice-blessed Adam fell asleep. They cut and sliced him to pieces; thus, with that death he brokered for himself a deathless life.

"Thus, this is how the fathers were taken. They were neither cowardly nor distressed; but rather, they were joyful and giving thanks to the Lord, as they filled and adorned the church with blood. Though their holy bodies remain here on earth as earthly, their spirits mounted to the heavens, where they rejoice together with the martyrs unto the ages.

The Massacre of the Fathers of Raithu

The Aftermath

"The barbarians, after they slew everyone, kept searching for booty in every imaginable place. They kept hoping to find something of worth in exchange for their fiendish work. Those mindless and demonized pagans were unable to comprehend that the venerable martyrs had no acquisitions in this world, save only their bodies by means of which they inherited the heavens. I, the least of all, who stayed concealed under the palms, was shaking and in terror, fearing that I might be discovered. I kept imploring the Lord to protect and shelter me, if that were His determination, as He is compassionate. Now those manslayers did come over to the palm branches where I was hiding. They looked at the pile but gave it no consequence; either that or God blinded them, lest they should take my life also. Those useless beings, not finding anything which they thought was of value, finally left. They went toward the sea only to find their boat in ruins, because one of the Christians, who stowed away, as a lover of Christ, overtook, in a clever manner, the barbarian on patrol and slew him. Afterward, he cut the ropes and cables, but he remained onboard. He had the ship drive straight for the rocks, where it was smashed, but he had already swum back to shore and fled. Thus, the barbarians, left with no means to return to their land, were enraged. In their anger they turned upon the captives—a considerable multitude of men, women, and children—and slew all of them. Next, they set fire to all the date palms.

"It was then that Ishmaelites and Pharanite men, elite warriors, numbering six hundred, arrived at dawn. Also, many male natives joined the brigade. Word of the massacre had reached them, and they made ready to encounter the barbarians. The stubborn barbarians, with the sea to their backs, having no hope of fleeing, fought strenuously, as much as they could, until the ninth hour when all were slain in that battle. Not one of them was taken prisoner. The fatalities among the Pharanites numbered eighty-four, with many wounded.

The Thirty-Nine Martyrs at Raithu with Abba Domnus

"Then I came forth from the pile of fronds. I examined all the bodies of the saints to see if anyone had survived. All were already dead, save for three: Fathers Domnus, Andrew, and Orion. Abba Domnus lay on thè ground in dreadful pain and suffering, having sustained a fatal wound to his side. Abba Andrew had suffered many wounds, but none of them were life-threatening; for that reason he survived. As for Abba Orion, he sustained no wounds. I say that because the barbarian ran his sword through the right side of his cassock, which passed through to the other side, only slightly touching his flesh, but leaving a little blood on the blade. The barbarian, thinking he had killed him, then hastened to run his sword through another. Meanwhile, Father Orion fell upon the other slain, as one dead, and remained motionless. He only rose up and came forward with me. He handled the bodies of the slain holy brethren and cried.

"Now after the Pharanites dispatched the barbarians, they left their bodies at the edge of the sea that they might be devoured by birds and wild animals, even as they deserved. Meanwhile, there had assembled the acquaintances, friends, and kindred of those who were slain during the first attack. There was lamentation and mourning, as they buried their dead in various caves of the mountain. Afterward, they came to us and beheld the bodies of the saints strewn about. Again they wailed inconsolably with us, gazing upon the sheep of Christ scattered on the ground. It appeared as though wolves had come, leaving mangled, hewn, and fragmented bodies. Next I saw the Christ-loving Ovedianos and the other notables of Pharan bringing costly and splendid garments, in order to honor and reverence the holy and righteous slain in burial, as was meet.

"The count for the dead among the fathers was then numbered at thirty-nine. But then, at evening, Abba Domnus, who hailed from Rome, also reposed, and we buried him. Now he was specially buried, since we did not wish to reopen the tombs of the other fathers. The saints thus completed their earthly sojourn all together, that is, a proper and full forty, on the 14th of January.

"Abba Andrew and Abba Orion remained but a short while there, since they had doubts whether to remain there to the end or leave. As for myself, I was unable to endure the wilderness and isolation. I therefore came among you for some consolation and comfort. I should also mention that many besought me to remain, including the Christ-lover Ovedianos. The latter, so as to help establish me there, also showed himself eager to supply me with whatever I might require. Ultimately, I could not oblige on account of the aforementioned reasons. Behold, brethren, at another time I shall recount the rest. For now, tell me how you have fared in this place."

Abba Ammonios Continues His Account

We then told him what I had written earlier. We marvelled at the extraordinary and mysterious wonders of God that even as the fathers ended at Raithu, so it was in this place for the same number of holy men, on the same day and in the same manner, forty. Then Abba Doulas rose up and exhorted the other brethren, saying, "Beloved, those fathers, as elect slaves of the Christ, were accounted worthy of Christ's kingdom and blessedness; they are truly blessed and happy. After so many struggles, afflictions, and temptations, they secured the crown of the contest. In the heavens, they, as martyrs, have received from God both great honor and glory. Let us then keep the commandments of the Lord diligently. Let us supplicate them that they entreat the Lord on our behalf that we may be numbered with them in His kingdom. To the good and man-loving God, let us give thanks, for He protected us and delivered us out of unholy hands in the most marvellous manner." When the venerable elder spoke these soul-benefitting words of admonishment, the fathers were encouraged and offered up thanksgiving to the Lord.

As for me, the lowly Ammonios, I returned to Egypt, not to Canopus but Memphis. I wrote down this account on paper, lest such a narration of compunction should be forgotten. I also recorded it that those born after us may read it and know—whatever may befall one—the meaning of zealous virtue, perseverance in afflictions, and giving of thanks and glory to the Lord, to Whom is due all glory, honor, and veneration, now and ever and to all ages. Amen.

On the 14th of January, the holy Church commemorates our venerable Father THEODOULOS of Sinai, the son of Saint Neilos.

Theodoulos, our venerable father, was the son of our righteous Father Neilos, who is commemorated by the holy Church on the 12th of November. Neilos, the former prefect of Constantinople, left the glory of the world. He went to Mount Sinai and became a monk, taking his son Theodoulos with him. While they were living in quietude and prayer, suddenly barbarians rushed upon them and began rounding up the holy fathers. Father Neilos managed to escape, but Theodoulos, together with another young man, was captured. The barbarians bound and dragged them away, leading them to their camp. The pagans then decided that the two young captives were suitable as sacrifice to the morning star of Aphrodite (Venus), which rises before the sun. The younger of the two brethren was able to flee, leaving Theodoulos alone.

The barbarians, after they had become intoxicated, were mastered by drowsiness and fell into a heavy sleep. They were only roused from their stupor well after sunrise. The pagans therefore missed sighting the morning star. They did not slay Theodoulos, but chose instead to sell him. When they brought Theodoulos to the marketplace at Elusius, and he could only fetch two or three gold coins, one of the barbarians was maddened by these offers. He brandished his

Saint Theodoulos

sword in preparation to kill the youth. This action was seen by one who, having taken pity on the young man, quickly offered to purchase him for more money. After the sale had been made, Theodoulos then was exchanged again and passed into the hands of a priest who immediately freed the young man.

The young man then came to the attention of the local bishop, who intended to place him in the service of the Church. After much inquiry, Father Neilos discovered his son was at Elusius, and wished to bring him back to the mount. But the bishop was also desirous of taking him and ordaining him. Nevertheless, both father and son yearned to return to their solitude in the wilderness. Perceiving this, the bishop ordained them both to the priesthood and permitted them to return to Sinai. The personal and detailed account of Father Neilos is given in the following pages.

Afterward, the two holy fathers lived in the wilderness of Sinai for a considerable time. Their manner of life was both wondrous and austere, as they exercised strict abstinence and extreme asceticism. Father Neilos, as one wise, wrote ascetical treatises which afforded his readers profound spiritual benefit. His numerous epistles and essays, filled with wisdom, incited many people toward divine love and denial of the world. After leading this type of life, which was equal to that of the angels, the holy Neilos reposed in peace and was translated to the Lord. He reposed in the middle of the fifth century, after spending sixty years in the Sinai wilderness. After this, Father Theodoulos also surrendered his soul in peace into the immaculate hands of the Almighty.

The relics of this saint and of his son Theodoulos, along with those of other ascetics, are preserved in the Church of the Holy Apostle Paul, at

Constantinople, which is found in the Orphanage,[9] where many miracles and wonders took place, to the glory of the Father, Son, and Holy Spirit, the Trinity one in essence, to Whom is due dominion, honor, and homage always, now and ever and to the ages of the ages. Amen.

Saint Neilos

**A Narrative of
Saint Neilos the Sinaite,
Concerning the Captivity
by the Barbarians of
Saint Theodoulos,
during their inroads against
the Venerable Fathers
of Sinai and Raithu.**

After the unholy barbarians captured and murdered the venerable fathers at Sinai and Raithu, I, Neilos, went to Pharan. I had heard some men praising the life of silence and solitude, lauding it as the cause of salvation for many. Such a conduct of life, they said, is toward the betterment of the soul, rendering it free of agitation or confusion. Thus the mind may mount to divine knowledge, that is, true blessedness and blessed rest. While I listened to them, I wept for my son Theodoulos. I could not help but bring to remembrance that on account of such quietude and solitariness, which they extolled, the barbarians seized my boy and deprived me of him. The Christians noticed that I was exceedingly sorrowful and shedding copious tears. They asked me the

---

[9] The most famous orphanage in Constantinople was that of Saint Paul in the Acropolis region. The Byzantines showed particular compassion toward orphans and widows, for whom the state had legislation to protect the rights of orphans. The complex in the capital included a school for the orphans, as well as a center for the blind, crippled, and elderly. This foundling home allowed the orphans to remain until they reached marriageable age. *Oxford*, s.v. "Orphanages."

cause of my sadness. I answered them, saying, "I also, beloved brethren, was of the same mind regarding silence, tranquility, and contemplation. But for the sake of such things, I suffered a great misfortune and deprivation with the loss of my son, who was the light of my eyes. Now I lament and wail. I am inconsolably grieved. I do not know what has happened. I kept thinking that those barbarians who seized my son would either offer him in sacrifice or keep him alive and torture him, to the peril of his soul."

The Christians then said to me, "Pray, tell us more particularly about this matter." I perceived that they desired to learn of my suffering, so I said to them, "I, the unfortunate one, had two children. I was desirous to depart for the wilderness that I might find my salvation. I came to an agreement with my spouse that I would leave one of our children with her as a consolation and would take the other that he might accompany me as my consolation. I therefore took my son, named Theodoulos, and received forgiveness from my wife. We each, weeping, went our separate ways. Believe me, there is profound pain when a couple separates. We had spent many peaceful years together with much carnal love, even as God had yoked together man and woman. She, as a fragile woman, was more afflicted at our leave-taking, but I comforted her with various words of the divine Scriptures, saying to her, that in the future we shall rejoice together in the heavenly kingdom with ineffable pleasure on account of this separation and parting. Thus with constraint, I persuaded her, and she fell silent. I thereupon came with Theodoulos to the wilderness of Sinai. The lad was a small child at the time. He, however, comported himself prudently and virtuously, so that I marvelled and gave glory to God Who enlightened and empowered him to preserve with exactness those hardships attendant with strict asceticism. We therefore laid anchor in the harbor of hesychasm for many years, abiding in peaceful and untroubled waters.

"Afterward, the envious hater-of-good incited the barbarians to come to the small monastic settlement, Skete, where there were many other hermits, in order to murder us. When those unholy creatures arrived in the midst of our venerable synaxis (assembly), those heartless beings slaughtered some and captured others, including Theodoulos. They took into captivity those who were young that they might serve them. I, together with others, fled, but again I saw my child from afar. I was sure that the barbarians had seized him. Though I did not have the heart to leave, yet I did not have any strength. I thought about going back, to see what I might do to contrive his deliverance, though they probably would have cut me to pieces to save themselves the trouble. Now Theodoulos saw me and made a motion with his eyes, thereby showing that I should flee as quickly as possible. Thus, I, the unfortunate one, found myself in a difficult situation. Without my wishing to do so, in my body I fled toward the mountain, followed by others who ran before me. But in my soul, heart, and mind, I was entirely with Theodoulos. I ofttimes looked back that I might catch a glimpse of him, until he was too far off.

"Then, when I no longer could see him, I cried before God, not only for my beloved child, but also on account of those venerable fathers who were murdered unjustly by the unholy barbarians. I then uttered these words in an address to them: 'O thrice-blessed fathers, where are the pangs of your continence and your perseverance in toils? These atrocities which have taken place, are they truly the rewards and the payment of your long contest and struggle? What has happened to your toil and trouble? Was it in vain and to no profit? Did divine providence leave you bereft of help, that you, as pious and righteous, might be massacred by the unjust and ungodly? How is it that fire did not fall from the heavens and consume those whose merits deserve vengeance? Or why did not the earth tear asunder and swallow them up into the abyss? What now has become of divine vengeance, which once submerged so many thousands of Pharaoh's men in the sea, that He should not rightfully punish those unrighteous, but permits them to unjustly lay low so many of the virtuous and righteous slaves of God? Thou, my child, Theodoulos, dost thou yet live, or have the barbarians put thee to death? If they have slain thee, what place has received thy blood? And what birds have eaten thy members? I should only be contented with one portion of thy holy relics for my own small consolation.'

"I spoke these words of complaint and a great number of other irrational things from my profound sorrow. In the meantime, the barbarians, after having done with the saints, looted as much clothing as they could find that had some value. Then they departed, taking the captives with them. We then descended from the mountain when darkness fell, and buried the holy relics of the saints. We found that one of the venerable fathers, whose name was also Theodoulos, was still breathing. He spoke these final words to us: 'Be not wondering at these tribulations, my most beloved brethren in Christ, for thus the demon is wont to do. He seeks from the Lord permission to tempt His slaves. The righteous Judge then gives leave to the hater-of-good to be put to shame, so that the saints might receive in His kingdom more glory and double the crowns.' Upon uttering these words and others for our edification, the goodly Martyr Theodoulos delivered his holy soul into the hands of God. We buried him with the other holy fathers who completed their martyric course on the 14th of January."[10]

---

[10] The name of Saint Theodoulos is not the only name left to posterity. Saint Neilos and the other fathers conducted investigations to locate the murdered and bury them

(continued...)

Even as I was relating these accounts to those Pharanites, we caught sight of one of those venerable ones who had been taken captive by the barbarians. Since he was known to me, I asked him, "How is it possible that thou didst escape?" He answered me, saying, "The barbarians had determined that with the rising of the morning star they would sacrifice both me and Theodoulos. Before nightfall, they prepared the wood, altar, and all that their profane worship required. Then the barbarians supped. They sated themselves and overdrank, which caused them to fall into a heavy sleep. At midnight, I dragged myself along the ground, until I was out of their sight. I then walked away softly, lest my departure should be sensed and I suffer being caught. Now I knew that they were about to offer us as sacrifice, due to the fact that one of the kidnaped brothers, who knew the tongue of these barbarians, overhead them taking counsel how they would sacrifice us on the morrow at dawn. Thy son, however, decided to remain behind, fearing recapture and torture. He left his end to God's will. I do not know whether they slew him or not, because, as soon as I was far enough away, I took to my heels. My fear was intense. As the Lord is my witness, my heart is still trembling, when I bring to mind the murders executed by those unholy ones. I should tell thee that in order to reach that place where the barbarians had taken us, we were dragged and bound. We did not traverse any good road, but rather went through the mountains and ravines.

"As we were going and night fell, we encamped in a plain which had delicious water. It was there that they put to death a youth. First they dealt him a knife blow to the neck. He fell to the ground convulsing for a long time. The intent of those merciless creatures was both to execute and tyrannize him simultaneously. Those bloodthirsty and beastly-minded men even rejoiced at the sight of his suffering. Thereupon, they cast him into the fire, wherein he suffered spasms and quivered as a fish. His hands and feet struck the coals. Many times he attempted to raise himself, but again and again he fell. Thus, he, of many great names, finished his earthly life.

"In the morning, I observed that there was a tiny cell just opposite the mountain. I then noticed that some of the barbarians hastened to enter into the cave, where there was one hermit. They pulled and dragged him outside. I could see that hermit's countenance. It was joyful and radiant, not downcast.

---

[10](...continued)

honorably. Among the slain, the following holy martyrs were identified in the places where they suffered: Proklos, killed at Bethrambos; Hypatios, at Getha; Isaac at the monastery of Salail; Makarios and Mark in the outer desert; Benjamin at Thola; and Elias at Aza.

The barbarians, not bearing their swords with them, then took up stones and murdered him as they shouted aloud in triumph.

"After that, a little further on, they encountered a younger hermit. He was pale of countenance, due to excessive abstinence. They put an end to him in like manner, with stones, as they themselves were verily of stone and heartless. That holy soul received the wounds from that stoning, giving thanks to his murderers, because his temporal death would usher in life everlasting.

"After these macabre incidents, they gathered up their gear and spoils. We then proceeded further on. We encountered a lad of about fifteen years of age. The barbarians questioned him, saying, 'Where are the monasteries in these parts? Show us; and for thy trouble, we shall grant thee thy life.' Though he was young in years, yet he had the mentality of an elder. He neither feared them nor cowered in the least. Instead, he censured them and said, 'I am not obliged to you Christ-fighters that I should betray the Christ-lovers to the likes of such Christ-haters as you.' Hearing these words, the barbarians were enraged. The insatiable cutthroats hacked him into little pieces. This homicide did not quench their anger. Those sadists had hoped to extend his torture, but that noble youth did not survive long.

"We then continued. Their bared swords were still dripping with blood. We then caught sight of two monasteries, at a distance of fifteen stadia (1.7 miles) from one another. One was toward the south, while the other faced the north. The barbarians then planned their attack. They would split into two groups, dispatching one to each monastery. I was kept with those barbarians who made their assault on the monastery lying toward the north. I tell you that howsoever many monks they found, they were massacred without mercy. There was one venerable father, extremely swift of foot, who attempted an escape. The barbarians, however, gave chase and riddled him with so many arrows that he collapsed to the ground. He was still breathing, so they rolled him over on his back and sliced him open, from his navel to his chest. All of his inward parts spilled out, which they cut to pieces and cast to the ground, in the manner of wild dogs."

After I, Neilos, heard these accounts, my heart was in pain. I feared that perhaps my Theodoulos had suffered such violence at their hands. The sorrow those stories implanted in my heart was excessive. The layfolk who inhabited Pharan, hearing the news of the shocking barbarities perpetrated against the monastics, were embittered. They were resolved to send an embassy with letters to the chieftain of the barbarians, Amaneen by name. In their messages they expressed their wish to live in peace and made an offer to pay them a yearly tribute, which was not without precedent. With those who were sent on this mission, I too volunteered. I thought that perhaps I might be able to ask about my son, whether he were alive or dead. After a few days we arrived at their camp. We presented them with gifts and the letters. We were received by them in a cordial manner and given hospitality. The chieftain gave us his promise that the manslayers would be punished as was fitting. They would also give back all that they looted. The others then returned to Pharan and reported all that had transpired in the negotiations. I tarried a little longer in their camp that I might conduct a thorough investigation regarding the whereabouts of Theodoulos. As a result, I questioned many of them. Only one was able to inform me that my boy was sold at a city called Louzin or Elusius, and that a priest had bought him.

I must say that this intelligence relieved some of my heart's sorrow. Therefore, upon receiving these tidings, I took two guides and traveled toward the aforementioned city. I felt very joyous and walked briskly, so that at times I even broke out running. We arrived and hastened to find the bishop. Some persons, hearing that I was the much-suffering and generally talked of father of the captive child, announced my presence to him. I finally then arrived at that habitation, where my son was staying. The moment we laid eyes on one another—I do not know what happened exactly—I suddenly collapsed to the ground, barely breathing. I am unsure whether my reaction was the mounting effect of my previous intense sorrow or the result of my rush of excitement and joy at seeing him. He took me into his arms and ardently kissed me, being the loving son that he is. With a concerted effort, I came to myself and also embraced him. Weeping uncontrollably, I began saying things, by way of proffering some excuse. But I scarce know why I uttered these words: "Forgive me, my beloved child, for I am the cause that thou hast suffered so many torments; for I separated thee from those maternal arms and embrace that would have kept thee safe. But I only wished, for the good of thy soul, to bring thee to the desert. But I beseech thee, tell me all that happened, from the moment thou wast taken captive. For just as health rejoices the heart after sickness, thus I am also gladdened after thy deliverance, though thy story should be filled with sorrows."

Theodoulos sighed deeply and began saying, "I imagine the first part thou hast already heard from that brother who slipped away and fled. All that took place afterward, I shall now speak of briefly. Now by evening, the barbarians had readied their abominable altar for sacrifice, upon which they decided to sacrifice me the following day. I should tell thee that I could not sleep a wink that whole night, but kept constant in prayer to the almighty Lord, having all my hopes of salvation in Him. I kept weeping but kept faith, saying these words: 'O Master and God, Creator of all creation, Thou hast authority over life and death. Even as Thou didst preserve Daniel from the mouths of lions and kept the holy Three Children unharmed in the furnace by Thine ineffable and invincible power, do Thou also deliver me, Thine unworthy slave, from a profane death which is soon expected. Thou knowest that to this day I have remained chaste and virginal, but now my body is to be given over as sacrifice to that defiled demon of licentiousness. Do Thou therefore change and tame the beastly hearts of these savages, even as Thou didst once curb the anger of the Median King Artaxerxes (Ahasuerus) before Esther, transforming it into sympathy and mercy [Esther 8]. Yea, O all-merciful Lord, save me, though I wish no evil to befall my murderers, yet return me to my father who is Thy slave. Though my fellow prisoner, being swift-footed, has escaped death, yet I take courage in Thy help and remain, having my hopes in Thee.' Thus, I kept vigil all that night, crying until dawn. When dawn came and I beheld the morning light, I felt consoled. I prayed with more fervor, shedding copious tears to the Lord, saying, 'Cause me to marvel in Thy mercy to me, O Master, and save me, even as Thou didst preserve from slaughter Isaac who was about to be offered as a sacrifice by his God-loving father of ready obedience. Keep me as once Thou didst Joseph who was rescued from the envy and fratricide of his brothers, and then years later, his father received pleasure upon seeing him as a king. So do Thou also for me, O almighty King, and grant me my life for the sake of my pious father, Thy slave, that he might glorify, even by means of my release, Thine all-holy and all-hymned name.'

"When the barbarians finally rose from sleep, they were confounded and in a tumult. The time for them to have offered sacrifice was passed. This is because they worship the morning star of Aphrodite, which rises before the sun. I am told that at its rising they are supposed to offer sacrifice. When they noticed that the other prisoner was missing from the camp, they asked me about him. I told them that I did not know what became of him. They accepted my answer and shrugged off his loss, not taking any retaliation against me. For this, I gave glory to God; inasmuch as He hearkened to my prayer. Then they commanded me to eat of their polluted food and to sport with their women, but I gave them no heed. Then we moved on and arrived at a village called Souvaita. They led me into the marketplace, attempting to incite the natives to purchase me. But no one would give them more than three gold coins. This maddened them. They took out a sword and put it to my neck, ready to swing it and lop off my head. I besought the bystanders, anyone, to buy me and give them whatever their price was for me, saying that I would repay them afterward. To whomsoever would deliver me from their clutches, I offered to slave for the rest of my life. Someone saw my weeping and took pity on my dire predicament. He purchased me, but thereafter he made another transaction when I was ransomed by a priest, who showed me love as one of his own children. Give glory then, my father, to the Lord, Who delivered me from death." I then said to him, "Thou, child, on the one hand, hast endured tens of thousands of perils and deaths which thou didst expect at any moment; but I, on the other hand, when thou wast taken captive, arranged with our Master that if He should vouchsafe me to enjoy seeing thee alive, I would pass the remainder of my life practising great abstinence and ascetical hardships. These things are what I had promised, and then I heard a voice saying to me, 'May God make firm thy word!' Well then, it is not proper that I should prove false to God, but I ought to fulfill my promise eagerly." Theodoulos then said to me, "I, O father, am willing and eager to become a partaker in this hardship, that I might help thee, as God may endow me, in the event thou shouldest suffer any ill plight, that I too may enjoy the grace and benefit that shall issue therefrom." I then uttered a prayer that it might be according to his words, that we should both come to a great recompense.

After we rejoiced together at being reunited, the bishop of the city offered us hospitality and demonstrated genuine love toward us, as a true lover of Christ of Whom he was an imitator. He was insistent that we remain in his diocese, and promised to supply us with whatever we might require. When we informed him of our desire to return to the wilderness that we might render to the Lord that for which we obliged ourselves, he no longer restrained us. He also did not wish to appear that he was exercising his authority over Theodoulos to remain as a recompense for the outlay made at his purchase. He retained us for a sufficient time that we might have a little rest and consolation. Afterward he let us go in peace, but not until he had constrained us both to receive the rank of the priesthood. Neither I nor my son wished this dignity, as we were perfectly sensible of the gravity and weight of the office. His opinion prevailed, since he believed that the pangs of asceticism vouchsafe a man to be worthy, as one having attained boldness before the Lord. Therefore, we were compelled to obey him. Then he munificently endowed us with whatever we might need for the road. After we received his blessing and pardon, we returned to the desert.

On the 14th of January, the holy Church commemorates our venerable Father STEPHEN, the Builder of the Monastery of Chenolakkos.

Stephen, our venerable father, hailed from eastern parts. He was of noble lineage. As the Righteous Job, from the beginning, he loved the ascetical life. For this reason, he traveled to those districts by the Jordan. He saw the monasteries and hermitages of the holy fathers dwelling in those parts. He also visited the renowned monasteries of Saints Efthymios, Theodosios, and Savvas. After he studied and learned the manner of life at each monastery, he went to Constantinople in 716. At that time, the iconomach, Leo the Isaurian (717-741) was reigning. Father Stephen was offered hospitality by the most holy Patriarch Germanos (716-730) and remained there for about one year. The patriarch then sent him into Bithynia to a place called Chenolakkos or "Goose Pond," northeast of Trigleia,[11] situated near Moudanion. Father Stephen built a monastery in that place, where he gathered a multitude of monks. He taught and instructed them in the fear of the Lord. He ascended the heights of perfection and came to the "measure of the stature of the fullness of the Christ [Eph. 4:13]." The monks of Chenolakkos always had icons and later supported the restoration of the holy icons by the Second Synod of Nicaea (787). After the ever-memorable Stephen had lived a God-pleasing life, being established and anointed by God Who sealed him and gave him the earnest of the Spirit in his heart [cf. 2 Cor. 1:22], he passed over to that future glory and blessedness. His soul flew from the lower realm to the upper and heavenly abode, being seen by his disciples to ascend in glory and to be conducted into the heavens.

On the 14th of January, the holy Church commemorates
the holy Martyr AGNES,
who finished her contest in a dark prison.[12]

On the 14th of January, the holy Church commemorates
our venerable Father SAVA,
Archbishop of Serbia,
Builder of Hilandar Monastery on Mount Athos.[13]

---

[11] Trigleia (Triglia; Turk. Tirilye) situated near Moudanion.

[12] This Saint Agnes is not to be confused with the other martyr of the same name, who is commemorated by the holy Church on the 21st of January and suffered martyrdom by fire.

[13] The Life of this saint was taken primarily from the *Neon Eklogion* of Nikodemos the Hagiorite, which text appears in *The Great Synaxaristes* (in Greek). Collateral sources are noted in the English version.

Father and son, Saints Symeon and Sava of Serbia, are considered the founders of the Hilandar Monastery, but their story does not end here. In addition to Hilandar, both are regarded as joint builders (*ktitores*) of Great Lavra, Iveron, and the main church at Karyes. Saint Sava is also considered one of the builders of other great Athonite monasteries, including Vatopedi, Karakallou, Xeropotamou, and Philotheou. He also built a church belonging to Vatopedi in Prosfori (modern Ouranoupolis) outside Athos, and flanked it with a tower. The donations that both he and his family lavished upon the Athonites are renowned.

Sava (Savvas), our holy father, was from Serbia. His father, Stefan Nemanja,[14] was the pious grand župan[15] of Raška, that is, Serbia.[16] His mother's name was Anna, who also was the scion of royal lineage. At that time, the Serbs attempted to gain their independence from the Byzantines. However, Emperor Manuel I Komnenos (1143-1180) managed to suppress these outbreaks. In 1166 or 1167, Nemanja had been appointed grand župan by Manuel I. With Hungarian and Venetian support, Nemanja rebelled against the Byzantines successfully. Then, in 1172, Manuel I, with a large Byzantine army, attacked Nemanja. Forced to surrender, he was taken captive to Constantinople.[17]

In 1183, Nemanja was restored to power as a Byzantine vassal. After the death of Manuel I, Nemanja again rebelled against Byzantium. In alliance with Béla III of Hungary, they invaded Byzantine territory. Though the allies sacked Belgrade, Braničevo, Niš, and Sofia, Nemanja kept control over Niš.

---

[14] The name Nemanja, where the *j* is pronounced as the *y* in yes, is the same as the Hebrew prophet's name Nehemias (Nehemiah). In 1113, Nemanja was born in Ribnica in Diocleia and reposed at Hilandar on the 13th day of February, in the year 1199.

[15] Grand župan means "satrap" in Byzantine terminology. Note: *ž* is pronounced like *s* in pleasure or Asia. This title is used by the Greek historian Niketas Choniates when referring to Stefan Nemanja. Dimitri Obolensky, *Six Byzantine Portraits*, p. 115.

[16] Serbia was a medieval Balkan state. In Latin sources it is sometimes referred to as Rascia (Rassia, Raxia), derived from the Slavic name Raška. The term "Serbian" appears in 9th C. Latin texts in the form *Sorabi* describing a people living in Dalmatia. Note: *š* is pronounced *sh*.

[17] Nemanja was deserted by his allies, the Venetians and Hungarians. Niketas Choniates comments that when Nemanja observed the emperor was in pursuit, the župan "showed himself in battle...and then hid in the cover of mountain caves which he sealed with stones." It is then recorded that Nemanja surrendered, having prostrated himself at Manuel's feet. Pleading not to be handled cruelly, he was further filled with anguish at the prospect of losing sovereignty over his people and of having his political power transferred to those whom he previously overcame. *Historia*, ed. I. van Dieten (Berlin, 1975), 158. See Obolensky, loc. cit.

Another contemporary historian, John Kinnamos, records that "Nemanja asked that he might gain an audience with him (Manuel) without personal risk. So when the emperor assented, he came and approached the tribunal, with head uncovered and arms bare to the elbow, and feet unshod; a halter was about his neck, and a sword in his hand. He offered himself to the emperor for whatever treatment the emperor willed. Having mercy on him for this, he (Manuel) set the accusation aside. After this success, the emperor departed Serbia, and the grand župan went with him." Joannes Cinnamus, *Historiae*, bk. 6, ed. A. Meineke (Bonn, 1836), 287, 288; *Deeds of John and Manuel Comnenus by John Kinnamos*, tr. C.M. Brand (New York, 1976), 215. See Obolensky, pp. 115, 116.

The grand župan expanded his territory to the east and south, and united Zeta with Raška.

Saints Sava and Symeon

Prince Rastko of Serbia

The imperial couple, Stefan Nemanja and Anna, were devout Orthodox Christians. They had two sons, Vukan and Stefan (born ca. 1165). However, the queen took sick and was no longer able to bear children. Though they had a kingdom and many riches, nonetheless, with tears and fasting, they entreated our holy God to bestow another child unto them. Circa 1170 or 1175, the Lord hearkened unto their supplications and granted them a third child, the ever-memorable Rastko, or Sava in the monastic tonsure.

From his earliest youth, Rastko was first educated in the sacred writings. After a little while, he was instructed in all the ecclesiastical books available in his native tongue. He manifested such qualities as understanding, prudence, discipline, continence, humility, and a cheerful disposition, so that all who beheld him loved and revered him. Hence, as the prince increased in age, the more so did his love toward God intensify. He gave himself over entirely to divine love. Nought occupied his mind other than how to please his Creator and Fashioner, God. Day and night he continually prayed, undertaking struggles with fasting, vigils, and diverse voluntary hardships.

One medieval biographer writes that when Rastko was fifteen years old, Nemanja gave him a province to govern near the western borders of the state (Hum or Hercegovina). The pious young man was its provincial governor for two years.

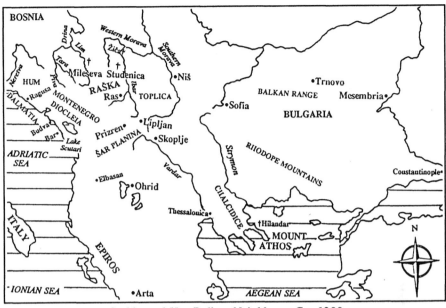

Serbia and Her Balkan Neighbors, Ca. 1200

Then, when he was seventeen years old, since he loved virginity, he besought God to vouchsafe him a life according to Christ. The man-loving God would grant the desire of his heart at the appropriate time.

In the early 1190s, Nemanja attempted to improve relations with Byzantium.[18] He achieved this by having his second son, Stefan, marry

---

[18] By this time, the territory of the Serbian state extended from the lower reaches of the rivers Morava and Drina in the north to Šar Planina in the south, while in the southwest it included the coasts of Southern Dalmatia and Montenegro. The stretch of the Adriatic coast and its interior was first known as Diocleia and later as Zeta. This annexation in the 1180s added to Raška a sizeable minority which owed allegiance to Rome. A Latin presence in this predominantly maritime region was balanced by Greek jurisdiction over the interior, in the person of the Bishop of Ras, capital of Raška, near Novi Pazar, who was a suffragan of the autocephalous Archbishop of Ohrid.

Moreover, this dualism is reflected in Nemanja's own life. In his native Diocleia, as an infant, he was made to receive the Latin sacrament of baptism by a Latin priest. Later, while still a young child, he was received into the Orthodox Church by the Orthodox Bishop of Ras. See Obolensky, pp. 117, 118. Evidence is at variance whether he was received by the Orthodox Mystery of holy Baptism or by the Orthodox Mystery of Chrismation.

Evdokia, a niece of Emperor Isaac II Angelos (1185-1195).[19] Stefan received the Byzantine title *sebastokrator*.[20] Greek monks that arrived in Serbia as part of the entourage of Evdokia drew some Serbs to the monastic life. However, let us return to Saint Sava and how God opened the path to eternal life for him.

Saints Symeon and Sava

Certain fathers from the Holy Mountain of Athos, hearing of the virtues of Stefan Nemanja and, especially, that he was exceedingly merciful and generous toward the poor, resolved to journey to Rastko's homeland. Therefore, to collect alms, the Athonites entered Ras (present-day Novi Pazar), a mountain town and the capital of the grand župan.

Stefan Nemanja, as we mentioned earlier, was a God-fearing man. Though he could well afford to live luxuriously, both he and his family led a simple life in a modestly appointed residence. When Nemanja was younger, in 1183, he founded the Studenica Monastery in a wooded valley of a tributary of the Ibar near Ušće, in south central Serbia. The church, with its white polished marble, combined architectural features of the Byzantine and Romanesque traditions. Within the monastery enclosure, he had been responsible for commencing the building of the Church of the Virgin and the independent Chapel of Saint Nicholas. Hence, the Athonites chose to request donations of this man. Among the traveling brethren were those of the Russian Monastery or Monastery of the

---

[19] Nemanja's first military engagement with Byzantium took place in the autumn of 1190, when Emperor Isaac II's army vanquished his troops on the river Morava. Ibid., p. 119.

[20] The *sebastokrator* was the highest title, following that of co-emperor and later *despotes*, conferred on the emperor's sons and brothers. *Oxford*, s.v. "Stefan Nemanja" and "Sebastokrator."

   This title, no less than the marriage, marked Serbia's incorporation, as an autonomous state, into the Byzantine cultural commonwealth. Obolensky, loc. cit.

Thessalonian, which came to be known as Saint Panteleimon Monastery.[21] The monks, of Russian descent, were very virtuous.

When the blessed Rastko gazed upon them, he was desirous to enter into conversation with them. After he had done so, he asked them about the monasteries of the Holy Mountain. He also wished to learn of their order and rule, and the conduct of life of the monastics, and whatever else was useful toward his ultimate aim. When he was informed by them, concerning the divine life of the monastics, this promoted further warmth in his heart, so that tears streamed forth from his eyes. After he had wept sufficiently, he said to the elder of the group, "I see, O father, that God knows the depths of my heart and my intention. He has sent thee here to me, the sinner, that thou mayest direct me toward the divine path, because my soul rejoices upon hearing thy divine words, so that I am unable to abide any longer in this erring and misguided world—neither do I wish to behold its fallacies, deceits, and imaginations. Therefore, I beseech thee to instruct me how to leave the vanity of this world, and attain to the same manner of life that thy holiness lives, because my parents are considering having me marry shortly. For this reason, I decided one hour earlier to depart hence and repair to the Holy Mountain. In this matter, O holy father, I ask thine advice."

After listening to him speak, the elder answered, "I perceive, my child, that thine intention is excellent and appointed of God; moreover, I see that the love of God dominates thy soul. Indeed, what thou dost contemplate, thou must do as quickly as possible. I shall be thy traveling companion and guide, until I take thee to the Mountain." Then, contriving a method of escape, Rastko arranged with the elder to meet at a certain place. Rastko then went to his parents, and said to his father, "I heard that such a mountain has much game; and I beg you to give me leave and your blessing to go hunting that I might amuse myself for a short while. I beseech you not to become angry with me." After his father granted him permission and gave him as many menservants as he required, Nemanja blessed him.

The blessed Rastko, with unbounded joy, anticipated his meeting with the elder who went ahead, where he waited for the young prince at a prearranged place. In the meantime, Rastko commanded those in his hunting party to sit a while and wait for him. Rastko then departed and went with the elder into a hamlet, where he changed his imperial garb. They entered some poor home, and Rastko donned beggarly clothing. Thereupon, Rastko and the

---

[21] The Russian Monastery then stood about two miles northeast of the present Saint Panteleimon Monastery.

elder set off for the Russian Monastery on the Holy Mountain.[22] Once there, Rastko was instructed and trained by that same elder in the monastic conduct of life. The young man, revering his elder, as was befitting, performed with great eagerness and obedience all that was commanded of him.

His parents, in the meantime, wept inconsolably. To every quarter, they dispatched men who were ordered to make an elaborate search, because the parents could not endure being deprived of such a comely, wise, and prudent son whom his father intended to make successor to his kingdom. The grand župan's men were sent everywhere. Among them, three leading men were sent to Athos to conduct an exact examination. It was not long before they learned that a group of recently-arrived Serbs was at the Russian Monastery. Nemanja's armed men sought and found the young prince at this monastery. Though Rastko, with tears, pleaded to be left alone, the Serbian officers would not withdraw. At this juncture, Rastko contrived another plan to elude his father's persistent agents. He told them to rest and wait until the following day.

Then, by night, secretly, the blessed Rastko entered the monastery tower, where he importuned the elder to tonsure him to the Angelic Schema of the monastics. He received the tonsure and was renamed Sava, after the great Palestinian father, Saint Savvas the Sanctified, commemorated by the holy Church on the 5th of December. Afterward, he composed a lengthy epistle to his parents, concerning the end of the age and the blessedness of the saints. He also wrote about the vanity of this world and unending punishments. The following morning, when the Serbs sought Rastko and could not find him, they laid blows upon the other monks to make them reveal his whereabouts. Sava, hearing the shouts and cries of the brethren, appeared before them as a monk. He cast down his gold-embroidered princely robes,

---

[22] The flight of Rastko and the rest of his life are told in four medieval Church Slavonic documents, but with several discrepancies. We, too, will refer to the following:

1. *The Life of Stefan Nemanja*, by Rastko-Sava (ca. 1208). See *Spisi*, s.v. "Save," ed. V. Ćorović (Belgrade-Sremski Karlovci, 1928), 151-175.

2. *Vita of Nemanja*, by son Stefan (1216). See V. Ćorović, "Medjusobni odnošaj biografija Stevana Nemanje," *Svetosavski zbornik*, i (Belgrade, 1936).

3. *Life of Sava*, by Athonite Monk Domentijan (Vienna, 1242/3; St. Petersburg, 1253/4). See Domentijan, *Život svetoga Simeuna i svetoga Save*, ed. Dj. Daničić (Belgrade, 1865).

4. Teodosije Hilandarac, *Život svetoga Save*, ed. Dj. Daničić (Belgrade, 1860; repr. Belgrade, 1973). Cf. C. Müller-Landau, *Studien zum Stil der Sava-Vita Teodosijes* (Slavistische Beiträge, 57 Munich, 1972). The Athonite Monk Teodosije wrote in the late 13th or early 14th C.

together with the hair shorn at his tonsure, and said, "Take these signs away with you: Show them that you found me alive, as a monk of God, with the name of Sava."[23] He then presented the epistle to be given to his parents. Nothing more could be done by the Serbian agents. They remonstrated with the new monk, so that the Serbs and even Sava himself shed tears.

Though Sava was quickly made a monk, this did not occasion prideful thoughts on his behalf. Considering himself the least member in the brotherhood, he submitted to all. However, he remained only a few months at this monastery when, at the Feast of the Annunciation, the hegumen of the great Athonite Monastery of Vatopedi invited the hegumen of Panteleimon to attend. Sava was asked to accompany him. The young Serbian monk made a favorable impression upon the hegumen of Vatopedi, who invited him to remain at the Greek monastery. With the Russian abbot's permission, Sava left for Vatopedi, where he would dwell and struggle for twelve years.

This sudden move to a Greek monastery was God's providence working in young Sava's life. At Vatopedi, since Greek was all that was spoken and chanted in the services, at length, Sava learned the Greek tongue perfectly. He also read at the divine offices and sang in the choir. As a result, he immersed himself at the monastery's rich library where manuscripts of the Greek fathers were preserved.

Returning for a moment to the day of Sava's tonsure, we resume with the Serbian officers who returned to Ras and the royal couple, to whom the chief officer presented Sava's epistle. Upon reading the epistle, they wept exceedingly and mourned the loss of their son; yet the letter also made an indelible impression upon his aged and doting parents. By his God-inspired words, he drew his beloved parents to compunction, so they too began to contemplate the monastic life for their final years.

After Nemanja composed himself, he responded to Sava by asking that he return home for a visit. Moreover, out of his love for God and his son, Nemanja desired that his son succeed in his chosen life and new country. Therefore, he sent him gifts for distribution among Sava's fellow ascetics on Athos.

After receiving the blessing of Vatopedi's hegumen and that of the *protos* (the head of the monasteries),[24] the holy Sava distributed his father's largess among the great coenobitic monasteries, but he did not overlook the hermits and the dwellers in the cells and small monasteries (kellia). As a bee

---

[23] Panagiotes Christou, *The Holy Mountain*, p. 75.

[24] The *protos* (lit. "the first monk") of Mount Athos was elected by an assembly of monks at Karyes. Assisted by the *hegumenoi* (abbots), he administered justice and had disciplinary powers over the monks of Athos.

collecting honey amid the choice flowers, so Sava stored up for himself the precious teachings and experiences of the monks and the monasteries that he visited. He not only showered gifts upon them, but also partook of their way of life. The imperial donations included gold, liturgical vessels of gold and silver, rich embroideries, and brocades. Though Sava preferred traveling barefooted, yet he did not neglect to give as gifts beasts of burden for riding and transporting goods.

The brotherhood of Vatopedi, of course, also benefitted greatly. Saint Sava not only oversaw the construction of residences, buildings, and three chapels, but also participated by laboring physically.[25] In fact, Sava built a place to dwell for both father and son. Though ten of his twelve years had already passed at Vatopedi, Sava had not laid eyes on his father. They did, however, correspond, wherein each would ask the other to come for a visit. Then, in a final letter, Sava was stern with his father, warning him not to set aside his invitation another time, or "abandon the hope of seeing me in the next life."[26]

The many seeds of piety that Sava planted in the souls of his mother and father, God granted to come to fruition. Anna resolved to become a nun, and received the Angelic Schema at a women's monastery. As the Nun Anastasia, she lived a God-pleasing and sanctified life up to the time of her blessed translation unto the Lord. The saint's father, Nemanja, in March of 1196, abdicated in favor of Stefan the First-crowned, while giving the governance of Zeta to Vukan. The latter ruled them as king of Dalmatia and Diocleia. Nemanja then received the monastic tonsure from Bishop Kalinik, taking the name Symeon. He thereafter repaired to the monastery that he founded, Studenica. After Nemanja's abdication and tonsure, Stefan's ascendancy as grand župan would later be opposed by Vukan, the elder brother of Stefan and Saint Sava.

While abiding at Studenica for about eighteen months, Symeon followed the rule and order of the monastery. His stay was not without benefit to this monastery. Symeon gave it a sound economic base, appointed Hieromonk Dionysios as abbot, and also arranged for his own grave. The temple of the Virgin at Studenica, as his burial church, was built of finely dressed local marble. After he had arranged all these things, the holy Symeon set his mind toward the Holy Mountain and his beloved and youngest son Sava. In November of 1197, the elderly Monk Symeon, at eighty-four years of age,

---

[25] Saint Sava endowed Vatopedi with many other things, too difficult to enumerate, so that he was accorded the title of "The second founder of Vatopedi," after Emperor Theodosios the Great in the 4th C. See Velimirović, *The Life of Saint Sava*, p. 22.
[26] Ibid., p. 23.

arrived at Vatopedi. He was welcomed with great rejoicing and reverence by the brethren. The old man, indeed, had not come empty-handed. He brought rich presents from Serbia to distribute to everyone, including gifts for the churches, useful articles for the brethren, and horses and mules.

All the years that Sava spent building, he did not neglect his asceticism. As he practised mental prayer, calling upon the name of our Savior, saying, "Lord Jesus Christ, Son of God, have mercy upon me," the demons were scourged, as he sought to be brought "to a perfect man, to the measure of the stature of the fullness of the Christ [Eph. 4: 13]." Yet, now, after ten years of waiting and praying, at twenty-seven years of age, he would behold his aged father again. Upon meeting, overcome with emotion and longing, they fell into each other's embrace, shedding a torrent of tears between them. However, not only those of Vatopedi greeted the former and renowned grand župan and soldier, founder of the Nemanjid Dynasty

Saint Symeon Nemanja

and the independent Serbian state, but also the *protos*, abbots, and monks from all the monasteries came to greet the Monk Symeon.

It was Symeon's desire to live with his son who, years earlier, prepared a dwelling place for the both of them.[27] Thereupon, both holy men remained and dwelt together a sufficient time and led wondrous lives. Through their generosity, Vatopedi was also a recipient of many improvements, including three more churches, new hospices, and new vineyards. This

---

[27] There appears to be a discrepancy regarding when the Monk Symeon took his monastic vows. Bishop Nikolai Velimirović (p. 25) records that Bishop Kalinik tonsured Nemanja on the 25th day of March, in the year 1196. However, Nikodemos the Hagiorite states that Nemanja received the Angelic Schema from his own son; he even remarks that as Symeon was Sava's physical father, yet Sava was Symeon's spiritual father. See *The Great Synaxaristes* (in Greek), vol. i, p. 306 and vol. ii (5th ed., 1978), p. 334, n.1. Perhaps what is meant is that Symeon received the highest monastic grade, the Great and Angelic Schema, from Saint Sava.

did not distract Symeon and Sava, who struggled daily with fasting, all-night vigils, and prayers. In a little while, both became masters of continence and temperate in the passions of the flesh. They attained the summit of virtue, more so than all the fathers found on the Mountain. Thus, they became worthy vessels of the All-Holy Spirit. Since the good report of their virtue incited many Serbians in their former homeland to join them as monastics, it could be seen, every day, that the Serbian group on Athos was increasing. It soon became evident that they needed to build their own monastery.

Hence, the holy fathers fasted a sufficient number of days and kept vigil with fervor to our Lady Theotokos. They invoked her that she might direct them to the holy will of God and where to build the monastery. By divine vision, this was revealed unto them. The new Grand Župan Stefan II requested the fathers at Vatopedi to give his father and brother the ruined settlement of Hilandar,[28] in an area about twelve miles northwest of Vatopedi called Meleon, not far from the north coast of the peninsula. The gift was ratified by the chrysobull of Emperor Alexios III (1197), who was their in-law.[29] By special edict, Alexios transferred Hilandar and its surroundings from the jurisdiction of the *protos*, and placed them under Vatopedi's hegumen. Protos Gerasimos and the abbots of many of the minor monasteries were against the assimilation of the small monastic houses by the large monasteries. Therefore, they intervened in favor of Hilandar remaining independent. Emperor Alexios was persuaded and made it an independent monastery, stipulating that it should be a gift in perpetuity to the Serbs.[30] Therefore, in June of 1198, Alexios III canceled his earlier *sigillion*, an imperial document with his seal, submitting Hilandar and its surroundings to Vatopedi, and placed it under the authority and management of Symeon and Sava. Hence, they now had a monastery that was independent and self-governing for their people on the northeastern side of the peninsula.

As soon as father and son settled at Hilandar by July of 1198, they commenced the reconstruction and expansion of the existing buildings. Stefan II also contributed an enormous amount of gold and silver toward enlarging the coenobium. Though the strength of the aged Symeon was waning quickly, they both built a new church and added a refectory. Sava, of course, hired

---

[28] The name Hilandar or Chelandari first appears at the end of the 10th C. Its founder was probably George Chelandrios ("the Boatman"), the author of an official Act of the Mountain dating from that period. By 1015, it was deserted and had been handed over to the Kastamonitou (Konstamonitou) Monastery, located in the interior of the peninsula, between Docheiariou and Zographou. *Oxford*, s.v. "Hilandar."

[29] The wife of Stefan II, the grand župan, was Evdokia, Alexios' daughter.

[30] Sotiris Kadas, *Mount Athos*, p. 87; Christou, loc. cit.

many artisans to build not only the church, but also the cells and other needful structures. Symeon, in 1198, probably with Sava's input, drafted the monastery's earliest foundation-charter. In 1199, at Sava's kellion in Karyes, he composed a *Typikon* based on the rule of the Evergetis Monastery at Constantinople,[31] which is still in force at Hilandar. Sava, with his father's approval, appointed Hieromonk Methodios as the superior. The new and beautiful church, which they built from the foundation at their own expense, was dedicated to the Entrance of the Virgin Mary into the Temple, which the holy Church celebrates on the 21st of November.[32] Not much time passed before other Serbians, both noblemen and menservants, took their monastic vows at Hilandar.

The holy Elder Symeon was now eighty-six years old. He lived a righteous and God-pleasing monastic life. Knowing that his translation was imminent, he instructed his son to bury him, in due time, at the grave that he had prepared earlier at Studenica. Saint Sava, writing his father's biography, gives us the following account: "My father said, 'My child, bring me (the icon of) the most holy Mother of God, for I have made a vow to yield up the

---

[31] When Saint Sava traveled to Constantinople, at his father's behest, to secure the chrysobull of Alexios declaring Hilandar independent, he stayed at the Monastery of the Holy Virgin Evergetis, that is, the Benefactress, which is located outside the city walls. See Velimirović, p. 33. Moreover, Evergetis regarded both Symeon and Sava as among their monastery's greatest benefactors and builders (*ktitores*). See Obolensky, p. 132.

The *Typikon* or Constitution, drawn up by Sava, using Evergetis as a model, appointed two overseers, the hegumen (abbot) for spiritual matters, and the *œconomos* (steward) for administrative and business affairs. Upon the repose of the abbot, he was to be replaced by the steward, and the brotherhood would elect a new steward. See Christou, p. 76. Saint Sava's *typikon* included detailed rulings on the Liturgy, Confession, Communion, fasting, clothing, conduct inside church and the refectory, and the monastery's autonomy. See Obolensky, loc. cit.

[32] The katholikon (main church) of Hilandar is reputed to be one of the most lovely churches on Athos. The original katholikon, built in 1198, was replaced in 1303 by a new and larger church erected with the donations of King Milutin (1282-1321). The last addition to the main church, from 1396, was an exonarthex donated by Prince Lazar Hrebeljanovich (d. 1389). Frescoes in the main church were painted in 1303 by iconographers who adorned churches in Serbia at that time, though now they are under more recent layers of frescoes. Icons in the exonarthex were executed in the 19th C. Adjacent to the katholikon, east and slightly to the north, is the Tower of Saint Sava. Today, only the lower portion is from his time; whereas, the upper part is from the days of King Milutin. Saint George's Tower is also from the time of the saint. Mateja Matejic, *The Holy Mount and Hilandar Monastery*, pp. 30, 31.

Saint Symeon

spirit in front of her.' And when his command had been carried out, toward the evening, he said, 'My child, do me a service of love; clothe me in the rason appointed for my funeral and place me in the same sacred position in which I shall lie in my coffin. Spread matting on the ground. Lay me upon it and place a stone under my head, that I may lie here until the Lord should come to visit me and take me hence.' I did all this, even as he commanded. And all of us who looked on wept bitterly....He received the salutations of all the brethren and, with love in his heart, asked everyone's forgiveness and blessing. When night had fallen, they all took their leave of him; and, after receiving his blessing, they returned to their cells to do what they had to do and rest a little. I and a priest whom I had kept with me remained by his side all that night. At midnight, the blessed father fell silent and spoke to me no longer.

"When morning came and the singing of the Praises began in the church, the blessed father's face was suddenly illumined, and he looked up to heaven, and said, 'Praise God in His sanctuary, praise Him in the firmament of His power [Ps. 150:1].' I said to him, 'Father, whom dost thou see as thou speakest these words?' He looked at me and said to me, 'Praise Him for His mighty acts, praise Him according to the multitude of His greatness [Ps. 150:2].' And when he had said this, he, straightaway, yielded up his godly spirit and reposed in the Lord."[33] The date of his repose was the 13th day of February, in the year 1199.

With the death of his father, Sava went into seclusion and increased his ascetic contests with extreme fasting. In Karyes, the holy man had purchased a hermitage, a hesychasterion, where, in the company of one or two other monks, he retired to a life of solitary prayer. Though he was vouchsafed heavenly visions, he also succumbed to a perpetual disease of the spleen. In one of his visions, his father appeared to him and said, "Thou shalt be honored with two crowns, one ascetic and the other apostolic; and both of

---

[33] Sava, pp. 169, 170; Obolensky, pp. 138, 139.

us shall enjoy everlasting bliss. "[34] By this sacred appearance, Sava understood that he should return to Hilandar for the one-year memorial of his father.

In the spring of 1199, Sava undertook a trip to Constantinople seeking to increase Hilandar's revenues. In June, Alexios issued another chrysobull confirming the rights of the builder Sava and the full autonomy of Hilandar. The monastery also received land and the buildings of the abandoned monastery of Zygon on Athos' western edge. Hilandar also was granted permission to own a tax-free boat to help transport supplies.[35]

At his father's one-year memorial, the blessed Sava invited the *protos* of the Mountain and the reverend fathers. They conducted a vigil on behalf of the blessed soul of Sava's father. Then, during the doxology, such an ineffable fragrance emitted from the grave of Saint Symeon that it permeated all of the monastery. The fathers approached the grave and beheld myrrh gushing from out of the tomb. Thereupon, they glorified God Who glorifies those that glorify Him. The sacred Sava received great joy in his soul, because the blessed repose and sanctified relics of his father were glorified.

Thereafter, he gave himself over to even greater fasts and vigils; and, in a prodigious fashion, he applied himself in other contests of asceticism that are impossible to describe. Since it was not meet that such virtue should be kept concealed, by God's œconomy, the righteous Sava was made manifest unto all. Daily, many came seeking his spiritual teachings and instructions. Among those that came for counsel was Protos Dometios of the Mountain, though he, too, was a virtuous and Spirit-bearing elder. Not only Dometios, but the other monastery heads as well, regarded the venerable Sava as their chief counselor. Indeed, without his opinion, no matter was decided, since the grace of the Holy Spirit, dwelling within Sava, enlightened his mind so that he uttered all that was beneficial to the soul and toward salvation. In fact, he was so beloved that they enjoined him to accept the dignity of the priesthood. Though they attempted to compel him, the humble-minded Sava would simply say that he was unworthy; and, ofttimes, he would even conceal himself. Finally, so as not to appear disobedient, and perceiving that it was God's will, he said, "Let the Lord's will be done." As a result, he was ordained a deacon and a priest in his monastery by the then Bishop of Ierissos, Nicholas.[36]

Then, the Archbishop of Thessalonike, Constantine Mesopotamites, hearing of the virtues of the priest-monk from Hilandar, after much entreaty,

---

[34] Velimirović, p. 40.

[35] *Acts de Chilandar*, no. 5, pp. 11-15.

[36] The Bishop of Ierissos had no jurisdiction over Mount Athos. However, he was authorized, if requested, to ordain Athonite monks to the diaconate and priesthood. Obolensky, p. 133.

brought him to Thessalonike. They conversed for a number of days, whereby the hierarch received immense spiritual profit. Not only Constantine, but also

Saint Sava

other bishops, clergy, and layfolk were instructed thoroughly by Sava's soul-benefitting teachings. Hence, the archbishop, in concert with his bishops and all the clergy, decided to elevate him to a higher dignity on one Sunday. Therefore, while the saint was preaching to the people in the main church of the city, Hagia Sophia, suddenly, though he did not want it, he was made an archimandrite by three bishops and Archbishop Constantine. The holy man, due to the excessive honor and reverence they bestowed upon him, departed secretly and returned to his monastery.

In the year 1204, when the Crusaders plotted to assassinate Emperor Alexios V Doukas Mourtzouphlos (1204), they failed. After planning another assault on the city, on the 12th of April, both Crusader and Venetian forces attacked the sea walls of Constantinople on the side facing the harbor of the Golden Horn. The Byzantine defenders successfully beat them back, but the Latins returned. After they had scaled the walls, they entered the city and cruelly sacked it. Thousands of Orthodox were slain or taken captive; thousands more fled the capital. A Latin emperor was crowned, Baldwin of Flanders (1204-1205).

Then, in 1205, a young Byzantine nobleman, Theodore I Laskaris,[37] the son-in-law of former Emperor Alexios III Angelos,[38] rallied the remnants of Constantinopolitan aristocracy and the hierarchy. He organized a government-in-exile across the Straits of Nicaea.[39] After the Latin takeover

---

[37] Theodore Doukas Laskaris (d. 1221) composed the famous Service of the Great Supplicatory Canon to the Most Holy Theotokos, as well as another salutary canon to her, published in the *New Theotokarion* of Nikodemos the Hagiorite.

[38] Laskaris married Anna Angelina, Alexios III's daughter.

[39] Nicaea, a city of Bithynia, is the modern Turkish city of İznik. It is situated at the eastern end of Lake Ascania (İznik Lake), fifty-eight miles southeast of Istanbul.

of Constantinople, Theodore, circa 1208, was crowned as "Emperor of the Rhomaioi (Romans)," in order to perpetuate the Byzantine monarchy.[40]

After the fall of the City, the *protos* of Athos sent the blessed Sava and the heads of the monasteries to Laskaris, the founder of the empire of Nicaea and its emperor, with regard to necessary matters facing the Holy Mountain Athos. Though the precise nature of these matters is unclear, more than likely, the inroads made by the Latins were necessarily a main topic. This is because Boniface of Montferrat, and now marquis of Thessalonike, wielded his authority over Athos by the first half of 1205. Italian clergy pressured the monks to accept papal authority and practises of the Latin Church. In the summer of 1205, Cardinal Benedict, Innocent III's legate at Constantinople, placed the monasteries under the jurisdiction of the Latin bishop of Sebasteia. Then, after he had built himself a castle (Frangokastro) on Athonite territory, he pillaged and terrorized the monks with the help of Frankish barons. Unarmed monks were tortured in the hope of uncovering monastery treasures.[41]

The emperor, with the entire senate, and even the patriarch and the body of priests, were then situated in Nicaea, the new capital of Byzantine power. When Saint Sava arrived in Nicaea and met with Laskaris, his kinsman through marriage, the emperor desired not so much to meet Saint Sava due to their kinship, as because he was extremely desirous to behold this preeminently virtuous man. Therefore, he rejoiced exceedingly upon beholding the holy Sava, whom he rendered great attention. As Laskaris conversed with the holy elder, marvelling at his virtue, he regarded him with profound reverence.

Despite the Athonite embassy to Nicaea, the Athonites were made to endure four years of unconscionable spoliation and injury by the Latins. Saint Sava tells us that the Latins "even invaded us and that holy place; and there

---

[40] Serbia, meanwhile, had within her borders Orthodox and Roman Catholics. Her coastal provinces were under the Latin archbishopric of Bar; the interior, including the bishoprics of Ras, Prizren, Lipljan, and Niš, belonged to the Archdiocese of Ohrid. The center of the autocephalous archbishop, Ohrid, lay inside the Greek principality of Epiros, which was founded after 1204 by the Byzantine nobleman Michael Angelos Komnenos. Though Michael owed a token allegiance to the emperor of Nicaea, his half-brother and successor Theodore challenged the Nicaean leadership. In December of 1224, Theodore seized Thessalonike from the Latins. Soon after, he was crowned "Emperor of the Rhomaioi," by Archbishop Demetrios Chomatianos. Hence, a second Byzantine empire-in-exile was founded. Obolensky, p. 149.

[41] Ibid., pp. 134, 135.

was great turmoil."[42] Only after the joint action of Innocent III (1198-1216) and the Latin Emperor Henry of Flanders was the Bishop of Sebasteia deposed and exiled for the enormity of his crimes against the Athonites. In 1213, the Athonite monasteries even appealed to the pope for protection. Though it was no more than an administrative formality, the Mountain was granted the protection of both Innocent III and Emperor Henry, until their deaths in 1216. Afterward, the Athonites looked to Nicaea for protection, much to the dissatisfaction of the new pope, Honorius III (1216-1227).[43]

Oddly, the fall of Constantinople in 1204 made it possible for the Serbian state to grow. Vukan, Nemanja's eldest son, urged on by his Roman Catholic wife and court dignitaries, resented that his younger brother Stefan was made grand župan. Civil war erupted when Prince Vukan attacked Stefan with a mercenary army and Hungarian support. The assaults took place on a number of occasions, until Vukan thrust Stefan out of their homeland. Desiring to be crowned, Vukan had promised Pope Innocent III fidelity to the papacy. By the grace of God, the Hungarian archbishop, due to internal strife within Hungary, was prevented from entering Serbia to crown Vukan and bring the Serbians under the papacy. Thereupon, thanks to an invasion by his Bulgarian allies, Stefan struck Vukan again and succeeded in driving him back to his coastal provinces. Stefan regained his throne after four years of fratricidal struggle.[44] At length, Stefan and Vukan desired to declare a permanent reconciliation. In order to bring this about, they decided to invite their youngest brother, Sava of Hilandar, whom they also asked that he return with the miraculous relics of their father, Saint Symeon.

Twenty years had passed since Sava left home. Directed by God, the holy man was resigned to return at his brothers' behest. Moreover, Sava had promised his father, when the latter was living, that he would return his relics to Studenica Monastery. After eight years, the tomb of his sanctified father was opened. Saint Symeon's august relics were found intact. Therefore, Saint Sava made the journey to Serbia during the winter of 1206-1207. Once there, early in 1207, the relics were escorted with great solemnity by Saint Sava and Stefan to Studenica. Prince Vukan and his family were also present when the relics were interred in the marble tomb that Nemanja prepared many years prior to his entry on Athos. Saint Sava tarried awhile at Studenica, where he became reconciled with his two older brothers. When the 13th of February arrived, the day of commemoration of Saint Symeon, holy myrrh began to flow from the relics, from which many miracles were wrought.

---

[42] Ibid., p. 135.
[43] Ibid.
[44] Velimirović, p. 47.

Now it was Stefan's wish that his brother Sava remain as superior of Studenica. Sava was the senior non-Greek churchman in Serbia. He agreed and set about building the spirituality of the Serbian people. As an apostle, to combat the inroads of the papists and the Bogomils,[45] he went preaching and proclaiming Orthodoxy to his people. Stefan, prompted by Sava, also decided to build a great new monastery of his own at Žiča, near the confluence of the Ibar and the Morava. Saint Sava brought architects and marble workers from the Greek land.[46] During the years that Sava was in Serbia, he not only compiled his saintly father's biography and composed a service in his honor, but also maintained a correspondence with the brotherhood at Hilandar and with Serbian princes. Also, during those ten years in Serbia, the holy man wrought miracles, healing people by prayer or laying on of hands or anointing them with the sweet-smelling holy oil that suffused the relic of Saint Symeon.[47]

During this time, Stefan divorced his first wife, Evdokia.[48] For reasons of state, he later married the fanatical Roman Catholic Anna, the granddaughter of the Venetian Doge Enrico Dandolo (d. 1205), who played a leading role in the conquest of Constantinople in 1204. Prompted by his new bride to be a crowned king, and surrounded by the antagonistic Latin kingdoms of Constantinople, Hungary and Bulgaria, the grand župan agreed to be crowned by Pope Honorius III. Thus, in 1217, Pope Honorius III sent a special delegation with royal insignia and crown that he might confer upon Stefan the title of king. Sava strived to prevent his brother's coronation by a papal legate. He understood that his sister-in-law, Anna, planned to have her husband crowned a Roman Catholic king and, thereby, hoped to convert the Serbs to Roman Catholicism. Though it is not clear, it appears that, in protest,

---

[45] Bogomils were a dualist and neo-Manichaean sect that denied most of the basic doctrines of Holy Orthodoxy, including the incarnation.

[46] Later, as archbishop, he brought trained iconographers from Constantinople to adorn the temple at Žiča. There is no doubt of the saint's personal share in the building and decoration of the church. Žiča was to become the model for other great 13th C. churches of the Raška school. Also, as the first seat of the Archbishop of Serbia, it became the country's most hallowed shrine. Teodosije, 97, 98, 141; Obolensky, p. 137.

[47] Velimirović, pp. 64, 66.

[48] Stefan repudiated his Byzantine wife. According to Choniates, both parties accused each other of infidelity. Stefan turned his wife out of the house, virtually naked, dismissing her in disgrace to go forth as a wanton. It was Stefan's brother Vukan who provided her with clothes and an escort to Dyrrachium. She returned to Constantinople with a splendid retinue dispatched by her father, Emperor Alexios III. See Niketas Choniates, 531, 532; Obolensky, p. 140.

Sava departed.[49] When he left Serbian soil for Hilandar, the miraculous and healing myrrh of Saint Symeon ceased to flow.

Not much time passed before Stefan sent a letter to Sava at Hilandar, requesting his return; for he believed only then would the myrrh continue flowing. Saint Sava responded by writing an epistle that was to be opened and read over the tomb of Saint Symeon at Studenica. It was only then that the myrrh resumed flowing.[50]

Next, Stefan wrote Sava another letter expressing his aim toward the independence of the Serbian Church. A Latin patriarch was set up in Constantinople, and another was in Bulgaria during the reign of Kalojan (1197-1207). After the Fourth Crusade, Boniface of Montferrat became marquis of Thessalonike. His territory encompassed Macedonia and western Thrace, and he had interests as distant as the Peloponnesos. Moreover, after this crusade, Greece was easily conquered by the Franks. The following Frankish states were established: the principality of Achaia (Morea), the duchy of the Archipelago, the lordship of Athens and Thebes, and Evia (Euboea, Negroponte). Serbia was surrounded, because the Vatican ofttimes incited her northern neighbors to conquer and latinize her. The Serbs needed their own independent Orthodox Church, especially since the œcumenical patriarch was living in exile at Nicaea. Stefan needed strong Church backing.

---

[49] Both ancient hagiographers, Domentijan and Teodosije, describe the coronation at length. Obviously, Sava and Stefan did not mention it in their biographies, dated 1208 and 1216, respectively. Domentijan (pp. 245-248) contends that Sava sent Bishop Methodios, a disciple, to Rome. He was instructed to request a royal crown that Sava might crown his brother. The pope is alleged to have complied.

Teodosije (pp. 141-152) leaves out all reference of Rome and the pope. According to him, only Saint Sava crowned his brother at Žiča in 1220. See Obolensky, pp. 142, 143.

Bishop Nikolai Velimirović (p. 69) remarks, "Some modern historians maintain that Sava left Serbia because of his conflict with his brother's court." Though ancient hagiographers record this scene differently, we agree with Bishop Nikolai who says, "Nevertheless, we think the modern historians may be right."

Most historians have concluded that Saint Sava was completely unsympathetic with Stefan's pro-Roman policy, and this prompted his departure from Serbia and return to Athos. See Obolensky, pp. 146, 147.

[50] At Hilandar, today, behind the abbot's throne, among the elders' prayer-stalls, is the silver tomb of Saint Symeon, from which a vine has sprouted. Its fruit, dried by the brotherhood, exerts a miraculous influence against barrenness for those who partake of it with faith and reverence. Even to the present day, many have begotten children in this manner. Christou, p. 78; Andrew Simonopetritis, *Holy Mountain: Bulwark of Orthodoxy and of the Greek Nation*, pp. 59, 60.

After much prayer, Sava, with a group from Hilandar, entered a ship and sailed to Nicaea to see Emperor Theodore Laskaris and Patriarch Manuel I Sarantenos (1215-1222). The Byzantines, meanwhile, were combating the crusaders on one side and the Seljuk Turks on the other. Nonetheless, during Theodore's lifetime, he dealt both enemies crushing blows; therefore, neither dared crossing the Sea of Marmara. When Saint Sava and the emperor met again, their meeting was cordial. Sava spoke to him about the Serbian people and their need for an independent church and their own archbishop. The emperor then called in the patriarch, who spoke with the saint concerning Serbia and how it lacked an archbishop. Sava urged him to ordain one of his monks from Hilandar as archbishop. Now the patriarch and Sava discussed this matter for a

The Consecration of Saint Sava

sufficient number of days. The patriarch then went to the emperor, and the two of them decided that the holy Sava should be Archbishop of Serbia. Though Sava did not seek the office for himself, they were insistent that he be elevated to the apostolic dignity of the episcopacy. Indeed, many days passed, and Sava would not give place. Finally compelled to do as they wished, Sava was ordained by the patriarch. This consecration gave great joy to the emperor on that day. The new Serbian archbishop's first request was that future Serbian archbishops might be elected and consecrated by Serbian bishops. Though at first they hesitated, Archbishop Sava received a *grammata* (official document) from Patriarch Manuel authorizing this in 1219. Only one condition was imposed: in Serbian churches, the Byzantine patriarch was to be given precedence over all other bishops in liturgical commemoration.[51]

The new archbishop then gave himself over to even greater struggles and contests. First, he stopped briefly at Athos and then Thessalonike in the autumn of 1219. He stayed at Philokales Monastery, where he was considered

---

[51] Obolensky, p. 151.

one of its builders. It was here that he copied many books of law and compiled his *Nomocanon*.[52] It was to become the basic constitution of the Bulgarian and Russian Churches.[53] Archbishop Sava returned to his see where he instructed his flock daily, teaching them the word of the Gospel and a life according to Christ. The Orthodox faithful were strengthened by his sermons and the example of his virtue. Many heretics, by the grace and sweetness of his teachings, turned from their heresy to piety. Thus, in but a little while, the unbelievers and heretics of his see became Orthodox. All revered Saint Sava as their only shepherd and teacher.

Saint Sava

His episcopacy was not without troublesome incidents. With determination and subtlety, he defended the autocephalous Serbian Church against papal claims. He protected Bosnia from Bogomil influence. The archbishop also warded off the continuing efforts of Demetrios Chomatianos, Epirot Archbishop of Ohrid, to place Serbia under his diocese. When Saint Sava organized his archdiocese in Žiča, his first act was the selection and consecration of bishops from among his disciples. He set up eleven bishoprics, and some of them were based in monasteries. Three of them—Ras, Prizren, and Lipljan—were claimed by the Archdiocese of Ohrid. The Greek incumbents were replaced by Sava's Serbian bishops. Other disciples were ordained archpriests, acting as his "exarchs" or delegates. They were sent into the provinces to stamp out pagan traditions among the rustics.[54] Together with defending the Church from outside attack, he was busy building and adorning the majestic monastery church at Žiča, dedicated to Christ the Pantocrator. The Feast of Ascension was the day on which the monastery church celebrated.

In 1220, at Žiča, Saint Sava persuaded the Serbs that Stefan should receive the crown of kingship. The holy Sava maintained his father's policy of creating a viable Serbian state. As the archbishop performed the divine Liturgy, he consecrated, anointed, and crowned his brother, crying aloud, "Long life to Stefan, the first-crowned King of Serbia!" The following day,

---

[52] *Nomocanon* (*Krmčija* or *Kormčaja Kniga*, "Book of the Pilot").
[53] Ibid., p. 155.
[54] Domentijan, 243-245; Teodosije, 151; Obolensky, p. 156.

when the saint served Liturgy, he made more comprehensible to the people the word of the Gospel. He then exhorted King Stefan and the nobles to recite the Creed and pledge obedience to the canons of the holy Seven Œcumenical Synods and two local synods. All complied.

Circa 1220, Archbishop Sava, as a well-reputed diplomatist, persuaded King Andrew of Hungary not to attack Serbia. At the same time, Archbishop Demetrios Chomatianos of Ohrid, whose see lay in the principality of Epiros, challenged Sava as Nicaea's man. In a letter, he refused to recognize Sava's elevation to the episcopacy. He charged the holy man with luxurious living instead of showing stability on Athos. He also cited canons which, he believed, Sava broke. Though Chomatianos was civil to the patriarch, he was hostile to the Nicaean government throughout the 1220s. He questioned the legitimacy of Laskaris, though nearly every former Byzantine citizen, with the obvious exception of the Epirots, admitted that the empire, for the time being, was in Nicaea, until the Laskarids could regain their heritage, Constantinople. At length, the embroilment between the patriarchate, Chomatianos, and Sava gradually dissipated. The autocephaly of the Serbian Church was recognized by other Orthodox Churches.[55]

In 1228, King Stefan's health deteriorated. It was his desire to become a monk as his father and two brothers had done.[56] Nearing death, he called out for his brother Sava to come to Ras. However, the archbishop arrived too late, for Stefan already passed away. Sava then prayed to God to restore the soul of his brother that he might tonsure him and that his brother might name his successor. The Lord hearkened unto His faithful slave and returned the soul of Stefan. Stefan arose and spoke, naming Radoslav, his eldest son, as successor. The archbishop then garbed his brother with the Angelic Schema of the monks and changed his name to Simon.[57] The relics of the Monk Simon and first-crowned King of Serbia were laid to rest near his father Saint Symeon. The coronation of Radoslav was performed by Archbishop Sava at Žiča in 1228.

In 1230, Saint Sava resolved to make that long-desired pilgrimage to the holy land. Leaving his diocese in good order, he traveled southward.

---

[55] Obolensky, p. 161.

[56] Vukan, or the Monk Theodosios, took monastic vows. He was buried at Studenica beside his father. See Velimirović, p. 106. Thus, within the royal family, the youngest son, then mother and father, with two other sons, became monastics.

[57] Saint Stefan (in monasticism Simon) is commemorated by the holy Church on the 24th of September. Circa 1231, Saint Sava, at the annual memorial service for his brother, opened the tomb. The relics of the monk-king were found intact and fragrant, attesting to his sanctity. Saint Sava translated the relics to the Monastery at Žiča.

Visiting the Mountain again, he enjoyed the company of the fathers at his monastery. After a few days, he gathered all the brethren and told them of his great yearning to worship at the all-holy Tomb of our Lord. After he taught them and received their prayers, he set sail for Palestine. With God's help, he arrived within a few days. He was received by the Patriarch of Jerusalem, Athanasios II (1224-1236), who concelebrated with the saint that Sunday. The patriarch asked the archbishop to bless the people and preach unto them. The patriarch, clergy, and faithful possessed such love and reverence toward Sava that they did not want to be separated from him. Every day, they came to hear his soul-benefitting teachings.

Tricherousa

While the archbishop was in the holy land, with much devotion and compunction, he venerated all the churches, shrines, and sacred sites. The holy man bestowed many alms and worked charitable deeds in the holy land.[58] At the all-holy Sepulcher of the Lord, he shed an abundance of hot tears. The saint then left the holy city and went toward the Judaean Desert and the lavra of his namesake, Saint Savvas the Sanctified. In accordance with the prophecy of Saint Savvas the Sanctified, it was foretold that, in the distant future, his namesake, an archbishop of a western country, would come to the monastery. Saint Savvas the Sanctified had bequeathed his staff and two precious icons of the Theotokos, known as "The Theotokos of the Three Hands" (Tricherousa)[59] and "The Milk Giver." Thus, Archbishop Sava of Serbia received these precious gifts.

Afterward, the saint left the holy land and entered a ship bound for Nicaea. Emperor Theodore and Patriarch Michael had reposed. The new

---

[58] Of his many benefactions and charitable works, Saint Sava bought the Latin-held Church of Saint George at Acre, belonging to the Monastery of Saint Savvas the Sanctified. In Jerusalem, the saint bought, after expending a great deal of gold, the Islamic-held Upper Room wherein our Savior celebrated the Mystical Supper. See Velimirović, p. 110.

[59] The Theotokos icon, known as "She Who Has Three Hands," now hangs behind the abbot's throne at Hilandar. This is the icon before which Saint John of Damascus prayed when his hand was severed upon the instigation of the notorious iconoclast Leo; the hand was miraculously restored. In honor of this restoration, Saint John fashioned a hand to the icon, as a votive offering of thanks to the Theotokos. See the Life of Saint John of Damascus, commemorated by the holy Church on the 4th of December.

emperor, Theodore's son-in-law, was John Doukas Vatatzes (1222-1254).[60] When John succeeded him to the imperial throne, he was an ardent protector of all victims of wrongdoing, a bastion of justice, and a fount of mercy, so that he was surnamed "the merciful." Likewise, he was a zealot of piety and Orthodoxy, and was the cause of many Jews receiving holy Baptism during his reign. Having a desire to unite east and west, he called for a dialogue. Pope Gregory IX (1227-1241) sent legates to a meeting presided over by Germanos the New, Patriarch of Constantinople (1223-1240). Peace between the groups was thwarted when the westerners refused to remove the addition of the Filioque from the Symbol of the Faith.

Vatatzes rejoiced at beholding Saint Sava, and received him with exceeding reverence and honor. He glorified God that he was able to receive his blessing. His wife, the Empress Irene Laskaris, also reverenced the elder. Thereupon, the royal couple named Saint Sava their spiritual father. After the saint tarried a few days at Nicaea, he decided to go again to the Mountain. Since Sava was his spiritual father and distantly related, Vatatzes vouchsafed him a portion of the honorable Cross, other sacred relics, and precious vessels. Vatatzes then commanded that the archbishop be borne to his monastery by a royal ship. By divine help, Saint Sava arrived at Hilandar. He presented the honorable Cross with the other holy relics, and whatever else was bestowed by Vatatzes, to the brotherhood of the monastery.[61] He also brought the Icon of "The Theotokos of the Three Hands" and gave it to the brotherhood, to be regarded as the "Hegumene (Abbess) of Hilandar." After abiding there a sufficient time, he guided and instructed the fathers in a God-pleasing manner. Saint Sava appointed a virtuous monk as hegumen to shepherd the flock, and then returned to Serbia.

The holy man went to his jurisdiction, where he shepherded the flock in a God-pleasing fashion. He illuminated all of Serbia with the bright beams of his virtues and his divine teachings. He preserved and kept them unharmed from the noetic wolves, wisely directing them into the heavenly sheepfold. However, since that area of the Balkans was so riddled with heresies, the saint entered into other provinces where he taught them apostolically. Going from place to place, he led both the heretics and impious to true piety.

---

[60] Saint John is commemorated by the holy Church on the 4th of November.

[61] Among the treasures at Hilandar, there are two crosses incorporating fragments of the true Cross, a gift of the Emperor John III Vatatzes, and another cross studded with precious stones. The first is a silver and gilded cross with precious stones; the other is an ancient Byzantine cross with transparent gems within which are seen icons of the Lord and the Theotokos. Also from our Lord's Passion, Hilandar possesses tiny slivers of the relics of the crown of thorns, the reed, and the shroud.

However, Serbia and the Balkans were changing, and a new generation came into power. King Radoslav, brought up by his Greek mother Evdokia, married a Greek princess, Anna Doukas, daughter of Prince Theodore Komnenos Doukas Angelos of Epiros, in 1228.[62] The people despised both him and his wife. Therefore, when his father-in-law was taken prisoner and blinded by Asen II, the royal couple fled. After his wife abandoned him, Radoslav sought his uncle's help. Archbishop Sava made him a monk, and Radoslav took the name of John.

Now the former King Stefan, the first-crowned, also had three other sons, Vladislav, Uroš,[63] and Predislav.[64] Hence, with Radoslav out of the country, the group around Vladislav desired to make him king. Though the saint was far from enthusiastic about Vladislav becoming king, he desired to preserve the unity of his nation; therefore, he crowned his nephew. A marriage between Vladislav and the daughter of Asen II, Bjeloslava, was also arranged.

In 1234, Saint Sava was again contemplating resigning and making a second pilgrimage to the holy land. He also desired to select a successor. Enlightened by God, he selected Arsenije, a worthy priest-monk and ecclesiarch whom Sava had trained from his novitiate at Žiča. Archbishop Arsenije would shepherd the flock in a wise and God-fearing manner for the next thirty years.

Thereafter, the saint entered a vessel bound for the holy land. When his ship experienced a raging storm at sea, the saint prayed and, making the sign of the Cross, he commanded aloud in the name of Jesus that the winds and sea be calm. God hearkened to his request, and therefore they were able to sail without incident to Acre in Palestine. Upon arriving in the holy land, the saint, for a second time, worshipped at the Holy Sepulcher. Whatever cities the saint passed through, he taught and strengthened the Christians there through many miracles. Once again, he bestowed alms upon the poor and those in need. However, for the sake of brevity, we cannot narrate the miracles that he wrought.

---

[62] After conquering Thessalonike (1224), Adrianople (1225), and Thrace, and taking them from the Latins, Theodore Angelos was crowned as emperor by Archbishop Homatijan of Ohrid, an enemy of Saint Sava who desired to be patriarch. Theodore would have gone on to take Constantinople, but, in the battle of Klokotnica (1230), he was defeated and captured by the Bulgarian tsar, John Asen II (1218-1241), who allowed the Bulgarian Church to remain under papal auspices.

[63] Stefan Uroš would succeed to his deposed brother Vladislav's throne and become King of Serbia from 1243-1276.

[64] Predislav took monastic vows and, at length, became Archbishop Sava II of Serbia.

The saint also visited the Patriarch of Alexandria, who received him as a brother. While the saint was in Egypt, he visited all the important churches and bestowed alms and gifts among the poor. The saint also made a pilgrimage to Sinai and Saint Katherine's Monastery. After he had dwelt there for a short time, he left a large sum of money. Afterward, the saint again went through Jerusalem and then on to Baghdad, Antioch, and Armenia, leaving gifts at the monasteries. From there, he passed through the dangerous territories of Kurdistan and of the Seljuk Turks.

Finally, the saint and his entourage set sail for Nicaea. The sea passage proved difficult for Saint Sava, who suffered from seasickness and physical exhaustion. Finally, they were received by Emperor John Vatatzes and the empress. Again, the holy man preached in the Nicaean churches and bestowed alms upon the poor. He persuaded both emperor and patriarch to agree to recognize the Bulgarian patriarch.[65] Moreover, he pleaded for the pardon of King Asen who, previously, turned to Roman Catholicism, but later abjured his apostasy.

The last country that Saint Sava would travel through was Bulgaria. When he landed at Mesembria, the Nesebŭr promontory in the Black Sea, King Asen sent servants and horses to escort the Serbian party to Tŭrnovo (Türnovo), the royal capital. Upon their arriving in the capital, Sava and his entourage were greeted warmly by Asen and Patriarch Joachim. The archbishop was quick to inform them of the willingness of the Nicaeans to grant amnesty to Asen and recognize the Bulgarian patriarchate. Saint Sava also gave them rich ecclesiastical presents from the east. The holy man was rendered exceeding honor and genuine love by the Bulgarians. As the saint tarried among them, he wrought no small benefit among the people through his gifts and charities.

While the saint was at Tŭrnovo, the Feast of the Theophany was approaching. Asen requested that the archbishop serve and bless the waters. While the saint chanted the Service for the Great Blessing of Waters, the following miracle took place. As he immersed the honorable cross, the waters divided in the midst and stood as a wall on the right hand and a wall on the

---

[65] When John Asen II sought patriarchal status for the Bulgarian Church, he turned to John III Vatatzes, the Nicaean emperor. The latter was willing to arrange this in return for a joint undertaking against the Latins of Constantinople. The alliance was sealed with the marriage of Asen's daughter, Helena, to Theodore II Laskaris, heir to the Nicaean throne. As a result, the Bulgarian Church was duly accorded patriarchal rank by a Church council meeting at Kallipolis (1235). *Oxford*, s.v. "John Asen II."

left.[66] All the spectators who beheld this phenomenon glorified God. The king greatly revered the saint and besought him to tarry there until Pascha, though he would be busy elsewhere with some other matters.

Saint Sava indeed remained, but, after a few days, he fell ill. Foreknowing his repose, he summoned his disciples and instructed them toward salvation. He placed in their care what he had stored up and brought back from the east, including whatever holy relics and other sacred ecclesiastical vessels that he possessed. He then bade them to return to Serbia with the goods for the Serbian churches, King Vladislav, and Archbishop Arsenije.

When the hierarch of Tŭrnovo heard of the saint's illness, he went to see him. Beholding the severity of his sickness, Joachim wished to send a message to King Asen. However, the saint would not permit it but said, "O brother, I beseech thee, neither inform the king nor trouble thy holiness to come here; only go in peace and pray on my behalf that the merciful God bring us together in the upper Jerusalem." Saturday evening, the saint communicated the undefiled Mysteries. His face then shone brightly, and he was filled with gladness and rejoicing. Then he uttered thrice: "Glory to Thee, O God." Afterward, he surrendered his holy soul into the hands of God on the 14th day of January, in the year 1235.

In the morning, as the hierarch, clergy, and people prepared to bury his relics, they perceived an indescribable fragrance. All marvelled and were at a loss where to inter him. Though the king was absent, when he was informed of their quandary, he ordered the interment of the holy one's relics at his own monastery Church of the Forty Martyrs in Tŭrnovo. Thereupon, they buried him there with all due reverence. A few days later, Asen arrived and first went to the tomb of the saint. He placed there a beautiful marble top and an oil lamp, and commanded that it always be lit. God also glorified His servant, when those who suffered from diverse infirmities hastened with faith to his tomb and were vouchsafed cures.

When King Vladislav of Serbia, the son-in-law of Asen, and Archbishop Arsenije, whom the saint ordained his successor, learned of the saint's repose, they sorrowed exceedingly. Yet, when they heard of the miracles worked by the saint, they decided to seek his sacred relics. Therefore Vladislav wrote a letter to his father-in-law, beseeching him to return his saintly uncle to Serbia. Vladislav had his epistle delivered by several Serbian noblemen, so they might take up the relics. However, Asen would not release the relics. Vladislav wrote a second time, imploring Asen for the relics. This time he sent even higher-ranking officials, bearing great gifts. Again, Asen refused and simply answered, "Since the good God, in His œconomy, has

---

[66] Cf. Ex. 14:21, 22.

permitted the saint to repose here, it means that He has granted us this treasure; and, therefore, who am I to oppose the will of the Lord?" Therefore, he sent back the nobles, who failed in their mission.

Then Vladislav took his most select nobles and functionaries and went himself to seek the relics of the saint. When they arrived in Bulgaria, Vladislav first went to the tomb of the saint. He wept warm tears, saying, "O saint of God and most revered father of ours, why hast thou loathed us sinners and dost not wish to come to thy homeland where thou hast stood not only as shepherd, but savior also? Thou hast delivered us from the error of the devil and hast directed us to the truth. Thou hast freed thy flock from heresies. Thou hast healed the sick; thou hast delivered us from spiritual death; those in peril hast thou raised up; thou hast adorned the Church with spiritual services, with sacred order, and given laws that were soul-saving.[67] Therefore, how shalt thou leave us now, O holy one, bereft of the sanctity of thy divine relics? How shalt thou leave us in utter want of the never-emptying treasure of thy divine grace? Shall we waste and pine away, deprived as we are of the sweet fountain of thy wonders? Let it not be, O father, most compassionate! Pity me and overlook my iniquities and those of thy people who have failed thee;[68] and come unto us, though we be unworthy and sinners; and leave us not bereft of thy presence and protection."

Having prayed thus, Vladislav, afterward, went to his father-in-law. That night, Asen beheld a vision wherein he saw the saint as a lightning-like angel. Saint Sava then commanded Asen to give his relics to his son-in-law to take back to his country. In the morning, King Asen gathered the people, the clergy, and the metropolitan, and revealed what had taken place. Taking his son-in-law, they went chanting, bearing candles and incense, to open the tomb of the saint. O Thy wonders, Christ King! The entire area was filled with an ineffable fragrance. The saint's face shone as the sun. All marvelled and cried aloud, "Lord, have mercy!" Then, making a great procession and offering up supplicatory prayers, the two kings walked and bore the relics outside of Tŭrnovo. Vladislav, sensing tremendous joy that day, continued toward Serbia. As they proceeded, thousands flocked to pay their respects.

To confirm the reconciliation between him and his holy uncle, Vladislav had the relics of Saint Sava interred at a church the king built in

---

[67] Saint Sava edited monastic *typika*, liturgical texts, and the Serbian *Nomocanon* (compilations of secular laws and ecclesiastical regulations).

[68] Bishop Nikolai Velimirović (p. 150) suggests that King Vladislav feared the growing consternation of his people who blamed him for making Archbishop Sava leave Serbia. Vladislav grieved the saint by creating havoc in the royal family through his intrigues and the overthrow of his elder brother, the former King Radoslav.

Hercegovina, called Mileŝovo (Mileŝeva) in the valley of the Lim in western
Serbia, dedicated to the Pantocrator.[69] At Mileŝovo, the precious and august
relics were a source of countless cures, both physical and spiritual, for those
that flocked there in faith, to the glory of Father, Son and Holy Spirit, the
All-Holy Trinity, to Whom is due dominion, honor, and worship unto the
ages of ages. Amen.

Hilandar Monastery

By the early thirteenth century, Hilandar was inhabited by ninety
monks. The monastery prospered for centuries, receiving colossal contributions from Serbian rulers. Stefan Uroŝ II Milutin (1282-1321) sought the
support of the Church by founding many monasteries and making generous
donations to them. Among the fifteen churches and monastic buildings he
assisted, in 1303, he replaced the late twelfth century katholikon at Hilandar
with a new triconch church with narthex. He also restored the refectory and
strengthened Hilandar's fortifications by adding a tower (Tower of Milutin)
at the harbor. Originally, the holy Saint Symeon (Nemanja) endowed Hilandar
with fifteen Serbian villages. Thus, the monastery became exceedingly
wealthy and, by the mid-fourteenth century, owned one-fifth of the Athonite
peninsula, plus lands from Macedonia to Serbia, totalling 360 villages or parts
of villages! Saint Symeon and Saint Sava also obtained Zig and Prosphora,
which they restored. Later, they acquired Saint Basil (Hrusia), Strovilaia,
Komitissa, Paparnikion, Kalyvae, and Omologiton. They made sure there
would be no problem in supporting Serbian monks. Other benefactors
included Palaiologan emperors and Stefan IV Duŝan (1345-1355). Prince
Lazar Hrebeljanovich (d. 1389) also provided assistance, as did his son Stefan
Lazarevich (d. 1427).[70]

---

[69] After the conquest by the Turks, the Ottomans tolerated for more than a hundred
years the following of faithful who were dedicated to Saint Sava, whom even the local
Turkish population came to revere. On the 27th of April, in the year 1595, by order of
the grand vizier Koca Sinan Pasha, the relics of Saint Sava were taken to Belgrade,
and his wooden reliquary burned on a pyre. A huge flame that soared into the heavens
illumined the city by night and could be seen from beyond the Danube. Ibid., p. 159;
Obolensky, p. 171.

[70] In the 15th C., help came from the Brankovi dynasty. Due to the lavish donations of
Mara Brankovi, wife of Sultan Murat, the monastery was always filled with Serbian
monks. The monastery was completely independent of the authority of both the
Byzantine emperor and the *protos* of Athos. Ofttimes, Hilandar's hegumen became
Archbishop of Serbia. During the Turkish occupation on Athos, Hilandar received
support from the Ukraine, Russia, and Moldavo-Wallachia (present-day Romania), and
from enslaved Serbia.

(continued...)

On the 14th of January, the holy Church commemorates our holy Mother NINA, Equal-to-the Apostles, Enlightener of Georgia.[71]

[70](...continued)

The monastery was the chief religious center for the Serbian nation. When Serbian monks achieved a reputation for wisdom and learning, they were also ordained as patriarchs, archbishops, and bishops for the Serbian Church. Many books were translated or written in Slavonic. The Serbian variant of Old Church Slavonic was developed at Hilandar, which housed a scriptorium, a center for translation, and a bilingual library. Most of the approximately one thousand two hundred manuscripts at Hilandar are in Slavonic.

During the Ottoman occupation, Hilandar continued to thrive, owing to the beneficence of the Russian tsars and rulers of the lower Danube countries. The Serbs flocked not only to Hilandar, but to the other Athonite monasteries as well; therefore, during this period, it was not unusual to find a Serb as *protos* of the Mountain.

In the 17th C. and, especially after 1675, when the Serbian patriarchate was abolished and the Serbian Church was placed under the œcumenical patriarchate (Constantinople), Hilandar declined. At one point, Hilandar was largely occupied by Bulgarians. This occurred when Serbs migrated north or, worse, converted to Islam. In 1722 and 1891, Hilandar suffered two fires from which it recovered. By the end of the 18th C., the font, with a dome supported on eight columns, was built in the center of the courtyard.

In 1896, when King Alexander I Obrenovich of Serbia visited the monastery, he was moved by God to buy back the monastery from the Bulgarians and provide funds for rebuilding. More important, he sent Serbian monks to live at Hilandar that the monastery might again come into Serbian control. With the liberation of Macedonia in 1912, when the *protos* was a Serb, the monks of Hilandar led the efforts of the Holy Mountain for it to be included in the area under Greek sovereignty. Moreover, during the Second World War, the Serbs at Hilandar were on the side of the Greeks against the occupying Axis forces.

The monastery's sacred treasures include two crosses embodying the true Cross, articles from our Lord's Passion, part of Prophet Esaias' skull, Saint Panteleimon's right foot, part of Saint Nikephoros the patriarch's right hand, and relics of Saints Barbara and Katherine, and many others. Of the famous icons, Hilandar possesses Tricherousa, Papadiki, Galaktotrofousa, and Akathistou, each with its own story of derivation.

Today, Hilandar has thirteen small chapels, of which eleven are found within the monastery walls. After Great Lavra, it is the monastery with the largest land holdings on the Mountain. From its foundation, Hilandar has occupied fourth place in the hierarchical order of Mount Athos. See Kadas, p. 58; *Oxford*, s.v. "Hilandar"; Christou, pp. 76-80; Simonopetritis, p. 60.

[71] The Life of this saint was taken from two Greek pamphlets: "The Life of the Holy and Equal-to-the-apostles Nina, Enlightener of Iberia-Georgia," published by

(continued...)

Nina (better known in Georgia as Nino), our holy mother, and her mission among the Georgians, also known as the Iberians, were foretold on the day of Pentecost. This land today is situated in western Transcaucasia, bounded by the Black Sea, Azerbaijan, Armenia, and Turkey.[72] According to

---

[71](...continued)
Hieromonk Efthymios of the Kellion of Saint George Kerasia (Holy Mountain Athos, 1987), which text originally was translated into Greek from the original Russian publication of the Holy Monastery of Panteleimon, Holy Mountain, printed in Moscow in 1900; and, "Saint Nina, Equal-to-the-apostles," published by the Holy Monastery of the Paraclete (Attike, 1999). The Life of the saint, together with notes, is also discussed briefly in *The Great Synaxaristes* (in English), under the date of the 27th of October, in a narration concerning the Iberians.

Recensions of the Life of Saint Nina (Nino) reached the west ca. 395 when Tyrannius Rufinus met in Palestine the Georgian Prince Bakar (Bakur), the former hostage at Rome, and heard the story of the saint. Rufinus' narrative in his Church chronicle [*Historia Ecclesiastica*, composed as early as ca. 403] was copied by Sozomen, Socrates of Constantinople, and Theodoret [*The Ecclesiastical History*, Bk. I, Ch. 23]. It was translated early, often with additions and alterations, into Greek, Syriac, Armenian, Coptic, Arabic, and Ethiopic. While there was certainly a strong oral tradition about the saint in Georgia, it was not until the 10th or 11th C. that the Georgian biographies took shape. Rufinus' work probably was not known in Georgia until the 11th C., through Ephraim the Younger's translation of Theodoret. A discovery was made recently which may further contribute to Georgian hagiography. In 1975, after a fire was put out at Saint Katherine's Monastery on Mount Sinai, an account of the life of this saint was discovered in an ancient manuscript [Sin-48] of Georgian composition, entitled "The Conversion of Georgia." Nina is the popular Western version of Saint Nino, the Georgian form of her name used in most of the literature about her. Butler's *Lives of the Saints* includes a note that the Roman Martyrology called her "Christiana" because her name was unknown. It mentions also that in Egypt she was sometimes known as "Theognosta" ("Known to God"), which Butler supposes arose from a misunderstanding of the Greek text of Rufinus, who does not record the saint's name. In the footnotes of Theodoret's *The Ecclesiastical History*, there is speculation that "Nina" is a title for a rank of a nun, because Moses of Chorene gives her the name Nunia.

[72] The modern term "Georgia" refers to two areas: eastern Georgia (K'art'li, Gr. Iberia, Arm. Virk', Pers. Gurgan) and western Georgia (Gr. Colchis, later Lazika; Georg. Egrisi, later Abchasia). These were united politically in Byzantine times only in the years 978-1258 and 1330-1491, but had a common language and similar social structure. King Mirian converted to Christianity in the 330s. There were Christian settlements on the Black Sea coast by the 4th C. Western Georgia accepted Christianity in the same century, but as in Armenia, the populace was not fully converted until much later. *Oxford*, s.v. "Georgia."

Georgian tradition, the Apostle Andrew first preached Christianity in those parts, leaving as his successor Saint Nina.[73]

The Lot of Iberia-Georgia Falls to the Mother of God

Св. Раб-

ноаn. Нина

Stephen the Hagiorite records the following narrative. After the descent of the Holy Spirit at Pentecost [Acts 2], the apostles cast lots that they might determine where each should go and preach the Gospel. The Virgin-Mother also requested a lot for herself, so that she might share in the preaching. Therefore, she said, "I, too, desire to take part in the preaching of the Gospel and wish to cast my lot with you to receive the land which God shall show." Then

Saint Nina

with fear and reverence, they cast for the Theotokos; and her lot fell on the Iberian land. The most pure Mother of God then joyfully accepted her lot.

After the day of Pentecost, the Theotokos was planning to set out for Iberia at once, but the Archangel Gabriel appeared to her, restraining her, saying, "Virgin Birth-giver of God, Jesus Christ Who was born of thee, thus commands: 'Thou shalt not depart from the land of Judaea, that is, Jerusalem. The place assigned as thy lot is not Iberia but Macedonia's peninsula, Mount Athos. After some time thou wilt have the work of preaching in the land to which God will guide thee. This place shall be greatly blessed and illuminated in the light of thy countenance.'" The archangel then revealed to her the following about the Iberian land: "The land which fell to thee will be enlightened in the latter days, by another woman, and thy dominion will be established there." These words were fulfilled three centuries later when the Virgin Mary sent Saint Nina, "Equal-to-the-apostles," whom she blessed and helped in proclaiming the Gospel to the Iberians.

---

[73]In Saint Nina's time, Western Georgia comprised the provinces of Colchis, Abchasia, and Lazika, which had been evangelized by missionaries in the Greek colonies along the Black Sea coast. The Synod of Nicaea (325) had been attended by bishops from Trebizond, the principal seaport of Lazika, and from Bichinta, the metropolitan see on the borders of Colchis and Abchasia. See D. M. Lang's *Lives and Legends of the Georgian Saints*, p. 13.

Saint Nina and Her Family

Nina, our holy mother, hailed from Cappadocia. She was the only daughter of pious parents. Her father, Zabulon, was a Roman general and a kinsman of Saint George the Great-martyr.[74] Zabulon originally came from Cappadocia, but was stationed in various places. Nina's mother, Susanna, was also from Cappadocia. Susanna's parents had reposed early and left two children, unprotected by human means. Susanna and her brother Juvenal decided to take the long journey to the holy land and Jerusalem. The two orphans found refuge in the Church of the Resurrection. At length, Juvenal was appointed as steward (*œconomos*) of the Holy Sepulcher of our Lord Jesus Christ. Susanna went into the service of the most pious Deaconess Niofora (Sara-Niofora) of Bethlehem.

Now before Zabulon married, he served under Maximian (306-308) at Rome. He quickly moved up the ranks and was appointed general. At that time, there was an insurrection among the Franks against Rome. The Franks crossed over the Alps and encamped by the river Po. Zabulon was commissioned to go out and meet the enemy. With the help of God, he vanquished them and took many prisoners, including the rebel king. While Maximian rewarded his general, he condemned to death the captives. In the meantime, the prisoners of war, before they were executed, asked Zabulon if they might receive holy Baptism. They came to believe in Christ, for they saw His great power working in the general. Zabulon not only had them baptized, but also secured their lives from the emperor. He then took the newly-illumined with him back into Cappadocia. Within ten days' time, the priests baptized the people of that place on the banks of the river Gantamar.

Zabulon then left the priests to minister to the people, while he went to venerate the shrines of the holy land. Zabulon also shared his wealth with the poor. While there, he became acquainted with Juvenal, former steward of the Holy Sepulcher in Jerusalem. It was also at that time that the Deaconess Sara-Niofora counseled Juvenal, who was then bishop, saying, "Give thy sister Susanna as wife to Zabulon. He is not only a glorious general, but also, and more importantly, he is a God-fearing man, who helped the Franks come to the knowledge of the Christ!" Juvenal was pleased with the deaconess' recommendation.[75] Therefore, the marriage between Zabulon and Susanna

---

[74] One old account records that Saint Nina was Saint George's cousin who suffered under Diocletian (284-305).

[75] Giving an exact date for Saint Nina's life proves interesting. One source records that her father served under Emperor Maximian (306-308) [Paraclete, p. 7], while some identify the patriarch as Juvenal (422-458) [Kerasia, p. 8]. The account also mentions

(continued...)

took place soon. The newlyweds decided to return to their homeland of Cappadocia.

This blessed couple gave birth to the blessed Nina, the enlightener of Georgia. When Nina was twelve years old, she accompanied her parents to the holy city of Jerusalem. Her father Zabulon, for the great love which he bore God, decided to become a monk. With the consent of his wife and with the blessing of the bishop, Zabulon took refuge in the wilderness of Jordan, where he remained concealed as a hermit. No one learned where he settled in the desert. His burial place was also unknown. When he bade farewell to his young daughter, it was a tearful parting. Zabulon commended her to the care of God, the Father and Protector of widows and orphans. Zabulon then said to Nina, "Fear nothing, my girl. Be emulating with much zeal the examples of Mary Magdalene and Mary the sister of Lazarus. If thou wilt love Christ as they did, then His grace shall never depart from thee."

Susanna took her daughter and went to her brother at the patriarchate in Jerusalem. Juvenal made Susanna a deaconess, and she served in the Church of the Resurrection. Her duties including ministering to the poor and giving assistance to women in need of help. Nina, for her rearing and education, was assigned to the pious Eldress Niofora, who knew well Christian truths. She continually taught Nina, who showed much zeal and obedience. Nina was intelligent, quick-witted, and attentive. After two years of study under Niofora's tutelage, the apt Nina, with the grace of God, was well versed in the doctrines and canons of the Faith. Diligent study of the sacred Scriptures on a daily basis bore much fruit.

The Question in Saint Nina's Mind Regarding the Tunic of the Lord

Nina's heart leaped with love and gratitude for Christ Who endured so many sufferings for the sake of man's salvation. With tears she read the Gospel accounts concerning the crucifixion of the Lord. Her thoughts would always become immersed in the question of our Lord's tunic.[76] She then asked her eldress, Niofora, "Where then is the garment of the Lord? Where is that

---

[75](...continued)
her acquaintance with the holy Virgin-martyrs Rhipsimia and Gaïane (d. ca. 312), commemorated by the holy Church on the 30th of September, who had been persecuted by Diocletian and were slain by Tiridates, Arsacid king of Armenia (ca. 298-ca. 330). In order to coincide with the traditional date that King Mirian (265-342) of Iberia was converted in the 330s by Saint Nina, the patriarchs of Jerusalem at that time would necessarily have been Imeneos (260-298), Zamvdas (298-300), Eerman (300-314), and Makarios I (314-333). If the name of Saint Nina's uncle Juvenal is correct, he either may have had a second name or alias which is unknown to us or may have been residing at Jerusalem as a bishop but not as patriarch of that see.

[76] Cf. Mt. 27:35; Mk. 15:24; Lk. 23:34; and Jn. 19:23.

earthly purple of the Son of God? It is impossible that such a sacred article should not be found somewhere in the earth!" Niofora answered, "I shall answer thee according to what tradition has bequeathed to us, which is that it is found in the city of Mtskheta (Mc'xet'a) of Iberia, which is northeast of Jerusalem. It was conveyed there by a rabbi of Mtskheta, one Elioz, who obtained it from the soldier who had won it by lot at the foot of the Cross.[77] The people of that land are known as the Kartvelians (Kartvelebi), whose neighbors include the Armenians and other tribes. The Kartvelians to this day remain in the darkness of idolatry." The words of the eldress entered the holy Nina's heart, where they were deeply engraved.

The Theotokos Gives Saint Nina Her Apostolic Mission to the Georgians

Day and night the holy maiden kept constant in fervent prayer to the most holy Theotokos, entreating her and saying, "Vouchsafe me, O Lady, that I might go to the Iberian land, that I might venerate thy beloved Son's tunic which thou didst fashion with thine own hands!" The Panagia or all-holy one heard the maiden's supplication and appeared to Nina in her sleep, saying, "Go to Iberia, since thou dost so desire it! Moreover, thou shalt preach the Gospel of Jesus Christ to the people who inhabit that land, for they are unenlightened. Christ shall grant thee an abundance of grace, and I shall also help thee." The humble Nina replied, "I am just a weak maiden. How can I be vouchsafed such an important ministry? How shall I perform such a great work?" The Theotokos answered, "Take this cross. It shall be a shield and guard against enemies both visible and invisible. Thou shalt raise up this saving sign of the Faith. By the power of the Cross, thou shalt lead the land of the Iberians to faith and belief in my beloved Son 'Who willeth all men to be saved and to come to a full knowledge of the truth [1 Tim. 2:4].'" When the holy maiden awakened from her sleep, she beheld that marvellous cross in her hands. Even as in the vision, it was fashioned from vine shoots. With tears, she began kissing the cross. She next cut a portion of her tresses and braided it to the cross.

Nina was then resolved to go and visit her uncle, Juvenal. She related in detail all that had transpired in the vision. When she recounted the holy command she received from the Theotokos to preach the Gospel in Iberia, the bishop discerned that this was truly God's will and His clear command. He did not hesitate in the least to give his blessing to the young maiden to march forward and struggle for the Gospel. When the proper time came for her departure, he led her before the holy altar. Placing his hand upon his niece's

---

[77] The soldiers did not wish to tear Jesus' tunic (χιτών), which "was seamless, woven from the top throughout," so they said, "Let us obtain it by lot for whom it shall be [cf. Jn. 19:23, 24; Lk. 23:34]."

head, he uttered the following prayer: "O Lord God and our Savior, into Thy hands I commend this orphaned maiden and send her forth to the service of Thy divine preaching. In Thy good pleasure, O Christ, wheresoever her lips should proclaim the Gospel of Thy holy name, do Thou be her guide and protector. Give her to know what to speak. May the words be filled with Thy power and wisdom, so that none may be able to resist or gainsay them. And do thou, O Panagia, Virgin-Theotokos, the help and succor of all the Christians, aid Nina whom thou hast chosen to preach the good tidings of thy Son, our Christ and God, to the idolatrous peoples. Endow this maiden with thy strength and firmness against enemies both visible and invisible. Become for her always a shelter and invincible champion. Do not deprive her of thine assistance, until she should fulfill thy holy will."

Saint Nina Accompanies Saint Rhipsimia

Now during that time, more than thirty[78] nuns were fleeing persecution from Diocletian, who sought to marry the beauteous Nun Rhipsimia. The consecrated women had originally left Rome, under the leadership of their spiritual Mother Gaïane. They departed to make a pilgrimage from Ephesus to the holy land, before they entered their final destination of Armenia, at Ararat. Saint Nina accompanied them, until they came to the capital of Armenia, Vagarshapat. The account of the sufferings and terrible mutilations of the nuns is given fully under the date of their commemoration, the 30th of September. As a result of their sacrifice, the land of Armenia was converted to Christianity.

Now Saint Nina was the only one in their company who was miraculously preserved from the pagan executioners. With the help of God, she was guided by an invisible hand and hid inside the branches of a wild rose bush which had not yet budded. From that position, she witnessed the terrifying martyrdoms of the other women. She raised her eyes heavenward and prayed fervently on their behalf. An angel clad in a shining white orarion, like a deacon's stole, and a censer in his hand, was accompanied by a multitude of the heavenly host. Concurrently, the souls of the women martyrs were seen ascending from the earth, joining the choir of heavenly citizens, so that together they rose to the heavenly heights. Nina then cried aloud with tears, "Lord, Lord, why hast Thou left me alone in the midst of these vipers and serpents?" An angel answered and said, "Cease sorrowing. Be a little patient and thou shalt also be directed to the kingdom of the Lord of glory, whenever this wild rose bush should put forth fragrant and tender roses,

---

[78] There exists a discrepancy in the number of nuns; some give their number as high as fifty-three virgins.

which have been planted and cultivated in a garden. Now, however, rise and proceed to the north, where a great harvest awaits."

The saint walked for a long while, until she arrived at the banks of a great and unknown river by the village of Hertvisi (Khertvisi). This was the river Kura (Mtkvari), which waters central Georgia (Kartli), flowing from the west and then southeast up to the Caspian Sea. At that time, on the riverbank, there were some shepherds tending their sheep. She asked them for some food, because she was feeling exhausted and worn out. They gave her food, responding to her in the Armenian tongue. She understood them well, because she had been taught that language in the schoolroom of Eldress Niofora. She then asked, "Where might be found the city of Mtskheta? Is it far from here?" One of them replied, "Seest thou this river? On the banks of this river, a great distance off, lies the great city of Mtskheta, where our gods predominate and our kings reign."[79]

The Divine Vision and Message

Nina then continued walking further on that road. At one point the holy pilgrimess grew weary and stopped to rest for a minute. She sat down all alone on a rock and began reflecting on what she was doing. She said to herself, "Where is God taking me? What might be the fruits of my toils and sufferings? Am I laboring in vain with such a difficult mission?" Weighed down with all these thoughts, she fell asleep and beheld a vision. There appeared to her a majestic man. His hair spilled down to his shoulders. In his hands he was bearing a scroll. He unrolled it, and Greek letters could be discerned. He then handed the scroll to Nina and said to her, "Read this carefully!" Instantly he vanished, and the saint was awakened. She was astonished to see that in her hands was that mysterious scroll. Nina then began reading and saw that what followed were Gospel verses:

"Verily I say to you, wheresoever this Gospel shall be proclaimed in all the world, also what she did shall be spoken of for a memorial of her [Mt. 26:13].

"There is neither Jew nor Greek, there is neither slave nor free, there is neither male and female; for ye are all one in Christ Jesus [Gal. 3:28].

"Cease being frightened. Go and bring tidings to My brethren [Mt. 28:10].

"The one who receiveth you receiveth Me, and the one who receiveth Me receiveth the One Who sent Me forth [Mt. 10:40].

---

[79] Mtskheta, the ancient capital and ecclesiastical center of Georgia, is located twelve miles northwest of Tbilisi, at the confluence of the Mtkvari and Aragvi rivers. Towering above the town stands the Church of Djvari (Holy Cross), at the very site where Saint Nina first set up the cross over the Georgian land.

"I will give you a mouth and wisdom, which all those who oppose you shall not be able to contradict nor withstand [Lk. 21:15].

"And whenever they bring you in before the synagogues and the rulers and the authorities, cease being anxious how or what ye should speak in defense, or what ye should say; for the Holy Spirit shall teach you in the same hour what things it is needful to say [Lk. 12:11, 12].

"Do not become afraid because of those who kill the body, but are not able to kill the soul [Mt. 10:28].

"Go therefore and make disciples of all the nations, baptizing them in the name of the Father, and of the Son, and of the Holy Spirit, teaching them to observe all things whatsoever I commanded you; and behold, I am with you all the days until the completion of the age. Amen [Mt. 28:19, 20]."

The divine vision strengthened the saint who, with renewed zeal, continued her difficult journey. She was exceedingly tired from both hunger and thirst, together with suffering perils from wild animals. She finally arrived in the ancient Iberian city of Urbnisi. She tarried in the Hebrew quarter for one month, during which time she was offered hospitality in their homes, since she knew their language well. In the meantime, she learned the manners, customs, and language of the indigenous people who only now had become known to her.[80] The most-praised, Nina however, came to understand the language of tribes foreign to her, being given wisdom from the Holy Spirit, so that she might bring the people of that land to Christ.

The Entrance of the Saint into the Capital
and the Destruction of the Idols

After one month, the men of the city and those in the outlying districts were preparing to go to the capital of Mtskheta, that they might pay homage to their shamefully ridiculous and foul gods. Saint Nina also was borne along by the crowd. As she entered the city by the bridge Pobeev, she encountered the chariot of King Mirian (265-342)[81] and Queen Nana (Nanno). The royal couple were accompanied by a throng of people going to offer veneration to the soulless idol, named Armaz, which was set up opposite the city on a high

---

[80] According to tradition this city was build by Urblosa, son of Mtskhet, great-grandson of Japheth (2340 B.C.) [cf. Gen. 10:2; 1 Chr. 1:5].

"The Georgian language (with Mingrelian, Laz, and Svan) belongs to the southern Caucasian, or Kartvelian, group." *Oxford*, loc. cit.

[81] Contemporaneous with Iberia's conversion to Christianity was the inauguration of a new dynasty in eastern Georgia. The Iberian Arsacids had recently become extinct, and Mirian was the first ruler of the new Chosroid dynasty, who were themselves a branch of the Iranian Mihranids, one of the seven Great Houses of the Persian Empire. See D. M. Lang, *The Georgians*, p. 95.

mountain. Until the afternoon the sky was cloudless. This day was to be the last one of the domination of the idol in the Georgian land. With the arrival of Saint Nina, Christianity would dawn this day in Georgia. Nina was inside the press of people and was carried along to the mountain. Standing at a vantage point, she caught sight of the disgusting statue. It resembled a man of supernatural build and size. It was cast of gilded copper. The image was clad in a gold coat of mail and a gold helmet. One eye of the statute held a sapphire and the other a pearl. Both stones were of an extraordinary size and brilliantly shone forth. To the right of Armaz was a smaller idol of gold named Katsee (Gatsi), and to the left, a silver idol named Gaïm, both with human faces. The king, together with all his subjects, stood before these gods with mindless reverence and even trembling. The king was also frightened, believing that should anything go wrong he would be struck by the idol's sword. In the meantime, the pagan priests were preparing the sacrifice. When they finished setting up, they burnt the offering and shed blood. When this occurred, the trumpets and cymbals were sounded. This gave the signal for all, including the king, to fall down prostrate before the inanimate idols. As soon as they heard the sound of the instruments, they all fell on their faces to the ground.

Then the heart of the saint was kindled with the zeal of Prophet Elias. She sighed deeply, as tears streamed down her eyes that were looking heavenward. She then fervently prayed and said, "Almighty God: Bestow Thy mercy on this multitude of people that they may come to know Thee as the one and true God. Destroy and cause to vanish these idols, even as the air makes ashes and dust to disappear from the face of the earth. In Thy love for mankind, look upon these people whom Thy mighty right hand has fashioned and has honored with Thy divine image. Thou, O Lord, didst love Thy creation so much that Thou didst give Thine only-begotten Son for the salvation of those who had fallen. Do Thou deliver the souls of these people from the ruinous authority of the prince of darkness who, lest they should see the true path of salvation, has blinded their eyes. Do Thou, in Thy good pleasure, O Lord, grant that I might behold with my eyes the absolute destruction of these idols which stand here so proudly. Do Thou make it so that the people and all the ends of the earth might behold Thy salvation. May it be that the north and the south rejoice in Thee, and that they might venerate Thee as the one eternal God and Thine only-begotten Son, our Lord Jesus Christ, to Whom belongs eternal glory."

The saint had not yet finished her entreaty when suddenly black clouds appeared out of the west and began moving toward the multitude quickly, even as swiftly as the current of the river Kura. The king and the people perceived the danger and turned to flee. Nina did not run but hid herself in the cleft of a rock. A storm cloud burst with thunder and lightning over the city and the site of the idols. The images were consumed and turned to ashes. The walls of the idol temple were completely demolished. The resulting floods from the storm washed away into the river all trace of the temple and the idols. Saint Nina, protected by the right hand of God, remained unharmed in the cleft of the rock. She calmly observed from that concealed place the elements of nature rage around her. Then the sky cleared, and the sun shone radiantly. This event took place on the day that the holy Church commemorates the Feast of the glorious Transfiguration of the Lord, when the true light shone forth on Tabor. Now, for the first time, the true light shone forth on the mountains of Georgia. This would mark the change from idol-worshipping darkness to the light of Christ.

The following day, the king and the people set about in vain, trying to find their gods. When no one found any trace of the idols, each became frightened and was saying to one another, "Great is the god Armaz; but is there perhaps Another Who is greater than he and has overcome him? Is this not perhaps the God of the Christians Who dishonored and put to shame the gods of the Armenians and moved King Tiridates to become a Christian? But in Iberia-Georgia there is no one who has heard anything regarding the Christ. No one has proclaimed that the Christ is God above all the gods. What is this that has occurred to us? What else should we expect?"

Saint Nina at the Capital and the Beginning of the Miracles

Some time after the catastrophe that befell the idols, the saint went about the city of Mtskheta. She was as a pilgrim, though she called herself a captive. She was inspired to go directly to the imperial garden. There she encountered the gardener's wife, Anastasia. As though Nina were already known to her and she had been awaiting her arrival, Anastasia hastened to overtake her. She then reverenced Nina and brought her into her home. Anastasia washed Nina's feet and anointed her head with oil. She then set before her bread and wine. Anastasia and her husband both begged her to abide with them as a sister, since they were childless and sorrowed on account of their loneliness. Nina consented to the arrangement. At length, Anastasia's husband, in accordance with Nina's wishes, built a small cell for her in the corner of the garden. At the time of this writing, this had become a small chapel, dedicated to Saint Nina, in the enclosed area about a woman's monastery known as Samtavro. In that small cell, Nina placed the cross which had been given into her hands by the Theotokos. Nina spent her time in prayer and psalmody.

In that cell and from that corner in the garden began the illuminating struggles of Saint Nina and the miracles and wonders to the glory of Christ. The first members of the Church of Christ in Iberia were Anastasia and her husband, who received the slave of Christ and offered her shelter. By the prayers of Saint Nina, Anastasia was loosed from the bonds of childlessness. She was to become a mother of many children, beautiful to behold. She was the first believer before any of the other women or men of Iberia-Georgia.

On another occasion, a woman went about the streets of the city wailing and crying out. She was bearing in her arms her dying young son, appealing for help. Saint Nina took the child and laid him upon her bedding, which was put together with leaves. Nina then offered up prayer and placed the cross of vine shoots upon the boy. She then returned him to the mother well and cured.

The Commencement of the Divine Preaching

From that day, Nina began boldly and openly preaching the Gospel word. She invited the Iberians, both the idolaters and Jews, to come to repentance and believe in Christ. Her piety, righteousness, prudence, and pure manner of life were known to all, so that they willingly heeded her preaching. Many, especially among the Hebrew women, were ofttimes going to her that they might listen to her words and new teaching concerning the kingdom of God and everlasting salvation. As a result, many of them became secret Christians, among whom were Sidonia, the daughter, though some say the sister, of Abiathar, the high priest of the Jews in that land, together with six other Jewesses. At length, Abiathar himself came to believe in the Christ, upon hearing the explanations and interpretations of Saint Nina on the ancient prophets concerning Jesus Christ and how the prophecies were fulfilled in Him, as Messiah. "The law of Moses and the prophets," she concluded, "led to the Christ, Whom I preach." Abiathar concurred and confessed openly, saying, "This Jesus is the end and fulfillment of the law. Beginning with the creation of the world, this strange and wonderful woman has explained all to me, regarding how God prepared the salvation of men before the ages by means of the promised Messiah. This Jesus Christ, born seedlessly of a virgin, is truly the One Whom the prophets named. Our fathers, out of envy, raised Him upon a Cross and slew Him, but He arose and was taken into heaven and shall come again to earth in glory. He is the expectation of the nations and the glory of Israel.[82] The holy Nina has wrought signs and wonders before my very eyes, which only the power of God can work."

The Tradition Concerning the Tunic of the Lord

Saint Nina had many occasions to discuss spiritual matters with Abiathar. She even learned the following tradition of the Lord's garment from Abiathar, who said, "I heard from my parents, who heard from their parents and grandfathers, that when Herod reigned in Jerusalem, the Hebrews

---

[82] Gen. 49:10; Ezekiel, passim; Lk. 2:32.

inhabiting Mtskheta and all Kartli (a province of Georgia) received the news that Persian kings came to Jerusalem, conducting an investigation that they might locate a newborn Infant of the tribe of David, born of a mother without the seed of man, and named the King of the Jews. They found Him in Bethlehem, in the city of David, in a poor lodging [Mt. 2:11]. They offered Him royal gifts of gold and frankincense and myrrh. After they paid Him homage, they returned to their own land.

"After the passage of some thirty years, my great-grandfather Elioz received a letter from the high priest Annas which read: 'He, Whom the Persian kings came to render homage with their gifts, has come to a mature age. He preaches that He is the Christ, the Messiah and Son of God. Do come to Jerusalem that thou mightest behold His death, to which He shall be subject in accordance with the law of Moses.' When Elioz, together with a company of fellow travelers, was preparing to take the road to Jerusalem, then his mother, the godly Vasilissa, who was of the lineage of the high priest Elias, said to Elioz, 'My son, go forth in compliance with the royal invitation, but I beseech thee not to take part in the assembly of the impious against that One Whom they have resolved to put to death. He is the Logos of the prophets and the One spoken of by them. He is the Enigma of the wise. He is the Light of the nations [Lk. 2:32; Jn. 1:4] and the Eternal Life [1 Jn. 1:2; 5:20]. This is God's hidden Mystery, foreordained before the ages [1 Cor. 2:7].'

"Elioz then went in the company of Longinos the Karenikon. They entered Jerusalem and were present at the crucifixion of the Lord Christ. Vasilissa, who had remained in Mtskheta, on the eve of the passover suddenly heard within her heart the sound of the strokes of a hammer driving in nails. With a mighty voice, she cried out, 'Now is the kingdom of Israel lost, because they have delivered to death the Savior and Redeemer of their people. Moreover, this people is guilty of the blood of their Creator and Lord. O my misery! Why had I not died before this took place? Then I would not have heard that fearful hammering. There shall no longer appear on earth the glory of Israel.' Upon uttering these words, she then surrendered her soul.

"Elioz, who was at Golgotha, purchased the garment from the Roman soldier who had won the garment by lot, and returned with it to Mtskheta. Elioz understood that the clear perception of his mother had been made manifest before his own eyes at the Lord's crucifixion. When he was seen to arrive home safely, his sister, Sidonia, greeted her brother joyously. She then recounted to him the wondrous and sudden death of their mother and the words she uttered before her death. Elioz confirmed the words of his mother and showed Sidonia the Lord's tunic. Sidonia took the garment and soaked it with her tears. When she hugged it to her breast, she suddenly fell down dead. No human power was able to wrest that sacred garment from the hands of the deceased. At that time, even Aderkios (Aderc) the king and his court of nobles came that they might pay their respects to the maiden on account of her unexpected death. They too attempted to remove her hold on the garment, but were unable. Elioz then committed his sister to the earth. He buried her together with the garment, wrapped tight in her embrace. But the place of burial was kept secret, so that no one to this day knows the grave of Sidonia. According to the conjectures of many, in all probability, it is located in the midst of the royal garden. Since that time there has grown up a shady cedar at that place. Of its own accord, it was planted and increased; and to this day, the root and trunk are whole. Around that tree people have gathered, deeming that tree to be possessed of some great power. Beneath the cedar's roots, it is very probable that the grave of Sidonia is located. But again, we are not sure beyond a doubt."

After Nina learned this history, she began to go by night and pray under the shadow of the cedar tree. She was uncertain, however, whether or not the Lord's garment was hidden underneath. In that place, however, she was vouchsafed revealing visions that assured her that the spot was holy and would be glorified in the future. Then one night, as she was praying, at the completion of her midnight prayers, she beheld, from all the surrounding parts, hundreds of black birds enter the royal garden. She then observed that the flock flew to the river Aragvi, where they immersed and washed themselves in the waters. She then noticed that they rose up out of the waters and flew, but that they were as white as snow. The flocks then flew to the branches of the cedar and filled the garden with paradisiacal melodies. The vision was a clear sign that the neighboring nations would be illumined by the waters of holy Baptism. In the very place where the cedar stood there would be built a church to the everlasting glory of the almighty and true God.

Saint Nina also saw that the mountains Armaz and Zanten, which lay opposite to one another, shook and fell. At other times, she heard warlike shrieks and wild cries of the demons. They were uttering insults and blasphemies. They appeared in the form of Persian soldiers, who seemed to have fallen upon the capital. She then heard the terrifying cry of their king who gave orders that all be exterminated. The vision vanished the moment that Nina raised up the cross and then signed the air with it, saying, "Keep silence, O demons! The end of your authority is come. Behold the victor Christ!"

Queen Nana's Conversion

Saint Nina was assured by these signs that the kingdom of God and the salvation of the Iberians were nigh. She did not cease preaching the word of God to the people. In this holy labor, she toiled together with her disciples, especially Sidonia and her father Abiathar. He contended zealously for the sake of Christ against his old coreligionists, the Jews, so that he became the subject of persecutions at their hands and was even condemned to death by stoning. However, King Mirian intervened and delivered him from death. The same king kept pondering the Christian Faith within his own heart. He had learned that the neighboring Armenians had accepted this Faith, and also that the Roman Emperor Constantine I (306-337) had become a Christian. He had also been informed that Constantine had undertaken the protection of the Christians in neighboring Persia and elsewhere. By the name of Christ and the power of the Cross, the autocrat Constantine had vanquished his enemies. Now Mirian knew of the holy Nina's ministry and preaching of the Gospel of Christ. He in no wise impeded her freedom of speech to teach Christ in all the cities of his kingdom. Furthermore, Mirian's own son, Bakar (Bakur), was at Rome, as a kind of hostage or pledge, so he in no wise was about to harass the saint. Nevertheless, the king's consort, Queen Nana, a gravely ill woman, was harsh and a fanatical devotee of the inanimate idols. She had been responsible for the erection of the statue of the shameless Aphrodite in Iberia. She also condemned the Christians in a private capacity. But the grace of God which heals all sicknesses and weakness and fulfills all that is lacking, quickly cured even Nana of her disease.

This came about when Nana had become extremely ill. The greater the physicians' efforts to treat her and ward off death, the more her condition worsened. The women of her circle, recognizing the great peril, besought their queen to invite the pilgrimess Nina who, by means of prayer to her God, cured every sickness and weakness. The queen gave the order to have her brought. The saint, however, in order to prove the queen's faith and humility, replied to the messengers, "If the queen wishes to become well, let her come to me in this small chamber; and I believe that here she shall find healing through the power of Christ our God." The queen conformed and bade her servants to convey her on a litter to the holy woman's home. The queen was also escorted by her son Rev and a great company. When the royal party arrived, Nina bade those close to the queen to place her on the bed of leaves. Saint Nina then knelt down and offered up fervent prayer, entreating the Lord, the Physician of souls and bodies, to heal the queen. Then the saint took her cross and placed it on the head of the sick woman. She repeated this on the queen's feet, shoulders, and sides. Thus she traced over the queen the sign of the Cross. After this had been done, the queen rose up from that bed healthy. The queen then gave thanks to the Lord Jesus Christ and boldly confessed to Nina, the people, and then her husband, that Christ is true God. Nana made Nina her particular and trusted friend and her only confidante. Nana's soul was nourished with the holy words of Nina's instruction. The queen also had as her close adviser the wise elder Abiathar and his daughter Sidonia, from whom she learned much regarding the Faith and godliness.[83]

King Mirian Comes to the Knowledge of God

The queen then returned to the palace and excited the admiration of her consort by the suddenness of her cure. King Mirian, however, still would not confess Christ as God and Lord. On the contrary, he presented himself as a zealot of idolatry. On one occasion, he even planned to exterminate all those who confessed the Christ, including the holy Nina. Then the following incident occurred. A close kinsman of the Persian king, a Zoroastrian possessed of all kinds of learning, came to visit Mirian. It happened that the Persian guest fell victim to a severe demonic illness. Mirian became fearful that the Persian king might retaliate should his kinsman perish while his guest. Compelled to find a speedy solution, Mirian quickly sent a message that Nina come and cure the prince. Nina bade them to bring the ill man to the cedar, which was in the center of the royal garden. She positioned the sick prince so that he faced east with his hands raised toward heaven. She then commanded him to recite the following thrice: "I renounce thee, Satan, and join myself to Christ, the Son of God." After he uttered this thrice, he who was lorded over by that wicked spirit was convulsed and cast down to the ground as a dead man. But that foul spirit could not bear the prayers of the holy virgin, and so he departed from the sick man. The prince recovered, came to believe in Christ, and returned to his homeland as a Christian. This outcome caused more terror to Mirian than if the prince had died, for he feared that the Persian king, a fire-worshipper, would extract some terrible punishment for the conversion of his kinsman to the belief of Christ. Mirian then turned upon Nina and threatened her with death and all the Christians with annihilation.

Such were the evil thoughts which troubled the soul of Mirian. In such a spiritual state, he decided to divert himself with hunting in the forest known as Mukhrani (Georgian for "oak"). He was having a discussion with his hunting companions and said, "We have drawn down on ourselves the wrath of our gods, because we permit these Christian enchanters to run rampant in our land, proclaiming their Faith. But I shall soon cut them off. I shall put to the sword all those who venerate the Cross and the crucified One

---

[83] Upon her repose, the people honored their queen as a saint, commemorating her on the 1st of October. There may be found to this day, at Mtskheta in the Church of Samtavro, the graves of King Mirian and Queen Nana. King Mirian was interred by the southern corner of the pillar, in which there is a piece of the divinely raised pillar. The following year, Queen Nana reposed. She was buried on the west side of the pillar, close to her husband. After their repose, Mirian's son Bakar reigned and converted many of the Caucasian peoples.

on it. I shall even command the queen to renounce the Christ. Indeed, should she refuse, then I shall eliminate her with the rest of the Christians." The king then ascended to the summit of Mount Tkhoti. Then suddenly, that sunny day changed to unexpected darkness. A violent storm arose, much like that which occurred and destroyed the idol of Armaz. A flash of lightning blinded the eyes of the king. The frightening peals of thunder caused his hunting party to disperse. The king was left alone, and despaired. He called upon the help of his gods, but they were deaf to his prayer. Then the thought took hold of him that the living God was punishing him for his wicked disposition. Thereupon, he cried out with a great voice, "O God of Nina, lift the darkness from my eyes and I shall confess Thee and shall glorify Thy name!" The compassion of God was not slow to reveal itself to Mirian the supplicant. His sight returned, and the storm ceased. Mirian was astonished at the power of only invoking the name of Christ. The king then turned himself around and faced east. He raised his hands heavenward and with tears called upon God, saying, "O God, the One Whom Thy slave Nina proclaims, in truth Thou art the only God above all gods! Now I perceive, O God, Thy great mercy toward me. My heart feels thanksgiving, consolation, and Thy closeness to me, O most glorified One! On this spot I shall raise the tree of the Cross, and may it be an everlasting memorial and sign for that which has taken place for me."[84]

The king, his sight restored, then returned to the capital. As he walked the streets, the king thundered forth, "All people, give glory to the God of Nina, the Christ; for He is the God of the ages, and to Him solely belongs all glory unto the ages." The king was seeking the holy Nina and kept asking, "Where is that woman, the pilgrimess, whose God is my Redeemer?" Now at that moment, the saint was in her tiny habitation conducting her evening prayers. The queen in the meantime had come to meet her husband. Together they went to Nina's dwelling, followed by a multitude of people. After they came to the saint's cell and beheld her, the king dropped to his knees, saying, "My mother! Teach me to invoke the name of thy great God and my Savior." The saint, instead of giving voice to an answer, shed an abundance of tears from her joy. The king and queen, together with all those bystanders, also began weeping. Sidonia, who witnessed this event and recounted it later, would say, "Whensoever I bring to mind that moment, tears, without my wishing it, stream forth from my eyes. They are tears shed in joy." The conversion of the king to Christ was decisive and firm. Thus, Mirian was to Iberia what the autocrat Constantine was to Byzantium and Rome, and also what the Great Prince Vladimir was for the Russian land.

---

[84] At the summit of Mount Tkhoti there still stands, to this day (1904), a church built by Mirian.

King Mirian, a Fervent Laborer of the Gospel

The Lord chose Mirian to lead the people by the hand to salvation and the true Faith. Mirian then very soon dispatched envoys to Emperor Constantine, requesting that he send forth hierarchs and priests that the people might be baptized and taught the canons of the Faith and piety, for he desired that the holy Church of God should be planted and established in Iberia. Saint Nina also composed a letter to Empress Helen, Constantine's mother, recounting the miracles that had taken place and begging that priests be sent to baptize the newly converted people. Until the return of those envoys with clergy, Saint Nina, with tremendous zeal, untiringly preached to the people the Gospel of Jesus Christ. She showed them the true path for the salvation of souls. She revealed the inheritance of the kingdom of the heavens. Nina further catechized them by teaching them prayers to Christ. In this way, she prepared them in advance for holy Baptism.

The Raising of the Sacred Church and the Mysterious Cedar

The king desired, before the arrival of the priests, to build a church of God. He chose that place in the garden, indicated by Saint Nina, where stood the aforementioned cedar. Mirian then uttered, "Would to God that this perishable and temporal garden might be converted to one that is imperishable and spiritual, which would produce fruit for eternal life!" The cedar was then felled, and from it six branches were hewn into six columns. All six were set in their assigned places without the least difficulty. Now from the very trunk of the cedar, the builders fashioned a seventh column. When they attempted to raise and set it in its place, as the main support of the temple, all were amazed that by no exercise of strength was it possible to move it from its place. When the sun set, the distressed king went to his home crestfallen and bewildered. He kept pondering the dilemma and saying to himself, "What does this signify?" The people also were disappointed.

Now Saint Nina, together with twelve women from among her disciples, stood by a section of the construction site all that night. Her tears watered the tree stump. Then that morning, very early, there stood before her an extraordinary youth, girt with a fiery belt. He spoke to Nina secretly, whispering three mysterious words. When she heard them, she fell to the ground and venerated him. Afterward, the youth went to the trunk (the seventh column) and uprooted it. He then clasped it in his arms, lifting it with himself high into the air. That trunk shone forth as lightning and illumined the entire city. The king and the people gathered together quickly at that spot. All wondered and were in awe at such an unexpected appearance, thinking and saying, "How does that heavy trunk, with no one holding it, rise up so high? Why, if twelve men were to line up and stretch out their arms, that would be its height from the ground." Then they observed that the trunk began descending until it touched the stump from whence it sprouted. Then it was seen how the trunk finally rested in its place and stood immovable. From the root of the trunk there began gushing forth an aromatic and healing myrrh. Sick folk approached and received that medicinal ointment with faith, and they were all cured.

Then a Jew, a man born blind from birth, approached and touched the trunk. He immediately received his sight. He gave glory to God and came to believe in the Christ.

A child who had been gravely ill for seven years was brought by his mother to the life-bearing trunk. She besought Saint Nina to heal her son, and confessed her belief that Jesus Christ, of Whom Saint Nina preached, was true God. The saint stretched forth her hand to the life-bearing trunk and then placed her hand on the sick child, and he became well. The great press of people compelled the king to protect the column, so a special fence was built. Now from that time not only the Christians revered that spot, but also the idolaters. After this, the building of the first wooden church in Iberia was accomplished quickly. That church came to be dedicated to the Twelve Apostles, but also acquired the name of The Life-giving Pillar (Sveti-Tskho-veli).

The Arrival of Efstathios of Antioch and the Baptism of the Iberians

The envoys sent forth by Mirian to the emperor were received with great honor. On their return to Iberia they bore many gifts from Constantine. Empress Helen sent a letter of praise and encouragement to Nina. The emperor also sent Bishop Efstathios of Antioch (325-331, d. 337), commemorated by the holy Church on the 21st of February, who was noted as an ardent opposer of Arius at the First Synod of Nicaea (325). The embassy also included two priests and three deacons, carrying with them all the ecclesiastical vessels necessary to perform the Mysteries.

Not much time passed before Mirian dispatched orders to all provincial governors, military commanders, and courtiers, that they were to come to him in the capital. When they all assembled before the king, Mirian, before all those present, received holy Baptism. Next, the queen and their children received illumination. This took place at the bridge on the river Kura, where of old had been the house of the Hebrew Elioz, and later the house of idolatrous priests. The bishop then baptized the commanders of the army, the nobles and lords, so that the spot came to be named "The Font of the grandees" or "The place where the princes received Baptism" (Mtavarta sanitavi or Mtavart Sanatlo). Downstream from this place, two priests were baptizing the people who presented themselves for divine illumination with great enthusiasm and joy. This was due to their remembrance of the words of Saint Nina who told them that Jesus said that "unless one should be born of water and the Spirit [Jn. 3:5]," such a one could not behold life and light eternal, but rather that soul would come to perish in the darkness of Hades. Afterward, the priests went about the cities and villages, baptizing the people. In this manner, the country of the Kartvelians received Baptism in one year's time.

The Caucasian mountaineers were one exception, as they continued to abide in the darkness of idolatry. The Jews living in Mtskheta were the other exception, excluding of course Abiathar the high priest. Abiathar received holy Baptism, together with all those of his house. There were also another fifty Hebrew families who received the Mystery of divine illumination. According to tradition, it is said that they were descendants of the robber Barabbas.[85] As a token of his good will, Mirian gave them a special place, which is situated high above Mtskheta, called Tsichenteli. Thus, with the help of God, the word of the Gospel soon took hold in Iberia. In this work of God, Archbishop Efstathios toiled with Saint Nina for the enlightenment of all of Iberia. After the archbishop established the order for divine services in the Greek language, he consecrated the newly built church in Mtskheta. It was dedicated to the name of the Twelve Apostles, being modeled on the church in Constantinople. Efstathios then blessed the newly established Church, commending the faithful to the peace of Christ, and made plans to return to Antioch. He consecrated for the new Church the priest John, as Archbishop John I (335-363), who was dependent on the see of Antioch. He proved himself an excellent preacher and teacher to that nation of the knowledge of God. He wrought wonders and miracles, together with his teaching, and drew the people to the Faith of the Christ, baptizing them. Sacred churches were built in various places, and priests were ordained. Thus, at length, the Iberians received the knowledge of the true God.

King Mirian Sends Another Legation to Constantinople

During that time, Mirian sent another legation to Emperor Constantine, beseeching him to send forth to Iberia yet more priests that they might be able to bring all the people to the obedience of the word of salvation and open an entrance to all toward the blessed and everlasting kingdom of Christ. The king also requested that architects be sent to Iberia for the design and construction of stone churches.[86] Constantine, with holy love and joy, fulfilled the petition of Mirian. The emperor donated a part of the life-creating Cross, where Christ's feet had been nailed. Now the Cross had just been discovered

---

[85] Cf. Jn. 18:40; Mk. 15:7; Mt. 27; Lk. 23:18.
[86] Some maintain that Mirian himself eventually met with the great Constantine. They believe that Mirian also traveled to Jerusalem and asked for a place called Lot, where he then built a monastery to honor the precious Cross.

by Constantine's mother, Saint Helen (326). The emperor also entrusted Mirian's envoys with one of the nails by which the immaculate Lord's members were affixed to the Cross. Not only an enormous amount of gold and silver was sent, but also crosses, icons of the Savior Christ and the most holy Virgin Mary, and sacred relics of the holy martyrs for the consecration of churches. It was also at that time that Mirian's son, the hostage Bakar, was released from Rome and was free to return to his father.

An epistle from Emperor Constantine to King Mirian was also sent, which read: "I, the autocrat Constantine, who have become the servant of the heavenly King Who delivered me from the bonds of the devil, do now write to thee, King Mirian who, of late, even as myself, has been guided to the Faith. May joy and peace be with thee, even as with those who know the infinite God. It is no longer necessary to detain thy son as a hostage. It is sufficient for me that we have a common Master, the Christ, the Son of God. I therefore commit thy child into thy hands. Do thou take pleasure in him. May the angel of the peace of God be with thee! May God the Creator drive out for all time wicked Satan from thy land!"

Thereupon, the embassy returned to Iberia with a company of priests, architects, and master builders. The first church for which they laid the foundation was in the village of Erusheti (Eranset), on the border of Kartli, the embassy saving for that church the nail from the Lord's Cross.[87] They founded a second church in the village of Manglisi (Mangli), some fourteen kilometers from Tiflis, renamed, as in Georgian, Tbilisi, the chief town of Transcaucasia, situated on both banks of the Kura River.[88] It was there that they left the relic of the life-giving Cross, which we mentioned earlier. In Mtskheta, in accordance with the wish of King Mirian and the direction of Saint Nina, the foundations of a church were laid in the royal garden, close to the cell of Saint Nina. The church was fashioned from stone and dedicated to the glorious Transfiguration of the Lord. Saint Nina did not see the completion of this august church. She did not wish to countenance the glory and honor that was being accorded her, for she only desired the glorification of Christ's name.

Saint Nina took herself out of the populated city and repaired to the mountains, to the arid heights of Aragvi. There, with fasting and prayer, she prepared herself for new toils and sufferings for the sake of bringing the

---

[87] This nail, during the mid-13th C., was incorporated into the crown of an episcopal mitre, from King David of the 9th C. In 1781, the nail was brought to Moscow, where it was kept until the time of this writing (1904) in the Church of the Dormition.

[88] The foundation of Tiflis (41°41′N 44°48′E) dates from the 4th C. after Christ, but it succeeded Mtskheta as the capital of Iberia (eastern Georgia) in the 5th to 6th C.

Gospel to the neighboring provinces. As she wandered through the mountain, she discovered a small cave, camouflaged with tree branches. She settled herself therein, spending her time in tear-filled prayer. Water for her was miraculously made to gush forth from the barren rock of the cave. The spring that was created there, today only flows in drops of water, almost like tears, which is why it was called by the local population the "Spring of Tears." It is also known as the "Milk Spring," for the waters bring milk to mother's shriveled breasts.

The Vision of the Illumined Cross

At that time, the inhabitants of Mtskheta beheld a wondrous vision. They observed in the sky an illumined cross with a crown of stars shining upon the first-built church. With the arrival of dawn, the four most brilliant stars withdrew and went to different sides of the sky. One went to the east and the other to the west. The third star shone over the church, the bishop's residence, and the entire city. The fourth shone over the refuge of Saint Nina and rose to the summit of a crag on which was found a great tree. Neither Bishop John nor the king was able to interpret this vision. But Saint Nina bade them to cut down the tree and fashion four crosses from it. According to Saint Nina's command, the one cross was to be placed on the steep crag. Another cross was to be brought west of Mtskheta and set on Mount Tkhoti, where King Mirian was blinded and converted to the true God. A third cross was to be given to the king's daughter-in-law, Salome, the wife of Rev, that she might raise it up in the city of Udzarma.[89] The fourth cross was assigned to the village of Bodbi, in the Kakhetian domain of Queen Sophia (Sudzhi). To the last-named place, Nina, being filled with zeal, purposed to go quickly and convert it to the light of Jesus Christ.

The Saint Preaches the Gospel in Other Parts

Saint Nina took with her the Priest Iakovos and one deacon. She ascended the surrounding mountains, to the north of Mtskheta, by the upper regions of the Aragvi and Iori rivers and ravines of the Caucasus. In these places she continued proclaiming the Gospel to the mountaineers and highlanders. These wild inhabitants of Tsaleti, Ertso, and Tsoneti (Tioneti) bowed before the divine power of the Gospel word and the miracles which were wrought by the prayers of the holy announcer of the Gospel. Thereupon, they accepted the Gospel of the kingdom of the Christ, destroyed their idols, and received holy Baptism from the Presbyter Iakovos.

From these parts, Saint Nina went toward Kokabeti. She converted to the Faith of Jesus Christ all who dwelt there. Then she moved in a southerly direction toward Kakhetia, to the village of Bodbi, where she

---

[89] Udzarma or the ancient town of Ujarma, northwest of Patardzeuli.

settled. This was the last station. It was in this village that her holy struggles and earthly sojourn would be brought to a close. She built herself a hut on a mountainside, where she spent her days and nights in prayer before the precious cross. Her neighbors soon noticed her and gave her heed. They daily attended her that they might hear the sweetest teachings concerning the Christian Faith and the path of everlasting life.

At that time, Queen Sophia of Kakhetia lived at Bodbi. She heard of the curious preacher who had come into their midst. Sophia wished to hear the holy woman speak, so she went with a party of others. Not much time had passed before she perceived the divine grace of the preaching and no longer had any desire to depart. Shortly thereafter, the queen and all the courtiers, together with a multitude of people, received holy Baptism from Presbyter Iakovos.

The Repose of Saint Nina

After all these events took place in Kakhetia, which was the site of her final missionary labor in the land of Iberia, Saint Nina received a divine revelation of her approaching end. Concerning this, she informed King Mirian by letter. The saint invoked upon the king and his kingdom the blessings of God and the all-holy Virgin. She also supplicated God to send for their protection and fortification the invincible power of the Cross of the Lord. She also wrote: "As a pilgrimess and wayfarer on the earth, I am leaving this world and am going the way of my fathers. I beseech thee, O king, to ask Bishop John to come to me that he might prepare me for the everlasting course, because the day of my death approaches."

Queen Sophia herself delivered the message to Mirian. The king read the letter and informed the others. Thereupon, the king and all his court, together with the bishop with his sacred clergy, quickly set out and directed their steps that they might overtake the saint who was near death. They reached her and found her alive. The people had collected around her deathbed and were weeping. Many sick folk, after they approached and touched her bedding, received cures. On the last day of her earthly sojourn, her greatly grieving disciples asked that Saint Nina speak to them concerning her origin and life. It was Salome of Udzarma who recorded the narrative, which account herein is the basis of the life of this holy evangelist. The blessed Nina then said, "Let my insignificant and sluggish life be written down that it may be made known to your children. Let it be written so that your descendants may learn of your Faith and the love with which you encompassed me. Let it be written so that the divine signs which you beheld with your own eyes may be remembered." She then continued speaking of life eternal. Afterward, with much compunction, she communicated the Mysteries of Christ from the bishop. She then bade them to inter her body in that poor habitation where she was then sheltered, lest the newly planted Church of Kakhetia should remained orphaned. Then in peace, after years of serving an apostolic ministry, she surrendered her soul into the hands of God. Saint Nina reposed on the 14th day of January, in the year 338. She was sixty-seven years old. The king, bishop, and people mourned her passing and the deprivation of such a great light of faith and piety. They were then desirous to translate the precious relics of their teacher to the Cathedral of Mtskheta, so they might bury her by the life-bearing trunk of the cedar. But try as they might, they were unable to move the bier of the saint from the place which she chose for herself. For this reason, the body of this evangelist of Christ was buried in that poor habitation in the village of Bodbi.

In the year 342, King Mirian laid the foundation of a church at her grave. It would be dedicated to her kinsman, Saint George the Great-martyr. The church was completed by Mirian's son, King Bakar (342-364).[90] This church has been renovated many times over the centuries, but it was never destroyed and stands to this day (1904). Near this church, the metropolitan see of Bodbi was built, which is the oldest in all of Kakhetia. From that vantage point, the Gospel spread to the mountain regions of the eastern Caucasus. The all-good God glorified Saint Nina, preserving her body incorrupt. But the precious treasure remained hidden "under the bushel," in accordance with her command that the coffin remain sealed. After her repose, it was not the custom in Georgia to open the relics of the saints. Now signs and wonders took place without ceasing at her tomb. It was not only her supernatural miracles, but also the account of her angelic life and apostolic labors, which guided the newly established Church of Iberia to proclaim, with the blessing of the Antiochian Church, Saint Nina as the equal of the apostles and enlightener of Iberia. Thus, she was accounted worthy to be added to the choir of the saints and to have established in her honor the day of her repose as her feast day, the 14th of January.[91]

Thus, the Georgian Orthodox Church justifiably honors Saint Nina as an equal to the apostles, for she enlightened all of Georgia from her major

---

[90] Much later, a convent, dedicated to Saint Nina, was established in that place.

[91] Though we do not know exactly in which year this feast was first celebrated, it was undoubtedly very early, immediately after the blessed virgin's repose. In her honor, a church was built which stands to this day. It is a small stone structure, situated opposite Mtskheta, built by King Vakhtang Gorgaslani (446). It was in that location that the saint, by her prayer, demolished the idol of Armaz. Many Iberian monastic institutions were founded in her name. Her divine office was translated from Georgian into Slavonic by Metropolitan Isidore, which service was printed with the blessing of the Holy Synod of the Russian Church in 1860.

city to the most remote mountain region. She converted thousands of souls to Christ and holy Baptism. Hearken to the words of the Apostle Iakovos, who wrote: "Brethren, if any one among you should be led astray from the truth, and someone should turn him around, let him know that the one who turneth a sinner from the error of his way shall save a soul from death and shall cover a multitude of sins [Jas. 5:19, 20]." Prophet Jeremias also said, "Therefore thus saith the Lord, 'If thou wilt bring forth the precious from the worthless, thou shalt be as My mouth [Jer. 15:19].'" In view of this, then how much more is she worthy of honor who turned to God an entire nation from the destructive deceit of the idols to the true God and taught them how to worship properly? In truth, she showed herself to be as the mouth of God. Meet it is that she should be joined with all the saints in the kingdom of our Christ and God, to Whom, with the Father and the Holy Spirit, is due honor, glory, thanksgiving, and veneration, now and ever and to the ages of the ages. Amen.

Appendix I: Concerning the Tunic of the Lord

Concerning the tunic of the Lord, which Saint Nina was desirous of finding when she was in Jerusalem, the Georgian chronicles transmit little. According to the narration given, she undoubtedly discovered only its hiding place, that is, the tomb of the virgin Sidonia, with whom the tunic was buried. Although the cedar that grew above that grave was cut down by Saint Nina's command, the root remained intact, as did the grave and the garment of the Lord. It appears that the light-bearing man, who is mentioned as appearing to the saint while she was in prayer that night over the root, spoke three mysterious words. Although it is unknown what the divine messenger uttered, we still may presume from the saint's reaction that she never thought to cut the root of the cedar or open Sidonia's grave. The saint also did not continue her investigation or excavate another place.

On another occasion, King Mirian, who was saddened that his envoys had not returned to Mtskheta with the life-giving Cross and nail, but rather had chosen to leave these treasures for Manglisi and Erusheti, was comforted by the holy Nina who said, "Cease grieving, O king! It was necessary that it should be so. Thy kingdom's boundaries are protected by the power of the Cross of Christ, so that the Christian Faith may flourish. For us who are in the capital, grace is sufficient, for here lies the most precious tunic of the Lord." There, in Saint Nina's time, the presence of the Lord's garment was demonstrated by the flow of fragrant myrrh with healing properties. The

Catholicos (patriarch) of Georgia,[92] Nicholas I (1150-1160), renowned for his holy life, indicated that many had doubted the tradition of the tunic, because no one had excavated the site or seen the tunic. Nevertheless, he said that the flowing myrrh from the trunk and the miracles that resulted therefrom, before the eyes of all, were surety enough that these manifestations emanated from the tunic of the Lord. The miracles indeed were without number. Those who disbelieved and attempted to dig up the garment, met with death. The Catholicos Nicholas recalls how the Turkish sultan occupied Mtskheta, and that one of his wives, a curious woman, wished to open Sidonia's tomb. After she had done so, she fell down when flames leaped forth from around the stump. The grave-violating Tartars were also dealt blows by an invisible force.[93] Many witnessed these incidents. The myrrh only stopped flowing in the thirteenth century, at which time, by God's permission, the tunic was extracted from the earth. An unknown Georgian writer records: "This was a difficult period for Georgia. We suffered from the inroads of the barbarian hordes." The invasions of Transcaucasia by Genghis Khan of the Mongols (d. 1227), from 1220 onward, brought Georgia's golden age to an end. Later, Tamerlane or Timur (1334-1445) conquered Georgia in 1394. The writer continues and says, "Cities and churches were destroyed, and holy objects were desecrated. Nearly one hundred thousand people were utterly destroyed. Many of the Christians were forced to flee on foot. Some hid in the forests or mountain ravines. Observing the wretched end that awaited Mtskheta, one pious man, not wishing to leave behind the sacred treasure of the church to the demonic madness of the barbarians, offered up prayer to God and then opened the tomb of Sidonia. He took up the precious tunic of the Lord, which he then entrusted to a hierarch. Soon thereafter, the Cathedral of the Apostles at Mtskheta was demolished to its foundations."

    During that period, the Lord's tunic was kept in a special reliquary, until the rebuilding of the first solemn Church of Mtskheta, by Alexander I, who reigned in Georgia from 1514 to 1542. Afterward, the tunic was transferred to that cathedral, where it remained until the seventeenth century,

---

[92] The Catholicos-patriarch of Georgia was dependent on Antioch, probably until the 11th C. Over the years, the catholicate became part of the Russian Church. With the slaying of the tsar, the national church with the catholicos was established on the 18th of May, in the year 1918. With the Bolsheviks in power, the Church came under the control of Moscow, leading to the imprisonment of the catholicos and several of his bishops. The catholicos now has the title "Archbishop of Mtskheta and Tbilisi, Catholicos of All Iberia" and lives at Tbilisi.

[93] Catholicos Nicholas composed a service to honor the tunic of the Lord and the life-bearing trunk. Later this text was revised and edited by two of his successors, Bessarion and Anthony.

hidden in the church cross. By that time, the Moslem Turks had partitioned the country and persecuted the inhabitants. In 1578, the Turks overran all of Transcaucasia and seized Tbilisi. They were subsequently driven out by Shah Abbas I (r. 1587-1629), who deported many Georgian Christians to the distant regions of Iran. The shah, wishing to secure the friendship of the Russian imperial court, placed the Lord's tunic in a gold chest and sent it to Patriarch Philaret, who also happened to be the father of the reigning Tsar Michael Feodorivich. Both patriarch and tsar received this great gift with joy, more so than if they had received every earthly gift. The authenticity of the gift was verified by many miraculous healings. The command was then given that a special place be built in a corner within the Cathedral of the Dormition in Moscow to house the Lord's garment. This was done, and the relic was deposited therein. To this day (1904), not only is the tunic found at that shrine, but also miraculous cures are wrought. Patriarch Philaret then had established a feast day, the 10th of July, for the deposition of the Lord's garment.

Appendix II: Concerning the Cross of Saint Nina

The history of the cross of vine shoots, given to Saint Nina by the Theotokos, is also known. Until 458, the cross was kept in the cathedral church at Mtskheta. During the time when the Christians were persecuted by the fire-worshipers, a monk, named Father Andrew, took the holy cross from Mtskheta and conveyed it to the province of Taron of Armenia, since at that time the Georgians and Armenians were of one belief.[94] The cross was kept in the Church of the Holy Apostles, which is called by the Armenians Gazar-Bag, that is, "The Temple of Lazarus." Afterward, on account of persecution from the Persian Magians, who were exterminating anything Christian, the cross was taken south of Tbilisi and hidden at Armenian fortresses at Kapotsi, at Banai, at Kars, and the city of Ani. These movements took place up until the mid-1230s, when the queen of Georgia, Rusudan (Rousouda, d. 1237), and her bishop besought the Mongolian overlord Tsarmagan (Jamukha), who occupied Ani, that she might return the cross to Georgia from whence it came. Permission was granted, and the cross was placed at the Cathedral of Mtskheta. However, it remained there only for a short time. On account of the frenzied madness of the barbarians, it was necessary for the cross many

---

[94] In 505-506, at the Council of Duin, both the Georgians and Armenians rejected Chalcedon and went into the Monophysite camp. However, in 607, under Archbishop Kyrion I, the Armenians and Georgians split, and the Georgians returned to communion with the Greeks, which resulted in close contacts between Byzantium and Georgia, while relations with the Armenians were often strained. *Oxford*, s.v. "Georgia"; Lang, *Lives and Legends of the Georgian Saints*, p. 5.

times to be taken and hidden in the mountains. On one occasion it was taken to the Church of the Holy Trinity, which exists to this day on the small mountain of Kazbek, north of Tbilisi toward Chechnia. On another occasion, it was at Kastro Ananour in the old temple of the Theotokos.

In 1749, Metropolitan Romanos of Georgia fled from Georgia to Russia, secretly taking Saint Nina's cross and giving it to Queen Bakar Baktanovitch, who was then staying at Moscow. The cross then remained in the village of Liskovo for fifty years with princes from Georgia, who were the descendants of Baktan and had migrated to Russia in 1724. Prince George Alexandrovitch, the grandson of Bakar, in 1801, brought the cross of Nina to the autocrat Alexander Paulovitch, who thought it good at that time to return the great and holy treasure to Georgia. To this day, it is the symbol of the apostolic toils of Saint Nina.[95] The vine cross was deposited in a silver case at the Sion (Sioni) Cathedral of Tbilisi, next to the north pillar of the sanctuary. On top of the case may be seen engravings of scenes from the saint's life and miracles wrought by the cross.

<blockquote>
Through the intercessions of Thy Saints,
O Christ God, have mercy on us. Amen.
</blockquote>

---

[95] The faithful of the Georgian Church interpret, in a typological manner, the cross of vine shoots given to Saint Nina by the Theotokos at her commissioning. The grape vine, a multivalent symbol, is pictured in many Georgian icons, engravings, and frescos. Christ says, "I am the vine, the true one,...and ye are the branches [Jn. 15:1, 4, 5]." An example of Georgian symbolic thought is that the vine branch connects Saint Nina with the fruit-bearing vine of the Gospels. It is a symbol of evangelical teaching—the new wine. Furthermore, it refers to the Eucharist and the cup of martyrdom. In Georgia, a nation known for its vineyards, the vines extend to the mountaintops, symbolizing the enlightenment of their land. In addition, the Georgians believe that when Saint Nina wrapped her hair about the cross, it was a sign that she became a slave of God, and not of men, and that she would deny herself, offering her life in service to God.

**On the 15ᵗʰ of January,
the holy Church commemorates
our venerable Father
PAUL of Thebes.[1]**

Saint Paul

Paul, our venerable father, hailed from the Egyptian city of Thebes.[2] He lived during the time of Emperors Decius (251-253) and Valerian (253-259). He witnessed the fierce persecutions waged by Decius against the Christians. Since he feared an encounter with their punishments and torture, he began thinking about fleeing to a secret place. Saint Cyprian, in his *Letter 33*, remarks that the martyrs longed to be put to death, but were not permitted a swift one. The deaths contrived for the Christian martyrs in Egypt and the Thebaid were slow and cruel, for the cunning enemy was more keen to slay their souls than their flesh. Thus in those days men sought death and desired to die, but death fled from them [Rev. 9:6].

At the age of fifteen, Paul was orphaned and left as the heir to great wealth in the Lower Thebaid. He received a good education in both Greek and Egyptian letters. He possessed a deep love for God and a compassionate disposition. He had one sister who was married. Now his brother-in-law contrived to betray him to the pagan authorities that he might take charge of the paternal estate. Though the sister knew of her husband's plot, she could not dissuade him in spite of her tears and remonstrations. The brother-in-law

---

[1] The Life of this saint was recorded in Greek by Saint Symeon the Metaphrastes. The text is extant in the Athonite monasteries of the Great Lavra, Iveron, and in other places. The text was rendered in simpler Greek by Agapios the Cretan, who published it in his *Neon Paradeison*, which was included within the life of Saint Anthony, who is commemorated on the 17ᵗʰ of January. Blessed Jerome's well-known Latin version [*P.L.* 23:17] was translated from the Greek. Other versions are found in Syriac, Arabic, and Coptic manuscripts. The Greek original may have been written as a supplement to the Life of Saint Anthony the Great, by Saint Athanasios. Other English translations include those of H. Waddell's *The Desert Fathers*, pp. 29-39, and C. White's *Early Christian Lives*, pp. 75-84.

[2] Thebes, the former capital of ancient Egypt, became in the late Roman period the heart of monastic development and a center of settlements.

decided to carry out his crime. He went and betrayed Paul to the authorities. Though God Who looks down from on high and sees all did not thwart the plot, He gave Paul discernment, so that in a timely manner he fled into the wilderness and desert, even as David did of old. With the passage of time, what was enjoined upon Paul became his own choice. There were times that he would double back, but then he would turn around and go further into the desert. At length, as the fear of torture was diminishing in his heart, it was being replaced with the fear of God and the sole desire to please Him.

Consequently, he continued going deeper into the interior desert. He came to a rocky mountain, where he found a small cave at its foot, but the entrance had been blocked by a stone. He wished to know what was hidden on the other side, which is the natural human desire for discovery. He managed to move the stone with God's help and eagerly took to exploring within. He came upon a spacious courtyard that was open to the sky. The wide-spreading branches of an ancient palm provided shelter. Finding such a tree meant that water must be there. Indeed, there was a spring of clear water, which gushed forth a stream which was drunk up again by a small crack in the ground. He then observed that there were a number of chambers, dwelling places, in that hollow mountain. Paul, moved to further investigate, found the remains of hammers, chisels, and anvils, which had been utilized to stamp coins. Egyptian records show that this spot was a mint for coining counterfeit money during the time of Cleopatra and Antony. Paul was overwhelmed at finding such a place of quiet beauty, which provided a ready supply of water and palms. He decided that he would abide in that place. He felt certain that the Lord had guided him to that retreat for the benefit of his soul. He thereupon abided in that place for thirty years. He fed himself on grass and the date-palms, and dressed himself with a tunic made of palm leaf fronds, tightly woven. God then pitied him and dispatched daily one-half loaf of bread. He spent those years with God as his abode, living in hymnody, abstinence, prayer, and vigil.

The great Anthony, commemorated by the holy Church on the 17th of January, spoke of the venerable Paul, calling him blessed in three ways, saying, "He had dwelt in a quiet and wilderness place; he had patiently endured and shown stability for many years; he had completely departed from this world and its attractions." It should be known that, among the venerable fathers, this Paul was first to venture into the deepest part of the desert. He was the first to exert himself for such a long interval on the path of asceticism. He did after all leave the world and all its comforts and provisions at a young age. When the holy Paul reached the age of one hundred and thirteen, Saint Anthony was then ninety years old and living in another part of the desert. At that time, Anthony ofttimes kept pondering to himself, "I

wonder if there is another monk like unto me in the inner desert?"[3] Then one
night, while he was meditating upon such things, there came to him an angel
of the Lord who said, "Go quickly to the innermost desert. There thou shalt
find Abba Paul, more virtuous than thou, and from him thou shalt receive
great benefit." When Anthony heard these words, he did not postpone a visit
with him for some later time. Instead, Anthony thought little of his advanced
age and a long journey with all of its attendant discomforts. That very
morning he set out, taking his walking stick to support his feeble limbs.
Although by noon the scorching sun was overhead, this still did not dissuade
him from pressing forward. He walked all that day, hoping that the Lord

would show him that living treasure. He
said to himself, "I trust that God shall show
me my fellow slave, even as He said He
would."

Abba Anthony traversed the desert
for three days. He only observed the tracks
of irrational animals in the sand. He then
encountered a demonic apparition, which
some have compared with the mythological
hippocentaur, that is, a creature that appeared as half man and half horse. He then
beheld another creature, the mythological
satyr, having the form of an ape and horns   *Saint Anthony's Encounter*
on its head, with feet shaped as a goat's.
Since Anthony had firm faith in God, he in no wise cowered before these
creatures, but instead armed himself by making the sign of the Cross. He
remained constant in prayer that God might guide him to that which he
desired.[4] Thus the saint continued his trek. He was unsure which way to go,

---

[3] Blessed Jerome records that, one day, Anthony suddenly had the thought that there
was no other monk in the desert more perfect than he.

[4] Blessed Jerome records that the saint questioned the creature, "In what part of the
country does the slave of God abide?" The creature grunted something and then
pointed with his right hand, thus indicating the direction. The creature then swiftly
made across the open plains and vanished. Jerome then said, "Whether the devil had
assumed this shape to terrify Anthony, or whether the desert breeds such monstrous
creatures, we have no certain knowledge." Jerome then reports that Anthony then
beheld a dwarfish figure, sprouting horns, and whose lower body ended in goats' feet,
who offered dates as tokens of peace. Anthony questioned him, to which the creature
replied that he was mortal, but that the pagans, deluded by various errors, worshipped
fauns, satyrs, and incubi. The creature asked for Anthony's prayers and spoke of
(continued...)

but he remained confident that God would reveal the way. Anthony spent the dark night hours in prayer.

Then at dawn on the third day he noticed a lion[5] which hastened to the foot of a mountain. The saint perceived that God had hearkened to him and sent that creature. He followed the beast, up until it entered a cave. Anthony stood outside and began to peer inside, but that dark cave would reveal nothing to his eyesight. Nevertheless, even as it is written in the Scriptures, "Perfect love casteth out fear [1 Jn. 4:18]," so Anthony entered the cave, holding his breath and proceeding carefully. He could not see where he was going, so he would keep stopping to catch a sound of something, anything. But then as he kept going forth with faith, he discerned a light in the distance. He hastened to meet it, and as a result struck his foot against a stone. Anthony made a noise, which reverberated in the cave. This sound alerted its occupant, Abba Paul, of Abba Anthony's approach, so he quickly shut the door. Anthony then besought him from outside, saying, "I entreat thee for the Lord's sake, O holy father, open up to me that I might see thy venerable countenance." The holy Paul, wishing to test him, did not open the door. Thereupon, the blessed Anthony lay down flat on the ground; for on account of the toil of his journey and the blow to his foot, he could not stand up straight. He lay there prone on the ground for six hours, entreating Paul. He then observed that the sun was near setting, so he increased the intensity of his request to the saint, "Open the entrance, holy father!" Abba Paul then asked from within, "From whence art thou? What seekest thou?"

Saint Paul spoke in such a manner that he might see the patience of the divine Anthony, because in truth he already knew, by the Spirit, the answers to his own questions. Anthony replied and spoke the whole truth: "Who I am and whence and why I have come, thou knowest." Then Anthony added at the end, "I know, O man of God, that I am not worthy to see and converse with thee, but thou knowest that I shall not depart until I should take pleasure in thy countenance and most sweet words. I am an old man who has undertaken such a long journey. Dost thou not take into account the toil, suffering, and trouble I have endured, besides the fear of beasts? O namesake and imitator of the elect vessel, the most blessed Paul! I have observed that though thou dost receive and treat wild animals hospitably, yet a man, made in the image of God, though a sinner, thou dost turn away and dost not even

---

[4](...continued)

Christ Who came for the salvation of the world. Anthony rejoiced upon hearing these words; but he rebuked Alexandria for worshipping monsters in the room of God, while teratoids speak of Christ. The creature then ran away as if borne on wings.

[5] Blessed Jerome records the creature to have been a she-wolf.

account him deserving to see and speak with thee that we might rejoice together in the Spirit. Woe to me, the wretched one! Moreover, how canst thou overturn the divine words: 'Keep on asking, and it shall be given to you; keep on seeking, and ye shall find; keep on knocking, and it shall be opened to you [Mt. 7:7; Lk. 11:9]'? If thou wilt not be prevailed upon, then know I shall die before thy very door. Then thou shalt need to bury my corpse." Now the great Anthony spoke these words tearfully. At this point, Abba Paul answered him pleasantly, but in a jesting manner, saying, "No one pleads like this who comes to threaten; no one comes to condemn in tears. Shouldest thou marvel that I did not open to thee, if it is thine intention to die?"

Paul then opened the door and said with a smile, "It is good that thou hast come, O brother and fellow laborer, Anthony!" Then the two men embraced one another with a holy kiss. They spoke of divine matters and rejoiced spiritually. After this introduction, the great Paul remarked, "Why hast thou undergone such hardships to come as far as here? Was it to see one decaying elder who is about to end his earthly sojourn in a short

A Raven Brings Bread to Saints Anthony and Paul

time? But since the divine Paul teaches us that love 'endureth all things [1 Cor. 13:7],' it is manifest that love empowered thee and led thee to me. Therefore, I beseech thee, tell me, how are men faring in the cities and the nations? Are they at war or at peace? Before all, give me tidings whether those who govern are still found in the grip of idolatry?" Anthony answered all these questions and spoke of many other things as well. The venerable Paul gave thanks to God that piety had spread everywhere. As the two saints conversed, they noticed that in the branches of a tree a raven had settled. In its beak it clasped a pure loaf of bread. The creature then swooped down from the tree, delivering the bread in the midst of the two elders. Now the holy Anthony marvelled at this extraordinary incident. The great Paul commented, "In truth, brother, the merciful Lord exceedingly loves man. He is the One Who 'supplieth seed to the sower and bread for eating [2 Cor. 9:10; Is. 55:10].' For, 'Thou openest Thy hand and fillest every living thing with Thy favor [Ps. 144:17].' This raven has brought me bread every day for sixty years, but only half of a loaf; but today, at thy coming, I see that our good God and Master has doubled our rations."

Saint Paul

After the great Paul finished speaking, they both gave thanks to God and went to the spring to eat. But then each vied with one other for a long time, as both were extremely humble and desirous that the other should cut the loaf and bless the table. The great Paul then said to the divine Anthony, "Thou, as my guest, shouldest take precedence. This is the custom. Moreover, thou art the superior of many monks and a teacher." The great Anthony replied, "I much prefer that thou shouldest do this, as thou art the elder." Then they compromised by having each take one end of the loaf and pull toward himself. Each would then retain that portion that remained to him in the pulling of the bread. They did this, invoking the name of the Lord. Each one gave thanks, as he ate the bread and was satisfied. They drank a little of the water while bending over the stream.

Anthony then said to Paul, "Tell me, father, from whence comest thou? And from the beginning, how didst thou come to this untrodden wilderness?" Abba Paul then recounted all that we have written above. Then the fathers offered to God the sacrifice of praise and passed the night in vigil, giving thanks and glorifying the Lord. In the morning the venerable Paul said to the great Anthony, "It is many days since the Lord has revealed to me that thou dwellest in this wilderness, and He promised me that I should see thee before my end. Now, according to the promise, God has sent thee forth that thou mightest bury my body. I have a desire to depart and to be with Christ, for that is very much better [Phil. 1:23]. There is laid up for me the crown of righteousness, now that I have finished the course [cf. 2 Tim. 4:7, 8]."

When the great Anthony heard these words, tears streamed down from his eyes. He lamented their separation and besought Paul fervently to make an entreaty to the Lord that he accompany him on the journey. To this request, Paul answered, "It is not fitting, brother, that we should seek only our own advantage, but rather that of our neighbor. 'Love seeketh not its own [1 Cor. 13:5].' It then is not the time for thee to go to the most-desired One, but it is necessary that thou support and strengthen the brethren that they might be like unto thee in virtue. Therefore, I beseech thee for love's sake, unless it be too great a trouble, go and fetch the mandya (cloak) given thee by

Athanasios the Great, for whom I have profound respect, that I might be buried with that garment wrapped around me." These words of Abba Paul, however, did not signify that he was interested in having his relics clothed—for what were garments to one who dressed in woven palm leaves?—but that Anthony should be absent and spared the grief of his death. As for Abba Anthony, he marvelled at Abba Paul's clairvoyance in regard to the archbishop's garment. Since Anthony revered Paul as an angel, after he wept and embraced him, kissing his eyes and hands, he bade him farewell and began the return to his own cell.

The feet of the elderly and emaciated Anthony could barely keep pace with his resolve to return as quickly as possible. As he approached his cell, worn out and gasping for breath, his two disciples, Isaac and Plousianos, who had ministered to him as he grew old, ran to overtake him. "Where hast thou been, O father? Why hast thou gone for so many days?" Saint Anthony replied, "Woe is me, the wretch! For I, my children, falsely wear the garb of a monk and have not practised even one virtue. By my clothing, I feign that I am a monk. I have just seen Elias the Thesbite and John the Forerunner. I indeed beheld another true Paul, as in Paradise, dwelling in the wilderness." The disciples questioned him, but he gave no answer except, "There is a time to be silent, and a time to speak [cf. Eccl. 3:7]." He then quickly collected some food for the return journey, took up the aforesaid mandya, and began running to Paul, for whom he thirsted and whom he desired to see with his eyes; for whom his soul was refreshed and in whom he took delight. As Anthony hastened as much as he could through that wasteland, he kept fearing that he might not arrive while Paul was among the living so as to receive his blessing.

Abba Anthony walked all that first day and part of the second day. Then, while on the way, with the noetic eyes of his soul, he beheld an angelic host, choirs of prophets and apostles, and companies of martyrs, righteous, and venerable. In their midst was the soul of Paul, radiant and whiter than snow. They were escorting him as they ascended into the heavens with much good cheer. After Saint Anthony beheld this vision, he fell prone to the ground. He cast sand over his head, struck his face, and bewailed his misfortune. After he wept for a long while, he then rose up and began running. He felt much strength in his members, even more than when he was a youth. After he arrived at the cave, Anthony observed that the holy man was kneeling down. Both his face and hands were raised heavenward. He then thought that Paul was among the living and praying. He did not wish to disturb him, so he watched him carefully. After the passage of a long time, during which Anthony observed that Paul had not stirred in the least, nor sighed, nor done anything else that might lead him to think that he was alive, he came to acknowledge the truth. Since no movement was made by Abba

Paul, Abba Anthony perceived that the end had come while the holy man was at prayer. He approached with much reverence and embraced those august relics, ardently kissing them and lamenting his loss. He kept thinking that he had known Abba Paul for only a short time and was now deprived of further spiritual benefit from him. Anthony then set about preparing the precious relics for burial, wrapping them in the mandya. He recited the customary psalms and as many hymns (troparia) proper to the occasion as he knew. He then wished to inter the holy man but had no spade with which to dig the ground. He had taken no tools with him when he left his cell. In such a quandary, he began thinking, "If I should return to the monastery, it will take four days. But if I remain here, what more can I do? Therefore, O Christ, let me die beside Thy warrior."

Saint Anthony Buries Saint Paul

As he stood there exceedingly saddened, he began thinking he would not leave until the Lord should send help from on high. Anthony then espied two lions. They were fearsome-looking and running at great speed with flying manes toward him. As a man, he initially became frightened, but then he strengthened his heart toward the Lord and stood there without the least dread or tremor. The lions drew closer but went up to Abba Paul, wagging their tails. They crouched before his relics and licked his feet. When they perceived his final departure, they began roaring loudly. This was their way of lamenting his loss, for which Abba Anthony marvelled at this display by wild beasts. Then with their paws, as though in a rivalry with one another, they both, in a furious manner, began to dig a grave for the saint in the sand. The size of the hole they left was adequate for one man. Then Anthony observed that the lions bent their ears back, shook their tails, lowered their heads, and licked his hands and feet, as though requesting some reward for their labor. The saint perceived that they were asking for his blessing. The saint marvelled that even these beasts instinctively knew that God exists. Abba Anthony then raised his hands to heaven and prayed, "O Lord God, without Whose command no leaf may light from the tree, nor may a single sparrow be brought down to the ground, do Thou grant that reward, O Lord, which Thou knowest to be best for these creatures."

After the saint uttered these words, making a sign to the beasts with his hand, he bade them to depart. The lions turned, abased themselves before Abba Paul, and departed. Then venerable Anthony took the sacred relics and interred them on the 15th day of January, in the year 341. Now the great Anthony tarried there the rest of the day that he might see whether the raven might come with bread; but it did not appear. The saint then became the heir to Saint Paul's tunic woven by himself out of palm leaves, resembling the work of a weaver of baskets. He took the tunic of palms and returned to the monastery, where he recounted this history to the monks. As for the garment of Saint Paul, Abba Anthony wore it at Pascha and other great feasts.[6]

On the 15th of January, the holy Church commemorates our venerable Father JOHN the Kalyvite (Hut-dweller).[7]

Saint John

John, our venerable father, surnamed the Kalyvite or Hut-dweller, lived at the time of Emperor Leo (r. 457-474). John's father, Eftropios, was an extremely wealthy nobleman.[8] His mother was Theodora, the wife of Eftropios. Both of his parents were godly people. They were circumspect not only in things pertaining to the world, but also in their moral character and in the ways of virtuousness, equity, and kindness. This pious couple gave birth to three children. Two of them were men in high office and prosperous in the things of this life. The youngest son, the goodly John, remained with his parents. He applied himself to the study of sacred letters, rhetoric, and philosophy, by which he preferred to be enriched rather than with money. He did not set his eyes on vain and false glory. When he was twelve years of age, his marked preference for the divine words rather than his other lessons, resulted in frequent visits to Church both day and night.

---

[6] Blessed Jerome records that the saint wore Saint Paul's tunic on Pascha and Pentecost.

[7] The Life of this saint was recorded in Greek by Saint Symeon the Metaphrastes, whose manuscript begins, "A good life, and virtuous, and a man undefiled, righteous and perfect..." [*P.G.* 114:567-582]. The text is extant in the Athonite Monastery of the Great Lavra. The text was rendered in simpler Greek by Agapios the Cretan, who published it in his *Neon Paradeison*.

[8] Saint Symeon the Metaphrastes [*P.G.* 114:568] identifies Eftropios as an exceedingly wealthy man of Rome, with the rank of *stratelates* (general) or *magister militum*. However, *The Great Synaxaristes* (in Greek), identifies Eftropios as a senator and gives Constantinople as the birthplace of Saint John and his parental home.

His soul, athirst for the word of God, was watered by such activities, so that he could be compared to "the tree which is planted by the streams of the waters, which shall bring forth its fruit in its season [Ps. 1:3]."

At about that time, a certain monk from the Monastery of the Akoimetoi (Unsleeping ones)[9] conceived the desire to venerate the holy places at Jerusalem. This monk started his journey on foot, passing through their city where he had some business. He lodged in a home near to that of the senator. Now the young John saw him and asked, "Father, from whence dost thou come, and whither art thou going?" The monk revealed his plan to make a pilgrimage. John then asked him, "Tell me about the order of thy monastery." The monk, perceiving the youth to be sincerely desirous to learn about such things and the brotherhood, described to him in detail the rule of his monastery. He spoke to him about fasting and chanting and the pursuit of the virtues. John found this discourse as the sweetest honey. His heart was smitten and consumed with desire for the ascetic life. He then took the monk aside, to a private place, and said to him, "I adjure thee by God, the Trinity, that whenever thou shouldest return to thy monastery, thou shalt come by here and take me secretly with thee. For I wish to become a monk as soon as possible, before my parents should learn where I might be. I am telling thee these things because they are thinking to have me marry. Moreover, they would also bestow upon me honors and rank, which are worldly illusions and vanity. I know these things because I hear the word of God read in Church. I have read these things myself and understand that all in this life is vanity. As for me, I have a great desire for the monastic conduct of life and thirst to be numbered in your synodia, because I believe these attainments to be true glory and honor, which are certain and a seal of that blessedness." The monk then promised to fulfill the youth's longing to give his life to Christ. Thereupon, that monk continued on his journey. In the meantime, divine love and yearning for Christ increased in the holy youth's soul, so as to kindle a mighty flame. John felt joy in every hour he spent with the Lord, conversing noetically with Him in prayer.

---

[9] The original idea was to have an unending cycle of twenty-four offices, one per hour, with a minimum amount of time allowed for unavoidable bodily needs and care. The cycle came to be performed by three choirs in succession, each one conducting an eight-hour shift per day. This was started in the time of Archimandrite Alexander. As a result of persecution, the brotherhood was compelled to move about to a succession of monasteries. By the mid-5th C., under Archimandrite Markellos (b. ca. 400-ca. 484), commemorated by the holy Church on the 29th of December, the Unsleeping ones had settled at Eirenaion on the eastern shore of the Bosporos.

The goodly John, reflecting on what he was about to do, then said to himself, "Before my departure, I should go to my parents and receive some blessing from them. I shall seek from their hands a Gospel that I might be able to learn the traditions of my Christ and perform His will." After meditating on these things, he went to his parents. He found a pretext by which to approach his mother and said, "I am unable to attend school, because all my classmates have a Gospel each which they all read. But I sit in contempt by myself, because I do not possess one. For this reason I beseech thee very much to have a Gospel made for me, so that I too may have one in my hands to read." His mother Theodora received joy at this information, because her son had such love for the divine and sacred writings. She said to him, "With all joy, my son, when thy father comes, I shall tell him to have a Gospel ordered for thee, even as thou dost wish." When his father Eftropios came, Theodora spoke to him of her earlier conversation with their son, saying, "I beseech thee, milord, have a Gospel copied out by a calligrapher for our son. Then give it to a goldsmith, so that he may produce a gold cover adorned with precious stones. Thus, by both its inward and outward beauty, our son's mind and desire shall be drawn to it. He shall thereby come to learn well the divine and sacred words." The blessed John's father straightway hearkened and commissioned a skilled calligrapher who transcribed the holy Gospel, exercising all care. Eftropios also gave a hundred gold coins, as well as precious stones and pearls, to the goldsmith for the work. When the commission was completed, Eftropios called his son John to him and said, "Receive, my beloved son, this holy Gospel, and know that on account of my love for thee, I spent five hundred gold coins in addition to the cost of these precious stones and pearls."

John took the holy Gospel into his hands. He saw that in every way it filled his every desire. He then kissed the hands of both his father and mother. The gift brought him great joy, and so he kissed it ardently. He brought it with him everywhere, reading it with great desire. He gave glory to God and thanks to his parents who fulfilled his wish. In the meantime, he bided his time until the abba should return from Jerusalem that they might depart together. The abba did return, and when John beheld him, he rejoiced and was glad both spiritually and bodily. John met with that abba and greeted him with much good cheer, saying, "Milord, thou knowest very well that if my father or my mother should learn that I wish to become a monk and enter into a monastery with thee, from the torrent of their tears and pleas, they shall attempt to hinder me and cut me off from the God-pleasing path which I have chosen for myself. For this reason, I beseech thee, abba, let us depart and exercise the greatest secrecy, lest anyone should learn of it." The abba, considering the great love of John for asceticism, said to him, "May God fulfill thy desire, my child, and do that which thou hast decided." John then followed the abba, and together they went down to the shore secretly. They found a ship and said to the sailing master, "We wish, brother, to hire thy boat that thou mightest take us to the holy Monastery of the Akoimeton." He answered, "That is why I am sitting here. I am looking for passengers or cargo by which to fill my ship. Certainly the fare of two passengers is hardly worth my sailing this ship. No, I shall wait until I receive the required sum." John then asked, "And how much might that be?" The sailing master said firmly, "One hundred florins." The saint then said, "Wait for me, brother, and in three days I shall pay thee thine one hundred florins." Thus they made an agreement with the sailing master.

The blessed John said to the abba, "Indeed, the passage-money is considerable, but so is my desire to depart. Nevertheless, may God and thy blessing pilot me to carry out my desire." The abba replied, "May God be with thee, child!" John then went directly to his mother, saying, "Milady and mother, who has nursed and reared me as few other mothers, I know your boundless love for me and how it pleases thee not to disappoint me. There is something I wish to request from thee and from father." She said, "Tell me, child, thou light of my eyes, what is it that thou dost want?" He answered, "O my beloved mother, thou knowest that many of my school fellows have ofttimes offered me handsome hospitality, expending much to spread a table with all kinds of dishes. But I never have been vouchsafed to return these social obligations in kind, so that now I am ashamed to go to school." She hearkened to his concern and responded warmly, "Is it for this that thou hast been pensive and exasperated, my son? Wait, child, and today I shall speak with thy father. Upon his return from the palace, I shall ask him to give thee whatsoever amount thou wilt need to treat thy friends; therefore, no longer be grieved."

When therefore Eftropios came home, his wife sat down with him. Theodora recounted the concerns of their much-beloved son John. Eftropios said, "We should give him one hundred florins and a manservant to escort and guard him on the road." This thought pleased both parents, and so John received the sum and the servant. When John took the money into his hands, he was filled with joy and gave glory to God. He then went out with the servant. On the way, John spoke to the abba, but not so that the servant could hear. John told the abba all that had transpired and said to him, "Milord, my father's manservant is with me. Let him sit here for a short spell and detain him." John then bade the servant, "Stay here while I go and find my friends. I shall return quickly. But I need to inform them that I shall be inviting them for dinner." John then went straight to the sailing master and said, "Brother, according to the agreement we have made, behold, I have come to give thee the one hundred coins, so that thou shalt set sail taking passage-money from only me and the monk. I only beseech thee that when the suitable time comes for our departure, thou wilt not be negligent or slack, but be ready to take us to that place I mentioned. I also implore thee, brother, by God, keep as a secret this voyage and speak of it to no one." The sailing master, since he had received his asking price in full, said, "Go with God, my master, for I shall do as thou hast bidden me; that is, I, with God's help, shall secretly take you away." Satisfied with his words, the holy youth returned to the abba. He disclosed to him what had passed between him and the sailing master and how all had been arranged. John also was careful that his father's manservant should hear nothing.

The following day, the blessed John said to the manservant, "Let us go to the shore and buy some fish." When they arrived at the docks, by God's good pleasure, the weather was fair and the wind favorable. John saw that the sailing master was standing on his boat looking about for him and the monk. He then caught sight of them from afar and made a motion for them to board. John perceived that the moment had come. The time to set sail was perfect, and the sailing master was waiting on them. He then needed to think how he might divert the manservant. John then said to the servant, "Go, I beseech thee, to the school and see what my schoolmates are doing. Then come here and tell me." The servant took his instructions and hastened to the school. John then acted quickly by running to bring the abba down to the boat. After this had been done, they boarded the hired vessel. The sail was hoisted, and they got under way. In the meantime, the manservant, having performed what he was told, returned to inform his master but could not find John anywhere along the shore. He then thought that his young master must have gone to the school, but by another path. He therefore returned to the school, seeking him. Not finding him at the school, he returned to the docks, where he spent considerable time asking around for him. Since evening had come and John was not seen or heard of, the servant returned to his master's home. When he entered, he reported to John's mother what had taken place that day.

When Theodora heard this alarming report concerning her son, she became terribly agitated, fearing lest some peril befell her boy. She quickly dispatched other servants, many of them, to make inquiries regarding her son. The servants searched out all of the city. Not being able to discover his whereabouts, they returned that night, saying, "Though we went throughout this entire city searching and making inquiries, yet we did not find the young master." By that time, Eftropios had come home and was waiting to hear news. When he heard the servants' report, he began weeping, lamenting, and saying, "O my beloved and most sweet child, the light of my eyes and the consolation of my old age! What more have I to do with this life without thee? Why hast thou not told me where thou wert bound? Why hast thou concealed thy departure? Why hast thou not in some quarter at least left word that I might learn some news from thee? Woe is me! Thou hast given a poisonous drink to me, for which my heart shall never again experience sweetness. Thou hast submerged me in one boundless sea of grief, on account of which tears shall never be absent from my eyes as long as I am found in this present life and remember thee. This was the party thou wast to have for thy fellow pupils? Why didst thou not at least tell me to give thee sufficient money that thou mightest have it with thee? What shall one hundred coins do for thee? Where art thou now found that I might come and see thee and be comforted?" These and many other heart-rending words were uttered by a weeping father who would not be consoled.

The search continued for many days inside the city and neighboring villages. Theodora could see that all hopes for the recovery of her son were being exhausted. There was no clue found to clarify the mystery of John's disappearance. Theodora kept crying and admitting no consolation, saying, "O my beloved child John, why dost thou despise thy beloved mother? Why hast thou deprived thy mother who feels for thee from her inward parts and loves thee so much? Since I never opened my mouth to utter a word that might grieve thee, why hast thou taken flight without so much as a 'fare thee well,' as though I were some deadly enemy? Why hast thou not permitted thy suffering mother to kiss thy most sweet face for the last time? What bad thing have I done that thou shouldest not even bid me goodby? Hast thou known of this departure? Into what inexorable sorrow has my heart been plunged! How shall I endure thy separation? How shall I look upon thy costly garments, which I had sewn for thee with great joy? But how could I have known that thou wouldest not be here? I see those garments, and a river of tears flows from eyes that have been deprived of the sight of thee, my child, the beloved. Why didst thou not ask me to at least prepare two changes of clothing for thee in that solitary place of thine exile?" She said this and much more. Thus both parents were left weeping and wailing for the loss of their much-loved son.

As for the ship conveying John and the abba, they were at sea for three days, until they arrived at the harbor where they disembarked for the Monastery of the Unsleeping Ones. When they arrived at the monastery, they first went inside the church in order to venerate and kiss the holy icons. Afterward, they went and made a prostration to the hegumen, kissing his right hand. They also greeted the other brethren in like manner. The abba then disclosed the entire matter to the hegumen concerning John. "The youth is of noble parentage and cherishes a great desire to receive the Angelic Schema." The hegumen, looking upon John, saw that he was young. He marvelled and said to him, "O my child, thou art very young. How shalt thou endure the ascesis and toils of the monks? For whosoever would be a monk, first must become a novice for a year that we might see and test his mettle and virtue. Then afterward we tonsure him with the cutting of his hair." John then replied to the hegumen, "My holy master and honorable father, I beg thee with all my heart, do tonsure me a monk this day; for I have a great longing and love to receive the Angelic Schema." He persisted in this manner with the hegumen, who then said, "My beloved child, thou dost wish to traverse a long and rough path, which requires thee to take heed at every turn, for 'narrow is the gate and straitened is the way [Mt. 7:14],' even as it is written in the Gospel. Again, thou art very young and not able to tread upon this path. But if thou wilt insist, at least attempt forty days here among us in our ascetic rule, and then we shall speak again of the tonsure." The goodly John, shedding tears, then adjured the hegumen, saying, "By the most holy Trinity, do thou tonsure me today, for I yearn to be clothed in the Schema of the monastics."[10]

Then the hegumen and archimandrite, seeing the youth's love and his stream of tears, took pity on him and made him a monk, garbing him in the Angelic Schema. He then blessed him, saying, "May God, the hope of all and the strength of the weak, vouchsafe thee, my child, to keep the confession which thou hast made before His angels, that thou mightest vanquish that serpent, the twisted dragon, the devil of many machinations." The holy John venerated him, asked for his prayers, and withdrew to his cell which they gave him. Who is able to describe the toils and diligence he applied to divine virtue, fasting, continence, keeping vigil, all-night entreaties and prayers, tears, and other virtues? Who can characterize his obedience to all and his humility? Who can recount his devotion to the study of the divine Scriptures? He attained such excellence in everything that he surpassed all others in asceticism, including those who had grown old in the monastic state.

Father John dwelt three years at that monastery. On account of strict fasting he became unrecognizable, which abstinence amazed the brethren in that monastery. The hegumen also observed the young man's austerities and guided him, saying, "The magnitude of thy struggles, child, that is, the severe fasts, have so weakened thy powers that soon thou shalt no longer have strength to fulfill thy prayer rule and glorify God, Who does not will that we should do what is beyond our strength." The hegumen counseled John in this manner, since the young monk ate nothing; that is, except on Sundays, when he would communicate the immaculate Mysteries. Afterward, he partook of a little bread and water, but not so as to sate himself. Father John consequently begged the archimandrite's forgiveness and prayers that he might start anew.

In the meantime, the envious devil was observing these practises. He was unable to endure being trampled upon and mocked by any man, much

---

[10] *P.G.* 114:573C.

less a youth. He then put in the saint's heart the remembrance of his parents
and a desire to go and see them. As often as he suggested such thoughts, the
saint would rise up and pray, supplicating God to dispel such sentiments. The
devil, however, kept tempting him and ventured to overcome him with the
recollection of ten thousand tender memories of his family and fellow
students, so that his heart was inflamed. The devil did not limit his suggestions to such fond images, but also brought to John's mind the good food and
excellent drink at his parents' table, as well as soft bedding and expensive
clothing. These reflections of his past created great warfare, so that a flame
of fire was kindled in his heart. He, however, continued to rise and offer
prayer, making the sign of the Cross and saying, "Get thee behind me, Satan;
for thou art an offense to me [Mt. 16:23]. I have Christ as a helper; for, 'The
Lord is mine illumination and my savior; in whom shall I be afraid? The Lord
is the defender of my life; from whom shall I cower in fear [Ps. 26:1]?'" The
saint endured this spiritual warfare daily from the devil. It had the effect of
exhausting his body further. The hegumen observed John's debilitation, as
though the shadow of death touched him. Therefore the hegumen again
admonished him, saying, "Did I not tell thee, child, that God does not
demand from His slaves more than what they can bear? Thou hast applied
thyself beyond measure, rendering thyself a shadow, by exhausting thy body.
Such excessive fasting and asceticism many times bring a man condemnation
as his own murderer." John then said, "I entreat thee, father, it is not the
fasting that is laying me low, but my sins are causing me to stumble. This is
because for many days the enemy of the good, a demon, has been agitating
my soul, inciting it with remembrances of my parents and my house.[11] He
suggests that I return and see my parents, so that when I remember such
people and places, my heart is set afire. Besides such memories, there are
many other things that the enemy recalls to my soul."

When the hegumen heard this explanation from John, he sighed and
said, "My child, John, was I not telling thee how thou wouldest not be able
to endure the labors and suffering associated with asceticism? This is due to
the devil's envy, malice, and subtleties. He has laid many snares that he might
succeed in the war against thee. Therefore, my child, what hast thou now in
thy mind?" The saint answered, "That thou mightest give me leave that I may
go to my parents and there conquer and trample upon his devices, being
supported and strengthened by the power of my Christ and thy holy prayers."
The hegumen, being a virtuous man, foreknew, by the grace of Christ, the
future of the holy John. Furthermore, when he looked upon Father John, he
saw how worn out he had become from the devil's warfare, so that he was in

---

[11] *P.G.* 114:576A.

danger of death. The handsomeness of his countenance had waned, his body was withered, and his eyes had sunk deep into his head. All that remained were skin and bones. The hegumen grieved and wept at such a sight, because he greatly loved Father John for his many excellent virtues. The following day, Father John went to the archimandrite. He fell at his feet, begging him for a blessing to go and see his parents, so that, with God helping him, he might trample upon the evil one. Thereupon, the archimandrite gathered all the monks and ascetics of his monastery. They conducted a Supplicatory Canon to God on behalf of Father John that he be granted power to conquer the devil. The hegumen then said, "In the name of the Father and of the Son and of the Holy Spirit, go in peace, having Christ as thy fellow traveler that He may strengthen thee and guide thee to do His will." Then Father John arose and made a prostration before the brethren, beseeching them to entreat God on his behalf. After they all blessed him, the saint then said to them, "Be saving yourselves, my brethren, my blessed synodia; well did your prayers and blessings restore me. But I am the least among you and am unworthy to be found in such a holy synodia."[12]

Thereupon, he tearfully went forth from the monastery, saying, "O God Who fashioned me, do Thou preserve and guard me from the snares of the enemy." After he was a little distance away from the monastery, he turned about and gazed upon its walls. He thereupon sat down and wept for a long time, kneeling and offering up prayer to God. He then rose up and continued walking the road that led to his parents' home. As he was going on his way, he encountered an indigent monk, clad in an old and shabby rason (cassock), and said to him, "Rejoice, brother and fellow traveler; dost thou wish to walk together with me?" The monk replied, "Gladly will I walk with thee." The holy John then remarked, "I see that thy garment is tattered and thou art not able to walk about. But remove thy garments, and exchange them with mine, that we might walk more easily." That poor monk straightway removed his ancient clothing and gave it to the holy John, who in turn put on the tattered rason. After they had walked that road for some days, they came to that juncture in the road where they would depart from each other in different directions. The monk then said to Father John, "Brother, take back thy garments and return mine." The holy man said, "Go, brother, in peace. These old clothes suit me fine. God shall also dispense in His œconomy what I need. Only do thou pray to God on my behalf that I be delivered from the snares of the enemy." They each blessed and bade the other farewell. Father John then continued on his way alone. When he beheld from afar his parental home, he knelt to the ground and with tears began saying, "O Son of God,

---

[12] *P.G.* 114:576C.

Jesus Christ, my God, do not forsake me or stand off from me, but do Thou help me even here in the home of my parents, that I might conquer the envious devil, that hater of good."

When he arrived at the door of his house, he was surrounded by the darkness of a very black night. He fell prostrate, pressed his forehead to the ground, and wept, saying, "Behold, thou hast arrived, O John, even at thy father's house!" He then began praying, "I give thanks to Thee, O Lord Jesus Christ, because Thou hast vouchsafed me to arrive at my father's house. I therefore entreat Thee, forsake me not. But do Thou strengthen me with Thy divine grace that I might utterly vanquish my enemy, the wicked devil; and do Thou vouchsafe that I complete my contest in this place." Thus, Father John remained in prayer all that night by his parents' gate. When dawn broke, the doorkeeper, according to custom, opened the gate. Then a servant of John's father emerged. As soon as he saw Father John, suffering hardship and clad in ragged garb, he remarked, "Man, who art thou and what seekest thou? Begone from here, because the master of the house shall be passing through to go to the palace. Indeed, if he should catch a glimpse of thee, he shall put thee down, and we shall suffer a reprimand." Little did that manservant know that he was addressing his master in Father John, for whom those of that household wept and lamented. The venerable John then said to that manservant, "I beseech thee, my good man, for the love of Christ, leave me in this corner. I shall neither trouble nor hinder anyone. Be assured that thou shalt have a reward from the Master Christ, because thou didst keep a poor man by this gate." The manservant pitied him and let him sit down in a corner.

When Father John's parents arose that morning, he caught sight of them from a distance. As soon as the holy John saw his beloved parents, his eyes filled with tears, and he said to himself, "Behold, O John, by the power of thy Christ and God, thou dost gaze upon thy parents! But do thou struggle to trample underfoot the treacheries and ruses of the devil." He then rallied and made another prayer to God, saying, "Lord Jesus Christ, abandon me not." It was then that his father was passing through the gate. He turned and observed Father John to be destitute, in tatters, and worn down by hardship and suffering. He in no wise recognized him to be his young son. Eftropios, however, pitied Father John's wretchedness and asked him, "Whence comest thou, O poor man?" He answered his father, "I am a stranger. I beseech thine illustrious person not to loathe me and find me repugnant, but perform an act of mercy and leave me to remain in the gateway." Eftropios replied, "Come into the courtyard and sit in a room." The venerable one answered, "Milord, this spot here is sufficient for me, for which I am glad. I only beseech thee that thou mightest instruct one of thy menservants to build a hut (*kalyve*)." Eftropios consented and bade his men to attend to it. That evening, when he returned home, he remarked to his wife, "I very much pity that pauper, the one who is at the gate, inasmuch as he endures the chill and ice of such a winter." Theodora had not yet seen Father John. Eftropios sent food out to the holy one and then continued saying to his wife, "However, perhaps God has sent him forth to us that we might also be saved through his prayers. If we are merciful, we can hope to find mercy from the Lord in that day. Only God knows if my boy is in similar dire straits as that man. And if he should be in such a predicament, we can hope that God shall have him kindly dealt with if we should attend to this stranger as we would wish our son to be treated."

Then, on one of those days, Father John's mother exited their home on her way to church. At that moment, Father John happened to be sitting outside of the hut. As Theodora looked upon him, she became frightened and trembled. She said to her servants, "Tell him to go inside. I see him living in a wild state and barefoot, and cannot bear to look upon his rough countenance." Straightway the servants did as their mistress bade them, saying, "Man, for this reason did our master make for thee a hut: that thou mightest suffer neither the cold nor the burning sun. Go thou therefore and sit within, for our lady mistress wishes to pass and fears to look upon thy fierce face." The holy John immediately went inside the hut and began weeping, saying, "I give thanks to Thee, O my Lord Jesus Christ, that even my mother, she who gave me birth, finds me disgusting. Do Thou grant me patience to the end that I may remain unknown to my parents." Thenceforth, Father John would only leave the hut when he wished to attend church. In the meantime, his father daily ordered that food and drink be brought to the lodger's hut from the master's own table. Thereupon, the servants would convey all kinds of foods and drinks to Father John's hut. He, however, was giving away the food to the servants and the poor, keeping only for himself a little bread and water. He nourished himself on the immaculate Mysteries. He so exhausted and humbled his flesh that his bones and the joints of his hands and feet stood out. He passed three whole years at his parents' gateway. Ofttimes the devil would cast stumbling blocks his way, attempting to compel Father John to reveal his identity to his father and mother. Father John remained vigilant and kept saying, "In no wise, O devil, shalt thou deceive and mislead me, because I have Christ as my helper."

The holy God, Who is glorious in His counsel, beheld the great contest of the saint, that is, his sufferings, hardships, and distress. Though Father John was half-dead from his struggles, yet he surpassed all in ascesis, so that he finished the good fight. After three years, the Lord appeared to him in his sleep and said, "Rejoice, John, that thou hast forsaken all corruptible and temporal things of this world and hast followed Me! The time of thine end has drawn near. Thy conduct of life may be likened to that of My disciple John the virgin, since thou hast left all and followed Me. But now the time of thine asceticism is fulfilled, that is, thy fasts, prayers, all-night vigils, continual tears, patience, the wounds sustained by the devil, and the dissolution of his snares. Rejoice and be glad from this day, because thy contest has been completed! Rejoice that thou hast vanquished and trampled upon the head of the dragon! Thou art verily blessed, and thy life shall abide as an example to the ages. Know that after three days thou shalt come to Me and rejoice forever with the angels and all the saints."

When therefore the holy John was awakened, he began weeping and praying to God and saying, "Glory to Thee, O Christ King, that although I am unworthy, still Thou, in Thy goodness, hast accounted me worthy of a place of repose among the righteous and numbered me with those who have been pleasing to Thee. But I yet entreat Thee, O Lord, that Thou also remember my parents, who not only gave me birth but also instructed me in the divine and sacred writings and brought me to know the path of Thy truth. Therefore, I supplicate Thee to forgive their sins. Take not their iniquities into account, but blot them out. Pardon their transgressions if they sinned in anything before thee out of human weakness. Tear up the handwriting of their sins, as Thou only art our God and the lover of man. Do Thou also turn them from this vain world." When he finished uttering this prayer, he called over one of the menservants, the one who had first received him and also made the hut for him, and said, "Milord, from the beginning thou hast shown mercy to me, the poor and pitiable stranger. I beseech thee that thou mightest do me one more favor, and the Master Christ shall recompense thee here in this life and in the kingdom of the ages." The manservant said, "With all joy, tell me what I may do for thee." The holy man said, "Go to your ladyship and, after thou shouldest deliver my respects, say that 'the poor stranger who dwells in the hut requests thine illustrious person to visit him, because he has something to say to thee. Do not disdain him for his poverty, for Christ impoverished Himself for sinners.'"[13]

The manservant went and related the words of the holy man to his mistress. She remarked, "What could that pauper wish to say to me? For God knows how I am unable to look upon his face." When Eftropios came in, Theodora spoke to him of the words of the hut-dweller. "He has asked me to go and see him, because he has something to say to me. But I fear his rough countenance," said she. Eftropios then said, "Well then go, wife, for to refuse is a sin. After all, the poor are God's chosen." What was spoken of by his mother was related to Father John by the manservant. Father John then

---

[13] *P.G.* 114:580B.

said to the manservant, "Go to her again and say that 'within three days, I shall die; and if thou wilt not come, later thou shalt repent of it much.'" When Theodora was informed that he would soon die, she said to the manservant, "Go to him, taking two menservants, and raise him up and bring him here." She also gave that manservant a muslin sheet to cover the hut-dweller's body, lest she should gaze upon him. The menservants went as she had directed and conveyed him to her. Father John completely covered himself. Theodora still had not recognized him as her most beloved son John, for whom she wept night and day. Father John then addressed her, saying, "Today is the Gospel word fulfilled which says: 'Insofar as ye did it to one of the least of these My brethren, ye did it to Me [Mt. 25:40].' Therefore the welcome, hospitality, and almsgiving which you showed me, the poor and pitiable stranger, you did for Christ Who shall recompense you. However, for now, I beseech thee to do what I am about to tell thee. But first of all, I adjure thee not to transgress my word."[14]

Theodora pledged herself to him that she would do what he requested. The saint then said, "Take heed, milady, that when I die thou dost not remove my raiment in which I am clad, nor do thou bury me in another place other than the hut where I am now living. This is because in that hut I conquered the wicked devil. Moreover, I am not deserving of a change of clothing or a more honorable burial place." After he spoke these words, he said, "Though I am poor, yet I have a precious and costly gift to grant thee for the kindness that you both have shown me." He then removed from his breast the divine and sacred Gospel, saying, "In this present life may this Gospel be a bond of union, and in the future one may it furnish both thee and thy husband with supplies for the everlasting journey. Receive this great gift, and may God grant love that is pure and firm, and spiritual joy and gladness, to thee and thy husband." After he spoke thus, Theodora received the Gospel, and he returned to his hut. Theodora looked over the Gospel from top to bottom and from side to side, "Bless me!" she exclaimed. "How it resembles the one made for my son John." Straightway her heart was consumed, and she hastened to show the Gospel to Eftropios, saying to him, "Milord, is this not the Gospel which we gave to our son John?" Eftropios examined it and remarked, "Yea, milady, in truth it appears like it." Eftropios then dispatched messages to the calligrapher and the goldsmith, who originally wrought the gift for John, that he might show them the work. Each confirmed his craft in producing that sacred book. When Theodora heard the assurances of both, she began to cry. Eftropios then said to her, "Let us go, milady, and put the hut-

---

[14] *P.G.* 114:580CD.

dweller under oath to tell us where he found it. Perhaps he even knows the whereabouts of our son!"[15]

Saint John

Then they went to him and said, "Brother and man of God, we adjure thee by the tri-hypostatic God of the heavens and earth, not to conceal the truth, but to confess to us where thou didst find this Gospel, since this is the very one that we gave to our son, named John; and from that time we have neither seen nor heard anything concerning him. Since this Gospel was found in thy hands, do tell us what thou knowest regarding our most desired John." As they spoke these words, they were weeping. John then, beholding his father and mother shedding tears, could no longer bear up. He forced himself to speak through his tears and their wailing, saying, "I am your son John. This Gospel is that very one for which I had asked and which you had made for me. But my desire was for Christ, and to bear His most light yoke." When the parents heard this admission, they beheld him anew. The truth swept over them and they fell on his neck. He recounted to them everything concerning the one hundred florins which he requested to treat his fellow pupils. He told them how he diverted the attention of the manservant whom they had placed to attend him. These and many other details he gave them regarding what had taken place. As his parents listened to these explanations, they gazed intently upon his features and characteristics. They carefully looked for other distinguishing marks and attributes. They listened attentively to his voice and speech. They knew it was their son in very truth. For a long time they remained speechless, as ones beside themselves. When they came to themselves, they were wondering what to do first. Should they rejoice at the discovery of their son or mourn for his death?

They kept embracing him and weeping and lamenting exceedingly, saying, "O most beloved child of many sorrows! O the grief in which thou hast plunged our souls this day! O how much more hast thou wounded our hearts now that we have found thee than when thou didst first leave us! Then

---

[15] *P.G.* 114:580D-581A.

we could venture to hope for thy return, which hope sweetened somewhat the intense bitterness of our sorrow. But now thou hast taken even these hopes of consolation and turned our little comfort into affliction. If thou hadst not informed us that thou wert alive, then our wound would not have been made wider and our suffering made more acute. O misfortune, finding thee only to be lost! O beloved face which has saddened those who longed for thee! Thou oughtest to have revealed thyself when thou didst first come. Then we would have had time to rejoice and be glad in thy return. But rather, thou camest in among us in a hidden manner, and we knew thee not. But now we hapless ones do not know what to do first. Shall we celebrate thy finding or mourn thy pending death? Of all, we are the most wretched. We had thee in our hands, and we put thee out, the very one whom we sought throughout the world with such effort and care. O what a fearful spectacle has been wrought under the constellations and the sun! How many sighs and fountains of tears can befit or assuage such hard suffering? What stone or iron or anything else as strong by nature could hold out against such an unbearable affliction?" These and many other plaintive cries were his parents voicing for four hours. Most especially was his much suffering mother made miserable, when she brought to mind her irrational aversion and the disdain which she had shown. She lamented then piteously and inconsolably, even tearing the hairs from her head and beating her breast and face.

The news of this event spread like lightning throughout all of the city, so that all partook of the sorrow and joy of the mother and father. Everyone mourned and suffered with the parents. They were also gladdened in their souls but struck with consternation at the unrivaled and inimitable patience of the saint. Father John then said, "I hear the hymnody of the angels, and I rejoice, for I am being delivered from this vain and corruptible life, that I might go to the place which the Christ has prepared for me on account of His extreme goodness. Only hearken to this, my father and most sweet mother. Enough of your tears! The time of my departure is nigh. Even as I told you earlier, take heed not to remove my garments. Bury me with them in this very place." Father John then raised his hands to heaven and uttered a prayer, saying, "O my Lord Jesus Christ and God, Who 'bowed the heavens and came down [Ps. 17:9]' and became perfect Man that Thou mightest deliver us from the hands of the devil, I thank Thy holy name which has empowered me to vanquish the wicked devil. I entreat Thee, hearken to me in this hour: give comfort and consolation to my parents. Teach them the word of Thy truth and bless the faithful who are standing here, and grant unto them those things conducive to salvation, accounting them worthy of Thy heavenly kingdom, for blessed art Thou to the ages of the ages. Amen." After he pronounced the "Amen," he delivered his soul into the hands of God.

His mother, overcome by her love for him, forgot her son's order and the oath she had made. She clothed his relics with splendid garments interwoven with gold. But O the wonder! O the fervent love toward Christ! Rather than his mother's costly array, the symbols of the ascetic's contests, his old garments, were what he had grasped at and more yearned for. Straightway, when the relics had undergone a change of clothing, there occurred a great earthquake and clap of thunder. A voice was then heard saying, "Put on my garments, which thou hast removed, that thou mayest not be greatly chastised." Upon hearing that voice, the saint's mother became paralyzed, speechless, and confounded in her mind for a long while. The father, seeing his wife completely immobilized, remembered the command of his child. He immediately ordered that the deceased be clad again in his tattered and old rason. Immediately, with the carrying out of that order, Theodora was cured. Thereupon, the parents demonstrated prudence and sober-mindedness. Thus, God made it manifest that not only are children obliged to keep the commands of parents, but also parents those of children when their commands are according to God's will.

The hour that Saint John surrendered his soul, boundless miracles occurred. The blind gained their sight, the lame walked, and many others were healed that day. Then the whole city assembled—the emperor, the entire senate, the patriarch and clergy—and interred the saint in the hut, even as he himself had directed. The burial was carried out with great honor and piety. The saint's parents spent much money and built a sacred church at the hut, dedicating to it one-half of their estate. The remaining half was distributed among the poor, including the creation of a hostel for strangers, in order that the tree should resemble the fruit. After Eftropios and Theodora had lived a virtuous and God-pleasing life, they were interred in the church they had built. Their souls were translated to the kingdom of the heavens, where they rejoice forever with their most holy and beloved son, John, and all the saints. The relics of Saint John later came to be in Rome. The saint's Gospel book is preserved at the Monastery of the Pantocrator on Athos.

We have described herein both the life and conduct of Saint John the Hut-dweller. He took up the good yoke of Christ from his youth. He spurned the riches of this life and loved poverty for the sake of Christ. He conceived a strange life, pursuit, and practise, as a homeless beggar at his parents' gate. He meekly endured afflictions and rejection that he might attain to dispassion. By his own volition, he chose to be a stranger to the world and to his own parents. Neither the love of parents nor attachment to riches and comforts did he prefer to Christ. Thus, by this path of asceticism, tears, fasting, and poverty, he trampled upon the adversary and won 'the prize of the high calling of God in Christ Jesus [Phil. 3:14],' to Whom is due glory and dominion unto the ages of ages. Amen.[16]

On the 15th of January, the holy Church commemorates the holy Martyr PANSOPHIOS.

Pansophios, the holy martyr, was from Alexandria. He lived during the time of Emperor Decius (249-251). The saint's father was Neilos, who held the office of proconsul. On account of Pansophios' great wealth and his natural dexterity and cleverness, together with his father's care, attention, and love for the beautiful, Neilos gave his son the best education. Pansophios achieved the highest degree in learning and instruction, both in the exoteric learning of the Greeks and in the esoteric doctrines of the holy Scriptures. Upon the repose of his father, Pansophios distributed his wealth to assist the poor. Afterward, he repaired to the wilderness, seeking to find the Lord that he might turn away from earthly things. He sojourned in the desert for twenty-seven whole years, devoting himself only to God by means of silence, solitude, and prayer. He was denounced to Augustalius, the governor of Egypt, who had been appointed by Decius for the purpose of carrying out the persecution against the Christians. Since the great virtue of the hermit Pansophios could not be hidden, he was brought before the governor. The saint began censuring the imposture and deception of the Greek pagans by citing examples from their own legends and mythology. The governor was refuted and frustrated by the arguments of the saint, who made the point that their pagan superstitions were based on natural phenomena and that their gods personified the passions. Since Augustalius suffered public disparagement in his own court, he ordered that the holy man receive a severe thrashing. Thus, the ever-memorable one received the amaranthine crown of martyrdom.

On the 15th of January, the holy Church commemorates the holy SIX FATHERS in the utter desert, who reposed in peace.[17]

Through the intercessions of Thy Saints,
O Christ God, have mercy on us. Amen.

---

[16] *P.G.* 114:581D.

[17] *The Great Synaxaristes* (in Greek) suggests that these six fathers could be identical with the six living martyrs who are commemorated on the 4th of January. The verse given in the *Menaion* for these souls is: "Six luminous souls shone forth from the smelting pot of life and now stand on the same threshold as the six-winged minds of the seraphim."

On the 16ᵗʰ of January, the holy Church celebrates the veneration of the honored CHAINS of the holy and glorious Apostle PETER.[1]

Saint Peter in Prison

Peter, the most glorious and chief of the apostles, whose chains are venerated by the Church this day, had suffered imprisonment for the sake of Christ, as we read in Saint Luke's account of Acts, Chapter 12.

"Now at that time, Herod the king put forth his hands to maltreat some of those from the Church [Acts 12:1]." The time is the early part of A.D. 44, since that is the date of Herod's death. The title "king" was also accurate during this period, since Herod Agrippa I, grandson of Herod the Great, was king of Palestine from A.D. 42 to 44.[2] Only those three years was he king over Palestine from the death of Herod the Great. Saint Bede (ca. 673-735) writes that this was not Herod Antipas (who slew John the Baptist and played a role in the Lord's Passion), for Josephus reports that Caius (Caligula), upon becoming emperor, immediately handed over the rulership of the Jews, together with the tetrachies of both Philip and Lysanias [Lk. 3:1], to this Herod, the son of Aristoboulos. He calls him, however, Agrippa. Caligula, in the fourth year, or last year, of his reign, similarly bestowed upon the same person the tetrachy of Herod Antipas.[3]

---

[1] The precious and honored chains of the Apostle Peter have been the subject of a number of homilies, including those of: Niketas the Rhetor, which text is extant in the Athonite monasteries of the Great Lavra and Dionysiou; Saint Symeon the Metaphrastes, which text is extant in the Athonite monasteries of Vatopedi and Iveron, though previously it had been at the Great Lavra; and Theodore the Prodromite, which is reproduced in *The Great Synaxaristes* (in Greek) and presented in part herein.

[2] Herod Agrippa I was an Idumaean through his grandfather Herod the Great and a grandson of Mariamne the Maccabean princess.

[3] The Venerable Bede, *Commentary on the Acts of the Apostles*, Ch. 12, p. 111. See also Eusebius/Rufinus of Aquileia, *Church History* 2, 4; *Die Griechischen Christlichen*

(continued...)

"And he killed Iakovos (James) the brother of John with a sword [Acts 12:2]." Apostle Iakovos, a son of thunder [Mk. 3:17], was the first of the apostles to die. His death had been foretold by Christ [Mk. 10:39 ff.; Mt. 20:23]. Saint John Chrysostom (ca. 347-407) writes that "so none may say that without danger or fear of danger they

The Veneration of the Chains

brave death, as being sure of God's delivering them, therefore He permits some to be put to death, and chief men too, Stephen and Iakovos, thereby convincing their slayers, that not even these things make them fall away and hinder them."[4]

And, "because he saw that it pleased the Jews, he in addition went on to seize Peter also—and they were the days of unleavened bread— whom after he laid hold of, he also put in prison, and delivered him up to four sets of four soldiers to guard him, purposing after the passover to bring him forth to the people [Acts 12:3, 4]." Saint Luke, author of Acts, notes the time of the year. He signifies that the occasion of the passover was a ploy by Agrippa to increase his favor among the Jews by a display of zeal against the Christians. Chrysostom exclaims, "O excessive wickedness! On whose behalf was it that he gratified them by doing murders?...Like a wild beast, he attacked all indiscriminately and without consideration."[5] The soldiers guarding the apostle consisted of four, a quaternion (*tetradion*), two on the inside, chained to the prisoner, and two on the outside, in shifts of six hours each, sixteen soldiers in all—the usual Roman custom. "Peter, therefore, on the one hand, was being guarded in the prison, but on the other hand, earnest prayer was being made by the Church to God on his behalf [Acts 12:5]." "Here," observes Chrysostom, "Peter also evinced his own manly courage. But hear how the faithful were stricken and attached to their teachers. No factions, no perturbation. They betook themselves to prayer, which is indeed invincible. They did not say, 'What? I, poor insignificant creature that I am, to pray for him!' for, as they acted out of love, they did not give these things a thought."[6]

---

[3](...continued)
Schriftsteller der esten Jahrhunderte (GCS) 9, 1:115, 14/19; Josephus, *Antiquities of the Jews* 18, 6, 10-7, 2; *Wars of the Jews* 2, 9, 6.
[4] Saint Chrysostom, Homily XXVI, *The Acts of the Apostles*, Nicene, 1ˢᵗ Ser., XI:168.
[5] Ibid., XI:168, 169.
[6] Ibid., XI:170.

An Angel of the Lord Awakens Saint Peter

"And when Herod was about to bring him forth, on that very night Peter was sleeping, bound with two chains between two soldiers; and guards also were before the door keeping the prison [Acts 12:6]." There were two chains, that is, one chain fastened to each soldier on either side of the apostle.

"And behold, an angel of the Lord stood by him, and a light shone in the chamber; and he struck the side of Peter, and woke him up, saying, 'Rise up quickly.' And the chains from his hands fell off of him [Acts 12:7]." The angel smote Peter on the side in order to wake him up. Saint Chrysostom observes that the apostle slept; he was not in distress or fear.[7] Saint Bede says that "the striking of his side was a remembrance of the Passion of Christ, from Whose wound our salvation poured forth. To those of us who are bound by the chain of persecution, the Apostle Peter himself gave this comfort: 'Since then Christ suffered for us in the flesh, arm yourselves also with the same thinking [1 Pe. 4:1].'"[8] Saint Chrysostom informs us that Peter was delivered at night, and that "the light shined in the prison that he might not deem it a fancy or apparition. None saw the light, but he only. This entire incident was so unexpected to the apostle—so prepared was he for death, so entirely had he made up his mind that he was to be put to death—that he thought it all a dream."[9]

---

[7] Ibid.
[8] Saint Bede, op. cit., p. 112.
[9] Saint Chrysostom, loc. cit.

"And the angel said to him, 'Gird thyself about, and bind on thy sandals.' And so he did. And he saith to him, 'Cast about thee thine outer garment, and follow thou me [Acts 12: 8].'" The girdle was worn about the tunic (*chiton*). The outer garment (*himation*) was placed over the tunic. Saint Bede remarks that "both the prophets and the apostles made use of waistbands. Peter had undone the ties of his on account of the chilliness of the prison at that hour, so that his tunic, lowered about his feet, might lessen somewhat the cold of the night. This provides an example to the weak—when we are tried by bodily affliction or unjust treatment by men, we are permitted to relax somewhat our intended rigor."[10] Saint Chrysostom observes that the departure from

Saint Peter Follows the Angel Out of the Prison

the prison was not done in haste, "for one who wishes to break out is not so particular as to take his sandals and gird himself."[11]

"And he went out and kept on following him, and did not know that it was real that which was happening by means of the angel, but he kept on thinking he saw a vision. And after they passed a first guard and a second, they came up to the gate, the iron one, which leadeth into the city, which was opened to them of itself; and having gone out, they advanced one street, and straightway the angel departed from him [Acts 12:9, 10]." Saint Bede comments that "the iron gate which leads to the heavenly Jerusalem was narrow indeed, but it now has been made passable for us by the footsteps of the apostles, who by their own blood prevailed over the enemies' iron."[12] Saint Chrysostom tells us that "when there was no hindrance, then the angel

[10] Saint Bede, loc. cit.
[11] Saint Chrysostom, XI:169.
[12] Saint Bede, op. cit., p. 113.

departed. For Peter would not have gone along, had there been so many hindrances."[13]

"And after Peter came to himself, he said, 'Now I know of a truth, that the Lord sent forth His angel, and took me out of the hand of Herod and all the expectation of the people of the Jews [Acts 12:11].'" Saint Chrysostom remarks that "the Lord would have the pleasure come to him all at once, that he should first be at liberty, and then be sensible of what had happened."[14]

"And having become aware, he came to the house of Mary, the mother of John who was surnamed Mark, where a considerable number of them were gathered together and praying [Acts 12:12]." Saint Chrysostom writes: "Observe how Peter does not immediately withdraw, but first brings the good tidings to his friends....Who is this John? Probably he that was always with them; for this is why he adds his distinctive surname of Mark. Also observe, 'praying' in the night, how much they got by it: what a good thing affliction is; how wakeful it made them! Do you see how great the gain resulting from the death of Stephen? Do you see how great the benefit accruing from this imprisonment? For it is not by taking vengeance upon those who wronged them that God shows the greatness of the Gospel; but in the wrongdoers themselves, without any harm happening to those, he shows what a mighty thing the afflictions in themselves are, that we may not seek in any wise deliverance from them, nor the avenging of our wrongs."[15]

"And after Peter knocked at the door of the gateway, a maidservant, by name Rhoda, came to hearken [Acts 12:13]." Saint Bede says that "it was also a woman who first announced to the disciples that the Lord had come forth from the confinement of the grave."[16]

"And having recognized the voice of Peter, from her joy she did not open the gateway, but she ran in and announced that Peter stood before the gateway [Acts 12:14]." Saint Chrysostom also notes: "Mark how the very servant girls were henceforth upon an equality with them. 'From her joy,' it says, 'she did not open.' This too is well done, that they likewise may not be amazed by seeing him at once, and that they may be incredulous, and their minds may be exercised. 'But she ran in,' just as we are wont to do. She was eager to become the bearer of the good tidings, for good news it was indeed."[17]

---

[13] Saint Chrysostom, XI:170.
[14] Ibid., XI:169.
[15] Ibid., XI:169, 171.
[16] Saint Bede, loc. cit.
[17] Saint Chrysostom, XI:171.

"And they said to her, 'Thou art mad.' But she was strongly affirming that it was so. And they kept on saying, 'It is his angel [Acts 12:15].'" Saint Bede says here that "each of us has angels, which fact is found in *The Book of the Shepherd of Hermas* and in many places in holy Scripture. The Lord said of little children that 'in the heavens their angels continually behold the face of My Father [Mt. 18:10].' Also Jacob, referring to himself, spoke of 'the angel who delivers me from all evils [Gen. 48:16].' And here the disciples believe that the Apostle Peter's angel was coming."[18]

"But Peter continued knocking. And after they opened, they saw him and were amazed. And having motioned to them with his hand to be silent, he set out in detail to them how the Lord brought him out of the prison. And he said, 'Relate these things to Iakovos and to the brethren.' And going out, he went to another place [Acts 12:16, 17]." It is plain here that Iakovos, the brother of the Lord and author of an epistle, who later presides over the synod, is shepherding the Jerusalem Church [Acts 15:13].

"Now it having become day, there was no small disturbance among the soldiers, what then was become of Peter. And after Herod sought after him and found him not, he examined the guards and commanded them to be led away to execution. And having gone down from Judaea to Caesarea, he was staying there [Acts 12:18, 19]."

The Apostle Peter then left Jerusalem and preached the Gospel in other places. News of his miraculous release spread throughout Jerusalem. The chains which fell from the apostle's body were collected by the Christians and reverently retained by them as precious relics. Those formerly base and ugly links of metal, used odiously for the detention of the apostle, became sacred treasures from the time they were clapped upon him. By means of those chains, he suffered the Lord's Passion in his own body through imprisonment and humiliation. Later, chains would also bind him on the path to crucifixion.

Later, when Emperor Nero (54-68) learned of the shameful end of his friend, Simon Magus [Acts 8:9], he blamed Peter. He grew exceedingly angry with the apostle and wanted him killed. Yet, as Saint Symeon Metaphrastes relates, the wrathful Emperor did not fulfill his evil intentions concerning the holy Apostle Peter immediately, but waited for several years. In the meantime, the apostle preached the Gospel in diverse places, including Spain, Carthage, Egypt, Jerusalem, Milan, and Britain.

In the twelfth year of Nero's reign, Peter arrived in Rome for the third time. At length, Saint Peter was arrested by soldiers, chained, and taken to his death. Saint Symeon the Metaphrastes says that Saint Peter was not

---

[18] Saint Bede, loc. cit.

taken alone, but with a multitude of the faithful. The tyrant condemned them to decapitation, but ordered Saint Peter crucified. Laying hold of the condemned, the soldiers brought them to the place of execution. The apostle requested that he be crucified head-downwards. Thus the great apostle of the Lord, the holy Peter, reposed, glorifying God in his death by the cross; enduring great torment from the nails in his hands and feet, he surrendered his blameless soul into the hands of God, on the 29th day of June, in the year of our Lord 67. Afterward, his disciple, the holy Clement, having begged for the body of the apostle, took it down from the cross and washed it. He then called together the remaining faithful and clergy, and they interred the relics with honor. Decent burial was also given to those who suffered with him. The chains by which the apostle was fettered were also kept as sacred heirlooms by the Church. Thus, today, in our celebration of the veneration of his chains, we are keeping faith with the faithful of generations past by this expression of unity.

In 438, Athenais-Evdokia (b. ca. 400-460), wife of Emperor Theodosios II, augustus from 402-450, fell from favor as a result of allegations of adultery. She thereafter went to Jerusalem, as an exile of her own volition, still retaining her imperial title. She constructed and adorned churches, for which Juvenal (ca. 422-458), Patriarch of Jerusalem, presented her with the gift of the spiritual treasure of the Apostle Peter's chains. For three centuries, the treasured chains were kept in Jerusalem, where many healings and miracles were wrought through them. The empress brought these relics back to Hagia Sophia in 439. She kept one set of chains and sent the other to the eldest of her three children, Licinia Evdoxia (b. 422), who had become the wife of Valentinian III, western emperor from 425-455. This Evdoxia built the Church of Saints Peter and Paul on the Esquiline Hill in Rome. Together with those chains she received as a gift from her mother, another set of chains was also placed within it, with which Saint Peter was shackled before his death under the Emperor Nero.

The account of Saint Bede[19] calls for the celebration of this particular day. Evdoxia, the wife of Emperor Valentinian, returned the chains from Jerusalem to Rome on the 1st day of August. She consulted with the pope, who then brought out the chains with which the same apostle had been bound under Nero. When the two chains were put down side by side, they miraculously joined together, as if there had always been one chain. The newly joined chains were placed in the Church of Saint Peter *ad Vincula*

---

[19] See J. de Voragine's *The Golden Legend*, II:37.

("Saint Peter's where the Chains are" or "Saint Peter in Chains").[20] The church was endowed with many gifts and privileges.

Thus, that church in Rome then held the chains from both the apostle's imprisonment in Jerusalem and his martyrdom under Emperor Nero in Rome. The holy Church established the 16th day of January as the feast of this wondrous deliverance of the Apostle Peter and the celebration of the veneration of his sacred chains. These chains wrought many miracles and cures. Even as the handkerchiefs and aprons from Saint Paul's skin were being put upon the sick at Ephesus, and diseases and evil spirits departed from the afflicted [Acts 19:11, 12], in like manner the chains which fettered Peter's body were divinely energized to work wonders. Indeed, not only the bodies and relics of the saints are filled with wonderworking grace, together with their articles and associated instruments, but even their shadows—as that of Peter [Acts 5:15, 16].

The *titulus Apostolurum*, the earliest name by which the Roman parish was known, possibly came into existence at the end of the fourth century. It referred to the two Apostles Peter and Paul, as inscriptions prove. When the church was rebuilt, it was consecrated by Pope Sixtus III (432-440). It then became known as the *titulus Eudoxiae*, in honor of the Byzantine princess who was the principal benefactress. It was not until a century later that we first find it referred to as Saint Peter *ad Vincula*, with reference to the chains wherewith the apostle had been bound while a prisoner at Rome. Later, the chains, which had fallen from Peter's hands in Jerusalem, were sent by Athenais-Evdokia to Evdoxia at Rome, where they had miraculously united with their fellow already there.[21]

The apostle's chains have been venerated in Rome from ancient times. The Feast of the dedication of the basilica of Saint Peter in Chains is celebrated on the 1st of August in the western tradition. The chains taken from the prison in Jerusalem were sent to Rome; then part of them was given to Constantinople, which account is described below.

Theodore the Prodromite, also known at Ptochoprodromos ("Poor forerunner"), who flourished in the twelfth century, also wrote a sermon

---

[20] In Rome, north of the Colosseum, down the Via Cavour, a staircase on the right leads to the Piazza and Church of San Pietro in Vincoli, formerly known as the Basilica Eudossiana. It was consecrated in 439. Later it was restored in the 8th and 15th C., and finally in 1958-1959. The façade has an elegant portico. Inside there is a nave with two aisles, separated by twenty marble pillars, ten on each side. See G. S. P. Freeman-Grenville's *The Beauty of Rome*, p. 25, which says that Michaelangelo's statue of Moses dominates this basilica.

[21] *Butler's Lives of the Saints*, s.v. "1st of August: Saint Peter *Ad Vincula*."

regarding the uncovering of the relics and chains of the Apostle Peter. Nikodemos the Hagiorite rendered the text into simpler Greek and revised it for incorporation into the *Neon Eklogion*, which is reproduced in part herein.

During the reign of Nero, the Apostle Peter suffered martyrdom on a cross, upside down, that he might prepare his feet for the path to the heavens. After his martyric end, no one requested the apostle's relics from Nero. Then certain pious persons, seeing that his precious relics were negligently flung aside, took them up. His body was secretly placed inside a basket-like hamper for honey, which they buried in the earth. They were ever conscious of being liable to repercussions from the murderous and savage idolaters. They feared not only violence against their own persons, but even that the relics might be consigned to the flames or the deep. The destruction of the relics would have been a great loss to the Christians. After the relics were interred safely, a church was built over them.

After the passage of many years, when an earthquake occurred, the formerly hidden relics miraculously returned to the surface. At that time, during the reign of the great Constantine (324-337), when the persecutions of the idolaters against the Christians had subsided, the godly Christians built a splendid church with arches, which was dedicated to the chief of the apostles. The saint's relics were deposited inside an inviolable asylum, that is to say, a hidden spot that was not accessible to all. A throne was crafted within, upon which they placed the holy relics. Two reasons have been proposed for fashioning a throne for the first-enthroned apostle. First, the apostle, though he is dead according to human laws, yet is alive and reigns with Christ. Second, the apostle shall sit upon a throne, in accordance with the Lord's words to His apostles: "Ye shall sit upon twelve thrones, judging the twelve tribes of Israel [Mt. 19:28; Lk. 22:30]." The rest of the church to the apostle was opened to all the faithful. As for the relics, they were viewed only thrice yearly, at which time the Christians could venerate them. High security was always maintained with double doors and locks, lest anyone should be tempted to steal the precious treasure. The foot coverings of the apostle were gilded with pure gold, embellished on top with pearls and precious stones. This brings to mind the words of Esaias: "How beautiful are the feet of those preaching the glad tidings of peace, of those preaching the glad tidings of good things [Rom. 10:15; cf. Is. 52:7]." The apostle's garb was interwoven with gold and adorned with pearls. Now outside of the sanctuary were kept the apostle's chains. They could be seen and venerated by all at any time. Diverse miracles took place for those who approached those chains with faith. Thus the very means by which the devil wished to put down the apostle, the same were exalted by God and wrought many good things for the faithful. There are so many wonders that can be recounted. We shall select a few, which shall not only bring delight to the readers but also clearly manifest the divine power energizing in those chains; for both physical and spiritual ailments were cured, even to the pardoning of sins, by means of these honored chains.

On one occasion, a certain man who had committed grave sins went with tear-filled eyes to the pope, at that time a marvellous spiritual father and wise in things divine. The penitent spilled forth copious tears, seeking forgiveness. The pope joyfully received his confession and repentance, but also gave him a canon to perform. He enjoined a penance upon him, telling him that, in so fulfilling it, by the authority of the chief of the apostles, he would be loosed from his sins. The pope bade him to bind his hands, feet, and body with the chains of the apostle. He was then to make a circuit around the grounds of the church seven times. Upon completing this labor, he then was to go to that closed part of the church where the sacred relics of the apostle are kept and tap his head on the closed door before the throne and relics. If the door opened to him, that would be a sign that his sins were forgiven. If the door did not open to him, then his penance was still in effect. That Christian soul did as the pope directed. He then struck his forehead against the door, invoking the help of the apostle. Straightway—O the sympathy of the chief of the apostles of Christ, Peter!—the seals broke, the locks unfastened, and the door opened to him. He entered therein, released from the bond of the chains and delivered of his sins. Thus gladdened, he returned to his house rejoicing. Why should this miracle seem incredible? Did not the Lord say to Peter, "And I will give to thee the keys of the kingdom of the heavens, and whatsoever thou shalt bind on the earth shall have been bound in the heavens, and whatsoever thou shalt loose on the earth shall have been loosed in the heavens [Mt. 16:19]"? What are earthly locks to one who has the keys to the heavenly kingdom?

Thereupon, the fame of this miracle spread, not only in Rome but also abroad. The pope was then known to enjoin this penance upon others. Now there was at that time another Christian man, a very wealthy merchant, who traded on the seas with his ships. Though he possessed vast wealth, he lost it all and became destitute when the sea swallowed up his cargo. With much difficulty, he battled the swells and managed to save his life. He sought assistance in many quarters, but could in no wise find any consolation. He then brought to mind the chains and relics of the Apostle Peter. He had heard of the fabulous treasure of precious stones and pearls with which the relics were adorned. As he pondered in his mind on the apostle, a stream of tears flowed from his eyes. He supplicated him with all his soul, saying, "When thou, O man of God, wast in this world, of thine own volition thou didst choose poverty, in accordance with the Master's command to the apostles 'not to procure for yourselves gold, nor silver, nor money in your belts, nor leathern pouch for the way, nor two tunics, nor sandals, nor a staff [Mt. 10:9, 10].' For that cause thou also didst cast out Simon Magus for offering money for the giving of the Holy Spirit [Acts 8:18 ff.]. Thou didst often by thy teachings show disdain for gold.[22] The Master has well said, 'It is easier for a camel to pass through a needle's eye than for a rich man to enter into the kingdom of God [Mt. 19:24; Lk. 18:25].' For the love of Christ thou didst endure all things. But now that thou are dead, what need hast thou of gold shoes and costly array, studded with jewels? When thou wert alive thou gavest all to the orphans, widows, and poor. Now I who was formerly wealthy am the poorest of men. I have been made wretched and miserable from my poverty. Therefore, I come to thee in my penury and hunger, asking for some consolation in my indigent state. There is no one else in whom I might entertain some good hope. No one wishes to see or hear me. If they do see or hear me, I am quickly shunned. Since no human remedy is available, I come to thy sacred feet. If I may make bold to ask, I shall now use those divine words spoken to Moses: 'Loose thy sandals from off thy feet [Ex. 3:5],' or should I say, the one sandal at least. Thou knowest, O divine apostle, my misfortune and the cargo I lost to the bottom of the sea. Thou also wast a man of the sea and made thy living with ships. Thou knowest how many times the sea puts man to the test. I know that at least twice thou wast in danger of drowning. Once, when the Master was sleeping on a cushion, a great storm arose, with waves being thrown over into the ship. You had awakened Christ Who then rebuked the wind and commanded the sea to be still and silent [Mk. 4:37-41]. Then on another occasion, thou didst come down from the ship and walked on the water to go to Jesus. But thou didst fear upon seeing the strong wind. When thou didst begin to sink, Jesus stretched forth His hand and laid hold of thee [Mt. 14:28-33]. Now I am not requesting of thee to give me thy sandal as a free gift but as a loan. I know that with thy sandal I shall have a successful voyage and the waves of poverty that have overwhelmed me shall subside. In thanks, I shall fashion for thee a splendid and more honorable foot covering. As for now, thy foot may remain bare, for it will not be cold or tread on thorns or stumble on any rock or become unclean from mud. That is because the place where thou art now is not only well appointed but also decorated with splendid marble slabs. Indeed, thou hast finished thine earthly course; there are no other earthly roads for thee to traverse by foot. Now thou mightest rest and remain still."

These were the words of that hapless merchant who persuaded himself that what he wished to do was allowed in his present condition. The problem

---

[22] 1Pe. 1:18; 3:3; 5:2.

still remained as to how to gain access to the relics and the treasure. He then addressed the apostle, saying, "If thou wilt ordain it, O first of the apostles, I shall feign that I committed some deadly sin. I shall go to the pope and confess, though falsely. I know very well that he shall give me a penance, and the usual one, as he has done so on previous occasions. Yes, I shall bind myself with thy chains and tap my head on thy door. At which time, do thou show me thy philanthropy and sympathy by opening up to me." The merchant spoke these words while weeping. He then fell asleep from exhaustion and beheld a vision. It appeared to him that the apostle came and bade him to carry out his plan. The merchant then went to the pope, confessed to such and such a sin, and received the much-desired penance. He followed through and bound himself with the chains and made a sevenfold circuit about the temple. He then went to the door of the relics and struck his forehead upon the door. The apostle—O who can describe thy power?—opened up to this sacrilegious plunderer. The apostle then gave over his sandal to his robber, by extending his foot slightly with the sandal. The merchant took the sandal and concealed it under his arm. He then exited very happy, giving thanks to his benefactor.

As he carried the sacred shoe in his hand, the door not only opened but also closed of itself. Why should this be so astonishing? Had not the sick been carried out into the streets on beds and pallets, in order that at least the shadow of Peter as he came might overshadow some of them? And all of them, even those who were troubled by unclean spirits, were healed [Acts 5:15, 16]. Now the theft went unnoticed for a little while, by both the Romans and the pope himself; that is, until, the appointed day when the relics were to be brought out for veneration. On that occasion, the pope observed that the one foot of the apostle was uncovered. He marvelled and sorrowed greatly. He could not fathom what had became of the one sandal. The locks and seals were untouched. "How was it possible that a grave robber entered?" he asked. He then perceived that this could not have occurred without it being God's will, because had not the apostle permitted it, this daring removal could not have taken place. The pope then was resolved to commission a similar sandal for the apostle's sacred foot.

In the meantime, the merchant succeeded very well. In exchange for the Apostle Peter's sandal, he received sufficient money by which to trade. As a result he became exceedingly wealthy. One would have thought that, in thanksgiving, the merchant would have made good on his loan, but he did not. Had his soul become corrupted from the flowing in of too many riches? Had he fallen into avarice? Perhaps he had heard that the pope commissioned a new foot covering and thought it superfluous to provide a third sandal. The reason is not known for his negligence toward his benefactor. But the divine Peter did not leave for long that merchant to be mastered by his carelessness and indifference. The apostle appeared to the merchant one night and reminded him of the obligation and sought the promised return. The merchant instantly commissioned the making of a brilliant foot covering. When the work was completed, the merchant entered a ship bound for Rome. After he truthfully confessed to the pope all that had transpired, he again bound himself with the chain and knocked at the door. It opened to him and—O the wonder!—the apostle stretched forth his foot. The merchant removed the sandal replaced by the pope, exchanging it for the one he had promised. The merchant then placed the pope's offering in between the two feet of the apostle, who had separated his feet a little to accommodate the third sandal. The merchant then exited, relieved and glad that he had fulfilled the terms of the agreement.

The relics of the apostle remained adorned in that manner for many years. Then, after the passage of much time—I (the author) do not know why—God dispensed in His œconomy that the precious relics should become detached. As it is written: "Who knoweth the mind of the Lord? Who shall instruct Him [1 Cor. 2:16; Is. 40:13]?" The relics were dismembered and entirely separated—the head from the body, vertebrae, arms, palms, feet, ankles, and fingers. This perhaps took place on account of the sins of the Romans. Then the throne, the garment, and the sandals were taken away. The apostle's relics were deposited in a chest and placed in the church. Many years again passed. A Constantinopolitan, distinguished in rank as the best of senators, God-loving in disposition, needed to go to Rome on some business. He was vouchsafed to see and venerate the apostolic relics. Since he loved both his homeland and God, he conceived a daring idea. He would venture to steal the relics of the apostle and return with them to Constantinople. Perhaps he would have succeeded in this endeavor had he performed what the previous merchant had done; that is, had he first confessed to the apostle his intention and then sought his permission, he might have received leave to carry out what he intended. But rather, he moved audaciously forward and committed the deed. After he stole the treasure, he placed the relics in a new and clean sack. He then loaded them on a mule and began his trek back to his home in Constantinople.

What, however, did the divine Peter dispense? ("I," says the author of this account, "admit that I do not know the reason why the apostle forbade the translation of his relics to Constantinople.") Was it because the translation did not take place with his permission? Or was it because he preferred to remain as the guardian and preserver of Rome? That same night, the apostle informed the pope of all that had transpired. The pope was greatly agitated by the vision and dispatched cavalry and soldiers to apprehend the thief. They sped off to carry out the commission and succeeded. The men arrested and scourged the Constantinopolitan perpetrator. They bound him and brought him with dishonor before the pope. "Who art thou?" demanded the pope. It was then learned that the Constantinopolitan was a man of high office and illustrious lineage. He made his case, stating his intention, saying that he was pious and a lover of the apostle. The pope then ordered that the Constantinopolitan be untied. He then spoke to him calmly, as would a spiritual father. The relics were then secured within the holy Table. As for the Constantinopolitan nobleman, he was granted a portion of the august chains, as a consolation not only for his sorrow and dishonor, but also for the love he cherished toward the apostle. Thus the chains were brought to Constantinople.

The chains proved to be a source of healing and comfort, both for the soul and body. We kiss those chains which the apostle wore for Christ and by which he had bound falsehood and the tyrant. Though he wore those chains as though he were a malefactor, yet he slew the devil and bound him by those very chains. We beg the apostle's intercession that we may be released from the chains of the passions and our transgressions. As he is the keeper of the keys of the kingdom, we beg him to open the gates thereof to us who reverence him with love.

On the 16th of January, the holy Church commemorates the holy brothers and Martyrs PEVSIPPOS, ELASIPPOS, and MESIPPOS, and their grandmother NEONILLA.

Pevsippos, Elasippos, and Mesippos, the glorious and holy martyrs, were triplets from Cappadocia. They were skilled in horsemanship and in taming small wild horses and running with them on level country. When a civil holiday of Nemesis, whom the pagans believed to be a goddess pursued amorously by Zeus, was being celebrated in their homeland, they invited their grandmother Neonilla to keep festival with them. The elderly lady, having been taught in the Faith of Christ, mocked the idols and spoke to her grandsons regarding God the Logos and the dispensation of the incarnation. This instruction came to be

The Martyrdom of Saints Pevsippos, Elasippos, and Mesippos in the Fire

the cause of their salvation and Faith. Now each of the brothers remembered a mystical dream, which they each recently had been vouchsafed. All of these events led them to believe in the Christ. Straightway, the triplets demolished the idols and boldly confessed Jesus Christ. They were denounced to the authorities and suffered execution by fire at the hands of the idolaters. The holy Neonilla was charged with confessing Christ and was taken to another city and beheaded. Thus, the blessed ones bore away the crowns of martyrdom.

**On the 16th of January, the holy Church commemorates
the holy Martyr DANAKTOS (DANAX), the Anagnost (Reader).**

Danax, the holy martyr, hailed from Avlon of Illyricum, which is now known as Albania. He was a clergyman of the holy Church of God. He put into safekeeping the ecclesiastical vessels that they might be preserved from the inroads of the unbelievers. He was arrested in one place where they attempted to compel him to offer sacrifice to the idols, especially Bacchus. Since he remained unpersuaded, they put him to death by plunging their daggers into him. Thus the ever-memorable one received the crown of martyrdom.

Saint Damaskenos

**On the 16th of January,
the holy Church commemorates
the holy New-hieromartyr
DAMASKENOS of Bulgaria (1771).**[23]

Damaskenos, the holy new-martyr, was born in a village called Gambrovo in the province of Tŭrnovo.[24] He left his country and came to Mount Athos, where he became a monk at the Monastery of Hilandar. At Hilandar he was ordained a deacon, then a hieromonk, and finally became the abbot. The fathers of the monastery sent Damaskenos to Bulgaria. Throughout the duration of his visit there, he stayed at a *metochion* (monastery holding) in the province of Sphistovi. Before his return to Hilandar, he gathered all his belongings and attempted to collect a certain sum he had lent to the Turks. But they were dishonorable and ill-disposed, refusing to give him the money; rather they decided to keep it, in addition confiscating everything that Damaskenos had in the *metochion*.

What else, in addition to this, did the devil inspire them to do? They chose a Turkish harlot and raised her by a ladder to the top of the *metochion*

---

[23] The martyrdom of Saint Damaskenos was taken from the *Neon Martyrologion*, 3rd ed. (pp. 98-101), and incorporated into *The Great Synaxaristes* (in Greek).

[24] Tŭrnovo, a city on the river Jantra in northern Bulgaria, which is not related to Tyrnovos in Thessaly.

and left her there. Then the Turks smashed the door down and broke into the *metochion*, finding the woman whom they themselves had put therein. Thereupon they seized and tied the saint, and dragged him to the judge, beating and kicking him all the way. Once they arrived, the Turks shouted accusations against Damaskenos, saying that he dared to take a Turkish woman and sin with her. But the judge knew that the whole matter was slander and sought to deliver him. The false witnesses and all the Turks that heard the judge's pardon, however, were opposed to it and cried out that Damaskenos was guilty of death. The pernicious ones prevailed and took the martyr away in order to hang him.

On the way, the Hagarenes asked the saint three times if he wished to become a Moslem and save his life. Then they would return all that they had taken away from him, giving him back even more. But the martyr of Christ replied, "I was born in the Christian Faith, and I will die in the Christian Faith, so take me wheresoever you wish." Therefore, they led him to the place of execution. Damaskenos asked their permission to say his prayers, in response to which request they loosened his bonds and allowed him to pray. The martyr then faced toward the east and prayed. After he made the sign of the Cross, he begged the murderers to tie him again. Afterward they hanged him, and the ever-memorable one received the crown of martyrdom in the year 1771. However, following the death of the saint, divine justice avenged those iniquitous manslayers. As they were crossing the Danube River, they drowned in its currents and received as retribution everlasting damnation. May we be delivered from such an end and be made worthy of the kingdom of the heavens, through the intercessions of the holy Priest-martyr Damaskenos. Amen.

Through the intercessions
of Thy Saints,
O Christ God,
have mercy on us.
Amen.

**On the 17ᵗʰ of January, the holy Church commemorates
our venerable and God-bearing Father ANTHONY the Great.**[1]

Saint Anthony the Great

Anthony (Antony),[2] our great father, was born in Egypt, during the reign of the most impious Decius (249-251). His parents were Christians who raised him in piety. He was modest, shy, and honest. He had no dealings with others apart from his kinsfolk. He did not wish to learn letters, because of the rough behavior of the lads at school. By nature he was guileless and had no desire to keep company with other children or engage in their games. His desire was to conduct his life according those words that have described the Patriarch Jacob; that is, that he was a simple, natural, and unaffected man, dwelling in a house [Gen. 25:27]. Anthony did not wish to have anxieties, concerns, and confusion. He did have a desire to attend church frequently with his parents,

---

[1] The complete Life of this saint was recorded in Greek by Saint Athanasios the Great, Patriarch of Alexandria (328-373). His Life was also recorded in Greek by Saint Symeon the Metaphrastes, which text was rendered in simpler Greek by Agapios the Cretan, who published it in his *Neon Paradeison*, which was incorporated into *The Great Synaxaristes* (in Greek). Collateral sources in English include: Saint Athanasios, *Life of Antony*, Nicene, 2ⁿᵈ Ser., IV:195-221, translated by Rev. H. Ellershaw, edited by P. Schaff and H. Wace; Carolinne White's *Early Christian Lives: The Life of Antony by Athanasius*, pp. 8-70; *The Life of Saint Anthony*, Ancient Christian Writers, No. 10, translated by Robert T. Meyer, Ph.D.; *Early Christian Biographies*, FC, 15:134-216, translated by Sister Mary Emily Keenan, S.C.N.; *The Paradise of the Fathers*, Vol. 1, translated from the Syriac by E. A. Wallis Budge; and H. J. Thurston & D. Attwater, *Butler's Lives of the Saints*. For further reading, see also the sayings of Saint Anthony in "170 Texts on Saintly Life" and "Directions on Life in Christ," from *Early Fathers from the Philokalia*, translated by E. Kadloubovsky and G. E. H. Palmer.

[2] There is no justification for the spelling "Anthony," other than its current popular usage as a variant of Antony or Antonius. Jacobus de Voragine, *The Golden Legend*, Volume 1, records that the name comes from *ana*, above, and *tenens*, holding, meaning one who holds on to higher things and despises worldly things.

to whom he was obedient. He listened attentively to the sacred readings, keeping in his heart the exhortations and admonitions from which he benefitted. He was neither idle in his parents' house, nor negligent toward them, nor did he despise them as they aged. Though he was reared amid moderate affluence, he did not pester his parents for varied or luxurious fare, nor was this a source of pleasure to him. He did not trouble them for costly array or other items which youths generally ask of their parents. He was satisfied with what his home offered him and sought nothing further. His manner of life showed discernment and understanding. His parents had no need to reprimand him, but he rather became a teacher to others. His attitude toward them was that of a man according honor to his parents, for which they treated him as the household steward.

When Anthony was about eighteen or twenty, his parents reposed. He was left with the care of not only his parental estate but also one little sister. Now it was not six months after the death of his parents that he continued his perfect attendance at church. On one such occasion, as he was going to church, he communed with himself as he walked, and reflected upon how the apostles left all and followed the Christ, even as did the martyrs and other venerable saints. He then meditated upon those words in the Acts of the holy apostles, about how the first Christians sold their possessions and brought and laid them at the apostles' feet for distribution to the poor [Acts 4:34, 35]. He thought how great was the blessing of such, and how great a hope in the heavens [Col. 1:5] was laid up for them who had in this wise obeyed the voice of Christ.

Saint Anthony's Call to Asceticism

As he entered the church, it happened that the Gospel was being read. The words of Jesus to the rich men sounded in his ears: "If thou art willing to be perfect, go and sell thy possessions, and give to the poor, and thou shalt have treasure in heaven; and come and keep on following Me [Mt. 19:21]." Upon hearing this admonition, the holy Anthony perceived those words of the sacred Gospel as a message to himself. After reflecting upon these words, he deemed them not to have been pronounced as a matter of chance, but instead that the righteous notion he had about the apostles might be confirmed. He forthwith departed from the church and donated to his neighbors, those who were poor, all of the beautiful property which he had inherited from his forefathers. He possessed three hundred fields, extremely fertile and productive. He shared them out among the poor villagers, lest any should harbor a grudge against him or his sister. He did not wish that either he or his sister should be encumbered or troubled with the cares of the land's cultivation, but that they might labor unhindered in spiritual contests. The remainder of the movable estate and possessions was sold. Anthony received a considerable sum of money from the sale, which proceeds went to the poor. He did, however, retain a sufficient amount for the maintenance of his sister, for he deemed her more vulnerable on account of her gender and age.

On another occasion, when it was Sunday, Anthony went to church. He inclined his ear carefully to hear what would come forth for him. Then the Gospel words of the Lord to His disciples were read aloud: "Do not become anxious for the morrow [Mt. 6:34]." He thereupon went out and gave away among the poor whatever else remained. He spoke to his sister lovingly, regarding truth and the fear of God. He brought her around to his way of thinking, that is, renunciation of the world for the sake of Christ. He then entrusted her to the care of certain virgins living there. Anthony then began his ascetic course in a place close to his house, where he built a cell. At that time, there were neither monasteries in Egypt nor any who knew of the inner desert. If one wished to give attention to his soul, he practised the ascetical life alone, usually not far from his village. Anthony therefore betook himself a sufficient distance from the village, so that he might be apart from the habitation and conversation of men.

Now there was in the neighboring village a certain blessed solitary who had taken up the ascetical life from his youth. Anthony had observed this man and desired to emulate his conduct and deeds; for "it is good to be zealous in a good thing always [Gal. 4:18]." If he heard of any other righteous men pursuing such a mode of life, as a wise bee which hovers and rests over flowers, Anthony went and strenuously sought out such persons. He would pay his respects and then obtain the gift of honey, whether it be spiritual instructions or the manner of asceticism of these hermits. He disciplined himself, and his resolve grew daily, lest his thoughts should wander to his previous inheritance and the remembrance of his kin. He directed all his energies to spiritual practises that he might be a pure offering to God. He also labored with his own hands, because he heard the apostle say, "This we commanded you, that if anyone is not willing to work, neither let him eat [2 Thess. 3:10]." With a small amount from the wages he received, he provided for himself, while the remainder he donated to the poor. He prayed continually, for he had heard the injunction to "be praying unceasingly [1 Thess. 5:17]." He also gave all his attention at the reading of the Scriptures, lest anything should escape him. Thereupon, not one word fell to the ground. He retained everything in his memory, which came to serve him in place of books.

Thus Anthony found "grace in the presence of God and men [Lk. 2:52]." He was beloved by all and loved all. He subjected himself in sincerity to those righteous anchorites he visited, learning thoroughly where each surpassed him in zeal and discipline. He hearkened to them in everything and showed them much love and reverence. If he were delayed in visiting them, their love was such that they would send after him; thus, they revealed their anxious care for him. They perceived in Anthony that he was the object of God's mercy. They understood that he was to be perfected as a chosen vessel. They also observed how he benefitted by trafficking in the riches of heaven. Each one of these righteous fathers therefore took him under his wing, according to the measure of the gift and power bestowed upon him by God. Consequently, Anthony carefully heeded those whom he visited, that he might imitate their virtues. He observed the graciousness and courtesy of one, and the constancy and unceasing prayer of another. He took knowledge of another's freedom from anger and another's loving-kindness. He attentively watched those who kept vigil and noticed their endurance and perseverance. He noted how another studied assiduously and with devotion. He regarded with respect another for his fasting, sleeping on the ground, and undergoing other hardships. He looked with pleasure upon those who were meek, even-tempered, and forbearing. In all these virtuous men, he noted their piety toward Christ and the mutual love which animated all. Thus filled with the knowledge of their pursuits and manners, he returned to his own retreat of philosophy and discipline. Once there, he would apply himself and assimilate as his own the qualities of each. He wished to possess in himself the virtues of all. With men of his own age, he was not given to engaging in any rivalry, but was concerned only that he should not be second to them in higher things. He in no wise had high thoughts about himself nor vied with another. He contrived in every way not to give offense. He toiled in his ascetic labors in such a way as not to make others envious of him; rather, they rejoiced and gave thanks to God Who wrought mightily in him. He was called by them a lover of God, that is, Theophilos. Some loved him as a brother, and others as a son.

Saint Anthony Strives with the Demons

The devil, who hates and envies what is good, could not endure seeing such eagerness and diligence in one so young. He saw Anthony's perfection and therefore endeavored to war against the saint, in a manner he was wont to effect against other young men. He first attempted to thwart his asceticism with the remembrance of the care and concern of his little sister, hoping by this anxiety and solicitude to shake his settled purpose. He whispered to Anthony about his former wealth, as he attempted to implant in Anthony a love of money and glory. He reminded him of those sweet and delightful things of the table and the relaxation and enjoyment of the flesh. He warned him of the toil and suffering entailed with striving for virtue and the rough path that lay ahead, involving many years of hardship. He then called to Anthony's mind the infirmity of the flesh and bodily sicknesses, and other such ailments that might issue from unchecked austerities. He tried to sow all these images in his mind that he might cut off his eagerness and enthusiasm. The devil, however, saw for himself that he was vanquished by the great faith and firm resolve of the venerable one. Though the devil was confounded by Anthony's prayers, he still had confidence in his own munitions, that is, in the weapons which are in the navel of man's belly. These he was wont to employ as his initial snares against the young. He disturbed and harassed the young man with all kinds of recollections, so that even the onlookers could perceive the struggle which was going on between Anthony and the adversary. But Anthony proved a strong combatant in that hard war of the flesh and the belly. The adversary not only attempted to put Anthony to the test and trouble him during the night, but during the day as well. The enemy began suggesting and scattering the seeds of unclean thoughts and carnal desires, but the saint countered such temptations with prayer. Ofttimes the thrice-accursed one would appear as a beguiling woman in his attempt to goad Anthony and draw him into sin. Thus he utilized every ploy to seduce and vanquish the invincible, but his craftiness was to no profit. The saint invoked the Christ, with Whom he filled his mind with the nobility inspired by Him and considered the spirituality suited for man's soul. Thus, with prayer and fasting, he quenched that coal of the enemy's deceit and remained wholly chaste. Now Anthony also employed anger and turned his thoughts to the everlasting fire and the gnawing worm. He set such thoughts in array against his adversary, and thereby passed through that fiery temptation unscathed. Though the foe fancied himself to be like God, now he was put to shame by a stripling of a man. The devil who boasted himself against flesh and blood was put to flight by a man in the flesh. This is because the grace of the Lord was working in Anthony. Verily the Lord, Who for our sakes put on flesh, gave the body victory over the devil. Therefore, whenever one repeated the triumphs wrought for Anthony, the saint would say, "I toiled,...yet not I, but the grace of God which was with me [1 Cor. 15:10]." Again, all those involved in this struggle should cite these words of the apostle.

The serpent then, seeing that by means of suggestive thoughts alone he was unable to overthrow Anthony, gnashed his teeth. He threatened to show the righteous Anthony his outward form, thinking to terrify him by his exterior appearance. He therefore assumed the likeness of that which revealed his blackened nature. He appeared to Anthony as a swarthy and malignant-looking child. Though the guileful devil did not ply Anthony with thoughts, yet he fawned and cringed as it were before him. He lamented at his being worsted, declaring, "I shall bring thee low, even as I have many." The saint then made over himself the sign of the Cross, which the enemy observed and from which he drew back, saying, "Many were they whom I have deceived and cast down, but in warring against thee I have proved weak." Anthony then inquired, "Who art thou who speakest thus with me?" The creature answered with a plaintive voice, "I am the spirit of whoredom, and have taken upon me incitements which lead to it against the young. I am called the spirit of lust. I have deceived and agitated many who wished to live soberly. I have attacked thee, but I was powerless before thee and thy works. I have persuaded many to return to their former foul lives who had sought to live chastely. I am he on account of whom also the prophet reproved those who had fallen, saying, 'They have gone astray in a spirit of whoredom [Hos. 4:12].' For it has been by me that they have stumbled. I am also the one who has so often troubled thee, but thou hast overthrown me." The venerable Anthony then gave thanks to the Lord and said to the demon, "I am not afraid of thee any longer. Nor do I assign thee any consequence, since thou art benighted in mind as some infirm and contemptible child. Henceforth, 'the Lord is my helper, and I shall look down upon mine enemies [Ps. 117:7].'" After the devil heard this, he shuddered and forthwith took flight, not daring to approach the holy man again.

This was Saint Anthony's first encounter against the devil, or rather this was the triumph of Christ working in Anthony; for Christ "condemned sin in the flesh, in order that the ordinance of the law might be fulfilled in us, who walk not according to the flesh, but according to the spirit [Rom. 8:3, 4]." The holy man, however, neither relaxed nor neglected his rule. He knew from the Scriptures that the ways of the enemy were diverse and wily. He knew that though the enemy had been vanquished for a time, he would not desist. He would look for other opportunities or some small negligence on Anthony's part to gain a foothold and overwhelm him. Saint Peter clearly taught that our "adversary, the devil, as a roaring lion, walketh about, seeking whom he might devour [1 Pe. 5:8]." Anthony also learned that we must put on the full armor of God, in order to stand against the wiles of the devil [Eph. 6:11]. The devices of the evil one are manifold. Reflecting upon this, Anthony reckoned that although the devil had not deceived his heart by bodily pleasure, still the adversary would lay snares to catch him by other means; for the devil's love is sin. Anthony thereupon decided to add toil to toil and mortify his flesh and keep it in subjection, lest haply having conquered on one side, he should be dragged down on the other. He therefore engaged upon a more severe mode of life. His readiness to serve God made every labor easy to bear. Many marvelled at how Anthony was able to endure toils easily. He was tireless in equipping himself for battle, that is, training himself with fasting, vigils, and every imaginable hardship. He endured all this preparation that he might be found ready, should the tempter attack from another flank. On account of his zeal, he participated in all-night vigils, not once or twice, but many times. He ate once daily, after the setting of the sun, or sometimes once in two days, and often even in four. His fare consisted of only bread and salt. His beverage was a limited amount of water. As for oil, it was not part of his diet. Of flesh and wine, it is superfluous even to speak. His bedding consisted of one rush mat, but he many times slept on the bare ground. He would not anoint himself with oil. He observed that it made the body soft and the members effeminate. He thought that the use of oil would hardly cause young men's bodies to grow strong, if they were being softened by oil. He advised young men to mortify their flesh as much as possible, saying that, whenever the pleasures of the body were diminished, then the soul was empowered, according to the apostle: "Whenever I am weak, then I am strong [2 Cor. 12:10]." Thought Anthony's struggles and contests were long in duration, he daily had renewed zeal, as one who had just begun the contest. He came to the conclusion that renunciation and retirement from the world and progress in virtue should not be measured by time, but by desire and fixity of purpose. He therefore took no account of the time that he had passed in the desert. Each day he began his life of ascesis (askesis) anew, as he had done at the beginning. He remembered the words of the apostle and would recite them: "Brethren, I count not myself to have apprehended; but one thing I do, forgetting the things which are behind, and stretching forth to those things which are before, I pursue toward the mark for the prize of the high calling of God in Christ Jesus [Phil. 3:13, 14]." The holy man was also mindful of that spoken of by Prophet Elias, "As the Lord of Hosts before Whom I stand lives, today I will appear before him (Ahab) [3 Kgs. (1 Kgs.) 18:15]," which words incited him to be worthy to stand before God daily. For he observed that in saying "today," the prophet did not reckon the time that had passed. But daily, as though he were ever commencing, he endeavored to appear fit before God, being pure in heart and ever ready to submit to His will alone. He thought that the manner and acts of the monk should be as one alien to this world but akin to the angels. Thus did the saint master and govern himself.

Saint Anthony Lives in the Sepulchers and Contends with Demons

Anthony then went out to the sepulchers. They were located some distance from the village. He entered and took up his abode therein that he might continue his ascetic struggle. He bade an acquaintance of his to bring him a morsel of bread from time to time. Anthony then had this same man shut and lock the door of that sepulcher, leaving him alone to pray. The enemy became frenetic at this juncture, surmising that in but a short time Anthony would fill the desert with the ascetic discipline. Thereupon, the devil came one night with a company of his minions. They administered such a thrashing to the saint that he was left lying on the ground from his wounds and excessive pain. He was half-dead, with little breath remaining in him.

Indeed, the enemy so cut him with stripes that Anthony lay on the ground speechless from the excessive pain. He later said that the pain inflicted had been so excessive that no blows inflicted by man could ever have caused him such torment.

Saint Anthony at the Sepulcher

Nevertheless, by the providence of God—for the Lord never overlooks those who hope in Him—the next day, his acquaintance came with the allotted loaves. He opened the door to the sepulcher, only to find Anthony lying on the ground as one dead. That man raised up Anthony and carried him to the main church in their village, and laid him upon the ground. When his kindred and neighbors learned of his brutal beating, they came running in grief. They then prepared to conduct funeral rites for Anthony. No small number of people collected to pay their respects, as he was laid out in their midst, and they all sat around him. Anthony, however, was in a deep sleep that was restful and sweet.

At about midnight, the saint regained consciousness. He looked about and saw that all of them were slumbering, with the exception of that acquaintance who attended to him. He had been sitting by Anthony's pillow and watching over him. Anthony then nodded at him, making a gesture that he carry him to the sepulcher without waking anyone. He said to him quietly, "Do this charity, lest these people should believe that the evil one still

Saint Anthony is Attacked by Demons

has power and they become afraid to counter him." That man hearkened and carried Anthony to the sepulcher and shut the door after him. As Anthony lay there, he kept constant in prayer. He would have stood, but he had not the strength from the wounds he sustained from the demons. After he had prayed, he said with a shout, "Where are you? Here am I, Anthony. I shall flee not from your blows; for even if you should inflict more wounds, nothing would separate me from the love of Christ [Rom. 8:35]." Then he began chanting,

"Though a host should array itself against me, my heart shall not be afraid; though war should rise up against me, in this have I hoped [Ps. 26:3]."

The fierce and savage enemy, marvelling not only at the words of the ascetic but also that he dared to return to the sepulcher, summoned his hounds. He emitted smoke and addressed them, saying, "Do you see how this insolent fellow challenges us? He treats us with contempt. Neither the spirit of fornication nor the pain of physical blows overcomes him. His heart is not afraid. Let us contrive a way to attack him in another fashion." Now changes of form and creating apparitions are easy for the enemy. The phantasms take on such a character that they seem real to the beholder. The demons then caused a phantom earthquake to rock the sepulcher, making such a din that it seemed to rend asunder the four walls of the chamber. Holes then appeared in the walls, and all kinds of different demons poured forth in the shapes of wild animals and reptiles. They filled the saint's chamber with specters in diverse forms—lions, bears, leopards, bulls, serpents, wolves, vipers, and other such creatures. According to the nature of each of these species, they made noises and moved according to the assumed shape. The lion began roaring as when it is about to slay; the bull was ready and tossing its horns to gore Anthony; the panther was preparing to pounce; the snakes and vipers were writhing and hissing, appearing ready to strike; the scorpion was scuttling into position to sting him; and the wolves seemed to be rushing at him. The noises and the faces of these creatures were terrible, but Anthony was in no wise perturbed. Though the saint groaned as he was pummeled and goaded by them, they could in no wise slay him. He lay there watching them and, although he experienced worse pain, still his mind was unafraid and vigilant. So unshaken in his soul was he that he then laughed and mocked the demons, saying, "There is no power in you. If there had been any power in you, it would have sufficed had only one of you come. But since the Master has deprived you of your strength, you attempt to terrify me by your numbers. Indeed, a proof of your weakness is that you take the shapes of brute beasts." Then with very great boldness of heart, he said to them, "If you have received authority against me, be not negligent. Delay not to attack. But if you are unable to do anything, why trouble yourselves in vain? For faith in our Lord is a seal and a wall of safety to us." The demons then gnashed their teeth against him, because they were mocking themselves rather than him.

Now the Lord was not forgetful of the venerable Anthony's contests, but instead was at hand to help him in his wrestling. The saint then looked up and beheld the roof, as it were, to have been opened. A ray of light came down upon him. Then the demons suddenly dispersed and vanished, the pain of his body forthwith ceased, and the chamber was again whole. There was no sign or trace of the wounds sustained by Anthony. He perceived the divine visitation and the help of the Lord. After he recovered somewhat and rejoiced in that revelation, he lifted up his voice and entreated the Lord, saying, "O Lord, I give thanks to Thee for Thy gracious help. Where wert Thou, O my most sweet Jesus? Why didst Thou not appear at the beginning to halt my pain and tribulations?" And a voice came to him: "Anthony, I was here, but I waited to look upon thy fight. Therefore, since thou hast endured and triumphed, not being worsted or broken with sadness in thy tribulations, I will ever be a succor to thee. I will make thy name known throughout the world." After he had heard this, Anthony arose and prayed. He receive such strength that he perceived that he had more power in his body than formerly. He was then about thirty-five years old.

Saint Anthony Crosses the Nile for Solitude in the Desert

The following morning, Anthony departed from the sepulcher. He went forth with even greater love for God, and increased zeal and commitment. He went to see the ancient elder, the solitary who dwelt by the side of the village. Anthony attempted to persuade him to accompany him into the desert. Though he beseeched the old man, the latter declined and asked to be excused. He put forth as his reasons the infirmity of old age and that there was no custom of monks living in the desert. Anthony did not press him, but instead rose up and prayed with him. By their joint prayers, he hoped that God might make blessed the path that lay before him. Afterward, Anthony went alone into the desert. As he went toward the mountains, the enemy followed after him and looked for an opportunity to diminish his zeal. After traversing a great distance, to the edge of the desert, Anthony grew tired. It was then that the enemy began contending with him. In his attempt to thwart the ascetic, he projected the illusion of a large silver plate cast down in the road. The blessed man perceived this was another wile of the evil one. He then said, "The evil one wishes to do me harm by means of this great plate. Indeed, a silver plate in the desert! How did it come to be here? This road is not a frequented path. There is no trace of any wayfarer. There are no habitations nearby. This is not the ground of thieves. If it spilled out from someone's baggage, something this large could hardly have dropped and lain here unnoticed. Moreover, the owner would have returned looking for it. He certainly would have discovered it gleaming in this desolate place. This must be the handiwork of the enemy. Thou shalt not, O adversary, pervert my mind or mock my resolve by means of this silver. Let it go with thee into perdition!" As Anthony brought his words to a close, the silver plate vanished, leaving in its place smoke.

Anthony thereupon proceeded on the path. The evil one then showed him some gold littering the ground. This time, the sighting of gold was real.

The saint fell into deep thought. "What is this? A lump of gold scattered in the way? Is this a trick of the devil or it is temptation from divine power, that God—may He be blessed!—might try me by real gold and prove me before the evil one?" Though Anthony marvelled at the quantity, he utterly disdained it and was not overthrown. He passed it by as though he were going over fire. He uttered a prayer and signed himself with the sign of the Cross. He did not turn to gaze upon it, but dashed off that he might then lose sight of it. Afterward, neither he could say, nor could we know, whence that gold came.

The saint was then more determined than ever. He came to the mountains, where he discovered a deserted and ancient fortress on the far side of the river. It had been so long abandoned that it was infested with all kinds of creeping things, many of them venomous, on the other side of the river; he crossed over to it and dwelt there. The reptiles, as though someone were chasing them, immediately left that habitation. The saint barricaded the entrance with stones and dwelt within that walled stronghold, where he laid in a supply of bread every six months. The Egyptians had the custom of baking bread every six months, since at one time they make enough bread for a six month's supply. The Thebans find that the bread often remains unspoiled in the dry desert air for a whole year. There was water in the place, so he took up his abode, as if in a shrine, alone, for one year. Anthony never went forth, nor did he look upon any who passed by. Thus he was a long time training himself. His solitariness was such that when he took in his bread supply through the roof twice yearly, he did not converse with those who brought provisions to him. Thus, he made his abode for many years in that remote place, far from any inhabitants. Those of his acquaintances who did come to him, he would in no wise admit within the fortress. They would remain outside for one or two days. When they strained their ears, they would hear the din of a mighty multitude of people or confused sounds, like that of clamoring and lamenting men. Among the shrieking sounds, they could discern voices saying, "Begone from our habitation! What dost thou want in this desert? Thou canst not endure our assaults and attacks." At first, those outside the fortress had the impression that there were some men quarreling with Anthony. They thought that men had entered through the roof. They went around the fortress and found a small opening in the wall. They went up with ladders and peered through, only to find the holy man alone. They became frightened, accounting the noise to be that of demons warring against him. In their dread, they called out to Anthony. The blessed man came to the door and spoke to them graciously, saying, "Be not afraid, beloved, of these noises and conjured-up specters. The devils are wont to act thus before those who are timid. Seal yourselves rather with the sign of the Cross and return to your homes with boldness and faith in God. Leave these creatures to play and make laughingstocks of themselves." They therefore fortified themselves, making the sign of the Cross, and departed. The saint was left unharmed by the demons. He was not wearied by the struggle, but rather he gained strength and courage through heavenly visions and the defeat of his foes. Now the report of this occurrence reached his friends and acquaintances. Thereupon, they began to come periodically to see if he were dead or alive. When they arrived outside, where they wished to be, they would strain their ears for any sound from within. Then they would hear Anthony chanting melodiously: "Let God arise and let His enemies be scattered, and let them that hate Him flee from before His face. As smoke vanisheth, so let them vanish; as wax melteth before the fire, so let sinners perish at the presence of God [Ps. 67:1, 2]." And then, "All the nations compassed me round about, and by the name of the Lord I warded them off [Ps. 117:10]."

The Saint Becomes a Father of Monks

The saint passed twenty years at the fortress, seldom seen by any human. He had not exited in all that time nor visited with anyone. With the passage of time, his fame reached other solitaries in Egypt. Monks, seculars, and men of distinction came in large numbers to see him. Some monks came who were committed to emulating his deeds, while others were wishful to imitate his discipline. Suffering laity came that he might pray over them and heal them. They called out to him, but he answered them not. His friends also came and forcefully wrenched off and broke down the door, removing it and the wall of rocks. Then Anthony, as from a shrine or divine sanctuary, came forth as one initiated in the mysteries and filled with the Spirit of God. This was the first time in twenty years that he was seen outside of the fortress. The sight of him, like unto an angel of light, inspired wonder in all. Those who knew him noted that he had the same frame and weight as he had before his retirement. They observed his dignified bearing and the beauty of his countenance, which had not altered. He was neither fat or flabby, like a man who had been without exercise, nor lean or emaciated from fasting and striving with the demons. His body had not been weakened, and his understanding suffered no enfeeblement. Anthony beheld the large concourse of people and was not disturbed. What purity of mind! Frivolity and pleasure did not make him burst out laughing. The thought of past sins or grief or dejection did not cause him to frown. The high praise of those present did not lift him up with conceit. Neither did he feel any elation upon being saluted by so many. His voluntary solitude had not rendered him uncivil. Daily strife with the evil adversaries had not brutalized him. His mind was calm, guided by reason, and his attitude was equable in all situations. The people came forward with their petitions. He showed no irritability or impatience or anger. With the living God working in him, he was in a placid and thoughtful state, as he listened to many who were suffering terribly. By the hand of Anthony, the Lord healed them, delivering both those afflicted with bodily ailments and cleansing others from unclean spirits. God also granted grace to Anthony's speech. He consoled the sorrowing and distressed, and he restored peace and unity to those set at variance. Those who were afflicted became long-suffering, the haughty became humble, the arrogant were brought low. The saint exhorted them and would say that nothing—neither kin or possessions or our lives—was to be esteemed of value but the love of Christ. He urged them to remember the good things to come and the loving-kindness of God toward us 'Who indeed spared not His own Son, but delivered Him up for us all [Rom. 8:32].' He then said, "How much more reasonable is it for us who have tasted and known such divine grace to deliver up our lives on behalf of our own souls?" The holy man persuaded many to embrace the solitary life, which resulted in cells arising in the mountains. Therefore, the desert was colonized by monks, who came forth from their own people, and enrolled themselves for citizenship in the heavens.

On another occasion, when the blessed man needed to visit the brethren, he was obliged to cross the Arsenoitic Canal. It was named after the city of Arsinoë and linked the Nile and Lake Moeris, but it was full of crocodiles. The saint uttered a prayer while in the boat. All those with him passed over and remained unmolested. They also returned safely. The saint then returned to his monastery, struggling valiantly as he had previously. By his frequent discourses, he increased the eagerness and zeal of those who were already monks and drew many others to take up that life and discipline. Thus, the monasteries multiplied under his fatherly affection and guidance. He therefore became their holy father and hegumen.

The Saint Gives a Discourse to the Monastics

Then on one of those days, when the brethren had assembled, they besought the holy man to speak to them words of salvation. He spoke to them in the Egyptian tongue, that is, Coptic, as follows: "Sufficient are the Scriptures for our instruction, but it is a good thing to encourage one another in the Faith with soul-saving words. Therefore you, as children, carry that which you know to your father; and I, as your elder, shall share with you what knowledge and experience have taught me.

"Let this be the first rule for you and the common aim of all of you, my children, that none should weaken or become fainthearted in his commitment to this ascetic way of life he has chosen. Let no one say, 'I have lived in this ascetic discipline for a long time.' Rather, each should strive to renew his earnestness and zeal daily, as if he were just starting out. Consider our human life and its shortness when compared to the ages to come. Our time here is as nothing when compared to everlasting life." The holy man then paused a moment and resumed, saying, "Look at this present life. Everything is sold at its price, and a man exchanges one equivalent for another; but the promise of eternal life is purchased for very little. For it is written: 'As for the days of our years, in their span they be three-score years and ten. And if we be in strength, mayhap fourscore years; and what is more than these is toil and travail [Ps. 89:10, 11].' There-fore, if we should live eighty or even a hundred years in the disci-pline, we shall not reign for that same measure of time in the future;

Saint Anthony Discourses

instead, we shall reign forever and ever. And though we have fought and struggled on earth, we shall not receive our inheritance here. The promise of those good things abides in the heavens. 'For it is needful for this corruptible to put on itself incorruption and this mortal to put on itself immortality [1 Cor. 15:53].' Therefore neither grow weary, nor think you have been labor-ing for so long, nor be puffed up thinking you have done anything great. 'For...the sufferings of the present time are not worthy in comparison to the future glory to be revealed in us [Rom. 8:18].' Let not our mind revert back to the world, thinking we have renounced anything of much consequence. This is very small when compared to all of the heavens. Even if we chanced to be lords of all the earth and forsook it all, still it would be not be worthy of comparison with the kingdom of the heavens. For it is even as a man who thinks slightly of one copper drachma that he might gain a hundred gold ones. In like manner, if a man were lord of all the earth and were to renounce it, that which he has abandoned is little, since he receives a hundredfold. Therefore, if not even the whole earth is equal in value to the heavens, what then are a few acres that one leaves? Nothing. Even if one has forsaken a great house or much gold, this is no cause for boasting or being dispirited. Furthermore, if we do not voluntarily relinquish such things for the sake of virtue, afterward, at death, we shall certainly leave them behind. Consider the words of the preacher in the book of Ecclesiastes: 'And I hated the whole of my labor which I took under the sun; because I must leave it to the man who will come after me [Eccl. 2:18].' And, 'For whom do I labor, and deprive my soul of good? This is also vanity, and an evil trouble [Eccl. 4:8].' And, 'Strangers shall devour it [Eccl. 6:2].' We are enjoined to give to those to whom we do not wish. Why then should we not give them up for the sake of virtue, that we may inherit even a kingdom?

"Therefore, let the desire of possession take hold of no one, for what gain is it to acquire these things which we cannot take with us? Why not rather pursue those things which we can take away with us—that is, love, charity, sober-mindedness, righteousness, justice, temperance, fortitude, understanding, faith in Christ, freedom from wrath, hospitality? If we come to obtain these virtues, we shall find them before us preparing a welcome in the land of the meek.

"Let no man make light of these things, especially if he considers that he is himself a servant of the Lord, and owes service to the Master. Therefore, as a servant, he would not dare to say, 'Since I labored yesterday, I need not work today.' A servant does not count up the times of past service and then claim rest for them that he might be released from the tasks that lie ahead. No, even as it is written in the Gospel, he waits on his lord.[3] He daily shows readiness to please his lord, lest he should incur great loss and injury. Let us therefore persevere, knowing that the Lord shall not pardon us for the sake of the past if we end in negligence. We have heard the Prophet Ezekiel speak of this, saying, 'When the righteous turns away from his righteousness and commits a trespass, and dies in the trespass he has committed, he shall even die in it [Ezek. 18:26; cf. 3:20].' Bring to mind also Judas, who undermined all his previous toil in one night [Jn. 6:71, 72].

"Therefore, my children, let us hold fast to our ascetic discipline. Let not carelessness creep in. Know this: the Lord is our fellow worker. Even as it is written: 'We know that to those who love God all things work together for good, to those who are called according to purpose [Rom. 8:28].' That we might not succumb to indolence and negligence, let us ponder on the apostle's words: 'I die daily [1 Cor. 15:31].' For if we too should live in this manner, we shall not sin. The meaning therefore is that, as we rise day by day, we should think that we shall not tarry in this life till evening; and again, when about to lie down to sleep, we should not assume that we shall rise up on the morrow. For our life is naturally uncertain and unpredictable. We should understand that God's providence governs our lives insofar as it is measured out to us daily. If we are disposed to carry on our daily life as our last day, we would neither fall into sin, nor lust for anything. We would not bear any grudges or stay angry. We would not heap up treasures here on earth. After all, to one who lives each day with the expectation of death, what is wealth? We would forgive all things to men. Even our desire of women or any other carnal lust would be extinguished. We would deem it transitory and turn away

---

[3] Cf. Lk. 12:35-47; Lk. 17:7-10.

from it as past and gone. We would be thinking of the day of judgment, holding in our mind's eye that coming final retribution. For the fear of judgment and dread of punishment withers the lusts of the flesh and dissipates evil desire.

"Since we have already begun and have set out in the way of virtue, let us strive the more that we may attain those things that are before. Let no one turn to the things behind, as did Lot's wife [Gen. 19:26], especially since the Lord has said, 'No one, having put his hand upon the plow, and looking to the things behind, is fit for the kingdom of God [Lk. 9:62].' To look back means nought else but to feel regret, and to be once more worldly-minded. But fear not to hear of the word 'virtue,' nor be astonished at the name. For it is not far from us, nor is it outside ourselves, but it is within us, and is easy if only we are willing. That they may get knowledge, the Greeks live abroad and cross the sea. But we have no need to depart from home for the sake of the kingdom of the heavens, nor to cross great watery expanses for the sake of virtue. The Lord has already told us, 'The kingdom of God is within you [Lk. 17:21].' Therefore we need only to will perfection, since it is within our power and is developed by us. Who can doubt the natural purity of the soul, were it not tainted by filth from outside? When the soul keeps the understanding in its natural state, that is, when it remains as it was created, perfection is confirmed. When the soul came into existence, it was fair and exceedingly honest. For this cause Jesus, the son of Navee, in his exhortation, said to the people, 'Set your heart right toward the Lord God of Israel [Josh. 24:23].' And John the Baptist said, 'Be making His paths straight [Mt. 3:3].' For rectitude of soul consists in its having its spiritual part in its natural state, its original soundness, as created. If the soul swerves and turns away from its natural state, that is called vice of the soul. Thus the matter is not difficult. If we abide as we have been made, we are in a state of virtue; but if we think of ignoble things, we shall be accounted evil. If, therefore, this thing had to be acquired from without, it would be difficult in reality; but if it is in us, let us keep ourselves from foul thoughts. And as we have received the soul as a trust or deposit from Him, let us preserve it for the Lord, that He may recognize His creation as being the same as He made it.

"And let us strive that wrath rule us not nor lust overcome us, for it is written: 'Man's wrath doth not work out God's righteousness [Jas. 1:20].' And after a man 'conceiveth the desire, it bringeth forth sin; and sin, after it is fully formed, bringeth forth death [Jas. 1:15].' Living in this manner, let us keep guard carefully, and as it is written: 'Keep thy heart with the utmost care; for out of these are the issues of life [Prov. 4:23].' For we have terrible and crafty foes—the evil spirits—and against them we wrestle, as the apostle said that 'for us the wrestling is not against blood and flesh, but against the principalities, against the powers, against the cosmic rulers of the darkness of this age, against spiritual hosts of evil on account of the heavenly things [Eph. 6:12].' In the air around us, their number is great; they are not far from us. Now there are great distinctions among them; and concerning their nature and distinctions much could be said, but such a description is for others of greater powers than we possess. But at this time it is pressing and necessary for us only to know their wiles against ourselves.

"First, therefore, we must understand this: that the demons have not been created demons as we understand that name; for God made nothing evil, but even they have been made good. Having fallen, however, from the heavenly wisdom, since then they have been groveling on earth. On the one hand, they deceived the Greek pagans with their apparitions and displays; but on the other hand, out of envy toward us Christians, they move all things in their desire to hinder us from entry into the heavens, lest we should ascend thither from whence they fell. Hence, there is need on our part of much prayer and discipline. When a man has received through the Spirit the gift of discerning spirits, he has been empowered to recognize their characteristics: which of them are less and which more evil; of what nature is the special pursuit of each, and how each of them is overthrown and cast out. For their villainies and the changes in their plots are manifold. The blessed apostle and his followers knew of such things when they said, 'We are not ignorant of his designs [2 Cor. 2:11].' Moreover, we, from the temptations we have suffered from them, ought to guide one another. Therefore, having had proof of them, I speak to you as my children.

Guises of Demon Attacks

"The demons, therefore, if they see all Christians, and monks especially, laboring cheerfully and advancing, first make an attack by temptation and place snares and hindrances to hamper our way, to wit, evil thoughts. We, however, need not fear their suggestions; for by our prayer, fasting, and faith in the Lord, their attack immediately fails. But even when they fail, they do not retreat or desist, but knavishly, by subtlety, they come on again. For when they cannot deceive the heart openly with foul pleasures, they approach in another guise. They change their shapes and forms, displaying themselves as women, wild beasts, creeping things, gigantic bodies, and troops of soldiers. But not even then need we fear their deceitful displays. For they are nothing and shall quickly vanish, especially if a man should fortify himself beforehand with faith and the sign of the Cross. Yet I tell you that they are still very bold and shameless; for if thus they are worsted, they make an onslaught in another manner. They pretend to prophesy and foretell the future, or they show themselves of a height reaching to the roof and of great breadth. They do these things that they may stealthily catch by such deceptions those who could not be deceived by their arguments. If here also they find the soul strengthened by faith and a hopeful mind, then they bring their leader to their aid."

Saint Anthony then went on to say that "they often appeared as the Lord revealed the devil to Job, who said, 'His eyes are as the appearance of the morning star. Out of his mouth proceed as it were burning lamps, and as it were hearths of fire are cast abroad. Out of his nostrils proceeds smoke of a furnace burning with fire of coals. His breath is as live coals, and a flame goes out of his mouth [Job 41:9-11].' When the prince of the demons appears in this wise, the crafty one, as I said before, strikes terror by making great claims. Again, the Lord described him, saying to Job, for 'he considers iron as chaff, and brass as rotten wood....He regards the sea as a pot of ointment, and the lowest part of the deep as a captive: he reckons the deep as his range [Job 41:18, 22, 23].' Through the prophet, the devil boasts, 'I will pursue, I will overtake [Ex. 15:9].' And through another, he says, 'I will take with my hand all the world as a nest: and I will even take them as eggs that have been left; and there is none that shall escape me, or contradict me [Is. 10:14].' In this way, by speaking such deadly words, the evil one ensnares some of those who live a good life, but we the faithful ought not to believe—not even give the appearance of believing—his promises or fear his threats. He ever deceives, and none of his promises are true. He is a liar and never speaks the truth. Although he speaks so many words in his boldness, without a doubt, as a dragon was he drawn with a hook by the Savior's Cross, and as a beast of burden was he bound with a halter round his nostrils, and as a runaway slave were his nostrils pierced with an iron ring, and his lips bored with an armlet. He was bound in the net by the Lord as a sparrow, that we should mock him. He now groans with his fellows who have been trampled underfoot by Christians, like serpents and scorpions [Lk. 10:19]. The proof of all this is that we now live opposed to him. Look at him who threatened to destroy the sea and take the world into his hand. He cannot stay our discipline, nor even me speaking against him. Let us then heed not his words, for he is a liar. Let us not fear his visions, seeing that they are deceptive. For that which appears in them is no true light, but they are rather the sign and semblance of the fire prepared for the demons who attempt to terrify men with those flames in which they themselves shall be burned. Doubtless they appear; but in a moment they vanish again, hurting none of the faithful, but bearing with them the likeness of that fire which is to receive them. Thereupon, it is unfitting that we should fear them on account of these things; for through the grace of Christ all their practises come to nothing.

"They are treacherous, ready to transform themselves into every appearance and shape. At times they feign singing psalms or reciting Scriptures. At other times, while we are reading, they repeat many times, like an echo, what we have read. They rouse us from our sleep to prayers; and this constantly, hardly allowing us to sleep at all. At another time they assume the appearance of monks and simulate pious speech of holy men, that by their assumed likeness they may deceive and thus drag their victims where they will. But we ought to pay them no heed, even if they should arouse us to prayer or counsel us against complete abstinence. We ought not to pay attention to them, if they should accuse and revile us for what they once approved and in which they were our accomplices; for this is a pretense on their part of seemingly admirable behavior. They do this not for the sake of piety or truth, but that they may gain the confidence of their victims and then carry off the simple and guileless into despair. They wish to drive their victims to say that the ascetic discipline is useless. They would have it that men should come to loathe the solitary life as burdensome. Their aim is to hinder or trip up those who would lead such a life in spite of them.

"The Lord therefore sent the prophet to declare these creatures as wretched, saying, 'Woe to him that gives his neighbor to drink the thick lees of wine, and intoxicates him, that he may look upon their secret parts [Hab. 2:15].' For such devices are subversive and seduce people from the path that leads to virtue and heaven. Note that even the Lord Himself, although the demons spoke the truth—for they said truthfully that 'Thou art the Christ, the Son of God [Lk. 4:41]'—still bridled their mouths and suffered them not to speak, lest haply they should sow their evil along with the truth. He wished to accustom us never to give heed to them, though they should appear to speak the truth. For it is unbecoming that we, having the holy Scriptures and freedom from the Savior, should be taught by the devil who has not kept his own order but has changed his mind now to one thing, now another. Therefore, even if the demon should use the language of Scripture, Christ would forbid him, saying, 'But unto the sinner God hath said, "Why declarest thou My statutes and takest up My covenant in thy mouth [Ps. 49:17]?"' For the demons are wont to practise all kinds of pretenses—they prate, they confuse, they dissemble, they confound—in order to deceive the simple. They may make a din, or laugh madly and senselessly, or whistle, or hiss; but if no heed is given them, they weep and lament as ones vanquished.

"The Lord therefore, because He is God, stayed the mouths of the demons. It is fitting that we, taught by the saints, should do as they did and emulate their courage. For when they saw these things, they were wont to say, 'I set a guard for my mouth, when the sinner stood up against me [Ps. 38:2].' And, 'I became as a man that heareth not, and hath in his mouth no reproofs [Ps. 37:14].' So let us neither hear them, as they are strangers to us, nor give heed to them even though they should rouse us to prayer or urge us to fast. But let us rather apply ourselves, because it is part of our way of life. Let us not be deceived by them who do all things in deceit, even though they should threaten death and attack us. For they are weak and can do nought but threaten.

"I know that I have already spoken of these things, though only in passing, yet now I must not shrink from speaking at greater length; for to put you in remembrance will bring greater security for you. Since the Lord came, the enemy and his power have been weakened. Therefore, although he can do nothing, still, like a tyrant, he did not bear his fall quietly, but utters threats, though they be words only. Let each one of you consider this, and he will be able to despise the demons. Now since our enemies are not clothed in flesh, they cannot give as an excuse for their inability to overcome us that they are unable to enter because we have closed the door to them. If they possessed our fragile bodies, when the entrance was closed, access would be denied them. But since they are free of this burden and can penetrate what has been closed and fly about without hindrance, it is clear that because of their weakness the body of the Church remains unharmed. We should not be terrified of them. We should not be afraid of their voices. The Savior affirms that the devil was 'a manslayer from the beginning, and hath not stood in the truth, because there is no truth in him. Whenever he may speak the lie, he speaketh out of the things which are his own; for he is a liar and the father of it [Jn. 8:44].' Despite all their attempts and threats, we are still alive, spending our lives opposing them; therefore, it is plain that they are powerless. But be circumspect: no place is a hindrance to their plots, nor do they look on us as friends that they should spare us; nor are they lovers of good that they should amend. But on the contrary they are evil, and nothing is so much sought after by them as wounding them that love virtue and fear God. Since they have no power to effect anything, they do nought but threaten. But if they could, they would not hesitate in working evil—for all their desire is set on this—and especially against us. Behold now, we are assembled here and continue speaking against them. They know that when we advance they grow weak. If they had the power, they would permit no Christian to live, for 'a righteous man is an abomination to an unrighteous man, and the direct way is an abomination to the sinner [Prov. 29:27].' But since they can do nothing, they afflict themselves with greater wounds; for they cannot fulfill even one of their threats. Then this also is to be considered, that we may have no fear of them: if they had power, they would not come in great numbers, nor conjure phantoms and apparitions, nor change forms and frame deceits. It would suffice that one only should come and perpetrate what they will. If the devil had authority, he would make full use of it as he wished. But the demons, as they have no power or authority, are like actors on the stage. They transform themselves so as to frighten children with specters, apparitions, and various forms. From all this, they should be despised as blazoning their ineptitude. At least the true angel of the Lord sent against the Assyrian host had no need for tumults nor displays from without, nor noises nor rattlings; but in quiet he exercised divine power and straight-way destroyed a hundred and eighty-five thousand Assyrians [4 Kgs. (2 Kgs.) 19:35]. But demons like these, who have no power, try to terrify at least by their empty phantoms and displays.

"Should anyone, however, bring forward the history of Job and say, 'Why did the devil go forth and accomplish all things against that blessed man? He stripped him of his belongings, slew his numerous children, and smote him with dreadful bodily sores, did he not?' I say that such who make this objection should recognize that it was not the devil who was the strong man, but God Who delivered Job to him to be tried. This power is granted against us either for our glory, if God approves of us, or for our punishment should we do wrong. Certainly the devil had no power to do anything. He needed to ask, and that twice, demonstrating his weakness and want of power. Upon receiving leave, he did what he did. So also from this, the enemy is the more to be condemned; for although willing, he still could not prevail against this one righteous man. For if he had power, he certainly would not have asked permission to carry out his plot. Indeed, not only could he do nothing against Job, but even against Job's cattle he required permission. We know he has no power over swine, for so it says in the Gospel: 'The demons besought Him, saying, "If Thou cast us out, permit us to go away into the herd of swine [Mt. 8:31; cf. Mk. 5:12]."' Therefore, if they have not power even against swine, much less have they any authority over men made in the image of God.

"My dear friends, we ought to fear God only, and despise the demons, and be in no fear of them. A pure life and faith in God are great weapons against the demons. I have personal experience of this; for they fear our fasting, keeping vigil, prayers, meekness, quietness, contempt of money and vainglory, humility, love of the poor, alms, freedom from anger, and, chief of all, piety and pure love toward Jesus Christ. The foul serpent knows that it is God's command that he should lie beneath the footsteps of the just, even as the Lord said, 'Behold, I give you the authority to tread upon serpents and scorpions, and upon all the power of the enemy; and nothing in anywise shall injure you [Lk. 10:19].'

"Furthermore, if they pretend to foretell the future, let no one give any heed to their divination. Ofttimes, they may announce beforehand that the brethren are coming to visit us; and in fact they do come. The demons, however, do this not from any care for the hearers, but to secure their confidence and thereby gain admittance. Then, at length, after they have them in their power, they may destroy them. Consequently, we must give no heed to them, but ought rather to confute them when speaking, since we do not need them. For what wonder is it, if with more subtle bodies than we, when they have seen them start on their journey, they surpass them in speed, and announce their coming? Likewise a horseman, outstripping a man on foot, announces the arrival of the latter beforehand. So in this there is no need for us to wonder at them. For they know none of those things which are not yet in existence; but God only is He Who knows all things before their birth. But these creatures, like thieves, running off first with what they see, proclaim it. Indeed, to how many already have they announced our business, before any one of us could go forth and tell of this assembly? I mean that we are here gathered together to discuss measures against them. This in good truth a fleet-footed boy could do, getting far ahead of one less swift of foot. Let me give you an example. Before anyone begins to walk from the Thebaid, or from any other district, the demons do not know whether he will walk. But when they have seen him walking, what do they do? They run ahead and, before he should arrive, report such-and-such's approach. And so it falls out that after a few days the travelers do indeed arrive. But then again, it also happened that the walkers turn around, rendering the demons purveyors of falsehoods.

"Another example of their idle talk regards the Nile. With respect to the water of the river, they sometimes make foolish speculations. For example, they have seen that there has been considerable rain in sections of Ethiopia. They know that the overflow of the river originates there, and so they run on ahead to Egypt and announce it. Now even men could make these predictions, had they as great a facility of running as the demons. Blessed David's scout [2 Kgs. (2 Sam.) 18:24] ascended a lofty place and was able to spy out those who were coming, before the people down on the plain caught sight of them. Thus the forerunner announced not those things which had not taken place, but those things which were already on the way and were being accomplished. In like manner do the demons prefer to declare what is happening, simply for the sake of deceiving the gullible. If, however, providence meantime plans anything different for the waters or wayfarers—for providence can do this—the demons are deceived, and those who gave heed to them are cheated.

"This is how, in days gone by, there arose the oracles of the Greek pagans. Thus they were led astray by the demons. Now their deception was brought to an end by the coming of our Lord. Silence was enjoined upon those demons. Their devices were brought to nought. For they know nothing of the future, but, as thieves, what they get to know from others they pass on, and guess at rather than foretell things. Therefore if sometimes they speak the truth, let no one marvel at them. Consider experienced physicians. They observe the same malady in different people. They can foretell what it is, discerning it by their familiarity with the symptoms. Navigators, too, and farmers, from their regular acquaintance with all kinds of weather conditions, often can tell at a glance the state of the atmosphere and forecast whether it shall be stormy or fair. Now no one would claim that they make these declarations, based on either practical experience or education, by inspiration. No one would sanctify such persons as gods. So if the demons should at times do the same by guesswork, let no one wonder at it or heed them. Even if for the sake of argument we should say that the demons do predict true things, what use to the hearers is it to know from them what is going to happen before the time? Or what concern have we to know such things, even if the knowledge be true? For it is not productive of virtue, nor is it any token of goodness. For none of us is judged for what he knows not, and no one is called blessed because he has obtained learning and knowledge. But each one will be called to judgment in these points—whether or not he has kept the Faith and truly observed the commandments.

"Therefore, it behooves us not to set much value on these things, nor for the sake of them to impose on ourselves a life of discipline and labor. What is important is that by living piously, we may please God. And we ought neither to pray to know the future, nor to ask for it as the reward of our asceticism. Much rather, our prayer should be that the Lord may be our helper in gaining victory over the devil. But if even once we should conceive a desire to know the future, let us be pure in mind. For I believe that if a soul serves God, and is perfectly pure and in its natural state, it is able, being clear-sighted, to see more and farther than the demons. For in the case of such persons, their souls have the Lord Who bestows revelations. Such was the soul of Eliseos who beheld what was done by Gehazi [4 Kgs. (2 Kgs.) 5:26], and beheld the armies standing nearby [4 Kgs. (2 Kgs.) 6:17].

"When, therefore, the demons use other means of deception, coming by night and wishing to tell the future, give them no heed. Even if they should say, 'We are the angels,' know that they lie. Yea, even if they praise your discipline and dedication and call you blessed, promising future rewards, give them no attendance. Have no dealings with them. Rather, seal yourselves and your houses with the sign of the Cross, and pray, and you shall see them vanish. For they are cowards and greatly fear the sign of the Lord's Cross. As it is written: Christ, 'having put off from Himself the principalities and the powers, He made an example of them openly, triumphing over them in it [Col. 2:15],' that is, the Cross. But if those creatures should shamelessly stand their ground, capering and changing their forms of appearance, fear them not, nor cower, nor heed them as though they were good spirits. For, by the help of God, the presence either of the good or evil can easily be distinguished. The vision of the holy ones is not fraught with distraction. Remember what is written: 'He shall not strive nor cry out, nor shall anyone hear His voice in the streets [Mt. 12:19; cf. Is. 42:2].' Thus the holy angels come quietly and gently, instilling joy, gladness, and courage in the soul. For the Lord Who is our joy is with them, and the power of God the Father. And the thoughts of the soul remain unruffled and undisturbed, like a waveless sea, so that it, enlightened as it were with rays, beholds by itself those who appear. For the love of what is divine and of the things to come possesses it, and willingly it would be wholly joined with them if it could depart along with them. But if, being men, some fear the vision of the good, then those angels who appear, being that they are so kind, immediately take fear away. This was also the case when the Archangel Gabriel spoke to the Prophet Zacharias [Lk. 1:13], or when the angel appeared to the women at the holy sepulcher [Mt. 28:5], or when the angel declared to the shepherds, 'Cease being afraid; for behold, I announce to you good tidings of great joy [Lk. 2:10].' For their fear arose not from timidity or mental terror, but from the recognition of the presence of such superior and mighty beings. Such then is the nature of the visions of the holy ones.

"However, the inroads and the appearance of those most wicked creatures is fraught with confusion, and terrifying sounds, such as the disturbance of boorish youths or robbers would occasion. They strike fear in the heart and usher in confusion of thought. They produce dejection, lethargy, indifference, and despair. They instill hatred toward those who live a life of discipline. They promote a disregard of virtue, unsettled habits, and a desire for evil things. If terror and trembling should be replaced by joy, love, and trust in God, together with cheerfulness, courage, renewed strength, calmness of thought, and all those I named before, then take courage and pray. For joy and a settled state of soul show the holiness of Him Who is present. Thus Abraham, seeing the day of the Lord, rejoiced exceedingly and was glad [Jn. 8:56]; John, at the voice of Mary Theotokos, leaped in Elisabeth's womb [Lk. 1:41]. But should there be confusion, noise, worldly display, threats of death, and the like, such an appearance would signal an onslaught of evil spirits.

"And let this also be a token for you. Whenever the soul should continue fearful, there is a presence of the enemies. For the demons do not

take away the fear of their presence as did the great Archangel Gabriel in the
case of Mary and Zacharias [Lk. 1:13, 30], and as he did for the women at
the tomb [Mk. 16:6]; but rather, whenever the demons should see men afraid,
they increase their delusions that men may be terrified the more. Then, at last,
Satan mocks such persons, saying, 'Fall down and make obeisance to me [Mt.
4:9].' Thus they deceived the pagan Greeks; and thus, by them, they were
considered gods, though falsely called. But the Lord did not suffer us to be
deceived by the devil, for He rebuked him whenever he framed such
delusions against Him, saying: 'Get thee behind Me, Satan. For it hath been
written: "Thou shalt make obeisance to the Lord thy God, and Him alone
shalt thou worship [Mt. 4:10; cf. Deut. 6:13]."' More and more, therefore,
let the deceiver be despised by us. For that which the Lord spoke was done
for our sakes. The power conveyed by these words has been granted to us,
so that when the demons should hear like words from us, they might be put
to flight through the Lord Who rebuked them by those very words.

"We must not boast of casting out demons. This is not fitting for us.
We should not be uplifted by the healing of diseases. Be more concerned
about your way of life than performing miracles. If any of you should be
vouchsafed to work wonders, he should neither be lifted up with pride nor
look down on those who do not. But rather consider each person's discipline
and conduct. It behooves each to emulate the perfect and supply what is
lacking in himself. It is not for our humble selves to work miracles, but for
the power of God. Be mindful of the Savior's words to the disciples: 'Cease
rejoicing in this, that the spirits are being made subject to you; but be
rejoicing that your names were written in the heavens [Lk. 10:20].' The fact
that our names are written in the heavens is a testimony to our virtuous life;
but to expel demons is a free gift of the Savior Who bestowed it. Therefore,
to those who boasted in signs, but not in virtue, and said, 'Lord, Lord, we
prophesied in Thy name, and cast out demons in Thy name, and did many
works of power in Thy name, did we not [Mt. 7:22]?' then the Lord will
profess, 'I never knew you; depart from Me, ye who work lawlessness [Mt.
7:23].' For, 'the Lord knoweth the way of the righteous, and the way of the
ungodly shall perish [Ps. 1:6].' But we ought always to pray, as I have said
before, that we may receive the gift of discerning spirits; that, as it is written
that we 'cease believing every spirit, but keep on putting the spirits to the test,
if they are of God; because many false prophets have gone out into the world
[1 Jn. 4:1].'

"I should have liked to speak no further and to remain silent regarding
things that happened to my humble self. But lest you should think that I was
speaking of things at random, of which I have no experience, or that I was
beating the air with stories of events which could not possibly happen, for this

cause—even though I should become as a fool, yet the Lord Who hears and knows my conscience, and that it is not for my own sake, but on account of your affection toward me and at your request—I again shall tell what I saw of the practises of evil spirits. How often have these foul creatures called me blessed and I have cursed them in the name of the Lord! How often have they predicted the rising of the river Nile, and I answered them, 'What have you to do with it?' Once they came threatening and surrounded me like soldiers in full armor. At another time they filled the house with horses, wild beasts, and creeping things and scorpions, but I challenged them and sang: 'Some trust in chariots, and some in horses, but we will call upon the name of the Lord our God [Ps. 19:7].' And at that prayer, by Christ's compassion, they were turned to flight. Once they came in darkness, bearing the appearance of a light, and said, 'We are come to bestow our light upon thee, Anthony.' But I closed my eyes, refusing to gaze at that light, and prayed. Immediately, the light of the wicked ones was quenched. Then, after a few months, they came as though singing psalms and quoting the words of Scripture: 'And I became as a man that heareth not [Ps. 37:14]'; but in actuality they were babbling. Once they shook the cell with an earthquake, but I continued praying with an unshaken heart and unmoved mind. After this, they came again producing noises. They whistled, hissed, and pranced about. But I continued constant in prayer, chanting psalms as I lay on the ground. Then they began to weep and lament, as if their strength had failed them. But I gave glory to the Lord Who humbled those creatures and made an example of their brazenness and madness.

"On another occasion, the monastery was shaken, and there appeared a demon of very large stature, who dared to declare, 'I am the power of God. What dost thou wish that I should grant thee, O Anthony?' I blew my breath upon him, calling on the name of the Lord, and he forthwith vanished. On yet another occasion, as I was fasting for a number of days, that cunning deceiver came to me as a monk. He began offering me loaves of bread and saying, 'Do thou partake. Do not be fasting so much, lest thou shouldest fall ill, as thou art human.' By the grace of God, I perceived that serpent's artifice and ghoulish face; so I rose up and prayed, and he vanished like smoke wafting through an open window. Then how many times in the desert has he attempted to trap me with what resembled gold, that I should only touch it and look on it! There were other times that the demons dealt me blows, but I would chant such words as, 'Who shall separate us from the love of Christ [Rom. 8:34]?' Upon hearing this, those creatures turned on one another in their rage. They were put to flight at the Lord's command, not mine. It was also the Lord Who put them to nought, even as He Himself spoke: 'I was beholding Satan as lightning having fallen out of the heaven [Lk. 10:18].'

Therefore, let us be mindful of the apostle's words: 'These things, brethren, I transferred in a figure to myself [1 Cor. 4:6],' so that you neither grow fainthearted in the ascetical life nor fear the delusions of the devil and his demons.

"But since 'I speak as being beside myself [2 Cor. 11:23],' by recounting many of these experiences for your benefit, I should like to tell you this, but let no one doubt the truth. On still another occasion, a demon knocked on the door of my cell. I exited only to behold a creature of enormous height. I asked, 'Who art thou?' He answered, 'I am Satan. Why do you monks and the other Christians condemn me unjustly?' I answered, 'Why dost thou tempt them and put them to the test?' He replied, 'Who, me? Nay, not I. I do not do anything. It is they who cause each other agitation and trouble. Much rather, I am to be pitied. I ask thee, hast thou not read, "The swords of the enemy have utterly failed, and his cities Thou hast destroyed [Ps. 9:6]"? Look at me now. I have no longer a place, a weapon, a city. The Christians are spread everywhere. Even the desert is crammed full with monks. Let them take heed to themselves, and let them not curse me undeservedly.' Then I marvelled at the grace of the Lord, and said to that odious creature, 'Thou art ever a liar and never speakest the truth. But here, against thine own will, thou hast been forced to admit this truth without lying. For Jesus Christ, having put on flesh, stripped thee naked of every power.' Now I had hardly finished the sentence when that huge figure collapsed and vanished, being unable to bear the burning caused him at the sound of our Savior's name.

"Therefore, brothers, if Satan himself confesses to his infirmity and owns up to his lack of power, we ought utterly to despise both him and his minions. Since the enemy with his hounds has but devices of this sort, we, having got to know their weakness, are able to deem them contemptible. Therefore, let us not become disheartened, nor succumb to cowardice, nor frame fears for ourselves, saying, 'I fear, lest a demon should come and overthrow me. I fear lest he should lift me up and cast me down. I fear lest rising against me on a sudden he should confound me.' Dispel such thoughts. Let us not be sorrowful as though we were perishing; but rather let us be courageous and rejoice always, believing that the Lord is with us and has vanquished our enemies and broken their power. Let us take to heart that while the Lord is with us, our foes can do nought against us. For when they approach, they come in a form corresponding to the state in which they discover us. They adapt their delusions to the condition of mind in which they find us. If, therefore, they find us timid, confused, or dissatisfied, they forthwith beset the place, like robbers, having found it unguarded. Indeed, what we of ourselves are thinking, they do, and more also. For if they find us fainthearted and cowardly, they mightily increase our terror, by their delusions and threats. Thus, the unhappy soul is thenceforth tormented. But if they see us mindful of the Lord and deeming all things in His hand, or rejoicing in Him and contemplating those future good things, no evil spirit has any strength against the Christian, nor any power at all over anyone. For when they behold the soul fortified with these thoughts, they are discomfited and retreat. Thus the enemy, seeing Job fenced round with these thoughts and strengthened by the Lord, withdrew from him; but finding Judas unguarded, him he took captive. Therefore, if we are to despise and overcome the enemy, let us rejoice in hope and have constant recollection of the Lord in our souls. Then we shall see the snares of the demon driven out like smoke. Thus, instead of pursuing, these evil creatures shall be put to flight. For they are, as I said before, exceeding fearful, ever anticipating the everlasting fire prepared for them [Mt. 25:41].

"Now to bring my discourse to a conclusion, I shall mention one more thing. Whenever there is any apparition, be not prostrate with fear. But whatsoever it be, first boldly ask, 'Who art thou? And from whence comest thou?' Now if the apparition is holy and a vision of angels or saints, they will assure you and change your fear into joy. But if the apparition should be anything diabolical, immediately it becomes feeble, beholding your firm purpose of mind. For merely to ask, 'Who art thou? and whence comest thou?' is a proof of coolness. On the one hand, Jesus, the son of Navee, learned who his helper was, asking, 'Art thou for us or on the side of our enemies [Josh. 5:13]?' On the other hand, the enemy, that is, the two wicked elders, did not escape the examination of Daniel [Susanna 1:51 ff.]."

Monasticism Flourishes

These things and many others were spoken of by the great Anthony to the monastics that had gathered. They marvelled at the grace given him by the Lord, in the discerning of the spirits, which put the monks in a joyful spirit and enhanced their desire to advance in virtue. Thus the desire for virtue increased in some, while carelessness was cast aside in others. Those with flagging faith were rejuvenated. Previously false opinions maintained by some were cast out from their minds. Those who feared the devil and his schemes, after taking Anthony's advice, came to despise that creature and his devices. So then, on that mountain, monastic cells were like tents, filled with divine choirs of men chanting psalms, reading, and praying. The saint's discourse had inspired them to persevere, pray, and fast, in their desire for those future good things. There was no self-conceit, only love and compassion among themselves. It was a land to itself, removed from worldly concerns, and filled with godliness and righteousness. There was no evildoer, no one who suffered wrong, no pesky tax collector. There were only ascetics, all of one mind and one set purpose, which was the attainment of virtue. If one could view these solitary cells and the good order of the monks who rivaled one another in carrying out their duties, he would lift up his voice and exclaim, "How goodly are thy habitations, Jacob, and thy tents, Israel! As shady groves, and as gardens by a river, and as tents which God pitched, and as cedars by the waters [Num. 24:5, 6]."

Thus, the commitment of the brethren grew with each new day. The saint, however, according to his practise, returned alone to his own cell and increased his ascetic discipline. He meditated on, and sighed daily for, those heavenly abodes [Jn. 14:2]. He reflected upon the shortness of man's life, deeming that which he had already achieved to be of little value. When his human condition enjoined him to partake of some food or sleep or any other necessities of nature, he was overcome by an extraordinary sense of shame. He believed that the physical needs and limitations of his poor flesh restricted his spiritual freedom. He would ponder upon spiritual food, so that ofttimes, while sitting at the communal meal, he would ask to be excused. He would then withdraw, far off from them, deeming it a matter for shame if he should be seen eating by others. However, when by himself, he used to eat through bodily necessity. But there were many times that he did take his meals with the brethren. Though covered with shame on these occasions, yet he admonished them that the body must not be completely starved, nor should it be overfed, lest it should lose its mobility and facility contrary to the Creator's will. He used to say that it behooved a man to give all his time to his soul rather than his body, yet to grant a short space to the body through its necessities. He exhorted them that the body should be in subjection to the soul, as spoken of by the Savior: 'Cease being anxious for your soul, what ye shall eat; nor for the body, what ye shall put on....And ye, cease seeking what ye shall eat or what ye shall drink, and cease being anxious. For all these things the nations of the world seek after; and your Father knoweth that ye need these things. But be seeking the kingdom of God, and all these things shall be added to you [Lk. 12:22, 29-31.].'

Martyrdom Under Maximinus

After these events, the Church came under siege. The cruel persecution which took place under Maximinus (Maximin, 308-314) brought many holy martyrs to Alexandria. Anthony also followed, leaving his cell, and said, "Let us go too that, if called, we may contend or behold those who are contending and triumphing." In his love for Christ and those suffering, that blessed man was already a martyr. Though he longed to suffer martyrdom, yet he was unwilling to give himself up. In the meantime, he ministered to the confessors in the mines and in the prisons. Anthony stirred up the Christians to zealously confess Christ in the judgment hall, lest they should be compelled by the violent persecutors to deny Christ. Those who were sentenced and were on their way to receiving martyrs' crowns, he accompanied to the execution site, as though he were the victor. The judge, vexed at the fearlessness and interference of Anthony and his companions, commanded that no monk could appear in court or even in the city. So all the rest thought it good to hide themselves that day, but Anthony gave so little heed to the command that he washed his garment and mandya (cloak), and stood deliberately all the next day on a raised and prominent place, before the pagans. He was dressed in white to be sure to catch the judge's attention as he walked by with his retinue, for Anthony also had a desire to suffer martyrdom. His conduct demonstrated that Christians ought to persist in an attitude that disdains death. When he was not granted to undergo martyrdom for the name of God, he did grieve that he had not borne witness with his blood. The Lord, however, was preparing a leader to shepherd His flock. Anthony was being preserved so that the monastic life, still in its infancy, would be developed and strengthened not only by the memory of his words, but also by his personal presence and example. For many, by just beholding his manner of life, became zealous to emulate his ways. So he again ministered as usual to the confessors, as though he were their fellow captive. Thus he labored with all his heart in this ministry, blessed by God. Indeed, on account of his genuine love, sympathy, and anxious concern, he suffered more than they until they should triumph. With the martyrdom of Archbishop Peter, who was beheaded in 311, on the 24th day of November, the storm of persecution subsided. Now Anthony, for his part, was a martyr by disposition and confession, so that he could say with the apostle, "I affirm,...I die daily [1 Cor. 15:31]." But again, his intense hardships and sufferings incurred by his ascesis—wearing a thick hair shirt directly on his skin and a garment of animal skin on top, which articles were left uncleaned, and never washing his head or his feet—were a living martyrdom. Indeed, no one ever beheld Anthony's flesh until his repose when he was washed for burial.

There was an occasion when the saint withdrew for a considerable time from all and immured himself in his cell, refusing all visitors. There came to his retreat a Roman officer of the military, named Martinianos, who interrupted Anthony's solitude. He kept knocking at the door, begging the elder to emerge and offer up prayer on behalf of his dear daughter who was being tormented by an evil spirit. The father persisted in knocking and calling out the saint's name for a long time. Although Anthony had no wish to exit, the officer's persistence could not go ignored. The saint then, not bearing to open his door, looked out from above and said, "Man, why dost thou call on me? I also am a man even as thou art. But if thou wilt believe on Christ Whom I serve, go, and according as thou believest, pray to God, and it shall come to pass." Therefore, he obeyed the saint's word, by believing and calling upon the name of Jesus. Straightway, his little daughter was restored to him, cleansed from the unclean spirit. Many other miracles were wrought by the Lord through His servant Anthony, which deeds are spoken of in the holy Gospel by the Lord Who said, "I say to you, keep on asking, and it shall be given to you; keep on seeking, and ye shall find; keep on knocking, and it shall be opened to you [Lk. 11:9]." For many of those who were smitten and suffering from ailments, when Anthony would not open his door, slept outside his cell; and they, by their faith and sincere prayers, were cured.

Saint Anthony the Great

Saint Anthony Retreats to the Inner Mountain

Before long, the saint perceived himself beset by many visitors. Not only was his solitude being penetrated, but he also feared what the miracles, which the Lord wrought by him, might lead to: either that he should become puffed up or that some should be induced to think of him above what he warranted. Thereupon, he was resolved to set off toward the upper Thebaid and abide among a people to whom he was unknown. After the brethren gave him some loaves of bread, he sat down by the bank of the river. He kept looking to see whether a boat would go by, that, after he had embarked thereon, he might go up the river with them. While he was considering these things, a voice came to him from above, "Anthony, whither goest thou and wherefore?" But he in no way was disturbed, for he was accustomed to being called often thus. He gave ear to the query, answering, "Since, my Lord, the people permit me not to live in stillness and contemplation, and they also demand of me things beyond my powers, I repair to the upper Thebaid." But the voice said unto him, "If thou goest into the Thebaid, or, as thou hast in mind, down to the Bucolia, the marshy district close to Alexandria, thou shalt surely endure more, aye, double the burden as the present one. But if thou wilt truly be in quietude, depart now into the inner desert." And Anthony said, "Who will show me the way to that difficult place? For I am acquainted with neither the terrain nor any guides." Immediately, the voice pointed out to him a caravan of Saracens, engaged in trade, who were about to go that way. So Anthony went forth and drew near them. He inquired if he might go with them into the desert. They, as if commanded by divine providence, received him willingly. After he journeyed with them for three days and three nights, he came to a very lofty mountain near the Red Sea (Inner Mountain or Mount Kolzim, about one hundred and sixty kilometers southeast of present-day Cairo). At the foot of that mountain ran a clear spring, whose waters were most sweet and very cold. Outside there were a plain and a few palm trees.

Anthony, seeing the beauty before him and moved by God, loved the place; for this was the spot which He Who had spoken with him by the banks of the river, had pointed out. After he received loaves from his fellow travelers, he dwelt in the mountain quite alone. He perceived it to be his own home. The Saracens, for their part, saw the earnestness of Anthony and deliberately used to pass that way, glad to bring him more loaves. The palm trees also afforded him a meager and frugal relish. But after this, the brethren, having learned of the place, like children mindful of their father, took care to send supplies to him. At length, Anthony, seeing that the dispatch of bread to him was a source of hardships to others, thought to spare them the trouble of traversing so long a path. He was resolved to ask some of those who came to bring him a spade, an axe, and a little grain that he might sow and thereby feed himself. When these tools and grain were conveyed to him, he went around until he located a small plot of ground, at the foot of the mountain, suitable for cultivation. Since the place was endowed with a plentiful supply of water, he sowed. Consequently, he got his bread from this planting, rejoicing the more that he should no longer be a burden to anyone, but rather would eat by the work of his own hands. He produced a crop large enough for a year's supply of bread, which pleased him. After this, seeing again that throngs were coming to him in that place, he cultivated a few herbs and vegetables, that he might offer some little fare to solace visitors after they had made that difficult journey. At first, however, the wild beasts in the desert, coming because of the water, often injured his seeds and husbandry. But he, gently laying hold of one of them, said to them all, "Why do you injure me, when I hurt none of you? Go in the name of the Lord, and come nigh no longer!" Henceforth, as though fearful of his command, they no more trespassed the place.

So Anthony was alone in taking possession of the Inner Mountain, spending his time in prayer and ascetic labors. The brethren who served him asked that they might come every month and bring him olives, pulse, and oil, as a concession to his old age. It was on account of the visits of others to him that we came to learn of the many wrestling matches he endured, "not against blood and flesh, but against the principalities, against the powers, against the cosmic rulers of the darkness of this age, against spiritual hosts of evil on account of the heavenly things [Eph. 6:12]." Visitors reported hearing tumults, many outcries, and, as it were, the clash of arms. Terrified eyewitnesses gave descriptions of how the entire mountain was seen to be overrun by fiery phantoms and flashing spears. Now at night, they saw the mountain become full of wild beasts. They observed Anthony also fighting, as though against visible beings, and sending up prayer against them. On the one hand, Anthony offered encouragement to those who came to him; but, on the other hand, he contended with the adversaries as he knelt and prayed. Anthony, comforting his visitors, would say, "They are empty apparitions which perish, as if they never existed, at the name of Jesus and the sign of the Cross." Surely it was a marvellous thing that a man, alone in such a desert wasteland, was not terrified out of his wits. He feared neither the demons who rose up against him, nor the fierceness of the four-footed beasts and creeping things, though they were so many. But in truth, as it is written: "They that trust in the Lord shall be as Mount Sion [Ps. 124:1]." Thus his mind remained unshaken and undisturbed; so that the demons and wild beasts rather fled from him, as it is written: "For the wild beasts of the field shall be at peace with thee [Job 5:23]."

The devil, on another occasion, observing Anthony standing fast and chanting the psalms of David, kept gnashing his teeth against him. The blessed man was consoled by the Savior and continued unhurt by the devil's wiles and varied devices. As he was watching in the night, the devil sent wild beasts against him. Thus, almost all the hyenas in that desert came forth from their dens and surrounded him. Anthony was encircled by them, as each beast threatened to tear him apart. Seeing that it was a device of the enemy, he addressed them all: 'If you have received power from God against me, well then, I am ready to be devoured by you; but if you were sent against me by demons, remain not, but depart quickly, for I am a slave of Christ,[4] the Master of creation.' When Anthony spoke the name of Christ they fled, driven by that word as with a whip.

A few days after, as Anthony was laboring at his handiwork, for he was careful to work hard, some creature stood at his door. That monster then pulled the plait which he was working, for Anthony used to weave baskets, which he gave to those who came, in return for what they brought him; for Anthony would not eat his bread for free. Anthony then leaped up and beheld a beast, resembling a man from his head to his thighs, but having legs and

---

[4] Saint Paul also frequently calls himself a slave of Christ [Rom. 1:1; Phil. 1:1; Gal. 1:10].

feet like those of an ass. The blessed man quickly sealed himself with the sign of the Cross and said, "Christ's slave am I. If thou art sent against me to do evil, behold I am here." But that monster fled so quickly that it burst asunder, from which the evil spirits with it vanished. Thus, the demons strived in all manner of ways to overcome and drive out Anthony from the desert, but they were unable to do so.

Saint Anthony Visits the Brethren Along the Nile

Now some monks came and requested that the saint visit them in their abodes. After a time, compelled by love, he yielded and journeyed with those who had come to him. A camel was laden with provisions of bread and water for them. This was done because they needed to traverse a desert wasteland, having no water fit for human consumption. In fact, the only water available was in that mountain, where Anthony had his cell. On their way, the water supply gave out. The blazing heat of the sun was intense, imperiling all of them. After they went searching round those parts and found no water, those with the saint became weak and could walk no further. They stretched out on the ground, despairing of their predicament, and then let the camel go. The old man, perceiving that all were in jeopardy, groaned in deep grief. He departed a little way from them and knelt down. He then stretched forth his hands in prayer, uttering, "Consider, O Lord, at this time also the prayer of Thy slave." Straightway, as soon as tears fell from his eyes, the Lord made water spring forth where Anthony had been praying. Therefore, all drank and were revived. After they filled their water skins, they sought the camel and found her; for the rope, by God's dispensation, came to be caught in a stone and held fast the beast. They gave the camel water, and then placed their bottles on its back and finished their journey safely.

As they approached an inhabited district, many rushed forward and venerated him as a righteous man. When the holy man came to the outer cells, all saluted him and gazing upon him intently as a father. They vied with one another to respectfully kiss and embrace him. He exhorted and helped them spiritually by his instructions and practical experience, so that there was great joy in the mountains. They were gladdened at the triumphs of the blessed old man whom they beheld renewing his youth "as the eagle's [Ps. 102:5]." Anthony also rejoiced when he beheld their earnestness. He lauded their discipline, stimulated their zeal for improvement, and comforted them through their "mutual faith [Rom. 1:12]." Anthony also joyfully embraced his very own sister who had grown old in virginity, and saw that she herself also was the leader of other virgins.

The Brethren Visit Saint Anthony

After some days, the saint then hurried back to his mountain. Henceforth many resorted to him, and others who were suffering ventured to go in. To all the monks therefore who came to him, he continually gave this precept: "Believe on the Lord and love Him; keep yourselves from filthy thoughts and fleshly pleasures, and as it is written in the Proverbs, 'Neither be deceived by the feeding of the belly [Prov. 24:15].'" He urged them, before all, to freely confess the true Faith of Christ, and love it with all their strength. He also admonished them to not to give heed to evil thoughts and the lusts of the flesh. He encouraged them to avoid vain boasting. He counseled them to hold in contempt the things of the world. He instructed them to pray continually, chant psalms, and recite the Church offices before they slept. He advised them to meditate upon the acts and lives of the apostles. He told them to recall the deeds of the saints. He urged remembrance of the Faith's spiritual heroes, so that the souls of his disciples might be inspired and trained by the zeal and deeds of the saints. By their sacred examples, the saint hoped that his disciples would keep in mind the Lord's commandments and His holy Faith unadulterated. He counseled them to bear in mind continually the apostle's words, 'Be ye angry, and sin not: let not the sun set upon your provocation [Eph. 4:26; Ps. 4:5].' Anthony considered that this was spoken of all commandments in common. The sun should not go down, not only on our anger, but on any other sin of ours. For it was good and needful that neither the sun should condemn us for an evil by day nor the moon for a sin by night, or even for an evil thought. That this state may be preserved in us, it is good to hear the apostle and keep his words, for he says, 'Be putting yourselves to the test if ye are in the faith; be examining yourselves [2 Cor. 13:5].' Let each become an honest examiner of his own thoughts, before the righteous Avenger comes and renders to each according to his manner of doing [Mt. 16:27]. Those who have waged war against sins shall be encouraged by Christ. If one has sinned, let him cease from it. If one stands in the truth, Christ will urge him on, lest he should be swept away with boasting or despoiled by over-confidence or come to despise one and love another or justify his own soul. Let us practise these things, even as the Apostle Paul said, 'until the appearance of our Lord Jesus Christ [1 Tim. 6:14],' Who shall 'bring to light the hidden things of darkness and make manifest the counsels of the hearts [1 Cor. 4:5].' For often, unawares, we do not know our own manner of life and works. Although we have lost this knowledge, still it is manifest before God Who 'shall judge the secrets of men [Rom. 2:16].' Therefore, let us commit judgment to Him. Let us have sympathy one with another. Let us 'keep on bearing one another's burdens, and thus fill up the law of the Christ [Gal. 6:2].' Let us examine our own selves and hasten to fill up that in which we are lacking. As a further safeguard against sin, let the following be observed. Let us each write down both his actions and thoughts upon the tablet of his heart, as if he were obliged to read them aloud to every man. For when he considers the disgrace he could incur should these things come to light, he will abstain from sin and harbor no base thoughts. For who wishes to be seen while sinning? Who will not rather lie after the commission of a sin, through the wish to escape notice and shame? Therefore, let that which is written be to us in place of the eyes of spectators, our fellow hermits, that blushing as much to write as if we had been caught, we may never think of what is unseemly. Let us do as Paul who said, 'I buffet my body and bring it into bondage, lest, having preached to others, I myself should become unapproved [1 Cor. 9:27].' Thus fashioning ourselves, we shall be able to please the Lord and trample on enemy devices."

These and many other words of advice were given by the saint. He encouraged and inspired those who came to pursue the rigors of asceticism. He sympathized with those who were suffering. The Lord wrought mightily through Anthony, delivering many from their ailments. Such achievements did not cause him to become lifted up in his heart. If it happened that his prayers were not hearkened to that moment, he did not murmur against God but rather gave thanks. He persuaded those who were smitten with afflictions to bear them with greater patience. "Remedies such as these," he was saying, "belong to God Who grants healing to those whom He chooses and at a time which He knows best. Neither I nor any other man has power to grant such relief which only God could do." He continued to console them, which also was a relief and lightened their burdens, by these and other words. The sufferers were happy even to receive his words as a cure. They understood the lesson not to give up but to continue being long-suffering. Thus, he taught the down-hearted sufferers to bear their trials with equanimity. Those who were delivered from demonic possession were instructed to return their gratitude to God only, as the almighty One, and not to Anthony.

Saint Anthony Performs Miracles in the Desert

Now there was a nobleman, Fronto by name, who was an officer of the palace. He suffered terribly from a demon. Fronto was given to biting and gnawing at his tongue. He had a further complication involving his eyesight, which was nearly destroyed and about to leave him totally blind. This man had heard of the wonderworkings of the great Anthony. He went to the mountain and besought him that he might be healed. The saint uttered a prayer, "Depart and thou shalt be healed." Fronto, however, did not wish to leave. He insisted on remaining there for some days, waiting for help. The saint again said to him, "Until when shalt thou sit here to no benefit? Therefore, do thou go forth, and whensoever thou comest into Egypt, thou shalt behold the wonder wrought in thee." He finally believed and departed. Straightway, from afar, as soon as he set eyes on Egypt, his sufferings and possession ceased and he became whole, according to the word of the venerable Anthony, as our Savior had revealed to the abba in prayer.

There was also a maiden from Busiris Tripolitana, who had a terrible and very loathsome disorder. The discharges of her eyes, nose, and ears, when they fell to the ground, immediately became worms. Together with this general condition of putrefaction, she also suffered from paralysis and a nerve disorder to her eyes. Her parents, having learned that a group of monks was going to the great Anthony, asked permission to accompany them with their daughter. These parents believed in the Lord and the miracle He performed on the woman with the issue of blood [Mt. 9:20]. The monks granted their petition. In due course, the parents, together with their maiden daughter, remained outside the mountain with Paphnutios, the confessor and monk. In the meantime, the monks of that party went to see Anthony. They greeted the saint and wished to inform him first of all about the damsel, but the man of God anticipated them. Anthony himself gave details of her sufferings and how she, together with her parents had journeyed with them. But when they asked permission that she might be admitted, Anthony did not allow it, but said, "Go and, if she be not dead, you will find her cured; for the accomplishment of this is not mine, that she should come to me, pitiful man that I am, but her healing is the work of the Savior Christ, Who in every place shows pity to them that call upon Him. Now know this: the Lord, in His love for man, has revealed to me that He shall heal the damsel where she now rests." Indeed, so the miracle took place. The monks went out and found the maiden cured. Then all together they returned rejoicing to the parents' homeland.

On another occasion, two brethren were coming to see the saint. On the way, the water supply failed. One died, and the other was at the point of death. The surviving brother had no strength to go on, but lay upon the ground expecting to die. In the meantime, as Anthony was abiding in the mountain, he called two monks who chanced to be there, and said to them, "Take a vessel of water and hasten on the road toward Egypt. There were two brethren who were coming, but one is already dead and the other is in danger of dying, unless you should overtake him speedily. For this has been revealed to me by the Lord, even as I was praying." The monks therefore made haste. After one full day, they found the one lying dead and buried him. They also came across his companion, whom they revived with water, and brought him to the old man. But if anyone should inquire why Anthony had not spoken up before the other had died, the question ought not to be asked. For the judgment of death was not Anthony's decision but that of God, Who also judged the one and revealed the condition of the other. But the marvel here was only in the case of the watchful Anthony: that he was sitting in his mountain retreat with a heart pure and vigilant, when the Lord showed him things happening afar off.

Having this blessed spiritual gift, the saint on another occasion was again sitting on the mountain. He gazed upward and beheld a soul being borne upward into the heavens. There was much joy among those who met him. Then wondering and deeming such a soul to be blessed, he entreated God that the identity of that holy one might be revealed to him. Immediately a voice came to him, saying, "This is the soul of Ammoun, the monk at Nitria." Now Ammoun, commemorated by the holy Church on the 4th of October, had persevered in the ascetic discipline to ca. 356, when he reposed at the age of sixty-two. In order to traverse the distance from Nitria to the mountain where Anthony sojourned, a thirteen-day journey was required. The companions of Anthony therefore, seeing the old man amazed, asked to learn the cause of his state of wonder. The blessed elder said that Abba Ammoun had just reposed.

Now the holy Ammoun was a famous ascetic. Moreover, he used to visit and stay there very often among them. He also wrought many signs and wonders, of which one shall now be recounted. On a certain occasion, Ammoun, together with his disciple Theodore, wished to visit with the great Anthony. Ammoun and Theodore went and found themselves before the river called the Lykos ("Wolf") or Dâbhâ. Ammoun was abashed to remove his clothes in order to swim across unhampered. Hence, both men agreed that each should go away a short space from the other, lest they should see each other's nakedness as they swam across. The blessed Ammoun then was agitated by thoughts of shame and did not even wish to gaze upon his own nakedness. While he was engaged in such a quandary, suddenly, an angel of the Lord came and bore him aloft over the river and safely set him down upon the other side. Theodore, in the meantime, had already stripped and swum across. He was startled to find his elder had overtaken him, since he entered the river well before the elder; yet now he observed his elder's hair, beard, feet, and clothing were utterly dry. His elder had passed over the river by the might of the Holy Spirit. The righteous ascetic Theodore repeatedly asked, "How didst thou cross over, my father?" Ammoun kept making excuses, but Theodore was convinced that divine grace was at work here. Theodore then fell down before the holy man's feet and took hold of them, saying, "Yes or no, holy father: was it divine grace? I will not desist until thou hast shown me how this came to pass." When Ammoun observed that there was no way to conceal the matter from his disciple's persistence, he said, "I shall disclose it to thee, but do thou promise not to reveal it until I shall have departed from this world." Theodore agreed, and Ammoun revealed to him how he had been carried over by an angel, and that his feet never at all touched the water. He then cited how, as the Lord empowered his disciple Peter to walk upon the water to go to Jesus [Mt. 14:29], so also did he by the command of the Lord. The holy Theodore kept his promise and did not reveal the matter until the old man's repose, even as they agreed.

Now the monks to whom Anthony spoke concerning Ammoun's repose made a note of that day and the hour in which the God-bearing Anthony advised them of Saint Ammoun's repose. Not much time passed before certain brethren from Nitria were passing through. The brethren who had been with Saint Anthony inquired, "Tell us of the repose of the blessed Ammoun. When did it happen?" The traveling monks acknowledged his repose and said that it occurred on such a day and at such an hour, which exactly matched the time when Saint Anthony communicated what was made manifest to him in the Holy Spirit. The brethren marvelled at the holy Anthony's divine vision, which allowed him to see clearly what had taken place at a distance of some thirteen days' journey.

In another instance, the court functionary (*comes*) Archelaos found the blessed elder in the Outer Mountain. He asked him to pray for Polycratia of Laodikeia, an excellent virgin dedicated to Christ. She was suffering terrible pains in her stomach and side. This was brought about by her austere manner of life, which left her weak and exhausted. Anthony offered up prayer on her behalf, at which time Archelaos recorded the day and hour. After the blessed man dismissed him, Archelaos departed for Laodikeia. He found the virgin wholly restored. He immediately inquired when and by what means was she relieved of her infirmity. He then found that the time of her cure corresponded to the time he had written down. He then produced the paper on which was written the same time. All wondered when they knew that the Lord had relieved her of her pain at the time when Anthony made a prayer on her behalf, invoking the goodness of the Savior.

Now concerning those who came to see the holy man, he often foretold their arrival, sometimes days and even months beforehand. Some came only for the sake of seeing him, others on account of illness, and still others because of sufferings incurred from evil spirits. All deemed the labor of the long journey neither trouble nor loss. For each one returned aware that he had received benefit and relief greater than any toil. When anyone exulted in these triumphs and wished to narrate them, the blessed Anthony would entreat them not to marvel at the deeds, but rather at the divine grace of God. For this grace not only vouchsafed unworthy men such great care, but also brought knowledge of God to men according to their capacity.

Afterward, on another occasion, Anthony came down to visit the outer cells. He was asked to embark in a boat and to cross over the river. The saint perceived a foul and fetid odor that smote him only. He asked what might be the cause of the smell, but no one knew. They were answered by others, "Perhaps what thou art smelling comes from the fish and salted meat on board." He replied, "The stench does not arise from those things." Then, while he was speaking, a youth, possessed by an unclean spirit, was found on the boat. He had slipped in beside the hull and stowed himself away. Then the youth cried out at the sight of the holy man. Saint Anthony rebuked the demon in the name of our Lord Jesus Christ. That spirit forthwith departed, leaving the young man whole. All on board, in a state of wonderment, were then persuaded that the evil smell arose from the demon.

Another man, a person of rank, who was sorely tried by a demon, was brought to the saint. The demon was so terrible that the man's mind was carried away, so that he could not understand any question that was put to him. He did not even know that he was being taken to the great Anthony. His whole body was covered with bites from his own mouth. Those who brought him to Anthony besought the saint for his prayers. The elderly Anthony looked upon the young man and was moved to pity. He was resolved to keep watch with the sufferer all that night. Anthony had the young man stand up while he knelt in prayer the whole night. At dawn, the young man approached Anthony from behind, getting ready to smite the saint. He then pushed Anthony, which action received a quick rebuke from others who were present. When Anthony saw that they had become wroth with the youth, he said, "Be not angry with the young man; for it is not he, but the demon which is in him. Since that demon was rebuked and commanded to exit and return to his place, it was the demon who became incensed and did this. Instead, give glory to the Lord, since by this He has given you a sign that the demon was driven forth." When Anthony had said this, straightway the young man became whole. He came at last to his right mind and knew who he was, and through whom deliverance had been wrought. He then began embracing the blessed Anthony and loudly giving thanks and praise to God.

Visions of Saint Anthony

Many monks have related, with the greatest agreement and unanimity, other such accounts done by Anthony; but these do not give rise to as much amazement as the following wonders. Once, when about to eat a biscuit, Anthony rose up to pray at the ninth hour according to his custom. It seemed to him that angels came and bore him aloft. In the air he encountered dreadful and gloomy demons who attempted to prevent his higher ascent. The angelic beings who escorted him contended with those demons who demanded a defense for Anthony's deeds which he committed from birth. The angels rebuked them. The demons attempted to set forth Anthony's sins from birth, but the angels shut their slanderous mouths, saying, "Anthony's sins have already been blotted out through Christ's goodness. You have license to examine whether he kept his promises, the ones which he gave when he took the holy Schema, to preserve sobriety, poverty, and the other virtues, which he has practised. Therefore, concerning them, you might examine." The demons continued lying, in a shameless manner, accusing Anthony of many things, which they could not prove. Therefore, the saint's ascent lay open and unobstructed. But then he returned to himself and saw himself once more as he had been, in the very place where he had been standing. The saint kept pondering on the vision, so that he forgot to eat. He kept sighing and praying, bringing to mind the words of the apostle regarding "the prince of the power of the air [Eph. 2:2]." He thought upon the great army of enemies against our race and how much we must endure and struggle. He then brought to mind that for this cause we are told, "Take up the full armor of God, in order that ye might be able to withstand in the day, and having counteracted all things, to stand [Eph. 6:13]." Thus, anyone opposing us "might be ashamed, having nothing bad to say about us [Tit. 2:8]." Now, my beloved, in connection with this account, let us be mindful of the apostle when he says that "whether in the body I know not, or whether out of the body I know not, God knoweth—such a one was carried off as far as the third heaven [2 Cor. 12:2]." But Paul was "caught up into Paradise and heard unspeakable words [2 Cor. 12:4]," and then he came down; while Anthony was borne away to the place to which he ascended, received a pledge for his toils, and returned and took up his abode.

Saint Anthony was also granted this spiritual grace that while he was living in solitude on the mountain, should he ever be in perplexity regarding his meditations, the Lord would reveal the answer to him in prayer. Thus, that happy man, as is it written, was "taught of God [Jn. 6:45; cf. Is. 54:13]."

After this, when he once had a discussion with certain men who had come to him, concerning the state of the soul and of what nature its place will be after this life, the following night One from above called him, saying, "Anthony, rise, go out, and pay attention to what thou seest." He went out, knowing that the voice was from God. He looked up and beheld a huge and horrid giant, standing and reaching to the clouds. He also saw that around that giant, on all sides, were numerous beings; some were flying about, and some soared above the giant and escaped heavenward. The giant meanwhile was putting forth his hands that he might lay hold of some of them, but he failed. Those who were borne aloft, free from care, caused that son of perdition to gnash his teeth. Although he rejoiced over those who fell back, he still would have preferred that every man perish with him. Forthwith a voice came, saying, "Consider the matter, understand the vision [Dan. 9:23]." Then was Anthony's mind thoroughly opened to understand [cf. Lk. 24:45]. The one standing in the midst was Satan, the enemy of righteousness, who envies the faithful. He attempts to stay the passage of souls, but is unable to seize those who have not yet yielded to him, as they pass above him. So, after he had seen this, Anthony was incited to triumph in his old age, "forgetting the things which are behind, and stretching forth to those things which are before [Phil. 3:13]."

Now he was unwilling to speak of these visions. The brethren enjoined him, after they observed that he was sighing during his lengthy prayer to God. By this sign, they perceived the old man had seen something. They therefore pressed him with inquiries to reveal what he had seen. Therefore, as a father who cannot withhold things from his children, he first examined his mind and perceived that it was free of boasting. He then decided to speak to them, so that his spiritual sons might stand up like mighty warriors against the enemy, lest they should be caught by him. He thought that the disclosure would be beneficial to them and show them what the fruit of their labors might be.

Saint Anthony's Reverence for the Clergy

Anthony was also meek in spirit. In all things he preserved scrupulously the Church canons. He responded to the clergy according to each one's rank, honoring them above himself. Toward bishops and priests, he was not ashamed to bow his head at the time of the blessing. Toward deacons, if ever one came seeking help, he discoursed with him on what was profitable. Although as a father he spoke to them words of admonition, during the time of prayer he gave place and would set them in front by reason of the authority which had been given them by God. He not only sought that another should hear the word, but also rejoiced to hear it himself. Though he was an old man and famous, he was never ashamed to do so. On several occasions, he would even ask questions of those who were with him at all times. He would also acknowledge whenever he had been benefitted therefrom.

Now the saint's countenance had a great and wonderful grace, which was a gift also from the Savior. For if he were present in a great company of monks, and one who had never made his prior acquaintance should wish to see him, all the newcomer had to do was quickly gaze over those present, and he would be drawn to distinguish Anthony above the rest, as though attracted by his appearance. It was not that Anthony was taller or of a larger build or more comely than most that he should appear conspicuous, but rather that the serenity of his manner and the purity of his soul radiated from him. He possessed a soul free from disturbances, which was reflected in his outward calm. One could perceive the state of his soul by his outward movements, so that the words of Scripture applied to him which say, "A glad heart promotes health; but the bones of a sorrowful man dry up [Prov. 17:22]." Thus Jacob discerned by Laban's countenance that he was mediating some fraud and so commented to his wives, saying, "I see the face of your father, that it is not toward me as before, but the God of my father was with me [Gen. 31:5]." In like manner, Samuel recognized David, for the beauty of his eyes, and that he was "very goodly to behold [1 Kgs. (1 Sam.) 16:12]." Thus, by such indications, was Anthony known. He was never disturbed, for his soul was at peace. He was never downcast, for his mind was joyous.

Saint Anthony, Confessor of Orthodoxy

The saint was also firm in the Orthodox Faith, to which he held fast with honor and discernment. He never held communion with the Meletian schismatics,[5] knowing their dissensions, wickedness, and apostasy from the beginning. The saint also had no friendly dealings with the Manichaeans or any other heretics; or, if he had, only as far as advice that they should convert to piety. For he thought and asserted that intercourse with these would be harmful and destructive to the soul, and said as much: "Neither in the discussion of them nor in their result is there any advantage." Similarly, he detested the heresy of the Arians, and exhorted all neither to approach them nor to embrace their erroneous belief. Once, when certain Ariomaniacs came to him, he questioned them that he might ascertain their impiety. When he learned of their godlessness, he drove them from the mountain, saying that their words were worse than the poison of vipers.

Once the Arians falsely asserted that Anthony held their opinion. The saint was displeased by this slander and moved to righteous indignation. Since the wickedness of the Arians was prevailing and their report against the saint circulated throughout the city, the bishops and other faithful Orthodox besought the saint to come as far as Alexandria, to lend his support to the faithful against the dangerous presence of the heretics. He thereupon descended from the mountain and entered Alexandria (ca. 335), where he denounced the Arian impiety and blasphemy, teaching the people that the Son is coessential (*homoousios*) with the Father and coeternal. But they, even as the heathen, worshipped the creation rather than the Creator. In a loud voice he warned all to beware of the Arian error, saying, "This Arianism is the essence of all heresies. Keep away from them, lest you should be corrupted

---

[5] The schism, named after Meletios, Bishop of Lykopolis (ca. 325), is not to be confused with that of the Antiochene bishop, which occurred some fifty years later. The Nicaean Synod took action against the Egyptian bishop. He disagreed with Archbishop Peter of Alexandria regarding the lapsed during the Decian persecution. He was deposed for his irregular behavior and arrogation of the right to ordain clergy to replace those who had been imprisoned. His followers later went with the Arians, among whom they became prominent adversaries against the present hagiographer, Saint Athanasios.

by them. God forbid that the Son of God should be proclaimed to be a creature that hath been made, or that He should be brought into existence from non-being. For He is of one essence with the Father, and He is His Son and Logos. It is therefore great wickedness for a man to say that there was ever a time when Christ was not; for the Logos of God existed at all times. Therefore, flee from association with them, lest you should have a portion in their blasphemy; for 'what communion hath light with darkness [2 Cor. 6:14]?' You must have no connection or association whatsoever with them. For you are in the righteousness of your Faith. Those who say that the Son of the living God is a created thing are in no wise different from the heathen. Believe me, beloved brethren, 'the whole creation groaneth together and travaileth together until now [Rom. 8:22],' in the face of the Arian madness, because it sees its Lord, 'of Whom, and through Whom, and to Whom, are all things [cf. Rom. 11:36]' made, being accounted as one of the creatures."

Saint Anthony the Great

The faithful rejoiced, hearing the saint anathematize that Christ-fighting heresy. The citizens flocked to hear the great elder of the desert. Not only layfolk and heathen, but even the priests of the Greek pagans sought to behold the man of God, even as he was called, for he wrought many miracles and wonders. Therefore, many came to believe in the Christ and to receive Baptism during those few days that he spent in the city. His virtues were conspicuous, and his great knowledge and understanding were extraordinary, though it was known that he had not received a formal education. Then when some observed that the elder was being thronged by the crowds and in danger of asphyxiation, they went forth and began dispersing the crowd. The blessed man, not in the least annoyed at the human press, responded to this quietly and with a smile, remarking, "Let the people have their way. For what do think? Is it not easier for me to bear with this crowd of believers than with the more numerous army of demons inhabiting the desert?"

"When he was leaving, and we (Saint Athanasios and those with him) were accompanying him on the way, as we arrived at the gate, a woman from behind, running with all her strength, called out, 'Wait a little for me, O man of God, for my daughter is grievously vexed by a devil. Stay, I beseech thee, lest I too should harm myself with this hard running.' Now the old man, when he heard her, paused. We too asked him to stay, but he wished to do so in any event. When the woman drew near, the child was placed on the ground. Then Anthony prayed and called upon the name of Christ. The damsel was restored and raised whole, for the unclean spirit had gone forth from her. The mother rejoiced and blessed God, and all gave thanks. Anthony himself also rejoiced, for he was departing to the solitude of his mountain as a man about to return to his home after a long absence."

Saint Anthony and the Greek Philosophers

Saint Anthony was exceedingly prudent and wise. The wonder to many was that although he had not had formal schooling, he still was a ready-witted and sagacious man. At all events, two Greek pagan philosophers once came, thinking they could try their skill on Anthony and outwit him. While the old man was in the Outer Mountain, he recognized who they were from their garb and appearance. He went forth to meet them, addressing them by means of an interpreter, "Why, O philosophers, have you troubled yourselves so much to come to a foolish man?" When they said that he was not a foolish man, but exceedingly prudent and wise, he said to them, "If you came to a foolish man, your labor is superfluous; but if you think me wise, become as I am; for at all times we ought to imitate what is good. Had it happened that I had come to you, I should have been moved to become as you. But since you have come to me, become Christians even as I am." The philosophers marvelled at his words. They departed in awe of him, for they saw that even demons feared Anthony and were subject to him.

On another occasion, others such as these met with Anthony in the Outer Mountain. They came thinking to treat him scornfully, as if he were a simpleton, only because he had not received schooling. Anthony said to them, "What do you say? Which came first, the mind or letters? And which is the cause of the other? Is learning the source of the mind, or the mind of learning?" They answered, "The mind is the prince of learning, for it has discovered learning and invented letters." Anthony then said to them, "Does not the man whose mind is enlightened and bright surpass greatly him who has only learning? Therefore, he who has a sound mind has no need of letters." This answer amazed both the bystanders and the philosophers. They departed marvelling that they had seen so much understanding in an unlettered man, that is, one who did not know Greek. He was not boorish, and his manners were not rough, as though he had been reared in the mountain or desert where he had grown old; much rather, his mannerisms were gracious and polite. His speech was seasoned with the heavenly salt, so that no one was envious or angry, but rather all his visitors rejoiced over him.[6]

After this, certain other philosophers also came. They were men who were deemed wise, and gladly received, among the Greeks. They asked the elder questions concerning faith in Jesus Christ. When they attempted to dispute and confound him concerning the preaching of the divine Cross, Anthony paused a little, bearing with them and pitying their ignorance, and then spoke, through an interpreter who could skillfully interpret his words, saying, "Which is more beautiful, to confess the Cross or to attribute to those whom you call gods adultery, fornication, parricide, incest, and the seduction of boys? For that which is chosen by us, the Christians, is a sign of courage and a sure token of the contempt of death. That religion which you preach is a service to impurity, the teacher of obscenity, and cultivation of the passions of licentiousness. Next, which is better, to say that the Logos of God was not changed in His divinity, but, being the same, He took a human body for the salvation and restoration of man, that having shared in human birth He might make man partake in the divine and spiritual nature? Or do you think it better to liken the divine to senseless animals and consequently to worship four-footed beasts, creeping things, and the likenesses of men? For these things are the objects of reverence of you wise men. Our belief proclaims the incarnation of Christ took place for the redemption of men, and that it should not be for a cause for fornication, falsehood, injustice, gluttony, drunkenness, lasciviousness, and the rest of the practises of the world. We exhort men to shun these things, for a penalty has been decreed for those who dare to transgress in respect of one of these things. Now you, through the fable of error, labor in abominable works. We, however, trust in the power and mercy of God, believing that the preaching of the Cross is the best for us to follow.

---

[6] Saint Anthony is quoted as saying, "People are generally called intelligent through a wrong use of this word. The intelligent are not those who have studied the sayings and writings of the wise men of old, but those whose soul is intelligent, who can judge what is good and what is evil. They avoid what is evil and harms the soul. They intelligently care for, and practise, what is good and profits the souls greatly thanking God. It is these alone who should properly be called intelligent. A truly intelligent man has only one care—wholeheartedly to obey almighty God and to please Him." Kadloubovsky & Palmer, "170 Texts on Saintly Life," §§ 1, 2, *Early Fathers from the Philokalia*, p. 21.

But you, without any discernment, ascribe all kinds of hateful deeds to your gods, so that you without any further thought may do everything that pleases you. The Christian Faith, in regard to the almighty God's mercy, believes that the incarnation was possible for God, but in such a way that this condescension had not caused Him to lose dignity.

"But you, who proudly announce that the soul issues from the purest source of God, say that the soul has shamefully fallen. Furthermore, you say that the soul is an image of the mind and proclaim that the soul is unborn. When you have meditated well upon this subject, you change back and say that it shall be dissolved. Because of this opinion, which comes from your study, you lay it down that the mind itself will be broken up and changed. Thus, after proudly claiming that the soul issues from the purest source of God, you say that it has shamefully fallen. Thus, you desecrate this nature by your insults. Now, of necessity, the image must in its form and similitude be exactly like that of which it is the copy. Consequently, the image which according to you retains the natural likeness and substance of its maker, sends back its own humiliation and injuries to its origin. So beware: your insults to the soul will, as a result of your blasphemy, redound to their father, as you call him.[7]

"Now let us discuss the Cross of the Lord our God. I ask you, how is it an obscenity of religion? Is it not better to endure the Cross or a death of this kind at the hands of wicked men than to bewail the Egyptian mythical tales which have spread to the Greeks and Romans, regarding the dubious wanderings of Isis in search of her husband Osiris, or the plots of Typhon, who murdered Osiris, or the banishment of the Titan Cronus, who mutilated his father and seized world dominion, and then swallowed his children, except for Zeus (Jupiter), but later regurgitated them? You ought to be put to the blush at Zeus' murder of his father and his incest or even at his ravishing of both women and boys. He flowed into Danae's lap, sought the embraces of Leda, and corrupted a boy with birds as his accomplices. These are the fables you believe and worship. These are the accounts that decorate your temples. These things are not wisdom. Therefore, weigh our words with impartial justice. Is all or nothing to believed in the sacred books of the Christians? Why do you make a mockery of the Cross only and not keep silent regarding the resurrection? Those who have written of the latter also wrote the former. When you make mention of the Cross, why do you not also recount the resurrection from the dead? Why do you omit speaking of the miracles, I mean, the restoration of the blind, the hearing of the deaf, the cleansing of the

---

[7] Saint Anthony here refutes the teaching of the Neo-Platonists, especially Plotinos, who maintained that the Mind, or *Nous*, was the first emanation from the One.

lepers, and the healing of the paralytics? There are also the accounts of the walking upon the water, the flight of demons, the raising from the dead, and the return from Hades of those who were dead. Your judgment therefore is not just, for you do not judge matters rightly. You do not read the Scriptures in the proper manner. But read and see that the deeds of Christ prove Him to be God come upon earth for the salvation of men. You do not deal fairly in this matter when you clearly accept certain things, but reject those things which are akin to them.

"But do you tell us your religious beliefs, that is, if you are not ashamed to do so. What can you say of these disgraceful creatures except senselessness, grossness, and ferocity? But, as I hear, you now wish to say that these cruel and obscene things are spoken of by you as legends, and so you veil them in allegory. According to you, the rape of the maiden Persephone (Libera) is allegorized as that of the earth; the lameness of Hephaestus (Vulcan) represents fire; Hera (Juno), the air; Apollo, the sun; Artemis (Diana), the moon; Poseidon (Neptune), the sea; and Jupiter, the foremost of lechers, the sky. You call the elements gods, that you may mislead men from the one God Who is the Creator of the universe. Now if the beauty of the elements has drawn you to write such stories, you should have limited yourselves to admiration, and not to have gone so far as to make gods of creatures and creations, by offering them the worship that is due to the Creator only. Your logic is distorted. You divert to the house the honor that is due the architect; you ascribe glory to the household that is due to the king; and you heap upon the soldiers honors which are due to the general. You do not worship the Creator Himself, but serve the creature. Is it not time to have done with this error and deceit? What then can you possibly reply to these things, that we may know whether the Cross has anything deserving of mockery?"

The philosophers were at a loss, turning hither and thither, in their embarrassment. Anthony smiled and spoke through an interpreter, saying, "Sight itself proves that the elements are in servitude. But since you go about collecting things for dialectical proof, of which you are masters, you would force us to use this ploy to affirm our religion. You take refuge in guileful words, skillfully utilized, so that others should journey on without the truth, devoid of worship of the true God. But since you prefer demonstrative arguments, answer me this: how is knowledge of God truly comprehended and proved more clearly? By means of demonstrative arguments or by the working of faith? Which comes first: an active faith or verbal proof?" They answered that the working of faith takes precedence and is true knowledge. Anthony remarked, "You have answered well, for faith arises as the sign of the love which is made perfect in the soul. Dialectic depends on the skill of those who invent strings of words. For those who have active faith, demonstrative argument is needless, or even superfluous. For what we know through faith, this you attempt to prove through words; and often you are not even able to express what we have comprehended. No matter how many comparisons and similitudes you may contrive, you shall never be able to narrate the things of the truth which we have perceived. Therefore, it is evident that our faith, which is expressed in works, exceeds in excellence your wisdom which consists of a discussion of words. Your professional sophisms cannot by any means be rightly compared with active faith which is superior.

"We Christians therefore hold the mystery not in the wisdom of speech [1 Cor. 1:17] or Greek arguments, but in the power of faith, richly supplied to us by God through Jesus Christ. In proof of this claim, behold how, without having learned letters, we believe in God. We possess understanding concerning His creation. From His works, we recognize His providence and mercy over all things. We have confidence that our faith in Christ is effective, which supports us, whereas you rely on your words which are full of contention. God's words are sufficient for us to attain to the knowledge of God. The portents of the idols among you are being done away with, but our Faith is expanding in every place. In your case, although you have an abundance of words and arguments, still you have no power to convert even one Christian to Greek paganism. While our faith is effectual, your well-cultivated sophistries and polished words are powerless against the teaching of Christ. We who teach the Faith of Christ have crushed the worship of idols. We have exposed your superstition, since all have come to acknowledge Christ as true God. The preaching of the Cross and Christ crucified, though despised by you, has put to flight the demons, whom you fear as if they were gods. Where the sign of the Cross is placed or named, cunning error has been brought to an end. Whether it be divination or oracles or magic or sorcery, it has been brought to nought.

"Tell us therefore where your legendary oracles are now? Where are the charms and incantations of the Egyptians? Where the delusions of the magicians? When did all these things cease and grow weak, except when the Cross of Christ arose? Is then the Cross worthy to be despised? Much rather, should not the things brought to nought by it and convicted of weakness be deserving of mockery? Now this is a marvellous thing, that your religion was never persecuted, but even was held in honor and magnified, while the followers of Christ are persecuted, and still our side flourishes and multiplies over yours. Our religion was held in contempt and harassed, though it was great and glorious in its operation, and yet it spread and filled the universe while your religion perishes. For when has the knowledge of God so shone forth? When have sobriety and the excellence of virginity appeared as now? When has death been so despised, except when the Cross of Christ has appeared? Now no one doubts this when he sees the martyr scorning death for the sake of Christ, when he sees for Christ's sake the virgins of the Church keeping themselves pure and undefiled.

"These are signs sufficient to prove that faith in Christ alone is the true religion. But still you seek for conclusions based on reasoning. We however make our proof 'not in persuasive words of human wisdom [1 Cor. 2:4],' as our teacher has it, but we persuade by faith which manifestly precedes argumentative proof."

The saint then said, "Behold there are here some vexed with demons." Now there were certain people, disquieted by demons, who had come to the blessed man. Anthony brought those suffering souls into the midst and said to the philosophers, "Draw nigh and cleanse these afflicted sufferers by whatsoever means you may wish, whether it be arguments, calling on your idols, working sorceries, or pronouncing your enchantments. But if you are unable to give them any relief, put away your strife with us and stand aside that you might see the power of the Cross of Christ." The philosophers, struck with amazement, drew back. Anthony then called upon Christ and made the sign of the honorable Cross over the sufferers three times. Straightway, the men stood up whole and in their right mind, giving thanks to the Lord. The philosophers marvelled at what they had witnessed and were also astonished exceedingly at the understanding of the holy man. But Anthony said, "Why do you marvel at this? Which is better, tell me, words or works to show forth with certainty what is true knowledge of God? Is a demonstration of the true Faith to be made through talk or action? Which is to be preferred? Surely the proper response is a demonstration of efficacious action. But know this: we are not the doers of such works, but Christ Who wrought them by means of those who fear Him and believe on Him. Believe, therefore, also yourselves, and you shall see that with us there is here no handicraft of the devils or trick of words, but faith and love being energized, which can take place in you. If you would possess this love, there shall no longer be any need for you to seek after demonstrative arguments. You will consider faith in Christ sufficient." These were the words of Anthony to the philosophers. They stayed to hear him whom they put to the test, only to receive ample proof of the spiritual and mental adornments of the old man. After they accorded the venerable elder a respectful farewell, they openly confessed that their meeting with him had been of immense benefit to them. With great honor, they embraced and kissed him. After they acknowledged that they were benefitted by him, they returned to their own country.

Emperor Constantine and His Sons Correspond with Saint Anthony

The fame of the saint also came to the ears of Emperor Constantine and two of his sons, Constans (337-350) and Constantius II (337-361). Though Abba Anthony lived in obscurity, he was held in honor by the imperial court, which heard of his deeds. They besought the holy man to reply to them as a father would his children. They wrote frequently and entreated him that he might offer up prayers on their behalf and correspond with them by letters. The saint in no wise became puffed up at this singular distinction from the rulers. He preserved his humility and sweet disposition. Now the saint was not a quick writer. When he communicated with the emperors, with all meekness, he offered them soul-saving counsels, exhorting them to leave off any arrogant thoughts that their present glory in this life might usher in. He admonished them to be mindful of the future recompense and that the Christ, the only true and everlasting King, was to be emulated by earthly kings. He went on to say that they should imitate Christ's love for man with philanthropic deeds, care of the poor, and meting out righteous judgment. After the imperial letters arrived, which Anthony preferred not to receive, he would assemble the brethren and those who happened to be present, and remark, "I suppose that you marvel that the emperor and princes should write to us poor men in the desert. But what need is there to wonder at this? In truth, what we have here is one man writing to another man. What is truly deserving of wonder is how God not only wrote the law for the children of men, but also spoke to us through His only-begotten Son." He then read out the epistles received from the palace. He would say, "It is not within my ability to craft such letters as they write." Since Constantine and his princes were deemed Christians, he deemed it rude not to respond, or to treat the epistles lightly. If he did not answer, they might become displeased at being snubbed.

The saint was beloved and venerated by all. Many entreated him to become both their father and teacher. During this phase, the saint was ninety years of age. It was at this time that a divine revelation came to him and led him into the inner desert and to the venerable Abba Paul of Thebes, whom Abba Anthony interred. The account of their meeting is given in its entirety on the day of Saint Paul's commemoration, the 15th of January.

Saint Anthony Prophesies of the Beastly Acts of the Arians

The holy man returned to the Inner Mountain and resumed his wonted discipline. On another occasion, as the saint was sitting and working on palm leaves, he beheld a fearful and solemn revelation as he was in a state of ecstasy. He was seen to tremble and sigh. Now on other occasions, when people came to him, as he was sitting or walking, as it is written in Daniel, Anthony also turned his face toward the ground and kept silent [cf. Dan.

10:15]. Then, after a season, Anthony resumed the thread of what he had been saying before to the brethren who were with him. It was evident to his companions that Abba Anthony was seeing a vision. Wrapped in a vision, Anthony, while on the mountain, would often see what was happening in Egypt. Afterward, he disclosed what he had seen to Serapion the bishop,[8] who was indoors with him. But on this particular occasion when Anthony came into a state of ecstasy, he kept sighing deeply and groaning. Then after some time, he turned to those present with groans and trembling. He then prayed and fell on his knees, where he remained a long time. After he arose, he wept. His companions, then beginners in the monastic life, began to tremble, and fear gripped them. They desired to learn from him what he had seen. Since they importuned him greatly, he was compelled to speak. After many groans, he said, "O my children, it were better to die before what has appeared in the vision should pass."And when again they asked him, he sighed deeply and said sadly, "Great wrath is about to seize our Church, and it is on the point of being given up to men who are like irrational beasts. For I saw the holy Table of the Lord and wild mules standing around it on all sides in a ring. These creatures were kicking not only the things therein, but they were also kicking the faithful. And you saw," said he, "how I groaned, for I heard a voice saying, 'My altar shall be made an abomination.'" These things the old man saw, which took place after two years (ca. 343), when the Arians held sway in the Church. These things came to pass with the Arian spoilation of the churches, when they violently plundered the vessels and made the heathen carry them. They even forced the heathen from their workplaces to join in their services, and in their presence did upon the holy Table as they would. Then we all understood that these kicks of the mules signified to Anthony what the Arians, senselessly like beasts, are now doing. The profane and depraved acts perpetrated by the Arians and their minions cause every sober Christian's mind to recoil in horror. Virgins and honorable married women were raped, the faithful were slaughtered in the churches, and abominations were committed in baptistries. All of these events were accurately seen by Abba Anthony. But when he saw this vision, his sharp eye also beheld other future events. He consoled therefore the brethren, saying, "Be not grieved, my children; because speedily again shall the Church take up her previous good order and shine forth brilliantly; for in a short time, impiety shall vanish and the splendor of piety shall shine forth as before. You shall behold those who were persecuted to have been restored. The horn of the righteous, those who hold to the true Faith, shall be exalted. They shall

---

[8] Bishop Serapion (339-ca. 360), surnamed "Scholasticus," of Thmuis in the Nile Delta, was also a correspondent of Saint Athanasios the Great [cf. *P.G.* 26:530].

proclaim the truth boldly and freely in every quarter. The evil one, together with those who work his will, shall turn on his heels. The time of these things shall be short. The Lord shall send redemption to His people, and the just shall live by faith.[9] As for yourselves, beware that you do not defile yourselves with the Arians; for their teaching is not that of the apostles, but that of demons and their father the devil; yea, rather, it is barren and senseless, the product of perverse minds, like the senselessness of the mules."

Saint Anthony the Wonder-worker

The Wonderworkings of Saint Anthony at the Outer Mountain

These were the accomplishments of the venerable Anthony. Such were the words of this blessed man. We ought not to doubt whether such miracles and wonders were wrought by the hand of this man; for it is the promise of the Savior Who says, "If ye have faith as a grain of mustard, ye shall say to this mountain, 'Move from here to there,' and it shall move; and nothing shall be impossible to you [Mt. 17:20]."

And again He said, "Verily, verily, I say to you that whatsoever ye shall ask the Father in My name, He will give it to you....Keep on asking, and ye shall receive [Jn. 16:23, 24]." The Lord also said to His disciples and to all those who believe in Him, "Be healing the sick, cleansing lepers, raising the dead, casting out demons; freely ye received, freely give [Mt. 10:8]."

The blessed man healed all manner of sickness. The cures were not wrought by him as one giving commands, but by praying and invoking the name of Christ, so that it was manifest that it was not he who was working the cures, but that God wrought them by his hands. The old man was triumphant in all such matters; for the Lord fulfilled his desire with good things, and his strength was renewed as the eagle's [Ps. 102:5]. Anthony's part in the miracles consisted of prayer and discipline. Although he possessed love for his fellow man and was cheerful in showing it, still he came to be grieved and afflicted by reason of the continual flux of people coming to see him. Now he had settled on the Inner Mountain for the sake of rejoicing in the contemplation of divine things. At length, he was troubled by so many people that in order to have some respite he was compelled to repair to the Outer Mountain. It should be known that his good fame spread in every level of society, not only among private individuals, but also among the nobility and those in the judicial system. Now the judges used to ask him to come down from the

---

[9] Cf. Ps. 110:8; Hab. 2:4; Rom. 1:17; Gal. 3:11; Heb. 10:38.

mountain that they might consult with him and enjoy his wise judgments. It was not possible for them to go to the holy man, on account of their large following of people, that is, those involved in lawsuits, and also on account of the general fatigue which ensued from the journey to the saint's habitation. Though Anthony avoided such encounters and excused himself, yet they remained firm and persisted. Thereupon, in order to bring Anthony into their midst more often, the judges and governors also craftily contrived to send Greek pagans and other people who had been arrested and charged. The judges had dispatched, under military escort, their prisoners in chains, so that, on account of these and their pitiable circumstances, Anthony might come down. These defendants would then implore the saint to intercede on their behalf, for which Anthony, as one sympathetic, did not wish to turn them away without hope. Thus by these means and pretexts, the judges often had occasion to confer with the holy man. Thereupon, the saint, constrained by necessity and seeing the defendants lamenting, did not wish to reject them or turn them away empty and despairing. He came into the Outer Mountain; and again, his labor was not unprofitable. For his coming was advantageous and serviceable to many. He was of profit to the judges, counseling them to prefer justice to all things. He admonished them to fear God and bring to remembrance that "with what judgment ye judge, ye shall be judged [Mt. 7:2]." But of all things which he did, he loved more than all his sojourn in the mountain. Therefore, after he had been compelled by those who begged his help and performed for them his kind offices by speaking with either the governor or military commander, he hastened back to his philosophical retreat.

On another occasion, when he was importuned by those prisoners in distress, the military commander (*doux*) sent numerous messengers requesting that the saint come down from the mountain. Moved by the tears of those prisoners in their wretchedness, he went and gave advice that was beneficial for salvation. He commended the prisoners, acquitting some of them. The saint then began to hasten away toward his mountain hermitage. The military commander implored him to remain another day or two. Abba Anthony entreated him courteously to be allowed to return, and offered this pithy simile, saying, "Just as fish, if they should remain long on dry land, perish, so do monks suffer injury and loss if they tarry long with those of the world." He then said, "Therefore, it is meet that as fish spend their lives beneath the waters, so should we monastics carry out our lives and works in the wilderness. Therefore as fish must hurry to the sea, so must we hasten to the mountain, lest we should forget the things within us." The military commander, after he had heard this and many other things from Abba Anthony, remarked, "He speaks that which is given to him from heaven and not from himself. How could this simple man possess such a wealth of knowledge and understanding, unless he was beloved by God and instructed by divine love?"

During the reign of Constantius, the Christians were persecuted bitterly on account of the Arians—that name of ill-omen. Now there was a certain official at Alexandria, the profane Gregory, who perpetrated many atrocities against the Orthodox faithful, which exceed the power of language to describe, and which anyone who should hear would think to be incredible. How many monks were stripped and scourged! How many bishops were wounded and banished! How many virgins were beaten in public! All this occurred as Gregory sat by with Valacius (Balak), the military commander of Egypt (340-345). The reason why this Gregory acted thus was because he had not received his ordination according to ecclesiastical rule, nor had he been called to be a bishop by apostolical tradition. Instead, this Gregory had been sent out from court with military power and pomp, as one entrusted with a secular government. He therefore boasted rather to be the friend of governors, than of bishops and monks. Whenever, therefore, our Father Antony wrote to him from the mountain, as godliness is an abomination to a sinner, so Gregory abhorred the letters of the holy man. But whenever the emperor, or a general, or other magistrate, sent Gregory a letter, he was as much overjoyed as those in the Proverbs, of whom it is written: "Alas for those who forsake right paths, to walk in ways of darkness; who rejoice in evils, and delight in wicked perverseness [Prov. 2:13, 14]." So Gregory honored with presents the bearers of these letters. Now Abba Anthony sent a final letter to Valacius, stating: "I see God's wrath coming against thee. Cease, therefore, persecuting the Christians. If thou desirest thy health, desist and accept correction, so that the angel of wrath may be restrained against thee. Behold, he is set to come. Do this therefore, lest divine justice should apprehend thee and thou wailest to no benefit." Valacius laughed and spat upon the letter, casting it from him. He insulted those who bore the message, bidding them to tell this to Anthony: "Since thou takest thought for the monks, soon I will come after thee also." And five days had not passed before divine justice came upon him. For Valacius and Nestorius, the prefect of Egypt (345-352), went forth on horseback to the first halting-place from Alexandria, which is called Chaereu of Lower Egypt, some seventeen miles southeast of Alexandria. The horses belonged to Valacius, and were the quietest of all his stable. But the men had not gone far toward the place when the horses began to frisk with one another as they were wont to do; and suddenly the quieter beast, on which Nestorius sat, with a bite, unseated Valacius and attacked him, and tore his thigh so badly with its teeth that he was borne straight back to the city. Three days later, the mocker Valacius expired. All were sore astonished, because what Anthony had foretold had been so speedily fulfilled.[10]

These therefore are the things which Abba Anthony was wont to say to the judges of this world. His manner of counsel was loving. He exhorted them not to be puffed up in their minds or magnify themselves over the people. There was none among the governors at that time who did not gladly hearken to Abba Anthony, so that they repented of their evil deeds. Abba Anthony also demonstrated great care for those who were treated unjustly or were plundered. He would bear all their troubles. His words were comforting and soothing, so that many forsook their possessions and occupations and enrolled in the rank of monks. The saint admonished the disorderly and supported the wronged. He became the general physician of all Egypt who was sent by God. All who were grieving or mourning on account of their dead or some other loss or injury, he sent away consoled. The poor and needy were encouraged and comforted, so that many among the poor, though broken by poverty, left the saint despising riches. Those who were angry or indignant, he caused to be filled with love, graciousness, or long-suffering. Those who were licentious or intemperate, he brought to sobriety. Those who were possessed by demons or troubled by perverse thoughts, he marvellously cured. Monks who were sorrowing or being neglectful departed from him full of strength as mighty men of war. Young men, burning with lust and desire for pleasure, went away from the abba with their lusts quenched and mortified. When they beheld the old man triumphant, they henceforth contended in the forefront of the battle of self-restraint. Those who were troubled in their minds went away composed and rational. In a word, all those who met with the venerable elder were greatly benefitted.

The saint had the grace of being able to distinguish and understand the wiliness of the demons. By this gift of discerning of spirits [1 Cor. 12:10], he comprehended not only those things wrought by the adversary, but also the causes by which men were troubled and tempted. Thus those who were suffering from the devices of the evil one were given both armor and shield by Anthony. Even virgins who beheld the holy man from afar, left those to whom they were betrothed and betrothed themselves to Christ. Not only Egyptians sought out the holy man, but also many others came from afar with their questions, which he answered suitably. Needless to say, with his repose, all the people mourned their orphanhood. His memory in fact never died from among the people. Each encouraged himself by the repetition of Abba Anthony's triumphs and sayings.

---

[10] See also Saint Athanasios, *History of the Arians*, Part II(12, 14).

The Repose of Saint Anthony

"It is worthwhile that I (Athanasios) should relate, and that you, as you wish it, should hear the account of his repose, which is worthy of imitation." According to his custom, he visited the monks in the Outer Mountain. The matter of his repose was not hidden from him. Having learned from divine providence that his own end was nigh, he said to the brethren, "This is my last visit to you which I shall make. I have come to bid you farewell, for I would be surprised if we should see each other again in this life. At length, the time of my departure is at hand; for I have exceeded a century by five years. In but a few days, I shall go to Him Whom I desire." When they heard his announcement they wept, embraced, and kissed the elder, as though he were departing from them that very moment. But he, as though sailing from a foreign city to his own, spoke joyously, and exhorted them, saying, "Do not become negligent or careless in your asceticism, but conduct yourselves daily as though it were your last day. This is how each one of you ought to struggle. Guard yourselves against sordid thoughts. 'Keep on desiring earnestly the better gifts of grace. Keep on pursuing love and emulously desiring spiritual gifts [1 Cor. 12:31, 14:1].' Guard yourselves against associating with the Meletian schismatics and the heretics. You know the cause of their schisms and their profane and cunning ways. With all your might, flee from the doctrine of the Arians. Their wickedness is now patently obvious to all. Be free from all communion with them, so you shall be able to take good heed to the preaching of the truth of our Lord Jesus Christ and to receive the true doctrine of our fathers. Be not troubled if you see the judges protecting them, for their mortal and short-lived pomp shall cease. Therefore, keep yourselves untainted by them and observe the tradition of the fathers. Preserve and uphold chiefly the holy Faith in our Lord Jesus Christ, which you have learned from the Scriptures, and of which you have often been put in mind by me."

Now when the brethren were urging him to abide with them until he should repose, he suffered it not, for many reasons. He showed his refusal by keeping silence. He was especially adamant regarding the undue and age-old honor in the funeral rites accorded to the dead by Egyptians, who were wont to wrap in linen cloths the bodies of good men, and especially of the holy martyrs. The Egyptians did not bury their relics underground, but rather placed them on couches kept in their houses, thinking by these means to honor the departed. Anthony often urged the bishops to give commandment or issue an ecclesiastical decree to the people addressing this practise. In like manner, the blessed Anthony taught the laity and reproved the women, sternly saying, "This habit was neither lawful nor holy in the least. The burial places of the early fathers, the prophets, and the apostles, are known to you this day. Their bodies, until now, are preserved in tombs. Indeed, the very body of the Lord was laid in a tomb, and a stone was laid upon it, and hid it until He rose on the third day." And thus saying, he showed that he who did not bury the bodies of the dead after death transgressed the law, even though they were sacred. He would argue, "For what is greater or more sacred than the Master's body which was buried?" Many therefore having heard this explanation, henceforth buried the dead underground, and gave thanks to the Lord that they had been taught rightly.

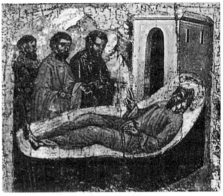

Saint Anthony Falls Sick

But he, knowing the tyranny of long and accepted custom, and fearing that his body would be treated this way, hastened away. After he bade farewell to the monks in the Outer Mountain, he entered the Inner Mountain, where he was accustomed to abide in his cell. After a few months he fell sick. He summoned those who were there with him, his two disciples, Makarios and Amathas. They had been with him in the mountain for fifteen years, practising the discipline and attending on Anthony on account of his age. The elder said to them, "I go the way of my fathers, for I perceive that I am called by the Lord. I also ask that you be watchful and grow not weary of your long discipline, but as though now making a beginning, zealously preserve your readiness and determination. For you know the plots and assaults of the demons, how fierce they are, but how little power they have. Therefore fear them not. Be faithful, trusting in the Lord and being ever renewed in Him. Live as though dying daily [1 Cor. 15:31]. Give heed to yourselves, and remember the admonition you have heard from me.

"Again, have no communion with the schismatics, nor any dealings at all with the heretical Arians. For you know how I shunned their strange doctrines and deemed their blasphemy as filthy and hostile to Christ. Therefore be the more earnest always to be found with the Lord and His saints, that after death they also may receive you into the everlasting tabernacles [Lk. 16:9] as well-known friends. Ponder over these things and think of them. You know that I have never held a conciliatory conversation with them on account of their perverted will and their continual war against Jesus Christ.

"Moreover, if you have any love for me and are mindful of me as of a father, suffer no one to take my body into Egypt, lest haply they should embalm me and lay me up in their houses;[11] for to avoid this I entered into the mountain and came here. Furthermore, you know how I always put to rebuke those who had this custom, and exhorted them to desist. Bury my body, therefore, and cover it with dirt yourselves. Let my words be observed by you that no one may know the place but your dear selves alone. For at the resurrection of the dead, I shall receive it incorruptible from the Savior.

"Furthermore, I would have you distribute my garments as follows. To Athanasios the bishop, give one sheepskin and the garment whereon I am laid.[12] Now he had of course given me that garment new, but over the years it has grown old with me. To Serapion the bishop, give the other sheepskin; and for yourselves, keep the hair garment. Be working at your salvation and saving yourselves in the Lord, for you shall no longer find Anthony in your midst; for I am being translated to Him Whom I desire. For the rest, my children, God be with you, for Anthony is departing and is with you no more."

After Anthony spoke those words, his disciples ardently kissed him as they sobbed. The saint then stretched out his legs, as he beheld his friends, the holy angels, coming to him. The sight of them made him exceedingly joyful, but this signal caused the disciples to weep and cry out for their elder. The saint's countenance was that of a man who sees a friend whom he rejoices to meet. Abba

The Repose of Saint Anthony

Anthony said nothing further. He quietly reposed and was gathered to his fathers. He had surrendered his soul into the hands of God in the year 356, during the reign of Constantius II.

Afterward, according to the saint's commandment, his disciples, without hesitation, resolutely prepared him for burial underground. They wrapped his relics round in the garment in which he was clad. They dug a hole in the ground, carried him outdoors, and interred him in the earth. No

---

[11] The saint enjoins that he should not be mummified in accordance with pagan Egyptian custom.

[12] The garment mentioned here is the same referred to in the Life of Saint Paul of Thebes, who, on the point of death, requested it of Saint Anthony, saying, "I beseech thee for love's sake, unless it be too great a trouble, go and fetch the mandya (cloak) given thee by Athanasios the Great, for whom I have profound respect, that I might be buried with that garment wrapped around me."

one knows to this day where the relics were buried, save those two disciples only. But each of those who received any one of Saint Anthony's garments regarded it as a most valuable possession, nay, a precious treasure. Indeed, even to look upon any of the great abba's garments, one could imagine that he was looking at the blessed man in it. Whensoever anyone put on one of those garments, such a one felt as if he were arrayed in the abba's commandments and promises, so that he would take up the blessed Anthony's counsels with great joy.

This closes our account of the life of the blessed old man, Anthony, in the body, while the previous narrative spoke of the beginning of his deeds and labors. If what has been recorded appears to be too small in comparison with the number of the triumphs of the blessed man, still from what has been set down, one can imagine how great was this divine man of God. Abba Anthony, from his youth to so great an age, ever showed constancy in the ascetical life. It should be noted that neither through old age did he yield to the desire for costly food, nor through the infirmity of his body did he change the fashion of his clothing. He was not urged by bodily infirmity even to wash his feet with water. While he maintained his discipline, keeping his body in restraint, God preserved him entirely free from harm. Abba Anthony's eyes, despite his old age, were undimmed. They were quite sound, and he saw clearly. As for his teeth, he had not lost one, but they had become worn to the gums through the great age of the old man. Both his hands and his feet were sound and healthy and remained strong, contrary to the laws of nature for centenarians. His ability to walk was unhampered. His head never ached. While other men were feeding on dainty meats and costly foods, taking baths, and donning fine clothes, he possessed strength which was out of all proportion to his aged body, and maintained a cheerful disposition.

A clear proof of his virtue, his perfect love toward God, and God's love for Anthony, may be seen in his good fame being blazoned in every place. All beheld him with wonder. Those who have never seen him long for him. His faith and love spread throughout all the provinces. It was not from discourses, or writings, or worldly wisdom, or crafty arts and schemes, that he gained renown; but God performed this work. This was Christ's gift. For from whence into Spain and into Gaul, how into Africa and Asia, and Rome herself, was this secluded man heard of who abided hidden in a mountain, unless God had made Him known everywhere? For God had also promised this to Anthony at the beginning when He said, "I will make thy name known throughout the world." For even if they work secretly, even if they wish to remain in obscurity, yet the Lord shows such persons as lamps to enlighten all, that those who hear may thus know that the precepts of God are able to make men prosper and in this way be zealous in the path of virtue.

Epilogue to the Life of Saint Anthony

Read these words, therefore, to the rest of the brethren that they may learn what ought to be the life and conduct of a monk. Let them hear and believe, that they might believe that our Lord and Savior Jesus Christ glorifies those who glorify Him. Let them know that the Lord leads those who serve Him not only to the kingdom of the heavens, but even here, though they should hide themselves and seek withdrawal, He makes them known and spoken of everywhere on account of their virtue and the help they render others. And if need be, read this account among the heathen, that even in this way they may learn not only that our Lord Jesus Christ is God and the Son of God, but also that the Christians who truly serve Him and piously believe on Him, not only prove that the demons, whom the Greek pagans themselves think to be gods, are no gods, but also trample on those deceivers and corrupters of mankind, and cast them out and put them to flight, through Jesus Christ our Lord, to Whom is due dominion, honor, and veneration, together with His unoriginate Father and the all-holy and good and life-creating Spirit, now and ever and unto the ages of the ages. Amen.

Saint Anthony the New

On the 17th of January, the holy Church commemorates our venerable and God-bearing Father ANTHONY the New and Wonder-worker.

Anthony the New, our venerable father, hailed from Verea (Berroia) of Macedonia.[13] He was the scion of virtuous and prosperous parents. He received a liberal education and rearing, which led him to desire a life of virtue. The ever-memorable one, even from his childhood years, was consumed with love for the divine. He therefore left behind dainty living and every luxury, together with the vain pleasures and pastimes of this life, and repaired to the Monastery of Peraia, situated by a running river. At that time, a multitude of monastics flourished and labored at virtue in that holy precinct.

---

[13] Berroia in Macedonia is a city at the west end of the central Macedonian plain.

He renounced all the things of this world, so that he might be clothed in the Schema of the monastics. He shrank from no labor, but instead resolutely carried out every task and obedience enjoined upon him. He became for the other brethren a standard and rule of conduct. At length, he besought the hegumen to give him leave to struggle alone in a nearby mountain that he might live the life of an anchorite in silence and solitude.

After he received a blessing from the monastery superior, he went exploring all about that mountain. He found a precipitous spot with a cave located by the mouth of the river. The terrain was very difficult to traverse. No man knew of the place except one priest. He would come at appointed times, traveling on an unmarked and narrow path, bearing the holy Mysteries, so that Father Anthony might commune. In that solitary abode the venerable man dwelt fifty whole years. He partook of nothing but grass, weeds, and herbs, all of which he found growing around the cave. He drank nothing but water from the river that flowed through that tranquil wilderness.

It should be told that the blessed man endured great temptations from the demons, even as it was reported by that priest who brought the Mysteries. At times, the demons approached the venerable Anthony as though they were thieves, administering such a thrashing to him that they left him nearly dead. At other times, they appeared as wild beasts. On some occasions, they made it appear that the river was rising up to such a level as to submerge the saint's cave. The demons, however, were unable to drive away Christ's athlete from his habitation. They therefore departed in shame. Now the saint lived to the advanced age of ninety. He reposed in that very cell, which he made the site of his contests and struggles.

After his earthly sojourn came to an end, the following miracle took place. There came into that mountain retreat some hunters. They found themselves before the river, opposite the cave wherein the relics of the saint were resting in peace. As they stood, their dogs began baying. The hunters looked about and caught sight of a man's hand beckoning to them amid the foliage that covered the entrance of the cave. The hunters were thinking that someone from their party found good game and was summoning them. They therefore forded the river hastily and followed the sound of the dogs, which led them outside of the cave. They entered but found no one living there; instead, they discovered the holy relics of the saint. Saint Anthony was on the ground, lying in an orderly fashion. The hunters also observed a lamp, which was lit, above the relics. Thus they easily discerned the sacred relics of a man in that cave. They venerated the holy anchorite, fervently and piously kissing his feet. Afterward, they returned to the city and revealed the matter to the hierarch.

The hierarch, taking the priests and a crowd of Christians, went to the cave. They carried out the relics reverently and accompanied the saint with lamps, myrrh, hymns, and odes. But then a point of contention rose up among the Christians. Two rival parties began vying for the anchorite's relics. One party consisted of the inhabitants of Peraia, and the other party was made up of the natives of Verea. The issue of which group would claim the relics led to a disagreement between the country folk and those of the city. It therefore seemed blessed to allow the saint to decide for himself. Therefore, the sacred relics were placed on a wagon, in imitation of the ark of the covenant [1 Kgs. (1 Sam.) 6:10-12]. Two pair of oxen were yoked to it and left to go as the saint willed. The oxen took off speedily on the road, passing the river, and heading straight for Verea, without tarrying by the roadside, or turning aside to the right or left, or losing sight of their destination. When the pair entered the city, they bore along the relics until they came to the saint's paternal home. Not long after, that home was converted into a church honoring our Lady Theotokos. But immediately after the arrival of the relics, it was dedicated to the saint. At that very place where the oxen halted with their precious cargo, the faithful believed that the saint wished to have his relics laid to rest. Now we should mention that his holy skull is a source of healings, especially for deliverance from demons. Various wonders and miracles are energized for those who hasten with faith to Saint Anthony. As for the mountain retreat where he contested, a monastery was established there. In that place, which was named the Skete of Saint Anthony the New, many ascetics came to struggle.

On the 17th of January, the holy Church commemorates the pious Emperor THEODOSIOS the Great.[14]

Theodosios the Great, augustus from 379-395, was known as a pious emperor of rare courage. He was born in Spain on the 11th day of January in the year 346 or 347. He was the son of the Spanish-born general Theodosius the Elder, military commander in Britain, who died in Carthage ca. 375, after he had received Baptism before he was executed on a charge of unclear nature. After the battle of Adrianople, when the Roman army was defeated by the Goths in August of 378, the young Theodosios was promoted to the rank of general by western Emperor Gratian (Flavius Gratianus, r. 367-383), son of Valentian I. Later, on the 16th day of January, in the year 379, Theodosios was proclaimed emperor in the east by the same at Sirmium. When he ascended the throne, his exceptional concern for enhancing the

---

[14] Concerning the great Theodosios, *The Great Synaxaristes* (in Greek) recommends reading Meletios, Vol. 2, p. 403, and Dositheos' *Dodekavivlos*, p. 246.

Orthodox Faith was evidenced from the first moment of his reign, when he immediately ousted the Arian Patriarch Demophilos. He then elevated to that throne the great Gregory the Theologian. According to Meletios, even in political matters, Theodosios displayed skill as a statesman. He differed from the other kings slightly in virtue, as he was possessed of a sharp temper, and this is evident from the many unjust executions and killings that he ordered in Thessalonike because of the murdered Buthericus (Butheric). In 390, during a riot in Thessalonike, he supported the barbarian soldiers against the citizenry. He would have repeated the same act in Antioch because of the destruction by the mob of the statues of the Empress Flaccilla (Plakilla), his consort, who is commemorated by the holy Church on the 14th of September. She was his first wife and the mother of their children, Arkadios, Honorius, and Pulcheria. Later, as a widower, he married Galla, who bore to him Galla Placidia.

However, he was first corrected by Saint Ambrose, the Bishop of Milan (373/374-ca. 397),[15] who prevented him from entering the church and gave him a canon. Not only did Theodosios accept the canon for the sake of repentance, but he also enacted a law, to wit: those who were sentenced to death would not be immediately condemned, but only after thirty days to allow for leniency or pardons. In the second reprimand, he was prevented by the intercessions of the Patriarch of Antioch, Flavian (384-404), and by the intercessions of the ascetics surrounding Antioch, states Saint John Chrysostom in his sermon, *On the Statues*, and as Nikephoros Kallistos brilliantly elaborates. His repentance was such that the ever-memorable one even wrought miracles. This is confirmed in the history given by Kedrenos, who also says that the emperor, wishing to worship in the holy land in Jerusalem, went dressed as a common citizen. When he came to the Church of the Resurrection, he knocked on the door. A certain servant opened it from within, and when the emperor answered—lo, and behold the miracle!—even though all the lamps were unlit, they all ignited at once, as if during a festival. As the servant was astounded by this miracle, he reported it to the patriarch, and the latter alone realized his identity and blessed him. Kedrenos describes the emperor as a gracious man with blond hair and an aquiline nose.

In 380, Theodosios, a staunch supporter of Orthodoxy, declared Orthodoxy the true Faith. He thereupon had Arianism condemned at the second synod held in Constantinople. This emperor was fortunate in the

---

[15] In the Life of Saint Ambrose, commemorated by the holy Church on the 7th of December, more information is given regarding the massacre and the emperor's penance.

following situations. (1) During his lifetime, the Second Œcumenical Synod was convened in A.D. 381, declaring that the Holy Spirit was also God, and the subsequent theology concerning the *homoousion* (one in essence) of the Holy Trinity. (2) At that point in history, there appeared many wise and holy men in both the east and the west. (3) He became a strong adversary against the heretics and idolaters. This emperor had copied the holy Gospel in its entirety in his own handwriting and read it every day. He issued strict laws prohibiting pagan rites of sacrifice. He reigned for seventeen years; according to some, for sixteen. At the age of 50, he was translated to the Lord in Milan on the 17th day of January, in the year 395. He was succeeded by his sons, Arkadios and Honorius; one ruled in the east (395-408) and the other in the west (395-423), respectively. His relics were transferred for burial in Constantinople. According to Augustine of Hippo, this king would often say that he was more fortunate to be a member of the Church of Christ than to rule on earth. By the mid-fifth century, the Church had endowed Theodosios with the title "Great."

On the 17th of January, the holy Church commemorates the venerable ACHILLAS (ACHILLES) of Sketis, who reposed in peace.

Achillas, our venerable father, was an anchorite. He struggled in asceticism in the desert of Egypt. He is mentioned in the Greek edition of *Evergetinos*, in regard to his encounter with Abba Esaias. On one occasion, Abba Achilles went to the cell of Abba Esaias and found him eating. As he came in, there was a basin of water and salt, which Abba Achilles saw him hide behind a mat. He did this lest the great old man Achilles should be scandalized, since it was not the custom in Sketis to partake of such dishes. But then Abba Achilles asked Abba Esaias, "Tell me, father, what hast thou been eating?" Abba Esaias replied, "Forgive me, father, I was cutting some palm leaves. After suffering under that scorching heat, I partook of a morsel of bread and salt. My throat however had become so parched, that I was unable to swallow my food. Since it caused me pain when I swallowed, I therefore cast a little salt in the water that I might dip my dry bread into it and continue eating. But forgive me this." Abba Achillas then exclaimed, "O fathers of Sketis, come and see Abba Esaias who eats broth in Sketis!" He then said, "If thou wilt partake of soup, then get thee to Egypt." He said this because all of the monastics kept such strict abstinence then in Sketis.[16]

---

[16] See *Evergetinos* (in Greek), Vol. II, p. 146, § 3; and also, E. A. Wallis Budge, *The Paradise of the Fathers* (in English), Vol. II, p. 210(260).

Though he may have been an austere ascetic, he strived with all his soul and body to keep brotherly love and peace. It happened that when someone addressed him with an insulting word, he did violence to himself by not making a retort. The restraint he applied to ward off any feeling of resentment resulted in his mouth filling up with blood. Now at that time a certain elder happened to have seen Abba Achillas spit out blood, and asked, "What is this?" The abba answered, "This blood is the hard word of one brother who grieved me. And how I struggled not to reveal it to anyone else! I implored God that He might take away the remembrance of it from me. Thereupon, that word became blood in my mouth. Now that I have spat it out, I am at rest and have forgotten my sorrow."[17]

Once when a certain brother came to him and began whining about the power that the demons exercise over us, he commented, "The only power they possess is derived from our own dissolute will. Thus, they act as an axe to cut us down."

On the 17th of January, the holy Church commemorates the holy New-martyr GEORGE of Ioannina (1838).[18]

George, the blessed new athlete and martyr of Christ, hailed from Ioannina[19] of northern Epiros, situated on a peninsula on Lake Ioannina. He was born in 1810, in a village called Tsourchli,[20] in the province of Grevena. He is the boast of Ioannina and has shown himself to be a river of miracles. He has become the downfall of the unbelievers and the resurrection of the faithful. His parents, Constantine and Vasilo, were extremely poor farmers. When George was eight years of age, he was left orphaned of both parents. He then became the charge of his elder brother and sister. During those years,

---

[17] See *Evergetinos* (in Greek), Vol. I, p. 253, § 14.

[18] The martyrdom of this new-martyr was taken from the second edition of the *Neon Martyrologion* (Athens, 1856), published at the expense of Constantine Skatharos, which included the accounts of the new-martyrs from 1794-1838. The first edition was published at Venice in 1794. A festal divine office, together with a Supplicatory Canon, was composed in honor of Saint George of Ioannina by the hymnographer, Father Gerasimos Mikrayiannanites.

[19] Ioannina, built by Justinian I (r. 527-565), fell to Stefan Uroš IV Dušan circa 1348, and passed to Symeon Uroš after 1355. The tyrannical Thomas Preljubović ruled in the city from 1366/1367 onward. As he struggled against the Albanians, he summoned Ottoman assistance in 1380. Since the citizens were frightened by Albanian attacks, they acknowledged Carlo Tocco as their ruler. After his death in 1430, Ioannina was ceded to the Turks. *The Oxford Dictionary of Byzantium*, s.v. "Ioannina."

[20] Tsourchli was the Turkish name, which village has been renamed Saint George in honor of its new-martyr.

the people of Epiros were subject to tumultuous vicissitudes and the hostilities of the Albanians and other military forces which beset Epiros. The Albanian,

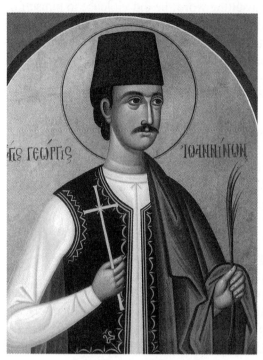

Ali Pasha, known as the "Lion of Ioannina," had broken with the Ottoman sultan and formed an independent state of Albanians and Greeks. George's village of Tsourchli was on the road that connected Korytsa in Albania with Trikkala in Thessaly. This road was also used by the Ottomans and Albanian Muslim mercenaries. It was during this period that the blessed George, at the age of fifteen, came into the employment, as a groom, of a Muslim agha (ruler), who had originally come to George's hometown to rest. Wheresoever the military duties of the agha took him, George necessarily accompanied him.

Saint George of Ioannina

After the passage of some years, when George was twenty-two years of age, he was in service to groom horses for Hatzi Abdullah, an officer of Imin Pasha, who had succeeded his father Kioutachi as *vali*, that is, governor of Ioannina in 1830, when the latter was made grand vizier. The Hagarenes, according to their custom and for reasons of their own, were not in the habit of calling George by his Christian name. Despite his adherence to the Orthodox Faith, the Muslims nicknamed him "Giaour Hasan," which meant "unbelieving" or "infidel" Hasan. Therefore, with the passage of time, most persons ignorantly assumed that the groom was not a Christian but one of the Ottomans. Now what do you suppose came to pass? In the year 1836, when Imin Pasha became governor of Ioannina for a second time, he brought with him Hatzi Abdullah and the blessed George. Shortly thereafter, at the prompting of some of George's friends, he was betrothed to a certain young woman named Helen. She too was orphaned of her Orthodox parents, Basil and Peristera, and had become the ward of an aunt, named Theophano, and an uncle, named Zapheires, a teacher. Helen also had two brothers, Alexios and Constantine. Although the maiden was rather poor in this world's material things, she was most wealthy in spiritual virtues. All who were acquainted with Helen bore witness to her soberness, prudence, and fear of God. Hearken, however, to what took place on the very day that Helen's aunt betrothed her to the blessed George.

A certain Turkish hodja, that is, a teacher of the Koran, who was from Ioannina, had recognized the saint. He had known George when his coreligionists dubbed their groom Giaour Hasan. Since he was a fanatical Muslim, the hodja began to denounce the blessed George, saying to him, "How is it that thou, a Muslim, should wish to take a Christian woman?" The saint said to him, "I, as a Christian, seek to take a Christian wife." But that thrice-accursed one hastened alone to the judge and slandered the blessed George, charging, "Some Turk seeks to take to wife a Christian woman, while I know him to be a Turk, that is, a Muslim." Consequently, George was brought to the courthouse, where he was questioned. He answered forthrightly from his heart, "I am a Christian." The *cadi* (judge), attempting to frighten him, bellowed, "Here, the hodja testifies that thou art a Turk." The holy man replied, "Nay, I was and I am a Christian." As he made that response, he sealed himself with the sign of the Cross. It happened at that time that a sincere friend of the saint was in the courtroom. As one studied in the Turkish language, he spoke fluently and with exceptional daring, opposing all the words of the accuser and judge, since the saint was a man of few words.

The judge, observing all these developments, did not know how to proceed. But then he decided to remand the case to the governor, who interrogated the saint. He received the same answers from George that the latter gave before the judge. When the governor learned that the defendant was in service to Hatzi Abdullah, he summoned him and inquired, "Is the defendant a Christian or not?" He answered, "From the start I knew him to be a Christian." Thus cleared by his employer, the governor then dismissed the charge and released George. The governor then commanded that the judge register George as a Christian in the records.

Now that very same week, the first Sunday after his release, on the eve of Saint Demetrios, he wore the wedding crowns with Helen, and they were joined in matrimony in 1836. During that same time, Imin Pasha departed for Prusa, followed by Hatzi Abdullah and George himself. George, however, remained only a short time, having receiving permission from his employer to return to Ioannina. Only a few days after his return, he was hired as a groom by Moutselimi of Philiates, who had been posted there by the new governor, Mustafa Pasha. George remained three months in Philiates, then returned to Ioannina in the company of Moutselimi's superior on the last Wednesday of December. During that same night, as Thursday was dawning, Helen, his wife, gave birth to their son. It was due to this, that when his superior was about to leave the city, George received permission that he might take leave and be by his wife and child in Ioannina.

On the 7th day of January, the son of George and Helen was baptized. While the saint was vouchsafed to become a father, his heavenly Father, during those days, was preparing an amaranthine and gloriously plaited crown of martyrdom. The following Tuesday morning, George fell into such a deep sleep that he did not awaken that whole day. Many times his relatives attempted to stir him from his bed, but he was utterly unmindful of his surroundings. Finally, toward evening, he arose and began to eat. Instead of pronouncing the customary words we are saying before eating, that is, "in the name of Christ," the blessed one said, "Glory to Thee, O God." When one of his kinfolk inquired why he spoke thus, he said, "O blessed one! Again would you not all say that it is good that I know even this much?" The following day, Wednesday morning, he asked for his best attire and dressed himself. As he was leaving, he gave the pretext that he was going to find his fortune. It was assumed he would be searching for other employment. As he went to the door, he looked back with deep entrancement upon his son, his wife, and his other relatives. They, observing this state, wondered and said, "Why do you gaze upon us so?" He replied, "Why should it trouble you?" He uttered this twice.

After these incidents at home, George went directly to the market-place. As he was going through and passing the plane tree, behold, there appeared that thrice-accursed hodja who had troubled George earlier with his false accusation. In the hodja's company there happened to be a certain judge, Bouloumbases. The hodja immediately took hold of the holy George, even as he had earlier, and threatened him, saying, "Until when shalt thou make fun of the faith? Art thou a Turk or a Christian?" George, as a man, became afraid. He then, in some suitable way, asked him to unhand him and leave him alone. Now it also happened at that moment that Alexios, the brother of George's wife, was passing by. Alexios came to George's defense and attempted to break free the hand grip of that betrayer of the innocent. As this took place, many Hagarenes heard the clamor and gathered around. Many Christians also came to see what was drawing attention. Among those present were two notables from the market-town of Konitsa. The one was George Diamantes and the other Adamos, originally from Spadae. Both men were of irreproachable character. They provided the author of the present narration with eyewitness accounts of the events as they unfolded. The strife took place by the house of Daout Pasha, commander of the armed forces.

Seeing from his house the commotion taking place, Daout Pasha dispatched his men to bring before him the involved parties. When Daout questioned them, the saint's slanderers answered, "This fellow was a Turk, and we all know him. Now, however, he has returned and become a Christian, as his fez plainly indicates, bearing the symbol which shows forth the Christians."[21] Daout then turned to George and questioned him. The saint boldly answered, "I was born a Christian; I am a Christian; and a Christian I will die." Since the judge, Bouloumbases, was present, the commander of the armed forces delivered up George into his hands. The commander then had one of his men escort George and the judge to the Turks' abominable Mahkeme (Court of Justice).

After this was accomplished, the saint was led before the same judge from the first inquiry when he was denounced. The judge opened the questioning, asking in Turkish, "Thou art a Christian?" The saint answered courageously, "Yes." The judge continued and said, "No. At one time thou wast a Christian, but now thou art a Moslem." The saint, empowered by divine grace, spoke with boldness, saying, "No, no! I am a Christian, even as thou thyself didst corroborate last year when thou hadst it marked down in thy records." The judge came back with this rejoinder: "At that time there was only one witness, but now there are many witnesses, testifying that thou art a Turk. Consequently, with their evidence against thee, thou hast two options from which to choose: either come to be a Turk or be put to death." The saint answered him dryly, saying, "Do whatsoever thou wilt."

It happened at that hour that a pernicious old man, aged seventy, who had apostatized from the Orthodox Faith, was present. At such an advanced age, the wretched man espoused Mohammedanism on account of his vain and light-minded opinions. That odious man looked upon the saint and said, "Look here, I spent seventy years in the Faith, which I forsook and became a Muslim." The saint, seeing this new Lucifer, was in no wise afraid, though he was as a sheep in the midst of wolves; for he was filled with divine zeal. As one empowered by providence and foresight from on high, he said to the wicked old man, " O wretched one, I shall ignore these shameless ones who are present and tell thee as much about my Faith as I know, for it is more radiant than the sun; but thou, O thrice-miserable one, with what conscience didst thou separate thyself from thy family and thy three sons of whom—indeed now!—thine eldest is a priest? Does not thy soul ache to depart from them, thou filthy and evil old man?" So the valiant athlete of Christ spoke. O courageous testimony! O what eagerness and readiness, deserving of heavenly praises! (Now it happened that a certain other George, the judge's scribe, a nephew of the steward of Doliana, recounted these events to us.) When the Turks heard such language they were wroth. Then they set about to examine

---

[21] According to the command of Imin Pasha, all the Christians were enjoined to wear this symbol, which was black.

George if he had received circumcision, and soon uncovered that he was uncircumcised. The shameless ones then took hold of the lamb of Christ and brought him to the proconsul. George answered the identical questions with the same answers, which resulted in the proconsul commanding George's incarceration.

In the prison George discovered that there were many other Christian prisoners. Two in particular, Haralambos and George, of Vourbianitsa, asked George for what reason was he being imprisoned, whereupon the holy man recounted his case. As George spoke and informed them of the events, it was obvious to his listeners that George was by nature a man of few words. Nevertheless, they perceived that he was being persecuted because of his Faith. Haralambos and George began by offering words of advice, inspiring him and making him enthusiastic for martyrdom. On the next day, Thursday, the Muslims led the saint before the judge who sought, together with those who sat with him, to incite George to become a Turk and Muslim. George simply stated, "A Christian I am; a Christian I will die." Thereupon, he was brought to the dungeon. His feet were placed in wooden stocks. A stone slab, weighing approximately one hundred and forty pounds,[22] was placed upon his body. Despite the obvious discomfort that this would have ushered upon anyone, George slept very sweetly and soundly. He did not feel the weight in the least, for it seemed to him to be a light and soft blanket. When he awakened, the others asked him, "Brother, how didst thou pass the night? We were afraid that perhaps thou didst die from the weight of the stone!" The saint replied, "I did not feel any pain or discomfort. Indeed, I beheld a vision of one who strengthened me. He appeared to be a youth, clad in white, who came and spoke to me in Turkish, saying, 'Cease fearing, O George!'"

That Saturday he was again made to stand before the judge, at which time he once more proclaimed the Holy Trinity. The judge asked, "What hast thou decided? Know that the hour of thy death has come, for such is the sentence I shall hand down." The saint, however, was not in the least intimidated and answered boldly, "Do what thou wilt with me. I was born a Christian; I am a Christian; and a Christian I will die." The judge, observing such valor, then decided to release him. But that thrice-accursed, barbaric, and superstitious race of the Turks, dwelling at Ioannina, began crying out for the death of the reviler of Mohammedanism. One bloodthirsty, misanthropic, and most defiled soul, named Sheikh Ali, who was greatly esteemed by all the Ottomans, appeared before the vizier twice, promoting the death of George. The vizier consented out of reverence to his own vile religion. Therefore, the

---

[22] Oke or oka is a unit of measure, around 2.8 pounds, used in Greece, Turkey, and Egypt. The slab weighed fifty of these units of measure.

decision was given, and the saint was led to prison. It is said by some that at that very moment that the judge pronounced the sentence, a great bolt of lightning struck, the din of which was terrifying. The waters of the nearby lake also seethed so that people trembled.

Now the Christians learned of these activities and made every effort to obtain George's release. The bishops, Joachim of Chios (who eventually became Joachim II, Patriarch of Constantinople), and Neophytos of Arta and Grevena, together with notables of the city and the saint's relatives, attempted to intervene on George's behalf, but they were unable to succeed with the Turks. They also went before the vizier, before whom they testified that it was shown that George was uncircumcised. They hoped by this discovery to secure his release. The vizier replied, "That piece of evidence is for the judge to decide upon. In any event, I am unable to revoke his sentence."

In the meantime, the Christians did not fail to keep sending individuals into the prison to encourage George for martyrdom. The aforementioned Haralambos and George did not ever cease from exhorting their fellow prisoner. But he said to them, "Cease being excited or scared, brothers. Indeed, I will eagerly suffer martyrdom for the sake of my Christ." The blessed George was calm, as his wife also noticed, and she remarked that he was calm as no other. It should be noted as many days as he was kept in prison, those thrice-accursed Muslims were going and inciting him to become a Turk. The saint, true to his reticent character, continually responded with only these words: "I am a Christian." The other Christians who were also found in that prison with him urged him to rebuke them, but he kept saying to them, "Now should I break my head shouting at them? I told them that I am a Christian." The accursed prison guard never ceased from harassing the holy man, saying, "Hey, George, become a Turk for now, that thou mightest escape death, and afterward go into those parts of Greece which are free or someplace else and become a Christian again." The saint, endeavoring to guess the meaning of those soul-destroying words, would answer with his natural simplicity, saying, "I die a Christian. With that, what does anything else matter?"

When therefore it was Monday morning, the 17th of January, the feast day of Saint Anthony the Great, at about the third hour (9:00 a.m.), behold, five executioners entered the prison. Other Christian prisoners, who were also condemned to death, saw them entering. They were in terror and began to say their prayers, as much as they were able. The saint, however, was sitting by the fire, undisturbed at the sight, with his chin in his hand. Since it happened that the prison guard was not present at that moment, Haralambos saw a youth, named Tasoulas, and made a motion of his head in such a way that meant, "Why have the executioners come?" The youth then nodded with his head toward George. Then the other condemned prisoners, with much secrecy, began whispering to George and saying, "Do not be afraid, brother, but play the man. The pain is short, but afterward thou shalt rejoice to the ages forever." The blessed George, upon hearing the death sentence read out to him, rejoiced exceedingly. He gave glory to God Who accounted him worthy to die on behalf of His holy name. The saint's fellow pious Christian prisoners then said to George, "Guard thyself well, brother, because they shall employ every means to make thee take back thy words. Therefore, attend carefully, lest thou shouldest be made a laughingstock."

As they were saying these things, the prison guard opened the door and told the saint to rise up. The guard then began to bind George in the usual manner for those who have been condemned to death. When he finished, George exchanged a kiss and embrace with the other Christians in that place. Then the executioners led George to the slaughter. The blessed one hastened with such eagerness "as the hart panteth after the fountains of water [Ps. 41:1]," according to the words of David. The executioners said to George, "We are going to hang thee." The saint, scorning them and turning up his nose, bravely answered, "Whatsoever you do, do it an hour earlier." It was a wonder to behold him hastening beside the executioners with such readiness and rejoicing, so that he seemed to be airborne on wings. His face appeared grace-filled and altogether radiant from the joy of his soul.

They brought the saint to a place called Kouramanio. The executioners again questioned him, saying, "What art thou?" The saint answered, "A Christian. I venerate my Christ and my Lady Theotokos." George then requested of the executioners to untie his hands. When they loosed him, he made the sign of the Cross and addressed those Christians present, saying: "Forgive me, brethren, and may God forgive you also." The executioners placed the noose around the martyr's neck and drew him up. Saint George surrendered his soul into the hands of God. His earthly sojourn ended most courageously at the age of twenty-eight.

According to the custom of the Hagarenes, the sacred relics were left hanging at the end of the rope for three days. Every evening the guards beheld a heavenly light shining radiant about the Martyr George's body on the gallows. They kept thinking it was lightning, which was sent to burn him because he was an infidel. Thereupon, they called the judge that he might see the spectacle. He came and marvelled at the phenomenon, resulting in his sending for the vizier. The vizier was of the opinion that the body would suffer burning by that light, leaving only ashes by the following day—that is, the 18th of January, the same day that the Christians celebrate their feast of Saint Athanasios the Great at the cathedral. When the 18th had arrived, the relics of Saint George were still whole, incorrupt, radiant, and fragrant, to the glory of Christ, our true God.

After three days, at the beseeching of the Christians, the vizier called Metropolitan Joachim and gave him permission to inter the sacred relics. Thereupon, the Christians took the relics and brought them to the cathedral church. In opposition to the Muslims, the Christians, with much ceremony and pomp, had gathered. All the hierarchs and crowds of Christians from Ioannina were present. Tears were shed, and joy filled the faithful on account of the glory of our blameless Faith. The Muslims had been put to shame, not having gained what they had demanded. With splendid chanting and zeal for the Faith, the Christians interred the holy relics of Saint George at the left side of the church, next to the gate of the holy bema, in a Christian and magnificent manner.

As many Christians that had received a portion of the rope which was used for the hanging, or a swatch from the saint's clothing, became witnesses of great healings. Also, all those sick folk who hastened to the tomb of the saint were vouchsafed their health. The mute received their voices, while the lame were able to run a straight course. The withered hand of a certain woman was completely restored and set right. Many cures took place merely by touching his tomb. Saint George also was seen by many in dreams. He also appeared to his wife, consoling and comforting her with these words: "Cease fearing, for I shall ever be visiting thee." The fame of his miracles and wonders spread in every place. Consequently, multitudes of the infirm without number came and continue to come to the saint's tomb. Those who come receive their health according to their faith.

Now a certain priest-monk, a lover of the martyrs, hearing these things concerning the saint, was moved by divine zeal. He sent to Ioannina and commissioned an icon of the saint with notable scenes from his life and martyrdom. This icon has wrought many miracles to this day.

Let us therefore also, O brethren, give glory to God Who has vouchsafed us to see with our own eyes the valor of the holy martyrs from all ages past endure even to our own days. Let us glorify God, I say, because the death of the holy New-martyr George became a resurrection of the faithful and a falling of the unbelievers who, having spoken with venomous tongues against our holy Orthodox Faith, suffered great embarrassment. By the intercessions of the holy new-martyr and of all the saints, may we also be deemed worthy of the kingdom of the heavens and that everlasting blessedness. Amen.

Through the intercessions of Thy Saints,
O Christ God, have mercy on us. Amen.

**On the 18th of January, the holy Church commemorates
our holy fathers among the saints,
ATHANASIOS and KYRIL, Archbishops of Alexandria.**

Athanasios and Kyril, the most holy archbishops of Alexandria and
our divine fathers, were from Alexandria. The great Athanasios lived during

Saints Athanasios and Kyril

the years of Emperor
Constantine the Great (306-
337). He attended the First
Œcumenical Synod in
Nicaea (325), which put
down the profane Arius.
This saint also suffered numerous exiles on account of
the Arians. Saint Kyril lived
during the time of Emperor
Theodosios II the Younger
(408-450). He attended the
Third Œcumenical Synod in
Ephesus (431), which de-
nounced the blasphemies of
Nestorios. Kyril champi-
oned the Virgin Mary's title
of Theotokos. Saint Athanasios addressed those questions pertaining to the Trinity, while Saint Kyril wrestled with Christological
problems. Both fathers left
the Church many religious
writings. Today the Church
celebrates the synaxis of these two holy fathers. This feast was observed from
ancient times by our holy Mother Church. Saint Athanasios is individually
commemorated by the holy Church on the 2nd of May, which has been
assigned as the day of the translation of his relics. Many are of the opinion
that this latter date should be the main feast day, maintaining it was the day
of the saint's repose. The shared date of the 18th of January is believed by
them to be in response to the feast day of the Three Hierarchs, commemorated by the holy Church on the 30th of January. The special feast day of Saint
Kyril is commemorated by the holy Church on the 9th of June, the day of his
falling asleep in the Lord. The histories and sayings of Saints Athanasios and
Kyril have been popular with many writers. Those who have written about

Saint Athanasios include Saint Gregory the Theologian, Saint Symeon the Metaphrastes, Theodoretos of Kyros, Socrates Scholasticus, Eusebius, Rufinus, Saint Epiphanios, Sozomen, and other ancient chroniclers. Two hagiographies of Saint Athanasios are extant, which are kept at the Athonite Monastery of the Great Lavra. An elegant encomium by Saint Gregory the Theologian has also been preserved. The biography in *The Great Synaxaristes* (in Greek) is taken from *Neon Thesavron*, upon which the English version herein was based and enhanced with other sources. The biography of Saint Kyril was composed by Nikodemos the Hagiorite, taken from Nikephoros and Sozomen and other ecclesiastical histories, and placed in the *Neon Eklogion*, from which the account in *The Great Synaxaristes* (in Greek) is taken. An encomium to Saint Kyril was composed by Zonaras, which is preserved at the Great Lavra, Vatopedi, Dionysiou, and Iveron. Father Gerasimos Mikrayiannanites composed twenty-four stanzas to honor this saint, together with a complete divine office for the 9th of June.

The Life of Saint Athanasios the Great

The homeland of our holy father Athanasios the Great (ca. 296-373) was Alexandria of Egypt. He was described as being very small of stature, somewhat stooping, and emaciated by fasting and many troubles. Nevertheless, he had a fair countenance with a piercing eye and a personal appearance of great power even over his adversaries.

He was the offspring of pious Orthodox Christians who surpassed others in both their wealth and nobility. Straightway, from his earliest years, the saint showed in which state he would labor later in life. Even as a youngster Athanasios did not engage in disorderly play as other children, nor did the youth busy himself with improper pastimes and playthings. Generally, he remained indoors where he prudently hearkened to the admonitions of his parents.

One day in the year 313, however, Athanasios went with a group of other Orthodox companions to the seashore. The city walls of Alexandria were situated nearby the sea. Athanasios and his friends began to imitate the order of the baptismal service of the Church. Although this was recreation to them, it proved to be a prophecy of the future. Some of the lads took the part of Church readers, others as deacons, and others as priests. The young Athanasios was appointed as patriarch by his fellows. Now there were other children also playing down by the seashore. Those that were unbaptized were brought before Athanasios, who then baptized them in the sea.

That same day was the anniversary of the martyrdom of Bishop Peter of Alexandria (311). The then Patriarch of Alexandria, Alexander, after the service, was expecting some clergy for dinner in a house by the sea. The patriarch happened to gaze out the window looking toward the sea when he observed the boys playing on the shore. He was struck with astonishment how

they performed the sacred rite of the Church with such exactitude. He then came to the opinion that the children were really exceeding the bounds of playacting in their imitation. He sent off his attendants to fetch the youngsters and bring them before him.

When the little fellows came face to face with the patriarch, they were alarmed at his questions. At first they denied it out of fear, but Alexander—feigning a stern countenance—threatened them with punishment. The patriarch finally drew out of them the details of what he had witnessed from afar. He learned that one of them acted as bishop and baptized the others. The children confessed that Athanasios was their bishop. Alexander ascertained that all points and the exact order of the Church had been accurately observed by the children in performing the baptisms. He decided to confer with his clergy over the episode.

It was decided that it was unnecessary to rebaptize the children who were immersed in the sea. On account of the Orthodox children's simplicity, they had been judged worthy of divine grace. The baptisms were deemed valid. Indeed, as many children as the holy Athanasios baptized in the sea, the patriarch only performed upon them such offices as it is lawful only for those who are consecrated to initiate when celebrating the Mysteries. Thus, Patriarch Alexander completed the baptisms and then dismissed them in peace, but summoned the parents of the boys. He counseled

Saint Athanasios

them to hand the lads over to tutors that they might be educated for the sacred profession and holy orders.

Now Alexander was especially impressed with the fourteen-year-old boy-bishop, Athanasios. He singled Athanasios out, perceiving his future ability and devotion. He spoke to Athanasios' parents and foretold that their son would become great and marvellous in the future. He commanded them to give the youth over to teachers that he might learn sacred Scriptures, and added that when he should reach eighteen years of age they were to bring Athanasios to him; but not long afterward he had Athanasios as his able companion and secretary.

Athanasios' education was liberal and that of a Greek. Egyptian religion, monuments, and history had no special interest for him. Nowhere did he betray a trace of Egyptian nationalism. He studied sacred Scriptures from his earliest years, and the Scriptures saturated his mind. He did not know Hebrew, which limited his knowledge of the Old Testament to the Septuagint. With the passage of time, especially during his future exiles, his knowledge of Latin grew considerably. His command of both the Old and New Testaments was formidable.

The holy youth did well in his studies—a combination of scriptural study and of Greek learning at the famous Alexandrian School. He also frequented classes of grammar and rhetoric. It was the school of Clement, Origen, Dionysios, and Theognostos; yet, it was from Patriarch Alexander of Alexandria that Athanasios received much of his molding in true Orthodox belief. Saint Athanasios' study and work in the bishop's household bore fruit. Although trained in Alexandrian theology with its influence of Origenism, Athanasios revealed early on that he achieved an independent grasp of Orthodox theology. He was a thinking man, conspicuous among his classmates, and something more than what the school was capable of graduating.

According to Saint Gregory the Theologian (ca. 329/330-390) the young Athanasios was brought up, from the first, in pious customs and practises, after a brief study of literature and philosophy, so that he might not be completely unlettered in such subjects, or ignorant of profane learning and such matters which he had chosen to despise. He had a generous and eager soul that could not brook being engaged in vanities. He meditated upon every book of the Old and New Testaments, "with a depth such as no one else had ever applied even to one of them," says Saint Gregory.[1] He grew up rich in contemplation, using both life as the guide of contemplation, and contemplation as the seal of life. He understood that the fear of the Lord is the

---

[1] Saint Gregory the Theologian, *Oration XXI: On the Great Athanasios*, ¶¶ 7, 8, Nicene, 2nd Ser., Vol. VII. Also in this Life, extracts are taken from Saint Athanasios' *Defence Against the Arians*, *Discourses Against the Arians*, *Defence Before Constantius*, *Encyclical Epistle to the Bishops of Egypt*, *Defence of the Nicene Position*, *Defence of His Flight*, *History of the Arians*, and his *Epistles*, in Select Works and Letters, Nicene, 2nd Ser., Vol. IV.

beginning of wisdom; but when wisdom has burst the bonds of fear and risen up to love, it makes us friends and sons of God instead of slaves.

When Athanasios attained his majority, his parents brought him to the patriarch, who foresaw in the Spirit the virtue of the holy young man before him. With holy joy he received him, and enrolled him in the sacred clergy: first to the office of Reader, followed by the ranks of Subdeacon and then Deacon after he reached twenty-five years of age. Numerous are the exploits of the saint. Many are the toils which he undertook. Varied and sundry are the temptations he suffered for the sake of the Orthodox Faith, due to the machinations of the Arians. Hearken now with attention to some of his deeds, as he passed through all the offices of holy orders, until he was finally entrusted with the throne of Saint Mark.

Arius Enters Alexandria

During that time, one named Arius (250-336), a native of Libya, settled in Alexandria. Spurred on by ambition, he sided at first with Meletios, a schismatic, and then with Archbishop Peter of Alexandria (d. 311), who ordained him a deacon. He was reconciled with another schismatic, Achillas, who raised him to the presbyterate. Arius was put in charge of the parish of Baucalis, one of the principal urban churches at Alexandria. He was not so well versed in understanding Scripture as he was crafty and a vessel of the devil, skilled at instigating scandals. As he was a popular preacher, his teachings began to incite controversy, because he said that Christ was not coeternal with the Father. He was a vigorous advocate of subordinationist teaching about Christ, and his vile doctrine quickly spread, and he made many disciples.

At first, he privately made known his brand of theology; but then he made bold to declare openly that the Son and Logos of God is a creature, and that there was a time when He was not, and that the nature of God the Father is different than that of the Son. Arius conceded that Christ is a God-bearing man, but not God incarnate. These and other blasphemies, which agitated the Orthodox faithful, were spewed forth by the deceitful Arius. His beliefs circulated in the mouths of many. Daily his teachings put every city and land in confusion, because many hierarchs and priests, together with highly placed men, were succumbing to his doctrines. He filled Egypt with tumult and confusion.

After the repose of Archbishop Peter, Arius was disappointed at the election of Alexander to the see of Alexandria. His ill will reached a climax when he opposed Alexander's Orthodox teachings. Archbishop Alexander was at first conciliatory, and agreed to give Arius a patient hearing. Arius was intractable. He canvassed for support and won it. By the concoctions of the enemy of our salvation, his ideas were widely accepted among layfolk, virgins, deacons, presbyters, and the bishops of Antioch and Ptolemais in Pentapolis.

A synod at Alexandria, under Archbishop Alexander, condemned Arius. In September of 324, Emperor Constantine the Great sent Saint Hosius of Cordova the Confessor (ca. 257-357), as his acting ecclesiastical advisor, to Alexandria. He investigated the dispute between Alexander and Arius. He reported his findings—which strongly favored Alexander—to the emperor, who decided to convene an œcumenical synod. This was something new. Although local councils were a recognized organ of the Church for legislation and judicial proceedings, there was no precedent—no ecclesiastical law or theological principle—which established the "general synod" as the supreme expression of the Church's mind. They would attempt to bear witness before all of their consensus in the Faith handed down from apostolic times. Brother bishops of different languages, races, and civilizations were to meet and deliberate, without fear.

The First Œcumenical Synod

In 325, the emperor summoned the bishops of the empire by a letter of invitation, putting at their service the public conveyances, and liberally defraying from the public treasury the expenses of their residence in Nicaea and of their return trip. The clergy were to meet in Nicaea of Bithynia from the end of May until the 25th of August. The year was 325. Each bishop was entitled to bring with him two presbyters and three servants. They traveled partly in the public post carriages, partly on horses, mules, or asses, and even on foot. The number that attended was three hundred and eighteen, about one-sixth of all the bishops of the empire (approximately one thousand for the Greek provinces, and eight hundred for the Latin). The Eastern Church was strongly represented. The Western Church had only seven delegates which included Saint Hosius of Cordova. A Persian and a Gothic bishop were also present. The discussions were held part of the time in a church or some public building, and part of the time in the emperor's residence.

The formal opening of the meeting was made by the emperor's entrance. The moment the approach of the emperor was announced, all rose from their seats. The emperor, very tall, slender, handsome, and majestic, walked in. He united the spiritual ornament of the fear of God with modesty and humility. His eyes were downcast, his face bore a blush. When he reached the golden throne prepared for him, he halted, and would not sit until the bishops gave him leave. After him, they all took their seats. The emperor then delivered the address in the Latin tongue, which was immediately translated into Greek. Afterward, he gave way to the ecclesiastical presidents of the synod, and the business began. The emperor, however, repeatedly took an active stance, and exercised much influence.

Saint Athanasios was a young deacon when he attended that great and holy synod meeting. Deacon Athanasios was acting as the representative of the Patriarch of Alexandria, who was feeling ill. His convictions were secure. His grasp of the issues made him the backbone of his bishop's party. The young archdeacon from Alexandria was noted for his fervor, intellect, and eloquence.

Among the prominent men at the meeting was Evsevios of Caesarea, noted for his historical writings. Some who attended were confessors from the time of the persecution, who still bore the marks of Christ upon their bodies: Paphnutios of the Upper Thebaid, Potamon of Herakleia (whose right eye had been plucked out), and Paul (who had been tortured with red-hot irons under Licinius, and crippled in both hands). There were illustrious ascetics present: Iakovos of Nisibis and Spyridon of Cyprus. But it was Hosius of Cordova, whom Athanasios calls "the Great," who had the most influence with Constantine.

The Orthodox party held firmly to the deity of Jesus Christ. At first they were in the minority, but in talent and impact they were certainly the more weighty. At the head of the party stood Archbishop Alexander of Alexandria, Efstathios of Antioch, Makarios of Jerusalem, Markellos of Ankyra, Hosius of Cordova (the court bishop), and above all our Alexandrian archdeacon. According to then current practise, he was not admissible to a voice or a seat in the synod meeting; yet he exhibited more exuberance and insight than all others. He showed promise already of being the future head of the Orthodox party. Indeed, this would be the very thing that would engage his attention.

The Arians or Evsevians numbered some twenty bishops, under the head of the influential Evsevios of Nikomedia (later of Constantinople). He was allied with the imperial family, and the presbyter Arius, who was commanded by the emperor to attend, so that he might explain his views. Also in that ill-famed group were Theognos of Nicaea, Maris of Chalcedon, and Menophantos of Ephesus. Evsevios of Caesarea took a middle ground. Many had an Orthodox instinct but little discernment. Many were disciples of Origen or preferred simply biblical expression; others had no firm convictions. The Arians first proposed a creed, which was rejected and torn to shreds.

A middle-of-the-road confession was introduced but avoided the term *homoousios* (*omo-ousios*, of the same essence). The Arians hated the word *homoousios*, declaring it unscriptural. Hosius of Cordova then announced that a confession was prepared, and that Deacon Hermogenes of Caesarea, the secretary of the synod, would read it aloud. It is in substance the well-known Nicene Creed or Symbol of the Faith, with some additions and omissions.

Almost all subscribed to the Creed, Hosius at the head, and then the two Roman Presbyters Vito and Vincentius as delegates of the aged Pope Silvester I (314-335). Evsevios of Caesarea signed after a day's deliberation. Evsevios of Nikomedia and Theognos of Nicaea signed without the condemnatory formula of the Arian heresy. Only the two Egyptian bishops, Theonas and Secundas, refused to sign. They were banished with Arius to Illyria.

At the synod, those that had rallied around Alexander in formal opposition to the Arians might have been about thirty. Between this assembly and hardened Arians sat those bishops, numbering about two hundred, mostly from Syria and Asia Minor, who only desired that they might deliver the Faith to their successors as they received it at holy Baptism. This middle party, while untainted with Arianism, either failed to grasp the nature of this cancer which attacked the body of the Church, or else held to the view of the need for an adequate test if it were to be banished. There was a mood of uncertainty, sympathy, or unwillingness to put Arianism to the test. The Arian party could only hope for their toleration and indulgence. The spokesman of the middle party, a devoted Origenist, was Evsevios of Caesarea—and his theology was vague.

The two other points which this œcumenical synod discussed and decided were the paschal question and the Meletian schism.[2] The synod issued twenty canons in reference to discipline. Canons 1, 2, 9, and 10 dealt with the conditions of ordination. Canons 4 through 7 dealt with hierarchical structures. Canons 3 and 15 through 17 dealt with the life and status of clerics. Canons 11 through 14 concerned the penance and the reconciliation of lapsed Christians. Canons 8 and 19 set out the ways to admit dissidents. Canons 18 and 20 settled two points of liturgical discipline. The Creed and canons were written in a book, and the bishops signed the document. Imperial edicts were sent to the churches, and the decrees which were reached through divine inspiration were set forth as the law of the realm. A splendid banquet was then hosted by the emperor in his palace. The bishops were remunerated in a lavish manner and dismissed with a suitable valedictory, with letters of

---

[2] Meletios, Bishop of Lykopolis, was accused of having sacrificed during the persecution in 301. He was condemned by a synod under Patriarch Peter of Alexandria. He carried on schismatical intrigues under Peter, Achillas, and Alexander. He even attracted a large following, especially in Upper Egypt. Many cities had Meletian bishops. He also managed to secure the confidence of many hermits and some monasteries. The Meletian account of the matter differs from this. Meletios had been in prison with Peter. They differed on the question of how to deal with those who lapsed from the Faith. Meletios maintained a sterner point of view. This created a schism in the Egyptian Church. An alliance of Meletians and Arians belongs to a later date. See Saint Athanasius, "Letter LVI," Nicene, IV:xv.

commendation to the authorities of all the provinces on their way home. Thus ended the Synod of Nicaea, the first of the œcumenical synods.

Saint Athanasios remarked, "It was a true monument and token of victory against every heresy." Athanasios indeed was a man of God and a mighty trumpet of truth. He was energetic and eloquent. Though not ranked among the episcopate, he held the first rank among the members of the synod; for preference was given to virtue as much as to office.

The synod testified that Arianism was a novelty, subversive of Orthodoxy. The Orthodox Church annually celebrates the memory of this event on the Sunday before Pentecost. The eternal deity of Christ abides. Thus the Orthodox Faith was proclaimed and confirmed, through the God-inspired word and right dogmas of Athanasios. Arius was censured, and the Orthodox Faith was made manifest. The hierarchs and other fathers then returned to their own cities and sees. In like manner the great Athanasios returned to Alexandria. The word *homoousion* was everywhere proclaimed, that is, that the Father and the Son and the Holy Spirit are of the same essence.

After 326, Arius spent the next few years in Illyria. At court, on account of the influence of one Arian sympathizer, Evsevios of Nikomedia, Arius was returned from exile by Constantine. Arius went to Alexandria.

Saint Athanasios had thrown himself wholly into the cause which he advocated. However, the truth is that the synod's triumph was a victory only in appearance. Some of the bishops had subscribed to *homoousion* with reluctance, or out of regard to the emperor, or with the reservation of a broad interpretation. If circumstances changed, some undoubtedly would have made a turnabout. A controversy could not be restrained. Council was held against council, creed was set forth against creed, anathema was cast against anathema. Saint Athanasios rebuked the restless flutter of the clergy, who journeyed the empire over to find the true Faith. The Arians became increasingly intolerant and violent. They contested elections of bishops, which would often end in bloody frays. The pagans watched and ridiculed the Christians with scorn. Imperial intervention only aggravated the parties.

Evsevios of Nikomedia and Theognos of Nicaea, filled with notions of their own importance, used all their influence against the advocates of *homoousion*. On account of the maneuvering and sophistry of Evsevios of Caesarea, many were swayed who went on thinking that they were in accord with the Orthodox view and the Nicene Creed. The substance of the mischievous controversy was, to many, misrepresented and never fully explained.

The Repose of Saint Alexander

Saint Athanasios was always on hand as Saint Alexander's assistant. He behaved toward him as a son would to his own father. On his deathbed Alexander summoned Athanasios. With God's help, he believed the succession was to devolve upon Athanasios. When Saint Alexander was at the point of death, he wished to entrust Athanasios with shepherding the Church. He called upon Athanasios, who was then out of town. It was believed he fled to escape the proposed honor. At the time, however, there happened to be another deacon of that same name who answered the summons. When that other Athanasios entered the room of Saint Alexander, the latter kept silent, since he was not summoning that man. Again Alexander called out for the absent Athanasios while the one present kept still. At length, the blessed Alexander then made a prophetic utterance, "O Athanasios, thou thinkest to escape, but thou shalt not escape! It cannot be." The meaning of these words was that Athanasios would be called to the conflict. Not much time later, by the help of God, Saint Athanasios was discovered in the place of his concealment. Bishop Alexander of Alexandria (commemorated on the 29th of May) reposed in 328—the year the fire of schism broke out again.

Elevation to the Episcopacy

Saint Athanasios succeeded to the high-priesthood of the episcopacy on the 8th of June. Though Alexander had nominated him, Athanasios was elected bishop by general consent and popular opinion. He was viewed as good, pious, a Christian, one of the ascetics, and episcopal material. He did not at once, after taking possession of his throne—as do men who unexpectedly seize upon some sovereignty or inheritance—grow insolent. This is the conduct of illegitimate and intrusive priests, who are unworthy of their vocation. They are the ones who only have just begun to study religion, and now are appointed to teach it.

Now Alexandria was the second see in all of Christendom at that time. Athanasios went on to become the head of the Nicene party and teacher of the world. He adamantly refused to admit persons who were condemned of heresy at the œcumenical synod. This stance brought down upon the new hierarch a threatening letter from the emperor. He wrote that he would depose Athanasios by imperial mandate, unless he should freely admit all who might desire communion. Saint Athanasios abided steadfast. He answered that "the Christ-opposing heresy had no fellowship with the Church."

From the first, the Arians were unable to endorse the idea of Athanasios on the throne. When they beheld the man of God sitting upon the throne of Alexandria, they lost no time—after being goaded by their father the devil—in exhibiting their malice. They did not cease, on a daily basis, creating stumbling blocks, with the intention of not only having the saint exiled from his throne, but also from the city, and if possible even to deprive him of life itself.

Saint Athanasios the Great

Now chief among those who would snare the saint was the aforementioned Evsevios, whose piety existed only in name (in the Greek language his name means "piety"); for he was in reality utterly impious. Of like mind with Evsevios was Metropolitan Theognos of Nicaea, Ision, Evdaemon and Kallinikos. They believed that if they could remove Athanasios, they would impose Arianism upon the people of God. They enlisted whomever they could in Alexandria to defame the archbishop by accusing him of three crimes: 1) that Athanasios compelled the bishops and priests of his jurisdiction to hand over as a kind of tax a certain number of vestments, veils, and coverings on a yearly basis; 2) that Athanasios was plotting treachery against the emperor; and, 3) that Athanasios was avaricious, and that for safekeeping he deposited with a friend a chest filled with gold florins. (These charges of course were false.) The calumniators wrote down these three charges against the saint and made them known throughout the city. These written charges were then given to a pseudo-priest, Ischyras by name. He was supposed to go into Nikomedia to Evsevios, who kept audience with the emperor. The sorry story of this imposter, is told below.

The Case of Ischyras

While Saint Athanasios was at Nikomedia, the following tale was reported to Emperor Constantine regarding a clergyman of Archbishop Athanasios, one named Makarios, who was sent to Ischyras, a presbyter whose canonical standing was questionable.

The background and truth of this story is as follows. Ischyras desired to become a priest, but he was unworthy of the dignity. The bishop at that time knew this, and refused to ordain him. Ischyras departed for a time. Then, without the fear of God or reverence for the divine canons, he returned, claiming to be a presbyter ordained by one named Kollynthos, and performed priestly ministrations. If in fact he had been ordained a presbyter by Kollynthos, then his ordination would have been invalid. Every ordination of Kollynthos during the schism had been pronounced invalid at the Alexandrian Synod of 324. That being the case, Saint Athanasios maintained that Ischyras was to be ranked among the laymen. Nonetheless, Ischyras persisted in performing priestly functions in a very small private house where he lived with the orphan child Ision. Out of the few inhabitants of his village, only his seven relatives were attending his services.

Now during a visitation of his diocese, a report of Ischyras was submitted to Athanasios by the presbyter of the township. Saint Athanasios sent one of his clergymen, Makarios. He was to ascertain if Ischyras was really an ordained presbyter by finding out who performed the ordination and where. He was also to bring Ischyras back to the archbishop for an examination. Makarios found Ischyras living in poverty, sick in bed, and unable to accompany him. He discovered that Ischyras was not ordained. Makarios exhorted Ischyras' father to prevail upon his son to desist from holding such irregular gatherings. However, Ischyras had other ideas and joined the Meletians. He feared that the archbishop might punish him as a traitor for disdaining the canons. He then plotted against the holy archbishop by taking the written accusation and bringing it to the enemy of the saint, Evsevios. The latter then took the written charges to Constantinople and showed them to Arian-minded bishops, who were overjoyed by the prospect of creating a great scandal against Athanasios. They received Ischyras as a legitimate priest.

Ischyras contended that Makarios burst into his cottage, smashed the chalice, upset the holy Table, and cast the holy books into the flames. The Arians wasted no time bringing the accusations to the ears of Emperor Constantine. To advance their designs, they kept trying to stir up the emperor against the saint by charging Athanasios with disobedience to the emperor's edict to accept Arius into ecclesiastical communion. Nonetheless, Constantine the Great, a meek and gentle emperor, had no desire to provoke a scandal either among the hierarchs or in the Church. Hence, with peace-filled words, he sought to reconcile the disputants.

The Council of Tyre

At that time, already some thirty years since Constantine began his reign, the bishops of the east and the west and Africa were gathering together in Jerusalem for the consecration of the great Church of the Resurrection of Christ, scheduled for the 13th of September. His mother, the illustrious Saint Helen, had raised this church from the foundation. The emperor did not wish to condemn the holy Athanasios, so he decided to bring the case before those bishops attending the solemn dedication of the church. After the dedication, the hierarchs were summoned to Tyre to examine the charges against Athanasios. The issue of Arius was also on the agenda. They would investigate the proceedings of his excommunication, whether it was out of malice, and if Arius was preaching true Orthodoxy. If his excommunication proved unjustified, he was to be received back.

At the synod meeting, the prefect was summoned, and also the Priest Makarios was brought bound in chains. Makarios was to present his defense in answer to Ischyras' allegations that he trampled upon the body and blood of Christ. Saint Athanasios was also summoned to appear. Now the saint was planning to attend and make his defense concerning the alleged crimes, but what did God dispense on his behalf? The Arian contingent had a considerable representation at the council, including Evsevios of Nikomedia, Narcissus, Maris, Theognos, Patrophilos, George of Laodikeia, Ursakios, and Valens. Evsevios of Caesarea headed a large party of conservative malcontents. Of the total number of one hundred fifty bishops, those who rallied for Athanasios were outnumbered by two to one. The proceedings were passionate and chaotic. Wildly indiscriminate accusations were hurled from side to side. The president himself was even accused of sacrificing to idols, while against the holy archbishop every charge that could be contrived was laid at his door. The saint was accused primarily of harshness and violence in dealing with those who took up Ischyras' cause. They charged that those who refused to be in communion with Archbishop Athanasios were beaten and imprisoned. It was lamentable that most of the bishops in attendance were prepared to believe the worst concerning Athanasios. The saint could scarcely believe that he should ever find justice in this conclave. His enemies then wished him to answer to the charges of taxing Church linens and also avarice. As God was helping him, the slanders were immediately proven false.

At the proceedings, Saint Athanasios entered into evidence an exhibit that showed in the following manner that the person who was his accuser was not even a presbyter. When Meletios was admitted into communion, Athanasios' blessed predecessor Alexander—who perceived Meletios' craftiness—required of him a registry of the bishops whom he claimed to have in Egypt, including the presbyters and deacons in Alexandria herself, and if he had any clerics in the country districts. The purpose of Patriarch Alexander's demand was as follows. In the event Meletios, after he received the freedom and sanction of the Church, should develop the habit of imposing many undeserving clerics upon the Church, thus foisting upon her whomsoever suited him, this registry would fix the name and number of his clergy. The schedule was presented personally by Meletios to Archbishop Alexander and did not have among its enrollment any person named Ischyras. In fact, he did not profess to have any clergy even in the region of the Mareotis from which Ischyras hailed. With impudence, however, the enemies of Athanasios shamelessly and boldly persisted.

The Case of Arsenios

In the meantime, the Bishop of Hypsele, Arsenios, received a sizeable bribe from one of the Meletians, John Arcaph. Arsenios was prevailed upon by Arcaph to go missing and hide himself among certain Meletian monks in the Thebaid of Egypt. Reports circulated that Athanasios contracted to have him slain. After the slaying, it was alleged that one of the victim's hands was severed for use in magic ceremonies. This ridiculous rumor was bruited about, until a report was drawn up for Emperor Constantine, together with an updated rendition of the Ischyras incident.

Constantine was moved to anger. Even though he expressed his previous sentiments to condemn their injustice, as soon as he heard this accusation, he straightway became incensed. Saint Athanasios, as a result, was not granted a hearing. The confused and disordered proceedings were never examined. The angry emperor could not keep his countenance. Jolted after receiving the bizarre intelligence of a severed hand, he bade his half-brother Dalmatos, a high official at Antioch, to investigate the particulars of the case. The latter suggested a council convene in 334 in Caesarea, under the presidency of Evsevios. Saint Athanasios received a summons but refused to appear before a judge who was patently prejudiced against the defendant. Nonetheless, the venue was fixed for Tyre, and the date postponed till the following year. A peremptory summons was issued by Constantine to Athanasios that he must put in an appearance. Though unwilling, Saint Athanasios obeyed the imperial writ compelling his appearance.

Commenting upon the conspiracy contrived against him, he said, "There are in Egypt, Libya, and Pentapolis nearly one hundred bishops. Not one of them has ever laid anything to my charge. Not one of the presbyters has ever found fault with me. However, the Meletians—ejected by Peter, and the Arians—divided the plot between them: one party is claiming the right of accusing me, while the other sits in judgment of the case." The saint objected to having Evsevios and his minions sit in judgment, regarding them as biased and, moreover, heretics and not even presbyters. The high functionary Dionysios was to represent the emperor.

In the meantime a trusted deacon of Saint Athanasios was doing investigative work behind the scenes in the Thebaid, to locate the missing Arsenios. The deacon's detective work traced the bishop to a Meletian Monastery of Ptemencyrcis in the nome (province) of Antaeopolis in Upper Egypt. But the elder of that community, one named Pinnes, a presbyter, also had his own informants. He received intelligence that Athanasios' deacon had learned the whereabouts of Arsenios. Pinnes caused Arsenios to embark on

a vessel, thus smuggling him down the Nile, where he made his way toward
Tyre. The deacon with others then suddenly entered the monastery, took hold
of Pinnes, and bore him away to Alexandria before Dionysios. In the
presence of Pinnes, the very monk who stole Arsenios away was brought
before him. Pinnes and that monk were compelled to confess their mischief.
Pinnes wrote John Arcaph that the plot had been exposed, and recommended
that all charges be dropped.

Meanwhile, Arsenios was reported to have been seen at an inn in
Tyre by the servant of some magistrate. In fact, Arsenios learned of the false
accusations laid at the feet of the holy man, and was saddened. He betook
himself secretly to Tyre. This same magistrate took Arsenios into custody.
Thereupon, Athanasios was notified of Arsenios' recovery. The saint rejoiced
and gave glory to God. The brash audacity of Arsenios was almost too absurd
when he continually refused to acknowledge his own identity. But the Bishop
of Tyre knew better, and identified Arsenios for all. Unable to maintain the
charade, Arsenios acknowledged his true identity. The holy Athanasios visited
him, and said, "Grant me one favor, Arsenios. Do not present thyself before
my accusers and the witnesses before I go into the synod meeting, lest they
should slay thee. But when the perjury of the witnesses is exposed, then thou
shalt present thyself before them in order to censure them as slanderers and
false witnesses."

While this was taking place, the enemies of the saint were not
satisfied with the crimes already charged. Unwilling to adhere to the facts and
ignoring all civility, they fabricated another story against Orthodoxy's bright
ornament. A certain brazen woman, who was willing to give false testimony,
was hired for a handsome sum by the saint's opponents to accuse the holy
man of sinning with her. When the trial recommenced, they set propriety at
nought and led in the shameless woman. Summoning up her tears, she began
to wail before the judges, accusing Athanasios, who in fact she never even
had met, but had only heard of him. "For the Lord's sake I received the
bishop into my house, in the hope of receiving his blessing. However, I
suffered adversely when, in the middle of the night, he crept into my chamber
and forced himself on me. No one could rescue me, since the entire
household was asleep." As the unabashed perjurer continued, Father
Timothy, a prudent priest and friend of the hierarch, could no longer bear to
hear her filthy account, and wished to reveal her as a liar. He entered into the
court, assuming the character of his bishop. He approached her, and said,
"Was it I, O woman, who sinned with thee?" The woman, assuming him to
be Athanasios, exclaimed aloud, "This is the man, O holy hierarchs, the
abominable and unclean Athanasios, who committed the iniquity! He is the
one unworthy of the episcopacy. He is the one who rendered me violence in

exchange for my hospitality." The judges then howled with laughter, for she continued with her blatant pretense, not realizing she had been discovered. The charges were dismissed. The Arians' hatred only sharpened when their attempt was turned against them. They proceeded to examine the charges against Athanasios dealing with the crime of sorcery.

The discussions grew heated. Then, at one point, a severed hand, alleged to be that of Arsenios, was actually produced as evidence. The accusers raised it and showed it to the holy man, shouting, "This hand, O Athanasios, rebukes thy magic. This hand, O impious and unrighteous one, reveals thee a sorcerer, a conjurer, a trickster! What kind of magic didst thou perform?" Saint Athanasios, never losing his composure, humbly questioned them, asked, "Among your reverences, who did know Arsenios?" There rose up five of the hierarchs, and then from many sides there echoed, "We knew him." These were men of no conscience who set themselves up as judges, accusers, and witnesses. The holy man asked them again, "Who knoweth for certain that the hand which is being displayed is that of Arsenios?" The same answered again, "We knew him." Athanasios, unwilling to allow the truth to be maligned, cried aloud to Arsenios to enter into the midst of the synod. Straightway, Arsenios was escorted in their midst, clad in an ample cloak that concealed his arms entirely. Saint Athanasios then addressed them, "Is this one Arsenios, holy hierarchs, or someone else?" The spectators, speechless, were struck with astonishment at this unlooked-for spectacle. The council members then expected an explanation of the way he had lost his hand. Saint Athanasios then turned up Arsenios' cloak revealing that at least one hand was present. All were spellbound. Moments of intense expectation passed, as the onlookers waited to see what might be exposed at the end of Arsenios' other wrist. Then the other hand, intact, was unveiled. Saint Athanasios then said, "Do ye seek two hands from Arsenios, or a third? Behold the right hand! Lo, the left!" At that dramatic juncture the accusers were requested to answer from where the third had been severed. The accusers were brought to shame, and the synod meeting broke down.

But the trial proceeded when an imperial epistle was brought into the proceedings. The defamers of the holy man were rebuked. Athanasios was acquitted, and summoned to meet with the emperor in Constantinople. The wicked hierarchs, since they were unable to fulfill their will against the holy man, followed after Athanasios, threatening, insulting, and reviling him, saying, "Magician, swindler, charlatan, hypocrite, mischief-maker!" From that hour there was such rage and commotion from the multitude and the attendants and friends of the bishops, that if the imperial magistrate Archelaos had not been not present, there surely would have been scenes unpleasant and violent. Although this same Archelaos was no friend of Athanasios, nonetheless he knew that his duty was to keep order. He also did not wish to be accountable for any civil disobedience. Therefore, he took hold of Athanasios and escorted him safely outside the city limits. He advised the archbishop to betake himself far away.

Saint Athanasios wrote afterward: "The grace of God prevailed. For they could not convict Makarios in the matter of the chalice. Arsenios, who was reported to have been murdered by me, stood before them alive, with both his hands joined to his body, thus openly showing the obvious falseness of their accusation. Nonetheless, when they perceived that they were unable to convict Makarios, Evsevios and his fellows became enraged that they had lost the prey of which they had been in pursuit. They persuaded Dionysios, who is one of them, to send to the Mareotis, in order to see whether they could not find out something there against the presbyter, or rather that they might at a distance patch up their plot as they pleased in our absence; for this was their aim. However, we protested that the journey to the Mareotis was a superfluous undertaking. Yet if they must go, then at least the suspected parties ought not to be sent. Dionysios was convinced by my reasoning with respect to the suspected persons. But they would do anything rather than what I proposed. For the very persons whom I objected against on account of the Arian heresy, they were the very ones who were promptly dispatched. In the meantime, Makarios, the accused party, was to remain behind in custody under a guard of soldiers, while they took with them the accuser. Now who after this does not see through this conspiracy? For if a judicial inquiry is to be made, the accused ought not to have been sent thither."

The commission of enquiry with the apostate prefect of Egypt and heathen soldiers were not to have their way. The presbyters of Alexandria found fault with them, because they were by themselves in their proceedings. Their evil design had not escaped detection. The presbyters of the city and of the Mareotis addressed letters to the investigators. They protested that both Archbishop Athanasios and Father Makarios ought to have been brought. Hence, they rightfully wrote: "Your coming was only the act of a cabal and conspiracy."[3]

The clergy of the Mareotis also wrote, affirming that "Ischyras was never a presbyter of the Church. In fact, he never had a church. But since he has falsely accused our Archbishop Athanasios of breaking a cup and overturning a table, we are necessarily obliged to address you on this point. We have said already that he never had a church in the Mareotis. And we declare before God as our witness, that no cup was broken, nor table overturned by our bishop, nor by any one of those who accompanied him. But

---

[3] Saint Athanasius, *Defence Against the Arians*, Part II, Ch. VI, Nicene, Vol. IV.

all that is alleged respecting this affair is mere calumny. Now we do not say this as if we were not present with the bishop, for we are all with him whenever he comes on a pastoral visit of the Mareotis. He never goes about alone, but is accompanied by all of us presbyters and deacons, and by a considerable number of people." Thus the whole charge was proved a false invention.

The Saint in Constantinople

The Evsevians attempted to recover themselves, unwilling to let Athanasios clear his name. When they prevailed upon Dionysios to dispatch a commission, made up mostly of Arians, to the Mareotis to investigate the Ischyras case, Athanasios himself escaped in an open boat with four of his bishops. They managed to find their way to Constantinople, and arrived on the 30th of October.

Emperor Constantine describes his chance encounter with the archbishop: "As I was entering our all-happy home of Constantinople, all of a sudden Bishop Athanasios, with certain others whom he had with him, approached me in the middle of the road, so unexpectedly as to occasion me much amazement. My servants informed me both who he was, and under what injustice he was suffering, though I should have been able to recognize him at first sight. I, however, did not enter into any conversation with him at that time, nor grant him an interview. When he requested to be heard, I refused, and all but gave orders for his removal. With increased boldness he persisted and claimed only the favor that the bishops who had assembled at Tyre should be summoned to appear before me, that he might complain before me in their presence of the ill-treatment with which he met. I deemed this a reasonable request and suitable to the time."

The emperor wrote to Jerusalem and summoned all who had been at the Council of Tyre, in order that they might render in person a true account of the proceedings. Constantine wished to learn if the judgment passed was impartial and incorrupt.

When Evsevios and his cohorts read the emperor's letter, sensible of their outrageous behavior, they hindered the other bishops from going, and only went themselves, namely, Evsevios, Theognos, Patrophilos, the other Evsevios, Ursakios, and Valens. They did not dare bring up the matter about the cup or Arsenios, but invented some other vicious charge. They alleged that Athanasios levied a precept upon Egypt for Church expenses. It was generally known that the Archbishop of Alexandria had command of large funds, which were used for Church purposes and almsgiving. Evsevios and his fellows went up and falsely charged Athanasios, that he deliberately detained the vessels laden with corn exports from Alexandria to Constantinople every autumn.

As soon as Constantine heard this, he was incensed and exiled Athanasios to Gaul. Certain friends of Athanasios, the two Alexandrian Presbyters Makarios and Apis, were in the palace that day and heard the emperor's threats. The emperor observed them and questioned them concerning the allegations made by Evsevios and the other bishops against Athanasios. They made as good a defense as possible for their archbishop. These priests, being God-fearing, told the truth. They said that the charges were lies, and those alleging them were calumniators. The emperor discerned their integrity and sincerity, and believed them. The emperor straightway issued a decree to those bishops that in whatever hour they were to receive the imperial command, they were to desist and leave Athanasios free and on his throne. Those bishops, however, together with Arius, stirred up trouble, demanding that the case of Ischyras be tried, and that Athanasios be made to answer for the grain losses.

When Athanasios heard the account of the false report, he cried out against the calumny. He positively declared it to be a lie, for how, he argued, should he, a poor man, and in a private station, be able to do such a thing? Evsevios, waxing bold, went public with the accusation. He swore that Athanasios was wealthy and powerful and could do anything he chose. By now Constantine was no longer disposed to hear about the broken chalice or Arsenios, but the allegations of stopping grain ships struck him sorely.

The emperor was now persuaded that the profane hierarchs were being instigated by the devil. He ordered that Athanasios, for his own safety and well-being, should be sent away to Gaul. He left on the 5th day of February, in the year 336. Thus, he was condemned and deposed for false accusations by two Arian councils: one at Tyre (ca. 335) under the presidency of the historian Evsevios, and the other at Constantinople in 335/336.

It was the emperor's desire to bring an end to the ongoing scandal, and for this reason he thought it wise to dispense with the problem by removing Athanasios out of the sight of his slanderers. Constantine wished to unite the churches, since these bishops would have created a schism in the Church, giving idolatry a strong hold on those weak Orthodox who might fall back to their old ways. Thus, the grace of God proved superior to the wickedness of the Arian madmen.

The Repose of Emperor Constantine

The emperor, at sixty-five years of age, after reigning thirty-one years, reposed at Nikomedia in May of 337. None of his three sons was present, so couriers were dispatched to notify them. Constantine left his legacy and empire to his three sons, Constantine, Constantius, and Constas. In the articles of his will, he disposed of the empire as follows. Constantine was to reign in Constantinople and all her prefectures; Constantius was to reign in Spain, and Constas in Rome. The dying emperor furnished instructions to the Priest Efstathios to deliver the will to his eldest son Constantine. That vile man, however, filled with Arian madness, had waited for the appropriate moment to further the cause of Arianism. Therefore, he was quite determined not to hand over the will to the firstborn son, but gave it instead to the middle son, deeming him impressionable and one who could be easily persuaded. He knew that he could move Constantius to support the dogmas of Arianism. He also believed that Constantius would not revoke the exile of the holy man Athanasios. Evsevios and his confederates also supported him in this, as did several of the imperial eunuchs. Not many days had passed when, after the chief eunuch was converted, the others followed him. The emperor's consort was also convinced to change her Orthodoxy after listening only to a few blasphemous words. It would not be long thereafter that Constantius should prove himself inconstant, and be won over.

Constantine, the eldest son, keenly aware of the long and unjust exile of the saint (then two years and four months), was grieved for him. Being a devout Orthodox Christian, he decided to return him to his patriarchal throne. On the 17th day of June, in the year 337, he wrote a letter to the Alexandrian clergy and people proclaiming the restoration of Athanasios as their archbishop. He wrote: "The victor Constantine, to the Church of Alexandria and to the people: I suppose that it has not escaped the knowledge of your pious minds of the temptations which came upon the splendid preacher, the great Athanasios, the interpreter of the precious law, who was sent away into Gaul, to the city of Treveri (Trier) for a time. The object of that was that the fierceness of his bloodthirsty enemies might not persecute him, unto the peril of his holy life. In order to escape this, he was ordered to pass some time under my government. Now it was the fixed intention of our master Constantine Augustus, my blessed father, to restore the said bishop to his own place, and to your most beloved piety. Before his repose he ordered me, his eldest son according to the succession, to give Athanasios his episcopal throne. Now he went to his rest before he could accomplish his wish, so I believe it is incumbent upon me to fulfill that intention of the emperor of sacred memory. Therefore, receive Athanasios with all honor and reverence, as a hierarch, shepherd and teacher of piety. Then, after a time, send him to me, that I may honor him also as I should." By this epistle, a way was opened for the saint to enter Alexandria.

Constantine with his two other brothers, Constantius and Constas, then hastened to meet together in Sirmium. They agreed upon the division of the empire, so that Constantine took the Gauls and Africa, Constantius took the east, and Constas took Italy and Illyricum. By the 9th of September, they each formally assumed the title of augustus. Saint Athanasios had accompanied Constantine on his way eastward to Sirmium, when he met Constantius for the first time at Viminacium.

Not much time passed afterward when the Ariomaniacs culminated their influence on the mind of the middle son, Constantius. In a very short space of time, he, too, became a militant Arian and engulfed in the darkness of impiety. After he professed and championed Arianism, he issued a decree that every city and province was to believe in what Arius taught. He also said that any bishop or priest who did not accept the dogmas of Arius would be cast out and exiled.

At that time, the Patriarch of Constantinople was Alexander, that of Antioch Efstathios, and of Jerusalem Maximos. The Alexandrian flock still recognized their absent Archbishop Athanasios as the legitimate shepherd. Alexander of Constantinople was commanded to concelebrate the divine Liturgy with Arius; otherwise, he was to relinquish his throne. But we are getting ahead of ourselves. Here is some background on Arius.

The Decease of Arius

In 335, Arius was formally acquitted of the charge of heresy by a council at Jerusalem. From Jerusalem he went to Alexandria, but he did not succeed in gaining admission to the Church. He decided to return to the capital. The Evsevians did not wish him to be repelled, so Arius satisfied the emperor by a sworn profession of Orthodoxy.

Saint Athanasios was not in Constantinople when Arius died, so he received the account from Makarios. Arius had been invited by the Emperor Constantine, through the interest of Evsevios and his fellows. When he entered the presence of the emperor, inquiry was made of Arius whether he held the Faith of the catholic Church. He declared upon oath that he held the right Faith, and submitted an account of his belief in writing, suppressing the points for which he had been cast out of the Church by Bishop Alexander, and speciously alleging expressions out of the Scriptures. When he swore that he no longer professed the opinions for which Alexander had excommunicated him, Constantine dismissed him, saying, "If thy belief be right, thou hast done well to swear; but if thy belief be impious, and thou hast sworn, may God judge thee according to thine oath."

Evsevios now wished to bring Arius into the Church. A day was fixed for his reception. But Alexander, the Archbishop of Constantinople, was greatly distressed. He resisted them and said that the inventor of the heresy ought not to be admitted to communion. Evsevios and his minions threatened, and declared, "We have caused him to be invited by the emperor, in opposition to thy wishes. Tomorrow, though against thy desire, Arius shall have communion with us in this church."

It was the sabbath when Bishop Alexander heard this. He was understandably distressed, and entered into the church. He stretched forth his hands to God and bewailed himself. As he lay prostrate in the sanctuary, his tear-stained face rested upon the pavement. Makarios was present and prayed with him. He was a witness to the bishop's words. Alexander asked God for two things: "If Arius is brought to communion tomorrow, let me, Thy servant, depart, and destroy not the pious with the impious; but if Thou wilt spare Thy Church—and I know that Thou wilt spare—look upon the words of Evsevios and his fellows, and give not Thine inheritance to destruction and reproach. Take Arius away, lest if he should enter into the church, the heresy also may seem to enter with him, and henceforward impiety be accounted for piety."

The bishop then arose and retired in great distress and anxiety. Then an extraordinary circumstance took place. On the evening before the intended reception and procession from the imperial palace to the Church of the Apostles, Arius suddenly died. The year was 336 when he was over the age of eighty. He died while attending to the necessities of nature. God hearkened to the bishop's entreaty in the following manner; for at Arius' withdrawal to attend to this need, suddenly, "he fell headlong and burst asunder in the midst [cf. Acts 1:18]." For his daring criminalities, there was a violent relaxation of the bowels. Soon afterward a faintness came over him, and together with the evacuations, his bowels protruded, followed by a copious hemorrhage, and the descent of the smaller intestines. Portions of his spleen and liver were discharged in the effusion of blood, so that he almost immediately died in the back of Constantine's Forum.

Though Saint Athanasios knew in the Spirit that this was God's judgment upon that detractor of Jesus, others ascribed his death to magic or even heart disease. His spiritually diseased condition proved stronger than any remedy. Regrettably, many drank from the turbid waters of his impiety. Afterward, Athanasios wrote to the bishops of Egypt about the significance of that evil agitator's death: "Death, it is true, is the common end of all men,...but the end of Arius was not after an ordinary manner. Evsevios and his fellows threatened to bring Arius back into the Church, and Archbishop Alexander of Constantinople resisted them. Now it was the sabbath, and he was expected to join communion on the following day. There was a great struggle between them; the others threatening, Alexander praying. But the Lord, being the Judge of the case, decided against the unjust party; for the sun had not set, when the necessities of nature compelled him to that place, where he fell down, and was forthwith deprived of communion with the Church and his life. The blessed Constantine, hearing of this, at once was struck with wonder to find him thus convicted of perjury....The Arian madness was rejected from communion by our Savior both here and in the Church of the Firstborn in heaven." Such was the end of Arius. Alexander then celebrated the divine Liturgy with piety and Orthodoxy. Now Alexander himself reposed very soon afterward. Paul was elected in his place but was banished on some charge. Then Evsevios of Nikomedia was brought to the capital some time between 336 and 340.

The Saint's Banishment in Gaul

Saint Athanasios stated the reason why he was sent to Gaul by Emperor Constantine, in a letter written from Treveri (337). "Who does not plainly perceive the intention of the emperor, and the murderous spirit of Evsevios and his fellows, and that the emperor had done this in order to prevent their forming some more desperate scheme? The emperor listened to them in simplicity."

The holy hierarch remained at Treveri at the noble home of the emperors on the banks of the Mosel. He made his abode there for about one year and spent Pascha in the unfinished church where construction was still proceeding. In this exile Athanasios did not suffer from want, and even had certain Egyptian brethren with him. Bishop Maximinus of Treveri was compassionate and befriended him. Though friends of the saint viewed the banishment as an act of royal clemency, the punishment was what might have been handed down to one who was an agitator, a disturber of the peace, and one charged with treason.

Behind the scenes all the while, Evsevios was still seeking imperial approval for the proposed election of a successor to Athanasios. He failed at this. Therefore, on Athanasios' return after the death of Constantine, Athanasios found his see unoccupied. At length, Arsenios made peace with the man of God, and in due time he even succeeded to the sole episcopate of Hypsele. John Arcaph met with disgrace, confessed his role in the intrigue, and disavowed his schism. Afterward he was invited to court, but his obedience was never stable.

With regard to answering this fabricated charge, it should be noted that Saint Athanasios left Alexandria on the 11th day of July, in the year 335, and was absent for two years, four months, and eleven days from his see. Later, those who lived with Arsenios gave testimony that he was kept in concealment that they might pretend his death.

At length, the relatives of Ischyras persuaded him to retract his accusations. The bishop was then given a statement by Ischyras, wherein he declared that he slandered Makarios on account of the violence that he suffered. Ischyras was pardoned but placed under censure. However, instead of truly repenting, he became increasingly embittered. He made new and more fantastic charges. Later at the Councils of Tyre and Philippopolis,

Athanasios himself was accused of breaking the chalice in a basilica, which he allegedly razed to the ground. Ischyras was unable to prove anything. The holy hierarch was vindicated as a result of this frivolous charge. The Arians temporarily retreated, but regrouped.

Saint Athanasios Returns From Exile in Gaul

In 338, months after Saint Athanasios was recalled from his banishment by Constantine II, he was received by the people with great enthusiasm, more joyously than even an emperor. Joy and cheerfulness prevailed, and the people ran together, hastening to obtain the desired sight of Athanasios. The churches were full of rejoicing, and prayers of thanksgiving were offered up to the Lord in every place. All the clergy gazed upon him with such profound feeling that their souls were filled with delight, and they esteemed that day the happiest of their lives. Saint Athanasios had returned from Gaul triumphant!

The saint, adorned with gentleness and modesty of spirit, possessed an extraordinary love for his neighbor. He showed the constancy of his affection for the people. Athanasios, as one not besotted with power, was described as follows by Saint Gregory the Theologian: "Everything was done harmoniously. For immediately on his restoration to his Church, he was not like those who are blinded by unrestrained passion. Such ones, under the dominion of their anger, thrust away or strike at once whatever comes in their way, even though it might well be spared. But thinking this to be a special time for him to consult his reputation—since one who is

Saint Athanasios of Alexandria

ill-treated is usually restrained, and one who has the power to requite a wrong is ungoverned—he was resolved to treat mildly and gently the very ones who had injured him, so that even they themselves, if I may say so, did not find his restoration distasteful."[4]

In 339, Saint Athanasios held a synod meeting of nearly one hundred bishops in Alexandria. In the encyclical issued as a result thereof, the following was urged upon the bishops throughout the world: "In order that the ordinances which have been preserved in the Churches from times of old until now may not be lost in our days, and the trust which has been committed to us required at our hands, bestir yourselves, brethren, as being stewards of the Mysteries of God and seeing them now seized upon by others."

The Nicene doctrine was vindicated, but again the triumph was temporary for Athanasios. Arianism still prevailed in the east. Constantius, ruler of the east, and his whole court maintained a fanatical Arianism. Evsevios of Nikomedia was elevated to the throne of Constantinople (338) and became the leader of both the Arian and moderate parties.

Reappearance of Troubles for the Saint

The Nikomedian Evsevios, a long-time opponent of Saint Athanasios, was Archbishop of Constantinople, and had Emperor Constantius' ear and found him a willing patron. The malcontents also gained the sympathy of Jews and pagans. The evil rumor that even Anthony the Great sided with the Arians was soon proven false, when the illustrious ascetic left his desert retreat at the request of the Orthodox. He entered the strife-filled city, and his presence attracted both Christians and pagans. They wished to catch a glimpse of him or to receive some physical benefit from his touch. Saint Anthony condemned Arianism as the worst of heresies. He was then escorted out of the city on the 27th day of July, in the year 338, but his impact was felt. He showed himself also wonderful in many other things, including healing many of the sick.

Saint Gregory the Theologian writes about the reform brought about by Saint Athanasios: "The saint imitated Christ and cleansed the temple of those who made merchandise of God [Jn. 2:15] and trafficked in the things of Christ. He did not bring this about by the use of persuasive words, nor with a twisted scourge. He reconciled those who were at variance, both with one another and with himself, without the aid of any coadjutor. Those who had been wronged he set free from oppression, making no distinction as to whether they were of his own or of the opposite party. He also restored the teaching which had been overthrown, and the Trinity was once more boldly spoken of."[5]

Athanasios' enemies harped on the fact that he had been deposed, and by a council. They maintained that the see of Alexandria was legally vacant,

---

[4] Saint Gregory the Theologian, *Oration XXI*, ¶ 30.
[5] Ibid., ¶ 31.

and that the restoration of Athanasios was against ecclesiastical order. The proceedings at Tyre, however, were not considered by Saint Athanasios as canonical. Saint Athanasios considered himself—as did his flock—the sole and rightful Bishop of Alexandria. Those who were Arians remained hostile and persecuted the hierarch. The holy man was accused of treachery, slayings, and exiles.

One day a rabble of Arians surrounded the saint, insulting him and threatening his safety. The saint, by the grace of God, passed through them, and left the city by secret means. The Arians sent letters everywhere, citing his deposition and illegal occupation of the throne without conciliar decree. They denied him access to all cities and churches in the empire. In the meantime, the protector of the hierarch, Emperor Constantine II, was slain by soldiers in Aquileia. The Arians lost no time by inciting the hatred of the middle brother Constantius against the saint.

New charges were fabricated. The saint was accused of embezzling corn that had been set aside by the imperial bounty of the emperor for the needy widows of Egypt. Repeated wranglings between the parties, barren of results, continued until a council in 339. Athanasios' deposition was pointed out, so the Evsevian party consecrated Gregory the Cappadocian as the new bishop for Alexandria. There was some violence at Gregory's installation, but he was protected by the prefect of Egypt, also a Cappadocian.

In a circular letter of Saint Athanasios, he mentions the violent and uncanonical intrusion of Gregory. "Such proceedings tend to the dissolution of all the ecclesiastical canons, and compel the heathen to blaspheme, and to suspect that our appointments are not made according to divine rule, but as a result of traffic and patronage. Our schools of religion have been turned into a markethouse and an exchange."

The Saint Hides in a Well

For a long time the holy man hid inside a deep and dry shaft of an abandoned well. No one knew of his hiding place, except the God-fearing woman who provided for him. Though that fountain was dry, in that pit hidden in the earth, his pen gushed forth streams of inspiring words in a powerful appeal to the bishops of all the Churches. He described the ungodly excesses which he witnessed. He gave his opinion decidedly and besought help for his beleaguered Church of Alexandria, which was under attack by Arian madmen and mobs—all of whom received the sanction of Emperor Constantius.

The search for Athanasios in the meantime was relentless. Not finding him, those wicked hierarchs issued a second excommunication. Still not satisfied, they continued their search in a meticulous manner throughout every quarter. The emperor also did his part, and offered a huge reward, estates, and imperial esteem to anyone who would reveal the whereabouts of Athanasios, whether he were alive or dead—and if he were dead, his head would suffice. Some soldiers then learned that he was in a certain neighborhood, hiding in a pit. The night before the morning on which they were determined to arrest him, the great Athanasios was enlightened by divine grace to flee to another well. There he was concealed for many days, but the soldiers were informed of that location also. He was then led by the Spirit to the Western Empire, and to Rome, to see Emperor Constas and Pope Julius I (337-352).

The Second Exile of Saint Athanasios

The second exile of our holy father falls into two periods: the first of four years to the time of the Council of Sardica (339-343); the second of three years, to his return in October of 346.

In the spring of 339, Saint Athanasios again withdrew from his see with a few of his clergy. He betook himself to Rome and Pope Julius, where he found sympathy. The holy man was at leisure to give himself entirely to Church services. He bore the solitude cheerfully. In general the whole Western Church was more inclined to Nicene Orthodoxy, and even honored Athanasios as a living martyr of the true Faith. Indeed he was highly regarded by the west. His personal sojourn in Rome and Treves, together with his knowledge of the Latin tongue, contributed to the people's high esteem of him. Above all, it was his adherence to fundamental Orthodoxy that gave him a good reputation in the west.

He was cleared of the charges made against him at Tyre, pronounced innocent on all counts, and admitted to communion as the lawful Bishop of Alexandria. However, at the same council, Markellos of Ankyra, accused of heresy, was also admitted to communion. As a result, issues were obscured. At length, Athanasios broke communion with Markellos.

In 341, a synod at Antioch, presided over by the Evsevians, issued twenty-five canons. Four creeds were promulgated which rejected Arianism but avoided the Orthodox formula and the usage of *homoousion*.

In his *Defense Before Constantius*, Saint Athanasios comments about his stay in Rome: "When I left Alexandria...I went only to Rome; and having laid my case before the Church—for this was my only concern—I spent my time in public worship. I did not go to thy brother Constas' headquarters, or to any other persons. I did not write to thy brother, except when Evsevios and his fellows had written him to accuse me; and I was compelled, while yet at Alexandria, to defend myself. And I also wrote him when I sent to him bound volumes containing the holy Scriptures, which he had ordered me to prepare for him.

"After three years elapsed, he wrote to me in the fourth year (342), commanding me to meet him in Milan. I did not know the reason for this (the Lord is my witness), so I made an inquiry. I learned that certain bishops had gone up and requested him to write to your piety, desiring that a council might be called. Believe me, sire, this is the truth of the matter; I lie not. Accordingly, I went to Milan, and met with great kindness from him. He condescended to see me, and said that he dispatched letters to you, requesting that a council might be convened. While I remained in Milan, he sent for me again in Gaul, for Father Hosius was going there, that we might travel from thence to Sardica."

Though Constas was busy at that time campaigning against the Franks, he still found time to think about the business surrounding Archbishop Athanasios' case. He was persuaded that only a synod meeting would air both sides. He wrote to his brother Constantius to make the arrangements for a general council. When Saint Athanasios visited him in Milan, he was informed of this by Constas himself, who admired the holy man. He had already received the Scriptures from the saintly bishop, so he was well-disposed toward him. After their meeting, Constas took the road to Gaul and later called Athanasios to follow him there. The saint did go to Gaul, and he met with Saint Hosius and others.

The east and west were in opposition. It was a time of rival theories of Church authority and ecclesiastical battles fought through creeds and formulae. Emperor Constantius of the east and Emperor Constas in the west successfully summoned the general council at Sardica (now Sofia, Bulgaria) in Illyria (August-September 343), in the hope of correcting the division, and to hear the cases of Athanasios and Paul. The Nicene party and Roman influence prevailed. Saint Athanasios records there were about one hundred and seventy bishops. In attendance were about ninety-four occidentals and seventy-six orientals or Evsevians, including the infamous Ischyras of the Mareotis. Pope Julius was represented by two Italian priests. The Spanish Bishop Hosius presided.

Nicene doctrine was confirmed. Also, twelve canons were adopted, some of which are very important since they refer to the discipline and authority of the Roman see. The Arianizing oriental bishops were annoyed at the admittance of Athanasios, and even of Markellos. They demanded that the accused bishops should not be allowed to take their seats in the council. The majority responded that, pending the present inquiry, all previous decisions against them must be considered suspended. The eastern bishops would not abide the consensus.

On the pretext of congratulating Constantius in his victory over the Persians, they withdrew by night and took no part in the proceedings. They sent their excuses by the Sardican Presbyter Efstathios. They held an opposition council in the neighboring city of Philippopolis in Thrace, where they confirmed the decrees of Antioch. They anathematized both Athanasios and Markellos, their western supporters, with Pope Julius and Hosius of Cordova. They proclaimed anathema to the dogma of the coessentiality of God the Son with God the Father. Instead of healing the division, these two councils exacerbated the contention.

The Synod at Sardica continued. The fathers at this synod anathematized the blasphemous heretical council at Philippopolis for its godless confession. The Sardica Synod also vindicated Athanasios and Markellos, after the exiles were examined. All the charges were carefully examined and dismissed. Those who had seized their sees were deposed. This synod also granted the Bishop of Rome important, but limited, appellate jurisdiction in disputes among bishops. The synod addressed an encyclical letter to all Christendom, embodying the synod's decisions and announcing the depositions of those bishops involved in Arianism.

The people of Adrianople would not have communion with the deposed bishops. Savage cruelties and barbarisms ensued, instigated by the deposed and those who fled the synod. Saint Athanasios was closely observed, to see if he should attempt to return to his see by reason of this synod's acquittal. The deposed carried their complaints to Emperor Constantius, and this act led to the beheading of ten of the laity. Plots were also perpetrated against the Orthodox at Antioch. During this time, Emperor Constas of the west took up the cause of the Sardican Synod. In 344, he communicated to his wayward brother Constantius the propriety of restoring the Orthodox exiles. By this time Emperor Constantius began to feel remorse, especially since Constas threatened to use arms, if necessary, against him. Constantius as a result accepted Patriarch Paul of Constantinople and sent him to his see in honor. Constas gave orders that the presbyters and deacons who had been banished from Alexandria into Armenia should immediately be released. He also wrote (August of 344) an open letter to Alexandria, commanding that the clergy and laity who were friends of Athanasios should suffer no further harm. Thereafter, the saint passed that winter and spring at Naissus.[6] During the following summer, the saint received an invitation from Constas to come to Aquileia (345).

In June of 345, Gregory, who supplanted Athanasios on the Alexandrian throne, died. Constantius then sent for Athanasios with every mark of honor, writing to him a very friendly letter, exhorting him to pluck

---

[6] Naissus, a Roman city on the river Nišava, is near modern Niš in southeastern Yugoslavia.

up courage and come. A presbyter and deacon were also sent to encourage Athanasios' return. The saint hesitated and stayed on at Aquileia. After receiving a third invitation from the emperor, he committed the whole matter to God Who moved the conscience of Constantius to act in this manner. Athanasios then went to Rome to bid farewell to his friend Julius. After that, he went to Trier to take leave of Constas. He then traveled by way of Adrianople to Antioch, where he went to see Emperor Constantius.

When Saint Athanasios visited Constantius, he received a favorable audience. The interview was brief. The emperor assured Athanasios of his future goodwill. He implored the holy man to allow the Arians at Alexandria the use of one church. Athanasios agreed that he would permit it if the Efstathians of Antioch, with whom Athanasios alone communicated during this visit, might receive the same entitlement. Constantius then sent Athanasios away, writing at the same time to the magistrates in several places, that they should grant the bishop free passage. Nonetheless, Bishop Leontios of Antioch forbade the arrangement. Thus it came to nothing. Athanasios stopped over in Jerusalem, where he was detained by the welcome of a council which the holy confessor Maximos of Jerusalem had convened to congratulate him.

Upon the return of Saint Athanasios (October of 346), the Alexandrians received him with enthusiasm and love. The bishops of Egypt and the Libyan provinces, and the laity of both those countries with those of Alexandria, assembled. They met him a hundred miles distant, filled with indescribable delight that they received their bishop. They were also relieved to have been delivered from the tyrannical heretics. The change among the people was remarkable. Many women decided to remain virgins for Christ. Young men were inspired to take up monasticism. Fathers and children wished to practise asceticism. Husbands and wives gave themselves up to prayer. Widows and orphans, who before were hungry and naked, now found that they were fed and clothed. All wished to emulate virtue. In the churches there prevailed a great peace. Many who formerly hated Athanasios now showed him affection. Enemies were reconciled. Those who were forced to side with the Arians came by night and sought forgiveness for themselves. They anathematized Arianism and besought pardon. Saint Athanasios, now forty-eight years old, was to enjoy undisturbed peace for nine years, three months, and nineteen days (346-356).

The Alexandrian Church Flourishes

The next decade was to witness true reform among the faithful of the Alexandrian Church: an increased strictness of life, the sanctification of home, greater assiduousness in their prayer life, almsgiving and charity, and the desire for the monastic life. Saint Pachomios (d. 346) had already organized the coenobitic life in Egypt. Saint Athanasios was welcomed by monks and solitaries of Tabenne and became the head of the monastic communities. Saint Athanasios often filled up vacancies in the episcopate from among the army of monks, as in the case of Serapion of Thmuis. The saint consecrated bishops not only for Egypt, but also for the Abyssinian kingdom of Auxume. The saint was truly established in Alexandria.

In 350 Constas was murdered. Certain charges were made against Athanasios to the emperor. The saint was accused of poisoning the mind of Constas against his brother Constantius. The holy man replied that he had never spoken to the late emperor, except in the presence of witnesses. The second charge was that the saint was in communication with the treasonous and irreverent General Magnentios. Yet everyone knew of Saint Athanasios' affection toward Constas, who fell victim to the plotting of Magnentios, resulting in the loss of the sovereign's life.

The third charge against the saint was that he used the new church in the caesareum before it was completed or dedicated for the paschal festival of 355. This charge the saint acknowledged, but pleaded necessity and precedent, adding that no disrespect was intended toward the donor, nor any anticipation of its formal consecration. He explained that there was a want of room during the season of the Great Fast. He added that there had been a great number of children, older women, and young men suffering from the pressure of the crowd, and some were obliged as a result to be carried home, but no one died. Nonetheless, there was great discontent and murmuring in the midst of the congregation on account of the crowd. By this the saint justified his use of the building. He indicated that there was no dedication, only a prayer service.

The fourth charge was that Athanasios disobeyed an imperial order to leave Alexandria for Italy. The saint replied that he never received a written command. In this latter instance, when Athanasios began to apprehend the danger that was looming with the establishment of Constantius as sole ruler of the empire, he sent a deputation to Constantius in Milan, headed by his trusted suffragan Serapion. An officer of the palace refused the legates but granted an alleged request of Athanasios to be allowed to come to Italy. No request of this kind was ever made by Athanasios, so the holy man suspected a ruse to draw him from his see.

Second Arian Persecution Under Constantius

After the murder of Constas (350), Constantius, bent to a sorry purpose, convened three successive councils in favor of a milder Arianism. One council was at Sirmium in Pannonia (351), one at Arles in Gaul (353), and one at Milan (355). Patriarch Paul of Constantinople and Bishop Maximos (333-348) of Jerusalem were expelled from their sees. The decrees of these councils were enjoined upon the Western Church. Orthodox bishops were deposed and banished, such as Liberius of Rome, Hosius of Cordova, Hilary of Poitiers, and Lucifer of Cagliari (Calaris). They all resisted, as did Saint Athanasios. It was at the councils at Arles and Milan that the bishops were pressured to stand against Athanasios.

However, the banishment of the western bishops helped greatly in spreading the knowledge of the truth. They had threatened the emperor with the day of judgment, warning him against infringing upon ecclesiastical order and mingling Roman sovereignty with the order of the Church. They counseled him against introducing the Arian heresy into the Church of God. He would not hearken to them, nor permit them to speak further. Instead, he threatened them so much the more and even drew his sword against them. He gave orders for some of them to be led to execution. He repented of this afterward. The holy men left, shaking off the dust and looking up to God, for they neither feared the threats of the emperor nor betrayed their cause before his drawn sword. They accepted their banishment as a service pertaining to their ministry. As they traveled about, they preached the Gospel in every place and city, even though they were in bonds. They proclaimed the Orthodox Faith, anathematizing the Arian heresy. Thus the wanderings of these holy men actually evinced the impiety of the emperor and the evil-minded bishops. All that saw these bishops enter into exile greatly admired their courage and fortitude, deeming them confessors. The onlookers believed the emperor and his minions to be impious men, executioners and murderers, and anything but Christians.

Persecution of the Church of Alexandria

After Constantius did all he desired by exile and violent oppression, he succeeded in filling every place with fear. Finally his fury shifted toward Alexandria. The enemies of Christ now removed any possible bishop to whom Athanasios might complain, thus leaving him alone in persecution.

The emperor first wrote a menacing letter. He then sent the military commander (*doux*) Syrianos and his soldiers with some notaries. Their arrival in Alexandria ushered in terrible and cruel outrages committed against the Church. A great number of bishops, partly by threats, and partly by promises, were forced to declare, "We will no longer hold communion with Athanasios."

On the 6th day of January, in the year 356, Syrianos reached Alexandria. Athanasios questioned him if he came with any orders from court. Syrianos replied in the negative. Syrianos then remained quiet until he referred the matter to the emperor.

Then on the night of 7th/8th of February, in the year 356, Saint Athanasios was presiding at a vigil in the Church of Saint Theonas, when he was driven from the cathedral during the divine office. Five thousand armed soldiers, under the command of Syrianos, had one mission—remove one man, Athanasios. Suddenly they surrounded the church and broke down the doors. It was just after midnight when Syrianos and the notary Hilary entered with a great force of soldiers.

Saint Athanasios later wrote that "Arians were mixed with the soldiers in order to exasperate them against me, and, as they were unacquainted with my person, to point me out to them. It was night. Some of the faithful were keeping a vigil, preparatory to holy Communion in the morning. The commander Syrianos suddenly came upon us with more than five thousand soldiers, having arms and drawn swords, bows, spears, and clubs." Other witnesses attest to this, saying that he came with many legions of soldiers, armed with naked swords and javelins and other warlike instruments, while wearing helmets.

"He surrounded the church," continues Saint Athanasios, "stationing his soldiers near at hand, in order that no one might be able to leave the church and elude them. I deemed that it would be unreasonable for me to desert the people during such a disturbance, and unacceptable not to endanger myself in their behalf." Saint Athanasios then declares, "I sat down upon my throne, exhorting all to pray. I desired that the deacon should read a psalm, and the people to respond, 'For His mercy endureth forever [Ps. 135],' and then all to withdraw and depart for their homes. The general, having made a forced entry with the soldiers, surrounded the sanctuary for the purpose of apprehending us. The clergy and those of the laity who were still there, cried out and demanded that we too should withdraw. I refused, declaring that I would not do so, until they had retired one and all. Then I stood up, and having bidden prayer, I then made my request of them, that all should depart before me. I said that it was better that my safety should be endangered, than that any of them should receive harm. Thereupon, the greater part departed. The monks who were with us and certain of the clergy then came up and dragged us away. Thus, while some of the soldiers stood about the sanctuary, and others were going round the church, we passed through, under the Lord's guidance (Truth is my witness). With the Lord's protection we withdrew without observation! We greatly glorified God that we had not betrayed the people. but sent them away first. Then were we able to save ourselves, and escaped the hands of those who sought us."

Other witnesses related that "when the doors were burst open by the violence of the multitude, Syrianos gave command, and some of the soldiers began shooting. Others were shouting, their arms rattling, and their swords flashing in the light of the lamps. Virgins were slain; men were trampled down. Others were falling over one another as the soldiers dashed upon them.

Several were pierced with arrows and perished. Some of the soldiers even began to plunder. Others were stripping the virgins, who were more afraid of being touched by them than they were of death.

"The holy man, superb in a crisis, was delivered by providence in a wonderful manner. It was only at the last moment that a group of monks and clergy took hold of their archbishop and managed to convey him in the confusion out of the church in a half-fainting state. Those who witnessed the miraculous escape commented, 'The bishop was seized, and barely escaped from being torn to pieces. He fell into a state of insensibility, and appeared as one dead. He disappeared from among them, and went where we know not. The perpetrators were eager to slay him. But when they saw that many had already perished, they gave orders to the soldiers to remove out of sight the bodies of the dead. The most holy virgins who were left behind were buried in the tombs, having attained the glory of martyrdom. Deacons who were beaten with stripes inside the church were also interred therein.'"

Pierced in his soul on account of the sufferings of his flock, the saint was somewhat relieved that most of the people escaped safely. After that incident, Athanasios disappeared from the public eye. In the pandemonium, the holy hierarch went through their midst. He escaped to the monasteries of Upper Egypt, where he was to hide for six years and fourteen days (356-362). He hid himself for a little season, until the indignation should pass away [cf. Is. 26:20].

The Church in Captivity

The time of Saint Athanasios' involuntary vacancy of church and home was used by him in a prudent and agreeably engaged manner, as he allotted the time to beneficial undertakings. His quick mind had time to galvanize into a flurry of writing activity. More than half of his extant works were the fruit of his seclusion, wherein he did every subject justice. He was not too far from Alexandria, but virtually impregnable to the uninitiated. He found safe anchorage in the vast sands of Nitria. The monks harbored their holy refugee zealously, and not once was there any whisper of betrayal.

The people of the Church of Alexandria, who were loyal to Archbishop Athanasios, wrote two public letters of protest and added their signatures. They inveighed against the nocturnal assault upon themselves while in the Lord's house. They made known the fact that the bodies of the slain which were discovered were exposed in public. Evidence was ample, as the bows and arrows and other arms strewn about in the church pointedly proclaimed the outrage. When the faithful went to complain to Syrianos, and request him not to do violence to any, nor to deny what occurred, he chose not to listen. Attend to how he added to his audacious crimes. He ordered those Christians to be beaten with clubs, which only served to strengthen the faithful's accusation concerning the assault in church that night. Objecting to the heinous offenses committed in church, the Christians were resolved to take the matter directly to the emperor. First they made their request known to the prefect and controllers of Egypt to relate these matters to the emperor. They wished to inform the emperor that war had been waged against the Church, and that Syrianos had caused virgins and many others to become martyrs.

The faithful also made known in their protest letter that after all this had taken place, whosoever pleased broke open any door that he could and searched and pillaged what was within. The soldiers entered even into those places where not even all Christians were permitted entry. The evidence of their hostile assault was well documented with the javelins and swords left behind and hung up in the church. The Christians testified that the duumvirs at the head of the police force at Alexandria, as well as the commander of the city police, were desirous to remove the implements of war, but the faithful would not allow it, until the circumstance was made known to all.

They wrote: "Now if an order has been given that we should be persecuted, we are all ready to suffer martyrdom....We also desire by this petition that they may not attempt to bring in hither any other bishop: for we have resisted unto death, desiring to have the most reverend Athanasios, whom God gave us at the beginning, according to the succession of our fathers, and whom also the most religious Augustus Constantius himself sent to us with letters and oaths."

Council of Milan (355)

Desiring to depose Athanasios, Constantius convened a council in the Italian city of Mediolanum (Milan). If Arianism were to prevail, Athanasios needed to be permanently removed. Truly Orthodox bishops declined to attend the profane council, and later refused to uphold its decision to depose Athanasios. Those who refused to attend included Eusebius of Vercelli, Dionysius of Milan, Rhodanus of Toulouse, Paulinus of Trier, and Lucifer of Cagliari. As a result, they were sent into exile in Ariminum (Rimini). The account of this council is unedifying. All those who were present yielded and registered their names to condemn Athanasios. The number of bishops was very small. There were protests and then open coercion. When the deposition was handed to each bishop for his signature, if he should refuse, the sentence of banishment was immediately pronounced. The emperor was present, sitting with the velum drawn. This council put forth no creed, since its only business was to depose Athanasios.

The saint was informed by God through an angelic vision of an impending assault by the procurator's forces, who were empowered by the emperor to dislodge him. The holy hierarch fled the episcopal residence by night and hid in the dwelling place of a certain Christian virgin adorned with hospitality. Some hold the tradition that this godly virgin was our holy mother among the saints, Syncletike, commemorated by the holy Church on the 5th of January.

The virgin was endowed with such extraordinary beauty that those who beheld her regarded her as a phenomenon of nature. The bloom of grace induced all to admire her. Nonetheless, men who possessed prudence and continence avoided her that no suspicion might be attached to their names. She was in the flower of youth, and extremely modest and prudent. Saint Athanasios sought refuge in her home by the revelation of God Who foreordained to save him in this manner. Also, the saint did not want to bring any danger or distress upon his own relatives for harboring a fugitive. She had the courage to receive him, and through her prudence preserved his life. She was his most faithful keeper and assiduous handmaid. She washed his feet, brought him food, and served in every other necessity. Books that the saint needed, she managed to secure through the agency of others. While all this took place, none of the inhabitants of Alexandria knew anything about it.

Saint Athanasios eluded all their search parties. He bore his toils nobly and energetically. During part of the year (357-358), he was actually in the city itself, though it is believed that he also was able to spend some time in the cells of Upper and Lower Egypt.

Writings and Sayings of the Saint

Saint Gregory the Theologian comments, "Saint Athanasios was the first and only one, or with the concurrence of but a few, to venture to confess in writing, with entire clearness and distinctness, the unity of the divinity and essence of the three hypostases."[7]

His *Four Discourses Against the Arians*, written between 356 and 360, were comprehensive treatises refuting the Ariomaniacs, Christ-opposers who contended with God.[8] We also, for the edification of our readers, cite some of the saint's God-benefitting utterances regarding the coeternal Son and and the incarnation.

Speaking to the Arians in his writings, Saint Athanasios says: "You say that He made for Himself His Son out of nothing, as an instrument whereby to make the universe. Which then is superior, that which needs or that which supplies the need? Or does each supply the deficiency of the other?"[9] The saint then tells the Arians that it is a grave error to call God's Logos a work. "God shall bring every work into judgment." He then asks

---

[7] Ibid., ¶ 33.
[8] Discourse III.
[9] Saint Athanasios, *Discourse I Against the Arians*, Ch. VII(26), Nicene, Vol. IV.

them, "What room is there for judgment, when the Judge is on trial?"[10]
Elsewhere he declares, "Arius raves in saying that the Son is from nothing
and that once He was not."[11] Comparing the Arians to Jews, he writes: "The
Jews said, 'How, being a man, can He be God?' And the Arians, 'If He were
very God from God, how could He become a man?' These are Ariomaniacs.
Let them openly confess themselves scholars of Caiaphas and Herod, instead
of cloaking Judaism with the name of Christianity."[12] He then speaks of them
as heretics, characterizing heretics for us: "A heretic is a wicked thing in
truth, and in every respect his heart is depraved and irreligious. They invent
for themselves other questions Judaic and foolish, as if Truth were their
enemy, thereby to show rather that they are Christ's opponents in all
things."[13]

In his letters, the saint wrote: "How can men be called Christians who
deny Christ? And how can men be admitted to church who do evil against the
churches?"[14] "For whom do Arians spare, who have spared not even their
own souls?"[15]

Speaking about the coeternal Son, He writes: "Christ the Logos is
'the effulgence of the glory and impress of His hypostasis [Heb. 1:3].' It is
irreligious to say that once the Son was not. For when did the Father not see
Himself in His own Image?"[16] "Now beholding the Son, we see the Father;
for the thought and comprehension of the Son is knowledge concerning the
Father, because He is His proper Offspring from His essence."[17] "Is it not
blasphemous, God being Maker, to say that His framing Logos and His
Wisdom once was not? For if the Logos is not with the Father from
everlasting, the Triad is not everlasting; but a Monad was first, and afterward
by addition it became a Triad."[18] Therefore, "He cannot be called Father,
unless a Son exist."[19]

In his *Second Discourse*, he speaks of the relationship between Father
and Son: "The Son is begotten not from without but from the Father; and
while the Father remains whole, the expression of His subsistence ever exists,
and preserves the Father's likeness and unvarying image, so that he who sees

---

[10] Ibid., *Discourse II*, Ch. XIV(6).
[11] Ibid., *Discourse IV*, § 6.
[12] Ibid., *Discourse III*, Ch. XXVI(28).
[13] Ibid., *Discourse III*, Ch. XXX(58).
[14] Ibid., "Epistle XLVII, To the Church of Alexandria," Nicene, Vol. IV.
[15] Ibid., "Epistle LI, Second Letter to Bishop Lucifer."
[16] Ibid., *Discourse I*, Ch. VI(20).
[17] Ibid., *Discourse I*, Ch. V(16).
[18] Ibid., *Discourse I*, Ch. VI(17).
[19] Ibid., *Discourse I*, Ch. VIII(28).

Him, sees in Him the subsistence too, of which He is the expression."[20] He then explains, "'I and the Father are one [Jn. 10:30],' saying, 'I am in the Father and the Father is in Me [Jn. 14:10],' by way of showing the identity of the divinity and the unity of essence. For They are one, not as one thing divided into two parts. But They are two, because the Father is Father and is not also Son, and the Son is Son and not also Father; but the essence is one. He and the Father are one in propriety and peculiarity of essence, and in the identity of the one Divinity. For the radiance is also light."[21]

In his *Third Discourse*, Saint Athanasios then explains the word "firstborn"[22] with relation to the Son, saying, "When the Son is called Firstborn, this is done not for the sake of ranking Him with the creation, but to prove the framing and adoption of all things through the Son."[23] He then speaks of the Jews: "The Logos of God is Himself the image of the invisible God, being the effulgence of the glory and impress of His hypostasis [Col. 1:15; Heb. 1:3]. The Jews did not receive Him Who spoke to them; thereby they did not receive the Logos, Who is the form of God."[24]

The saint then explains very clearly about the incarnation of our Savior. "He divinized that which He put on, and gave it graciously to the race of man."[25] When we read that "on behalf of them I sanctify Myself, that they also may be sanctified in truth [Jn. 17:19], and "Now God anointed Him with the Holy Spirit" [cf. Acts 10:38], He Who sanctifies Himself is the Lord of sanctification. "If then for our sake He sanctifies Himself, and does this when He is become Man, it is very plain that the Spirit's descent on Him in Jordan was a descent upon us, because of His bearing our body. For when the Lord, as Man, was washed in Jordan, it was we who were washed in Him and by Him. And when He received the Spirit, it was we who by Him were made recipients of the Spirit."[26]

When we read He became a curse for us [Gal. 3:13], Saint Athanasios explains, "He hath made Him sin for us Who knew no sin. We do not simply conceive this, that the whole Christ has become curse and sin, but that He has taken on Him the curse which lay against us."[27]

---

[20] Ibid., *Discourse II*, Ch. XVIII(22).
[21] Ibid., *Discourse III*, Ch. XXIII(4).
[22] Rom. 8:29; Col. 1:15, 18; Heb. 12:23.
[23] Saint Athanasios, *Discourse III*, Ch. XXIV(9).
[24] Ibid., *Discourse III*, Ch. XXV(16).
[25] Ibid., *Discourse I*, Ch. XI(42).
[26] Ibid., *Discourse I*, Ch. XII(47).
[27] Ibid., *Discourse II*, Ch. XIX(47).

When we read He received our infirmities [cf. Is. 53:3; Heb. 4:15], "He is said to be infirm Himself, though not Himself infirm, for He is the power of God, and He became sin for us and a curse, though not having sinned Himself, but because He Himself bore our sins and our curse."[28]

When Jesus is said to have "kept on advancing in wisdom and stature, and in grace in the presence of God and men [cf. Lk. 2:52]," the saint explains, "To men then belongs advance, but the Son of God, since He could not advance, being perfect in the Father, humbled Himself for us, that in His humbling we on the other hand might be able to increase. Thus, to advance in wisdom is not the advance of Wisdom Itself, but rather the manhood's advance in it."[29]

When some say that the Christ was terrified at death [cf. Mt. 26:39, 42], the saint counsels, "It is irreligious and unseemly to say that Jesus was terrified at death or Hades, Whom the keepers of the gates of Hades saw and shuddered. But these affections were not proper to the nature of the Logos, as far as He was Logos, but in the flesh which was thus affected was the Logos....For Christ's enemies are given to see how He Who did the works is the same as He Who showed that His body was passable by His permitting it to weep and hunger, and to show other properties of a body. For while by means of such He made it known that, though God is impassible, He had taken a passable flesh." And, "He let His own body suffer, for therefore did He come, as I said before, that in the flesh He might suffer, and thenceforth the flesh might be made impassible and immortal."[30]

He explains the purpose of the Christ's becoming Man in this letter: "He put on the creature, that He as Creator might once more consecrate it, and be able to recover it. But a creature could never be saved by a creature."[31]

Third Exile (356-362)

During his exile, the saint struggled in his mind that the emperor would renege upon his pledges, which he gave voluntarily after the death of Constas. The archbishop composed a *Defense Before Constantius*, which dealt with four charges that were drawn up against the hierarch. After he finished his defense, he learned of reports confirming the indiscriminate banishment of Liberius (352-366) of Rome and the great Hosius of Spain. Pope Liberius was the successor to the holy Julius I (337-352), who was heir to Saint

---

[28] Ibid., *Discourse II*, Ch. XX(55).

[29] Ibid., *Discourse III*, Ch. XXVIII(52).

[30] Ibid., *Discourse III*, Ch. XXIX(58).

[31] Ibid., "Epistle LX, To Bishop Adelphius," ¶ 8.

Silvester. After exiling Liberius to a certain island, they had the presumption to replace him with an Arian pope, named Felix.

Saint Athanasios knew that they had been banished because they refused to endorse his own banishment. Soon thereafter other sad tidings overtook him of the oppressive measures taken against his Church. Ninety bishops were under persecution, and their churches were given up to the Arians; sixteen bishops were banished, while others fled. Saint Athanasios addressed an epistle to the bishops of Egypt (ca. 356) warning them to shun any Arian formula or creed, even if it meant becoming fugitives. He stated clearly and briefly the original Arian position, and confuted it with the Scriptures. He urged the bishops to become true confessors.

One report of appalling injuries was especially disturbing to the Orthodox. While the brethren were praying during Pascha in a desert place near a cemetery, the general pounced upon them with more than three thousand soldiers, with arms, drawn swords, and spears. The unprovoked attack was even launched against women and children, who were only offering prayers to God. Virgins were stripped, and even the bodies of those who perished from the blows were not buried, but cast out to the dogs. The relatives of the slain, at great personal risk, came secretly and retrieved the relics. Much effort was needed to accomplish this successfully.

Saint Athanasios then received a copy of one of the letters sent from the emperor to him. The letter denounced him to the Alexandrians and recommended a new bishop, one George. It was evident to Athanasios that a personal interview with Constantius was not in order. He returned to his retreat, believing that in the future he would be enabled to address the emperor.

The Arian madmen abruptly installed the uninstructed and greedy George of Cappadocia (356/357), a blackguard and one well acquainted with the ways of the world. He could not attract anyone by a single grace of personal address, other than those of similar mean character. A zealous and wealthy Arian, he made his name as a profiteering fraud and pork contractor in the army. The alliance between George and the Arians was reprehensible. In his arrogant presumption, when he seized the throne, he used violence against the supporters of Athanasios and delivered up the churches to the Arians. Even in exile, the faithful adherents to Nicene theology suffered harassment. George's crude manner, expression, and conduct could not be tolerated indefinitely. His tyrannizing rapacity and affronts against pagan worship also earned him their intense hatred. He abominably abused many hapless souls. One history that was well documented is as follows. He scourged forty men with sticks, thorny and fresh from the palm tree, which necessitated that some of them undergo surgical procedures, but others died from their sufferings. Those that perished were left unburied. Those whom they took away were banished to the great Oasis.

In addition, the following bishops were cruelly driven from Egypt and Libya: Ammonios, Muius, Gaius, Philo, Hermes, Plenios, Psenorsiris, Nilammon, Agathos, Anagamphos, Markos, Ammonios, another Markos, Drakontios, Adelphios, Athenodoros, and the Presbyters Hierax and Dioscoros. Some died on the way, while others perished in exile. The persecution caused more than thirty bishops to take flight.

In his *Encyclical Epistle to the Bishops of Egypt* (356), written after Syrianos expelled him and the nomination of George the pork contractor for the Alexandrian see was accomplished, the saint warns them, "According to the Arians, God was not always a Father."[32] And, again, in his *Defense of the Nicene Definition*, he challenged the Arians: "Let them dare to say openly what they think in secret, that God was once wordless and wisdomless."[33]

Saint Athanasios also writes in *Defense of His Flight*: "Although they have done all this, yet they are not ashamed of the evils they have perpetrated against me. Now they even accuse me, because I escaped their murderous hands. They bewail themselves that they have not put me out of the way; so they pretend to reproach me with cowardice, not perceiving that by this they turn the blame upon themselves. For if it is a bad thing to flee, it is much worse to persecute."

George stirred up such resistance against himself that he feared for his own life. He, too, withdrew from Alexandria in 358. Although George went missing, the holy man was unable to return to his see, because the emperor opposed him. The saint refused to accept the emperor's rule in all matters. In this he was supported by the west, which was unwilling to recognize the emperor as a kind of "bishop of bishops." Constantius still begrudged the use of the word *ousia* (essence), favoring those who upheld that the Son was like the Father.

In his written *Defense Before Constantius*, Athanasios defended his flight into the desert. He wrote: "I fled, not because I feared your piety—for I know your long-suffering and goodness—but because from what had taken place, I perceived the spirit of my enemies, and considered that they would make use of all possible means to accomplish my demise, from fear that they would be brought to answer for what they had done contrary to the intentions of your excellency....Now neither was it from fear of death that I felt—let none of them condemn me as guilty of cowardice—but because it is the

---

[32] Ibid., *To the Bishops of Egypt*, Ch. II(12) and Ch. III(9), Nicene, Vol. IV.
[33] Ibid., *De Decretis* or *Defence of the Nicene Definition*, Ch. IV(15), Nicene, Vol. IV.

injunction of our Savior that we should flee when we are sought after, and not expose ourselves to certain dangers, nor by appearing before our persecutors inflame still more their rage against us. For to give one's self up to one's enemies to be murdered is the same thing as to murder one's self; but to flee, as our Savior has enjoined, is to know our time, and to manifest a real concern for our persecutors, lest if they proceed to the shedding of blood, they become guilty of the transgression of the law, 'Thou shalt not murder [Ex. 20:13].'"[34]

The saint then informed the emperor of the conduct of the Arians against the holy virgins, the brides of Christ. "First they stripped them, and caused them to be suspended upon a rack, and scourged them on the ribs so severely there several times, that not even real criminals have ever suffered such abuse. Pilate, to gratify the Jews of old, pierced one of our Savior's sides. Now the limbs of the virgins are in an especial manner the Savior's own. And these men scourged both their sides. All men shudder at hearing the bare recital of these misdeeds. These men not only did not fear to strip and scourge the virgins, solely dedicated to Christ, but when they were rebuked by all for such excessive brutality, instead of showing any embarrassment, they also pretended that it was at thy command. Such a deed as this was never heard of in past persecutions. Even if it had occurred before, yet surely virginity never suffered such outrage and dishonor in the time of your majesty, a Christian. Such wickedness belongs only to heretics, to blaspheme the Son of God, and to do violence to His holy virgins."

After explaining such enormities perpetrated by the Arian maniacs, he mentions his life in exile, saying, "I endured everything; I even dwelt among wild beasts, that your favor might return to me, waiting for an opportunity to offer to you this my defense, confident as I am that they will be condemned, and your goodness manifested to me."

Now Athanasios was also a man of his age. This is why he wrote to the emperor, who was considered the first personage in Christendom. He honestly hoped against hope that the emperor would renew his solemn assurances. Athanasios did so as long as there was any chance of bringing Constantius back to a sense of piety.

Nonetheless, the emperor imposed his rule upon the Church and despotically interfered. Constantius delivered the Alexandrian churches to the heretics. A change of governor was made for Alexandria: Maximos of Nicaea reached Alexandria with the functionary Herakleios. They conveyed with them a letter from Constantius threatening the heathen with severe measures if they did not begin hostilities toward the Athanasian party. Herakleios then

---

[34] Ibid., *Defence Before Constantius*, § 32, Nicene, Vol. IV.

made this announcement: "The emperor disavows Athanasios, and has commanded that the churches be given up to the Arians." All wondered at these words, asking, "What! Has Constantius become a heretic?" All magistrates, including heathen functionaries of the temples, were to sign agreements to the persecution and receive the emperor's nominee for new bishop. The heathen were threatened with starvation, slavery, and the destruction of their idols if they did not consent. Therefore, the pagans reluctantly complied with the imperial incitements. The more abandoned among their tradesmen and workmen took part in the persecution.

Soon after, when the faithful were assembled in the great church, it was the time of dismissal. Most of the congregation had departed, except for a few women. The women had just finished saying their prayers, and sat down to rest. Suddenly, youths that were urged on by the Arians attacked them with stones and clubs. Some women escaped, but others were stoned to death. The virgins consecrated to Christ had their veils torn off and were scourged. Those that resisted were kicked by the feet of the youths. They were assailed with obscene language. Saint Athanasios said, "This was dreadful, exceedingly dreadful."

The youths then seized the seats, the throne, the table, and the curtains of the church. They carried them out into the great street and burned them, casting frankincense in the flames. They sang praises to their idols and exclaimed, "Constantius hath become a heathen, and the Arians have acknowledged our customs!" Now one of those perverse youths sat down upon the throne and gave voice to some lascivious ditty. He then attempted to rise up and drag the throne toward himself, when divine justice chastised that impudent fellow. The wood of the throne penetrated his own bowels. Instead of carrying out the throne, he eviscerated himself by this blow, and the throne ushered in his death. The day after he died, another heathen entered the church with boughs of trees, and waved them in his hands and mocked. He was immediately struck with blindness. He needed to be supported and removed by his rowdy comrades. The pagans were gripped with fear due to these occurrences. The Arians, on the other hand, were not even touched by them.

The general persecution at Alexandria was urged on by one heathen, the vulgar Faustinus. The enormities that he and his minions committed at the instigation of the Arians surpasses the bounds of all wickedness. They went from house to house, searching for Athanasios. What family did they not ravage and plunder? What garden did they not trample upon? What tomb did they not open, pretending they were seeking Athanasios, though their sole aim was to take spoil of all that came their way? Soldiers who assisted them were given the contents of the lodgings of private citizens. Many changed their residence, moving from street to street, from the city into the suburbs. Some were dealt severe fines, and, when unable to pay, they borrowed, so as to escape this wickedness.

The profligate young Manichee, military commander Sebastian, who succeeded to the military command of Syrianos, also used violence. More bishops were driven into exile, and Arian bishops and clergy were installed. Those virgins that condemned their impiety were hauled from their houses. They were insulted and stripped of their head coverings by Sebastian's young men. The Subdeacon Eftychios was scourged on the back with a leather whip, till he was at the point of death. He was then sent away to the mines without having his wounds dressed. He was unable to finish the journey to the mines, and on account of the pain of his stripes, he reposed on the way, obtaining the glory of martyrdom. The poor also suffered ill-treatment. When the military commander delivered the churches up to the Arians, the destitute and widows no longer received aid. When the brethren attended to the needs of the poor, the Arians descended and persecuted the widows, beating them on the feet. Those who performed the acts of kindness upon the poor were brought to trial. The sufferers neither betrayed nor denied the true Faith in Christ. Even the heathen protested these proceedings, calling them cruel and barbaric. But these men lost even the common sentiments of humanity. Even Gorgonios, the commander of the police, caused the soldiers to ill-treat the presbyters and deacons.

Saint Athanasios asks, "Who would call them even by the name of heathen—much less by that of Christians? Would anyone regard their habits and feelings as human, and not rather those of wild beasts, seeing their cruel and savage conduct? Persecution was the weapon of Arianism....This heresy is altogether alien to godliness. It acts contrary to our Savior, seeing also that it has enlisted that enemy of Christ, Constantius, as it were Antichrist himself. He has endeavored to emulate Saul in savage cruelty." The holy man urged the duty of separating from heretics, saying, "Depart ye, depart, go out from thence, and touch not the unclean thing; go ye out from the midst of her; separate yourselves, ye that bear the vessels of the Lord [Is. 52:11]."

In Defense of His Flight and Seclusion

Saint Athanasios in his *Defense* says of his persecutors that "neither their thoughts nor their words are according to the Gospel, but that after their own pleasure, whatsoever they themselves desire, and they think to be good....Where is there a place that has not some memorial of their malice?...So zealously did they endeavor by all means to prove that they were not truly Christians....

"They pretend themselves to be friends, while they search as enemies, to the end that they may glut themselves with our blood, and put us also out of the way, because we have always opposed and do still oppose their impiety and confute and brand their heresy....

"They even reproach men for hiding themselves from those who seek to destroy them, and accuse those who flee from their persecutors. What will they do when they see Jacob fleeing from his brother Esau, and Moses withdrawing into Midian for fear of Pharaoh? David for fleeing from his house on account of Saul,...Abimelech, the great Elias? The disciples also withdrew and hid themselves for fear of the Jews. Paul was sought by the governor at Damascus. For there was a command under the law that cities of refuge should be appointed. But when they persecute you in this city, flee to another [Mt. 10:23].

"The Logos Himself condescended to hide Himself when He was sought after, that is, His flight into Egypt, and when He withdrew from the Pharisees. Jesus therefore was walking no longer openly among the Jews; but went away from that place into the country near the wilderness [Jn. 11:54].

"He hid Himself when He was sought before that time came, as we do; when He was persecuted He fled; and avoiding the designs of His enemies He passed by, and so went through the midst of them. He neither suffered Himself to be taken before the time came, nor did He hide Himself when it came....

"Therefore, the blessed fathers thus regulated their conduct also; they showed no cowardice in fleeing from the persecutor, but rather manifested their fortitude of soul in shutting themselves up in close and dark places, and living a hard life."[35]

Persecution of the Western Bishops

A mild Arianism then gained the ascendancy in the whole empire. In place of *homoousion* (same in essence) the doctrine of *homoiousian* (*omoiousian*, similarity of essence) was adopted, instead of the militant Arian view of hetero-ousianism (difference of essence). Rome and the papacy itself also fell prey to this heresy, after the deposition of Pope Liberius. As we mentioned earlier, the Arian Deacon Felix II, "by antichristian wickedness," as Saint Athanasios describes it, was elected as his successor.

The Romans wished to recall Liberius, forcing Constantius to restore him. Some claim that Liberius was prevailed upon to apostatize by subscribing to an Arianizing confession, for which he was restored to the papal throne (358), but later repented. He was said to have denied the Faith through weakness, but not from conviction. The allegation he lapsed from the Faith is admirably refuted on the day of his commemoration, that is, the 27th of August.

---

[35] Ibid., *Defence of His Flight*, §§ 1, 2, 11, 15, 17, Nicene, Vol. IV.

After the lapse of Liberius, the impious thought they had accomplished nothing, so long as the great Abraham-like Hosius did not fall prey to their craftiness. They exerted their fury upon that great old man who served in the episcopate some sixty years. The Arians recognized him as the president of the council, and acknowledged that his letters were everywhere carefully heeded. It was he who put forth the Nicene confession and proclaimed the Arians as heretics. Ancient though he was, they began to persecute him. Constantius wrote to him, "Wilt thou continue as the only person to oppose? Be persuaded and subscribe against Athanasios; for whoever subscribes against him thereby embraces with us the Arian cause." Hosius remained fearless and was ready for persecution. He wrote the emperor a letter expressing his determination to remain steadfast, saying, "I will not unite myself to the Arians; I anathematize their heresy. Neither will I subscribe against Athanasios, whom both we and the Church of the Romans and the whole synod have pronounced to be guiltless. And thou thyself also, when thou didst understand this, sent for the man, and gave him permission to return with honor to his country and his Church. What reason then can there be for so great a change in thy conduct?...Cease then, I beseech thee, O Constantius, and be persuaded by me."

The emperor was not persuaded and did not desist from his designs. He threatened the venerable elder, with a view either to bring him over by force, or to banish him if he refused to comply. His officers were unable to invent any charge against the old man, for his blameless life was known to everyone. Constantius sent for the elder and detained him a whole year in Sirmium. The emperor neither feared God, nor regarded his own father's affection for Hosius, who was now a hundred years old. He used such violence toward the old man, and confined him so straitly, that at last he broke him by means of his disorientating sufferings. He was brought, though with difficulty, to hold communion with the Arian bishops Valens, Ursakios, and their fellows, though he would not subscribe against Athanasios. How the enemies of the Faith drew such a prize would distress anyone in the telling of it. But his falling victim to them should excite our compassion.

Yet there is cause for cheer. Do not, dear readers, make yourselves uneasy. At the approach of his repose, as it were by his last testament, he bore witness to the force, imprisonment, and imperial threats which had been used toward him. Consistent with piety and honor, he anathematized the Arian heresy and gave strict charge that no one should receive it.

Nicene Orthodoxy was discomfited. Yet even the heretics fought among themselves and were divided into factions. The Evsevians or Semi-arians, represented by Basil of Ankyra and Gregory of Laodikeia, maintained that the Son was not of the same essence (*omo-ousios*), yet of like essence (*omoi-ousios*) with the Father. Many who belonged to this group wished to agree with the Nicene Faith but either harbored prejudices against Athanasios or misunderstood the term *homoousios*. Many did not understand the distinction between *ousia* (essence) and hypostasis (subsistence), or substance and person as the Latins interpreted such words. The decided Arians, under the lead of Evdoxios of Antioch and his Deacon Aetios, together with Bishop Evnomios of Kyzikos in Mysia (after whom they were called Evnomians also), taught that the Son was of a different essence *(hetero-ousios)*, and even unlike the Father *(anomoios)*, and created out of nothing (*ex ouk onton*). They were also known as Heterousiasts, Anomoeans, and Exukontians.

A number of councils attempted to deal with these internal schisms: two at Sirmium (357, 358), one at Antioch (358), and one at Ankyra (358); a double council at Seleukeia and Rimini (359) and one at Constantinople (360). No compromises could be reached, and Constantius was unsuccessful in unifying the factions. No one was allowed to mention either *homoousios* or *homoiousios* in a sermon. All that any preacher could say was that the Father is greater than the Son in dignity, honor, splendor, and majesty. In time people were dissatisfied with the lack of formula.

In the spring of 358, Basil of Ankyra, who used *homoiousios*, emerged as the leader of those who restored *ousia* to the rolls of religiously correct vocabulary, and anathematized both Aetios and Markellos.

Emperor Constantius, Sole Ruler of the Eastern and Western Empires

In 359, Magnentios, the usurper to the throne, committed suicide in Lyons, leaving Constantius the sole emperor in the Roman world. Constantius was wary and distrustful of Athanasios, whom he believed to have received an emissary from the late Magnentios. Constantius wished to be rid of Athanasios. He now had political reasons to bolster his condemnation of the prelate. Arianism had not yet contaminated Gaul, but of the Gaulish bishops, only Paul of Trier, where the holy exiles had been banished some eighteen years earlier, repudiated the emperor's request to condemn Athanasios.[36]

On the political level, Saint Athanasios recognized that the emperor had powers to summon synod meetings and to legislate to protect the Church against pagans and heretics. However, he, together with many of the western bishops, opposed imperial attempts to integrate the Church within the state, lest the state sit in judgment on ecclesiastical law and decisions.

---

[36] At the Council of Milan (355), those who refused to condemn and banish Saint Athanasios were Dionysius, Bishop of Alba, the metropolis of Italy, Eusebius, Bishop of Vercelli in Liguria, Paulinus, Bishop of Treves, Rhodanus, and Lucifer of Cagliari in Sardinia. Saint Hilary of Poitiers also would not condemn the saint.

Saint Athanasios thought Constantius to be heterodox. If imperial power were to defend the Church, that protection would be based on Constantius' belief regarding what constituted the Church. Constantius' priority was to establish tolerable religious unity around a creed acceptable to as many of his subjects as possible. Saint Athanasios deemed the emperor's course of action as serving political peace and cohesion, instead of proclaiming the truth and the Faith.

Another creed was promulgated at Sirmium where *ousia* was cast out, since it was deemed an unscriptural term. A version of this creed was placed before the bishops of the east and west—in Seleukeia, in Isauria, and in Ariminum. The west asserted that Christ was like the Father. In October of 359, the east adopted the same resolution. Both east and west then ratified their conclusion at Constantinople in January of 360. Aetios refused to accept the Constantinopolitan Creed of 360, and he was deposed and exiled.

In 361, with Constantius' death, the second and lasting victory of Nicene Orthodoxy was soon to be ushered in. In his *History of the Arians*, Saint Athanasios wrote: "Constantius was worse than Saul, Ahab, and Pilate."[37] Julian the Apostate (361-363) recalled Orthodox bishops, in the hope that the intolerance among the warring Christian factions might bring about their self-destruction. The usurper George returned to Egypt only upon hearing that Constantius had died. He was attacked by the pagans with shouts and reproaches. They put him in prison. Early, the next morning, they rushed upon him in the prison, slew him, and flung the corpse upon a camel, making sport with it. After exposing it to ridicule and every imaginable insult during the day, they burned the cadaver at night. The Arians asserted that the followers of Athanasios slew him, but this is unfounded.

The Saint Returns to His See

In accordance with the permission granted by Julian for bishops exiled by Constantius to return to their sees, our beloved Athanasios went home to Alexandria on the 21st day of February, in the year 362. His unexpected appearance by night in the church at Alexandria struck all with amazement. No one knew from whence he came. The people rejoiced at his return and restored his churches to him. The Arians were expelled and compelled to meet in private houses. With the death of their Arian bishop George, they now had Lucius, who had nothing to recommend him.

Straightway, Saint Athanasios convoked a synod meeting to deal with the questions which stood in the way of the peace of the Church. On the agenda were four issues: 1) The terms on which communion should be vouchsafed to those Arians who wished to reunite. (They were to ask for

---

[37] Ibid., *History of the Arians*, § 68, Nicene, Vol. IV.

nothing beyond the Nicene test, and they were to anathematize Arianism, including the belief that the Holy Spirit is a creature.) 2) The question of Arian Christology. 3) The state of the Church of Antioch. 4) Theological terminology, and the uses of "essence" and "hypostasis."

The synod members included saints and confessors, and Egyptian bishops who had suffered under the Arian madman George. Also attending were Lucifer of Cagliari, Apollinarios of Laodikeia, Eusebius of Vercelli, and Paulinus the presbyter who shepherded the Efstathian community at Antioch.

Supporters of both *homoousios* and *homoiousios* made ready to reexamine the causes of discord. "Like in all respects" was taken to imply *homoousios*, but with two conditions: the acknowledgment of the hypostases of the Trinity, and that no Sabellianism was inferred. The Holy Spirit's coessentiality with the Father and Son was acknowledged. Another issue that was discussed was how the Son is co-essential with the Father and yet one with us. As a result, former Homoiousians became Homoousians. Those bishops who out of fear signed the creeds of the Councils of Seleukeia and Ariminum were pardoned. Terminology was also discussed, but the rift was not completely healed between the two anti-Arian groups. The council was yet another jewel in the heavenly crown for the saint. Its Orthodox resolutions proceeded from him.

Saint Gregory the Theologian comments about the Alexandrian Synod of 362, writing: "We use in an Orthodox sense the terms one essence and three hypostases, the one to denote the nature of the Divinity, the other the properties of the Three. The Italians mean the same, but, owing to the scantiness of their vocabulary, and its poverty of terms, they are unable to distinguish between essence and hypostases, and therefore introduce the term 'Persons,' to avoid being understood to assert three essences. Now there was danger of the whole world being torn asunder in the strife about syllables. Seeing and hearing this, our blessed Athanasios, the true man of God and great steward of souls as he was, felt it inconsistent with his duty to overlook so absurd and unreasonable a rending of the word, and applied his medicine to the disease. In what manner? He conferred in his gentle and sympathetic manner with both parties. After he had carefully weighed the meaning of their expressions—and found that they had the same sense, and were in nowise different in doctrine—he permitted each party to employ its own use of terms, and bound them together in unity of action.

"This in itself was more profitable than the long course of labors and teaching....This again was of more value than his many vigils and acts of bodily mortification, the advantage of which is limited to those who perform them."[38]

Saint Athanasios was a source of vexation for Julian the Apostate. Julian's anticipated results of recalling the exiles were very different from what was taking place. The hierarch was ordered to leave the city immediately on pain of severe punishment. The people appealed the order, but without effect.

Though Julian worked to unite his empire, he could not overthrow his ancestral imposture of idol madness. Begrudging his own salvation, in a brazen manner, he openly denied and blasphemed the Christ. Borne hither and thither by the demons, he paid homage to senseless idols, reconstructed the pagan temples, and decreed that sacrifices were to be offered to the gods, thus blazing his degradation to the world. Bestirring themselves, the Orthodox clergy and laity protested. Julian, whose behavior was vulgar and offensive in the extreme, responded by raining down a wave of acute persecution against the faithful. The deranged defector, seeking council with his confederates and sorcerers, sought to eradicate the name of Christ and Christianity from his realm. All those with Julian concurred that Athanasios must be the first to be removed. He was the lodestone that needed to be crushed. They believed that the removal of that popular hero and living martyr was the most expedient way to lead others to idolatry, because if one destroys the foundation of the house, then out of necessity the entire structure falls.

"Although Julian," says Sozomen, "was anxious to promote paganism by every means, he acknowledged the imprudence of employing force or vengeance against those who refused to sacrifice. There were so many Christians in every city throughout the empire that it would have been no easy task even to number them. He did not forbid them to assemble, but he expelled the clergy and presidents of the churches from all the cities, in order to put an end to their gatherings. He believed that on account of their absence and with none to convene the churches, surely the gatherings would be effectually dissolved. He reasoned there would be no one to teach or celebrate the Mysteries. Thus, their religion should fall into oblivion. The pretext he used was that the clergy were leaders of sedition among the people."[39]

Although the pagan temples were opened and sacrifices were being offered, and Julian was forever prating about the glories of the gods, Christianity still prevailed among the populace. Julian was particularly provoked when he discovered that the wives, children, and servants of many

---

[38] Saint Gregory, *Oration XXI*, ¶¶ 35, 36.
[39] Sozomen, *Ecclesiastical History*, Book V, Ch. XV.

pagan priests had been converted to Christianity. The standard of the Roman armies, since Constantine's time, was the Cross. Exercising imperial privilege and irrational hostility, Julian indulged himself and changed the ancient form of the standard to display pictures of the gods and even himself. Every soldier was commanded to sacrifice and was promised gold if he did so. Christians were then prohibited from the markets and the judicial seats. They were not allowed to share in Greek education. Christian children were forbidden entry into public schools. Julian granted permission to the Jews to rebuild the temple at Jerusalem. Every attempt to put their hands to the work of the temple resulted in fire springing upward and killing many. The sign of the Cross miraculously appeared on the clothing of many who had exerted themselves in this work.

The Saint's Fourth Exile (362)

The emperor was informed that Saint Athanasios held meetings in the Church of Alexandria. His informants also notified him that Athanasios taught the people boldly and even converted many pagans to Christianity. The latter activity, in Julian's mind, signed the death warrant for the archbishop. In his deluded view, nothing now would acquit the hierarch.

Julian wished to humble the hierarch and have him publicly put down and humiliated before the Alexandrian Church. In October of 362, Julian sent an indignant letter to Prefect Ekdios Olympos, threatening Athanasios with a heavy fine if he refused to leave not only the city, but even the country. He then made a complaint about how Athanasios baptized some Greek pagan ladies of rank. The hierarch was charged as an "enemy of the gods." The emperor again commanded Athanasios, under the most severe penalties, to depart from Alexandria. Another excuse which he used was that after Athanasios had been banished by Constantius, he resumed his episcopal see without the sanction of the reigning emperor. Julian said that he never had contemplated restoring the bishops exiled by Constantius to their ecclesiastical functions, but instead only to their homelands. In December, he sent a letter to the Alexandrians with arguments in favor of Serapis and the other pagan gods. He wrote against Christ and repeated his command for Athanasios to exit Egypt, calling the holy man "a contemptible little fellow."

The beacon of virtue, Athanasios, was again subjected to an illegal and criminal trial. With a deadened conscience and conduct so carelessly unguarded, Julian dispatched a military force of two hundred armed soldiers which was again ordered to enter Alexandria. They surrounded the cathedral and commenced a search for the archbishop, that they might put him to death.

Imitating the Master's love for man, the saint implored the Christian multitudes: "Be of good courage; let us retire for a little while, friends; it is but a cloud which shall speedily be dispersed." After uttering these words on the 23rd of October, he bade them farewell. He commended the care of the Church to his most zealous friends. By the grace of God he was enveloped by so many Christians that he was able to pass through the crowd undetected by the soldiers.

The hierarch went to the Nile. He found a ready boat and set sail for Upper Egypt and the Thebaid. But this time the holy man had been observed. He was closely pursued by those who sought to lay hold of him. When the saint understood that his pursuers were not far distant, his attendants began to beseech him to retreat into the desert again. The saint then, moved by the Holy Spirit, told the captain to turn the vessel around and sail toward their adversaries! Though quite surprised at the unexpected words of the archbishop, he did as he was bidden. As the enemy vessel closed the gap between them, the archbishop called out to the soldiers, saying, "What are ye seeking, and why do you make haste so?" They replied, "The Patriarch of Alexandria, Athanasios. Have you seen him?" The hierarch answered, "He is before you as you go; only hurry to overtake him!" They did not recognize the archbishop. God had allowed this delusion to befall the soldiers. Those rascals accelerated their hot pursuit, but to no avail. The man of God made good his retreat, by God's good pleasure, and returned secretly to Alexandria. Again, however, he remained concealed. He is said to have returned to Chaeru, the first station on the road eastward from Alexandria. After the danger of being caught had passed, he ascended to the upper parts of Egypt, as far as Upper Hermoupolis in the Thebaid and as far as Antinoupolis.

As the saint approached Hermoupolis, about one hundred bishops, clergy, and monks of the Thebaid lined both banks of the Nile to welcome their archbishop. He then greeted Abba Theodore, who was great among the Tabennesian monks, and asked after the brethren. "By thy holy prayers, father, we are well," he was told. The hierarch was mounted on an ass and escorted to the monastery with so many lit torches that they nearly burned him. Abba Theodore walked before the archbishop on foot. The saint inspected the monasteries and gave his approbation of what he saw and heard.

Meanwhile, the governors of the province then took advantage of the emperor's command and committed more grievous outrages upon the Christians than their earthly sovereign had decreed. At times they exacted more money than they ought to have done, and upon others they inflicted corporal punishment. The emperor learned of these excesses, and instead of punishing the offenders, he entered into collusion with them. Indeed, the emperor was not blameless. When the victims appealed to their emperor against their persecutors, he tauntingly replied, "It is your duty to bear these afflictions patiently; for this is the command of your God." Surely Jesus warns of offenses, and says to Julian and those like him: "Woe to the world because of the stumbling blocks! For it must be that the stumbling blocks come, yet woe to that man by whom the stumbling block cometh [Mt. 18:7]!"

About midsummer Saint Athanasios was near Antinoupolis. Loyal couriers warned him that his enemies were on his trail. Abba Theodore brought his covered boat to escort the archbishop up to Tabenne. Traveling with the archbishop at that time was also the friend of Abba Theodore, Abba Pammon, who was an old man of a cheerful disposition. The vessel made its way slowly against contrary winds and tide. Though completely concealed, Saint Athanasios became apprehensive about the unfavorable conditions. Having continual recourse to prayer, he besought divine assistance. The monks with Theodore then got out and began towing the boat. Abba Pammon began to encourage the archbishop. But the seasoned fugitive had not given any thought to repining, and replied, "Believe me when I say that my heart is never so trustful in time of peace as in time of persecution. For I have good confidence that suffering for Christ and strengthened by His mercy, even though I am slain, yet I shall find mercy with Him." Saint Athanasios then observed that while he was saying this, Abba Theodore looked on Abba Pammon and smiled. The other one then barely restrained a chuckle. The saint asked, "Why dost thou laugh at my words? Dost thou censure me for cowardice?" Abba Theodore then said to Abba Pammon, "Tell the archbishop why we smiled." Abba Pammon said, "It is thee that ought to tell him." Abba Theodore then said to his archbishop, "In this very hour, Julian hath been slain in Persia, for so God hath declared beforehand concerning him. The haughty man, the despiser and boaster, shall finish nothing. But an illustrious Christian emperor shall arise. However, he shall live only a short while. Do not, therefore, trouble thyself by departing into the Thebaid. Secretly, go to the court, for thou wilt meet the new emperor along the way. Thou shalt be kindly received, and thou shalt return to thy Church. And he shall soon be taken by God." And thus it all came to pass. Julian was killed in Persia on the 26th day of June, in the year 363. While Saint Athanasios was sojourning in Upper Hermoupolis in the Thebaid, and as far as Antinoupolis, it was learned that the Emperor Julian had died.

Saint Gregory the Theologian writes of Julian: "Envy could not brook all this, or see the Church restored again to the same glory and health as in her former days. Therefore, it was, that the enemy (the devil) raised up the emperor against Athanasios. This Julian was a rebel like the enemy himself, and his peer in villainy—inferior to him only from lack of time. He had the infamous distinction of becoming the first of Christian emperors to rage against Christ. From the time he was proclaimed emperor, he showed himself to be a traitor to the Emperor Christ—Who had entrusted him with the empire—and a traitor to the God Who saved him. Julian devised the most inhuman of all persecutions. The honor achieved by the martyrs in their struggles only heightened his cruelty and envy. He called into question the reputation of the martyrs for their courage, by making verbal twists and quibbles a part of his character, or, to speak the real truth, buckling down on them with an eagerness born of his natural indisposition, and imitating in varied craft the evil one who dwelt within him. The subjugation of the whole race of Christians he thought a simple task; but found it a great one to overcome Athanasios and the power of his teaching over us. This crafty perverter and persecutor, clinging no longer to his cloak of illiberal sophistry, laid bare his wickedness and openly banished the bishop from the city. Brief was the interval before Justice pronounced sentence and handed over the offender to the Persians; thus sending him forth an ambitious monarch, but bringing him back a corpse for which no one felt pity."[40]

Emperor Jovian

After the death of Julian the Apostate, Jovian (363-364), a Christian, came to power. He was a soldier by profession, very tall in stature, and well known for his bravery. During the reign of Julian, he removed his officer's belt on account of the Faith of the Christ, and resumed the life of a civilian. When he was about to be garbed in the imperial robe, no garment of sufficient length was to be found in the entire imperial wardrobe, on account of his great height.

Saint Gregory the Theologian describes the new emperor and the beginning of his reign, as follows: "Another king arose—not shameless in countenance like the former, not an oppressor with cruel tasks and taskmasters—but most pious and gentle. In order to lay the best foundations for his empire, he inaugurated his reign, as is meet, by an act of justice: he recalled from exile all the bishops. And in the first place, he restored Athanasios, who stood first in virtue and had conspicuously championed the cause of piety. For Jovian made inquiries into the truth of our Faith which had been torn asunder, confused, and parceled out into various opinions and portions by many. He intended, if it were possible, reducing the whole world to harmony and union by the cooperation of the Spirit."[41]

The archbishop entered Alexandria secretly. He made haste to meet Jovian that Church affairs might be settled, since Jovian was on a march from Persia to Antioch and was passing through Alexandria briefly and privately. There was another reason for his haste: the Arians were rising up against him again. Evzious, bishop of the Arian heresy in Antioch, endeavored to install a eunuch named Provatios in Alexandria. Lucius, a citizen of Alexandria,

---

[40] Saint Gregory, *Oration XXI*, ¶ 32.
[41] Ibid., ¶ 33.

who had been ordained presbyter by the usurper George, undertook defaming the hierarch, by claiming he was accused of various crimes and had been banished by preceding emperors as the author of dissension in the Church concerning the divine Being. Lucius wanted Jovian to appoint another bishop, even himself, over the Church of Alexandria. Jovian, well aware of the conspiracies against Athanasios, cast a friendly eye upon the hierarch and gave no credence to the slander. He both threatened Lucius and commanded him to withdraw quietly. The emperor, deeming the eunuchs as troublemakers, also ordered Provatios and the other eunuchs to act more advisedly. Thenceforth Jovian exhibited the greatest friendship toward the man of God. He sent him back to Egypt with directions to govern the churches and the people as he deemed proper.

Thus Athanasios was recalled from hiding in the desert. Jovian had written him a letter. "To the most pious and friend of God, Athanasios: Admiring exceedingly the achievements of thy most honorable life, and of thy likeness to the God of all, and of thine affection toward our Savior Christ, we accept thee, most honored bishop. And inasmuch as thou hast not flinched from all labor, nor from the fear of thy persecutors, and, regarding dangers and threats of the sword as dung, holding the rudder of the Orthodox Faith which is dear to thee, are contending even until now for the truth, and continue to exhibit thyself as a pattern to all the people of the faithful, and an example of virtue, our imperial majesty recalleth thee, and desireth that thou shouldest return to the office of the teaching of salvation. Return then to the holy churches, and tend the people of God, and send up to God with zeal thy prayers for our forgiveness. For we know that by thy supplication we, and all who hold with us the Christian Faith, shall have great assistance from the supreme God."[42]

As a result, the saint was able to resume his throne in relative peace. However, this would only last for seven months. On his way to Constantinople, Emperor Jovian died in his sleep in Galatia. It is unknown whether this was an act of God or human treachery.

The Saint in Exile a Fifth Time (365)

In early 364 Jovian died, after reigning only eight months, and was succeeded by Valentinian I (364-375), an officer of Pannonian birth, who was elected emperor in the west by the army. He appointed his brother, Valens (364-378), as emperor in the east. Valens was steeped in the sottishness of Arian impiety. He agreed with the creeds promulgated at Seleukeia and Ariminum. He in turn was supported by two successive Bishops of Constanti-

---

[42] Saint Athanasios, "Epistle LVI" (Copy of a letter of the Emperor Jovian, sent to Athanasios, the most holy Archbishop of Alexandria), Nicene, Vol. IV.

nople, namely, the Arians Evdoxios (d. 370) and Demophilos (370-380). Valens strove to put these creeds into effect upon the bishops in his eastern realm. The Arian Bishop Evdoxios baptized Valens in 367. Saint Athanasios, speaking of the baptism of heretics, said in his *Discourses Against the Arians*, "There are many other heresies too, which use the words only, but not in a right sense, as I have said, nor with sound Faith, and in consequence the water which they administer is unprofitable, as deficient in piety, so that he who is sprinkled by them is rather polluted by the irreligious than redeemed."[43]

Those bishops who had been exiled by Constantius and recalled by Julian were to be expelled from their sees. Meletios, Archbishop of Antioch, was driven out. If the civil authorities did not follow the injunction, heavy fines were imposed on them, and also the threat of corporal punishment. The announcement was vehemently opposed by the people. The faithful contended that the order should not apply to Archbishop Athanasios, since he had been restored by Constantius, expelled by Julian as an anti-idolater, and reinstalled by Jovian's command. The majority of Christians in the city assembled and besought the governor not to eject Athanasios without further consideration of the terms of the imperial letter. The governor could not be persuaded. Riots ensued which lasted one month, and an insurrection was anticipated. The governor, however, restrained himself and did not use force against the populace. The prefect restored order only by announcing that the matter had been referred to the augustus. The issue was referred to the emperor, and the bishop was allowed to remain in the city. Some days afterward, when the excitement appeared to have diminished, the holy hierarch secretly departed the city at dusk.

The very same night, the governor of Egypt and the military chief seized possession of the Church of Dionysios, where Athanasios lived most of the time. They searched every part of the building and the apartments of the clergy—even the roof, but to no avail. The truth is that they had counted upon seizing Athanasios when popular feeling had subsided. When the city was asleep, they were to execute the emperor's mandate and to transport Athanasios quietly out of Alexandria. The saint dreaded the irrational impetuosity of the multitude. He feared lest he should be regarded as the author of the excesses which might be committed. Some attributed the archbishop's escape to divine revelation, others to the advice of his followers. The holy man fled that October night (365) and retired to the country.

The saint actually hid in the family sepulcher, where he remained four months, until the death of the Alexandrian governor, Tatianos, who was

---

[43] Ibid., *Discourse II*, Ch. XVIII(43).

seeking to slay him. The people's love for their archbishop was so impassioned that on account of their affection for him, they became seditious in impatience over his absence. In the meantime, the rest of the empire was experiencing civil unrest as a result of a revolt instigated by one named Prokopios.

There were also signs and portents, permitted by God, as a warning to the Arians. There were earthquakes. The sea also exceeded her bounds, flooding and covering many cities and countries. Places that were once bereft of water were covered, and those that were once covered with water were now dry. Lakes vanished. Cities in Crete completely disappeared. Peradventure by these signs the Arian emperor would quit his blaspheming? But instead of considering all that befell his realm, he only wished to enforce his own will.

However, fearing where the agitation might lead in an Alexandria already in turmoil, the emperor deemed it expeditious to allay the public anger. Wishing to avoid upheaval, he decided to repeal the edict of banishment against the archbishop. By his letters he issued an imperial order allowing Athanasios to preside unmolested over the churches. In February of 366, a notary publicly announced the recall of Archbishop Athanasios. The notaries then went out to the suburb personally and escorted the archbishop in state to the Church of Dionysios.

Thus, the Alexandrian Church was to partake of a few years of tranquility until the death of the saint. The Arians' faction took possession after his repose, but that is another history.

The Final Years

The last seven years of the holy man's life were spent in Alexandria. These years were relatively peaceful for his Church. As long as he lived, the Orthodox Church was secure from molestation in Alexandria and Egypt. Even the emperor, restrained by God's providence, abstained, for he also was cognizant that the multitude maintained a strong attachment to their archbishop. Therefore, he was unwilling to risk public displeasure and civil unrest due to his beliefs.

Athanasios' almost omnipresent activity, his rapid and mysterious movements, his fearlessness, and his clairvoyance were attributed by his friends to divine assistance, but by his enemies to demonic powers. Yet our holy father possessed prophetic foreknowledge through his perpetual intercourse with God. His flock in Alexandria and the monks of Egypt were attached to him through all the vicissitudes of his tumultuous life. They deemed him a venerable and pure person, superior in character and clear in his judgments. His zeal for the purity of the Orthodox Faith often placed him in the midst of theological controversies. His Church writings in the Greek tongue are in a magnificent, antique style, and yet they are most readable, natural, and direct. His language is mighty when expressing great thoughts. He pursued and drove out the arguments and sophisms in the secret hiding-places of the Church's enemies with his eloquent pen. It was his life-work to vindicate the deity of Christ. For this truth he spent the best years of his life and strength, often either suffering deposition or spending some twenty years as a refugee. He suffered persecution as a living martyr. He would not practise persecution. He believed Orthodoxy should persuade one to faith, not compel it.

However, in 367, Lucius, who was ordained by the Arians as their Bishop of Alexandria, tried to enter the city. He was especially covetous of the episcopate of Athanasios. He arrived secretly one September night, after a long absence from Alexandria. He sojourned in a small house, where he hid for one day. After he went to visit his mother in the city, the faithful learned of his appearance among them. The news spread quickly, and civil unrest was menacingly close at hand. The military commander and the prefect were displeased at his arrival. Officials were sent to escort him out of the city. The officials hesitated to remove Lucius from his house, fearing the angry multitude that had gathered outside. A report was made to the judges. It was necessary for the prefect and the military commander to remove Lucius themselves. Lucius obediently and cautiously followed after the judges, and all the people after them. Both Christians and pagans were in the crowd. They shouted, and hurled charges and accusations at Lucius. The people cried out, "Let him be taken out of the city." Nevertheless, the military commander took him to his own home, where he stayed for one day and night. Early in the morning he was sent as far as Nikopolis, where soldiers escorted him out of Egypt.

On the 22nd day of September, in the year 368, Saint Athanasios began to build a church in the quarter known as Mendidium. It was dedicated on the 7th day of August, in the year 370.

Information about the last years of his life is scanty. There was a case involving the young officer Siderios. He was appointed as a bishop by only one bishop, Philo, without the canonical number required for a consecration. This of course was also done without the knowledge of Athanasios. Evidently Philo felt pressed when two large villages of the diocese were clamoring for a bishop when their own Bishop Orion was becoming senile. In view of the utility of the appointment, Athanasios overlooked the irregularity. Later he even promoted Siderios as Metropolitan of Ptolemais, merging the two villages upon Orion's death once more into their proper diocese.

There was also the matter of Saint Basil corresponding with Saint Athanasios over the matter of the schism at Antioch. Saint Basil respectfully requested Saint Athanasios' mediation. He wished for Saint Athanasios to compose a letter addressed to the bishops in communion with Meletios, that he might use his influence with Paulinus and prevail upon him to withdraw. Nothing came of the application. However, Saint Basil obtained the good offices of Athanasios in his attempt to induce the bishops of Rome and the west to give him some support in his efforts against heresy in the east. The westerners, however, showed themselves arrogant and self-serving. Thus, they failed with Saint Basil.

Saint Basil was also put out by the continued refusal of Saint Athanasios and the western bishops to repudiate Markellos of Ankyra. Saint Athanasios wished to be indulgent toward Markellos after he and his followers submitted a statement of the Faith, emphatically adhering to the Nicene Creed and condemning Sabellios. Saint Athanasios accepted his confession. Saint Basil regretted Saint Athanasios' generosity. Nonetheless, both Athanasios and Basil, though they never personally met, held each other in veneration and high esteem.

Saint Athanasios had a commanding personality which rose to decisive, epoch-making influence. He was scarcely more than twenty-seven at the Synod of Nicaea. His election as bishop was accomplished when he was barely of canonical age. His rapid rise in Egypt and Libya, the enthusiastic loyalty of his clergy and monastics, and his great popularity among the lay people, even the pagans (except the more abandoned among them), were prodigious. He would not compromise with Arius or Arianism, and he wrote to the bishops of Egypt, "We are contending for our all"; while with wayward friends he restrained himself and was even lenient. The glory and welfare of the Church was his major concern. The emperors recognized him as a true political force of the first order. He was brave, self-sacrificing, humble, steady in his resolve, versatile, resourceful, and sympathetic. He often treated subordinates as equals, asking Serapion and the monks to correct or alter anything incorrect in his writings. He was not a systematic theologian, nor a speculative one. He did not play the schoolmaster or philosopher. His brilliance lay in his tight grip on soteriological principles. His solid character, strength of mind, and firmness of purpose rendered him fit for such holy service.

To the last, the man of God Athanasios was active. His eye was not dim, nor his natural force abated. When he perceived in the Spirit that the end of his earthly sojourn was drawing near, he followed his predecessor's example and named the devout and eloquent Peter as the most able to become his successor. He reposed in a wonderful manner on the 2nd day of May, in the year 373. His life and habits represented the idea of what ought to constitute a true bishop. As for his teaching the law of Orthodoxy, what reward does he not win for his piety? At a good old age he closed his life and was gathered to his fathers, the patriarchs, and prophets, and apostles, and martyrs who contended for the truth.

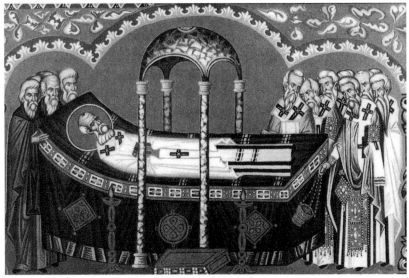

The Repose of Saint Athanasios

Saint Athanasios presided over the flock as a bishop for forty-six years. His fame extended through the east and west. Seventeen of those years he sojourned in exile. In summary, the first exile was from 335 to 337, a result of the Council of Tyre; the second exile was from 339 to 346; the third exile was from 356 to 362; and the fourth and fifth exiles were from 362 to 366, during the time of Julian and his successors. His sojourn in Rome and Treveri, and his knowledge of the Latin tongue, endeared him to the west. He was held in high esteem in the Western Church during the fourth century, and even helped transplant monasticism to the west. Embodying the dignity of patriarchs, and splendidly adorned with action and vision, he departed this life during the second consulate of Gratian and Probus after having piloted the Alexandrian Church through some of the roughest waters of its history.

Slowly the Nicene Faith gained ground despite the interference of politics in theology. At length it prevailed first in the Latin Church, which held several Orthodox synods in Rome, Milan, and Gaul. Synods were then held in Egypt and the east, through the labors of Saint Athanasios, who was inflamed with love for the Trinity and emerged as victor. Later in the fourth century, Nicene Orthodoxy was supported by the three great Cappadocian Fathers: Saints Basil the Great, Gregory the Theologian, and Gregory of Nyssa.

On the 18th of January, the holy Church commemorates the holy Martyr THEODOULE of Anazarbos.

Theodoule, the holy martyr, was from Anazarbos,[44] a city of Cilicia.[45] She lived during the reigns of Emperors Diocletian (284-305) and Maximian (286-305).[46] The emperors sent Pelagios to assume the governorship of Anazarbos, with orders to punish the Christians. At that time, Theodoule was apprehended for being a Christian and made to stand before the judgment seat of Pelagios. Before all, the holy woman professed Christ as true God. As punishment for her confession of the Faith, she was suspended by the hairs of her head from cypress wood. Then they wounded her breasts with burning skewers. The governor observed that the martyr did not even regard such torments; but rather, she derided him and the idol of the Roman Emperor Hadrian (117-138). By her prayers, she demolished the idol and then restored it at the governor's request; for he had promised to become a Christian if she returned the idol to its former place. Instead, however, that wretched and thrice-accursed man became indignant. Confounded by what he had seen, he did not know what to do. At this point, the court clerk (Lat., *comment-ariénsis*), Elladios, who was in attendance, addressed Pelagios, saying, "Grant me the authority to deal with her. If I do not prevail upon her to sacrifice to the idol of Hadrian, then strike off my head!" Straightway, Pelagios remanded the prisoner to Elladios to do with her as he willed.

Elladios made five nails, two of which were driven into the saint's ears. One nail was embedded in her forehead, and two others were thrust into her breasts. When she had been thus pierced in five places, Theodoule raised the eyes of her mind and fixed them upon heaven. She entreated God to grant her patience to withstand this hideous torture. Not much time passed before God meted out the favor, and the saint was vouchsafed the patience she sought. The court clerk, in the meantime, beheld her long-suffering fortitude and stout-heartedness in the midst of such sufferings, which seemed as nought

---

[44] Anazarbos (Anazarbus, now Anavarza) was later named Diocaesarea and Caesaravgousta; now it is called Ak Isar or Ak Serai by the Turks. It is a city in the eastern plain of Cilicia on a tributary of the Pyramos. It was the civil and ecclesiastical metropolis of Cilicia II.

[45] Cilicia in ancient geography was the maritime country between Pamphylia on the west and Syria on the east, lying south of the Taurus Mountain range along the extreme northeastern boundary of the Mediterranean Sea. The capital of Cilicia was Tarsus, the birthplace of the Apostle Paul [Acts 21:39; 22:3]. In present-day Turkey, the entire district is known as Lesser Armenia.

[46] Diocletian and Maximian were joint emperors (augusti). Maximian was adopted by Diocletian as his colleague in 286. Both abdicated in 305, in favor of Galerius and Constantius I, respectively. Later, in 306, Maximian reassumed power.

to her. He then began to reason that should he fail to induce her to renounce Christ, his own life would be in danger by reason of the pledge he gave. Elladios then summoned the saint to appear in his home. He besought her to sacrifice with him before the idols. Theodoule, perceiving the terror he suffered from his vow, made a prayer on his behalf to God. She then taught Elladios divine matters and persuaded him to become a Christian.

Saint Theodoule

A now calm court clerk, together with the holy woman, presented himself before Pelagios. Elladios then announced, "I was unable to persuade the handmaiden of the true God to turn aside from the good and straight path which she now treads. Instead, she converted me and delivered me from the darkness of ignorance wherein I was found. She enlightened the noetic eyes of my soul through her divinely-spoken words and brought me to my Lord Jesus Christ, the true God." These words only kindled the anger of Pelagios. The governor then ordered that the court clerk's head be severed and his body discarded into the sea. Hence, the blessed Elladios completed his martyrdom and ascended, crowned, into the heavens. Pelagios then commanded that Theodoule be flung into a fiery furnace. As she prayed and glorified God in the midst of the flames, He preserved her intact.

The governor, bewildered, shouted aloud, "What shall I do with this woman who defies death?" One of the bystanders, named Voëthos, declared, "Give her to me, O governor, that I might coerce her; because I am not foolish and ignorant as was the court clerk." The governor then remanded her to Voëthos, who brought the saint to his house. She also instructed him in the Faith and brought him to piety, as had happened with the court clerk. That same day, Voëthos went before the governor with the saint, and said, "I came, O governor, to reveal to thee a matter concerning me. Know this: I also confess Christ as true God. The hopes I harbored in my promises seem vain and empty to me. It is far preferable that I should appear untrue to my previous pledge, so I might have a portion with Christ, rather than fulfill my vow to thee and inherit the Gehenna of the fire! O governor, much more shouldest thou believe, as thou didst formerly promise, and offer thanks to the true God Who has delivered thee from death. However, not only hast thou not performed thy word, but thou dost show thyself an ingrate before thy benefactress Theodoule, whom thou hast delivered up to horrible torments!"

When Voëthos had finished, Pelagios ordered the decapitation of that honorable head. Turning to Saint Theodoule, Pelagios then charged that she be stretched upon a burning rack. Beneath the red-hot rack, they sprinkled pitch, oil, and wax to intensify the heat. In the meantime, Voëthos finished his course of martyrdom and was translated unto the Lord. Theodoule, praying, ascended atop the rack. As soon as the rack received her, it was reduced to powder and scattered, burning most of the spectators. The saint was then cast into prison. The following day, a large furnace was lit. Together with Saint Theodoule, other confessors of the Faith were hurled into the flames. Their names included those of the holy Evagrios, Makarios, and many other holy confessors. Immersed in prayer, the holy woman stretched forth her hands and, thanking God, surrendered her soul. Their resolve and love for Jesus abiding inextinguishable, Theodoule and her companions persevered to the end of their blessed martyrdom and received imperishable crowns from the Lord.

Saints Evagrios, Theodoule, and Makarios

On the 18th of January, the holy Church commemorates the holy Martyrs and companions of Saint Theodoule: **EVAGRIOS and MAKARIOS**, who were cast into a fiery furnace; and **ELLADIOS and VOËTHOS,**[47] **who were slain by the sword.**

On the 18th of January, the holy Church commemorates the holy Martyr XENE, who was burned to death.

On the 18th of January, the holy Church commemorates our venerable Father MARKIANOS of Cyprus.

Through the intercessions of Thy Saints,
O Christ God, have mercy on us. Amen.

---

[47] Within the account given in some ancient *Synaxaria* and *Menaia*, the court clerk is anonymous and Elladios is his assistant (Gk., *voëthos*). In the version given in *The Great Synaxaristes* (in Greek), Voëthos is presumed to be the assistant's first name.

On the 19th January, the holy Church commemorates
our venerable Father MAKARIOS the Great,
Anchorite of Egypt.[1]

Makarios the Great, who was from the Thebaid of Egypt, has a contemporary of the same name who was known as Makarios the citizen of Alexandria. Both holy fathers are commemorated by the holy Church today. They were close friends and disciples of Saint Anthony the Great. The biography of Makarios the citizen, who was priest in a monastery in the desert of Kellia (Cellia) which adjoined Sketis (Wadi-el-Natrun), shall follow the present account of Makarios the Great.

Makarios of Egypt was born about the year 301. Since he loved virtue from an early age, when a firm foundation in piety was laid, he conducted his entire life in a manner blameless and irreproachable. When he reached twenty years of age, though according to other accounts he was thirty years old, he withdrew from the world. The ever-memorable one demonstrated such endurance and patience in ascetic toils and hardships that in a few years he was vouchsafed to receive the gift of discernment. He also attained authority and power over demons, foretold the future, and wrought miracles. When still a young man, he was called "the boy elder" or "the youth elder." It is said by some that he was a disciple of Anthony the Great. After many supplica-

---

[1] The Life of Saint Makarios of Egypt was recorded in Greek by Saint Symeon the Metaphrastes. The text was rendered in simpler Greek by Agapios the Cretan, who published it in the *Eklogion*. This same saint was known as "the Great." He attained to the measure of his abba, the great Anthony, assimilated his teachings, and recorded his own meditations in his work, entitled *Fifty Spiritual Homilies*. His writings speak chiefly of divinization and communion with God. Together with his *Homilies*, there are seven *Ascetic Treatises*.

Saint Makarios the Great also penned several prayers which have entered into Orthodox Church usage: From the "Prayers Before Sleep," the first prayer, "O eternal God"; and, the fourth, "What shall I offer Thee." And, from the "Morning Prayers," the first prayer, "O Lord, cleanse me"; the second, "Having risen from sleep"; the third, "To Thee, O Lord"; the fourth, "O Lord, Who in Thine abundant goodness"; and, according to Greek manuscripts, the ninth also, "O holy angel." His works have been translated into English. See *Fifty Spiritual Homilies: Macarius the Great*, translated by A. J. Mason, Willits, CA: Eastern Orthodox Books, 1974; and, *The Fifty Spiritual Homilies and the Great Letter*, translated by George A. Maloney, NY/NJ: Paulist Press, 1992.

A service to Saint Makarios of Egypt was composed by Father Gerasimos Mikrayiannanites. Father Gerasimos also composed one service to all four famous fathers having the same name: Makarios of Egypt, Makarios of Alexandria, Makarios of Rome, and Makarios of Corinth.

tions by the bishop, who could not bear to see the lamp hidden under the bushel, he received the rank of the priesthood. He was then forty years of age.

Saint Makarios the Great

Our venerable father had two disciples. One of them abided with the elder in order to take in the sick for safekeeping, whom he brought daily before Makarios that he might treat and heal them. The other disciple sojourned in another cell found far distant. Now the righteous one observed that his subordinate, who was in obedience to him, received silver from the infirm. He forewarned his disciple that if he should choose not to correct himself, he would be the recipient of wrath and chastisement from the Lord. Indeed, this disclosure of the future became reality, since that same brother did not amend his ways, and was rendered a leper.

At one time they were trying to bring to the holy man a certain youth who was possessed by a legion of demons. At times he could not be satiated, but at other times he discharged his food as though a fire were in his belly. Then again, at other times his stomach emitted a foul stench. Sometimes, if he had no bread to eat, the wretched man ate his own dung. The mother of this youth came and fell before the feet of the venerable elder. With ardent tears she entreated Makarios to cure her son, knowing him to be a sympathetic elder. Thereupon, the saint offered up prayer for seven days. At the end of this time he gave the youth back to his mother healed and possessed of a sound mind. The youth thereafter partook only of thirty-six ounces of bread daily.

At one time there was a man who was slain secretly. When the body was found and the murderer unknown, an innocent man was pronounced guilty. Knowing that they intended to deliver him up to the authorities in order to punish him, the innocent man fled arrest and took refuge at the cell of our holy Father Makarios. The soldiers, hastening, pursued him there, and placed him in bonds. The innocent man let out loud cries and shouts, swearing his innocence. The saint pitied him and went to the grave of the murder victim, accompanied by all the people present. Makarios fell to his knees, so as to pray, saying to the bystanders, "The Lord now doth wish to make manifest to you if this man is guilty." With faith, the saint cried out to the dead man, saying, "I adjure thee by the Master Christ, to tell us the truth, whether this man who stands accused murdered thee?" The dead man—O the wonder!—as though he were only asleep, was roused and answered him, "No, honorable father, this one is not at fault, but another murdered me." After the bystanders heard this declaration, they feared and trembled. They therefore besought the saint to question him again and ask who had slain him. The all-wise elder said to them, "It is enough that I established this man as innocent and that you desist from punishing him. But I am not a judge to punish the transgressor."

Palladius narrates the following account of righteous Makarios the Egyptian. A certain intemperate man sought to draw a prudent maiden into a satanic love. Unable to attract her, he resorted to diabolical magic that she might appear as a mare to the people. Her parents went and took refuge in Makarios, saying, "This mare that we have led forth to thy holiness was our daughter. And by the sorceries of a certain man she was transformed into this shape. Therefore, we beseech thee to entreat the Lord, so as to return her to her former state." The saint answered, "As for me, I behold a woman and not a mare, as you declare. This transformation is not to her body, but only to your eyes. It is a delusion of the devil." After he had said this, they took the maiden into his cell, where he made a prayer and anointed her with holy oil. Henceforth she again appeared to all who beheld her as a woman by nature, since through the entreaty of Makarios the apparition vanished.

At a later time they brought another maiden who had a dread illness which caused her flesh to putrefy and emit an incomparably foul stench. Makarios spoke to her, saying, "Keep on having patience, daughter; God has allowed this illness for the benefit of thy soul." The holy man then offered up prayers for her sake during the next seven days. At the same time, he anointed her with holy oil. He cured her completely, and all were amazed.

One day, Makarios in the company of Abba Sisoes and five other monks went to harvest in the cool of the morning dew. Now a certain woman followed them and collected the ears of grain which remained, but all the while she was weeping and sighing bitterly. The venerable elder questioned the master of the field, "What has taken hold of this woman and afflicted her so?" He replied that she was a widow whose late husband, when he was living, was entrusted with a valuable deposit by a certain man. Thereafter, her husband suddenly reposed, never speaking of the matter to her. Thereupon, the owner had the woman summoned to court. Since she was poor, he sought to hold in servitude both the woman and her children. Makarios was moved to sympathy at the suffering widow's plight. He repaired to the grave of her husband, where he inquired of the dead man, "Where hast thou concealed the deposit?" O Thy wonders, Christ King! He answered that he hid it by burying it beneath the foot of his bed. The saint related this to the woman, who in turn found the deposit. She handed it over to the rightful owner and was thereafter left untroubled.

The venerable man was so patient and persevering in fasting and continence that for twenty years he never satiated himself with bread or water or sleep; but daily, he ate according to a set weight in ounces, together with three cups of water. While leaning against a wall, he slept a little lest he should injure his mind from much vigil and excessive hardship. Whenever the brethren came to see him, he sat down with them at table, eating and drinking, in order to flee pretentiousness. But when his guests departed, depending on how many cups of water or wine he partook of, he would then deprive himself of water for such a number of days. He did this so he might bring his flesh under subjection. This observance alone, with regard to his body, bears witness of the extreme continence he practised.

On a certain day the holy Makarios went to visit Saint Anthony the Great. He knocked at the door, and Anthony from within asked who it was and what he sought. Makarios answered, "It is thy countryman Makarios, and I came to speak with thee." The great Anthony, wishing to prove Makarios' patience, secured the door further. Despite this seeming discourtesy, Makarios was not offended, but stood patiently and meekly outside for a long time. Thereupon, Anthony, perceiving Makarios' marvellous patience, opened the door and received him rejoicing, saying, "It is a long while that I have heard of thy good fame. I had a great desire to behold thee. Glory be to the Lord Who fulfilled my desire!" After they greeted and embraced one another in the Lord, Anthony laid a table, and they became fast friends. After he had said the prayer of thanksgiving, Anthony took up his handiwork of weaving palms, lest he should sit idle as he conversed to the benefit of the soul. Now Makarios requested that he himself might perform a little handiwork. After the great Anthony observed how he wove most beautifully in a row, he kissed Makarios' hands, saying, "These blessed hands are full of much kindness and virtue."

After these events, Makarios returned again to his cell and gave himself to contemplation, so that his mind and soul were most of the time in the heavens rather than on the earth. Therefore, in order to attain greater attention toward God, he opened underneath his cell a subterranean chamber. He then dug out for a distance of one-half a stadium or about three hundred and three English feet. The passageway, as a spiral shell, had turns hither and thither; but, at the end, he dug out a cave with his own hands. When many people came and troubled him, he passed over secretly by means of the underground stoa and concealed himself inside the cave. Then, no one was able to find him.

At another time, during a certain feast day, he repaired to the Mount of Nitria, where he went to the monastery of Abba Pambo, who is commemorated by the holy Church on the 18th of July. The monks there besought him to teach them with a view to spiritual benefit. As one humble-minded, Makarios answered, saying, "I am not yet a monk; however, I saw some monks, and on account of them I shall speak to you of a few things toward edification." He began to say the following:

"Once, while sitting in my cell, a thought gave me warfare, which said, 'Arise and get thee to the desert.' And I, fearing that perhaps this was a demonic suggestion, in order to confound and agitate my silence, warred against this thought for five years. After I perceived that my thought remained steadfast, I came to the knowledge that it was from God. I hearkened and obeyed, walking about a long way into the desert. I found a lake at which wild beasts and other creatures came and drank water. In the midst of the creatures, I observed two hirsute men. I felt frightened and fainthearted, presuming that they were demons. Beholding my terror, they spoke to me, saying, 'Cease fearing, for we are men also.' Consequently, I was filled with fresh courage and drew closer to them. I inquired of them where they were from and how they managed to support themselves. 'We, O brother, persevered in one monastery. And after we received forgiveness and consent from the hegumen and the other brethren, we took our leave. We came to this desert, where we have already sojourned in silence for some forty years. One of us is from Libya, and the other from Egypt. The Lord has graciously bestowed upon us the gift that we should feel neither the burning summer heat nor the winter cold.'" Saint Makarios then broke off his account, and said to the monks of Abba Pambo's monastery, "For this cause, brothers, I told you that I am not yet a monk."

At another time again, while the righteous one was on the road coming from Sketis, night overtook him. He therefore entered one of the sepulchers of the idolaters that he might sleep for the night. He took up the skull of one of the deceased and used it as a cushion for his head. Now the demons bore Makarios much malice, because he did not frighten when they attempted to make him act cowardly. At that time, Makarios was hearing one of them saying to some woman who was laid in the tomb, "Bestir thyself, O woman, let us be off to the bath that we may work." And another demon answered from the skull used as Makarios' pillow, saying, "One foreign abba has me as a cushion, and I am not able to go forth." Despite all this chatter,

Saint Makarios and the Skull

the holy man did not fear, but was saying, "If thou art able to rise up, go thy way." Put to shame, the demons then fled and said, "Thou hast prevailed over us, O Makarios!"

Once, a certain heretic went to the saint and contended that there was no resurrection of the dead. Therefore, the great Makarios raised a dead man in order to persuade and fully assure the heretic. The resurrected man was a pagan Greek who came to believe in Christ and was baptized. He then became a monk, taking the name of Miles.

At another time, the venerable elder was saying that there are two orders of demons. The one order wages wars against humans in diverse ways, by means of the passions of anger and desire. The other order, which is named "the ruling order," contends against the people and casts them into various heresies, blasphemies, and errors. Satan, the leader of this order of demons, sends his minions to sorcerers and to heresiarchs.

One time the saint saw the devil having his contrivances and tools inside a casket used for unguents. Makarios observed that he was sitting down quietly, having taken the form of a man dressed in linen. His garment revealed many holes, and from each opening there was hanging one small gourd. The holy man asked him whither he would go and what was he holding in the vessels. The devil gave answer, "I am going to the monastics who hold out in the lower gorge. I am bearing different drinks, in order that each of them may drink for whatever he yearns." After he disclosed these things, the demon vanished. The elder remained in that place, offering up prayer that he might see the outcome. When the demon returned, Makarios asked him what he wrought at the monastery. He replied that he prevailed only over one monk, but the rest fought courageously. The saint said, "I adjure thee by the Master Christ, that thou tellest me the name of the monk whom thou didst overtake." The demon said, "He is named Theopemptos."

After hearing this, the saint went to the aforementioned monastery. All the brethren received Abba Makarios with reverence. The holy man then inquired, "In which cell might I find Theopemptos?" After he learned where

Theopemptos was located, he went to him. He questioned him regarding spiritual things and how he was faring in the spiritual life. Keeping his reply short and restricted, Theopemptos answered, "Well, with the power of God, father." The most wise Makarios, perceiving he was ashamed to confess his sin, as a practical and effective physician, in a skilled manner, said, "I, the wretched one, though I have so many years in the desert and though I have acquired such a celebrated name, yet again am unable to flee shameful and sordid thoughts. If the Lord did not help me, I should be in danger of being conquered." Upon hearing these frank words, Theopemptos took courage and confessed the truth, saying, "I also, honorable father, am suffering in like manner, and am in danger of death!" Then the spiritual physician explained what Theopemptos should practise and how much he should fast. He expounded on how to pray in order to prevail against the one who tempts him. After he had corrected him as was meet, he returned to his own cell. A certain number of days later, Makarios saw the same demon, as he was returning from the monastery with the gourds. Makarios inquired how he passed his time with the monks. "Badly and with reverses," said he, "inasmuch as all fought against me, and more so did Theopemptos resist, he whom I had for my friend! I do not know what happened and how he became the harshest toward me!" Thus, the great knowledge and virtue of Makarios delivered Theopemptos out of danger.

Saint Makarios of Egypt

Once the saint was returning from out of Egypt. He went to his cell and found thieves who were taking whatever Makarios possessed. Now just as he arrived, they were loading the donkey. Makarios feigned that they were not his own things. Thereupon, he not only did not speak badly to them, but he even helped them to load his belongings. He then uttered, "Naked came I out of my mother's womb, and naked shall I return thither: the Lord gave,

and the Lord hath taken away; blessed be the name of the Lord [Job 1:21]."
Saying these things, he was able to abide undistressed at the deprivation of his
possessions.

Not only did Makarios endure this loss of his few possessions with
long-suffering, but even earlier in his life, as a young man in the coenobium,
he endured a terrible slander. Hearken to this account, though the charge was
false. Now Makarios neither pleaded any excuse nor shuffled about when the
accusation was laid at his door. But for the sake of the love of God he
remained silent. Later, when the truth came to be known, he was marvelled
at even more. This incident took place thus, even as Makarios himself
narrated with these very words: "When I was a beginner in the monastery,
they were intending to ordain me as a deacon, though I had no wish for this.
Now I adjudged myself unworthy, so I fled from the lavra to a hidden place,
where a layman attended to me. He would take my handiwork, plaited
hand-baskets; and, in exchange for these wares, he brought me food. There
happened to be in those parts a maiden who fell into sin with a certain man.
Consequently, that foolhardy girl came to be with child. Her parents
questioned her about the matter, and the devil advised her to say that I
ravaged her. Her parents, filled with wrath, hastened to me and seized me as
wild beasts. They hung clay vessels all over my body in order to show their
scorn and contempt. They struck me mercilessly, making me a spectacle and
putting me to shame. They kept on shouting aloud throughout those parts,
'This monk overpowered our daughter.' Even the layman who attended me
they subjected to insult, saying, 'Behold what has been accomplished by the
virtuous monk whom thou didst laud so highly! Indeed, all thy words to us
falsely represented him as a holy man. But know this: we shall not leave him
until he should remit all the expenses and the future support of the child that
she shall bear, because he corrupted her virginity!'

"Then I made a gesture, motioning the layman that he might become
my guarantor without drawing back. He accepted and took me, half-dead
though I was, from their hands. Arriving at my cell, I recovered somewhat
and set about weaving, saying, 'Work, lowly Makarios, that thou mightest
feed the woman and thyself.' Thus, I toiled night and day. I gave my straw
baskets to that layman that I might feed that pitiful woman. When the time of
her giving birth arrived, she remained in painful labor for many days. But the
unfortunate one was unable to deliver the infant. By means of those birth
pangs, which put her life and soul in peril, she acknowledged her sin. She
confessed to those present the truth and said, 'I suffer now justifiably; for I,
the unjust one, slandered that virtuous man, the monk, saying that he forced
himself upon me. Know in truth that I sinned with that other man, my
neighbor.' Having spoken thus, the woman was finally delivered of her

womb's burden, suffering no complications. Those present came running to me. They shed tears and begged my forgiveness. Henceforth, they greatly revered me. Then I, in order to escape the praise of men, fled from that place and came to this desert."

Makarios the Great was once asked which way is the easiest to be saved. he replied, "Whosoever leaves the world and goes to a quiet place and cries over his sins finds his salvation."

Once, as Saint Makarios was returning to his cell from another place, he met the devil coming toward him with vehemence, carrying a sickle and making gestures to cut and slay him. But that weak creature was incapable of doing anything to the holy man. Explaining his action, the devil said, "I suffer greatly due to thee, Makarios. I never manage to defeat thee, even if I exceed thee in certain excellences. Though thou dost fast on certain days, yet I never eat. Though thou keepest vigil, yet I never sleep. Nevertheless, there is one virtue in which thou dost excel me, on account of which I exercise no power over thee." The saint asked, "What might that be?" Hurriedly, the devil replied, "Humility." Then that foul creature vanished.

Saint Makarios the Great

A virtuous Egyptian man had a paralyzed son who could in no wise move his limbs. He lay abed as still as a rock. The father took his ailing son and quietly deposited him outside the cell door of Saint Makarios. He then departed in silence. When the abba emerged from his cell and beheld the young man, he queried, "Who has brought thee here?" The young man answered, "My father has lain me here and left." The saint then said to him, "Rise up and overtake him!" Immediately—lo the miracle!—the formerly motionless one arose, venerated the physician, and returned to his home rejoicing.

It is said that the heavenly Makarios spent more time during his early sojourn contemplating noetic union with God than giving thought to the things of this world which is under the heavens.

With such wondrous and God-pleasing labors did the great Makarios, whose name means "blessed," shine forth. Saint Makarios went forth to the Lord in the year 391 at the age of ninety, though some claim he was sixty years of age. He has left for us his wise *Fifty Homilies*, which some maintain that the great Anthony authored in the Syriac, but which the venerable Makarios translated into the Greek tongue.

On the 19th of January, the holy Church commemorates our holy Father MAKARIOS of Alexandria, known as the citizen.[2]

Makarios, our venerable father of Alexandria, was also surnamed "politikos" or "citizen." He had been a shopkeeper in Alexandria, providing cakes and dried fruit to the public. At the age of forty, he received holy Baptism. He thereafter renounced the world and retired from city life to the desert of the Cells (Cellia, Kellia)[3] between Nitria and Sketis.[4] He became a good friend of the venerable Makarios the Egyptian. Together, they were disciples of Saint Anthony the Great. With the other fathers of the desert, he suffered persecution at the hands of the Arians.

Makarios the Alexandrian attained to the height of self-mastery, continence, and patience. Since he had spent most of his life in the city as a civilian and was very familiar with a citizen's everyday life in the community, he was made a priest for the brethren of the Cells. His broad background and general knowledge in dealing with all kinds of people was perceived as useful for the correction and exhortation of the brethren. As for himself, whensoever he heard of any beautiful deed or extraordinary act of asceticism, he would

---

[2] In 390 or 391, when Palladius went to Cellia, where he sojourned for nine years, he met with Abba Makarios the Alexandrian, and wrote of him in *The Lausiac History*, § 18. A service to Saint Makarios of Alexandria was composed by Father Gerasimos Mikrayiannanites.

[3] The Cells had become a settlement of some six hundred anchorites. Their cells were out of earshot of one another. As they were scattered over a wide area, some of the residents had to travel as much as three miles to church. They had their own priest and church. They were dependent on Nitria for bread. See D. J. Chitty, *The Desert a City*, p. 29.

[4] The Wadi-el-Natrun is the Desert of Sketis. Nitria, as Palladius tells us, is some forty miles away, and was approachable in his day by boat from Alexandria. The term "Sketis" is sometimes used to cover Nitria as well, but the term "Nitria" is never used to cover "Sketis." The natural approach to Sketis is not from Nitria, but from the nearest point on the Canopic branch of the Nile at Terenuthis, some twenty miles away. Ibid., p. 12.

quickly put it into his own practise, but in a fuller form, and surpassed it to perfection.

Saints Makarios of Egypt
and Makarios of Alexandria

Father Makarios of Alexandria was also vouchsafed by God the gift of working miracles. On one occasion, as he was going to see the great Anthony, he observed that the great father was bearing beautiful palms in his arms. Makarios asked the elder to give him some fronds. But the holy abba answered, "It is written in the divine Scripture that 'thou shalt not covet anything that is thy neighbor's [Deut. 5:21].'" As soon as Abba Anthony spoke those words, all of the palms which he was carrying were consumed as if they had caught fire. Though the great Anthony suffered no harm, yet this phenomenon brought him to prophesy to Father Makarios: "Behold, the Holy Spirit shall rest upon thee, and thou shalt become an heir of my struggles."

Afterward, as Father Makarios was walking through the desert, he encountered the devil. That foul creature observed that Makarios was extremely tired and took the opportunity to comment to him: "Behold, thou hast received the grace of Anthony. Why dost thou not make use of this dignity and boldly ask from God that He send thee food and drink that thou mightest have strength for thy journey on foot?" The holy Makarios replied, "For me, power and glory are of the Lord. As for thyself, thou hast no authority to trouble the slaves of God." The vile devil brought about an apparition of a camel heavily laden with provisions. The animal seemed to have lost its way in the wilderness and was shown wandering about before the saint. As soon as the creature gazed upon the venerable man, it went and knelt before him. Makarios perceived this to be a demonic illusion. The saint straightway offered up prayer, and the camel instantly was swallowed up into the earth.

An occasion arose when both holy fathers, Makarios the Egyptian and Makarios the Alexandrian, were traveling together down the river Nile. Among those on board were some distinguished imperial officers. One of them commented to the fathers, "Blessed are you, who have disdained the world." The venerable Makarios of Alexandria answered him, saying, "We on the one hand have disdained the world; but on the other hand, the world has defrauded thee. But I see also that thou hast called us 'blessed.' Without being consciously aware of it, thou hast spoken by prophetic inspiration. I say this because we are both named Makarios, which means 'blessed.'" That man was brought to profound compunction by what he heard, to such a degree that he too came to scorn the splendid things of this life. He thereupon renounced his position, gave away all his belongings to the poor, and became a monk.

On another occasion, Abba Makarios received some fresh grapes, the beauty of which could spur anyone's appetite. Now the sober Makarios was mindful that one of the brethren was ill. He thought to deny himself and send the tasty fruit to him whose health could benefit therefrom. When the ailing brother received the grapes, he did not wish to lay aside his continence, though the sight of those beautiful grapes opened his appetite and made his mouth water. Nevertheless, he decided to make them a gift to another brother who was confined to his bed. That brother was most desirous to have the grapes and was filled with delight when he received them. But before he stretched forth his hand to pluck one, he thought it better to send them to another, saying, "Perhaps that other brother shall appreciate them"; and so he sent them off. When the next brother received the present, though he himself was bereft of any kind of fruit, he too passed them on to another brother. Now these grapes passed through the hands of many monks, but no one sampled even one grape. Then after making the rounds in the brotherhood, the grapes, by God's providence, were finally offered to the holy Makarios. When he received the grapes, he certainly recognized them to be the same grapes that he had earlier dispatched. When he observed that every grape was still in its place on the cluster, he gave glory to God for the self-control that prevailed among the brethren, and, of course, the love that was shown among them—inasmuch as each one preferred to please his neighbor before himself. For these reasons, neither did he taste of the fruits, that the wound to the demon might be complete.

Now the ascetical practises of the saint were considerable. As we mentioned earlier, whenever he heard that anyone accomplished some great feat, he was filled with a good zeal in his soul to imitate the deed. Now he had heard that the monastics found at Tabenna, known as the Tabennesiotes, never partook of any food that had been cooked by fire during the entire Great Fast. Abba Makarios wished to follow their example. He therefore did not partake of any food cooked by fire. This form of abstinence did not last forty days but for seven years, during which time his diet consisted only of wild herbs, raw vegetables, and soaked legumes.

On yet another occasion, the venerable Makarios learned that another monk was subsisting on one litra or twelve ounces of bread. Father Makarios straightway decided to take up this practise, but consumed only four to five ounces daily. In like manner, his consumption of water was very little, commensurate with the few pieces of bread he was eating. In order to vanquish the desire to eat more, he devised a way to curtail his intake. He broke his bread into small morsels and dropped them into a vessel with a narrow mouth, which allowed him little. He was resolved that he should eat nothing that his hand could not draw out the first time he would put his hand through the narrow opening. This was not a simple matter. He used to recount later that "indeed, once I managed to push my hand down, I could fill it easily enough, but it was another matter to withdraw it. It was not possible to remove my clenched fist, filled with bread, through that slim neck. Thus I could only extract what amounted to a small handful." Without the least trace of vexation, he would say in a nice way that "I ofttimes felt that I, with a hungry belly, was dealing with a difficult officer in customs who would not let me pass." This strict rationing and regimen of little water continued for three years. A pint of olive oil would last him one year. The truth be told, he only used oil on certain feasts: Pascha, Pentecost, Nativity, Theophany, and when he received the Mysteries during the Great Fast.

The divine Makarios also heard the report that the Tabennesiotes had a lofty conduct of life and that their ascetic struggles were not to be imitated anywhere else. Father Makarios then conceived the notion to disguise himself in secular apparel as a laborer and apply as a novice at their monastery. He walked through the desert for fifteen days. When he entered the Thebaid, he went directly to the monastery of the Tabennesiotes. Straightway he asked to see the great Pachomios, who was then superior of that monastery. This hegumen was imbued with the grace of God and the spirit of prophecy. However, at that time, God, in His œconomy, did not dispense a revelation to Pachomios regarding Makarios. When the venerable Makarios set eyes upon the great Pachomios, he said to him, "I entreat thee, father, receive me into thy flock, so that I too may become a monk." Pachomios answered, "Now that thou art advanced in years, art thou able to endure the ascetical life? Here we have brothers who have been accustomed from their youth to endure the hardships of this discipline. But thou art an old man and unaccustomed to such austerities. When thou canst no longer bear the toils of the monastic conduct, thou shalt leave and speak badly of us." Now the superior did not receive Makarios immediately. After seven days of persevering outside the monastery, without anything to eat, Makarios again approached Pachomios and said, "Do thou receive me, O abba; and if I should not fast and labor together with the brethren, drive me out of the monastery." With these words Pachomios was able to persuade the other brethren, who numbered fourteen hundred fathers, to receive Makarios. Not much time passed before the Great Fast was upon them. Now Makarios observed that some fathers ate once daily but only after Vespers; others partook of something every two days, while others every three days, and still others every five days. Some fathers stood all night in prayer. Some sat down during the day, while others labored throughout the daylight hours. As for the blessed Makarios, he took a large quantity of leaves of date palms and brought them to his cell. He soaked them and stood in one corner, working at them. He showed much perseverance, laboring and standing throughout the Great Fast, all the while keeping utterly silent until the arrival of Pascha. Now during all those days, he neither bent his knee, nor sat, nor stretched out on his bedding. Moreover, all that time, he neither ate bread nor drank water. Only on Sundays did he appear to be eating moistened cabbage leaves, so that he might give the appearance of consuming something. Whensoever he exited his cell for some needful reason, he quickly returned, stood in his place, and continued weaving rope from the palm leaves. He spoke to none and prayed in silence.

The brethren at the monastery, beholding such superhuman ascesis, began murmuring against Makarios. They complained to the hegumen, saying, "From whence hast thou brought this bodiless man into our midst? Was it to judge us or that we should be mocked before him? Either send him away, or we shall go." The head of the monastery had also heard of the fasting and rule of life kept by Makarios. He believed the matter now before him required further examination. He therefore offered up prayer to the Lord that it might be manifested to him who this newcomer might be. The Lord hearkened to the entreaty of His slave and revealed to him that it was Makarios the Alexandrian. Upon receiving this revelation, Pachomios went to the venerable Makarios. He took him by the hand and brought him to the holy sanctuary in the main church. Pachomios then gave Makarios a kiss in Christ and said, "Come, father, thou art Makarios; and yet thou didst not reveal this to me? I, for a long time, had been hearing of thy virtues, and was earnestly desiring to behold thee. I am sensible of thy sanctity, brother, and my gratitude is considerable, because thou hast taught my children by thy toil that they ought not be vainglorious that they perform such great contests of asceticism. Now however, I beseech thee, do thou depart, brother, to thine own cell and pray on our behalf. Thou hast sufficiently corrected us." The brethren then learned that the newcomer was in truth Makarios, the holy elder of the Cells. They hastened to kiss him farewell. Thus, Makarios took leave of the hegumen and the brothers.

Now there was another time when the blessed man would not enter under the roof of his cell or take shelter in any other place. He remained outdoors for twenty days, determined to vanquish sleep. He did not sleep or doze in the least during that period. During the day, he bore with the scorching heat of the sun. From sunset to sunrise, he endured the sharp chill of the night. After this labor, he remarked that "had I not taken shelter and rest, after passing twenty days deprived of sleep, I should have gone mad. As far as it was possible for me, I overcame sleep. But I was overcome against my will. Although the nature of the body has been overcome, yet I rendered to it what it required."

In another instance of self-denial but of another kind of contest, he describes it, saying, "There came upon me the desire that my mind should not be separated from God, if only for five days. I wished to fly above the care and anxieties attendant with material things. As I thought upon this, I shut the door of the courtyard and that of my cell. I was resolved not to answer anyone. I stood upright and constrained myself to remain in contemplation. I began on the second day of the week, Monday, enjoining my mind noetically in this manner: 'Be attentive to things on high and utterly leave lowly and earthly thoughts. Thou shalt not descend from the heavens where thou hast angels, archangels, cherubim, and seraphim, and all the hosts of the heavens, and the summit of all that is desired, the Most High and God of all.'

Then, after I had passed two days in such lofty contemplation, the devil was so inflamed that he became a flame of fire. He set fire to everything that I had in my cell. Even the mat upon which I stood was ablaze with fire. I then had the thought that should I remain still, I also would certainly be consumed. I then noticed that flames were all around me, about to envelop me. I became very frightened. It was in such a manner that my mind and thoughts descended on the third day. That wondrous contemplation came to a halt, because I lost my recollection. But I think this all came about by God's œconomy, lest I should come to prideful thoughts."

There was one time that the blessed man was troubled by thoughts to go to Rome that he might benefit those found there with cures for their sicknesses. He had received this grace from the Lord, that is, to heal every infirmity and to cast out demons from men. Though this matter greatly troubled him, yet he did not depart. On the contrary, he cast himself to the floor inside the door of his cell, but his feet were on the threshold. He then was saying, "Drag me, you demons, for I, by my own feet, shall not go to another place." Now he lay at the threshold till evening. If the brethren had not come, he declared, he would not have moved from that position. At length, when night fell, he stood up. But again, these same thoughts kept mounting up in his mind and pressing him. Since he was troubled by his thoughts, he decided to put himself to work. He began by filling with sand a basket which held two or three bushels. He then lifted this weight upon his shoulders and went out into the desert, going in one direction and another. In this manner, by the grace of Christ, he vanquished those bothersome thoughts about leaving. Now a kinsman, Theosevios the Antiochian, happened to notice him trudging about with that great weight. He naturally inquired, "What is this, father? What art thou bearing on thy shoulder? Surely thou art tired. Allow me to take thy load from thee." Makarios answered him, "By means of this weight, I am bringing under subjection my body. I am putting to work that which made me work, for it would have me go forth." Then after Makarios had walked about for a considerable time, he returned exhausted to his cell. Though he depleted his strength, yet his mind was renewed, and the temptation was overcome.

The following is an account given by Makarios himself, for he was a priest. "I observed," said he, "that whenever I was celebrating the Liturgy and Abba Mark drew nigh to commune, an angel of the Lord communicated the holy Communion to him. All that I was able to see were the knucklebones of the minister's hand." What we know of this Abba Mark is that from early manhood he knew by heart the Old and New Testaments. He was the most gentle and reserved of men.

There was even a time when the holy man was troubled by the demon of fornication. He therefore repaired to the utter desert, the Great Desert, and entered into a marshy wasteland at Sketis. He tarried and struggled in that place for six months. The place was woefully infested with blood-sucking mosquitoes, very large ones, much like wasps. These voracious insects could pierce the hides of wild boars. Therefore, when the blessed man sojourned, he suffered from bites to every bodily member. The reaction therefrom was manifested in swelling throughout his body. He thereupon returned to his cell. His appearance was so altered that no one recognized Makarios but for the sound of his voice. It was remarked that the deformity both to his face and body gave him the appearance of a leper.

Another account tells of how the holy man was sitting in his cell one day, when a gnat bit him on the leg. Makarios felt the painful sting and crushed the gnat in his hand. He immediately despised his impulsive response, for he had avenged himself on that tiny creature. Thus, he passed upon himself the sentence that he would enter the inner desert of Sketis, and sit naked for six months in the marsh. There were many large gnats and mosquitoes, so savage that they could pierce the skins of swine. Upon his return, his flesh was swollen and tough as elephant hide. Again, he could only be recognized by his voice.

There was a time when the brethren were digging a well. The blessed man was also present and suffered a bite to his hand from a deadly asp. Makarios seized that reptile, taking hold of its upper and lower lip with his two hands. Then he tore the creature in half, from its head to the tail, saying, "Since God has not sent thee, how didst thou dare to bite me?" The venom from that asp had no ill-effects on the holy Makarios.

On another occasion, as it is related by the saint's disciple, Paphnutios, the blessed man was sitting in the courtyard and conversing with the brothers on edifying subjects. It happened that a knock was heard at the courtyard door. A female hyena struck her head at the door and then entered with her blind whelp. She moved directly toward Abba Makarios and dropped the whelp at his feet. He took up the afflicted whelp and prayed for it. He then spat into the whelp's large eyes with longitudinal pupils, and the creature's sight was restored. The mother then took her offspring, gave it suck, and departed. The following day, however, she returned eagerly to the blessed man with a large skin, which had been stripped from a sheep. She offered the skin as a coat or covering. The blessed man then spoke to that carnivorous mammal and said, "I do not receive things taken by wrongdoing. If thou didst slay a sheep, I will not accept it." The mammal drew closer and left the skin before the blessed man. He then said to her, "I will in no wise take it unless thou shouldest leave off slaughtering the sheep of the poor from henceforth." The creature showed her submission by groveling before the blessed man. He then took the fleece, but later he gave the sheepskin coat to Saint Melanie the Roman, commemorated by the holy Church on the 31st of December, who was visiting the desert fathers from time to time. She received it from him as a blessing. Thus God Who subdued the hungry lions for Daniel [Dan. 6:22], also tamed and enlightened this hyena mother.

Abba Paphnutios said that "Abba Makarios had not spat on the ground from the day he received holy Baptism." He then added, "The blessed man lived for sixty years after his illumination."

Now the saint wrought many other cures and wonders. There was a case concerning a certain village priest. He had gone to the cell of Abba Makarios. His whole head was consumed with cancer, which disease had eaten holes into his scalp and exposed the cranial bone. But Abba Makarios declined to see the priest, which rejection led the sufferer to lie outside the blessed man's cell. The priest was seen by Palladius, who went in to see Makarios and said, "I beseech thee, have mercy. At the very least say something to that unfortunate man." Abba Makarios answered, "He is undeserving of healing. This grievous punishment was permitted by God as a means to bring him to repentance. If thou wilt see him healed, then persuade him to immediately resign his ministration in the divine Liturgy of the immaculate Mysteries." Palladius asked, "But why, abba?" The blessed man answered, "One cannot serve at the holy altar and also commit fornication. In this he has sinned, and for this he has received this dreadful punishment. Therefore persuade him to vacate the altar, and God will heal him." Palladius went and spoke to that priest, who pledged that he would never minister in the sanctuary again. Only then did Abba Makarios receive him and say, "Dost thou believe that God exists?" The priest answered, "Yes, milord." Abba Makarios then asked, "Dost thou believe that God is omniscient and that He makes manifest the hidden things [1 Cor. 4:5]?" Again, the priest, brought to compunction, affirmed this. Abba Makarios then said, "Perhaps thou wast thinking to mock God?" The priest answered, "Nay, milord." Abba Makarios then said, "If thou wilt acknowledge thy sin, for which thou art being punished by God and which punishment is fitting for thy deeds, then take care to correct thyself." He then confessed his sin and promised not to continue fornicating. He pledged that he would quit officiating as a priest and would retire to the rank of layman. The blessed Makarios then placed his hand on the sufferer's head. Straightway, all the pangs vanished. The skin began to grow and bind together. In but a few days hair appeared on the skull that had been ravaged by disease. He then received full health, glorifying God and thanking the blessed man. Palladius then saw him, completely restored, return to his own house.

There was another case of a noble-born maiden who suffered a number of years from paralysis. She came from Thessalonike to see the saint that she might be healed. By means of prayers and by anointing with holy oil, she was cured in twenty days. She then returned completely well to her own city and home. After she had departed, she sent to him both gold and goods of all kinds.

On another occasion, a lad, who was swollen in his bodily members and troubled by an unclean devil, was brought to the blessed man. The abba placed his right hand on the boy's head and his left hand on the sufferer's heart. On the child's behalf, Abba Makarios offered up supplication to God. The child then breathed out his breath and uttered a loud cry. Fluid thereupon flowed from all parts of his members, until he returned to his former size. The blessed man then anointed the boy with holy oil of the martyrs and sprinkled him with holy water. The abba at last returned the boy healthy to his father, but enjoined him, saying, "Let not thy son partake of flesh or drink wine for forty days, until he should be completely healed." Thus, after that time of fasting and prayer,[5] the demon completely left the boy. The multitude of demonized healed by the blessed man is without number.

The blessed man at another time took to the road that he might visit the garden-tomb of the brothers and magicians, Jannes and Jambres. The blessed man wished to confront the vile demons inhabiting that place. Now the divine Paul wrote that these brothers "stood against Moses [2 Tim. 3:8; cf. Ex. 7:11]." Having stood against the truth, they were utterly corrupted in mind and gained renown by serving Pharaoh. By their magic arts, they attained power and riches. They built an ornamented tomb of marble, filled with gold treasures, which was four feet square. They made a garden in the desert, digging a well and planting all kinds of trees and plants. Though Abba Makarios did not know the way, yet he was able to read a course by following the stars, thereby traveling through the desert, as those do upon the sea. Since the tomb was deep in the desert, Makarios contrived a way of marking his path. He brought a bundle of thin reeds. At the end of each mile, he drove a reed into the ground that he might track his way back. After he journeyed for nine days and came close to the spot where the tomb was located, Satan, who wages war against the athletes of Christ, collected all the reeds which Makarios planted in the earth. Since night had fallen, while the saint took his rest, the enemy, out of malice, placed the reeds under the blessed man's head as he slept. Thus, about one mile from the tomb, Makarios found the reeds under his head as a pillow. The blessed man immediately recognized the reeds

---

[5] Mt. 17:21; Mk. 9:29.

and the wickedness of Satan. Nevertheless, Makarios in no wise was troubled. God permitted this to occur not only to His glory, but also that the saint should triumph. It was better that Makarios trust in God and not put his confidence in the reeds, and so the saint recognized this. For the same God Who led the children of Israel through the wilderness for forty years by means of a pillar of cloud would also guide the blessed man.

Now the blessed man went forth and entered into the garden-tomb. Abba Makarios told us afterward that "seventy demons, in diverse forms, came forth against him. Some were shouting, others were leaping about, while others were gnashing their teeth. They were vexed and angry with me. Some, appearing as ravens, flew about and fluttered in my face, saying, 'What seekest thou here, O Makarios? What, are the demons of the desert insufficient to keep thee and thy monks sufficiently tempted? Perhaps we went and bothered some of those monks? Was it not enough that thou didst take possession of our desert, that which is our habitation and those who are with us, and drove us from that place? What have we to do with thee? Why hast thou encroached upon our territory? Thou art an anchorite, art thou not? Abide in the desert. This place, however, is for us, given to us by the men who built it. Thou art not able ever to dwell in this place. What then seekest thou in this garden-tomb? From the time we buried the brothers, to this day, no living man has entered this precinct.'" These and many other things did the demons screech and cry out in their extreme agitation. The venerable Makarios said, "I am come only that I might view it and then go back again." The demons then said, "This we would have thee promise on thy conscience." The blessed man gave his word that he intended to depart after having a look about. The demons then vanished from his sight. The saint then entered an extraordinary garden of trees, but soon encountered a devil brandishing a naked sword, to whom Makarios said, "Thou hast come against me with a bare sword, but I oppose thee in the name of the Lord Sabaoth, the God of Israel." The evil creature was then put to flight.

The saint entered the garden-tomb. He told us that "I looked about and took in everything. I observed suspended over the well an iron chain with a brass bucket, but they were both badly rusted with age. The hanging pomegranates were shriveled and burnt by the intense desert sun. The tomb had dedicatory objects and was lavishly decorated with pure gold. After seeing these things, I departed for my cell."

The blessed man had been traveling some twenty days when his supply of bread and water was exhausted. His life was in grave peril. He was on the verge of sinking into that vast sea of sand. It was at that point that he caught sight of a maiden. She was clad in a most pure white dress. In her hand she was bearing a cup dripping over with the coolest of water. He thought to himself that she could not be further than six hundred feet or so. Now he beheld her for three days. She called him to come and drink, but he could not overtake her. For three days, he followed her, intensely hoping to satisfy his raging thirst. When he had been brought very low that he had not quenched his thirst, there suddenly appeared a herd of buffaloes. One of the females with her little sucking calf halted before the blessed man. He then heard a voice from on high commanding him, "Go, O Makarios, to the buffalo and suck." He obeyed and drew close to her and sucked milk from her, from which he was strengthened. Thus God manifested His solicitude to His slave. Afterward, Makarios commented, "The Lord wished to teach me, in my infirmity, that I should trust in His care." Now the buffalo followed the blessed man in the desert until he came to his cell. Even then she yielded and gave him milk to drink, not letting her calf suck from her those days that she ministered to Abba Makarios.

We should mention that the blessed man had various cells. He had one in Sketis in the inner desert, a second in Libya, a third in the place called the Cells, and a fourth in Mount Nitria. Two of these cells were without windows. In them, he would sit in darkness for the forty days during the Great Fast. Another cell was so narrow that one could not stretch out one's legs. But there was one that was wide and spacious, where he used to receive the brethren who visited him.

On another occasion a monk, Herakleides, went to the blessed man. Herakleides himself explains what happened: "I complained to him, saying, 'I find myself, abba, in a state of indifference and in the midst of confounding thoughts. I keep saying to myself, "Thou hast not accomplished even one good thing, so why art thou tarrying in this place? Get thee hence!"' The blessed man then said to me, 'Whenever such thoughts should assail thee, prompting thee to leave, address them and say, "I, for the sake of Christ, shall remain and guard these walls."'"

An account which took place toward the end of Abba Makarios' life was recorded by Palladius: "Once, as I was sitting in my cell, the thought came to me to pay a visit to the ancient man, for he was then already a centenarian. I remember that at his advanced age he had lost all of his teeth. But impertinent fellow that I was in my younger days, I went and sat outside the ancient elder's door. I could hear him moving about and conversing. He was contending with both himself and the devil. I overheard him reprimanding himself: 'What now, old and gluttonous greybeard? Thou hast had oil and wine. What more wilt thou want?' The blessed man then remonstrated with the devil, saying, 'Do I still owe thee anything? Thou wilt find nothing! Begone!' Then I heard him humming, saying, 'Come, O white-haired glutton; until when shall I be with you?'"

It should be noted that in appearance the saint was bent over slightly. His frame was small and short. The iconographer Photios Kontoglu in his *Ekphrasis* (A:338) notes that Saint Makarios had a scanty beard, perhaps the result of years of austere asceticism. The miniature presented in the *Menologion of Basil II* (folio 334), made after 979, depicts the aged saint in monastic garb, with a pointed medium-length beard, and a full head of short hair with a slight wave. The icon presented herein of the two Egyptian saints named Makarios is from the Philanthropinon Monastery, Ioannina, the north wall of the exonarthex, frescoed in 1560.

The author acknowledges that he has recorded only a few deeds out of numerous accounts of both Abba Makarios and the brethren with him. What has been recorded is sufficient to show forth his marvellous conduct of life. Saint Makarios the Alexandrian, Christ's priest, wonder-worker, and soldier, reposed in peace, after fighting the good fight as confessor and ascetic. He surrendered his soul into the hands of the Bestower of prizes, Christ our God.

On the 19th of January, the holy Church commemorates the holy Martyr EPHRASIA of Nikomedia.

Ephrasia, the holy martyr, was from Nikomedia.[6] As the daughter of a notable family, she lived during the reign of Emperor Maximian (286-305). This devout maiden, moreover, was adorned with a sound and wise mind. In 290, when Ephrasia was reported to be a Christian before the emperor, she was apprehended. Since the pagans were unable to coerce her into offering sacrifice to their evil deities, she was severely beaten. As she remained steadfast in the Faith of Christ, her tormenters resolved to dishonor her by delivering her to a certain barbarian. Ephrasia, however, outwitted him in the following expedient manner. The holy maiden promised the barbarian that if he would not defile her, she would give him a certain elixir, which would continually make him invincible against every sword and javelin of the enemy. After saying this, she added that if he desired to be sure that what she uttered was the truth, he could experiment upon her own neck. Straightway, she stretched forth her neck as a specimen. The barbarian, believing her, mightily struck her throat and cut off her head. In this manner, empurpled with streams of blood, the blessed Ephrasia safeguarded the inviolate treasury of her bodily purity and received the crown of martyrdom.

---

[6] Ancient Nikomedia (modern Izmit or Ismid) of Bithynia is now a town in Turkey, capital of the Kocaeli vilayet, fifty-four miles east of Constantinople (Istanbul).

On the 19th of January, the holy Church commemorates
the translation of the relics of our holy father among the saints,
GREGORY the Theologian,
to the Church of the Holy Apostles, during the reign of
Emperor Constantine VII Porphyrogennetos (945-959).

On the 19th of January, the holy Church commemorates
the miracle wrought by Saint BASIL the Great who,
by his prayer, opened the doors of the church
of the Orthodox at Nicaea.[7]

On the 19th of January, the holy Church commemorates
our holy father among the saints, ARSENIOS,
Archbishop of Kerkyra (Corfu).

Arsenios, our ever-memorable father, was born during the years of the Emperor Basil the Macedonian (867-886). Arsenios was the scion of pious and God-loving parents. His father hailed from Jerusalem, while his mother was from Bethany. They had been lawfully joined in marriage, but had no child for a long time. While they conducted their lives together in a virtuous manner, performing good works, they kept beseeching God to heal them and grant them a child. God indeed hearkened to their entreaties and bestowed upon them the worthy fruit of their request, the blessed saint whom we now com-

Saint Arsenios

memorate. The excellent Arsenios was born in Bethany. From his swaddling clothes he was dedicated by his parents to God.

When Arsenios came to be three years of age, his parents took him and went to a monastery in those parts. As a votive, Arsenios was handed over to the monastery superior that the lad might bear fruit in those things beneficial to the soul in the monastic life. He was reared in the monastery and lived a life according to God with the brethren. That precious child was also well instructed in letters and advanced in every virtue. Then, twelve years after his birth, he was clothed in the monastic Schema.

---

[7] The full account of this seizure of the cathedral by the Arians is given in the Life of Saint Basil the Great, who is commemorated by the holy Church on the 1st of January.

At length, he wished to acquire further learning and instruction. He went to Seleukeia (Seleucia). He distinguished himself in his studies and shone forth in moral excellence and integrity. These virtues came to the attention of the bishop, who persuaded Father Arsenios to accept ordination to the priesthood. Father Arsenios was also longing to behold Jerusalem again. He embarked on a ship, which fell into the hands of Hagarene pirates. By the grace of God, Arsenios was delivered from captivity. He softened and pacified the ungodly by his mild manner and the sweetness and reverence of his words. After he was released, he went to the holy land and venerated the sites, thus fulfilling his desire. He then repaired to Constantinople, where he was offered hospitality by the most holy Patriarch Tryphon (927-931). Patriarch Tryphon entrusted the stewardship of the churches of the capital to Arsenios.

The patriarch's successor, a young Theophylact (933-956), the son of Romanos I Lekapanos (920-944), found in Arsenios a confessor of the Faith and a man of virtue. Moved by God, he consecrated Arsenios as hierarch of the great church of the Kerkyraeans. Thus the lamp was put upon the lampstand, that it should give light [Mt. 5:15]. After Arsenios was enthroned, he first adorned his life and steps by preserving his ordination pure and blameless. He assumed his ecclesiastical responsibilities and duties with much forethought and consideration. He became a father of orphans, champion of widows, protector of the wronged, nourisher of the hungry, provider of the poor, helper of the oppressed, consoler of the sorrowing, and physician of the sick. Simply put, he became what the divine Paul has described, "To the weak I became as weak, that I might gain the weak. To all these I have become all things, that by all means I might save some. But this I do on account of the Gospel, that I might become a joint partaker of it [1 Cor. 9:22, 23]." For this cause, God recompensed him with the gift of working miracles.

It was at that time that nomadic Scythians came against the island and passed through it, making inroads. They took prisoner the archbishop, but he gave no consequence to his capture. The Scythians in a piratical manner kept him and departed in canoes. The Kerkyraeans learned of the abduction and made ready to set sail on the straits. They encountered the Scythians at sea. By the prayers of their holy chief shepherd, the Kerkyraeans recovered their courage and advanced bravely. With God working mightily on the Kerkyraeans behalf, the Scythians were put to flight. Some of the infidels perished by the sword; others drowned in the waters. Still others were hotly pursued and engaged in combat at a place called Tetraneeson, where they were scattered. It also happened in that place that, by the intercessions of the saint, water sprang forth from a barren rock; the water flows to this day. Thus all of those of his faithful flock were able to quench their burning thirst after the battle. The distinguished archbishop was then escorted back and returned to his throne.

During his time as their shepherd, he wrought many other wonder-workings. By his entreaties, the heavens were brought down, so that the rays of the scorching sun were abated and the island was bedewed with rain, resulting in an abundance of crops. On one occasion, the child of a notable personage on the island was dreadfully troubled by a demon. The holy Arsenios delivered the child from this unclean possession by his prayer alone and the sprinkling of holy water. On another occasion, the wife of a certain clergyman, Andronikos, was in the throes of hard labor. The mother and child were in peril of dying. By the prayers of the saint, the mother's life was granted. She then was delivered easily and gave birth to a healthy infant. Also, there was a woman, semi-paralyzed, whom the saint anointed with holy oil. She too was restored to complete health.

After the sons of Romanos were deposed in 945, Romanos' son-in-law, Constantine Porphyrogennetos, known as the emperor of the Macedonian Dynasty (945-959), came to power. He was the offspring of Leo VI and his fourth marriage to Zoe Karbonopsina. Now Constantine waged an unjust persecution against certain notable persons of Kerkyra and summoned them to the capital. He who had received the imperial appointment to govern Kerkyra, as one avaricious, bore false witness against them. The hierarch, putting aside old age and infirmity, braved the perils of a sea voyage during the winter season. He sailed to Constantinople and brought about peace with the emperor and the Kerkyraeans. On his return, the chief shepherd arrived on the island of Skyros, some twenty-four nautical miles from Evia, where he fell ill. He, however, did not tarry long there. He sailed onward until he reached Corinth. Near Corinth, the holy hierarch surrendered his blessed soul into the hands of God in the year 953.

The saint was buried there in an honorable manner, by those who traveled with him and others in that place who had come to pay their respects. Afterward, the Kerkyraeans came and transferred the sacred relics to Kerkyra. It was then that a miracle was wrought by God Who glorified His household servant. Now the virtue of the saint and his fame as a wonder-worker were well known. Someone, for the sake of receiving sanctification, dared to secretly cut off a considerable portion of the saint's beard. Nevertheless, by the grace of God, the hair of his beard was miraculously restored whole. Many miracles and cures of every kind were wrought by the saint to the praise of our God, to Whom is due glory and dominion, together with the unoriginate Father and His all-holy and good and life-creating Spirit, to the ages. Amen.

**On the 19th of January, the holy Church commemorates
our venerable Father MELETIOS the Confessor of Mount Galesios.**[8]

Meletios, our venerable father, hailed from the coastal region of the Black Sea, from a village called Theodotos. He was born circa 1209, to George and Maria. They were God-fearing and virtuous people who loved to give alms and offer hospitality. As much as they shared their wealth with the poor, the more so did the Lord multiply their substance and add to their praise among the people. George held the rank of general in the imperial service but was better known for his generosity to the poor and strangers. Maria was known for her goodness, kindness, and moral excellence. She was a godly woman whose life was a blessing and doxology to God. These wondrous virtues were cultivated in their fruit, the wondrous Mel-

Saint Meletios   etios, who received the name Michael in holy Baptism. Meletios became his name later, in the holy tonsure, when he became a monk. Together with that name change, which bespoke his name and the life which he maintained, he gave himself over to the study and practise of contemplation. Thus, he received a name which proved justified, when he joined actual deed and activity to it.

After the child was baptized, his father sought divine guidance for his son's education. This was due to a dream he was vouchsafed, wherein an august and reverent man approached him who was sent forth by the king. He requested of George a gold pectoral. George was roused from his sleep, perceiving that what he had seen in his sleep pertained to his son. He understood that his son would become in the future that gold pectoral, that is, an elect vessel of the heavenly king. He committed his son to God's care, as to One Who loves us more than any father according to the flesh. For his part, George did all that was required to ensure a proper upbringing for the child.

The father, therefore, had his son tutored by a virtuous and excellent teacher that Michael might learn the sacred writings and be instructed in

---

[8] The Life of this saint was taken from the *Neon Eklogion* of Nikodemos the Hagiorite. An earlier version was written by Makarios Chrysokephalos, Bishop of Philadelphia (1336-1372). Saint Meletios' writings *On Prayer* were later translated by Saint Paissy. An English version of an extract ("The Letter Eta, On Prayer") of the saint's writings from *The Alphabetalphabetos* appears in the English periodical *Living Orthodoxy*, Vol. XII, No. 4, July-August 1990, p. 16.

virtue. Meanwhile, George was not negligent in admonishing and exhorting the child at home; for many parents leave the more serious parts of their child's upbringing to others. Michael was not to receive a haphazard or incoherent education, but one that continued in his home life, with the continuing example of both his parents' words and actions. They chose to conduct their home and lives in a God-pleasing manner, preferring to spend their time in Church twice daily, that is, with attendance at Orthros and Vespers. They kept this as their family rule that they might hear the teachings of the divine Scriptures and advance in the fear of God. The young Michael, sober-minded, prudent, obedient, orderly, and disciplined, did more than what was commanded of him by his father. For this reason, he excelled all his peers in virtue and made progress in all his studies. The holy youth gradually moved forward in the performance of good deeds and undertaking struggles. Later, Michael also beheld a vision, wherein he was ordered, even as Abraham of old, to flee his country and kin and go wherever God guided him.

Therefore, without losing any time, he quit everything—homeland, parents, relatives, comrades, his wealth and possessions—that he might follow God Who had called him. He therefore lifted upon his shoulders the Cross of Christ. He was resolved to make his way to Jerusalem. He desired to venerate the shrines of the holy land, where the Son and Logos of God condescended to become Man and live and walk among us. Michael yearned to see those places where Christ endured the Cross, death, and burial, and then arose on the third day and ascended into the heavens. The time that he fixed to go was January, in the heart of winter. He walked the distance, without any accompaniment or covering or convenience for the road. The deprivations he suffered on the road caused him much hardship. He also suffered from the inclement weather—snow, rain, and mud. He had to exert all his strength on account of the overflow of the river onto the roads, which greatly impeded his mobility. But none of these troubles truly touched him, as the venerable one was ever mindful of his desire for Christ.

After he passed by Lydda, he came to the river Paktolos. Since it was still winter, there was flooding. The river also had waves, comparable to those found at sea, which made crossing difficult. Michael looked about and saw no one. He looked for a passable spot along the riverbank, but found nothing. What did the man of God decide to do? He took refuge in God, with Whom all things are possible. He raised his hands, eyes, and mind heaven-ward. He wept and sighed from the depths of his heart, supplicating the Lord to send down help from on high. Then—behold, the wonder!—he was straightway borne aloft in the air and transported to the other side. After experiencing this extraordinary conveyance, he hastened along the remaining path to his goal with greater eagerness.

When he arrived in Jerusalem, he venerated all the shrines and sites with profound piety. He also desired to converse with the venerable fathers who were struggling in the desert and desolate places, that he might have them as models and receive from them the rules of the ascetic conduct of life. He repaired to Mount Sinai, where he beheld marvellous holy fathers, who had been struggling in asceticism, some for more than eighty years and others for their entire lives. Michael was in awe at their superhuman mode of living. He besought them with tears to receive him into their fellowship and synodia. He was received by them and immediately removed his secular clothing. Together with his garments, he also put off his secular name. He was garbed in a monastic hair shirt and renamed Meletios in the tonsure. With the donning of that rough clothing and the harshness of asceticism, he applied himself to laboring in every kind of virtue and moral excellence. During the day he ministered to the needs of the brotherhood. His nights were spent in prayers, doxologies to God, and the reading of the divine Scriptures. The saint also read the writings of the holy fathers, which later were reflected in his teachings. He was familiar with the sayings of Saints Anthony, Makarios the Great, Mark the Ascetic, John of the Ladder, Theodore the Stoudite, and John Cassian. His knowledge of the dogmatic writings of Saints Justin Martyr, Basil the Great, Gregory the Theologian, John Chrysostom, Maximos the Confessor, and others, was formidable. At times, he would partake of a little sleep for the unavoidable needs of human nature. Since he did not wish to lie down or take his ease on soft bedding, sometimes he kept himself vertical with a rope, while at other times he lay on desiccated ground. Now he did this because he wanted no bed, mattress, second garment, or any other covering. At times, he spent the whole night keeping watch. He also kept vigil for whole weeks, such as the Great and Holy Week of our Lord's Passion and other feasts of the Master.

After Meletios had passed considerable time among those divine fathers, laboring courageously in the practical virtues, he mounted up to lofty contemplation, so that he was vouchsafed spiritual gifts. Thereupon, what took place? The others marvelled at Father Meletios' feats, which could not be concealed easily. His name became well known, and his virtues were spoken of even in faraway places. This renown dismayed and saddened Father Meletios, who feared the praise of men, lest he should lose the reward of God for his struggles and then have labored in vain. He decided to depart from that place. He fled by night, leaving the monastery for Jerusalem, where he desired to stay for a time at the Holy Sepulcher of the Lord. One reason was his longing to behold the holy fire, which miraculously issues forth from the tomb of our Savior every year on Holy and Great Saturday.

After seeing the holy fire, thankful to God that he had been vouch-safed this sight, he longed to proceed toward Egypt and Alexandria. After he made a tour of these places, he went through Syria and Damascus. His intention, as an industrious bee, was to gather up the honey of virtue from different fathers. He then left Damascus, since he could not bear to dwell in the midst of the impious, and went to Mount Latros, where he sojourned for a long time. Next, he went to Mount Galesios[9] of western Asia Minor, outside of old Ephesus. The monastery located there was of a goodly size and was established by our holy Father Lazarus the Galesiot, who reposed in 1054 and is commemorated by the holy Church on the 7th of November. The Lord increased and glorified the monastery, embellishing it with the deathless adornment of virtue, because this monastery put forth venerable men who shone forth as luminaries and illumined the universe.

Meletios went to this monastery, where he observed the resident fathers. He esteemed their ascetic conduct and conceived the desire to dwell among them. He besought them to accept him that he might be a member of their united brotherhood. In this holy place, he was clothed with the Great Schema of the monastics. He submitted himself in obedience to one elder, named Mark, who was also called Amiselle. Who can recount thine excessive humility, O Father Meletios? Who could possibly present thy readiness in every ministration? Who can reveal thy tireless and receptive disposition? Though thou didst toil but a few years, yet thou didst accomplish many works. In whatever thy spiritual father commanded, thou didst carry out his orders eagerly. Thy services were exceptional; thy ministrations were sweet. Thy customary hardships and austerities, whether by thy labors during day or

---

[9] Mount Galesios (Turk. Alamandağ) was a monastic center north of Ephesus, on the right bank of the river Kaystros (Küçük Menderes). Monks first came to this holy mountain in the 11th C., in order to flock around Saint Lazarus the Stylite who is commemorated by the holy Church on the 7th of November. Under one hegumen, three monasteries were built around the stylite's pillar: those of the Savior, reserved for twelve eunuchs; the Theotokos, for twelve monks; and the Anastasis (Resurrection) for forty monks. A fourth monastery, the Theotokos of Bessai, was imperial and had its own hegumen. Though it housed three hundred monks in the 11th C., it rapidly declined. There was also the convent of Evpraxia. After the repose of Saint Lazarus, Galesios entered a period of obscurity. In the 13th C., with the establishment of the empire of Nicaea, the Galesiot monastery gained prominence. Two former Galesiot fathers, Joseph I (1266-1275; 1282, 1283) and Athanasios I (1289-1293; 1303-1309), became patriarchs. The monastery had an impressive library and active scriptorum. Its history came to a close with its capture by the Islamic Turks. *The Oxford Dictionary of Byzantium*, s.v. "Galesios, Mount."

thy vigils at night, in no wise made thee careless or negligent. Thy gift of tears was ever with thee, so that not one moment of any hour passed when thy heart was not meditating on, or thy mouth was not uttering, the name of Jesus Christ, reciting, "Lord Jesus Christ, Son of God, have mercy on me."

Father Meletios sojourned with that elder for a long while. He subjected himself in extreme humility to him. This brought him the praise and wonder of not only those with him, but also others who kept company with the Elder Mark. The elder did not conceal the virtues of his disciple Meletios, but made his virtuous life and conduct an example to all the other brethren in that place. Now the divine Meletios had the custom of immuring himself in his cell and keeping a forty-day fast, in imitation of Moses and Elias and even the Master Christ. Those who ministered to his needs supplied a jar of water and a measured amount of dry figs. At the end of that allotted time, they found him again whole, sound, and unfailing in any of his faculties. But they also discovered that he had not partaken of anything to eat. Thereupon, all the inhabitants of Mount Galesios were astonished. All the surrounding parts of Asia learned of his fame, which caused many to come and behold the ascetical contest.

Since, however, this hindered his solitude and asceticism, the venerable man was most grieved. He kept considering what he might do to flee the glory and praise of men. For this reason he was supplicating God day and night that he might discover the most desirable solution. On one occasion, at midnight, while he was entreating God concerning this matter, the cell was filled with divine and heavenly light. Christ also appeared, radiantly clad in brilliant white robes. He was flanked by youths who were most comely, and in His hands He held a scepter. Even as Meletios beheld this divine vision, he remained ecstatic and fell to the ground. Then one of the youths took Meletios by the hand and raised him up, saying, "It is the Master Christ, O Meletios. What fearest thou?" The Lord then said, "Thou didst call upon Me; and for this reason, behold, I am come." The venerable man was still fearful and quaking. He could neither speak a word nor raise up his eyes and gaze upon the Lord. The Lord then said to him, "Go to Constantinople and proclaim the truth, because there is war in the city." After Christ uttered these words to the saint, He ascended into the heavens in the company of those youths.

After the vision, the divine Meletios, filled with inexpressible joy, was considering how to obey the command of God. He deemed it prudent to notify his elder of his intentions to depart. He did not tell him about the vision he saw, but only asked for permission to leave. The elder, cognizant of the value and usefulness of such a man as Meletios, did not wish to give him leave. In all kinds of ways and with many words, the elder attempted to hinder Meletios. He brought to Meletios' remembrance how life in the cities and dealings there were entirely in opposition to the monastic conduct. The elder's negative response saddened Meletios. Thereupon, he again was brought to entreat God concerning the matter. The Lord indeed hearkened to his request. While Meletios was contemplating his departure, the elder heard a divine voice saying, "Do thou not prevent him. But give leave to My slave to go to Constantinople, where he shall benefit many souls." After Elder Mark heard this divine voice, he offered his blessing and prayers to the venerable Meletios and sent him forth.

The holy man managed to arrive in the capital. He did not wish to have his presence made known to any of the city's leaders, that is, the emperor, nobility, dignitaries, and all the rest, but he could not conceal his arrival. Thereafter, news of his appearance spread throughout Constantinople, so that countless people, on a daily basis, were seeking out the venerable Meletios. This was due to the grace of God which shone forth in Father Meletios, so that those who hastened to him were receiving great spiritual benefit. The saint's manner was humble, and his speech bore fruit. His mind was ever attentive. Simply put, his comportment, appearance, and movements inspired profound spiritual gain to onlookers. People were running to hear his teachings and record his words on the tablets of their hearts. There were some who wrote down his sayings that they might be remembered. The meek Father Meletios provided a remedy to the spiritual ills prevailing in the city, because political and civil unrest and instability were attacking the Church. Social evils and immorality pervaded the upper classes. Foreign presence and exploitation had negative effects. Worldly abbots, devoted to fine dress, high living, and keeping company with the aristocracy, demeaned the clergy in the eyes of many. The steady depopulation, spread of illness, lack of provisions, and companies of homeless and adventurers wandering the streets, seriously depleted the city's resources and infrastructure. Superstitions, astrology, and occult practises crept in and gained hold of the simple in every walk of life. Therefore, Father Meletios, as a genuine Orthodox monk, was received with reverence. He confirmed many in true Orthodox piety and worship.

At length, all of these distractions brought Meletios more sorrow than before, because he loved to maintain silence and solitude. He abhorred the people's glorification of him, for he was convinced that a man's mind was purified by means of stillness granted by God. He felt any other method to attain to divine grace was difficult. For this cause, he perceived it wise to depart Constantinople. He repaired to the mountain called Great Afxentios, where he found an especially small cave in a desolate place. He entered therein, where he dwelt for a long period, homeless and naked. He also did not have the benefit of fire for heat and light. Afterward, he fashioned a small hut before the entrance of the cave.

Father Meletios engaged in manifold ascetic struggles. He demonstrated eagerness and diligence in these contests, even as he had from the beginning. He fasted for many days, kept extreme vigilance, made many prostrations, and mortified his flesh with all kinds of hardships. A fellow monastic commented to him that he ought not labor with such severity, lest he should suffer death. The saint remarked, "Hast thou not heard, my child, that Abraham shall be remorseful when he beholds the superabundance of God's gifts at the time of reward on the day of judgment, because he had not struggled more?" When the visiting monk heard these words, he marvelled and respected the answer, so that he kept silence before the saint. The visitor, however, went about proclaiming, to both monastics and seculars, the nature of the blessed man's wondrous life. It was then that people began hastening to his retreat to converse with him. These bothersome distractions interrupted his much desired quietude and hesychasm. Exceedingly grieved by this intrusion into his solitude, he again sought refuge in God's intervention. After his supplicatory prayer, he went and opened the book of the prophets, that he might learn which path was the will of God. He then found this verse: "Behold, I have given thee for...a light of the nations [Is. 49:6]." By this declaration, Father Meletios understood that he should abide in the same place. Thereupon, he received the pilgrims who were coming, curing them of their weaknesses and infirmities, and addressing their needs. Those who were ignorant or seeking answers found solutions to their perplexities, anxieties, and dire circumstances. He kept teaching soul-benefitting instructions and admonitions, so that he helped in every way all those who came to him.

Through all these incidents, the venerable Meletios received great acclaim. There was no Christian who did not call upon his holy prayers. He was besought by mariners and wayfarers, that they might be rescued from their infirmities. He was petitioned by both sick folk and healthy, that they might be healed of their infirmities and problems. Those who were suffering illness indeed were healed, while those of sound bodies maintained their health. No one was neglected or shunned by the saint: neither soldiers, nor farmers, nor shepherds, nor huntsmen. Fishermen testified of the saint's divine grace, because as soon as they invoked his name with their mouths, they caught fish without number. Once, as he was walking along the shore with a disciple, he commanded the sea to give up a fish. He struck the water with his staff, and a large fish leaped forth onto the beach. The disciple took hold of the fish and prepared dinner. What more can be said? Even the animals and wild beasts testified to the grace of the saint. Indeed, even to these creatures did he exhibit great sympathy. Though the saint wrought many wonders, did he overlook the spirit of hospitality? Not in the least. Though he had very little bread, whatever he did have satisfied all—and they were many who came. He also shared abundantly with those who had need. Meanwhile, he nourished their souls with his godly and wise teachings.

On one occasion, as the blessed man was walking and the sun was beginning to set, his traveling companion said, "Father, hast thou noticed that dusk is closing in upon us? Let us therefore remain here, because the village is still a long way off and we shall not reach there before dark." The saint then lifted his eyes heavenward and said, "My God and Savior, Thou Who art the light of the world, Who had the sun stand still for the sake of Thy people Israel [Josh. 10:13, 14]: Do Thou stay the sun for our sakes that we might arrive at the village while it is still daylight." Then—O Thy boundless wonders, O Christ King!—the sun did not set until the saint arrived at the place he wished.

At the foot of the Mountain of the Great Afxentios, a little further from the mainland, there is an islet called Apostle Andrew. It is quite small in length, but delightful for contemplation. It was there that the venerable man built hermitages, oratories, and other needful structures. Afterward, he gave himself over to excessive ascetic struggles and toils. He engaged in standing all night, vigils, fasts, prayers, and tears. Moreover, this little island was not deprived of his wonderworkings. The testimony of witnesses, who hastened to him that they might be recipients of his help, abounds. However, since his quiet life was thrown into turmoil from the confluence of Christian petitioners, he decided to move to Mount Afxentios. As the saint prepared for his departure, there appeared before his eyes, in the middle of the day, the great and holy Afxentios himself, who had reposed circa 470. He greeted Father Meletios and even offered generous thanks for the church built in that place. Concurrently, Saint Afxentios notified Father Meletios that he had a great recompense for him, similar to that received in the year 766 by the venerable Martyr Stephen the New (commemorated by the holy Church on the 28th day of November), who enhanced the renown of his coenobitic monastery. This prophetic vision proved true when the divine Meletios later received the crown of a confessor.

"How can I," the narrator, "recount the rest of this narrative without tears? I say this because, at that time, even as a cloud full of hailstones threatens injury and harm, in like manner the Latin-minded in favor of union rained down persecutions upon the Church of Christ. The devil, the prince of evil, after much warfare directed against the flock of Christ, also advanced this last attack, the change of the Symbol of the Faith, that is, the Creed. Thus the Church of Old Rome was taken into captivity by the enemy, which caused the other Churches to weep and lament for the departure of the first among sisters from the Faith, for which loss even the angels, the guardians of the Church, mourned. The devil, however, rejoiced at the division and separation of the Christians.

Now from the time of the sack of Constantinople during the Fourth Crusade (1204), the Latin Empire had established itself in the city. Attempts were made to bring the Orthodox to submit to the papacy. Therefore, there was urgent need for the saint to lend his assistance to the Orthodox in the capital. The true Faith was being compromised by Emperor Michael VIII Palaiologos (1259-1282) in order to extract promises from the Latins. The Filioque and other cacodox dogma pervaded the west and arrived in the east when Emperor Michael, called "the azymite," reigned, who tyrannized the Eastern Church for years.

In the summer of 1261, Constantinople reverted from Latin rule to Orthodox hands. But on the Feast of the Nativity, in 1262, Emperor Michael blinded the rightful heir to the throne. He then had the youth imprisoned, which act brought upon Michael the excommunication of Patriarch Arsenios Autoreianos (1254-1260; 1261-1265). The emperor subsequently deposed the patriarch and had his father confessor, Joseph I, a monk of Mount Galesios, installed as patriarch (1266-1275; 1282, 1283). This action divided the Orthodox, since many faithful chose to remain with the unjustly deposed Arsenios. Joseph was deemed a usurper. While this division took place among the Orthodox, Emperor Michael attempted to impose his policy of Unia with Rome in order to advance his political agenda. Persecutions then arose against the opponents of the union. Soldiers of Christ, on behalf of the truth, were not missing in this struggle. Father Meletios took up spiritual arms and went to defend Orthodoxy in the midst of the embattled Church. He decided to seek not his own benefit, but rather that of his neighbor. He left his solitude and went all about the province of Bithynia, strengthening and supporting the Christians in Orthodoxy. He bade them to guard and preserve piety. He exhorted them to diligently distance themselves from this novel and perverse dogma, which was named Latinismos or Latinism.

In 1275, the Unia of Lyons was proclaimed. After some initial wavering, Patriarch Joseph denounced the Unia, and this act resulted in his deposition. Thereupon, John XI Vekkos was installed (1275-1282). Together with the emperor, he championed the union and persecuted the anti-unionists. Vekkos ordered the commemoration of Pope Gregory (1271-1276), so that at his services could be heard, "Gregory, the supreme pontiff of the apostolic see and universal pope." As for the Filioque, the addition of the blasphemous words "and from the Son" was introduced not only into the Creed, but also into liturgical exclamations, so that one could hear, "And to Thee do we send up glory, to the Father and to the Son and to Him Who proceedeth from Both, the Holy Spirit...."

Now when Emperor Michael the azymite presented corrupted Latin dogmas to the Great Church and sought the union between the Eastern Church and that of the west, he needed to expel the Orthodox patriarch from his throne. As we said, he appointed John Vekkos, who would champion the cause of union. Thereupon, the Orthodox were imprisoned, ill-treated, and subjected to manifold torments. It was then that the blessed Meletios thought to speak to Emperor Michael. Father Meletios mentioned this to the divine Galaction, a certain priest-monk with whom he struggled in the ascetic life on Mount Galesios. Father Galaction was expressive with language, at the summit of virtue, and worthy of respect. The two monks went together to Constantinople, where they gained an audience before Emperor Michael. They confessed the Orthodox Faith boldly. They declared themselves defenders of the Faith and said that they would suffer no intercommunion with the heresy of Latinismos, which had been censured and rebuked by the divine fathers. They explained that the holy œcumenical synods confessed to, and upheld, that article of the Symbol of the Faith which pronounces that the Holy Spirit proceeds from the Father. Those who dared to alter the Creed with either additions or subtractions of even the tiniest detail were subject to excommunication. After saying this and many other edifying explanations, they added, "Why then dost thou, O emperor, look askance at the words of Christ, which are recorded in the holy Gospel [Jn. 15:26], as is attested to by both the holy apostles [Gal. 4:6; Eph. 1:17] and fathers, and the sacred canons of the universal Church? Why hast thou given thyself over to deception and error? Why hast thou sought to displace the apostolic traditions? It is impossible that this should happen. Do not then undertake to move the immovable. For it is better that we should lose our lives than lose our Orthodoxy."

This boldness of the two confessors was deemed as a pointed and personal insult by the emperor. He delivered both men up to prison. These valiant soldiers of Christ endured the hardships of prison with joy. After a few days of confinement, the command came that they be removed from their prison cell and brought before the emperor. Michael was hoping that the sufferings and ills of prison life would have undermined the resolve of the monks. He was thinking that as wax, they might have melted from the fire of temptation. Nevertheless, these holy men had not softened their position. On the contrary, their resolve was hardened as iron, being fired by the warmth of their faith. Therefore, like iron hammers, they pounded the cacodox. At this second examination, they displayed even more courage and daring than at the first. The emperor waxed hot with anger. He sentenced the two holy monks to banishment on the island of Skyros, off the coast of Evia in the Aegean. This island, however, was under the metropolitanate of Athens. From Skyros, Father Meletios was remanded to Rome in chains for the purpose of entering into discourse with the pope's theologians. The pope consigned Father Meletios to bonds and a dungeon for seven long years. The holy confessor was then returned to Skyros, according to an imperial command, where he was incarcerated with the goodly Galaction.

The dungeon where the saints were detained was as the land of "darkness and the shadow of death [Ps. 106:10]." They were put to the test with many days of hunger, for by starvation had the authorities on Skyros determined to put the confessors to death. But those venerable fathers, and especially the divine Meletios, decided to keep a fast. This brought to Meletios' remembrance his old custom of fasting for many days. He therefore utilized this doleful torture as another occasion to mount the ladder to Paradise, by keeping a strict fast for forty days. Now the warden of the prison observed their abstinence and greatly marvelled, so that he mentioned the matter to his wife, saying, "O woman, we are lost, fighting against God. I say this because those two imprisoned monks possess such virtue that they appear to be angels rather than men." He then recounted to her their many days of fasting and their frequent prayers and vigils throughout the night. His wife was brought to a state of astonishment and wonder at these feats. In the morning, the warden's wife took their only daughter and went to see the holy prisoners. She entered and prostrated herself before their feet, asking for their blessings.

The saints, though they were found in the midst of such terrible hardship, nonetheless rejoiced in their tribulations. They were giving glory to God at all times and in every place. The emperor had a mania to spread Latinismos. To do so, he drew many to him, not only by employing threats and punishments, but also by bestowing offices and dignities. Whatever might advance his position, even if it meant utilizing treacherous and fraudulent means against what was just and true, he perpetrated. Some became his friends and followers of the moment and accepted Latinismos. All the Orthodox whom the emperor could not persuade, were either exiled or put to death. By employing such tyrannical ways of achieving his goals, he removed from his presence those who would not consent to his Latin way of thinking, for he believed that by such methods of disposal he would overcome all. He then at some point summoned his nobles and assumed a pleasant tone with them, saying, "It seems to me that the Church now has great peace, which gift profits the patriarch, because there is nothing to trouble the world." After hearing these words of the emperor, some of those present, seeking to ingratiate themselves with him, had one among them speak for the rest. He said, "Sire, there are those who have been banished to Skyros, who are reputed to be more discerning and knowledgeable than the rest, but who resist thy sovereignty and rule." The emperor inquired, "And who are these persons?" The nobleman answered, "Meletios and Galaction, the Galesiots." The pronouncement of these names wounded the emperor's heart, because these men were renowned for their virtue.

Straightway, a royal ship was fitted out. The emperor's men were dispatched to bring the two Galesiots to Constantinople. They were brought to the capital and placed in the prison known as Noumeron. In the meantime, many days passed. The emperor gave pretexts against hearing their case, saying that other matters of great import demanded his attention rather than to hear some churchmen. Thus, their examination before the emperor kept being postponed. But evil hierarchs and especially the patriarch slandered the saints persistently within the palace walls. O just and long-suffering God, how was this to be endured? These evil men used every means to persuade the godly Meletios and Galaction to subscribe to Latinismos, for death was the only other option. At length, by imperial command, the stout-hearted ones were taken from the prison and made to appear before the emperor. Once again, they demonstrated boldness and valor, but to a greater degree than before. The saints this time were subjected to greater punishments than those administered previously. Forthwith, they were submitted to a long and cruel thrashing with staves, until their bodies lay prone upon the ground, barely showing life and breath. Afterward, when they came to themselves, the sacred Galaction was cast into prison. The divine Meletios was suspended from ropes and a piece of wood. Then—behold, the miracle!—straightway, that wood blossomed forth and was covered with leaves.

The emperor heard of this miracle and changed his mind regarding his dealings with the two prisoners. By the mediation of others, the emperor conversed with the blessed man. He asked Father Meletios to have communion with Latinismos. The saint, having disdained the imperial request, then took flight as an eagle to the clouds, not to be caught or vanquished by the snares and machinations of these evil men. The emperor was in a state of wonderment. He knew not how to react to the fathers. Since he could not overcome their resolve, he though to subject their bodies to tortures. The emperor had his executioners blind Galaction and sever the tongue of Meletios. He chose these particular mutilations so that neither could Galaction serve or liturgize again, nor could Meletios speak on the theology of the Holy Trinity. But no matter how the emperor contrived to disable them, his will did not prevail. The divine Meletios, even with the cutting of his tongue, spoke clearly and distinctly. Galaction, when peace was established in the Church, returned to liturgize and celebrate the bloodless sacrifice. In 1282, Michael

Palaiologos died, under excommunication by Patriarch Arsenios. Michael was also under excommunication by Pope Martin IV (1281-1285) for being "the protector of the schismatic and heretical Greeks." Among his countrymen, he was unpopular for his subservience to Rome and persecution of the Orthodox. His son and heir did not give him a funeral, but rather had his body buried by night in a secret manner in the corner of a provincial monastery. Thereupon, pious Andronikos II (1282-1328) became emperor of the Romans. He repudiated all efforts toward union with Rome. The transgressor and lawless one, Vekkos, retired to a monastery. Joseph, a true shepherd and unshakeable tower of Orthodoxy, was recalled to the patriarchal throne in the midst of a popular celebration. Both Fathers Meletios and Galaction were removed from prison, together with many others who had refused to espouse Latinismos. They took part in the initial decisions toward the restoration of the Church. On the 1ˢᵗ day of January, in the year 1283, Father Galaction conducted a service for the blessing of water at Hagia Sophia, which was reopened for Orthodox services. Father Meletios, although he was enjoined by both the emperor and the aristocracy to accept the dignity of the priesthood, still refused, ever wishing to insulate himself from receiving glory among men, which he deemed to be injurious. He therefore returned to his beloved solitude, where a number of disciples gathered around him.

The saint lived to a deep old age. He then fell ill for some three years. He ate, during this illness, neither bread nor any other food except vegetables, the intake of which he monitored strictly. When he was about to be translated to the Lord, he called together the entire brotherhood and counseled them as was meet. He consoled and comforted them with joy. He gave to each of the brothers the final farewell and embrace. Together with all of them, he confessed and gave thanks to God. Afterward, he lifted his hands and eyes heavenward, saying, "Lord, into Thy hands I surrender my spirit." Straight-way, he went forth to the Lord. There was one monk, named Gerasimos, who was sleeping in his own cell during the moment of the elder's release from his body. This monk beheld a vision of the divine Meletios, that he had raised his hands and ascended with joy into the heavens. This vision awakened him from his sleep. He rose up and ran to the elder's cell. He found that the saint had reposed and that his countenance shone forth more brightly than the sun.

There was another priest-monk, Father Theokletos, who, out of the great love he bore Father Meletios, conducted forty liturgies from the time of the saint's repose. At the completion of this liturgical cycle, it also happened to be the Sunday of Orthodoxy. Father Theokletos, at that time, besought God that He might reveal to him what the soul of the divine Meletios was accounted worthy to receive. When Father Theokletos had fallen asleep, he beheld a vision. He found himself in a huge and beautiful church, according to the design of those built in the east. The height of the temple reached to the heavens, and it was illumined by one ineffable light. Within that holy precinct, he observed holy fathers who were chanting one angelic hymn in a wondrous manner. There was also present a sacred preacher who was giving a sermon. He was speaking of how the venerable Meletios, when he was among the living, built that very church to the honor of the Holy Trinity. Upon receiving the message of these words, Father Theokletos was elated by what he had seen and heard. Afterward, it seemed to Father Theokletos that he was going to the sepulcher of the saint, which happened to be opened. He saw within that there were two radiantly clad men, holding wondrous censers of great beauty, who were censing the chamber. Next, he even beheld the divine Meletios, who rebuked him, but in a playful manner that was graceful, saying, "Whilst thou, friend Theophilos, hast left my sepulcher uncared for, God sent forth these, whom thou seest before thee, that they might visit me." As Father Theophilos was ruminating upon what he had seen and heard, he kept thinking that though the saint spoke yet he was dead. He then heard a voice from heaven saying, "The one who believeth in Me, though he die, he shall live [Jn. 11:26]." The relics of the saint remained incorrupt and became the source of many miracles.

The Miracles of Saint Meletios

One day, as the great Meletios was walking along a narrow strip of land on the city seashore, he came upon some fishermen. As they were spreading out their nets on the sand, Father Meletios inquired if they had caught any fish. They answered that they had been fishing all that night but caught nothing. The saint was saddened for them and then said boldly, "Children, again cast your nets; but this time, do it in the name of our Savior God." They obeyed the words of the holy monk, and cast their nets. Then—O Thine ineffable grace, my Christ!—such a multitude of fish ran into the nets, that only with the application of much force were they able to drag in the catch to the shore. Thereupon, they gave glory to God and offered thanks to the venerable man, marvelling at his boldness before God.

When he built on the islet the divine Church of Andrew the First-called, as we mentioned earlier, it happened on one occasion that the cellarer approached Father Meletios and disclosed that there was no food for the builders. The holy elder then took up his staff and said to him, "Do thou follow me." They went down to the sea, at which point Father Meletios, calmly and gently, tapped the water and said, "In the name of the Master Christ, give to us what we need for this day." Then—behold, the miracle!—forthwith, there jumped out onto the shore a great and excellent fish. As the cellarer went to take hold of the creature, another fish, no less fine than the first, leaped forth from the waves onto the beach. The cellarer then took up the two fish and prepared them. Thus, by God's loving-kindness, both the brotherhood and the builders partook of a good and tasty meal.

During the time when the Orthodox Emperor Andronikos held the scepter, he invited the great Meletios to the palace. He wished to consult with Father Meletios on an ecclesiastical matter. The saint went and was received with great honor by the emperor. Now one of the nobility, whose name was Surmourinos the chief chamberlain, reproached the saint in his thoughts. He accused the saint of loving temporal glory, and said to someone sitting by him, "Leave off that monk, as he seems to seek that which he ought to have not sought, that is, he lives at present for the glory of men and rejoices in this." That evening, Surmourinos went to his house and fell on his bed to sleep. He beheld a vision wherein he found himself inside the royal palace. The emperor was garbed in both imperial and hierarchal robes. All about the emperor stood armies without number. It seemed that the emperor was angered greatly with Surmourinos, because he insulted his personal slave. The emperor then commanded his retinue to take vengeance on Surmourinos. In but a short time, they bound the hands and feet of Surmourinos. He was cast into a place reserved for those condemned of blasphemy. It was then that the great Meletios interceded on Surmourinos' behalf before the emperor to take pity. The vision so frightened Surmourinos that in the morning, very early, he straightway went to the saint. He prostrated himself before his feet and confessed how he had condemned the blessed man. He then went on to describe the vision he was vouchsafed to see. Then, with tears, he fervently besought Father Meletios' pardon, which he immediately received from the saint. Surmourinos departed with a happy heart. He recounted with praises the many accomplishments of the saint.

Thus, my dear brethren, this is as far as I, the narrator, have given an account of the life of Saint Meletios. We remember his surpassing zeal for Orthodoxy and the many wonderworkings wrought by him. He lived seventy-seven years, until he was translated to the Lord. He now, for our sakes, supplicates the All-Holy Trinity, to Whom is due all glory, honor, and homage to the ages of the ages. Amen.

On the 19th of January, the holy Church commemorates
our holy father among the saints, MARK EVGENIKOS,
Metropolitan of Ephesus,
single-combatant, champion, and guardian of Orthodoxy.[10]

Mark Evgenikos, our holy and God-bearing father, was born ca. 1392. He lived the greater part of his life in Constantinople. The father of the saint, George, was at first a deacon and later *proto-ekdikos*, *proto-notarios* and great *chartophylax* of the patriarchate.[11] The saint's mother, Maria, was the daughter of the well-known physician Loukas. Both of Mark's parents were the scions of renowned and devout families. In all likelihood, the saint's ancestors hailed from Imvros or Trebizond. When the saint first beheld the light of the sun, his home was in Galata of Constantinople.[12]

---

[10] This English version was taken from our publication, "The Life of Saint Mark Evgenikos," in *The Lives of the Pillars of Orthodoxy*, compiled from *The Great Synaxaristes* (in Greek), and other sources given herein. The triumphs of this saint have been praised in the writings of the Great Ecclesiarch Sylvester Syropoulos, Theodore of Gaza, Gennadios Scholarios, Nectarios and Dositheos the Patriarchs of Jerusalem, Athanasios Parios, and others. Particularly to be commended is the Greek publication of many pages by the Hagiorite Monk Kallistos of Zographou, formerly of Ephesus, entitled *Biography and the Superhuman Achievements Against the Latins of our Father among the Saints, Archbishop Mark Evgenikos of Ephesus, and the False-Council of Florence* (Βιογραφία καὶ τὰ ἐν τῇ Φλωρεντινῇ...), published in Athens, 1887. This work has also been incorporated into *The Great Synaxaristes* (in Greek), both in the January volume and the overflow into the February volume. The saint's brother, John, also penned a work, entitled *Biography of the Ever-memorable Mark* (in Greek), an anecdote of which has been included herein, which is extant in the Synodal Library of Moscow (No. 393, p. 119).

A divine office has been composed by Nikodemos the Hagiorite (1749-1809), published at Constantinople in 1834, and includes at least four editions. Father Gerasimos Mikrayiannanites composed a Supplicatory Canon to the saint.

[11] This means that George Evgenikos, at diverse times, was the inspector of convents, the chief notary, and then the director of all patriarchal correspondence and of the library. Nicholas P. Basileiade, *Saint Mark of Ephesus and the Union of the Churches* (in Greek), 3rd ed. (Athens, GR: The Brotherhood of Theologians of Sotir, 1983), p. 35.

[12] Ibid. "Saint Mark of Ephesus," January Volume of *The Great Synaxaristes of the Orthodox Church* (in Greek), pp. 470, 471; and, Archimandrite Amvrossy Pogodin, M.Sc Eccl., D.D., "Saint Mark of Ephesus and the False Union of Florence," *Orthodox Word* 3, No. 1(12) (January-February 1967): 9.

Before he embraced the monastic life, the young Mark was named Manuel. Up until the age of thirteen, Manuel's teacher was his father, who maintained a type of lecture-hall and place for meditation (φροντιστήριον). From his earliest youth, the lad distinguished himself in his studies. He was also a pupil of other acclaimed educators, under whom he advanced in his studies and knowledge. When Manuel was thirteen, his father reposed. The loss of his beloved father did not cause him to mourn unduly or to wane in his studies. In fact, he dedicated himself even more assiduously to his scholarly pursuits. In the field of liberal arts, he studied with the prominent professors of that time, such as Metropolitan Ignatios of Selymbria and the philosopher George Gemistes Plethon.[13] A brilliant student, he surpassed all others with his abilities. Yet, soon he would concentrate all his efforts on the study of theology and rhetoric.

Saint Mark Evgenikos,
the Pillar of Orthodoxy

The all-lauded Mark's principal biographer, his brother, John Evgenikos, writes about him: "In a short time, Manuel acquired the greatest knowledge, owing to his utmost diligence, attention, and sharp mind. Moreover, his conduct was gracious and sedate, more like that of a kind old man. Indeed, even his manner of dress, his glance, the way he bent his head, and his unsurpassed and eloquent conversations made my brother not only the marvel of his fellow students and peers, but even of the teachers themselves. In general, all esteemed Manuel."[14]

In time, the holy Manuel received a complete education. While still a young man, he became principal of the Patriarchal School. He acquired so much renown for his sermons that many people, even from other provinces,

[13] Basileiade, pp. 35, 36.
[14] Pogodin, pp. 9, 10.

often asked him to prepare a sermon for a specific holy day. He was admired and loved by all, causing young people to flock to him. Among his pupils were the renowned George Kourtesis Scholarios (the future Patriarch Gennadios II of Constantinople) and Theodore Agalistos. Both of these men, as they progressed, valued their teacher's profound and pious influence upon their souls. This is because Mark was not only a man of learning and letters, but was also adorned with a holy manner of life that evinced his dedication to Orthodoxy.[15]

All his biographers—his brother, the famous orator John, and George Scholarios—agreed that, while still a layman in his early youth, Manuel led a monastic and ascetic life. As if he were an angel living on earth, Manuel daily attended the divine Liturgy. When he was not at the divine offices of the Church, the holy man immersed himself wholeheartedly in the study of the sacred Scriptures and the holy fathers of the Orthodox Church. He spent his evenings in prayer, meditating upon God. He became as a diligent bee, wisely examining and searching the meadows of holy Writ and the works of the wise and sanctified fathers of the Church. Since Manuel loved God, the Master Christ gave him strength and power to oppose the serpent in every way. Later in life, this gift would serve him in resisting the evil confounding of the Faith and the violation of dogmas.

Thus, in the words of George Scholarios, "The holy young man, who was spiritually pure, behaved more like a desert dweller than like one who dwelt in the capital, the 'Queen of Cities.'" Manuel's demeanor and manner of life was foreign to the world about him; indeed, he was bound to nothing earthly.[16]

The sterling qualities of the holy youth were noticed by both Patriarch Efthymios II of Constantinople (1410-1416) and Emperor Manuel II Palaiologos (1391-1425). Thereupon, the emperor, who was devout and cultured, wished to draw the brilliant youth into his own service. He appointed Manuel as his personal secretary and entrusted him with editing his own writings. Indeed, a preeminent position in government already awaited Manuel, together with the honor and admiration of the world.[17]

Nevertheless, the world weighed heavily upon the blessed man. Among his many qualities, he possessed humility; and, therefore, he sought neither glory which is vain, nor riches that fade, nor the favor of the imperial

---

[15] Ibid., p. 10.

[16] Ibid.; George Scholarios, "Apanta ta Evriskomena," *Oeuvres Completes de Georges Scholarios* (Paris: Louis Petit, pub., 1928-1936; H.A. Siderides; M. Jugie), Vol. I, pp. 248, 249.

[17] Pogodin, loc. cit.

court. The young Manuel desired monastic perfection in the eremitic life, so that he might concentrate his soul and heart in prayer and in the remembrance of God. He believed there could be no greater good than unceasing joy in the Lord and in the illumination that comes only from the remembrance of God. He understood that to be vouchsafed such heights in the world was almost impossible, because joy and illumination immediately depart amid the unceasing distractions of vain cares that assail the mind and body. He brought to remembrance the words of Christ to Lazarus' sister, "Martha, Martha, thou art anxious and troubled about many things. But there is need of one thing, and Mary chose the good part [Lk. 10:41-42]." And what is that good part that Mary chose? She sat down beside the feet of Jesus and was listening to His word [Lk. 10:39].

Pondering upon that occupation that would enable him to attain to "Mary's part," Manuel resolved to quit everything—Constantinople, his distinguished position in the emperor's service, and his promising career. After having slightly tasted the fruits of the ascetic life, while he lived in the world, he betook himself to Abbot Symeon, a remarkable elder and ascetic, whose dwelling was outside the city. It is unfortunate that no other information concerning Abba Symeon has been preserved for posterity.

Manuel's brother, John, speaks thus about Manuel's departure from his home and friends: "When my brother was twenty-six years old, he unselfishly and generously distributed all his possessions among the poor. Manuel then took up the yoke that he yearned for from childhood and embraced the life of the fathers in the desert, a life beloved to both Prophet Elias and the Baptist John. Those whom he left behind, our relatives, household and friends, were filled with inconsolable sorrow. Emperor Manuel, who was very fond of Manuel, felt the loss of my brother's wisdom and learning. Moreover, even among the clergy his absence was felt. Then, of course, there were the many young people, his pupils, whom he had instructed and even raised. Simply put, his departure from our midst was the cause of universal mourning for all who knew my brother."

The Saint Pursues the Monastic Life

Manuel was now able to pursue the silence that he so desired, and to attain to inner quietness, peace and, ultimately, ascent to God. The holy young man betook himself to Antigone, a small and charming island of the Propontis (Sea of Marmara), where he dwelt for two years. Manuel subjected himself to harsh asceticism and to the prudent administration of his elder.[18] Manuel, however, was not to remain long outside the capital. At that time, the

---

[18] Basileiade, p. 37.

Turks were constantly attacking the area about their monastic dwelling. Therefore, Manuel's elder, Symeon, considered it imperative to relocate behind the massive city walls. This would ensure some type of defense against both the Turks and robbers.[19]

In Constantinople there was a renowned monastery called Mangan, built in the eleventh century and dedicated to the holy Great-martyr George the Trophy-bearer.[20] It was here that both Manuel and his elder went to dwell. The monastery at Mangan was nearby the palace of Mangan and was renowned throughout the capital as a center of theological studies. The monastery had an extensive library and a multitude of precious relics of the saints.[21]

Shortly after their settling in the monastery, the godly Symeon was translated to the heavenly mansions. After his novitiate, Manuel received the name Mark at his holy tonsure.[22] What a prophetic name that would prove to be! Mark's namesake was the evangelist who, iconographically, is symbolically depicted as a lion; for, roaring like a lion, Mark would disperse the arrays of the papophiles.

Living as a monk in this holy and eminent monastic enclave, Mark gave himself up entirely to silence. He disliked leaving the monastery and his cell, because it disrupted his inner attention and remembrance of God. So zealously did he guard his thoughts from distraction that he would not come out to meet with acquaintances or even members of his family.[23]

Mark was wholly engrossed in one activity, of which he never tired both day and night: studying the divine Scriptures and enriching himself with their understanding (which his writings clearly reveal). The young ascetic's other works consisted of heavy labor, extreme fasting, sleeping on the floor, and all-night vigils. Through all these holy labors, as one who had become the dwelling place of unceasing prayer, he was emboldened by God and given endurance in his wrestling against spiritual adversaries. Indeed, by God's grace, he remained invincible against the enemy's darts.

George Scholarios comments, "Father Mark was a spiritually pure person. Even as a young man, before he became a monk, he was wise in the

---

[19] Pogodin, p. 12.

[20] January Volume of *The Great Synaxaristes* (in Greek), p. 472. The monastery at Mangan was built by the Emperor Constantine IX the Monomachos (1042-1055).

[21] Basileiade, p. 37, n. 5.

[22] Several maintain that Manuel had been tonsured Mark at Antigone, before he entered the Monastery of Saint George at Mangan.

[23] Pogodin, loc. cit.

struggles of asceticism. He dwelt as though in the desert. When he renounced
the world for Christ and placed on his neck the yoke of holy obedience, he
never overthrew his promises before God. He never again took interest in the
clamor of the world, so that he might not be overturned by the vanity of
worldly glory. Till his death he would remain steadfast in his love for
Christ."[24]

Upon the brotherhood's constant urging and insistence, Mark, with
heaviness of heart and against his will, accepted the dignity of ordination. In
1420, at twenty-eight years old, the monk Mark was made a deacon. Then,
two years later, he was ordained to the priesthood.[25] His brother, John, makes
this comment about Mark and how he served the divine offices: "When
Father Mark celebrated the divine Liturgy, he was filled by divine inspiration
to such an extent that all who beheld him said that he appeared to be outside
of himself, outside even the earth, and completely immersed in God, like an
angel in the flesh."[26]

On account of the saint's exceptional learning and theological knowledge, he was adept at understanding sacred Scriptures and the mind of the
holy fathers. He also showed himself an excellent interpreter of the kontakia,
canons, troparia, and hymns of Orthodox ecclesiastical music. This might be
seen in his work, entitled *An Explanation of Ecclesiastical Services*, wherein
he drew upon his profound knowledge of Orthodox worship. In a concise
manner, he attempted to enlighten the faithful by expounding upon the Church
services, so that Christians might enter into true prayer. He desired for all to
experience that sweetness and ineffable enlightenment that enter the heart
upon remembering unceasingly Jesus Christ. In this work, he also reveals his
admiration for the melodist, Saint Romanos, commemorated by the holy
Church on the 1st of October. Saint Mark also wrote ecclesiastical canons in
all the eight modes of Byzantine music which, again, exhibited his thorough
knowledge of this sacred art. In addition to his musical talents, the saint also
wrote epigrams, poems, essays on dogma, and other theological themes, and
even on classical Greek literature.[27]

---

[24] Scholarios, loc. cit.

[25] January Volume of *The Great Synaxaristes* (in Greek), p. 474.

[26] Pogodin, loc. cit.

[27] Basileiade, pp. 40, 41. A copy of the canons composed by Saint Mark is extant in
the library at Vienna; see also P. N. Trembela, *Ekloge Hellenikes Orthodoxou
Hymnographias* (in Greek) (Athens, GR: Sotir, 1978), p. 414.

Troubles in the Empire

The deteriorating situation within the Byzantine Empire brought many, including Emperor Manuel, to the recognition that the empire was on the brink of ruin and collapse. The Turks had conquered and taken the empire to the east. Geographically, all that remained was the fortified capital of Constantinople. Emperor Manuel hoped to save his empire by entering into negotiations with the pope, with the idea of attaining a union of the Churches through an œcumenical synod. It was his hope that a council could solve all points of dissension between the Churches, by exercising the authority of holy Scriptures and holy Tradition. Then, when east and west had made peace with each other as to matters of dogma, he hoped that all western Christians would arise to the defense of their brothers in the east and do battle against the infidel. Simply put, the emperor believed that the pope and the western monarchs would send their armies to fight and destroy the Turks. This was the real motive for assembling the council.

Pope Martin V (1417-1431) was averse to councils and the theory that popes were subject to them. Moreover, he always felt that the emperor's demands had been too far-reaching; therefore, negotiations dragged on.[28] However, just when negotiations between Constantinople and Rome concerning the convocation of a council for the union of the Church were about to be finalized in September of 1422, the emperor suffered a stroke.

1. Emperor Manuel II Retires in Favor of John VIII

In June of 1422, the Ottoman Sultan, Murad II (1421-1451), launched a siege on the capital. Once more the strength of defenses saved the Byzantine capital, but it was the beginning of the last death struggle of the empire. After the siege, Manuel's son John, the heir to the throne, visited the western courts in an attempt to get help, but to no avail. Two years later, Emperor Manuel, taking to his bed, retired from active politics. He was obliged to entrust all state affairs to his son and successor, John VIII Palaiologos (1425-1448). Broken in mind and body, the aged Emperor Manuel II died on the 21st day of July, in the year 1425, as the Monk Matthew. After all he had experienced with the west, Manuel had come to regard union with them with quiet skepticism. On his deathbed, he is said to have expressly warned his son against placing any hope in the possibility of union. He thought that Latin pride and Greek obstinacy would prevent a union from ever being genuine. In spite of his father's advice, John VIII was convinced that the salvation of the empire depended upon union. He tried to press for a council, but was initially unwilling to have it take place in Italy.

---

[28] J. N. D. Kelly, *The Oxford Dictionary of Popes*, p. 240.

The political atmosphere in the Christian east was very serious. Events at that time included the sack of Serbia and Bulgaria by the Turks, the defeat of the crusaders at Nikopolis, the fruitless journey of Manuel II through western Europe and, finally, the conquest of Thessalonike by the Turks in 1430. Economically, the dismembered and enfeebled empire lay in complete ruin. Therefore, from 1431 onwards, fresh negotiations began to work toward a union with the Church of Rome when the former Venetian cardinal, Gabriel Candulmer, that is, Eugene IV (1431-1437), was pope. He had been an Augustinian hermit and was characterized as a man of inordinate zeal, but wanting in tact and gentleness.[29]

The autocrat of the "Romans (Rhomaioi)," as the Byzantines preferred to call themselves, John VIII, ruled Constantinople and the surrounding countryside. Districts on the Black Sea and in the Peloponnesos, once part of the empire, were governed independently by John's imperial brothers, all of whom took Latin brides. Theodore II married the charming Cleope Malatesta, who, although the cousin of Pope Martin V, to his fury, joined the Orthodox Church.[30] Constantine XI married Magdalena Leonardo Tocco, christened Theodora. Thomas married Catherine Zaccaria, heiress of the last Frankish prince of Achaia.

Emperor John VIII was hard pressed by the Turkish advance. In despair, he resolved to conclude negotiations between the two Churches. Again, he hoped to obtain the frequently promised western help against the infidel, even at the cost of ecclesiastical submission to Rome. Rome demanded recognition of her supremacy as essential and, in return, promised help against the oncoming Turks. However, she was not actually capable of supplying Latin military power in the east—only, perhaps, to a very limited extent. Prudently, John VIII spent all the money that the state could spare on repairs to the great land-walls of the city, so that they might be ready for the inevitable Turkish onslaught.

2. The Pro-union Party in the Capital

Although previous attempts at union ended in disillusionment and offered little encouragement, there was still an influential circle in Constantinople which favored a policy of agreement with Rome as the only hope in their hour of danger. The emperor put himself at the head of this group, in

---

[29] Joseph Gill, in *Eugenius IV, Pope of Christian Unity and Personalities of the Council of Florence*, paints a bright picture of Eugene IV. A negative image emerges in Philip Hughes, *The Church in Crisis* (London: Burns and Oates, 1961), p. 309: he characterizes Eugene as none "so weak a character as this particular pope."

[30] Sir Steven Runciman, *The Fall of Constantinople 1453*, p. 48.

spite of the very strong Orthodox nationalistic party against the union. The latter feared the loss of the purity of Greek Orthodoxy and also felt that western aid, bought by the price of union, would result in the political supremacy of the west over the east. Consequently, in their apprehension, they believed that the impending domination of the Turks would only be replaced by that of the Latins, who, as Crusaders, had already once sacked the city in 1204.

Nevertheless, envoys were sent to the Patriarchs of Alexandria, Antioch, and Jerusalem, requesting their presence at a council with the aim of uniting the east and west. The envoys returned with letters, replying that the patriarchs declined to appear personally at the council. They did, however, grudgingly comply and name their representatives, but allowed them no plenipotentiary powers. As delegates to the proposed council, the Patriarch of Alexandria chose Metropolitan Anthony of Herakleia and Priest-Monk Mark Evgenikos. The fame of the blessed Mark had been heard abroad, for he was distinguished in virtue and wisdom.[31] The Patriarch of Antioch chose Ioasaph of Ephesus and the emperor's confessor, Gregory Mammas. Gregory's egotistical character was depicted as that of a mean man, given to irritability, and with no set rules of conduct. The Patriarch of Jerusalem appointed Dionysios of Sardis and the Russian Metropolitan Isidore, formerly abbot of the Monastery of Saint Demetrios. These initial choices conformed with the emperor's wishes, but not with the preliminary consent of Joseph II, Patriarch of Constantinople (1416-1439).

The Patriarch's Prophecy

Then, one day, as Patriarch Joseph was sitting in his cell with other bishops, he made a perceptive statement. He said, "They desire the council to convene in Italy and that the Latins should subsidize our entire trip. If we are to expect daily rations solely at their hands, we have already become their servants and hirelings, and they the lords. The servant is obliged to do the bidding of his lord, as the hireling must perform that for which he is being paid. If the hireling does not fulfill his task, then he will not receive payment. If the Latins sever our provisions, what shall we do? If they will not provide for our expenses or furnish us ships, what shall we do? Hence, what profit is there for us, the poor ones, to submit to the rich and proud foreigners in their own territory? It is clearly to the Latins' advantage. Then, if we attempt to

---

[31] January Volume of *The Great Synaxaristes* (in Greek), loc. cit.

discuss and instruct them on the fathers or on piety, in my opinion, it will not be to our advantage."[32]

Although the patriarch uttered these prophetic words, after a secret meeting with the emperor and the legates of the pope, he changed his mind and made ready to travel abroad. He was assured that the Latins would receive them with much honor and love, and that the Greeks could freely, without hesitation, expound their views. The Eastern Church would be able to reveal her right beliefs and teachings, which the Latins would accept. They would return home victorious with the prize.[33] Patriarch Joseph then packed the most splendid vestments and holy vessels of Hagia Sophia.

The Priest-monk Mark Elevated to Metropolitan

At that time, Emperor John looked upon Saint Mark with much love and respect. In fact, many of the saint's theological works were written at the emperor's request. The emperor respected the holy Mark's thorough knowledge of the principles of Orthodoxy. He also appreciated his clear and disciplined mind, which quickly perceived the errors of the enemies of Orthodoxy.

The emperor was anxious to depart for Rome. The time was fast approaching for the Greek delegates to leave and meet with the Latins in council. During this period, there was another outstanding thinker among the Orthodox, Metropolitan Bessarion of Nicaea. Bessarion, formerly named John of Trebizond, had been a younger classmate of Mark and studied under the same teachers. Though a favorite of the emperor, Bessarion was more of a humanist than a theologian, and lacked firmness of character. With the death of Metropolitan Ioasaph of Ephesus,[34] and for many other reasons, the emperor insisted that the holy Mark accept the see of Ephesus and be ordained metropolitan.[35] He understood that Mark had a pure and incorruptible love for the truth and could develop sound ideas. It was the emperor's desire that Saint Mark attain to this rank, so as to occupy a suitable place among the Greek representatives, namely, the place of chief theologian of the Orthodox.

The holy man did not wish to accept such a high rank; for when he took the monastic tonsure, he had fled the world. He sensed that the office of

---

[32] "Saint Mark of Ephesus at The False-Council of Florence," February Volume of *The Great Synaxaristes* (in Greek), 5th ed. Athens: Matthew Langes, pub., 1978, p. 626.

[33] Ibid., pp. 626, 627.

[34] Ibid., p. 625; Basileiade, p. 36.

[35] January Volume of *The Great Synaxaristes* (in Greek), loc. cit.

Bishop was beyond his worth and powers. Nevertheless, he was enjoined by many respected persons, including the œcumenical patriarch. All pressed Mark to accept, asserting that his presence was indispensable for the imminent discussions with the west. They asserted that the title of metropolitan would be a rank that the Latins would esteem. Therefore, obedient to the patriarch, the emperor, and to the genuine need of the true and only Church of Christ, he submitted to the synod and its decision for his elevation. Thus, it was plain that he accepted this high ecclesiastical rank solely for the defense of Orthodoxy, which he loved. Indeed, the power and genius of the holy man's words were needed by the Orthodox, so as not to be led astray by the innovators who were already preparing a wayward path.

Shortly after his elevation, at forty-six years of age, the new metropolitan prepared to depart for Rome. Mark held high hopes for the possibility of union with the Latins. He profoundly believed in the potentiality of restoring the former unity between the two sides. Indeed, he believed in this warmly and fervently. He would labor inexhaustibly toward this aim. He said, "I followed the œcumenical patriarch and the God-given Emperor John to the council in Italy. I did not consider my own infirmity, nor the difficulty and enormity of the undertaking. I placed my hope in God and in the common saints shared between the Eastern and Western Churches. Indeed, I believed all would proceed well with us and that we would achieve something great and worthy of all our labor and hopes."[36]

Saint Mark, however, was a cautious man. Desiring to receive enlightenment and help from above for the mighty labor that lay ahead in Italy, Mark, in prayer, invoked the Holy Trinity, and begged the intercessions of God's holy angels and the Lady Theotokos. He prayed that God would put "His fear into his hard heart."[37]

The quiet and solitude that Mark treasured at the monastery at Mangan were now interrupted. The newly-appointed metropolitan made ready to depart. The truth, however, is that he was feeling physically poor. His previous austerities were taking their toll on his body. Though he felt weak, yet, by the grace of God, he would become as granite rock.[38]

The emperor was far from wishing the Greeks to give way to the Latins without a dispute. Therefore, it was determined that the works of former defenders of Orthodoxy, written during their disputes with the Latins

---

[36] Pogodin, p. 13.
[37] Basileiade, p. 50.
[38] Ibid., p. 55.

(especially the writings of Saint Photios the Great, Saint Gregory Palamas, and Metropolitan Neilos Cavasilas of Thessalonike), be examined.

In the West

During this period, Turkish successes were already a serious menace to Europe. The necessity of a common Latin-Greek struggle against the Turk was strongly felt. In the west, after the Councils of Pisa and Constance, Pope Martin V (1417-1431) opened the Council of Basle in 1431 and appointed Cardinal Giuliano Cesarini (1398-1444) to preside over it.[39] The celebrated Spanish theologian and Dominican, Juan de Torquemada (1388-1468), was appointed papal theologian at the Council of Basle.[40] Pope Martin, however, died on the 20th of February of that same year, leaving as his successor Pope Eugene IV (1431-1447).

The council had announced as its program the reform of the Western Church from the pope on down, and the settlement of the Hussite movement, which, after the death of John Huss, had spread very widely. However, because of poor attendance, a revolt in Bohemia, a war between Austria and Burgundy, and the prevalence of the above mentioned program in Basle, Pope Eugene, advised by John Beaupere, the emissary of Cardinal Cesarini, issued a bull on the 18th day of December, in the year 1431, dissolving the council. Needless to say, Pope Eugene IV was not in sympathy with this council at Basle; in fact, he feared and dreaded it. The council acted independently of the pope, backed by the Emperor Sigismund's authority, in the interest of all the German princes and of France. In the summer of 1433, Pope Eugene convoked a council at Bologna.[41]

Cardinal Cesarini, meanwhile, protested the closing of the council. He did not want to postpone union with the Greeks. Since the council had already held its first solemn session, it rejected the bull of dissolution. On the 14th of February, in the year 1432, the council declared itself an œcumenical council over the pope. The council ordered the pope and cardinals, under threat of a trial, to appear in Basle within three months.

The Council of Basle and the pope—simultaneously, yet independently of each other—opened negotiations with Emperor John by exchanging embassies. Emperor John, notwithstanding that he had already begun negoti-

---

[39] For the Bull of Martin V, *Dum onus*, see J. D. Mansi, *Sacrorum Conciliorum Nova et Amplissima Collectio* (Florence/Venice, 1757-1798, reprinted and continued by L. Petit, J. B. Martin (Paris, 1889-1927), vol. 29, 12A; Joseph Gill, *The Council of Florence* (Cambridge, England, 1959), 43, 44.

[40] *The Oxford Dictionary of the Christian Church*, s.v. "Torquemada."

[41] For the bull of Eugene IV, *Quoniam alto*, see Mansi, 29, 561-567.

ating with Eugene, recognized the advantageous proposals of the Council of Basle. He sent his ambassadors to Basle, with letters from both himself and the patriarch (dated the 15th day of October, in the year 1433), authorizing his people to agree to anything decided upon by the council that was conducive to the peace of the Churches. Numbered among the ambassadors was Isidore, Abbot of the Monastery of Saint Demetrios and later Metropolitan of Kiev.

After fruitless disputes concerning the place of a future council, the participants at the Council of Basle decided to first settle the Hussite quarrel and then consider the Greek "problem." The Byzantines were bitterly offended at being put on the same footing with the "heretic" Hussites. Since the council scored a major victory by reaching an agreement with the Hussites, under pressure from the newly-crowned Emperor Sigismund, Eugene IV issued the bull *Dudum sacrum* on the 15th day of December, in the year 1433, in which he recognized the Council of Basle.[42] Nevertheless, the council became annoyed with Eugene's decisions concerning the papacy, and reconciliation was no longer possible.[43]

In the intervening time, Emperor John was nearing agreement with the pope, who was taking over the leadership in negotiations for union. The pope wished to have negotiations take place in the northern Italian city of Ferrara, where the emperor himself would attend. Deciding the location of the council and where to find adequate funding to host the Greeks created the final break between Basle and Pope Eugene. The majority had favored Basle, Avignon, or some city in Savoy; whereas the minority favored some Italian city. The deputies of the Greek emperor preferred the minority decision. Political considerations prompted Eugene to confirm an Italian city, for he feared that the French might seize the papacy. The council then declared that Pope Eugene was contumacious. He was then summoned to stand trial. Pope Eugene responded by a bull *Doctorus Gentium* on the 18th of September, in the year 1437, officially transferring the council to Ferrara.[44] Since all efforts at reconciliation had collapsed, the loyal papal party withdrew from Basle and joined Pope Eugene at Ferrara.

The radical conciliarist group at Basle continued to maintain that it was the only lawfully constituted œcumenical council. Under the presidency of the only remaining cardinal, the ambitious Louis d'Allemand, Archbishop of Arles, the Basle assembly in 1439 declared: (1) a general council was

---

[42] For the document, see Mansi, vol. 29, 73.

[43] Sessio IV-XVIII *Conciliorum Oecumenicorum Decreta* (hereinafter referred to as *COD*).

[44] Bihlmeyer-Tuchle, *Church History*, Vol. II, p. 399.

superior to a pope; (2) a pope cannot protract or dissolve a general council; and, (3) that whoever denies these propositions is a heretic. Since Pope Eugene denied the decisions of Basle, on the 25th day of June, in the year, he was deposed as "a stiff-necked heretic and schismatic."[45] On the 5th day of November, in the year 1439, they elected the widower, Duke Amadeus VIII of Savoy, as Pope Felix V (1439-1449).[46] Discontented members of that council left Basle and sided with Eugene. Among the disgruntled was Giuliano Cesarini, who would play a prominent part in the future council with the Greeks.

In reality, the pope had worldly motives for assembling the council. Far from wishing the causes of disagreement between his church and the Eastern Church to undergo lawful investigation or careful scrutiny on the basis of the former œcumenical synods, he hoped to subject the Eastern Church to his rule. His ideas, theological training, and ecclesiological thinking were dominated by monarchical, centralist, and exclusivist Latin categories, which made the realization of a true union virtually impossible. The object of convening a council with the Greeks in Italy was to give it the appearance of an œcumenical synod and to oppose the one at Basle. Furthermore, by inviting the Byzantine emperor to his side, he felt it would terminate disputes. Pope Eugene and his Latin contemporaries thought that union with the Orthodox could be achieved merely by political manipulation, legal papers, theological agreement, and the acceptance of Eugene as pope. It never fully entered Eugene's mind that union had to rest on mutual acts of brotherly love and a respect for the rights, traditions, spiritual theology, and autonomy of each of the Eastern Churches. The weightiest difficulty to union would be the question of the primacy of the pope. There is no doubt that the western and eastern leaders attached different meanings to the rights and privileges of the Pope of Rome and to those of the eastern patriarchs.

The ecclesiological part of the Bull *Laetentur caeli* reads: "We likewise define that the holy apostolic see and the Roman pontiff hold the primacy throughout the world; and that the Roman pontiff himself is the successor of blessed Peter, the chief of the apostles, and the true vicar of Christ. The pope is the head of the entire Church, and the father and teacher of all Christians; and that full power was given to him in blessed Peter by our Lord Jesus Christ to feed, rule, and govern the universal Church, as is

---

[45] Ibid., p. 403.
[46] J. G. Rowe, "Amadeus VIII of Savoy (Felix V, antipope)," *New Catholic Encyclopedia*, 1:363; J. Grisar, "Amadeus VIII," *Lexicon fur Theologie und Kirche*, 2nd ed., 1:413.

contained in the acts of the œcumenical council and in the sacred canons....Moreover, we renew the order of the other venerable patriarchs, which was handed down in the sacred canons, and decide that the Patriarch of Constantinople will be the second after the holy Roman pontiff. Third, indeed, is Alexandria; fourth, moreover, is Antioch, and fifth is Jerusalem,...without infraction of all their privileges and rights."[47]

To the Latins, the primacy would be a dogmatic question of the first rank. To them, to be the "visible head of the Church" was to have universal and direct jurisdiction over the whole Church, including the Eastern Churches. The medieval tradition of "caesaro-papism" and centralism was so strong that all rights and privileges in the Church of Christ were seen as coming from its visible head—the Pope of Rome. As a result, all patriarchal rights and privileges were gifts bestowed by the pope on individuals chosen by him.

Both the Pope and Representatives from Basle Approach the Greeks

The pope sent some galleys with a legate to Constantinople. Grand Ecclesiarch Sylvester Syropoulos records that, before the Greeks left home, God permitted several episodes to befall them. When Commander Anthony Countloumera (Candulmer), the pope's nephew, dropped anchor at the imperial port, a great earthquake occurred.[48] Those that were prudent interpreted the event as a message from God, whereas others believed it was simply a physical phenomenon of nature.[49]

Then, four days after the arrival of the papal ships, galleys sent by the Council of Basle entered the Bosporos also. Indeed, the papal representatives deceived the emperor when they said there would be no representatives from Basle. They declared that the pope had united with the council members of Basle, giving Pope Eugene "all rule and might."[50] In fact, Countloumera told of his receiving a command from his uncle that anywhere he might encounter Basle vessels, he was to strike them. Immediately, the emperor interfered and sternly said, "If thou hadst encountered these vessels anywhere else, if thou

---

[47] *COD* 504, edidit Centro di Documentazione, Instituto per le Science Religiose-Bologna (Basle, 1962).

[48] February Volume of *The Great Synaxaristes* (in Greek), p. 627.

[49] Sylvestre Syropoulos, du Grand Ecclésiarque de l'Église de Constantinople, Les "Mémoirs" sur le Concile de Florence (1438, 1439) (Paris: V. Laurent Publications de l'Institut "Français d'Études Byzantines, Éditions du Centre National de la Recherche Scientifique, 1971), Vol. III, ch. 12, pp. 172(11-14); Basileiade, 63.

[50] Ibid., ch. 13, pp. 174(11-17); Basileiade, loc. cit.

hadst so desired, thou couldest sink the Basle ships. However, in my harbor, thou hast no license to spark a war."[51]

Indeed, the Italian rivals would have engaged each other in a naval battle had not the emperor restrained them. Both legates attempted to press the Greeks to their side, and it was then that the Greeks understood the real state of western affairs. Puzzled as to which party to join, many residents of the city attempted to incline both emperor and patriarch not to go to either Basle or Italy. Even the Emperor Sigismund sent a courier to the city requesting the emperor to delay union until internal dissension in the west could be resolved. Sultan Murad also counseled Emperor John to rely more on the stability of an alliance with him than to seek one with the Latins. Despite all the counsel and advice, Emperor John rejected the proposals of Basle. He gave orders to get ready to set sail—to Pope Eugene IV.

Departure for Italy

After many supplications to God for their safety and success, Emperor John, Patriarch Joseph II, the bishops, abbots, priest-monks, priests, and laymen, set sail on the 27th day of November, in the year 1437, using ships and funding provided by Pope Eugene IV. Immediately, when the emperor set foot on board the trireme, another message from God became apparent. Straightway, a terrible earthquake took place, causing the vessel to reel over raging waves that seemed to be boiling.[52] Making light of this occurrence, the emperor simply dismissed this divine warning also. When they were ready to set sail, the emperor's vessel was followed by Venetian vessels, which carried many of the emperor's party.

Among the passengers with the patriarch were twenty-two bishops: Metropolitan Mark of Ephesus, Dorotheos of Trebizond, Anthony of Herakleia, Metrophanes of Kyzikos, Bessarion of Nicaea, Makarios of Nikomedia, Dionysios of Sardis, Ignatios of Tŭrnovo, Dositheos of Monemvasia, Methodios of Lakedaimon, Ioasaph of Amaseia, Dorotheos of Mytilene, Esaias of Stavropol, Damianos of Moldovlachia, Nathaniel of Rhodes, Matthew of Melenikos, Dositheos of Drama, Gennadios of Ioannina, Kallistos of Dristas, Sophronios of Anchialos, and Gregory of Georgia.[53]

---

[51] Basileiade, p. 64.

[52] Syropoulos, "Memoirs," Vol. IV, ch. 1, p. 196(14-15); Basilciade, loc. cit.; February Volume of *The Great Synaxaristes* (in Greek), loc. cit.

[53] February Volume of *The Great Synaxaristes* (in Greek), pp. 625, 626. See Sylvester Syropoulos, "Apomnemonevmata" or "Memoirs" in *History*, edit. Hagae Comit (1660), in folio. The beginning of the *History* is lost, and therefore its real title is unknown. When dividing his *History*, Syropoulos called his work "Apomnemonev-

(continued...)

Isidore, elevated to Metropolitan of Kiev only a short time before, had been ordered, on his departure from Moscow to Constantinople, to bring Russian legates and bishops with him.

Other notables in the entourage were: Deacon Theodore Xanthopoulos, the *skevophylax* (keeper of the vessels); Archdeacon Michael Balsamon, the *great chartophylax*; Ecclesiarch Sylvester Syropoulos, the *dikaiophylax* (subaltern judge); Deacon George of Cappadocia, the *proto-ekdikos*; Manuel Chrysokokkes, the *great sakellarios* (patriarchal comptroller); and, John Evgenikos, the *nomophylax* (guardian of the laws), together with senators, and the learned and distinguished philosophers George Gemistos of Lakedaimon, George Scholarios, and George Amiroutzes of Trebizond.[54] Also, the imperial officer Manuel Jagaris was present. The total number comprising the grand Byzantine delegation was seven hundred ecclesiastics and laymen.[55]

The emperor, therefore, leaving behind his wife, who was a princess of the Roman Catholic faith (but had received the pope's consent to marry), had in his entourage his brother, the despot Demetrios, a strict upholder of Orthodoxy.

With elevated hopes, the Greeks weighed anchor. Indeed, with no less elevation of soul did the Latin clergy and people of Italy await their arrival. It was the universal belief that the much-desired union would be achieved. Nearly four hundred years before this council in Ferrara, from the time of Patriarch Michael Keroularios (1043-1059) and Cardinal Humbert, it had been a primary aim of popes and emperors to restore ecclesiastical communion. Negotiations with this object in view had, in fact, been conducted on approximately thirty different occasions.[56]

They underwent a difficult voyage on a stormy Mediterranean Sea, which portended what lay ahead. After sailing through Kallipolis, they arrived in Madytos, where they received a third divine message. Suddenly, a great

---

[53](...continued)
mata." The title given by the editor is "Truthful History of an Unjust Union." This work is the principal source for the history of this council.

[54] Ibid., p. 626.

[55] Deno J. Geanakoplos, *Byzantine East and Latin West: Two Worlds of Christendom in Middle Ages and Renaissance*, p. 94.

[56] L. Brehier, "Attempts at Reunion of the Greek and Latin Churches," *Cambridge Medieval History*, IV (1936), 594 ff.

earthquake occurred which startled all passengers on board. Nonetheless, the emperor did not consider these signs as a mark of divine displeasure.[57]

Arrival in Venice

Indeed, in view of the unfortunate position of the Greeks, the outcome was a foregone conclusion. After three months, the Greek delegation reached its destination, Venice, on the 8th day of February, in the year 1438. The emperor's vessel arrived first and was met by the papal representatives, including Cardinals Nicholas Albergati (Cardinal of the Holy Cross of Jerusalem) and Giuliano Cesarini.[58] The nobility and people of Venice, who had always been well-disposed toward the Greeks, also flocked to greet them.

Patriarch Joseph II, with the rest of the clergy, arrived in Ferrara three days after the emperor. Though they were also enthusiastically welcomed by the Venetians, the patriarch was indignant that the emperor landed before him. He commented that either they should have put into port simultaneously or the clerics of the Orthodox Church should have preceded.[59]

The Greeks then went aside that they might perform the divine Liturgy at a church. The Venetians gathered to observe and listen to the order of the divine Liturgy, as it was performed in the Eastern Church. With tears the people exclaimed, "Before we beheld the Greeks, we thought them barbaric. Now, however, we recognize and believe that they are the firstborn of the Church and that the Spirit of God speaks through them!"[60]

In the next three weeks, many of the Greeks and even some of the bishops considered Venice as the crossroad between east and west, and as the "promised land." In comparison with the miserable state of their own empire, then nearly overpowered by the Islamic hordes, Venice impressed them with its luxury, liberty, and the comforts of western life. This proved to be a temptation for weaker Greeks.[61] As part of their city tour, the Greeks visited the Church of Saint Mark, where they beheld excellently crafted Orthodox treasures, seized during the Crusades and Latin rule in the Byzantine capital

---

[57] February Volume of *The Great Synaxaristes* (in Greek), p. 627; Syropoulos, "Memoirs," Vol. IV, ch. 4, p. 200(5-7).

[58] Ivan N. Ostroumoff, *The History of the Council of Florence*, translated from the Russian by Basil Popoff, Saint Petersburg Ecclesiastical Academy, Aleksandr Vasilevich Gorskii, and edited by Rev. J. M. Neale, D.D. (London: Joseph Masters, 1861), p. 37. See https://archive.org/ details/historycouncilf00nealgoog.

[59] Basileiade, p. 69.

[60] Archim. Andron. K. Demetrakopoulos (Leipzig), p. 109, cited in "False-Council," February Volume of *The Great Synaxaristes* (in Greek), loc. cit.; Douka, *Historia Byzantine* (in Greek) (Bonn: Imm. Bekker, 1834), p. 213.

[61] Ostroumoff, loc. cit.

in 1204. Neither did the sight of this past crime cause the Greeks to withdraw from Venice.[62]

In February of 1438, Pope Eugene issued a papal bull excommunicating all those at Basle. The Council of Basle, for its own part, declared the Council of Ferrara illegal. Finally, they demanded that all the bishops assembled in Ferrara should come to Basle, under pain of ecclesiastical punishment. Thus, there was tremendous dissension in the Western Church in the first half of the fifteenth century.

A Question of Protocol

On the 4th day of March, in the year 1438, Emperor John, with his company of attendants, then proceeded first to meet Pope Eugene, who, with his cardinals, bishops, and abbots, awaited him in the palace of Ferrara. Upon the emperor's entrance, the pope, a tall and thin man, arose and embraced him. The pope then gave the emperor his hand, which the emperor kissed. After a private conversation, the emperor retreated to the palace prepared especially for him.[63]

The day after his arrival, the frail Patriarch Joseph received a messenger from the emperor, informing him that Pope Eugene expected him and all the clergy to bend their knees before him and kiss his slipper, the customary western manner of greeting the pope.[64] The patriarch immediately declared, "With such a kiss I shall not greet him. The pope and I are brothers; and as brothers we should embrace and kiss one another—any other way, I shall not do it."[65] When the Greek hierarchs met in council to discuss this distasteful matter, Metropolitan Dorotheos of Trebizond, quickly commented to the patriarch, "Now thou dost tell us these things? In Constantinople, thou didst say that the Latins await us with open arms and would receive us with exceeding honor and love!"[66]

This formality was to be the first cause of dispute between the Orthodox and the pope. The arrogance of Pope Eugene deeply grieved the patriarch and the bishops. Despite this, the pope persisted in sending his many messengers to persuade the Greeks. Joseph is said to have remarked to the pope's clergy that were sent to him, "Whence has the pope this right? Which

---

[62] Basileiade, pp. 65, 66.

[63] Ostroumoff, p. 38.

[64] Basileiade, p. 69; February Volume of *The Great Synaxaristes* (in Greek), loc. cit.; Syropoulos, "Memoirs," Vol. IV, ch. 30, p. 230(9-13).

[65] Sylvestrum Sguropulum, *Vera Historia unionis non verae inter Graecos et Latinos, sive Concilii Florentini exactissima narratio, Graeca Scripta* (Hagae: Robertus Creyghton, 1660), Vol. IV, ch. 19, pp. 92, 93; Basileiade, pp. 69, 70.

[66] Ibid., p. 70.

synod gave it to him? Show me from what source he derives this privilege and where it is written. The pope claims that he is the successor of Saint Peter. If he is the successor of Saint Peter, then we too are the successors of the rest of the apostles. Did they kiss the foot of Saint Peter?"[67] To these remarks the Latin bishops replied that it was an ancient custom for all to kiss the pope's foot—"bishops, kings and even the emperor of the Germans and the cardinals who are holy and superior to the emperor" have done so.[68]

Patriarch Joseph, with great resolve, kept to his former demand of only a brotherly welcome with the pope, saying, "This is an innovation; I will not follow it....If the pope wants a brotherly embrace in accordance with ecclesiastical custom, I will be happy to embrace him. If he refuses, I will abandon everything and return to Constantinople."[69] In fact, the patriarch not only spoke for himself, but for his entire entourage.[70] Finally, after two days of resistance and wrangling over how the Greek clergy were to meet him, on the 8th of March, the pope yielded to the patriarch's demand, feigning only a genuine desire for peace.[71] However, the pope would receive the patriarch in a separate chamber, to conceal his acquiescence to the Greeks and where few western eyes could witness the omission of this perceived mark of subordination.[72] Though he greeted Patriarch Joseph in a proper manner, the pope then immediately sat down when meeting and greeting the remaining Greek clergy.[73] Eyewitness Syropoulos describes the meeting chamber: "The throne of the pope was elevated, so that to his right the cardinals sat at the level of his feet. Then, to the left, and much lower, sat the Patriarch of Constantinople. The Greek clergy that followed the patriarch venerated the pope by kissing his hand and then his cheek."[74]

Desiring to employ the aid of the western monarchs, Emperor John explained to Eugene that not only their bishops should preside, but also the European sovereigns or their representatives. At first the pope refused, perceiving it as an impediment, because of the dissensions between the different kingdoms. However, John persisted, so the pope sent his legate to

---

[67] Sguropulum, Vol. IV, ch. 19, pp. 92, 93.

[68] Ibid., 95.

[69] Sguropulum, Vol. IV, ch. 21, pp. 94, 95; Syropoulos, "Memoirs," Vol. IV, chaps. 31-33, pp. 230-234.

[70] Dositheos, *Dodekavivlos*, p. 903.

[71] Ostroumoff, p. 39.

[72] February Volume of *The Great Synaxaristes* (in Greek), pp. 627, 628.

[73] Basileiade, p. 71, 72.

[74] Syropoulos, "Memoirs," Vol. IV, chaps. 34, 35, pp. 234(16-32)-236(1-29); Basileiade, p. 72.

the kings and princes of Europe with invitations to the council, though few would respond.[75]

1. Allocation of Monies

Moreover, the emperor prevailed upon the pope, with great difficulty, to allocate monies to the Greeks for their maintenance. The pope provided the emperor with thirty florins (gold coins), the patriarch with twenty-five florins, the Despot Demetrios with twenty florins, and the remainder with three or four florins each. This was not enough to provide for their basic needs. Syropoulos records that the emperor sold his weapons and pledged his robes. The patriarch, in order to eat, sold his cuffs.[76]

The Greeks were receiving daily rations like beggars. Although this treatment was quite against the treaty, this complaint was to persist continually during all council sessions. However, the pope had his reasons and motives; for, through deprivation, he was able to extract obedience and conformity from the Greeks. His cruel method was simple: when the Greeks refused to obey, their salaries ceased; but when they complied, wages were given out as a reward for obedience. In many instances, some Greek bishops were compelled to sell their clothes that they might eat.[77]

Negotiations Begin

The Latins arranged the seating so that they would sit on one side and the Greeks on the other, with the pope between them. The Greeks rejected these seating arrangements. After much discussion and debate, the Latins conceded to have the pope sit with the Latins to the right of the altar and the Greeks to the left.[78] No one was to sit on a high throne; instead, the Gospel was placed on it. On either side of the Gospel were placed candle stands, while on the floor were placed silver gilt statues of the Apostles Peter and Paul. The patriarch, pleading illness, declined to be present, though he gave his consent for the opening.[79]

Another problem cropped up with the arrangement and height of the seats and thrones. This entire affair provoked the emperor to say, "Now I understand the truth of these discussions concerning the throne and the seats. This is not a matter of synodical order and protocol, but much rather that of pride and worldly fantasy, which is far from our spiritual condition." The

---

[75] Ostroumoff, p. 41; February Volume of *The Great Synaxaristes* (in Greek), p. 628.
[76] Basileiade, p. 88.
[77] Ostroumoff, p. 42.
[78] February Volume of *The Great Synaxaristes* (in Greek), loc. cit.
[79] Basileiade, p. 73; Ostroumoff, p. 44.

emperor, though indignant, never thought to quit the talks, but remained a papal captive.[80]

On Holy Wednesday, the 9th day of April, in the year 1438, after the Latins finished Mass and the Greeks the divine Liturgy, a meeting was arranged in the Ferrara Cathedral of Saint George to discuss the question of the union of the churches. The pope was the first to enter the cathedral; he immediately went to the northern aisle and sat down on his throne—a throne that was elevated above those of the patriarch and the emperor, and constructed of richer materials.[81]

The council commenced with the reading of a papal bull and an encyclical of the patriarch. After the council formally opened, when the pope was questioned about participation of the members from Basle, he simply replied, "That matter has encountered difficulties."[82] Thereafter, for about another four months there passed a period of inactivity. All this time, the Emperor John was anxiously waiting for the western princes to assemble. He desired to meet with them and arrange a military alliance against the Turks. This, in reality, was the true motive of the Byzantine emperor for devising the entire affair of uniting the Churches. However, the political situation in the west at that time did not allow this.[83]

Although the pope had sent decrees to the western monarchs urging their attendance, all expectations proved fruitless. Basle continued to threaten the pope's throne and the council he had convoked. The Greeks delayed talks, awaiting other western envoys. However, after Pascha, on the 13th of April, Eugene required that the talks commence. Therefore, committees of both Latin and Greek theologians were organized for discussing the disputes between their Churches.

During this period, Patriarch Joseph requested of the pope that he furnish the Greek delegation a church that they might celebrate the divine Liturgy on Sundays and feast days. The pope responded that he personally could not provide them with a church, because it depended upon the permission of the bishop of the city. The Greeks believed this to be a strange answer coming from one who proclaimed himself chief over all in his Church.

---

[80] Syropoulos, "Memoirs," Vol. IV, ch. 40, p. 244(8-10).

[81] Ostroumoff, pp. 43, 41.

[82] *Praktika* (*Actorum Graecorum*), Concilium Florentinum Documenta et Scriptores, Series B, (Rome: J. Gill, pub., Pontificum Institutum Orientalium Studiorum, 1953) Vol. V, fasc. 1, p. 10(16-24); Basileiade, p. 74.

[83] Archimandrite Amvrossy Pogodin, M.Sc Eccl., D.D., "Saint Mark of Ephesus and the False Union of Florence," *Orthodox Word* 3, No. 2(13) (March-May 1967): 45.

Nevertheless, the bishop of that city claimed he could not lend the Greek Orthodox a church, simply because he did not have any available that was large enough. He insisted that a small church would not please the dignity of the patriarch. This also struck the Greeks as paradoxical. They hoped to reach a union of the Churches, only to find the doors of the churches closed to them![84]

The Contestants

There were about two hundred and thirty representatives present, of which two hundred were on the Latin side. Main Latin speakers included the skilled diplomat, Cardinal Giuliano Cesarini; Cardinal Nicholas Albergati; Archbishop Andrew of Rhodes (a Greek who had gone over to the Roman Catholics); Juan de Torquemada (1388-1468); and, later in the disputes, Fra John of Ragusa, and some other abbots. The Latin delegates to the council were a formidable team, but the actual head of the committee for the Latins was the pope. Soon to become apparent was the pope's aim to subordinate the Orthodox Church to himself.[85]

At the head of the Orthodox debaters were Saint Mark of Ephesus, exarch of the Patriarch of Antioch, and Metropolitan Bessarion of Nicaea. The latter, who had great facility in speaking, at first supported Saint Mark and the cause of Orthodoxy. Mark was most grateful for Bessarion's help, and even commented, "A brother helped by a brother is as a strong and high city [Prov. 18:19]."[86] In his zeal, Bessarion told his colleagues, "The words of the holy fathers alone are sufficient to resolve any doubt and persuade every soul. We will not be convinced by Latin syllogisms, probabilities, or arguments, but by the naked words of the fathers." Yet because of his egotistical character, Bessarion could never be a trusted coadjutor. Perceiving Mark as his rival, he would soon break friendship with him and become his opponent. Although Bessarion secured the confidence of the emperor, he actually harmed the Orthodox position. He would end his sorry life in apostasy, as one of the leading cardinals of the Latin Church.

Although the Greek delegates numbered thirty in their committee, most were not permitted to enter into the debates. It was evident that there was little team spirit among the individualistic Greeks. At the outset there was no coherence and no fixed policy among the Greeks. On the other hand, the Latin delegation was composed of highly trained controversialists who worked

---

[84] Syropoulos, "Memoirs," Vol. IV, chaps. 46, 47, pp. 250, 252; Basileiade, p. 88.
[85] Ibid.
[86] Syropoulos, "Memoirs," Vol. V, ch. 29, p. 282(16-18).

together as a formidable team.[87] The emperor remarked more than once that his best theologians were monks and laymen. In fact, as we already know, the three most active delegates of the council—Mark Evgenikos, Bessarion, and Isidore—were consecrated bishops on the eve of the council. In reality, though, Emperor John was the head of the committee of Greeks. The main thrust of his aim was to conclude an agreement profitable for the Byzantine state.

After the preliminary prayers, Saint Mark was permitted to address all present and to thank the pope for assembling the council. Saint Mark also made it clear that the Orthodox hierarchs had not come to Italy to sign a capitulation. The Orthodox would not sell the Faith for the benefit of their crumbling state. Their purpose in attending the council was for the confirmation of true doctrine. Mark, the star of the Church of Christ, made it clear to the west that the purity of Orthodoxy must be preserved. He indicated that negotiations could end in failure if Rome did not concede and renounce her innovations. The westerners had introduced dogmas and liturgical practises unknown to the ancient Church, which had led to schism between Rome and Byzantium. The fiery teacher of piety then said that if the Church of Rome desired to finish as well as she had begun—that is, from the time of the apostles—then she must retract her doctrine on the procession of the Holy Spirit and not perform the Liturgy with unleavened wafers (*azymes*). Furthermore, Saint Mark pointed out to them that union was just as necessary to the west, because all Christians had a common enemy—the Moslem Turks.[88]

It was visibly apparent that the pope and his committee received Mark's address with cold disdain. When Emperor John and others among the Greeks, who were not present, learned of Mark's words, they, too, were indignant. They did not wish the differences between east and west to be mentioned. As a result, the emperor almost surrendered Mark, the ornament of bishops and priests, to the judgment of the Greek council for daring to express such opinions before the western delegates.[89] As the real head of his committee, the emperor authorized only certain persons to speak with the Latin delegates. He bade them not to reject the Latin opinions, even if they were contradictory to Orthodox doctrine, but merely to look upon every question as not yet having been decided. A solution would be reached by taking the opinion of all as final and decisive. Thereupon, it was gradually

---

[87] Steven Runciman, *The Great Church in Captivity* (NY: Cambridge University Press, 1968), p. 104; Idem, *The Fall*, p. 17.

[88] Pogodin, "Saint Mark," *Orthodox Word* 3, No. 2(13), p. 46.

[89] Syropoulos, Vol. V, 2; Ostroumoff, p. 46.

revealed to the spiritual eye of the saint that his hopes for a holy and proper union would not, nay could not, be realized.

Subjects of the Debates

The purpose for which the council should have been held was not likely to be realized, because Emperor John would not allow his delegates to carefully examine Rome's unsound dogmas, fearing this would sow dissension with the west. The emperor realized that it would be impossible to reconcile Orthodoxy with Latin doctrines, but he did not want this to become evident too soon, that is, before he had attained the aim of his scheme. Not wanting to provoke or vex the west, he hoped to conclude the union on the basis of certain vague propositions.

The pope then took the initiative. In the third sitting of the council, Cardinal Giuliano Cesarini listed the principle points of dispute in doctrine, as follows: (1) the procession of the Holy Spirit; (2) the question of *azymes* in the Eucharist; (3) Purgatory; and, (4) the primacy of the Pope of Rome. The west then asked which of these points the Orthodox preferred to discuss first. The emperor decided that either of the last two points might be discussed. However, he forbade his representatives even to touch upon the question of the procession of the Holy Spirit.[90] The Latins agreed to discuss the issue of Purgatory. Matters such as the marriage of the clergy and divorce were left to be settled at a later time.

Since the Latins numbered more than two hundred and the Greeks only thirty, in preliminary discussions it was decided that to make a determination on any issue required the general assent of one or the other side, and not by majority vote. Thus, irrespective of their number, the Greek vote would have as much strength as the Latin vote. Sylvester Syropoulos records that any member of either party that crossed over to the opposition was to be strictly punished.[91] "Syropoulos," comments John Evgenikos (the saint's brother), as the eyewitness reporter of the proceedings, "clearly and genuinely related those matters involving my holy brother, the universal father and guide."[92]

Purgatory

On the 4th of June, in the year 1438, the discussion on Purgatory commenced.

---

[90] Ibid., Vol. V, 7, 8; Ostroumoff, p. 47.

[91] Ibid., Vol. VI, 9, 10.

[92] Spyridon Lambros, *Paleologia and Peloponnesiaka* (in Greek) (Athens, GR: 1912-1923 and 1926-1930), vol. 1, p. 193.

1. The Latin Statement

Cardinal Giuliano gave the Latin definition of their doctrine. He affirmed that, from the time of the apostles, the Church of Rome had taught that when the souls of the saints depart this world, pure and free of every taint, they immediately enter the regions of bliss. However, the souls of those that after baptism have sinned and later sincerely repented and confessed their sins, but were unable to perform the penance laid upon them by their spiritual father or to bring forth fruits of repentance sufficiently to atone for their sins, would be purified by the fire of Purgatory—some quickly, some slowly, according to their sins. Then, after their purification, they depart for the land of everlasting bliss.[93]

For the Latin defense, Cardinal Giuliano cited scriptural quotations from the Old Testament. It is written that Judas Maccabeus gathered up a collection to be sent to Jerusalem as a sin offering, to make reconciliation for those men slain in battle, that they might be delivered from sin; it is recorded that this was a good and holy thought on his part [2 Mac. 12:42, 45].[94]

They also quoted the words of our Savior when He said, "Whosoever shall speak against the Holy Spirit, it shall not be forgiven him, neither in this age nor in the coming one [Mt. 12:32]." However, the one verse that they believed defended their point involved the words of the divine Paul: "For no one is able to lay any other foundation beside the One being laid, Who is Jesus Christ. Now if anyone build upon this foundation gold, silver, precious stones, wood, grass, straw, the work of each shall become manifest; for the day shall declare it, because it is being revealed in fire; and the fire shall put to the test the work of each, of what sort it is. If the work of anyone abide which he built upon, he shall receive a reward. If the work of anyone shall be burned, he shall suffer loss, but he himself shall be saved, but so as in the midst of fire [1 Cor. 3:11-15]."[95]

2. The Orthodox Response

Saint Mark and Bessarion, both excellent speakers, had an opinion on this issue. In explaining the differences in belief, Bessarion said that the Latins claim that from now till the day of judgment, departed souls are purified by fire and are thus liberated from their sins, albeit, the amount of time needed for purification varies. He then explained that the west calls this purgatorial fire, but that in the future life they allow the everlasting, and not

---

[93] Ostroumoff, loc. cit.

[94] Ibid., p. 49.

[95] Ibid., p. 50.

the purgatorial fire. Thus, the Latins conceive both a temporal and everlasting fire.[96]

Bessarion continued by explaining that there is one everlasting fire only. The temporal punishment of sinful souls consists in that they, for a time, depart into a place of darkness and sorrow where they are punished by being deprived of the divine Light. However, they can be delivered from this place of darkness and sorrow through the prayers of the Church, the holy Eucharist, and deeds of charity done in their name—but not by fire. The Greeks also maintained that, until the resurrection and the rejoining of the soul to the body, neither do the souls of sinners suffer full punishment, nor do the saints enjoy full bliss. Although the Latins agreed that sinners presently do not suffer full punishment, yet, they claimed, the saints enjoy entire bliss and reward.[97]

The written answer, introduced by the Greeks countering the Latin defense of their doctrine of Purgatory, was either entirely or principally authored by Saint Mark. In answer to their scriptural quotations, Saint Mark gave a clear and satisfactory rebuttal. The Greeks remarked that the verses from the Book of Maccabees and Christ's words in the Gospel only prove that some sins will be forgiven after death. By what means this is accomplished, however, is not clear. The Greeks maintained that forgiveness of sins versus punishment by fire and tortures is inconsistent. Both cannot coexist; there is either forgiveness or punishment, not both simultaneously.

In explaining the Apostle Paul's words, the blessed Mark quoted from many eastern fathers, including Saint John Chrysostom (ca. 347-407), who, when using the word "fire," gives it the meaning of an everlasting fire and not one that is temporal and purgatorial. The words "gold, silver, precious stones [1 Cor. 3:12]" signify the virtues. Saint Chrysostom explains the words "wood, grass, straw" in the sense of bad deeds, destroyed in the everlasting fire. The word "day" implies the final judgment; and the words "saved, but so as in the midst of fire," means the preservation and continuance of the sinner's existence while suffering punishment. Therefore, Saint John finds and explains two punishments revealed in the Apostle Paul's words: "He who abides in wickedness shall suffer loss, in that his works perish into nought, leaving him naked of all defense, and that such a one shall abide in the fire."[98] The apostle divides all that is "built upon this foundation" into two parts, that is, gold,

---

[96] Ibid., p. 48.
[97] Ibid., p. 49.
[98] Saint John Chrysostom, Homily 9, *First Corinthians*.

silver, and precious stones versus wood, grass, and straw. There is no suggestion of any third or middle part.

Addressing the Latins, the Greeks said, "Your doctrine would perhaps have had some foundation if the Apostle Paul had divided bad works (hay, wood, and stubble) into two kinds, and had said that one kind is purified by God and the other is allotted everlasting damnation. However, the apostle made no such division. He simply contrasted two works: virtues that usher one into everlasting bliss and sins deserving everlasting damnation." The apostle does not divide sins into mortal and venial; he distinguishes between good and bad deeds. He attributes to fire the power of destroying evil actions, but not the evildoers. By the foregoing, it is obvious that the inspired theologian Paul was not describing a purgatorial fire.[99]

The apostle says, "The work of each shall become manifest; for the day shall declare it [1 Cor. 3:13]." This "day" is the day of the second coming of Christ, the coming age. The word "day" is used in a special sense, in that it is opposite the present life which is "night." We have the testimony of holy Scripture when we read that, in that "day," the Lord shall come in glory, and a fiery stream shall precede Him: "A stream of fire rushed before Him [Dan. 7:10]"; "Fire shall go before Him, and shall burn round about His enemies [Ps. 96:3]"; and "...the coming of the day of the Lord, by reason of which the heavens, being set on fire, shall be dissolved, and the elements, being burned with intense heat, shall be melted [2 Pet. 3:12]!"[100]

Consider the verse, "If the work of anyone shall be burned, he shall suffer loss (ζημιωθήσεται) [1 Cor. 3:15]." The apostle here speaks of everlasting punishment. The sinner's "loss" is to be deprived of the divine Light. This verse then cannot possibly refer to those who, according to Latin doctrine, are being purified in purgatorial fire. To the Latins, those being purified do not "lose" anything; indeed, they gain immensely when delivered from evil and clothed in purity.[101]

To defend their point, the Latin team then introduced the writings of Bishop Augustine of Hippo (354-430), especially since the foundation of the medieval doctrine of Purgatory is found in his works. He held that the fate of an individual soul is decided immediately after death, and he taught the absolute certainty of purifying pains in the next life.[102] Saint Mark rejected the explanation given by Augustine. This African bishop understood the words

---

[99] Ostroumoff, pp. 52, 53.

[100] Ibid., p. 53.

[101] Ibid., p. 54.

[102] *De Civ. Dei*, xxi. 13 and Ibid., 24.

"shall be saved (σωθήσεται) [1 Cor. 3:15]" to mean bliss and, therefore, gave quite a different meaning to this quotation. The Greeks, however, understand Greek words better than foreigners. The expressions σωθῆναι, σωζέσθαι, and σωτήρια connote continuance and existence. Hence, sinners doomed to everlasting fire are not destroyed but continue in fire. They are preserved and continue to exist.[103]

3. The Vision of Saint Niphon

In a vision of the future Judgment, Saint Niphon (4th C.), Bishop of Constantia, heard the righteous Judge declare, "Go from Me, ye who have been cursed, into the fire, the everlasting one, which hath been prepared for the devil and his angels: For I hungered and ye did not give Me anything to eat; I thirsted and ye did not give Me anything to drink; I was a stranger and ye did not bring Me in, naked and ye did not clothe Me, sick, and in prison, and ye did not visit Me [Mt. 25:41-43]." And, "these shall go away into everlasting punishment [Mt. 25:46]."

Saint Niphon then records, "As soon as the Judge pronounced that decision, at once, an enormous fiery river spilled over from the east and went rolling violently toward the west. It was broad like a big sea. When the sinners on the left saw it they were stunned and began to tremble, frightened in their despair. Nonetheless, the impartial Judge ordered everyone—just and unjust—to pass through the flaming river, so the fire could try them. Those at His right hand started first. They crossed and came out gleaming like solid gold. Their deeds did not burn, but instead proved to be brighter and clearer with the test; that is why they were filled with joy. After them, those at His left hand came to pass through the fire, so that their deeds might be tried. However, because they were evildoers, the flame began to envelop them and kept them in the middle of the river. Their deeds were burned like straw, whereas their bodies remained unharmed, to burn for endless ages along with the devil and the demons. No one was able to come out of that fiery river. The fire imprisoned all of them, because they deserved condemnation and punishment."[104]

4. The Latin Counterattack

In answer to all the arguments propounded by the Greeks, the Latins attempted to bring forward several eastern fathers. The Orthodox responded that the quotations introduced by the Latins did not support their position. When they brought forward the testimony of Saint Gregory of Nyssa, the Greeks restricted their words by the expression "such was his idea."

---

[103] Ostroumoff, p. 52.
[104] *Stories, Sermons, and Prayers of Saint Nephon: An Ascetic Bishop*, pp. 67, 68.

Moreover, "We must view the general doctrine of the Church, and take the holy Scripture as a rule for ourselves, not paying attention to what each has written in a private capacity."[105] When the Latins attempted to assert the weight of the opinion of the Church of Rome, the Greeks found this to be inconsistent with the present subject.[106]

With the course of the dispute becoming more difficult for the Latins to deal with, they drifted off, putting forward many light and abstract questions, such as, where and how do the angels fly? What is the substance of hellfire? The last question was wittily answered by the imperial officer, Jagaris, when he said, "The inquirer will receive a satisfactory answer when he experiences the nature of that fire personally!"[107]

5. Conclusion to the Issue on Purgatory

Very little remains of the council's discussions on Purgatory. However, false doctrine's stouthearted enemy, Mark, composed two treatises on purgatorial fire. These works are superb and constitute the most complete treatment of this question in Orthodox patristics. Even western critics have designated his treatises as "an excellent work and not to be neglected." The other Greeks at the council found the Latin doctrine too over-sure and disliked Latin phrasing and formulas. Indeed, the delegates from the west, having formulated their teaching on Purgatory just at that council, produced serious complications for themselves in the future.[108]

As negotiations on the subject of Purgatory deepened, it became evident that the Latin theologians could neither find firm proofs for their opinions, nor give them up—even after the Greek answer made evident the unsoundness of their newly-invented doctrine. The parable of Lazarus was also brought forth, where mention is made of Abraham's bosom [Lk. 16:23], the place of bliss—and of Hades and being in torments. The parable makes no mention of an intermediate place for temporal punishments. Therefore, the steadfast Orthodox, firm in the Faith handed down to them by the apostles and holy fathers, refused to accept Latin sophistries and a doctrine that was not founded on any good proofs.[109]

6. The State of the Departed Souls of the Righteous

Since the question of Purgatory went unanswered, another question was introduced: do the departed righteous attain entire bliss? The difference

---

[105] Ostroumoff, p. 54.
[106] Ibid., p. 55.
[107] Syropoulos, Vol. V, 16, 18; Ostroumoff, loc. cit.
[108] Pogodin, "Saint Mark," *Orthodox Word* 3, No. 2(13), p. 49.
[109] Ostroumoff, loc. cit.

of opinion between the both parties had been previously alluded to by Bessarion. The Greeks found it necessary to take a recess and confer privately on the subject.[110]

On the 15th of July, the Greeks gathered within the patriarch's cell to read the writings of the fathers. The emperor then called upon each to cast his vote. Those that gave a negative answer based their decision on the Apostle Paul's words, when he spoke of the works of the ancients who "having been approved by testimony through faith, received not for themselves the promise, God having foreseen some better thing concerning us, that they should not be made perfect without us [Heb. 11:39, 40]." Then, for the rest of that day, the Greeks gave arguments back and forth. The following day, all the Greek bishops unanimously agreed that the souls of the righteous are already in the enjoyment of bliss, but at the general resurrection, when they shall be joined to their bodies, their bliss shall be greater when they shall shine like the sun.

Factions Among the Greeks

To the detriment of Orthodoxy, the Greek party became divided. Bessarion became more passive and imagined Mark as a rival speaker, and not as a brother. He became jealous and was no longer very aggressive in the defense of the Faith. Why? This is because Mark was commissioned to write the Latins an answer about Purgatory, and not Bessarion, though he gave an answer also. Gregory Mammas, resentful that Mark had replaced him as vicar of the Patriarch of Antioch, did his utmost to set Bessarion against Mark and fan the flames of jealously in Bessarion.[111]

In one instance, Bessarion rose from his chair by Mark and went to sit with the senators, leaving Mark to contend alone with the Latins. At first the holy man was shaken by his former classmate's abrupt action, but he did not lose his courage and composure. The other Greeks were quick to perceive this rift between the leading debaters.[112] The Greeks then urged the patriarch to reconcile the misunderstanding; but, unfortunately, the invalid Patriarch Joseph refused to intervene in this matter—though by a meek reproof, he might have ended the quarrel.[113] Furthermore, a hypocritical Gregory Mammas often found fault with Mark, and would mock Mark's words. Yet, on the other hand, he secretly esteemed him. For example, Gregory sat down lower in the council, though he had the privileges of a higher patriarchal throne. When Gregory's opinion concurred with that of Saint Mark's, he

---

[110] Ibid., p. 56.
[111] February Volume of *The Great Synaxaristes* (in Greek), p. 633; Ostroumoff, p. 57.
[112] February Volume of *The Great Synaxaristes* (in Greek), loc. cit.
[113] Ibid.; Ostroumoff, pp. 56-58.

would say, "I am of the same opinion as the holy Metropolitan of Ephesus."[114] This was mere outward display, though, because in the presence of Bessarion and the emperor, Gregory would place Mark lower than the Archbishop of Nicaea. Bessarion did not care about the obvious self-contradiction in his behavior.[115] Therefore, as soon as the Greeks began discussions, there arose men who were to betray Orthodoxy, because of petty jealousies and rivalries; whereas, others sacrificed the Church for their own passions and gain.

More than three months had elapsed since the opening of the council. The dispute on Purgatory ended, and the Greeks, remaining inactive and suffering want in everything, began to feel sad, regretting having left their homes. They still had not received their stipend.[116] Due to their discontent, the emperor feared that some might abandon the talks. Therefore, no Greeks were to receive passports without the emperor's permission and signature; furthermore, he ordered the city governor not to allow any Greeks to depart.

George Scholarios, favoring union—though he later changed his mind—freely admitted that his compatriots were no match for the Latins in erudition and dialectic skill. Although the Greeks had the true Faith, they disagreed among themselves; and the emperor, who had his own motives, did not make their task any easier. He insisted that the Greeks not touch upon the matter of the divine energies. When the Latins raised the question of the energies, the Greeks, obedient to the emperor's wishes, had to reply with embarrassment that they were "unable to discuss it." Indeed, it is hard to see how a council that shirked the main issues of discord could hope to achieve concord!

An Epidemic Strikes Ferrara

During this time in Ferrara, the Greek delegates were kept in closed quarters. The emperor settled in a monastery not far from town and spent a good deal of time hunting.[117] He was still waiting for the ambassadors of the western monarchs, although the numbers of the council were diminishing, not increasing. Many fell before the frightful epidemic. Others, fearing disease, retreated to their homes. Nevertheless, the Greeks received proof of divine protection, because not one of them suffered from the epidemic. At the com-

---

[114] Syropoulos, Vol. VII, 10; Ostroumoff, p. 57; Basileiade, p. 81.
[115] Ostroumoff, p. 58.
[116] Ibid.
[117] February Volume of *The Great Synaxaristes* (in Greek), p. 634.

mencement of the solemn sessions, five out of eleven cardinals remained, and only fifty out of one hundred bishops attended.[118]

Isidore, Metropolitan of Kiev

Metropolitan Isidore of Kiev arrived in Ferrara on the 15th of August, in the year 1438. When he was in Moscow, he disclosed to the Grand Duke Vasili Vasilievitch that the Byzantine Church intended to unite with the Church of Rome, and that a council was being convened. The grand duke answered, "Our fathers and grandfathers would not even consider a union of Greek and Roman laws. I myself do not wish it." Nevertheless, Metropolitan Isidore insisted that he had given an oath that he would attend. The grand duke then advised him, "Remember the purity of our Faith, and bring it back with thee!" Isidore then swore to remain true to Orthodoxy.[119]

Isidore left Russia with an entourage of one hundred members, comprising of both clergy and lay people. His traveling party included Bishop Abraham of Suzdal, a representative of the grand duke, Archimandrite Bassian, and the Priest Symeon of Suzdal. Upon departing holy Russia, Isidore quickly revealed a strong inclination to side with the Latins, for when he was received by both Roman and Orthodox clergy in Livonia, he first saluted the Latin cross and afterward kissed the icons. His company was horror-struck at this display and from that moment lost their confidence in him.[120]

The Solemn State Sessions Commence

The pope then received disappointing news from his legate in France. The French had secured themselves from the pope's influence by a pragmatic sanction on the 7th of July, in the year 1438, founded on the decrees of the Council of Basle. Concurrently, the King of France, Charles VII (1403-1461), prohibited his bishops from attending the council at Ferrara.[121]

The pope then focused his attention on prodding the Greeks to commence formal discussions, and said, "You have been in Italy seven months. During that time you have signed only one paper, the one opening the council."[122] The emperor then returned from hunting. After he had several

---

[118] Syropoulos, Vol. VI, 3; Ostroumoff, p. 59.
[119] Ostroumoff, pp. 59, 60.
[120] Karamzin, *History of the Russian Empire*, ed. t.v. Ernerling, pp. 161-165.
[121] Ostroumoff, p. 60, 61.
[122] Syropoulos, Vol. VI, 5.

private interviews with Eugene, it was determined that the opening of the state session of the council be on the 8th of October.[123]

Emperor John VIII, however, created a minor stir when he announced that he intended to enter on horseback and ride the entire length of the council hall. This peculiar entrance into the hall owed to the fact that the emperor was severely crippled and did not want to make the long walk to his seat before the entire council. The Latins recoiled at his proposal, but a concession was reached: A passage would be opened and a door cut just behind the emperor's throne, so that he need only take a few steps to reach his seat.[124]

The Greeks then met privately to determine which of two questions should be discussed first: is the western doctrine of the procession of the Holy Spirit orthodox, and was it right that the Western Church made this addition to the Symbol of the Faith? Saint Mark and the philosopher Gemistos chose the latter question, and most of the others then joined them, including the emperor.[125]

There would be three council sittings per week, in the pope's palace chapel, commencing an hour and a half after sunrise and continuing until midday. The Greeks appointed Metropolitans Mark of Ephesus, Isidore of Russia, and Bessarion of Nicaea, together with Gemistes the philosopher, the *chartophylax* and the *skevophylax*. The Ecclesiarch Syropoulos was also appointed to be a speaker, but he urgently requested leave not to participate.[126] In reality, however, the emperor exclusively chose Mark and Bessarion, forbidding the civil officers to take part in the affair. The Latins chose Cardinals Giuliano Cesarini and Nicholas Albergati, the Bishops Andrew of Rhodes and John of Forli, and two monastics. One of the monastics was John de Montenero (also known as de Montenegro), a celebrated divine (papal theologian) of his time and the Provincial of Lombardy.[127]

In 1438, the first session commenced on the 26th day of September, the feast day of Saint John the Evangelist's repose. Surrounded by crowds of people, all the bishops assembled in the papal palace. In the center of the chapel, between Emperor John and Pope Eugene, two benches were arranged opposite each other. Each respective side would seat twelve Greek and Latin speakers. To the speakers' sides stood reporters and translators. Bessarion opened the meeting with a speech praising the members and advising them not

---

[123] Ostroumoff, p. 61.
[124] Gill, *The Council of Florence*, pp. 142-146.
[125] Syropoulos, Vol. VI, 12.
[126] Ibid., Vol. VI, 13.
[127] Ibid., Vol. VI, 14.

to spare any means to reach a successful end. A corresponding address was made by the Latin bishop, Andrew of Rhodes.[128]

Select Canons are Read in Council

After these preliminary speeches, the Metropolitan of Ephesus introduced the principal topic of the talks. He said, "Love was bequeathed by our Lord Jesus Christ to His disciples, and His peace He left them. However, the Church of Rome began to neglect the commandment of love and broke the peace. To date, this same Church, by assembling this council, manifests a desire to reinstate the peace. She can only realize this by repudiating the opinion which has been and continues to be the basis of the dispute between the Churches. When the present council acknowledges the canons of the former œcumenical synods, it shall meet with success." The firm pillar of godliness and the holy Faith, Mark, then made the justified demand that those canons connected with the subjects at hand should be read aloud before anything else.[129]

In October of 1438, the Latins, fearing exposure, would not agree to Mark's demand for the reading of the Church canons. Both Cardinals Giuliano and Nicholas, with several bishops, went to the patriarch's cell to urge him, the emperor and the Greek bishops to postpone the reading of the canons or, at least, to change their solemn reading into a private investigation of them.[130] The Greeks rejected both proposals. The Latins were compelled to yield, but rejoined that the reading would be for the Greeks alone. Hence everything was done to detract from the solemnity of that reading. People were not allowed to enter in so great a number as previously. The Gospel on the desk was closed. The statues of the Apostles Peter and Paul were placed face downward, and no candles were lit before them.[131]

1. The Addition of the "Filioque" to the Creed

Finally, the question of the Filioque was to be discussed. The word Filioque means "and the Son," which the Latins added to the Symbol of the Faith, or the Creed, saying that the Holy Spirit proceeds from the Father "and the Son." Indeed, this was the most painful question between the Orthodox and the Latins. The Greeks, led by Saint Mark, insisted that any introduction

---

[128] Synod Florence, pp. 44-49. *S. Gener. Florentina Synodus*, 4. The author's name is not given, though it appears to be written in Greek by Metropolitan Dorotheos of Mytilene, a participant; Ostroumoff, pp. 3, 6, 65.

[129] Syropoulos, loc. cit.; Synod Flor., pp. 60-75.

[130] Ibid., Vol. VI, 18; Ibid., p. 84.

[131] Sguropulum, Vol. VI, chap. 19, pp. 169, 170; Syropoulos, "Memoirs," Vol. VI, chaps. 30, 31, p. 330(2-10).

into the Creed—Filioque or not—was uncanonical. Some popes prior to Eugene would not sanction this addition; and, at other times, other popes supported it. However, it gradually became a permanent part of the Creed in the west, and succeeding popes reinforced this heretical teaching, declaring that the Holy Spirit proceeds from the hypostases of God the Father and God the Son: that is, His existence is from both hypostases. In an attempt to combat Arianism, the west created two Causes. The Orthodox affirm that the Father is the only source of the Son and the Spirit—the One begotten eternally from Him and the Other proceeding eternally from Him. God, therefore, is one because the Father is the source of divinity and that which makes the unity. The Filioque addition had been gradual, yet the Third and Fourth Œcumenical Synods enacted a strict decree that, in the Creed, no word could be changed, added, or subtracted—not even a syllable. Upon those that dared to make alterations, terrible condemnations were laid.

2. The Third Œcumenical Synod (Ephesus, 431)

The Third Synod, called by Emperor Theodosios II (408-450), numbered upwards of two hundred fathers, including papal legates. This holy synod deposed Nestorios from his see of Constantinople and excommunicated him. His doctrines were condemned, and the Creed of Nicaea was reaffirmed. The synod also delivered the sacred injunction that the Ever-virgin Mary be properly and truly called the Theotokos.

On the 16th of October, Saint Mark, the tongue that upheld all the patristic doctrines, said, "Let us begin with the acts of the Third Œcumenical Synod...and by the decree of the Ephesian fathers on the preservation of the Creed in its original condition." The *referendius* then read, under Mark's guidance, while Nicholas Secundini translated into Latin. The seventh canon of the holy Œcumenical Third Synod, in part, states: "...The holy synod decrees that no one should be permitted to offer any different belief or faith, or in any case to write or compose any other, than the one defined by the holy fathers who convened in the city of Nicaea, with the Holy Spirit. As for those who dare either to compose a different belief or faith, or to present one, or to offer one to those who wish to return to recognition of the truth, whether they be Greeks or Jews, or they be members of any heresy whatever, they, if bishops or clergymen, shall be deprived as bishops of their episcopate, and as clergymen of their clericate; but if they are laymen, they shall be anathematized."[132]

---

[132] "Concerning the Holy and Third Œcumenical Synod," *The Rudder* (*Pedalion*), p. 229.

At the close of the above reading, the divine mouth of right piety, Mark, commented, "The fathers of the synod, in passing this canon have, by their own example, exhibited a profound respect for the Nicene Creed; for they would not allow the addition of 'Theotokos,' an appellation so necessary in the dispensation of our salvation." Saint Mark then quoted Saint Kyril of Alexandria (d. 444), commissioned by Pope Celestine I (422-432), who presided over the Synod of Ephesus. "We prohibit any change whatsoever in the Creed of Faith drawn up by the holy Nicene fathers. We do not allow ourselves or anyone else to change or omit one word or syllable in that Creed."[133]

3. The Fourth Œcumenical Synod (Chalcedon, 451)

The Fourth Synod took place during the reign of Emperor Marcian (450-457) and the energetic virgin Empress Pulcheria (399-453), who took pains to assemble six hundred and thirty bishops. They upheld the decrees of the Third Synod but condemned the teaching of the union of the two natures of the Logos merged in one; for the two natures of Christ are "without confusion and without change."

The decree of the Fourth Œcumenical Synod of Chalcedon, in the fifth act, was then read, commanding that all receive the Nicene Creed and the Nicaean-Constantinopolitan Creeds as one, in which the dogma of the procession of the Holy Spirit is developed. Saint Mark said that the holy fathers, including the legates of Pope Leo I (440-461), who assembled at the Fourth Œcumenical Synod, declared: "This holy Creed is sufficient for the full knowledge of the truth. It contains in itself the full doctrine on the Father, the Son, and the Holy Spirit." The holy Metropolitan of Ephesus then had the exhortation of Patriarch John II of Constantinople (518-520) read, which is contained in the acts of the Synod of Constantinople (518). "We must keep to the holy Creed of the Synod of Nicaea, drawn up by the grace of the Holy Spirit, approved by the Synod of Constantinople, and confirmed by that of Chalcedon."[134]

4. The Fifth Œcumenical Synod (Constantinople, 553)

The Fifth Synod, called by Emperor Justinian I (527-565), with one hundred and sixty-five bishops present, condemned the writings of Diodoros of Tarsus, Theodore of Mopsuestia, Theodoret's work against the "Chapters" of Saint Kyril of Alexandria, and the letter of Bishop Ibas of Edessa. It further anathematized Origen, Didymos, Evagrios, and their detestable tenets.

---

[133] Acts of the Council of Basle, Binii Concil. t. xi., par. 1, 252.

[134] Ibid., t. ii., par. 1, p. 732; Ostroumoff, pp. 68, 69.

This synod also anathematized Anthimos of Trebizond, Severos, Bishop Peter of Apameia and Zooras.

Taken from the acts of the Fifth Œcumenical Synod was the epistle to Pope Vigilius (537-555), written by Patriarch Eftychios of Constantinople (552-565; 577-582), who wrote: "We always kept and do keep the Faith explained by the fathers at the four synods, and we follow those synods in everything." Though Pope Vigilius pleaded illness, he refused to attend the synod for fear of violence. In February of 554, he accepted the Fifth Synod and the previous four synods.[135]

5. The Sixth Œcumenical Synod (Troullos, 680)

The Sixth Synod, called by Emperor Constantine IV Pogonatos (668-685), was held in the secret chamber of the Troullos in the palace. According to Photios, Nikephoros, and Neilos, the fathers who attended numbered one hundred and seventy, but three hundred and eighty-nine fathers according to others. This synod dogmatized that our Lord Jesus Christ, though but one hypostasis, after His incarnation possessed two natural wills and two natural energies, as He also possessed two natures—that is, a divine will and energy and a human will and energy, both of them being at the same time indivisible and not conflated.

Then, in 692, Emperor Justinian II (685-695), summoned a synod in Constantinople, again in the lustrous palace called the Troullos. Papal ambassadors residing in the capital attended. This synod was known as the Quinsext Synod, because it was considered as a continuation of the Fifth and Sixth Synods. It ratified all the decrees of previous œcumenical synods, canons of the holy apostles, canons of the accepted regional synods, and canons of some fathers of the Church. Canons XIII, XXX, and LV were accepted by the papal legates without dispute. Canons XIII and XXX dealt with the marital state of those men accepted into ecclesiastical orders; whereas, Canon LV admonished members of the Church of Rome concerning fasting on sabbath days of the Great Fast. Pope Sergius (687-701), rejecting the canons, refused to sign.

Saint Mark also ordered the reading of that canon from the Sixth Synod in the Troullos which confirmed the Creed drawn up by the two first synods, and received as a rule of Faith by the three following ones. While these extracts were read, the Metropolitan of Ephesus, now and then, would interrupt the readings with his remarks. Then the two epistles of Pope Agatho (678-681) to the Greek Emperor Constantine IV (668-685), contained in the acts of the Sixth Synod, were read. Pope Agatho, having held a synod at

---

[135] Ibid., t.xi., par. 2, p. 48.

Rome (680) in which the doctrine of the two wills of Christ was again affirmed, sent his delegates to the Byzantine Emperor Constantine IV (668-685) with letters expounding this teaching.

In one epistle, Pope Agatho writes: "The Church of Rome upholds the Faith bequeathed by the five œcumenical synods, and takes special care that all that is defined by the canons should continue unaltered; nothing is to be added or taken away, but it is to be kept inviolate both in words and thoughts." In another epistle, Pope Agatho writes: "The apostolic seat preserves the Catholic and Apostolic Faith. We believe in God the Father, and His Only-begotten Son, and the Holy Spirit, the Lord and Giver of Life, Who proceedeth from the Father, Who with the Father and the Son is together worshipped and together glorified."[136]

6. The Seventh Œcumenical Synod (Nicaea, 787)

In agreement with Pope Hadrian I (772-795), the Seventh Synod was called by Empress Irene (780; 797-802) during the reign of her son, a minor, Constantine VI (780-797). Of the fathers who attended, three hundred and fifty were Orthodox, including the papal legates, but seventeen others joined the proceedings who had formerly been iconomachs. Later, they repented and were accepted by it, so that in all there were three hundred and sixty-seven. The synod originally met on the 17th of August, in the year 786, at the Church of the Holy Apostles in Constantinople, but was immediately dispersed by iconoclast soldiers. The synod members did not reassemble until the 24th day of September, in the year 787, this time in the Church of Haghia Sophia at Nicaea. The synod declared its adherence to the doctrine on the veneration (προσκύνησις) of images expounded by Pope Hadrian I in his letter to Empress Irene, adding that the icons are honored with a relative love (σχετικῷ πόθῳ), whereas absolute worship (λατρεία) is reserved to God alone, the honor given to the image passing on to the prototype.

Saint Mark then had the definition read of the Seventh Œcumenical Synod, in which the Nicaean-Constantinopolitan Creed was repeated. The Latins then presented a parchment which, in their opinion, was a very old Greek copy of the acts of the Seventh Synod. It showed the Nicaean-Constantinopolitan Creed with the Filioque. Except for this addition, the Greeks found the copy to correspond exactly. By this transcript, the Latins judged that the fathers at the Seventh Synod read the Creed with the Filioque addition. But how could this addition be made without any reasons for it mentioned anywhere in the acts of that synod? And how could this be valid, when in the

---

[136] Pope Agatho was a Greek from Sicily who was elevated to the papal throne. See Mansi 31A, 545AB; Ostroumoff, pp. 69, 70.

very Church of Rome the Creed was read without the addition for a long time after the Seventh Œcumenical Synod?[137]

The philosopher Gemistes Plethon quickly exhibited the error of the Latins' conclusion. He remarked, "Why do your Thomas Aquinases and other divines use so many arguments to prove the validity of the Filioque, when they might have simply referred to the addition made to the Creed at the Seventh Œcumenical Synod? However, your divines are silent about this addition."[138] The Greeks then surmised that what the Latins produced was a forgery. Saint Mark then concluded, saying, "The Greeks, therefore, obeying the decrees of the synods and the exhortations of the fathers, and mindful of their oath, cannot admit the addition to the Creed to be a right and lawful one. Nevertheless, they are ready to listen to the proofs brought forward by the Latins to justify their addition."

Many of the Latin monks present at the council, after hearing the decrees and acts of the œcumenical synods, together with Mark's explanation, confessed that they never heard anything like it previously. They exclaimed that the Greeks taught more correctly than their divines, and marvelled at Mark of Ephesus.[139]

The Latin Argument for the Addition to the Creed

There were, however, Latins that came forward, affirming that the Filioque was meant to be an explanation of a sound dogma. The talks on the "procession of the Holy Spirit" caused the most trouble. Discussions on it took up more time than any other issue at the council. Innumerable texts were brought up and disputed. In this matter, the problem of translations was particularly acute.

Through Bishop Andrew of Rhodes, the Latins argued that the insertion of the words "and the Son" was not an addition to the Creed, but purely explanatory, and that there was no prohibition of this in the synods. Further, he asserted that the Church of Rome had a right to make this "explanation" and "insertion" in the Creed. Then he began to argue about the sense of the words "addition" and "explanation."[140] Andrew brought forward the words of Saint Kyril of Alexandria which, in his opinion, supported the procession of the Holy Spirit from the Son, as well as from the Father. Commenting on John 14:16, "And I will ask the Father, and He shall give you another

---

[137] Ibid., pp. 70, 71.

[138] Syropoulos, "Memoirs," Vol. VI, ch. 31, pp. 330-332; Syn. Flor., 85-117.

[139] Sguropulum, Vol. VI, ch. 19, p. 171; Syropoulos, "Memoirs," Vol. VI, ch. 32, p. 332(10-14); Syn. Flor., 114, 115.

[140] Ostroumoff, p. 73.

Paraclete, that He may abide with you forever," Saint Kyril writes: "The Son is a partaker of the essential goodness of God. The Father also has the Holy Spirit, Who is understood as being of the Father, and not an addition or something extra; as each of us has within himself his spirit which he brings out of himself. This is why our Savior breathed Him forth corporeally [Jn. 20:22]; so also is the Spirit breathed forth from the divine essence in a manner worthy of God."[141] Examination of Saint Kyril's words suggests that the Holy Spirit is united essentially to the Son, being of one essence with Him. Saint Kyril admits that the Spirit, proceeding from the divine essence, is poured forth by the Son, but we do not read of an eternal procession from the Son.[142]

Bishop Andrew was even inclined to think that Saint Basil supported the Latin position. Though Andrew referred to this holy father's *Epistle XXXVIII* to his brother, Saint Gregory of Nyssa, Saint Basil does not support dual procession. Saint Basil writes that "there is no vacuum of interval, void of subsistence, which can make a break in the mutual harmony of the divine essence....He who perceives the Father, and perceives Him by Himself, has at the same time mental perception of the Son. Moreover, he who receives the Son does not divide Him from the Spirit, but in sequence, insofar as order is concerned, confirms his own faith in the Three united, One in essence. He who makes mention of the Spirit alone, embraces also in this confession Him of Whom He is the Spirit. Saint Paul writes that since the Spirit is 'of Christ [Rom. 8:9]' and is 'of God [Rom. 8:9; 1 Cor. 2:12],' then, as a person taking hold of one end of a chain must as a matter of course pull the other end along with it, so he who attracts the Spirit (εἵλκυσα Πνεῦμα), through Him attracts the Father and the Son also." Therefore, from the foregoing, a close study of this Epistle and the saint's other writings does not reveal a belief in a procession from the Father implies procession from the Son.[143]

Bishop Andrew of Rhodes could find no better arguments, though he made use of these and many others which had no bearing on the subject at hand. He claimed that many additions were made to the doctrines of Scripture, contrary to Saint Paul's warning that "even if we, or an angel from out of heaven, should preach a gospel to you besides what Gospel we preached to you, let such a one be anathema [Gal. 1:8]." Andrew then reminded all that the Nicene Synod added much to the Creed of the Apostles.

---

[141] In *Johnann. Lib.* 9, t.iv., p. 810.

[142] Ostroumoff, pp. 73, 74.

[143] See Saint Basil, *Epistle XXXVIII, To His Brother Gregory*, Nicene and Post-Nicene Fathers, 2nd Ser., VIII:138, 139.

He also said that the fathers at the Second Œcumenical Synod added to the Nicene Creed, to which the Third Synod added many other things not found in the Creed at the Second Synod. In his summation, Andrew concluded that the synods forbade the addition of false opinions to the already definite doctrine of the Church, but it did not extend to the addition of explanatory expressions. He felt that the Church is one and maintains the right to make additions to the Creed, since the apostle says, "one Lord, one faith, one baptism, one God and Father of all [Eph. 4:5, 6]." Also, the Church must oppose all heresies, whenever they arise, by means of her doctrine. She has the right to add explanations to the Creed which might help protect her children from heresy. He again insisted that the procession of the Holy Spirit from the Son is merely an explanation.[144] The Latins also founded their opinion on the quotation: "All things whatsoever the Father hath are Mine [Jn. 16:15]."

1. The Rights of the Papacy

Bishop Andrew then claimed the right of the Church of Rome and the supreme authority and power of the papal throne to make this necessary addition to the Creed. To support his arguments, he referred to many fathers of both the west and east. Nevertheless, none of these quotations truly supported the Latin doctrine.

The Greeks, forbidden by their emperor, did not introduce the question of whether the pope had any right to make an addition to the Creed. The Latins kept insisting that the pope had full disciplinary powers over the whole Church. Furthermore, as regards to doctrine, he should have the right on his sole authority to summon a council to deal with doctrine and to bind the whole Church to its findings.[145] The Greeks tried in vain to have some mention made of the rights and privileges of the eastern patriarchates.

Andrew then attempted to explain the events that enjoined the Church of Rome to add the Filioque. He said that a pope and a council of western fathers, before the Sixth Œcumenical Synod, added the "explanation" in order to refute the Nestorians, who said that the Holy Spirit does not proceed from eternity. This "western council," however, is not mentioned in any historical records. It is a well known fact that Pope Leo III (795-816) forbade any addition to the Creed. This same pope also had the Nicaean-Constantino-politan Creed engraved on two silver tablets, in Greek and Latin, and without the Filioque, at the tomb of Saint Peter.

---

[144] Ostroumoff, pp. 75, 76.
[145] Runciman, *The Great Church*, p. 108.

The Rebuttal of the Greeks

The Greeks then gave an answer to Bishop Andrew and Cardinal Giuliano. George Scholarios wrote a refutation and presented it to the emperor, who then gave it to Metropolitan Bessarion. In early November, at the emperor's bidding, Bessarion presented the rebuttal before the council. At the outset, the metropolitan demonstrated that the Filioque was not an explanation, but an actual addition to the Creed. Moreover, since the holy Third Œcumenical Synod, all additions are prohibited.

Metropolitan Bessarion brought forward the example of the name "Theotokos" which was not added to the Creed, though the meaning of this word is a short explanation of the doctrine contained in the Creed. Indeed, the addition of this word to the Creed would have proved effective in refuting the Nestorians. The Nestorians maintained that Mary ought not to be called "Theotokos" but "Christotokos," since, they said, she gave birth not to the Christ Who is God, but to the Christ Who is a man.

Another example wherein a synod did not allow an addition is that doctrine concerning the two natures and two wills in Christ, which would have been useful in the conflict against both Monophysites and Monothelites. Bessarion demonstrated that when the Church stood in need of new expositions, the fathers did not insert terms and definitions (ὅροι) in the Creed, but published them apart. The synod prohibits any addition to the Creed, even in the most urgent circumstances. The interdict of the Ephesian Synod, however, does not diminish the authority of the Church; much rather, it proves her unity, in that she remains true to her former rulings, thus preserving herself.[146]

Bessarion then said, "We know well enough the rights and privileges of the Church of Rome. We are aware of her power, as well as the limits of her power. How can an individual Church arrogate to herself the right of making an addition to the Creed, when the same right is refused by the synods even to the universal Church?"[147]

A Barren Outcome

As a result of this refutation, between the 11th and 15th of November, the Latins had Bishop Andrew of Rhodes answer the Greeks. His wearisome oration proved immaterial to the issues. In the following sitting, Bishop John of Forli only iterated the Latin argument that the Filioque was a simple

---

[146] Ostroumoff, p. 80.
[147] Ibid.

explanation.[148] Finally, the Latins grasped that at the center of the Greeks' reasoning was the interdict of the Third Œcumenical Synod. The Latins, through Cardinal Giuliano, stated that the Third Synod prohibited only unorthodox creeds when it condemned a Nestorian Creed. At that council, the confession of faith submitted by Priest Charisios of Philadelphia was not condemned. His creed was a defense of his Orthodoxy when he was wrongfully excommunicated.

The precious vessel of true discernment, Mark, however, was quick to point out to the Latins that Charisios' creed, though not identical to the Nicene Creed, was simply an Orthodox confession of a private individual. The Church never prohibits one from professing his faith, in his own words, as long as the confession of faith is Orthodox. However, it cannot be distributed as the Confession of the Faith for the entire Church. Mark pointed out that many examples of confessions of faith may be found. He cited as an example the epistles of Pope Agatho and Patriarch Sophronios of Jerusalem (634) that were read and approved at the Sixth Œcumenical Synod. In fact, in the east, every newly-ordained bishop sends to the Church representatives a written confession of faith, as proof of his Orthodoxy.[149]

Contentious to the end, Cardinal Giuliano, objecting to Mark's exegesis of Canon VII from the Third Œcumenical Synod, stated that the canon applies only to heterodox creeds. Giuliano succeeded only in wearying everyone by his long arguments. The Greeks found that all their efforts to persuade their opponents only met with the obstinate repetition of the Latin arguments. Giuliano, being unable to refute the Greek opposition, thought to change the subject of the debates. He said to Mark, "Holy father, let us examine the very dogma itself. If the addition to the Creed proves to be contrary to Orthodox doctrine, why, then we will drop the subject and remove it from the Creed. If, on the contrary, it shall be proved that the Holy Spirit proceeds from the Son, then we shall conclude that the addition is a correct one, and must retain it in the Creed."[150]

The Saint Censures the Latins

At some point during the fourth session in 1438, Saint Mark addressed the pope with his cardinals, archbishops, and bishops. The Russian priest, Symeon of Suzdal, records that "in a sweet voice, Mark said, 'Hearken, O reverend Pope of Rome and teachers of the Latins, how you speak and name this synod as the Eighth Synod! By doing so, you allude to

---

[148] Syn. Flor., pp. 216-242.
[149] Ostroumoff, p. 82.
[150] Syn. Flor., pp. 287, 289; Syropoulos, Vol. VI, 22.

the First Synod....You number your synod as the eighth, yet you deny the other Seven (Œcumenical) Synods. You do not consider the patriarchs as your brothers; and you have designated the Orthodox Church after the Latin Church.'" These words greatly angered Pope Eugene and created no small stir among the Latin cardinals and bishops.[151]

Calmly, the Orthodox Metropolitan of Ephesus continued, saying, "O Latins, how many more years shall you be in the grip of the demons and teach evil? How long shall you speak of the Seven Synods, yet deny their decrees as set forth by holy popes and the holy fathers, who have ordered us, the Orthodox Christians, to follow and preserve the Seven Holy Synods? First there was Pope Sylvester I (314-335) who supported the First Œcumenical Synod (Nicaea, 325) and its decrees. Pope Hadrian I (772-795) gave his full support to the Seventh Synod (Nicaea, 787), sending to it not only two representatives, but a dogmatic treatise....How is it now, Pope Eugene, that not only hast thou added something, but thou hast denied the Seven Synods? Thou namest this synod 'eighth,' and thou namest thyself 'first,' without naming or mentioning the holy fathers."

With the truth of these words ringing in their ears, the pope, the cardinals, the Italians, French, Milanese, Germans, Hungarians, Czechs, Poles, and other followers walked out of the meeting, leaving behind only the Greek Orthodox.[152] "I," wrote the Priest Symeon, "was astonished at this incident. When I beheld Metropolitan Dorotheos simultaneously weeping and laughing, I asked him, 'Eminence, why dost thou cry and laugh?' He answered, 'O Symeon, if thou didst see and hear that which the honorable Mark, Metropolitan of Ephesus, said to the pope and to all the Latins, thou too wouldest also laugh and cry. As thou dost see, the holy Mark of Ephesus is equal with the great Basil and Gregory the Theologian. See for thyself that the Latins dare no longer to contradict the holy Mark. The pope has departed, taking his words with him; that is, they took all their books with them.'"[153] Not much time elapsed before the Latin servants assigned to the Greeks also departed the council chamber.

Emperor John, however, had a few words to say. He turned to the Metropolitan of Ephesus and said, "My father, honorable teacher, why dost thou speak so harshly to the pope and the cardinals, causing all of them to leave? I, my holy father, have not come with that purpose. If thou hadst

---

[151] Symeon de Suzdal, "Les Russes au Concile de Ferrare-Florence," in the periodical *Irenikon*, 1974, No. 2, pp. 196-199; Basileiade, p. 91.

[152] Ibid.; Ibid., pp. 91, 92.

[153] Ibid.; Ibid., p. 92.

spoken in a humble manner, without hatred, there would not be even one accusation from any of us." Though the emperor accused Mark of speaking with hatred, this simply was not true. With boldness and holy pain Mark spoke the truth, after having witnessed the egotism and contempt exhibited by the Latins. The emperor then admitted that he desired union simply to create a military alliance with the pope.[154]

Saint Mark then addressed both the emperor and the patriarch, saying, "Hearken, O holy autocrat Lord John and holy Patriarch Joseph,...and bring to mind your words to us in Constantinople. You spoke of how the pope sent to you to discuss the matter of the return of the Christians to their ancient union, so the Church and Christians might be one, as the Christians of the first centuries. Remember how you agreed to these words. Now, therefore, O emperor and Patriarch Joseph, attend to what has now been declared by the pope. He speaks of an eighth synod, yet never mentions the previous Seven Œcumenical Synods. He names himself first and calls this synod his own. Concerning thee, the emperor, he never mentions thee; concerning the patriarchs, he does not call them brothers. He does not mention the Orthodox Christians first, but the Latins...."

Thereupon, both the emperor and the patriarch remained silent, and then left for their apartments. Soon after, to quickly curry Greek favor, the pope followed up by dispensing a great deal of money to the emperor, the patriarch, and the bishops. Mark censured all of them for being "bought" by the pope.[155] Now Saint Mark always desired peace and love. At the tenth session on the 18th day of November, in the year 1438, he spoke about this, saying, "We neither came here to contradict one another nor to display skills of refutation. We came here simply to discuss union peacefully and with love, until we uncovered the truth about them." Unfortunately, the Latins did not have the same spirit of peace and love. Their chief speaker, Cardinal Cesarini, declared he would counter every word of Metropolitan Mark Evgenikos of Ephesus.[156]

In the autumn of 1438, thirteen sessions were held, yielding no real results. On the 8th of December, in the year 1438, Metropolitan Mark, inspired by the Holy Spirit, reaffirmed the Orthodox position. "The testimonies of the western fathers and teachers that speak concerning the procession of the Holy Spirit from the Son, I neither recognize nor accept. I surmise that they are corrupt. There can be no compromise in things of the Orthodox

---

[154] Ibid.; Ibid., pp. 92, 93.
[155] Ibid.; Ibid., p. 93.
[156] *Praktika*, Vol. V, fasc. I, pp. 187(4-11), 214(16-17).

Faith....Do not accept them into your communion, as long as they abide in this novelty."[157] The saint's closing words at the Ferrara Council bespeak a man filled with the love of Christ. He said, "We beseech you, fathers, brothers, honorable sirs, as we besought you earlier, in the bowels of compassion of our Lord Jesus Christ,...come back into good concord with us and the holy fathers, which we possessed when east and west were the same, when there was no schism and we considered one another as brothers. Let us revere our common fathers and honor their decrees and fear their threats; let us preserve the traditions. Let us all together, with the same Faith, perceptions, and dispositions, with one mind and heart, glorify the all-honorable and majestic name of the Father and the Son and the Holy Spirit, now and ever and unto the ages of ages. Amen."[158]

In response to Mark's closing words, Cardinal Cesarini made a reply at their fourteenth and final meeting, on the 13th day of December, in the year 1438. His words were filled with passion and anger, as he ended the Ferrara sessions with these unforgettable words to the Ephesian: "Even if thou wilt put forward ten points, I shall counter with ten thousand!"[159]

New Subject for the Talks

After two months, the Greeks, weary of it all and deliberately kept short of food and comforts, wished to go home. But they lacked the means for a homeward journey, and the pope refused to pay their salaries. The Latins were hoping that an examination of their dogma of the procession of the Holy Spirit would ensue. They easily manipulated to their side the emperor, who still harbored hopes of Latin aid for his crumbling realm. The emperor then had the difficult task of persuading his bishops to enter into further talks. The Greek bishops felt that the Latin addition to the Creed was indefensible, and that the insertion must be removed before they examined the dogma itself. Metropolitan Bessarion then declared, "Why should we not discuss that dogma with the Latins? We can tell them many good things." This was actually Bessarion's sentiment from the outset of the council.[160] Nonetheless, the Greek bishops genuinely believed that the Latins would reject their arguments and rely on papal authority to say whatever they liked.

---

[157] "Saint Mark of Ephesus" (Marci Evgenici, Metropolitae Ephesi), *Opera anti-unionistica*, ed. ab L. Petit, Vol. X, fasc. II (Rome: Pont. Inst. Orientalium Studiorium, Concilium Florentinum Documenta et Scriptores, Series A), pp. 127(8-9), 130(18-24), 132(5-8, 34-35), 133(1-6); Basileiade, pp. 102, 103; *P.G.* 160: 69C, 97C.
[158] J. D. Mansi, *Sacrorum Conciliorum Collecti* (Paris-Leipzig, 1901-1927), Vol. 31A, 689D-692AB cited in Basileiade, p. 107.
[159] *Praktika*, Vol. V, fasc. I, p. 217 and fasc. II, p. 490; Basileiade, loc. cit.
[160] Syropoulos, Vol. VII, 3, 6.

Emperor John, counting upon the promised aid of the Latins, attempted to revitalize the group. Although he was against a strict investigation of the doctrine on the procession, he still maintained that it was "the very reason for our coming to Italy." He asserted that they must discuss this subject with the Latins. After a spirited, yet pleading talk with the bishops, he managed to carry the majority of votes. Saint Mark yielded, saying, "As thou dost deem it good to move on to the discussion of the dogma itself, I shall consent if the others wish it."

1. The Pope's Desire to Move to Florence

The pope harbored a desire to transfer the council to Florence. He considered using as an excuse the fear of the plague that had broken out in Germany. It is not known whether the fear of the plague influenced a change of location. Moreover, the pope complained that he could not pay the Greeks for their expenses in Ferrara, claiming to have been deceived by the people of that town. On the other hand, the rich Florentines promised to lend the pope forty thousand gold pieces if he transferred the council to their town. The pope insisted, saying, "We must go there to continue the discussions. If you will follow me, I promise to aid endangered Constantinople with twelve thousand gold florins and two triremes." Having held back the monies due to the Greek bishops, he now promised to pay. Although the emperor was long aware of a possible transfer to Florence, he still did not disclose the matter to his bishops. He now acted to persuade the Greek bishops to transfer to Florence.[161]

From the outset, the Greeks did not wish to transfer to Florence, for they had misgivings concerning their treatment and accommodations. The emperor implored them not to leave matters undone. He further enticed them with the promise of payment by a Florentine bank, at any time they desired. He then pleaded for the empire and added that they lacked the means to return to their capital. The bishops were then persuaded to prepare for the journey. It was the 12th of January, in the year 1439. The pope was the first to leave for Florence. Curiously, Patriarch Joseph ordered that extra luggage be sent on to Venice, and that only vestments were to be brought to Florence, as the union would take place there. The Greeks were exceedingly perplexed and troubled at this strange action. In view of what had taken place previously in their talks, no one could be sure of future developments.

Saint Mark urged the emperor to collect the views of each bishop on the Latin dogma. The righteous man then said, "If all shall agree, I am prepared to commence the struggle in defense of Orthodoxy. If not, I shall sit

---

[161] Basileiade, p. 108.

down with them that always keep silence in the council." Seething with envy, Gregory retorted, "Your majesty, did you appoint him as head of the council? If so, tell us, so that we might all obey him." Metropolitan Bessarion also expressed dismay at Mark's declaration. The emperor responded by heaping reproaches upon the holy man.[162] This all came about because the emperor was working behind the scenes. He had promised the pope that he would discover the means to achieve union. This explains the patriarch's prophetic words and the emperor's censure of Metropolitan Mark. The Greeks were paid their stipends and expenses for the trip to Florence. The emperor then took measures to prevent the Greeks from absconding and returning to the capital.

The Council at Florence

Among the Greeks, the emperor was the first to arrive in Florence, the home of Dante, Petrarch, Boccaccio, and Giotto. The aged patriarch arrived on the 12th day of February, in the year 1439, thoroughly exhausted, and was met by the officials of the city with great pomp and music. They escorted the patriarch to his living quarters, as the bells of the city rang out joyously.

A preliminary meeting was scheduled on Cheesefare Sunday, the 15th day of February, in the year 1439.[163] On that day the street was lined with joyous Florentines. As the emperor left his quarters and approached the city gates of Florence, it began to drizzle. When the emperor passed through the city gates, the rains were so strong that the crowds were forced to flee to find shelter. The emperor, thoroughly drenched, walked through the empty Florentine streets, escorted by only two cardinals. Instead of being met by an

---

[162] Syropoulos, Vol. VII, 14.

[163] As no official acts survive for the Council of Florence, our information is mainly drawn from three accounts by the participants themselves. First is the so-called *Praktika* or *Acta Graeca Quae Supersunt Actorum Graecorum Concilii Florentini necnon Descriptionis Cuiusdam Eiusdem*, ed. Joseph Gill (Rome, 1953), written in Greek most probably by the pro-unionist Latinophile, Bishop Dorotheos of Mytilene. Second is the Latin account in dialogue form by the papal advocate, Andrea of Santa Croce, in J. D. Mansi, *Sacrorum Conciliorum Collectio*, 31B, cols. 1431ff. (Florence/Venice, 1759-98). Finally, the third source is the Greek history or memoirs of the Grand Ecclesiarch Sylvester Syropoulos, whose work is well known in the east but often rejected in the west. See also Joseph Gill, *The Council of Florence* (Cambridge, England, 1959).

admiring and cheering crowd, the emperor encountered a chilly and damp reception.[164]

The first session officially commenced on the 26th day of February, in the year 1439. The atmosphere was extremely tense. The emperor was much more attentive in Florence than he had been in Ferrara, and abandoned his pastime of hunting. Mark knew in his heart that the pope and his followers would not be persuaded. However, he was determined, with all his strength, to oppose their erroneous beliefs. The Latins, sore displeased with Metropolitan Mark's words at Ferrara, remained impervious to his counsels. Realizing they could not contend with Mark's brilliance when it came to expounding on the decrees of the œcumenical synods, the discussions no longer involved the validity of adding "and the Son" to the article of the Creed, but instead whether the Spirit actually proceeded from the Son.[165] Nearly the only person among the Greek delegates to keep up the discussions was the lone combatant and warrior of the Orthodox, Mark, who met a skillful opponent in the dialectician John de Montenero, a Dominican provincial. At first, John declared that all of his arguments and deductions would be based on the authority of the Scriptures and the fathers. Yet, in reality, his speeches were merely a display of scholastic reasoning. Mark strictly followed the expressions and definitions of the Greek theologians that the Holy Spirit proceeds from the Father.[166]

When the patriarch was asked his opinion about the progress of the debates, he said, "I see that the Latins are contentious, vainglorious, and never to be persuaded, though our arguments are mighty against the addition of the Filioque. It is plain that anything we say, they refuse to agree with or to be persuaded by the truth."[167]

1. The Latin Position

The Dominican proved to be a wrangler and given to quibbling. It was not unusual for him to change the subject to unrelated matters when confounded by the words from Mark's lips that thundered as if from heaven, accurately confessing the Faith. Although the Greeks comprised a ten-man team, the emperor authorized only Mark and Bessarion to speak. However, once more Bessarion deserted his Orthodox brother. Both Bessarion and Gregory Mamas presumed that Mark would be routed by the Dominican, but

---

[164] Syropoulos, "Memoirs," Vol. VII, ch. 36, pp. 388(15-17); Basileiade, pp. 113-114.

[165] Basileiade, p. 109, 114.

[166] Ostroumoff, p. 93.

[167] Syropoulos, "Memoirs," Vol. VII, ch. 22, p. 372(17-21); Basileiade, p. 109.

were frankly amazed at the words of Mark.[168] Moreover, the bandying about of texts back and forth still proved unsatisfactory. Some points in the texts were completely different in the Greek and Latin versions. Therefore, the question of translations added to difficulties.[169]

John de Montenero stated that the verb "to proceed" means "to receive existence." From a Latin version, with questionable accuracy, he quoted two places in the works of Saint Epiphanios (ca. 315-403), Bishop of Salamis. One selection read: "The Father names Him—the Son, Who is from Him—and the Holy Spirit—Him, Who is from both."[170] Another quotation reads: "'Who (the Spirit of truth) proceedeth from the Father (ὅ παρὰ τοῦ Πατρὸς ἐκπορεύεται) [Jn. 15:26],' and 'shall receive (λήψεται),' saith the Lord, 'of Mine (ἐκ τοῦ ἐμοῦ) [Jn. 16:14].' 'Even as the Father knoweth Me, I also know the Father [Jn. 10:15]'; thus, I dare to say, no one has seen (ἑώρακεν) the Holy Spirit except the Father and the Son, from Whom He (*singular*) proceedeth, and from Whom He (*singular*) receiveth. And no one has seen the Son and the Father, except the Holy Spirit, Who of a truth glorifies [Jn. 16:14] and teaches all things [Jn. 14:26], and shall testify of the Son [Jn. 15:26], and Who is 'from (παρὰ)' the Father and 'of (ἐκ)' the Son."[171]

With these quotations John de Montenero concluded that the procession of the Holy Spirit from both Father and Son was a doctrine of Saint Epiphanios. However, if we consider the words in their full meaning, it is evident that Saint Epiphanios is borrowing words out of the Gospel, such as the Spirit "proceedeth from the Father" and "shall receive of Mine (Christ)," and uses them in that sense at the end of his statement. This must be the explanation, because there is no other possible reason for him to use two different prepositions, "from (παρὰ)" and "of (ἐκ)," if he were describing the procession of the Holy Spirit.

2. The Orthodox Response

Saint Mark, without examining the Greek text, said that Saint Epiphanios' words do not lead to the conclusion that the Spirit proceeds from the Son. He explained that the expression "to be from one" does not imply "to proceed from one." Saint Epiphanios is not saying that the Spirit receives existence, but "He shall receive of Mine [Jn. 16:14]." Mark then pointed out that when Saint Epiphanios said, "from Whom He proceedeth, and from

---

[168] February Volume of *The Great Synaxaristes* (in Greek), loc. cit.

[169] Runciman, *The Great Church*, pp. 105, 106.

[170] Opp. S. Epiph. Ancoratus. t.ii, p. 75.

[171] Ibid., p. 78.

Whom He receiveth," he twice employed the singular pronoun "Whom," placing the conjunction "and" between them. This indicates that Saint Epiphanios gave one meaning to the word "proceedeth" and another meaning to "receiveth." Furthermore, the preposition "from" does not always express "procession," but only a similitude or reception of attributes and nature.

To further explain the meaning of our Savior's words used by Saint Epiphanios, "He shall receive of Mine," Saint Mark quoted Saint Kyril of Alexandria[172] and Saint John Chrysostom. In his *Homily on the Gospel of Saint John*, Saint John Chrysostom explains that when Christ said, "He shall receive of Mine," it is as though He were saying, "'Whatsoever things I have told you, He shall also tell you'...and the verse 'of Mine' means 'of what I know,' 'of My own knowledge,' 'for the knowledge of Me and of the Spirit is one'...and 'the Holy Spirit shall speak in unison with what is Mine.'"[173]

The manuscript of Saint Epiphanios was then brought into evidence. Saint Mark showed that the text had been altered by the insertion of new matter, and said, "Concerning your books, I have accurate information that they have been corrupted and forged."[174] John de Montenero then read, "The Holy Spirit...Who is from both (ὅ μόνον ἐξ ἀμφοῖν ἐστίν)," but Saint Mark read the correct version, saying, "The Holy Spirit Who is known of Both (παρ' ἀμφοῖν νοεῖται)."[175]

3. The Orthodox and Saint Basil

Saint Mark then quoted Saint Basil who, in no uncertain words, says that the Spirit proceeds from the Father. "God gives birth not like man, but truly gives birth; He from Himself manifests a birth—the Word (Logos), not a human word, but shows this Word to be truly from Himself. He produces the Spirit by His mouth, not like man, for God's mouth is not corporeal, but the Spirit is from Him and not from aught else."[176]

Saint Mark then brought forward the epistle of Saint Basil to his brother, Saint Gregory of Nyssa, wherein he writes: "The Son, by Whom are all things, and with Whom the Holy Spirit is inseparably conceived of, is of the Father. It is not possible for one to conceive of the Son, if he is not previously enlightened by the Spirit. Thus, the Holy Spirit, from Whom all the

---

[172] *Thesaurus*, c. 14.

[173] Saint Chrysostom, Homily LXXVIII, *Homilies on the Gospel of Saint John*, Nicene, 1st Ser., XIV:288.

[174] *Praktika*, Vol. V, fasc. II, p. 386(8-10); Basileiade, p. 116.

[175] Ibid., p. 275(10-13).

[176] *Works of the Holy Fathers* (in Russian), Year 4, bk. 1., p. 199; see also Zoernikoff, *Tractatus Theolog.*, p. 26.

supply of good things for creation has its source, is attached to the Son, with Whom He (It) is inseparably apprehended (received), and has His being from (attached to) the Father, as Cause, from Whom also He proceeds. The Holy Spirit has this note of His peculiar hypostatic nature, namely, that He is known after the Son and together with the Son, and that He has His subsistence of the Father."[177]

Commenting on Saint Basil's words, "the Holy Spirit...attached to the Son, with Whom It is inseparably apprehended (received)," John de Montenero gave the meaning of "attached" the sense of procession by existence. Saint Mark quickly answered that the sense of the verb is defined by the nearest words, "is inseparably apprehended (received) with Him (the Son)."[178]

The Latins refuted everything with their faulty texts, poor translations, and private interpretations of what the Greek fathers meant when they wrote in Greek. The subject then drifted to whether spiritual gifts were created or not. Obedient to the emperor, three times Mark evaded answering the Latins regarding the divine energies.

Metropolitan Mark's Summation

In his summation, Saint Mark also mentioned Saint Dionysios the Areopagite (1st C.), who wrote: "There is one source of the pre-essential divinity—God the Father."[179] To represent the personal attributes of the divine hypostases, Mark said that we introduce the Unoriginate, the Only-begotten, and the Proceeding One from the Father.

Mark, the divine fragrance of theology, then mentioned the last discourse of Christ to His disciples when He imparted to them the secrets of theology, saying, "Whenever the Paraclete should come, Whom I shall send to you from the Father, the Spirit of the truth Who proceedeth from the Father, that One shall bear witness concerning Me [Jn. 15:26]." Commenting on this, he said to the Latins, "Here, by three expressions, our Savior has placed the three divine hypostases in their relation to each other. Of the Spirit, He says, 'Whenever the Paraclete should come'; of Himself, with the Father, He says, 'Whom I shall send to you from the Father'; and then, of the Father alone, He says, 'Who proceedeth from the Father.' Do you not see a strict exactness in the divine doctrine?...He did not say, 'The Holy Spirit Which

---

[177] Saint Basil, "Epistle 38, to His Brother Gregory," op. cit., p. 138.

[178] Ostroumoff, p. 103.

[179] *De div. nominib.* c.2.

proceedeth from Us.'...Consequently, no Filioque can be implied here."[180] Evgenikos then said that the addition to the Creed was "the first cause of schism."[181] He felt that to ever achieve union, this innovation must first be removed. It should also be noted that Mark, during this time, was suffering physically, yet he continued to speak at length. He then read select definitions from the œcumenical synods that confirm Orthodox doctrine.

1. The First Œcumenical Synod (Nicaea, 325)

The First Synod, called by the sainted Emperor Constantine I the Great (306-337), with 318 bishops present, condemned Arius. Hosius of Cordoba was president. Two papal legates of Pope Sylvester, together with other western bishops, were also present. A method of calculating Pascha was also determined, and canons were made referring to the ordination of clergy and other aspects of ecclesiastical order. It also proclaimed the first seven articles of the Creed.

From the *History* of this synod, Bishop Leontios of Caesarea said, "Receive the one divinity of the Father, Who hath produced the Son, and of the Son born of Him, and of the Holy Spirit proceeding from the very Father and proper to the Son, as the divine apostle says, 'Now if anyone doth not have the Spirit of Christ, this same one is not of Him [Rom. 8:9].'"[182] Saint Mark explained that the words "proper to the Son" mean that though the Holy Spirit does not proceed from the Son, He is not strange to Him and is His own by essence, co-essential with Him. Saint Basil the Great also teaches saying, "The Spirit is called Christ, as essentially united to Christ."[183]

2. The Second Œcumenical Synod (Constantinople, 381)

The Second Synod, called by Emperor Theodosios the Great, with 150 or 180 bishops present, condemned the semi-Arians and Patriarch Makedonios (Macedonius) of Constantinople (d. 362). This synod formulated the last five articles of the Creed.

The article in the Creed that says, "I believe...in the Holy Spirit, the Lord, the Giver of life; Who proceedeth from the Father; Who with the Father and the Son together is worshipped and glorified," must be understood in its context. The Second Synod desired to state the co-essentiality and the equality in honor of the Holy Spirit with the Father and the Son.

Mark, the mighty thunder of holy grace, then said to the Latins, "If that synod wished to state the Spirit's procession from the Father and the Son,

---

[180] Ostroumoff, pp. 108, 109.

[181] Mansi, 31A, 510A; Basileiade, p. 116.

[182] Gelasios Cyz. in the *History of the First Œcumenical Synod*.

[183] *On the Holy Spirit*, to Amphilochios, chap. xviii.

then why did it not speak as they further on spoke declaring that the Spirit is worshipped and glorified with the Father and the Son? In the first case, the fathers do not mention the Son when speaking of the cause of the Spirit's procession, but they do mention the Son when showing the Spirit's equality of honor and co-essentiality....The synods have prohibited and reproved, by their decrees, any addition. It is as if they prophetically foresaw what would happen among you." Mark then quoted Saint Gregory the Theologian (ca. 329-ca. 391), who said, "Everything the Father has belongs to the Son, with the exception of causality."[184]

3. The Third Œcumenical Synod (Ephesus, 431)

A father of the Third Synod, Saint Kyril of Alexandria, was called upon to answer accusations that he declared the Son's procession from the Spirit. Saint Kyril, complaining of being slandered, wrote to Bishop Eftropios, "Though the Spirit proceeds from the Father, still He is no alien to the Son, for the Son has everything jointly with the Father." In his epistle to Bishop John of Antioch (d. 441), he wrote: "We do not allow ourselves or others to change a single expression in the Symbol of the Faith, to omit one syllable, ever mindful of him who said, 'Remove not the old landmarks which thy fathers have placed [Prov. 22:28],' for it was not they who spoke, but the Spirit of God the Father, Who proceedeth from Him, but is not alien to the Son, as regards His essence."

Saint Mark then commented, "We teach in conformance with holy Scripture and the holy fathers and teachers, and do not change or misrepresent dogmas handed down to us. We do not add to them or take from them."[185] Although John de Montenero interrupted Mark in several instances with digressing comments, the holy man said that the manner in which the talks were being conducted could not last indefinitely. He urged them not to offer up arguments from extracts of spurious, interpolated or little known documents. Saint Mark concluded his statement advocating that concrete arguments should be based on holy Scripture and universally accepted passages of the fathers.

The Statement of John De Montenero

John then found it beneficial to make a formal statement, and said, "The Church of Rome does not admit of two Principles or Causes in the Trinity, but only one Cause and one Principle, anathematizing all who think

---

[184] Ostroumoff, p. 112.

[185] Ibid., p. 114.

to the contrary."[186] This, however, was a superficial proclamation, because
a full explanation of what he truly meant was avoided. John had not
disavowed that the Son was the Cause of the Holy Spirit. What he did say was
that though the Father is the original Cause of the Spirit, the Son receives
(λαμβάνει) power from the Father to educe (προβάλλειν)—or put forward
or project— the Spirit not from Himself, but from the Father.[187] Nevertheless,
John's words were to have an enormous impact.

The Greeks Consult with One Another

The emperor, impatient at the little progress made at the sessions, in
a private meeting with the bishops, found it expedient to exhibit and declare
an exposition written by Brother John de Montenero, acknowledging the
Father as the one Cause of the Son and the Holy Spirit. The bishops, however, were not convinced, having perceived the ambiguity of John de Montenero's words. They desired that the basis of union be built on an established
foundation.

1. Saint Maximos the Confessor

The Greeks found an epistle of the theologian and spiritual writer,
Saint Maximos the Confessor (ca. 580-662), written well before the schism
(ca. 1054), speaking of the western Christians: "Adducing the statements of
the western fathers and Saint Kyril of Alexandria,[188] those of the Church of
Rome do not affirm that the Son is the Cause of the Spirit, for they know that
the Cause of the Son and of the Spirit is the Father: One by generation and the
Other by procession. They only show that the Spirit is sent through the Son,
and thereby express the connection or unity (συναφὲς) and the exact likeness
or indistinguishability (ἀπαράλλακτον) of Their essence."[189] It is known that
the western fathers of the first eight centuries taught in agreement with the
eastern fathers regarding the procession of the Holy Spirit from the Father
alone. The Latins now, however, would not concede to the words of Saint
Maximos, and demanded the continuance of the sittings.

Florence proved to be different from Ferrara. As Saint Mark put it,
the Latins "threw off their masks." Severe pressure was brought to bear upon
the Greeks to capitulate to the Church of Rome. The Latins demanded that the
Orthodox accept all of Rome's doctrines and completely subordinate
themselves to the Vatican in all administrative affairs. Again the Greeks found
themselves in an intolerable situation, which was aggravated by the lack of

---

[186] Syn. Flor., pp. 511-550.
[187] Ibid., p. 493 ff.
[188] Saint Maximos, *Exposition on the Gospel of Saint John*.
[189] Zoernikoff, p. 409.

funds for their subsistence. It is only fair to report that the Vatican had its own financial difficulties at that time. Both Mark and Syropoulos wrote that the Greeks were exhausted from hunger. The Vatican allowed all this in order to manipulate and force the Greeks into submission and surrender.[190]

In addition to their personal deprivation and suffering, the Greek delegation was further burdened with genuine concern for the empire and its people, who were on the brink of destruction. In order to save Byzantium, many within the delegation felt that the end justified the means, that is, they should agree to everything if it were necessary. This attitude, in fact, was not the "salvation" of Byzantium, but instead the insidious cause of her destruction.[191]

"Many Are They That Persecute Me and Afflict Me;
from Thy Testimonies Have I Not Declined [Ps. 118:157]."

Since he could no longer control the anti-unionists, the emperor prohibited the reappearances of the two combatants for Orthodoxy, Mark of Ephesus and Anthony of Herakleia. At one of the sessions, when Anthony of Herakleia observed the partiality and the continued rivalry and contention of the Latin-minded (Greeks) who contradicted Mark, he exclaimed, "You all speak with passion." These words greatly incensed Bessarion of Nicaea and Isidore of Russia. The emperor, instead of acting as a peacemaker, snapped at the venerable Bishop Anthony, and sternly said, "Thou art illiterate, vulgar, a common rustic, insensible, and shameless!" These words greatly shocked everyone, as it was evident that the Greek team was crumbling.[192] The temper of the emperor swayed many of the Latin-minded Greeks deeper into deception.

Before the final two sittings on the 21st and 24th of March, the emperor had Mark confined to his cell and went so far as to post guards at the door in the event the metropolitan desired to leave. Though the pope did most of the talking, the absence of Mark was profoundly felt.[193] One of Mark's many adversaries, John, the Latin provincial, repeatedly demanded that his energetic opponent return. The emperor, preferring that a monologue should ensue, answered him, "We do not wish to renew the dispute; therefore, Mark is not present. We are present here only to satisfy your demands. Say what

---

[190] Pogodin, "Saint Mark," *Orthodox Word* 3, No. 2(13), p. 51.
[191] Ibid.
[192] Syropoulos, "Memoirs," Vol. VIII, chap. 14, p. 402; Basileiade, p. 126.
[193] Praktika, Vol. V, fasc. II, pp. 393(25-26), 397(4-5); Basileiade, p. 124.

you will, we will give no answer."[194] Therefore, John was the only speaker. The emperor's will was that none of the Greek delegates respond; hence, the solemn session ended. Eugene sent word to Joseph, saying that since the Greek delegates refused to continue the talks, two alternatives lay open to them: to consent to the doctrine of Rome or to go home by Pascha (the 5th of April).

The Emperor Uses Different Means

At this juncture, a painful conflict took place within the emperor's conscience to reconcile the demands of the Latins. The emperor, ever mindful of the care for his earthly kingdom, thought that the salvation of Byzantium, now on the verge of collapse, could be attained only by union. Emperor John knew that the issues demanded extreme circumspection.[195] He did not want a forced union,[196] because if abuse or injury resulted, he feared the vexation of his people would befall him. He was resolved, therefore, to do nothing without consulting the bishops, but meanwhile maneuvered people so that he might reach his goal.

He, therefore, became close with those of his delegation that were inclined toward, and even resolved upon, union with the Church of Rome: Bessarion of Nicaea, Isidore of Russia, and Gregory the *synkellos* (chancellor). The emperor soon pressed certain bishops to terminate the disputes and become reconciled with the west. The Latin arguments managed to win over Bessarion, who allowed himself to be persuaded because of his desire for union. He also desired to integrate Byzantine and western culture. Isidore of Kiev followed his lead, as did the lay philosophers, except Gemistos Plethon.[197]

It was with supporters of union that the emperor took counsel, and by them that he inclined the minds of the others to his aspiration. Thus, in a short time, the Greek delegation became divided. The only members to stand firmly for Orthodoxy were the vicars of the three eastern patriarchates, a few bishops, and some of the emperor's civil officials.

The far-shining star of the spiritual firmament of the Church, Mark, more daring than the rest, proclaimed to all that the Latins were not only schismatics but heretics. "Our Church," said the true spokesman of the eastern sees, "has kept silence on this, because the Latins are more powerful

---

[194] Ostroumoff, p. 117.
[195] Syropoulos, Vol. VIII, 7.
[196] Syn. Flor., pp. 590, 595.
[197] Runciman, *The Great Church*, p. 107.

and numerous than we are; but we, in fact, have broken all ties with them for the very reason that they are heretics!"[198]

In the meantime, the pope, keeping them longer in Florence than in Ferrara, did not supply the promised comforts and help. After four months, they still had received no stipends and were starving. When monies were finally approved, they were for only two months' back pay. The distributor of the papal largesse even had the impertinence to command that Metropolitan Mark receive no stipend, saying, "He eats the pope's bread, and opposes the pope, as a Judas. What the Ephesian needs is a rope, so that he might be hanged!"[199]

The New "Formula"

Private talks among the Greeks continued even after Pascha. The Latins desired to recommence the discussions. Initially, the emperor refused. Later, however, he agreed to appoint a committee of ten members. He chose Mark of Ephesus, Anthony of Herakleia, Isidore of Russia, Dositheos of Monemvasia, Bessarion of Nicaea, and several others.

Concerning the procession of the Spirit, the Latins found that the Greeks placed great stress on two expressions: "through (διὰ) the Son" and "from (ἐκ) the Son." To facilitate matters, the Latins wrote a formula for the Greeks, hoping that they might accept it. It read: "We (Greeks) do proclaim that, though we admit the procession of the Holy Spirit from the Father, still we do not deny that the Holy Spirit proceeds and receives from the Son, as from the Father. Since we have heard that the Latins avow the procession of the Holy Spirit from the Father and the Son, as from two Principles, for this very reason have we avoided this expression. However, we (Latins) affirm that, though we avow the procession of the Holy Spirit from the Father and the Son, still we do not deny that the Father is the source and origin of all divinity, that is, the Son and the Holy Spirit. In like manner, avowing the procession of the Holy Spirit from the Son, we do not deny that the Son has this from the Father, and do not admit two Principles or two proceedings of the Holy Spirit, but one origin and one procession."[200]

All the Greek bishops rejected this formula, except Isidore, Bessarion, Dorotheos and Gregory. The Latin partisan Bessarion endeavored to prove that the words "through (διὰ) the Son" are identical with the Latin "from (ἐκ) the Son." Using the words of Saint John of Damascus (ca. 676-ca. 750) in his

---

[198] Ostroumoff, p. 122.
[199] Syropoulos, "Memoirs," Vol. IX, chaps. 4-5, pp. 436(20-37)-438(1-8); Basileiade, p. 132.
[200] Ostroumoff, pp. 127, 128.

Exposition of the Orthodox Faith, Mark opposed Bessarion, saying, "Saint John wrote that 'the Spirit of the Father proceeds from the Father. We speak also of the Spirit of the Son, not as though from Him, but as proceeding through Him from the Father—for the Father alone is Cause.'"[201] The Latins have "introduced two Principles in the divinity...but for the Orthodox the only source, that is to say, cause of the super-essential divinity, is the Father, and this distinguishes Him from the Son and the Holy Spirit."[202] Saint Mark said that if "we accept that the Holy Spirit proceeds also from the Son, then we abolish the monarchy in the divinity and accept two Causes of the divinity." Saint Mark then mentioned what was said by Saint Gregory the Theologian and Saint Gregory of Nyssa.[203]

Maintaining his deep respect for the apophatic traditions of the Church, Mark proved ineffectual against his opponents, both from within and without his camp. He was further hampered by restrictions imposed on him by the emperor, by the difficulties in the translations, and by his ignorance of Latin. Notwithstanding, Orthodoxy was more precious to Mark than the state; Orthodoxy was the eternal treasure, the true Church of those being saved. The Byzantine state is of the earth; it was born, flourished, and would die. Yet Orthodoxy is eternal and must be preserved as an eternal light. Such were the thoughts of Saint Mark. Contrary to this, for the sake of his throne, Emperor John endeavored to press for the union at all costs—even at the cost of Orthodoxy. He ordered that a formula be composed in which both the Latin and Greek parties retained their own doctrines without rejecting the contrary opinion.

Many unnecessary discussions ensued on the two Greek words ἐϰ (from) and διὰ (through). The Greeks then came up with the following formula: "We (Greeks) do believe and confess that the Holy Spirit proceeds from the Father, but is as His own to the Son and flows out (ἀναβλύζον) from Him; we also affirm and believe that He essentially flows from both, that is, from the Father and through the Son."[204] They believed that through this formula each party could retain its own doctrine without rejecting the contrary

---

[201] Saint John of Damascus, *Exposition of the Orthodox Faith*, Book I, Ch. 12, Nicene, 2nd Ser., Vol. IX.

[202] *Confession of Correct Faith Exhibited in Florence*, Concilium Florentinum Documenta et Scriptores, Ser. A, Vol. X, fasc. II, pp. 128-130(14-17, 35), 131(8-9); Basileiade, p. 120.

[203] Basileiade, pp. 120, 121.

[204] Ostroumoff, p. 130.

opinion. Ambiguous as it was, Saint Mark, supported by several hierarchs, rejected this proposal.

Those with Metropolitan Mark knew that the addition of the Filioque phrase ("and Son") to the Symbol of the Faith was the essential dogmatic difference between Orthodoxy and the Church at Rome. They knew that this difference was a distinguishing mark not only of Ferrara-Florence, but also from long ago. The Church of Constantinople condemned this addition first adopted by the two Latin Councils of Toledo (547 and 589). It surfaced in the Frankish creed in about 769. Its introduction by Frankish monks in 807 into their monastery on the Mount of Olives aroused strong opposition from the Orthodox monks of Saint Savvas Monastery. The matter was referred to Pope Leo III (795-816), who strenuously resisted this addition as unwarranted and uncanonical.

Moreover, Saint Photios criticized those clerics—organs of the pope—that made inroads into Bulgaria and introduced the Filioque phrase into the Symbol of the Faith.[205] This heretical addition was condemned at the Synod of 879, convened by Patriarch Photios. It was to this synod that Pope John VIII (872-882) sent Cardinal Peter and Bishops Paul of Ancona and Eugene of Ostia, who recited the holy Symbol of the Faith without the addition of the Filioque. At this council it was declared that any clergyman who added to the Creed would be deposed, whereas a lay person would be anathematized. To these decisions, not one of the three papal legates brought forward any objection. When they returned to Rome, and Pope John read the acts, he wrote Emperor Basil I (867-886) of Constantinople and Patriarch Photios of his agreement.

In 1009, Pope Sergius IV (1009-1012), on taking possession of the papal throne, had the addition of the Filioque phrase to the holy Symbol in his enthronement letter. When his successor, Pope Benedict VIII (1012-1024) also yielded to this addition to the Creed, the Orthodox Church strictly opposed it. Concurrently, Patriarch Sergios of Constantinople (999-1019), the nephew of Photios, after a synodal decision, condemned the wilful stubbornness of the pope. In the diptychs, he then drew a line through the name of the Bishop of Rome which, from that date, has never been mentioned again. Each time the Church of Rome has made an attempt to pervert the holy Symbol of the Faith, whether it be from the pope or other Latins, there have been

---

[205] "Epistle of Photios to the Patriarchs of the East," see Ioannes Valettas, Photiou Epistolai (London, 1864), chaps. V, XXIV, pp. 169, 175.

counteractions. However, in every circumstance, the Eastern Orthodox Church has always strenuously opposed it.[206]

Therefore, Metropolitan Mark insisted that the Scriptures and the fathers reveal that the phrase "from the Son" and "through the Son" are different.[207] He said that if the Lord Jesus would disclose to His disciples that the Holy Spirit proceeds from the Son, then He would have said that the Spirit proceeds from Himself, that is, (τὸ ἐξ ἡμων ἐκπορευόμενον).[208]

The emperor, nevertheless, disregarded the prudent advice of Mark Evgenikos, Anthony of Herakleia, Sophronios of Anchialos, and Dositheos of Monemvasia. The emperor did his best to increase the number of votes favorable to the new formula. He also attempted to persuade Sylvester Syropoulos the ecclesiarch, Michael Balsamon the *great chartophylax* and George of Cappadocia the *proto-ekdikos* to accept Bessarion's view, that is, there was no essential difference between the phrase "through the Son" and "from the Son."

Death of the Papal Theologian

The Russian Priest Symeon of Suzdal then records an unusual incident, which is not mentioned by any of the other writers. Father Symeon wrote that one of the papal theologians, named John (probably de Monte-nero), began vehemently to slander and contradict the holy metropolitan. Mark, however, answered nothing. Later, when he was alone, coming out of the palace of the pope, Mark said to John: "Go, and prepare thyself that henceforth thou dost not reason falsely concerning the Seven (Œcumenical) Synods of the holy fathers." After Mark uttered these words, he returned to his apartment. The papal theologian John then went to his hotel room, where he immediately died.[209]

---

[206] Basileiade, pp. 117-119; Panayiotes N. Trembela, *Theoria Aparadekte Peri Tin Unam Sanctum* (in Greek) (Athens, 1964), p. 42; Idem, *Epi Tis Ecumenikes Kineseos ke ton Theologikon Dialogon Emiepisema Engrapha* (in Greek) (Athens, 1972), p. 20; Idem, *Dogmatike tis Orthodoxou Catholikes Ekklesias* (in Greek), Vol. I (Athens, 1959), pp. 278-298.

[207] *P.G.* 161:165C, 173BCD; Syropoulos, "Memoirs," Vol. VIII, chaps. 31-32, p. 418.

[208] Basileiade, p. 120.

[209] Symeon of Suzdal, "Les Russes au Concile, etc.," p. 201; Basileiade, p. 115, n. 5. The three chief Latin contenders against Orthodoxy and Saint Mark were the Dominican Provincial John de Montenero, the Spanish theologian Juan de Torquemada (1388-1468) and the Dominican theologian John of Ragusa (d. ca. 1443).

"They Are Heretics"

Saint Mark, describing the papists, again said, "They are not only schismatics, but heretics....Therefore, we must not have union, until they remove the addition from the Symbol and confess the Symbol as we do."[210] Unable to counter the words of Metropolitan Mark, before the patriarch, Bishops Methodios of Lakedaimon and Dorotheos of Mytilene rose up from their seats and, unabashed, approached Mark, uttering threats to break him, and said, "Who art thou that thou dost call the Latins heretics? How long shall we endure thee? We shall inform the pope concerning thee, so he may punish thee as thou dost deserve!"[211]

The Emperor's Dog

Syropoulos then records an event that is worthy of mention. As an eyewitness, he writes that when the emperor was promoting the union, he made an address to a standing assembly. By his side was a large hunting dog which always accompanied him, and even slept at his master's feet. The moment that the emperor opened his mouth to speak in favor of the union, the animal suddenly was roused and began to howl in a frightful manner. The servants attempted to silence the animal by raising their voices to frighten it and even resorted to using rods. Nothing would make the animal cease from wailing and whimpering in an almost tuneful manner. As long as the emperor spoke, the animal matched sound for sound, and only stopped when the emperor finished speaking.[212]

All present interpreted the event as a bad omen. Doubtless, some brought to mind the biblical account of Balaam and his ass [Num. 22:21-24]. The dumb she-ass of the prophet understood what was hidden to the befuddled prophet. In like manner, Emperor John VIII Palaiologos was blinded by the promises of the pope. The emperor should have spoken to the pope using the words of the Apostle Peter: "May thy silver be with thee for destruction, because thou didst think to acquire the gift of God by means of money. There is neither part nor lot to thee in this matter, for thy heart is not straight before God [Acts 8:20, 21]." Unfortunately, the emperor would not think or say such words. The emperor, however, managed to get a majority of twenty-one votes against twelve. While the Latins considered this a victory, Saint Mark and Anthony of Herakleia were continually harassed by their Latinizing brethren.

---

[210] Mansi, 31A, 885DE; *Praktika*, Vol. V, fasc. II, p. 400(25-33); Basileiade, p. 121.

[211] Syropoulos, "Memoirs," Vol. IX, chap. 10, p. 444(4-23); Ibid., p. 133.

[212] Ibid., Vol. X, ch. 8, p. 458(7-23); Ibid., p. 137.

Signatures for Sale

Dorotheos of Mytilene remarked, "If the pope wishes, let him give me florins, so I may distribute them to those that know what is to the pope's advantage. In that way, I shall prepare the way for the signing of the union." Somehow these words were repeated to the pope, who immediately acted upon the offer by giving Bishop Dorotheos gold florins. Syropoulos notes, "I do not know exactly how much he received, but, according to some, the amount was two hundred florins." Bishop Dorotheos then did as he pledged and shared the money with certain hierarchs. Syropoulos records that even the Great Chartophylax Michael's vote was bought with nine florins.[213]

Saint Mark Does Not Capitulate: "Incline My Heart unto Thy Testimonies and Not unto Covetousness [Ps. 118:36]."

Those in favor of union thought it might facilitate matters if the pope were to inform the Greeks of the tangible benefits which Byzantium could hope to gain by a union. The pope, quickly perceiving the "material" angle of the query, promised the following. At papal expense, the Vatican would provide the means for the Greeks' return to Constantinople. Rome would also provide three hundred soldiers to be stationed in Constantinople and two ships on the Bosporos for protection against the Turks. Eugene also made two other offers of a purely theoretical nature: the pope would summon the western sovereigns to aid Byzantium, and he would preach a crusade that would be made to pass through Constantinople.[214]

The Latins, however, were still unhappy with the duplicity in the Greek formula. They knew that in the Greek tongue the words "proceed from (ἐκπορευόμενον)" and "flow out from (ἀναβλύζον)" have different meanings, with the latter referring to the temporal mission, not the eternal procession of the Holy Spirit from the Son. No, the Latins wanted the Greeks to receive their formula, their confession, and put aside the Orthodox formula. More futile discussions between the Greeks only kindled anger and resentment. Bessarion even went so far as to declare that Mark was possessed by an evil spirit.[215] Dorotheos of Mytilene and Methodios of Lakedaimon threatened to tell the pontiff that Mark viewed him as a heretic. Some slandered Mark and, taunting him, said, "He has a demon and is mad. Why do you listen to him?" The imperial officer, Jagaris, observing how Mark acted toward those that contended with him, noted how the holy man was able

---

[213] Ibid., Vol. X, ch. 8, p. 482(8-19); Ibid., p. 135, n. 64a.

[214] February Volume of *The Great Synaxaristes* (in Greek), p. 650.

[215] Basileiade, pp. 133, 134.

to give convincing arguments and prevail over them. Jagaris wondered how they could not contend with one, yet he struggled with all.[216]

The Latins, meanwhile, were awaiting an answer. Bishop Dorotheos of Monemvasia said to the emperor, "Therefore, what dost thou desire? Dost thou wish that we betray our Faith, so the pope might give us the aid that we need to return to Constantinople? I should prefer to die than to be Latinized!"[217] The Greeks were sundered. All the emperor could do was to plead with the pope that his bishops were "confused and divided." Thus, the pope persuaded the emperor to invite the Greek bishops to his palace for a personal conference.

On the 27th of May, the pope threatened the Greeks that if they did not conform, they could hope for no aid from the Christian monarchs of the west. He complained that after he had underwritten all the expenses of the Greeks for two years, they were obligated to him to submit and give their signature for union. Straightway, George Scholarios perceived that the pope and the Latins were not so naive as to spend money without hoping to gain from the council. He understood that they had steered the council and anticipated all along that everything would end completely in favor of their desires.[218] Soon afterward, votes were collected in favor of the formula and the infamous union which would follow. The bishops anathematized all those that were adverse to union.

The Greeks Slowly Concede

The old Patriarch Joseph, the illegitimate son of a Bulgarian tsar and a Greek lady, possessed no great mental powers.[219] With his physical health quickly failing, he was absent from most of the sessions. When he was present, essentially, he contributed nothing. Though reluctant to consent, he put aside his vows to preserve the Faith, and at last conceded, saying, "Let there be some dispensation (οἰκονομία), some condescension. Both the union and the peace of the Churches are beneficial and needful."[220] Thus, the lukewarm patriarch wished for union and was prepared to admit that the Orthodox view of "through" the Son and the Latin "from" the Son mean the same. George Scholarios much later scornfully remarked that after Joseph

---

[216] Syropoulos, "Memoirs," Vol. IX, ch. 6, p. 438(9-21).

[217] *Praktika*, Vol. V, fasc. II, p. 400(4-8); Basileiade, p. 129.

[218] Scholarios, "Apanta," Vol. III, p. 87; *P.G.* 160:721C; Ibid., loc. cit.

[219] Runciman, *The Great Church*, p. 104.

[220] Syropoulos, "Memoirs," Vol. VIII, ch. 28, pp. 414-416; Basileiade, pp. 129, 130.

muddled his prepositions, there was nothing left for him to do but die.[221] The patriarch, seeking support for the union, also spoke to the Metropolitans of Moldovlachia, Tŭrnovo, and Amaseia, rebuking them for ingratitude and insubordination. The patriarch even had a private meeting with Mark to entreat him to sign, but the holy man remained firm. He was even asked to agree just for the sake of the others, to which Mark responded, "In matters of the Faith, there must be no concessions and no wavering."[222] The patriarch, betrayer of his own salvation and piety, persisted, but to no avail.[223]

Mark, for a time, was again subject to house arrest. The emperor, on his part, won over others by various promises, yet many bishops were adamant against the Latin formula. The emperor's brother Demetrios refused to vote and departed from his presence. He saw himself as a champion of the Greek Faith against the Latinizing tendencies of his emperor-brother. The aged and eccentric neo-Platonist, George Gemistes Plethon, also managed to withhold his signature. He considered the Latin Church to be more hostile to free thought than the Greek.[224] Therefore, he attended very few of the meetings, preferring to spend his time in Florence, giving lectures on Plato to enthusiastic audiences.[225] Syropoulos indicates that the lay delegates were required to make statements supporting the union. Yet, somehow, Plethon managed to evade making a statement. Much later, after Plethon's repose, the Platonic Academy of Florence, founded in 1449, would be dedicated to his memory.[226]

"O God, Transgressors Have Risen up Against Me, and the Assembly of the Mighty Hath Sought After My Soul, and They Have Not Set Thee Before Them [Ps. 85:13]."

As negotiations continued on the "formula," those bishops who were wholeheartedly for the union, Metropolitans Bessarion and Isidore, boldly stood up against Saint Mark. Little by little, through various means and favors, the bishops were being won over. Saint Mark realized that he would soon be alone. The holy man feared for his very life, and remarked, "I fear that the Latins will lay murderous hands upon me." Mark also suffered from an excruciating disease, a form of cancer of the intestines, which worsened in Italy. Thus, he was exhausted, persecuted, and in disgrace among those

---

[221] Runciman, *The Great Church*, p. 108.

[222] Syropoulos, "Memoirs," Vol. IX, ch. 6; Basileiade, p. 130.

[223] Ibid., Vol. IX, ch. 17, p. 452(9-12).

[224] Runciman, *The Fall*, p. 17.

[225] Idem, *The Great Church*, pp. 107, 108.

[226] Basileiade, p. 85.

who, in fact, disgraced themselves. Mark, the spiritual giant, to whom there is none to compare, represented in his person "a pillar of Orthodoxy."

1. A Formula is Derived

Finally, the opinions of the bishops were gathered and the following formula was derived: "We believe that the Holy Spirit is ever and essentially from the Father and the Son, ever and essentially proceeding from the Father through the Son." The Latins suspected the words "through the Son" lacked precision about the procession of the Spirit in time or eternity. They perceived it as an attempt by the Greeks to reconcile the "transcendent Trinity" of the Nicene Creed with the order of the "economic Trinity" as It acts and relates to the Church and the world. Many Church fathers, of both the east and the west, said the Spirit proceeds from the Father through the Son. Saints Kyril of Alexandria, Gregory the Theologian, John of Damascus, and others confessed the eternal procession of the Spirit only from the Father, though He "abides" in the Son. Nevertheless, the cardinals demanded that the words "through the Son" should be omitted in the Greek confession. After disputing long over this, the Greeks were at last obliged to change these expressions. Consequently, on the 8th of June, in the year 1439, the confession was read in the presence of the pope, in both Greek and Latin.[227] The Latins then gave the Greeks the kiss of love.[228]

More Disputes on Latin Doctrines

The pope then pressed harder and reminded all that it remained for them to define the doctrine on Purgatory, on the authority of the papal throne, on the bread in the Eucharist, and on the consecration of the host; after these points were settled, all disagreement would be done. After some argument, they were settled by compromise. The Greeks prevailed upon the pope to admit the validity of the Eucharist when performed with leavened or unleavened bread. The Latins agreed that the Greek use of *zeon* (hot water) was permissible. The Greeks could continue to utter the invocation of the Holy Spirit (ἐπίκλησις) in the divine Liturgy, but they were required to acknowledge that it was unnecessary.

In answer to the pope's proposal to discuss the issue on Purgatory, the Greeks replied, "We confess that the souls of good men receive their full reward, and those of sinners full punishment, whereas those in a middle condition are subjected to agonies in prison; but what is the exact cause of their agonies, whether it be fire, or darkness, or anything else, we cannot positively affirm."

---

[227] Ostroumoff, p. 141.
[228] Syn. Flor., pp. 621-624.

In regard to papal authority, the Greeks agreed that the pontiff ought to retain the rights he had before the schism. The Greeks were then required to give a definition of the divine essence and energies. Mark did not utter a word, though his fellow Greeks answered unsatisfactorily.[229] The pope then wished the Greeks to put into writing their acceptance of all papal demands, including the recognition of all privileges of the pope as the "Vicar of Jesus Christ." The pope also desired the Greeks to admit the addition to the Creed, to admit the doctrine on Purgatory, and to examine the doctrine on the divine essence and energies. The bishops, afraid of lingering disputes, only verbally acquiesced before the emperor and patriarch. This took place on the morning of the 10th of June.

The Patriarch Dies

The patriarch had been complaining of his suffering with dropsy and severe tremors. On Wednesday, the 10th day of June, in the year 1439, another affliction was laid upon the apostates from pristine Orthodoxy when, in the evening of the same day, Patriarch Joseph died during the evening meal.[230] Only eight days earlier, after Patriarch Joseph agreed to the union, he had expressed how anxious he was to return to Constantinople. He therefore sent his baggage on to Venice and said, "I will tarry a few more days here till the signing of the decree; then I will immediately leave Florence."[231] Admittedly, he was no champion of Orthodoxy and deserves much reproach, yet deep in his heart he grieved for the future of the Church. To his credit, he would never allow himself or anyone in any way to injure the holy and brilliant Mark.

The alleged last will of the patriarch appears to be spurious, admitting Purgatory and avowing the pope to be the blessed father of fathers and the supreme pontiff and vicar of Christ.[232] It reads: "Joseph, by God's grace, Archbishop of Constantinople, New Rome, and Œcumenical Patriarch. Whereas I have attained the limits of my life, and shall soon pay the universal tribute: I do now, with God's help, announce my opinion to all my children. I do myself confess and agree to everything held and taught by the catholic and apostolic Church of our Lord Jesus Christ, the senior Rome. I avow the pope of the elder Rome to be the blessed father of fathers, the supreme pontiff

---

[229] Ibid., p. 620-626.
[230] Syropoulos, "Memoirs," Vol. IX, chap. 38, p. 472(9-14); Basileiade, p. 139.
[231] Ibid., p. 472(6-9).
[232] Archimandrite Amvrossy Pogodin, M.Sc Eccl., D.D., "Saint Mark of Ephesus and the False Union of Florence," *Orthodox Word* 3, No. 3(14) (June-July 1967): 89.

and vicar of Christ. I certify this before all. I admit the Purgatory of souls. In assurance of which it is signed, June 9, indict 2nd, year 1439."[233]

Why should the patriarch affirm more than that which was required by the Church of Rome, especially since he was always so slow in giving his opinion? Neither the emperor nor the pope required him to make such statements. In any event, death rescued him from the countless and sharp humiliations to which the Church would now be subjected. He was interred in the Dominican Monastery of Santa Maria Novellae, where the pope resided in Florence.[234] The absence of the patriarchal signature on the Act of Union was later to give occasion for the defenders of Orthodoxy to contest the pretensions of the Florentine Council to be œcumenical. For they contended, saying, "How could it be an œcumenical synod when the Act of Union was not signed by the œcumenical patriarch of Byzantium?"[235]

The emperor now saw himself as completely answerable to the Church for all that had taken place at Ferrara and Florence. Upon Joseph's death, the emperor, self-appointed, moved in and took the direction of the Church into his own hands. This uncanonical act was strictly condemned by Saint Mark, the defender of the Faith. In one of his epistles, he expressly condemns this action, writing: "Let no one dominate in our Faith: neither emperor, nor hierarch, nor false council, nor anyone else, but only the one God, Who both Himself and through His disciples has handed it down to us."[236]

On the 13th of June, the emperor invited the Greek council to discuss the new demands of the pope. The emperor avoided speaking about Purgatory and the Eucharist. He did, however, want to bring matters to a close on the wafer, papal authority, and the Filioque.

Saint Mark Remains Adamant: "I Spake of Thy Testimonies Before Kings, and I Was Not Ashamed [Ps. 118:46]."

Mark, Orthodoxy's invincible advocate, knew that his brethren were ready to sign. He appealed to the emperor's brother, Demetrios, to thwart it; but it proved useless. Under Emperor John Palaiologos' direction, the "formula" became the "decree of the Florentine Union," in which the Orthodox capitulated to the Latins. Therein, the Orthodox were obliged to accept the papal teachings of the Filioque, the use of unleavened bread in the

---

[233] Syn. Flor., p. 627-630.
[234] *Praktika*, Vol. V, fasc. II, p. 445(21-35); Basileiade, p. 140.
[235] Statement made by the philosopher Gemistes Plethon. Pogodin, "Saint Mark," *Orthodox Word* 3, No. 3(14), p. 90.
[236] Pogodin, "Saint Mark," loc. cit.

divine Liturgy, the authority of the pope as supreme pontiff over the world, and Purgatory. The Greeks acknowledged the Latins to be in the right and admitted themselves to be in the wrong, though in reality the truth was on their side. The Latins acceded to nothing, yet the Greeks were obliged to accede in everything.[237] In exchange for this union, the Greeks were promised funds and ships for their return voyage to Constantinople. In addition, if the European monarchs would help, a fleet and an army would be sent to defend Byzantium.

The emperor, far from elated at the signing, viewed the Latins as obstinate persons who always sought to have their own way. He then said before his bishops that the Greeks conceded to the Latins more than what was right. In fact, Emperor John nearly despaired and understood that he had fallen into a trap. He knew that the Latins merely wrangled with words and were consumed with a spirit of contradiction; in disgust, he commented, "If one of us declared that Christ is our true God, in just one or two days, they (the Latins) would pursue by every means possible to refute our statement and declare that Christ is not our true God!"[238] By these words we may perceive the impression made by the papists upon the emperor. "How tragic a figure I am," thought the emperor.

Furthermore, the emperor also found revolting the adulation the pope paid the Greek bishops. The emperor lost all confidence in his bishops and turned to Mark. He commissioned the holy man to make an exposition of the Orthodox doctrine on the holy Eucharist.[239] The emperor, however, still bewildered and flustered, summoned those metropolitans, who were pro-unionists, in the hope that they might persuade Mark to consent to the union. The indefatigable Mark simply would not hear of it, and repeated that he would not compromise or condescend in matters of belief. He said, "There exists no little or worthless word in matters of the Faith; and that which appears insignificant contains the most important meaning."[240] When asked again about signing, Mark raised his voice, and said, "I will not sign. I will never do that which thou dost ask, even if you put my life in peril."[241] After

---

[237] Ostroumoff, p. 157.

[238] Syropoulos, "Memoirs," Vol. X, chaps. 1, 6, pp. 474(15), 480(15-19); Basileiade, p. 146.

[239] Syropoulos, Vol. X, 2.

[240] Ibid., "Memoirs," Vol. IX, ch. 11, pp. 444-446.

[241] Ibid., Vol. X, ch. 9, p. 484(5-6); Syn. Flor., p. 539, 641; Basileiade, p. 147.

this, Mark remained silent, but sensed a profound pain in the depths of his heart and soul from all the events that had transpired.[242]

The pope then, wishing to settle the matter of his authority and privileges, assembled the Greek bishops. The Greeks ultimately acquiesced to the privileges of the papal throne. The pope would not surrender his right to convoke an œcumenical synod without imperial consent and to judge the patriarchs in cases against them. The pope rejected all the Greeks' exceptions to his appropriated privileges, desiring only to exact their full submission to his will. The emperor, greatly wearied, uttered, "Make all the arrangements necessary for our departure." This took place on the eve of the Nativity of Saint John the Baptist, the 24th of June. Meanwhile, unknown to the Greeks, the Council of Basle, supported by western princes and the great universities, deposed Pope Eugene on the 25th of June, in the year 1439.

On the 27th of June, after some people prevailed upon both the pope and the emperor, the Greeks agreed to write that they admitted the pope as supreme pontiff, vicar of Jesus Christ, pastor and teacher of all Christians. Furthermore, they agreed to write that it was he who governed God's Church and the rights and privileges of the eastern patriarchs, so that the Patriarch of Constantinople was second to him, followed by the Patriarchs of Alexandria, Antioch and, lastly, Jerusalem.

The Betrayal of Orthodoxy

At last the end came. On the 5th of July, in the year 1439, by the signing of the Act of Union, Orthodoxy was betrayed and sold. The pseudo-Orthodox renounced Orthodoxy and espoused all the Latin formulas and innovations. A dispute arose at the very beginning as to whose name was to be placed first in the decree. The Latins obviously desired to have the pope's name first, but the emperor demanded his own name be prefixed. The solution found was to add to the pope's words, "with the emperor's consent."[243] The decrees were then written up in Latin by Ambrose Traversari and translated into Greek by Metropolitan Bessarion of Nicaea. Metropolitans Isidore and Bessarion then suggested that a list of anathemas be appended to the decree against all that opposed the union of the Churches. Emperor John straightway disapproved of this.[244]

After the emperor, all delegates, many of whom were reluctant, accepted and signed the Act of Union, whether for themselves or, in the case of some, for the eastern patriarchs, whom they had been entrusted to

---

[242] Ibid., Vol. X, ch. 9, p. 482(31); Ibid., loc. cit.

[243] Ostroumoff, p. 153.

[244] Syropoulos, "Memoirs," Vol. X, ch. 10, p. 484.

represent. Syropoulos mournfully notes that after the *great protosynkellos*, wardens, and hierarchs, the others attached to the Greek company were also made to sign, including himself. Though the emperor allowed no one other than those he appointed to participate in the discussions, the emperor enjoined the laymen to sign. Syropoulos labels himself and the others as "wretched cowards" and "unwilling volunteers" that were suffering from near starvation and fearing the specter of death. He writes that most "sighed from the depths of their hearts and signed weeping." Though Syropoulos was the last of the laymen to sign, he wrote: "I sign out of necessity in order to fulfill the decree and will of the emperor," though he comments, "I knew the union would not help the Church at all." He acknowledged that if he refused to sign, he knew that he would be punished. He remarks that God, Who knows the heart and reins and the secret things and thoughts, knows how each signed and who accepted money. Syropoulos then writes: "God knows the disposition of my soul, that neither do I accept this (union), nor do I sign voluntarily."[245] Syropoulos then closed the door to the emperor's room at the Peroutsi Palace and looked intently at each Greek signatory as a kind of Latin hierarch.[246] Though in their hearts many did not wish to sign, yet they trampled on their Orthodox conscience for fear of death or for the sake of money, food, or to appease the emperor. After the Greek delegates kissed the pope's knee, they were lavishly entertained by the pope.

Those Who Did Not Wish to Sign

When the pope learned that the Russian Bishop Abraham of Suzdal had not signed, he dispatched his own Bishop Christopher Garatoni of Corona to secure his signature. After this attempt failed, the Russian Bishop Isidore of Kiev had Abraham arrested and incarcerated for one week. After that he released Abraham who, under much pressure, agreed to sign.[247]

Metropolitan Anthony of Herakleia was absent because of illness but was enjoined to sign the decree while lying in bed. Even those who were not formerly allowed to vote were made to sign. The only exceptions were those who had either died or managed to escape Florence. None of the Greeks bothered to ask or disturb Mark; all were convinced of his firmness.

---

[245] Ibid., Vol. X, ch. 12, p. 492(11-20); Basileiade, p. 151.

[246] Ibid., Vol. 10, ch. 13, pp. 492-494; Ibid., p. 150.

[247] Symeon of Suzdal, "Les Russes au Concile," p. 203; Basileiade, loc. cit.

To avoid signing, those who definitely managed to flee to Venice were Esaias of Stavropol and the Bishop of Tver.[248] When Bishop Esaias learned that the Latins planned to murder him because of his refusal to sign, he secretly left the city. The Georgian Bishop Gregory also left Florence undercover in order to avoid signing the decree.[249] The Despot Demetrios departed four days before the death of Patriarch Joseph. Accompanying the Despot were George Gemistes Plethon who disliked the Latin Church, George Scholarios who left in protest, and John Evgenikos, the resolute champion's brother.[250] Also, the deacon and archphylax of the Great Church quit Florence. Curiously, the signature of Methodios of Lakedaimon is nowhere to be found.[251]

More Pressure Applied to Saint Mark

The pope then spoke to the emperor, provoking him to persuade the Ephesian to sign the union. Emperor John said, "If thou dost wish to speak to Mark the same improper and unreasonable words which were uttered by thine own theologian John, who then immediately died, do thou, O pope, choose one of thy company. Send him on thine own behalf, not mine, if thou dost wish to communicate something."[252] The moment Pope Eugene heard these words from the emperor's mouth, he was afraid and sent a papal representative to Mark, not to rebuke him but to pay homage to him. The representative, ordered to take a large tray laden with gold florins and a golden vase, was to beseech Mark to accept the gifts and accept an invitation from the pope, who would receive him with honor. It should be noted that, shortly before, the pope had spoken many evil remarks against Mark and threatened to cast him into the flames. Now, the pope changed his tactics and hoped to bribe the righteous man with gold and flattery. The holy man not only rejected the gifts, but also refused entry to any papal representative to his apartment. He said, "Tell thy lord, the pope, has he not ever heard what the Lord said to the scribes and Pharisees? 'Hypocrites! For ye cleanse the outside of the cup and the dish, but within they are full of plunder and incontinence [Mt. 23:25].' In like manner hast thou, O pope, gathered

---

[248] The *Acta* does not mention the flight of Bishop Esaias, but his signature is missing from the tomus, and Syropoulos, 292, explicitly mentions his secret departure before the signing of the union.

[249] Syropoulos, "Memoirs," Vol. IX, ch. 26, p. 462(5-10); Basileiade, loc. cit.

[250] Basileiade, loc. cit.; Fr. Petro B.T. Bilaniuk, "The Council of the Revolving Doors: Basle-Ferrara-Florence-Rome 1431-1445," *Studies in Eastern Christianity*, vol. 3 (Munich-Toronto: The Ukrainian Free University, 1983), p. 126.

[251] February Volume of *The Great Synaxaristes* (in Greek), p. 651.

[252] Basileiade, pp. 147, 148.

unclean gold. Therefore, give it to whomever thou dost wish, 'for where your treasure is, there will your heart be also [Mt. 6:21].' Thy council will not be a council, and all of you shall perish."[253]

The pope then sent another one of his representatives, Ambrogio Traversari (ca. 1386-1439), General of the Camaldolese Order at the Monastery of Santa Maria degli Angioli at Florence. Fra Ambrogio was fired by his possession of a splendid collection of Greek patristic manuscripts that he wished to translate into Latin.[254] Unfortunately, this was merely a scholarly pursuit for him and not a desire to learn the truth. When he came to Mark's door, Mark uttered, "If thou dost also slander the Seven (Œcumenical) Synods of the holy fathers, thou, in the same manner, shall die within forty days." Indeed, Ambrogio died in that time.[255]

Saint Mark Confronts the Pope: "Sinners Have Waited for Me to Destroy Me; But Thy Testimonies Have I Understood [Ps. 118:95]."

When the Greek bishops had affixed their signatures to the council's decree, the emperor sent ten bishops to witness the signing of the pope. When Eugene took up the document, he closely studied the signatures of the Greek bishops. Then, while Eugene was signing the decree, he asked whether the Ephesian had signed. When he was told that Mark had not, he involuntarily exclaimed, "Then we have accomplished nothing!"[256] He then stood up and demanded that Saint Mark be forced to sign the union, or be delivered up to judgment as a stubborn opponent to the decree. The emperor defended him, saying that since he was a metropolitan of the Eastern Church, he could be judged only by the eastern bishops. Nevertheless, the pope insisted that the emperor send Saint Mark to him to receive at least a private reprimand.[257]

The emperor then summoned Saint Mark of Ephesus, and said, "Because the pope has two and three times bidden thee to appear before him, thou must go. However, do not be timid, because I informed him about many things concerning thee. I still care about thee and shall see that nothing harsh shall befall thee. Go and hear whatever he has to say. As needed, boldly make a complete defense."[258] These final words were superfluous, since the brave-

---

[253] Ibid., p. 148.

[254] *The Oxford Dictionary of the Christian Church*, s.v. "Traversari."

[255] Symeon of Suzdal, "Les Russes au Concile," p. 202; Basileiade, p. 148.

[256] Syropoulos, "Memoirs," Vol. X, ch. 15, p. 496(19-20); "Saint Mark," January Volume of *The Great Synaxaristes* (in Greek), p. 475.

[257] Basileiade, p. 161.

[258] Ibid.

spirited Mark had already decided upon this. What is evident, however, is that the emperor regarded Mark with respect and affection.

Saint Mark of Ephesus and Pope Eugene

Sitting on his throne, flanked by his cardinals and bishops, Pope Eugene met the adornment of Ephesus, Mark, with rebukes and threats. The pope reminded him of the punishments appointed by the œcumenical synods for those who dare to disobey their decrees. Mark, observing everyone else sitting, told the pope that his kidneys and feet were causing him much pain, and that he could not stand. Metropolitan Mark, without waiting for an answer from the pope, immediately took a seat. By this action he also exhibited his fearlessness before Pope Eugene. Once again, the pope attempted to persuade Mark to sign the decree. Perceiving the utter hopelessness of convincing the Ephesian, the pope then threatened to depose him if he did not sign.[259]

Then, undaunted, the defender of Orthodoxy, Mark, gave the pope a decisive answer, saying, "The synods condemn those who will not obey the Church and maintain opinions contrary to what she teaches. I neither preach to my own glory, nor have I said anything new or unknown to the Church. I keep intact the pure and unadulterated teachings which the Church has received and preserved, and continues to preserve, from Christ our Savior. This doctrine was also clung to by the Church of Rome, unanimously with that of the Eastern Church, until the beginning of the schism. Even during the present synod, you have lauded this exact pious worship of the past. No one can censure or condemn this pious teaching. Therefore, if I remain steadfast in this teaching and do not desire to deviate from it, how is it possible to judge me as a heretic? First, one must judge the teaching which I believe, and then judge me. If, however, the confession is holy and Orthodox, how can I justifiably be judged?"[260] These bold and daring words, however, were spoken in a spirit of humility. They were not difficult for Mark. If his answer dissented from that of his emperor, why should he not speak out against the senselessness of the pope? Mark truly was a hero. Though he appeared physically weak and debilitated by cancer, God's power was manifest in him.

The pope, perceiving Mark's inflexibility, finally understood there was no hope of dissuading the lone and brave guardian of Orthodox truths. He bade Mark to leave his presence. The emperor also had much to do with preventing Mark from being further threatened by the pope and his organization.[261]

A Celebration of Union

On Monday, the 6th of July, in the year 1439, at the Church of Santa Maria del Fiore in Florence, the festival attendant with the union was concluded by celebrating the Mass according to the Latin Rite, though no Greek bishop participated or received the wafer. The Greeks only exchanged the kiss of peace among themselves. The reading of the Creed was executed in both Latin and Greek with, of course, the addition of the Filioque. When

---

[259] Ibid., p. 162.
[260] Syropoulos, "Memoirs," Vol. X, ch. 23, pp. 508-510; Basileiade, pp. 162, 163.
[261] Ibid., Vol. XI, ch. 4, p. 524(27-29); Ibid., p. 165.

the decree of the union was read, both Bessarion of Nicaea and Cardinal Cesarini embraced. The Byzantine emperor was then seen to bow before the pope, causing many to weep and repeat, "Lord, we have sinned."[262]

Peace was proclaimed, but later the Latins refused to be present at the Greek Liturgy. The pope was even so bold as to say that he wished to view the liturgical service of the Greeks for his approval. This bitterly offended the emperor, who said, "We had hoped to correct the errors of the Latins. Now I see that the Latins who have introduced new dogmas, defiled the Faith, and sinned in many things, wish to correct us who have in no way changed anything, but have kept the holy Faith intact and unadulterated."[263] After that, the emperor never again expressed his wish to have the Liturgy performed before the pope.

The pope, taking full advantage of his self-proclaimed right as head of the Church, also posed questions to the Greeks on the holy Eucharist, holy Chrism, divorce, and the election of a patriarch. The pope then desired that a new patriarch be appointed, and even offered a cardinal as his own candidate, saying, "He is a good man, useful, noble, elderly, and rich. If you accept him as patriarch, he could be most useful to thy Church, because he is quite old and will not live much longer; thus, thy Church shall inherit his wealth."[264]

The emperor refused to name a patriarch while in Florence, for he must be elected with the consent of all the dioceses under his jurisdiction, and ordained in Hagia Sophia. On the matter of divorce, the emperor remarked, through the bishops, that the Orthodox had sufficient reasons to allow it.

The pope was not willing to recall Latin bishops from Greek dioceses, but chose to leave the Latin and Greek bishops in their dioceses, though two might sit on one throne. He decided that successors would be chosen from the group of the surviving bishop.[265] The pope, though deposed at Basle, sent epistles to all in the west, proclaiming that the Greeks, Emperor John, and his metropolitans had bowed before him and signed the decisions of the council.[266]

---

[262] Symeon of Suzdal, "Les Russes au Concile," p. 203; Basileiade, pp. 153, 160.

[263] Syropoulos, "Memoirs," Vol. X, chaps. 16-17, pp. 500-502; Basileiade, p. 161.

[264] The editor of Syropoulos' "Memoirs," Vol. X, ch. 18, p. 503, notes that the candidate selected by the Pope was Cardinal Giovanni de Contarini. On the other hand, Ostroumoff, p. 158 and *Praktika*, Vol. V, fasc. II, p. 471(12-15) identify the candidate as the Pope's own nephew, Cardinal Franciscus Candulmer.

[265] Syropoulos, Vol. X, 14.

[266] Symeon of Suzdal, "Les Russes au Concile," loc. cit.; Basileiade, p. 154.

A False Union

"The decree of union was as a spider's web," Saint Mark later wrote to Scholarios.[267] This council can be call neither "holy" nor "œcumenical," for the following reasons: The document was not the fruit of brothers coming freely in Christ to discuss matters of the Faith. Forced measures were employed against the Greeks to reduce them to fear and trembling that they might sign. Bishop Abraham of Suzdal was even imprisoned. Others also were wearied from starvation and the threat of death; whereas others were pressured by the emperor and his pleas for aid to their homeland. Some shamefully accepted the bribe money, while others were actually persuaded by the Latin arguments.

Saint Mark identified this synod as the "assembly of Caiaphas [Mt. 26:3, 57]," that is, there were clandestine meetings and agreements in cells and apartments, not out in the open as is proper to an œcumenical gathering. When it came to the signing, "Many did not know the exact contents of the document they were signing," declares Syropoulos.[268] This is also confirmed by John Evgenikos, George Amiroutzes, Michael Balsamon, and Manuel the Rhetor. The important issues were not discussed in an open session. There was no voting of the general assembly. Most signed without ever publicly giving their opinion. It was not a union of free theological debate, but one that served political aims. Syropoulos remarked that the "magnitude of this appalling situation is the folly and shame of the Greek race."[269] George Scholarios observed, "There was nothing that was holy about this synod, neither from head to toe nor from commencement to ending."[270]

The manuscripts and texts brought forward by the Latins to support their views were often corrupted and forged. Furthermore, there was the decision of the Council of Basle that condemned Pope Eugene. When Pope Eugene signed the decree of the union in July, he had already been condemned on the 25th day of June, in the year 1439.

The Greeks in Venice

The Greeks were permitted to leave with "honors" toward the end of August. Before Emperor John arrived in Venice, Bishop Metrophanes of

[267] Mark of Ephesus, "Epistle to George Scholarios," Concilium Florentinum Documenta et Scriptores, ed, Concilio et Impensis Pontificii Instituti Orientalium Studiorum, Series A (Rome, 1953, 1977), Vol. X, fasc. II, p. 154(17-18); Basileiade, loc. cit.
[268] Syropoulos, "Memoirs," Vol. X, chaps. 28-29, pp. 518(12-32)-520(1-2); Basileiade, p. 156.
[269] Ibid., Vol. III, ch. 21, p. 182(8-10); Ibid., p. 157.
[270] Scholarios, "Apanta," Vol. III, pp. 136-139; Basileiade, loc. cit.

Kyzikos performed the divine Liturgy in a papal monastery of the city, wherein he commemorated the pope. His conduct was observed with indignation and displeasure by the other Greek bishops and the Despot Demetrios, who was astounded at this act.[271]

Emperor John and Metropolitan Mark arrived in Venice on the 6th of September. On the 17th of September, the Greeks celebrated the divine Liturgy at the Church of Saint Mark's in Venice. Emperor John was ill and therefore absent. Next to his brother, the Despot Demetrios, stood the Venetian Doge Foskari, who desired to observe a Liturgy. Latin clergy did not participate, and the name of the pope was not commemorated. Syropoulos comments: "Some criticized us for celebrating a Liturgy in a Latin church; yet, they wrongfully judge us. We celebrated upon our own Antimension (Corporal) and used our own holy vessels. Everything was performed according to our own ecclesiastical order. Furthermore, our Church recorder, with a great voice, recited the holy Symbol (of Faith)...without the addition (Filioque); neither was the name of the pope commemorated."[272] This incident is mentioned to exhibit that a true union never took place, but only a parody of a union.

The Greeks Leave Italy

After spending some time in Venice, the Greeks departed on the 19th of October, 1439, sailing on two Venetian vessels. Though the pope had promised to provide them with large and comfortable sailing ships, Syropoulos describes the vessels as "freight ships, suitable only to Circasian and Scythian slaves."[273] Mark, desiring safe passage home, asked the emperor to guarantee his safety, to which the emperor complied. Therefore, Mark traveled in the same galley with the emperor and had his comforts supplied by him.[274] The emperor treated Mark with reverence and love, which may seem paradoxical to most. It was the Holy Spirit that spoke to the emperor's heart in a mysterious way, so that he might perceive that Mark was a God-bearing hierarch. George Scholarios confirms this when he characterized the emperor as "beholding Mark with wonder as a virtuous and wise man."[275]

When the Greeks passed through Kerkyra (Corfu), Methone of the Peloponnesos, and Evia (Euboea), the Orthodox Christians of these places received them. However, when they were informed about the union made by the Greek bishops, Syropoulos describes them as "exceedingly disgusted and

---

[271] Syropoulos, "Memoirs," Vol. XI, ch. 3, p. 524; Ibid., p. 165.
[272] Ibid., Vol. XI, chaps. 5, 9, pp. 526(11-12), 530(14-26); Ibid., loc. cit.
[273] Basileiade, p. 166.
[274] Syropoulos, "Memoirs," Vol. XI, ch. 4, p. 524(29-30).
[275] Scholarios, "Apanta," Vol. I, p. 252; Basileiade, p. 167.

repulsed." They exclaimed, "It would have been better had you not attended the synod!" Syropoulos records: "The zealous Orthodox of Methone reproached us, saying, 'Till now we upheld our Faith against the Latins and condemned them....Now, however, we have nothing to say to them. You have worked a great evil for us in what you have done at Florence!'"[276]

On the 18th day of December, in the year 1439, the pope appointed the former Orthodox metropolitans, Isidore and Bessarion, to the rank of cardinal, to reward their zeal for the cause of the union. Meanwhile, the poor and defeated travelers who had been away from their homes and sees for about two years arrived in Constantinople on the 1st day of February, in the year 1440.

Metropolitan Isidore

At the closing of the Council of Florence, the assignment of prevailing upon the Russians and Lithuanians to accept the false union was delegated to Isidore of Moscow, now a cardinal of Pope Eugene. Isidore found no resistance in Poland. In 1440, when Isidore arrived in Vilna, the capital of Lithuania, he was compelled, on the basis of the Florentine Union, to settle various canonical problems. This included the rights of various bishops which had been altered because of it. After Vilna, he went on to Kiev, where he remained several months, commemorating the pope in the divine Liturgy and preaching the union. Isidore then journeyed to Smolensk, where he heard the report that Deacon Symeon, who had accompanied him to Florence, was disseminating anti-union literature in Novgorod. When the deacon was in Italy, he had come under the profound and holy influence of Saint Mark. Therefore, Cardinal Isidore ordered the authorities to arrest the deacon and bring him in chains to Moscow in March of 1441. However, news brought by those that had heard Deacon Symeon had already reached Moscow. Upon entering the city, Isidore was proceeded by an advance of Latin crosses and crosiers that made their way down the street to the Ascension Cathedral in the capital. During the divine Liturgy, he commemorated the pope; and afterward, he read the decree of the union. Four days later, Grand Duke Basil II had the cardinal and his papal legates cast into the Tchoudov Monastery on the charge of heresy. Basil described Isidore as a "ravening wolf" and the Greeks as "apostates." Isidore, however, managed to escape, fleeing to Italy in June of 1443.

This was a major turning point in Russian Church history, because, from that point on, Russians would choose their own metropolitan. They

---

[276] Syropoulos, "Memoirs," Vol. XI, chaps. 11, 13, 14, pp. 532, 534, 536; Ibid., p. 166.

turned their backs on apostate Byzantium, since she had forfeited all claims to leadership in the Orthodox world by betraying the true Faith. On account of this, Byzantium lost an embittered Russia. In her judgment of the Florentine Union, the Church of Russia had shown herself to be a worthy daughter of Orthodoxy.

Subsequent Reunions

Pope Eugene IV used a "divide and conquer" policy by dealing with each of the Eastern Churches as an isolated unit. The union with the Greeks was reached on the 6th day of July, in the year 1439. After their departure, the Armenians were led in and reunited on the 22nd of November, in the year 1439,[277] and the Copts of Egypt together with the Ethiopians signed the decree of the union with Rome on the 4th day of February, in the year 1442.[278]

After the transfer of a council of Rome,[279] union was concluded with the Syrians, that is, the Monophysites of Mesopotamia, on the 30th of November, in the year 1444.[280] After their departure, union was made with the Nestorians of Chaldea and the Maronites of Cyprus on the 7th of August, in the year 1445.[281] Thus, the Council of Florence led to a series of political manipulations by the pope. As a result of the Council of Florence, the prestige of Pope Eugene IV and of the see of Rome was enhanced. This contributed significantly to averting a new and prolonged western schism and led to the ultimate defeat of the anti-council of Basle and of the anti-pope Felix V, who eventually abdicated.[282]

All subsequent "unions" were clearly formulated as an unconditional surrender to the Church of Rome. The shrewd Latins, choosing the Greeks first as their negotiation partners, broke them down. Rome used this fact as an argument in their severe negotiations with the other churches, from whom they extracted complete submission.[283]

The Greeks Return to Constantinople

On the 1st day of February, in the year 1440, ships carrying the Greeks sailed into the Golden Horn. Through the merchants that had been in

---

[277] *COD* 510-535; Confer A. Balgy, *Historia doctrinae catholicae inter Armenos unionisque eorum cum Ecclesia Romana in Concilio Florentino* (Vienna, 1878).

[278] *COD* 543-559; Confer: G. Hofmann, "Kopten u. Athioper auf dem Konzil von Florenz," *Orientalia Christiana Periodica*, 8 (1942), 5-29; E. Cerulli, "Eugenio IV e gli Etiopi al Concilio di Firenze," *Reale Academia dei Lincei*, 6, 9, (1933), 347-368.

[279] Sessio XII, *COD* 559, "Eugenius, Indictio concilii Lateranensis."

[280] *COD* 562-565.

[281] Ibid., 565-567.

[282] Rowe, loc. cit.

[283] Bilaniuk, pp. 123, 124.

Ferrara and Florence, the fame and achievements of Mark arrived before him in the capital. After hearing of his valiant steadfastness, the people were waiting to applaud and cheer their hero.[284]

When the delegation arrived on shore, the Constantinopolitans overwhelmed the bishops with questions, asking, "How did the synod end?" and "Have we gained the victory?"[285] Bishop Anthony of Herakleia and others answered sorrowfully, "We have sold the Faith; we have exchanged piety for impiety; we have betrayed the pure religion; we have exchanged Orthodoxy for heterodoxy, and betraying our former undefiled sacrifice, we have become *azymites.*" The people then asked, "But why then did you sign?" With much regret, they replied, "We feared the Franks;...they forced us." The people pressed further, asking, "Did the Latins beat you or cast you into prison?" They answered, "Nay, but may our right hands which signed the unjust decree be cut off and may our tongues which acquiesced be plucked out."[286]

The people were justifiably angry. The selling of Orthodoxy really amounted to two ships and three hundred men from the pope. How the consciences of the bishops scorched them![287] One described the people's behavior toward Mark thus: "The Ephesian beheld that the crowd glorified him because he did not sign. The multitudes venerated him as the Israelites of old did Moses and Aaron. All lauded him and called him 'saint.'"[288] Even those that were against Mark said, "He received neither gifts nor gold" from the pope.[289]

Horrified, the faithful avoided the bishops that had signed and even cast insults at them. The clergy that remained in Constantinople also would not concelebrate with the unionists. In due time, the eastern patriarchs announced that they were not bound by anything that their representatives had signed. The venerable Mark was called a new Saint Athanasios and Saint John the Theologian. He was considered a confessor and martyr by almost the entire body of the Greek Church. He was met with universal enthusiasm and respect.

Upon his arrival, John VIII was troubled by the public's dissent. He was told of the death of his adored wife, the Lady Mary of Trebizond, from

---

[284] Basileiade, p. 171.

[285] Ostroumoff, p. 164.

[286] Douka, *Historia Byzantine*, p. 216A; Basileiade, loc. cit.

[287] Basileiade, p. 172.

[288] Description by the Latin-minded Joseph Methone, *Concerning the Events of the Holy Council of Florence*, *P.G.* 159:992C; Basileiade, loc. cit.

[289] Ibid., "Defense in Writing of Lord Mark Evgenikos," *P.G.* 159:1024C; Ibid., loc. cit.

the plague, which added to his sorrow.[290] The emperor's brother Demetrios was also informed that he was a widower with the death of his wife, Lady Evgenia.[291]

The negotiations at Ferrara and Florence had no positive political results. In fact, Murad II (1421-1451) was suspicious, and the emperor had to pacify the Ottoman Sultan by explaining that the negotiations were purely of a religious nature. The Turks did not really believe the emperor. By their shrewd political intrigues, at all costs, the Turks tried to keep Christendom divided politically and ecclesiastically. The authority of the Metropolitan of Ephesus and the machinations of the Turks contributed to the rejection by the Patriarchs of Antioch, Alexandria, and Jerusalem of the union at Florence.

The emperor then found that it was easier to sign the union than to enforce it. Influenced by his aged mother, Helena Dragases of the Serbian Dynasty in eastern Macedonia, the emperor did not force it on his people. However, he personally remained loyal to the union, but was hard pressed to find anyone to accept the empty patriarchal chair. The Byzantines did not accept the union and ignored all exhortations by the partisans of the union. An almost painful silence enshrouded the Church when, during the Great Fast of 1440, the churches were empty and there were no services. No one wanted to serve with the bishops who had signed. Nevertheless, almost the whole court and almost the entire episcopate were in the hands of the unionists.[292]

The Lay Population of the East

Throughout the history of the Eastern Empire, there was a large lay population that was as well educated as the clergy. The professors, the government servants, and even the soldiers were usually as cultured as the priests. Many of them were highly trained in theology, and most felt themselves perfectly competent to take part in theological discussions at any time, even in the streets and marketplaces. No one in Byzantium thought that theology was the exclusive concern of the clergy. It was probable that, because there were in Byzantium so many zealous theologians, amateur as well as professional, right worship, right belief, and traditions were jealously safeguarded by the lay people. The Byzantines were fiercely devoted to their Liturgy. The Liturgy was something in which the whole congregation participated. In fact, even the decoration of the church building was involved in it; the icons and mosaic figures, too, were participants. To both the lower clergy and lay people, bitter resentment was the response to any criticism of

---

[290] Douka, p. 215.
[291] Syropoulos, "Memoirs," Vol. XI, ch. 20, p. 542; Basileiade, pp. 172, 173, n. 5.
[292] Pogodin, "Saint Mark," *Orthodox Word* 3, No. 3(14), p. 94.

their holy rituals and practises, and they were suspicious of any attempts at innovation or alteration. They had an articulate public opinion that would not hesitate to criticize both the emperor and the hierarchy.

Lay Population of the West

Almost from the outset, east and west held incompatible views about ecclesiastical authority. The whole attitude of the medieval west was different. Christianity had spread more slowly in the west than in the east, and paganism lasted much longer there, particularly in cultivated circles. The Church of Rome was obliged, for its self-defense, to insist on the need for unity and uniformity of belief. At the same time, there was less general interest in speculative philosophy and theological debate. Political circumstances also harnessed the legalistic quality of Latin civilization to the service of the Church. When imperial authority broke down in the west, under the strain of barbarian invasion, the only organization to survive was the Church of Rome. Although the imperial viceroys and governors vanished, the pope and his bishops remained to negotiate with the new barbarian conquerors, and they even assumed the administration of the cities. Therefore, in time, the Bishop of Rome gradually inherited a position as an autocrat and the source of law. The Western Church eventually became a centralized body under an autocratic and "divinely inspired" head, a body directed by experienced administrators and lawyers, whose theology reflected their outlook. Thus, the west had a simpler, stricter, and more legalistic and logical conception of right and wrong belief.

On the other hand, the west had neither an educated laity nor a public opinion that was articulate on religious matters. If there was any criticism, it was directed toward the behavior, not against the beliefs, of the clergy. The only education that survived was conducted by the Church of Rome. In the early Middle Ages, there were few laymen in the west that could even read. The level of culture had been generally lower in the west than in the east, because the barbarian invasion had a very destructive effect on secular education in the west. Therefore, this gave the Western Church a position in society that the Eastern Churches never possessed.

Unlike the Eastern Liturgy, the Western Mass was an office performed by the priesthood, and the lay congregation did not have the same intimate feeling of participation. Only in the Eastern Church did the laity receive both the Body and the Blood of Christ. Moreover, while the language of the Byzantine Liturgy was roughly intelligible to the average Byzantine, the Latin of the Mass was a foreign language to most of the faithful in the west. In addition, whereas Greek is a subtle and flexible tongue, admirably suited to express every shade of abstract thought, Latin was far more rigid and uncompromising, a perfect medium for lawyers. Western layfolk were seldom permitted to interfere in any matter of religion. On the other hand, the western clergy, an intellectual elite, continually interfered in the affairs of state. Therefore, it is not surprising that the Latin Church could impose, with little or no resistance, innovations such as the addition of the Filioque upon a lay population that was generally ignorant and illiterate.

The Turban or the Tiara?

As the new Zorobabel, Mark raised up the Faith. The people of Byzantium quickly perceived the righteousness of Saint Mark. They rallied behind him, for they knew that earthly life was only a prelude to the everlasting life to come. To buy material safety here below at the price of eternal salvation was not to be considered. The Greeks were faithful believers in God's providence. If disaster was to befall them, it would be God's punishment because of their sins. Moreover, many surmised, with good reason, that the west would be neither willing nor able to send sufficient help to check the superbly organized military power of the Turks.

Others, especially churchmen, correctly speculated that the Caucasian, Danubian, and Russian Orthodox would not follow and join the union. The Russians, in particular, were known to regard the Latin Church with hatred as the assembly of their Polish and Scandinavian enemies. Union with Rome would, therefore, probably cost the Patriarch of Constantinople the loss of many of his dependent bishops. Furthermore, the sister-patriarchates of the east made their disapproval quite clear.

Since the majority of the Greeks were under Turkish domination, Greek integrity might well be better preserved by a united people under Moslem rule than by a fragment attached to the rim of the western world. Behold the remarks of the last great minister of Byzantium, Lucas Notaras: "Better the sultan's turban than the tiara of the pope."[293] This was not idle talk, since it was observed that the Turks in Asia Minor, in accordance with their Koran,[294] had generally permitted the conquered Orthodox to exercise their religion and retain their ecclesiastical hierarchy.[295]

Saint Mark, the Hero

Meanwhile, all zealots for Orthodoxy, Athonite monks, and even village priests, flocked around Saint Mark and revered him as a hero. The

---

[293] Ducas, *Historia Turco-Byzantina*, ed. V. Grecu, p. 329, cited in Runciman, *The Great Church in Captivity*, p. 111; Geanakoplos, p. 105.

[294] Qur'an (Koran) 9, 29 rules that the peoples of scripture will be attacked unless they pay a special tax for protection and maintain an inferior place.

[295] The Koran prescribed toleration to Christianity; see L. Brehier for Albin Michel's *Vie et Mort de Byzance* (Paris, 1947), 498.

holy man continued to shatter the strength of the apostates and the Council of
Florence by his writings and addresses directed against the union. Although
George Scholarios tolerated the union and was fond of the works of Thomas
Aquinas, he was soon convinced by Mark, the joy of Christians and the
sacred urn of the Spirit's grace, that he had been in the wrong.[296] Thus,
Scholarios could say with the Prophet David, "I have thought on Thy ways,
and I have turned my feet back to Thy testimonies [Ps. 118:59]."

As had been expected, Mark refused the dignity of the patriarchal
throne. Anthony of Herakleia, bowed with remorse, openly rejected the
union, declaring it contrary to the ancient tradition of the holy catholic
Church. He, also, refused the honor of being the patriarch, deeming himself
guilty.

Patriarch Metrophanes

On the Lord's Feast of the Ascension, the 4th day of May, in the year
1440, Metrophanes II of Kyzikos (1440-1443), who had signed the Act of
Union and had exhibited his servile adulation of the pope in Italy, ascended
the patriarchal throne. Those bishops and people who did not accept the
decree of the union insultingly nicknamed Metrophanes "Metrophonos,"
(Μητροφόνος) which means "matricide," that is, he was a "murderer of the
Mother Church." Another play on words was also derogatorily used to
characterize the council at Ferrara. In the Greek language, the word
"Ferrara" reminded the Orthodox of their word (φέρω) meaning "to bear" or
"to carry," and (ἀρά) meaning "curse." Hence, Ferrara was mockingly
referred to that which brings a curse.

At the divine Liturgy, on the 15th day of May, in the year 1440, at the
enthronement of Metrophanes, Metropolitan Mark was not in attendance. He
had no desire to concelebrate with the Latin-minded Metrophanes. Moreover,
he accepted neither Metrophanes nor his followers.[297] In fact, not only was the
holy Mark absent from the divine Liturgy, but also missing were Anthony of
Herakleia, Dorotheos of Trebizond, Sylvester Syropoulos, Michael Balsamon,
and crowds of layfolk. Those that attended were irritated at the presence of
the Latin bishop, Christopher Garatoni, who always stood at the right of
Metrophanes.[298]

Anticipating troubles, before the enthronement on the 14th of May,
1440, the day of Pentecost, the blessed Mark and Anthony of Herakleia
secretly fled the capital. They made their way to Prusa (Bursa), situated at the

---

[296] Runciman, *The Great Church*, p. 110.
[297] Mark of Ephesus, *Apologia*, *P.G.* 160-536C.
[298] Syropoulos, "Memoirs," Vol. XII, chaps. 8, 10, pp. 554, 556.

foot of Mount Olympos, about sixty miles south of Constantinople. From there, Mark planned to go on to Ephesus. Mark left for his see, in all probability because of his pastoral concern for his flock, which found itself under the Turks. Mark's escape made an impression on the emperor, who now feared that others would join in the flight. Soon after his elevation, Metrophanes attempted to compel bishops opposed to the union to officiate with him. Both he and the emperor commenced laboring in behalf of the union by appointing their friends to the vacant dioceses and disturbing the peace of the Church with their corrupt doctrines. As evinced in Mark's correspondence and in his talks, unrestrained zeal for Orthodoxy flamed up in his soul. The radiant luminary of the east, Mark, as a flaming cautery of the west, declared there could be no compromise in matters of the Orthodox Faith.

The Activities of the Saint

Saint Mark, the bright adornment of ascetics, now forty-nine years old and afflicted with terminal cancer, was still strong in spirit and would not remain silent. In his letters to all Christians, he encouraged them to depart from the Florentine Union, as a union offensive to God. He wrote: "These people admit with the Latins that the Holy Spirit proceeds and derives His existence from the Son. Yet, with us, they say the Spirit proceeds from the Father. The Latins imagine that this addition to the Creed is lawful and just, but we will not so much as pronounce it. They state that unleavened bread is the body of Christ, but we dare not communicate it. Is this not sufficient to exhibit that they came to the Latin council not to investigate the truth, which they once possessed and then betrayed, but simply to earn some gold and attain a false union? Behold, they read two Creeds as they did before. They perform two different liturgies—one on leavened and the other on unleavened bread. They perform two baptisms—one by triple immersion and the other by aspersion; one with holy Chrism and the other without it. All our Orthodox customs are different from those of the Latins, including our fasts, Church rites, icons, and many other things. What sort of union is this then, when it has no external sign? How could they come together, each retaining his own?" In a letter to Hieromonk Theophanes of Evia, Mark wrote: "Flee, brethren! Flee communion with the incommunicable and the commemoration of the uncommemorative. Behold, I, Mark, the sinner, tell you that whoever commemorates the pope as an Orthodox prelate is guilty. Moreover, one who minds the dogmas of the Latins will be judged with the Latins, and will be deemed a betrayer of the Faith."[299]

The venerable bishop's words and influence had an enormous impact on both the ignorant and the learned, inclining them to the defense of Orthodoxy. From all sides, voices were raised against the Florentine Union, and many saw its failure due to the writings and activities of Saint Mark. The secret motives of the Greeks and the actions of the council were brought to light in the writings of Syropoulos and Amiroutzes. Together with them, the philosopher Gemistes Plethon, who had defended the Orthodox position at the council, also published a defense of the Orthodox doctrine on the procession of the Holy Spirit. The saint's brother, John, regarding the Florentine union, also wrote a refutation.

Saint Mark traveled all about the regions where the far-famed evangelist and Apostle John had labored. Although chronically ill, the zealot for Orthodoxy spent long and difficult periods in laboring for his flock. Not only did he undertake the building of the cathedral church with its adjoining buildings, but he also visited the much ailing churches of his diocese and the ordained priests. Those among his flock, including orphans and widows, that had suffered injustices by reason of persecution or trial from the unrighteous, he defended, strengthened, and comforted. As for their tormenters, he would shame, interdict, appeal to, or exhort them. In the words of the holy Apostle Paul: "To the weak I became as weak, that I might gain the weak. To all these I have become all things, that by all means I might save some [1 Cor. 9:22]."

The holy man's brother, John, said that Mark had a constant desire for monastic solitude and seclusion and yearned to retire on the Holy Mountain. Although Mark, the unexcelled shepherd of Christ's sheep, had sacrificed himself for his flock, he knew that he had no approval from those in authority to serve in Ephesus. He mentioned this in one of his letters and then pointed out that his stay in Ephesus could be construed as "unauthorized." Hence, for political reasons and because of his desire for monastic solitude, Mark felt compelled to retire and leave his flock.

The Island of Limnos

The holy man departed and set sail for Mount Athos. His ship put in at Limnos, an island in the north Aegean which was still a Byzantine possession. Emperor John wasted no time in issuing a directive to the police of Limnos for the arrest of Metropolitan Mark. Upon his arrival, the author-

---

[299] "Epistle of Lord Mark of Ephesus to Theophanes," *P.G.* 160:1096-1100; Concilium Florentinum, pp. 172-174; Basileiade, p. 177.

ities recognized, arrested, and imprisoned Mark. The blessed man was made to suffer two years of confinement.

Commenting on this period of the saint's life, his brother writes: "Who would not marvel at or acknowledge the magnanimity of soul and perseverance in misfortune that Mark showed? He suffered from the burning sun and struggled with the deprivation of the most basic necessities. He was tormented by diseases that followed one right after the other. In the meantime, he was made to endure harsh confinement while the fleet of the God-hating Moslems surrounded Limnos. Once, when the island was threatened with a raid from the Turkish fleet, the danger unexpectedly passed. The delivered inhabitants attributed their salvation to the prayers of the holy prisoner Mark in their fortress."[300]

The true athlete of Christ never complained about his miserable conditions. In an extract of a letter addressed to the Prohegumen of Vatopedi Monastery, he writes: "We have found great consolation from thy brethren that are here on Limnos, including the most honorable ecclesiarch, the *megas œconomos*, and others. We behold them as inspired images of thy love and piety, for in showing us love, they have calmed and strengthened us. May the Lord grant them a worthy reward for their labor and love!"[301]

Ever vigilant, the holy man continued writing letters in his battle for Orthodoxy. In one of his letters, he wrote: "I have been arrested. However, the power of truth and the word of God cannot be bound [2 Tim. 2:9], but flow and prosper stronger. Many of the brethren, encouraged by my exile, have overthrown the reproaches of those lawless violators of Orthodoxy and the traditions of the fatherland."[302]

The holy Mark viewed his confession of the Faith as indispensable. He writes: "If there had been no persecution, the martyrs would not have shone forth. Also, the confessors who, by their exploits, strengthened and gladdened the Orthodox Church, would not have received the crown of victory from Christ."[303]

One characterization held by many, describes Saint Mark as follows: "Mark was truly a wonderful man, adorned with all spiritual gifts and replete with all divine knowledge. Even before his elevation to the episcopacy, he lived a righteous life. Having completely dedicated his life to God, he spurned every passion. He never sought to satisfy his flesh. This man had no fear of

---

[300] Pogodin, "Saint Mark," *Orthodox Word* 3, No. 3(14), pp. 95, 96.

[301] Ibid., p. 96.

[302] Ibid.

[303] Ibid.

exile or hunger, and gave no thought to thirst. He neither trembled before the executioner's sword nor dreaded prison. In fact, he viewed death as a benefaction."[304]

Encyclical Letter

During the period of his confinement in Limnos, he wrote his famous *Encyclical to All Orthodox Christians on the Mainland and in the Islands* (July of 1440), in which he exhorted the faithful to remain loyal to Orthodoxy.[305] It was an Orthodox position paper against the heresies of the Church of Rome and those who "desire to lead us away into the 'Babylon' of Latin rites and dogmas." To his readers, he describes the Greek Latinizers as having captured the true Orthodox and delivered them into captivity by concluding a false union. "What kind of unity is this, when there is no apparent or clear sign of it?...Just as before, two different Creeds;...and dissimilar Liturgies are performed—one with leavened bread, the other with unleavened bread; and two baptisms—one by triple immersion, the other by pouring water over the head—and one with the anointing of Chrism, the other without it; likewise the fasting and ecclesiastic order is divergent."

Mark then accused the unionists of duplicity, because they remained somewhere in the middle, unable to completely abandon what was canonical and blessed. He wrote: "They desire also to preserve their own...and at the same time do not follow the traditions of the fathers." The holy man declared that the holy canons state that one is a heretic and subject to the canons who departs even slightly from Orthodoxy. He then says, "If the Latins have not departed from the correct Faith, then we have cut them off unjustly. However, if they have departed from the Faith in regard to the theology of the Holy Spirit, Whom to blaspheme is the greatest of all perils, clearly, they are heretics; and we have cut them off as heretics."[306] There can be no middle ground concerning the procession of the Holy Spirit.

In quoting the wise Theodore Balsamon, Patriarch of Antioch, he said, "We must not sanctify one of the Latin race through the divine and most pure gifts given by priestly hands, unless that one shall first resolve to depart from Latin dogmas and customs and shall be catechized and joined to the

---

[304] This quote is taken from Theodore Agallianos, of holy memory, in a discussion with a certain monk. Kallistos Vlastos, *Dokimion Historikon Peri Tou Schismatos Tis Dytikes Ekklesias Apo Tis Anatolikes* (in Greek) (Athens, 1896), p. 121.

[305] *P.G.* 160:112-204; Concilium Florentinum, pp. 141-151.

[306] "Epistle to All Orthodox Christians," Concilium Florentinum, p. 144(29-33); Basileiade, p. 122.

Orthodox."[307] He concludes that by maintaining a middle ground, the Greco-Latins have become buyers and sellers of Christ, who suppose "piety to be a means of gain [1 Tim. 6:5]." The apostle advises "to be fleeing these things [1 Tim. 6:11]." Those people went over to the Latins, not to secure a legitimate union but for gain. "What communion hath light with darkness? And what consonance hath Christ with Belial? Or what portion hath a believer with an unbeliever [2 Cor. 6:14, 15]?"

Metropolitan Mark solemnly stated that the Orthodox, together with the fathers, do not say that the Spirit proceeds from the Son. Together with Saint Gregory the Theologian, we distinguish the Father from the Son in His capacity of being Cause.[308] The Greek unionists, together with the Latins, have united the Father and the Son into one capacity of being Cause, despite the fact that Saint Maximos (d. 662) said that the western fathers, till his time, "have not made the Son the Cause of the Spirit."[309] Nevertheless, in the Act of Union, the Greek unionists proclaim the Son as the Cause of the Spirit, and the Latins proclaim the Son as Principle. "However," Saint Mark says, "we, together with the philosopher and Martyr Justin (ca. 100-ca. 165), affirm, 'As the Son is from the Father, so is the Spirit from the Father.'"[310]

As a true Palamist, Mark also asserted, in agreement with the fathers, the will and energy of the uncreated and divine nature are uncreated. The Greek unionists, however, with the Latins and Thomas Aquinas, say that "will" is identical with "nature," and that the divine energy is created.[311] The theologians of the heterodox west, denying any distinction between essence and energy in God, declared the energies to be created. Then they reassigned the positive and moral qualities which belong to those energies—mercy, goodness, love, patience, etc.—to the divine nature as attributes.

Refuting this, Saint Mark of Ephesus wrote: "We must not be surprised if we do not find among the ancients any clear and defined distinction between the essence of God and His energies. If, in our time, after the solemn confirmation of this truth, the partisans of profane wisdom have created so much trouble in the Church over this question—and have accused her of polytheism—what mischief would not have been perpetrated in earlier

---

[307] *Reply to Mark, the Most Holy Patriarch of Alexandria*, P.G. 138:968; February Volume of *The Great Synaxaristes* (in Greek), p. 658-660; "Encyclical Letter of Saint Mark of Ephesus," trans. by Archimandrite Amvrossy Pogodin, M.Sc Eccl., D.D., *Orthodox Word* 3, No. 2(13) (March-May 1967): 54-57.

[308] *P.G.* 36:252.

[309] *P.G.* 91:136.

[310] *P.G.* 6:1224.

[311] February Volume of *The Great Synaxaristes* (in Greek), p. 660.

times against this truth by those puffed up with vain learning? This is why our theologians always insisted on the simplicity of God more than the distinction which exists in Him. It would have been inopportune to exhibit the teaching concerning the essence and energies before those who had enough trouble admitting the distinction of hypostases. Thus, by a wise œconomy this sacred teaching has become clarified in the course of time, God using for this purpose the foolish attacks of heretics."[312]

Speaking of Purgatory, the Orthodox champion reiterates that neither do the saints receive the kingdom and those ineffable good things prepared for them, nor are sinners cast into Gehenna; for both wait to be rendered their due in the future age after the resurrection and judgment. As expressed in their Act of Union, the unionists desire to receive and enjoy their reward immediately upon death. They also erroneously say that those in a middle state, who have reposed in repentance, they place in a purging fire, though not the same as Gehenna. Once purified, they may enjoy the kingdom with the righteous.[313]

In speaking of liturgical practises, Mark says that we obey the apostles when we turn away from the Jewish unleavened bread. The unionists, on the other hand, recognize what is used in the services of the Latins as the body of Christ. The unionists also affirm that the Filioque is allowed and blessed, though we consider it unlawful.

Commenting on the papacy, Metropolitan Mark writes: "For us, the pope is as one of the patriarchs—and only if he is Orthodox; whereas, they proclaim him vicar of Christ, father and teacher of all Christians."[314]

The illustrious confessor again admonishes: "Flee from them, O brethren, and from communion with them." Then, in the words of the divine Paul, he says, "For such are false apostles, guileful workers, transforming themselves into apostles of Christ. And a marvellous thing it is not; for Satan himself transformeth himself into an angel of light. Therefore it is no great thing if his ministers also transform themselves as ministers of righteousness, of whom the end shall be according to their works [2 Cor. 11:13-15]." In another place the Apostle Paul writes: "For such serve not our Lord Jesus Christ, but their own belly; and by smooth speech and fine speaking, they deceive the hearts of the simple [Rom. 16:18]....Nevertheless the foundation of God standeth firm, having this seal: 'The Lord knoweth those who are His

---

[312] Quoted in M. Jugie, "Palamas," *The Dictionary of Catholic Theology*, vol. II (Paris, 1931), p. 1759f.
[313] February Volume of *The Great Synaxaristes* (in Greek), p. 661.
[314] Ibid.

[2 Tim. 2:19].'" And in another place, "But even if we, or an angel from out of heaven, should preach a gospel to you besides what Gospel we preached to you, let such a one be anathema [Gal. 1:8]." Moreover, "Note what has been said prophetically, 'though...an angel from heaven...'; this means no one may cite in justification of oneself an especially high rank." Listen to the beloved disciple John: "If anyone come to you and bring not this teaching, cease receiving him into the house and saying to him fare-thee-well; for the one who saith to him fare-thee-well partaketh in his evil works [2 Jn. 1:10, 11]."[315]

Mark, the mouthpiece of theologians, then reminds all of the seventh canon of the Second Œcumenical Synod, which states: "As for those heretics, such as the Arians, Makedonians, Sabbatians, Novatians, and those calling themselves Cathari, Aristeri, and Fourteenists (the latter otherwise known as Tetradites), and Apollinarians, who betake themselves to Orthodoxy and to the lot of the saved,...we accept when they offer recantations in writing (*libelli*) and anathematize every heresy that does not hold the same beliefs as the catholic and apostolic Church of God, and are sealed first with holy Chrism on their forehead, eyes, nose, mouth, and ears. In sealing them we say, 'The seal of the gift of the Holy Spirit.' As for the Evnomians, however, who are baptized with a single immersion, and Montanists, who are here called Phrygians, and the Sabellians, who teach that Father and Son are the same Person, and who do some other bad things, and those belonging to any other heresies,...all of them that want to adhere to Orthodoxy, we are willing to accept as Greeks (pagans). Accordingly, the first day we treat them as Christians, and the second day as catechumens. Then, the third day, we exorcize them with the act of blowing thrice into their face and into their ears. Thus do we catechize them, and make them tarry a while in the church and listen to Scriptures; then, we baptize them."[316]

In closing, he wrote, "This is what has been commanded you by the holy apostles: 'Brethren, be standing firm and holding fast the traditions which ye were taught, whether by word or by our epistle [2 Thess. 2:15],' that you be not deprived of your firmness and be led away by the delusions of the lawless. May God make them to know their delusion. May He gather us into His granaries like pure and useful wheat, in Jesus Christ our Lord, to Whom is due glory, honor, and worship, together with His unoriginate Father

---

[315] Ibid.

[316] Ibid., p. 662. See "Concerning the Holy and Second Œcumenical Synod," *The Rudder (Pedalion)*, op. cit., p. 217.

and His all-holy, good, and life-creating Spirit, both now and ever and unto the ages of ages. Amen."[317]

Mark's period of affliction at Limnos was to come to an end. After two years, Emperor John ordered that the holy man be released with leave to go wherever he pleased. The day of his release was the 4th of August, when the holy Church celebrates the memory of the martyred Seven Youths of Ephesus. In thanksgiving, Saint Mark dedicated a poem to them.

Future Repudiation of Florence

April of 1443 marked the first official judgment against the false council of Ferrara-Florence, which was initiated by the Patriarch Joachim of Jerusalem (1431-1450). At Jerusalem, he met with Patriarch Philotheos of Alexandria (1435-1459), Patriarch Dorotheos of Antioch (1435-1451), and Metropolitan Arsenios of Caesarea in Cappadocia. They all condemned the Florentine Council as "vile" and only for "the glory of the Latins together with Pope Eugene."[318] Also, Patriarch Metrophanes II of Constantinople was condemned as a heretic. A letter was then sent to Emperor John VIII, warning him not to retain the Latin-minded Metrophanes.

Another wave of repudiation of signatures against the Council of Florence came after the failure of a Crusade—of deep concern to Eugene—which ended in defeat at Varna in 1444. In the end, only a very few were faithful to the council, such as the Œcumenical Patriarchs Metrophanes II and Gregory Mammas Melissenos Strategopoulos (1446-1450), and two eastern cardinals, Isidore (formerly of Kiev) and Bessarion (formerly of Nicaea). In 1447, on the 23rd day of February, Pope Eugene IV died.

Officially, the Union of Florence was recalled by Patriarch Symeon I of Constantinople (1466, 1471-1474), in the Synod of 1472. The Latins were once again denounced as heretics during the Synod of 1484, held under the presidency of the same Patriarch Symeon, during his third occupation of the patriarchal throne.[319]

The Saint Returns to Constantinople

After exile, the holy man lacked the physical endurance for asceticism on the Holy Mountain. Having become quite feeble, he departed for his home in Constantinople. The remaining years of his life were spent with the painful

---

[317] February Volume of *The Great Synaxaristes* (in Greek), p. 663.

[318] Chrysostom Papadopoulos (Archbishop of Athens), "To Proteion Tu Episkopou Romes" (in Greek), 2nd ed. in the periodical *Ekklesia* (Athens, 1964), p. 283; Idem, *Historia Tis Ekklesias Ierosolymon* (in Greek) (Jerusalem, Alexandria, 1910), p. 439ff.; Basileiade, p. 183.

[319] Bilaniuk, p. 126.

symptoms and complications of his disease. However, the persecution from the Uniate episcopacy and the court did not cease. Nevertheless, by his personal influence, the holy man restored many to holy Orthodoxy once more.

Patriarch Metrophanes II died on the 1st day of August, in the year 1443, leaving the see vacant until 1445. Although the emperor still could not make up his mind to break relations with the pope, the vacant see was given to the *protosynkellos* and pro-unionist Gregory Mammas until 1450. He wrote rebuttals against Mark's writings, for which writings the pope commended him for his zeal in the Latin cause. In Constantinople, significant attempts were made to strengthen the union. Permanent representatives of the Vatican, including Cardinal Isidore, ensured official loyalty to the union. The danger to the Church was far-reaching. Mark was clearly aware of this when he said, "Murdered souls have been tempted concerning the mystery of the Faith." Mark was the leader of the battle, though he was scarcely able to walk, exhausted by disease and harassed by the wiles of men. However, the power of God is accomplished in weakness [2 Cor. 12:9]![320]

The Repose of Saint Mark: "He Being Made Perfect in a Short Time, Fulfilled a Long Time [Wis. of Sol. 4:13]."

Long before his death, the saint, as a father, gave instructions to those present concerning the direction of the Church and our correct Faith, by admonishing many to turn away from every innovation. However, the time of his earthly translation approached, that he might receive the everlasting reward. In 1444, having retired to his boyhood home in Galata, a section of Constantinople, the holy man suffered terribly for fourteen days prior to his repose.

His brother, John the *nomophylax*, relates: "From his youth to the holy Schema of the monks, Mark ever dwelt with the love of God. He excelled in everything he undertook: in the most holy Schema, in the degrees of priestly service, in hierarchal dignity, in arguments for the Orthodox Faith, and in his devout and passionless confession of the Faith. Then, having attained fifty-two years of age, on the 23rd of June, he departed rejoicing. Like unto the divine Paul, he wished to depart to be with his much-desired Christ, Whom Mark glorified by good works, theologized in Orthodox fashion, and pleased his whole life long. He was ill for two weeks, and the disease itself, as my brother himself said, had the same effect as those iron instruments of torture applied by executioners to the holy martyrs. The cancer metastasized, girdling his ribs and internal organs, pressing upon them and

---

[320] Pogodin, "Saint Mark," *Orthodox Word* 3, No. 3(14), p. 97.

thereby causing unbearable pain. Hence, what men could not do to his sacred and martyric body, disease fulfilled. This was in accordance with the unknowable judgment of divine providence, so that Mark, the confessor of truth, the martyr, the conqueror and victor of all possible sufferings, might appear before God as one who had undergone every misery, even to his final breath. Thus, as gold is tried in the furnace, the holy Mark would receive for eternity even greater honor and reward from the just Judge."

The saint, knowing that his death was imminent, was concerned that the patriarch or his hierarchs and clergy might make a display of feigned respect at his funeral, thereby confounding people into believing that Mark was in communion with them. Therefore, before trustworthy men, he addressed them in no uncertain terms, saying that he had never accepted communion with the pro-unionists and that he rejected the union and Latin dogmas. He then said, "I am absolutely convinced that the farther away that I stand from him (the patriarch) and those like him, the nearer I am to God and all the saints."[321] The blessed man then commanded that none of that party were to approach either his burial or his grave. Further, he ordered that none of them that were with him were to concelebrate with the patriarch and his clergy in the divine services. He said that it absolutely befits them not to mix with the unionists, but to remain apart from them, until God shall grant correction and peace.

On the day of his blessed repose, the last thoughts of the saint were not for himself but for Orthodoxy, to which he had devoted his whole life. He especially addressed one individual, his former student and spiritual son, George Scholarios, recommending and entrusting him with the position of defender of the Church. Later, Scholarios became an ardent champion of Orthodoxy. Now George Scholarios wrote a very revealing description of his feelings toward the great Mark: "Who else, other than thyself, knows my desires, aims, and plans? I believe that even my parents, who know me well, could learn about these things from thee. Just as they understand their physical offspring from the time of birth, so it is with thee, through words, education, and good leadership. Though they once gave birth to me, yet thou hast cultivated and poured thyself out for me all these years."[322] Meanwhile, let us listen to Mark express his feelings for Scholarios: "I have known him

[321] Idem, "Address of Saint Mark on the Day of His Death," *Orthodox Word* 3, No. 3(14) (June-July 1967): 104.
[322] "Epistle to Mark of Ephesus," *P.G.* 150:746A.

from earliest youth. I nourish sincere feeling and great affection toward him. He is as my own son and friend...."[323]

Albeit the holy man's agony was extremely painful, death came easily and joyfully when he surrendered his blessed and radiant spirit, saying, "Lord Jesus Christ, Son of the living God, into Thy hands I commit my spirit."[324] Having excelled in good deeds, Mark then departed for the endless life, where he beholds the sacred light of the triune Sun. Although the date of his death is a matter of disagreement, his brother John notes that Saint Mark was fifty-two years old when he reposed on the 23rd of June. Manuel the Rhetor affirms the year to be 1444.[325]

The Saint's Funeral: "His Soul Pleased the Lord: Therefore, Hastened He to Take Him Away from Among the Wicked [Wis. of Solomon 4:14]."

The saint's precious relics were then interred by the altar window in his beloved Monastery of Saint George at Mangan, amid a throng of people, after numerous marks of respect.[326] George Scholarios writes of the saint's repose: "Our sorrow was increased more by the fact that he was taken away from our embrace before he had grown old in the virtues, which he had acquired, and before we could sufficiently enjoy his presence during this passing life. No cunning had the power to shake his mind or lead his soul astray, so strongly was it nourished and tempered by virtue. Even if the vault of heaven should fall, even then the righteousness of this man would remain unshaken, his strength would not fail, his soul would not be moved, and his thought would not be impaired by these difficult trials."[327] From the funeral address of George Scholarios, we may understand the depth of sorrow that overcame the Orthodox at the loss of such a great pillar of the Church; for Mark was learned, meek, and easy to approach, in that he drew all to himself as a magnet attracts iron.

The Last Emperor

Wearied and disillusioned, Emperor John VIII died childless, at fifty-seven years of age, on the 31st day of October, in the year 1448. Manuel the Rhetor records that, on his deathbed, John repented of his dealings in Ferrara-

---

[323] *The Ephesian to Scholarios*, Concilium Florentinum, p. 179(2-6).

[324] Pogodin, "Saint Mark," *Orthodox Word* 3, No. 3(14), p. 98.

[325] Manuel the Rhetor, *Logos Peri Markou*, Concilium Florentinum, p. 213(26-27).

[326] January Volume of *The Great Synaxaristes* (in Greek), pp. 477, 478.

[327] Pogodin, "Saint Mark," *Orthodox Word* 3, No. 3(14), p. 97.

Florence and rejected all union with the Church of Rome.[328] He had acknowledged before his death that the union with Rome only brought turmoil and dissension to his subjects. Before his repose, Saint Mark also mentioned that the emperor "openly repented of the event (the union)."[329]

The next in line to the throne was Theodore II, but he had recently died. Therefore, Emperor John VIII was succeeded by the Despot Constantine Dragases, who was married to Magdalena Leonardo Tocco. Before Constantine XI Dragases Palaiologos (1448-1453) succeeded his brother to the throne, George Scholarios proposed that his coronation be conditional on his pledge to remain faithful to Orthodoxy. However, the new emperor threatened him with reprisals, whereupon George took refuge in the Monastery of the All-possessing God, where he was tonsured and given the name Gennadios.

The next year, 1449, three eastern patriarchs (Philotheos of Alexandria, Dorotheos of Antioch, and Theophanes of Jerusalem) held a synod in Jerusalem where they again condemned the Council of Florence as "tyrannical and foul." The following year, they met again in Constantinople at the Church of Hagia Sophia. At this council (1450), under the influence of the Monk Gennadios Scholarios, they again denounced the "union" and deposed Patriarch Gregory Mammas, replacing him with the pious monk Athanasios (1450-1453). Mammas had held the post for more than six years and had been shunned by most of the clergy. Deprived of his throne, he fled as a fugitive to the more friendly atmosphere of Rome in August of 1451.[330]

As Turkish forces began the long preparation for what was to be the final assault on Byzantium, Pope Nicholas V (1447-1455) sent an ultimatum to the emperor. The infamous Cardinal Isidore delivered it to the capital on the 12th of December, in the year 1452. The pope demanded three things: (1) that Constantine solemnly proclaim the "Union at Florence" valid, and enforce it; (2) that Gregory Mammas be received back as Patriarch of Constantinople; and, (3) that all the Greek clergy be compelled to commemorate the pope's name in the divine Liturgy. In exchange for this, Nicholas promised his aid against the infidel invaders. The emperor, stricken with terror and fearing the massive attack of Mohammed II, acquiesced to the pope's demands. He sent an embassy to Rome, petitioning for help and inviting the fugitive Gregory Mammas back. The populace was divided. Half

---

[328] Kallistos Vlastos, *Dokimion Historikon Peri Tu Schismatos Tis Dytikes Ekklesias Apo Tis Anatolikes* (in Greek) (Athens, 1896), p. 224; Basileiade, p. 181, n. 22.
[329] "Epistle of Lord Mark of Ephesus to Theophanes," *P.G.* 160:1097D; Concilium Florentinum, p. 173(33-37); Basileiade, p. 181.
[330] Runciman, *The Fall*, p. 18.

the people agreed with the emperor, which situation caused Gennadios to seclude himself in his cell, affixing on his door a message that read, "O miserable citizens, you have ruined everything, and now you have abandoned your religion...." The remaining half of the people disagreed with the emperor; and, they, with the clergy, were furiously indignant and ran through the streets shouting, "We want no aid from the Latins!" Cursing the union, they cried aloud, "We want no union; let us be rid of the *azymite* worship!" Nevertheless, Constantine XI proclaimed the "union" in the Great Church (Hagia Sophia) in the presence of the papal legates. Gennadios, of course, took no part in the ceremonies. Thus, during the last few months of the empire's existence, the Cathedral of Hagia Sophia was desecrated again by the hands of the Latins and Latin-minded clergy.

Any effective aid from the west was doomed at the outset, because of conflicting interests among the western rulers. The most powerful prince in the Mediterranean at that time was Alphonso V of Aragon and Naples. He had hoped to found a new Latin empire in Constantinople, with himself as emperor. The very modest resources of Eugene's successor, Nicholas V, for the defense of Constantinople were swallowed up by the aggressive policy of the King of Naples, whose continual demands for money from Rome were met. Even if Rome had actively intervened to save the city, its aim certainly would not have been to rescue the Byzantine Empire for the Byzantines—but neither was there any possibility of founding a new Latin empire in the east.[331]

The Glorification of Saint Mark

The solemn commemoration of Saint Mark was first celebrated by his family. When Scholarios was elevated to the episcopacy as Patriarch Gennadios, there was a wider glorification of Mark. Following the capture of Constantinople (1453), the saint's relics were transferred to the Monastery of Lazarus at Galata. After centuries, many devout people in monasteries and churches preserved the memory of Saint Mark. There have also been many miracles of healing recorded and attributed to Saint Mark.

Nearly three centuries after his repose, in February of 1734, the holy Synod of the Church of Constantinople, under the presidency of Patriarch Seraphim I (1733-1734), brought forth a decree for the glorification of Metropolitan Mark of Ephesus, instituting the 19th of January as the date of his commemoration. They wrote: "All of us of the holy Eastern Church of Christ acknowledge the holy Mark Evgenikos of Ephesus. We honor and receive this saintly, God-bearing, and righteous man as a zealot of ardent piety, who was a champion of all our sacred dogmas and correct piety. He is an emulator of

---

[331] George Ostrogorsky, *History of the Byzantine State*, p. 505.

and equal to the holy theologians, and those who adorned the Church of ancient times."[332] Through his prayers, may Christ our God have mercy on us. Amen.

Through the intercessions of Thy Saints,
O Christ God, have mercy on us. Amen.

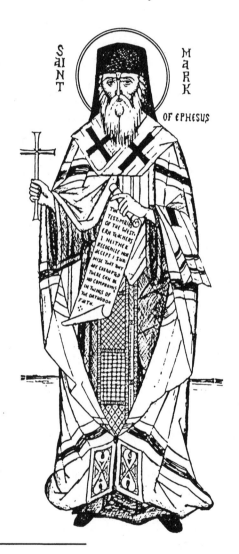

SAINT MARK OF EPHESUS

THE TESTIMONIES OF THE WESTERN TEACHERS I NEITHER RECOGNIZE NOR ACCEPT I SURMISE THAT THEY ARE CORRUPTED THERE CAN BE NO COMPROMIS IN THINGS OF THE ORTHODOX FAITH.

---

[332] See the periodical, *Byzantinische Zeitschrift*, Vol. II (Leipzig-Berlin, 1902), pp. 65, 66; Mansi, 37, 1003; see also service composed by Nikodemos the Hagiorite (Constantinople, 1834), p. 27 and service and Supplicatory Canon by Gerasimos Mikrayiannanites (Athens, 1964); Basileiade, pp. 208, 209, n.38.

**On the 20th of January, the holy Church commemorates
our venerable and God-bearing Father
EFTHYMIOS the Great.[1]**

Efthymios the Great, our father, desert-dweller and ascetic, was born about the year 377, in Melitene of Armenia near the Euphrates, during the reign of the Emperor Gratian (367-383). His father's name was Paul, and his mother's was Dionysia; they were both eminent and virtuous. They, however, were ever distressed and grieved that they were childless, and often went to the Church of the Holy Martyr Polyefktos,[2] which was nearby, and entreated God to give them an inheritance and to assuage their sorrow. As they prayed on one particular night, they beheld a certain divine vision in which it was disclosed to them: "Be of good cheer, you servants of the Lord, and rejoice! Behold, the Lord has hearkened to your prayer and will give you a child

Saint Efthymios the Great

to be named Efthymios (Cheerfulness), for the birth of the child given by God shall bring the Church gladness and joy." Then they returned to their home rejoicing, readily promising to dedicate to God the child to be born. Thereupon, Dionysia was elated when she conceived. In time, the child was born, and they named him Efthymios according to the vision.

---

[1] The Life of this saint, in its entirety, was written in Greek by the disciple of Saint Savvas, the Monk Kyril of Skythopolis [*P.G.* 114:595-734], who also wrote the Life of Saint Savvas, who is commemorated by the holy Church on the 5th of December. He was urged to do so by the two saints, who appeared to him in a vision. It was copied by Saint Symeon the Metaphrastes and included in his Collection. The text is extant in the Athonite monasteries of the Great Lavra, Iveron, and in other places. The text was rendered in simpler Greek by Agapios the Cretan, who published it in the *Eklogion*. Some collections (Delehaye) record the day of the saint's commemoration as the 19th of January. Also, according to the Patmian Codex 266, the translation of Saint Efthymios' relics is celebrated on the 7th of May. Father Gerasimos Mikrayiannanites wrote twenty-four stanzas (*oikoi*) to the great Efthymios.

[2] Saint Polyefktos is commemorated by the holy Church on the 9th of January.

When the saint reached three years of age, his father reposed. His mother took him and went to her brother, Evdoxios, who was the counselor to Metropolitan Eftropios of Melitene. Dionysia besought her brother to give Efthymios to the above-named hierarch and to offer him just as Hannah did Samuel in former times [1 Kgs. (1 Sam.) 1:25-28]. When Eftropios saw the child and heard of the vision, he prophesied and said, "In this child the Spirit of the Lord shall rest!" Afterward, they baptized the child; and later he was installed in the office of Reader. His mother, who was virtuous and most reverent toward the holy things, was ordained a deaconess. In this manner, the divine Efthymios devoted his first years to God.

As he studied the sacred writings, Efthymios stored up for himself, like a bee, as many divine examples of men worthy of emulation as he could find in holy Scriptures. They spurred his soul toward divine love, and he yearned to emulate them. He accustomed himself to every good deed and devoted himself to what was beneficial for the soul. Efthymios spent most of the years of his youth in reading the Holy Scriptures and the accounts of the virtues of the saints. He especially became zealous in his service to his excellent and very virtuous teacher Akakios, who became the Bishop of Melitene.[3] Therefore, as a wise disciple, not only of the lessons but also of his teacher's virtues, he became a diligent and active follower.

His teacher rejoiced on beholding Efthymios' wisdom and piety. His fare was simple and balanced. His sustenance was spiritual words, in which his soul delighted rather than in bodily and perishable food. He was devout in all the liturgical order of the Church, rendering complete mental concentration and a contrite heart with such contemplation that he never laughed, and stood with great devotion as if looking straight at the Master and King of Creation. During the remaining years in his house, he devoted himself to study of, and meditation on, the divine law day and night. He never said an idle or vain word, but as a fruitful and useful tree planted in the waters of psalmody, he used every moment profitably. In time of anger and wrath, he

---

[3] Akakios also participated in the Holy Third Œcumenical Council, which was convened in 431 at Ephesus, and was a great champion of the dogmas of Orthodoxy. He defended Saint Kyril of Alexandria and condemned Nestorios, whom he formerly attempted unsuccessfully to persuade to return to the Orthodox Faith, because he happened to be a personal friend. He also fought Theodore of Mopsuestia, sending to the Bishops of Armenia an encyclical, in which he condemned Theodore's opinions. He was held in great honor among the fathers; in Melitene a synod was convened in 458, naming him "father" and "teacher." The year and circumstances of his repose are unknown. Accordingly, on the 31st of March, he is commemorated with another Bishop of Melitene of the same name, who suffered martyrdom and was tortured to death during the reign of Decius. He has no connection with the above-named.

brought forth the fruit of love and meekness. Against pleasure or gluttony, he brought forth continence; the thoughts of vainglory he countered with voluntary poverty. And thus, with every virtue, the most prudent one conquered all the opposite vices.

Because of his godly conduct, he was ordained against his will by his teacher to the rank of presbyter. He was given charge over all the monasteries that existed within the diocese. But the saint loved quietude more, and he frequently went to the city of the martyrium and the Church of Saint Polyefktos, and there he passed most of his time. He left the city once a year, after the Feast of the Theophany (Lights), and would retreat to a certain mountain in the wilderness and remain there until Palm Sunday, when he would return.

But the oversight of the monasteries did not afford him the opportunity for the solitude for which he yearned in his heart. He went out secretly from his country when he was twenty-nine years old. He had a desire to make a pilgrimage to the holy land, to converse with the holy fathers, and to take from them models in virtue and to emulate them. So he hastened with all speed, as on an eagle's wings. Therefore, after he had worshipped at the holy places and taken heed of each elder's divine conduct of life, he became an ardent zealot of solitude. He found a cell near the Lavra of Fara,[4] which dwelling place was exceedingly quiet. He remained there, plaiting the fronds from the palm trees. Since the profit earned from these was in excess of what he needed for his sustenance, the remainder he gave as alms to the needy, so as not to eat of another's labors, but rather that others would be supported by his handiwork. In this land he found rest, and his soul was freed from all earthly cares, and only upon those good things of the future did he meditate.

Saint Theoktistos

Nearby him was another ascetic named Theoktistos, commemorated by the holy Church on the 3rd of September, of similar virtue and state as himself. Eventually, they nurtured such great affection and godly love for each other that their souls and bodies were almost as one and, as one would have a certain sentiment, likewise the other would also. In this manner, as spiritual

---

[4] Ain Fara is the one plentiful perennial spring in the Judaean wilderness, about seven miles northeast of Jerusalem beyond Anatoth. At Fara, as we shall see later, Efthymios spent the first five years (406-411) of his monastic life in Palestine. The word "lavra" and its monastic use appear to have originated in Palestine. The organization it connotes is a row or cluster of solitary cells around a common center, including a church and a bake house, where the ascetics would assemble for Saturdays and Sundays, spending the rest of the week in their cells. See D. J. Chitty, *The Desert a City*, p. 15.

brothers, they went every year into the desert. In that place, they remained in solitude, bereft of all human company and association, from the octave of the Theophany until the Feast of Palm Sunday,[5] when they would return again to their cells, each bearing his wealth of virtues and dedicating it to the risen Christ. Indeed, it was a wealth more precious than the gold offered by the Magi. Efthymios surpassed Theoktistos in goodness of character, simplicity of manner and humility; therefore, he grew in everything before God with boldness, and the great grace of the Holy Spirit came upon him.

In Fara, Saint Efthymios remained with Theoktistos for five years. When the fifth year arrived, according to their custom, they went into the desert. After traversing a deep river and precipitous area, they came upon a large cave,[6] which before was probably a refuge for beasts; later, however, it became a holy church and dwelling place of angels. They believed that God had directed them there, and they remained in solitude for a considerable length of time, without having any human assistance. Nourishing themselves only on wild herbs, they rejoiced in the hope of future fulfillment and eternal rest.

Inasmuch as the Lord wished to reveal their virtue and to benefit others through them by His œconomy, they were discovered in the following manner, so that the garden would not be closed, nor the fountain of their wisdom and sanctity sealed; but on the contrary, they would enlighten others by their divine state of life. Hence, it chanced that shepherds with their sheep from the village of Lazarus (Bethany) came to the wadi, and, as they saw the saints, suddenly were terrified and began to run in their confusion. But the saints called to them, saying, "Brethren, fear not, for we are men, and it is for our sins that we have come to this land for solitude." Then the shepherds took courage and came into the cave, and not finding any food or other provisions for bodily necessity, they marvelled and went into their village revealing what had taken place.

As the monks of Fara learned these things, many came to visit Efthymios and Theoktistos, and some stayed, captivated by the sweet and irresistible words of those heralds of the truth, by whom they were thoroughly instructed in every monastic practise. The saints became well known in that vicinity, and afterward, they built monasteries, the head of which was the wondrous Theoktistos. Due to the fact that the good reputation of Efthymios reached almost every place, all rushed to him and stayed in obedience to him for their salvation. For this reason, they made the cave into a holy church,

---

[5] Saint Efthymios brought with him from Melitene a practise that was to have a considerable influence on the future of Judaean monasticism. Ibid., p. 82.

[6] In 411, Efthymios set out with his friend Theoktistos for the Utter Desert of Coutila toward the Dead Sea, the region of Qumran. Ibid., p. 82.

and they built over it a lavra, similar to that of Fara, since it was impossible for it to be in the cave because of the steepness and rough landscape.[7] Efthymios made Theoktistos hegumen of the lavra and retired into seclusion inside the cave. However, this expert caretaker and physician of wounded souls accepted whomever came to him, and he confessed every one of them. And according to the injury to their souls, he also applied the appropriate medicine with wisdom and discernment. He taught them to renounce the world and to have, principally, obedience and humility, and to have death always in remembrance, and to labor for their food with their own hands. He taught the young men especially to exhaust their bodies, in order to obtain obedience in spiritual labors, and never to violate the commandment of the divine Paul: "If anyone is not willing to work, neither let him eat [2 Thess. 3:10]." He bade them to keep before them the apostle's words: "These hands ministered to my needs, and those who were with me. These hands have ministered unto my necessities, and to them that were with me [Acts 20:34]." Inasmuch as they of the world labor to feed wives, children, and all in the house, and to pay taxes and rent, and in addition to give alms, so it is absurd and improper that we, the monastics, do not have compassion on our brother and neighbor. He ordered the young men to keep silence diligently, so that none dared to speak in church or in the refectory. But come, let us enter into the wonders that the all-good God wrought through the intercessions of the great Efthymios, that we might know his great prominence and sanctity.

The Saracens

A ruler of the Saracens, named Aspebet (Aspebetos),[8] had a son called Terevon, who, from demonic complicity, was semi-paralyzed, so that the right side of his body was atrophied. This child had a certain vision and told it to his

---

[7] It is to these remote gorges that the focus of monastic activity would presently move from the neighborhood of the villages. While passing down one of the most beautiful of the gorges, the Wadi Mukellik, the two monks came upon this great cave in its northern cliff. The danger of passage for the night service from the other caves in that precipitous valley to the main cave, which was marked for the church, persuaded them not to make the place a lavra, but instead to gather the brethren together in a coenobium built along the edge of the last drop into the torrent-bed, at the foot of the cliff in which was the cave. A tower (since fallen) was built up against the cliff-face to give access to the church-cave, in which Efthymios would stay through the week, making himself approachable only on Saturdays and Sundays. Ibid., pp. 82, 83.

[8] "The sheik himself had been in command (his name, Aspebet, is a Persian title—'master of the horse') over the Arabs under Persian suzerainty. Reported for protecting Christians in their flight from the persecution which was renewed in the last year of Yazdgird (420), he had taken refuge with the Romans and had been appointed to a similar command by Anatolios. He was still a pagan." Ibid., p. 83.

father, who took the sick boy with many barbarians in his company and immediately departed Arabia. They came to the cave of Saint Efthymios, just as the revelation commanded in the vision. They approached and inquired of Theoktistos the whereabouts of the great Efthymios. Theoktistos answered that Efthymios was in seclusion, and by no means was he allowed to speak to him until Saturday. Terevon told him the details of the matter, saying, "Servant of God, I have availed myself of all the magicians and physicians of Arabia, to whom I paid great sums; however, not one benefit of any kind did I obtain. Afterward, I went into Persia and suffered similarly, but a cure I have not known. From this, I observed that all that we esteem are myths, so I prayed to the true God that if He healed me, I would become a Christian. Then after praying in this manner, I beheld a certain monastic elder with a long beard, who inquired about my sickness, and I showed him my affliction, and he said to me, 'If thou art healed, thou must perform whatever thou hast promised to the true God.' I said to him, 'Yea, master, verily I will.' And revealing himself, he said to me, 'I am Efthymios, and I dwell by the Torrents, ten miles outside of Jerusalem. If thou desirest to be cured, come to me, and the Lord will heal thee.' These things that I saw, I related to my father, and behold, we have left everything and have come swiftly to the place shown in the vision."

When Theoktistos heard all these things, he interrupted the solitude of Saint Efthymios and related the matter to him, and the blessed man perceived that it was the œconomy of God. He descended at once and met the barbarians; and while the saint was praying over the youth—O the wonder!—that very hour, he was completely cured. The barbarians were amazed at the miracle, and they believed in Christ and sought Baptism from the saint. The holy one, seeing their great eagerness, was not negligent; but straightway, he formed out of the corner of his cave, a small baptismal font. And indeed, the first baptized was Aspebet, whose name was changed to Peter; then afterward, his wife's brother, Maris, who was not only eminent and wealthy, but also knowledgeable and virtuous; then Terevon and all of the rest. They kept the fast for forty days, and Saint Efthymios admonished and taught them to preserve their piety inviolate. Then all received from the saint permission to depart. But Maris, the uncle of Terevon, under no circumstances would remove himself from the monastery, but offered all his fortune and renounced the world and became a monk, remaining till the end in obedience to Efthymios.[9]

Dometian the Steward

Word of this spread to all the surrounding areas. From everywhere, whosoever had a sickness found cures without fee. All returned healthy,

---

[9] "When Theoktistos reposed forty years later (466), Maris succeeded him as head of the coenobium." Ibid., 85, 95.

glorifying God and thanking the saint. And the great father, observing that so many people were coming to him, grew sorrowful because of the honor they accorded him and because of all the clamor, due to which he no longer had any tranquillity as before. For this reason, he thought to leave for Rouba secretly, to avoid being troubled. However, the godly Theoktistos perceived what he had in mind and gathered all the brotherhood and ardently besought the saint not to leave them orphans, but to have pity on his flock and not leave the enemy to rend it to pieces by his departure. Thus they entreated him, but the blessed one, out of irresistible love for solitude, departed secretly with a virtuous disciple named Dometian. They came to the Dead Sea near Rouba, and ascended Mount Mardan,[10] which was higher than all the others. There was water there, and there were ruins from which they built a church; and they settled therein. In the interim, they ate wild weeds and afterward traversed over to the Wilderness of Ziph, to see the cave in which David hid when persecuted by Saul [1 Kgs. (1 Sam.) 23:15]; and, because Efthymios liked the place, he rested there.

Saint Efthymios the Great

However, the all-good God made him famous there also, and in this place, a monastery was erected in a marvellous manner. A youth from the village of Aristobol had a demon which tormented him, and he would call upon the name of Saint Efthymios without even knowing him. His parents learned who the great Efthymios was and where to find the saint. Therefore, they took their child and went to discover him. However, before they arrived at the cave, the demon foreknew its own

---

[10] "It appears to be on the top of the old Jewish stronghold of Masada, where a ruined church still remaining is probably that set up by him. Even he seems to have found a prolonged stay here impracticable, and he moved up to establish a monastery." Chitty, pp. 83, 84.

feebleness before the blessed man's power. Losing courage, the demon went out of the youth, violently convulsing him, but leaving him whole and sound. Of this miracle certain others heard, and they came from the above mentioned village and built a monastery there. To the monastery, many gathered who were attracted to the wondrous virtue of the saint, as iron to a magnet. Learning that in this place there were certain heretics entrenched in the Manichaean madness,[11] he went over to them alone and, through his good instruction, restored all to Orthodoxy.

But the saint, seeing again that many gathered there, took Dometian and returned to the blessed Theoktistos who, with the rest of the brothers, hearing of his arrival, received exceeding joy, just as when one thirsty finds cool water. But the blessed man stayed about three miles away from the coenobium in a wholesome and secluded place, where he found a cave to dwell in. Theoktistos went there, too, and did not wish in any way to depart from Efthymios, because of the great love that they had between them. Hence, Theoktistos begged him with many supplications to keep him there with him. But the saint thought of the monks at the lavra, and would not agree; he promised only to come down frequently to visit them.

Peter the Saracen

When the pious Peter, formerly Aspebet, heard of the return of Efthymios, he assembled many Saracens, whom he had catechized to piety, and hastened to meet him, in order to enjoy his most delightful and cheerful presence. The saint received them joyously and blessed them, baptizing all

---

[11] "Manichaeism is a religious system based on the doctrines of Manes, a Persian religious leader born about 215 (some say 240). Manes combined the Christian theory of salvation and the Zoroastrian concept of dualism, or belief that two opposing principles govern the universe. According to this system, the world originated as a mixture of light and darkness, which represent good and evil. Manichaeans believe that man's soul, which arose from the Kingdom of Light, wants to escape from the body, which represents the Kingdom of Darkness. They believe that the soul can attain release only through wisdom, not through the renunciation of material or sensual things. They also believe that a savior will provide the wisdom necessary for release." *World Book Encyclopedia*, Vol. 13, 1976, s.v. "Manichaeism." "He set up his own organization and claimed to be the incarnation of the Holy Spirit. Although put to death by Zoroastrian priests, his ideas were widely proclaimed in spite of great hostility in the Roman Empire." M.A. Smith, *The Church Under Siege*, p. 266. Saint John Chrysostom writes: "He taught that God was the cause of good, and matter the cause of evil. The theory about matter led him to hold that the body of Jesus was an incorporeal phantom. He eliminated the Old Testament from the Scriptures and held himself at liberty to reject such passages in the New Testament as were opposed to his own opinions." *On The Priesthood*, Nicene, 1st Ser., IX:65, note 3.

who were catechized by Peter. And the latter brought skilled men and built into the hermitage of the saint three cells, a large cistern in the garden, a church, and whatever else was necessary. Every day there came large crowds from the Hagarene belief to hear his delightful teachings. Therefore, in order not to be deprived of his beloved quiet, he ordered them to build, near the two monasteries, a church and huts for them to abide in, and he often visited there, diligently counseling and strengthening them in the Faith. Saint Efthymios' words were so sweet and wise that, in a short while, multitudes of pious people assembled in that place and built huts and dwelt there. Thereupon, he wrote about this to Juvenal, the Patriarch of Jerusalem, who ordained Peter, the father of Terevon, as bishop,[12] and subsequently, the number of faithful increased daily.

Three Brothers

Indeed, the saint had a yearning to remain quiet and undisturbed by people, but the Lord wished to populate that land with reason-endowed sheep. After a short while, there came three brothers according to the flesh, born in Cappadocia but reared in Syria. They were very virtuous individuals, respectively named Kosmas, Chrysippos, and Gabriel, who came in order to become monastics. The blessed one initially did not want to keep them there, because they were young, especially Gabriel, who was a beardless boy. However, at night he saw a vision of a wondrous man who told him, "Receive the brethren, for God has sent them." Therefore, he arose that morning and told Kosmas, for he was the eldest among them, "Because the Lord has commanded me, I accept you gladly. However, be careful never to leave Gabriel to converse with anyone, and make certain that he always remains closed up in the cell until he should grow a beard, inasmuch as the enemy greatly makes war against the monastics with the womanly faces of the beardless. And, on account of this, it is necessary to safeguard everyone from such a great danger." After he said this to Kosmas, he also predicted the future to him, that he would be Bishop of Skythopolis—which came to pass.[13]

---

[12] Peter was consecrated bishop for his tribe, by that time distributed in a number of camps. He was to play a conspicuous part in the Synod of Ephesus. He was appointed to a delegation to call on Nestorios and reported on the result. Chitty, pp. 84, 98, note 12.

[13] Kosmas became Bishop of Skythopolis [=Beth-Shan]. He was previously *stavrophylax* (Cross-warden) in Jerusalem. He was succeeded in this office by his brother Chrysippos, who left us a number of rhetorical sermons. The third Cappadocian brother,...Gabriel, became hegumen of Evdokia's Church of Saint Stephen: he could speak and write in Greek, Latin, and Syriac. Ibid., p. 85.

The Lavra Grows

From that time, the saint received all that came with great joy. Consequently, through the gathering of so many from different lands, within a short period of time there began another lavra as that at Fara. And the patriarch, observing this progress, decided to come himself and to visit Saint Efthymios, who was then fifty-two years old. He also renovated the church and ordained deacons.[14] As time passed, thus did the brothers multiply, but they suffered great privation as a result. However, the Lord, Who bestows favor and goodness, in His œconomy, sent them aid in the following marvellous manner.

In those days, there descended from Jerusalem to the Jordan four hundred Armenians, who had wandered from the original path and come upon the lavra of Saint Efthymios. The blessed one, upon seeing them, called the aforementioned Dometian, who had the stewardship, and told him to offer them hospitality, as much as possible. But he replied that not even one day's food could they find. Nonetheless, the saint had hoped in the merciful and benevolent God and answered him confidently, "Go child, and see how the thoughts of men differ from the grace and power of God!" Thereupon, he went to the storehouse, and—O the unutterable wonder! O Lord Who loves man!—it was overflowing, so much so that it was impossible to open the door. Then he shouted to the brethren that he might summon them there. With great difficulty, they opened the storehouse and found it filled with whatever they required. There was an abundance of bread, wine, and oil. Seeing these things, Dometian perceived the power of divine grace, and he fell at the feet of the venerable Efthymios, asking forgiveness. But the saint raised him up and answered, "My child, thou sowest with blessings, and with blessings thou dost harvest. Whosoever ministers to strangers and receives the poor benefits himself even more. Thus shouldest thou do, if thou dost wish God to bless thee to be strong enough in this present world and to enjoy life everlasting in the age to come."

Afxentios the Monk

In a short period of time, the number of brethren increased to fifty. Hence, pack animals were in demand to transport the required provisions. Now, there was a monk from Asia named Afxentios, whom Dometian, as the monastery steward, frequently begged to treat the animals kindly, for this was Afxentios' obedience; and he was very suited for the requirements of this all-important service. However, this disobedient one did not wish to obey the elders. As a result, Dometian made this known to the holy elder, who

---

[14] "Domitian of Melitene and Domnos of Antioch were ordained as deacons for the lavra; Domitian continued to serve there as such until his death." Chitty, loc. cit.

likewise entreated Afxentios to bring about a change of mind, but not even then did the imprudent one hearken. Afxentios said that he did not wish to listen, for fear that he would suffer some spiritual sickness if he were obedient to the elders! Then the saint replied, "All of us pray to the Lord that thou wilt not fall into error; only go with faith." But the shameless one did not obey. Consequently, the saint was somewhat offended and told him, "O child, indeed, we advised thee for thine own welfare, but, as incorrigible, thou wilt know the fruit of thy disobedience in a little while." These things the saint uttered and—alas!— Afxentios was seized with great fear and collapsed to the ground, a pitiful sight to the onlookers and worthy of many tears. Then, those present begged the saint quickly to revive him, that both his body and soul should not perish. And the saint, being meek and not bearing resentment, instantly forgave him and completely cured him. From that hour Afxentios progressed in obedience and no longer dared to disobey the saint, but ministered diligently in his service of the mules.

Two Monks Decide to Leave

Two other brethren, named Maron and Klematios, had in mind to leave the monastery. But the saint, possessing divine grace, knew the secret when he saw in a vision the devil, who was putting a bridle on the heads of these two and attempting to cast them into a trap. Therefore, understanding the meaning of the vision, he warned them, instructing them with various examples concerning obedience, saying that when one departs from one land to another, desiring to attain virtue, he is mistaken, because it is the manner of life and not the place that saves a man. And just as a frequently transplanted tree does not thrive, in like manner also, the monk who often goes from place to place never succeeds in virtue. As proof, the saint related the following example of an angry monk who went out of the coenobium, thinking that, being independent, he would not be angry or have any temptations. When he was a few days alone, he filled a cup with water and put it on the ground. It then rose up of itself and poured out the water, not only once, but thrice. So again, he grew angry and cast the cup to the ground and completely shattered it. Hearing these things, Klematios laughed. Therefore, the saint was scandalized and said to him, "Instead of weeping, thou laughest, O shameless one? Dost thou not know that the Lord rebukes those who laugh, and blesses those who mourn? Know this, O ignorant and senseless one, that outspokenness is the mother of all the passions." After he had reprimanded him thus, the saint entered into his cell, and Klematios fell to the earth, rolling and trembling all over and seized with terror. Then Dometian and certain other bystanders sympathized with the sufferer and begged the saint to forgive Klematios' indiscretion; therefore, he healed him in both soul and body and dismissed him with a warning.

The Struggles of the Saint

The hermit, Kyriakos, who had been in obedience to the saint from his youth and knew his austere conduct of life in everything, verily assured us of these and other similar narrations. Also, he never saw the saint eat food or speak a word at all five days out of the week—except Saturday and Sunday—unless there occurred some great necessity; nor did he sleep lying down on his side, but instead sat, or was suspended upon a rope in one corner of his cell, where he took a little sleep, saying to himself, "Come, wicked servant." In this and other things, Efthymios zealously emulated the life and virtue of the great Arsenios, commemorated by the holy Church on the 8th of May. When a certain brother began to tell of the attributes of Arsenios,[15] he recorded them, so as to imitate them; that is, his withdrawal, humility, silence, worn garments, abstinence, vigils, compunction, tears, sympathetic nature, discernment, intense prayer, readiness, and endurance. And in all these things, Efthymios also excelled. Furthermore, he foresaw the future as it was to happen, just as it is evident below.

Anastasios the Sacristan

A true and zealous disciple of Saint Passarion,[16] the sacristan of the Church of Saint Anastasia, had a desire to converse with the divine Efthymios. He was accompanied by Bishop Pheidon of Joppa, Kosmas the *stavrophylax* (Cross-warden), and certain others; and they went to the monastery to meet him. Now Efthymios knew of their coming, by divine

---

[15] "Arsenios was born in Rome about 360. A well-educated man of senatorial rank, he was appointed by the Emperor Theodosios I as tutor to the young princes, named Arkadios and Honorius. He left the palace in 394 and sailed secretly to Alexandria. From there he went to Sketis. He was renowned for his austerity and silence, and this, combined with his learning, made him seem somewhat forbidding to the Egyptian monks." See Benedicta Ward, SLR, *The Sayings of the Desert Fathers*, pp. 7, 8.

[16] Passarion, Archimandrite in Jerusalem. "When Juvenal came down to consecrate the church of Saint Efthymios' lavra, he brought with him the theologian Hesychios and the *Chorepiscopos* Passarion. He was 'Archimandrite of the monks'—that is to say, 'Archimandrite in the special sense given that word in Jerusalem, referring to those who had oversight of all the monks in the diocese. Hence his coming down for the consecration of Saint Efthymios' church.' He died less than seven months later, toward the end of November. He was remembered as a primary figure in the monastic life of Jerusalem, where he founded a famous almshouse outside the east gate of the city, and a great and beautiful coenobium within the walls of Holy Sion for the 'devotees' of that shrine, 'for the service and psalmody of them that without ceasing glorify the Lord.' The stress on liturgical order once more marks a contrast between Palestinian and Egyptian monasticism. In this, in his coenobitic order, and in his attention to the poor, Passarion seems to be in the tradition of Saint Basil." Chitty, p. 86. Saint Passarion is commemorated by the holy Church on the 11th of August.

revelation, and that the sacristan, Anastasios, was about to become the patriarch. For this reason, he summoned Chrysippos, the monastery steward, and said to him, "Make ready beforehand the necessary arrangements, for the patriarch is coming to us with thy brother." When they arrived at the monastery, and Chrysippos saw that it was not the patriarch, but the sacristan Anastasios, he told the saint. In order to prove it, they showed him the garments of the sacristan, which were silken and costly, whereas the patriarch was not permitted to wear any, save humble and moderate garments. So the blessed one answered, "Believe me, I saw him clothed in white, vested as the patriarch; and I believe that I am not deceived. But God, Who knows the future, revealed the truth to me." And according to the prediction of the saint, so did it occur, to the wonder of all.[17]

A Childless Couple

A ruler of the Saracen race, named Terevon (not the aforementioned), had a barren and childless wife. For this reason, they led an unhappy life, and both had profound grief. Therefore, they appeared before the saint and besought him to dissolve their sorrow with his supplications, which were acceptable to God. Thereupon, the blessed man made the sign of the Cross thrice, touching the belly of the woman and saying, "Go rejoicing, for the Lord will grant thee to beget three children." They believed these words unhesitatingly and departed joyfully; and, in time, the first son was born, and they named him Peter. With the ensuing years, there were also born two others, according to the trustworthy promise of Efthymios.

Emilian the Monk

A certain brother in the lavra, named Emilian, of the Roman race, who exercised virtuous conduct from his youth, was also especially pure in body and wise of mind. The devil envied him and, on one Sunday, unleashed such a difficult and fierce carnal warfare that he was unable to endure it, and, inclining to shameful thoughts, he also assented to them. When the saint went at dawn to Orthros, he happened to be close by the aforementioned brother, and he sensed such a stench exhaling from him that he realized it was a plot of the demon and rebuked the impure spirit. The supplanter of men, the devil, cast the brother to the earth and convulsed Emilian. The afflicted one spewed foam from his mouth. Then the saint requested that a light be brought, as the place was dark, and he said to the other fathers, "Behold, brethren, how this one from childhood was wise and virtuous, but now is prostrate from his defiled thoughts, a frightful sight and worthy of tears. Let everyone strike wicked thoughts and drive them from the mind at the start, when they are not strong. For if we entertain them kindly, concurring and taking pleasure even

---

[17] Anastasios, Patriarch of Jerusalem (459-478). Chitty, p. 182.

though we do not come into contact with another body, in our soul we have sinned nonetheless. Therefore, according to the teaching of the Lord, like adulterers, we will be condemned on that fearful day when the hidden and unseen shall be revealed."

Then the blessed one told the following example which was related by certain Egyptian elders: "There was a man in the city, thought by all to have a marvellous life and appearing to possess great goodness. However, secretly he angered God with his depraved thoughts and movements of his heart, to which he consented. Although he never sinned in actual deed, he ofttimes committed adultery in his mind. When he had contracted a grave and mortal sickness, all those of the city wailed and lamented inconsolably, considering his death a general calamity. There happened to be in that city a clairvoyant elder who, upon hearing the common misfortune and beholding such sorrow in the faithful, went with haste also to take his blessing and receive forgiveness from him. When he arrived, he saw the bishops with all the clergy and the rest of the rulers, who held lit candles, awaiting the departure of his soul. Unobserved by others, the saintly elder came before the barely breathing man and saw a frightful phenomenon, which to the others was hidden. He saw in a vision a certain fearful giant, which held in his hands a fiery trident pinned into the man's heart, mercilessly forcing the departure of the soul. Afterward, he heard a voice from above which said, 'Just as this soul did not give me rest even for one day, be thou never negligent, neither cease this torturous and dreadful punishment!'"

The saint taught the brethren ever and always to be cautious and reflective at the departure of the soul, and to learn from the example of Emilian and others, lest they should suffer similarly. He admonished them thus, and said a prayer over the afflicted one; and instantly, all the nearby area was filled with an intolerable stench as that of burning sulphur. Close upon the foul odor there followed a voice saying, "I am the spirit of fornication." Thenceforth, Emilian was sober and sensible and became a chosen vessel.

The Drought

At that time there occurred a drought, and the entire lavra was parched and needed water. The brethren endured immeasurable grief, for which reason all gathered together (and in their company also was the blessed Theoktistos), imploring the saint to intercede with the Lord, that He would send water to the thirsty ground and refresh men and the offspring of all living creatures, which were in great danger. But the saint did not wish to make the entreaty, and replied, "This, my children, is a chastisement of God for our sins; therefore, if I entreat His goodness, He will not heed me, just as it was said to the Prophet Jeremias: 'Therefore pray not thou for this people, and intercede not for them to be pitied, yea, pray not, and approach Me not for them, for I will not hearken unto thee [Jer. 7:16].'" Indeed, these things the divine Efthymios said through modesty and extreme humility. And the drought continued for many days. Hence, all the faithful people of those parts could not suffer the pain of this dreadful scourge and assembled outside of the lavra, bearing crosses in their hands and crying out in a pitiful voice continually, "Lord have mercy"; they did so not only with their mouths crying aloud, but also with their hearts, in deep and profound compunction.

Now the saint, sympathetic and compassionate wherever he was, grieved for them. He emerged and said, "My children, I do not have this boldness before the Lord, as I am a sinner and unworthy; yet rather, I am praying for the loving-kindness of God, especially also at this time of the righteous wrath and anger of God on every one of us. It appears to be daring and impudent that I should make such an entreaty, insomuch as with our iniquities, we have soiled every image of Him, the Lover of men, and polluted His temple with desires and pleasures, as He hates our malice, greediness, and inhumanity. However, because He is compassionate, let us fall down before Him with tears, begging, and perhaps He will pity us with heartfelt fatherly love and fulfill our request." These things the saint proclaimed, and all with one tongue and voice said, "Thou art sanctified, O venerable father; therefore, make a supplication in behalf of us before the Lord, Who does the will of those who fear Him." Therefore, so as not to grieve them, the saint ordered the entire multitude to make a supplicatory prayer outside. In the meantime, he, with all the monastics, entered into the church and fell prostrate to the ground, offering up a fervent and tearful prayer. As soon as the tears of Saint Efthymios fell to the ground, God hearkened to the petition of His servant. Clouds filled the air. A violent wind was heard, together with thunder and lightning. Consequently, rain fell in such a downpour that the earth was drenched.

Then the blessed one came out of the monastery and, prophesying to the people, declared, "Behold, brethren, the Lord has hearkened to our prayer and visited the earth and saturated her farms. He wishes to bless the crops of this year more abundantly than all the others, to fill the plains with richness, for the fields to yield fruit, to fill up the valleys with wheat and to gird the mountains with rejoicing!" After he had uttered this, he dismissed the people; and his prediction was fulfilled, when such an abundant downpour fell into all that region, that all rejoiced.

Defender of the Faith

But now, let us speak of the remaining astounding and remarkable accomplishments of the saint, as they were told by Saint John the Hesychast, Bishop of Koloneia, and Thallalaeos the presbyter, who served in the lavra of Saint Savvas, and who claimed that not only the others, but even the divine Savvas himself, admired the great Efthymios and held him in utmost respect, not only for the aforementioned miracles that he wrought, but also because he was an ardent zealot of the true Orthodox doctrines and combated the Manichaeans, the Arians, and the other heretics, whose mythological theories of pre-existence and reconciliation he proved wrong, refuting them mightily with arguments from the holy Scriptures. Furthermore, all the heretics that he entered into discourse with, he wounded mortally, and they were defeated by him as foxes by a lion, for many scandals were created at that time by them, and they misled many people. But the disciples of Saint Efthymios, having been counseled by him, never strayed.

The Divine Liturgy

When the saint reached the age of seventy-six, he came down from Rouba to the lavra and served the divine Liturgy that Saturday. Dometian stood on the right side of the sanctuary. The Saracen Terevon was also there, and so was Gabriel. Some stood near the sanctuary, while others were further away. When the doxology of the Trisagion was done, they suddenly saw—great is Thy grace upon Saint Efthymios, O Christ!—fire which descended from above, and it enshrouded the saint and Dometian, from the beginning of the Trisagion until the end of the divine Liturgy. Terevon was terrified, as he was most pious; and, not daring to stand near there, he left the church and stood outside in a state of ecstasy and wonderment at this marvel, as Kyriakos described it later, having heard it from Terevon and Gabriel. They also added that the Lord had given Efthymios such grace that, from the appearance alone, he knew everyone precisely and, as from a mirror, understood also the inner movements and passions of the soul, and from which passion one was defeated and in what passions one defeated the demons.

They also related this about the saint, as he himself said in private to certain brethren for their benefit, that many times he saw frightening angels who liturgized with him and served as deacons. And when he gave Communion to the brethren, he observed some of them to be bright and fair, while others were black and dismal, for they were unworthy of holy Communion. Therefore, he counseled them often and enjoined that they should always be vigilant and prepared according to the apostle, and thus with a clear conscience, they should receive the holy Mysteries, simply because whosoever receives unworthily will be judged unto the ages. For this, the priest safeguards the people, beforehand saying: "Let us lift our hearts unto the Lord." In other words, let us turn our souls and thoughts to the heavens and away from earthly cares. Then the celebrant receives the response from the people: "We lift them to the Lord," and completes with assurance the divine

Liturgy. Afterward, he raises his hands heavenward, so as to show that the Mystery was instituted for our salvation, and says: "Holy things for the holy," indicating "that, since I too am a man with passions like yours, and am not aware of your acts, for this I urge and caution all of you that each one should examine himself; and, if he is subject to some passion, either enmity or pride or envy or any other, he should not dare to approach if he is not cleansed of the contagion, for these Mysteries are not given to the unworthy and impious, but to the pure and holy. Therefore, all that have a clear conscience come forth and receive light," and the rest.

Saint Savvas

When Saint Efthymios was eighty-two years old, the blessed Savvas came to him. He was then a beardless youth, but asked to be allowed into his synodia or company. The saint, by foresight, knowing his future state and virtue, gladly received him; but because of his age, he sent him to Theoktistos until he grew a beard. He wrote to him: "Receive this young boy and counsel him and lead him carefully in asceticism and the monastic life with precision, for it seems to me that he will progress immensely in the ascetic life and shall enlighten many with his superb and wondrous accomplishments." Saint Efthymios prophesied this about Saint Savvas; and, as he had foretold, it all happened. For today, there is no city or desert where the divine accomplishments of Saint Savvas are not recounted with spiritual joy. But these have been recorded on the day of his memory, that is, the 5th of December. Therefore, let us say a few more things about the great Efthymios, that we may not leave our subject.

Patriarch Anastasios

In those days, Patriarch Juvenal (ca. 422-458) reposed in the Lord after many years on the throne. Anastasios (458-478) was ordained, according to the prophecy of Efthymios. Anastasios then ordained a certain Pheidon as deacon and dispatched him with the *stavrophylax* to the great Efthymios, reminding him of the prophecy that he had made and asking him to allow the patriarch to go to the lavra and visit Efthymios, that the two might rejoice. And the saint answered him thus: "I have always had a desire to see his beatitude the patriarch; and I believe that I will spiritually gain by thy presence. Inasmuch as formerly thou didst visit me without a procession and excitement, but thou must now come according to the dignity of a hierarch, this is too much for my weakness. Therefore, I beg of thee not to take the trouble, for I will greet thee gladly if thou choosest to come, but later I will be obliged to greet the others. Therefore, afterward, being unable to receive so many crowds, I will perchance depart from here and seek out a place to afford me more solitude." Upon hearing this, the patriarch did not dare go, lest the saint should be troubled and consequently be forced to leave.

Saint Efthymios the Great

Empress Evdokia

The Empress Evdokia[18] erected a great number of churches, monasteries, hospitals and shelters for the poor, as she was pious and God-loving. She also constructed a splendid church dedicated to Saint Peter, directly opposite the lavra of Saint Efthymios, where she constructed a fountain for the refreshment of the brethren. On a certain day, she went to visit the saint. After observing that the cells of the monks were built separately, she was struck with great contrition of soul. The augusta sent Gabriel to the saint, beseeching him to permit her to go and to speak with him about a pressing matter. She also expressed her desire to bestow a great sum of money for the needs of the monks. The saint wrote a note to the augusta as follows: "Do not trouble thyself any further, my child, for in a few days thou shalt go to the Lord, to Whom thou shouldest pray for the forgiveness of thy sins. We will pray to the Lord for thy soul and will not be negligent in this." As she heard this, she was completely astonished by his foreknowledge, and she departed for the holy city and related to the patriarch all that he had told

---

[18] "Athenais-Evdokia wrote to Saint Symeon the Stylite about her doubts, her hesitations—that is, her insistence on Monophysitism. The saint answered: 'Know, my child, that the devil, seeing the wealth of thy virtue, is determined to plunder thee like the grain, and that ravager, Theodosios, (her husband), receptacle and instrument of the evildoer, has clouded and confused thy soul beloved of God. I have marvelled greatly at this, that, having a well-spring near and not knowing it, thou dost try to bring water from afar. Thou hast the godly Efthymios. Follow therefore his teachings and admonitions, and thou shalt be saved.'" See Jeanne Tsatsos, *Empress Athenais-Eudocia*, pp. 117, 118. Saint Evdokia, the consort of Emperor Theodosius II, for her virtuous life, was declared a saint and is commemorated by the holy Church on the 13th of August.

her. Later she donated tremendous amounts to all the churches she had built, and she visited them with the patriarch, restoring and furnishing them generously. After a period of four months, she was translated to the Lord.

Saint Theoktistos Reposes

In those days, the blessed Theoktistos, having reached a very old age, became gravely ill. Saint Efthymios, being elderly himself, ninety years of age, went to visit him and to minister to his needs, knowing that Theoktistos was to depart for what he desired. When the patriarch learned this, he went to bury the blessed Theoktistos and also to behold the great Efthymios. As they met after the funeral, Anastasios kissed the holy hands of the saint with the utmost respect, saying, "I had a great desire, O servant of God, to see thee, and I thank God that He has made me worthy. I pray that thou wilt beseech the Lord that the true prophecy thou madest on behalf of me will remain to the end. Write to me, if thy reason-endowed flock is ever in need, and I will obey all thine orders as a child its father." These and many other similar things said the pious patriarch with much humility. The saint, practicing self-restraint, answered, "It is I, O master, who need thine intercessions before the Lord." And he said to him again, "I, O holy father, shall obey thee in this, even though I am unworthy. But do thou, who art filled with divine gifts and have found favor before the Lord, cease not to pray for thy children." Again, the saint responded with meekness and humility, "Forgive me, O master, but do thou provide for this monastery and all the brethren, as thou art the leader of our Church." And the patriarch said, "Insofar as thou hast been the leader of this desert, which thou hast embellished with thy virtue, and hast caused it to blossom like another Jerusalem, thus mayest thou now be the guardian of all the monks and guide of their souls and bodies."

At the end of their conversation, the patriarch departed to the church in the city. Meanwhile, the saint chose as hegumen the uncle of Terevon, Abba Maris, who was superior in virtue, but he lived for only two years in the ascetic settlement. Thereafter, he chose the praiseworthy Longinos. Later on, Kosmas the *stavrophylax* was ordained Bishop of Skythopolis, and Chrysippos was appointed *stavrophylax*, as Saint Efthymios had foretold. The blessed Kosmas lived as a hierarch for thirty years, accomplishing a great number of praiseworthy deeds. His brother Chrysippos served as *stavrophylax* for twelve years, ending his life in a God-pleasing manner. Their brother Gabriel erected a monastery dedicated to the holy ascension; and because he was studious and a friend of virtue, emulating the great Efthymios, he retreated from the monastery after the Feast of the Holy Theophany and returned on Palm Sunday. In the eightieth year of his life, Abba Gabriel departed for the heavenly mansions, having performed great feats. His holy relics were buried in the tomb of Saint Theoktistos.

A Retreat During the Great Fast

More than anything else, the saint desired solitude. Therefore, he took Dometian and Savvas—the latter was very zealous in the monastic life—and they retired into the inner desert, where they lived on the roots of wild plants and had no other bodily comfort. As they proceeded through the arid desert, Savvas could not stand on his own feet and collapsed from the burning thirst. The saint then went some distance away from the others and made a prayer to the Lord, saying, "Give water, O Lord, to the parched earth for the relief of our brother." After the prayer, he took the hoe, with which they dug up roots of plants to eat, and dug a little into the soil. Then—O the wonder!—refreshing, sweet water sprung forth. As Savvas drank, relieving his suffering, he glorified and offered thanks to God Who works signs and wonders through His servants.

The Saint's Farewell

Thus, the holy Efthymios, having such authority before God, foretold not only his blessed departure to the Lord, but also all that was to happen to the lavra that he had erected with much toil. Eight days after the Feast of the Theophany, many of the fathers gathered in the cell of the saint, some of them to bid him farewell, others to follow him into the desert. Among them were Elias and Martyrios, who saw that he had prepared nothing for the yearly departure, and they asked if he would depart on the morrow. He said to them, "Throughout this week, I shall remain with you, and at midnight on the sabbath, I shall leave you." But he said this of his final departure. However, they did not perceive what he meant. Three days later, it was the Feast of Saint Anthony; so he ordered them to conduct an all-night vigil in the church.

After the celebration, he called the clerics together into the sacristy and said to them, "Know this, O brethren, that the Lord has called me from this life to the future one. Tomorrow, therefore, let all the brethren be gathered together, that I may tell you how to continue conducting yourselves after my departure." In the morning, they all came together with great urgency, and the saint said to them, "Fathers and brethren, beloved in the Lord and dearest children, in three days I will tread the final road of my fathers. You in turn must firmly keep all the commandments that I leave you, so that your piety and love toward me may be revealed. The foremost of all the virtues that you should possess is love, without which it is impossible to accomplish anything. All the virtues are known through love and humility. Humility exalts the virtuous to the heights of accomplishment, while love does not allow him to fall from the heights. We must always confess our sins before God, and we should always praise Him, especially we monks, as we have vowed before the precepts of the holy Gospel, and as we are free from daily concerns and lead a life without distraction. Therefore, always remain pure in your souls and bodies. Always maintain the rule that I have given you and also perform the doxology during the gatherings. You must care for the suffering as much as possible. All the brethren that are disturbed by foul and adverse thoughts should confess them immediately and be corrected by the more experienced fathers with instruction and examples, so that they will not be undermined by the devil. This last commandment I bid you to keep with diligence: never shut the gate to those who come forth, but let it be open to the weary travelers and the poor; and may all the things that you possess be open to them that need them, if you wish for the Lord to send all the things you require in abundance."

After he enjoined these things, he asked them whom they desired to have as their superior and leader. They all unanimously asked that Dometian be chosen, as he was the most virtuous of all. But Efthymios answered them, saying, "Choose another, for Dometian has only seven days left in this world after my repose." This announcement shocked all those that stood about, as he said it with authority and did not hide it. As they did not succeed in having Dometian, they asked for a certain Elias of the lower monastery, who hailed from Jericho. Then the saint turned to him and said, "Know this, that God has ordained that this lavra shall soon become a coenobium." The next day, the saint instructed the new hegumen where to erect the coenobium and how to organize it. He exhorted him about the care of visitors and the order of chanting and the remaining functions, that is, how to care for the brethren and especially how to counsel those that are tempted by adverse thoughts and are burdened. Later, he said to them, "If I find boldness before God, I will ask of Him that I always remain with the synodia in spirit." After he said these things, he dismissed all of them, except for Dometian, who stayed with him for three days; and on Saturday evening, the great Efthymios reposed in peace and departed to the heavenly bliss, a presbyter full of days, at the age of ninety-six on the 20th day of January, in the year 473.[19]

---

[19] "That night in the coenobium of Saint Gerasimos, young Kyriakos, who was then serving as cook, was staying up to clean vegetables for the fathers, when, about 11:00, Gerasimos summoned him to put on his cloak and sandals and follow him. When they came near Jericho, Kyriakos asked what was happening, and Gerasimos told him that about the third hour of the night he had seen a lightning-flash from heaven to earth, which remained as a pillar of light from earth to heaven, and had been told it was the soul of Efthymios being taken up." Chitty, p. 96.

The Saint's Burial

News of the holy man's repose spread throughout the countryside. The result was that a vast multitude of monks and layfolk assembled, including Patriarch Anastasios with his entourage of ecclesiastics and military men. Chrysippos and Gabriel were there, and so were Pheidon the deacon and all the anchorites of the desert along with the great Gerasimos. In other words, so great a multitude of people gathered that it was impossible for the priests to entomb the holy relics. When the patriarch realized that it was the ninth hour of the day, he ordered the soldiers to turn the people away by force. As this was done, they were, with great difficulty, finally able to perform the traditional service of the divine fathers and to place the great athlete's most venerable relics on the blessed bier, while chanting the appropriate hymns and praises. Everyone wept and lamented the loss of the great Efthymios. Martyrios and Elias especially mourned inconsolably, and the patriarch comforted them, promising that he would always send them the necessary assistance for the maintenance of the brotherhood.

But his genuine disciple and emulator of his virtues, Dometian, who had served him for fifty years, never left the tomb of his teacher. Seven days later, the venerable Efthymios appeared to him, bright and radiant, saying, "Behold, God has deemed us worthy of this: that we rejoice together eternally as we were inseparable in the transitory life. Come and receive the glory and honor that have been prepared for thee." Dometian made this known immediately to the brethren and, with joy, departed to the heavenly mansions and was buried with honor by the fathers. Later, the patriarch returned with many followers and, with deep reverence, took up the holy relics of Efthymios; and, with lighted candles and incense, they brought the relics to the structure that he had erected and placed them securely within a sacred receptacle, so that no one would be able to take any part of them.

The Saint's Appearance

You should know this, O brethren, of the holy Efthymios: by nature he was inherently mild-mannered and resolute; he was of fair complexion; his cheerful face was round and comely, graceful in age; his beard was long, down to his thighs, and even lower. All his parts were healthy and sound; none of his bodily members were missing, not even his teeth. He was born, as we indicated, according to divine revelation and was dedicated to God in the third year of his life and, at the age of ninety-six, was translated to the heavenly bliss.

But let us recount a few of the miracles that he performed after his holy repose, including an exceptional and incomprehensible one of which Hierodeacon Pheidon was the recipient, and because of which the lavra of the saint became a coenobium. Attend, therefore, to the entire matter, so that you will perceive how great the authority of Saint Efthymios is before God.

Pheidon the Deacon

One year after the repose of the saint, the pious Emperor Leo[20] also reposed and was succeeded by his grandson Leo (the son of his daughter by Zeno), who was but a child, and who lived only one year, leaving as successor his father, Zeno. However, Zeno was driven from the throne by a plot of the overbearing Basiliskos, who became a tyrannical ruler and adhered to the heresy of Eftyches and Dioscoros, believing that Christ has only one nature, and uttered other blasphemous things about Him, which the holy Fourth Œcumenical Council anathematized. In those days, the leaders of that heresy assembled in Jerusalem and elected their own patriarch. In the meantime, Zeno gathered constituents from Isauria and came to put Basiliskos to death and to seize his throne. The Patriarch Anastasios had reposed by then, and Martyrios (478-486) sat on his throne. Martyrios sent a letter to

Saint Efthymios the Great

Emperor Zeno and to Patriarch Akakios of Constantinople concerning the aforementioned heretics, to censure them, so as to prevent scandals. Therefore, he gave the letters to Deacon Pheidon, who went to Joppa. Upon finding and boarding a ship there, he sailed on its maiden voyage on the open seas. But he was caught in a storm, and the ship capsized. Some of the people drowned, while others clung to wreckage. He also seized some wreckage and managed to stay afloat, but with great difficulty, anticipating an almost certain death.

---

[20] This was Leo I, the Thracian, also called the Great, who reposed in 474. He was declared a saint and is commemorated by the holy Church on the 20th of January for his struggles in behalf of the Church.

As he grieved in this misfortune and excessive exhaustion, which was dreadfully painful, Saint Efthymios came to his mind, and he cried out in faith to him thus: "O saint of God, Efthymios, hasten and save me from this difficult danger!" And as he prayed in this manner, he saw the saint walking on the waves, and saying to him, "Fear not, for I am Efthymios, the servant of the Lord Christ, and know this, that God was not pleased with the journey which thou hast made, and this is why thou wast shipwrecked. Therefore, return to him that sent thee, and tell him not to be concerned about the schism of the Aposchists;[21] for, in a few days, before his repose, there will be a union in the Church, and all the Jerusalemites will have one shepherd and leader. Go to my lavra and level all the cells from the foundations and create a coenobium there where the cemetery is, as it is the will of God that the lavra become a coenobium." After this, the great Efthymios took off his mantle and covered him, snatching him up at once. Pheidon at once—O the wonder!—found himself on land; moreover, in the midst of the holy city of Jerusalem. Then he removed Saint Efthymios' cloak, whereby he had traversed the sea like an eagle, and put on his usual clothes.

One miracle followed the other, for the mantle was seized again by an invisible hand, and vanished. Pheidon, meanwhile, meditated in secret over what had occurred and how he was rescued from that great danger. Thereupon, he glorified God and thanked the wondrous Efthymios, saying, "Now I see that the great Efthymios is a true servant of God!" He also related this to the patriarch, who marvelled, saying, "A true prophet was the God-inspired Efthymios. Everything that has taken place at the lavra had been foretold by the holy man before his repose!" After this, he ordered Pheidon to do as the saint commanded, and he gave him every assistance. Within a short period of time, they constructed the coenobium with all the required necessities. But as they attempted to consecrate the church, they lacked water. In those areas, it rained only in winter, and the water that gathered in crevices in between rocks served their needs for the remainder of the year. During summer there was a severe shortage of water.

To this end, they brought mules from many directions to carry water, but at midnight, the great Efthymios appeared to Hegumen Elias and said to him, "Why hast thou not entreated the Lord to send thee water, O thou of little faith, but instead thou hast burdened the pack animals? From the jawbone of an ass [Judg. 15:19], God caused water to spring forth and quenched the thirst of Samson, and from the surface of the rock He satisfied

---

[21] The Aposchists were heretics who were cut off from the Church because they did not recognize the canonical clergy, nor did they accept the holy Mysteries and holy Traditions, that is, the sign of the Cross, icons, etc.

a disobedient and ungrateful people—the Israelites [Num. 20:8]; believest thou that He will leave thee helpless at such a time? Fear not, for within three hours, all the ditches shall be filled with water." He awakened and revealed the vision to the others. Straightway, a great cloud appeared in the heavens, and it rained so much that they did not need any water except what had fallen. The miracle was heard of throughout the desert. Therefore, Archbishop Martyrios went there, and they held a vigil and performed the consecration on the 7th of May. In the holy Table, they placed the relics of the Martyrs Provos, Tarachos, and Andronikos.[22] At that time, it was twelve years since the repose of Saint Efthymios.

After all this, Pheidon became bishop of the city of Dora.[23] Patriarch Martyrios assembled all the bishops and monks, and peace returned to the church according to the prediction of Saint Efthymios. At the monastery of the saint, after the repose of the blessed Elias, Symeon became hegumen, but lived for only three years. Later, the monastics elected Stephen from Arabia, who had a brother named Prokopios, who donated six hundred gold pieces to the monastery.

Caesarios and Leontios

A certain prefect by the name of Caesarios came to the holy city and fell gravely ill. The doctors could not help him, so he went to the tomb of Saint Efthymios. After Caesarios was anointed with oil from his lamp, he was immediately cured. Therefore, he donated to the Church all the gold that he could find. He furthermore promised to donate other large sums. After returning to his house, he went to Tripolis and disclosed this miracle to Bishop Stephen. Meanwhile, the bishop's nephew, Leontios, younger in age, as he heard this, felt contrition in his soul and, from divine love, forsook the world and every physical pleasure and went to the Monastery of Saint Efthymios, where he was tonsured. Thereafter, he became not only the hegumen, but also successor to the see upon his uncle's repose. At the monastery, they voted for another hegumen by the name of Thomas. Out of piety, Caesarios came again to worship at the monastery of the saint, and they opened the sacristy so that he could venerate the holy Cross and other precious relics.

---

[22] Martyrs Provos, Tarachos, and Andronikos at Tarsus (304) are commemorated by the holy Church on the 12th of October.

[23] Dor or Dora was a fortified city in Palestine which lay in the foothills of Mount Carmel near the modern town of Tantoura. At the time of the Canaanites, it was the seat of a king, and during the Christian period, the seat of a bishop.

Theodotos the Monk

A certain brother, Theodotos, a Galatian by birth, while serving in the sacristy, saw the six hundred pieces of gold donated by Prokopios and, overcome by avarice, stole the gold with such cunning that no one noticed it. On the next day, he pretended that he was going to a secluded place, but left and went to Jerusalem. While he was passing by the Monastery of Martyrios, he took out fifty florins from the sack and hid the rest under a great rock, marking the spot. Later, he went to Joppa, where he rented a team of horses and then returned to the rock where he had hidden the treasure and—behold God's judgment!—he saw a terrifying and awful sight. Under the rock there was a dreadful and frightening serpent which, as if it were ordered to keep watch over the gold, would not permit him to approach, and he left in terror. Later, he returned again, but always found that terrible sentry of the gold, who was vigilant and advanced toward him, driving him away so that he could not come near.

The final time that he attempted to approach, he was struck by an invisible force as if by a heavy club. From this, he fell to the earth nearly dead. Certain Lazariotes, who were on their way to Jerusalem at the time, found him and lifted him up and brought him to the hospital. As he lay there for many days, he fell asleep and saw an elderly man who was very angry and said to him, "If thou dost not return the money that thou hast stolen from the monastery, thou wilt never get well!" Then he summoned the innkeeper and confessed the sin. When the matter was disclosed to the hegumen, he went to the holy city and took Theodotos and carried him back on a mule to the rock. Behold the true miracle! That terrible guard, as it caught sight of the true owners of the treasure, withdrew, leaving them to take what was theirs. Theodotos, meanwhile, was immediately cured, recovering completely.

Kyril of Skythopolis

"Thomas served as hegumen for eight years and reposed on the 25th of March, having lived altogether seventy years. After the repose of Thomas, Leontios assumed the direction of the brethren in those days, and I (Monk Kyril of Skythopolis) was there and wrote this biography, as a lamb of that flock. Thereupon, all that the holy fathers told me about the wonderful Efthymios, I did not conceal his wonders from their children or the next generation. Now I will write of all the miracles that I witnessed with my own eyes, and from which I became convinced of the previous ones.

Paul the Possessed

"In the sixteenth year of the Emperor Zeno, I put on the holy Schema and went to Jerusalem to worship at the holy places, where I found John the Hesychast; and I asked him where I should go to find salvation for my soul. As I inquired of him, he sent me to the Monastery of the holy Efthymios. At that time, the aforementioned Leontios was hegumen, and he received me gladly. While I was there, a certain monk, a Cilician by birth, whose name was Paul, was possessed of a demon. He was from the Monastery of Martyrios, and his relatives had brought him to the tomb of Saint Efthymios, who appeared to him at midnight and at once cast out the demon. After the monk was healed, he came to the Orthros service and chanted with me. The monks of Martyrios heard this, and they came to take Paul, because he was tonsured in their monastery. However, Paul was so grateful to the great Efthymios that he did not wish ever to leave the coenobium of the saint. Therefore, he remained and served us all with eagerness. Hearken to another similar story.

Two Cisterns

"At a distance of two stadia from the coenobium, we had two cisterns. The saint had constructed them, one of which he gave to the Hagarenes, whom he had baptized, and the other was left to us. But in the summer, it was always locked, as there was a dearth of water. On a certain occasion, a barbarian went to the cistern to water his camels, but finding it locked, he was incensed and, with a single rock, smashed the gate. Immediately he was demonized, and he fell down foaming at the mouth and rolling on the ground. After a while, the barbarian was brought to the monastery by a Christian named Thalavas, who related the matter to us. Therefore, I felt pity for the barbarian; so we took him and carried him to the tomb of the saint, who had punished him for his audacity, for he was the only one who could cure him; and again, through his philanthropy he bestowed healing. However, the barbarian received much more than that, for not only was he cured in body, but his soul was enlightened by divine grace, and he accepted holy Baptism.

"Furthermore, the saint also cured the niece of the above mentioned Thalavas of a foul demon, when she was brought from Bethany and drank a little sanctified water.

"The son of a certain Hagarene named Argod was grazing his sheep when a vehement demon entered into him and tormented him. He lost his mind and suffered distortion to his eyes and face. They also brought him to the tomb of Saint Efthymios, and he was cured within a short period of time.

The Woman of Vitavoudisa

"A woman from the village of Vitavoudisa, who wed, was possessed by a furious demon that tormented her for seven months. Her husband was very sad and, not having any other recourse, brought her to the monastery and left her outside, as women were not permitted within. She stayed there for three days fasting and praying. Finally, Saint Efthymios appeared to her saying, 'Behold, thou hast been cured. Therefore, return to thy home.' And straightway, she found herself totally healthy and departed, glorifying God and thanking the saint. Not only then did she do so, but every year she also went to the monastery with gifts; however, she remained outside kissing the earth with much piety. She also received the brethren into her home, offering them hospitality as she could.

Prokopios the Monk

"Another brother who was with us, named Prokopios, was by birth a Galatian of noble lineage. Before he became a monk, he was possessed by a demon that secretly tormented him. But when he came to the tomb of Saint Efthymios and put on the rason, then the demon revealed itself, as a thief is exposed by light. The unfortunate Prokopios began to rend his flesh, and he fell to the ground tormented dreadfully and became speechless. But the saint had compassion on him and in turn healed him from that demonic madness and also loosened the bonds of his tongue. He is with us to this day, not only healthy, but also adorned with prudence and patience, bearing the wonderful yoke of Christ, according as he has been able.

A Stranger at the Gate

"How can I not mention the miracle that happened to the stranger that came on a certain day, as we sat at the monastery gate working at our handicrafts? He shouted aloud, as he was tormented by a demon that cried out saying, 'Why dost thou drag me before my enemy who persecutes and burns me? What is there between thee and me, O servant of God? Where art thou taking me by force? I will not come out from here!' After he said this, he threw him before the gate, and he lay there before them that saw him, a most lamentable sight. As we witnessed this, we felt pity for him, and, with difficulty, I lifted him up with the help of the doorkeeper, Babylas, and took him to the saint's sepulcher. And he cried again, saying, 'Alas! I shall not go with you, but I will depart from this man, and will never enter him again!' As we arrived with much difficulty at the tomb of the saint, the demon shook him again and tore at him so severely that he remained speechless throughout the night. But in the morning—behold the miracle!—he was found healthy and of sound mind, so much so that everyone was amazed. I then asked him why he shouted the previous day, creating such a disturbance. He said that he remembered nothing: neither how he came there, nor that he had created any disturbance.

Romanos the Monk

"From the village of Vetagavaion, there was a priest in the monastery by the name of Achthavios, who was with us for forty-five years and who kept the commandments of God with diligence and precision. This priest had a brother, named Romanos, in that village, which is near Gaza, who was spiritually poor and impious of soul, but according to temporal life rich and prosperous. For this he was envied by some, and they attempted to harm his progress through sorcery. As a result, he fell grievously ill and suffered from dropsy. He lay at home, moaning and distended with water, so that the physicians gave up on him, and his friends mourned over him as one at death's threshold. As he lay in this dreadful state awaiting death, he made a sign to them that stood around him to leave the room, and then he turned to the wall and, like another Ezekias [4 Kgs. (2 Kgs.) 20:2], with contrition of heart, he prayed, 'O Lord of Hosts, look down, look down upon me and deliver me from this dreadful calamity and need by the intercessions of Thy servant Efthymios!' As he said this, he saw an elderly monk with a white beard who said, 'I am Efthymios whom thou hast called upon. I am come to cure thee of thine ailment. Be not cowardly, but show it to me.' Thereupon, Romanos uncovered his stomach. The saint then made an incision with his fingers and cut away the infected part, as if with a scalpel. Out of his stomach, he excised an object shaped like a tin horseshoe with distinct markings, and he showed it to the ailing man, placing it on the table before him. He then closed the incision, thereby curing him altogether. Afterward, he revealed to Romanos the sorcerous plot and cautioned him to strive diligently for the salvation of his soul, lest he should suffer unto the ages. He also said, "This has happened to thee, Romanos, because thou hast neither attended church nor received the Mysteries for a long time. Someone has hired demons against thee, who prevailed against thee on account of thy negligence." Then Romanos arose, healthy and joyful, and cried out to his relatives, telling them of the miracle; and he came to us also, and related to his brother the priest the great benefaction, which the saint had performed on his behalf. In addition, he still commemorates him every year to the glory of God."

Kyriakos the Perjurer

"I did not wish to mention a certain wonder that was wrought recently, fearing that some people might not believe it, as being adverse to the loving-kindness of the saint. But, I write it as an example, in order to instill fear into whomever swears falsely. In a village called Faran, situated toward the east, there was a shepherd by the name of Kyriakos, to whom an impoverished neighbor entrusted ten sheep to watch along with his own. Not long afterward, a need arose, and the poor man had to sell his sheep; so he asked Kyriakos for them, but the latter returned only eight, keeping the other two for himself. The poor man demanded that he give back all his sheep, but Kyriakos insisted that he was given only eight to tend. The poor one continued, 'If thou art willing to take an oath before Saint Efthymios, I do not care if I lose them!' Kyriakos consented to do so; and, as they approached the tomb, the one who had been wronged, seeing that the other was about to perjure himself, feared the iniquity and said, 'Let us turn back, brother, for it is as if thou hast already taken the oath.' Yet, that senseless one did not turn back, but he approached the sacred reliquary of Saint Efthymios and took a false oath audaciously and later returned to his house. As he lay in bed the following night, it appeared to him that the door opened and a monk came in with a rod in his hands, followed by five young men. Suddenly, the entire house was filled with infinite light. The saint, with a stern look, shouted at him, 'O vain one, how darest thou take a false oath on the tomb of Efthymios?' And Kyriakos became speechless and unable to answer. The saint then ordered four of the young men to seize him and gave the rod to the fifth one saying, 'Strike him with all thy might, that he no longer dare scorn God and perjure himself and take what does not belong to him!' After they had thrashed him sufficiently, the saint took hold of the hand of the youth, so that he would no longer strike Kyriakos, and said to the perjurer, 'Didst thou not know, unrighteous one, that there is a God and that He judges the unrighteous on earth justly? He imposed this punishment upon thee, not for thine own good, as tomorrow thou shalt die and others will take what thou hast gathered unjustly; but for the correction of others, to escape the peril of perjury and, furthermore, even to avoid the taking of a truthful oath according to the commandment of the Lord [Mt. 5:33-37].'

"After the holy one had said these things, he departed, but Kyriakos was unable to bear the pain and began to cry out. His neighbors gathered round, and he showed them the wounds, confessing the perjury and begging them to take him to the tomb of the saint, that he might take pity upon him, as a disciple of the all-loving Christ, and cure him. As they stood about and beheld the terrible sores, they were frightened and would not lift him, so they filled two sacks with straw and placed him between them, and thus they transported him to the monastery. They related the whole matter to us in detail and showed us the frightful wounds that he had sustained. They that saw or heard of this wonder were terrified, and no one dared take an oath on the saint's tomb again, true or false. After two days, the relatives of Kyriakos observed that he was near death, as his stomach burst open, and he vomited continually. They took him back to his house, and the next day he died.

"These are a few of the many marvels that the great Efthymios performed, as we have witnessed them with our eyes and have heard from many others. And I too received much help from him and great benefit of body and soul, and witnessed numerous miracles that occurred daily at his tomb, which I did not record, for the sake of brevity. For this reason, I often wondered in astonishment, saying, 'How did God bestow so much authority on Saint Efthymios?' Therefore, I asked many ascetics of this desert who knew him and spoke with him many times, and also with Saint Savvas, and they narrated to me all that I wrote earlier, to the glory of God Who is wondrous in His saints."

About the Author

At the conclusion of the life of Saint Efthymios, his biographer, Kyril of Skythopolis, adds, "May they that read this account forgive me if my style does not suit them, for Bishop John the Hesychast (commemorated by the holy Church on the 3rd of December) urged me to do this; and I, being aware of my unworthiness and meager knowledge of letters, did not dare to attempt what was beyond my powers, and remained idle and fruitless. I sojourned in the lavra for two years after I had been instructed to do this work, desiring all the while to write this salutary account, but again I was hesitant for the above mentioned reason and besought God with tears to enlighten me.

"One day, as I sat on a chair in sadness, I had a scroll in my hands but did not know how to commence, and was overcome by sleep. It was the second hour of the day, and in my vision I beheld the divine Savvas and the great Efthymios wearing the same garments. Saint Savvas said to Saint Efthymios, 'Behold thy Kyril, who clasps the papyrus roll in his hands and still has not begun to write!' And Saint Efthymios replied, 'How can he fulfill such a task, if divine grace does not descend upon him from above and guide him?' The blessed Savvas continued, 'Do thou bestow upon him that grace, O holy father!' Then the great Efthymios put his hand in his bosom and took out a handsome silver alabaster phial, into which he dipped an instrument having a flat blade, and drew a trace of liquid three times and put it in my mouth. It appeared like olive oil, but in taste—behold the divine grace!—it was so sweet that if I likened it to honey, I should understate its worth. Then, from the untold delight, I awakened, and traces of that divine flavor were still in my mouth. And as I was filled with the divine and sublime pleasure, I began the present edifying narration; and after I finished that of Saint Efthymios, I wrote that of Saint Savvas, by whose intercessions may we be deemed worthy to emulate both of them as much as possible; may we become partakers of their glory through Jesus Christ our Lord, to Whom is due all glory, honor, and worship, with the Father and the Holy Spirit, unto all ages. Amen."

**On the 20th of January, the holy Church commemorates
the holy Martyrs BASSUS, EUSEBIUS,
EUTYCHIUS, and BASILIDES, Senators of Rome.**

Bassus, Eusebius, Eutychius, and Basilides, the holy martyrs, flourished during the reign of Diocletian (298). They were men of wealth and rank, holding the office of imperial senators. They came to believe in Christ and received holy Baptism, since they had witnessed the struggles and

martyric feats of Theopemptos, Bishop of Nikomedia, who is commemorated
by the holy Church on the 5th of January. Though the holy hierarch manfully
endured many terrible tortures at the hands of the unbelievers, yet with the
power of Christ he wrought marvellously before Diocletian and his minions.
Thus, when the four Christians, Bassus, Eusebius, Eutychius, and Basilides,
were denounced before Diocletian, they too appeared bravely before him and
confessed Christ as God. Consequently, Diocletian deprived them of their
belts, a sign of their exalted office. He then subjected them to heinous
punishments, which only brought shame to the persecutors.

(L. to R., top to bottom):
The Martyrdoms of
Saints Eusebius, Eutychius,
Bassus, and Basilides

Saint Bassus was cast inside a pit up to his thighs.[24] The executioners
then severed his hands and then cut up his entire body, thus causing him to
breathe his last. Saint Eusebius ended his life in martyrdom when he was
suspended upside down and the torturers chopped him to pieces with an axe.
Saint Eutychius completed his contest when he was stretched between four
stakes and hacked into three parts. Saint Basilides surrendered his soul when
his abdomen was torn open with a knife. Thus, all four confessors received
the crowns of martyrdom.

---

[24] In the *Painter's Manual* (p. 76) of Dionysius of Fourna, Saint Bassus is described
as an older man and the others as younger men with incipient beards.

On the 20th of January, the holy Church commemorates the holy Martyrs INNAS, PINNAS, and RIMMAS.

Innas, Pinnas, and Rimmas, the holy martyrs, were from a certain land situated in the northern regions.[25] After converting many Goths, they were detained by barbaric idolaters who brought them before the chief of their place. When it was observed that the holy ones professed Christ, they were commanded to deny Jesus and burn incense to idols. The three martyrs answered, "We worship neither wood, nor marble, nor stone. Our Lord Jesus Christ is God through Whom all things were made." Thereupon, they were condemned to end their lives exposed to the cruel elements of cold weather. The saints were bound together in an upright position upon wood and thrust into the midst of the river Danube. Now it was wintertime, when congealed water and slippery ice could not support their mass of motionless weight. As they endured those freezing depths, their souls were at peace and warmed by the grace of the Holy Spirit. Thus, by this fierce torment, the blessed ones, in the second century, surrendered their souls into the hands of God and received the crown of martyrdom.[26]

The Martyrdoms of Saints Innas, Pinnas, and Rimmas

---

[25] The *Synaxarion* of the *Menaion* for January records that they were from a land nearby the Arctic region (Athens: Apostolike Diakonia, 1979). Bishop Nikolai Velimirović (*The Prologue From Ochrid*, Part One, p. 81) writes that they were of Slavic origin and disciples of the Apostle Andrew. They are reputed to be the first group of Slavic martyrs recorded in ecclesiastical history. See Father Daniel Rogich's *Serbian Patericon*, p. 145.

[26] The three saints had already reached a great age when they became martyrs on the other side of the Danube, near Varna (Bulgaria) on the west shore of the Black Sea. See Velimirović, loc. cit.

**On the 20th of January, the holy Church commemorates
the Blessed PETER the tax collector.**[27]

**On the 20th of January, the holy Church commemorates
the holy Martyrs THYRSOS and AGNES.**

**On the 20th of January, the holy Church commemorates
the most pious Emperor LEO the Great,
who was called Makelles and Thracian.**

Leo I, called Makelles ("the Butcher") or "the Great," became emperor on the 7th day of February, in the year 457. He was of Bessian origin, born in Illyrian Dacia ca. 400. He had been a low-ranking officer, commanding a garrison in Selymbria, a city of Thrace on the north shore of the Sea of Marmara: hence his other surname, "the Thracian."

An event which took place before he became emperor is worthy of repeating here. The Life-giving Spring (Zoodochos Pege), the ancient sanctuary of the Virgin, located outside the Theodosian walls, was opposite the Silivri Gate. It had miraculous waters with curative powers. Before Leo had become emperor, on one occasion as he was walking and meditating in the forest surrounding the city, he met a blind man who was thirsty. Leo attempted to lead him to water in the forest but was unable to find any. As he searched for water in the forest, he suddenly heard a voice from on high saying, "Emperor Leo, thou shalt find water deep in the forest. Wash the blind man with this water, and thou shalt behold the power of the Lord." Leo was amazed, not only because of the voice, but also because he had been addressed as "Emperor Leo." He obeyed the voice and found the spring. As he bathed the eyes of the blind man, the sufferer received his sight. Leo was astonished by this and the course of events that eventually led him to the throne of the vast Byzantine Empire.[28]

---

[27] The account of the Blessed Peter is given in its entirety in the Life of Saint John the Merciful, Archbishop of Alexandria, who is commemorated by the holy Church on the 12th of November [see our *November Synaxaristes* (in English)]. Blessed Peter lived during the time of Justinian I (530). He reposed peacefully in the Lord at Constantinople in his old home. He was interred in a place called Voos.

[28] The shrine that was eventually built grew in fame, and thousands made pilgrimages there to receive healing from their illnesses. Afterward, when Emperor Justinian (527-565) was healed, he also built a church and monastery at the Spring, which received its name "Life-giving" in the 11th C. At that time, a pilgrim from Thessaly died before reaching the Spring. His dying wish was to be anointed with water from the sacred Spring and then buried in the forest nearby. His fellow travelers fulfilled his request,

(continued...)

Now Leo had been in the service of Aspar and his son Ardabourios, functioning as a *kourator* or manager of estates. Aspar, an Alan, representing the Germanic soldiery, had been consul, *patrikios*, and *magister militum*. He also exercised considerable influence over the eastern court after the death of Emperor Marcian in January of 457. Since Aspar was an Arian, he could not hope to attain to the throne himself, so he secured the elevation of Leo, whom he thought he could manipulate. Leo was crowned by Patriarch Anatolios (449-458), in the first case of imperial coronation by a patriarch. Before his crowning, Leo was married to Verina. Together they had two daughters, Ariadne and Leontia, and a son who died in infancy. Leo's reign saw many disasters, including earthquakes and the great fire in the capital (465). He lowered taxes and curbed official abuses. He prohibited working and trading on the Lord's day. The maritime expedition of 468 against the Vandals failed on account of his commander and brother-in-law Basiliskos.

By 468, Leo began extricating himself from the tutelage of Aspar and the Ostrogoths, employing the warlike Isaurians and their chieftain Zeno, which alliance caused a rupture between Aspar and Zeno. Leo married his daughter Ariadne to Zeno in 466. Aspar's son Patricius received the hand of the emperor's second daughter, despite his Arian leanings. He was made heir presumptive and received the title of Caesar. Anti-German feeling in the capital, however, put an end to any further ambitions. In 471, Aspar and his son Ardabourios were assassinated, while Patricius was wounded and fled. He was divorced from the emperor's daughter and stripped of his rank as Caesar. Predictably, Zeno and Isaurian influence dominated. When Leo I reposed in 474, he was succeeded by his grandson Leo II, the son of Ariadne and Zeno, with Zeno as co-emperor. The autumn of that same year, the young boy died, leaving his father as sole possessor of the throne.

Orthodox tradition depicts Leo I and his wife Verina as pious sovereigns, devoted to the Virgin Theotokos. They ordered a gold *soros* (reliquary casket) for a relic from Palestine of the Virgin's maphorion (veil), which is a garment covering the head and shoulders. He commissioned an icon of the Virgin enthroned, being venerated by members of the imperial family. Leo had installed the Virgin's mantle in a round chapel adjoining the

---

[28](...continued)

but after anointing he returned to life. Since that time, the Spring has become known as Zoodochos Pege or Life-giving Spring. Today it is outside the ancient walls of the city. Adjacent to this shrine is a Greek Orthodox hospital, Valoukli, for the sick and afflicted. Though the church has been destroyed many times by both earthquakes and Muslims, it was always rebuilt. The Church has appointed the Friday after Pascha for the feast of its dedication.

Church of the Virgin of Vlachernai. The chapel was known as Hagia Soros, which was inaccessible to layfolk.[29]

**On the 20th of January, the holy Church commemorates
the holy Martyr ANNA of Rome, who desired the noetic Bridegroom.**

**On the 20th of January, the holy Church commemorates
the holy New-martyr ZACHARIAS, who suffered martyrdom
in Old Patras of the Peloponnesos (1782).[30]**

Zacharias, the new athlete, was from a village of the Arta district.[31] An incident occurred wherein he renounced Christ and became a Moslem, for which he left for ancient Patras.[32] Since he was a furrier by trade, he established a workshop in which he manufactured furs. He kept hidden away a book, entitled *The Salvation of Sinners* (*Amartolon Sotiria*), which he oftentimes read. This book brought him to utter contrition, causing him to cry bitterly for the evil he had committed. Therefore, he fervently implored our Lord Jesus Christ to grant him the chance of salvation. Upon questioning a Christian friend, he learned that there was a virtuous and experienced father confessor in the area. At night he paid him a visit and confessed his sin, together with his intention to make a public appearance professing Christ Whom he had previously denied. The spiritual elder answered, "Although thy thoughts have captured and occupied thy heart, we must not hastily put them into action. The devil has the custom of frequently deceiving people by 'approaching from the right' and suggesting good thoughts. Therefore, let us put these thoughts to the test, my child, to see if thy thoughts verily are from God. Go to thy shop and immure thyself for forty days in constant prayer and fasting. Read the book thou hast in thy possession. I, too, will do the same in my cell, out of my love for you. Then we shall meet again."

Zacharias received the advice of the elder gladly. He shut himself in his shop and hastened to fulfill the elder's commands. However, he could not contain himself for more than twenty days. A flame was ignited in his heart,

---

[29] See *The Oxford Dictionary of Byzantium*, s.v. "Leo I" and "Aspar" and "Pege"; G. Ostrogorsky's *History of the Byzantine State*, pp. 56, 57.

[30] The Life of this new-martyr was taken from the *Neon Martyrologion*, and incorporated into *The Great Synaxaristes* (in Greek).

[31] Arta (ancient Ambrackia), capital of the state of Epiros of northwestern Greece, is a mountainous area between the Pindos and Ionian Sea. Arta fell to the Ottomans in 1449.

[32] Patras, a city in the northwestern Peloponnesos, is at the mouth of the Gulf of Corinth. The city fell to the Turks in 1460.

which brought him to the loftiest height of love for Christ. Zacharias was inspired with an unquenchable desire to be sacrificed for his Christ's holy name. (Indeed, if it were possible to live ten lives, Zacharias would have offered them all up to our Savior.) He therefore went to his confessor. Falling before the elder's feet, with hot tears rolling down from his eyes, he began saying, "Father, bless me to go to martyrdom; for I can no longer withstand the fire which burns in my heart." The confessor replied, "The time has not yet come." Zacharias continued, "Father, it has come, and it has passed. It is a great sin to hinder me." Then the elder asked him to confess all his transgressions which he had committed in his lifetime. Zacharias stood erect with his hands crossed and compunctionately confessed all his sins. Nevertheless, the elder found him quite pure (except for the denial) and even worthy of the priesthood.

Again, the elder, as a practical and prudent man, thought it judicious to test Zacharias. Therefore, he ordered him to sit down as he addressed him, saying, "Consider well, my child, the consequences of what thou art about to undertake, because from the time of the war, when the Albanians overran the Peloponnesos,[33] they taught the native Turks a diversity of tortures to inflict upon the Christians. Frankly, the tortures mentioned in the lives of the ancient martyrs are not to be compared with those executed by the odious Albanians. Therefore, do not think that whensoever thou shouldest appear before the authorities, they will cut off thy head at once. Nay, thou must think of everything that thou wilt encounter. Unless it is too late, I tell thee, my child, give up this idea which thou hast conceived, so as not to merit greater punishment and bring us temptation and trouble. It is possible to obtain thy salvation through more secure means. I promise thee that thou wilt find forgiveness for thine apostasy; for there is no sin which cannot be vanquished by the compassion of God." The blessed Zacharias smiled while the elder said these things. Then he felt slightly gloomy, sighing from the depths of his heart, and commented, "I marvel, father, that with the profound wisdom thou dost possess, thou dost speak the words of small children. I have come to the point where I have dedicated my entire being to my Christ, so that I no longer

---

[33] In this case, the author refers to the catastrophe that visited the Peloponnesos from Albania after the revolt of 1769. The Sublime Porte (Pasha's Gate) sent Albanians to the Peloponnesos to suppress the insurgents. For one decade, these Turko-Albanians caused terrible destruction and oppressed both Christians and Turks to such a degree that the Turkish admiral, Gazi-Hasan Pasha, was dispatched against them. He was accompanied by a Greek interpreter of the fleet, Nicholas Mavrogenes. After extreme difficulties, Gazi-Hasan Pasha succeeded in annihilating the Albanians, assisted by armed Greeks, to liberate the Peloponnesos from that fearful scourge.

belong to myself, but to Christ. I exceedingly thirst to suffer for His love, so much so that I am desirous of receiving more punishments than those thou hast indicated were practised by the Albanians. Therefore, I implore thee to give me thy blessing to go forward, because I can no longer endure the flame which burns in my heart."

The spiritual father glorified God that the saint was, by God's grace, divinely inspired. He read the prayers of absolution according to the order of the Church. Then, after chrismating Zacharias, he administered the holy Mysteries. Thus the elder strengthened Zacharias with spiritual food and armed him with spiritual weapons. Together they recited the Supplicatory Canon to the most holy Theotokos. The elder then blessed and sealed him with the sign of the life-giving Cross and sent him off with instructions not to censure in excess the religion of the Turks, because it was important that he make a denial of that religion with as few words as possible while declaring himself a Christian. Thereupon, the saint kissed the elder's right hand and left for his workshop. First he sold all his belongings, the value of which he gave to the poor, keeping only five and one-half piasters and some change. Then he went to his landlord's residence, giving him the rent and the shop's key. Straightway he headed for the municipal judge, saying to the Christians he met on the way, "Forgive me, my brethren, and may God forgive you as well."

As the saint rushed to the judge's quarters, he chanced upon a poor youth on the way who did not possess a belt, so Zacharias took off his own silk belt and gave it to the lad. Then he purchased a piece of rope with the change he had left and used it as a belt. Zacharias arrived at the judge's quarters and entered his house saying, "Long life to thee, effendi!" The judge was acquainted with Zacharias, because he used to make his furs, and addressed him: "Where is thy *selam*, *zavalli* Mehmet?[34] Come up here and sit down. Tell me, what has happened to thee?" Blessed Zacharias answered with much authority and courage, saying, "I am not Mehmet, but Zacharias. I had been deceived and denied Christ, the true God, in Whom I believed from the cradle until the day I accepted your religion. But now that I have come to my senses, recognizing that I was deceived, I have come before you to deny your religion and to put on Christ, Whom I had disdained. Therefore, take back these white clothes and dispatch your officer to the poll tax bureau (*harac*)[35]

---

[34] *Selam* means greetings or salutations. The Turkish epithet *zavalli* means poor, miserable, or unlucky. As for Mehmet, that was Zacharias' Muslim name.

[35] *Harac* was the poll tax bureau for the tribute paid by foreign countries and non-Muslims.

to bring me a certificate stating that I am a *raya*[36] of our sultan of many years, like the rest of my fellow Christians."

Observing the martyr's daring, the judge attempted to lure him with flattering words: "My child, Mehmet Pasha, if something unfortunate has happened to thee and thou hast lost thy bearings, I am prepared to call upon the aghas (lords) that we may assist thee as much as possible. Only do thou tell me, what is in thy heart?" The martyr replied, "I, effendi, sold all my belongings and gave them to charity. Therefore I do not need white clothes." The judge interrupted and said, "Then thou must be drunk." The martyr answered, "May Christ bestow my heart's desire. It has been three days since I put anything in my mouth—that includes bread, water, or the usual coffee. There is no other reason why I am doing this, except that which I told thee in the beginning. So take the white clothes that I have put on thy desk and send them to the tax bureau that I may obtain my certificate." When the judge saw Zacharias' irreversible stand, he sent him to the civil authority under custody with a letter explaining everything. The martyr appeared in his presence and said the very same things that he had said to the judge.

After that, the civil authority summoned the aghas and apprised them of the situation. They decided to put Christ's confessor in jail. They would take him out three times a day and harshly beat him with rods in the courtyard, until he should either return to Islam or expire from the torture. They wished to avoid spilling any blood, so that the Christians might not rush in and take the soil which was soaked with his blood. The Turks knew that a disturbance would ensue if they restrained or threatened the Christians from gathering the soil. Thus they spoke and meted out. Meanwhile, the martyr of Christ was lashed and beaten about the stomach and chest with a slungshot, which was a small, heavy weight attached to a thong, used by Ottoman soldiers as a weapon. Undaunted, he remained adamant and unshakeable in the Faith of Christ. Not only did he do this, but in a joyous spirit he also recited unceasingly within himself the prayer, "Lord Jesus Christ, Son of God, have mercy upon me who denied Thee, and help me." One day, at dusk, the blessed one was tortured to such an extent that he could not recite the prayer any longer, but only raised his eyes heavenward as he was beaten without mercy.

Finally, the chief officer in charge of the Turks, who was called Bouloumbases, ordered the jailor to torture the Christian to the utmost during the night, so that he would expire, and so that they would not have to afflict him any longer with torture. The jailor at once put the saint's feet in the

---

[36] *Raya* was a term denoting the non-Muslim subjects of the Ottoman Empire, which literally means "cattle people."

stocks and tormented him exceedingly. Then he climbed up to a bed where he was elevated and sat there to eat his supper. The martyr, in the meantime, lay in dire pain and exclaimed, "Alas!" In response, the jailor said to him, "Wait till I drink all my wine, O infidel, and I will sever thy limbs one by one." The martyr replied, "If thou art a real man, do not only talk but act; so that I might owe thee a favor." Enraged by the words of the martyr, he climbed down and stretched Zacharias' feet on the rack to such an extent that he tormented him intensely, and then he clambered back up again to finish his supper, threatening to cause him worse pain later. At this point the martyr of Christ shifted a little, and wrenched his spine. Then he made the sign of the Cross over his entire body and said with a great voice, "Lord, into Thy hands, I commit my spirit." He then surrendered his holy soul into the hands of God, to acquire the imperishable crown of martyrdom. The year was 1782. Straightway—lo, the miracle!—the jail was filled with an unspeakable fragrance; so much so, that the jailor was put to shame and left that part of the jail without a word and retired to another area in order to sleep.

At dawn, the Christians learned that the saint had completed his martyrdom. They were all filled with joy and glorified God. The bishop sent people to the governor, demanding that they turn over Zacharias' relics for burial. The latter said, "He is neither one of you, nor one of us, because he ridiculed both religions. Therefore he is not worthy of burial." Immediately, the governor ordered two soldiers to bind the holy relics by the feet and drag them through the streets to a dry well near the Church of the Holy Trinity. As the saint was dragged through the streets, his arms lay open. Even when he was dropped into the well, he landed upright on his knees. The following night the Christians saw a radiant light over the well. They hastened, making a clamor, to venerate the saint and to observe him. When the Turks heard the commotion, they sent men to cut grass and shrubs and throw them into the well. Then they brought dirt and soil and filled the well. The saint remained secure in that state. By the intercessions of the New-martyr Zacharias, may God save and have mercy upon us! Amen.

Through the intercessions of Thy Saints,
O Christ God, have mercy on us. Amen.

**On the 21ˢᵗ of January, the holy Church commemorates
our venerable Father MAXIMOS the Confessor.**[1]

Maximos, our holy father, a Constantinopolitan, was born in 580 to a prosperous and pious Orthodox family of noble lineage. His baptismal name was Moschos.[2] From an early age, Maximos displayed good conduct and a pure disposition. He was provided with an education in philosophy, rhetoric, and grammar. Possessed of a sharp mind and diligent character, he learned his lessons quickly. In short, he was prepared for a career at the Imperial Court. The young Maximos successfully

Saint Maximos the Confessor

completed his curriculum, excelling in expounding upon the philosophical and theological foundations of Orthodox spirituality. He pursued what was good and useful, leaving behind what was injurious and useless to the soul. His soul was smitten with divine love. He only wished to please God. He was humble-

---

[1] The Life of this ever-memorable saint was recorded in Greek by Saint Symeon the Metaphrastes, whose manuscript begins, "Herakleios held the scepter of the Roman Empire...." The text is extant in the Athonite monasteries of the Great Lavra, Iveron, and in other places.

   The text was revised and edited for incorporation into the *Neon Paradeison*. At the aforementioned monasteries, there is extant a sermon of Saint Maximos, which begins, "All those who wish to conduct their lives according to God...."

   The Life herein is taken from *The Great Synaxaristes* (in Greek), and *Maximos the Confessor* (in Greek), compiled by Hieromonk Efthymios and synodia from the Kellion of Saint George at Kerasia, Mount Athos (1997).

   The text is extant in *P.G.* 90:109-129, which includes Saint Maximos' explanation in the senate and before the *sakellarios*; in *P.G.* 90:131-133, which regards the Monk Anastasios, Saint Maximos' disciple; and, in *P.G.* 90:135-172, which includes the dialogue between Saint Maximos and Bishop Theodosios.

   The translation of Saint Maximos' relics is commemorated by the holy Church on the 13ᵗʰ of August. The right hand of Saint Maximos is venerated today at the Monastery of Saint Paul on Mount Athos.

   See also the 20ᵗʰ of September, when Saint Maximos and his disciples (Anastasios, Anastasios, Theodore, and Efprepios), together with Saint Martin, are commemorated by the holy Church.

[2] Moschos, from two Greek synonyms, means "calf or young bull" or "musk."

minded and moderate. He was not puffed up due to his family's nobility. He was not proud on account of his own wisdom and virtue.

By the time Maximos reached his early thirties, he achieved a respected name in the senate for his competence in government matters. Herakleios had heard good reports of Maximos and therefore retained him as a secretary, entrusting him with official palace documents. He became head of the Imperial Chancellery or First Secretary to Emperor Herakleios (610-640).[3] He would often take counsel with Maximos, on various matters. Now the emperor was an able general, who was married twice: first to Fabia-Evdokia and then Martina. He fought the Slavs, Avars, and Persians. In 627, Herakleios invaded Persia, overthrew Chosroes II, and recovered the true Cross which had been captured by the Persians. Immediately following the recovery of the relic of the true Cross, after an eighteen-year war with the Persians, the atmosphere at the Byzantine court was zealous.

Maximos also lived and flourished under Herakleios' successors: Herakleios Constantine III (641),[4] Heraklonas (641),[5] and Constans II Pogonatos (641-668).[6] The patriarchs of Constantinople during that time

---

[3] Herakleios was the son of the exarch of Carthage and Epiphania. He fought the Slavs and Avars. In 636, the Arabs invaded Syria and crushed the Byzantines at Yarmuk. Herakleios commanded the army in person, but was unable to resolve religious disputes. Monoenergism seemed to him to be only a middle way between the Chalcedonians and Monophysites. *The Oxford Dictionary of Byzantium*, s.v. "Herakleios."

[4] Herakleios Constantine was the son of Herakleios and Fabia-Evdokia. Upon the death of his father, he inherited the throne with his half-brother Heraklonas. His stepmother, Martina, opposed him. He died in 641.

[5] Heraklonas or Herakleios II was the son of Martina and Herakleios I. Heraklonas was co-ruler with his half-brother Herakleios Constantine. Upon the death of Herakleios I, Heraklonas ascended the throne, but his mother ruled *de facto*. She attempted to remove Herakleios Constantine. Her chief adviser was Patriarch Pyrrhos. She upheld a Monothelite policy. Opposition from the senate and troops in Asia Minor brought about the surrender of her son. Heraklonas had his nose slit, an impediment to taking up the scepter. He then left with his mother and brothers for exile in Rhodes. *Oxford*, s.v. "Heraklonas."

[6] Constans II Pogonatos was the son of Herakleios Constantine and Gregoria. He became sole emperor after Heraklonas and Martina were deposed. He was continually occupied with the empire's external enemies: Arabs, Slavs, and Lombards. His religious policy was an attempt to put an end to the Christological arguments. His *Typos* angered the western bishops, which brought about the trials of both Pope Martin and Saint Maximos. He was murdered and then buried in the Church of the Holy Apostles in Constantinople. *Oxford*, s.v. "Constans II."

included Sergios I (610-638),[7] Pyrrhos (638-641),[8] Paul II (641-653),[9] Pyrrhos (second term, 654), and Peter (654-666).

In 638, the imperial power was again attempting to direct the dogma of the Orthodox Church for its political advantage. Prior to this, there were three religious movements in an attempt to find a solution to the problem of the God-Man relationship in Jesus Christ. All were compromises and heretical: Monophysitism, Monoenergism, and the eventual refinement, Monotheletism (Monothelitism). Imperial involvement in the Church lay in the need for stability in the realm. There was significant turmoil among the various Churches of Rome, Alexandria, Antioch, Jerusalem, and Constantinople. Emperor Herakleios had strived to reorganize and ready his empire for a counter-offensive against the Persians, by issuing administrative and military reforms. He had grave concerns about the loyalty of the Monophysites in the Middle East province. He suspected that they might turn to the Persians or to the Arabs. Thus a dogmatic formula acceptable to the Monophysites was invented by Patriarch Sergios, who chose to obey the imperium rather than Church tradition.

Thus, while Maximos was in the imperial service of Emperor Herakleios, the heresy of Monotheletism, first defended by Patriarch Kyros of Alexandria (631-642)[10] and then Patriarch Sergios of Constantinople (610-638), seems to have drawn Emperor Herakleios into its nets.[11] From 626

---

[7] Patriarch Sergios I had crowned Herakleios and attempted to dissuade him from marrying Martina, the emperor's niece, deeming it incestuous. When several of their children were retarded, it was deemed a divine judgment. He approved the use of church treasures for the Persian expedition. Sergios was later condemned at the Synod of 680 for Monotheletism. *Oxford*, s.v. "Sergios I."

[8] Patriarch Pyrrhos supported Monotheletism and confirmed the *Ekthesis*, which brought him formidable adversaries in Stephen of Dor in Palestine, Maximos the Confessor, and Pope John IV (640-642). The conflict was further intensified with the arrival in the exarchate of Africa of Monothelite refugees from Egypt. With the death of Herakleios and the banishment of Martina, the emperor's second wife whom he supported, he departed for Carthage. He returned to Constantinople and resumed a second patriarchate which lasted only a few months. He was condemned at the Synod of 680. *Oxford*, s.v. "Pyrrhos."

[9] Paul II was a Monothelite who supported Constans II. Paul could not achieve a compromise with anti-Monothelite Popes Theodore I (642-649) and Martin I.

[10] Kyros, Patriarch of Alexandria, former Bishop of Phasis in Kolchis, was an initiator of Monoenergism, through which he reached an accord with some Monophysites, despite resistance from Sophronios, future Patriarch of Jerusalem.

[11] The *Great Synaxaristes* (in Greek) reports that Herakleios was misled by Patriarch Athanasios (594-630) of the Jacobites, followers of Jacob Baradaeus (d. 578), who

(continued...)

until 633, Saint Sophronios, Maximos' spiritual father, who was located in a
monastery near Carthage, guided his studies on the Chalcedonian doctrine,
the confirmed Orthodox confession in the Synod of 451 which upheld two
natures, distinct and unmingled, within the person of Christ. Saint Maximos,
within three years of his appointment in the imperial service, began to have
fears that he might be led astray. In order to better understand the diverse
parties and beliefs at that time, we include a brief history.

Historical Background

In the seventh century, two theological movements dominated talks
in political and Church circles: Monotheletism and Monoenergism. Monotheletism, from the Greek words meaning "one will," was bequeathed the
problems inherent in Monoenergism "one energy." This novel phrase "a
single will (*thelima*)" in Christ was proposed by Patriarch Sergios I and
developed by his supporters Patriarch Makarios of Antioch (656-680/681) and
Patriarch Pyrrhos. Sergios tried to enlarge a theological compromise to
promote unity in the empire. Together with Kyros of Phasis, the future
Patriarch of Alexandria, and Theodore of Pharan, he developed the formula
of Monoenergism in 633. It was later altered into the concept of one will in
Christ (Monotheletism). His alliance with Pope Honorius I (625-638) and the
idea of one will in Christ formed the foundation of the *Ekthesis*. Herakleios
viewed Monotheletism as a means of compromise and unity between
Chalcedonians and Monophysites.[12] Prior to these movements, the Fourth
Œcumenical Synod, held in the Church of Saint Ephemia of Chalcedon in
451, defined Christ's two natures as inviolably united without confusion,
division, separation, or change, in one person or hypostasis.

With a view to unifying his subjects, in 638, Herakleios proclaimed
the *Ekthesis* or exposition of the Faith. It was a document penned by Patriarch
Sergios, who clearly attempted to end disputes concerning Monoenergism, by
forbidding any discussion of the energy in the person of Christ. The formula
asserted by those who thought as Sergios was that the two natures of Christ

---

[11](...continued)
were Syrian Monophysites. Jacob Baradaeus had been a disciple of Monophysite
Bishop Severos (d. 538) of Antioch. When Herakleios was in Verea (Berroia) of Syria
(present day Aleppo of Syria), Athanasios, with twelve of his bishops, went to meet
the emperor.

[12] The Monophysites, from the Greek words meaning "one nature," had two responses
with regard to the divine and human nature. The followers of Eftyches accepted a
doctrine of the union of natures, whereas the moderates, as Severos of Antioch,
construed the *physis* (nature) as close to the concept of *prosopon* (person) or hypostasis
and saw in Christ a new *physis*, possessing both perfect divine and human qualities.
Oxford, s.v. "Monophysites."

were joined by a single will (free will). The formula of "one will" had been proposed by Pope Honorius in a letter to Sergios. The *Ekthesis* was accepted by local councils in Constantinople (638 and 639). Saint Maximos, the major opponent to one will in Jesus, elaborated upon the concept of a variety of wills: the natural will, a property of nature, desires good; free will (*proairesis*) involves a choice and therefore presupposes the possibility of error or sin; finally, *voulesis* is imaginative desire (*phantastike orexis*).[13] Christ, having two natures, had to have two natural wills. Herakleios soon perceived that his attempt to reconcile the parties was futile. The compromise was rejected by the Chalcedonians, headed by Saint Sophronios I of Jerusalem (634-638). Staunch Monophysites also rejected the *Ekthesis*. It would be in 648 that Constans II would withdraw the *Ekthesis* and replace it with the *Typos*. Later, the *Ekthesis* was condemned at the Third Synod of Constantinople in 680.

Monoenergism, from the Greek words meaning "one energy," assumed that Christ had a single energy attributed to His individual hypostasis. This idea had been implied in Monophysitism, which presumed that one nature presumed a single activity. Patriarch Kyros of Alexandria, in 633, attempted to reconcile the parties on the basis of the formula "the single Christ and Son operating as God and man in the single theandric activity."[14] Sophronios, future Patriarch of Jerusalem, resisted the formula. When he became Patriarch of Jerusalem (634-638), he single-handedly protested, in his enthronement speech and synodical epistle, the doctrine of Monoenergism or the Monothelite heresy to the Patriarch Kyros and Patriarch Sergios. During his discussions with Patriarch Sergios I of Constantinople, they came to a compromise: Both phrases "single activity" and "two activities" were prohibited. Instead, one had to speak of "the single Son acting upon both divine and human things." Pope Honorius approved of the compromise. Sophronios soon brought up discussions against it. However, since the *Ekthesis* of Herakleios in 638 banned the *energeia* formulas, the debate devolved upon the problem of the single will or Monotheletism.[15]

The *Typos*, an imperial edict of Constans II, was drafted in order to mollify opposition to the *Ekthesis* and end debate over Monotheletism. It was Patriarch Paul who persuaded Constans II to sign the *Typos*. Monotheletism was not directly condemned in the *Typos*, but the text of the *Ekthesis* was ordered removed from Hagia Sophia. The *Typos* did not define official dogma. It forbade discussion of Christ's wills and energies. It commanded

---

[13] *P.G.* 91:13B.
[14] Mansi 11:565D.
[15] *Oxford*, s.v. "Monoenergism."

acceptance of Scripture and the doctrinal definitions of the five œcumenical synods.

The Saint's Renunciation and Writings

Maximos took courage in the words of the psalmist: "For better is one day in Thy courts than thousands elsewhere. I have chosen rather to be an outcast in the house of my God than to dwell in the tents of sinners [Ps. 83:10, 11]." He, therefore, resigned his post and repaired to the Monastery of the Theotokos at Scutari,[16] across the Bosporos, that he might fulfill his love for quietude and prayer. He received the monastic tonsure and the name Maximos, and became thoroughly engaged in the ascetical life. He overcame the tyranny of the passions by daily meditation on the holy Scriptures and study of the writings of the holy fathers. Clad in but a hair shirt, he mortified his flesh with hardships, vigils, and all-night prayers. He was held in high regard among the brotherhood of that monastery, surpassing all the brethren in ascetic struggles. After a few years, when the superior of the monastery reposed, a vote was taken. Father Maximos was then asked to take up the office of hegumen. The ever-memorable one wished to avoid that rank and the governance of the brethren. He deemed it a most heavy burden. Out of love, he accepted the office. He now no longer had the care of his own soul's salvation but also that of others, which role he took seriously in the knowledge that he would answer for his charges before Christ. All now looked upon Father Maximos as their rule and standard. The divine man knew this and ceased not in every time and place teaching his disciples by deed and words. At times he was gentle and at times he was stern, depending on the time and situation, that he might instruct in that which was needful and profitable. The holy man spent twelve years at the Theotokos Monastery. His many ascetical contests, and practise of silence and contemplative prayer, trained him to meet future great trials. The man of God also meditated upon the great mystery of our Lord's dispensation regarding man's salvation and divinization, and the recapitulation[17] of all things in the Christ [Eph. 1:10].

---

[16] Chrysopolis in Bithynia (Scutari, modern Üsküdar) is a harbor on the eastern shore of the Bosporos, and a suburb of Chalcedon.

[17] Saint Maximos the Confessor: "The human race, having the power to naturally unite every division at the mid-point of every extreme, was last introduced into the world of beings as a sort of natural link,...in itself bringing into one all things that are segregated in nature,...so as to unite everything in a comprehensive unity in God—as Cause. Humanity has its own division (i.e., into female and male), but in its dispassionate relationship with divine virtue, there is no division....Thus did the incarnate Jesus cancel the difference between male and female and the partitioning of nature....'There is neither male and female; for ye are all one in Christ Jesus [Gal.

(continued...)

Maximos had come to be known as "Maximos the Wise" not only among fellow monastics, but also with the diplomats and government officials with whom he had served. He would now prepare to defend the apostolic Faith through God-inspired words. In both the east and west, he is acknowledged as the most significant theologian of his times. He expounded and acted upon the traditions handed down to him, that is, Mysteries, divine offices, Scriptures, synods, saints, and writings of the fathers.

Saint Maximos in Kyzikos

In the year 624, Father Maximos began preaching about the hypostasis of Jesus Christ, the Logos of God. He had a constant disciple, Father Anastasios, who would accompany him even to martyrdom. Now on account of the Monothelite heresy, Father Maximos left Scutari and dwelt in the small Monastery of Saint George at Kyzikos.[18] In that sacred precinct, he produced many spiritual works. The most influential of his early writings were *The Ascetic Life*, a catechetical piece on the two great commandments,[19] and *The Four Centuries of Love*, consisting of practical discourses on the Christian life and prayer, and the practise of the virtues. Father Maximos taught that the virtues are natural. By nature we have an appetite simply for what is good. Nature impels us to desire and move toward obtaining these virtues. They exist in all men because of the identical nature of men, but we do not all practice what is natural to us to an equal degree. With regard to asceticism, he comments that it was devised in order to ward off deception, which establishes itself through sensory perception. When deception is completely expelled, the soul immediately exhibits the splendor of its natural

---

[17](...continued)

3:28].'...With our complete nature, He united it all, having demonstrated the convergence of the entire creation into one, in Himself, according to His own most sovereign and complete Rationale (*Logos*), which is entirely undivided and unsevered. And He first united us in Himself by the removal of the difference between male and female; and, in place of men and women, He properly and truly exhibited just human beings—entirely transfigured to become like Him and bearing His integral and completely authentic image (icon)....Thus did He divinely recapitulate everything in Himself, having shown the entire creation to exist as one....Now the whole creation can reveal itself as having one and the same wholly undifferentiated rationale (*logos*), based on its Creator." [*P.G.* 91:1305B-1309D.]

[18] Kyzikos, present-day Balkiz near Erdek, a city on the southern coast of the Sea of Marmara.

[19] "Thou shalt love the Lord thy God with all thy heart, and with all thy soul, and with all thy mind, and with all thy strength. This is the first commandment. And the second is like this: Thou shalt love thy neighbor as thyself [Mk. 12:30, 31]."

virtue.[20] Father Maximos perceived the Scriptures as foretelling man's purpose, since it was God Who said, "Let Us make man according to our image and likeness....And God made man, according to the image of God He made him, male and female He made them. And God blessed them....And God saw all the things that he had made, and, behold, they were very good [Gen. 1:26-28, 31]." Saint Maximos said that we are taught to speak to ourselves of the grace of adoption. In his commentary on the Lord's Prayer, *Our Father*, he writes that "we are also taught to speak to ourselves of the grace of adoption, since we are by grace worthy to call Father the One Who is our Creator by nature. Thus by respecting the designation of our Begetter in grace, we are eager to set on our life the features of the One Who gave us life. We sanctify His name on earth in taking after Him as Father, in showing ourselves by our actions to be His children."[21]

While dwelling at Kyzikos, Father Maximos began to expound upon the union between God and man through the person of Jesus Christ, the Logos of God. Moved by His infinite love for mankind, the Logos condescended to unite Himself to our nature, which had been separated from God and divided against itself by means of self-centered love. "'Christ took hold of the seed of Abraham. In all things it behooved Him to be made like His brethren, that He might become a merciful and faithful High Priest in things pertaining to God, in order to be made an expiation for the sins of the people. For having Himself been tempted in that which He suffered, He is able to help those who are tempted [Heb. 2:16-18].' Now His divine power has 'freely given to us all the things for life and piety, through the full knowledge of Him Who called us by glory and virtue, by which He hath freely given to us the very great and precious promises, that through these ye might become partakers of the divine nature [2 Pe. 1:3, 4].' God made us so that we might become 'partakers of the divine nature' and sharers in His eternity, and so that we might come to be like Him [1 Jn. 3:2] through divinization by grace. It is through divinization that all things are reconstituted and achieve their permanence; and it is for its sake that what is not is brought into being and given existence."[22]

In his work, entitled *Four Centuries of Love*, our holy Father Maximos makes clear in the first letter, "First Century," that a Christian trains in love (agape): "Love is a good disposition of the soul by which one prefers no creature to the knowledge of God. It is impossible to attain to a

---

[20] See "The First Opuscule (ca. 645-646): A Dogmatic Tome to Marinos the Priest," *The Theological and Polemical Works*; and *Disputation with Pyrrhos*, Nos. 85 and 95.
[21] Saint Maximus, *Selected Writings: A Commentary on the Our Father*, § 4, p. 106.
[22] Saint Maximos the Confessor, *First Century on Various Texts*, ¶ 42, *The Philokalia, the Complete Text*, Vol. II:173.

lasting possession of such love if one has any attachment to earthly things." Saint Maximos encourages us, writing: "Love is begotten of detachment, detachment from hope in God, hope from patient endurance and long-suffering; and these from general self-mastery; self-mastery from fear of God; and fear of God from faith in the Lord."[23] In the "Second Century," he instructs us that "pure prayer is from one who truly loves God and so prays entirely without distraction."[24] In the "Third Century," Saint Maximos reminds one of the Christ-like response to passions, for example, resentment, by saying: "If thou dost harbor resentment against anyone, pray for him and thou wilt prevent the passion from being aroused; for by means of prayer thou wilt separate thy grief from the thought of the wrong he has done thee. When thou hast become loving and compassionate toward him, thou wilt wipe the passion completely from thy soul. If someone regards thee with resentment, be pleasant to him, be humble and agreeable in his company; and thou wilt deliver him from his passion."[25]

In the "Fourth Century," he wrote: "The one who loves Christ thoroughly imitates Him as much as he can. Thus Christ did not cease to do good to men. Treated ungratefully and blasphemed, He was patient; beaten and put to death by them, He endured, not thinking ill of anyone at all. These three are the works of love of neighbor, in the absence of which a person who says he loves Christ or possesses His kingdom deceives himself."[26]

As an important sign that we are beginning to free ourselves from self-love, we practise loving our enemies. "Why did the Lord give you the command to love your enemies, to bless those who curse you, to do well to those who hate you, and to continue praying for those who persecute you [Mt. 5:44]? To free you from hatred, grief, anger, and resentment, and to make you worthy of the supreme gift of perfect love. But you cannot attain such love if you do not imitate God and love all men equally. For God loves all men equally and wills that all men be saved and come to a full knowledge of the truth [1 Tim.2:4]." [27]

God, in His divine providence, began preparing Saint Maximos as a confessor first through his ascetic labors and compassionate works as a writer. As his baptized name, Maximos, implies "greatest," so were the depths and effects of his expositions on the transforming power of contemplation of divine love—the purpose for which man was created. His later works included

---

[23] "The First Century," *The Four Hundred Chapters on Love*, ¶¶ 1, 2.
[24] "The Second Century," ¶ 1.
[25] "The Third Century," ¶ 90.
[26] "The Fourth Century," ¶ 55.
[27] "The First Century," ¶ 61.

Questions to Thalassios, Books of Difficulties (commentaries on difficult passages in the holy fathers, especially from Saint Gregory the Theologian and Saint Dionysios the Areopagite), *Mystagogia* (Eucharist as the cosmic Liturgy leading the entire universe to perfection in Christ, the God-Man "Theanthropos"), and *Centuries on Theology* and the *Incarnate Dispensation*. For Saint Maximos, as for all the holy fathers, many heretical ideas were confounded by the Scriptures. Basing his treatises on holy tradition, Saint Maximos would often refute heresies (Apollinarian, Nestorian) by enlisting the help of Saint Gregory the Theologian and Saint Irenaeos. He stated in his defense of the God-Man Christ: "For that which He has not assumed He has not healed; but that which is united to His divinity is also saved. If only half of Adam fell, then that which Christ assumes and saves may be half also; but if the whole of his nature fell, it must be united to the whole nature of Him Who was begotten, and so be saved as a whole."[28]

Saint Maximos would continue to clarify throughout his life that a man-made or composite Christ was not of God nor to be found in the Scriptures. "The incarnation," he wrote, "is the ineffable and incomprehensible hypostatic union of the divine and humanity. This is the great and hidden mystery. This is the blessed destiny for which all things have been constituted....It is the cause of all things and caused by none of them. With this purpose in view, God brought into being the substances of all things. This is the primary object of the prescience and for thoughts according to which all things made by God are recapitulated in Him [Eph. 1:10]. This mystery encloses all the ages, showing forth the infinite great counsel of God that surpasses infinity and preexists the ages eternally....For Christ and in the mystery of Christ, all the ages and all things in them received their being and purpose. The union of the limitation and limitlessness, of measure and measurelessness, of finiteness and infinity, of the Creator and creation, of stillness and motion was deliberated prior to the ages. And in the last days, this union was revealed in Christ, in itself giving fulfillment to the foreknowledge of God."[29]

On account of Christ's two natures, fully human and fully divine, He could neither sin nor choose something in error as being good, because in His divinity He knows what is truly good. "I hold," Saint Maximos wrote, "that, according to nature, the humanity of the Savior is no different from our own, but it is the same in essence without any differences, because He took it from our nature by the ineffable assumption from the undefiled virginal blood of

---

[28] Saint Gregory the Theologian, "Epistle 101: To Kledonios the Priest Against Apollinarios."

[29] *To Thalassios, P.G.* 90:620, 621.

the most holy Theotokos. United to this blood, as to a seed, the Logos became flesh, without ceasing to be God by essence. He was thus made perfect Man, sin only excepted. We, however, often rebel against and oppose God by means of the faculty of will, which in our case inclines both to the one side and to the other; but He, being by nature free from all sins, as being not a mere man but enhominized God, has nothing in Him that opposes God. He has rather preserved our nature undefiled and completely pure. It is as He Himself said, 'The ruler of this world is coming, and hath nothing in Me [Jn. 14:30]'; that is to say, nothing of the things whereby we demonstrate the opposition of our will to God, thus distorting our own nature....To confirm the truth of this enhominization, He became, and voluntarily did, all things for our sake, not repudiating our essence or any of the natural and innocent things that belong to it. Rather, He divinized it with all its characteristics, entirely permeating it through the union and becoming one with it without confusion by means of the one unique hypostasis, rendering it totally capable of acting in a divine way. Therefore, the humanity that is proper to Him differs from that which is ours, not in the rational principle of its nature, but in the new mode of its genesis. For it is the same as ours by essence but it is not the same in its seedless generation. It is not the nature of a mere man, but the human nature of God the Logos Who was enhominized for our sake. In the same way, His human will was a genuinely natural will just like ours. But it was molded in a divine manner which transcends us."[30]

Father Maximos frequently agrees in his treatises with the writings of Saint Gregory the Theologian and Saint Dionysios the Areopagite,[31] concerning natures, wills, and the establishment of the rationale for our existence. No other Church father before him had treated the subject so deeply regarding the doctrine of the incarnation and human freedom and of its union with God in Christ. It only remained for Saint John of Damascus to present it later in a more accessible manner.

Saint Maximos in Carthage (646)

Father Maximos desired to depart from among the heretics who had established themselves in Constantinople. He wished to live among those who firmly preserved the Orthodox Faith. As a youth, he had considered living in Jerusalem, but with the Saracen invasion of Palestine, he was compelled to alter his course for Old Rome. As he grieved in spirit and wept incessantly for the state of the Church, he heard that the Monothelite heresy had been completely rejected in the west. He was resolved to depart, despite the fact that the brethren of his monastery were sorrowed by those tidings. Father

---

[30] *Theological and Polemical Works* 4, *P.G.* 91:57D–60D; see *Free Choice*, 170.
[31] Saint Dionysios, *P.G.* 3:716A, 716C, 732CD.

Maximos counseled them sufficiently and strengthened them in true piety. The brethren did not wish to appear disobedient, so they did not attempt to thwart him; for both they and he perceived his departure was God's will.

As Father Maximos traveled toward his goal, he stayed in the north African region of Carthage, finding opportunities to confirm the Orthodox bishops there in the Faith and to avoid heresy by all means. To some who were far away, Father Maximos sent letters. He taught all with love and clarity of thought. He urged the faithful to shun the words and writings of the heretics, who laid subtle linguistic snares. He also advised the faithful not to succumb to promised perquisites by the government as a reward for compliance. While still producing many of his most spiritually profitable works (634-645), Saint Maximos entered the dogmatic struggle in support of his spiritual father, Saint Sophronios of Jerusalem.

Patriarch Pyrrhos, a favorite of Herakleios, had been hegumen of the monastery of Chrysopolis before he mounted the throne of Constantinople. He supported the Monothelite program of Sergios and confirmed the *Ekthesis*. With the death of Sergios, Pyrrhos became Patriarch of Constantinople in 638. Then with the death of Herakleios in 640, he was succeeded by Herakleios Constantine, the son of his first wife Fabia-Evdokia. But then Constantine died of poisoning by his stepmother Martina, who would have her own son Heraklonas rule. Pyrrhos elevated her son to the throne. After six months, those opposed to mother and son cut off Heraklonas' nose and slit Martina's tongue, which were deemed impediments to the scepter. They were then exiled to Rhodes. Then Constans II, the son of Herakleios Constantine and grandson of Herakleios, popularly known as Pogonatos for his thick beard, ascended the throne. Pyrrhos as a result was most unpopular with the people on account of his support of Martina and Heraklonas. Consequently, when her party lost, he laid his episcopal attire on the altar of Hagia Sophia and left for Carthage, without having been canonically deposed. When the Monothelite Patriarch Paul II could not achieve a compromise with Popes Theodore I (642-649) and Martin I, the exarch of Carthage, named Gregory, contrived to use this conflict to gain the support of Pyrrhos. Gregory organized a disputation between Pyrrhos and Maximos.[32] Father Maximos, basing his proofs on Scripture and the holy fathers, decisively demonstrated that as Jesus has two natures, so there must also be two wills and energies (operations), though indivisible in the one person.[33]

---

[32] *P.G.* 91:287-354.

[33] "*Gnomie* is nothing else than an act of willing in a particular way, in relation to some real or assumed good, that is, a gnomic use of will implies that the willer can err

(continued...)

The discussion then turned to Jesus in Gethsemane, when He prayed and said, "O My Father, if it is possible, let this cup pass from Me; however, not as I will, but as Thou wilt [Mt. 26:39]." In Saint Maximos' disputation with Pyrrhos, he explained this passage: "Since the God of all hath Himself become Man without change, it follows that the same One not only willed appropriately as God in His divinity, but also willed appropriately as man in His humanity. For the things that exist came to be out of nothing, and have therefore a power that impels them to hold fast to existence, and not to non-existence, which power is simultaneously an inclination towards that which naturally maintains them in existence, and a drawing back from things destructive to their existence. Consequently, the super-essential Logos, by virtue of His humanity, had of His humanity this self-preserving power which clings to existence. And in fact, He exhibited both aspects of this power, willing the inclination and the drawing back on account of His human energy. He exhibited the inclination to cling to existence in the natural and innocent use He made of a great many things, and the drawing back at the time of the Passion, when He drew back from the voluntary death. The Church confesses that along with His human and created nature, there existed also in Him those principles inserted creatively in that nature by Him, without which that nature could not exist....Fear is proper to nature when it is a force that clings to existence by drawing back from what is harmful, but it is contrary to nature when it is an irrational dread. The Lord did not have that type of fear that is contrary to nature....Rather, He assumed, as good, that which is proper to nature and which expresses that power, inherent in our nature. Those natural things of the will are present in Him, but not exactly in the same manner as

---

[33](...continued)

as regards what is good, ultimately choosing what appears or is assumed to be good, rather than solely what really is good....Thus, those who say that there is *gnomie* in Christ, as this inquiry is demonstrating, are maintaining that He is a mere man, deliberating in a manner like unto us, having ignorance, doubt, and opposition, since one only deliberates about something that is doubtful, not concerning what is free of doubt, that is, perfectly or certainly known. By nature we have an appetite simply for what by nature is good, but we gain experience of the goal in a particular way, through inquiry and counsel. Because of this, then, the gnomic will is fitly ascribed to us, being a mode of employment (of the will), and not a principle of nature, otherwise nature itself would change many times (with the change of its principles). But the humanity of Christ did not simply subsist in a manner similar to us, but divinely, for He Who appeared in the flesh for our sakes is God." *Disputation with Pyrrhus*, Nos. 85-95.

they are in us. Thus, He truly was afraid, but not as we are, but in a mode surpassing us."[34]

Saint Maximos also discussed how each nature, divine and human, demonstrated its proper energy, by means of the miracles from the Gospels. "These—the resuscitation of the child, or the restoration of sight to the blind, or the blessing of the loaves of bread, or the cleansing of the leper—were effected by means of an omnipotent word and decree, and also corporeally by the sense of touch, as was proper to each nature, so that He might demonstrate that the flesh was life-giving flesh in that it was truly His own, and not that of any other, in its unmixed union with Him. The divine energy was made known in His deeds in both of these—I mean the command and the touch—and did not in any way impair the natural, passable, human energy of the flesh proper to us....For the stretching out of the hand, the touch, the grasping, the mingling of spit and clay, the breaking of bread, and simply, anything which is brought to pass by the hand or any other part or limb of the body, proves the existence of the natural energy of Christ's humanity. Accordingly, He Who is by nature God Himself was active also as man, naturally working divine things, so that through both He might be believed to be both perfect God and perfect Man—sin only excepted—both being subject to true demonstration." [35]

At the symposium, African bishops were also in attendance. Father Maximos so successfully defended the Faith against the ex-patriarch and monoenergistic Pyrrhos, that Pyrrhos not only repented of heresy and

---

[34] Saint Maximos, *The Disputation with Pyrrhus*, ¶¶ 33, 35, pp. 16-18.

Elsewhere Saint Maximos writes: "What do you suppose the prayer indicates? Dread or courage? The highest agreement of His human will with the divine will or its utmost separation from it?...The sentence, 'However, not as I will, but as Thou *wilt* [Mt. 26:39],' excludes all opposition, and demonstrates the union of the human will of the Savior with the divine will of the Father, since the whole Logos has united Himself essentially to the entirety of human nature, and has divinized it in its entirety by uniting Himself essentially to it....Since He had become what we are for our sakes, He spoke these words in a manner fitting to His humanity, to God the Father, because He, Who was by nature God, had as man a faculty of will wholly in accord with the Father's will. Wherefore, according to both natures from which, in which, and of which His hypostasis was constituted, He was made known as desiring and effecting our salvation: On the one hand, as consenting to it with the Father and the Spirit; on the other hand, the human as becoming obedient unto death, to the Father, even the death of the Cross, Himself bringing to pass the great mystery of the œconomy towards us by means of the flesh." See *Theological and Polemical Works*, 6, *P.G.* 91:65B-D, in *Free Choice*, 172.

[35] *The Disputation with Pyrrhus*, ¶ 187, p. 64.

confessed Orthodoxy but he also composed a book confessing the Orthodox Faith and the synods. Pyrrhos offered to go to Rome that he might place his written anathema against Monothelitism on the tomb of the apostles. Pyrrhos' confession of the true Faith, however, was temporary. When the Emperor Constans II sent for Pyrrhos, as a "dog returned to his vomit [2 Pe. 2:22]," Pyrrhos recanted his confession of Orthodoxy and became worthy of the anathema which the holy fathers subsequently laid upon him and his fellow Monothelites. Pope Theodore I responded to the apostasy of Pyrrhos by excommunicating him immediately and condemning Paul II, his successor to the throne of Constantinople.

Following the excommunication of two Constantinopolitan patriarchs, imperial reaction in the person of Constans II was swift and lethal. The emperor feared that an open breach with Rome could destabilize the political situation in the empire, especially after the invasion of Egypt by the Arabs. Thus, Constans II published the *Typos* in 648, forbidding all Christians, on pain of severe punishment, to discuss two natures and two wills in Christ. This vile document ushered in the persecution of Christians, especially the monks and friends of Father Maximos.

Saint Maximos in Rome (648)

Thereupon, Saint Maximos went to join Pope Martin I in Rome. Upon reaching land, he walked to Rome, undergoing much hardship. Constans II wanted Pope Martin to approve of the *Typos*, but he refused saying, "If the entire world should embrace the new heresy, I would not. I will never renounce the doctrines of the Gospels and the apostles, nor the traditions of the holy fathers, even if I am threatened with execution." Saint Maximos had found papal support for the defense of Orthodoxy during these Christological and imperial crises. Neither the late Pope Severus of Rome (d. 640) nor his successor Pope John IV (d. 642) had accepted the imperial *Ekthesis*. The latter pope had even anathematized it. However, it was Father Maximos' friend, Pope Martin I, who would suffer imperial persecution for defiantly convening a council on the advice of Saint Maximos. Martin had previously served as papal *apokrisiarios* (legate or delegate) in Constantinople and all along had supported Father Maximos. When he was elected pope, Martin did not receive confirmation from Emperor Constans II.

In October of 649, at the Lateran Basilica, Pope Martin convened a synod, during which sessions both the *Ekthesis* and *Typos* were condemned as heretical pieces of work. Present at this council were Saint Maximos, Bishop Stephen of Dor of Palestine, and thirty-six Greek abbots and monastics. Reaction to the document was strongest in the west. The text is preserved in the acts of the Lateran Council. In spite of the presence of the exarch Olympios, that council denounced the *Typos*, excommunicated

Patriarch Paul, and issued a letter to Constans which blamed the patriarch for endorsing Monotheletism. The synod's Latin acts bear the signatures of one hundred and six bishops who condemned the *Ekthesis* and *Typos*. Hence, the doctrine of Chalcedon was reaffirmed. Though personal condemnation of Emperors Herakleios or Constans did not take place, their heretical decrees were formally condemned and many heretics anathematized. Constans considered opposition to the *Typos* as treasonous. This charge would be prominent in the trials of both Pope Martin and Maximos the Confessor.

Though the *Typos* forbade any further discussion, Saint Maximos defied the royal edict and energetically continued the fight against Monotheletism. Constans accused Maximos of treason, since Maximos supported Pope Martin I. Imperial response to papal resistance was harsh. Saint Maximos and those who stood with the Lateran Council were persecuted. They were also charged as traitors and heretics who blasphemed the Mother of God.

In 653, exarch Theodore Kalliopas entered Rome with an army. He was instructed to force the pope to submit to the imperial will or seize him and bring him back to the capital. Upon his arrival in Rome, Theodore publically accused Pope Martin of being a traitor and a heretic. Without even listening to his defense, Theodore pronounced Martin guilty of all charges. Although the blessed and innocent Martin denied these crimes, he was then secretly arrested. Even though Pope Martin was in poor health at this time, he was carried away to Constantinople, suffering much ill treatment along the way. Within that same year, Pope Martin was made to stand before the Byzantine senate, where he was condemned as a traitor. He attempted to discuss the *Typos* but was not permitted to do so. In his defense at the odious tribunal in Constantinople, presided over by the Monothelite Patriarch Peter, the pope again refuted the malicious slanders of treason and heresy, saying, "I have never made any agreement with the Saracens to invade the Roman Empire and to make war against the emperor. I have sent alms only to the Orthodox who live in poverty and destitution among the Saracens. I have kept the Faith handed down by the holy fathers. And if anyone does not confess and venerate the most pure Mother of God, let him be accursed in this present age and in the age to come. It is not we who are incorrectly observing the Faith entrusted to us by the holy apostles and fathers, but those who think otherwise." Pope Martin was deposed and stripped of his episcopal vestments. He was then sentenced to death. Instead he was taken and exiled to Cherson in the Crimea. While he was in those parts, he died of starvation in Cherson. He reposed in the year 655. He is commemorated by the holy Church on the 20th of September.

Saint Maximos in Constantinople Before the Senate (653)

As for our holy father, Saint Maximos, and his faithful disciples Anastasios and another Anastasios, the one being the pope's *apokrisiarios*, they were all arrested shortly before Pope Martin. Anastasios the *apokrisiarios* would later provide us with the details of the many trials of Saint Maximos. The emperor knew who had been influential in supporting the pope's calling of the Lateran Council. In 653, he ordered the arrest of Father Maximos and his two disciples. The holy man was transferred by sea to Constantinople. Upon his arrival, he was brutally treated. He was without shoes or clothing. He was bound with fetters and dragged through the streets by two imperial officials and ten palace guards. This was done to set him forth for public mockery and humiliation. The holy man was about seventy years of age.

In June of 654, our holy father was locked in a dark dungeon. He was alone and kept separated from his disciples. They were finally reunited at the royal palace, just before their interrogation before the senate and a large gathering of the public. Father Maximos was suffering from bodily weakness, as a result of ill treatment in isolation. He was still in chains and rags when his first trial commenced. The emperor chose not to preside. Instead, one of the dignitaries, the *sakellarios*[36] (treasurer) was entrusted with the interrogation of the prisoner.

The treasurer began the interrogation by addressing Father Maximos with much anger and passion, "From what thou hast previously perpetrated, it has become clear to everyone that thou hatest the emperor and his realm. Thou hast favored the Arab conquest of Egypt and Africa. Thou hast betrayed to the Saracens not only Alexandria, Pentapolis, and Tripoli, but also all of Egypt and Africa." Saint Maximos calmly replied, "And where is there proof of these things? What have I, a monk, to do with the conquest or defense of lands and cities? Furthermore, why should I, a Christian, aid the Saracens? My only desire is the bestowal of God's blessing on our Christian cities."

Without recognizing the idiocy of their charge, the treasurer continued with fresh falsehoods. They accused Father Maximos of belittling the emperor, by saying that Maximos declared the western emperors more worthy of honor. Our blessed, humble, and devout monk answered, "I thank God that

---

[36] *Sakellarios* was the title of both an administrative and ecclesiastical official, the functions of which varied with the times. Herakleios set his *sakellarios*, Theodore, at the head of an army. Constans II had his *sakellarios* conduct the examination of Saint Maximos. Patriarch Nikephoros (806-815) called the officers of that post "treasurers of the imperial funds." The functions were not always financial, but by the end of the 8th C. the office had acquired fiscal duties. *Oxford*, s.v. "Sakellarios."

He has allowed me to fall into thy hands. I, moreover, hope that by enduring these afflictions, my voluntary transgressions might be purged. Regarding thy last charge, I should like to know: didst thou hear me condemning the emperor, or did others tell thee what I said?" The saint received this answer: "We heard it from others, who heard it from thy very lips."

After several more slanderous statements were introduced into the session, which were hearsay and without written evidence, the saint demanded that those who heard him speak against the emperor be brought forward to testify. For the saint would meet his accusers. When Father Maximos was informed that the witnesses for the state were deceased, he asked, "Well then, why was I not questioned while they yet lived? Think how much trouble thou wouldest have been spared! But now thou must produce evidence and witnesses! The truth is that I have committed no crime and my accusers have no fear of God, Who searches out the hearts of men. May I cease to be reckoned among the Christians if I have committed any of the despicable deeds which thou hast attributed to me!"

Though the frustrated treasurer's anger mastered him, he was not about to give place to the defendant. A false witness, named Gregory, was summoned. He then testified, "While in Rome, I heard Father Maximos' disciple, Anastasios, declare that he and his teacher held that Emperor Constans II claimed priestly authority." Father Maximos answered the allegation, saying, "This man was in Rome with us at the same time; but we discussed with him Monotheletism. He pressed us to accept the *Typos* document, but we refused, mindful of Christ's judgment. God is my witness that neither I nor my disciple have ever charged the emperor with assuming the role of priest. What I did say, not to Father Anastasios but to Gregory himself, was that to expound upon dogmas of the Faith is not the work of emperors, but ministers of the altar. Ministers both anoint and lay hands on the emperor, stand before the altar, and perform the Mystery of the Eucharist and other divine Mysteries. I spoke these words then, and I stand by them now. Gregory remembers these words of mine. Should he deny them, then he must think there is some advantage for him. In any event, this is the truth as I have spoken it. Judge me as thou wilt." The prosecutors, hoping to base their verdict on the testimony of the false witnesses, were unclear how to proceed. They dismissed Father Maximos from the proceedings.

Afterward, they summoned Father Maximos again. They charged him with being a follower of Origen's teachings. This accusation was refuted when he proclaimed that Origen and his followers were cut off from communion with Christ and the Church.

The prosecutors then questioned Father Maximos regarding Patriarch Pyrrhos. They also raised the matter of why Maximos separated himself from the patriarchate of Constantinople. After the saint answered them, they privately acknowledged that there was no one who could best Maximos in argumentation. The imperial representatives threatened that unless he should submit to imperial authority and accept the imperial *Typos* and the Mono-thelitist belief as stated therein, he would be publically humiliated, anathematized, and put to death. With meekness, Father Maximos humbly said, "May God's will be done in me, unto the glory of His holy name."

Unable to convict the confessor on the basis of false witnesses, the saint's enemies attempted to prevail over the truth by violence. They brought in for questioning Anastasios, the disciple of Maximos. They employed harsh language and threats against him, so that he would testify that his elder, Father Maximos, had only prevailed over fallen Patriarch Pyrrhos by means of torture. Anastasios was intimidated by neither beatings to his head, face, and neck nor threats of death. He relied on his faith in God and his disciple-ship of thirty-seven years under Hegumen Maximos. He categorically refused to confirm the slanderous charges against his elder.

Saint Maximos Receives Patriarchal Representatives in Prison

Visitors then went to see the saint in prison. They claimed that they had been dispatched by the patriarch. These perverse interrogators demanded that Maximos explain why he had separated himself from communion, not only with the Patriarch of Constantinople but also the patriarchates of Antioch, Alexandria, and Jerusalem. They said to Father Maximos that "all these churches and the provinces under them are in concord. If thou wouldest belong to the catholic Church, thou must enter into communion with us at once, lest thou shouldest forge a new and strange pathway and fall into unexpected disaster." Our blessed confessor replied, "On what basis have all the churches entered into communion? If it is on a foundation of truth, as that professed by blessed Peter, I do not wish to be separated from them."

The representatives answered, "We confess both operations in Christ by reason of His distinct natures, and one operation because the two natures are united in one person." Saint Maximos then said, "You say that you confess two operations. If you say that the two operations have become a single operation in consequence of the unity of natures in one person, this means that you recognize a third operation, beside those two, which is fused or Theanthropic, at once divine and human." The messenger said, "No, we recognize only two operations, but speak of one by reason of their being united." The humble Confessor Maximos then demonstrated the futility of the emperor's position and said, "You are devising an ill-founded faith for yourselves. For you assert that God can exist without being. If you fuse the two operations into one, by reason of the union of natures in one person, and then divide by two this unity of operation by reason of the natures being different, there shall be neither unity nor duality of operations. For duality is excluded by the union, and union is excluded by the division. These contrivances make that in which the operations dwell completely ineffectual. The union of God and man in Christ is rendered ineffectual, or rather altogether the union is abolished, since each nature does not manifest activities proper to it. An essence that is not manifested in its own operation has no being. So God would not have being according to your formulation. This is why I will never agree with your interpretations. It is contrary to everything I have learned from the holy fathers and the canons. With regard to my temporal fate, do with me as you please: you have power over my body."

The visitors could not gainsay Father Maximos. They went to the patriarch and reported all that had transpired. In 653, on the Sunday following the conclusion of the first trial of the saint and his two disciples, the officials of the Church met with the emperor. They selected a place of exile for Father Maximos, as the punishment befitting one whom they deemed a traitor and blasphemer. Just as in days of old with Pilate and the Jews, the state and religious leaders consulted each other to eliminate those who would resist.

Saint Maximos in Bizye (653)[37]

For Saint Maximos, they chose Bizye,[38] a town in Thrace, as his place of exile. His disciple, Anastasios, was banished to a bleak and barbarian place, Perveris (Pervera), on the border of the empire. The other Anastasios, the former *apokrisiarios* of Rome and author of the biography of Maximos, was sent to the Thracian city of Mesembria[39] on the western shores of the Black Sea. The banished fathers were not permitted visitors. Thus, they were alone, naked and hungry, having only God's help. They exhorted all Christians, crying aloud, "Pray that the Lord God might perfect His mercy with our lowliness, and that He might teach us that those who sail along with Him experience a savage sea, like a ship which is driven about by winds and waves but stands firm and unshakeable."

In exile, Saint Maximos persisted as a censure and embarrassment to both the emperor and the patriarch. Before Father Maximos was exiled, Patriarch Paul died. Pyrrhos was then appointed patriarch; but, after four months, he also died (654). Peter, the Monothelite, then ascended the throne of Constantinople.

---

[37] For this section see *P.G.* 90:135 ff., which is also found in the pamphlet of Hieromonk Efthymios' Μαξίμου τοῦ Ὁμολογητοῦ (*Maximos the Confessor*), Athonite Kellion of Saint George, pp. 24-33, §§ Α΄-Ε΄, Ι΄-ΙΓ΄, ΙΣΤ΄-ΙΗ΄, ΚΓ΄.

[38] Bizye (41°48'N 27°49'E) is in present-day Turkey.

[39] Mesembria (42°39'N 27°43'E, Nesebur) is in present-day Bulgaria.

A considerable amount of time passed. On the 24th of August, in the year 656, there were sent to the fortress at Bizye three men of high rank: Bishop Theodosios of Caesarea in Bithynia, on behalf of Patriarch Peter of Constantinople; and Paul and Theodosios of consular rank, on behalf of Emperor Constans II. They were dispatched to ascertain if Father Maximos had altered his opinion. They were commissioned to find out if he were now willing to accept Monothelitism and the *Typos*, that he might be in communion with the see of Constantinople. They went and Bishop Theodosios inquired, "How art thou faring, milord abba?" The faithful slave of God replied, "Exactly as God knew I would before the ages. He foreordained the circumstances of my life, which life is guarded by providence." Bishop Theodosios remarked, "What art thou saying? That God foreknows and foreordains the acts of each of us before the ages?" Father Maximos answered, "Since He certainly foreknew, He also foreordained."[40] Theodosios asked, "What dost thou mean by 'He foreknew, He foreordained'?" Father Maximos answered, "God's foreknowledge pertains to our thoughts, words, and deeds that are within our power. But foreordaining pertains to those things, not in our power, which befall us." Theodosios continued and said, "And what is and what is not in our power?" Father Maximos replied, "Despota, thou knowest these things. Dost thou inquire that thou mightest try thy slave?" Theodosios then said, "In truth, I know not. I desire to understand what things are in our power and what are not. I should like to know how one pertains to God's foreknowing and the other to His foreordaining."

Father Maximos then took up his request and gave this response: "Our virtuous and bad deeds depend on our own will. But chastisements and disasters which come upon us, as well as their opposites, are beyond our

---

[40] "For whom He foreknew (οὓς προέγνω), He also foreordained (καὶ προώρισεν) to be conformable to the image of His Son [Rom. 8:29]." Saint Symeon the New Theologian: "God knows all things beforehand, both past and present at once, and everything which is going to happen in the future up to the end of the world. He sees them as already present, because in and through Him all things hold together [Col. 1:17]....It is not God's foreknowledge of those who, by their free choice and zeal, will prevail which is the cause of their victory, just as, again, it is not His knowing beforehand who will fall and be vanquished which is responsible for their defeat....All those who have believed in Christ are foreknown and foreordained, and become conformed to the image of the Son of God. And all of them, as foreordained, are called; and, as called, they are also justified; and, as justified, they are glorified. Because, while those perish who, after being baptized and believing in Christ, and becoming conformed to the image of the Son of God, do not keep themselves in this state, all who abide in it are saved." See "The Church and the Last Things," *On the Mystical Life: The Ethical Discourses*, Vol. 1, Second Discourse, 86-89.

power. We are not empowered to be in health or sickness, though we do contribute to those conditions which are likely to lead to one or the other state. In like manner, we cannot determine whether we shall attain the kingdom of the heavens or be cast into the Gehenna of the fire, though keeping God's commandments is cause for our attaining the kingdom, and not observing them is cause for our being cast into the Gehenna of the fire."

Theodosios then asked, "Why dost thou afflict thyself with this exile and incarceration?" Father Maximos answered, "I pray God that, castigating me by means of these sufferings, He may forgive my transgressions." Theodosios then interjected, "Do not afflictions come that one may be tried and his manner of life may be made manifest among men?" Father Maximos said, "The saints are tried so that their secret virtues may be made manifest to all. Job was tempted to reveal his perseverance and patience, while Joseph was put to the test that his chastity and temperance might shine forth. If God permits the saints to suffer in this life, it is because He would have us vanquish the devil, the ancient serpent. The patience of the saints was a consequence of their trials."[41]

At this point, Theodosios remarked, "Thou speakest well. I should very much like to converse with thee always on such matters. But I and my traveling companions, the honored consuls here, have come a very long distance to discuss with thee another matter. We have a proposal to offer thee. We hope that thou wilt consent and bring joy to the whole world." Father Maximos asked, "What is it, despota? Who am I that I should usher in joy to the world? Speak on." Theodosios then said, "It is the express wish of both the emperor and patriarch that thou shouldest explain why thou hast cut thyself off from communion with the see of Constantinople."

Father Maximos then explained, "Thou knowest the novelties introduced by Patriarch Kyros of Alexandria twenty-one years ago. He published the *Nine Chapters*,[42] which the patriarchate of Constantinople approved. There have also been other documents which have proposed

---

[41] Saint Maximos, from his *Commentary on the Our Father*: "The evil one mischievously uses other types of temptations, voluntary and involuntary, the first by sowing and greatly provoking the soul with bodily pleasures and scheming first to take away the desire of divine love. Then he cunningly works on the other type, hoping to corrupt our nature by pain so as to constrain the soul, struck down by the weakness of sufferings, to set in motion the attitudes of hatred of the Creator. We pray to avoid voluntary temptation, so that we will not turn aside our desire from divine love. As far as involuntary temptation is concerned, let us endure it nobly as coming with God's consent, so that we may show that we prefer the Creator of nature to nature itself." Saint Maximus, *Selected Writings: Our Father*, § 6, Classics, pp. 118, 119.

[42] The *Nine Chapters* introduced Monoenergism.

innovation and perverted the definitions of the synods. I include the *Ekthesis* and the *Typos*. The novelties found therein were devised by the primates of the Church of Constantinople: Sergios, Pyrrhos, and Paul. These documents and the circumstances surrounding them are known to all the churches. As long as the scandal of heresy persists in the Church of Constantinople and her bishops are miscreants, I will not enter into communion with her. It would be a transgression. There, I have given you my reasons. Let the offenses and stumbling blocks brought in by these men into the Church be removed; and let those who introduced them be deposed. The Lord spoke through the prophet and said, 'Make a way for My people; and cast the stones out of the way [Is. 62:10].' Then shall the path of salvation be cleared. Then shall you walk the smooth path of the Gospel purged of all heresy. When I see the Church of Constantinople as she was formerly, then shall I enter into communion with her. I shall not need any urging on the part of men. But as long as the scandal of heresy persists in her and her bishops are heretics, there is no argument, no deed, no persecution, which can ever persuade me to enter into communion with her."

Bishop Theodosios then asked, "But what mistaken profession is in our confession that thou shouldest shun communion with us?" Father Maximos then expounded on the meaning of a quaternity instead of a trinity, saying, "It is confessed by you that the Savior's divinity and humanity have one energy (μίαν ἐνέργειαν, operation). But the holy fathers teach that each distinct nature had its own distinct energy. You are then confessing the Holy Trinity not as a trinity but as a quaternity. By positing one operation of the Savior's divinity and humanity, you are saying that the Logos assumed, not our flesh and that of the pure Virgin Theotokos, but flesh having the qualities of the divine nature. You have implied that His flesh has ceased to be completely akin to human nature and that a new essence was formed, of one essence with the Logos to the same extent that the Logos is of one essence with the Father and the Spirit. Thus, you have invented a quaternity, because you deny that Christ had a true human nature. Thus, you allege that the nature formed in the incarnation was actually coessential with that of the pre-eternal Logos, as the Logos is coessential with the Father and the Spirit.

"Again, by denying the two energies and declaring that Christ's divinity and humanity share a single will, you deprive and belittle His independent actions in doing good as God and man. If nature should lack its proper and intrinsic operation, it is incapable of doing anything at all. Then if each nature in Christ does not have its own energy, then even if one of the natures should wish to do good, it cannot, since its ability to act had been taken away. Indeed, without the ability to act and without the operation proper to its nature, nothing can work or do anything.

"You recognize the incarnation of the Christ and acknowledge His two natures. And though you have made His flesh beginningless according to its will, yet you also admit that, according to its nature, His flesh was created in time. In other words, you say that the flesh is without beginning, just as Divinity can have no beginning. But according to the nature of flesh, it was fashioned in time. This is not only senseless but godless. You are not simply saying that there is one will in Christ, but you call it divine. But a divine will, as Divinity Itself, has neither beginning nor end. Moreover, you also take away from Christ the Lord all the properties and manifestations by which His divinity and humanity are known.

"In the *Ekthesis* and the *Typos*, you demand that there should be no discussion regarding one will or two wills in Christ. You demand that there should be no talk of His operations or His natures. And yet, you have abolished the notion of a single will and operation by insisting on their duality, that is, you acknowledge that this will is twofold by your very admission that the human will is subject to the divine. Therefore, you contradict the truth that there are two wills and operations; for you have fused them into one."

These words and many more words were uttered by Father Maximos, according to Father Anastasios, his disciple and biographer. After the way that Father Maximos explained that a quaternity had been created by the Monothelites, Bishop Theodosios and the patricians began to realize their error. But then Theodosios quickly checked himself and said, "Accept the emperor's *Typos* not as a confession of the dogma of the Faith, but as his personal expression and means of quelling controversy. Be mindful of the fact that what was written by Emperor Constans II was not issued as a law, but simply his written decision of the Faith."

Father Maximos then said, "If the *Typos* is neither a law nor the prescribed dogma, establishing the unity of will and operation of our Lord, then why have you exiled me to a land of barbarians and pagans who know not God. Why have I been exiled to Bizye? Why have my two fellow laborers been banished, one to Perveris and the other to Mesembria?" After giving no answer, Father Maximos reminded them of the Lateran Council, saying, "A synod was convened in Rome by Pope Martin. The Monothelites were condemned." Theodosios then said, "But that synod had no significance. It had not been summoned by the emperor's decree. It is his imperial summons which bestows authority to a synod."

Father Maximos looked at Bishop Theodosios and remarked, "If that were true, then the Orthodox Faith should have come to an end long ago. If the only synods to be confirmed were those initiated by an imperial summons, well then, where would be the Orthodox Faith? Consider those synods which were summoned by royal decrees against the coessentiality (*homoousios*) of the Son of God and God the Father. Recall the first one held in Tyre, the second in Antioch, the third in Seleukeia, the fourth in Constantinople under Evdoxios the Arian, the fifth in Nike of Thrace, and the sixth in Sirmium. Then there was the seventh council under Dioscoros, who presided, which took place in Ephesus. I remind thee that all of these were convened by an imperial summons, but came to be rejected and anathematized on account of their godless decrees. If thou believest that a synod is valid solely if the imperium convenes it, then on what basis dost thou accept the synod which condemned and anathematized Paul of Samosata? As thou knowest, that synod was presided over by Gregory the Wonder-worker. Its decrees were confirmed by Pope Dionysius of Rome and Dionysios of Alexandria. I remind thee that no emperor convened that synod, yet its resolutions are irrefutable. The Orthodox Church recognizes those synods which profess true dogmas. Despota of course is already aware that the canons require that local councils meet twice yearly in every Christian land for the defense of the Faith and the administration of the Church. However, the Church canons mention nothing about imperial decrees convening synods.

"The apostle says, 'God set for Himself some in the Church: first apostles, second prophets, third teachers [1 Cor. 12:28]'; this is for the building up of the Church and the faithful. In the Gospel, we hear those words, spoken by Christ Who said, 'Now what I say to you, I say to all [Mk. 13:37]....The one who receiveth you receiveth Me, and the one who receiveth Me receiveth the One Who sent Me forth [Mt. 10:40].' And, 'The one who rejecteth you rejecteth Me, and the one who rejecteth Me rejecteth the One Who sent Me forth [Lk. 10:16].' Let us examine one other thing. God sent forth apostles, prophets, and teachers for the setting aright of the faithful. The devil has dispatched false apostles, false prophets, and false teachers to war against the Church. Only heretics find a place in the formulations of these false apostles, false prophets, and false teachers, whose thoughts and words pervert others. If we examine the innovations of our time, we enter into the meaning of the apostle who said that 'this is that spirit of the antichrist, which ye have heard that it is coming, and now already it is in the world [1 Jn. 4:3].' It is evident that novelties and alien dogmas have been introduced into the Church. This being so, we ought to heed David who says, 'Blessed are they that search out His testimonies; with their whole heart shall they seek after Him [Ps. 118:2].' Together with this searching to find God, we need to pray these words: 'Give me understanding, and I will search out Thy law, and I will keep it with my whole heart [Ps. 118:34].' This discovery leads to knowledge of the law; and desire for knowledge persuades those who are worthy to guard it in their hearts to perform the commandments of God. 'Wonderful are Thy testimonies; on this account did my soul search them out [Ps. 118:129].' The Lord Himself directs His apostles and us, saying, 'Keep on searching the Scriptures, for in them ye think to have eternal life; and these are they which testify concerning Me [Jn. 5:39].' The chief of the apostles, Peter, exhorts us, saying, 'Concerning which salvation the prophets sought and searched out, who prophesied concerning the grace toward you [1 Pe. 1:10].' The divine Paul says, 'But even if our Gospel is being veiled, it is hidden in those perishing, in whom the God[43] of this age blinded the minds of the unbelieving, so that the illumination of the Gospel of the glory of the Christ, Who is the image of God, should not dawn on them [2 Cor. 4:3].' Let us not immerse our minds, as do the Jews, in just the naked words. They pursue solely the letter of the law. They have fallen outside of the truth. They have a veil over their hearts, lest they should give thought to the true Spirit hidden in the words; 'for the letter killeth, but the Spirit maketh alive [2 Cor. 3:6].' Therefore, despota, do thou be informed about me: I shall not become as the Jews. We ought not, therefore, to invent novelties and use formulas ungrounded in Scripture and the words of the Fathers. Find me any father who enters into the meaning of what thou hast spoken and those of like mind."

Bishop Theodosios then said, "What, then? We ought not to impute one energy in Christ?" Father Maximos answered, "According to the Scriptures and the holy fathers, it is as we believe: Christ has two natures. Thus we believe and confess that He has two natural wills and energies, appropriate to each." Theodosios said, "Verily, abba, we profess His natures and energies in a different manner; that is to say, divine and human, even the will of His divinity and the will of His manhood, since His soul was not without a will. But we simply do not say that He possesses two wills, lest we should create a conflict in Him." Father Maximos said, "What art thou saying? That two natures present a conflict on account of there being two?" Theodosios said, "No." Father Maximos continued, "Well then?" Theodosios said, "Absolutely, the fathers do speak of wills and energies, but they wished to avoid division." Father Maximos said, "Thou sayest one thing and meanest another." Theodosios said, "I know what I mean, but I will not say two." Father Maximos took up the book containing the minutes of the holy apostolic synod. He then pointed out to Theodosios a particular section and said, "The

---

[43] 2 Cor. 4:3 "the God of this age," according to Saint John Chrysostom [Homily 8, *P.G.* 61:493 (col. 455)] and Blessed Theophylact [*P.G.* 124:263A (col. 840)], is the God of all.

holy fathers, in this section, unreservedly speak of the two wills and energies of our Savior and God Jesus Christ." Consul Theodosios then took hold of the book and began reading the minutes of the fathers' words.

At length, the bishop and the patricians could not gainsay Father Maximos. They sat in silence for a long while, pondering the holy man's explanations and examples. They finally were moved to contrition, hung their heads, and wept. After a while they rose up. They bowed to Father Maximos, who returned their gesture with a bow. Bishop Theodosios then said, "As the fathers confess, so do I." Theodosios then immediately put in writing his affirmation of the two natures, and two wills, and two energies of Jesus Christ. He then urged Father Maximos, saying, "Commune with us and let there be union." Father Maximos replied, "I do not dare to receive thy document concerning such a matter. I am but a simple monk. But if God has given compunction to thy heart, so that thou hast received the words of the holy fathers, thou shouldest dispatch, as the canons demand, this written confession to the Pope of Rome, the emperor, and the patriarch. For I cannot commune unless these events come to pass. I urge thee to speak to the emperor and patriarch, that they too may follow thine example." Bishop Theodosios gave his word to speak to them.

As further confirmation of their conversion, the three visitors kissed the holy Gospels, the honorable cross, and icons of Christ God the Savior and our Lady Theotokos. They then discussed for some time other edifying subjects. After they exchanged a kiss of peace in the Lord, Father Maximos bade them farewell. Consul Theodosios then said, "Behold, I have done everything; but will the emperor be persuaded?" Father Maximos said to him, "Thou must speak to him by all means, if thou desirest to be an imitator of God Who by His extreme humility brought about our salvation." Consul Theodosios then said, "I hope that God keeps in my memory all these words that passed between us, that I might recite them to the emperor and persuade him." Then they embraced one another. Bishop Theodosios and the two consuls departed in peace. The bishop then left Father Maximos with an old cassock.

In his dealings with heretics, Father Maximos wrote: "What is more pleasing to the faithful than to see the scattered children of God gathered again as one? Neither do I exhort you to place harshness above the love of men. May I not be so mad! I beseech you to do and to carry out good to all men with care and assiduity, becoming all things to all men, as the need of each is shown to you. I want and pray you to be wholly harsh and implacable with the heretics only in regard to cooperating with them or in any way whatever supporting their deranged belief. For I reckon it hatred toward man and a departure from divine love to lend support to error, so that those previously seized by it might be even more greatly corrupted."[44]

Saint Maximos in Constantinople for a Second Examination (654)[45]

Now Bishop Theodosios and the two patricians returned to Emperor Constans, who became infuriated at their report. The three men feared imperial wrath and disfavor, so they reverted to Monotheletism. Constans then commanded the Patrician Paul to go to Bizye and transfer Father Maximos to Constantinople. Father Maximos was to be treated humanely and assigned a cell in the Monastery of Saint Theodore, near the emperor's palace, in the suburbs of the capital. Paul carried out this transfer on the 8th of September.

The following day, the patricians Epiphanios and Troilos were also dispatched to see the saint. Therefore, the patricians, with Bishop Theodosios, and a company of soldiers and servants, returned to Bizye and met with Father Maximos. They traveled with much grandeur. Meanwhile, Father Maximos had been waiting and hoping that Bishop Theodosios had succeeded in changing the beliefs of the emperor.

It was not long before Father Maximos perceived that Bishop Theodosios preferred his earthly king to the heavenly King and His Church. They convened in the catechism chamber of that monastery's church. The emperor's men sat down. They persuaded Father Maximos to also take a seat. Then the patrician Troilos opened the discussion by saying, "The emperor, the God-appointed master of the inhabited world, has commissioned us to proclaim the royal pleasure. But first, tell us, wilt thou obey the emperor's will?" Father Maximos replied, "Milord, first I will hear what his majesty wishes and then I shall respond. For how can I offer a reply to that which I know not yet?" Troilos, however, persisted and said, "We shall not apprise thee of the imperial will unless thou shouldest first announce that thou wilt submit to the emperor." Perceiving their sharp insistence and malice in their countenance, Father Maximos answered them, saying, "Since you are unwilling to inform me, your slave, what is pleasing to our master, the emperor, and what he wishes of me, I therefore state before God and His angels that if the emperor should command me to perform something of temporal and transitory significance, and such a command is not opposed to God or detrimental to the salvation of my soul, I would gladly fulfill the command." Troilos, leaping up from his seat, made as if to leave and said, "It is obvious that this fellow has no intention of fulfilling the royal will."

---

[44] *P.G.* 91:465C.

[45] For this section, see also Hieromonk Efthymios' *Maximos the Confessor* (in Greek), pp. 33–37, §§ ΚΔ΄-Λ΄.

In the meantime, a clamor arose among those present and the crowd of onlookers who had gathered. A great noise and commotion arose. Bishop Theodosios then intervened and said to Troilos, "Declare unto Father Maximos what is the will of Emperor Constans, and let us hear his reply. How can we possibly justify our departure without having spoken a word to Father Maximos about what would please the emperor? It would be nonsensical." The patrician Epiphanios then declared, "Hear his majesty's words: 'May the Lord grant thee compunction, so that thou wouldest accept our *Typos* and enter into communion with us! The schismatics in both the east and west are causing disturbances on account of thee. They have become apostates from the Faith. They refuse communion with us. Be assured that we shall receive thee with love at Chalke, escort thee to the Great Church (Hagia Sophia) with great honor and glory, and place thee beside us where royalty sits. Together we shall communicate the Mysteries. We shall then proclaim thee as our father. There shall then be joy not only throughout our Christ-loving city, but throughout all Christendom. It is our firm belief that shouldest thou be persuaded to enter into communion with the Church of Constantinople, then all those who, by thine example, have cut themselves off from communion with us shall be reunited. We are certain of these things. Thou mayest depend on what has been promised thee.'"

Father Maximos' eyes welled up with tears. He then sighed and looked upon Bishop Theodosios, saying, "Despota, we all await the fearful day of judgment. Hast thou forgotten what thou didst promise when thou didst lay thy hand upon the Gospel, the life-giving cross, and holy icons of our Savior and God and the Ever-virgin Mother and Panagia (all-holy one)?" Bishop Theodosios, ashamed, lowered his countenance and answered with a broken voice, saying, "There was nothing I could do to guide the emperor to change his mind. The most devout emperor had already reached the conclusion that with thee as the guide of the schismatics throughout the east and west, they have risen up against us. They ever increase in number and incite disturbances, cutting off communion with us. If thou wilt accept our *Typos* and enter into communion with us, all who have cut us off because of thy teaching shall come to be united with us." Father Maximos then asked, "But why didst thou and thy companions place your hands on the Gospel, if you were not resolved to fulfill that which you vowed? Truly, all the hosts of the heavens could not persuade me to do what you have proposed. How would I answer—I do not say God—my conscience, if I were to reject the true Faith for the sake of empty glory and the praise of men, which are of no worth?"

The emperor's men then jumped to their feet. In a rage, they lunged at Father Maximos, raining down blows and insults. They dragged him about the floor with the hairs of his head. They kicked and trampled upon the aged elder. From head to toe, he suffered wounds and bruises. Without a doubt, such an assault would have led to Father Maximos' death had not Bishop Theodosios intervened. When they finally desisted, they covered the holy man with so much of their malodorous spittle that his clothes were soaked. Bishop Theodosios then chided them, saying, "You ought not to have done so. We were only required to hear his answer and report it to the emperor. The canons do not sanction such abuse. Matters subject to Church canons are judged differently." It was only with difficulty that Bishop Theodosios persuaded them to take their seats again. They hearkened to the bishop but hurled crude insults at Father Maximos.

The patrician Epiphanios could not master his resentment toward the holy man. He spoke angrily to the saint, saying, "Speak to us, thou wicked dog: why dost thou reckon the emperor and the Constantinopolitans as heretics? We are more Christian than thou art, and more Orthodox too." Epiphanios then collected himself somewhat and continued, saying, "See here, we do acknowledge in our Lord Jesus a divine will, a human will, and a noetic soul. It is intrinsic in every rational being to have the power to will and the capacity to energize. We also recognize that the Lord has the power of willing according to His divinity and His humanity. We do not deny that He has two wills and two energies." Father Maximos then said, "If you believe as the Church of God teaches, then why are you compelling me to accept the *Typos*, which utterly does away with that which thou hast just spoken?" Epiphanios answered, "The purpose of the *Typos* is to provide a form of expression to that which is not entirely comprehensible. This shall protect the people from falling into error as a consequence of what they little understand, due to the subtlety of expression used in theological speech. As a result, this shall also prevent controversies from erupting."

Father Maximos wished to correct their suggestion that the *Typos* was merely a general instruction on theological matters difficult to comprehend, so as to end controversy and unite the Church. The zealous confessor countered Epiphanios, saying, "On the contrary, the *Typos* is opposed to a correct confession of the Faith, as defined at the Synod of Chalcedon, which Faith sanctifies every person. The *Typos*, in fact, by suppressing the proper confession of the Faith, has denied the Faith." Epiphanios then interjected, "But I am telling thee that the *Typos* does not deny the two wills of Christ. It simply orders that one not speak of the two wills, for the sake of preserving peace in the Church." Father Maximos said, "Suppression of the Faith is a denial of it. The Holy Spirit has spoken through the Prophet David, saying, 'There are no tongues nor words in which their voices are not heard [Ps. 18:3].' Thereupon, if a word is not spoken, it is no word at all."

Troilos said in retort, "Believe what thou wilt in thine own heart. No one cares nor forbids thee to do so, only do not foment disturbances." Father Maximos corrected his suggestion, saying, "Salvation does not depend alone on faith of the heart. Hearken to the words of the Lord: 'Whosoever shall deny Me before men, him will I also deny before My Father Who is in the heavens [Mt. 10:33].' The holy apostle also exhorts us, writing: 'For with the heart one believeth unto righteousness, and with the mouth one confesseth unto salvation [Rom. 10:10].' If God, and the prophets and apostles, command that the great mystery of the Faith, which brings salvation to the world, should be preached, then our salvation and that of others is being hindered when the proclamation of the Faith is prohibited."

Epiphanios, irritated at these words, then reverted to another subject, asking, "Didst thou put thy signature to the *libellus*, that is, the defamatory resolutions set forth in the synod held at Rome?" Father Maximos answered, "Yes, I did sign." Epiphanios then asked, "How didst thou dare to sign and anathematize those who confess the Faith in a sound manner, even as the catholic Church teaches?" Without waiting for an answer, Epiphanios threatened Father Maximos, saying, "Verily, we shall drag thee through the streets and bind thee in the forum. We shall give free access to actors, mimics, harlots, and the rabble that they might administer to thee a thrashing and spit in thy face." Father Maximos said, "Let it be as thou sayest, if we should anathematize those who acknowledge two natures and two corresponding wills and energies in Christ the Lord, Who in His divine nature is true God, and in His human nature, true man. But milord, I urge thee to read the minutes of the Lateran Council held in Rome. All those who signed have anathematized those who, like Arius and Apollinarios, acknowledge one will and one energy in the Lord. They pronounced against those who do not confess that our Lord Jesus has a distinct energy and will for each of the two natures by which He wrought our salvation."

Those who were present then complained, "If we should let him speak on, we shall have no opportunity to eat or drink. Let us go in to supper. Afterward, we can tell the emperor and patriarch what we have heard from his lips. The wretch has evidently sold himself to Satan." They all arose and went forth to eat and drink. It was then the eve of the Feast of the Exaltation of the Cross. The vigil was about to commence. After they supped, they left the suburbs and went into the city. The visitors were all very angry at the results of their encounter with Father Maximos.

The following day, the 14th of September, consul Theodosios went to see Father Maximos alone. He undertook this commission at the emperor's behest. He entered the holy man's cell, confiscated all of the elder's books, and said, "Since thou didst not wish honor and put it far from thee, then thou shalt be vouchsafed of that which thou dost deserve, even the same sentence as thy disciples; for the one is found in Mesymbria and the other in Perveris. We shall, however, convey them from their places of exile that we might make a determination in their cases."

Saint Maximos in Selymbria (September of 654)[46]

Soldiers seized Father Maximos and led him away. They first brought him to Selymbria[47] of Thrace, on the north shore of the Sea of Marmara, west of Constantinople. Father Maximos spent two days in that city, during which time a Selymbrian recruit started a vile rumor in the army camp that Father Maximos had blasphemed the Theotokos. It was bruited about into the ears of the Selymbrians. The military governor, moved by God to treat the prisoner humanely, was sympathetic toward Father Maximos. The military governor invited the leading clergymen of Selymbria to assemble and examine Father Maximos, for the purpose of ascertaining whether or not the rumor were true. As the clergy and monks approached Father Maximos, our holy father rose up and made a prostration before them. They then bowed themselves in return. Afterward they all sat down. Then a venerable elder from among those who came, with a meek and respectful tone, addressed Father Maximos and said, "Father, certain individuals have erred concerning thy sanctity. They were scandalized by a rumor that thou hast denied our Lady, the all-holy Virgin, by not addressing her as Theotokos. I, therefore, adjure thee, by the coessential and life-creating Holy Trinity, to dispel from their hearts this absurd report by stating the truth. We should not wish to think of thee unjustly." Father Maximos then made a full prostration to them. He then rose up and lifted his hands toward heaven. With tears in his eyes, he solemnly declared: "In the name of the Father, Son, and Holy Spirit, the coessential and supra-essential (ὑπερούσιος, beyond all being) Trinity, and of all the heavenly hosts, the choir of the apostles and prophets, the immense multitudes of martyrs and righteous souls who have reposed in the Faith." Some of those who assembled, then began weeping. Father Maximos paused and said, "Whosoever does not confess our Lady, the all-hymned one, the most holy and immaculate Virgin, who is the most honorable of rational beings, to be the true Birthgiver of God 'Who hath made heaven and the earth, the sea and all that is therein [Ps. 145:6],' let such a one be anathema, now and ever and unto the ages of ages."

Upon hearing such a solemn affirmation, the monks and clergy wept. They blessed Father Maximos and said to him, "May God empower thee, O

---

[46] For this section, see also Hieromonk Efthymios' *Maximos the Confessor* (in Greek), pp. 37, 38, § ΛΑ´.

[47] Selymbria (41°05′N 28°15′E) was at the end of the Via Egnatia.

father, and vouchsafe thee to worthily complete thy course without stumbling." Now many soldiers had stood by that they might hear some edifying exhortations. Some of the military governor's officers observed their men listening carefully. The soldiers next began censuring the government for banishing Father Maximos. Thereupon, the officers quickly gave the order that Father Maximos was to be removed from their midst and the camp. The holy man was then made to march two miles farther in the direction of Perveris, as that place is called by the natives, where he was to continue his exile. The clergy and monks standing by, out of love for Father Maximos, accompanied him on the road. When the time came to depart, they embraced the saint with tear-filled eyes. After they mounted Father Maximos on a beast of burden, they returned to Selymbria. The saint was taken, under guard, to Perveris where he was imprisoned.[48]

Saint Maximos in Perveris (654)

Father Maximos, with his disciple Anastasios, spent five years in Perveris. Emperor Constans II finally recalled Father Maximos and his two disciples to Constantinople. They reached the city by ship, arriving as the sun was setting. When the ship docked, the prisoners were placed in the custody of two captains of the guard and ten soldiers.

Saint Maximos in Constantinople for a Third Examination (659)[49]

Father Maximos and his disciples disembarked half-naked and without anything on their feet. The confessors were incarcerated in separate cells. Several days later, the prisoners were taken to Constans' palace. Both of the saint's disciples were left outside and under guard, while Father Maximos was escorted into the senate, which was in session. The senators were present but not the emperor. The elder was then presented to the seated nobles. The first to address the holy man was the *sakellarios*. His voice betrayed his anger when he asked, "Art thou a Christian?" Without pride, but in great humility toward our God and Savior, Saint Maximos replied, "By the grace of Christ the God of all, I am a Christian." The treasurer replied, "That is not true!" The slave of God calmly responded, "Thou sayest that I am not, but God says that I am and will remain a Christian." The imperial representative maliciously continued, "But how, if thou art a Christian, canst thou hate the emperor?" The saint disarmed the interrogator's advance with this reproof: "And how can this be evident? For hatred is a hidden disposition of the soul, just as love is." The treasurer then said, "But from thy deeds it has become

---

[48] The account rendered by Father Anastasios the *apokrisiarios* ends here. The subsequent text is based on what is found in *P.G.* 90 and 91.

[49] For this section see *P.G.* 90:109 ff., which is also found in Hieromonk Efthymios' *Maximos the Confessor* (in Greek), pp. 11-16, §§ A´-E´.

known that thou art an enemy of his majesty and the realm. Thou hast betrayed Egypt and Alexandria and Pentapolis and Tripoli and all of Africa to the Saracens!" Father Maximos asked, "Where is there proof of this charge?"

Father Maximos was also maligned as a critic of Herakleios I and his family. The allegation maintained that Father Maximos claimed that God was not pleased to give the royal family the rule of the empire. The treasurer then produced his witness, a man named John. He had been secretary to Peter, former general of Numidia.[50] The treasurer then had his witness give testimony against Father Maximos. The *sakellarios* John then began: "Twenty-two years ago, the grandfather of our Emperor Constans II, that is, Herakleios I, ordered the general, the blessed Peter, to lead his army into Egypt against the Saracens. I remember that Peter had complete confidence in Father Maximos, whom he deemed as a servant of God. Peter wrote Father Maximos and requested his advice regarding the campaign. Father Maximos answered, 'It is not God-pleasing that thou shouldest fight for Herakleios and his heirs.'" John claimed that this statement was put in writing. Father Maximos answered, "If thou art telling the truth, then thou must surely be able to produce this correspondence. Let the correspondence be brought forth in evidence; and I shall be subject to the punishments prescribed in the law." The ignominious John answered, "I do not have in my possession any letters, nor have I ever seen any pertaining to this case. But I do know that everyone in the camp spoke of these things to each other at the time." Father Maximos then said, "If the whole camp talked about this exchange, why art thou the only one to libel me? Hast thou ever laid eyes on me?" The treasurer answered, "Never." "I, too," said Father Maximos, "have never laid eyes on thee prior to this."

The unjust nature of the proceedings therefore was exposed. The man of God then turned toward the senate and addressed the members saying, "Judge for yourselves if it is just to have such accusers or witnesses brought forward. 'For with what judgment ye judge, ye shall be judged; and with what measure ye measure, it shall be measured in turn to you [Mt. 7:2].' Thus speaks the God of all."

The prosecution did not rest. It brought in its next witness, one Sergios Magudas, who stated: "Ten years ago, Abbot Thomas of Rome related to me that Pope Theodore had dispatched him to Gregory, the patrician, exarch of Carthage, who had rebelled against the Rhomaioi. The pope commissioned Abbot Thomas to assure Gregory that he should not fear

---

[50] Numidia was a province situated to the west and south of Africa Proconsularis, that is, the region about Carthage.

to attack the empire, because God's servant, Father Maximos, had seen a dream. Father Maximos had seen a multitude of angels in the heavens. Some were positioned in the east, crying aloud, 'Constantine[51] Augustus, thou shalt conquer!' Some were standing in the west, crying aloud, 'Gregory Augustus,[52] thou shalt conquer!' Father Maximos declared that the voices of the angels in the west were louder and stronger than those in the east." After Magudas spoke, the treasurer, acting as prosecutor, made a comment to Father Maximos and said, "And I suppose now that God has brought thee to this city to be burned alive."

Father Maximos replied, "I give thanks to God Who is cleansing my sins, both voluntary and involuntary. But 'Woe to the world because of the stumbling blocks! For it must be that the stumbling blocks come, yet woe to that man by whom the stumbling block cometh [Mt. 18:7]!' It is shameful to speak disparagingly of someone unjustly, as thou hast. It is no less shameful to leave unpunished those who speak such things merely to please men. All of these charges should have been brought forth when the exarch Gregory was alive. Then the patrician and general, Peter of Numidia, Abbot Thomas, and the holy Pope Theodore could have been summoned or sent their affidavits. Were they here, I should ask the exarch Peter, 'Tell me, milord, didst thou write me, as thy secretary claims, or did I write thee?' I should then have inquired of the blessed pope, 'Master, had I ever disclosed one of my dreams to thee?' Even if the pope were to say that I had related to him such a dream, the guilt would lie with the one who encouraged the rebellion, which I did not. Moreover, a dream is not a matter of will. Certainly one cannot be punished by law for something he dreamed. The law punishes those deeds which depend upon a man's free will."

Troilos the patrician then said to the elder, "Abba, art thou playing? Dost thou know where thou art?" Father Maximos said, "I am not playing; rather, I am mourning that my life has come to this point here that I should be in peril from such fantastic allegations." The patrician Epiphanios then said, "God knows and is not mocked if this is not the truth." The secretary became angry and said to Father Maximos, "Simply put, thou art saying, art thou not, that everyone else is lying, but only thou art speaking the truth?" Tears filled the eyes of the slave of God as he said, "Thou hast authority, permitted by God, to grant me life or to put me to death. However know this:

---

[51] Constantine is Constans II.

[52] Gregory, exarch of Carthage, and relative of Herakleios supported the anti-Monothelite position of Saint Maximos. In 646, Gregory rebelled against Constans II. In Africa, support for Pope Theodore and Father Maximos was strong. Gregory was defeated by the Arabs. He died in 647.

if these allegations should be true, then Satan would be God by nature; but since that is not so—of course it is not!—neither are the allegations true. May I be right opposite the Christians and the supra-essential God, Maker, Creator, Producer, Foreknower, Judge, and Savior of all, if ever I recounted such a dream, or heard another narrate it."

The prosecution continued introducing other false accusations, which Father Maximos refuted wisely and humbly. In every instance, he was able to demonstrate his innocence. The prosecution pressed the allegation that Father Maximos and his disciples censured the emperor while the three men were in Rome. Theodore, a false witness, was brought forward. He was the son of John Kandidatos, who also bore the second name of Hila, who was then the brother-in-law of Lord Platon the patrician. This Theodore claimed that he met with Father Maximos in Rome. "In a discussion," said Theodore, "which took place between us in Rome, the subject of his majesty arose. Father Maximos began mocking the emperor to make his majesty look ridiculous. What I mean is that he was telling offensive jokes that injured the royal person." The slave of God responded to this charge, saying, "Not ever have we had such a conversation. We spoke together only once, in the company of the most reverend elder and Lord Theoharistos, the brother of the exarch, regarding a church officer, at which time thou didst urge me to write some letters on his behalf. If thou shouldest find me uttering a falsehood, let me be punished."

Next they brought in Gregory, the son of Photinos, who stated: "I went to the cell of Abba Maximos in Rome. Abba Anastasios, his disciple said to me that 'the emperor plays even the priest; may he never be accounted worthy to be a priest.'" The slave of God answered this straightway, saying, "Milord Gregory, dost thou fear God? For such a conversation was never held by either me or my disciple." Father Maximos then bowed to the senators and said, "Exhibit patience toward thy slave, and I shall tell thee all that was spoken between us. Then you might judge me with all the facts."

Father Maximos then commenced, "Milord Gregory, when he came to Rome, paid me, your slave, the honor of visiting me in my cell. As soon as I caught sight of him, I made a prostration, as I am wont to do. I then greeted and embraced him. We then sat down and I asked him, 'What is the reason for this visit from my master, the emperor?' He said to me, 'Our good and God-supported master desires to bring peace to the Churches of God. He has issued a decree to the God-honored pope that there be unity with Constantinople on the basis of the *Typos*.' I said, 'I know that it is impossible. The Romans are not about to prefer the unclean voices of heretics to the illuminating teaching of the holy fathers. They are not going to extinguish the light and exchange it for darkness. For there will be nothing left for us to ascribe veneration.' He then said to me that 'the *Typos* was not advanced to be a document on divine teaching, but a means to maintain silence on such teaching that we might regulate peace.' I then said, 'Does the sacred Scripture write of maintaining such silence? Did not God speak through David, saying, "There are no tongues nor words in which their voices are not heard [Ps. 18:3]?" But if the word of God is neither spoken or heard, then it is no longer in our midst.'

"He then said, 'Do not put me in a difficult position. I ascribe to the holy Symbol of the Faith, the Creed.' I then said, 'And how is it possible that thou shouldest ascribe to the holy Symbol, while accepting the *Typos*?' He said, 'What harm is there in accepting the *Typos* and pronouncing the Creed?' I answered, 'It is patently clear that the *Typos* eradicates the Creed.' He exclaimed, 'For the Lord's sake, how is that so?' I explained, 'Recite the Creed to me, and learn how it confutes the Creed. I tell thee, recite it now!' He then began, 'I believe in one God, Father almighty, Maker of heaven and earth, and of all things visible and invisible.' Then I interrupted and said, 'Pause here for a moment. See how the Faith of the fathers of Nicaea is destroyed. For He would not be Creator if He were in want of natural will and energy. For it certainly was by His will that He made heaven and the earth, even as David says in the Spirit: "All that the Lord hath willed He hath done, in heaven and on the earth, in the seas and in all the abysses [Ps. 134:6]." If now, for the sake of regulating peace, the saving Faith is ill-conceived, this is complete separation from God and not union. For tomorrow, the ill-famed Jews shall say, "Let us arrange a peace amongst us and let us unite. We shall remove circumcision and you shall take away Baptism; only let us no longer have any strife in our midst."'

"'Similarly, the Arians made this offer to the great Constantine, writing: "Let us do away with the terms *homoousion* (same essence) and *heteroousion* (different essence), and let our Churches unite." This proposal was not accepted by our God-bearing fathers. They preferred death to remaining silent and setting aside the supra-essential divinity of the Father, the Son, and the Holy Spirit. Though Constantine may have been well-disposed, as some have recorded in history, for the political advantage to be achieved by consenting to such a union, yet neither he nor any one of the emperors may act as an intermediary and compel the God-bearing fathers to compromise with heretics regarding such issues. The Church fathers continue professing the pure and true dogma, pronouncing categorically that discussions and determination of the saving doctrines belong to the priests.'

"Milord Gregory then said to me, 'What then? Is not every Christian emperor a priest?' I said, 'He is not. He stands not in the sanctuary. And after the consecration of the bread, he does not elevate it and say, "Holy things for the holy." Neither does he baptize, nor anoint with Chrism, nor ordain, nor consecrate temples. He does not take upon himself the symbols of the priesthood, the omophorion and the Gospel, but the diadem of the kingdom and the red cloak.'

"But why should we speak of so many things?" Father Maximos then said to the senators. "At the sacred Anaphora[53] in the Liturgy, above the holy Table, the high priest and deacons and all the priestly ranks, commemorate the emperors and lay people. After the consecration, in secret prayers, there takes place the commemoration of the dead and the living: 'Remember those who have fallen asleep in faith, Constantine,[54] and the rest.'"[55] Upon hearing this, one named Menas cried out in the chamber, "Speaking such things tears apart the Church." Father Maximos denied that the words of sacred Scriptures and the holy fathers tear apart the Church.

The holy man was then questioned about Origen. He was accused of misleading all with the dogmas of Origen. The slave of God answered in the presence of all, "Anathema to Origen and to his dogmas, and to all those of like mind." The saint, therefore, was able to overturn every charge.

The guards then brought in Father Anastasios, the elder's disciple. The interrogators laid snares for him that he might incriminate his teacher. It was soon evident to the prosecution that the witness would not speak falsely or implicate his teacher. Maddened by Father Anastasios' responses, they began beating him with their fists. The prisoner was then taken away. Both fathers were then returned to their cells.

Saint Maximos is Visited by the Envoys Troilos and Sergios Efkrates[56]

The following evening, the patrician Troilos and the steward of the imperial table, Sergios Efkrates, came to visit the venerable Maximos in his cell. They brought food with them, so as to offer something to the holy man.

---

[53] The Anaphora is that portion of the Liturgy in which the eucharistic elements are offered as an oblation.

[54] According to Stratos, Herakleios Constantine (d. 641), son of Herakleios I and Fabia-Evdokia, was called Constantine II. Constantine III, whom Stratos maintains is Constans II, was crowned co-emperor as Constantine III in 641 by his uncle Heraklonas.

[55] After the consecration, the clergy prays for "those who in faith have gone to rest before us—forefathers, fathers, patriarchs, prophets, apostles, preachers, evangelists, martyrs, confessors, ascetics, and for every righteous spirit in faith made perfect." Then we hear aloud, to the Theotokos, "Especially our all-holy...." Afterward, the priest says, "Remember all those who have fallen asleep in the hope of resurrection."...Then the priest remembers the departed. After that commemoration, he says, "And grant them rest...."

[56] For this section, see also Hieromonk Efthymios' *Maximos the Confessor* (in Greek), pp. 16-19, §§ ΣΤ´-ΙΑ´.

They then asked him, "Milord abba, do tell us the conversation thou hadst in Africa and Rome with Pyrrhos. With what proofs hadst thou persuaded him to recant his own dogma and accept thine?" Father Maximos answered, "Were I to have the book in which I recorded the details of our discussions and arguments, I should be delighted to tell you. But my books and tablets were removed from my possession, leaving me to rely on what I can remember." The elder then recounted as much as he was able, closing with these words: "I have no dogmas of my own. I only hold to those common to the catholic Church. Not a single word in my confession of the Faith may be designated as my own invention."

Troilos and Sergios then posed another question: "Then we are to understand that thou wilt not enter into communion with the throne of Constantinople." Father Maximos replied, "I will not commune." They inquired further, asking, "For what reason wilt thou not commune with the patriarchate?" Father Maximos answered them with a serious countenance, saying with a sigh, "On the one hand, there is nothing more onerous than the reproach of one's conscience; but, on the other hand, there is nothing more desirable than the approval of one's conscience." They pressed the holy man to give them an answer for his lack of communion with them. Father Maximos then explained: "I cannot enter into communion with the throne of Constantinople, because the leaders of that patriarchate have rejected the resolutions of the four œcumenical synods. Instead, as their rule, they have accepted the Alexandrian *Nine Chapters*. Thereafter, they accepted the *Ekthesis* of Patriarch Sergios and then the *Typos*, which rejects everything that was proclaimed in the *Ekthesis*, thereby excommunicating themselves many times over. Together with having excommunicated themselves, they have been deposed and deprived of the priesthood at the Lateran Council held in Rome. What Mysteries can such persons perform? What spirit comes upon what they celebrate or those ordained by them?" The saints' visitors then asked, "Then thou alone wilt be saved, while everyone else perishes?"

Father Maximos said, "When Nebuchadnezzar made a golden image in the province of Babylon, he summoned all those in authority to come to the dedication of the image [Dan. 3:1, 2]. The holy Three Children condemned no one. They did not concern themselves with the practises of others, but looked only to their own business, lest they should fall away from true piety. When Daniel was cast into the lions' den, he did not condemn those who prayed not to God that they might obey the decree of Darius [Dan. 6:12 ff.]. Instead, he concentrated on his own duty. He preferred to die than to sin against his conscience and transgress God's law. God forbid that I should judge or condemn anyone or that I should claim that I alone shall be saved!

I should much prefer to die than betray the Faith in any way or go against my conscience."

Troilos and Sergios presented a new development, saying, "But what wilt thou do when Rome unites with us? Thou shouldest know that only yesterday two papal legates arrived in the capital. Tomorrow, the Lord's day, they shall partake of the Mysteries with the patriarch. Thou wilt be accused of perverting Rome. After thou didst depart Rome, the Romans came to an agreement with us." Saint Maximos replied, "Even if those legates should commune tomorrow, they did not bring with them any preliminary judgment from the throne of Rome. They bear no epistle to the patriarch. Even if they should partake tomorrow, I am not persuaded that the Romans shall unite with you, unless they do not confess that our Lord and God has two natures, each with its corresponding will and energy." They then asked, "And what if the Romans should come to terms with us? What wilt thou do?" Father Maximos answered, "Were the universe to enter into communion with the patriarch, I should never commune with him. Take heed of the words of the Holy Spirit through the apostle: 'Even if we, or an angel from out of heaven, should preach a gospel to you besides what Gospel we preached to you, let such a one be anathema [Gal. 1:8].'"

The envoys then asked, "Is it truly needful to confess two wills and operations in Christ?" Father Maximos replied, "It is absolutely needful, if we are to remain Orthodox in doctrine. Every nature has its corresponding action. By the operation is the nature known to exist. If the nature is not revealed in the operations, how are we able to know that Christ is true God and true man by nature?" The envoys conceded this and said, "We understand what thou art saying and know it to be the truth. But we must not oppose the emperor. He issued the *Typos* for the purpose of bringing peace to the Church, not in order to deny any of Christ's attributes. The emperor only commanded that there should no longer be any discussion of the properties of Christ, lest controversies should be engendered by it. It is for the sake of maintaining peace that he has promulgated this document."

Tears filled the venerable's man's eyes. He prostrated himself on the floor and cried aloud, "Though I do not wish to grieve our dutiful emperor who is a good man, yet I fear God's judgment by keeping silence about those things which God commands us to confess. The apostle says, 'God set for Himself some in the Church: first apostles, second prophets, third teachers [1 Cor. 12:28].' It is clear that God speaks through them. All of Scripture, the writings of the Church teachers, and the synodal decrees teach that Jesus Christ, our incarnate God, has power to will and to act according to both His divinity and His humanity. He lacks in no property pertaining to divinity or to humanity, except sin.[57] It follows then that He is perfect in both natures, having no deficiency in anything proper to either of them. It is evident, therefore, that should one not confess that Christ has all the innate properties of each nature, such a one distorts the mystery of Christ's incarnation." Saint Maximos spoke these words and many more. The envoys marvelled at the wisdom of Father Maximos. They understood that it would be futile to refute the irrefutable.

Nevertheless, Sergios Efkrates, said, "Only thou, O father, hast caused consternation. On account of thee, there are many who refuse communion with the Church of Constantinople." Father Maximos countered this statement, saying, "Who is able to prove that I have ordered anyone not to have communion with the Constantinopolitan Church?" Sergios answered, "Since thou hast refused communion with us, therefore others will not commune with us."

Troilos then asked Father Maximos, "Dost thou deem it a good thing that the *Typos* of our pious emperor has been anathematized and despised throughout the west?" Father Maximos said, "May God grant forgiveness to those who recommended that the emperor issue the *Typos*." Sergios then asked, "And who were they?" Father Maximos answered, "The primates of the churches urged Emperor Constans. The nobles gave their assent, thereby putting all the responsibility for their impiety on our ruler, who is a stranger to all heresy. I should advise his majesty to follow his grandfather, Herakleios, of blessed memory. When Herakleios learned that many holy fathers refused the *Ekthesis* on account of the heresy it promoted, he dispatched letters to the churches disclaiming all responsibility for the document. He explained that the *Ekthesis* was not his invention, but that of Patriarch

---

[57] Saint Maximos: "Sin is a certain incorrect use of nature by the mode of the incorrect use of the motion proper to nature. But sin is not a rational principle or power proper to nature, because it is contrary to that rational principle and law of nature....The will of the Savior's humanity, even though natural, was nevertheless not 'naked,' as is that natural will proper to us, but was divinized to the uttermost, that is, made to subsist in the most divine manner, as it was the human will of a divine, omniscient person, and in a manner beyond our power by dint of the union, to which its sinlessness may also be correctly ascribed. But our will is 'naked' and, because of its capacity for alteration, by no means sinless. Not that nature alters, but that natural motion is capable of being turned to different courses (diverted)....So it is clear then that sin is an error from the choice elected out of many alternatives, that is, multiple 'goods' from which to choose, but this in no way changes the nature into an irrational essence nor diverts it from its innate existence, which is rational." See "The Twentieth Opuscule (by 640): The Dogmatic Tome to Marinos the Priest," *Theological and Polemical Works*.

Sergios. If our lord Constans should elect to imitate Herakleios in this matter, he would be exonerated." Troilos and Sergios pondered a long while on the venerable man's suggestion, and then said, "Father, it would be troublesome, nay, rather not feasible, to follow such a course of action." The subject, therefore, was then changed. Troilos and Sergios Efkrates then departed on cordial terms with the holy man.

Saint Maximos and His Disciples are Interrogated at the Royal Palace[58]

A week later, on a Saturday, Father Maximos and his two disciples, both named Anastasios, were summoned to the royal palace for further questioning. Father Anastasios, the former legate of the Church of Rome, was left outside. The other Father Anastasios, whom the saint knew longer, was brought in and presented to the senate and two patriarchs, Peter of Constantinople and Makarios of Antioch. Father Maximos' enemies began hurling slanderous charges against the elder. While Father Maximos was being falsely accused, those present desired to have Father Anastasios cooperate with them and corroborate the charges. Father Anastasios refused to collaborate with them against his elder. He, therefore, bravely stood against the patriarchs and the senate. Two of the prosecutors, Constantinos and Menas, led the inquisition. Father Anastasios then declared before all, "You have brought in Constantinos. And have you introduced him as the secretary of the palace? He is neither a presbyter nor a monk; rather he is the supervisor of persons of the theater. The Africans and Romans know which women he maintains." When Constantios was thus discovered, some said that the women attached to him were his sisters, while others said that the women traveling with him came that they might commune with the Church of Constantinople. Constantios was then exposed for his shameless gain of money and sordid pleasures. After he was discredited, questioning resumed regarding the *Typos*.

The dignitaries then asked Father Anastasios, "Hast thou anathematized the *Typos*?" Father Anastasios answered, "Indeed, I not only have anathematized it, but also have written a *libellus*, a little book, denouncing it." His questioners then asked, "Dost thou acknowledge that thou hast done badly by this?" Father Anastasios replied, "May God forbid that I should deem it an error to have upheld the ecclesiastical canons!" With God helping him, Father Anastasios answered his interrogators wisely. The dignitaries, however, were frustrated and drove him out.

Father Maximos was then brought into the chamber. Patrician Troilos addressed the venerable elder, saying, "Tell the truth, abba, and the Master Christ shall be merciful with thee. Thou art about to be legally examined in

---

[58] For this section, see also Hieromonk Efthymios' *Maximos the Confessor* (in Greek), pp. 19-22, §§ IB´-IΔ´.

accordance with the laws of this realm. If even one of the charges is proven, thou wilt be sentenced to death." Father Maximos gave answer and said, "I have already spoken, and again I say, that all I have affirmed is the truth. As it is not possible for Satan to become God, so it is not possible to prove even one of your accusations against me. Since Satan is not God, but an apostate, so the accusations against me are untrue and cannot become true. In spite of that, you would have it as you wish. Since it is God Whom I revere, I am not wrong."

Troilos opened his questioning as follows: "Didst thou not anathematize the *Typos*?" Father Maximos answered, "Ofttimes, I have affirmed this." Troilos then pursued this line of questioning further, asking, "If thou hast anathematized the *Typos*, thou hast anathematized the emperor." Such was the logical consequence to the mind of Troilos. But Father Maximos objected and said, "I have not anathematized the emperor. I have anathematized the document which is alien to the Orthodox Faith of the Church." Troilos then queried, "Where was the *Typos* anathematized by thee?" Father Maximos answered, "It was anathematized at the local council in the Church of the Savior and Theotokos at Rome."

The prefect, who was presiding over the interrogation, then interjected, "Wilt thou or wilt thou not enter into communion with the Church of Constantinople?" Father Maximos replied, "I will not enter into communion with your Church." The eparch then demanded, "Why?" Father Maximos answered, "Because your Church has rejected the rulings of the Orthodox synods." The prefect then asked, "If that is the case, then why is it that the fathers of those synods have retained our Church in their diptychs?"[59] Father Maximos asked, "What is the profit in commemorating them, when you throw out their doctrines?" The prefect then asked, "Tell me, canst thou prove that our Church has renounced the dogmas of the holy synods?" Father Maximos replied, "I can demonstrate it very easily, if thou shouldest command it and give me leave."

As all fell silent in the chamber, the secretary then interposed this question: "Why lovest thou the Romans, and hatest the Greeks?" Father Maximos replied, "Our God commands us not to hate anyone. I love the Romans since they hold the same Faith (ὁμοπίστους) as I; and I love the Greeks because we speak the same language (ὁμογλώσσους)." The treasurer then inquired of Father Maximos, "How old art thou?" The elder answered, "Seventy-five." The treasurer then asked, "And thy disciple, how long has he been with thee?" Father Maximos answered, "Thirty-seven years."

---

[59] The diptychs are a two-leaved tablet listing the names of Orthodox dead and living commemorated in eucharistic services.

Then suddenly, one of the clergymen present shouted aloud, "May God render to thee what thou didst bring upon blessed Pyrrhos!" Father Maximos did not answer that derisive comment. The interrogation continued, though neither patriarch spoke a word during the proceedings.

Demosthenes, who appointed himself to be the saint's adversary, injected his mistaken assertions about the Lateran Council held in Rome, saying, "That was not a true council, because he who convened it, namely Martin, was deposed." Father Maximos, the slave of God, corrected Demosthenes—for the ecclesiastical sanctions against Pope Martin, who confessed the Orthodox Faith, were to be deemed invalid—and said, "Pope Martin was not deposed, but persecuted. What synod or canonical act deposed him? If he were canonically deposed, where is the official judgment according to the sacred canons? After all, his predecessor, the holy Pope Theodore, excommunicated Patriarch Pyrrhos and condemned Monotheletism." When Troilos heard this, he merely said, "Thou knowest not what thou art saying, abba; that which happened, has happened."

The interrogation then was completed. A summation of the proceedings was then given. The senators sent out Maximos, while they deliberated upon his case. The decision was made that it would be too humane to allow him to return to exile. They were resolved to hand him over to cruel punishments and torture. Father Maximos and Father Anastasios were therefore given into the custody of the city prefect.

Saint Maximos in the Praetorium and Before the Prefect

In that doleful place, the iniquitous torturer had the holy elder stripped naked and flogged with sharp, ox-hide thongs. The heartless tormentors were not put to shame by Maximos' advanced age and emaciated body, wasted by ascetic labors and lengthy imprisonment. The prefect's executioners left the holy man's body bloodied and torn, and the floor reddened with his blood. Not one single part of his body was left unwounded. The prefect then administered the same brutal punishment to both of Father Maximos' disciples. While this was taking place, a herald kept repeating: "Those who disobey the imperial decrees and those who persist in their insubordination, are justly liable to such punishments." The prisoners were then dragged to their cells. They were nearly half-dead.

The Martyrs Suffer Mutilations[60]

The following day, at dawn, Father Maximos, together with Father Anastasios—the disciple who had been with him longest—were brought before the prefect's tribunal. The holy man, hardly breathing and covered with blood

---

[60] For this section, see also Hieromonk Efthymios' *Maximos the Confessor* (in Greek), pp. 38, 39, § ΛΓ˘.

and ghastly wounds, was a sight that should have inspired compassion if not horror, but which incited the malignant prefect and his minions to devise new punishments. The prefect decided that the penalty for blasphemy was removal of the tongue. The venerable Maximos' tongue was torn out from the very root. In this way, the heretics thought to render the elder silent. Father Anastasios also suffered the same. Both holy men were then cast into prison. The Physician of bodies, Christ, Who of old "perfected praise out of the mouths of babes and sucklings [cf. Ps. 8:2; Mt. 21:16]" and bestowed speech upon the dumb,[61] also then granted speech to His faithful slaves, Fathers Maximos and Anastasios. Though tongueless, they miraculously received the ability to speak

Saint Maximos the Confessor

more clearly than when they had tongues. The heretics were roundly ashamed by this wonderworking. In their anger and malice, the heretics took a knife and plunged it through the elder's right wrist, which stroke severed the hand. The heretics then cast to the floor that hand which wrote divinely inspired wisdom. They justified this amputation as fitting for one whose hand penned blasphemies. They also said that it was traditional punishment for those who had spoken and written against the emperor. Then they went to Father Anastasios, stabbed his right hand in the same manner, and severed it. As for the other Anastasios, the former legate, he did not suffer these gruesome mutilations. Since his right hand had once been employed as the imperial notary, they decided he could keep that member.

The lurid crimes perpetrated against the prisoners did not end with dismemberment. The prefect contrived further sufferings. Father Maximos and Father Anastasios were removed from the praetorium. They were dragged and maltreated through the marketplace and all twelve quarters *(tmeemata)* of the city. Their amputated tongues and hands were displayed to clamoring crowds.

---

[61] See Mt. 15:30, 31; Mk. 7:37.

Saints Maximos, Anastasios, and Anastasios in Their Final Exile

That Sunday, the emperor was persuaded to banish the prisoners. The prefect's men then prepared to take the three prisoners to separate places of exile. The prisoners were unshod and nearly naked. They received neither medical treatment, nor food, nor drink, nor covering. Who can describe the hardships, sufferings, pain, and hemorrhaging? Our Father Maximos was unable to sit in an upright position on either a horse or in a carriage. The jarring of a moving wagon for the elder was excruciating. The soldiers, thereupon, wove a basket of switches, making for the elder a bed of sorts. The holy man was placed within the basket. With great difficulty, he was conveyed far away to the place of his banishment, the Schemarion fortress in Lazika, by the southeast shore of the Black Sea.[62] This would be his final earthly separation from his disciples. The younger Anastasios was taken to Thrace, to a desolate fortress. He underwent such cruel treatment and suffering while being transported, that he reposed after a few days in his place of exile. The other Anastasios, the former *apokrisiarios*, was banished to the land of the Albanians. He was also made to endure many torments for twenty years until he departed to his much-desired Lord. Anastasios the *apokrisiarios* had written the lengthy biography of his Elder Maximos, describing his labors and sufferings.

Saint Maximos in the Fortress at Schemarion

The thrice-blessed Maximos lived another three years in the fortress at Schemarion, confined to a dungeon. With only one hand, the ailing elder was compelled to care for his own needs. He bore with many hardships, afflictions, and ill treatment to the end. Father Maximos withstood all for the sake of the person of Christ and His body, the holy Orthodox Church.

The Repose and Grave of Saint Maximos

Before the venerable elder completed the course of his earthly sojourn, the Lord comforted His much-suffering servant with a divine visitation. The Master summoned Maximos to the heavenly Jerusalem, by revealing to him the day and hour of his repose. This ushered in great joy for the martyr and confessor, who then gladly surrendered his soul into the hands of Christ God, Whom he had loved from his youth and for Whom he had suffered so greatly. The heavenly man and earthly angel, Saint Maximos,

---

[62] Schemarion or Schiomaris (Tsikhe-Muris), near present-day Tsageri in Georgia. The Laz fortress was near the frontier with Alania, which was in the western Caucasus, not far from the Black Sea. Schemarion was situated near two Byzantine trading centers, Sotirioupolis and Sebastopolis. The Alans guarded the Darial pass in the middle of the Caucasus range, through which caravans on the silk route passed from China to Constantinople.

reposed in Lazika on the 21st day of January, in the year 662, at the age of eighty-two.[63]

Saint Maximos and His Tomb

After the interment of the relics of Saint Maximos in Schemarion, there appeared every night three lamps over his tomb. They miraculously burned and illuminated the entire place. This wondrous phenomenon confirmed for many how much boldness the venerable Maximos found before the Master Christ, to Whom is due all glory, honor, and veneration, together with the Father and the Holy Spirit, forever and ever. Amen.

Epilogue

Within twenty years of the repose of Saint Maximos, the Sixth Œcumenical Synod was convened in Constantinople. The sessions took place between the 7th of November, in the year 680, to the 16th of September, in the year 681, during the reign of Constantine Pogonatos, in the Troullos (Trullo). The fathers who attended numbered one hundred and seventy, according to Photios, Nikephoros, and Neilos. Others count three hundred and eighty-nine members. George of Constantinople distinguished himself at this synod, as well as the Presbyters Theodore and Sergios, and Deacon John, who acted as exarchs of Agatho of Rome. Monk Peter represented the Archbishop of Alexandria, and Presbyter George represented the Archbishop of Jerusalem. There were also present three bishops representing the westerners. The synod condemned the following bishops for heresy: Pope Honorius of Rome; Patriarchs Sergios, Pyrrhos, Paul, and Peter of Constantinople; Patriarch Kyros of Alexandria; Patriarch Makarios of Antioch; Bishops Theodore of Pharan and Apergios of Perga; Priest Polychronios of Antioch; Hegumen Stephen of Antioch; and many others who were in error.

This synod dogmatized that our Lord Jesus Christ, though but one hypostasis, after His incarnation, possessed two natural wills and two natural energies, just as He also possessed two natures—that is to say, a divine will and energy and a human will and energy, both of them being at the same time indivisible and inconflatable. "In Christ there are two natural wills and two natural energies—indivisible, inconvertible, inseparable, unconfused." For neither the divinity nor the humanity, the two natures of Christ, remained without a will and an energy after the union. For if the peculiarities of the natures should be refuted, which are the will and the energy, the natures themselves should inevitably be refuted too, along therewith. For every nature consists of and is identical with its natural peculiarities, and without these it

---

[63] As a point of interest, in 668, Constans II, while in Syracuse of Sicily, was murdered while bathing. It is unclear whether he was struck in the head by a servant or stabbed by conspirators.

could not become existent. Accordingly, this synod dogmatized, in brief, that "in the hypostasis of the God-Man Logos, each form acted in communion with that of the other one, which it had had as its own." This means, in other words, that the Logos wrought that which was the function of the Logos, whereas the body performed that which was the function of the body—just as the Fourth Œcumenical Synod had dogmatized, that is to say, previously by means of Pope Leo's letter. Now these two wills "are not contrary the one to the other,...but His human will follows and that not as resisting and reluctant, but rather as subject to His divine and omnipotent will....For as His flesh is called and is the flesh of God the Logos, so also the natural will of His flesh is called and is the proper will of God the Logos." The bishops concluded, "Therefore, we confess two wills and two energies, concurring most fitly in Him for the salvation of the human race." The decisions of the synod were embodied in an imperial edict hung up in the atrium of Hagia Sophia. On the 23rd of December, in the year 681, the decisions were promulgated to all the bishops of the empire. Since Pope Agatho had already reposed, his successor, Leo II, approved the definition of the synod and had it translated into Latin and sent for subscription to the bishops of the west.

The earlier opponents of Monotheletism—Saints Maximos the Confessor, Pope Martin I, and Sophronios of Jerusalem—were thus vindicated. Jesus Christ is to be confessed as one single hypostasis with a divine will and energy and a human will and energy, united without confusion. The incarnate Logos has joined two natural wills and two natural energies, a circumincession (*perichoresis*), but has preserved the characteristics of each nature. Thus, our humanity has been divinized in its totality. To complete the synod's work and to issue disciplinary canons, the Trullo Synod again convened in 691-692. The holy Church commemorates the Sixth Œcumenical Synod on the 14th of September.

On the 21st of January, the holy Church commemorates the holy Martyr NEOPHYTOS.[64]

Neophytos, the wondrous ascetic and martyr, was truly a heavenly "new plant," which is the interpretation of his name in the Greek language, and an evergreen tree that blossomed forth during the years of the profane

---

[64] The Life of this saint was recorded in Greek by Saint Symeon the Metaphrastes, whose manuscript begins, "The notables of the city...." The text is extant in the Athonite Monastery of Iveron and in other places. Another manuscript of the saint's martyrdom is preserved at the Great Lavra and begins, "Not only many but...." This latter text was rendered in simpler Greek by Agapios the Cretan, who published it in his *Neon Paradeison*; it was then incorporated into *The Great Synaxaristes* (in Greek).

Emperors Diocletian and Maximian (290). Hailing from Nicaea, he was the scion of wealthy and pious parents of noble birth. His father was called Theodore and his mother Florentia. The two of them were virtuous Christians and zealots of the Faith. Neophytos emulated his parents' good example. As a result, from his early youth, moral excellence and virtue characterized his way of life. It indicated beforehand the interior state in which he would attain perfection. He loathed proud thoughts and boasting. For this reason he did not wish to keep company with vainglorious and silly companions, but only with those who were humble-minded. Such persons generally were often poor in this world's wealth. Neophytos was moved to compassion for

Saint Neophytos

them and ofttimes distributed bread given to him by his parents for his own sustenance. Therefore, the thrice-blessed youth on many occasions went hungry. Such was the conduct of the enlightened and divine Neophytos from an early age.

"How can I," asks the biographer, "recount his hidden and inexplicable life, which was truly marvellous?" Even in the first bloom of his youth, he wrought a wonder like unto that of Moses [Ex. 17:6]. On one occasion, the goodly Neophytos was in the company of other children. He was then only nine years of age in the flesh, but an old man in understanding. Neophytos uttered a prayer at the door of the church and struck a rock with one finger. Straightway—O Thy boundless power, Logos!—as though a spring were sealed and then opened, a vast supply of water and milk poured forth. Later, great crowds were able to partake and quench their thirst. The drink from that rock was extraordinary. The children satisfied both their souls and bodies, so that they ate and drank nothing else. As for the humble-minded Neophytos, wise beyond his years, he in no wise became vainglorious on account of this mysterious and exceptional wonder. Neither did he ask of his companions any wage or money for that excellent draft. He did, however, ask that they not report what had taken place.

Howsoever carefully the blessed youth attempted to conceal this virtue and excellence, so much more did the Lord make him known in every place and reveal what was hidden and unknown. Now his mother Florentia beheld a mysterious dream, which revealed the virtue of the child and his uncommon achievements. His mother was in such a state of wonder regarding her child that she was at a loss how to understand what she beheld and what it might portend. Was it real, or was it an apparition or a phantom? She therefore entreated the Lord with tears, uttering such words as these: "Master and God, Who knows all things before they come to pass and Who foreordains what comes to be, reveal the vision to me that I might comprehend its meaning, so as to know the future progress of my child." So spoke Florentia; and the all-good God, Who works wonders and extraordinary signs so as to affirm the truth of our belief and entices us to what is to our benefit, hearkened to her prayer. For she had beheld a dove, verily having wings but gold on the broad of its back. She had also observed that it entered into Neophytos' chamber and flew around the bed and then sat upon it. Florentia was amazed at what she witnessed and was sure that such a dove was not some irrational creature, but instead a divine visitation and heavenly promise. She then received an explanation when she spoke to the dove as though it were innately rational: "For what reason hast thou perched upon the bed of the lad?" The dove replied—O the miracle!—in a human voice, saying, "The Holy Spirit sent me to hover over the bed of Neophytos, so that I should cast out every assault of the enemy and preserve his bedding pure and blameless."

As Florentia clearly heard this divine voice, an ineffable light descended, so that she could not bear it. It was as if a great bolt of lightning had struck her. She had become so stirred at the sights and sounds about her that she fell to the ground and expired. "I think," writes the biographer, "that she beheld a vision of angels. Their intense light and sublime majesty were too much for her to endure and understand." Thus, she remained without breathing and speaking. She was discovered by the neighbors, who determined that she had expired. Since they could not know what was about to take place, they carried on with the customary preparations for burial. Now Neophytos in no wise grieved for the death of his mother, but rather was happy and would not leave them to inter her. He insisted that they cease grieving, and said, "Leave her until my father should come." Then a man, a friend of Theodore, named Leivadios, who was a leader of the senate, sent a message to Theodore of the sudden and unexpected death of his wife. Theodore had been in a field. When he heard the mournful news, he ran toward the city. He was in great distress and anguish, as copious tears streamed down his face. As he was on the road, he was met by Leivadios, who attempted to console him lest he should become embittered. When Neophytos caught sight of his father approaching their home, he went forth and said, "Cease sorrowing, father, that mother has finished her course. For even though she appears to be dead to those present, yet I am able with divine help to raise her up." Neophytos then returned to the house. He took the hand of his dead mother and said, "Rise up, O mother, forasmuch as the Lord has willed it, thou hast slept enough."

O the exceptional wonderworking! How wonderful and awesome was the appearance of our Savior Jesus Christ Who brought death to nought and brought to light life and incorruption through the Gospel [2 Tim. 1:10]. Before the divine took on flesh, Hades was terrifying to us, and death was not to be evaded. But after the death of the immortal One, death was put to death, and Hades was despoiled of those held captive. Thus, the soul of Florentia, upon hearing the command of Neophytos, returned speedily to her body. She awakened as one from sleep and recounted her vision to Theodore. When she began speaking of the dove, all present then beheld that very dove above the bed of Neophytos, commanding him to depart as once did the Patriarch Abraham. He was bade to leave all earthly things and kinfolk and go after the true land and everlasting life. Now this voice the bystanders also heard, but only the pious, those acquainted with divine operations, believed the words. Neophytos thereupon bade them farewell and kissed them sweetly. These supernatural occurrences became the talk of the blind and mindless idolaters, some of whom, that is, those who thought more deeply and were noble-minded, converted from their ancestral impiety and came to believe in the Christ and receive Baptism.

The highly exceptional Neophytos took to heart all that had tran-spired, and also heard of the conversions. He believed it was God's will that he had conceived the desire to go to Olympos, which is a mountain near Nicaea. It is a wilderness place, inspiring awe and wonder, and is the home to earthly angels and the most holy of men. Now Neophytos was only a ten-year-old lad when he left the city to go to Olympos. At that time, the dove also accompanied the youth and guided him on the road, until he arrived at the mount. After he made a tour of nearly all the cells of the fathers and received from each one counsel to his soul's benefit, Neophytos ascended a lofty height, a rock projecting into the air, which had a hollow in its side, something like a cave. The dove entered first and then Neophytos. Once inside, the holy youth encountered a fearsome lion, which was sufficient to strike terror in an army camp and cause all to scatter in fear and trembling. The saint, however, in no wise cowered; but rather, he took hold of the beast by its mane and said, "Thou hast dwelt herein long enough. Give to me thy den and find another habitation; for thus it is commanded by the Holy Spirit." Then that wild beast—lo, the miracle!—as though it were a rational and cognitive man, rose up on its hind legs and kissed the chest of the youth, turning its head with much gentleness. After the animal licked Neophytos' feet, it swept the ground carefully. The creature then bowed its head in a gesture that seemed to say, "Pardon me," and then it departed to fulfill the saint's command.

Neophytos lived there for one year, sustained on heavenly bread and supported by a divine spirit, for every day a holy angel came and brought him a fixed ration. At the close of one year, the angel, together with the food, gave the saint a book in which were written the following words: "Holy, Holy, Holy, Lord of Sabaoth, thus I command thee, Neophytos, and enjoin: the number of thy parents' years approaches the end. Therefore leave the mountain and go to thy homeland for the maintenance of thine elderly parents. After thou hast given them burial, return again to Me, thy heavenly Father." The blessed youth read what was written in the book and understood that he was being commanded to descend the mount, to do which was as bitter as leaving Paradise. At first, in his thoughts, he hesitated to comply and did not know whether to go or remain. He then thought better of it, after he pondered on the perils wrought by disobedience. He deemed it unseemly to disobey the divine command, so he descended the mountain, hoping in the Lord's providence that all would come about according to His holy will. Neophytos then entered into Nicaea. He went to his parents to whom he ministered in accordance with the divine ordinance. He in no wise relaxed his ascetic conduct of life, nor did he leave off his remembrance of God. Even as Saint Paul wrote, Neophytos could say with him, "I have been crucified with Christ; and I no longer live, but Christ liveth in me; and the life that I now live in the flesh I live in faith [Gal. 2:20]." As it was foretold to him, he buried his parents. He then set about distributing the estate to the poor. Neophytos then returned to the mountain and resumed his former life, which was equal to that of the angels. Thus we have now spoken a little about the accomplishments of Neophytos in his youth and his ascetic contests. Now let us speak of his toilsome life and martyric bouts, for which he received a rich reward and became the recipient of a double crown, that is to say, of asceticism and the martyric contest.

At that time, Diocletian and Maximian, the antichrist emperors, were reigning. They posted to the province of Bithynia one harsh and inhuman governor, named Maximos. Even his appearance was ferocious, and his way of thinking more beastly than that of the beasts. The tortures he inflicted upon the Christians were savage and merciless. He sent little children to be burned to death or cut up into small pieces or to be drowned at sea. In his evil and perverse mind, he was seeking new ways and means, together with unspeakable machines and appliances of punishment, to put to death the soul before the body. By these means, that most vile man was able to vanquish some by the employment of the harshest tortures imaginable and bring them to offer incense to the senseless idols. Such persons preferred—alas!—temporal life and everlasting torments rather than the everlasting kingdom and life—for which preference the profane Maximos honored them with the rewards of corruptible wealth and soon withering glory. But there were others who readily gave over their flesh to diverse torments and ten thousand punishments. These all-wise contestants chose to disdain transitory prosperity that they might enjoy the everlasting good things.

An angel from on high then came to Neophytos. He relayed his commission from God, which was a command that Neophytos enter far-famed Nicaea to participate in a soul-saving martyrdom. Neophytos hastened eagerly, taking the helmet of salvation and the sword of the Spirit [Eph. 6:17]. Then suddenly, as lightning, he leaped into the theater and was as radiant as the sun. All who beheld him were astonished at the unexpected sight of this dazzling and beardless youth. The tyrant interpreted his presence as a desire to sacrifice to the idols. But afterward, when he heard Neophytos censuring the ignorance and vanity of idol worship, and preaching Christ as true God, the wretched Maximos was infuriated and threatened to chastize Neophytos harshly if he did not quickly offer sacrifice. The wise Neophytos laughed and said, "Is not thine own perdition enough, O Maximos? Must thou, O ignorant one, constrain with violence even the wise to participate in thy deception?" The tyrant's anger waxed so hot that he forgot to take pleasure in the festal events planned that day in the theater. Putting aside the day's program, he ordered that Neophytos be stripped naked and suspended from a rope. He then bade his executioners to scrape and flay the Christian's flesh and to administer a pitiless thrashing.

These orders were carried out. Behold the profound perseverance of the martyr! He received five hundred blows from rods. He was taken down and subjected to further scraping and carving of his bodily members. Then the executioners applied vinegar and salt to his wounds, so as to usher in bitter pain. The saint kept praying to Christ to enlighten these Greek pagans, that they might come to piety and thirst for their salvation. As for himself, the saint did not leave off teaching them. He continued preaching and saying, "Men, brothers, neglect not your salvation. But come to know that there is one true God Who made man, whom He made anew with His taking on of flesh. Do not therefore be venerating the wicked demons who are leading you into everlasting punishment, but leave the darkness and the guileful and vain demons and come forth to the light. Do not fear Maximos, neither his craftiness nor beastliness. Cower not before the various torments, for the Master Christ shall stand by you and empower you. He shall lighten the pains of the punishments and prepare for us everlasting blessedness."

These and many more counsels were uttered by the saint. For the sake of brevity, we cannot impart all that he said, but we will say that he urged those godless men to come to repentance. He exhorted them not to offer sacrifice to the lifeless images or the demons that dwell in them. He spoke of the incarnation and redemption. As for the unfit governor, it was observed that his rage increased against the lover of Christ. The tyrant therefore ordered worse torments. Whatever flesh remained from the previous torture was to be scraped with iron claws. This detestable mutilation was carried out, leaving exposed the bones on each side of the martyr. Now some of the Greek pagans, observing this extreme maiming, approached and thought to offer their sympathy, saying, "Take pity on thy youth, O Neophytos, and offer sacrifice to the gods that thou mayest be delivered from these fearsome tortures." The saint, rather than suffering from his bodily wounds, was more pained over their soul-injuring counsel. He thereupon wished to show he had overcome the punishment and eagerly sought martyrdom, and began saying, "I have sacrificed my flesh to God, and I also wish to offer a sacrifice of praise. I desire to render my prayers to the Most High Who became incarnate for the sake of His many tender mercies and Who was crucified of His own will that He should bring to nought and utterly destroy the abominations of the idols before which you, as those without sense, fall down and worship. As the almighty One, He has put an end to your repugnant and profane sacrifices."

The words of the martyr inflamed the tyrant to the extent that he bade his men to exchange the iron claws for cutting instruments, which were able to cut through bone, not only the martyr's ribs, but his hands and feet also. Thus the torturers were able to render damage and dismember all bodily members, leaving nothing uninjured. The heinous atrocities that were performed left the martyr a most pitiable sight. The mindless tyrant, however, still attempted to pervert the martyr's resolve by flattery and promises of honors and gifts without number. The saint, not heeding Maximos' words in the least, gave forth the appropriate answer, saying, "I am ready to undergo, and happily, tens of thousands of deaths for the sake of Christ. I therefore tell thee not to entertain any hope that I might deny piety for temporal pleasure and enjoyment or out of fear of punishments, even if they were more harsh than what has already been done." The tyrant, as a result, gave up in despair. He was saddened and depressed because he was unable to vanquish, with so many methods of torture, one beardless boy.

The governor kept going over in his mind what he might execute next. It then came into his mind to inform the emperors regarding this case, so that they too might also wonder at this monstrous report. He therefore submitted a description of all events and sought their guidance on how to proceed. The emperors, upon receiving Maximos' account of the proceedings, wrote back that the prisoner should be cast into a fiery furnace. The ferocious Maximos did not wish to put the martyr to a quick death, but rather ordered that there be a great celebration and that costly, sweet smelling spices be offered to the gods. Thus, great amounts of incense were brought to the place of sacrifice. Maximos thought that perhaps the saint might change his mind and venerate the idols. The sacrifice was to take place at the pillar of Hercules, a gymnasium filled with statues of the emperors. The abominable altar was decorated according to pagan taste when the martyr was brought forth. Maximos incited the young martyr to sacrifice before the image of Hercules, so that Neophytos might be endowed with strength. The martyr answered this ludicrous suggestion, saying, "I revere and pay homage to only one trihypostatic God—Father, Son, and Holy Spirit—to Whom I solely offer sacrifice, not with oxen and bulls and birds. 'A sacrifice unto God is a broken spirit; a heart that is broken and humbled God will not despise [Ps. 50:17].' I offer to my God my entire self, that is, all my heart, soul, mind, and strength [Mk. 12:30]. As for your Hercules, I deem you deceived and unhappy, because you worship a dead and insensate idol." The tyrant finally perceived the immovable stance of the saint, so he ordered the firing of a great and terrifying furnace. The amount of wood thrown within could not be estimated. This stoking was followed by the saint being cast inside. The portal of the furnace was carefully shut off. It was decided that Neophytos would be left therein for three days so that his bones would also be consumed.

On the third day, the impious were thinking that the martyr had been burned to ashes. They believed that the furnace had been extinguished, so they prepared to open its door. As this was done, straightway, there leaped out from the furnace mighty flames which burned all those standing about. The saint—O heavenly might! O divine wonderworking!—emerged from the fiery furnace healthy and uninjured. Not even one hair of his head or a thread of his garment had been singed. To the censure of the lawless, the martyr was chanting in a loud voice to the almighty God Who works wonders. The tyrant, put to shame as one impotent and weak, then ventured to contrive another form of death.

Therefore, he who was more mindless than the wild beasts, ordered animals from the wild to be brought forward. Those animals were left five days without being fed anything. After this was done, the first creature set loose upon the martyr was a fierce bear. At first it moved toward the saint, but then as it drew closer it began licking the martyr's feet. By the grace of God, the bear was made to forget its hunger and ferocity and behaved as a tame lamb. The tyrant then had a leopard released into the area. In the same manner as the bear, it behaved gently as though it possessed a rational nature, and kissed the martyr's feet. Even after this attempt failed, the tyrant loosed a ferocious lion against the saint. But this was the very lion which had deferred to the divine Neophytos and left its den.

As the lion came up to the saint, the creature recognized him and began ardently kissing his body. He shook his tail, and then was seen leaping about, showing obvious signs of joy at the discovery of an acquaintance and friend. The saint then bade the lion to return to its old habitat, but without injuring any man on the way. Thus the creature endowed with an irrational nature changed its wildness into rational understanding. As for the mindless and most profane Maximos, since he could succeed in no punishment against the martyr, he became more irrational than the wild animals. He commanded his soldiers to pierce the martyr's body all over with spits until he should surrender his spirit. When this was done and Maximos observed that Neophytos, although filled with tormenting spits, still stood upright and fearless, he became so filled with wrath that he took hold of a spear and rushed against the holy Neophytos, penetrating his heart. In this manner then, the adamantine man completed his martyrdom. He offered himself as an acceptable sacrifice, winning a double crown after struggling with the hardships attendant with asceticism and enduring the unspeakable tortures of the tyrant, including the bonds, iron instruments, mangling, wounds, fire, flayings, wild beasts, and spear. He went forth bearing crowns to the Lord, to Whom is due glory, honor, and veneration to the endless ages. Amen.

On the 21st of January, the holy Church commemorates our venerable Father ZOSIMUS, Bishop of Syracuse, who reposed in peace.

Zosimus, our venerable father, hailed from the island of Sicily. He was the son of godly and faithful parents, who were self-supporting landowners and performed good works. They had a property near the Monastery of Saint Lucia the Virgin, who is commemorated by the holy Church on the 13th of December. After they gave birth to Zosimus and he was weaned from his mother's milk, the parents dedicated the boy to that very monastery located in Syracuse and to the service of Saint Lucia (Lucy) located in Syracuse. The reason for this dedication was the fulfillment of a vow which the parents made before their child's birth. Together with their son, they also donated to the monastery that property mentioned earlier. Thus, from an early age, about seven years old, Zosimus was reared at Santa Lucia's by the abbot himself, Faustus, who brought up the lad in the instruction and fear of the Lord, teaching him diligently the canons and traditions of the Church. Since the lad was quick of mind and applied himself diligently to his lessons and studies, in but a little while he achieved all that was morally excellent and virtuous. In all that he undertook, he demonstrated

Saint Zosimus

patience and perseverance. He was also humble-minded and meek, being enriched by obedience and purity.

Since the venerable one achieved such an excellent conduct of life, he was charged with the care of the relics of their patroness, Saint Lucia. He therefore was assigned as *prosmonarios* to attend to the pilgrims who came to the church and venerated the relics. He was still a youth when given this charge. During the time of this commission, he kept bringing to remembrance his parents and was desirous to behold them. Vanquished by his yearning, he went to see them. The parents, however, quickly escorted him back and reprimanded him, saying, "There, child, thou art obliged to remain, in the place where thou wast dedicated." They finally arrived at the monastery, and the seriousness of his lapse was impressed upon him. That night, Saint Lucia came forth from her reliquary and frightened Zosimus. She was just about to administer a severe spanking when there appeared another woman, glorious to behold and clad in imperial purple. It was she, perhaps the Lady Theotokos, who shielded him. Though Saint Lucia had just begun the punishment, she desisted, somewhat embarrassed, before the great Lady. Saint Lucia then commanded him not to leave the monastery again for such a reason. He promised to guard her relics, and verily he did, as he settled down to a life of prayer, contemplation, and work.

The blessed Zosimus also gives an account of a certain woman, the daughter of a house of noble lineage, whose mind and purpose were bent toward shamelessness and uncleanness. As a result, she had received a beating by her husband. She then went to the Monastery of Santa Lucia in order to spread abroad her affliction, claiming she was a woman much tried under the wrath of her husband and required medical treatment. Then, when night fell, Saint Lucia cried out, making a sound that pierced the ears of a sleeping Zosimus. He heard the saint say, "Cast out that rank smell from the monastery." He then saw Saint Lucia pointing with her finger. Zosimus, although very frightened, went and spoke to that woman's handmaidens, saying, "Rouse thy mistress quickly and take her, together with her bedding, outside." The handmaidens approached their mistress and began trembling, for they could see that she had expired.

At length, the abbot of the Monastery of Santa Lucia was translated to the Lord. Consequently, there arose great uncertainty regarding the choice of a successor. The fathers of that brotherhood, as one body, went to Bishop John of Syracuse with the intention of having him make the appointment for them of another worthy abbot. They left behind Zosimus to guard the monastery and shrine, and to answer the door. The bishop gazed upon them and asked, "But is there another brother in the monastery?" They answered, "There is none other except one whom we left to attend to the monastery."

The bishop then replied, "I know that he is the one who is worthy to become abbot." Therefore Father Zosimus was summoned. The bishop sealed his appointment and presented him to the brethren, saying, "Behold, brothers, the one whom God has chosen to be thy master and superior."

Not much time passed before the venerable Zosimus was also ordained to the priesthood. He governed the monastery for forty years with all meekness and forbearance. He was renowned for his pure love and excessive sympathy. He governed the monastery with such love, wisdom, and prudence that no predecessor or successor ever surpassed him. He never assigned an obedience or task which he himself had not previously undertaken.

Now when the see of Syracuse fell vacant circa 647, the people elected Zosimus, but he declined the dignity. As for the clergy, they selected a priest called Vanerius, a rather vain and ambitious man. The petitions of the people did not go ignored when an appeal came before Pope Theodore I (642-649), who decided in favor of the abbot of Santa Lucia. Bishop Zosimus shepherded the flock of his see in a venerable and God-pleasing manner for thirteen years. He wrought many miracles and maintained his ascetical conduct of life. He was renowned for his liberality to the poor and his zeal in preaching the word of God to the people. He brought many unbelievers to belief, and converted the wicked to the paths of virtue. He healed many sick folk, ailing from various diseases, before his own interment and after. He delivered sufferers from demonic possession and restored sight to the blind. There was a certain Christian whose spouse had a condition of hemorrhaging. When a portion from the saint's clothing was taken and given to her as a blessing, by means of that swatch the flow of blood was immediately halted, and she was healed of her sickness. Saint Zosimus reposed in peace at the age of nearly ninety, in about the year 660.

On the 21st of January, the holy Church commemorates the holy Martyrs EVGENIOS, VALERIAN, KANDIDOS,[65] and AQUILAS (AKYLAS) of Trebizond.[66]

---

[65] In other *Synaxaristae* the name Kandidos (Candidus) is given as Kanidios.

[66] Trebizond (mod. Trabzon, 41°00′N 39°43′E) was the greatest city of Pontos because of its harbor. It was restored by Diocletian after a Gothic attack. It was made into a legionary base. It became an archbishopric in the 8th C. and a metropolis of the diocese of Lazike in the early 10th C. Later, the Trapezuntine Empire became one of the three successor states to the Byzantine Empire, lasting from 1204 to 1461. *Oxford*, s.v. "Trebizond."

Saint Evgenios

Saint Aquilas

Evgenios and those holy martyrs with him suffered during the years of Diocletian and Maximian, the ungodly emperors, when Lysias (Lysios) was military commander, in 292. A bloody and cruel persecution had been launched against the Christians, which caused many of the faithful to flee into the mountains of Trebizond of Pontos. First among those arrested were Valerian, Kandidos, and Aquilas, who confessed the Christ as the only true God. They were banished to the narrow fortress, named Pityous, in the land of the Lazes known as Lazika.[67] From thence, they were brought to Trebizond and made to stand before Lysias. He ordered that they be flogged with the sinews of oxen. After this torture, the three martyrs were suspended and made to suffer the scraping and flaying of their flesh with iron claws. This punishment was followed by burning with lit torches.

---

[67] "Lazika, at first, was the southwest region of ancient Colchis lying along the east shore of the Black Sea. It included the mouth of the Phasis River. In the 4th C., the Lazes extended their suzerainty northward toward Abchasia and Svaneti (Suania)." Ibid., s.v. "Lazika."

Saint Valerian

Saint Kandidos

It is to be noted that the executioners administering this punishment became exhausted and fell prostrate to the ground. The sight of his men collapsing agitated Lysias, who then ordered that the saints be incarcerated.

Within days, the holy Evgenios was discovered and arrested. After he confessed the Christ, the pagans gave him a merciless thrashing. Next he was taken with Lysias to the temple of the idols. By the lever of the martyr's prayers, the images were toppled, shattered, and turned into dust. The pagans took hold of Evgenios and stretched him out, binding ropes to his hands and feet. Making use of thick rods, they struck him repeatedly. Then they suspended him and employed all their strength scraping his sides with iron claws. This was followed by the application of lit lamps to burn his body. Then they utilized both salt and vinegar to introduce the most bitter of pains as they rubbed his wounds. After they implemented all these tortures, they placed Evgenios with the other three martyrs, Valerian, Kandidos, and Aquilas, into a red-hot furnace. The four confessors survived this fiery ordeal unscathed. The impious then struck off the martyrs' heads, and thus the blessed ones received the incorruptible crowns of martyrdom.

On the 21ˢᵗ of January, the holy Church celebrates the SYNAXIS of Saint IRENE, the most holy church by the sea.[68]

On the 21ˢᵗ of January, the holy Church commemorates the holy Martyr AGNES of Rome.

Agnes, the holy martyr, was from the city of Rome, which was also the place of her triumph. She was the offspring of illustrious and prominent parents. Her Greek name, meaning "pure," also bespoke the manner of her blameless life. At the time of her glorious death, Agnes was a young maiden. She would teach and exhort other women to take hold of faith and love in the Savior. Her riches and beauty caused her to be one of the most sought out young ladies, and many young noblemen of the first families in Rome contended as rivals for her hand. Nevertheless, Agnes answered them saying she had consecrated her virginity to a heavenly Husband, the Master Christ.

Saint Agnes

In 303, the cruel edicts of Diocletian against the Christians were published. Agnes' suitors, finding her resolution unshakable, accused her before the governor as a Christian. It was their hope that since

---

[68] Saint Constantine the Great (324-337) enlarged this church and gave it the name of Eirene (Peace), before the inauguration of Hagia Sophia in 360. It was burned down in 532, and rebuilt by Justinian I (527-565). It was destroyed by the earthquake of 740, and probably rebuilt by Constantine V (741-775). The church is the second largest standing in Constantinople. It has the form of a domed basilica with a flat, second dome covering the west bay. The lower part is Justinianic, but the upper part dates from after 740. The Turks altered the colonnades and made it an arsenal. There are some remnants of mosaics in the narthex. *Oxford*, s.v. "Irene, Church of Saint." See also the Life of Saint Marcian, commemorated the 10ᵗʰ of January.

allurements made no impression on her, the threat of torments would prove more effective against one of her tender years. At first, the judge employed the mildest expressions and seductive promises, but Agnes paid no heed. She would only repeat that she could have no other spouse but Jesus Christ. He then made use of threats, but she was endowed with much courage and was even eager to suffer torment and death that she might gain a better resurrection and enter into everlasting bliss. At that juncture, they decided to display before her a blazing fire, iron hooks, racks, and other instruments of torture, all the while threatening to employ them upon her. However, she appeared undismayed and displayed good cheer in the presence of the fierce and cruel executioners. She was so far from betraying the slightest symptom of terror that she even expressed her joy at the sight and offered herself to the rack.

They then dragged her before the idols, and the Roman governor commanded her to offer incense. Nonetheless, they could not compel her to move her hand to sacrifice, for she would continue to make the sign of the Cross with it. The governor, seeing his measures proven ineffective, threatened to send her to a house of prostitution, where what she prized so highly (that is, her virginity) could be exposed to the insult and outrages of the licentious men of Rome.[69] Agnes remarked that her Christ was too jealous of the purity of His chosen one to suffer it to be violated in such a manner, for He was her defender and protector. Then she said, "Thou mayest stain thy sword with my blood, but thou shalt never be able to profane my body, which is consecrated to Christ! Moreover, I will not offer sacrifice to thy gods, even though thou shouldest threaten me with a house of ill-repute, because I have

---

[69] In this manner, Christian virgins were treated as objects of public contempt, for no greater shame can be inflicted upon maidens than to be viewed naked by lustful and wanton eyes. Therefore, Christian maidens, to the insult of the holy Faith, were given over to panderers or to wanton youths, or taken to public brothels to have their maidenhood violated. Though these injustices were permitted by the Romans, by way of insult to the Christian religion, there was a long established custom of the Romans (so saith the Roman historian Suetonius in his *Life of Tiberius*) that it was unlawful for a virgin to be violently put to death, except first she had been deflowered by her executioners or by whoremongers. Suetonius' actual words are: "Unripe girls, forasmuch as by established custom it was forbidden that virgins be strangled, were first violated by the hangman and then executed."

God, however, by Whose nod all things are ruled, willed otherwise. The goodness and power of Christ Who knows how to safeguard His genuine brides when they are so exposed to evil, not only preserved their virtue intact that they might be offered to Him as unstained sacrifices, but also liberated them from the hands of insolent and unbridled men of passion.

hope in my God, the almighty One, my sweetest Jesus Christ Who, by His help, will enable me to escape unscathed from thy snares!"

The unjust judge, incensed at this response, thereupon ordered her to be immediately led to the place of shame, wearing only a simple dress. The governor then gave the order that all had liberty to abuse her person. Therefore, many young profligates ran thither, full of wicked desires, but they were seized with such awe at the sight of the saint that they froze like dead men, unable to execute their base desires upon her. However, there was one, exceedingly proud and a braggart, who attempted to violate the virgin; but—O the wonder!—straightway, he fell down dead to the earth. His companions became terrified, for the dead youth lay there for a long time while Agnes sang praises to Christ, her protector. Beholding their dead comrade, they all cried out in unison, "Great is the Faith of the Christians! Great is the power of Christ!"

The wicked governor heard of this event and had Agnes brought before him, and said, "Tell me, O evil woman, how didst thou slay the youth?" Agnes answered, "When thou, O governor, didst order me to the brothel, I was accompanied by a splendid youth clad in white. He deadened the desire of the youths who sought to dishonor me; however, one more impertinent than the others attempted to approach me, and before he could utter anything shameless, he was cast down, as thou now canst see." The governor then said, "And who is this person who has helped thee?" The athlete of Christ answered, "The Lord my God sent His angel who protects me from all dishonor." The governor continued, "If thou canst prove thy words true, beseech thy God and raise the dead youth." The holy Agnes then raised her hands to heaven and, by her prayer—O the wonder!—she resurrected the youth.

Upon beholding this miracle, the impious were astonished and exclaimed, "Great is the Faith of the Christians, and great is this most noble woman of God!" Nonetheless, some within the crowd cried aloud, "Remove her from our midst, for she doth all these works by magic!" At this point, the governor ordered a huge fire to be made and Agnes cast therein. She then made the sign of the Cross and entered the flames with great courage and, all the while, she uttered a prayer on her lips. Her blessed soul then hastened into the heavens to join her Bridegroom Christ. The relics of the victorious virgin were then taken up secretly by the Christians and interred with honor a short distance from Rome, beside the Via Nomentana.

On the 21ˢᵗ of January, the holy Church commemorates the holy FOUR MARTYRS of Tyre, who were slain by the sword.

On the 21ˢᵗ of January, the holy Church commemorates
our venerable Father NEOPHYTOS,
Prosmonarios[70] of the Athonite Monastery of Vatopedi,
who heard the voice of the Theotokos
coming from the mouth of her holy icon, and reposed in peace.

On the 21ˢᵗ of January, the holy Church commemorates
our holy Father MAXIMOS the Greek.[71]

Maximos, our holy father, the namesake of greatness, was born in
Arta,[72] the capital of the Greek province of Epiros, in about 1470, during the
Turkish occupation. His secular name was Michael Trivolis. His parents,
Manuel and Irene, were Greek Orthodox Christians. He was from the well-
known and well-to-do Trivolis family, among whose members included one
Patriarch of Constantinople, Kallistos I,[73] and another who was in the
entourage of Theodore I, Despot of Morea (1383-1407) and received
correspondence from Emperor Manuel II (1391-1425). The city of Arta had
been captured about twenty years earlier. Many Greek families sought to

---

[70] *Prosmonarios* is the keeper of a church. He is also the one who waits for and
receives those who come to worship.

[71] Further reading of biographical data, times, and sayings of Saint Maximos the Greek
may be found in several English sources, including: Dimitri Obolensky's *Six Byzantine
Portraits*, pp. 201-219; and Isaac Lambertsen's "Our Father Among the Saints
Maximus the Greek," *Living Orthodoxy*, Vol. XIII, No. 1, Jan-Feb 1991, pp. 3-17.
Scholarly sources included in Obolensky's work are as follows: (1) E. Denissoff,
*Maxime le Grec et l'Occident: Contribution à l'histoire de la pensée religieuse et
philosophique de Michel Trivolis* (Paris-Louvain, 1942); (2) A. I. Ivanov, 'Maksim
Grek i Savonarola,' *Trudy Otdela Drevnerusskoy Literatury* xxiii (Leningrad, 1968);
(3) A. I. Ivanov, *Literaturnoe nasledie Maksima Greka* (Leningrad, 1969); (4) *Prince
Andrey M. Kurbsky's History of Ivan IV*, ed. with translation and notes by J. L. I.
Fennell (Cambridge, 1965), pp. 76-81, 90, 91; (5) *Sochineniya prepodobnogo
Maksima Greka*, iii (Kazan, 1862); (6) *Akty istoricheskie, sobrannye i izdannye
Arkheograficheskoyu Kommissieyu*, I (St. Petersburg, 1841), no. 122, p. 176; (7) J.
V. H. Haney, *From Italy to Muscovy, The Life and Works of Maxim the Greek*
(Munich, 1973), 114; (8) N. A. Kazakova, *Ocherki po istorii russkoy obshchestvennoy
mysli: Pervaya tret' XVI veka* (Leningrad, 1970); and, (9) V. S. Ikonnikov, *Maksim
Grek i ego vremya*, 2ⁿᵈ ed. (Kiev, 1915).

[72] Arta (39°09′N 20°59′E), the site of ancient Ambrakia, on the river Arachthos, is
about thirteen kilometers north of the Gulf of Arta. It was the capital of Epiros from
1205 onward. It fell to the Ottomans in 1449.

[73] Saint Kallistos (1350-1354; 1355-1363) is commemorated by the holy Church on the
20ᵗʰ of June.

make a new life in the west, away from the Islamic scourge. Not before long, Michael's family emigrated to the Ionian island of Kerkyra (Corfu), which was then under Venetian sovereignty. The title of Count was bestowed upon them by the Doge of Venice in 1770. The island was not only secure from the Muslims but also a refuge for a number of Greek scholars. Michael's father, an official with an important post, imparted an elementary education to his son. Since it was nearly impossible to receive higher education under the Ottoman yoke, many Greek youths were sent to European cities to continue their education.

Life on the Island of Kerkyra

At ten years of age, Michael was sent to his uncle, named Demetrios, who lived on Kerkyra. This uncle was not a staunch Orthodox Christian. He sympathized and recognized as valid the religion of the papacy, accepting their authority, as did some other emigres. It was not uncommon to find ecumenical concelebrations between Greek and papal clergy on Kerkyra. At about twenty years of age, Michael stood for election to the island's Governing Council. He lost the election: twenty votes were cast for him, seventy-three against.

By God's providence, Michael, while living with his uncle, also received his education from the scholar John Moschos, an oppo-

Saint Maximos the Greek

nent of Latinism and an upholder of true Orthodoxy. In 1491, when Michael was about twenty years of age, John Laskaris, the famous grammarian and philologist in the service of Lorenzo de'Medici of Florence, visited at the house of his uncle. The young Michael was so impressed with Laskaris' erudition that he attached himself to him.

Life in Italy

Michael then accompanied Laskaris to Florence and became acquainted with the latter's teacher, Demetrios Chalkokondylis of the Platonic Academy. Lectures were given regularly on Greek antiquity. While sojourning in Florence, the Greek expatriate Michael learned both Latin and Italian under Laskaris' instruction. The young man also came under the influence of the Italian reformer Girolamo Savonarola (1452-1498), who censured the decadence of both Florentine society and the papacy. Michael remained in Florence at the Studium, under the tutelage of Laskaris, for some five years. He also attended the Platonic Academy. Laskaris then entered into the service of King Charles VIII, taking up a post at the University of Paris. It is unclear if Michael accompanied him.

Michael, in 1496, went to Bologna, when he studied under the pagan scholar Cordrus Urceus, a humanist. This program of study lasted for a short time, until Michael repaired to Padua, Milan, and then to Venice. From 1496 to 1498, Michael took up employment with the printer of Greek classics, Aldus Manutius. Michael's duties entailed editing classical Greek writings for the Aldine Press. On account of financial difficulties in March of 1498, Michael left for Mirandola where he lodged in the home of the family of the late humanist Giovanni Pico. Michael found ample patristic literature in the library of that home. At Mirandola, Michael and his patron, Gianfrancesco Pico della Mirandola, an admirer of both Savonarola and everything Greek, received tidings of the torture and hanging of the Dominican friar Savonarola. Michael, bereaved, returned to Kerkyra. Not long after, he returned to Italy in 1500.

In 1502, though he did not renounce Orthodoxy,[74] he entered the Dominican Monastery of San Marco in Florence, the former place where Savonarola had been the abbot. Though the union of Rome and Constantinople failed, yet there were certain places where communion was taking place. This was especially true in both Venice and Kerkyra, where tolerance toward the Latin Church prevailed and concelebrations and intercommunion were

---

[74] Maximos did not speak to the Russians of his time in the Dominican order, but he severely criticized Latin beliefs and practises. He denounced their religion as heretical in his Russian writings. He attacked the Filioque and the claims of the papacy. See Obolensky, p. 205; *Sochineniya*, iii. 182-194. On Saint Maximos' views of the Filioque, see B. Schultze, 'Maksim Grek als Theologe,' *Orientalia Christiana Analecta*, clxviii (1963), 245-255; on his attitude toward papal claims, see same, pp. 283-290.

permitted and took place. Alexander VI (Borgia) was then pope (1492-1503). Not much time passed before the young postulant Michael perceived the fallen state of Latinism. Sin and faithlessness abounded in Italy. Belief in fate, chance, astrology, and no life after death were prevailing pagan ideas. Religion was deemed man-made and the preoccupation of old women and the unenlightened. Thus, after two years as a candidate in the monastery of his celebrated hero Savonarola, Michael quit and left Italy forever.[75] He took away with him a secular education and a thorough knowledge of ancient Greek and Latin, and Italian and French. He was resolved to become an Orthodox monk on Mount Athos.

Life on Mount Athos at Vatopedi

On more than one occasion, Michael heard Laskaris comment upon the fabulous libraries on Mount Athos. He especially made mention of Vatopedi, one of the larger monasteries, located above a small inlet on the northeast side of the peninsula. Thus, Michael went to that monastery dedicated to the Annunciation. He arrived in 1507 and was tonsured at Vatopedi, taking the name Maximos. Father Maximos was able to immerse himself in Byzantine works, both patristic and secular. The inventory of books and manuscripts deposited in the libraries of Mount Athos became greater after the fall of Constantinople. Father Maximos studied in depth Saint John of Damascus and Saint Gregory the Great, his favorites. Among secular works, the one he used, and which was the most translated in Russia, was the encyclopedia and lexicon known as *Souda*. Mount Athos, at that time, was a pan-Orthodox center of monasticism. Byzantine texts were being translated into Slavonic. Cultural cooperation between the Greek monks with those from Serbian, Bulgarian, Romanian, and Russian backgrounds continued, creating a Graeco-Slav environment.

Father Maximos' superiors could not possibly have been ignorant of his past life in Italy. There is no evidence that he felt either isolated or ostracized on Athos. Now Father Maximos spent ten years attached to Vatopedi, though his obedience was to leave the monastery and collect alms for the brotherhood. The semi-coenobitic brethren at the Vatopedi Lavra no longer had the means to support themselves. Thus, Father Maximos went about, from city to city, begging alms after delivering sermons, urging his listeners to maintain the purity of their Orthodoxy.

After that period, in 1516, Grand Prince Vasily (Basil Ivanovich) III of Moscow decided to have translated a collection of ancient Greek manu-

---

[75] A note in an unpublished chronicle of the Monastery of San Franco in Florence states that, in 1502, Michael was professed as a monk of that monastery. See Obolensky, pp. 204, 205; Denissoff, 95, 458; Ivanov, 163.

scripts, which had been untouched on shelves in his palaces. His father, Tsar Ivan III, had married Sophia, the scion of the Palaiologos dynasty of Constantinople. The grand prince had a love and desire to make these Byzantine treasures available to his subjects. Vasily consulted with his spiritual father, Metropolitan Varlaam. As a result of this counsel, Vasily wrote to Patriarch Theoleptos of Constantinople and the Protos Symeon of Athos, requesting that they send to the grand prince a learned man to examine Greek manuscripts.

In March 1515, the Tsar's envoy, Vasily Kopylov, was dispatched with a message requesting that the Elder Savva of Vatopedi, a famed and competent translator, accompany Kopylov. The written request indicated that the work would be but for a time. The Russians promised to send him forth again to Athos, if God should grant it. Elder Savva, however, declined the invitation on account of his advanced years and poor health. Thereupon, Hegumen Anthimos of Vatopedi recommended Father Maximos for the work, commenting that Maximos, one most worthy and experienced in the Scriptures, was competent in the interpretation of both ecclesiastical and Hellenic books. He remarked that Father Maximos had grown up in them and had been instructed in the virtues, not as one who merely had read some works.[76] Following this suggestion, Protos Symeon also approved the selection of Father Maximos. As for Maximos, he had a kind of foreboding regarding the mission. He made known to his superiors his wish not to leave Mount Athos. Hegumen Anthimos spoke gently to Father Maximos, reminding him that to supply spiritual food for the starving is not only a holy labor but an act of great love. Father Maximos finally relented and submitted to God's will. He departed for Russia with the tsar's envoys.

Hegumen Anthimos dispatched a letter to Metropolitan Varlaam in behalf of Father Maximos, indicating that though Maximos was unfamiliar with the Russian tongue, it was the hope of both him and others that Father Maximos would acquire that language quickly. Father Maximos was also accompanied by Hieromonk Neophytos, who had already been to Russia collecting alms, and Monk Laurence. Both of these Greek fathers had some command of the Russian tongue. The journey required two years, since the envoys spent time in Constantinople and then in the Crimea. This time was not ill spent by the saint who applied himself to learn Russian. Doubtless, when visiting the patriarchate, Father Maximos was briefed on two issues: the wish of the Constantinopolitan patriarchate to establish its authority over the Russian Church and the hope of receiving aid, material or political, from Moscow for the Greek Orthodox subjects of the Ottoman sultan.

---

[76] See Obolensky, p. 208; *Akty istoricheskie*, I, no. 122, p. 176.

Life in Moscow Under Metropolitan Varlaam

The party arrived in Moscow in the early part of 1518. Grand Prince Vasily arranged for Father Maxim, as he was called by the Russians, to lodge within the Kremlin walls at the Chudov Monastery. Father Maximos also received an allowance. Metropolitan Varlaam, first hierarch of the Russian Church, was pleased to have Father Maximos, whom he deemed a saintly and erudite man. The library shelves of the grand prince were truly a treasury. Rare manuscripts and books were plentiful. The multitude of books that had been collected, much more than what Father Maximos had seen on Athos, required an inventory of the entire collection. A list was provided, recording the untranslated works. The grand prince consulted with the metropolitan and his boyars. Father Maximos was then assigned his first work: the translation of an annotated Psalter, since it was the kind of book which was in widespread use.

Father Maximos earnestly applied himself to assimilate Church Slavonic grammar. He had not yet attained adequate competency in the system and structure of that language.[77] The Russians were cordial and assigned him two assistants, Dimitri Gerasimov and Vlasy, both skilled in Latin and Church Slavonic. Two monastic scribes from the Trinity-Saint Sergios Lavra were also appointed: Fathers Mikhail Medovartsev and Silouan. Dimitri and Vlasy took turns translating into Slavonic what Father Maximos had translated from Greek into Latin. The scribes took down what was spoken by either Dimitri or Vlasy. The annotated Psalter had twenty-four commentators. The work on this title continued for seventeen months. This cumbersome procedure could hardly fail to produce some error. Upon completion, the translation was presented to the grand prince who offered it to Metropolitan Varlaam. The metropolitan was pleased with the work and commended the firstfruits of Father Maximos in the cathedral.

Vasily gave gifts to Father Maximos who in no wise was misled by them. His premonition of suffering still plagued him. In his heart, the holy man was uneasy about the translation, not having final control of what was transcribed from the patristic Greek. He could not help sense that Russians lacking a proper education would either misunderstand or have difficulty with the Slavonic. Father Maximos, a modest and humble monk, felt compelled to write a letter to the grand prince, claiming the work to be imperfect. Father Maximos protested that a translator of greater experience and literary ability ought to have been engaged for such a profound book. He complained that the

---

[77] In Saint Maximos' old age, one of his disciples informs us that the holy man came to know Russian, Serbian, Bulgarian, and Church Slavonic. See Obolensky, pp. 208, 209; Ivanov, 43.

Greek, due to its many shades of meaning, proved difficult to translate. He also voiced displeasure at the ignorance and errors of copyists. He expressed his own discontent at not having spent more time and effort. He mentioned that ancillary books and sources were required to assist in properly understanding damaged texts. His letter was self-effacing. He did not deny that there might be errors in his translation, either from oversight or misunderstanding. He commended all his assistants and requested that they be duly rewarded for their efforts. He then concluded by requesting permission, on his behalf and that of Fathers Neophytos and Laurence, to return to Mount Athos. He frankly disclosed that he and his fellow visitors desired to return to where they made their monastic vows before Christ and His angels. The closing lines of the letter praised the tsar as another Constantine and Theodosios the Great. He then said, "May God be pleased to free the New

Saint Maximos the Greek

Rome (Constantinople), cruelly tormented by the godless Muslims, through the pious majesty of your tsardom; and...may we, the unfortunate ones, receive through thee the light of freedom."[78]

The grand prince, seeing the excellent quality of the translation of the annotated Psalter, besought Father Maximos to continue his holy activities in Moscow. He could not refuse. Father Maximos then commenced translating an ancient commentary on the Acts of the Apostles, and the homilies of Saint John Chrysostom on the Gospels of Saints Matthew and John. After the Grand Prince Vasily and Metropolitan Varlaam discerned that Father Maximos had by now learned the Slavonic language adequately, he was given the task of revising the Church service books. Though this endeavor was arduous, Father Maximos could not refuse this commission. Once again he applied himself diligently to the work at hand.

By and by, jealousy and misunderstanding arose among some Russians. Father Maximos had not hesitated to express his criticisms against incorrect practises and custom long in use among those in his host country.

---

[78] See Obolensky, p. 218; *Sochineniya*, ii. 318, 319; translated by Haney, 163.

This provoked some to slander the holy man, by calling him a heretic who did not correct the books but rather corrupted them. Father Maximos was also known to take up the causes of boyars, whose plights required his mediation before the grand prince. Father Maximos, zealous for the purity of the Faith, advised the spiritual council to move against those who opposed the Faith, especially the Judaizers.[79] The Judaizers maintained a disbelief in the Trinity, a repulsion of icons, and a strong dislike of the Church hierarchy.[80] Russian society was divided into two parties. One party wished to deal with the heretics by bringing about their extermination, while the other party preferred milder measures.

Father Maximos also offered to review the books of the Church's canon law (*Nomocanon* or *Kormchaya knyga*). While he corrected the Church's service books and translated books on canon law, comparing it with the original Greek, he always consulted with the hierarch whenever he uncovered contradictions or inconsistencies. Some of the clergy resented and were disturbed by his labors, though Father Maximos carried out his work in private. Nevertheless, Metropolitan Varlaam remained unwavering in protecting his august guest.

Life in Russia Under Metropolitan Daniel

In 1521, Varlaam was forced out of the Moscow cathedra, after having fallen into the disfavor of the grand prince. Varlaam's replacement, Daniel, a monk of Volokolamsk Monastery, was installed. He was not an admirer of Father Maximos.

Father Maximos, prior to this, had remonstrated with a clause which had been added to every Russian's hierarchal oath at the time of consecration. The clause stated that no one from the patriarchate of Constantinople was to be considered a brother. This article could have been justified during the time of the spurious union with Rome at the Council of Florence (1439). With the fall of Constantinople in 1453, after which Patriarch George Scholarios served, the Church of Constantinople was unquestionably Orthodox. The inserted clause could no longer be justified. Father Maximos challenged the

---

[79] When the heresy of the Judaizers first afflicted Novgorod in 1470, and then Moscow ten years later, Saint Joseph of Volokolamsk (d. 1515, commemorated the 9th of September) and Archbishop Gennadios of Novgorod (commemorated the 4th of December) secured its condemnation at the synods held in 1490 and 1504. The militants who wished to execute the heretics took the name "Josephians." Public burnings were opposed by laymen and ecclesiastics beyond the Volga. According to Archbishop Gennadios, the Judaizers corrupted the book of Psalms. This was another reason why work on the Psalter was Saint Maximos' first work among the Russians. See Obolensky, pp. 209, 210.

[80] See Obolensky, p. 209.

change of metropolitan without the prior consent of the Greek patriarch. The Russians insisted that they had the consent of the Greek patriarch, so that they could install the Russian metropolitan upon the authority of their own Russian bishops. Try as he might, Father Maximos was not given access to this document from the Constantinopolitan patriarchate. Needless to say, Metropolitan Daniel was displeased with Father Maximos for initiating such disquiet at the time of his consecration.

After Metropolitan Daniel's elevation, he asked Father Maximos to translate the *Ecclesiastical History* of Theodoretos of Kyros. The holy man politely declined, claiming that the acts of the heretics were contained therein, which might harm an unsuspecting or unlearned reader. The metropolitan was maddened by the refusal.

In other places, high and low, Father Maximos was shunned or denounced. The holy man spoke out against injustices and social evils. His cell in the Simonov Monastery came be a meeting place for dissidents. Critics of Muscovite society, mostly of the nobility, were gathering before Father Maximos to air their grievances.[81]

Father Maximos also criticized the acquisitions of monks and monasteries, while praising mendicants. He reminded monastics of their vow of poverty.[82] In central areas, large coenobitic houses owned land. Such monasteries came to be known as "Josephian," after Saint Joseph who was the hegumen of Volokolamsk. The northern sketes of the forest believed landowning and monasticism to be mutually antagonistic. The leader of the Non-Possessors was the former general and diplomat Vassian Patrikeev, who fell into disgrace and was compelled to become a monk. Vassian gained influence with Grand Prince Vasily III and became a close friend with Maximos. However, with the installation of Metropolitan Daniel, a leader of the Possessors, the Non-Possessor Vassian's influence at court was greatly eclipsed.

At that time, the papacy, struggling with Luther's activities, attempted to entice the Russian Church into union. Saint Maximos refuted the papists

---

[81] Obolensky, p. 213; V. O. Klyuchevsky, *Kurs russkoy istorii, Sochineniya*, ii (Moscow, 1957), pp. 161-164.

[82] As monasteries were being established throughout Russia, wealthy donors were bequeathing to them both properties and goods. When the question was posed whether possession of lands and goods by monastics could be reconciled with the vow of poverty, Saint Joseph of Volokolamsk advocated this right for monasteries, provided that such wealth be used for serving the Church and the poor. This view was approved by the synods held in 1503 and 1504, a position also upheld by Saint Nilos of Sora (1433-1508, commemorated the 7th of May).

and the papal legate, Nicholas Shoenberg, in fifteen written discourses. He also fearlessly wrote against Jews, Moslems, and idolaters.

In 1524, Grand Prince Vasily Ivanovich, wishing to change his barren wife, the pious Solomonia, of twenty years, for another woman, did not have permission either from the Gospel or the Church canons to put away Solomonia and take up with Elena Glinskaya. Using this incident, Metropolitan Daniel found a way to scheme against Father Maximos and dispose of him. But Father Maximos was not alone. Vassian, his friend and scion of the princes of Lithuania, also respected by the grand prince, stood with him and the canons. Father Maximos wrote the grand prince, urging him to do what was right as a Christian and not to succumb to the passions, lest he should fall from being a living image of the earthly Master and become an anthropomorphic likeness of irrational nature. A conspiracy, meanwhile, was brewing. Father Maximos was accused of having communicating vital national security information to the Turkish ambassador, then in Moscow. Maximos' detractors alleged that he had written to the sultan, describing Russian military might as weak. They claimed that Maximos charged the grand prince with committing cruel acts. Then it was alleged that the Greek monk exhorted the Turks to attack the Russians. Father Maximos was slandered before the grand prince, who was also told that Maximos kept company with two disgraced boyars.

The Saint is Cast into Prison and Brought to Trial

In February of 1524, Father Maximos was suddenly seized, clapped into chains, and cast into the dungeon of the Simonov Monastery. Two regular visitors of the saint were also arrested, charged with high treason, and found guilty: one was decapitated; the other was sentenced to have his tongue cut out.

After several days, Father Maximos was brought forward to stand trial. He was questioned regarding his association with disgraced boyars. He answered all questions truthfully and candidly. He plainly stated that the boyars were disgruntled that the royal and national customs and duties fluctuated in price. When interrogated concerning his position toward the grand prince, he answered frankly that he was disappointed with the grand prince's disregard for the wife of his youth. He was then returned to prison. Solomonia was divorced that November, and the grand prince married Elena.

Since there was no palpable evidence against Maximos, his enemies thought to challenge the holy man in the arena of his translating work. They accused him of perverting the Scriptures and changing the tenses of verbs. In a sentence regarding Christ, they asked Father Maximos why he translated the verb as the simple past: "seated at the right hand of the Father." Why did he not rather use the continuous action of the verb? They then inquired: does he, Father Maximos, wish to imply that possibly the Son of God no longer sits at the right of the Father? Father Maximos recognized his errors and fell prostrate before the synod thrice. He confessed to them that, at that time, he had required further study of the language with its nuances and declensions. He reminded them of the procedure by which the translation was achieved, that is, he was made to convey Greek thought into Latin for Russian interpreters. He said that he repeatedly asked if this or that expression were proper. Though Father Maximos wept and begged forgiveness for his ignorance and errors, the spiritual council judged that Father Maximos had not only distorted the Scriptures but also had fallen into heresy.

This court, presided over by Grand Prince Vasily III and Metropolitan Daniel of Moscow, convened in May of 1525. The metropolitan also acted as chief prosecutor. The long list of charges raised eyebrows, especially that of sorcery and holding heretical views.[83] Both charges were absurd. The charge of sorcery was groundless. The evidence presented to substantiate the charge of heresy was no more substantial than some grammatical errors in Father Maximos' translations. Among the other charges listed, we discover that the prosecution had found Father Maximos engaging in treasonable relations with the Turks, being critical of the grand prince, upholding the claim that the Russian Church's independence from the Constantinopolitan patriarchate was illegal, and denouncing the Possessors for owning land and peasants. No correspondence or evidence were presented linking Father Maximos with any Ottoman authorities. With regard to the Russian Church electing her primates without reference to the Patriarch of Constantinople, Father Maximos expressed his opinion that the Russian Church should return to her mother-Church.[84] The saint also did not deny that he had denounced the activities of the Possessors, which activities included amassing lands and riches, exploiting the peasants, and practising usury.[85] Father Maximos' friend, Vassian, was tried and sentenced to imprisonment in the Volokolamsk Monastery.

The Monastery of Volokolamsk Under the Josephians

The saint was excommunicated and taken away to the Monastery of Volokolamsk, the stronghold of the Possessors. This was done in a secret manner, so that none of his friends knew what had happened to him or if he were dead or alive. He was kept captive at the monastery. He was denied visitors, books, and writing paper. He was not allowed to attend monastery

---

[83] See Obolensky, p. 214. The Trial Record (*Sudnyi spisok*) is not a copy of the proceedings but a pamphlet based on an official transcript of Maxim the Greek's trials. See the discussion of this document, and other relevant sources, by Kazakova, *Ocherki*, 177-187.

[84] See Obolensky, pp. 214, 215; Kazakova, 196-203; Haney, 75-77, 82.

[85] *Sochineniya*, ii. 5-52, 89-118, 119-147, 260-276, iii, 178-205; Ivanov, 156-160.

services. He endured deplorable living conditions, smoke, foul odors, beatings, and bonds. An angel appeared to him and encouraged him to endure, saying, "Take courage and be patient, elder. By these tortures wilt thou be delivered from everlasting torments." He spent his nights chanting sweetly and melodiously. He composed a canon to the Holy Spirit, the Paraclete, that he might be comforted. Since he was given no paper, he wrote out the canon on the wall of his cell with a piece of coal. Now the superior of that doleful precinct was the forbidding Father Niphon, a disciple of Metropolitan Daniel. Father Maximos spent four terrible years in chains and deprivation. He suffered much from certain pernicious monks who were called Josephians. Father Maximos' friends were allotted the same punishment, but they were taken away to other monasteries and dungeons.

After five years, in 1531, Father Maximos was again summoned to stand trial in the capital. Archbishop Makary of Novgorod, who was occupied with compiling the hagiographies of the saints, brought a translation of Father Maximos to Metropolitan Daniel's attention. The manuscript, on the life of the Virgin Theotokos, was presented in court as evidence. It was filled with inaccuracies and blasphemies. Father Maximos rejected the manuscript as being corrupted with spurious interpolations. He even anathematized whosoever created the forgery. Two perjurers also testified that Father Maximos uttered the blasphemies that had been found in that manuscript. The saint therefore was not released. He was also denied the Mysteries and moved to another monastery.

Imprisonment at the Monastery of Otroch

The saint was remanded to Tver and the Otroch Monastery. He was kept under strict surveillance by Bishop Akakios. The conditions of this confinement were not barbaric and cruel. Bishop Akakios was a humane man. He often invited Father Maximos to his table and allowed him books. Father Maximos was allowed to continue his theological work and maintain an extensive correspondence.

In 1534, the odious grand prince died. Father Maximos composed a confession of the Faith that he might refute his calumniators. In anticipation of his adversaries, he answered their predictable retort: "Thou, O Maxim, dost insult the wonder-workers of our land. With the very sacred books which thou hast corrected, they pleased God and performed miracles." Saint Maximos addressed such words of protest with the words of Saint Paul: "But to each one the manifestation of the Spirit is given to the profit of all: for to one is given by the Spirit a word of wisdom; and to another a word of knowledge according to the same Spirit; and to another faith in the same Spirit; and to another free gifts of healings in the same Spirit; and to another operations of works of power; and to another prophecy; and to another discerning of spirits; and to another kinds of tongues; and to another interpretation of tongues; but the one and the same Spirit energizeth all these things, distributing to each separately as He will [1 Cor. 12:7-11]."

Saint Maximos the Greek

When a conflagration occurred at Tver in 1555, the great church built by Bishop Akakios was destroyed. When the bishop began spending enormous sums for the rebuilding of the church, Father Maximos cried out that there were widows and orphans who required his assistance. This reproof from Father Maximos caused him to lose the friendship of that bishop.

In the meantime, the regent Elena died. Metropolitan Daniel, after fifteen years, was deposed and imprisoned in the Volokolamsk Monastery. Since Daniel had fallen so low, Father Maximos felt impelled to be reconciled with him. He learned however that a man who was close with the banished hierarch continued his dislike toward him. Despite this, Father Maximos wrote to Daniel. He attempted to comfort his chief persecutor on his fall from power. He also offered him the hand of reconciliation.[86]

Father Maximos then decided to send his confession of the Faith to the new Metropolitan Joseph. He wished to comfort the living martyr and have him receive Communion, but seditious boyars thwarted him. He wrote Father Maximos saying that "we kiss thy chains, as we would those of the saints." Then, after thirteen years of being deprived of the Mysteries, he was allowed to communicate if he were seriously ill. Since he refused to feign illness, his enemies relented and allowed him to commune as he wished. In the meantime, seditious boyars overthrew Metropolitan Joseph. Father Maximos was not silent. Undaunted, he wrote of the wretchedness of the Russian land, by depicting her as a woman with a tattered dress, surrounded by ferocious animals, sitting at a crossroads. But in 1545, Moscow was

---

[86] See Obolensky, p. 217; *Sochineniya*, ii. 367-376; cf. Ikonnikov, 535; Haney, 85, 86.

miraculously saved by our Lady Theotokos from the horde of the Crimean khan.

The hierarchs of the east were not apathetic to the sufferings of their fellow Greeks in Russia. The Œcumenical Patriarch Dionysios and Patriarch Joachim of Alexandria, in 1545, wrote the young Tsar Ivan IV (later known as the Terrible), regarding the release of Father Maximos.[87] The hierarchs were denied their request, since the Russians felt that Father Maxim had seen too much in Russia to be allowed to leave the country. Thus, the man of God spent twenty years at Tver.

The Lavra of Saint Sergios

In 1551, Hegumen Athanasios of the Holy Trinity-Saint Sergios Lavra, a friend of Father Maximos, prevailed upon the sovereign to release the sacred prisoner. Father Maximos entered the Lavra of Saint Sergios of the Holy Trinity near Moscow, in present-day Zagorsk. His legs were weak, as well as his entire body, but his spirit was cheerful and filled with lofty contemplation. Although Father Maximos was more than eighty years of age, he labored over a translation of the Psalter from Greek to Slavonic. He enjoyed greater liberty and was permitted to work at his literary productions. Despite his diminishing eyesight, he continued to write and taught Greek to a fellow monk.

After two years at the Saint Sergios Lavra, the tsar visited the holy man. It was the spring of 1553 when the tsar departed his capital, for the purpose of making a pilgrimage to a monastery in the far north. He wished to offer up thanks for his recovery from a recent grave illness. The tsar was traveling with the tsaritsa and their newborn son Dimitri. They visited with Father Maximos, at which time, the holy man urged the tsar to abandon his pilgrimage. The man of God exhorted him, saying, "Return to Moscow. It would be far better to comfort the families of the Russian soldiers slain in the recent war against the Tartars." Father Maximos then cautioned the tsar that, if he persisted, his little son would die. The tsar would not turn back. On the road, the infant died. The tsar, thereupon, came to revere the Greek monk, both as a confessor and a prophet.

Father Maximos was then invited by the tsar to attend a synod in Moscow. The purpose of convening the synod was so that Matthew Bashkin's heresy, similar to Calvinism, should be condemned. Father Maximos, on account of his advanced age, wrote that he could not travel the road to the synod. The tsar then requested that Father Maximos compose an epistle and forward his opinion by messenger. This would be his last ecclesiastical deed. Within one year, in 1556, on the 21st of January, Saint Maximos reposed after

---

[87] See Obolensky, p. 216; Ikonnikov, pp. 507, 508.

forty years of labor and suffering in the Russian land, which expiated his youthful ecumenicity. He left translations from the Greek and hundreds of works on a variety of topics, including theology, grammar and lexicography, secular philosophy, statecraft, and social problems.[88] The holy man left many disciples, men of zeal and learning. Among them was Prince Andrei Kurbsky, who utilized the oral instruction of Saint Maximos that he might refute the Lutherans.

After the Repose of Saint Maximos

After the saint's repose, many came to the Lavra that they might venerate the holy man. Now, in 1559, Patriarch Joachim of Constantinople was in Moscow for the consecration of Metropolitan Job as the First Patriarch of All Russia. The archimandrite of the Lavra of Saint Sergios and many of the faithful also petitioned Patriarch Joachim to authorize the veneration of the holy Maximos. Patriarch Joachim consequently bestowed his own decretal of authorization for the confessor. Many miracles and wonderworkings occurred at the site of the saint's tomb, now an abode of grace. The saint appeared in visions and healed the sick. In the nineteenth century, Metropolitan Platon had a reliquary and shrine built over the grave. In 1840, Archimandrite Anthony of the Trinity-Saint Sergios Monastery, had a chapel built over the saint's grave. This was done with the blessing of Metropolitan Philaret of Moscow.

Bereft of home and homeland, as a stranger, the saint was a radiant lamp of Orthodoxy, excellent in the correction of the divine writings and filled with the grace of working healings. He was a prophet of repentance and an undaunted champion of Orthodox dogma. He proved himself a model of endurance in suffering and incarceration. The most prolific of all the writers of Old Russia, he prevented the penetration of western humanism into Russia. He was brilliant and decisive as an unhesitating struggler against the heretics and the unjust. His lack of acquisition and renunciation of the world caused him to be the father of monks. There was nothing that he touched that he did not adorn, so that the land of Russia came to be embellished with his wondrous discourses. He imparted the spiritual treasures and writings of Byzantium to his adopted home in Russia. At length, he was venerated not only as a martyr but also as an "Enlightener of Russia." As a Greek born under the Turkish yoke, with a Byzantine heritage, Italo-Greek connections, and links with Mount Athos, all of which he bridged to the medieval Russia of Tsars Vasily III and Ivan IV, he was certainly one of the last of his kind.

Through the intercessions of Thy Saints,
O Christ God, have mercy on us. Amen.

---

[88] See Obolensky, p. 210; Haney, 114.

**On the 22nd of January, the holy Church commemorates
the holy Apostle TIMOTHY.**[1]

Saint Timothy

Timothy, the glorious apostle of Christ, possesses a name that bespeaks one who honors God. He is first mentioned in Acts as dwelling in Lystra [Acts 16:1] of Lykaonia, the southern part of the central Anatolian plateau of Asia Minor. His mother was Evnike (Eunice), a Jewess [2 Tim. 1:5]; his father was a Greek pagan who may have died earlier in Timothy's life, as he is not mentioned later [Acts 16:1, 3]. Timothy had not been circumcised as an infant, possibly owing to objections made by his heathen father. Timothy's grandmother, Lois [2 Tim. 1:5], and his mother are commended by Saint Paul and mentioned by name. Saint Paul speaks of their unhypocritical faith, which first dwelt in these women and then in Timothy.

Timothy was one of the best known of the divine Paul's companions and fellow laborers. He is described by the Apostle Paul as "my child, beloved and faithful in the Lord [1 Cor. 4:17]"; and elsewhere, Paul writes to Timothy "my genuine child in the faith [1 Tim 1:2]" and also "my beloved child [2 Tim. 1:2]." When Saint Paul made his second visit to Derbe and Lystra, he perceived Timothy's unfeigned faith, conduct, and character. Timothy then joined with Saint Paul to work as a missionary, both to Jew and Gentile. In order to conciliate the Jewish Christians [1 Cor. 9:20], who would

---

[1] The Life of this saint was recorded in Greek by Saint Symeon the Metaphrastes, whose manuscript begins, "Timothy the great..." [*P.G.* 114:761-774]. The text is extant in the Athonite monasteries of the Great Lavra, Iveron, and in other places. Nicholas the Rhetor composed an encomium, which text is preserved at the Great Lavra, Dionysiou, Iveron, and Vatopedi. Hymns that had been lacking from his divine office were added by Nikodemos the Hagiorite. A service to the saint with a second canon by the hymnographer Father Gerasimos Mikrayiannanites was published by Metropolitan Timothy of Maronia (Athens, 1960).

otherwise have protested and stirred up trouble, which would have weakened Timothy's position and work as a preacher of the Gospel, Paul took Timothy and circumcised him.[2] Saint Paul then ordained Timothy [2 Tim. 1:6].

Saint Timothy left home at once to accompany Paul on that apostle's second missionary journey. He went with him to Verea [Acts 17:14], having evidently accompanied him also to Phrygia, the region of Galatia, Mysia, Troas, Neapolis, Philippi, Amphipolis, Apollonia, Thessalonike, and Verea. After Timothy accompanied Paul on the Macedonian tour, he and Silas stayed behind in Verea, when the apostle went forward to Athens. Afterward, Timothy went on to Athens and was immediately sent back [Acts 17:15; 1 Thess. 3:1] by Paul to visit the Thessalonian church. Timothy brought his report to Paul at Corinth [1 Thess. 3:2, 6; Acts 18:1, 5]. Hence both the epistles to the Thessalonians, written at Corinth, contain his name with that of Paul in the opening address.

During Paul's long stay at Ephesus, Timothy ministered to him [Acts 19:22]. Timothy was also sent before him to Macedonia and to Corinth. Paul desired to have Timothy remind the Corinthians of Paul's ways which were in Christ, even as he taught everywhere in every church; for Timothy was working the work of the Lord as Paul [1 Cor. 4:17; 16:10]. Since Timothy's name accompanies Paul's in the opening of the Second Epistle to the Corinthians, it reveals that Timothy was with Paul when he wrote it. Timothy was also with Paul the following winter at Corinth, when Paul wrote from thence his epistle to the Romans, sending greetings to them with that of his fellow worker Timothy [Rom. 16:21]. On Paul's return to Asia through Macedonia, Timothy went ahead and waited for Paul at Troas [Acts 20:4, 5]. At Rome, Timothy was with Paul during his imprisonment, when the apostle wrote his epistles to the Colossians [Col. 1:1], Philemon [Phile. 1:1], and Philippians [Phil. 1:1]. He suffered imprisonment with Paul but was later set free, as mentioned by Paul [Heb. 13:23].

On Saint Paul's third missionary journey, Timothy again accompanied him. He is mentioned when they reach Ephesus, where they spent two years. When Paul made plans to go on to Jerusalem, after passing through Macedonia and Achaia, he sent Timothy on before him, with Erastos [Acts 19:22]. In Saint Paul's epistle, he commended Timothy to the Corinthians and mentioned that Timothy was traveling to Corinth [1 Cor 16:10], apparently taking a longer route before entering into Macedonia.

---

[2] Saint Paul was willing to agree to this being done, on account of the fact that Timothy's mother was a Jewess. It was therefore quite a different case from that of Titus, a Gentile by birth, where Paul refused to allow circumcision to be performed.

After a riot occurred in Ephesus, Paul left Ephesus and went to Macedonia and Greece. In Macedonia, he was rejoined by Timothy, who accompanied him into Greece, where they stayed three months. From Greece, Saint Paul proceeded toward Jerusalem, with Timothy and others accompanying him [Acts 20:4].

Timothy then is mentioned as being found with Paul during his first imprisonment in Rome. He is mentioned in many notices of how he was occupied in the apostle's service. Paul also speaks of sending Timothy to Philippi that he might comfort the Philippians and that the apostle may receive a report of the condition of their Church. After Paul was set free, Timothy once again traveled with him. It is difficult to trace their travels together, but we are told that Paul left Timothy in Ephesus [1 Tim 1:3]. Soon thereafter, Paul wrote his epistle to Timothy, giving full instructions on how to conduct the affairs of the Ephesian Church, until Paul himself should revisit Ephesus [1 Tim 3:14].

Paul afterward summoned Timothy to Rome, where Paul was imprisoned for a second time. He wrote: "Hasten to come to me quickly [2 Tim 4:9]." It is noteworthy that Paul requested Timothy to be with him in his final hours, revealing the true affection which bound them together. No mention is made of whether Timothy was able to reach Rome before Paul's beheading. This last notice of Timothy also includes Paul's request to bring the cloak, books, and parchments [2 Tim. 4:13] and to do these things before winter [2 Tim. 4:21].

Timothy seems to have had bodily "infirmities," so that Paul had to urge him not to be drinking only water any longer, but to be using a little wine for his stomach and frequent infirmities [1 Tim. 5:23]. Saint Paul also encourages Timothy, saying, "Let no one despise thy youth, but keep on becoming an example of the believers in word, in behavior, in love, in spirit, in faith, in purity [1 Tim. 4:12]."

When Saint John the Theologian was exiled to Patmos by Emperor Domitian (81-96), the blessed Timothy was installed as Bishop of Ephesus,[3] after having been consecrated by the Apostle Paul. The heathen had dedicated their city to the goddess Diana or Artemis. Then on one occasion, the divine Apostle Timothy observed that the Greek pagans of Ephesus were celebrating a wild festival of their homeland, known as Katagogia, which had been established to honor the falsely-named deity of wine Dionysus, and which deteriorated into a citywide orgy. The blessed man witnessed all kinds of civil

---

[3] *The Church History of Eusebius*, Book III, Ch. IV(6). That Saint Timothy was the Bishop of Ephesus is stated also in the *Apost. Const.* (VII. 46) and by Nikephoros in his *Ecclesiastical History* III.II.

The Martyrdom of Saint Timothy

disorder. While the citizens, both men and women, masqueraded and sang through the city, holding idols in their hands, they plundered, despoiled, and committed murder. Beholding these terrifying spectacles, the divine Timothy was inflamed with divine zeal and could no longer bear to gaze on such destruction, which they deemed as service to their gods. Bishop Timothy went out among them and kept teaching them to cease from committing such crimes. The rage and violent emotions of the masqueraders, as savage and beastly minded creatures, were so stirred up against his censure of their festival that they slew the Lord's apostle. With wood and knives that they had in their hands, they rained down blows upon Saint Timothy. The Christians managed to drag their bishop from out of their hands. He was brought, barely alive, to a nearby hill, where he surrendered his noble soul to Christ. They interred him not far from the tomb of Saint John the Theologian.

Afterward, in the year 356, the holy relics of Saint Timothy were brought to Constantinople by the holy Artemios,[4] where they were kept treasured with the relics of the Apostles Luke and Andrew in the altar of the Church of the Holy Apostles, where their synaxis was celebrated together. Many miracles were wrought through the relics of the apostles, but their relics were stolen by the Crusaders who pillaged Constantinople in 1204.

On the 22nd of January, the holy Church commemorates the holy Martyr ANASTASIOS the Persian.[5]

Anastasios, the glorious holy martyr, a Persian by birth, lived during the reign of the Persian King Chosroes II (627) and when Herakleios was emperor of Byzantium (610-641). Anastasios' Persian name was Magundat.

---

[4] Saint Artemios is commemorated by the holy Church on the 20th of October, and his Life contains the account of the translation of the relics.

[5] The Life of this saint was recorded in Greek by Saint Symeon the Metaphrastes, whose manuscript begins, "The holy city of Jerusalem..." [*P.G.* 114:773-812]. The text is extant in the Athonite monasteries of the Great Lavra, Iveron, and in other places. The text was rendered in simpler Greek by Agapios the Cretan and published in *Eklogion*. A service was composed for the saint by Father Gerasimos Mikrayiannanites.

His father, named Vav, was a priest-magician, who thoroughly taught his son the magic arts. When Magundat reached a certain age, he was subject to military service; therefore, with many other young men, he was placed in a division with other recruits.

In 614, when the Persians had taken and plundered Jerusalem, the wood of the Cross of Christ, together with many other holy and precious vessels, was taken as spoil into Persia. The holy Cross, which is a weapon of salvation and invincible trophy, shone forth brilliantly in their land. Many desired to learn more about the captured treasure of the Christians and their Faith. The young soldier Magundat, upon hearing of the taking of the Cross by his king, also grew inquisitive concerning the Christian religion. Magundat was one of those who heard Christianity being preached, and straightway, a secret and divine flame was ignited in his soul. The spark of love grew in him, and he was desirous to learn more about this Faith: how God took on flesh; why He was crucified; and many other things. He discovered some pious people and from them he learned the mystery of the dispensation of Christ. He received all that they said with great joy, and the seed of faith multiplied in his heart.

So great an impression was made in his soul that when he finally reached home from an expedition, he resolved to abandon his homeland, wealth, family, and the military. There-

Saint Anastasios

fore, he retired to Hierapolis, where he lodged with a devout Persian Christian who was a goldsmith. Magundat pressed the goldsmith to have him baptized, for he desired to be cleansed of the mire and putridity of the magical arts; he now only desired to be a blameless servant of Christ and to be sealed with the sign of the Cross. However, the goldsmith hesitated out of fear of the

Persian idolaters. Undaunted, the young Magundat entered the local church
to pray. Once inside, he was completely absorbed by the icons and asked
about the lives of those who were depicted; for he was anxious to learn the
accounts of their struggles and contests. All the while, his heart was
consumed with divine love; and, as a hart panteth after the fountains of water,
he, too, conceived a strong desire to be baptized in Jerusalem.

Magundat then betook himself to the holy city, where he met a
Christian who was a silversmith. Magundat disclosed the purpose of his
pilgrimage, and the silversmith brought him to Elias, the presbyter at the
Church of the Resurrection. Elias then introduced the young Persian to
Patriarch Modestos II, who is commemorated by the holy Church on the 16th
of December, and who joyfully received the youth and baptized him, naming
him Anastasios. In Baptism, his Persian name was changed from Magundat
to that of Anastasios to remind him, according to the meaning of the word in
Greek, that now he had risen from death to a new and spiritual life. (Also,
when he was brought to the laver of regeneration, a compatriot of his was
also sponsored for holy Baptism. This Persian's name, unfortunately, is not
known to us; what is known is that he suffered martyrdom in Edessa.)

After his Baptism, Anastasios remained in the home of Elias for eight
days, as was the custom then for the newly-illumined. The presbyter then
asked Anastasios what his plans were for the future. The better to fulfill his
baptismal vows and obligations, Anastasios asked to be made a monk. Elias
did not refuse Anastasios, for he perceived the nobility of the youth's soul.
Later, when the holy Elias finished celebrating the divine Liturgy, he took
Anastasios, and they went to the Monastery of Saint Anastasios, which was
approximately four stadia or about one-half mile from the holy city. The
hegumen of the monastery was the enlightened and virtuous Justin, who
joyfully accepted the blessed Anastasios into his synodia. It was then the tenth
year of the reign of Herakleios (620 to 621).

Anastasios was given to an elder who made him first study Greek and
learn the Psalter by heart. In a short while, Anastasios fulfilled these
obediences, and the hegumen, noting the youth's excellent and God-pleasing
life, tonsured him to the monastic Schema. After this, Anastasios exemplified
virtue and humility in all his labors. He was also meticulous and thorough in
the two obediences that were assigned to him: gardening and cooking. He
executed these two offices expertly and, moreover, was never absent from the
monastery gatherings and divine offices, in which he also excelled. Indeed,
Anastasios was the first to enter the church when the divine Liturgy was to be
served. Whenever he would hear the lives of the saints, his entire attention
was completely focused on the readings; furthermore, he retained accurately
all the accounts in his memory. If there was a difficult word that he did not

know or understand, he would never tire of asking the others for definitions. However, he would read privately on his own the lives of the martyrs and their glorious accomplishments. The book from which he was reading became soaked with his tears; and all the while, he, too, wished that he might be vouchsafed such an end. Therefore, he supplicated God for this blessed end that he might valiantly shed his blood for the love of Him.

Anastasios dwelt in the brotherhood for seven years, which did not pass by untroubled. During that time, the father of envy could not endure to witness Anastasios' virtue, fervor, and love of Christ. Therefore, the demon assailed him with all kinds of temptations and memories of his father's love and his leisurely life in Persia with its worldly enjoyments and other such vanities. Moreover, the demon brought to his recollection the practises and superstitions which his father had taught him. Nevertheless, the wise youth understood all these suggestions and temptations to be demonically inspired. Thereupon, he invoked the name of the Lord for sure assistance and then betook himself to his spiritual advisor and laid bare, with tears and a frank disclosure, his thoughts and the machinations of the perverse "dragon." His confessor then summoned a gathering of the brethren who offered up a supplicatory canon of prayer on behalf of their brother; and, straightway, the temptations departed.

Shortly thereafter, the thrice-blessed one beheld a vision. In the vision, he had ascended a lofty mountain that seemed to be suspended in the air. When he reached the top, a man gave him a gold cup that was adorned with precious stones and filled with wine. He then said to Anastasios, "Take and drink this." The blessed Anastasios partook of the wine, which he found to be exceedingly delicious, and sensed a sweetness in his soul. Before he came out of the vision, he understood that the Lord was portending his future martyrdom.

After he emerged from the vision, he rejoiced and hastened into the church and found that all the fathers had assembled, for it was the great and holy eve of the Resurrection of Christ. Anastasios then took his spiritual advisor into the sacristy and, with tears, fell before his elder's feet, beseeching him to offer up prayer for his disciple who in a few days would come to his end. Then he said, "I wish thee to know, O holy father, that of the many benefits and labors that thou hast bestowed upon me, including enlightening me to the knowledge of truth, as thou art a genuine slave of Christ, do not neglect this: make supplication on my behalf!" But the elder replied, "How dost thou know that thou wilt soon depart to the Lord?" Anastasios then revealed the vision he had beheld and how he had perceived the cup to be death, of which he would soon partake. Whether it would be a death that is common to all or in a manner to his benefit, Anastasios said he did not know;

for he did not reveal to his elder his intense desire for martyrdom, fearing the elder might attempt to dissuade him or prevent him.

After hearing this, his elder offered him encouragement, and then they celebrated the feast. After the divine Liturgy, where all the brethren communicated the all-holy Mysteries, they all embraced in the trapeza (refectory). When all had retired to their cells in the lavra, Anastasios was unable to sleep, as he was all afire with the desire for martyrdom. Therefore, he secretly departed, without concern for bread, money, or additional clothing other than what he was wearing. He then repaired to the shrine of Saint George at Lydda (Diospolis), then to Gerazim and the holy places. Afterward he went to Caesarea of Palestine, where he entered the Church of the Ever-virgin Theotokos, where he prayed for two days that he might be directed to what was to the benefit of his soul. Next he went to the Church of Saint Ephemia where, outside, he descried a magician from Persia who was working his magic and enchantments. Anastasios, knowing the utter foolishness and vileness of this illicit art (for he formerly practised it), was moved by divine zeal and sternly rebuked and censured him. The magician was taken aback at the monk's audacity and asked why he had derided him. Anastasios then offered the appropriate response. He explained how he himself had formerly been deceived by these abominable and irreligious practices, but that, afterward, learning of the true Faith in Christ, he was cleansed by holy Baptism and now despised these superstitions and abominations. Anastasios said this and many other things, which the magician held in contempt; and he even attempted to convert Anastasios. It happened that standing nearby were other Persians, former comrades-in-arms of Anastasios. They swiftly apprehended Anastasios, in the manner of wild wolves, and put him in jail. Anastasios was then to be brought forward for examination before Marzavanes, the governor.

Anastasios spent three days in prison without eating, for he refused to taste their vile food. He was solely nourished with the hope of his pending trials, which he would suffer for Christ. Several pious people learned of his incarceration and called him blessed, offering their encouragement. They advised him not to cower before the dread tortures or before death that would only usher in eternal life in the kingdom of the heavens. When Marzavanes was ready to hear his case, Anastasios was brought in. However, the monk did not do obeisance to the governor, which was the Persian custom, but instead stood straight without a trace of fear, showing an unsubjected soul. Then, glaring with an angry countenance at Anastasios, Marzavanes inquired about the prisoner's identity. Anastasios then began to relate, in detail, everything concerning his Persian birth and former beliefs and his becoming a Christian. The governor then, by flattery, attempted to change Anastasios' mind, promising him the perishable and vain things of the world. Anastasios then looked heavenward and said, "May it never be, O Christ King, that I deny Thee!" The governor then ordered that the holy prisoner be bound with an iron chain to be attached from his neck to one foot. He was then condemned to lift and carry rocks for the building of the fortress wall. Some of Anastasios' former acquaintances and compatriots were present, and they questioned him why he spurned their beliefs, saying, "Why dost thou insult thy former noble people? Why hast thou become a contemptible Christian, only to be bound as a captive criminal, to the shame of thy people, O mindless one?" These and other reproaches were heaped upon him. Then they began to strike him and rain blows upon him.

After a few days, he was again examined by Marzavanes, who attempted to dissuade him by threatening to send him to the king himself, who would inflict cruel tortures upon him. Anastasios, nevertheless, remained steadfast and unmoved, and simply said, "Write what thou wilt. I am a Christian: I repeat it, I am a Christian." Marzavanes then ordered the prisoner to be beaten without mercy. The executioners were preparing to bind him on the ground, but the saint declared, "I will remain myself and endure bravely the strokes, for just as the man who, during harvest, is driven by a parched mouth and desires to quench his thirst with cool water, so do I, desire even more—unworthy though I be for my Christ—to receive the most bitter and harshest death!" The saint then begged leave to put off his monk's habit, lest it should be treated with contempt, which he felt only his body deserved. After he had removed his outer garment, he stretched himself on the ground and with great courage of soul endured the beating with clubs. Without holding on to anyone or anything, he did not stir but remained immovable. The marvellous athlete of Christ, in the midst of bitter and unbearable bodily pains, was consoled only by divine love and sustained by the hope of future blessedness.

Then the mindless governor again threatened to remand him to the king for worse tortures because of his obstinacy. But the wise one answered, "The king is a man subject to corruption just as we are subject, and he will die either today or tomorrow. Therefore, there is no need to fear him. He before Whom we need tremble is the heavenly and everlasting King Who made all things, visible and invisible." The tyrant then commanded the prisoner to return to the dungeon. Marzavanes nonetheless still had private hopes that Anastasios would change his stand.

Therefore, after a few days, Anastasios was brought before the governor. He demanded that Anastasios sacrifice to fire, since this was the Persian belief and custom. Anastasios answered, "To offer sacrifice to the fire, the sun, the moon, and the horse? What ignorance! Why dost thou not order me to prostrate myself before the mountains and cattle or any created thing, O miserable one? It is God Who hath placed man at the head of His creations that they might be subject to him. God is the only King to honor." This and many other true statements did the martyr utter, which rendered the tyrant speechless. Therefore, Anastasios was sent back to prison.

Meanwhile, his elder and teacher, Justin, at the Monastery of Saint Anastasios, learned of his disciple's boldness in rebuking the tyrant, and how he had undergone with great courage dreadful torments. Anastasios' elder was filled with holy joy over the victories of the contestant in virtue. He then decided to summon all the brethren that they might offer up a Supplicatory Canon on behalf of Anastasios. They prayed that God would empower His martyr to vanquish the tyrant and thereby gain the crown of victory. It was then decided that two of the brethren would be dispatched, carrying letters. The substance of these letters to Anastasios advised him not to fear the tyrant and to end the conflict as courageously as he began.

A number of days elapsed, and Anastasios was still bound in a cell. All that time, he did not leave off reciting his rule of prayer, even for one night, though this was not without difficulty, since he had been bound to a felon at both their necks and feet. However, Anastasios, in order not to disturb his cell mate at night, did not stand up completely but always prayed with his neck bowed downwards, keeping the chained foot near his companion so as not to disturb him, though the reciting of his service was achieved only with great discomfort and difficulty.

One evening, as Anastasios chanted, the jailer, who was a Jew, heard him. He was a good-willed man who noticed how Anastasios toiled all day conveying rocks and spent the greater part of the night at prayer; and the jailer marvelled at how the prisoner did not tire. He decided to go and have a look at the prisoner, so he peeked through an opening of the cell, only to see a most astonishing sight. He beheld in the cell some men who were clad in white garments, each resembling the stole of a bishop. They shone brilliantly as the sun. Anastasios was similarly enveloped in light, and standing next to him was a splendid youth who resembled a hierodeacon, and who was censing Anastasios. The jailer was in utter amazement, and he wanted to go and bring a companion of his who was a Christian from Skythopolis; but the jailer, from his great surprise, was unable to move his hands or feet. (By divine condescension was the unbaptized one permitted to see such a vision, so that he might later reveal it.) Finally, he forced himself to move and brought one that was nearby to share with him what he had seen, but the other man saw nothing.

The following day, a message was sent to Anastasios from Marzavanes. The governor indicated that he had written to the king concerning

Anastasios' case. The governor let the martyr know that the king could be satisfied by one condition: if only by word of mouth Anastasios would abjure Christ, thereafter he could choose whether to be an officer in the royal service or remain a Christian and a monk. He added that Anastasios could adhere to Christ in his heart, but that just once he would have to renounce Him, in words. It could be done privately, before two witnesses, "in which case," he declared, "there could be no harm nor any great injury to his Christ." The governor's words fell on deaf ears. Anastasios answered firmly that he would never dissemble or appear to deny his Christ, and also said, "May it never be, O Christ King, that I should violate the truth or make a pretense to deny Thee—no, not in my mind or thought or even in a dream!" Marzavanes, perceiving the monk's adamancy, bound him in chains to two other Christians; and all three were sent to the king. At this juncture, Anastasios was being followed by one of the monks whom Abba Justin had dispatched. (The acts of his martyrdom were afterward recorded by this monk.)

The Christian prisoners were then placed in the municipal prison for three days. Then, on the eve of the Exaltation of the Precious Cross (the 14th of September), the saint and his cell mates, together with other Christians who, out of love, when they learned of their plight, came to the prison, conducted an all-night service, which gave all the prisoners great joy. Also, the controller of customs, a pious and God-fearing man, requested of the governor that Anastasios be released into his custody for a few hours, so that he might attend the service the following day in the church; and permission was granted. In the church, when the Christians beheld the martyr in their midst, they were filled with delight and joy. They commended him and reverently kissed his wounds. All this only served to further inflame the martyr's zeal for martyrdom. At the completion of divine Liturgy, the controller of customs invited the saint to his home that he might offer hospitality and receive the blessing of his presence. So as not to grieve his host, he felt compelled to accept. Therefore, Anastasios went in the company of his two fellow prisoners and athletes; after which they returned rejoicing to the prison.

Soon afterward, Anastasios and his two fellow prisoners were taken out of Caesarea. Anastasios was followed by a throng of Christ-lovers who were weeping and praying to God to strengthen His athlete. Close by too was one of the monks that was sent by his former elder, and who was instructed to assist Anastasios in whatever he might need; he was also to stand as witness and relate all that had occurred to the brotherhood when he returned. The monk then followed Anastasios from city to city. He observed the local inhabitants coming out to meet and greet Anastasios. The truth is, Anastasios was sorrowed at the honor and respect paid to him and feared it was a result of some sin. Therefore, when Anastasios reached the Tigris River, he decided to write two letters to the Bishop of Hierapolis, asking him if he would make entreaties before the Lord on his behalf for two things: that he might complete the contest of martyrdom favorably, and that he not be judged for the temporal honor he received here from pious people.

When the holy martyr and his fellow prisoners arrived in Bethsaloe, six miles from Discartha (Dastagerd) in Assyria, near the Euphrates (where the king then was), they were immediately cast into a dungeon. One of the monks who was following close behind lodged in the home of a certain Christian, the son of Jesdin, who was pious and loved Christ. After a few days, Chosroes made his pleasure known and sent an officer to interrogate the saint. The officer asked the holy captive who and what he was, and why he had denied the faith of his fathers. Anastasios did not wish to converse in the Persian tongue, for when he abandoned the former beliefs and practices of his people, he also left off speaking his native language. Therefore, as he was speaking Greek only, an interpreter was brought in, and Anastasios replied, "Your religion is the delusion of devils and ushers in a dread death. It is by this religion that I, too, was once deceived. However, I fled the darkness and came to the light, and now worship the Creator of all things." The officer then commented, "But the Jews crucified thy God, so why dost thou not revere our religion, O miserable one?" The saint continued, "Of His own will was He crucified that He might redeem us from our sins, for He loves mankind. But you mindless ones worship fire and the moon and sun." The officer replied, "Cease uttering such foolish words and return to your ancestral piety, and thou wilt receive both honor and innumerable gifts!" Anastasios made the following answer to the officer's magnificent promises, saying, "For a long time I have held in contempt such things. I prefer this shabby garment, the holy and revered Schema of the monastics; it is through the angelic life that I hope to inherit the kingdom of the heavens. Therefore, how is it possible to exchange the imperishable gifts of the kingdom for the paltry and earthly gifts of a king, who must shortly die himself?"

The officer next attempted by flattery and afterward by threats of torture to alter the martyr's mind. When this had failed, he ordered Anastasios to be mercilessly beaten with rods. After the executioners finished, the officer said, "If thou wilt not worship the sun, daily thou wilt receive the same number of blows that thou hast received today, until thy bones are laid bare!" Anastasios answered, "Do thou execute thy pleasure without more ado, but I will never deny my Creator and Savior!" Then after the Persian manner, he was cruelly beaten with staves; the punishment lasted for three days. On the third day, after the officer made his report to Chosroes, it was then commanded that Anastasios be laid on his back and stretched, while a heavy beam was to be laid across his thighs and pressed down by the weight of two men, thereby crushing the flesh to the very bone. The martyr underwent this torture for a considerable time and endured great distress; he was then returned to the dungeon. However, the martyr's tranquility and patience astonished the officer, who went again to make his report to Chosroes.

It happened that the jailer, also a Christian, gave everyone access to the martyr that desired to assist him. Therefore, Christians filled the prison to visit Anastasios, including the children of the aforementioned Jesdin. They would fall before the holy martyr's feet and kiss his bonds, asking his blessing; they would also keep as holy relics whatever had been sanctified by contact with him. The humble Anastasios was sorrowed because he did not wish the praise of men, so he tried to hinder them, but could not.

After a few days, Anastasios was removed from his cell and brought before Chosroes. The holy man was then asked if he would bow down and worship their gods; otherwise, he could expect worse torments. The martyr, though greatly provoked, answered, "Why dost thou aimlessly waste thy time to try me with useless things? I have told thee many times that I will not deny my Master, even if thou shouldest chop my flesh into ten thousand pieces!" The martyr was then ordered beaten with clubs. All observed and marvelled how he courageously persevered under torture, as though he were a stone and not a man. He was then remanded to prison, only to be removed after several days. Once more they attempted to persuade the steadfast martyr to deny his faith, by employing flattery and then by threatening him with the use of fearful devices.

After they had taken him to the torture chamber, they attached a huge rock to one of his feet while he hung by one hand, as they hoped to break his limbs in this manner. However, by divine assistance, he bravely endured this trial that lasted for two hours. After this, the officer despaired of getting Anastasios to recant, so he had the saint thrown back into the dungeon. The officer left and went to report to Chosroes and to advise the king to discontinue any further attempts, because the prisoner remained unchanged. After hearing the report, Chosroes ordered that Anastasios and all the Christian captives should be put to death. Therefore, seventy prisoners were removed from their cells and marched to the river. All were to be strangled with a cord, one after another, on the riverbank. All were strangled before Anastasios; and when it came to his turn, they remarked, "Why dost thou not do the will of the king, but thou dost prefer to receive such a violent death?" But the saint offered thanks to the Lord for permitting him to die for the love of Him. Then he answered the executioners, saying, "I desired you to cut off my limbs and my flesh into small pieces for my most sweet Master, so that

I could receive the most bitter and grievous death. However, you will slay me with a death that is not very painful or evil." After this, they carried out their orders and strangled him. However, afterward, the executioners struck off the martyr's head as evidence before Chosroes that they carried out the slaying. This happened in the year 628, on the 22nd of January, during the seventeenth year of the reign of Herakleios.

Saint Anastasios

Meanwhile, the jailer desired to take up the relics of the blessed martyr, but the executioners would not permit him. However, the sons of Jesdin, after offering the executioners a sum of money, were told to secretly return at night to take the sacred remains. Therefore, the sons of Jesdin and the monk from Anastasios' monastery (who often ministered to the saint while he was in prison) came by night to take up the martyred body. Behold the miracle! They found the dogs devouring the bodies of the other dead, but the sacred body of the Martyr Anastasios they did not even approach! Therefore, with great reverence the Christians took up his relics and laid them in the Monastery of Saint Sergios, a mile from the place of his triumph, in the seventeenth year of the reign of Herakleios. (It is from the name of this monastery that the place was later called Sergiopolis, but it is now called Rasapha, in Iraq.)

The following day, two soldiers of the prison were discussing the events of the previous day. The one remarked to the other, "Yesterday, didst thou observe how the dogs devoured the bodies of the slain, but they did not approach the body of that monk? Indeed, the dogs sat about it and guarded it." The other soldier said, "I beheld something even more marvellous. There was a brilliant star, though lower than the other stars, that hovered brightly near the earth. I, therefore, went to take a closer look at the phenomenon, only to discover that it was not a star but a light that stood over the body of Anastasios; and I greatly feared!" As the soldiers talked, two imprisoned Christians, who understood the Persian language, overheard their discussion.

Then, after the passage of ten days, on the 1st of February, Herakleios' army arrived. The emperor, who had personally taken the field, after many brilliant successes against the Persians, practically defeated the dreaded Persian enemy. After the martyrdom of Saint Anastasios, Herakleios advanced and occupied Dastagerd, Chosroes' favorite residence from which he beat a hasty retreat. Before April was out, Chosroes II, as Anastasios had predicted, had been deposed and slain by order of his son, Kavād II (Shirū-ya), who opened peace negotiations with Herakleios. According to their agreement, the Persians returned to the Byzantine Empire the conquered provinces of Syria, Palestine, and Egypt, and the relic of the holy Cross. Finally, the victorious Byzantine Empire dealt the death blow to its constant enemy, leaving the Persian army prostrate. Herakleios then returned to the capital in great triumph.

Then on the 21st day of March, in the year 630, Herakleios left with his wife Martina for Jerusalem. Upon their entrance into the holy City, there was much joy: sounds of weeping and sighs, the burning of flaming hearts, the exaltation of the emperors, the princes, soldiers, and inhabitants. Hardly anyone could chant from their great emotion. The emperor then restored the holy Cross, to the joy of all Christendom, to its place and returned all the church objects, each to its place. He then distributed gifts to all the churches and to the inhabitants of the holy city.

However, as we said, after the death of Chosroes, the two Christian prisoners that we mentioned above were then released from their bonds. Upon their release, they made their way to Jerusalem, where they proclaimed the achievements of the saint and how he had predicted all that came to pass in the Persian land; for the martyr uttered the following on the eve of his death to these two Christians: "Know this, my brothers, that tomorrow I shall end my course. However, within a few days, you shall be freed by divine help, because the unjust Chosroes shall be slain. Then you must go to the Monastery of Abba Anastasios and relate to my elder and the brethren all that you have seen." On account of the saint's true prophecy concerning them, they fulfilled his order and went to Anastasios' monastery.

As for the monk that was sent by Abba Justin to follow Anastasios, after the relics were interred at Saint Sergios, he brought back the martyr's mantle. He waited several days, until an expedient time should arrive when he could travel safely, although it was evident that the new king was more humane and would not follow the practises of his father. Then, to the monk's great surprise, he beheld soldiers who were speaking Greek. He saw the Roman troops as bright lamps shining in the darkness and rejoiced exceedingly. The soldiers also asked the monk what he was doing in this strange land, and he explained everything in great detail. Straightway, the soldiers, with great respect, provided him with protection and took him into their camp.

Therefore, the monk traveled with the army back to Armenia; from that point, he left to go with a group that was traveling to the holy city. After almost two years' time, he arrived safely in his monastery and related to the hegumen and the brethren all that we have written above concerning the saint's courage and martyrdom. At that time, in the monastery, there was a young monk who was possessed by an evil spirit. The hegumen then took the mantle of Saint Anastasios and put it on the demonized monk and—O the instant therapy!—just as darkness flees at the presence of light, the demon fled the sufferer, unable to bear the holiness of the martyric rason (cassock).

Then, in the twentieth year of Herakleios' reign, the emperor sent a bishop to Persia. He brought back the precious relics of the saint to Caesarea in Palestine, leaving only a small remnant behind. Later, the saint's relics were removed to Constantinople, and at last to Rome. The saint's head, together with a miraculous icon, reputed to drive out demons and restore the ailing, were then translated and enshrined in the Church of Saint Vincent in Old Rome. The translation of the saint's relics is commemorated by the Church on the 24th of January.

On the 22nd of January, the holy Church commemorates the holy Hieromartyrs MANUEL, GEORGE, PETER, LEO, and PARADOS, and their companions in martyrdom, Generals LEO and JOHN, together with GABRIEL, SIONIOS, and 377 MARTYRS.

Manuel, the glorious hieromartyr, and those holy martyrs with him, hailed from various provinces and lands, but were all together in Adrianoupolis[6] where Manuel was bishop. Khan Krum (ca. 802-814) and his fierce

---

[6] Adrianoupolis or Adrianople, also Orestias (mod. Edirne), is a city of Thrace on the middle Hebros River. It was the major military road serving Belgrade-Sofia-Constantinople. It was considered a strategic northern stronghold in the defense of Constantinople. In the 9th-10th C., Adrianople was a strongpoint in wars against Bulgarians. Emperor Nikephoros I (802-811) attempted to defend the city, but to no avail. Krum and Symeon managed to seize Adrianople temporarily. *The Oxford Dictionary of Byzantium*, s.v. "Adrianople." In 811, Nikephoros invaded Bulgaria, not taking seriously the entreaties for peace offered by Krum, the Bulgarian khan. In July of that year, Krum destroyed the Byzantine army in a mountain pass and slew Nikephoros, and thereafter captured Develtos. In 812, he seized numerous Macedonian and Thracian towns and forts. In 813, he routed the Byzantine army at Versinikia, whereupon he marched on to Constantinople. He was wounded in an assassination attempt organized by Leo V. Krum still managed to devastate Constantinople's environs. He also captured Adrianople, deporting its inhabitants to Bulgaria. In 814,

(continued...)

Bulgarian followers, wanting in feeling, warred against the Rhomaioi or Byzantines at that time. These pagans captured Christians in Thrace and Macedonia before they moved against Constantinople. They came as far as Adrianoupolis, where they stood their ground for three days and captured the city. This occurred during the reign of the iconomach Leo the Armenian (813-820). Krum cast out forty thousand Christians, together with the most holy Bishop of Adrianoupolis. He pushed the bishop down upon his face, placing his foot on the holy man's neck. Krum died soon thereafter in 814, leaving as successor Dukum or Dicevg, a harsh Bulgarian who also loathed Christians.

The new khan proved to be inhuman and a brute. Upon arresting the holy Hierarch Manuel, he rent him asunder in the middle, and severed his hands and shoulders. He cast the dismembered body parts to wild animals for food. On account of his beastliness, he was wounded from on high, in an invisible manner, when he suffered blindness to both eyes. He was then assassinated by his own followers. His successor, another Bulgarian, Omurtag (814-831), murdered all Christians whom he could not compel to deny Jesus Christ. Some of the faithful he bound and subjected to all kinds of tortures on wheel and rack. There were also other punishments, equally savage and brutal. The holy Bishop George of Develtos[7] and Bishop Peter were first rent apart with staves and then had their holy heads removed. In like manner, three hundred and seventy-seven other Christians also suffered martyrdom.

Prisoners of war, the Christian Generals Leo and John suffered beheading. Bishop Leo of Nicaea underwent the sundering of his abdomen with a sword, while Gabriel and Sionios were decapitated. Parados, the most holy priest, was condemned to stoning. Many other Christians also suffered death in diverse ways. It should be known that not only Omurtag perpetrated

---

[6](...continued)
Krum perished from a hemorrhage. Ibid., s.v. "Krum." This is the background surrounding the lives of the martyrs commemorated this day.

[7] Develtos, or Deultum, was a city and fortress in Bulgaria about twenty kilometers southwest of Burgas. Develtos had been a major Byzantine defensive position against the Bulgarians. This city also had been captured by Krum in 812. A defensive earthen wall had been put up by Omurtag, from the Black Sea to the river Marica. The treaty of 846 restored the city to the Byzantines, but Symeon of Bulgaria took it again in 896. In 927, it once more became a Byzantine possession, but at the end of the 12th C. it went back to the Bulgarian Empire, until the Turks seized it in 1396. Ibid., s.v. "Develtos."

these atrocities against the Christians, but his Bulgarian chiefs also committed similarly cruel executions.[8]

On the 22nd of January, the holy Church commemorates our venerable Father JOSEPH the Sanctified of Crete, who was surnamed Samakos.[9]

Saint Joseph

Joseph, our venerable father, was born and raised on the notable island of Crete. He hailed from the village of Keramon and was the son of pious parents. When he became of school age, his parents entrusted his education to a learned and godly spiritual father. Joseph's teacher dwelt at one of the monasteries dedicated to the glorious and far-famed apostle and Evangelist John the Theologian, which was also surnamed by many "Dermata" for the Bay of Dermata or in Turkish, Koum-Kapi. The church stands by the sea at Chandax, the ancient name of Herakleion, the Cretan city on the northern coast. It was in this place that the young Joseph learned not only reading and writing, but also excellence and God-pleasing morals. In but a short time, he learned sufficiently those things needful for salvation. He was an avid reader of Church books and the holy fathers. Consequently, he not only came to an understanding of the vanity of this world, but also found repugnant the temporal and corruptible things of this life. His desire was only for those everlasting and imperishable good things of the heavens. He resolved to struggle with great eagerness in committing virtuous deeds. He also was determined to support himself by his own labors, which his skill in calligraphy allowed.

Joseph's parents, observing the piety and virtue of their son, were filled with profound joy and gave glory to God. However, not much time passed before both parents reposed. Since there were no other siblings, Joseph remained as sole heir. Joseph, for his part, neither was elated by the inheritance nor left its use to his own judgment. Instead, Joseph consulted

---

[8] By 864 the Christianization of Bulgaria was taking place. This evangelic work was followed in 885 by the disciples of those missionaries to the Slavs, Saints Kyril (826/7-869) and Methodios (815-885).

[9] The Life and divine office to this saint were first published in 1864 at Zakynthos. A complete service was composed for the saint by the hymnographer of the Great Church, Father Gerasimos Mikrayiannanites.

with his spiritual father and teacher. Acting on his counsel, Joseph distributed all of his acquisitions as alms for the poor. Thus he was delivered from that concern, and thereafter, with great humility, he placed himself in obedience to his elder. He tamed the flesh with fasting beyond measure, keeping vigil, making full prostrations, and unceasing prayer. He vanquished the force of nature with a small amount of bread and water, and very little sleep. In short, he entered every contest of asceticism, discipline, and self-control, becoming a pure vessel of the All-Holy Spirit. What was extraordinary about his ascetic life was that it took place in the middle of the city, amidst all the clamor and tumult of the world. Joseph, however, trampled upon the crafty devices of the demons, so that even the bodiless angels were amazed.

Joseph's spiritual father watched the progress of his disciple increase daily. He observed his ascetic labors and ascent from virtue to virtue. He therefore clothed him with the divine and Angelic Schema of the monastics. He was confident in Joseph's constancy, because he had put him to the test for a sufficient time. At length, the spiritual father judged it right that Father Joseph, as one worthy, should be elevated to the rank of the priesthood. Therefore, Father Joseph was sent to the bishop with a letter from his spiritual father. The bishop also marvelled at Father Joseph's understanding, ethics, and extreme humility. According to Church order, the bishop ordained Father Joseph to the priesthood, which ordination gave great joy all around. Father Joseph was then sent back to his elder, who was very grateful and happy to receive him. The elder then gave him every instruction in fulfilling the priesthood. Now the elder was advanced in years and retired from performing the divine service. The holy Joseph then resumed his elder's place in celebrating, blamelessly and purely, the divine Liturgy.

Not much time passed before Father Joseph's spiritual father became ill. The elder knew of his imminent death, so he called the holy Joseph to himself and said these things: "As for me, O child, I have arrived at my end. I am going to that place where each receives his due according to his works. As for thyself, keep a diligent watch over thyself and thy flock, because thou shalt need to make a defense before the righteous Judge. For that reason thou shouldest pray unceasingly. Seek to pass thy life quietly and without contention and strife. Do not neglect the divine offices and thy prayer rule. Be diligent in helping the poor. Assist as much as possible both the widows and orphans. In every way, attempt to console and comfort those in affliction and misfortune. And whensoever thou shouldest celebrate the divine Liturgy, have all of thy mind riveted to God, the great High Priest. Continue practising that small command which I enjoined, that is, the distribution of thy sustenance in thirds. Continue sending one-third to the Holy Mountain Athos and another third to holy Mount Sinai. As for the final third left to thee, use

that for thy maintenance and for the needs of the poor and those in want."
After the elder gave these counsels, he uttered a prayer to God on behalf of
his spiritual son and then departed to the Lord.

The holy Joseph grieved deeply at being orphaned from his spiritual
father. He mourned and wept as was meet, and then interred him reverently.
Father Joseph then repaired to the holy land, where he venerated the shrines
and sacred places. He distributed the belongings of his spiritual father,
according to his elder's stipulation. After his pilgrimage, he returned again
to Crete and to the Monastery of Saint John the Theologian. He resumed his
struggles and ascetic contests with heightened vigor. He put into practise
every God-pleasing virtue, but mostly he demonstrated love toward his
neighbor, especially in dispensing alms. In a matter of days, he had disbursed
to the poor and needy his own portion of maintenance and support left to him
by his elder. He himself came to such a state of destitution that he could not
even provide for a daily meal. In the meantime, many indigent were coming
to him and asking charity, but Father Joseph had nothing left to donate. The
thought of sending others away empty-handed grieved him exceedingly.
However, the Lord Who searches the hearts of men, knowing His servant's
sorrow, wrought a miracle by divine grace. The venerable father was led to
find a large basket filled with bread. He therefore gave out the bread to feed
the poor and even himself. Let us not be doubtful of this occurrence; for the
Lord Himself spoke in the Gospel and said, "Keep on asking, and it shall be
given to you; keep on seeking, and ye shall find; keep on knocking, and it
shall be opened to you [Mt. 7:7]." This is also spoken of by the prophet-king:
"Cast thy care upon the Lord, and He shall nourish thee; He shall not permit
unto the age for the righteous to waver [Ps. 54:23]."

Whensoever the blessed one conducted the Liturgy, the loaves of
prosphora[10] brought to him by the faithful were also distributed among the
poor. There were many occasions when the holy priest would go out late at
night and secretly leave much-needed bread at the doors of the impoverished.
He then would quickly dart off into the night, lest he should be seen by
anyone. He conducted himself in such a manner because he had read that the
Lord said: "When thou art doing alms, let not thy left hand know what thy
right hand is doing, so that thine alms might be in secret; and thy Father Who
seeth in secret Himself shall render what is due to thee openly [Mt. 6:3, 4]."

---

[10] Prosphora (lit. "offering") is the bread offered for use in the Liturgy by members
of the congregation. The bread is round, leavened, and somewhat flat and bears the
inscription IC, XC, NI, KA (Jesus Christ conquers) and the Cross. Some might have
an eight-pointed cross or a festal icon stamped on the bread. It is made of the best
quality wheaten flour, mixed with water and a little salt.

Day and night, Father Joseph made the needs of the poor his own concern. If it happened that he had nothing to hand out, he even went and borrowed so that he might dispense alms. His sphere of work was not only among the poor, but also among the imprisoned and sick. He offered alms to them as well as to the handicapped and impaired. Though he dealt much with the public, he was obedient to the civil authorities, mindful of the apostle's words: "Render then to all their dues: to whom the tribute is due, the tribute; to whom the customs duty, the toll; to whom the fear, the fear; to whom the honor, the honor [Rom. 13:7]." On another occasion, when it was the august Feast of the glorious John the Theologian, the Christians offered a multitude of prosphora, all of which were distributed by the holy man to the poor. That same evening not one loaf was left, so that Father Joseph needed to beg bread from another to eat.

There was another occasion, also a feast day, when the Christians brought oil for the lamps and incense and other offerings, but no one thought to bring prosphora. Consequently, at the hour for divine Liturgy, the sacristan observed that they were in want of prosphora. Since there was not even a loaf to celebrate the divine Mystery, he went to disclose the urgency of the situation to the priest, saying, "Honorable father, the hour for Liturgy is here, and there is no prosphora. Therefore, command me what I should do." Father Joseph gave him an answer in accordance with the voice and faith of Patriarch Abraham at Isaac's query, saying, "God Himself will provide the sacrifice, my son [cf. Gen. 22:8]." Then a short while later, Father Joseph said to the sacristan, "Come, child, into the holy sanctuary, and look to the right side. There thou shalt find that which thou wast seeking through the grace of my Christ." The sacristan entered the altar and turned to look toward the right side. And behold—lo, the miracle!—not one prosphora, but many were seen. They were large, too, and nicely stacked. The sacristan then let out a loud cry and proclaimed the wonder to all present. The venerable man, however, reproved him, ordering him to keep silent. Then Father Joseph immediately commenced the divine Liturgy. Afterward, the loaves of prosphora left over were distributed among the poor, even as Father Joseph was ever wont to do, to the glory of Him Who works great and extraordinary wonders without number.

There was a time when our Father Joseph had a need to visit another place. As a result, he was required to go through the neighborhoods of the Jews. Now it happened that he was on the road and encountered some Jews, who had already decided to have some sport with the Christian priest. The Jews filled a cup with wine and offered it to the venerable man, saying, "Drink, father, this wine." Father Joseph, without the least hesitation, took the drink from the hands of one of the Jews. He then proceeded to make the sign of the honorable and life-giving Cross over the cup, blessing it in the name of our Lord Jesus Christ. He drank a little of it and poured the rest into the wine jar. The Jews began shouting and making a tumult. They demanded that the venerable priest pay the full price of the wine. The holy man then spoke to them the truth, saying that he did not injure them in the least, and that they ought not ask for any price. Indeed, they instead should be giving thanks to him, inasmuch as he blessed their wine when they were not nonparticipants in blessing.

Now those Jews fomented a great contention against the venerable man. Some Christians who were present were drawn into the commotion. They rightfully extracted the priest from the Jews' clutches and roundly and deservedly rebuked them. The Jews, unwilling to countenance the public censure, hastened to the military commander (*doux*) who was in that city. They demanded that the priest be summoned, charging that they had been wronged by him. The commander had Father Joseph brought before him and asked him for what cause the Jews wished to make a case against him. The saint answered, "I was going on my way when I encountered these Jews, where there is the meeting of three roads. They had a jar filled with wine, from which they filled a cup and put it in my hands, saying, "Drink this wine." I received the cup from their hands, but did not wish to partake of a Jewish drink, but a Christian one. I therefore blessed the cup in the name of Christ and made the sign of the precious and life-giving Cross over it. I then drank as much as I wanted, and poured the remainder into the same jar from which they had served me. Therefore, by thine own sagacity, judge whether what I did was right or wrong."

The commander listened to the priest carefully and then turned to the Jews and said, "You ought not to have made an accusation against this honorable father, since he has shown love toward you by receiving your wine, that of the unbaptized, and in return he blessed it. You therefore should be thankful to him and not bring a charge against him. I say, therefore, take your wine and no longer trouble the holy elder with your fallacious reasoning." The Jews then answered, "We are not able to receive such wine in any way at all, since it received a Christian seal." Then the commander replied, "But you yourselves, against yourselves, but rightfully I might add, deprived yourselves of this wine. Since you are also bereft of blessing, receive a blessing in this manner: let the wine be given to poor Christians, without asking a price or anything else in return." Thus the wine was given to poor Christians, to the glory of Christ, Who overcame the Jews' craftiness by their own craftiness. The Jews, sad of countenance and put to shame, departed from the judgment hall, feeling the full failure of their unsuccessful ruse and the loss they suffered therefrom. There are other accounts worthy of wonder, which the saint accomplished; but, for the sake of brevity, we shall remain silent.

Saint Joseph lived a reverent and God-pleasing life to well over seventy years of age. After succumbing to a slight illness, he was translated to the Lord, rejoicing and glad, in the year 1511, on the 22nd day of January. The priests of the city gathered together and in a majestic manner interred his relics in the Church of Saint John. After the passage of a considerable number of years, by divine vision, it was revealed that his most honorable relics were whole and incorrupt. The vision proved true, and the relics were uncovered, with a heavenly fragrance wafting therefrom. The relics were transferred to a wooden chest inside the Church of the Theologian. All those who were sick and hastened with faith to the relics received healing. Thus God knows how to glorify those who faithfully glorify Him.

After the departure of the Venetians,[11] the War of Crete went on for nearly twenty years. Then Crete fell in 1669 to the Turks. Many Cretans fled and sought refuge on the Ionian island of Zakynthos. At that time, the august relics were taken by Saint Joseph's relatives and brought to Zakynthos on the 29th of August. A priest, Father Anthony Armakis, took the relics and brought them to the Holy Monastery of Saint John the Theologian near the village of Gaitaine. Presently, the relics are situated in the parish Church of the Pantocrator in that village.[12] On Zakynthos also, the Lord glorified the relics, which wrought miracles and signs, to the glory of His servant.

Through the intercessions of Thy Saints,
O Christ God, have mercy on us. Amen.

---

[11] After the Latin conquest of Constantinople in 1204, Crete was sold to Venice. The harsh domination of the Venetians prompted several revolts (1363, 1453) in which even some of the Venetian nobles participated. *Oxford*, s.v. "Crete."

[12] Metropolitan Titus of Rethymnon, *Cretan Saints*, p. 10.

On the 23rd of January, the holy Church commemorates
the holy Hieromartyr CLEMENT, Bishop of Ankyra,
and the holy Martyr AGATHANGELOS.[1]

Saint Clement

Clement, the blessed and God-inspired hieromartyr, was from Ankyra of Galatia.[2] He lived during the reigns of the Christ-hating emperors, Valerian (253-259), Diocletian (284-305) in the east, and Maximian (286-305) in the west. He was accounted worthy of the crown of martyrdom many times. In accordance with his name, Clement, signifying "branch" or "vine-twig," also possessed the corresponding deeds, for he was adorned as a fruit-bearing branch with the grapes of the All-Holy Spirit, for which his homeland gathered in the fruit after the accomplishment of his martyrdom. He was the scion of a distinguished and noble line.

His father, however, was an idolater who died—alas!—doubly, that is, not only physically but also spiritually. His mother, Sophia,[3] was a wise and pious Christian, and the daughter of Christians. She had married Clement's father against her better judgment but in obedience to her parents, who reminded her that "the unbelieving husband hath been sanctified in the wife, and the unbelieving wife hath been sanctified in the husband; for otherwise then your children are unclean, but now they are holy [1 Cor. 7:14]." This, however, was not written to Christians looking for marriage partners outside

---

[1] The Lives of these saints were recorded in Greek by Saint Symeon the Metaphrastes, whose manuscript begins, "After the year 250..." [*P.G.* 114:815-894]. The text is extant in the Athonite monasteries of the Great Lavra, Iveron, and in other places. The text was rendered in simpler Greek by Agapios the Cretan, who published it in his *Neon Paradeison*.

[2] Ankyra was both the civil and ecclesiastical metropolis of Galatia, the northern hilly region of the central Anatolian plateau of Asia Minor. It was a military base and center of trade on the main highway.

[3] *P.G.* 114:816A.

the Church, but to those husbands or wives who had converted while married to a spouse outside of the Church. In any event, the marriage had not brought about the results desired by Sophia's parents, for their son-in-law was a benighted idolater who remained entrenched in his deception. Sophia exhorted him, but his heart was closed to his own salvation. Sophia begged God to bring her marriage into a spiritual union or separate them physically. The Lord hearkened to her prayer and freed her from marriage with a pagan. The unbelieving husband departed of his own accord, leaving Sophia with their infant son. Thus, again Saint Paul speaks: "If the unbelieving separate himself, let him separate himself. The brother or sister hath not been placed under bondage in such cases. But God hath called us in peace [1 Cor. 7:15]." Sophia was then free to raise her son in a Christian manner. She brought him to Church in order to receive holy Baptism. By prophetic inspiration, she had her son named Clement, for she foresaw in the Spirit that he would become a fruitful branch on the true Vine, Christ, and produce rich grapes, that is, spiritual clusters of souls. It was also revealed to her that Clement would become a martyr of the Lord. He would be as a branch pruned by diverse tortures devised by many rulers. Thus, his religious education became a serious undertaking for her. She brought him up in the fear and admonition of the Lord, instructing him with holy books, and leading him to practise virtue. Thus, the lad "kept on advancing in wisdom and stature, and in grace in the presence of God and men [Lk. 2:52]."

When Clement reached ten or eleven years of age, his mother perceived that her repose was imminent. She was desirous of possessing those heavenly treasures rather then temporal riches. She then embraced her son and kissed him ardently, saying, "My child, beloved and most sweet, I, on the one hand, bodily conceived thee, but it was Christ through the Spirit Who gave thee birth. Therefore, know well thy heavenly Father, that thou mightest worship Him faithfully, for Christ is the only God. He is our immortality and salvation. He was crucified for our sakes, making us not only His sons, but also gods according to grace." The godly mother spoke these words with tears filling her eyes. She then prophesied to her son all that he would suffer in the future, saying, "I beseech thee to do me one favor, my child. Since the impious have kindled a persecution against the Christians, even thou shalt appear before kings and governors on account of Christ's name. They shall lay hands upon thee and persecute thee [Mk. 13:9; Lk. 21:12], even as they did the Master Christ, Who died for our salvation. I tell thee 'by means of patience, be running the course which is set before thee [cf. Heb. 12:1],' and so 'let patience keep on having a perfect work, that thou mayest be perfect and entire, lacking in nothing [Jas. 1:4].' Bring honor to thy race of the Christians and receive from God the incorruptible crown. Do thou prepare and train in advance, lest thou shouldest be captured early and the lawless vanquish thee. Therefore, play the man and contend courageously. Thou shouldest realize that one of two outcomes shall follow. If thou wilt endure the tyrants' tortures, thou shalt enjoy everlasting life and rejoice inside Paradise with the saints; but if thou deniest the Christ, thou shalt burn with the demons in the fire, the everlasting one [Mt. 25:41]. Since then it is necessary that mortal nature come to death, it is better that thou diest for the sake of Christ that thou mightest be glorified without ending."

With these and other exhortations, that most wise mother taught her child. She spoke to him all day, preparing his disposition toward martyrdom, so that his end should be most blessed. She then said, "These returns, my boy, do thou make to thy mother. Let them be the reward of my birth pangs and efforts in raising thee. The apostle has said the woman 'shall be saved through the childbearing, if they abide in faith and love and sanctification with sober-mindedness [1 Tim. 2:15].' This is my hope also. I bore thee, child, to suffer in thy flesh, which is my own. Spare not thy soul, but let thy blood flow and thy flesh bear wounds, that I may rejoice in the Lord, as if my members were suffering. Righteous Salome offered her seven sons to God and watched them as they were cruelly mutilated and slain, one by one for piety's sake [2 Mac. 7]. I have one son only whom I may present to the Lord. But thou shalt suffice me to win the King's favor, if thou wilt fight the good fight and finish the course [2 Tim. 4:7]. In thy martyrdom, I too shall rejoice in thy members. The roots of a tree drink up the same water which bedews its branches. My soul hangs with thine that it may suffer thy passion together with thee. I am leaving this world, even today; and though we shall be physically separated, yet not in spirit. Then we shall go together and pay homage to our Master, brilliantly arrayed with the radiance of thy contests." She then kissed her son's bodily members, saying, "I am blessed that I should have opportunity to kiss the members of a martyr, which shall become a sacrifice for the sake of the Lord." After she embraced her son and kissed him most sweetly, she surrendered her soul into the hands of God, leaving her body in the hands of her son. Clement had his beloved mother buried reverently and honorably. In the meantime, her divine words were preserved exactly in his heart.

Henceforth, that blessed youth denied himself any temporal enjoyments. He took up an austere and monastic lifestyle. Now his mother's friend, also named Sophia, had Clement come and stay in her home, where she treated him with love and care. Sophia, a most reverent Orthodox woman, had means and property but was childless. Now this new relationship for Sophia and Clement took place according to divine providence. Sophia was an educated woman. Her divine manner of life was spent in prayer day and night. She continued the young man's education, instructing him in the fear of the Lord. She also loved him as though he were her own genuine child. Clement also responded with similar feelings as though she were his mother. He obeyed her, keeping her commands strictly. As good earth, the crop of fruit was manifold. Now hear this account of the youth's almsgiving and divine virtue.

During that time a great famine struck Galatia. Clement was taking into Sophia's home those children of the Greek pagans who were destitute or orphaned. Their lives and physical needs were in a crisis. Clement dressed and fed them, providing them with shelter and better lives. He did not neglect their spiritual needs, but kept teaching them our holy beliefs, as much as he was able. The homeless children remained with him for a long time. He ate and slept with them, spending his time strengthening them in the godly Faith of the Christians. Whatever they needed for their physical well-being, he obtained from Sophia's substance. Whatever they needed for their spiritual benefit, he himself spent and treated them from his own God-given store of inner and spiritual wisdom. He watered their souls with the drink of his wonderful teachings. Together with all his other virtues, Clement exercised strict continence. The blessed young man ate no meat or animal products. He partook only of vegetables and bread. He drank no wine, only water. He was mindful of the holy Three Children who, by means of fasting and discipline, overcame the flames in the furnace and suffered no burns. Through the practise and acquisition of these virtues, his works of kindness among the Christian community in Ankyra endeared him to all. His knowledge and wisdom, though unusual in one so young, earned him the respect of all. The time then came for the lamp to be placed upon the lampstand, so that light could be given to all those in the house [Mt. 5:15]. He first received the office of Reader, then Deacon, then Priest. After two years this was followed by consecration to the episcopacy. He was compared to the Prophet Daniel who, while even a youth, demonstrated wisdom and discretion, especially in the unhappy case of Righteous Susanna. Thus, at the age of twenty, Clement was elevated to the office of Bishop. This of course took place well before the sacred synods and divine canons of the Church had prescribed mandatory ages for attaining offices in holy orders. Though Clement was young physically, he possessed a spiritual maturity and disposition which exceeded those of old men. As a bishop, Clement had a special and diligent ministry among the orphans and poor. He baptized children and ordained those adults who were worthy vessels for holy orders. The Church grew daily under his loving shepherding of the flock. Parents in those parts brought their children for catechism and stayed for a certain number of days. Afterward, the people received holy Baptism. These were the early fruits of Clement's ministry and divine achievements. In the meantime, events were coming to pass and bringing closer the saint's prophesied martyrdom. Indeed, the plaiting of this most precious crown was already in process.

Saint Clement in Ankyra Before Vicegerent Dometianos

At that time, some seven years after the prophetic words and repose of Clement's mother, the Christ-hating emperor of Rome, Diocletian, decreed to all those under him, that is, his governors and noblemen, to inflict merciless punishment upon the Christ-lovers. These sycophants, wishing to advance themselves with the emperor as faithful subjects, went to the height of pitiless treatment toward the Christians. One particular toady was vicegerent (*vicarius*)[4] and proconsul of Galatia. He heard reports concerning the blessed bishop, Clement, of how he baptized children, proclaimed Christ as true God, and mocked the idols. Dometianos (Domitianus)[5] ordered that Clement be apprehended and brought to him. When that vile man saw that Bishop Clement was young, decent, and honest, he thought that he would put him to the test and said, "The nobility of thy countenance and thy good order and discipline testify that thou art a thinking man and prudent. Reports that I have heard from those who would accuse thee appear exaggerated and incongruous, because they claim that thou committest childish and mindless deeds. Therefore, do thou speak concerning these charges that we might ascertain the truth." Bishop Clement said, "Our prudence and knowledge is the Master Christ, Wisdom Himself, the Son and Logos of God, Who made the cosmos and bestowed upon us reason and speech." Dometianos winced and retorted, "By the gods, thou hast embittered us with these opening words by uttering such nonsense. But if thou wilt have what is best for thyself, leave off this imbecility that thou mightest flee from punishments. Do thou also venerate the gods and receive from us significant honors and gifts. Look at me and what I achieved after paying my dues to the gods."

The saint smiled and remarked, "We Christians consider such gifts to be loss and injury. We deem whatever honor you might accord us to be to our dishonor. Therefore, do not have any hope that thou mightest divert us from piety with such threats." These words infuriated Dometianos, who cast a fierce eye upon the saint, saying, "It is I who made thee so audacious, because I spoke to thee compassionately and humbly. But this is nothing strange or extraordinary, since thou art a youth with little discernment. But know this: if thou wilt not pay homage to the gods, I shall submit thee to a harsh death—indeed, an unheard of one. To be more precise, I mean thou

---

[4] *Vicarius* or vicegerent (vīs jēr'ənt) was an officer appointed as a deputy by a sovereign.

[5] *P.G.* 114:825BC.

shalt be subjected to diverse and manifold tortures, after which thou shalt be put to death as a malefactor. By thine example other proud Christians shall think and behave more soberly." The blessed man answered, "More knowledge do the small children of the Christians possess than thou who art educated and old. For God has hidden these things from the wise and intelligent, and revealed true wisdom to babes [cf. Mt. 11:25]. I prefer to offer my God a rational sacrifice, but your priests hope in vain to appease demons with gore and fumes. Moreover, I beseech the true God that I might become a voluntary sacrifice, even as Christ Who became Man and sacrificed Himself on the Cross for me." The tyrant then cast off all pretense of civility and revealed his true ferocity and barbarity. He bade his executioners to suspend the Christian upon the wood. They were then to scrape and flay the bishop's sides, so as to expose his inward parts, thus rendering Clement a pitiful spectacle to onlookers.

The saint withstood these sufferings without cowering and without uttering a word. His countenance was not altered. He did not sigh in the least. He endured this dreadful mutilation with great magnanimity, even giving thanks to the Lord. As time passed and this savage destruction of his flesh caused onlookers to avert their eyes, the soldiers grew tired. The torture of Clement sapped their strength and left their hands debilitated and lifeless. Clement, for his part, remained unperturbed and even joyful. The odious vicegerent then said, "Do not take courage in the exhaustion of the soldiers, thinking that I too shall flag and let thee go. Indeed, be assured that I shall merely change as many times as is needed teams of executioners, until all thy flesh has been whittled away, leaving only bones." This in fact took place in both word and deed. As the groups of soldiers tired and were changed, they continued to rake his flesh, doing their worst, more so than the first group. When they were left utterly exhausted, Clement was taken down. There was nearly no flesh remaining upon him. He was nearly all bones and all but about unrecognizable. What remained was—alas!—a most pitiful and terrifying sight. Dometianos then thought to prove the martyr again. This time he used blandishments, but then threatened him with death if he should continue not to do his bidding. The saint answered, "My death, O judge, renders incorruption to my body and works immortality for my soul." Dometianos then replied, "Leave off these fables of enjoying everlasting life, which becloud the sweet light of the sun given to us by our gods. If thou wilt not obey me, then do thou expect more chastisements. I have now given thee a few days' reprieve to regain thy strength, so that thou mightest withstand future torture." The saint answered, "By using threatening words and committing savage acts, thou shalt attain nothing. I have already informed thee that as much as thou wilt inflict bitter torments to my flesh, the more so is my soul benefitted. Since then I have told thee what I think, do to me as much as thou art able." Thus, Christ's soldier spurned every torture.

The unjust judge, galled and incensed with what he deemed cheeky behavior on the part of the prisoner, commanded that the righteous man receive a beating to his mouth, cheeks, and jaw. "Buffet his impudent mouth! Strike him on the cheek and jaw! Put to silence those remaining members. Hit them hard and pound them to pulp, lest he should speak so brashly." Therefore, because only the saint's head was left intact, the soldiers did their worst. Some of the soldiers, however, after gazing upon his shredded and flayed body, came to pity him and were saddened to administer new tortures. Other soldiers, heartless ones, thought only to obey the tyrant. They struck the saint with stones, thereby shattering that truth-loving mouth, which spoke and said, "You do me honor by making me a partaker of Christ Who suffered slaps and buffets.[6] The imitation of His sufferings in my flesh lightens my pains." After he had spoken this, he then offered up prayer and gave thanks to the Lord. The tyrant, observing that the bishop could not walk about, ordered his men to lift Clement and convey him to the prison until further notice. God, however, empowered His athlete. No one was able to draw near to him. Clement then walked on his own and began saying, "As for the oil of a sinner, let it not anoint my head [Ps. 140:6]." Dometianos heard this and marvelled greatly at Clement's perseverance and courage. He then commented, "Such soldiers as Clement should the emperors have, who would have no cowardice in the face of dangers, and they would fight manfully. I shall remand him to the emperor who alone, as one experienced in such cases, can overcome him." Dometianos then sent a dispatch with the martyr to Rome. Now the blessed Clement, who had never exited his homeland, offered an entreaty to Christ: "O my Lord and God, guard and protect Thy city. I commit the care of this city to Thee. Let not the adversaries vanquish Thy faithful slaves. Do not have me become estranged from my homeland. But I entreat Thy dominion that even as Thou didst bring Jacob back to his father's house [Gen. 35:27] and didst return Joseph's bones and laid them to rest with those of his fathers [Ex. 13:19], do Thou also dispense in Thine œconomy that I should be brought back here to my homeland."

Saint Clement in Rome Before Emperor Diocletian

After the saint uttered this prayer, he was transferred to Rome. The Emperor Diocletian[7] observed the saint beaming with joy. He took notice of the bishop's nobility and good breeding. He read the report that accompanied the prisoner, but could discern no trace of Clement's previous ordeals. He

---

[6] Mk. 14:65; Jn. 18:22; 19:3.
[7] *P.G.* 114:833D.

pondered on how he might strike terror in Clement; for he wished to change his attitude toward torture and have him prefer that which is joyous and delightful. He bade his servants to bring forth beautiful articles, which were found in the palace, such as gold and silver vessels, costly garments, precious stones, and whatever else entices the eyes. All these objects were set forth in a place opposite the instruments of torture. The latter included iron beds heated to red-hot temperatures, wheels of torture, braziers, cauldrons, spits, stakes, plates, frying pans, and other such appliances. Even if one had not undergone torture by means of any of these, only to look upon them instilled terror and trembling. The emperor then pointed to the costly palace articles and said to Bishop Clement, "I shall bestow all of these upon thee, together with my friendship, if thou wilt act sensibly and fall down and worship the gods. If thou choosest to disobey, thou shalt experience these instruments of torture and others much worse." The saint then answered, "If it seems to thee that these gold and silver vessels are splendid and costly, how much more shalt thou deem those heavenly good things? And if these temporal chastisements appear to thee so terrible, how much more horrible shall the river of fire appear to thee, or Tartarus, or the other everlasting torments? This gold of yours is mean, cheap, and lifeless. Thieves can break in and steal it, and you suffer loss of precious metals shaped by fire and iron. Those costly garments are the offspring of worms, the cunning workmanship of barbarians, and the food of moths. You wear such array to adorn your bodies, but these silk garments soon are worse for wear and require mending and laundering. All those who esteem such fabrics are mindless. Those silk weavers are more estimable than those who clamor to wear their product. Consider that they at least create something of use, while their customers walk about with a vain and pompous bearing, showing off what comes of worms. Such things are coveted by those of this world, which shall perish in the end with your gods. But those everlasting good things are delightful and inspire good cheer. 'Even as it hath been written: "Eye hath not seen, and ear hath not heard, and neither hath it entered into the heart of man the things which God prepared for those who love Him [1 Cor. 2:9]."' These good things are imperishable and unending, even as the Creator and Master of all creation is without beginning and deathless. He is both perfect God and perfect Man. As God He is impassible, but as man He endured the Cross, burial, and resurrection on the third day, thereby raising us, as He is good and the almighty One."

The emperor was enraged by all he heard, and said, "Thou mayest be articulate, but thou understandest little. I have borne with thee long, and again I tell thee to trust in our gods. Do not put thy hope in this Christ Who was illtreated by the Jews and crucified. He suffered and died, but our gods do not undergo suffering and death." Bishop Clement then remarked, "Suffering and death cannot be experienced by the insensate and lifeless. Your idols are the works of the hands of men, who give them mouths, eyes, ears, noses, hands, and feet, but they do not speak, see, hear, smell, feel, or walk [Ps. 113:12-15]. Christ, however, voluntarily suffered, according to His human nature. In order that He might bring us up to God, He indeed was put to death in the flesh, but made alive in the Spirit [1 Pe. 3:18]. For He came that He might save the world [Jn. 12:47]. Since we, His children, have partaken of flesh and blood, He also Himself in like manner partook of the same, in order that through death He might bring to nought the one who has the power of death, that is, the devil [Heb. 2:14]." The tyrant became irritated with the martyr and summoned the executioners. He ordered them to bind Clement to the wheel, which spun with great vehemence. The saint was tied naked to the wheel and mercilessly beaten with rods as he went round and round. While the wheel turned with great violence and speed, the saint's flesh was being cut to shreds, and his bones were being broken. The martyr kept constant in prayer and said, "O Lord Jesus Christ, look down upon me and have mercy upon me. Do Thou come and help me. Lighten the burden of this punishment. 'The pangs of Hades encircled me, round about the snares of death have overtaken me [Ps. 17:5].' Therefore, redeem me for the glory of Thy name. 'Let all mine enemies be greatly put to shame [Ps. 6:9].' Grant me to be made whole that I may continue to bring to nought the devices of the ungodly. Strengthen Thou me. 'For in Thee have I hoped, O Lord; Thou wilt hearken unto me [Ps. 37:15].'" The wheel then came to a stop, as though halted by an invisible hand, which also loosed Clement's bonds. The hands of the soldiers became enfeebled and withered. They were not able to move them in the least. The saint then appeared unharmed and in health. Many witnessed these wondrous events. They were enlightened in their souls and cried out, "Great is the God of the Christians!" Thus, the blessed Clement, the branch on the vine which is Christ, brought forth beautiful fruit by means of his bodily members. He glorified the Lord and gave thanks to Him, as is meet, saying among many things, "I give thanks to Thee, O heavenly Father, that Thou hast permitted me to undergo torments for Thy name in this city of Thine only-begotten Son. In Rome both the Apostles Peter and Paul preached and suffered martyrdom. Here, my namesake, Clement, glorified Thee. They are now glorified in the heavens and on the earth. I pray Thee that the time be shortened until every nation shall praise them more than the kings of the earth. May emperors submit to Thy holy Faith and venerate Thy martyrs!" Thus Bishop Clement entreated God, for he believed that idolatry would soon be disbanded. The rage of the tyrant had waxed hot. He completely dismissed the miracles he had witnessed. He bade other soldiers to break the bishop's mouth and teeth with thick iron crowbars. The saint's mouth and jaw were broken and his teeth were fractured. The bishop was still able to proclaim God's praises. The emperor then ordered that the prisoner be fettered in the common prison. That night, all those men and women who came to believe entered the prison. They warmly besought the martyr to vouchsafe them holy Baptism. The saint perceived their fervent piety and baptized them all, chanting joyfully, "Blessed are they whose iniquities are forgiven, and whose sins are covered [Ps. 31:1]." The Baptisms were facilitated by the fact that as much water as they required was found in that prison.

At midnight, a most radiant light shone and illumined the entire dungeon. In the midst of that light there appeared a man, having large wings, who was all light. He offered the saint bread and wine, and then disappeared. The saint understood by these two elements, heavenly sent, that he was to perform the Mysteries. The bishop then recited the customary liturgical prayers and had as many as had received divine illumination in holy Baptism also communicate the immaculate Mysteries. At length, the prison became filled with faithful believers, who were offering up prayer and chanting. The guards, beholding such a transformation, went and made a report to the emperor, saying that the prison had become a church. The emperor then dispatched his men by night to ambush the assembled Christians. The troops then rounded up the faithful and brought them outside of the city to an execution site. Men, women, and children were to be slaughtered as sheep. The prisoners were given a choice: either suffer decapitation or pay homage to the idols. As the turn of each one of the faithful arrived to suffer decapitation, the executioner asked, "Wilt thou deny the Christ and save thy life?" The answer given by each believer was negative. Thus, a multitude suffered martyrdom. Only one youth remained alive. His name was Agathangelos, whose name means "good angel." He had not concealed himself out of fear of death, but on account of his desire to suffer many tortures, that he might be more glorified in the kingdom of God. Concerning his feats, we shall clearly set them forth hereunder.

The emperor then commanded that Clement be brought to him that he might try him again with blandishments, in the hope of vanquishing him. The emperor did not succeed with the blessed man. He then had Clement cast to the ground. Four mighty soldiers were selected to drag the bishop and then stretch him out by his hands and feet, as much as they were able. After they stretched him, they shook him violently in order to traumatize his members. By this procedure, they dislocated his joints and caused the saint bitter pains. Next, four men administered lashes with dry bullwhips. The saint endured all these chastisements manfully, as though someone else were suffering. The tyrant marvelled and commented, "Even as thou hast a contentious soul, Clement, so thy body refuses to be humbled. But I shall try again to put thee to the test. Since thou hast shown thyself hard, even as iron, then with iron claws shall I rouse the deep sensations of thy flesh." The saint replied, "Well hast thou spoken, O emperor, that my Master Christ gives me the most sweet sleep, putting to sleep these pains with the hope of those future delights." Clement was then suspended from a wooden pole. The pitiless executioners scraped and stabbed Clement's flesh, so that no flesh remained upon the martyr. This happened not so much on account of the savage tyrant's command, as at the instigation of the man-hating demon. Thus, our martyr appeared to be bones.

Despite this raking and laying bare of his bones, Clement informed the emperor, saying, "This flesh undergoing torture is not that with which I was originally covered by nature. That body of flesh was destroyed by previous tortures, which left not even the smallest patch of skin. My bones and joints were clothed in this flesh afterward by Christ. Therefore, even if thou shouldest destroy this flesh, the Lord shall provide me with a new one. The Potter, the Creator of man, never wants for clay." These and other statements were spoken by Clement. The tyrant then commanded that Clement's sides be consumed with burning candles. Once more, the emperor observed that Clement underwent all with marvellous perseverance, so that he was rendered awestruck and said, "I have punished many of these ill-named and hateful Christians. I have put to death countless among them, but I have never seen such resolute purpose or resiliency in another man." After he spoke these words, he sent the blessed man away. Clement was remanded to the prefect of Nikomedia. Diocletian sent a letter to the prefect and bade him to try with all his might to convert the prisoner to idol worship. In the event he did not succeed, he recommended that the prisoner either be cast as prey to wild animals or be subjected to some cruel demise.

Subsequent to this, as Clement was being led out of Rome, the faithful Christians were weeping. Some were kissing his hands and feet, while others anointed themselves with his blood. The faithful could not be separated from him. It was only by the use of force that the soldiers were able to get the bishop on board the ship. The bishop was then heard uttering a prayer on behalf of the Christians in Rome. The faithful on the dock also prayed on his behalf.·

The divine Agathangelos, whom we mentioned earlier, conceived a desire to suffer for the sake of Christ. He wished to accompany the holy Clement, so he entered the ship earlier. He had made a prior arrangement with the sailors and paid the passage-money. Agathangelos therefore kept to himself in a corner of the ship, praying and waiting for the bishop's arrival. He caught sight of Bishop Clement and waited for the proper moment. When Bishop Clement was alone and in prayer, Agathangelos approached and

Saint Agathangelos

disclosed the entire matter to him. He explained how he longed to suffer martyrdom and all that went with it. Bishop Clement gladly received Agathangelos as an angel of God, for which he gave glory to God and uttered this prayer: "I give thanks to Thee, O Master Jesus Christ, my only comfort and help. For neither in the earth, nor in the sea, hast Thou left me without help; but Thou hast consoled my soul, as Thou dost will, and hast sent me, as a good angel, my brother Agathangelos. I beseech Thee to strengthen him in his confession and glorify him, that Thou, O most merciful One, should be glorified by him."[8] Thus, they kept constant in prayer day and night. Neither did they taste of food, nor did anyone provide for them. They had their hearts not on "the meat which perisheth [Jn. 6:27]." They had heavenly bread and water upon which they were nourished, so that the bishop said, "I shall not hunger with the true Bread, Jesus Christ within me. I shall not ever thirst with the living water, the grace of Christ." The soldiers, observing that Clement and Agathangelos fasted so many days, began to pity them, and pity moved them to offer victuals. The saints thanked them for their kind disposition, but they did not accept the food. They said that God was nourishing them from on high. This indeed was the case. During the first watch of the night, the Lord from on high sent them what was fitting. He nourished men of earth with the bread of angels.

The ship put in at Rhodes. Some of the crew went ashore to stock up on provisions. The saints remained behind in the ship with a few of the guards. Now the bishop and Agathangelos were desirous to go to church that Lord's day, so as to commune the divine Mysteries. Photinos, the Bishop of Rhodes, learned of Bishop Clement's arrival. In the company of his clergy and many other Christians, Bishop Photinos went to the ship. Photinos requested the release of the prisoner into his custody. Since he pledged himself to the soldiers that he would return Bishop Clement in a timely manner, the captain of the guard gave his permission. Thus both Clement and Agathangelos went with Photinos to the church. The God-loving Bishop Photinos invited the Bishop of Ankyra to celebrate the divine Liturgy, to which the latter hearkened. When they came to the part where the holy Gospel is read, the faithful heard these words of the Lord: "Do not become afraid

---

[8] Butler adds that Saint Agathangelos was ordained deacon.

because of those who kill the body, but are not able to kill the soul; but rather fear the One Who is able to send away both soul and body into Gehenna [Mt. 10:28]." These words trickled sweetly into the souls of Clement and Agathangelos, so that from their joy they wept. The Christians present, moved to sympathy, also wept for the saints. Now when Bishop Clement was liturgizing, those who were accounted worthy beheld the following vision. A radiant man was seen with the saint at the holy Table. In the air there stood a multitude of angels, brilliant as flashes of lightning. Those who were vouchsafed this sight, prostrated themselves on the floor, for they were unable to gaze upon that ineffable light.

The news of this miracle was heard throughout the city. Not only the faithful gathered, but also many of the idolaters. This included sick folk, who were placed before the feet of the holy bishop with reverence and faith. When the saint laid his hand upon those sufferers—O the wonder!—each of them received healing. Now many of those benighted by the idols beheld these miracles and came to believe in Christ and request Baptism. In the meantime, the soldiers, viewing the popularity of their prisoner, began fearing that the local populace might seize the bishop and take flight. Therefore, the soldiers laid hold of Bishop Clement and returned him to the ship, where he was clapped in irons. The weeping faithful accompanied Clement and Agathangelos to the ship, and then bade them farewell. A fair wind followed and brought them quickly to Nikomedia.

Saints Clement and Agathangelos in Nikomedia Before Prefect Agrippinos

Once there, the saint was delivered up to Emperor Maximian, who was in Nikomedia when the ship came into port. Maximian read Diocletian's report and was astonished. He did not wish to become involved in the case, fearing being put to nought, so he turned the prisoner over to the prefect, Agrippinos, for examination. Agrippinos began the questioning, making a cold inquiry: "Thou art Clement, art thou not?" The bishop answered, "Yes. I am the slave of the Christ." This response alone angered the prefect. He ordered his men to buffet the bishop's face. Agrippinos then said explosively, "Say not that thou art Christ's slave, but the abject slave of the emperors." The saint answered, "Would to God that your emperors cried out that they were slaves of the Christ! The whole world would have them as their sovereigns, which would usher in peace. But since they are ungodly and perverse, those mindless ones contend among one another that they might destroy us."

Agrippinos was now enraged and was unable to give answer to the bishop. He then turned his face toward the other man who stood before him and said, "But thou, who art thou? Thy name is not in the imperial letter of indictment." Agathangelos, after gazing heavenward and then at the saint, answered, "I am a Christian. I was baptized by this Saint Clement." Agrippinos was in no humor to make further inquiries, but only retorted, "Then thou dost admit that this Clement deceived thee. In fact, he has now led thee to a painful death." He ordered his men to suspend Clement and have him struck with the flat of the sword. Agathangelos was cruelly flogged with bullwhips. Bishop Clement prayed for Agathangelos that he might persevere to the end, which he did bravely. After the two martyrs were thrashed for a considerable time, they were put in prison.

They spent that entire night in prayer. Angels from on high descended and encouraged them on their martyric course. Now there were other inmates in the prison. They too witnessed the descent of the angel and were moved to compunction and belief in Jesus Christ. They implored Christ's slaves to show them the way to God. The martyrs both taught the prisoners sufficiently, making them steadfast. Since there was plenty of water in the prison, they were baptized by the bishop. At the close of the Mystery, Bishop Clement opened the prison door. He had no key, but merely gained access by his word. He bade the newly-illumined to flee and save themselves from the ungodly. He then invoked the blessing of Christ upon them, and they departed, unhindered, rejoicing. Saints Clement and Agathangelos stayed behind. Now the prefect learned of this incident and became incensed.

The beastly-minded Agrippinos had lions rounded up and other wild beasts collected for the arena. The prosecutor let loose against the two saints those creatures, which in no wise harmed them. Much rather, they were licking the prisoners, wagging their tails, and making friendly motions, even as one might see dogs playing with their masters.

The saints were giving thanks to the Lord, saying, "Thou art glorified, O Christ, in that Thou hast enlightened wild beasts even to hold us in reverence, even as Thou once marvellously wrought for Thy slave Daniel in the lions' den." That brute, Agrippinos, however, did not acknowledge the cause of the animals' tame behavior, on account of his being senselessly benighted in extreme impiety. He then ordered that long skewers be fired to red-hot temperatures. When this had been done, he bade his executioners to thrust them into the fingers of Clement and Agathangelos. He then ordered that they be pushed through until they reached the martyrs' elbows. As the skewers were shoved into their bodies, the bitter pain that resulted therefrom to the martyrs defies description. Outwardly though, their flesh could be seen drawing back from the burning skewers. The spectators recoiled with a collective shudder, appalled at this blood-chilling spectacle. Greatly empathizing with Clement and Agathangelos, they kept shouting for the authorities to release the prisoners. Their displeasure at the barbarism caused the prefect's anger to wax hotter. Instead of rescinding the punishment, he bade his officers to heat other skewers. When this had been done, those skewers were made to pierce the martyrs' armpits, which then penetrated their shoulders. This heinous torment instilled deeper pain. The crowd, thoroughly indignant at the savagery and ferocity of Agrippinos, began casting stones at him as one unjust, who justly deserved death. All the while, they kept shouting, "Great is the God of the Christians!" The reason why they were exclaiming this so loudly was due to their astonishment and wonder that the saints had not perished under this harshest of tortures. Consequently, a great tumult and clamor resulted. The prefect fled, giving leave to the saints to go to Mount Pyramis, a place which concealed many idols of the Greek pagans. In that place, the idol-mad also offered up sacrifices.

After some days, the prefect sent men to apprehend the saints. Agrippinos then addressed the saints, saying, "With magic arts have you turned the crowd so that they raised their hands against me and shamelessly blasphemed the gods." They answered him, saying, "It was God who enlightened them to proclaim the truth; for if He were not true God, then He could not work such wonders. Therefore, do not be negligent. Render to us other punishments, even as thou hast been contemplating. In that way, again thou shalt behold the almighty One's deliverance of us from out of thy hands." The prefect wasted no time. He ascended with the saints to the pinnacle of the mountain, where a heathen temple was located. Agrippinos first had the martyrs' flesh cut to shreds and then—alas!—ordered the breaking of their bones with staves. Afterward, he had each martyr placed in a sack, together with large rocks. The sacks were then heaved from a sheer cliff at the mountain's summit. The sacks tumbled down the rocky slope and into the sea below, leaving all to believe that the martyrs had perished.

In the meantime, the lovers of martyrs went and stood on another part of the shore, waiting for the sea to yield those treasured relics by washing them ashore. With the passage of considerable time, the sacks were seen to arise from the sea and float on the waves. The Christians then embarked on a fishing boat in order to retrieve the sacks. As they opened the sacks and looked inside—O Thine ineffable marvels, Christ King, and Thine unutterable and mysterious power!—the saints were found alive. They had no trace of any wound upon them. It was midnight when a light came upon them from the heavens, and angels took the saints by their hands. They brought both Clement and Agathangelos out onto dry land and gave them heavenly food to eat. The saints partook of this nourishment and were empowered. The angels strengthened them so that they became mightier and more powerful than before. The saints then entered into the city. They stood in the square and lifted their hands heavenward, saying, "We give thanks to Thee, O Lord Jesus Christ, Who hast remembered those who put their hope in Thee. Thou hast delivered us from the evil devices of our enemies who gnashed their teeth against us. They would mock us, but Thou hast magnified Thy holy name in us." Thus they recounted to the faithful these wonders of God.

As the saints walked through the marketplace, they encountered two blind men in a room. One of them had a withered hand, while the other was completely paralyzed. The martyrs laid their hands upon those so sorely afflicted and cured them without toil or expense. These miraculous healings were seen by others, who started bringing forward their sick folk and those possessed by demons. Both Bishop Clement and Agathangelos healed all those suffering from diverse illnesses, by their prayer and laying on of hands. The prefect learned of these miracles but thought to himself, "Not only can I not put these men to death, but now they are injuring many idolaters by bringing them to Christ. I must therefore be rid of them. I shall send letters to the emperor. Let him dispatch them as he wishes." When the emperor learned of the magnitude of the tortures employed and that the prisoners had not died, he drew back from taking the case. He felt he could not afford public ridicule. He therefore wrote to the governor of Ankyra, one Kourikios. He reasoned to himself, "Since this is where Clement hails from, let him be sent there." This all took place by God's dispensation, that is, that the divine Clement should return to the place of his birth. He had already passed through land and sea, even as he prayed that he might be able to confess Christ before governors, rulers, and kings.

Saints Clement and Agathangelos in Ankyra Before Governor Kourikios

Consequently, Bishop Clement was returned to his home and see, where, filled with exceeding joy, he gave thanks to God, saying, "Glory to Thee, O Christ God! Thou hast hearkened to my entreaty and brought me back to my homeland, with this goodly addition and fellow athlete Agathangelos."

After some days, Kourikios sat on the judgment seat. The holy Clement and Agathangelos were brought forward. The guileful governor thought to try the bishop first with flattery. He started by praising the sacred Clement, acclaiming him a prudent and sensible man. However, it was not long before that wretched governor saw that the two saints had contempt for the idols. He became more wroth when he heard them say that tortures brought them joy. Kourikios said to them, "Since you rejoice in chastisements, I shall oblige you who are tormented by an evil genius." The governor thereupon heat a piece of metal to such a degree that sparks were flying from it in every direction. He then placed it on Clement's armpits in succession. A wooden post was then placed upright in the earth, whereupon Clement was bound with his elbows tied back. The executioners applied the fiery plate to his sides. Agathangelos, who was next to him, was suspended on high and encircled by the executioners, who were raking his sides and thighs. The governor then mockingly inquired if they felt the pain of their punishments. Clement answered, "We are not fainthearted; but even if our outward man is being utterly destroyed, yet the inward man is being renewed day by day [2 Cor. 4:16]." The tyrant contended that he might conquer extreme patience with an excess of punishments. He next contrived to fire an iron helmet, which glowed red-hot. It was placed on top of the martyr's head, so that smoke exited from his mouth, nose, and ears. Bishop Clement sighed deeply as he sought divine help, uttering, "O Well of living waters, Fountain of life, living Water, Torrent of salvation, heal me with the dew of Thy grace. As Thou didst deliver Thy slaves from the sea, do Thou deliver us from these fiery torments." It was then that the helmet miraculously cooled. At the same time, those who were flaying Agathangelos fell back in exhaustion. The tyrant beheld these sights and trembled. He wondered at their patience, and then commanded their imprisonment.

The wise Sophia, Saint Clement's foster mother, even after so many years when his existence was unknown and when hope seemed gone, still hoped to gaze upon him. She rejoiced to the depths of her soul when she learned of his arrival in the neighborhood. She went secretly by night to the dungeon, where she embraced him. She wept as she kissed his mouth, eyes, hands, and all his members. She asked him how he had passed his time abroad and how he struggled. She also inquired after his companion and fellow athlete. The saint answered all her questions, narrating from the beginning all that had befallen him. She was filled with motherly love and compassion, and began washing the saints' wounds. Sophia had brought herbs, bandages, and towels, together with as much food as they wished.

Kourikios, in the meantime, kept turning over in his mind how to deal with these martyrs. He acknowledged to himself that he could not overcome them. He then received orders from Maximian to send the bishop to the vicegerent and administrator of Amisos,[9] named Dometios (Dometius).[10] Sophia, the lover of children and martyrs, followed him to that city, accompanied by all those children that the boy Clement had previously brought to the Faith and who had received Baptism. When this incident was mentioned to the emperor at that time, he commanded that if the Christian believers should separate from Clement, they would be able to go wherever they might wish. If they should persist with the bishop, they could expect to

---

[9] Amisos (now Samsun) is a coastal city of Pontos, which later was a suffragan of Amaseia on the Lykos. Diocletian made Amaseia metropolis of Diospontus (later Helenopontus), which was Christianized early.

[10] *P.G.* 114:864A.

be relieved of their heads. The soldiers strenuously toiled to disband them, but they failed. Many of these Christian comrades who had flocked around the bishop, then prostrated themselves at the blessed man's feet. They took hold of them tightly, lest they should be parted from him. They were impervious to the sentence of decapitation for their show of loyalty toward Christ and His slave. Thus, they all demonstrated constancy to the end. This is the perfect gift of good purpose and pure intention. The divine Iakovos reminds us that "every good gift and every perfect gift is from above, coming down from the Father of the lights [Jas. 1:17]."

Therefore, the holy bodies of those children were executed together in the plain. The excellent Sophia took forgiveness from the holy bishop and Agathangelos and remained behind to carry out the interment, but said that she would soon follow them.

Saints Clement and Agathangelos in Amisos Before Vicegerent Dometios

The saints were brought to Dometios, with whom the divine Clement conversed most wisely on everlasting life, attempting to see if he might bring him to repentance and belief in the Christ. But that pagan did not put his mind to consider the words of the saints. Instead, he commanded that the prisoners be put in prison that he might examine them individually, thinking that in this way he should be able to overcome them with greater facility. The vain one, however, travailed for nought. Thereupon, he had filled one large asbestos pit with unslaked lime. He had the saints placed therein, while soldiers guarded the perimeter, lest any should attempt their rescue. God, however, preserved His slaves unharmed and intact, even as He once saved the holy Three Children in the Chaldean furnace. When night fell, a brilliant light came from the heavens and wondrously illuminated that place throughout the night, the fruit of which was to follow. Two of the guards, Phengos and Efkarpos,[11] beheld that light and leaped into the pit, invoking the name of Christ. Dometios, dead in soul, thought that they had died and ordered the removal of human remains from the pit. When the soldiers saw that all four men were still alive, whole and healthy, they were astonished. They reported their findings to the tyrant. He ordered that the two soldiers suffer impaling with stakes. Thus, those two blessed soldiers, Phengos and Efkarpos, the namesakes of "light" and "good fruit," received the amaranthine crown of martyrdom.

After these events, the holy Clement and Agathangelos were given a thrashing with staves throughout their bodies, until all their bones were broken. Next, two belts were strapped to the martyrs' spines. Each man was lifted up and conveyed to a red-hot iron bed. They were stretched out while

---

[11] *P.G.* 114:868A.

a great heap of lighted coals was stoked. As the martyrs lay on these beds, the executioners poured over them such an excess of boiling pitch, sulphur, and oil that a fire resulted, leading all to believe that the Christians had perished. The vicegerent then noticed that the martyrs did not move in the least, and that their eyes were closed. He thereupon bade his men to extinguish the fire and cast the remains into the river. The saints, however, were in the midst of a sweet and wonderful sleep, wherein they beheld Christ, the Judge of the contest, with a multitude of holy angels. Jesus spoke to them and said, "Cease fearing, for I am in your company." The saints were awakened, and each related his vision to the other, which proved the same. It was as if they were oblivious to their surroundings. They conducted themselves as those taking their ease in a bedewed grassland, rather than those fighting to survive consuming flames. Dometios, who witnessed this extraordinary spectacle and how the Christians mastered fire, utterly despaired. He was at a loss for devising another torture that might prevail over them. Exasperated, he decided to dispose of them by sending them to Maximian, who had just come to Tarsus.

The saints were sent to meet Maximian. On the road, as they were walking under a scorching sun, the land about them was arid and desolate. Not only the saints, but also the soldiers escorting them, were in danger of dying of thirst. The saints then bent their knees and inclined their hearts to God, uttering, "O Lord Jesus Christ, our God, Who commanded the waters of the sea to be divided and didst bring forth water out of the flinty rock, do Thou also cause water to gush out of this waterless place that our immeasurable thirst might be quenched; for Thou art able to do all things, as Thou art the almighty One." After they made this fervent and tear-filled entreaty—lo, the miracle!—from that dessicated spot of earth, the most clear and sweet water sprang out. All drank and were thereby cheered. Now the fame of this miracle was heard in the surrounding countryside. People began bringing their sick folk to the saints, who healed those who came to them. They did not use herbs and drugs on the sufferers, but instead wrought cures with the laying on of their hands. Now the most blessed Clement thirsted exceedingly to continue his sufferings for Christ. He earnestly desired to undergo other torments, not being satisfied with those previous feats; for he wished to say with the divine Paul, "I die daily [1 Cor. 15:31]." He therefore entreated God that he might be vouchsafed to be tortured for the sake of Christ's love throughout his life, and said as much when he supplicated Him: "O Master and God, the only King of the ages, do not yet take me to Thyself in the midst of my days, but grant me this favor, that is, that I might suffer chastisements all the days of my life for the sake of Thy love, until I should sacrifice all my members so as to enjoy them again more splendidly."

After he had made this prayer, Bishop Clement heard a voice from on high saying, "What hast thou asked to have, O Clement? Well then, be thou empowered and run courageously the course of the contest for the entire time of thy life, until thou shouldest finish with martyrdom, which thou hast desired to this day, covering a period of twenty-eight years."

Saints Clement and Agathangelos in Tarsus Before Emperor Maximian

They went forth to Tarsus and stood before the emperor, who engaged in blandishments for a long time that he might cajole and bring the prisoners to his perversity. Saint Clement discoursed with the emperor, without the least trace of cowardice or fear, censuring his ancestral impiety. The tyrant became so angry that he lost his voice. When he had composed himself somewhat, he had a furnace heated, hotter than that of Nebuchadnezzar in Babylon [Dan. 3:19]. The saints were cast inside that inferno. All believed that Clement and Agathangelos would suffer immolation and give up their spirits quickly. No one who saw the fiery furnace and knew its purpose could feel anything but genuine terror and trembling. The pagans left the saints within the flames for one day and night, lest even a bone should remain. Divine grace, however, bedewed the martyrs, even as it once preserved the holy Three Children. Thus, fire had no power against their bodies. Neither was their hair singed, nor were their coats scorched, nor was the smell of fire upon them. [Dan. 3:27]. From outside the furnace there could be discerned not only the sound of triumphant singing, but also the scent of a marvellous fragrance wafting forth. The following day, when the flames died down, the emperor himself went forth to see the results. O the magnitude of Thy wonderworkings, O Christ! The saints were found in the midst of their prayers. Not even a hair of their heads was burned. They were then conducted outside, at which point the foolish emperor said, "Tell me, I beseech you, what kind of sorcery have you wrought that the flames in no wise consumed you?" The saints replied, "We do not know magic. But the true God, the One Whom we venerate, exercises authority and power over the elements, and all obey Him."

Maximian then ordered that the Christians be tied from their feet and dragged throughout the city, until their bodies should be rent asunder and they give up their spirits violently. But once again, the emperor designed what would be to his own injury. Even as he saw the martyrs emerge from the fiery furnace unscathed, in like manner he witnessed their bodies being dragged and sundered, but they did not die. This was not witnessed by only a few, but by many who came to believe in the Christ and His unsurpassed power. All of these events left Maximian in a state of bewilderment. He was at a loss how to deal with them. He wished only to remove the martyrs from the public eye, so he confined them four years in a dark prison. He reckoned the hardship and distress attendant with prison life would dispose them to conform to his will. The vain one anticipated wrongly. The saints' desire for Christ and the hope of enjoying those future good things brought them joy in that prison, as though they were in a rich and brightly lit palace. The emperor received reports of how they were faring, but he neglected taking any action. He was neither eager nor willing to punish them further. He knew only too well their resolve. He therefore gave this pretext, saying, "The case of such fools is not worthy of my attention." Maximian then made some private inquiries and learned that the most cruel and harshest of his governors was Sakerdos, who had put many Christians to death by means of dreadful torments.

Saints Clement and Agathangelos in Tarsus Before Governor Sakerdos

Maximian remanded the prisoners to Sakerdos for further examination. Both Clement and Agathangelos were brought to the judgment hall and tried with different words, alternating between threats and flattery. The governor perceived that he was not making any progress by mere words alone, so he subjected the saints to torture, even as his tyrannical predecessors had done. The saints were bound naked to trees and thrashed without pity. The flesh of the saints became so torn and shredded that their joints, spines, and all their bones were left exposed. But they were strengthened and maintained by divine grace, enduring manfully this hideous torture. The governor admitted that this punishment had not succeeded in breaking their resolve. He ordered that they be returned to the prison. Once the saints were untied, they walked back to the prison, unassisted and without the least show of distress. Sakerdos, witnessing their serenity, was consumed with such sorrow and shame that he swooned and needed to be carried to the palace.

As the saints entered the prison, faithful Christians hastened to collect their falling flesh and flowing blood. For the sake of piety and reverence, they retained these relics as great treasures. Who can describe all of Sakerdos' artifices, clever tricks, ingenious contrivances, captious arguments, conjuring, superstitious means, mechanical devices, and engines? Although he stubbornly persisted in assailing the unassailable, he still was left ashamed and exceedingly grieved. When Maximian was apprised of all that had transpired, he mocked Sakerdos before the nobles, saying, "Behold, the famed Sakerdos, who has prevailed over armies of martyrs, has been taken down by these two hapless Christians!" It was then that a certain governor, named Maximos, declared to the tyrant, "Give them to me, O emperor, and I hope in the great gods to conquer or to put those wicked ones to an evil demise, so that they may no longer trouble us."

Saints Clement and Agathangelos in Tarsus Before Governor Maximos

The wretched Maximos, now the eighth tyrant to take up persecuting the two holy men, began his examination. The guileful nobleman initially feigned being their friend and spoke to them cordially and with affection. He engaged them in several conversations and spoke in a pleasant manner. His histrionic outpourings and use of all the stock and hackneyed phrases about the idols and the worship of the gods were tiresome and pointless. Did he really hope to shake the immovable resolve of the two martyrs with his claptrap appeals? Then, after a few days, he manifested his deceit and treachery, giving the cause of his pretense for friendship. He addressed Clement and Agathangelos, saying, "You should know that the immortal gods love you as their children, even as they informed me in my sleep. They are not angered with you, because they know that in the end you shall come to them. Again, even this morning, the great Dionysus told me to lead you to his altar that you might venerate him." The saints then said, "Which Dionysus dost thou name as immortal? There are two idols here, one of brass and the other of stone. If thou sayest the stone one, be informed that in but a few days thou shalt see Dionysus in pieces, which fragments shall be used either in the building of a stone wall or for the making of asbestos in a furnace. As for the bronze idol, thou shalt see him beaten with the edge of a hammer by a craftsman who shall turn him into a pitcher and frying pan."

The tyrant, upon hearing these prophetic words, was incensed. He cast off his pretense and revealed the inner Maximos. He bade his officers to wedge into the earth skewers, spears, knives, and pitchforks. They were turned about and diligently arranged, so that the tools were kept close together and the points jutted up from the ground about the length of one foot. Over this bed of sharp and piercing edges, the blessed Clement was spread out on his back. He was then beaten on his abdomen mightily with thick pieces of wood, so as to weigh and push his back down deeper into the sharp-pointed objects. As for Saint Agathangelos, they poured over his head boiling lead. Once more, the Lord empowered His slaves to manfully endure these deadly tortures as the previous ones. The idolaters especially wondered and marvelled how Saint Clement had not perished, for it was plain to all that the points from the skewers pierced his heart and the rest of his body. After this torture was ended, the officers were ordered to remove Clement. This was not easily done, as the bishop's body was impaled in many places. His body appeared as if he were wearing a tattered and shredded garment with holes. Every bodily member was penetrated and cut through. Only by his voice did they understand that he was still alive. Bishop Clement then addressed the idolaters, saying, "Do you now know that the God Whom I revere is the almighty One, and that He is the One Who has set at nought all your assaults, by not giving leave to my soul to exit from the body?" At this juncture, Maximos completely lost heart. He knew not how to continue. He sent tidings to the emperor, who also had no further hope in converting the two martyrs. Maximos was commanded to keep them jailed until they should expire.

Saint Clement and Agathangelos in Tarsus Before Nobleman Aphrodisios

After the passage of much time, it was seen that the saints had not died of natural causes. A certain nobleman, Aphrodisios, who was of Persian ancestry, then received imperial permission to try his hand against the martyrs. He was notorious as a diabolical torturer of the Christians, inventing all manner of hideous deaths. Therefore, the martyrs were released into his custody. He took them and prepared a rich banquet. Aphrodisios wished for them to have a slight reprieve before he subjected them to tortures. When they were invited to dine at table with him, they declined, saying to him, "We partake of heavenly bread, and whenever one should eat of it, he shall never hunger." The senseless Aphrodisios was incensed by this slight, because they refused his friendship and the invitation to break bread with him. What did this demented man contrive? He had two large millstones brought and fitted on the martyrs. He then had them dragged throughout the country town, while the senseless cast stones at the martyrs. The valiant martyrs endured these grievous punishments, not only with marvellous perseverance but with thanksgiving. Their conduct brought idolaters to believe in the Christ. Therefore, it was the mindless Aphrodisios who was vanquished.

He sent word to the emperor who gave his decision in writing that the prisoners were to be incarcerated in a dark dungeon, without any care or attention or food, until they should give up their spirits from hunger and excessive ill-treatment. This too was divinely dispensed that the time should pass and come to the allotted twenty-eight years, which revelation the Lord vouchsafed the blessed Clement when the same had requested a life of tribulations. Consequently, the saints were confined in prison for many years. Though they were bereft of all human aid, yet God helped and nourished them in an extraordinary and mysterious manner. During that period of their confinement, many other godly faithful suffered martyrdom.

Saints Clement and Agathangelos in Ankyra Before Governor Lucius

After the passage of many years, the guards, who knew very well that no one provided the two holy prisoners with any provisions, grew weary of their charges in that ward. When Maximian's successor, Maximin[12] or

---

[12] *P.G.* 114:884C. In 305, after joint Emperors Diocletian and Maximian, Constantius I (305-306) was in the west and Galerius (305-311) in the east. Then, Maximian (306-308), Flavius Valerius Severus (306-307), and Maxentius (306-312) became rival

(continued...)

Maximinus (308-314) came into power, these guards made mention of these two prisoners in their report. The matter so angered the new emperor that he began insulting his own deities, because they could not dispatch two wretched Christian enemies. The guards then said, "Sire, we have had these two men in bonds for years. Rulers, governors, and emperors tried them with diverse punishments, but they never succumbed. No one has fed or tended them, yet they are healthy and thrive. Indeed, those of us in the prison think they must be immortal. What wilt thou have us do?" Maximin then asked the warden what might be the background of Clement. When he learned that he was a native of Ankyra, Maximum changed the venue of the case to Ankyra. Thereupon, he wrote Governor Lucius of that city, instructing him to take custody of the prisoners and put them to death. All of these events, foreknown by the Lord Who does the will of those who fear Him [Ps. 144:20], allowed for His slave Clement to be returned to the place of his birth. Though Clement passed through so many perils in diverse cities and countries, yet he would repose in his homeland, even as he once requested of the Lord. Therefore, when they were taken from their dungeon in Tarsus and conveyed to Ankyra, they were gladdened.

When they entered Ankyra, the governor straightway had them imprisoned and put in wooden stocks. Heavy stones were tied to them, lest any should attempt to move either prisoner. Lucius first called Agathangelos and tried him with blandishments that he might deceive him. The mindless governor toiled in vain, for the saint rebuked him with much boldness and contemned the idols, as was meet. The tyrant perceived the immovable stance of the saint, so he thought to introduce tortures. He first arranged that long red-hot iron nails be forced into Agathangelos' ears, so that the nails passed through and pierced his brain. This resulted in dark smoke belching from his mouth and nose. As though this gruesome torture were not sufficient, those unbridled pagans also burned his sides with lamps.

The pain and suffering of these afflictions were born nobly by the glorious Agathangelos, who called upon the Lord for help and said, "O Master Jesus Christ, do not deprive me of the enjoyment of those everlasting good things, but strengthen me to finish the course of Thy confession, so as to number me with Thy slave Clement and Thine other martyrs; for my strength is failing me, and in Thee only does my soul hope." These are the words which the saint prayed; and God hearkened to his entreaty. It was then that the governor handed down the final judgment; for he perceived he could

[12](...continued)
augusti in the west. Constantine I was sole augustus in the west after 312. Licinius (308-324) and Maximinus in Asia (Maximin, 308-314) were augusti in the east.

The Martyrdom of Saint Agathangelos

not divert the prisoner's strong belief. Therefore, Agathangelos was taken to a place known as Krypton, not far from Ankyra, where his honorable head was struck off on the 5th of November. His blessed soul then went forth into the heavens that he might rejoice and delight with the holy angels to the ages. The God-loving and godly-wise Sophia, when she beheld the saint's end, was gladdened by his triumph. She took up his relics and interred them in a secret place, a cave, with much reverence. The Christians of that place, in times of persecution, attended Saint Agathangelos' grave site, which had become a chapel.

The athlete of many labors, the martyr of Christ, Clement, when he learned of his fellow contestant's glorious finish, gave profound thanks to God that Agathangelos completed the course in a holy manner. The governor ordered that the saint daily receive one hundred thrashes from rods, together with one hundred blows to his face. The stone to which he was bound in the dungeon and all the earth in his cell were reddened with his blood. The saint continued enduring this punishment, giving thanks to the Lord. Then, by night, a holy angel entered his cell, enveloped with boundless light, and healed him of all his wounds. This procedure followed day after day for the divine Clement, as he was bound to that stone in the prison, until twenty-eight years should be fulfilled, from the time of the commencement of his martyrdom. In the meantime, the infuriated executioners carried out their orders with increased vehemence. At length, his final slaughter took place in the following manner.

Saint Clement in Ankyra Before Governor Alexander

Governor Lucius was recalled by the emperor. In his place, Alexander became governor at Ankyra. Now, the God-loving Sophia had an intense longing to behold the blessed Clement liturgizing. Then one night, just as they were about to conduct the vigil of the holy Theophany, Sophia, that most modest woman, moved by divine zeal, ventured to commit a good but daring deed. She went forth with her servants and slaves, and those children whose souls she had nourished, together with Christian men and women, and secretly entered the dungeon. She bribed the guards and then had them loose the saint's bonds. She then garbed Bishop Clement in white vestments. Then all together they proceeded to the cave church with lamps and incense burning. Sophia herself also wore white garb, as a sign of her joy which she cherished in her adopted son Clement. The saint foreknew that his end was approaching. He held in his one hand the holy Gospel. He then raised his other hand and his eyes heavenward and offered prayer on behalf of his spiritual mother, for all the flock of Christ, and all those who wished to celebrate, that the Lord might grant salvation to their souls and whatever other request that was blessed.

After he uttered these petitions, the Christians kept prayerful vigil that night, with the doors carefully closed. Since dawn had come, the saint began celebrating the divine Liturgy. The faithful then communicated the divine Mysteries. Afterward, the divine Clement, the vine branch of the true Vine, Christ, who produced the wine of sweetest theology, gave drink to the rational sheep by giving a sermon. He then observed that the congregation became fearful when he said that soldiers would come and slay them. He calmed them when he then prophesied, "Cease fearing, brethren, but rather take courage, for none of you shall be murdered. Only I, together with the two deacons, Christopher and Chariton, shall

Saint Clement

suffer death. After this, the rage of the idol-mad shall be extinguished. Peace shall prevail in the world. The heralding of Christ shall be proclaimed from all the citadels and cities. The abominable altars of the Greek pagans shall be closed down, and all that pay homage to idols shall flee. All of this shall take place in but a short time, as many of you shall witness." These prophecies were clearly delivered by the saint and brought happiness to the wise Sophia and the assembly of widows and orphans whom she supported generously. The beginning of the fulfillment of these predictions came to pass in 313, when Constantine I (306-337) issued the Edict of Milan. Christians gained freedom of worship, and the Church was recognized legally by Constantine the Great. When Constantine became sole ruler, after the death of Licinius

(308-324) of the eastern provinces, he convoked the first œcumenical synod in Nicaea (325).

Now when the appointed day arrived, that is, Sunday, the saint liturgized, and all received holy Communion. During that moment in the divine service when the saint was bending his neck toward the holy Table, the nobleman Alexander, with a company of soldiers, suddenly burst into the church. Alexander then commanded one soldier to raise his sword and strike off the head of Clement. O Thy long-suffering, O Christ King! The martyr's most holy head became a pure offering. The ungodly and vile soldiers cast it to the floor and stepped upon it.

Thus, Saint Clement finally realized his most-desired end on that 23rd day of January.[13] Thus the sacrificer came to be an acceptable sacrifice to God. Some of the faithful left weeping, As for the two deacons who were celebrating with the bishop, they stood their ground at the holy Table and were slain. Then the faithful Sophia, who according to God was the great Clement's mother, nurturer, and tutor, lit the lamps and incense. She took Bishop Clement's much-suffering body of many labors, chanting spiritual hymns, as was meet, and wrapped the precious treasure of those relics in a pure linen sheet hidden away at Krypton. In that place, she buried Saint Clement with his fellow athlete Agathangelos, so that their bodies were in one chest. Thus their bodies were united in death even as their souls are together, resting and delighting in the Lord. As for the two deacons, Saints Christopher and Chariton, they too were buried in a place nearby where a little oratory was made.

Afterward, Sophia sat by the grave of Saint Clement and spoke to him with faith, saying, "O child, I, indeed, concealed thee at Krypton, but Christ has given thee rest in a manifest place, since it was for Him that thou wast punished. I have aged much and am now coming to thee, for God has preserved me until this day that I might bury you together; since for many long years you suffered martyrdom together and contended well to the end. But I pray to you both, entreat you, and supplicate you, my beloved children, for the sake of your mother, nurturer, and handmaiden, that the Lord might vouchsafe me, the sinner, a little boldness before Him that I might join your company, even as I served thee in the passion you suffered." So spoke this blessed woman with tears and faith. Her request did not fail, for the all-good Lord took her to Himself, by the intercessions of Saint Clement, and re-

---

[13] Various dates are given as to the year of Hieromartyr Clement's repose. Since one of the first of the tyrants to persecute Saint Clement was Diocletian, who reigned from 284 to 305, the bishop's twenty-eight year martyrdom could not have occurred before 312.

compensed her a hundredfold. For Christ said, "The one who receiveth you receiveth Me, and the one who receiveth Me receiveth the One Who sent Me forth. The one who receiveth a prophet in the name of a prophet shall receive a prophet's reward; and the one who receiveth a righteous man in the name of a righteous man shall receive a righteous man's reward. And whosoever shall give to one of these little ones only a cup of cold water to drink in the name of a disciple, verily I say to you, in no wise shall he lose his reward [Mt. 10:40-42]."

This, then, was the life of the corpse-raising Clement, who was dead to this world and alive to Christ. These were his contests and terrifying struggles. These were his superhuman achievements, which have been described briefly. O the manliness, fortitude, and valor! How many deaths had the ever-memorable Clement experienced? How many tyrants had he vanquished in the course of twenty-eight years? Actually, there were eleven rulers before whom he provided testimony and proclaimed the Gospel:

1) Vicegerent Dometianos at Ankyra;
2) Emperor Diocletian at Rome;
3) Prefect Agrippinos at Nikomedia;
4) Governor Kourikios at Ankyra;
5) Vicegerent Dometios at Amisos;
6) Emperor Maximian at Tarsus;
7) Governor Sakerdos at Tarsus;
8) Governor Maximos at Tarsus;
9) Nobleman Aphrodisios at Tarsus;
10) Governor Lucius at Ankyra; and,
11) Governor Alexander at Ankyra.

The living example of this saint's suffering and torments should be a lesson to the remiss and impatient who, if they should be pricked with a needle or bitten by a flea, have no patience; instead, they do something rash or blaspheme upon experiencing a little pain. Wherever the pain might be, in the ear or tooth or entrails or any other member, let us bear it patiently. Let us not show impatience and wish for death. Bring to mind the unspeakable torments of everlasting punishment, so that you might endure every temporal punishment. Even if the pain or punishment is greater than most, know that by means of that small chastisement you can be delivered from those terrifying ones that never end. By means of temporal sufferings one can inherit indescribable joy and everlasting rest, so that such a one may be glorified with Saint Clement, of many labors whose deadened body rose from the dead many times, together with the other martyrs who rejoice in the All-Holy Trinity, to Whom is due glory and veneration, always, now and ever, and unto the ages of the ages. Amen.

**On the 23rd of January, the holy Church commemorates
our venerable Father EVSEVIOS of the Monastery of Teleda.**[14]

Evsevios, our venerable father, was enclosed inside a small and dark cell, where he was exercising himself in every hardship and ascetic contest. His retreat lay east of Antioch and west of Beroea. There was a high mountain, called Barakat, in those parts, containing a village called Teleda. Above the foot of the mountain is a dale, where Abba Ammianos had built a philosophical retreat and brought together many men of virtue who eventually numbered one hundred and fifty fathers. This Ammianos, surpassing others in his modesty of spirit, out of humility, did not wish to become their hegumen. Though he was more than competent to govern the brotherhood, he would often visit the great Abba Evsevios and urge him to accept the office of superior. Now the windowless cell of Abba Evsevios was some twenty-five stades or three miles distant from the philosophical retreat of Abba Ammianos.

Abba Evsevios had been guided into the ascetical conduct and this form of solitude and silence by his abba and uncle, named Marianos, the faithful slave of God. Marianos persuaded not only Evsevios to love the ascetic life, but also his brother, father to Evsevios. Marianos could not reconcile the thought of bringing others to virtue while leaving his brother and nephew outside of the taste of divine love. He thereupon strived to imbue them with equal enthusiasm for such a conduct of life. At length, Marianos immured them both in a small cell. Marianos' brother, however, fell sick and reposed. Thereupon, in that dark cell, Abba Evsevios continued in silence and unceasing prayer.

Now Abba Ammianos was determined to have such an abba as the superior of his brotherhood. He went to Abba Evsevios and posed a question, asking, "Tell me, good friend, whom dost thou believe thou art pleasing by the austere life which thou hast adopted?" Abba Evsevios answered candidly, "God, the law-giver and teacher of virtue, of course, abba." The venerable Ammianos continued, "Well then, since thou lovest Christ, I shall show thee a more perfect way that shall kindle thy love and serve the Beloved." Ammianos then could see that Evsevios' interest was stirred. Evsevios then made a motion that he continue. Abba Ammianos then said, "If one were only to care for oneself, the charge of self-love would be difficult to evade, for divine law prescribes loving one's neighbor as oneself. If we are mindful of the words of Saint Paul who said that 'love is the filling up of the law [Rom.

---

[14] The Life of Saint Evsevios was recorded by Theodoretos of Kyros (Cyrrhus), in Number Four of his *Religious History*. See also *A History of the Monks of Syria*, Cistercian Studies Series: Number Ninety-Eight, pp. 49-56.

13:10],' then sharing one's wealth is love. This wealth is not only material but spiritual as well. The summing up of the law and the prophets, says Paul, is that 'thou shalt love thy neighbor as thyself [Rom. 13:9].' Bring to remembrance therefore also the words of our Savior to Peter, who professed to love Jesus more than the others; for our Lord commended him to tend His sheep. On the other hand, God, through Prophet Ezekiel, rebukes those who have not shepherded the flock. He asks the shepherds of Israel, 'The shepherds do not feed themselves, do they? Do they not feed the sheep [cf. Ez. 34:2]?' Thus, Ezekiel is called a watchman and charged to warn the sinners [Ez. 3:17-19]. But Jonas, who was unwilling to go where he was ordered, that is, Nineveh, was then sent as a captive." Thus, with these and like words—that is, the histories of Elias, Eliseos, and the Forerunner John, who were commanded to go about in the midst of the impious and preach—Abba Ammianos found a way to draw Abba Evsevios out of his voluntary imprisonment. Therefore, Abba Evsevios was entrusted with the care of the brethren at the monastery started by Abba Ammianos. He governed them with humility and wisdom.

The biographer, Theodoretos, comments, "I myself do not know which to admire the more, the modesty of Ammianos or the amenability of Evsevios." The truth be told, when Abba Evsevios came to the brotherhood, it was not necessary for him to use many words of instruction. Nay, Abba Evsevios' mere appearance was sufficient to move the most slothful of the brothers to enter the race for virtue. What were words before his living example? How could anyone dare not to know what was expected of him before that paragon of virtue? Those who have beheld Abba Evsevios' countenance remarked that he always maintained a grave aspect, which was enough to instill awe in those who saw him. The great man only partook of food every three or four days, but he did not enjoin this rule on his fellow contestants. He allowed them to eat every day, but exhorted them to always have God in remembrance.

Abba Evsevios was humble and discerning. He also strived to correct himself. One such occasion was when both he and Abba Ammianos were sitting on a rock. As Abba Ammianos was reading out the Gospel, Abba Evsevios explained the more obscure passages. But while this study was taking place, Abba Evsevios became distracted when he observed some ploughmen on the plain. Meanwhile, Abba Ammianos was waiting for an interpretation of a hard passage. When Abba Evsevios came to himself and saw his companion waiting for him, he asked to have the reading repeated. Abba Ammianos said, "I see that while thou wast distracted with the ploughmen, thou wast not hearkening to the pericope." As a result of that lapse, Abba Evsevios enjoined upon himself never to look out upon that plain again nor gaze at the beauty of the heavens and the stars. He only would look upon the narrow path that led to the house of prayer, never stepping outside of it. He continued with this rule for the next forty years. Lest he should suffer a moment of absentmindedness and look away, he bound his waist with an iron belt, which was attached by a chain to an exceedingly heavy collar about his neck. This truss forced him ever to be stooped over. Such was the penalty he imposed upon himself for a moment's inattention at the Gospel reading.

Now the great Akakios also spoke of this situation. He had seen how Abba Evsevios was bent over and asked, "Abba, what profit is there in not looking at the sky or the plain before us? What is the harm if thou shouldest walk outside this path to the church?" Abba Evsevios then explained that he contrived this method, lest he should succumb to the evil one's devices. He then said, "Therefore, I have submitted to this in order to prevent him from making war on me in those things that are of importance. I meant to say, I do this so that I might hinder his assault to steal my self-control. I persevere that I might prevent his provocations that might lead me to anger, or might kindle desire, or might make me puffed up with vanity. Thus I have moved the sphere of conflict with him to unimportant things, such as looking out on the plain or up at the sky. Even if he should win, I suffer no great injury. But if he should lose, he becomes all the more ridiculous in that he was not able to overcome this little contrivance. Therefore, since I perceive that this war is less dangerous—for really what is the harm at looking up at the plain or gazing at the sky?—I take up this position against the adversary. For from this position in the battle, he cannot deal me a mortal wound." Akakios was amazed at this strategy and the abba's experience in warfare. He often repeated the account to others for their edification.

The renown of Abba Evsevios spread everywhere, so that many others came and joined the brotherhood, including those already far advanced in the ascetical life. The ever-memorable Evsevios lived for many years until his blessed repose in the Lord. Abba Agrippa succeeded to the post of hegumen. Those holy fathers that lived on after the great old man, proved excellent disciples of their trainer, the divine Evsevios.

On the 23rd of January, the holy Church commemorates our venerable Father MAUSIMAS the Syrian.[15]

---

[15] The Life of Saint Mausimas was recorded by Theodoretos of Kyros (Cyrrhus), in Number Fourteen of his *Religious History*, whence his *Synaxarion* was compiled. A note in *A History of the Monks of Syria* (p. 113, note 2) identifies Mausimas as an

(continued...)

Mausimas lived in the vicinity of Kyros (Cyrrhus), which is nigh unto Antioch. For this reason, he spoke a Syrian dialect, and he had a peasant and rustic upbringing; even so, he excelled in virtue. Mausimas always wore the same garment, which eventually became threadbare, but he did not discard it. Rather, he sewed patches over the torn parts, and thus he covered his nakedness. He showed such care for strangers and the needy that he always opened the door of his cell to them. It is said that he had two earthen jars, one filled with wheat and the other with oil, from which he gave to all the needy. These jars were always replenished and never became exhausted, as God "is rich to all those who call upon Him [Rom. 10: 12]," according to Saint Paul. This occurrence may be likened to what had taken place for the widow at Sarepta, when the Lord spoke through Prophet Elias, saying that the pitcher of meal shall not fail and the cruse of oil shall not diminish [3 Kgs. (1 Kgs.) 17:

Saint Mausimas

16], thus rewarding her for the hospitality she showed the prophet. Similarly, God granted to this wonderful Mausimas this same gift as a reward for his generosity to others.

This holy Mausimas also received from God the gift to perform miracles. One such miracle took place for a certain noble and faithful woman and her young son who became gravely ill. The physicians had already abandoned his case as that of one terminally ill and about to die. She took her ailing son into her carriage pulled by mules and hastened to visit the holy man. She entreated him to assist her in her distress. He took the child into his hands and placed him at the foot of the altar. Mausimas then lay face downwards and offered up prayer to the Physician of souls and bodies. God granted the holy man's request, so that he restored the child in good health to his pious mother.

Now Mausimas also admonished Leetoyos (Letoius), the village chief and leading member in the council of Antioch, to be kind and merciful to his

---

[15](...continued)
ascetic village priest who reposed before Theodoretos became Bishop of Kyros in 423.

brethren. He was a tyrannical man who demanded heavy tribute from the farmers. Unrelenting as he was, Leetoyos ignored the wise words of the holy man and actually became harsher and more cruel. He, however, was to learn by hard experience the penalty for his obstinacy and indifference. While he was in his carriage, he ordered the muleteer to drive the mules. The wheels of the carriage, nevertheless, seem to be fastened and immobile. Even when the peasants attempted to budge the carriage from its fixed position, the wheels neither rocked in place nor made any revolution forward or backward. Someone who was in the carriage with Leetoyos commented, "I believe this phenomenon is taking place because the holy Elder Mausimas has laid a penance upon thee, until thou shouldest come to a reconciliation." At that conscience-searching moment, this information was timely. Leetoyos jumped from the carriage and made directly for the blessed man. He fell at Father Mausimas' feet, kissing his soiled garments and begging him to appease his displeasure. The holy one accepted his supplication and loosened the invisible bonds that held fast the carriage wheels; and thereupon they began to roll again. At that moment, Leetoyos corrected himself. He lived a good and righteous life thereafter on earth and was translated to the Lord.

On the 23rd of January, the holy Church commemorates our venerable Father SALAMANES the Hesychast.[16]

Salamanes, our holy father, hailed from a certain village called Kapersana, situated on the west bank of the Euphrates River and north of Zeugma. He had early fallen in love with the solitary life of the monks, and discovered a small cell in a village on the opposite bank of the river. In that retreat, the saint enclosed himself, making no allowance for a door, so that he would not be able to go out. There was also no window, so that light might not enter. Once a year, he dug a hole under the cell and came forth for a brief respite, gathering whatever food he would need for the remainder of the year; and this is how the blessed one lived for many years. As the hierarch of the neighboring city heard of the extraordinary virtue of this man, he visited him, wishing to ordain him a priest. Therefore, he dug a hole into the cell, and put his hand through it and onto the head of the saint, and he uttered the prayer of ordination. The bishop also spoke to him of the grace of the priesthood and many other things. But from the saint, the bishop heard not one word. He departed after this and ordered others to close the hole that he had dug into the cell.

---

[16] The Life of Saint Salamanes was recorded by Theodoretos of Kyros, in Number Nineteen of his *Religious History*, whence his *Synaxarion* was compiled.

At another time, his fellow Christians crossed the Euphrates River by night and completely razed his cell to the ground. Then they seized the saint and brought him to the village. This was done without Father Salamanes either hindering them or his telling them to do so. They had another cell in the village ready for him, and enclosed him within it. Once immured, he carried on as before and spoke to no one. A few days later, the Christians, those who dwelt in the village on the opposite side of the river, came by night and demolished that cell too. They seized the holy man, carrying him off to their village. He never opposed them, nor did he try to force them to leave him alone, nor did he go eagerly.

By these examples, the saint mortified himself utterly and became totally dead to this life. In accordance with the words of the Apostle Paul, he often said: "I no longer live, but Christ liveth in me [Gal. 2:20]." Thus, mortifying his being as no one else ever had, he passed his life, until he was translated to the Lord that he might rejoice in the heavens for all ages. Amen.

**On the 23rd of January, the holy Church commemorates
the holy TWO MARTYRS of Parion,[17]
who suffered martyrdom when cast into a pit.**

**On the 23rd of January, the holy Church commemorates
our holy father PAULINUS, Bishop of Nola.[18]**

---

[17] Parion was a city by the sea with a harbor, between Kyzikos and Lampsakos. Meletios maintains that it was built by the inhabitants of the island of Paros.

[18] The writings of Saint Paulinus were numerous. Only thirty-two poems, fifty-one letters, and fragments have come down to us. Although there is no proper Life of Saint Paulinus of early date, we have not only a letter by one named Uranius describing Saint Paulinus' repose, but also a short notice by Saint Gregory of Tours. Nevertheless, within the saint's own correspondence and the references of his contemporaries, enough biographical data is found to construct his biography. There is also a short history of Saint Paulinus by Saint Gregory, Pope of Rome (*The Dialogues*, Bk. 3, Fathers of the Church Series, Volume 39, pp. 111-115). Moreover, that which has only become available in comparatively recent times is the Life of Melanie the Younger, preserved both in a Greek and Latin text, which also speaks of Saint Paulinus.

The works of Saint Paulinus also appear in English: *Letters of St. Paulinus of Nola: Letters 1-22, Volume 1* and *Letters 23-51, Volume 2*, in the Ancient Christian Writers Series, Numbers 35 and 36. Translated and annotated by P. G. Walsh. NY, NY: Newman Press, n.d. The Letters were translated from the text by Harvel in *Corpus scriptorum ecclesiasticorum latinorum* 29 (Vienna, 1894). See also *The Poems of Saint Paulinus of Nola* in ACW Series, Number 40. See also *Butler's Lives of the*

(continued...)

Paulinus, also known as Pontius Meropius Paulinus, was born circa 355[19] at Burdigala (Bordeaux) in Aquitaine.[20] He was the scion of a wealthy and noble senatorial family that was related to the most illustrious in the empire. His father, prefect of Gaul, had lands in Italy, Aquitaine, and Spain. Paulinus was educated at Bordeaux by Ausonius (ca. 310-ca. 395), the tutor of Emperor Gratian (b. 359, r. 367-383). Ausonius was also a professor and poet of the famous Bordeaux School. He taught Paulinus before the latter's Baptism (390). Afterward, in 395, Ausonius tried to dissuade Paulinus from the ascetic life. At a young age, Paulinus, as a result of his assiduous scholarship, earned forensic success and the poetic laurel. He also made a name for himself at the bar. Blessed Jerome comments that everyone admired the purity and elegance of Paulinus' diction, the delicacy and loftiness of his sentiments, the strength and sweetness of his style, and the vividness of his imagination.

Now Paulinus held a number of public offices, but the precise duties entailed on each has not been left to us. We do know that his work necessitated extensive travel, during the course of which he made many friends in Italy, Gaul, and Spain. In 378, in his early twenties, he was appointed senator.[21] He then obtained a curule magistrature, the governorship of Campania[22] in 379. He was known to exercise that office with much humanity. By 383, Paulinus had married a virtuous and pious Spanish lady

---

[18](...continued)
Saints, Volume II, s.v. "June 22"; and, *Encyclopedia of the Early Church*, Volume II, s.v. "Paulinus of Nola."

[19] In ¶ 17 of Letter 4, written in 395, wherein Paulinus mentioned that he had recently passed his fortieth birthday, he gives the main evidence for his date of birth.

[20] Aquitaine, the name given to a region of southwestern France, applied at different times to different parts of the region or to the whole region. This vast territory had no single capital: Avaricum (Bourges), Limonum (Poitiers), Mediolanum Santonum (Saintes), Burdigala (Bordeaux), and Elusa (Eauze). The Roman poet Ausonius writes of Aquitaine as a rich country, producing corn and wine and exporting the marble quarried in the Pyrenees.

[21] There is little information preserved regarding Paulinus' secular career before 379, the year in which Ausonius was consul. Membership of the senatorial order was hereditary, so that Paulinus became senator by right. Since Paulinus held the curule office before Ausonius, he assumed it before 378. The tenure of Paulinus' governorship of Campania would have been preceded by a less exacting administrative office. See *Letters of Saint Paulinus*, Volume 1, p. 219, note 13, to Letter 5, ¶ 4.

[22] Campania, a region of southern Italy comprising the provinces of Avellino, Benevento, Caserta, Naples, and Salerno. The Samnites were the conquerors of the Etruscans in Campania. Nola was taken circa 421 or 428. Latin, Greek, and Oscan (a local dialect) were spoken.

named Therasia. After some years, he resigned his offices and retired in Aquitaine.

Saint Paulinus

At the same time, after the murder of Emperor Gratian (383), Valentinian II (b. ca. 371), his half-brother, became emperor of the west (375-392). Valentinian was still a child, so his mother Justina ruled in her son's name. The chief difficulties with her reign were religious conflicts and pressure from the Alemanni on the northern frontier. The latter were curbed by General Bauto, with the help of the Huns and Alans. Since Justina had strong Arian leanings, this was at variance with Bishop Ambrose of Milan who exercised a strong influence over the young emperor.

As we said, it was circa 383 that Paulinus returned to Aquitaine. He passed through Milan and met with Saint Ambrose (ca. 339-397, bishop from 374). There were subsequent encounters between the men, during which time Ambrose gave Paulinus his final instruction in preparation for holy Baptism. After the assassination of Gratian, then the Spaniard usurper and army man Magnus Maximus (383-388) was proclaimed augustus by his troops. Consequently, all of Gaul came under his control. He posed as a champion of Orthodoxy and condemned the heretic Priscillian and his followers. This procedure and interference by the state, however, was condemned by both Saints Ambrose and Martin of Tours. Theodosios I in the east and the young Emperor Valentinian acceded to Maximus' rule. Maximus invaded Italy in 387, forcing the court to flee to Thessalonike. It was Theodosios I who finally slew the rebel at Aquileia. In the meantime, the Arians persecuted Orthodox magistrates, especially those who supported the usurper Maximus in Gaul.

In 389/390, during Paulinus' period of retirement, he came to know the aged Bishop of Bordeaux, who became his spiritual father. Paulinus always adopted a tone of devoted deference in his letters to the bishop. He also made friends with Amandus, the priest who had been his catechist at

Bordeaux and became his friend.[23] Thereupon, Paulinus received holy Baptism at home from Bishop Delphinus, who was also a correspondent of Ambrose. Delphinus, who had been present at the Council of Arles in 314, also furthered the evangelization of his diocese. He encouraged and praised Paulinus' knowledge of the Bible. Delphinus was always proud of his convert and was ever seeking news from Paulinus regarding his activities and scriptural meditations. Now since Paulinus and Therasia had no children, they received destitute orphans into their home, supporting and catechizing them as if they were their own children.

It was also about this time that Paulinus suffered the news of the violent death of his brother in Aquitaine, which induced him to leave. The circumstances surrounding the murder are unknown, but Paulinus was hounded by the scandal. On a personal level, Paulinus was distressed at the death of his brother, who had died indifferent to his spiritual life and welfare.

On account of Arian persecution, Paulinus, Therasia, and Paulinus' family fled to the recesses of the Pyrenees. This self-imposed exile necessitated breaking connections with Paulinus' old circles and his friend and teacher Ausonius. In the autumn of 389 or in the year 390, Paulinus and Therasia went to live on her estate in Spain.

After years of childlessness, a son, Celsus, was born to them. The boy, however, died at the end of eight days and was buried at Complutum.[24] As a result of this, Paulinus and Therasia took up a more ascetical life. They lived strictly and performed alms. At length, they renounced their wealth and dispossessed themselves of much of their estate for the needs of the poor.

On one occasion when a beggar came to the dwelling of Paulinus and Therasia asking for alms, they had nought but a single piece of bread. Paulinus wished to give the suppliant this last piece and said to his wife, "God shall provide for us. We shall not miss that which we have given for the sake of our love for Christ." Therasia, nevertheless, hesitated and then refused to surrender the bread, since they had nothing to eat that day. Not much time passed before a messenger came to the blessed man bearing tidings that one of Paulinus' affluent acquaintances arrived by sea. The messenger also related that his master had dispatched a generous supply of provisions for Paulinus and his work among the poor. The blessed man was also informed that his rich friend lost at sea one of his ships, the last one, which was laden with food stuffs. Upon hearing this sad news, Paulinus said to Therasia, "See, my Therasia, if thou hadst given as alms our last piece of bread, the last ship with

---

[23] Letter 2, ¶ 4.

[24] Complutum, the modern Alcala in New Castille (cf. *Carm.* 31.599 ff.)

food should not have disappeared under the waves. God ofttimes punishes the unsparing by not sparing their goods."

A year later, Paulinus and Therasia went to Barcelona, the most important city in Hispania Tarraconensis, to make their way to Nola.[25] While at Barcelona, ca. 393, the citizens wished to have Paulinus serve as their priest. This outcry of the people was in response to Paulinus' great charities among the poor. On the Feast of Nativity, therefore, at the insistence of the congregation at the cathedral, the Bishop of Barcelona, Lampius,[26] forcibly ordained a reluctant Paulinus to the priesthood, though the latter had not been a deacon. The people of that city were anxious to keep such a holy man in their midst, especially since he gave away his immense wealth; for an enormous fortune had been distributed by Paulinus and Therasia to the Church and the poor.

Regarding this event, Saint Paulinus wrote to Severus, stating: "On the day on which the Lord deigned to be born as Man, I was ordained to the priesthood. It happened through the sudden compulsion of the crowd, but I believe that I was forced into it at the Lord's command. I confess that I was unwilling. Not that I despised the rank; for I call the Lord to witness that I longed to begin my holy slavery with the name and office of Sacristan (that is, the humblest level)....I therefore trembled at this strange and unexpected decree of the divine will that I should be enrolled with the priests."[27]

On the one hand, the liberality of Paulinus' charitable activities proved a stumbling block and scandal to many; on the other hand, Ambrose,[28] Jerome, Severus,[29] and Augustine praised Paulinus for his renunciation of the world. The Church of Barcelona, however, was not to realize its hope of retaining him. The holy Paulinus had already resolved to leave Barcelona and settle at Nola. Therefore, in 395, he departed Spain and went to the small town of Nola, where he still had property in that city.

As soon as the plans of Father Paulinus were learned, he found opposition. He attempted to dispose of his holdings in Aquitaine, as he had

---

[25] Nola (40°55'N 14°32'E), a town in Napoli province, Campania region, Italy, lies fourteen miles from Naples. Nearby is Cimitile where the bodies of Christian martyrs were interred, among them Saint Felix.

[26] Letter 3, ¶ 4.

[27] Letter 1, ¶ 10.

[28] None of the correspondence between Saints Ambrose and Paulinus has been preserved, but there was a close spiritual relationship. In a celebrated letter (Ep. 58), Ambrose extolled the conversion of Paulinus and the latter's decision to sell his ancestral possessions.

[29] Sulpicius Severus, following the death of his wife, made frequent visits to the monastery of Saint Martin at Tours. He then retired to a monastic life at Primuliacum.

done with those of Therasia in Spain. Friends and relatives voiced their disapproval. Paulinus, however, was not to be deterred. He left for Italy where he was received by the holy Ambrose and other friends. He passed through Rome, visited Pope Siricius (384-399) and his clergy, but was coldly ignored.[30] He then left for Nola with Therasia.

Since the years of his governorship, Paulinus came to dedicate himself to the service of the holy Martyr Felix the Confessor, who had been interred at Cimitile at Nola, in a cemeterial area.[31] The veneration of this third-century saint, commemorated on the 14th of January, drew many pilgrims. Miracles abounded, including deliverance from demonic possession. Paulinus dwelt in Nola until 409 or 410, living an austere ascetic life with Therasia and other companions. His lodging, a long two-storied building outside the walls, was next to the sanctuary of Saint Felix. Though he gave away vast amounts of his fortune, he still possessed means in Italy to support his wife. By and by, he gradually disposed of his Italian property to further religious and philanthropic endeavors. Paulinus' rejection of the contemporary world meant not only renunciation of wealth, arms, and political power, but also repudiation of its culture. He writes: "Let rhetoricians keep their literature, the philosophers their philosophy, the rich their wealth, the princes their kingdoms. Our glory, property, and kingdom is Christ."[32] Much like Blessed Jerome, Paulinus, steeped in classical poets and orators, did not divest himself entirely of the

---

[30] When Paulinus reached Rome in the summer of 395, the reason for the cold reception by the pope and his entourage of priests has been the subject of much speculation. Was it Paulinus' ordination by popular demand? Was it jealousy of the popular stir roused by the arrival of this celebrated convert to monasticism? Was it some vile rumor or evil suspicion of involvement in Priscillianism? But since Siricius was also hostile toward Blessed Jerome, it has been suggested that the pope distrusted the rapid development of monasticism in the west, as this movement had repercussions in the internal rivalries and factions within the Church. See *Letters of Saint Paulinus*, I: 221, n. 46, to Letter 5, ¶ 12. Saint Paulinus attributes the reception he received to jealousy, and states it in writing in ¶ 13 of Letter 5.

[31] It was devotion to Saint Felix that led Paulinus to establish his community at Nola. Felix was a native of that town but the son of a Syrian. Felix had distributed most of his possessions to the poor before being ordained. He was imprisoned during the persecution of Decius (250). After Decius' death, Felix refused a pressing invitation to become Bishop of Nola. His sale of property and renunciation of the world first directed Paulinus' thoughts to the monastic life when he was governor of Campania. It had been Paulinus' predecessor in that office who had persecuted Felix. The details of the life of Paulinus' patron are recorded by Paulinus in his *Carm.* 15, 16, 18, 21, 23, 24, 26, 27, 28, and 29. See *Letters of Saint Paulinus*, I:222, note 56, to Letter 5, ¶ 15. Saint Paulinus describes his patron as the "lord of his house." See Letter 5, ¶ 15.

[32] Letter 38, ¶ 6.

formative affects of his education, so that he apologized for quoting Virgil or Terence; and he said as much, writing: "Why do I use the language of foreigners, when our own tongue is sufficient for everything?"[33] When writing to Christian friends, his style is dominated by constant quotations from the Bible, especially the Psalms and the Epistles of Saint Paul. He constantly emphasizes the typological significance of biblical figures. For instance, he depicts the Queen of Saba (Sheba) [3 Kgs. (1 Kgs.) 10:1] as a type of the Church, or Samson as a type of Christ.[34] Saint Paulinus avoided the heretical doctrines of his day, and chose to present Christian dogma in an orthodox fashion. In one letter, he spoke scathingly of several heretical sects.[35] In both letters and poems, he gives a sound outline of the doctrine of the Trinity and indicates the orthodox teaching on Christ's dual nature.[36] "If men do not attain salvation, it is because with their God-given freedom they have refused the gift of that grace."[37]

In nearly every letter, Paulinus urges his friends to offer up prayer to God in praise or supplication. He also asks that they intercede on his behalf, that he may win forgiveness of his sins and grow in perfection. He stresses that we are the limbs of the one body, and that Christ is our head.[38] Intercession for fellow Christians has been made possible by Baptism. A kinship stronger than that of blood is created for Christians. In Letter 11 to Severus, Paulinus writes: "When Christ asked, 'Who is My mother? And who are My brethren [Mt. 12:48]?' Surely not those who are born of the will of the flesh and of intercourse in sleep, but those born of God [Jn. 1:13] through the Wisdom of God Who is Christ. He renews all things and gives men power to be made the sons of God [Col. 1:16; Jn. 1:12]. He took the form of our lowly bodies to transform it that it may become conformed to the body of His glory [Phil. 3:21], so as to tear us from our native land and our kin [cf. Gen. 12:1] and to bear us off to share His fortune and become His offspring. By this gift He has deigned to create us for Himself, and to link us with the chain of His love. He has replaced physical friendship, and He has advanced us to permanent kinship through a higher love. Thou, as my brother who art born of Him, dost outstrip, by thine immediate help and everlasting friendship, all the affection shown to me by my kin of the flesh; for thou art my brother sprung from a better Father than are those joined to me by flesh and blood

---

[33] Letter 7, ¶ 3.
[34] Cf. Letter 5, ¶ 1; Letter 23, ¶ 16.
[35] Cf. Letter 21.
[36] Cf. Letter 21, ¶ 3 and Letter 37, ¶ 5.
[37] Cf. Letter 38, ¶ 7.
[38] Cf. Letter 6, ¶2; Letter 2, ¶ 3; Letter 5, ¶ 9; Letter 18, ¶ 1.

alone. For where now are my blood brothers? Where are my former friendships and the companionship of old? I have vanished from all men and am 'become a stranger unto my brethren, and an alien unto my mother's children [Ps. 69:8 KJV]. My friends and neighbors now stand afar off [cf. Ps. 38:11].' They pass me like a river racing by or a wave passing over me. Perhaps they are troubled in my regard and are ashamed to come to me. So, by the Lord's doing, thou hast replaced my parents, brothers, and friends."[39]

Such passages as this show that Saint Paulinus' decision to renounce the world and enter the monastic life caused a rift not only with friends but also with his family. The saint repeatedly exhorts that we are the limbs of the one body and that, as members of the same body, we must all be of one mind, and must all feel the same joys and the same pains as each other.[40] The concept of Christian friendship transcending the most noble of human friendships held a key position in Paulinus' mind.[41]

In his letters, he exhorts the need for asceticism. Those who are rich are to be stewards of their wealth, being lent it by Christ. They are to lend support to the poor in this life, that there may be an equality, even as spoken of by Saint Paul: "Your abundance for their want, that their abundance also might be for your want, so that there might come to be an equality [2 Cor. 8:14]." He believed that by contributing their possessions to those in want, the rich were lending Christ His own gifts. He does not condemn riches, but the wrong and selfish use of them.[42] Though Paulinus himself renounced wealth, he stresses that the relinquishing of riches does not itself imply perfection, but only the beginning of the ascent toward surrender of self-gratification.[43] The saint also gives prominence to humility and that we are to humble ourselves before God. He who submits to God alone is subject to none. The soul cannot rise to heavenly things without mortification of the limbs. There are such things as saintly pride and wicked humility.[44] The one dominating thought throughout his letters is that of love. There is the material level shown in giving charity, but the giving must be invested with compassion and concern.

The saint also suffered with illness, though precisely what ailed him is not known to us. The notion of the mystical unity of Christians extended

---

[39] Letter 11, ¶¶ 2, 3.
[40] Letter 13, ¶ 3; Letter 14, ¶ 1; Letter 15, ¶ 1; Letter 18, ¶3.
[41] See Letter 11, ¶ 5.
[42] Letter 13, ¶ 20.
[43] Letter 40, ¶ 11.
[44] Letter 12, ¶ 7.

even to sympathetic illness is something that Paulinus believed.[45] He wrote to Severus: "I am still drained and weak. Yet Apostle Paul bids us to exult in this state. He proclaimed that weakness made him strong, because when the flesh, which wars on the spirit, is broken by ill health, it cannot with its strength crippled so easily take by storm the power of the spirit. So my bodily weakness advances growth in the spirit."[46]

The saint was aware of the pagan concepts of fortune and fate, which held an obsessive place in Hellenistic literature and philosophy, which consequently carried over into Roman thought as well. Since the saint was familiar with such discussions and the topic was taken up early by Christians, he wrote one named Jovius: "You attributed not only all the motions of the elements (in which only the hand of God can ensure the safety of men) but also our actions (which are guided by the power of the highest Lord, Who directs and governs them in accordance with our merit) to the concepts of fate and fortune, as though they were powers equal to God....We must have no doubt that all of God's acts, however obscure to us, are planned. So if God, Who created the whole world, also guides it, where will chance, fate, and fortune govern a single created thing? Through ignorance of God and lack of reason, men follow a long-standing error; with foolish imagination they endow these hollow names, as though they were deities, with bodily form, and more foolishly do they accord them honor....Rather we must heed the teaching of reasoning and truth. All that is around us, and of which we are a part, is God's achievement. All that guides and preserves us amidst the uncertainties of this frail and fleeting life is His gift."[47]

Paulinus' public works included, but were not limited to, a home which both he and his wife found for monks and poor folk, a church for Fondi, and a much-needed aqueduct for Nola. He supported a company of poor debtors, homeless, and indigent, many of whom lived in the lower level of his own home. He received friends and visitors who came from all parts to see him in Nola. Paulinus, Therasia, and a few friends occupied the upper story.

They conducted their lives in a semi-monastic fashion, reciting the daily office in common. Information on the monastic routine adopted can be gleaned from his letters. He mentions assembling in church in the latter part of the afternoon for hymn singing. They also conducted all-night vigils. In

---

[45] Letter 5, ¶ 11.
[46] Letter 5, ¶ 12.
[47] Letter 16, ¶¶ 2, 4, 5.

one letter he acknowledged the gift of a Gallic hymnary.[48] He also details the clothing which was worn. He writes of the symbolic importance of the monastic habit. The approved garment of goat hair or camel's hair is contrasted with the showy uniform of soldiers. He also speaks of the close-cropped head of the monk.[49] The saint also describes in some detail their meals. In accordance with general fourth-century practises in monasteries in both the east and west, only one daily meal was served at Nola, even those days outside of the Great Fast. The community assembled for the evening meal, at which the fare was always vegetarian. Paulinus, however, did permit a little wine for those at table.

Adjacent to his home, he had a building with a garden. It served as a guest-house for visitors, both male and female. Among those who enjoyed his amiable personality and hospitality were Saint Melanie and the missionary Bishop of Remesiana,[50] Nicetas, who stayed with him twice. There is no evidence either of the community's size nor their handicrafts. It appears that the holy Paulinus spent time at translating and working on Greek texts. It is likely that the less literary members of the community engaged in church-building.

Paulinus continued to correspond with bishops and other Christians. Most of his surviving letters and poems were composed at Cimitile. Those epistles which are extant include among his correspondents Jerome, Augustine, Rufinus, Jovius, Pammachius, Desiderius, Sulpicius Severus, Amandus, Delphinus, and others. In his writings, he shows himself to be warm-hearted and sociable. All of his sentiments are made pure and genuine by his spirituality and love for the Christian brethren and humanity. His letters reveal a vibrant and intense faith. He consecrated his poetry to Christ. From his letters, we find a man firmly rooted in the Scriptures. He deemed the writing of letters an indispensable part of his monastic life, for they entailed considerable meditation and study of the word of God.

Though generally thought to be a mild man on account of his sympathy for the humble and poor, and also from his friendly disposition in which he addresses his correspondents, he also knew when to be austere and decisive. He rejected Ausonius' rebukes for having abandoned secular poetry. He could be severe with the criticisms of his detractors. On one occasion, he reproved the citizens of Nola who had denied him water for his sanctuary. In every situation, his fervor for the Faith took precedence. This love and zeal

---

[48] Cf. Letter 41, ¶ 1.

[49] On clothing, cf. Letter 17, ¶1 and Letter 29, ¶ 1; on hair, Letter 22, ¶ 1 f.

[50] Remesiana is now Bela Palanka in Serbia. Bishop Nicetas was Saint Paulinus' guest (*Carm.* 17 and 27.333; Ep. 29, 14).

filled all his actions and literary activity. He showed love to his neighbor, which he offered as love and praise of Jesus Christ. Most of his poems were written for the annual celebration of Saint Felix.[51] Paulinus is known to still use the old classical forms with great skill, but he fills them with great Christian warmth, which is one of the greatest charms of his poetry. He is considered one of the most remarkable men of his age. He was eulogized in terms of great love and appreciation by Saints Martin, Ambrose, and Gregory of Tours, and other writers.

When Saint Paulinus settled at Nola there were already three little basilicas and a chapel grouped about the tomb of the former presbyter, Saint Felix. Paulinus added another, which he undertook to have adorned with mosaics of which he has left a description in verse. These three churches shared a common outside entrance. Yearly, at the Feast of Saint Felix, Paulinus offered a poem in the saint's honor, of which fourteen or fifteen of these poems are still extant. Tradition maintains that it was Saint Paulinus who brought bells into the church (ca. 400).

In the year 409/410, Bishop Paul of Nola reposed. In the meantime, Paulinus' beloved Therasia had reposed in 409. He deemed her his fellow servant in Christ.[52] As the obvious and popular choice to fill the place of Bishop Paul, Paulinus left the retirement of Cimitile for the vacant episcopal see of Nola. He occupied the episcopal throne until his repose. He shepherded his flock with wisdom, charity, and liberality. Once a year he left on a pilgrimage to Rome to celebrate the Feast of Saints Peter and Paul.[53] Apart from that excursion, he never left Nola. He was a loyal and great writer of letters, though he did not keep duplicates of his correspondence. The surviving letters are a fraction of the voluminous amount he actually penned, some of which he stated he did not recognize as his own when he saw them again. Since he did not keep copies, those that survived were kept by recipients who regarded them as of permanent value.

Saint Gregory the Dialogist (ca. 540-604), Pope of Rome (from 590), gives the following account of the saint. The Vandals, a Germanic people, who appeared in 406, crossed the Rhine, with the Alans and Suevi, and

---

[51] These birthday poems, addressed to Saint Felix, the patron of the monastery at Nola, are the *Natalcia*. Saint Paulinus wrote a poem every year to celebrate the anniversary of Saint Felix's repose on the 14th of January. Fifteen of these, one for every year between 395 and 409, have survived. See Letter 28, ¶ 6.

[52] Letter 5, ¶ 19.

[53] Each year from his arrival at Nola until ca. 406, Saint Paulinus visited Rome on the 29th of June. Later he changed the time of his annual pilgrimage to the period immediately following Pascha. Cf. Letter 45, ¶ 1; Letter 17, ¶ 2.

devastated Gaul for three years. In 409, their king Gunderic led them across the Pyrenees, at which time they settled in Spain. Saint Gregory mentions in his *Dialogue Three* that some came into Italy at that time. The Vandals abducted large numbers of the inhabitants and sent them to Africa. Bishop Paulinus was feeding the starving people who survived the ravages of the barbarian. He also was ransoming captives, the expense of which exhausted the funds of his diocese. The Vandals also tortured the Christians, compelling them to reveal where there was buried money and jewels. The holy Paulinus, filled with grief, cried out to God, "O Lord, Thou knowest that I have hidden my wealth in the hands of Thy slaves, the poor and needy. Let the unbelievers torture me for gold and silver."

Then it happened that a poor widow came to the holy bishop. She bewailed that her son was taken captive to Africa. "I have also discovered," she said, "that he has been placed in the home of the son-in-law of the Vandal chieftain. I implore thy holiness, give me something by which I may offer a ransom for my boy. The lad is my only future hope for support in my old age." Paulinus made a meticulous search throughout the dwelling to see what could be used to bargain for the youth's release, but there was nothing left to give away except himself. Paulinus spoke to her frankly and said, "Woman, I have nought to give thee save myself. Here, take me as thy slave and sell me or exchange me for him." The woman searched the bishop's countenance. She began thinking to herself, "How could this former patrician, a man so highly placed among God and men, utter such a suggestion? Is he mocking me or is he showing me compassion, that which only a saint could possibly possess?" Though she doubted that such a sacrifice was being made available to her, she at last was convinced by the bishop's demeanor and language. He urged her not to hesitate, but to hand him over to the slavers, bishop though he was, for the ransom of her son. They both then set out for Africa.

They drew near to the Vandal chieftain's son-in-law, even as he was passing out of his home. The widow cast herself at the Vandal's feet. Weeping profusely, she begged the Vandal prince that an exchange be made on behalf of her son. The arrogant barbarian scorned her request. She persisted and said, "Sir, take this man in my son's place." As she pointed to Bishop Paulinus, the prince looked carefully upon Paulinus and was favorably impressed with his fine features. The prince asked, "What is thy trade, man?" The bishop answered, "A craftsman I am not, but I can cultivate a fine garden for thee." The prince was pleased at this offer, since at that very time he required an experienced gardener. The barbarian accepted the offer and took Paulinus as his slave. The youth was released and returned with his mother to Italy.

Paulinus was then sent to take up his labors as gardener. He took up these duties carefully and labored assiduously in working the land. The Vandal, before long, perceived that his gardener was a very wise man on various matters. He therefore often visited the garden that he might consult with Paulinus. Not much time elapsed before the Vandal left the companionship of his former friends that he might enter into conversations with his new gardener. The Vandal enjoyed not only their talks but also the fresh supply of fragrant herbs on his table daily. In exchange, Paulinus received a portion of bread. These meetings took place frequently. On one such occasion, in the course of the conversation, the holy bishop said to the Vandal, "Consider well whether to make the journey thou art planning. Instead, be making preparation to assume thy father-in-law's place, for the chieftain shall die a sudden death. Therefore, do thou remain and make a proper disposition of the chieftain's domains, lest while thou art away another should seize his vacant place." The Vandal was startled at his gardener's prophecy and advice. He did not keep silent, but went to see his father-in-law, with whom none stood higher in favor. He spoke candidly to his father-in-law about Paulinus. Thereupon, the father-in-law showed a keen interest to see Paulinus. The son-in-law said, "He supplies my table with fresh herbs daily. Therefore, I shall bring him to thy table, at which time thou canst become acquainted with him."

The table was prepared and the chieftain sat down to his meal. As soon as the chief caught sight of the holy Paulinus, he trembled. Paulinus entered, bearing in his hands all kinds of fragrant herbs and greens for the table. The chieftain then beckoned to his son-in-law and said privately, "I have kept a secret from thee and all others till now. What thou, my son-in-law, hast heard from thy gardener is true. I tell thee that last night in a dream I beheld judges sitting opposite me in a court of law. This very man, Paulinus, was among them. By the verdict of the judges, the scourge which I had once held in my hand was then taken away. Do thou, therefore, find out who this gardener truly might be, for I suspect that a man of such merit is not the ordinary manservant he appears to be. Indeed, last night I beheld the very man in great dignity." The son-in-law then drew away Paulinus from the table and inquired, "Who art thou in truth?" The saint asked, "I am thy servant whom thou didst accept in the stead of the widow's son." The son-in-law would not be put off, but insisted and adjured the holy man, also saying, "Tell me not thy position which thou holdest in my household. Instead, tell me what thou wast in thine own land." The man of God, troubled by the unrelenting interrogation and unwilling to fall under the fearsome oaths sworn by the Vandal, no longer concealed his identity. He admitted that he was a Christian bishop. The Vandal was filled with reverential awe. He then said to the bishop, "Ask what thou wilt. If thou wilt return to thy homeland, then thou shalt have rich gifts from me." Bishop Paulinus answered, "The best gift thou canst confer upon me is to free all my fellow citizens from captivity here in Africa. Allow them to return to their homeland."

The Vandal did not delay in bringing together the requested captives, though many had been transported to other parts of Africa. As an added kindness, the Vandal arranged to have them all return on ships loaded with grain. Thus, the former captives, together with their saintly bishop, sailed to Italy. A few days later, the Vandal chieftain died, even as prophesied by Saint Paulinus. This was in fulfillment of God's plan. The Vandal chieftain lost the scourge he had wielded to his own condemnation.

As for Saint Paulinus, by surrendering himself into slavery, he came to lead a great multitude back to freedom. He did this in imitation of Christ, Who "emptied Himself and took the form of a slave, and came to be in the likeness of men [Phil. 2:7]," that the human race might be delivered from bondage to the devil. Paulinus, emulating Christ, did not spare himself. He freely chose the lot of a slave for a time, so that he might thereafter enjoy liberty with many. Paulinus became the good shepherd who laid down his life for the sheep [Jn. 10:11]. Saint Paulinus returned to Nola and tended the flock entrusted to him in a God-pleasing manner for many more years.

This Christian poet survived until 431. According to Saint Gregory the Dialogist, "The account of Paulinus' last days is contained in the annals of his church. There we read that his repose was caused by an inflammation of the side."[54]

The closing days of his life are described in the letter of an eyewitness named Uranius. Three days before Bishop Paulinus' repose, he was visited by two bishops, Symmachus and Acyndinus, with whom at his bedside he celebrated the divine Mysteries. It was then that the Priest Postumian arrived and announced that forty pieces of silver were due for clothing on behalf of the poor. The dying Paulinus smiled and said, "Someone shall pay the debt of the poor." Almost immediately, a messenger arrived, bearing a gift of fifty silver pieces. On the last day, at the hour for Vespers, as the lamps were being lighted in the church, the holy man, who had been quiet for many hours, stretched forth his hand and said, "I have prepared a lamp for my Christ." Some hours later, a sudden tremor was felt, as of a slight earthquake. It was at that moment, in the year 431, that Saint Paulinus yielded his soul to God. He was interred in the church which he had built for Saint Felix.

Saint Gregory also records that the chamber in which "Paulinus lay shook with an earthquake, while the rest of the house stood firm. All those

---

[54] Saint Gregory the Great, *Dialogue Three*, Fathers of the Church, 39:115.

present were terrified. Such were the signs that accompanied his soul's departure from his body, and the bystanders who were privileged to witness it were filled with awe. The virtue of Paulinus which I described above was of an inner, personal nature....His external acts of power, his miracles,...are well known and were described to me by persons whose sanctity confirms my belief in these wonderworkings."[55]

Later, Saint Paulinus' relics were translated to Rome. In 1909, however, Pope Pius X ordered that the relics be returned to Nola.

On the 23rd of January, the holy Church commemorates our venerable and God-bearing Father DIONYSIOS of Olympos.[56]

Dionysios, our venerable father, who lived as the bodiless angels, is commemorated today. Blessed is the Lord, the all-merciful and almighty One Who, even now, enables a few of His grateful and faithful servants to combat the adversary and to defeat him decisively, and thus obtain the laurels and trophies of victory, in that they have become inured to the censure and silence of those of little faith. In their prattling and railing, those of little faith maintain that the times induce people not to live in a godly way; but thereby deceive themselves. For we have seen with our own eyes and have been assured that many in our times have suffered martyrdom, and their honorable and sacred relics have become fragrant, and that others have lived piously as the saints of old, such as Anthony and Efthymios. Therefore, it is not the times that are the cause of the reluctance of many, but people's intention.

---

[55] Ibid.

[56] It has become evident that the memory of Saint Dionysios was erroneously assigned to the 24th of January, the mistake first having been made in the *Neon Paradeison*. Nikodemos the Hagiorite has also assigned the Life to the 24th of the month. All the other *Synaxaristae* (including that of K. Doukakes) have been affected, and have assigned his memory to that date. We have corrected this error by placing the date of commemoration on the 23rd of January, in accordance with the tradition at the Olympian monastery of the saint. The date of the 23rd is also overwhelmingly evinced by the divine offices that have been published in the saint's honor: (1) at Venice, 1728; (2) by George Constantine of Ioannina at Venice 1756-1757, revised edition; (3) at Venice, 1781; (4) by the Greek Patriarchal Press at Constantinople, 1816; (5) at Constantinople, 1901; and, (6) at Thessalonike, 1917, under the title, "The Sacred Patriarchal and Stavropegial Monastery of Saint Dionysios on Olympos." The Life was selected from the *Neon Paradeison* of Agapios the Cretan and was compiled and revised accordingly, reflecting the aforementioned corrected date. The saint's liturgical service is printed in a separate pamphlet. The hymnographer, Father Gerasimos Mikrayiannanites, has composed twenty-four *oikoi* (stanzas of a kontakion) to this saint.

Proof of this is the present, God-bearing Dionysios, who surpassed even the ancient fathers. For in those times there were many virtuous men, and each one emulated and vied to surpass the other. But now the elect are few in number, and even the very best fall into negligence.

Saint Dionysios

All those who live in these latter days, who are grateful to our common Lord and keep His salutary commandments, should be esteemed by everyone more than the ancient ones. "For this reason," writes the biographer, "I am recording the godly life and edifying account of the most wise Dionysios. I will relate the whole truth and shall not write even one word of my own, but only the things that the trustworthy and God-bearing fathers have disclosed to me. For it is neither proper nor just to conceal their God-pleasing accounts; rather, they should be heard by all, that we may emulate their works and accomplishments. Attend, therefore, to this most beautiful narration."

The Early Years of Saint Dionysios

The praiseworthy Dionysios was born at the close of the fifteenth century, in the village of Platina, in the province of Phanarion, in Trikkala of Thessaly.[57] His parents, Nicholas and Theodora, were poor but pious. In holy Baptism, they named their son Demetrios. They labored to raise the infant with the utmost care. Once, as he slept at night, wrapped in swaddling clothes, they witnessed over him a most wonderful prefiguration. They beheld the sign of the Cross shining as the sun, which portended his future state of virtue and saintliness; for he would renounce the world and all the desires of the flesh. In the words of the blessed Paul, he would be

---

[57] Elsewhere it is written as Sthlatena. The compilers of *The Great Synaxaristes* (in Greek) give the opinion that this is in all probability the same village that until the early twentieth century was called Sclatena. It has since been renamed Rizoma, and is located approximately fourteen miles north of the city of Trikkala (39°33′N 21°64′E).

crucified with Christ [Gal. 2:20]. As the parents beheld such a revelation over the child, they glorified God, hoping to see what was to come.

When he reached the age of seven, they sent him to school. Within a short period of time, he became enlightened and perfected by the Holy Spirit. The more he delved into the sacred Scriptures, the more so was his soul captivated by divine love. He also learned calligraphy and advanced each day from one level to the next. The saint was never given to any pleasures of the body, nor did he ever desire any harmful or vain thing, nor did he associate with ill-behaved children, lest he should be harmed by their conversations. Instead, he studied the divine Scriptures each day and increased in humility and meekness. He abstained beyond measure and, in short, maintained so many good practises that everyone marvelled at how such a young man was able to possess so many virtues and to spend almost the entire night in prayer.

Saint Dionysios at Meteora

Shortly thereafter, the parents of the saint reposed. Therefore, in order to meet his basic needs, Demetrios taught the children in the village; and thereby, together with the payment received for calligraphic services, he made his living. Some time after, he aspired to become a monk. As he pondered upon this, a certain hieromonk (priest-monk) named Anthimos happened to come to Platina from Meteora, and spoke with him. After they reached an agreement, Demetrios joined his synodia, that is, his company of brethren. He did not keep anything from his parents' property except a single silver cup which he gave to the aforementioned Hieromonk Anthimos.

Upon arrival in Meteora, he was placed under obedience to a righteous monk named Savvas. Demetrios served with utter humility, keeping good conduct with diligence and without sloth. In the meantime, Savvas gave him a rason (cassock) and named him Daniel. Following a short stay there, he desired to go to Mount Athos for greater solitude and austerity. But when he asked permission from the elder, the latter did not allow him, so that he would have Daniel as a help for his soul and body. Fearing lest Daniel should abscond, the elder shut the gate of the monastery and hid the ladder (for the monasteries of Meteora are built upon precipitous rocks). But in vain did the elder scheme. The young Daniel knew that his desire was God-pleasing, so he decided to disobey, as he had not yet taken the tonsure. Therefore, on a given night, possessing unwavering faith in the Lord Christ, he jumped from a great height and plummeted into a river outside. He did not injure himself, however, for divine grace helped him. He then fled to the Holy Mountain.

Saint Dionysios at Mount Athos

Once on Athos, he asked where he might find a virtuous elder. He was told about a respected spiritual father, a prominent Athonite, named Seraphim.

After the blessed one found him and conversed with him, Daniel was received by Seraphim, who was quite hospitable. Seraphim, who loved the brethren, exhorted Daniel to carefully observe the precepts of the monastic life. After the holy Seraphim kept Daniel in his synodia, he tonsured him a monk, naming him Dionysios. A bishop on the Holy Mountain ordained Dionysios to the diaconate, after which he served God with much piety and humility. His elder observed Dionysios' great virtues and was amazed by him.

On a certain Palm Sunday, after the divine Liturgy, Dionysios abandoned his cell and made his way into the forests to the Skete of Karakallou on Athos.[58] He fasted with severity and, as a bird of heaven, cared about nothing worldly. He remained there until Great Saturday of Holy Week and returned to his elder, who asked him where he had been and what he had eaten all those days. He answered that he had been at Karakallou and that he had eaten a few chestnuts and wild herbs. Again, the elder marvelled at his disciple's zeal.

Within a short period of time, his elder was chosen as *protos* (first monk) of Athos, and then was sent to Wallachia, as was the custom.[59] Thereafter, the monks of Athos had Dionysios ordained to the priesthood, that he might serve in the Protaton in his elder's stead. Later, when Seraphim returned from Wallachia, the saint stayed with him for a little while. However, soon thereafter, he pleaded with him to grant him permission to return to a secluded place and pray alone to God as he desired. Seraphim, though, was desirous to retain him in his synodia that he might serve him in his old age. But, on the other hand, he did not wish to prevent him from withdrawing into his much-desired solitude. Therefore, he permitted him to go wheresoever he wished. He also bade Dionysios to pray for him and to return occasionally, that they might converse. Seraphim desired to be kept

---

[58] A skete is a small monastic community of monastics living together in stillness, isolated from the world.

[59] During that dark period for the Greek nation, and especially for Christianity as a whole (first half of the 16th C.), when Hellenism gasped under the oppression of the Turk, and the Christians of the east experienced the harshest trials, the Holy Mountain enjoyed partial freedom, thanks to the privileges accorded it by the conquering sultans. However, that freedom was bought with vast amounts of gold and silver by the Athonites who procured it with great difficulty, because it was soon consumed by the greed of the conquerors. In order to meet their demands and pay the staggering tribute money, they were forced to go to the Orthodox Christians of free lands, one of which was Wallachia, also subject to the sultans, but administratively independent. The princes of Wallachia, from the time that Patriarch Niphon II (1486-1489, 1497-1498) visited there, contributed great sums to Mount Athos. For this reason, the *protos* traveled there at that time.

informed concerning how Dionysios withstood the temptations of the demons, of his thoughts, and of other encounters. Therefore, upon receiving the elder's permission to leave, the holy man sought a secluded place.

Saint Dionysios Goes into Seclusion

At the Skete of Karakallou, he found a spot that was inaccessible and cold. He resolved to build a small cell and dwell therein. The blessed one was so attentive to his spiritual struggle that, night and day, he never ceased laboring in the spiritual vineyard. He fasted, prayed, and was vigilant. He performed as many prostrations as possible. He kept with him the most excellent and edifying book, *Thekaras*,[60] which he always read. The saint did not concern himself with nourishment. His diet consisted of the study of holy Scriptures and a few of the chestnuts that abound on the Mountain. Of these, he would partake of no more than sixty, and only after the ninth hour. If he was taken to another *kellion*[61] to liturgize, he would partake of a morsel of bread in order to avoid praise. He practised such poverty and never put a key to his door, because he had nothing save the rason which he wore, and that was old and shabby. Otherwise, he owned no earthly possessions.

In that place he had constructed a small church, in the name and to the glory of the indivisible Trinity. He dwelt there for three years, praying to God and contemplating divine things. And since he was pure in heart, he became worthy of witnessing divine revelations.

Saint Dionysios in the Holy Land

While he struggled on the Holy Mountain, he conceived the desire to make a pilgrimage to the Holy Land where our Savior was crucified. (For it is the custom of those who have a dear one, when they do not see such a one, to desire to see the beloved's house or even his garments. For this reason, he wished to see the holy places where our blessed Lord Christ lived and suffered to redeem us from death.) Therefore, Dionysios departed with great haste. He offered up worship to God in the Holy Land and received much joy and exultation in his soul. While there, the Patriarch of Jerusalem showed the holy man much deference and desired to keep him there to nominate him as his successor. But the blessed Dionysios did not wish to stay. He then put to sea, bound for Mount Athos, and, upon returning to his cell, struggled as before.

---

[60] The *Thekaras* was a large volume which contained numerous contrite prayers, and it was used by Orthodox Christians as a prayer book or *Efchologion*. It was first published in Venice by Agapios the Cretan in 1683. Since then, it has been reprinted many times.

[61] On Mount Athos a *kellion* was a small monastery. The word is also used interchangeably for several types of monastic cells, whether a cell with one or two monks in a coenobium, or a cell at a lavra, or the cell of a hermit.

Saint Dionysios Returns to Athos and Enlarges the Church

The holy Dionysios decided to enlarge his church slightly. As he labored at this, a monk who was an acquaintance was coming to visit him. As the visiting monk approached, he saw two others who lifted up stones and carried them to where the saint was building. Therefore, he thought that they were actually men whom the holy man had summoned. But when he greeted them, they both vanished, and he alone remained. He then inquired of Dionysios what had happened to the others. The saint answered that no one else was there, save God Who is everywhere present. From this occurrence, the holy Dionysios understood that God was helping him in his undertakings. Dionysios rejoiced without falling into high-minded things about himself. Much rather, he humbled himself; and, as one being expert in the sacred Scriptures, he recited with the prophet: "O Lord, my heart is not exalted [Ps. 130:1]."

A Miracle During Cheesefare

But now, listen to another more beautiful miracle, that you may perceive the Lord's love and kindness toward us. As we said earlier, the saint had neglected all the things that are necessary for bodily sustenance; for he rejoiced and reveled solely in God. He lived only on wild chestnuts. However, the all-merciful and benevolent One desired to reward His servant generously and thereby reveal His concern for His servant.

Therefore, as Dionysios sat alone on Cheesefare Saturday, a certain monk came to him who appeared to be from the Monastery of the Bulgarians.[62] The stranger greeted him, saying, "It seems, honorable father, that the Great Fast is near, during which time the servants of God abstain. Thou must solace the weakness of the flesh during these days. Receive, therefore, this cheese and fish to thy fulfillment, and give thanks unto the Lord!" Dionysios accepted them gladly and asked him to remain that they might enjoy them together. But he replied, "I do not have the time now. Only partake of them and glorify God Who provides for His servants!" After he said this, he disappeared. The holy Dionysios then saw that the fish was still wriggling and the cheese dripped with thin milk. He was astonished and thanked God Who had bestowed them, acknowledging His great love for man and goodness. Dionysios never disclosed this miracle to anyone on Mount Athos. He wanted none to think highly of him. (However, later, when he built the monastery on Olympos, he did relate this miracle to his disciples, to assure them that God provides for His servants.) Now let us relate another miracle.

---

[62] The Monastery of Philotheou on Mount Athos was called thus because Bulgarian monks dwelt there.

The Thief

As the venerable one struggled in the aforementioned place, many monks from the Holy Mountain came to him and conversed with him to their benefit. However, a certain thief saw them and presumed that they had given alms to the saint. The thief plotted to slay him and take the money. Therefore, as the righteous one was going to his cell, the robber hid in a nearby creek bed to ambush him there. He waited for an entire day, but did not see Dionysios when he passed, because the Lord concealed His servant. Then the thief went up to the saint's cell to see if he were in that place. When he saw that Dionysios was indeed there, he was beside himself. He asked Dionysios how he had passed him. The holy man answered that he had passed by from the creek. The thief was shocked that he had been blinded thus and admitted his intent, saying, "I was lying in wait there to slay thee, but I realize that thou art a servant of God, Who protected and covered thee. Forgive my evil scheme which I had planned against thee. Beseech the Lord Christ to blot out my transgression and make me worthy to become a novice!" The saint answered him, "If thou shalt refrain from thy previous crimes and repent with all thy soul of thy felonies and strive for thy salvation, God will forgive thee, as He is merciful and compassionate." Upon hearing these words, the thief received them as divine seed in his heart. And, by divine inspiration, he went to the monastery and became a novice.

Elevated to the Abbacy

Dionysios remained in his cell for seven years, striving in prayer and abstinence, and all held him in reverence and respect. However, as the light should be on the lampstand, according to the Lord's command, and should not be hidden under the bushel [Mt. 5:15], God intervened. Dionysios, a humble and modest man, without seeking the honor, was elected hegumen (abbot) of the Monastery of Philotheou. After the election, the brethren approached him, begging and entreating him to take the monastery under his guardianship, lest it should decline and become deserted, thereby disappearing altogether. The saint, perceiving this change in his life to be the will of God, accepted the abbacy. Therefore, he withdrew from his solitude for the salvation of the brethren.

At that time, the monastery was under the Bulgarians, and it used the Bulgarian *Typikon* (order). However, the holy Dionysios replaced this with the Greek *Typikon*. He introduced Greek texts and procured all the necessities. To help increase their revenues, he undertook the task of going to Constantinople—since it was common to seek help there. The merciful God moreover granted success to his journey. The God-loving Christians gave him a large amount of money and accorded him much respect. Indeed, some followed the saint back to the monastery and became monks. The righteous man led everyone to God, exhorting them to attend the holy services and to have food and clothing in common.

Now there were certain disgruntled Bulgarians in the monastery who hated the saint for changing their *typikon*. Daily, they caused scandals for him and even plotted to slay the holy elder. Dionysios became aware of their scheme, so he bade farewell to his most trustworthy monks and departed. He did take, however, a few devout monks from his synodia.

The Skete of Verea

By the will of God, the saint went to the Skete of Verea (Beroea of Macedonia), where, at that time, there were twenty monks. At the Monastery of Saint Anthony the New, who is commemorated by the holy Church on the 17th of January, there were twenty or more monks; and the same number of monks were at the community at Panagia (the all-holy Theotokos). There were ten monks at the Monasteries of the Holy Trinity and Saint John the Forerunner. From the onset of the holy man's arrival, he converted the desert into a city. His virtue attracted many people as a magnet attracts iron. They came from everywhere to see that angelic figure, and some forsook the world and entered his synodia. He instructed and guided them to walk the narrow path of affliction, in order to enter Paradise.

At first, he restored the Church of Saint John the Forerunner. Even though he struggled in fasting and vigils, he never hesitated to do heavy labor. He would lift great stones and wooden beams, and participated in many other difficult tasks willingly, so as to fulfill the command of the divine Paul: "If any would not work, neither should he eat [2 Thess. 3:10]." Just as he labored in the earthly temple of the Forerunner to enlarge it, so much more did he struggle for the spiritual temple of the soul.

The people at the outskirts of Verea, observing all these things, gathered there, and many became monastics. The saint taught them, as they were his own natural children, to scorn the desires of the body, so as to inherit a heavenly reward. All the things that he taught them he also steadfastly guarded; for one that practises what one teaches will be called great [Mt. 5:19]. He fasted, prayed, and was always vigilant in his labors. He was meek and humble, and possessed many other virtues, which I will not mention for the sake of brevity. I will relate only three or four practises which were beyond nature, so that we may emulate him as much as possible. His meager fare during his seven-year stay at the Skete of Karakallou might be compared to that of the birds of the air which have no cares. At the time of the construction of the Skete at Verea, he ate nothing but fruits and never had a spare garment [Mt. 10:10]. He had such compassion and pity upon the poor that, whenever he returned to the monastery from Verea, where he traveled to hear the confessions of his spiritual children, all the alms that he received were distributed among the poor.

The Virtues of Saint Dionysios

One day, when a novice suggested to him to keep a little money aside for the needs of the monastery, he answered, "Monks do not need money. Remember that poverty is their training for salvation. Secular people who have children, wives, pay taxes, and bear many other worries and burdens, they should receive alms—not we who have no needs!" Not only this but many other uplifting virtues also did the saint possess. But mostly he exemplified humility, for he was obedient to everyone and served them all with utter meekness. He wore frayed and worn garments, for he desired to belittle himself in many instances. When he would write a letter or a testament, he would express the following: "I have been the recipient of a myriad of good things from God; I, the very least, even though I have committed many sins!"

The holy Dionysios always possessed love toward God and his neighbor. Now he did not only show his love by admonishing and inciting the monks to safeguard the vows of the Schema, but he also often went to the villages and cities, teaching all to keep the salutary commandments of the Lord. In general, he was the father of orphans and protector of widows, the supporter of the poor by almsgiving, and comforter to the afflicted. In the words of Saint Paul, the elder simply became everything to everyone that he might bring all to salvation [1 Cor. 9:22]. Though he possessed all these virtues, he also possessed the gift of tears, which were never absent from his eyes when he prayed or read or spoke with others about the holy Scriptures; furthermore, he made all those who listened also weep.

Hieromonk Matthew

The saint had converted the Monastery of the Forerunner into a coenobium and laid down the rules and order by which the monks were to abide. Many flocked to his monastery from the small hermitages of Verea when they heard of the feats of the saint, and sought his permission to build cells. He accepted everyone wholeheartedly and helped them in both body and soul. Though many of them were devout, yet a certain hieromonk named Matthew surpassed them all. Observing that the elderly Matthew was reverent, the holy man esteemed him. He placed the hieromonk in the cell next to his own, so that Matthew might hear the confessions of those who came. Now no one ever saw Matthew eating, as he was immured in his cell. He always mourned, as did Saint Arsenios the Great and Saint Ephraim the Syrian. He wept so often that he kept a swatch of his rason on his chest for drying the tears. His beard and stature were as those of Saint Gregory the Theologian. His appearance was so venerable and striking that whosoever met him dared not to look him directly in the face. But now, let us continue with the admirable Dionysios.

Saint Dionysios at Sea

In those days, Patriarch Jeremias[63] went to Jerusalem on urgent business, accompanied by two other patriarchs. The saint had a great desire to obtain letters of permission from the four patriarchs. Therefore, he departed for Thessalonike and there boarded a ship and sailed to Egypt and thence to Jerusalem. After he succeeded in this endeavor, he returned again by sea. As they sailed, there arose such a violent storm that the ship was about to capsize. The holy Dionysios, seeing the extreme peril, was grieved that he should perish with heathens. Thus, with unwavering faith, he prayed to the Lord Christ saying, "Save me, O Jesus Christ, as Thou didst save Thy disciples who were in danger. As Thou art the Master of land and sea, so calm its turbulent waves when Thou willest!" As he prayed thus with tears—lo, Thine indulgent love and care for them that entreat Thee, O Christ!—the stormy sea suddenly subsided. But the ungrateful barbarians, instead of thanking the saint, became suspicious and conspired to cast him into the deep, saying that he had bewitched the sea, because he raised aloft an icon of the Mother of God. However, divine grace, which guarded him to the benefit of all, prevented them from such an attempt. By the grace of God, one of the seamen, who was more humane than the others, advised them not to throw Dionysios overboard. Hence, they hearkened to their crew member, and thereby the righteous man was rescued from that peril by this intervention. Upon arriving at the monastery, all the monks rejoiced, for they still needed him to give them advice for their conduct and betterment. Thereafter, to the spiritual Elder Matthew, he related privately all that had occurred at sea.

Meanwhile, the cells increased in number, and the brethren progressed in spirituality by divine grace and power. Not only did the coenobia increase, but also a few *kathismata*[64] were formed, which had not existed before, and they grew daily. It must be remembered that, before our saint came to Verea, there were very few dedicated fathers. After his arrival, many desired to emulate his mode of life. The entire countryside was filled, not

---

[63] This was Jeremias I, who served from 1520-1545. During this trip, his enemies seized the opportunity and offered the Sultan four thousand golden dinars and succeeded in declaring Ioannikios I as patriarch (1523). When the other patriarchs who were still in Jerusalem learned of this, they excommunicated Ioannikios and succeeded in reinstating Jeremias to the throne.

[64] A *kathisma* (sing.) is a secluded cell located far from the monastery that it is dependent upon. Usually one or more monastics reside therein.

only with men, but also with women and young people who left their homes for the heavenly kingdom and became monastics.

The Saint Flees Ordination

In those days, the Bishop of Verea reposed, and everyone gathered and agreed to choose the saintly Dionysios as bishop. They sent representatives to the monastery and begged him to become their spiritual leader, but he refused, considering himself unworthy of such an honor. They insisted that he yield to their demand. In order that they not vex him, he bade them to wait till the following day for a response. Then, he opened the holy Gospel and read an isolated verse; and, knowing that it was not the will of God for him to become a hierarch, he fled to a secluded place. As a result, they returned very sad, ordained in his place another called Neophytos who, after a few years, was defrocked in dishonor.

Saint Dionysios at Mount Olympos[65]

The holy man had spent many years in the Skete of Verea, when he decided to go to the environs of Olympos to find a serene place to dwell, so that no one would distract him. Hence, he retired to a village called Malathraea, which was at the foot of the mountain.[66] He inquired of a certain man more precisely about the place, to wit, if it had water, trees, and vegetation. The man revealed to him that, in fact, the area was most beautiful, with many springs, tall trees, pines and delightful valleys. When Dionysios heard this description, he was extremely glad and pleaded with him for the Lord's sake to lead him thither. They departed for the site, where today stands the Monastery of the Holy Trinity. When the saint saw such a magnificent view, he was filled with joy and exhilaration. He tarried there a while, marvelling and observing the beauty of the location, including the

---

[65] Mount Olympos (40°05'N 22°21'E) is one hundred kilometers (sixty-two miles) southwest of Thessalonike, and seventeen kilometers (ten and one-half miles) southwest of Dion. It is the highest mountain in all of Greece. It is actually a conglomeration of thickly bunched summits. The highest peak, the summit of Mytikas, is 2,917 meters or 9,570 feet. Olympos is surrounded by seventeen hundred plant species and has a varied bird life. The lower slopes are covered with forests of holm oak, arbutus, cedar, and conifer. The higher elevations are adorned with oak, beech, and black and Balkan pine. If one hikes up Mount Olympos, when one comes from Prionia, the Monastery of Saint Dionysios is in the forest at the bottom of a turnoff to the right just below the refuge. During World War II, the monastery, suspected of harboring resistance fighters, was blown up by the Nazis. It is slowly being restored but was unfinished at the time of this notice (1999).

[66] Undoubtedly, this is the modern village of Malathria, belonging to the community of Dion in the province of Pieria (Katerini), lying on the northern slopes of Mount Olympos.

height of the two majestic peaks of the mountain, the numerous tall trees, the smoothness of the valley, and the crystal clear water which was refreshing and sweet to the taste.

Saint Dionysios

On observing all this, in the words of the prophet, Dionysios said to himself, "'Here will I dwell [Ps. 131:15],' for I am well pleased with this wonderful mountain!" He thanked the God-loving Christian man and said to him, "Go, O servant of God, to thy house, and I shall remain here and survey the whole mountain to see if it is good for habitation." Dionysios then tarried there for a number of days. Later, because he had no food, he bought a little flour and went down to the house of that man. Dionysios then baked bread which lasted for many days.

In a little while, it was noised about in the outlying district of Mount Athos that a certain venerable ascetic had appeared on the mountain. Therefore, another monk went to abide with him, whom the saint gladly received. After a few days, others came, and still others, so that they multiplied indeed. As a result, the saint contracted masons to build cells and a church for their spiritual and physical needs. While the monks built the cells, a group of Christians, out of innocence, went to Sakos, the Hagarene, who owned the mountain at that time, and mentioned to him that a holy ascetic had come there and was building a monastery. When Sakos heard this, he was incensed, because they were building without his permission, for he had purchased that land. So he went to the judge at Larissa, who had jurisdiction over that district, and obtained a writ to tear down the structures and to bring all the monks, including the saint, in chains before him.

Mount of Zagora

In the interim, the priest at Litochoro learned of this conflict. He sent a message to the holy man to leave immediately, lest he and those with him should be apprehended. The venerable Dionysios was saddened, because he was being exiled from such a soul-saving place. Weeping, he departed with the brethren, saying, "If it be Thy will, O my Christ, for a monastery to be erected here, show Thine invincible power, and grant that I return here soon!" As they left that district, they ventured to the mountain of Zagora, and, seeing that the location was suitable as a dwelling place for monastics, he decided to build cells and a church there to the glory and ceaseless praise of God. This he did within a few days. Such a great number of monks gathered together because of the good fame of the righteous one—some to see him, and others for the purpose of confession—that the entire area became as a populous city. He continued there for an entire year and led many to their salvation. Then he recorded the *typikon* by which they were to conduct themselves. Later, he returned to Olympos in a remarkable manner. Hearken to the cause, that you may exult and know of the boldness that the inspired Dionysios had before God.

Saint Dionysios Returns to Mount Olympos

From the time that the holy man was driven from Mount Olympos, it did not rain in that region. The inhabitants were ravaged with the resulting hunger and famine. On a certain day, many clouds were seen over the villages of Olympos, Malathraea, and Litochoro. The occupants of the other villages, seeing these clouds, blessed them, as they thought that much rain was imminent. But this was the wrath of God; for instead, great hailstones fell and destroyed the trees, vineyards, and crops. Moreover, the tiles on top of the houses were shattered, as if they had been struck with iron rods. Such intense rain fell, followed by lightning, that people fell to the ground on their faces. The hail that was on the ground accumulated to the depth of three hands' breadth. Then the villagers lamented their great calamity, not knowing the reason thereof. However, the pious and wise knew the cause, saying, "Because we cast out the ascetic and holy man, God has punished us justly!" The priest who had cautioned the saint to depart cried aloud, "Behold our misfortune! God's judgment is upon us! Because we exiled the righteous Dionysios, such a scourge has visited us suddenly! If we do not call upon him to make a prayer of forgiveness before the Lord, indeed, we shall perish all together!"

On hearing these things, the faithful prayed with tears for the Lord to forgive them. Now the governor, observing the destruction of the crops, was grieved; for he was unable to pay the taxes of the empire. He questioned the people as to the reason for the disaster and the ruin of the crops, and they answered him, saying, "We cast out a certain ascetic who was a holy man; and because of this, we have been visited with destruction. If we do not invite him and beg him to return to his cell again, the Lord will send yet greater losses and afflictions upon us." The governor responded, "Go then with a priest, a few prominent citizens, two of my servants, and my letter. Invite him to come without any fear to the mountain and dwell with his synodia."

After three days, they arrived at the outskirts of Zagora. They found the blessed man and greeted him, giving him the document with the governor's seal. Then they related the entire situation to him. However, the saint had doubts, fearing that perhaps they sought to plot against him and do evil; however, the priest swore to him that it was not treachery. They kissed his hand, and the servants of the governor said to him with great humility, "Our master sends many greetings and beseeches thee to come back to thy monastery to bless the place, for ever since thy departure, we have been terribly afflicted!" Then the saint took courage and consented to go. Thereupon, the Zagorans gathered before him, lamenting his departure. They said to him, "Do not leave us orphans, but think of us in thy holy prayers and supplicate God on our behalf!" The holy man promised to visit often for their edification. Thereupon, he returned to Litochoro.

Upon hearing this, all the natives came and gathered to welcome and reverence him. The governor also came on foot and greeted him, saying, "Hail, honorable father, and forgive us, inasmuch as we have transgressed against thee. We did not know that thou wast a servant of God. Ascend now, without any fear, upon the mountain. Take with thee as many builders as thou requirest. Build a church and resting place for thy monks, and glorify God, free from care." Then the holy Dionysios thanked him and promised to entreat the Lord on his behalf that He grant him many days. The saint then secured from the governor the written rights to construct a church and as many cells as he wished.

The saint then ascended the mountain. At first, he dwelt in a cave and built a small church. He did not think that many would join, but later, many more came. Those who came were not among the wealthy. Many of them were poor and needy, and due to their difficulties they became monks. Nevertheless, the saint received all as God-sent, calling to remembrance the verse: "All that the Father giveth to Me shall come to Me, and the one who cometh to Me in no wise will I cast out [Jn. 6:37]." Then he ventured into the countryside to seek assistance for the maintenance of the brethren. The townsfolk donated provisions; thus, through their almsgiving, the monastics were sustained in body. The saint applied all diligence to the saving of men's souls, becoming the mouth of God, just as the Prophet Jeremias declared: "If thou wilt bring forth the precious from the worthless, thou shalt be as My mouth [Jer. 15:19]." Also, the teaching of Saint Iakovos (James), the brother of the Lord: "Brethren, if anyone among you should be led astray from the truth, and someone should turn him around, let him know that the one who turneth a sinner from the error of his way shall save a soul from death and shall cover a multitude of sins [Jas. 5:19-20]."

The blessed one realized that there were three things with which to concern himself: solitude, the growth of the monastery, and what was beneficial to the Christians. At times, Saint Dionysios would rest in the cave of Golgotha or the Mount of Olives, and other times at Saint Lazarus, or at the Great Cave which gushed forth sweet water. He gave these names to places on Mount Olympos when he had returned from Jerusalem.

The ever-memorable one had the custom of ascending to the peak of the mountain to liturgize on the Feasts of the Holy Transfiguration of our Lord and God and Savior Jesus Christ (6th of August) and Prophet Elias (20th of July). He built the Church of Prophet Elias on that spot, and the monks go there to this day and every year celebrate with gladness.

After a while, the venerable elder saw that the brotherhood was increasing; so he desired to construct a central building and cells for the comfort of the brethren. He himself helped the builders with the heavier work. He carried wood to the furnace, as well as stones, and performed all the labors as did the workers, without his desire ever diminishing, for he was devoted. He built many churches of God which, for brevity's sake, we have not mentioned. Now with all these labors he did not neglect his abstinence. Although the others often ate fish and drank to strengthen themselves because of the effort they exerted, the saint ate only fruits and drank water. But let us recount a few of his many miracles, that you may understand how much boldness he had before the Lord.

The Unreasonable Shepherd

One day, the wondrous Dionysios went forth into a village for the saving of souls. While the holy man was absent, a shepherd came to the lower cave of the monastery. Upon observing that the place was suitable for the grazing of sheep, the rascal gathered wood and erected a small dwelling. The younger monks advised him not to attempt such a thing, lest he should trouble the saint. But he scoffed at them and did as he pleased. After three days, the blessed man returned. He sent one of the young men to bring water for drinking. Then the youth told him of the shepherd and how he had made a sheepfold. He also said that he feared being bitten by the shepherd's dogs. But the holy man said to him, "Go to the spring, and be not afraid." So he went. When he returned, the dogs bit him, and he went to the saint weeping. Thereupon, the holy Dionysios emerged and with meekness counseled the shepherd, saying, "My man, why hast thou come thither to vex us? Couldest thou not find a spot to make thy sheepfold other than here by the side of our monastery, to cause us annoyance? Withdraw thence with thy flock, lest thou shouldest discover the wrath of God!" But the shepherd, being a rude and ignorant man, answered, "I have brought no trouble here, old man, that thou shouldest hinder my sheep!" The blessed one said to him, "As unreasoning animals, thy sheep can find rest in any place; but we, the reason-endowed sheep of the Master, have no other suitable place that is God-pleasing!"

Indeed, these are the things spoken by the saint to the foolish and darkened mind of that shepherd. That wicked man indecently and shamefully insulted the venerable elder, saying, "I will not leave this place, where I was born and raised; rather take thyself away and begone! Thou camest here only yesterday and have no authority in this place, thou evildoer!" Then the holy man answered, "Blessed be God Who works everything to our advantage! If it is His will for me to build here, He will punish thee and thy sheep, that thou mayest understand Who God is, and how thou shouldest honor His servants!" After this exchange of words, Saint Dionysios repaired to his cell.

The miserable shepherd would not at all bear in mind the sincere resolution of the saint. He continued to graze his sheep at the foot of the mountain. However—O, the wonder and swiftness of God's vengeance!—a rock dislodged itself from the highest point on the mountain and killed many sheep. But again, the imprudent one failed to comprehend that the imprecation of the blessed man had overtaken him; nor did he think to seek forgiveness for the many foolish things he had uttered. Once again, he herded his sheep on the mountains of the monastery. Subsequently, in a few days, all the sheep were killed, and he fell into a grave illness and was bedridden. He was a pitiable and strange sight; neither was it possible for him to eat nor to drink, but he remained as a shadow. His face blackened; and, due to the dire pain he was experiencing, he desired death.

After a long time, he remembered the saint's rebuke and his own stubbornness toward him. He disclosed to his relatives the matter, and they advised him to go to the holy man and seek forgiveness and be cured, so as not to be further tormented, or die. They placed him upon a mule and went to the mountain. It so happened that the holy man was at that time coming down, and he inquired of them where they were going. They informed him of the matter in detail. The righteous man then took pity on him, being sympathetic and compassionate, and blessed him. He prescribed that they leave him in the monastery, and that he eat that of which the monastics partook, that is, the fruit of the cornel tree. In seven days, he recovered completely and returned to his home on foot.

The Village Elder

Another time, it happened that the saint was in the area of Kitros, in a village called Touria.[67] The Christians begged him to remain a few days to hear their confessions, and he consented. He tarried there three days and heard the confessions of many. Now there was a village elder who had an evil

---

[67] Touria or Tourgia is the old name of the modern village of Ganochora.

spirit dwelling within him. This man never went to confession; but rather, he mocked the others for confessing to a man of like passions and deeds, saying it was impossible for them to be benefitted by him. This and other unjustified charges and gossip did the faithless one utter. The holy one learned of this through a certain priest who sought the village elder to come that he might speak with Dionysios. He was finally brought forth to see the righteous man, who recited to him many verses from the holy Gospels, namely that the Lord commanded the bishops and priests to confess others of their sins, because they have been given the authority to forgive sins [Mt. 16:19], and that whosoever scorns confession will be condemned. These and many other things the saint said in his presence, in the hope of bringing him to repentance. But this unholy one derided and laughed at him. Consequently, observing his incorrigibility, the venerable man told him the following, in imitation of the great Paul: "Because thou hast made crooked the straight road of the Lord, and mocked my words and the precepts of Christ, O miserable one, behold, the hand of the Lord shall be upon thee, and merciless wrath shall come upon thy house, so that thou and others will see and turn to repentance!"[68]

After this, Saint Dionysios went his way. An infirmity befell the wicked man and all his house; and indeed, the others of his house met with evil deaths. He himself was bedridden and a pitiful sight; thus, the unrighteous one was justly punished. Then, certain of his kinsfolk sent word to the saint and besought Dionysios to help him. The blessed man was straightway alerted, but before the saint arrived at the ailing one's side, his wretched soul departed. At this, the saint was extremely sorrowful, because he had not been in time to bring him to repentance while still alive. But come, let us relate another similar account, that you may perceive the holy one's boldness before the Lord.

The Young Girl From Katerini

In the spring, the saint went to the city of Katerini. On the road, he met a group of young girls and boys, who were singing immodest and inappropriate songs, of the type that incites youths to shameful and improper desires. The blessed man was grieved at hearing these things, and he said to them, "Why do you say these things, being you are virgins? Such disgraceful and immodest words defile your virginity, exciting and inclining these youths to sensuality. Do you not call death to remembrance?" After the saint had spoken, they fell silent, except for one girl, who was very impudent. She retorted arrogantly, "You false monks fornicate yourselves; and wilt thou teach us, O hypocrite? Why dost thou not go thy way? What dost thou care

---

[68] Cf. 1 Cor. 5:5.

about us, since we are of no relation to thee?" Then the righteous man answered her, "Blessed be God Who works to the advantage of all! May He punish thy foolish and unbridled tongue, that thou mayest become to the others a model of morality!" Thus he spoke and left. That evening, the venerable man took shelter with a friend of the monastics.

However, the wretched girl, before she reached her father's house, became demonized, foaming at the mouth and kicking. Her parents were distraught and could not understand how this trouble had come about. But one of the young woman's companions related to them the matter in detail. Therefore, weeping, they ran and inquired throughout the city for the ascetic. They found the house where he was staying and fell at his feet, entreating him to forgive and not to bear resentment toward their ignorant daughter. The saint, never one to remember wrongs, then blessed the girl, and her soul was taught chastity, and her body was cured as well. Out of fear, she chose not to marry and ended her life in temperance.

The Unwary Monk

There was a monk at Verea who knew letters slightly. It so happened that a book on divination came into his hands, and he read it to test it a little, and thereby invoked the demons. One particular night, as he was sleeping, he saw in a dream a giant creature, blacker than any Ethiopian, who said to him, "Because thou hast called upon me, I am come. If thou wilt make obeisance to me, I will do what thou askest!" Now the monk recognized that this was the devil, and said to him, "I worship the Lord God, and Him only I serve!" Then in anger the demon smote him across the face, and said, "Since thou wilt not fall down and worship me, why didst thou summon me?" Then, on account of the pain, the monk awakened, shouting loudly, and cried out. Others gathered and saw his jaw and cheek very swollen and bruised. It was a very strange sight to behold. In a few days, the body tissues swelled further and blackened even more, to such a degree that his eyes could not be seen at all. Therefore, they sent a message to the saint to come and see this case. When the holy Dionysios saw him, he made a prayer to the Lord and chanted the Paraklesis (Supplicatory Canon) to the Theotokos. He anointed him with holy oil, whereupon he recovered and glorified the Lord.

A Mother and Her Two Sons

A widow named Zoe had two sons, Demetrios and Arsenios. A dreadful illness came upon the second son, causing his face to swell, which terribly distressed his mother. Demetrios then said to her, "If I do not take my brother to Olympos where Abba (Father) Dionysios is, he shall never be cured!" She said to him, "Go then, my son!" The two brothers went to the saint. After they told him of the entire matter, the elder received them gladly and read a prayer over the sick one and anointed his face with oil. In a few days, Arsenios recovered. Then Arsenios sojourned there for a little while and was so captivated with the life of the monastics that he resolved to become a monk. He, in turn, consulted Demetrios about this matter and encouraged him to do the same; the latter promised to become a monk also, but later on. Arsenios was then garbed in the rason. Demetrios returned to his house and related to his mother what had occurred. She then became so distraught that she began to pine away.

Now a certain evil woman advised Zoe to pay a sorceress to force Arsenios out of the monastery. The sorceress, in practising her evil craft, conjured the chief of the demons, whom she sent to Olympos to drive Arsenios out of the monastery. But the demon was unable to enter the monastery, for divine grace kept him at bay. Therefore, the evil spirit returned to Zoe humiliated, having had no success. He then seized her by the throat and beat her, saying, "Why didst thou send me to the ascetic and servant of God, whom I cannot approach? Now I will give thee thy just reward!" As the demon said these things, he repeatedly kicked and struck Zoe, causing her to scream. Her neighbors gathered around and asked her the reason for the commotion, and she confessed the truth. Then she sent Demetrios to call the saint; and, immediately, as he approached and uttered a prayer on her behalf before the Lord, she was restored whole and sound. Later, she so loved the Schema of the monks that she too became a monastic, as did Demetrios.

Paraskeve of Rapsani

A certain other woman named Paraskeve from the village of Rapsani was so severely hunched over that her head bowed until it reached down to her knees! She was a pitiful sight to behold, for she could neither sit, nor walk, nor lift her head up straight. Her husband was distraught and expended much silver on doctors, but to no avail. Paraskeve could not be cured by natural or human means. Only God could cure her; so that He dispensed in His œconomy that His servant Dionysios should pass by her village. The husband of Paraskeve entreated him with tears to come to his house and beseech the Lord on her behalf. The saint went and, after he prayed, touched her with his right hand. Behold the miracle! She stood up straight. The people that were present were astonished to see such a marvel, and they glorified our Creator and Savior, and thanked Dionysios who ministered this good act.

A Possessed Woman of Isvoron

In another village, called Isvoron, there dwelt a man whose daughter was disturbed by a demon. Her father felt more pain in his heart than did his daughter. He tried to heal his daughter through any means, but was unable to do so. At last he remembered the saint and went to him. Falling before his feet, he besought him to heal her for the Lord's sake. The holy man did not hesitate, but went immediately to the disturbed woman. As he prayed, the evil demon departed at once, as darkness is banished by light. This and many other deeds the God-sent one performed, which for the sake of brevity we cannot record. We shall mention a few lines only about the foresight he possessed, that you may perceive the prophetic gift he was vouchsafed as well.

The Priest of Portaria

When Saint Dionysios was at the Mountain of Demetrias, the steward of the monastery told him that there was no grain for the cattle. So, he traveled to a town called Portaria and lodged in the house of a certain priest named George. After the holy Dionysios uttered many kind and edifying words, he also added that he needed grain and desired to borrow from him until the spring. Now the priest had a whole barrel of grain in his storehouse, but he pretended that he had none and went to ask the neighbors for some. However, as he was leaving his house, the barrel overturned and fell, strewing grain everywhere. The saint knew this, and so he called the priest, saying, "Father George, return, the barrel has fallen over! Come and gather up the grain!" The priest returned and, beholding the barrel, was amazed and said to the saint, "Thy prayer, O father, has revealed the truth, because in my little faith I told thee that I did not have any, that my cattle might lack nothing. But because the Lord has revealed that which was hidden, take all thou needest and bless the remainder, so that it will suffice for my house." Afterward, the holy man departed, and there was enough for the priest from what remained.

Hearken to narratives of the saint's God-given foresight.

The Saint's Clairvoyance

When the saint built the monastery, he prophesied the following, "After my departure, a bishop shall come here who will build a tower on this spot." Thus it happened, for after the repose of the saint, Bishop Sophronios of Kitros raised up a tower, which can be seen to this day. He predicted the same for Golgotha, that a tower would be erected there too; and it was built by the Bishop of Platamon.

On another occasion, while he struggled alone beneath the monastery in a cave, he went by night, knocking at the gate of the monastery, saying, "Open, I say, O fathers, for we must pray for our brother Longinos who is in danger of death!" At daybreak, Longinos came in from the cow pasture and told them of a harrowing tale of what had taken place during that night. Thieves broke in and stole the gear and harness of the herd and the horse. They were about to cut him down with a sword, when a man suddenly appeared who bade them not to strike him; and so they left him alone.

At a later time, two monks came from the Monastery of Karakallou and said to the saint, "A certain monk of ill intent, a tailor by trade, came to us and joined the coenobium. One night he forced open our safe and stole the gold that we kept for the needs of our monastery." The blessed man felt pity for these brethren and sighed within. Then he comforted them, saying, "Remain here, that we may entreat the Lord to reveal to us the whereabouts of the sacrilegious one." The following morning, after they had a small vigil and supplication, Dionysios comforted them, saying, "The Lord has seen your poverty and hath revealed the one you seek. Go to the island of Skiathos, and there you will find the thief who is not a monk. But do not expose him publicly, lest the authorities should learn of it and take the money themselves; but speak to him, in a mild manner with meekness, that you may receive it." This they did; and after they received the money, they returned to Karakallou.

Once, as the saint sat in the Monastery of Zagora conversing with the brethren, he said to certain ones, "Go outside onto the road and see to it that the man who comes does not enter the monastery. He comes to harm us!" They went out only to find such a perverse man, who indeed was coming to revile the venerable elder. They did not permit him entry, so he departed in his embarrassment. A few days later, he fell before the saint's feet seeking forgiveness. He repented of his former sins and was reformed accordingly.

At another time, Dionysios sat at Golgotha with the brethren and said to them, "Behold, two monks approach!" Then he took a piece of paper and sketched them both, as he was an expert in painting, and drew one of them with a beard, and the other figure as a young man. The next day, two monks came. The first one was a deacon named Iakovos, and he was bearded. He remained in the monastery until his repose. The younger monk, a deacon also, was called Elias. He later became the hegumen and then Bishop of Platamon.

A certain elderly widow, who was ill, called upon the saint to make her a nun before her repose. He said to her, "Do not fear death, for after thou shalt become a nun, thou shalt live an additional twelve years." Thus it happened, as the divinely inspired man predicted.

On a certain occasion, a woman's only son, who had become a monk on Olympos, went to visit his mother, and she abruptly snatched the *kalymmafchion* (tall monastic hat) from his head and cast it down. She dressed him in secular clothes, keeping him in her house. In a few days, the saint visited that village, and the woman approached him with the intent of kissing his hand to receive a blessing. But he said to her, even though he had never seen her before, "Touch me not, O wretched woman, for thou hast trodden upon the Angelic Schema, conspiring to having thy son as an aid in thine old age! But woe unto thee, for tomorrow he dies an evil death, and thou shalt receive the penalty for thy foolishness!" The next day, her son fell from a high tree and died, as the saint had prophesied.

Another elderly woman, named Aegane, from the village of Platamon, encountered the saint and said to him, "It is impossible for me to work any longer; and I pray that the Lord will give me rest." But he replied, "Do not grieve over this, as today thou shalt repose; so take these three silver coins in order to pay for the priests to bury thee." He stated this and, in a little while, the woman fell ill. Her neighbors gathered about her, and she told them about the saint and his words to her. While Aegane narrated these things, she reposed according to his prophecy.

More Struggles of Saint Dionysios

But how can I recount his wonderworkings in order, as they outnumber the sands of the sea and the stars of the heavens? To many he foretold the future, and by his prayer many barren women became fertile. He led others to their salvation with his teaching and counseling. Much as did the all-praised Apostle Paul in his sufferings, Dionysios underwent many trials on land, at sea, and in every place at the hands of the Christ-hating Hagarenes and brigands. But the Lord kept him safe and unharmed.

The Bears on the Mountain

To this day, it is recounted on Mount Olympos that, at one time, our holy Father Dionysios was on a certain errand with a donkey. He grew weary and decided to lie down and rest. He fell into a deep sleep, whereupon a bear fell upon his animal and slew it. The saint awoke to find that his donkey had been devoured by a bear. Consequently, he rebuked the bear. In his denunciation, he prohibited bears from entering upon or inhabiting that side of the mountain. Henceforth, all the bears forsook that area and migrated to the other side of the mountain, never to trespass the invisible barrier set by the saint's word. Currently, the effects of this phenomenon are still in existence; for one side of the mountain is densely populated with bears, whereas the other side is completely devoid of their presence.

Saint Dionysios' Repose

However, because he too was made of flesh and was destined to repose as a man, the day of his departure came, when the saint was sojourning at the monastery on the Mount of Demetrias with Abbot Parthenios. As the brethren read the Midnight Service, Dionysios was unable to stand on his feet. Therefore, he sat in the kitchen to rest a little, while the others chanted. At that time, it was January, and he had not procured clothes to protect himself from the cold, but wore a thin and threadbare garment. After the brethren completed the service, the priest went and shook him to rouse him, assuming that the saint was sleeping. The blessed one, though, was enraptured in a vision and, barely breathing, lay there as senseless as a rock. After a long lapse of time, he cried aloud saying, "Glory be to Thee, O Christ King, our God, glory be to Thee! I thank thee, most holy Mother of God, that thou hast hearkened unto me!" The monks inquired of him what was wrong, and he said to them, "As I sat there, my soul was separated from my body, and I began to cry aloud, 'Most holy Virgin, as thou didst hearken unto me, I beseech thee now, hear thy servant, and raise me up that I may repent of my sins!' And thus, our Lady, the Theotokos, hearkened unto me. Therefore, take me to Olympos, that I may complete the remainder of my life there and instruct the fathers on how to conduct themselves." As he left, he bade farewell to the brethren, saying, "Know this, O brothers in Christ, fathers, and children: that the time of my repose is here, for God has disclosed this unto me. Therefore, I beg of you not to neglect your souls, but to repent of your sins as long as time allows, that you may be delivered from endless torments and attain everlasting joy!" As he said this, they mourned the loss of him.

He arrived on Mount Olympos, but did not go to the coenobium; rather, he repaired to his cell on Golgotha for the sake of solitude. The hegumen and the leaders were gathered there, and he said to them, "You know that in a few days I will be separated from you; and I caution you to remember that all temporal things vanish as a dream, which is why I have forsaken everything for the love of my Master." When his spiritual children heard this, they wept, but the holy man comforted them with his sweet words. He sent them to the monastery, retaining only two of them who were still novices. After three days, he departed for the Mount of Olives, a very secluded place. There he recited the hymns from the *Thekaras* day and night, as he was studious and learned. He stayed there for a few days, having neither a straw mattress nor fire nor any bodily comfort, even though it was midwinter and it was snowing. Consequently, he fell ill, and they bade him to go to the monastery to allow them to attend to him as they should. Therefore, in order not to confound them, he consented and went to the cave where he dwelt before he built the monastery. Then the monks gathered there and asked him, "The commandments and the rule that thou hast left us, O honorable father, are difficult for the brethren in certain applications and even unacceptable." And he replied, "Retain all the things that are good and practical, and pass over those things that are oppressive. Only this one thing I ask of you: follow the *Typikon* of Mount Athos and struggle as much as possible. And may the Lord direct you in my absence!"

Next, in bidding them farewell, he admonished them, saying, "Always possess love, patience and humility, my children. Love also the stranger, silence and prayer. The fasts, which the holy apostles have passed down to us, keep without grumbling. Let none of you be disobedient or idiorrhythmic, or rather demono-rhythmic, for this is the worst of all sins. For whosoever among the coenobites has silver or more garments than anyone else, he will never attain unto the divine glory. If there should be anyone among you like this, then drive him away from the monastery as a lamb with scabs, that the remaining sheep might not become infected. Confess your thoughts often, that the demons will not make their nests in your hearts. If some of you are scandalized, let them reconcile their differences before the sun sets, as the Lord commanded. Let everyone perform the handicraft he knows as much as he is able. Whosoever is able to work and does not work, let him not eat, as the apostle has admonished [2 Thess. 3:10]. Whosoever wishes to leave the monastery, let him tell the hegumen beforehand to receive permission; or, if he leaves in secret, let the sin be upon his soul; and I will be innocent of his perdition. The younger monks should be obedient to the elders, and they in turn should advise them with both good deeds and salutary words. Be ever mindful of the sick, as one of your members. One should not have a young friend, nor should one go into the cell of another. Always have love for one another. If you live in this manner, you shall attain the kingdom of the heavens and will rejoice with the Lord Christ and all the saints. Should I find boldness before Him, I shall beseech Him on your behalf always. A good sign for you that God has accepted my travail is that the monasteries, which I had built with so many pains, labors, and toil, shall increase and multiply."

At the conclusion of this, the blessed man uttered a prayer before the Lord on their behalf and sent them to the monastery, while he remained there for a few more days, wrestling with his illness. Then, on the 23rd of January, the divinely-inspired one surrendered his holy soul into the hands of God. They buried his precious relics solemnly and reverently in the narthex of the church that the blessed one had built with his own hands. After a few years, when they exhumed the righteous man's relics, they found them emitting a sweet fragrance stronger than that of myrrh, and they have remained fragrant to this day. The sanctified bones that survive perform many miracles for those who call upon Saint Dionysios with faith, to the glory of our glorious God Who exalts those who glorify Him. Amen.

Through the intercessions of Thy Saints,
O Christ God, have mercy on us. Amen.

**On the 24th of January, the holy Church commemorates
our venerable Mother XENE the Deaconess,
of Rome, Cos, and Mylasa, and her two handmaidens.[1]**

Xene, our wonderful mother, had a novel and strange life, brief though it may have been. The narration of it is plausible and plentifully sweet and filled with compunction, bestowing upon the pious spiritual benefit. The blessed maiden's name given at Baptism was Eusebia. The Greek name "Evsevia" betokens "pious." She was the daughter of prominent and noble parents who loved God, though they were wealthy and brilliant leaders in Rome. They nurtured in the young Eusebia a love for Christian virtue. When Eusebia attained the legal age for marriage, her parents sought a worthy bridegroom, equal to their daughter's fortune and gentry. Eusebia's parents, unaware of their daughter's true desire in this matter, arranged what they

Saint Xene

considered a suitable match. The profound and sober-minded maiden, however, dedicated all her mind to the heavenly Bridegroom, Who is truly comely and immortal. Her heart, too, smitten with divine love, was solely captivated by Christ.

When the holy Eusebia heard of her parents' plan for her marriage, she thought it was absurd and a jest. She then resolved to leave home secretly, so she might preserve her virginity. The holy maiden then decided to reveal the matter to two of her trustworthy maidservants, who promised never to repeat what she was about to tell them. Eusebia then disclosed to them the

---

[1] The Life of Saint Xene (pronounced "Ksenee") was recorded in Greek. The text is extant in the Athonite monasteries of the Great Lavra, Iveron, and in other places. The text was rendered in simpler Greek by Agapios the Cretan, who published it in the *Eklogion*.

following: "I, my beloved sisters, abhor the world as perishable and soon withering. Since I only desire my Master and Savior, I have resolved to secretly flee from my parents, so I may not be coerced into marriage. Now since I love you more than all my other maidservants, I have spoken my mind to you. If you desire to follow me, and for me to have you as my sister and mother, in the future life we shall partake together of that blessed glory. Have no fear that thou mightest suffer repercussions on account of this. I give you Christ as my Witness that I shall not change my mind, though they should subject me to ten thousand deaths." The sincere maidservants hearkened to their mistress' words. They promised never to separate from Eusebia, but instead to follow her eagerly, even unto death. They said that whithersoever she might lead them, they would love and protect her.

The three pious women collectively agreed to dedicate their lives to the universal Master. From that hour they prepared for, and accustomed themselves to, an austere life of toil and perseverance, in the event that weakness or sickness visited them. Exercising steadfastness and patience, they awaited the proper moment to depart without arousing anyone's suspicion. Whatever silver and gold, as well as expensive garments, the reverent Eusebia possessed, she quietly took from her parents. Then she gave them into the hands of her maidservants, who dispensed these goods among the widows and orphans, so that she might find those ineffable good things in the age to come.

Eusebia Leaves Home and Rome

The day of Eusebia's arranged marriage was approaching, so she decided that now was the time to put their plan into action. Eusebia, for the love of the kingdom of the heavens, rejected the vanity of wealth, passing glory, and fleeting entertainments. She spurned her earthly betrothed and abandoned pleasure for the heavenly Bridegroom, the most comely among the sons of men, so that she might partake of those ineffable heavenly delights. One evening, as they wept but rejoiced, all three donned men's clothing and departed their home. Eusebia later commented, "We were crying, not on account of sorrow, but for joy, because God enlightened us to forsake this vain and empty world and to gain our salvation. As we left, we prayed, 'Lord Jesus Christ, Son of God, enlighten us and direct us toward salvation, for it is Thee that we desire with all our souls.'" As they fled, Eusebia advised her companions, saying, "Preserve yourselves exactly and do not change your minds, because no other road but that of asceticism is blessed. Indeed, first of all, we have been delivered from the sorrow of the world and cares of this life. Secondly, we live in the hope of enjoying those future good things which are true and everlasting." By these and other soul-benefitting words, Eusebia encouraged her companions.

Eusebia on the Island of Cos

When the women arrived at the seacoast, by God's good pleasure, they found a ship and left that very hour for Alexandria of Egypt.[2] Their voyage ended in just a few days, because they had favorable winds. Once in Alexandria, they boarded another ship bound for Cos (Kos), one of the Dodecanese group of Greek islands in the southeastern Aegean, situated off the end of the Bodrum Peninsula in Asia Minor. The reason why Eusebia decided to travel to a remote island like Cos is because she knew that her parents would launch an extensive investigation in every convent to find her and bring her back home. Speaking to her two companions, she reminded them, "You must conceal our identities and confide in no one about our homeland. Also, you must not address me by my baptismal name of Eusebia, but you shall call me Xene, in Greek meaning 'stranger.' By calling me this name, you do not lie; forasmuch as I am become a stranger this day. I am in exile from my homeland and my beloved parents; and I have become poor and an outsider for our Lord Who also was a stranger." When they put in at Cos, Xene, therefore, searched for a place on the twenty-five-mile length of the island, whose surface rises partly into rugged hills, though a considerable portion is fertile and well cultivated. She finally found a suitable house and rented it for herself and her companions.

In Search of a Spiritual Father

Once they settled in their new dwelling, the grace-endowed Xene desired to locate an experienced spiritual father, so that she might be under obedience and never do her own will.[3] Xene then took refuge in prayer and, bowing her knees and her heart before the Lord, supplicated the Lord with tears, saying, "My God, as Thou dost behold and govern all, do not abandon us who have abandoned our homeland and relatives because of our love for Thee. Send unto us one who is an Orthodox advocate, a protector and guide, just as Thekla found Paul.[4] Thus, we, the humble ones, may be shepherded and not stray, either knowingly or unknowingly, before Thy magnificence."

---

[2] Alexandria is situated on a strip of land between the Mediterranean and Lake Mariut, about one hundred and twenty-nine miles northwest of Cairo by rail.

[3] Saint John Klimakos (ca. 570-ca. 649), in speaking about blessed obedience, says, "Obedience is absolute renunciation of our own life, clearly expressed in our bodily actions. Conversely, obedience is the mortification of the limbs while the mind remains alive. Obedience is unquestioning movement, voluntary death, simple life, carefree danger, spontaneous defense by God, fearlessness of death, a safe voyage, a sleeper's progress. Obedience is the tomb of the will and the resurrection of humility." See *The Ladder of Divine Ascent*, translated by Lazarus Moore, Step 4:3.

[4] The Life of Saint Thekla and her meeting with the Apostle Paul are given on the day of her commemoration, the 24th of September.

The young saint's soul-saving request was quickly heard by the all-good God, in the following manner. At length, Xene observed a certain worthy and holy elderly man approaching them. His appearance bespoke a man well initiated in asceticism. His countenance was bright and reverent, and his whole aspect was truly angelic. The virgin Xene rejoiced exceedingly and, weeping, fell at his feet, saying, "For the love of Christ, O holy master, do not reject us, the foreigners, but teach us and guide us to salvation." The reverend elder then asked Xene where she was from and how she came to the island. In a whisper she told him the truth. He then responded, "I, too, am a stranger in this place, for I am coming back from Jerusalem, where I worshipped at the holy places. I am now returning home." For some reason, known only to Xene, she thought that he was a bishop, so she asked him about his homeland and his clerical rank. The elder answered, "I am from Mylasa, a city of Caria, and my name is Paul; I am the hegumen in a small monastery."[5]

When the blessed Xene heard that his name was Paul (thinking of Saints Paul and Thekla), she marvelled at how the all-good Lord hearkened to her entreaty and sent him. Therefore, she rendered fitting thanksgiving unto God. She then besought the Elder Paul to become her spiritual father and to assume responsibility for the women. The holy man replied, "Here, in this strange land, it is not possible for me to guide you. It is needful that, straightway, you accompany me to my monastery. If you will join me in Caria, I shall be able to provide you with what you will need." These words were accepted joyfully by all three women, who hastened to depart for Mylasa.

Mylasa of Asia Minor

When they arrived in Mylasa, the Elder Paul gave the women a hermitage to dwell in that was close by his monastery. It was there that the holy Xene built a church and dedicated it to the Protomartyr Stephen, who is commemorated by the holy Church on the 27th of December. In time, the hermitage became a convent where other women desired to emulate the zeal of Xene. All this time, however, no one knew Xene's identity, because the blessed Paul would say that he brought her from Cos—and that was the truth.

The Struggles of Deaconess Xene

At that time, Bishop Kyril of Mylasa reposed, and the Elder Paul was elected to the episcopacy. He recommended that Xene be ordained as deaconess, as was the custom in those years. The humble-minded Xene,

---

[5] The ancient country of Caria formed the southwest corner of Asia Minor and was bounded on the south and west by the Mediterranean Sea. The inland city of Mylasa was northeast of the island of Cos.

however, did not wish to receive the burden of this rank. Nevertheless, against her will, Bishop Paul elevated her to the office of Deaconess. It is not possible here to describe her many labors and pains after she took up that dignity. In her youth, the holy maiden was accustomed to fine foods and a sumptuous table. However now, as Deaconess Xene, her conduct of life was almost immaterial and strange. It was a life that rivaled that of the angels and yet suffered extreme hardship. Even the enemy, the devil, fearfully kept away from her and dared not approach. When the spiritual warfare was relaxed, she would eat once every three days. When she contended in warfare, she would eat dry bread once weekly. She never partook of other sources of nourishment, such as wine, oil, greens, pulse, or cooked foods. Indeed, the little biscuit which she dipped in

Saint Xene

water was mingled with her tears and the ash from the censer. Thus, the consolation of food was taken with poverty and distress, in imitation of the Prophet David who wrote: "I ate ashes like bread, and my drink I mingled with weeping [Ps. 101:10]."

As much as possible, Xene concealed her asceticism from the others to flee praise. Her two former maidservants, however, had a good idea of the labors of Xene. From their deep reverence for their spiritual mother, they tried to emulate her as much as they were able. Regardless of the amount of fasting done by Xene, she never once deviated from her rule, but labored even more during the night with prostrations and prayers. Many observed Mother Xene to be kneeling in prayer from the setting of the sun, until the striking of the semantron for Orthros.[6] At other times, she spent the entire evening weeping while she prayed. The most marvellous characteristic of this holy woman, who was perfect in all the virtues, was that she always remained humble. In fact, when she prayed there were always tears in her eyes, as

---

[6] The semantron is a wooden board struck by a mallet to a certain rhythm in order to signal the nuns to prayers. It was either suspended by a cord or carried.

though she were a murderess, harlot, or perverse person. The venerable nun was truly meek and was never seen angry or irritated with anyone. She possessed love for all and served all. She always wore worthless and wretched garments, as those that are worn by prisoners. Simply stated, the ever-memorable one was accomplished in all the virtues and contested well, until she finished this life's course and went to Him Whom she desired.

Saint Xene Bids Farewell and Reposes

It was the Feast of Saint Ephraim, not the Syrian but another struggler for Christ, a bishop who hailed from Mylasa. At that time, Bishop Paul was invited to the village of Lefkeen, where the precious relics and Church of Saint Ephraim were located. Mother Xene then gathered the sisterhood and, with utter humility, addressed them: "I thank you, my sisters and ladies, for thy great love, compassion, and ministrations, which you rendered me, a stranger. I have sincerely guided you as sisters. However, now I beseech and entreat you much more to render me even greater love by not forgetting me. When you pray, on behalf of my soul, entreat God to forgive me, your unworthy slave. Then, on account of your holy prayers, I may hope for eternal life after death. I say this to you because today I shall end my earthly sojourn. My heart is distressed and filled with indescribable fear; for, if your holy prayers do not help me, I fear that my sins shall hinder my ascent to Christ. Also, I sorrow greatly and am oppressed because our spiritual father, Paul, is not here to help me in my need. But when he comes here, tell him not to forget Xene, since he gave his word to our Lord and Master Jesus Christ to lead us on the road of salvation when he gathered us here together."

While Mother Xene spoke to her nuns, all wept inconsolably for their orphanhood. However, more than all the rest, Xene's two former maidservants wept unceasingly, which caused Xene to weep also. Then Xene said to them, "Cease your wailing, O sisters. Be zealous as the wise virgins who took oil in their vessels with their lamps [Mt. 25:4]. Prepare yourselves, for the day of the Lord shall come as a thief [Mt. 24:43; Lk. 12:39; 1 Thess. 5:2; 2 Pe. 3:10]." After saying this, Mother Xene rose up and raised her hands and eyes heavenward, and uttered this tear-filled prayer: "My God, as Thou hast governed me, the stranger, with much love till this present hour, becoming my Father and Mother and my nourishment and sweet consolation, vouchsafe me to enter into Thy heavenly kingdom. Remember, O Lord, this sisterhood and deliver them from the machinations of the devil. Especially, as Thou art good, remember my two fellow slaves who were with me in the world and in the escape; for they partook of my labors and struggles without ever departing from my word. Grant us, O Lord, to remain inseparable forever."

After uttering this prayer, the blessed one asked forgiveness from all. She then went and enclosed herself in the church, where she prostrated herself in prayer. The two maidservants then caught sight of their spiritual mother, when they peeked through a crack in the double doors. Suddenly, a light and ineffable fragrance came from on high. The scent, most sweet and delightful, could not be compared to any earthly incense. The two nuns then opened the doors and went inside, where they found the blessed Xene had fallen asleep in the Lord. They then summoned the sisterhood, and all began to weep unceasingly. Now the Lord, Who glorifies those who glorify Him, glorified His beloved bride Xene in her divine translation, so that He might reveal to all the boldness that the saint was vouchsafed. It was about the sixth hour of a cloudless day when, suddenly, brighter than the sun, there appeared in the sky a crown of stars with an even brighter star-studded cross inside. This sight was beheld by all present.

This sign was seen by Bishop Paul, who was then in Lefkeen. By divine inspiration, he uttered, "The Lady Xene has fallen asleep, and that is why this wondrous sign has appeared." Divine Liturgy had just finished, and, without taking thought to eat, all hastened to the convent of the holy woman. Bishop Paul, without stopping to rest or refresh himself, gathered a large crowd of men and women, and all glorified the Lord with a great voice. Many of the women of the city cried aloud to the bishop, "Do not conceal the pearl, O Master. Do not bury the treasure. Do not cover the praise and glory of the city. Let us instead carry this radiant lamp, to the shame of the Jews and idolaters, so they might know the power of the crucified One." The bishop then went to the relics of the holy nun and, amid many lit candles and censers, venerated them. A procession was then formed that went into the middle of the city. As the procession moved, so did the starlit crown in the sky. When the procession stopped to recite the appropriate hymns and prayers of the Church, the crown also paused. On account of this strange wonder, many from the countryside flowed in to participate in the procession, which caused general consternation because of the overcrowding.

Everyone chanted and remained all night for the vigil. All sick folk, who with faith touched the sanctified relics of the deaconess, were healed. These included those who had been ill for many years. O the wonder! It was through the relics of our holy Mother Xene—not by means of herbs, money, or days of treatment—that all received healing within that hour. When the procession reached the southern section of the city called Sikinion, the righteous Xene was interred in a place that she had previously arranged. The crown of stars then descended and rested upon the holy relics. All believed that this meant that the holy Xene had followed her earthly temple, until it was buried. From the sheets that had been draped on her bier, the bishop reverently distributed swatches among the faithful as a spiritual boon for the soul.

Saint Xene's Two Companions

Not much time elapsed before the two former maidservants of Saint Xene reposed one at a time. In accordance with their mistress' command, they too were buried with her. Before the first maidservant reposed, she never divulged the identity of her mistress Eusebia. However, when she fell asleep in the Lord, the remaining maidservant was pressured into revealing everything. Since the two maidservants had promised Eusebia, under oath, never to reveal their mistress' true identity, it was Bishop Paul's rebuke and admonition that prodded her to speak and reveal all to the glory of God. Not wishing to be under a penance, she related every detail of the entire matter. She said that Xene was from the glorious city of Rome, that she was the daughter of a distinguished ruler, and that her baptismal name was Eusebia. In order to avoid marriage, for love of the Savior, the wise virgin left home and assumed the name Xene, meaning "stranger." She then lived and endured voluntary exile, poverty, and hardship. All that heard this account were astonished; and this served to enhance the veneration of blessed Xene.

Shortly thereafter, the ever-memorable and praiseworthy Bishop Paul went to the Lord. He was a good and God-pleasing shepherd of the rational sheep of Christ. His relics, too, wrought miracles. Thus, we close our account of the strange and praiseworthy life of the holy Xene.

Final Remarks

The Greek hagiographer of Saint Xene's life, who identifies himself solely as a priest-monk, then closes with a few words of instruction. He invites all brides of Christ to endure hardship in this life, by calling to remembrance the Passion of Christ and by remembering their own sinfulness. He also advises that, whenever men come to the convent, only the abbess and the doorkeeper should receive them. He warns that the younger nuns should never leave their cells to engage in conversations with the opposite sex, nor should any nun have a lengthy conversation even with the priest that serves the convent. Neither is any man or cleric, even if married, to enter the cell of a nun. He closes his narrative by exhorting all brides of Christ to preserve themselves blameless and to endure temporal privations; for if we sow in tears, we shall reap everlasting delights, rejoicing and co-ruling with the heavenly Bridegroom.

**On the 24ᵗʰ of January, the holy Church commemorates
the holy Martyrs PAUL, PAFSIRIOS, and THEODOTION.**

Paul, Pafsirios, and Theodotion, the holy martyrs, were brothers of the same parents, who lived at the time of Emperors Diocletian and Maximian (290), and when Areianos was governor in Egypt's Cleopatrid, known today as the Suez. Paul and Pafsirios became monastics in their youth, while

Theodotion abided in the mountains with thieves. The two brothers were seized by the governor, when Paul was thirty and Pafsirios twenty-five; and both confessed the Faith of Christ fearlessly. When their brother Theodotion learned of their capture, he left the mountains and the thieves, and went to bid them farewell. But seeing that they were being tried by the governor, he dared not draw nigh; rather, he withdrew to the side, pondering within himself what type of inheritance and glory would be bestowed upon his brothers. At that point, his heart was warmed by divine grace. He returned and stood before the governor, confessing that he too was a Christian. Then Theodotion lunged at him, picking him off his throne and dashing him to the pavement. Immediately thereupon, the men of the tribunal pierced Theodotion with glowing hot iron spikes in his sides and stomach, and later beheaded him; thus he received the laurel wreath of martyrdom. As for Paul and Pafsirios, they were cast into the river and completed their martyrdom in this manner.

On the 24th of January, the holy Church commemorates
the holy Hieromartyr BABYLAS of Sicily,
together with his disciples, the Martyrs AGAPIOS and TIMOTHY.

Babylas, our holy father amongst the saints, was of Near Eastern origin, born of noble and pious parents, in the famous city of Theopolis.[7] Babylas was trained and educated in the ways of God. He was instructed in the divine letters, which bring a man closer to God. After the repose of his parents, he distributed his wealth among the poor, widows, and orphans, thus disposing of his cares and burdens. The heavenly-minded one ascended a mountain, where he practised solitude in the company of his two disciples, Agapios and Timothy. He was also ordained a priest. Later, he departed from thence and sailed to Rome. But because wicked Greeks there attempted to deliver him up to the authorities, he departed from Rome and fled to Sicily with his two disciples. He dwelt there for a long time, converting many pagans to the knowledge of God by the grace of the Holy Spirit Who dwelt within him.

According to the words of the holy Gospel, "A city situated on the top of a mountain cannot be hid [Mt. 5:14]." For this reason, the blessed Babylas was unable to hide from the governor of Sicily. When the latter saw that he confessed Christ with boldness, he seized him, together with Agapios and Timothy. He subjected them to such a severe beating that their entire bodies turned red. The governor then ordered the soldiers to parade the martyrs around the city and simultaneously subject them to various harsh tortures. The

---

[7] Antioch was destroyed many times by earthquakes, and was rebuilt each time. During its reconstruction, at the time of Justinian, it was renamed Theopolis by him.

tyrant's purpose was twofold: to frighten the natives of Sicily and to satisfy the anger and malice which he harbored toward the saints. The holy martyrs drew strength from these inhuman excesses, setting their hopes and expectations on the everlasting rewards. The following day, he put the righteous ones to death by the sword. He then cast their holy bodies into a furnace. The fire, however, did not inflict any harm on the relics, and they remained safe and unscathed. Not long afterwards, certain Christians buried the saints with honor on that same island of Sicily.

On the 24th of January, the holy Church commemorates our venerable Father MAKEDONIOS.[8]

Makedonios, our holy father among the saints, roamed the mountains, and therefore the mountaintops became his home and the arena of his struggles. He dwelt in many areas, for he traveled from one place to another, that is, Phoenicia, Syria, and Cilicia. He wandered about in order to avoid the hindrance caused to him by those who visited him. The blessed one spent forty-five years without shelter over his head: that is, neither a hut or tent; but he stayed in a deep pit, for which cause he was called "Gouvas," which in the Syriac means "pit."

When he reached old age, he was convinced by his disciples to build a hut. He also used as a shelter certain cells which were not his own but those of others. He persevered in that state for twenty-five years, making the total number of his years seventy. He was known to have been a hermit on Mount Silpius near Antioch. Now on account of his diet consisting only of barley and water for over forty years, the Barley-eater, as he was called, turned ill and lived henceforth by partaking of a small piece of bread and little water daily. The biographer of this saint's life said that it was his very own mother who supplied Abba Makedonios with this ground barley for a long time. When he had experienced this weakness from his long-standing and unaltered diet, he thought it wise to yield somewhat to the infirmity of the flesh—not for the sake of luxury but out of need. "For the thought had occurred to me," he said, "that should I die, I would have to answer for my death before the

---

[8] The Life of Saint Makedonios was recorded by Theodoretos of Kyros (Cyrrhus), in Number Thirteen of his *Religious History*. See also *A History of the Monks of Syria*, Cistercian Studies Series: Number Ninety-Eight, pp. 100-109.

Among his other deeds, Saint Makedonios made it possible by his prayer for Theodoretos of Kyros to be born. His mother had been barren up to that time. When she gave birth (393), she named her son Theodoretos, meaning "Gift of God." She was in danger of suffering a miscarriage; and, when she was in labor with him, our saint gave her water to drink which he blessed, and she was preserved safe thereafter.

righteous Judge, as one having taken flight from the contest and having run away from the labors and contests of servitude." He therefore asked for some bread, though he would have preferred death by hunger to continuing in this life of toil.

When Flavian was Bishop of Antioch (ca. 384-404), he had heard of the pure and humble character of Abba Makedonios. The bishop feigned that a charge had been lodged against Abba Makedonios which required his descent from the mountain and attendance in church. While Makedonios was attending the divine Liturgy, Flavian led Makedonios to the sanctuary and enrolled him in the priesthood. Now the innocent abba was unaware that he had been ordained to the priesthood, until someone notified him after the divine office had taken place. The elder was grieved and remonstrated with those present, including the bishop, for he supposed that the ordination would likely deprive him of the solitude he so loved on the mountain. When the bishop invited him to attend another feast day for the Lord, the saint declined, fearing that he might be ordained again. Though he was assured that no one could receive the same ordination twice, still he would not attend. "I know," comments Theodoretos, "that some will not think this account so very admirable of the great old man, but I have recorded it as proof of his simplicity of thought and purity of soul."

Another time, one of the emperor's generals went hunting upon the mountain where Makedonios dwelt. He spotted the righteous one from a distance, but did not know him. The men in the general's hunting party told him about Abba Makedonios. The general then dismounted his steed and greeted the holy elder. After the general courteously inquired what he was doing there on the mountains, the saint replied with a question: "Why didst thou ascend this mountain?" The general answered frankly, "I came to hunt." The saint remarked, "I am also in pursuit, that is, of my God. I desire to find Him and have no intention of giving up this good chase." The general, hearing this pithy answer, marvelled; and acquiring benefit therefrom, he departed.

On another occasion, this saint rebuked the soldiers of Emperor Theodosios the Great (379-395), who were sent to punish those who had torn down the statue of his wife in Antioch. This was the notorious riot against the statues, the result of the populace's revolt against high taxes, which took place in 387 and had occasioned the famous homilies of Saint John Chrysostom on these very statues of the imperial couple. Makedonios left the mountain and confronted two generals in the marketplace. When they learned who he was, they dismounted their steeds and kissed his hands and knees. He bade them to carry a message to the emperor: "As a human being, he should not take vengeance because of the destruction of statues, by putting to death his fellow man who is in the image of God, since it is easy to restore inanimate images, but not possible to return slain bodies to life. And why should I say bodies? It is not possible to create a single strand of hair." He said this fearlessly in the Syrian tongue, and the generals reported the translated message to the emperor in Greek. The Antiochenes had been in terror that the emperor would lay waste to their city. At length, Theodosios granted amnesty to the Antiochenes, after the effective intercessions of Bishop Flavian, Saint John Chrysostom, and the monks.

Living with such remarkable abstinence, Makedonios was vouchsafed by God to perform miracles, such as to drive out demons out of people, to cure various ailments and diseases, and to work other paradoxical signs. On one such occasion, there was brought to the saint a nobleman's wife who, by demonic complicity, ate without ever being satisfied. She devoured thirty domestic hens daily and was still not satiated. Her relatives begged Makedonios to take pity on her and cure her of such voracious gluttony, from which she had not only spent her entire property trying to assuage her appetite, but also by which she was killing herself. Our saint took pity on her plight and prayed to God. Then he put his right hand in water, making the sign of the Cross, and advised the suffering woman to drink. Subsequently, the excess of her appetite was miraculously blunted, so that she consumed a normal amount of food, eating only half a chicken per day.

On another occasion, a girl became possessed by a demon, when she unwittingly fell under a magic spell, for which love was the cause of the enchantment. The father of the girl went before the provincial administrator (*comes*) and brought a charge against the man who laid the spell. The defendant went before the court and pleaded innocence, claiming he had been falsely accused. The father had no other witness, except the demon who served in the magic charm. He begged the judge therefore to call Father Makedonios to the courtroom. This was done, as the judge took a seat as a spectator and allowed the great Makedonios to act as judge and use the power within him to compel the demon to confess to the deed. The demon, under great duress, pointed out the man who cast the spell and the maidservant who dispensed the potion. As the demon confessed to this crime, together with arson, destruction of property, and assault, the man of God commanded him to exit the damsel and their city. The damsel was then restored. As for the man who had been accused by the demon, Abba Makedonios interceded for him before the judge, saying, "It is not right to inflict the death penalty on the evidence provided by the demon. It is better that the defendant be urged to repent." Therefore, the judge upheld the abba's judgment in this case.

The saint also cured a noblewoman who had lost her wits. She could no longer recognize her environment or family. She abstained from all food and drink. The husband, not finding help from the physicians, invited the saint into his home. Father Makedonios blessed cold water and ordered the sufferer to partake of it, despite the indignation and protests of the physicians. The husband sent all the physicians out of his house and gave his wife the blessed water. She immediately came to her senses and recognized the man of God. She implored him to bless her by placing his hands on her eyes and mouth, which he did. She then continued healthy and in her right mind.

On yet another occasion, a shepherd was searching for his lost lamb. When the shepherd came upon Abba Makedonios in his retreat, it was midnight, and thick snow was falling and covering the ground. The shepherd then observed how the abba lit a great fire by him. He then saw that two men, clad in white, were supplying wood for the fire. The shepherd then immediately found his little lost lamb after seeing the holy abba. The shepherd then departed, glorifying God and His saint.

The saint was also endowed by God with the gift of prophecy. The famous cavalry commander Lupicinus had been waiting fifty days for provisions to arrive from Constantinople. Since no word had been received, the commander was filled with anxiety. The saint, with the gift of clairvoyance working in him, said, "One ship, my commander, is lost, but the other vessel shall reach the harbor of Seleukeia tomorrow." Thus it came to pass, as the holy man foretold.

It is not possible to recount here all the marvels of the venerable elder, but the labors by which he drew divine energy have been sufficiently shown in these few accounts. He served God beyond nature for seventy years and was translated to Him. Officials, together with the nobility, citizens, and foreigners, came to pay their last respects at his funeral. Those holding high offices bore his sacred bier on their shoulders. His relics were conveyed to the shrine of the martyrs and interred with the holy Aphrahat and Theodosios.[9] The fame of Saint Makedonios abides inextinguishable, and no passage of time shall erase it.

On the 24th of January, the holy Church commemorates the translation of the relics of the venerable Martyr ANASTASIOS the Persian.

Anastasios, the glorious venerable martyr, suffered martyrdom during the reign of Emperor Herakleios (610-641). The full eyewitness account of Saint Anastasios' martyrdom, repose, and interment in the Monastery of Saint Sergios is given on the date of his commemoration, the 22nd of January. The

---

[9] Saints Aphrahat and Theodosios, venerable fathers and ascetics, are commemorated by the holy Church, respectively, on the 29th of January and the 5th of February.

translation of the saint's relics by a monk of his monastery, with the help of Roman troops, is also recorded therein. In the twentieth year of Herakleios' reign, a bishop was dispatched by the pope of Rome, and he brought the relics of Saint Anastasios to Caesarea of Palestine, leaving there a small remnant and keeping the rest. The holy skull of the martyr, together with his sacred icon, was deposited in a reliquary in Old Rome.[10]

---

[10] At the Roman Catholic monastery Tre Fontane in Rome, this ancient and wonder-working icon of Saint Anastasios, together with his sacred relics, was conveyed to Rome. The icon subsequently has been repainted in a western style by the Latins, which rendition bears the following inscription: "An icon of the holy Anastasius, monk and martyr, the appearance of which drives out demons and bestows healings to the ailing, as the Acts of the Second Council of Nicaea (Seventh Œcumenical Synod) bear witness." In the minutes of the Seventh Synod, held in 787, there is furnished therein, at the Fourth Session, among the proofs introduced into evidence to uphold the veneration of the icons, an extract from the narration of the martyrdom of Saint Anastasios and the miracles wrought through his icon:

"As the relics of the holy Monk Anastasios, who suffered martyrdom, were brought from Persia to Palestine, the entire populace went forth to meet them. A certain woman, named Areta, succumbed to doubt and said, 'I will not venerate the relics brought from Persia!' In a few days' time, the holy martyr appeared to her in a dream and asked, 'Art thou suffering from an illness in the hips?' She suddenly sensed that she was suffering from some ailment. She thereupon was afflicted for a long time with this malady. When she had some temporary relief from the pain, she pondered on what caused her to suddenly fall ill. After four days of reflecting upon her sufferings, on the fifth day, at dawn, the Martyr Anastasios appeared to her and said, 'Go to Tetraphilos. Pray to Saint Anastasios, and thou shalt be restored to health.' (During the 7th C. in Constantinople, at Tetraphilos, there was a church dedicated to Saint Anastasios with his relics and icon.) Areta went to the designated place and beheld the icon of the martyr, before whom she exclaimed, 'This is truly the one whom I beheld in my dream!' She then lay back on her cot and wept contritely for a long time. When she rose up, she found she had been miraculously restored to perfect health."

After the reading of this account in the synod meeting, Pope Adrian I of Rome (772-795), Peter, protopresbyter of the basilica dedicated to the Apostle Peter in Rome, and Peter, the abbot of the Monastery of Saint Savvas the Sanctified in Rome, declared that the very icon of the saint, together with his precious skull, was in one of their monasteries in Rome. Bishop John of Taormina added that he knew of a Sicilian woman, possessed by an unclean spirit, who walked to Rome in order to venerate the icon of Saint Anastasios. She too received miraculous healing from her affliction. "The Translation of the Precious Relics of the Holy Martyr Anastasius the Persian," *Orthodox Life*, Volume 35, Number 1, January-February 1985, p. 5.

**On the 24th of January, the holy Church commemorates
the holy Martyrs HERMOGENES and MAMAS.[11]**

**On the 24th of January, the holy Church commemorates
our venerable Father PHYLON, Bishop of Kalpasios,
who reposed in peace.**

Phylon or Philon, our holy father, was of unknown parentage and homeland. In the Life of Saint Epiphanios of Cyprus, who is commemorated by the holy Church on the 12th of May, it is mentioned that Phylon was a deacon. The sister[12] of Emperors Arkadios in the east (395-408) and Honorius in the west (393-423) had fallen ill. She heard that God healed those suffering from infirmity by means of Saint Epiphanios. She therefore dispatched to Cyprus this holy Phylon. When Phylon arrived, Saint Epiphanios, inspired by divine revelation, consecrated Phylon to the episcopacy, as Bishop of Karpasio or Kalpasio. This took place in 401. The holy Epiphanios also left Constantia in the competent hands of Bishop Phylon while he departed for an extended sojourn in Rome. Saint Phylon, according to the late tenth-century Greek lexicon *Souda*, also bequeathed to the Church his commentaries on the Pentateuch and the Song of Songs.

**On the 24th of January, the holy Church commemorates
our venerable Father PHILIPPIKOS
the Presbyter who reposed in peace.[13]**

**On the 24th of January, the holy Church commemorates
the holy Martyr BARSIMAS,
together with his TWO BROTHERS
who were slain by the sword.[14]**

---

[11] In some *Menaia*, the name Menas is given rather than Mamas.

[12] The first marriage of Theodosios I with the holy Aelia Flaccilla produced Pulcheria (d. ca. 385), Arkadios, and Honorius. Afterward, the widower Theodosios married Galla and had one daughter, Galla Placidia (b. 388), augusta (421-450) of the Western Roman Empire.

[13] In some *Menaia*, the name Philip is given rather than Philippikos.

[14] *The Great Synaxaristes* (in Greek) mentions that the *Synaxarion* of the *Menaia* places, after these three brothers, the holy Martyr Elladios, slain by the sword, who suffered with Saint Theodoule of Anazarbos, who is commemorated by the holy Church on the 18th of January.

**On the 24th of January, the holy Church commemorates
the venerable ZOSIMAS, who reposed in peace.**

Zosimas, our holy father, is not to be confused with the abba of the same name mentioned in the Life of Saint Mary of Egypt, who is commemorated by the holy Church on the 4th of April. Abba Zosimas whom we commemorate today was from Side, near Tyre in Phoenicia. He settled near Caesarea after spending time in the Lavra of Saint Gerasimos in the Jordan Plain. The historian Evagrius[15] records that while Abba Zosimas was at Caesarea, he had clairvoyant knowledge of the great earthquake at Antioch at the time of its occurrence in 528, some four hundred miles distant.

Evagrius also gives an account of how Abba Zosimas was traveling with a donkey laden with his possessions. A lion came and devoured the donkey. When the lion had finished his meal, Abba Zosimas complained to the lion that he had not strength to bear the donkey's burden. The lion obediently let the holy man load the burden onto his back. The beast then conveyed the burden to the gates of Caesarea.

Abba Dorotheos is responsible for the surviving collection of sayings of Abba Zozimas.[16] On one occasion, while discoursing on the Logos of God, Abba Zosimas said: "In taking flesh, the Logos has acquired such grace for those who believe in Him that, through the desire of our will and the grace energizing, it is possible, for those who so desire it, to consider the whole world as nought." Abba Zosimas then collected some straw, old clothes, and other bits and pieces, and remarked, "Would not one who contended, argued, bore resentment, or anguished over such things be deemed to have gone mad? In like manner the man of God ought not to make any ado about the whole world. In my humble opinion, it is not the having a thing which brings us harm, but being attached to it. Who does not know that the body is the most precious of all our possessions? How then are we bidden, when occasion demands, to despise it? And if the body itself, so much more those things that are external to us."[17] On yet another occasion, he spoke of the passion of anger. He counseled that we ought not to become distressed with those who treat us with contempt or mock us. We need to deem such persons as our benefactors and physicians. They have been sent by Christ for our benefit both in this life and the next. He said, "The beginning of victory over anger

---

[15] Evagr. *H.E.* IV.7.

[16] Abba Dorotheos' collection of the sayings of Abba Zosimas was published incomplete in *P.G.* 78:1680-1701. The only complete edition is that published at Jerusalem by the Monk Avgustinos (1913). Cited in Chitty's *The Desert a City*, p. 140.

[17] *P.G.* 78:1681AB.

is first not to make a retort when slighted." He also exhorted that the monk should examine and condemn himself.

On the 24ᵗʰ of January, the holy Church commemorates the holy Prophet, Forerunner, and Baptist JOHN, nearby the Taurus.

On the 24ᵗʰ of January, the holy Church commemorates our venerable Father NEOPHYTOS of Cyprus, the Enclosed or Recluse.[18]

Neophytos, our venerable father, was born in the year 1134 of pious parents named Athanasios and Evdoxia. He hailed from Lefkara, Cyprus, and lived at the time of the renowned dynasty of the Komnenoi. When the Saracens were permitted to take Jerusalem (for reasons known only to God), Cyprus also was subjected to numerous incursions by the Crusaders who were attempting to liberate the holy places.[19] They had converged from all parts of

---

[18] This biography was taken from John Hatzi-Iouannou's publication entitled *Interpretation to the Psalms, Part II, Hieromonk Neophytos, Recluse* (Athens, 1935); inserted therein are also two services to the saint. This text was revised and rendered into vernacular Greek. The aforementioned services are chanted in Cyprus: one is used on the 24ᵗʰ of January, celebrating his memory; and the other is used on the 28ᵗʰ of September, in commemoration of the translation of his relics.

[19] From the close of 1096 onwards, the great feudal lords of Europe and their followers gradually assembled, and Constantinople received the following knights, including: "Godfrey of Bouillon, the Duke of Lorraine, Count Raymond of Toulouse, Hugh of Vermandois, the brother of the French king, Robert of Normandy, the brother of the English king, and the son of William the Conqueror, Robert, the son of Count Robert of Flanders, and not least, the Norman prince, Bohemund, the son of Robert Guiscard. Although the undertaking upset his plans and was a positive menace to the Byzantine Empire, the emperor tried to make it serve his own interests, and those of his state as he could, by demanding that the Crusaders should take an oath of allegiance to him and pledge themselves to restore to him all captured towns which had formerly belonged to the Byzantine Empire. For his part, the emperor promised to supply the Crusaders with victuals and materials of war, and held out the prospect of taking the Cross himself and joining the crusading army as its leader with all his forces. With the exception of Raymond of Toulouse, all the Crusaders finally accepted the emperor's demands—even Godfrey of Bouillon gave in after lengthy negotiations. On this basis, agreements were made early in 1097 with individual leaders, including Bohemund, who not only gave his full consent at once, but tried to win over Raymond of Toulouse, and agreed to the emperor' terms, and offered his own services for the post of the *imperial domesticus* (an important functionary and bureau chief) of the

(continued...)

Europe, being motivated by the zeal of the kings of that continent. Saint Neophytos was eighteen years old at the time.

Saint Neophytos

His parents wished to have him marry. But when they made the customary preparations for the marriage, the blessed one learned of this, and secretly departed from his father's house. He came upon the holy monastery honored by the name of the divine John Chrysostom, also known as Koutsovendis (the mountain on which it was situated), and hid himself there. He forsook both his parents and the betrothal, and all vain worldly pleasures, albeit he never reflected upon them anyway, but cared only for the love of the Lord. Indeed, from childhood, he yearned for tranquility and desired the eremitical life, as is apparent from the annals of his monastery and from those who struggled there through the ages, to whom his godly mode of life was a living standard and example.

The holy Neophytos struggled devoutly in the monastery. After his withdrawal, his parents were left in inconsolable grief, being ignorant of the way of life he chose to pursue. They combed the entire island to locate him. Finally, they came upon the monastery wherein the blessed one was concealed and discovered him. Notwithstanding, he would by no means agree to follow them. They refused to leave and persisted in wailing and lamentation for days on end, until Neophytos was compelled to relent. Therefore, he returned to his home with them, inasmuch as it was impossible to do otherwise. As a result, he was enjoined by his parents to enter into marriage. He yielded to them, being constrained to fulfill the Gospel command. This was the cause of immense joy for his parents, kinsfolk, and friends alike. At the end of the reception, the relatives returned to their homes, as Neophytos remained alone

---

[19](...continued)
east." Ostrogorsky, *History of the Byzantine State*, p. 322.

with his bride in the bridal chamber. Suddenly, he took his wedding ring off. Then, after making a fitting prayer, he went out of his house and into the night. He took flight and repaired again to the Monastery of Koutsovendis.

On arriving there, he sought out the hegumen and begged him with tears to put the holy Schema of the monks upon him without delay. Therefore, they tonsured the righteous one and garbed him with the Angelic Schema. Then they sent him off to the hegumen of a certain skete called Stoupes, where he tended the vineyards. In this service, he remained for five years. During this interval, he never ceased to pray and meditate day and night. Furthermore, he was previously unlettered, yet there he learned to read expertly and could recite the Psalms of David by heart.

The holy one struggled in this fashion at the monastery, but in his heart burned the desire to cross over and worship in the holy land, at the most sacred and venerable sites made holy by the presence of our Savior. As a result, he embarked upon a ship sailing toward Jerusalem; and accordingly, he attained his desire and reached all those places and made his prayers. He then proceeded northward to the mountains of Magdala, Tabor, and Jordan. During his six-year stay, he sought out every cave and crevice, in order to find one to whom he could be in obedience, and practise asceticism. However, his wish was never fulfilled. Then, by divine motivation, he gave up this idea and returned to the aforementioned Monastery of Koutsovendis. Yet, he could not satisfy his love of silence there.

Thereupon, he left the monastery again and proceeded on to Mount Latros in Asia Minor, on the chance that God might grant that for which he had hoped. Now when Neophytos reached the fortress at the harbor of Paphos, the guards thought he was a fugitive. They arrested him and cast him, bound, into prison, for a sufficient length of time for him to be in dire straits. Certain pious people learned of this, took pity on him, and besought the island's rulers to release him from prison. As a consequence, the saint recognized that whatever intentions he had of going to another place, they were not propitious, and he suffered evil; so he set aside the undertaking altogether, perceiving that it was not God's will for him to remove himself from the beggarly condition of his country. The author of this present life concurs with this, saying that he believed that Cyprus "was bereft of virtuous men who led a devout mode of life, because it was then under the yoke of western overlords."

After he was released from prison, the holy one was in deep sorrow and doubt. He kept pondering upon which direction he should turn to fulfill his desire for solitude. As he meditated on this, he made the sign of the Cross and took a road at random in the name of the Lord. Finally, he reached the precipice which he later named Enkleistra (Enclosure), and ascended to the top. At that time, according to the saint's own record, it was the 24th day of June, in the year 1159. It was the celebration of the Feast of the Nativity of Saint John the Baptist. In the midst of that precipice, he found a cave, and began clearing it and leveling it out, at times with his own hands or with stakes. The location was extremely rugged and impassable, and it took him the better part of a year to make the cave suitable for habitation.

One may assume that Neophytos underwent considerable suffering and endured many hardships of the flesh. In that remote and confined spot he necessarily underwent exposure to the elements, hunger, privation, and all manner of physical strain. One must also consider his prayers, prostrations, vigils, and all-night standing for the love of Christ, as well as every austerity and restraint to which he subjected himself. Hence, owing to this, his fame spread everywhere, and many flocked to him for his prayer and blessing. Some even came to him with the purpose of becoming his disciples and to participate in his ascetical labors. At first, he did not accept them, not because he avoided human association and was indifferent to the salvation of others, but because he knew too well that one is more serene than two and much more silent.

Those who loved the righteous one came nearly every day and besought him fervently, thus affording him no rest whatsoever. Therefore, he consented to accept a few disciples (but not too many), about fifteen to eighteen. Thereafter, he instructed them in the acts of virtue. Due to this, the repute of his accomplishments increased, albeit the holy one avoided the esteem of men. Nevertheless, the all-merciful God does not only bestow upon His servants the glory of heaven, but also the present glory. Now hearken to the manner of it. In a divine vision, He commanded Basil, the hierarch of the city of Paphos, to elevate the saint to the rank of priest, as Neophytos was most worthy, and also commanded that they erect a monastery. Therefore, the hierarch bestowed upon Neophytos all the requirements necessary with a letter of authorization, doing everything precisely as he was ordered, ordaining the blessed one to the priesthood in 1170. The saint was then forty-six years of age.

After he had received the priestly rank, who can describe the efforts he exerted? Who can reckon the prayers, abstinence, and vigils which the blessed one performed? Near the cave, he constructed a monastery of uncommon beauty, naming it Enkleistra; and in his cave he inured himself to hardships for twenty-four years. Enkleistra was finally completed in 1183.[20]

---

[20] The church and the other buildings presently standing, even though they have been eroded with the passage of time and abnormal circumstances, appear to have been erected after the saint's repose. The construction funds were provided by the emperors and by various donations, as a patriarchal document which survives to this day, attests.

The saint instructed those who were with him to call themselves the Enkleistoi (the recluses or the enclosed ones)—not only in word but also in deed—having his life as an example. He established the brotherhood, often instructing them (as they were beginners) in all those things necessary for their salvation, and guiding them to the realization and fulfillment of virtue.

Saint Neophytos observed that the growing numbers of the faithful and those who desired to attend to his teaching were depriving him of his cherished solitude. Therefore, after a forty-year stay in the Enkleistra, he decided to found a new refuge beyond the Cave of the Holy Cross. This occurred in the year 1199. While he was engaged in excavating a small opening in the rock, which stood in the way of that impassable ravine, a great boulder was dislodged by demonic activity. As it fell, it carried Neophytos to the edge of the precipice. Nevertheless, divine grace intervened and rescued him, to the chagrin of the demon; for the boulder did not crush him, but the rock caught the saint's garment and hand, thereby preventing him from going over the edge. In this place also, the holy one converted the cave into a house of prayer and doxology to God. Therein, he accustomed himself to living in total silence, avoiding all noise, and struggling in fasts and hardships. Only on Sundays did Neophytos descend to the Enkleistra by a ladder which was brought to him. He would continue to counsel his disciples, leading them to virtue; and again ascended to the upper chamber of the cavern.

The holy one led this type of ascetical life for fifty years. He had been trained for five years in the study of the divine Scriptures and achieved the highest degree of virtue. However, he did not limit himself to the austere life, but also wrote many works for the edification of his students and for every Christian who wished to save his soul. The number of his works, as attested in the twelfth chapter of his *Typikas Diataxeis* (*Order of the Typikon*) are sixteen, of which the three major ones are: a panegyric; interpretations on the Psalms, the Song of Songs, the Hexaemeron, and other homilies and letters; and the *Typikas Diataxeis*. These texts are not the work of human wisdom, but are filled with the grace of the Holy Spirit, as is evident upon their reading.[21] Some survive in his monastery to this day, while others have been lost through the ravages of time.

---

[21] In the 12th C., Saint Neophytos was one of the first writers in the Orthodox Church who exposed the heresies of the Western Church. Prior to the 14th C. (which saw the official condemnation of the innovations of the Latins), there were no other Orthodox theologians who spoke out against these erroneous teachings except Saint Photios (9th C.), Patriarch Michael Keroularios (11th C.), Patriarch Gregory II (13th C.) and Emperor Theodore Laskaris (13th C.).

The saint struggled in this way for a long period, thus becoming a vessel of the Holy Spirit. He foreknew his translation to the Lord, which he did not hide from his disciples; instead, he summoned them. In his parting words, he advised them on the ascetic life and how to conduct themselves after his repose. He enjoined them to safeguard carefully all those things that he taught and urged, both by word and in writing. He also ordered that, after the funeral service, they bury him in the inner part of the cave, which he himself had excavated. He also stipulated that they enshroud him in the burial garments which he had sewn with his own hands. Then he exhorted them that they live in peace and harmony, and in a God-pleasing manner with brotherly love. He urged them to obey the abbot whom they would select for the monastery. He admonished them not to violate any of the ordinances he had written in his *Typikas Diatexeis*. After he uttered these things, he prayed for them and gave up his blessed soul into the hands of God.

Upon the repose of the saint, how can one adequately describe the lamentation and mourning by his followers and spiritual children, who had known his extraordinary life? It is impossible for us to explain fully. They performed everything as the holy one directed; interring his holy relics with the customary benedictions and prayers in the prepared tomb. Moreover, for many days they conducted all-night vigils in his honor. By Saint Neophytos' intercessions and entreaties, may we all be saved in our Lord Jesus Christ, to Whom is due all glory, praise and magnification unto the ages. Amen.[22]

---

[22] The Stavropegial Monastery of Saint Neophytos, with its three-aisled church and the famous holy cave of the Enkleistra, is situated in the Paphos district in the western part of Cyprus. About six miles from Paphos, following the road of the villages Mesoyi-Tremythous, the visitor arrives at this magnificent monastery, one thousand three hundred sixty feet above sea level. It lies in a scenic valley covered with green carob trees, olive trees, lofty pine trees, cypress trees, canes, and thyme. A high hill called Melissovounos stands by, silently mysterious, sheltering the monastery from winds and thunderstorms. The beauty of the scenery here is unique. One can see far away the Paphian Sea, vivid, restless, and shining like a sapphire.

The place where Saint Neophytos lived, taught, and died has been known as the "Enkleistra," from his times to the present. The visitor, passing up a rocky staircase, finds the narthex of the Church of the Holy Cross and a small courtyard with the entrance to the saint's grave and the Church of the Forerunner. The Enkleistra, with its exceptional Byzantine frescoes, depicting scenes from Jesus' life and the holy Bible, is a true gallery. The decoration with wall-paintings was executed in 1185 by Theodore Apseudes, the hagiographer, according to an inscription on the wall behind the saint's desk. On the western part of the ceiling, Saint Neophytos is depicted between the two archangels, Michael and Gabriel, whose wings are open. They are escorting him, holding him by the shoulders, up to Christ on the day of Judgment. On

(continued...)

Through the intercessions of Thy Saints,
O Christ God, have mercy on us. Amen.

[22](...continued)
the upper part of this wall-painting, there is the following inscription: "O holy twain, I fervently pray that this image shall be made reality." In another fresco, our Savior is depicted seated on a throne, holding a Gospel decorated with precious stones. The Virgin stands to His right and the Forerunner to His left entreating and gazing at Him. At the right foot of Jesus, Saint Neophytos is portrayed wearing a dark chiton, kneeling, turning toward Jesus. A tablet in front of him carries the following inscription: "Through the prayers of Thy Mother and Thy Baptist who stand reverently by Thy holy throne, be Thou merciful, O Christ, now and forevermore, to him that lies a suppliant at Thy divine foot."

Saint Neophytos

In the 16th C., the magnificent church in the monastery was built, owing to an anonymous royal donation. Its frescoes were executed by Cypriot hagiographers skilled in Byzantine art. The most important treasure in the large church is the sacred relics of Saint Neophytos. They are enshrined in a wooden sarcophagus. A silver case octagonal in shape holds his skull. It has a pyramid-shaped cover, and on it are depicted Saints Anthony, Neophytos, Savvas, and Efthymios. On the other side are the Virgin Mary, together with Saint Theodosios and Saints Constantine and Helen. The sacred skull can easily be seen by the visitors. The icon of the saint is to be found on the lower rank of the wood-carved iconostasion of the 16th C. The saint is represented as in the frescos of the Enkleistra. He has an oval face with a white beard. He is austere and impressive. In his right hand, he holds a silver cross leaning on his shoulder; while in his left hand, he holds a scroll. The icon was painted in 1806 by the Cretan hagiographer John Cornaros. See Charalambos G. Christodoulides, *Saint Neophytos Monastery*, pp. 4, 9, 20-22, 36.

**On the 25th of January, the holy Church commemorates
our holy father among the saints,
GREGORY the Theologian, Archbishop of Constantinople.**[1]

Saint Gregory the Theologian

Gregory the Theologian, our father among the saints, was born in Arianzos, near the town of Nazianzos,[2] in southwestern Cappadocia Secunda, in the year 329 or 330. His parents were wealthy, noble, honorable, and virtuous. His mother, Nonna, of a most illustrious line, was an Orthodox Christian from infancy, and had been brought up in right doctrine. Saint Gregory commented in a poem concerning himself and his parents that "she was herself still more pious, a woman in body, yes, but in character she eclipsed any man."[3] His father, Gregory, was an idolater, who converted to piety. In 330, he was ordained to the priesthood for Nazianzos. Saint Gregory the younger writes that, unlike his mother, Gregory the elder had been grafted in from a foreign olive [cf. Rom. 11:17], while she came from ancient and pious Orthodox roots. Gregory had a beloved sister, Gorgonia, and a younger brother, Caesarios, who became a physician. Saint Gregory was given a high

---

[1] The Life of this saint was recorded in Greek by a certain presbyter named Gregory, whose text is extant in the Athonite Monastery of the Great Lavra. The main sources of this Life include the saint's own writings, the epistles of Saint Basil the Great, and other fathers of the Church. The text was rendered in simpler Greek by Agapios the Cretan, who published it in his *Neon Paradeison*, which was incorporated into *The Great Synaxaristes* (in Greek). A divine office with twenty-four stanzas was composed by the hymnographer, Father Gerasimos Mikrayiannanites. The English version presented herein was taken from our publication, "The Life of Saint Gregory the Theologian," in *The Lives of the Three Hierarchs*, 2nd edition, pp. 69-112.

[2] Nazianzos, a minor station on the highway that led across Anatolia to Palestine. According to Socrates, it was a "shabby polis" near Caesarea [*Ecclesiastical History* 4:11.9]. In 325, it became a bishopric, which was suffragan of Caesarea, then Tyana, and eventually Mokissos. Romanos IV transformed Nazianzos into a metropolis. It fell to the Turks after the battle of Mantzikert in 1071. *The Oxford Dictionary of Byzantium*, s.v. "Nazianzos."

[3] Saint Gregory, *Three Poems: Concerning His Own Affairs, Concerning Himself and the Bishops, Concerning His Own Life*, Fathers of the Church, Volume 75.

quality of education; but Christian training, overseen by Nonna, began from his first consciousness.

It was after his father's ordination that Nonna conceived Gregory. She consecrated the child to God, even before his birth. Saint Gregory speaks of his mother's promise in a poem about his own life, writing: "Ever since the day she had yearned to nurse a man-child on her knee, she imitated the cry of the holy Hannah: 'O Christ King, that I might have a boy for Thee to keep within Thy fold! May a son be the flourishing fruit of my birth pangs!'" Saint Gregory also mentions that his mother was vouchsafed a holy vision wherein she knew her prayer would be answered and what the child should be called. "My likeness and my name appeared clearly to her." She was also told in the dream that he would become a genuine slave of God.

As a lad he remembers his mother's dedication of him to God. "With holy books," he recalls, "she sanctified my hands." Then one day she took him into her arms and uttered these words to God in the hearing of her son: "This beloved child, the gift of God, soon to become a sacred victim, is a precious charge under escort to the altar. He is the offspring of Sarah, late in motherhood. He is the root of the race, the product of hope, and the divine promise. The priest is Abraham, and the victim, an illustrious Isaac. Accordingly, in fulfillment of my promise, I offer thee, O child, as a living victim to God. It is for thee to implement thy mother's hope. Through prayer she gave thee birth, and now she prays that thou wilt fulfill it. My child, this is the noble inheritance I bestow on thee in this world—and in the world to come, which is by far the best." He understood and wished to fulfill his mother's wish, and his tender soul began to be shaped in the new mold of holiness.

Saint Gregory in a poem on his own affairs recounts a boyhood incident which he called "a stupid mistake which caused me great agony." As a lad, he foolishly toyed with a twig. Unwittingly, he drove the twig, as a thorn, into his right eye. It was bloodied, and his vision impaired. Until his death a scar could be discerned upon his right eye, though the ball of the eye itself was healed. He makes mention of this healing in the same poem, saying, "I could not use my hands to offer up the sacrifice of the Spirit, until my tears had healed the wound. For it is wrong to let anything unpurified touch what is holy, or to confront the burning sun with impaired vision."

Saint Gregory's Education

Early on, a tutor was engaged for Gregory and his brother. The tutor, named Carterios, later became a monk. The young Gregory had a passion for letters from boyhood. He attended school at Nazianzos and later went to Caesarea, the provincial capital of Cappadocia, to further his studies; there he also met Saint Basil the Great. The young Gregory had a sharp mind and was first in his studies.

After this period of schooling, Gregory and his brother chose the Christian school in Palestinian Caesarea, where they might also make a pilgrimage to the Church of the Holy Sepulcher of our Lord in Jerusalem. At length, Caesarios went on to Alexandria to attend its celebrated medical school, but Gregory was resolved to take up the study of rhetoric at the Palestinian School. Afterward, Gregory's love for learning also brought him to Alexandria, where Didymos was head of the famous Catechetical School. Gregory was also drawn to Egypt on account of his brother Caesarios, who was still studying medicine. When he entered Alexandria, Gregory soon discovered that his brother was a highly acclaimed student at the university. During this period, two great lights of the Orthodox Church shone brilliantly, Patriarch Athanasios and Anthony the Great. But Saint Gregory was dissatisfied with his life in Egypt, and decided to leave and study at Athens, famed for its literary school. He was then about twenty years old.

Shipwreck

Gregory could not wait for a suitable season to sail. He was determined to start at once. He took passage in November, when few venture to sea, on a ship bound for Aegina.[4] People skilled in such matters pointed out that it was dangerous. The voyage from Alexandria to Achaia began pleasantly enough, but when they were in sight of Crete, they were beset by a tremendous tempest. Everything became a great blackness. The ship was tossed by heavy seas and became waterlogged. The fury of the sea ruptured the water tanks, and they were scattered to the depths, leaving the ship's crew and passengers in dire straits without drinking water. For twenty days and nights Gregory lay prostrate in the prow, calling on the almighty God in prayers. From either side, like cliffs and mountains, the waves rolled upon the vessel. All the tackle was shattered as the wind whistled shrilly through the sheets. The heavens were black with lightning-flecked clouds. Thunder-claps resounded. Everywhere strident voices rose in clamor: cries of sailors, helmsmen, officers, passengers, all calling with one voice upon Christ, even the people who formerly knew not God. The question among them was whether thirst, or the sea, or the winds should cause them to perish woefully.

Now God sent speedy deliverance when Phoenician merchants unexpectedly appeared. "They were in fear themselves," remarks Saint Gregory, "but soon assessed from our entreaties how far more desperate was our emergency situation. They made fast our vessel using grappling hooks and manly strength, for they were exceedingly strong. They prevented the ship from practical shipwreck. The violence of the waves continued for several days." All continued to fear death, but more terrifying for Saint

---

[4] Saint Gregory, *Prolegomena*, Nicene and Post-Nicene Fathers, 2nd Ser., Volume VII.

Gregory was a hidden death. What exercised Gregory's mind the most was his lack of holy Baptism. In that moment he said he gave himself to God, and he made sacred promises which he believed later delivered him from the furious sea. In a poem on his own life, he later wrote: "I was fearful because my soul was as yet uninitiated in heavenly rites and lacked the salutary washing, which brings to human beings the grace and illumination of the Spirit....Those murderous waters were keeping me away from the purifying waters which divinize us."

Gregory sent up cries and stretched forth his hands. He lay prone with his garments rent. Then his fellow passengers, forgetting their own particular woes, joined their prayerful entreaties with Gregory's. He then brought to mind all the miracles of time past—when the sea divided and Israel passed through dry-shod, when enemies were defeated by hands raised in prayer, when plagues scourged Egypt, when city walls collapsed at trumpet blasts, and many other examples. Gregory then addressed the Maker of heaven and earth, saying, "If I escape this double danger of shipwreck and spiritual death, I shall live for Thee; if I am abandoned, Thou shalt lose a worshipper. At this moment Thy disciple is tossed upon the waves. For my sake, wake to me, and let the fear be stilled" [cf. Mt. 8:24-27]. These were his words, and then the clash of winds subsided. The sea grew serene, and the ship continued peacefully on course. The entire ship's company praised the great Christ. They passed Rhodes, and a little later struck sail in the harbor of Aegina.[5]

Saint Gregory at Athens

In Athens, Gregory renewed his earlier acquaintance with Basil. "In studies, in lodgings, in discussions," says Gregory, "I had him as companion." Their encyclopedic curriculum included grammar, rhetorical, ethical and metaphysical philosophy, dialectic, mathematics, astronomy, philosophy, physics, and theology. Students came from everywhere in the Greek world to study. Cliques and fraternities were formed, often by those of the same nationality. The most celebrated sophists of that time included the Armenian Christian Prohaeresios, the Arab Diophantes, and the Syrian Epiphanios.

Saint Basil's reputation had preceded him. Students mad upon Sophism were anxious to recruit him. Through the good offices of his friend Gregory, Basil was spared the rough horseplay of the fraternities. There was one incident with some Armenian classmates of Basil. They were jealous of him and began to beleaguer him with disputations and difficult sophistical questions. Saint Basil was more than competent to hold his own against them. Gregory, at first, did not perceive the envy and malice of the Armenian youths. He was naturally zealous and loyal for the prestige of his university,

---

[5] *Concerning His Own Life*, op. cit., pp. 80-83.

and took a stand with the Armenians so as to equalize the debates. It was not long, however, before Gregory perceived their true aim. He abandoned them and stood by his Basil. Victory for the side of Basil and Gregory was sure. It should be mentioned that Basil became disquieted when he saw that, as a result of Gregory's support, his friend became unpopular at school. Classmates of his own year deemed him a traitor to the school.

The bond of friendship between Gregory and Basil was profound, on account of their love for the philosophic and contemplative life. "We made a team," said he. "We had all things in common, and a single soul, as it were, bound together our two distinct bodies. But above all it was God, and a mutual desire for higher things. We reached such a pitch of confidence that we revealed the depths of our hearts, becoming ever more united in our yearning. There is no such solid bond of union as thinking the same thoughts." Their ascetic life as undergraduates attracted attention.

Athens in the fourth century was a city replete with worldly entertainments for young men. There were festivals, theaters, assemblies, drinking parties, and other distractions. The two young men from Cappadocia, however, rejected these pastimes, and allowed themselves only two directions: the path which led to church and its holy teachers, and the path which took them to their lectures at the university. Prince Julian, the future emperor and apostate, was also a student. Saint Gregory declares that he had foreseen, even at that early period, how matters would be from the time he was with him in Athens. Gregory says Julian came for two reasons. One was to visit Greece and her schools. But he also came to consult with the heathen priests and charlatans. Saint Gregory said he saw Julian's unevenness of disposition and the very unsettled condition of his mind, and said, "What an evil the Roman state is nourishing," though he prefaced this saying that he hoped he might be proven mistaken.

Saint Gregory spent about twelve years in Athens, from eighteen to thirty years of age. Later, in a poem about his own life, he commented upon his personal ambitions, saying that "marriage never bound me....I took no pleasure in the luxuries of the table. Living in great and brilliant houses did not please me. Christ is my best wealth. Human respect...never awakened need in me, nor glory that is doomed to perish. I did not seek to hold a high place in the royal court. I was not consumed by ambition for distinguished seats of justice; nor did I covet great influence in the state or among citizens. The fame that goes with letters was the only thing that absorbed me. I labored much for a long time in the craft of letters; but I laid this prostrate before the feet of Christ in subjection to the Logos of the great God."

Saint Basil left before him and went home to Cappadocia. The fellow students of Gregory and Basil importuned them strongly to remain in the city.

Basil persuaded the people only with great difficulty. Gregory began to weep. Suddenly he was encircled by everyone, including strangers, friends, classmates, and teachers. They protested and lamented his departure. They held Gregory tightly, insisting they would not release him. "It is not fair that Athens should lose thee, to whom we are prepared to concede by vote the primacy of letters," they shouted. They finally mastered Gregory's resolve to leave, for "only an oak tree could withstand such laments and entreaties," he later bemoaned. Therefore, Gregory lingered a while at Athens, and then, practically by stealth, he managed to elude his admirers.

Saint Gregory, Homeward Bound

Gregory left Athens and went to Constantinople, where Caesarios was practising as a court physician. Gregory persuaded his younger brother to accompany him home to Nazianzos. Upon arriving home, they found their parents still living and their father on the episcopal throne. Not long afterward, some people importuned Gregory to give a display of eloquence. Gregory speaks about this, saying, "It was, so to speak, a debt that I owed, because personally I placed no value upon vapid applause....Therefore, for my friends I gave a performance."

All the while, though, he maintained that his concept of the philosophic life was to sacrifice to God everything, as well as the labor of letters. He observed that those who are attracted by an active life do good to some of the people they en-

Saint Gregory the Theologian

counter, but they do themselves no good and are harassed by anxieties that wreck their serenity. On the other hand, those that stay detached are somehow more stable and turn with quiet mind to God. But their charity is narrow, and they are useful only to themselves. The life they live is somewhat unsocial and even harsh. Meditating upon his own path, Saint Gregory wrote: "I decided upon a middle way between the life without ties and the life of mixing, one which would combine the serenity of the former with the practical use of the latter." Saint Gregory acknowledged, however, that there was even a stronger consideration: the debt he felt he owed to his aged parents. He remarked, "It is a very pious duty to give prime respect, after God, to one's parents. They are responsible for our very knowledge of God. I supported them with all my strength. I led them by the hand, so that by showing consideration for old age, I might make provision for my own old age; because as we sow, we reap." Thus he wrote concerning his home life.

Thereupon, Saint Gregory spent some of his time at Arianzos with his parents, and the rest of his time with his friend Basil in Pontos in a monastic retreat. It is unclear whether Gregory was baptized while at school or during this period. In those years, it was customary for many young men to remain as catechumens until they finished school and attained the age of thirty. If he was not baptized then, he most certainly was in 360 when he returned to Nazianzos.[6] We do know that at his holy Baptism he made a solemn vow never to swear. He also pledged to commit his mind and strength to the glory of God and the defense and dissemination of the holy Faith.

Caesarios did not long remain home with a brilliant career beckoning him from the capital. His older brother was not in favor of his return, as he was cognizant of the perils and enticements of life at court. He did not hinder him, though he himself was powerfully inclined to the monastic life. Nonetheless, as the dutiful and elder son, he felt a keen responsibility and obligation to his aging parents. Therefore, Gregory could not give himself over entirely to the solitary life.

Saint Gregory's Ordination

In about 361, Gregory was prevailed upon by his father and was ordained to the priesthood during the Feast of the Lord's Nativity. His aged father's strength was failing fast, and he wished to have his son as a coadjutor in his pastoral duties. The younger Gregory remembers in a poem how his father exerted pressure to raise him to an auxiliary throne, so that he might constrain him by the bonds of the Spirit and pay him the highest honor in his power. "Why he did so," reminisces Gregory, "I cannot say. Perhaps he was moved by fatherly affection, which when combined with power is a considerable force." The elder Gregory finally persuaded his son, who was apprehensive about assuming the dignity of the priesthood. Gregory says that "my good father, under stress of years and yearning, kept beseeching me to

---

[6] *The Great Synaxaristes* (in Greek), p. 641.

respect what he called his last gasps." Saint Gregory assented, and comments, "I hastened into the abyss once more, something I should have never done. It was a crisis that saddled me with misfortune. I feared the reproach of an aged parent, lest the affection between us should issue for me in a curse; because simplicity, when angered and provoked, is able to do this."

Gregory was not slightly sorrowed by the ordination, which he describes as an act of tyranny, though he asks pardon of the Holy Spirit for his language. He says, "Tyranny of this kind—I can call it by no other name, and may the Holy Spirit pardon me for feeling thus—so distressed me that I suddenly shook myself free of everyone." About the season of the Feast of the Theophany in 362, he made his flight to Pontos and to the amiable society of Basil, mindful of the words of our Lord: "For where two or three are gathered together in My name, there am I in the midst of them [Mt. 18:20]." In their remote retreat, Gregory had the liberty and quiet needed for personal reflection on all the options before him. He owed obedience to his father, not only as a son, but now also as a priest to his bishop.

Thus he returned to Nazianzos for Pascha that year. He gave his first sermon as a priest, which included an apology for his former unwillingness. Although Pascha is considered the feast of feasts and usually draws very large crowds to attend church, this time the congregation was exceedingly small. Saint Gregory sensed it was a showing by the flock of their tacit disapproval of his departure. Gregory, the sensitive soul that he was, suffered the discourtesy sharply. In his next sermon, he made mention of their absence and how it saddened him. He frankly reminded them that for their sakes he felt constrained to forsake his quietude. He even chided them for their chilly reception toward him. The defense of his flight, however, did not end with one or two sermons. He committed his apology to writing. It was a long oration, wherein he makes clear his understanding of the responsibilities and obligations entailed upon the priesthood. He justifies his hesitation from accepting such a burden and awesome duty. It was published and later was used by both Saint John Chrysostom as the basis of his *Six Books on the Priesthood*, and Saint Gregory the Great and Dialogist in his *Pastoral Rule*.

Thus for some ten years, he spent his time aiding his elderly father and living intermittently the monastic life with Saint Basil in the latter's Pontic retreat by the Iris River. Both Gregory and Basil allotted their time wisely for prayer, psalmody, contemplation, study, and manual labor. It was during this time that Basil compiled and organized the monastic rule which is still in use. It is more than probable that his friend Gregory had a share in producing this work. The two friends were particularly fond of meditating and deliberating upon holy Scriptures. In their studies they were especially focused on interpreting the holy writings, not by their own personal deductions and opinions, but instead by applying the guidelines furnished by the authority of ancient interpreters. True, Origen was one of the commentators whom they consulted, but they avoided his errors. Together, the young men compiled a memorable book of extracts, which they published in twenty-seven books. They called it *Philokalia*, and it was an invaluable aid to the faithful and scholars. In the future, when the Arian supporters quoted Origen to support their errors, both Gregory and Basil, who were familiar with Origen's writings and meaning, were ready to confute them.

When he was at home, Saint Gregory also spent a little time ordering domestic matters. He was very concerned about his younger brother, who was by now a physician in the court of Julian the Apostate. In fact, Julian persuaded Caesarios to retain his position at court, even though he knew that his physician held different religious views from his own beliefs; but Julian was resolved to somehow overturn Caesarios. Gregory and his father felt intensely that Caesarios was in spiritual danger, and urged him to resign and come home. They did not wish to worry Nonna, so they managed to keep their apprehensions from her. Although he did not return, neither did he apostatize. After a little while, Gregory wrote a loving letter to his brother, encouraging him to retire. This time Caesarios resigned, and he withdrew when Julian left the capital for his campaign against the Persians.

Nazianzos, however, soon experienced the aggressiveness and bullying of the Arian emperor and his minions. The prefect of their province was dispatched with a military escort to take possession of the bishop's church. With the aid of Saint Gregory and the people, the bishop defied the imperial order. The prefect, quickly calculating the formidable resistance of the people, retreated and never renewed his demands in the neighborhood again.

The wicked Julian at one point contrived to deprive the children of learning to read and write in Greek, and the study of Christian writings. Since there was an imperial ban prohibiting Orthodox Christians from being instructors in rhetoric and grammar, Saint Gregory himself wrote a curriculum for the children. He composed beautiful poems, with verses holding up to public scorn the shameless myths of the pagan Greeks. He so thoroughly exposed the error of polytheism that even those with the slightest knowledge, after reading or hearing the saint's words, ridiculed the myths as vain and worthy of derision. Saint Gregory composed tragedies, comedies, and poems on many subjects, to the praise of virtue, and the importance of purity of the soul and body. His compositions spoke about prayer, theology, and many other matters, and were skillfully crafted, avoiding the prattling and foolery of the pagan Greek writers. Thus, he established for the Christians one wise teaching, ensuring that the children might properly learn both the Faith and their letters, and all the while be strengthened in godliness. The saint did this to the shame of the emperor, but to the strengthening of the Orthodox Faith.

This was not the first or last such encounter. In fact, both the elder and younger Gregory ofttimes clashed with the apostate during his stay in Cappadocia on his way to meet the Persians. But both father and son, together with the flock, made such a strong stand against Julian that he judged it better not to avenge himself at that time. He did declare that he would avenge himself after his victory against the Persians. By the grace of God, Julian never returned, as he was slain.

In 363 or 364, Saint Basil was also ordained a priest, despite his protests. Bishop Evsevios of Caesarea wished to have a priest in his entourage who was knowledgeable in theology, that he might assist him in countering the controversies of the times. Basil was his first choice. Saint Basil handled his duties competently and admirably, and grew in popularity. At length, a contention arose because Evsevios, though he was elected while yet a catechumen by an enthusiastic congregation, was unwillingly consecrated by the bishops. Some sought to place Saint Basil in his stead. However, Basil was not seeking rank or honor. He discreetly removed himself from the arena. He not did not wish to take up the episcopal throne, but he also sensed alienation from Evsevios. Basil retired to his community in Pontos and took his friend Gregory with him. Gregory did not stay long, because of the pleas of his father for aid and comfort. When Valens Caesarios, an ardent Arian, succeeded to the throne, Evsevios wrote to Gregory, imploring his presence and aid in Caesarea. Gregory courteously declined the call, out of regard for his friendship with Basil and for the wrong he had suffered. In fact, after several exchanges of epistles, Gregory even succeeded in effecting a reconciliation between Evsevios and Basil in 365.

In the interim, Saint Gregory's brother, Caesarios, who had been a physician for the court of Emperor Valens, received a choice piece of preferment in Bithynia. In the end of 368 or the beginning of 369 a powerful earthquake struck, placing Caesarios in jeopardy. He survived the danger but was moved to arrange for his final retirement. During that time, he fell sick and very soon reposed at forty years of age. Caesarios bequeathed his considerable estate to his brother, in trust for the poor. Caesarios was interred at Nazianzos in the Church of the Martyrs, in a vault which his parents had prepared for themselves. Saint Gregory gave the funeral oration. Shortly thereafter, Gorgonia also reposed, and he preached a sermon for his sister also. The settling of Caesarios' estate by his brother Gregory was troublesome. The considerable property he had accumulated was partly swallowed up by the gaping earth, when Nicaea collapsed in the earthquake. A good deal of his brother's property was stolen by rogues. Gregory admits that Caesarios revered him, as one would give respect to a beloved father. It was Gregory's desire, however, that what was left of the squandered property would be shared with the poor.

In 370, Evsevios of Caesarea reposed. Saint Basil, straightway, wrote his friend, imploring him to come to Caesarea. Saint Basil was contemplating having Gregory elected to that see. In the letter, without mentioning the death of the archbishop, Basil bade Gregory to come to him at Caesarea, saying that he himself was dangerously ill and even near to his last breath. Gregory, concerned and saddened by the news, shed a fountain of tears and wailed aloud. He was resolved to set off instantly. Gregory had not journeyed very far when he learned that Basil's health was as it always was, and that the bishops of the province were assembling at Caesarea for the election of a metropolitan. Gregory supposed that he perceived his friend's stratagem immediately. He presumed that Basil wanted him in Caesarea in order that his influence might bring about Basil's election! Gregory was indignant and wrote to his friend explaining how he felt; but after he had spoken with his father, they both agreed that no one was better suited to assume the vacant throne than Basil.

Therefore, Saint Gregory and his father worked to procure the election for Basil. Having his son as his secretary, the elder Gregory wrote two letters, one to the people of Caesarea and the other to the provincial synod, strenuously urging Basil's election. A third letter was written to Evsevios, Bishop of Samosata. Evsevios wrote back urging the elder Gregory, though he was in feeble health, to attend the synod in person, that Basil's election might be secured by their joint efforts. The elder Gregory, now very advanced in age and frail, managed to bring himself to the metropolis in time for the synod meeting where Basil was elected and consecrated. Saint Gregory the younger wrote a letter of congratulations to his friend, for he truly was glad to see Basil placed on that lofty throne.

Thus, in 370, Saint Basil became Bishop of Caesarea. In 371, Emperor Valens divided the civil province of Cappadocia into two administrations. At about the same time, Anthimos proclaimed for himself that the purely civil action of the state had *ipso facto* elevated him to the dignity of metropolitan of the newly formed province, with the capital at Tyana. Saint Basil opposed the division of his diocese. Anthimos' pretension was supported by the bishops of that district who were not very well disposed toward the great Basil. In order to assert his rights as metropolitan, and strengthen the Orthodox cause, Basil made several new bishoprics in the disputed province. To one of these, a village of little consequence named Sasima, a stopping place, he importuned Gregory to become bishop. Gregory's consecration was almost by compulsion and on account of his own father's wishes. Gregory was indignant at the treatment he received from Basil. Gregory felt that he had been ill-used, and did not attempt to disguise his reluctance.[7]

In a poem concerning his own life, he speaks about Basil and to Basil, saying: "He (Basil) showed himself another father to me, and yet a far more burdensome one. My real father, though he tyrannized me, I must shelter; but no such duty binds me in Basil's case, where friendship actually brought injury instead of deliverance from trouble. I do not know whether I should lay the blame on account of my own sins, which often indeed torture me, or on the high-handed style thou didst acquire the throne, O best of men!" Gregory agonizes over his past friendship with Basil, and dreads appearing to insult his honored friend; and yet his distress is a vexation for him. He brought to mind their days together at school and the pleasantness of their camaraderie. But, "What hast come over thee?" asks a disconsolate Gregory. "How was it that thou didst suddenly cast me off? Any style of friendship that so deals with friends ought to vanish from the earth. We were lions yesterday, and today I am an ape. But of course even a lion is trifling in thine eyes....I did not deserve this, I, the man whom thou didst set above thy friends....But what is the point of chafing?"

Meanwhile, Basil interpreted it as unkind of Gregory to be so reluctant to comply. Their relations were strained for some time, though Gregory submitted to the authority of the archbishop, yet with some reluctance. Saint Gregory described his diocese as an uncivilized and cramped little village: "There is a little station on a high road in Cappadocia, situated where the road is divided in three: without water, without vegetation, with nothing of freedom about it. It is a frightfully horrible and narrow little village; everywhere dust and noise and carts, weeping and shouting, lictors and chains. The people are all foreigners, passersby, and vagabonds. Such is my Church of Sasima! He (Basil) who was surrounded by fifty *chorepiscopoi*[8] was so magnanimous as to make me incumbent here!" Saint Gregory explains that the whole object of his appointment was to get the better of that intruder Anthimos through the founding of a new see. "And among Basil's warrior friends," wryly observes a dejected Gregory, "apparently I held first place."

As it happened, however, Anthimos occupied the village of Sasima with troops. This thwarted Gregory from taking peaceable succession of his see. Once, when Saint Gregory attempted to enter Sasima, Anthimos dispatched a company of armed soldiers to waylay the holy man and his

---

[7] *Prolegomena*, Nicene, VII:195.

[8] The *chorepiscopoi* (bishops of the countryside) were a rank of clerics which was formed in the latter half of the 3rd C. They were first seen in Asia Minor, to help provide hierarchical supervision in the larger dioceses.

attendants. Saint Gregory received intelligence about the ambush, and went another way, turning to a certain monastery where he made himself useful tending the sick. He then repaired to the wilderness for a little solitude.

Saint Gregory knew and admitted openly that the see could not be held without the spilling of blood. He described it as "a no man's land between two rival bishops." He adds, "The pretext was souls, but in fact, it was desire for control, and command—and I hesitate to say it—over taxes and contributions, which have the entire world in a miserable state." He then wrote a letter to Saint Basil, complaining: "I will not face the martial Anthimos, though he be an untimely warrior, being myself unarmed and unwarlike, and thus the more exposed to wounds. Fight with him thyself if thou dost wish, or look out for someone to fight when he seizes thy mules, keeping guard over a defile, and like Amalek of old, barring the way against Israel. Before all things, give me quiet. Why should I fight for suckling pigs and fowls, and those not my own, as though for souls and canons?...I shall gain this only from thy friendship: that I shall learn not to trust in friends, or to esteem anything more valuable than God."[9]

In fact, Saint Gregory never exercised any normal ministry in the tiny hamlet. He wrote: "I had not touched at all the church allotted to me, even to the extent of offering a single Liturgy there, or leading the congregation in prayer, or ordaining a single cleric." Therefore, he continued assuming his duties as coadjutor for his aged father. Saint Gregory asks, "In the name of God, where did the proper course of action lie for me? Acquiescence? Long-suffering of assaults by renegades? Blows at every hour? Suffocation by dust? Not to mention a place to rest my aging bones? Am I always to be driven from my house? Am I not allowed time to break bread with a guest? I am penniless, and have a penniless flock for my portion."

Gregory then remonstrates with Basil in his thoughts, reckoning, "Athens, our studies together, our sharing of roof and hearth, the single spirit animating two people, the marvel of Greece, the pledge that we made that we would cast aside absolutely the world and live the coenobitic life for God, placing our words in the service of the one wise Logos! This was the outcome of it all? Everything was shattered, abandoned on the ground, the old high hopes were gone with the wind. Where was one to turn,...bent as now I am, not in mind but in body?"[10] Elsewhere, he wrote to Saint Basil: "Thou dost accuse me of laziness and idleness, because I did not accept thy Sasima, and because I have not bestirred myself like a bishop, and do not arm thee against

---

[9] *Miscellaneous Letters*, Nicene, op. cit., Div. II, Epistle xlviii.
[10] *Concerning His Own Life*, 75:90.

the other like a bone thrown into the midst of dogs. My greatest business is to keep free from business."[11]

The contention about the Metropolitanate of Tyana went on. From the evidence extant, it appears that, at the request of Anthimos, Saint Gregory wrote a letter to Saint Basil, proposing a conference between the rival metropolitans. According to Saint Gregory, Saint Basil seems to have been annoyed with the proposal. Gregory wrote back to Basil, begging that his interference not be deemed officious. He explained to him that Anthimos came to visit Gregory the elder, though he believed it to be a pretext. Gregory then told Basil how Anthimos began sounding him out on a number of subjects: dioceses, the marshes of Sasima, his ordination, and other such matters. Gregory tells Basil that Anthimos was flattering, questioning, threatening, pleading, blaming, praising, and drawing circles, as though he ought only to look at him and his new metropolis, as being the greater. Gregory tells his friend that he defended him. He asked Anthimos, "Why dost thou draw thy line to include our city, for we too deem our Church to be really a Mother of Churches, and that too from ancient times?"

In the end, Anthimos went away without gaining his objective. He was out of breath and reproached Gregory for Basilism. Gregory then tells Basil that they followed up by sending him a synodal summons, which he declined, saying that it was an insult. He still took Saint Basil for his guide and teacher of the Faith, and for every honorable thing that can be said. He assured his dear friend that he had no desire to displease him or to curry the favor of Anthimos.[12] Ultimately, it was mainly Gregory's mediation that brought about a cordial settlement.

Gregory thought of escaping again to that beloved mode of life—solitude; yet he confesses, "Though I was schooled to bear all things, this one weakness do I possess: I cannot bear my father's wrath." The elder Gregory was bent on having his son settle in Sasima. His health worsened, and then he decided that it was better to have his son with him, and become his auxiliary. Gregory the younger characterizes his father's physical afflictions as severe. Touching Gregory's beard, the father entreated his son with outstretched hands, and pleaded with him, saying, "Thou art in the arms of the man who begat thee. As thou dost hope to find the one Father merciful to thee, do not, my child, rebuff me. The favor I request of thee is a good thing; and even if it were not, it is a father's request. Thy span of life does not yet measure the length of my sacrificial ministry. Let me have this favor, or let some other hand lay me in the grave. That is the punishment I

---

[11] Div. II, Ep. xlix, "To Saint Basil."
[12] Div. I, Ep. lviii, "To Saint Basil."

determine if thou wilt disobey. The few short days that remain, let me have. What comes henceforth, dispose of as it pleases thee." Hence, parental fear persuaded Gregory and brought him back again.

Therefore, even after the death of his father, Saint Gregory of Nazianzos (d. 374), the younger Gregory continued to administer to the needs of the Nazianzen Church for about a year, until the appointment of a legitimate successor. While he served there, he did not favor the arrangement. He kept on begging the bishops from the bottom of his heart to appoint some other bishop for the place, since he had not been assigned to it by any formal decree; and, moreover, he wished to relinquish all mundane affairs. Gregory failed to persuade his fellow hierarchs to relieve him.

Gregory also was a great favorite with the people. He, therefore, perceived his efforts to secure the appointment of another bishop would be fruitless. Again, the bishops would do nothing about this. At about the same time, in 375, Gregory became seriously ill, and he repaired to live the quiet life, unencumbered, at the Monastery of Saint Thekla at Seleukeia in Isauria. He reasoned within himself that they would tire of his delay and make haste to put someone else in charge. He dwelt there for about three or four years. His passionate desire for contemplation is expressed in his poem concerning his own affairs: "Would to God I had hidden myself in cliffs, and mountains, and crags!...Fleeing this world, this way of life and the anxieties of the flesh, I could have filled my mind totally with Christ."

Saint Basil implored his friend to return from seclusion, which he did. Saint Gregory then set about working in the poorhouses and hospitals, many of which were built by Saint Basil. About the same time, a new heresy came out of Arianism, that of the Makedonians (Macedonians) or the Pnevmato-machi (fighters against the Spirit). Some of the Makedonians blasphemed the Holy Spirit, calling Him a creature and not God, while others called Him neither God nor a creature. Saint Gregory considered them to be semi-Arians. Unfortunately, their sect grew and spread everywhere, so that they began persecuting the Orthodox. It appears that at Constantinople were the greatest concentration and tumult. At the behest of Saint Basil the Great, who knew firsthand of the preeminence in eloquence and purity of Faith of his friend, Saint Gregory the Theologian was sent to Constantinople, in the company of other hierarchs from their synod, to combat the heretics with all their might, so as to pull out the weed of heresy by its roots.

Nonetheless, even before Saint Gregory set out with his company, Saint Basil became ill, and reposed in 379. Who can describe the loss experienced by Gregory for his beloved childhood companion? He wrote a letter of condolence to the great Basil's brother, Saint Gregory, Bishop of Nyssa, saying: "This then was also reserved for my sad life, to hear of the death of Basil, and the departure of that holy soul, which has gone from us that it may be with the Lord, for which he had been preparing himself all his life. And among all the other losses I have had to endure, this is the greatest; that by reason of the bodily sickness, from which I am still suffering and in great danger, I am unable to kiss that holy dust, or be with thee....To see the desolation of the Church, shorn of such a glory, and bereft of such a crown, is what no one, at least no one of any feeling, can bear to let his eyes look upon, or his ear hearken to."[13] He also gave a magnificent funeral oration for his friend, and set out eagerly to fulfill the great Basil's last request to him.

Thereupon, when Gregory arrived in the city, he found the church greatly humbled and scorned by the imperial authority. The holy vessels had been seized and were trampled upon by the impious and evil-minded. As another David, Gregory moved against the enemy, using as a kind of sling his words of right doctrine and teaching so as to bring down the hateful theology of the heretics. Day by day, through his admonitions and counseling, the heterodox were caught by the holy bait of the wisdom of his words. Thus, not much time passed before they were drawn away from their wrong beliefs to knowledge of the truth. Who can describe the hierarch's labors and hardships, which no other bishop underwent at any time? Saint Gregory had not even finished uprooting that pernicious heresy when the devil brought in the profane impertinence of Apollinarios, who started his own heresy, blaspheming the Son of God as a kind of half-man. But more about Apollinarios and his followers later. In 381, the Synod of Constantinople condemned Makedonian views; thereafter, they declined and eventually ceased to exist as a distinctive sect.

Saint Gregory at Constantinople

In 379, the Orthodox congregation at Constantinople, the Nicaean group, prevailed upon Gregory to become their spiritual shepherd. For some forty years they were trampled upon by a ruthless parade of Arian pseudo-bishops. Under these wolves, the flock of Christ was nearly ravaged by the violent entry of other heresies, which Arian rule allowed to coexist, that is, the Evnomians, Makedonians, Novatians, Apollinarians, and others. During that time, since the imperial throne supported the Arians, the Nicaeans lost their influence and all ecclesiastical holdings in the metropolis. All Church properties were in Arian hands. But now, by the grace of God, there was a new monarch, and an Orthodox one too! Emperor Theodosios the Great (379-395) backed the petitions of the Orthodox flock of Constantinople, as did numerous bishops, to call Gregory the Theologian to Constantinople to help them amid their crises.

---

[13] Div. III, § 2, Ep. lxxvi, "To Saint Gregory of Nyssa."

*Saint Gregory
the Theologian*

Saint Gregory makes mention of his call to the imperial city in his poem concerning himself and the bishops, writing: "There was a time when I was set on high, above all things of perception; my mind was concerned with intelligibles only. Renown had been laid aside, as well as possessions, prospects, and eloquence. My luxury was to eschew luxury. I sweetened my life with frugal leaven. I was safe from contumely; because however wise one may be, one must expect anything." Indeed, the unexpected overtook Gregory when he was invited to Constantinople. He asks, "Was it the Holy Spirit, or just my sins, that I might pay the penalty of eminence?" True to character, Saint Gregory resisted for a long time, but eventually came to see that it was the will of God that he should help the Church at Constantinople, which was a scene of ecclesiastical strifes and partisanships. He acquiesced, though unwillingly, and went until such time as the Orthodox of the capital might elect an archbishop. Regarding this, he writes: "It was their protestations and prayers of every kind that swayed me; to have resisted them would have been unduly proud." Therefore, he left the land of Cappadocia, which he describes as "that bastion of Orthodoxy in the eyes of everyone," and arrived unequipped, according to his own testimony, with any of the things he needed. At the same time, his physical constitution was waning. He says, "This frame of mine, once stalwart, has withered under anxiety and grown bent already. My strength is exhausted, and even when I put forth every effort, I am less than adequate."

Upon entering the city, Gregory lodged with a relative. He arranged part of the dwelling as a chapel and dedicated it to the Resurrection, as the place where the Orthodox Faith should rise again. Divine services were conducted daily by him, together with his own excellent sermons. His constant theme was the worship of the Holy Trinity. It was his extraordinary oratorical skills and pristine theology which recommended this monkish provincial bishop to the sophisticated Constantinopolitans.

Men and women of every social class gathered to hear him discourse on the Faith. Even the famous blessed Jerome, who was already fifty years old, came from Syria to Constantinople to partake of his discourses. He also received private instruction from Saint Gregory in the interpretation of sacred Scripture. He called Saint Gregory his preceptor and catechist.

Saint Gregory's strength was not in administration, but in right doctrine. He was deemed by certain people to be somewhat naive and easily put upon by deceivers. For two years, the situation in Constantinople placed him in the forefront of the battle regarding ecclesiastical affairs. He himself comments, "In the midst of wolves I built up a congregation." During that intense time, it has been acknowledged that some of his best writings—and that of the century—on Orthodox Trinitarian doctrine flowed from his pen. His five *Theological Orations* secured him the title "Theologian."

His success in the Church of the Resurrection was not without incident. Once the Arian populace stormed the little domestic chapel by night and desecrated the altar. They mixed wine with blood, and Gregory barely escaped the fury of certain women and monks who came armed with clubs and stones. The following day Saint Gregory was summoned before the court to answer for the tumult. Our confessor skillfully defended himself, so that the episode actually reinforced the triumph of his just cause.

Maximos

The extraordinary and bizarre account of Maximos, a plausible adventurer and huckster, and how he came into Saint Gregory's life, we shall relate briefly. Maximos was a former Cynic philosopher who converted to Christianity. Saint Gregory later described him as a dandy of dubious sex, a street-lounger, an inarticulate nuisance, and a raging pest. He thought himself a person of consequence. He would preen himself meticulously, and gave special attention to the abundance of curls that fell about his shoulders. Was he fair or dark, curly or straight-haired? Saint Gregory remarks that "he had been one way, but recently he contrived to look another way—the coiffeur's art could do him all over again....He was a woman in hairstyle, and a man by reason of the staff." With the recommendation of the Alexandrian Church, he arrived in Constantinople and attached himself to the Orthodox. It happened that he got involved with a scheme for financial gain. A priest had come from Thasos with a purse full of money. He was sent by the Church at Thasos to Constantinople for the purchase of Proconesian tiles. With stealth, Maximos coaxed him and won him over as an accomplice for a scheme he was about to perpetrate. He misled that unhappy and deceived priest with all kinds of words and pledges. Maximos also persuaded another priest in Saint Gregory's flock to betray the hierarch. Saint Gregory later speaks of that particular man, saying, "He had never been overlooked or suffered any rebuff; but on the contrary, he had always held first place in honor and dignity."

In the meantime, Maximos slyly won the favor and confidence of Saint Gregory. He then bribed some other confederates, namely Egyptian bishops, including one of Gregory's clerics, and planned to have Gregory ousted, and have himself installed as patriarch. The arrival of the Egyptian fleet gave him further support. Gregory happened to fall sick during that time, so the deceivers planned to carry out the enthronement at night.

Gregory describes the scene in a poem about his own life: "At night, when I was indisposed, like thieving wolves in the fold, they suddenly made their appearance, bringing a gang of hirelings from the fleet; indeed, the sort who might make a typical Alexandrian mob." Continuing, he says, "They, with the sailors, burst into the church, without any previous notice to the congregation or the staff of the church—and certainly not to myself, who deserved at least a dog's treatment." They were bent on consecrating Maximos, and even alleged that they had been commissioned to act thus.

Saint Gregory then says that dawn came. "The clergy living nearby grew agitated, and the news spread quickly. A tumult ensued, with a large concourse of magistrates, strangers, and riffraff. They were foiled, but refused to abandon their purpose, even though during the consecration service they were driven from the church by a maddened flock. They repaired to the house of some flute player, where they finished the ceremony. There was no time to bind him as they tonsured him, or use any pressure. Oh no, Maximos was quite willing to presume upon higher things, only the coxcomb was undone by having his hair shorn. The Cynic was then proclaimed pastor.

"The city straightway was convulsed. Everyone was furious. Bitter accusations flooded in about his manner of life. The poor shorn dog was deprived of his beautiful hair and a flock to administer." If it had not been for Saint Gregory's intercession with the flock, Maximos would have been seriously hurt. Gregory admits that "the ignorance I displayed with regard to Maximos deserves censure....For a trusting person is the easiest in the world to persuade, since he is impulsively drawn to goodness, real or counterfeit." Saint Gregory discloses that when Maximos came to him from Egypt he did not know that his exile was for misdemeanors, for Maximos represented himself to Gregory as one suffering banishment for the Lord's sake. And though he was a rascal, he was made to appear as a hero to the holy hierarch. Later he admits, "He was in fact a reprobate, but I respected him as a decent man." He then asks, "If decent treatment fails to sweeten a person, is there anything else under the sun that could work? For in very truth my kindness to him constitutes his reproach."[14]

The commotion moved Gregory to retire into solitude; yet in fact it made him more popular with his flock. He did suffer, however, considerable negative comment for his gullibility and the manner in which he had been

---

[14] *Concerning His Own Life*, 75:98-104.

misled by the Cynic imposter. But the Gospel tells us to show love to all. Christ also says, "The one who cometh to Me in no wise will I cast out [Jn. 6:37]." Saint Gregory said: "Be not wroth with me in that I have done good to this man, failing to anticipate his craftiness. Are we to be guilty of failing to foresee someone's evil predisposition? Surely, only God is able to know the secrets of the heart. Are we not commanded by His law to open our hearts to all who come to us? For it was important to me that Maximos leave his error, and begin to worship the Holy Trinity. He appeared virtuous, although now I know it was hypocrisy. We cannot penetrate the thoughts of man. We do not know the future."

Saint Gregory also suffered from critics who reproved his simple life and serene demeanor. In fact, Saint Gregory was more than willing to retire, but he was prevented by the sincere protestations of his friends. Indeed, when the congregation learned of his wish to retire, they cried out in protest—men, women, girls and boys, old people, nobles, common folk, magistrates, soldiers on furlough. They truly believed that if Gregory left, the Faith might depart with him. He observes, "There I stood before them, speechless, beset by darkness. I neither could repress their shouting or promise anything that they requested." He then says that it was very hot—stifling hot with perspiration pouring down. The children were crying; mothers were hoarse in the panic. The flock refused to abandon their efforts, even if it meant dying in their tracks in the church itself. They protested, "Tell us then, art thou going to have the Trinity cast out with thyself?" Gregory says that he panicked, lest something awful should occur. He acceded to their remonstrances until, as he said, a fitter individual should be found. "I swore no oath," he says. "I said I would stay on until some of the bishops arrived, thinking that then I might extricate myself from this anxious situation....I really thought my stay would be brief." He himself commented he was not one to bend the knee to pressure, or to accept authority unless lawfully bestowed; but he also admitted, "I could not even be forced to accept it when it was lawful"—and how true that was, we know from his past.

Meanwhile, the wretched Maximos and the Egyptian rabble exited the city. They betook themselves to the camp of the eastern Emperor Theodosios, while he was on an offensive against barbarian tribes in Thessalonike. Maximos again attempted to instigate intrigues. He hoped to secure for himself a see by imperial decree. Theodosios cast him out like a dog, and the rogue scampered off to Egypt.

Emperor Theodosios' Entry into the City

The Orthodox Emperor Theodosios entered the city on the 21st day of November, in the year 381. Later Saint Gregory speaks of Theodosios, saying, "He was not a bad man, and he was wondrously devoted to the

Trinity. For this doctrine must be thoroughly ingrained in all those who presume to occupy securely a stable throne." The incident of the Maximos fracas tarnished the prestige of the Orthodox, though we know that when Maximos approached Theodosios in Macedonia, he was snubbed. The populace wondered how the emperor might deal with Bishop Gregory. On the 24th day of December, in the year 380, Theodosios entered the city and deposed the Arian bishop, Demophilos, with all his clergy, and transferred the Church of the Holy Apostles to Bishop Gregory. All uncertainty vanished when the emperor exclaimed, "God through me is handing over the Church to thee and thy labors." On hearing this declaration, the unorthodox party of the city was fully determined not to give way, even at the cost of incidents unpleasant to itself. Gregory thought to himself, "Coercing them would mean that their exacerbation would be vented on me, who am so easily intimidated."

God became the arbiter in His holy one's struggles. The emperor was empowered from on high to both expel the Arians from holding the churches and to restore the church properties to the Orthodox. Almost the first act of Theodosios was to put the holy Gregory in possession of the episcopal throne. The saint said, "I was suffused by a glow of pleasure not unmixed with apprehension." For the sake of security and safety, however, armed forces were drawn up in aisles, and made to encompass the church. An agitated mob drew forward, with their disposition changing repeatedly from hostility to entreaty. Saint Gregory notes: "They were hostile toward me, but made entreaty to the civil authorities." The places surrounding the church and the streets were teeming with all kinds of people who were shouting, groaning, weeping, and grumbling. Saint Gregory, depicting himself as sickly and decrepit, was solemnly escorted, as he marched between general and army, with his eyes raised heavenward. "Hope sustained me as we wound our way, until finally I stood in the church. I know not how." Though his triumphal procession took place at daybreak, Saint Gregory records that the orb of the sun was obscured by a cloud, so that night overlay the entire city. "My enemies," says Gregory, "were gleeful at this, as if God were showing His displeasure with the performance." But when the holy man of God and the purple-clad emperor entered the beautiful gates of the sanctuary of the Church of the Holy Apostles, at the invocation and the response of the people, the cloud was dispersed and sunlight was everywhere, bathing the old tabernacle in heavenly radiance.

At that stage, popular enthusiasm demanded that the imperial power place the holy Gregory on the episcopal throne. The demand came from both those in power and the common folk. The clamor of all the people was tremendous. Saint Gregory says that "I had no voice left, so tense was I and exhausted by fear. I made one of my retinue rise from his seat, and he made a pronouncement." He said, "Silence, O people, cease shouting! This is, above all, an occasion of thanksgiving. Later on there will be a suitable time for greater issues." Thus, Saint Gregory declined the patriarchal throne. Moderation appealed to the crowd, so they consented. The emperor commended Saint Gregory and took his leave.[15]

Saint Gregory remained indoors and kept to himself. The churches were in Orthodox hands. The tumult in the city ceased, though there were a few rumblings that required subduing. Saint Gregory continued to devote himself for the most part to God and the pursuit of perfection, leaving the doors of the mighty to others. There was one incident which Saint Gregory mentions when writing about his life, which we shall narrate.

The Saint's Conduct in the City

The venerable Gregory had been confined indoors at that time due to illness, which he notes was the invariable companion of his troubles. While he was laid up, some people burst in, hauling a young man with them. He was pale, long-haired, and poorly attired. Saint Gregory made an attempt to rise up. The people then began to thank God and the emperor for making this day possible. They also praised the hierarch, and took their leave. But the frightened youth, unable to speak, cast himself at the feet of Gregory, as if he were supplicating him. Saint Gregory kept on asking his name, where he was from, and what he wanted. The young man only cried louder. He swore, he moaned, he took hold of the hierarch's hands. Saint Gregory also felt himself close to tears amid that situation. Words were powerless, so the youth was dragged away by others. One of the bystanders finally disclosed the youth's identity, saying to the saint, "This man is thy would-be assassin. It is by the grace of God that thou art alive. He came of his own volition, to pass judgment on his own guilt, a kindly murderer, a noble accuser, who offers his tears as a penalty for blood." Saint Gregory remembers, "I was utterly broken by these words." The holy man hastened to say something to dispel all unpleasantness. "May God save thee. For me, who have been delivered, to be kind to my attacker is but a little thing. Thy courage hath made thee mine. See to it that thou mightest become a credit both to me and to God."

The Arians had hired this youth to assassinate the archbishop, hoping that, using the commotion his death would create, they might reinstall themselves. Yet God protected Gregory and hindered them and their hired killer. The young man admitted that he attempted to plunge a knife into the holy man's chest; but when he went to carry out this heinous deed, he was divinely prevented. He believed that God thwarted his plan, and he under-

---

[15] Ibid., 75:114, 115.

stood this intervention to have been miraculous. He was then gripped with fear at a dreadful recompense awaiting himself, and he repented from the depths of his heart. Saint Gregory, a true imitator of Christ, then counseled the young man, saying, "The Master Christ, Who guarded me, my child, may He also forgive thy transgression. Only do thou leave thy heresy and come to a right confession, so that thou mayest labor for Christ with a pure conscience." Word spread quickly throughout the city how the archbishop dealt with his would-be assassin. They were all astonished at his forbearance, and loved him the more for it.[16]

Another issue arose—and much to his dismay—when Saint Gregory uncovered irregularities in church funds. He could not find the slightest record among the papers of his predecessors of prodigious sums of money, treasures, and revenues from every quarter. Even in the files of the treasurers, who were responsible for such accounts, there were no records. Although others advised that he bring in an outside auditor, Saint Gregory chose to overlook the financial accounts, lest the cause of piety should be defamed by the probing and scrutiny of a public investigation. He said, "A man is responsible only for what he has, not for what he claims by right of inheritance."[17]

Another concern of the hierarch was that his enemies gossiped that the congregations of his churches were small, and would not reach even to the doors. Therefore, he made this his earnest concern, not to mention the work of administering to the poor, and to virgins, strangers, pilgrims, and prisoners. He also put in good order the psalmody and helped those practising continence.

The Synod of Constantinople

In the time that it took for the arrival of the bishops for the synod meeting which Theodosios convened, Gregory, though he had imperial force at his command, decided to be conciliatory with his enemies. Once more, he was criticized for his leniency in Orthodox circles. Saint Gregory states his methods in dealing with those who had gone astray from a pure confession of the Faith in this way: "Some were influenced by the force of what I had to say; others became tractable because of the way in which I said it. For I chose my language very carefully, avoiding controversy or ridicule. I was gentle and affable in my preaching, regarding myself as the proponent of a doctrine that is sympathetic and mild, and smites no one. For yielding is reasonable, and winning is much more commendable when someone is drawn to God by the force of persuasion."

---

[16] Ibid., 75:117; *The Great Synaxaristes* (in Greek), p. 646.
[17] Ibid., 75:118.

In the spring of 381, the Œcumenical Synod of Constantinople convened, which was attended by a representative body of eastern prelates, under the presidency initially of Meletios of Antioch. Saint Gregory describes him as "a saintly man, simple, straightforward, redolent of God, serene of countenance, impressing those who beheld him with his blend of courage and modesty, a true product of the Spirit."

Saint Gregory the Theologian

In May, in the early stages, Gregory was acknowledged as the legitimate Archbishop of Constantinople. In fact, this was the synod meeting's first item on the agenda: to sanction the translation of Gregory from the see of Sasima to that of the metropolis of the empire, and to enthrone him in Hagia Sophia. "On the august throne, then, the bishops installed me," says Saint Gregory. "I cried out and groaned; but, for one particular reason, was not altogether unwilling. The reason? Bear witness to it, O Logos, for it is not right to hide the truth....I thought, in my vain imaginings, that once I had control of this throne, since outward show carries great weight, I could act like a chorus leader between two choruses....I could blend them with myself and thus weld into a unity what had been so badly divided; for the division certainly ran deep....Between them there was a furious struggle for power and control....Concern about religion was not their real cause,...but rivalry about thrones. Why do I say this about bishops? I do not mean the bishops so much, as those partisans on either side."[18]

During that time, the Bishop of Antioch, Meletios, reposed in the Lord. Amid an elaborate ceremony, his relics were translated to his own diocese. Now the holy Meletios' rival for his see of Antioch, one named Paulinus, and the bishops in communion with him, were not in attendance at the synod meeting. A certain element was anxious to set up another bishop than Paulinus. With the repose of Meletios, Gregory presided at the sessions of the synod. Though Gregory was a supporter of Meletios, he attempted to

---

[18] Ibid., 75:119.

resolve the furious situation in Antioch by proposing that no successor be elected, but to leave the man who had held it thus far, that is Paulinus. And if Paulinus were recognized until his death, the problem would be resolved in time. The end of Saint Gregory's speech was the signal for screams on every side. There was anarchy in the synod meeting. The fathers went ahead and elected Flavian.

Saint Gregory says, "Fortunately, illness came to my rescue, because it kept me for the most part at home. I had only one idea in mind, to get away. There lay the solution to my problems."[19] He withdrew into privacy and actually changed the place of his abode. The congregation mourned Gregory, as if he were already dead. They feared that he would abandon them.

Then a further crisis was triggered with the arrival of contingents from Egypt and Macedonia, or, as Saint Gregory remarked, "a cold wind from the west." The Egyptian bishops on their arrival were disposed to take up the case of Maximos. They were determined to oust Gregory from the patriarchal throne. They made it clear that the measure was not directed against Gregory personally, but instead against those who enthroned him. They contested Saint Gregory's episcopal legitimacy in the see of Constantinople. They invoked Canon 15 of the Synod of Nicaea, which prohibited a bishop to go from one city to another. They argued that he was the Bishop of Sasima, and not of Constantinople. Though the act of another synod meeting rescinded the prohibition of translating bishops to other sees, Gregory was considering withdrawing. He had a gentle, softhearted soul; and he was hurt. The real reason for the Egyptians' protest was that the election had been made without them, and that Gregory would probably be unpleasant to them, on account of his reputation as a bold preacher of righteousness.

Disgusted with the operations of party passions in the synod meeting, Saint Gregory longed for freedom. He spoke to them, saying, "Now have I become Jonas the prophet. I am giving myself as victim for the safety of the ship, even though it shall be a case of the innocent encountering the waves. Take me then on the issue and cast me forth; the hospitable whale will welcome me from the depths. From now on begin to be of one mind, and then make your way toward everything in due order....When I was enthroned it was without enthusiasm, and now I take my leave with a will. My state of health, too, recommends this course of action. I have only one death to die, and that is in the hands of God. O my Trinity, Thou art all I care for....Fare-

---

[19] Ibid., 75:125.

you-well, gentlemen, and be mindful of my labors."[20] The synod was shocked at his words. Saint Gregory left, feeling both joy and some depression. He knew he had found some respite from trouble, but was pained at what might become of the people. He felt deprived of his children, and this caused him agony.

He offered his resignation in a speech to the synod, and only with difficulty secured the reluctant permission of the emperor. He said, "Let me have just this, permission to give way somewhat before jealousy. Let me with reverence look upon thrones, but from a distance. I am tired of being hated by everyone, even my friends, because I find myself unable to turn anywhere except to God. Enjoin upon these fathers a brotherly harmony." The favor was granted to Saint Gregory. Yet the task of having everyone accept it with a good heart awaited the saint. He coaxed, praised, and tried to reconcile himself with the disaffected element, the clergy, the administrators of flocks, the old Orthodox congregation, the recent converts, and those bishops who were especially stricken. Both relieved and saddened, he made his farewell and withdrew once and for all to his boyhood home of Arianzos, where he would cultivate contemplation unhampered.

From his retirement, he wrote: "All of you succeeded in defeating one man who wanted to be defeated." He wrote about his resignation in a poem about himself and the bishops, saying, "Envy rent apart those gentlemen, my fellow bishops....As for me, I propose to withdraw to God. It is for Him I live and breathe, to Him alone that I turn my gaze. Before I was born, my mother promised me to Him; and to Him dangers and a fair vision in the night have united me. To Him I shall offer in sacrifice the pure motions of the mind, conversing with Him, person to person, insofar as one can attain that state. Such then, on behalf of decent people, is my message for the miscreants." After his resignation, the catechumen and prefect of Constantinople Nectarios was elected in his stead.

Indeed, the fact that Saint Gregory removed himself from a volatile situation was praiseworthy. It is a laudable testimonial to his character; for other clergy of his time would not draw back from the intrigues and byways available to secure possession of such dignities as were offered to Gregory.

Retirement

From 381 and henceforth, he lived in retirement at his paternal home; though at a distance, he maintained his care for his native church in Nazianzos. He continued his austere asceticism, contemplation, and literary pursuits. When he retired there, he had been persuaded by the bishops of the province—especially Metropolitan Theodore of Tyana and Bishop Bosporios

---

[20] Ibid., 75:127, 128.

of Koloneia—and the earnest solicitation of the people, to undertake the administration of the diocese then vacant, until the vacancy should be filled. The bishops of that province, however, were desirous to retain Gregory altogether. Therefore, they made no haste to proceed to an election, despite the continual expressed wishes of Gregory that they find someone else.

Saint Gregory was a poet and a man of letters. Many of his epistles and poems were written during this period. He still participated in Church affairs through the operation of his numerous epistles. He maintained his sincere and active interest in the welfare and sufferings of others around him. He wrote prodigiously, mainly in verse, and kept up his correspondence with younger relatives and all sorts of other people, such as bishops, public officials, and rhetors. He also received letters from his correspondents, asking for advice. He himself, however, was happy, and nothing could induce him to reconsider entering public life again. He was active and alert to the end.

During his retirement, which was not so very quiet, his own city was set in turmoil by Apollinarian heretics, who attempted to establish themselves in the Church. Apollinarios had been Bishop of Laodikeia in the latter half of the fourth century. He maintained some heretical views on the nature of our Lord, which prepared the ground for various forms of the Monophysite heresy. He attributed to Christ a human body and a human soul, but not a reasoning spirit, whose place, according to him, was supplied by the Logos Himself. He even maintained that Christ's body was not really born of Mary, but was a part of the divinity converted into flesh. Saint Athanasios the Great also wrote against these innovations. In 377, a Roman council excommunicated Apollinarios and his adherents, and Saint Damasus (pope, 366-384) wrote a letter containing twenty-five anathemas.

As Gregory's illnesses gave him increasing discomfort, it became necessary for him to try the hot baths at the Monastery at Xantharis, on the advice of his physicians.[21] He went, but was suddenly stricken by illness. While the saint was away, a sect of Apollinarians, situated at Nazianzos, took advantage of his absence and ventured to procure the consecration of a bishop of like mind. True, technically, the see was vacant, but the administration of that Church had been committed to Saint Gregory by the bishops of the province. The truth, however, is that Saint Gregory did foresee that the heretics would attempt such a vile undertaking, which was another reason for his pressing the metropolitan and his co-provincials to fill the throne by a canonical election. Saint Gregory was in no way about to surrender authority of the Church entrusted to his safekeeping to an irregularly elected and uncanonically consecrated heretic.

---

[21] Div. I, Ep. cxxv, "To Olympius."

Saint Gregory also wrote some very important letters on the Apollinarian controversy, especially to Bishop Nectarios of Constantinople and the Priest Cledonios. He wrote to Archbishop Nectarios: "The care of God, which throughout the time before us guarded the Churches, appears to have completely forsaken us in these days. My soul is immersed to such a degree in these calamities that the private sufferings of my own life should hardly seem to be reckoned evils—though they are so numerous and great that if they befell anyone else I should think them unbearable—but I can only look at the common sufferings of the Churches. If some pains are not taken to remedy the present crisis, things will gradually come to a desperate condition. The followers of Arius or Evnomios—I cannot say who stirred them up to this folly—are making a display of their disease, as if they attained some degree of confidence and permission by collecting congregations. Those of the Makedonian party have reached such a pitch of folly that they are arrogating to themselves the name of bishops, as they wander about our dioceses. Evnomios is no longer content with merely existing. Unless he can draw away everyone with him to his ruinous heresy, he thinks himself an injured man. All this, however, is endurable. The most grievous time of all in the woes of the Church is the boldness of the Apollinarians."[22]

Saint Gregory wrote to the reverend and God-beloved brother and fellow priest Cledonios: "We do not sever the Man Jesus from the Divinity, but we lay down as dogma the unity and identity of Hypostasis (Person), Who of old was not Man but God, and the only-begotten Son before all ages, unmingled with body or anything corporeal. But in these last days, He assumed manhood also for our salvation; passible in His flesh, impassible in His divinity; circumscribed in the body, uncircumscribable in the Spirit; at once earthly and heavenly, tangible and intangible, comprehensible and incomprehensible; that by One and the same Hypostasis (Person), Who was perfect Man and also God, the entire humanity fallen through sin might be created anew.

"If anyone does not believe that holy Mary is the Mother of God, he is severed from the divinity. If anyone should assert that He passed through the Virgin as through a channel, and was not at once divinely and humanly formed in her—divinely, because without the intervention of a man; humanly, because in accordance with the laws of gestation—he is in like manner godless. If any assert that the manhood was formed and afterward was clothed with the divinity, he too is to be condemned....If any introduce the notion of two Sons, one of God the Father, the other of the Mother, and discredits the unity and identity, may he lose his part in the adoption promised to those who

---

[22] Div. I, Ep. ccii, "Against Apollinarius, the Second Letter to Cledonius."

believe aright. For God and man are two natures, as also are soul and body; but there are not two Sons or two Gods....For both natures are one by the combination, the Deity being made Man, and the manhood divinized or however one should express it....

"If any worship not the Crucified, let him be anathema and be numbered among the deicides. If any assert that He was made perfect by works, or that after His Baptism, or after His resurrection from the dead, He was counted worthy of an adoptive Sonship,...let him be anathema....

"If any assert that He has now put off His holy flesh, and that His divinity is stripped of the body, and deny that He is now with His body and will come again with it, let him not see the glory of His Coming. For where is His body now, if not with Him Who assumed it?...

"If anyone has put his trust in Him as a man without a human mind, he is really bereft of mind, and quite unworthy of salvation. For that which He has not assumed He has not healed; but that which is united to His divinity is also saved. If only half of Adam fell, then that which Christ assumes and saves may be half also; but if the whole of his nature fell, it must be united to the whole nature of Him that was begotten, and so be saved as a whole. Let them not, then, begrudge us our complete salvation, or clothe the Savior only with bones and nerves and the portraiture of humanity....For if He has a soul, and yet is without a mind, how is He man, for man is not a mindless animal?...

"But if you will look at what is mental and incorporeal, remember that I in my one personality can contain soul and reason and mind and the Holy Spirit....For such is the nature of intellectual existences, that they can mingle with one another and with bodies, incorporeally and invisibly. For many sounds are comprehended by one ear; and the eyes of many are occupied by the same visible objects, and the smell by odors; nor are the senses narrowed by each other, or crowded out, nor the objects of sense diminished by the multitude of the perceptions....The light is nothing compared with the sun, nor a little damp compared with a river, that we must first do away with the lesser, and take the light from a house, or the moisture from the earth, to enable it to contain the greater and more perfect.....

"And so the passage, 'The Logos became flesh [Jn. 1:14]' seems to me to be equivalent to that in which it is said that He was made sin [2 Cor. 5:21], or a curse [Gal. 3:13] for us; not that the Lord was transformed into either of these, how could He be? But because by taking them upon Him He took away our sins and bore our iniquities [Is. 63:7]."[23]

---

[23] Div. I, Ep. ci, "To Cledonius the Priest Against Apollinarius."

In 382, Saint Gregory received a summons to attend the synod at Constantinople. The retired hierarch wished to decline Emperor Theodosios' invitation, and wrote to Prefect Prokopios of Constantinople, saying that he disliked episcopal synods. Governor Olympios of Cappadocia also wrote him that he should attend. The archbishop then wrote: "It is more serious to me than my illness, that no one will believe that I am ill!" The saint wrote that when he considered the long journey, and being pushed into the midst of troubles—from which he formerly rejoiced to have withdrawn—it made him even think that he ought to be grateful for his bodily afflictions.

A little while after, the people of Nazianzos had in some way brought upon themselves the loss of their civic rights. The order for the forfeiture of the title of "city" had been signed by Governor Olympios. As a result, there was much civil unrest among the young people; and a revolt was fomented on the part of a number of them. The punishment determined by Olympios was that the entire populace should suffer with the total destruction of the place. Now Saint Gregory, hindered by his bodily ailments, was unable to put in a personal appearance before the governor. Undaunted, he pleaded eloquently and emotionally for the cause of his native city, using its official Latin name of Diocaesarea, in at least three letters which are extant, so as to procure a pardon. As a result, Olympios looked with a favorable eye upon the entreaty of the venerable man, and spared the citizens and their city.

Another situation arose in which the great old man was called in to provide a judgment. An honorable citizen of Nazianzos, named Verianos, was offended by his son-in-law. We are not told the nature of the offense, but, by reason of it, Verianos pressed his daughter to sue for divorce. Governor Olympios referred the unhappy matter to the episcopal arbitration of Saint Gregory, whom he sought not so much as a judge, but as a bishop. The holy man refused to even countenance the proceeding. Now the young woman was divided between reverence for her parents and affection for her husband. On account of her tears, Saint Gregory perceived that her words were with her parents, but her mind was with her husband. Denying any application for divorce, he wrote both the prefect and Verianos himself. He upheld in his letter to Olympios that it was contrary to Church law to grant such a divorce, though Roman law might determine otherwise. He pleaded for justice, and counseled that Verianos ought to overlook what took place. When he wrote the father, he said: "I have not time, for the sake of favoring thy friendship (though in all respects I have the highest regard for thee), to offend God, to Whom I have to give account of every action and thought. I will believe thy daughter—for the truth shall be told—when she can lay aside her awe of thee, and boldly declare the truth. At present her condition is pitiable; for she assigns her words to thee, and her tears to her husband."

Saint Gregory continued to press for the election of a bishop for Nazianzos. He desired that his cousin Evlalios the *chorepiscopos* should be nominated. The bishops felt some jealousy at what they took to be an attempt on Gregory's part to dictate to them. They refused him any part in the election. Saint Gregory protested. As it happened, Evlalios was chosen. Even then, Saint Gregory's enemies spread the vile rumor that Evlalios' election was against Gregory's wishes. Saint Gregory sent out an epistle to quash the false report. He explained that it was his wish that a worthy man of piety, such as Evlalios, be found. He gave as his reason his health, which rendered him unequal to the task, but more so because of his failing health he feared the responsibility of having the Church suffer neglect on his account. He reminded them that he was appointed not to Nazianzos but to Sasima, although for a short time out of reverence for his father, he says, "I, as a stranger, undertook the government."[24] Thus, Saint Gregory resigned the care of Nazianzos, and nothing could induce him to withdraw his resignation.

In his seclusion, Saint Gregory was rigorous in his self-denial, and his only indulgences were a garden and a fountain. His knees were worn from prostrations in prayer. He longed to depart and be with Christ. He kept a bed of straw covered with a sackcloth. He donned only a single rough tunic. He went about without shoes. He described himself as a breathing corpse. He had made a will before he left Constantinople, leaving all his property to the Deacon Gregory for life, with reversion to the poor of Nazianzos.

At sixty-two years of age he reposed on the 25th day of January, ca. 391. He is described as being of middle height and somewhat pale, though it became him. He had a graceful, charming, and even playful manner. His nose was somewhat snubbed and flat. He had thick hair which was blanched by age, though his short beard and conspicuous eyebrows were thicker. Later in life he was bald with white hair on the sides. He had a scar on his right eye, which may be seen in the sacred relic of his skull, which is kept at the Holy Monastery of Vatopedi on Mount Athos. His manner was simple, friendly, and attractive. His faith was zealous and fiery. His asceticism, used as a means of elevating and liberating the mind, was extreme, whereby he strained, if not injured, his health. He was a man of many talents and much cultivation, with noble affections and deep feelings.

Saint Gregory's Writings

The works of Saint Gregory the Theologian include orations, letters, and poems. Everything he penned bears the mark of a polished rhetorician. His forty-five orations were used as models in the schools of rhetoric. His five *Theological Orations*, which were preached in the Church of the

---

[24] Div. III, § 2, Ep. clxxxii, "To Saint Gregory of Nyssa."

Resurrection in Constantinople, wherein he explains the Nicaean doctrine of the Trinity, won him the title of "Theologian." The first oration is a preliminary discourse against the Evnomians. With the second oration he speaks of the existence, nature, being, and attributes of God, insofar as man's finite intellect may comprehend the Trinity. Both the third and fourth theological orations speak of the divinity of the Son. The fifth oration is on the Holy Spirit.

His most notable discourses and moral essays include a defense of his flight and treatises on his consecration to Sasima, on the plague of hail, on peace, on love of the poor, on the indissolubility of marriage, and on moderation in theological discussion, as well as a farewell discourse given at Constantinople. He also authored sermons for feasts, two for Pascha, one for the Nativity of our Lord, one for the Theophany, and one for the Pentecost. He wrote funeral eulogies on Saint Basil, and on his father, sister, and brother. His panegyrics on saints include those to Saints Cyprian and Athanasios, and on the Maccabaean brothers and their

Saint Gregory the Theologian

mother Solomonia. He also wrote political pamphlets, the two *Invectives Against Julian*. These were delivered at Nazianzos after the slaying of Julian. The orations mention the emperor's attempt to rebuild the temple at Jerusalem, and its failure, and his defeat in the Persian campaign. Saint Gregory illustrates the might of God's justice, and the consolation of His providence in our affairs.[25]

The *Patrologia Graeca* of Migne contains 243 epistles. They are finely written with his customary scrupulous attention to the rules of style, and elaborate Byzantine politesse, with dashes of wit and irony. His poems, written during the last ten years of his life, are filled with pertinent autobiographical data.

During his latter years, Saint Gregory also included a collection of Saint Basil's letters with his own, and gave his friend the first place. When asked the reason for this, Gregory explains: "I have always preferred the

---

[25] *Prolegomena*, Nicene, VII:200-202.

great Basil to myself, though he was of the contrary opinion; and so I do now, not less for truth's sake than for friendship's. This is the reason why I have given his letters the first place and my own the second. For I hope we two will always be coupled together; and also I would supply others with an example of modesty and submission."[26] Through his holy prayers, God have mercy on us. Amen.

On the 25th of January, the holy Church commemorates our venerable Father PUPLIOS of Zeugma.[27]

Puplios (Publius),[28] our holy father, was born in the city of Zeugma,[29] by the banks of the Euphrates River, into a family of statesmen. At an early age, he ascended a lofty mountain, which was a distance of thirty stadia (3.5 miles) from the aforementioned city, and there he built a small cell. Meanwhile, he distributed to the poor all those things that he had inherited from his parents, and lived in utmost abstinence and virtue. As a result, his fame spread everywhere, and many people flocked to him to share in his ascetic struggles. He ordered them to construct small cells. They built and lived within them, exerting themselves night and day.

The saint visited the brethren often and sought to discover anything superfluous in their cells. Even the very bread on which they subsisted was weighed in a scale; and if he ever found more than the allotted measure, he called that brother a glutton and a lover of the flesh. If, for instance, he ever saw a brother who cast out the chaff of the wheat, he would say to him that he lived on the food of the Sybarites,[30] who were known by historians to be pleasure-seekers. At night, he used to approach the door of every brother, and

---

[26] Div. III, § 8, Ep. liii, "To Nicobulus."

[27] The Life of Saint Puplios was recorded by Theodoretos of Kyros (Cyrrhus), in Number Five of his *Religious History*. See also *A History of the Monks of Syria*, Cistercian Studies Series: Number Ninety-Eight, pp. 58-62.

[28] Saint Puplios the monk and monastic founder lived around the time of Valens (364-378, emperor of the east. His monastery was probably founded circa 350.

[29] Zeugma was an ancient city in Mesopotamia, which was built by Seleucus the satrap, on the west bank of the Euphrates River, near the modern city of Bir. It was named Zeugma because in its neighborhood were built other bridges which joined the two banks of the river. On the opposite bank was built the city of Apameia, which today is called Biretzin. Theodoretos comments that Zeugma was where Xerxes, marching against Greece, crossed the Euphrates with his army, bridging the river by yoking many ships to one another. Xerxes therefore called the place Zeugma.

[30] Sybaris was an ancient Greek city in southern Italy, on the Gulf of Taranto. It was founded in 720 B.C. and destroyed in 510 B.C. It was noted for its wealth and luxurious living.

if he found that brother awake and praying, he left quietly. But, if he felt that he was sleeping, he would knock on the door of his cell and would verbally accuse that slumbering brother. Therefore, through these habitual visitations and diligence, many brothers absorbed all the virtues like sponges.

Observing Abba Puplios' concern for the welfare of the scattered brethren, some suggested one building that all might dwell together. They said to the elder, "Those who are scattered shall then live more strictly, which shall release thee from anxiety about them." Abba Puplios blessed the idea, and thus a coenobium was formed. "Live together," he said, "and urge each other onward. Thus, what one lacks, he shall receive from others. Thus, one can emulate the gentleness of another brother, who in turn can blend his gentleness with zeal. One can learn from another to keep vigil, while the other receives an example in abstaining, and so on. Thus the community life shall help fill what is lacking."

Now those brethren who spoke Greek, trained and offered hymnody to God in the Greek language. This same desire took hold of those who used the local Syriac language. Afterward, when the saint constructed a church, both groups were appointed to come together inside the church at the opening and closing of each day. They chanted, being divided into two choirs, the evening and morning hymns to God in both the Greek and Syriac tongues.[31]

Among the brotherhood were the Monks Theoteknos and Aphthonios, who, after the repose of this saint, received the labor of guardianship and governing of the brethren.[32] Thus, the ever-memorable Puplios, having struggled well, surrendered his soul into the hands of God.

---

[31]Greek was the language of Puplios' first disciples, as well as his own curial origins. This suggests that monasticism originated there among the educated, Hellenized class.

[32] Theodoretos mentions that in the coenobium formed by Saint Puplios there was another brother named Theodotos who, after Theoteknos, was entrusted with the guardianship of the brethren. He was adorned with so many virtues that he surpassed his predecessors in fame. He was stricken by so many arrows of divine love that, night and day, tears of compunction filled and ran from his eyes. Theodoretos also adds that Aphthonios became a hierarch afterward. Even as a hierarch, though, he did not discard the heavy and worn garment that he wore as a monk. He often came to the coenobium and remained there for many days, encouraging the brethren, resolving their grievances, and advising them toward their salvation. While he remained there, he was never idle, but either cleaned lentils or performed some other lowly task.

Theodoretos also mentions another brother of the same coenobium, named Gregory, who never, in his entire life, tasted the fruit of the vineyard, nor even in his old age did he taste raisins, milk, or cheese.

On the 25th of January, the holy Church commemorates MARIS the Chanter.[33]

Maris, our holy father among the saints, when young and in the world, had a comely appearance and possessed a good singing voice. In this manner, he adorned the feasts and celebrations of Christ and the saints with his sweet hymns and odes. The ever-memorable one loved God and always kept His commandments. He also safeguarded the chastity of his body and maintained the purity of his soul, albeit he was in the midst of worldly pleasures and associated with secular people. Finally, when he resolved to forsake the world, he traveled to a village called Homeros. Once there, he constructed a small cell, enclosing himself for thirty-seven years. Even though that cell was in a damp place and did not benefit his health, he never desired to move, but lived in it until he completed the course of his life.

This holy one loved simplicity and loathed the effete things and pretenses of life. He was more content in poverty than in wealth. For this reason, he wore garments woven of goat's hair, and his diet consisted of bread, salt, and a little water. However, since he lived in the wilderness for many years, he requested that a divine office be conducted in his cell. One day, Theodoretos of Kyros, the author of this saint's account, chanced to be there. Abba Maris pleaded with him concerning serving therein. The latter accepted gladly and sent people to a nearby village, where they obtained liturgical vessels; and using the hands of the deacons in place of a holy table, they offered the bloodless sacrifice upon them in Maris' presence.[34] Abba Maris, meanwhile, was filled with such grace that he believed he witnessed the throne of God. Of this, he said that he never enjoyed another similar spiritual delight. The holy one passed the remainder of his life in the paths of righteousness, and ascended to heaven, where he rejoiced amongst the saints in the courts of the Firstborn.

---

[33] The Life of Saint Maris was recorded by Theodoretos of Kyros, in Number Twenty of his *Religious History*.

[34] It is worthy of note that what Theodoretos of Kyros did, he was compelled to do, as was Saint Lucian of Antioch earlier, who performed the Liturgy on his own chest, while incarcerated in prison. This is because the hands of the priest or the deacon are more sacred than a holy table of stone, according to Saint John Chrysostom. This is done rarely and by necessity, and should not be performed by anyone else. See the footnote to Canon 31 of the Sixth Œcumenical Synod in the *Pedalion* (*The Rudder*), as well as the Life of the holy Hieromartyr Lucian, commemorated by the holy Church on the 15th of October.

**On the 25ᵗʰ of January, the holy Church commemorates
the venerable APOLLOS of Hermopolis in the Thebaid.**[35]

Apollos, the ever-memorable one, was only an adolescent of fifteen when he renounced the world. He repaired to the desert, where he heaped upon himself virtue after virtue. One day, Abba Apollos heard a voice, as that of an angel, from out of heaven saying, "Apollos, Apollos, by thy hands, I am about to put to nought the wisdom of the wise men of Egypt. I shall remove the knowledge, which is not knowledge, of the nations. The wise men of Babel shall be put to shame, and the service of devils shall be blotted out. Make haste now to get thee away. Thou shalt go near the habitations of men. Thou shalt beget for Me a holy people who shall be known by their good works." Abba Apollos answered and said, "My Lord, do Thou remove from me pride, lest I should become exalted over my brethren and lose all the blessing of grace and become as one without grace." The divine voice said, "Place thy hand upon thy neck. Whatsoever thou layest hold upon, cast it down and bury it in the sand. Thus thou shalt be delivered from pride." Apollos obeyed and laid his hand upon his neck. Then he observed a small dark being, like a dusky Arab boy, whom he threw to the ground. The creature laughed and said, "I am the demon of pride." The holy man then laid hold upon the creature and buried him in the sand. Apollos then heard a voice out of heaven repeating thrice, "Go from this place and cease fearing. For whatsoever thou shalt ask from God, it shall be given to thee."

Thus, Abba Apollos went forth, after being in one place forty years, to the inner parts where he found a cave for habitation. The location was in the Thebaid, on the borders of Hermopolis. This was where the Child Jesus, the all-holy Theotokos, and Joseph once took refuge, that the word of Prophet Esaias should be fulfilled: "Behold, the Lord sits on a swift cloud, and shall come to Egypt: and the idols of Egypt shall be moved at His presence, and their heart shall faint within them [Is. 19:1]." At the time of Abba Apollos, the house of the idols, wherein all the idols were toppled by God to the ground, could still be seen. In that place Abba Apollos dwelt without food. He devoted the time to raising his soul to the heavens. The garment in which he was clad, he had worn forty years without any trace of disintegration. He became famous in those parts, so that people were coming to him in his retreat. They came to hear his teachings and instructions, on account of which many made their dwelling with him nearby. He exhorted them to preserve the

---

[35] The Life of this venerable desert father was recorded by Blessed Jerome, which text is found paraphrased in the *Eklogion* by Agapios the Cretan. The triumphs of the blessed Apollos and Ammon are also recorded in *The Paradise of the Fathers*, I:340-353.

duties and obligations of the monastic and ascetic conduct of life. He counseled each to fast as much as he was able. The great man partook only of grass, herbs, benign weeds, or vegetables, but never did he eat bread.

During the time when he lived in the cave, which was by the base of a mountain near to Shaina, his conduct of life was as follows. He bowed his knees in unceasing prayer to God; that is, he prayed one hundred times in the night and also during the day. He had no care for food, but partook of what was given to him by God Who sent forth an angel. His apparel, a short-sleeved garment which covered his body, and a small napkin which he wore on his head, never wore out. By the grace and power of the Holy Spirit, he wrought miracles and healings. These cures were attested to by venerable elders in the brotherhood. Abba Apollos was considered a new prophet and apostle to their generation. His renown spread and attracted many disciples. He first of all showed them by his own example of ascetic excellence that which he exhorted in words. On Sundays he took his meal with the brethren. He tasted nothing but the herbs indigenous to the place. Again, he ate neither bread, nor pulse, nor fruits, nor anything that had been prepared by fire.

During that time, Julian the Apostate reigned (361-363). Both he and his governors persecuted the Christians. Now it happened that one of the monks was apprehended, whom the pagans not only wished to press into military service but also to renounce the Christ. The venerable Apollos went to the prison to offer counsel and encouragement to that brother. He urged him not to cower before temporal punishments, but to persevere and endure them manfully that he might win the heavenly crown. The elder strengthened the soul of that brother by these words, for the martyr was sorely tried by the temptation. The centurion in the meantime entered the prison and was dismayed at the sight of the holy man. In his anger, he shouted at Abba Apollos, "How dost thou dare show thyself herein?" He then turned and ordered his men to confine to a dungeon both the holy man and those who had accompanied him. The centurion then departed for his house, saying, "These men too are useful for military service." Then, in the middle of the night, an angel of the Lord, as radiant as lightning, came and opened the prison. The guards, out of fear, fell to the ground, imploring the prisoners to leave. The venerable elder, however, did not wish to leave and said, "Let us wait until he who enclosed us herein should come." And lo! the centurion came running into the prison. The centurion then ordered his men, saying, "Release the prisoners, for this same night a great earthquake struck, demolishing my house and killing all those who dwelt therein." Thereupon, the prisoners departed for their desert cells rejoicing and glorifying God with loud voices. The elder also returned and resumed his daily exhortations and admonitions before the brotherhood.

At another time, a certain virtuous and ancient ascetic fell asleep in the Lord. The venerable Apollos beheld a vision of that brother who had reposed. Apollos beheld him sitting in Paradise in the midst of the saints. Consequently, the saint entreated God that he too might go to the Lord and partake of that ineffable rejoicing. Christ answered him and said, "It is needful that thou shouldest abide for much more time in the world, for the benefit of many who shall emulate thy deeds and come to perfection; for a multitude of monks shall come and cultivate righteousness under thy direction. Then thou mayest receive a greatly multiplied recompense for thy labors." Thus it came to pass. A great monastery grew up about him in the mountain. At length, five hundred men came and dwelt together, holding all things in common. Thus were fulfilled the words of Scripture: "Be glad, thou thirsty desert. Let the wilderness exult and flower as the lily [Is. 35:1]"; and, "Rejoice, thou barren that bearest not. Break forth and cry, thou that dost not travail. For more are the children of the desolate than of her that has a husband [Is. 54:1]." Thus the land of Egypt was filled with true congregations of monastics, fulfilling the word of the apostle: "Where sin abounded, grace did much more abound [Rom. 5:20]."

Now there was a time when Egypt was filled with abominations and idols, more so than any other nation. They worshipped dogs and apes, and even onions, garlic, and herbs. These were considered gods. They worshipped the bull and the waters of the Nile. Why? Because they deemed such creatures and things to be the cause of their redemption. In the calamitous time of Pharaoh, when they suffered the plagues and the loss of one generation of their firstborn, they no longer cleaved to Pharaoh after his entire host was drowned in the sea while pursuing the Israelites. Each man did that which was right in his own eyes and made his own god, saying, "This is my god, and through this god I shall not perish with Pharaoh."

Around the monastery, there were ten villages of idol-worshipping inhabitants. Whensoever drought came upon their land, these benighted peoples made a procession with their wooden idol. There was dancing and leaping about by the pagan priests and the idol-mad natives. It happened also that Abba Apollos and a few of his disciples were by the bank of the river, where the pagans had congregated and begun their devilish sports in the hope of calling forth rain. The abba beheld them from a distance. He went to his knees in prayer on the very spot where he was standing by the river, offering up prayer to the God of the universe. There were thousands of pagans on the other side of the river. At the saint's entreaty, they all became bound with invisible cords. They could not move or even crawl away. By and by, they began to suffer from thirst. The scorching sun was beating down fiercely that day, leaving them parched. The pagans were sore astonished at what had taken place. Though they could not budge, they could speak to one another. The pagan priests then said, "There is a certain Christian in our borders. It is he who has done this to us." They of course meant Abba Apollos. Then the priests said, "If we are not to suffer tribulation, it would be right that we entreat Apollos." The saint heard their cries and shouts, and he came over to them. He offered up supplication in their behalf; and thus they were loosed from their bonds. All came to the knowledge that their former belief was leading them astray. They burned their idol, and all received holy Baptism. Some among them renounced the world and its sweet and delightful things that they might become monks. Consequently, the fame of the great old man went into every quarter, so that all who dwelt in those borders no longer observed idolatry.

Not long after, two of the villages began contending over certain fields. Abba Apollos went down to bring peace between them. One village was persuaded by the elder's words to end the quarrel peaceably. Though the other village might have come to terms, they did not relent; for they were relying upon a certain captain of a band of brigands who fought on their behalf. The elder observed the captain of the thieves contending mightily, so he said to him, "If thou wilt be persuaded by me, my child, I shall beseech our Savior to forgive thy sins." When the brigand heard this pledge from the elder, he cast his weapons down and fell before the knees of Abba Apollos. He then dispersed his band of thieves. Peace was thus achieved between the villages. The captain of the thieves, however, would not depart from the blessed elder, until he received fulfillment of the promise. Abba Apollos took the captain with him into the desert. He exhorted him to be patient. He assured him that God was able to grant him pardon. That night, both the elder and the thief beheld a vision. They were standing before the throne of Christ in the heavens, in the midst of angels and men worshipping God. They also fell prostrate before Christ. The voice of God then came to them, saying, "What partnership hath righteousness and lawlessness? And what communion hath light with darkness? And what consonance hath Christ with Belial? Or what portion hath a believer with an unbeliever [2 Cor. 6:14, 15]?" Then they heard, "Why is this murderer standing up with this righteous man? He is unworthy of this vision. Let him begone. But because he has taken refuge in thee, O abba, he shall find salvation." Now many other things were seen and heard, which cannot be uttered. Then both Apollos and the thief were awakened from that vision and each related what he had experienced, only to find that they beheld the same vision. The captain of the brigands then resolved to stay in the monastery. He took up the ascetic life and remained constant till his repose. Thus, the wolf became a gentle lamb. The prophecy of Esaias was fulfilled here: "And the wolf shall feed with the lamb [Is. 11:6]."

On another occasion, the idolaters were arming themselves to fight the Christians over the boundaries of certain districts. Abba Apollos again came and attempted to make peace between both parties. The chief of the heathen, a proud man, was boasting and saying, "As long as I live, there cannot be love between us. There shall never be peace until my death." The holy man then uttered, "According to thy word, so shall it be. No other man shall perish, on either side, except thyself. The earth shall not receive thy body, but the bellies of wild beasts." The following morning, it was seen that the remains of that heathen's corpse had been rent asunder by vultures and hyenas. When news of their chief's evil demise was circulated about the camp of the heathen, all marvelled but perceived that the venerable elder's words had become reality. They gave thanks to God and believed in the holy man's Christ, saying, "This old man is certainly a prophet." All of them then received holy Baptism.

On another occasion, while Abba Apollos and five of the brethren, who had been converted by him, were dwelling in a cave, they performed the divine office for Pascha in the cave. Afterward, they prepared whatsoever food they had, which was only a small quantity of dried-out bread and some vegetables. The venerable man said to his disciples, "O brothers, if we have faith in God, let each one request of God, the bountiful Giver, that He send forth what He will." The disciples thought themselves unworthy to receive a gift from God's munificence. But in obedience to their elder, they offered up their petitions. Now Abba Apollos meanwhile offered up entreaty with a gladsome countenance. At the end of his prayer, they all pronounced the "Amen." Then, at the conclusion of that prayer, it was observed by those in the cave that there were strangers standing at the doorway of the cave. These men, claiming to have come from a far country, were laden with all kinds of foods, many which did not exist in Egypt at that time or were out of season until August. They came with grapes, pomegranates, figs, nuts, almonds, honey in the comb, milk, butter, and dates. They also had ten loaves of bread fresh from the oven, which loaves were still hot. The foreigners told the monks they had been dispatched by their Master, Who was wealthy and honorable. As soon as those strangers brought in the food, they vanished. Apollos and his disciples first gave thanks to the Lord Who had filled them with so many good things. The excellent quality and purity of the gifts were such that they lasted until the holy Pentecost, fifty days later.

At another time, there was in the Thebaid a great famine and dearth of all that was necessary to support life. The natives, having heard that the blessed man and his monks dwelt without laboring for food, took their wives and children to see Abba Apollos. They, on the one hand, thought to plead with him for alms and for food; but he, on the other hand, received them with much compassion and handed over to them as much food as they could find. He was like a man who did not fear that food would be wanting for himself and his disciples. Three baskets of bread only remained, a day's fare for the monastic fathers who were with him. Many of the layfolk therefore who had gathered were not able to return with any food. As the crowd increased and the famine continued to be severe, the abba then commanded that the three baskets of bread be brought to him. This was said and done in the hearing of the crowds of hungry people and monks that had gathered before the holy man. The great old man offered up a prayer inwardly and then turned and addressed those who had gathered: "You believe, do you not, that the hand of the Master is able to multiply these remaining loaves of bread? For thus says the Holy Spirit: 'Bread shall not be wanting in these baskets, until the harvest when there is a new crop.'" Thus it came to pass. The multitude was fed daily from those baskets for the next four months. This was not the only occasion that the venerable man, by God's munificent grace, provided for so many. From time to time, this was done when there was a dearth of oil and wheat. The devil, bearing malice, came and tempted the elder, saying, "Peradventure, thou art Elias or another one of the prophets, or even one of the apostles, that thou shouldest dare to act thus?" The elder answered, "Why should I not act thus? The prophets and apostles were men, were they not? Have not the holy fathers handed down to us the tradition that the prophets and apostles were wont to act thus? God is the same now as He was then. He is able to perform such deeds at all times. Nothing is too hard for Him. If then our God is good, why art thou, O corrupt adversary, evil?"

The blessed elder also possessed the gift of clairvoyance. When Blessed Jerome, with two companions, came from Jerusalem to visit with the elder, they were intercepted by the elder's disciples. "The brethren," says Blessed Jerome, the biographer of the elder, "espied us from a distance. They recognized us by the accurate description which they had received from the elder." Although the elder and his disciples had never seen any of the three pilgrims, still Abba Apollos beheld them by the grace of the Spirit Who dwelt in him. Blessed Jerome continues and says, "They met us gladly and sang hymns of praise, which is the custom with all the brethren." The disciples then prostrated themselves to the ground before the three pilgrims and offered the salutation of peace. Jerome here says, "Then those disciples turned to their other companions and remarked, 'Behold, here are the three brethren of whom our abba spoke three days earlier. For he declared to us that, after three days, three brethren would come to us from Jerusalem.' Then we all marched together. The disciples were chanting the psalms antiphonally. Some who were following were chanting the refrains to those going on ahead. Now Abba Apollos heard their blessed chanting and came forth to meet us. When he saw us, he was first to bow low to the ground. He stretched out his hand, rose up, and gave us a holy kiss. He then escorted us inside, and we prayed together. The abba then washed our feet with his own hands. He had us take a rest and then eat something.

"The brethren did not eat, but first of all partook of the divine Mysteries together. This was their daily rule. Only after the ninth hour did they eat their meal. Afterward, some of the fathers were instructed by the abba, others went into the desert and recited Scriptures by heart the whole night long, while still others chanted psalms and hymns until dawn. Some of the fathers went without food for several days at a time, even from one Sunday to another. As for my companions and myself, we perceived their joy. There was nothing on the earth, no bodily delight, to compare with their inner joy. If any one of the fathers was afflicted or grieved, the old man knew the cause of it. He was granted by God to know the secret thoughts of each man's heart. He would counsel any who were sorrowing by saying, 'It is not seemly for us to be afflicted at our redemption. Remember that we are those who are about to inherit the kingdom of the heavens. Let the Jews weep, let men of iniquity take up mourning; but we, the righteous, ought to rejoice. They have their happiness in earthly things. Why should we not rejoice always, who have been vouchsafed such a blessed hope? Be mindful of those words of the blessed Apostle Paul who said, "Be rejoicing always; be praying unceasingly. In everything be giving thanks, for this is the will of God in Christ Jesus for you [1 Thess. 5:16-18]."'"

Blessed Jerome then relates how the abba exhorted them to receive the brethren. "He told us that when the brethren came to visit, it was proper to bow low before them. 'Not,' said Abba Apollos, 'that we bow down before them, but before the God Who dwells in them. Whensoever thou seest thy brother, thou seest the Christ.'" The abba then went on to speak of the custom of having the brethren come in that they might rest and refresh themselves. "We have derived this custom," said he, "from the Patriarch Abraham, and also from Lot, who invited angels to lodge in his home." The elder then urged daily partaking of holy Communion, saying, "It is fitting that the monks should partake each day of the immaculate Mysteries of Christ. Whosoever shall make himself to be remote from them shall remove himself from God. But whosoever shall receive them, shall receive our Redeemer always. Whosoever shall eat this body and drink this blood of the Lord, abides in Him. It is very helpful to monks to bring to remembrance the Passion of our Lord at all times. Therefore, it is right that we should always make ourselves worthy to receive the holy Mysteries."

The holy man then admonished that no man should set aside the fasts of Wednesday and Friday; the one being the day when Judas delivered up the Messiah and the Jews plotted to betray our Lord; the other being the day of our Lord's crucifixion. "Therefore," said he, "let us not become as one of the betrayers or a Jew." Blessed Jerome then complains that it was not possible for any man to write down fittingly all the teachings of the blessed man. "Then he blessed us," says Jerome, "bidding us farewell with these words: 'The Lord bless thee out of Sion, and mayest thou see the good things of Jerusalem all the days of thy life [Ps. 127:6].'" He then arranged an escort of three ascetics, learned in the languages of the Greeks, Romans, and Egyptians, to accompany through the desert the three pilgrims.

This, then, is a brief narration of that marvellous teacher Apollos, who had such wonderful boldness before God that, on account of the extraordinary wonderworkings wrought through him, all of Egypt came to believe in the Christ. The disciples of Abba Apollos gradually numbered five thousand. After fighting the good fight and struggling well, he departed to his Lord.

On the 25th of January, the holy Church commemorates the holy Martyr MEDOULE and her companions, who were burned to death.

On the 25th of January, the holy Church commemorates our venerable Father KASTINOS, Bishop of Byzantion.

Kastinos, our holy father among the saints, was born in Old Rome. In his earlier years, he was an idolater, a man of influence, and advisor to the emperor. Nonetheless, as it is recorded by the divine Paul in his Epistle to the Romans: "For whom He foreknew, He also foreordained to be conformable to the image of His Son, in order for Him to be the firstborn among many brethren [Rom. 8:29]." Therefore, by reason of His unsurpassing love for man, He foreknew the salvation of this saint. All those things that God permits to befall us, even though they do not seem to be in our interest, ultimately are conducive to our salvation. For example, as it is recorded in Scripture concerning the man of Corinth who had fallen into sin with his father's wife, the Apostle Paul turned him over to Satan that his soul might be saved [1 Cor. 5:5]. In like manner, by divine permission, our blessed Kastinos was tormented by a demon for many years, in order that he might attain salvation upon relinquishing the darkness of idolatry. Now Kastinos used all methods at his disposal to escape the torture of the demons. However, he did not succeed and, for this reason, gave up all hope for his salvation.

At that time, Bishop Kyrillianos of Argyropolis (217-230)[36] worked miracles near the town of Byzantion.[37] This news was related to Kastinos in Rome that the deeds of this wonderworking man could liberate him from the demon. Immediately, he left Rome and went to the area of Byzantion, where he met Saint Kyrillianos. He fell at his feet and implored the healing of his illness. The saintly bishop cured him, and thereafter, Kastinos was baptized. Following this, he distributed all his belongings to the poor and attached himself to Kyrillianos, serving him as a humble servant. The bishop, a clairvoyant, knew that Kastinos himself would one day take up the staff and shepherd people. Therefore, he imparted to him all the knowledge of the Church. Prior to the repose of Saint Kyrillianos, he ordained Kastinos as Bishop of Argyropolis and Byzantion (230-237) and instructed him as follows: "Behold, my son, thou hast become a bishop by the grace of God and by my hand. Therefore, strive to transfer the Church of Argyropolis to the opposite side of Byzantion. This was revealed a long time ago to me, the unworthy one, by almighty God."[38]

After the repose of Saint Kyrillianos, Kastinos built a church, in the northern sector of Byzantion, to Saint Ephemia, who had recently suffered martyrdom at Chalcedon. It is to this location that he transferred the diocese of Argyropolis. Therefore, Saint Kastinos was the eighteenth Bishop of Argyropolis and later of Byzantion.[39] In an apostolic manner, the blessed one shepherded the flock of Christ four years. He then ordained Titus[40] as his successor and was translated to the Lord.

---

[36] The memory of Saint Kyrillianos, otherwise known as Kyriakos, is celebrated by the holy Church on the 27th of October.

[37] Byzantion was the name of a Megarian colony at the southern mouth of the Bosporos. Constantine I chose Byzantion as the site of his capital, though the official designation was Constantinople. Thus Byzantion was absorbed into Constantinople. Argyropolis was south of the Keration Gulf, opposite Byzantion on the European promontory, which was later called Stavrodromion, while Chrysopolis (now Scutari) is found on the Asiatic promontory.

[38] Argyropolis (Argyroupolis) was relocated to south of the Golden Horn opposite Byzantium on the European side. Chrysopolis was located east of Byzantium on the Asiatic side.

[39] According to the patriarchal register of Zacharias N. Mathas, Saint Kastinos became the eighteenth patriarch of Byzantium, and not the second as written in other *Synaxaristae* (Nikodemos the Hagiorite and K. Doukakes). Meletios, however, in his *Ecclesiastical History* (Volume 1, p. 358), lists the saint as the seventeenth from Stachys the apostle (38-54), who is placed after the Apostle Andrew.

[40] After Saint Kastinos, some archives list as successor Evgenios I (237-242), and then Titus (242-272).

**On the 25ᵗʰ of January, the holy Church commemorates
our venerable Father DEMETRIOS the Skevophylax.**

**On the 25ᵗʰ of January, the holy Church commemorates
the holy New-martyr AFXENTIOS at Constantinople (1720).**[41]

Afxentios, the new-martyr of Christ, was a native of Vellas in the metropolis of Ioannina in Epiros, being the son of pious Christian parents. While still young, he left his home for Constantinople, where he worked as a furrier in the workshop of Mahmut Pasha. However, the enemy of good, the devil, who never ceases in his attempts to beguile youths in diverse ways, could not bear to behold the purity of this young man. The unclean spirit implanted thoughts in his mind to pass this life in pleasure and revelry. He succeeded in deceiving Afxentios into leaving his trade and securing employment in the imperial ships. As a seaman, Afxentios caroused with his friends, who betrayed him, saying that he had abandoned Christianity and embraced Islam. Afxentios secretly fled out of fear that he might be reported to the admiral. He returned to Constantinople in tattered garments. Later he procured a small skiff and earned a living by ferrying items to and fro. In time he repented of his former transgressions, and his heart was inflamed with a desire for martyrdom. Afxentios beseeched God night and day, with warm tears, to lead him to an experienced elder, to whom he could confess his sins and reveal his desire to partake of the cup of martyrdom. The all-benevolent God did not overlook his entreaty, and granted his desire.

The occasion arose when the *synkellos* (chancellor) of the Great Church of Christ, Gregory, an Athonite from the Monastery of Xeropotamou, happened to be traveling from Karakoy to the Phanar. By divine providence, he chartered Afxentios' boat. Seeing the venerable *synkellos*, the youth decided to disclose his intention to him. When they arrived at the Phanar, he revealed the great desire which he harbored to suffer martyrdom on behalf of Christ. The *synkellos* lauded him, but he also feared that Afxentios might weaken before the trials. He therefore admonished Afxentios, saying, "Hear me, O my son: the assaults of the devil are manifold. I fear that perhaps thou mightest weaken under tortures and, in the end, lose our most sweetest Jesus Christ. But depart from here and become a monk, that from henceforth thou mightest lead a virtuous life. I have hope in the goodness of our Jesus that God shall number thee among the choirs of holy martyrs that rejoice endlessly." Upon receiving this counsel, the youth kept silent, out of respect for the spiritual elder, but his heart burned with the love of martyrdom.

---

[41] The martyrdom of Saint Afxentios was taken from the *Neon Martyrologion*, 3ʳᵈ ed. (pp. 109-112), and incorporated into *The Great Synaxaristes*.

Therefore Afxentios resumed his labors as a ferryman. Afxentios kept only enough of his earnings for his immediate needs; the remainder he distributed to the poor. He passed the days of his life with fasting and all-night vigils. On many occasions, he visited the Church of the Most Holy Theotokos of the Life-giving Spring (Zoodohos Pege). There, throughout the entire night, he offered up supplication to the all-immaculate Mother of God that he might be empowered to complete his life in martyrdom.

Armed in this manner with the grace of the Holy Spirit, he returned and paid a visit to his previous ship in the imperial service. Immediately his shipmates recognized him, swarmed about him and beat him, raining down kicks and blows. They brought him to the courthouse, claiming, "He had espoused our faith and now denies it." But he replied courageously, "I was and am a Christian. Moreover, I am prepared to suffer a myriad of tortures for my Christ." One of his former friends, observing his courage, dealt him a blow to the forehead with an iron bar, dislodging his right eye. But the martyr thanked the Lord Who made him worthy to suffer for His name. The villain, however, then struck Afxentios in the mouth with such force that he knocked out two teeth. Nevertheless, the martyr once more proclaimed Christ as true God in a resounding voice. Then they went to the mullah's court, where the judge inquired as to why Afxentios changed his faith and espoused that which he earlier denied, as declared by the witnesses. The saint then lifted up his mind to God and sought divine assistance, replying forthrightly, "I, O judge, never renounced my sweet Christ, but believe and confess that He is the almighty God, the omnipotent One and Creator of the universe; and I am ready to shed my blood and not become a Moslem—God forbid!"

The judge became enraged at this declaration and ordered Afxentios to be thrashed immediately. No fewer than three hundred blows were administered to the bottoms of his feet; the blood ran profusely from his toenails. But the saint greatly thanked the Lord, entreating Him to strengthen him to complete the contest successfully. Afterward, the judge commanded that the martyr be remanded to Kapisi Prison and be confined there until the second hearing, because it was Friday. His spiritual father, the aforementioned Gregory, learned of the saint's daring and tribulations which he endured for Christ. He succeeded in entering the prison. With spiritual words, Father Gregory emboldened Afxentios not to weaken in the trials. He exhorted him to withstand them courageously, putting the devil to shame and obtaining the radiant crown of victory from the Prize-bestower, God. The martyr requested to receive the immaculate Mysteries, which the elder saw to immediately and fulfilled his request.

Five days later, the Turks brought the martyr before the court, bound in chains like a criminal. But Afxentios stood there very happy, as if he were at a festival. The judged glared at him with an angry and murderous eye, asking him, "Why is it that thou wilt not admit that our faith is true and good, but rather thou hast chosen to abhor and disdain it?" The martyr replied, "I was born a Christian and will die a Christian. I will not deny my Faith, even though thou shouldest subject me to ten thousand afflictions; for my Faith is good and true. May it be also that thou, sir, mightest come to believe, lest thou shouldest be condemned in the end." When the judge heard this, he became infuriated. Seeing that the martyr was unshakeable, he issued the final decision against him: death by the sword. The executioners seized the blessed Afxentios and brought him to the site of execution. The martyr prayed to God for the concord and peace of the Orthodox Christians and the world. Then he knelt, bidding the executioner to carry out his order. The latter severed his head on Tuesday, the 25th day of January, in the year 1720, at the second hour of the day. In this manner, the ever-memorable one received the crown of martyrdom at the age of thirty. On Wednesday, at dawn, a divine light descended upon the martyr's relics, which sight many Christians witnessed as well as many Turks.

The following day, a devout nobleman and powerful official, named Michael, bearing the title "the Royal Tertzimbasis," who possessed authority before the sultan, pleaded with him and obtained the martyr's body. Michael anointed the relics with myrrh and various spices (as did Nikodemos to the sacred body of Christ). Then Michael and the faithful Christians transferred the relics with utmost piety, accompanied by the patriarch and many hierarchs, to the Church of the Life-giving Spring, where they buried the martyr with honor. Out of deep respect for the martyr, Michael conducted the uncovering of Afxentios' relics two years later. As they opened the tomb, a divine fragrance wafted forth, so that all the participating Christians marvelled and glorified God, Who honors those who honor Him. The nobleman took the blessed skull of Afxentios to his house. At that time, his sons were afflicted with a grievous illness. So they kissed the holy skull with faith and piety. Then and suddenly—lo, the miracle!—they arose from their beds sound and healthy, glorifying God and His saint. Another man, a tailor named Nicholas, suffered from a dread disease. The physicians diagnosed his condition as terminal. However, he had heard of the miracle that the martyr wrought for the sons of the nobleman and sent someone to bring the sacred skull to him. When they laid the holy relic on him—O, the wonder!—he recovered instantly, glorifying God and the Martyr Afxentios.

The aforementioned *synkellos*, Hieromonk Gregory of Xeropotamou, hearing of the miracles of Saint Afxentios and having veneration for the saint, went to the nobleman, who was also a friend of his, and begged him to dedicate the blessed skull to his own Monastery of Xeropotamou. The nobleman, both out of great respect for the monastery and as a favor to his friend, offered it as a precious gift to the monastery. The sacred relic is treasured to this very day. The New-martyr Afxentios pours forth numerous miracles, saving many victims of terminal illnesses who, with devotion and fervent faith, seek refuge in him, to the glory of our Lord Jesus Christ to Whom is due all glory, honor, and veneration to the ages of ages. Amen.

Through the intercessions of Thy Saints,
O Christ God, have mercy on us. Amen.

**On the 26th of January, the holy Church commemorates
our venerable Father XENOPHON, his wife MARY,
and their children JOHN and ARKADIOS.**[1]

Saints Arkadios, Xenophon, Mary, and John

Xenophon, our venerable father, lived during the years of Emperor Justinian (527-565). He was a man of wealth, rank, and distinguished lineage, who hailed from Constantinople. He possessed a soul redolent with piety and the fear of God. His wife, Mary, was his equal in moral excellence, virtue, and the pursuit of godliness. There issued forth from their lawful union two sons, John and Arkadios. Their sons were trained not only in secular studies, but also in keeping the commandments of God. The parents sent their children for further education in Beirut of Phoenicia, which was reputed for its fine schools. The young men lived and studied there for some time, but never neglected the virtuous example that their parents had instilled in them from their boyhood.

It was during this period that Xenophon became ill and sent word for his sons to return home, lest he should repose without having seen and counseled them one last time. They arrived in the capital, which greatly heartened his parents' spirits. Xenophon then addressed John and Arkadios, saying, "I, my children, perhaps shall soon repose. You know very well my manner of life, pursuits, conduct, and treatment of others. You also know that for the love of Christ and His commandments, I have exerted myself to

---

[1] The Lives of these saints were recorded in Greek by Saint Symeon the Metaphrastes, whose manuscript begins, "Xenophon, the wondrous..." [*P.G.* 114:1013-1014]. The text is extant in the Athonite monasteries of the Great Lavra and Iveron. At Great Lavra another hagiographical account is preserved. These texts were rendered in simpler Greek by Agapios the Cretan and published in the *Eklogion*.

uphold the precepts of the Gospel and also, by my example, to instill this love in you also. I have struggled never to insult or outrage my fellow man, or reproach or mock anyone. Neither have I wilfully judged, nor borne malice or envy, nor injured or embittered any. I have made an effort not to be absent from Church services. No stranger, foreigner, or poor person has ever been driven from our home; but rather, we gave as much as was in our power. I advise thee, as I have myself, insofar as not allowing your gazes to dwell upon a beautiful woman. I have known no woman other than your mother. Moreover, after the birth of Arkadios, we mutually consented to preserve our chastity for the Lord's sake. I urge you to diligently uphold the Orthodox Faith, even to death. I ask you therefore to observe and do all these things, if you desire to have God bless you that you might live long. I counsel you to help the orphan and widow. Honor those in holy orders. Visit the sick and imprisoned. Assist the aggrieved. As for those who live in the mountains, caves, and holes of the earth, be mindful of them and revere them, for through them the Lord has mercy on the world. You know that a table set for monastics was never missing from my house. Protect and guard the monasteries. Do not absent yourselves from church. Honor your mother and obey all of her commands with fear and reverence, for she also labors at keeping the commandments of the Lord. Love the servants of our household as your children. Those that come to old age, nourish and maintain until death. Give alms to the poor. Such works have never left us in want of anything. Though you have ample wealth and shall lack for nothing in this transient life, yet, if you wish to inherit the kingdom of the heavens, strive to keep all the commandments of God, even as you have seen me do."

These and many other good counsels were spoken by the holy elder, yet not in a pharisaical manner, but as a father exhorting his children. John and Arkadios wept and lamented, saying, "Do not leave us, father, but do thou supplicate God that thou mightest be granted some more time. We believe that God shall hearken to thee. We are young and still require your guidance." Xenophon wept and then dismissed them from his bedside. In the morning he called his sons to himself and announced, "God has remembered me upon my bed of sickness. I have prayed to Him, from the time this condition befell me, that He might extend my days for your sakes that I might better establish you on the path of righteousness and see you perfected in everything, lest I should repose with this care on my soul. Now this very night, God fulfilled my requests; for He gave forth the command that I am to abide in this world until His dominion should ordain otherwise." When his sons heard this revelation, they were filled with joy and gave thanks to the Lord. Thereupon, when Xenophon rose up from his bed of sickness, he sent his sons back to Beirut to finish their education.

While John and Arkadios were at sea, the ship encountered a storm
and rough waves. Shipwreck appeared to be imminent. Both young men
invoked God and His saints for help, praying, "O Master Lord Jesus Christ,
God almighty, look down upon our affliction and deliver us from danger, that
we might be able to do Thy will and be accounted worthy of Thy kingdom.
Remember, O Lord, the deeds of our parents and do not take us in the middle
of our days, but vouchsafe us life that we may labor for Thee. For 'the dead
shall not praise Thee, O Lord, nor any that go down to Hades. But we the
living will bless the Lord from henceforth and for evermore [Ps. 113:26,
27].'"

The sailors, quick to perceive the peril, secretly prepared the one
lifeboat. This was not made known to the passengers, since there was not
adequate room to hold everyone. The storm showed no signs of abating. As
the passengers heard the terrifying sound of the ship's timbers breaking apart,
the crew deserted her and frantically rowed away. John and Arkadios,
together with their menservants, were left alone on board. Without divine
intervention, it was inevitable that the ship should sink. As it quickly filled
with water, the brothers removed their outward garments in anticipation of
entering the swells and taking hold of any piece of wreckage. While they
awaited their departure from each other, the atmosphere was dark, the wind
was howling in their ears, and the air was filled with droplets of water. They
then cried out as loud as they could to their dear parents, as though they were
present, saying, "Be saving yourselves, beloved parents, and all those of our
household! Be saving yourselves, most affectionate of parents!" John and
Arkadios, then viewing the general abandonment of the ship, asked forgiveness of one another. They then embraced and wept, saying to each other,
"How difficult it is to be parted from one another. But do thou save thyself,
brother dearest!" Then they said to one another, "Where now are the goods
of our father that were given to the poor? Where are his philosophical and
spiritual instructions? To what have come the good deeds and virtues of our
parents? Where are the prayers of the monks whom they assisted and gave
alms? Do not any of these things count? Are they to be reckoned as nought?
Have all these things become invalid? Have not any of the prayers of our
parents or those to whom they were generous and hospitable reached Thee,
O Lord, that we might be rescued through their prayers? Has the multitude
of our sins surpassed their charity? Yea, my brother, they are all good people
and counted among the worthy, but we are unworthy of this present life. Our
sins have surely outweighed the virtues of our parents, and for this reason
God has forsaken us. At home we were grieved at the possible loss of our
father. Who would have expected that they should be left mourning for us?
Although the burial and death of children are bitter events, still worse for any

parent is not to know the end of a child and never be able to visit a grave." This and many other forlorn statements were made by the brothers. After they embraced one another, the ship was rent in two. Before they entered the dark waters below, they said, "O King and Master of all creation, if it be not Thy will to deliver us from the sea, then separate us not as we die. Let one wave cover us." Then they shouted to the others, "Save yourselves, brothers," and leaped into the waves, each taking hold of whatever piece of wooden wreckage was at hand. Each swam as much as he was able. By the grace of God, each one was invisibly piloted to a different section of Tyre. John floated toward Melfethan, while Arkadios found himself at Tetrapyrgia. Neither knew anything of the other brother's survival, so each mourned more over the death of his brother than he rejoiced at his own escape from the watery depths.

When John emerged from the waves, he began deliberating on his miraculous survival, saying to himself, "Where shall I now go in this naked state? Where shall I pass the remainder of my life? I ought to give glory to the name of God. Better is a life of poverty and humility than one of wealth and vanity. I think now I understand the reason God hearkened not to my entreaty. He allowed this fearsome trial by sea in order to call me to Himself. If all went as was anticipated, my parents would have arranged our marriages and left us a great inheritance. Not that this still could not happen, but, on account of what has just befallen us, I perceive that we would have perished in this vain world sooner than the turbulent sea would have swallowed us. No, this incident was permitted by the good God Who knows what is profitable for us. In His wisdom and providence, He has dispensed all in His œconomy. But we, not knowing what is to our advantage, ask and seek for those things that are not to our benefit. His grace, however, grants to us those soul-saving and benefitting things that are fitting. I believe I should betake myself to a monastery." After giving thanks to the Lord, he uttered a prayer on behalf of his brother Arkadios, praying that he too would be delivered and give a good account of his life by becoming a monk. "Bring Arkadios to dry land, O Lord," he prayed, "that he might give thanks to Thee and give thought to serving Thee. And O Lord, do Thou also preserve our menservants who traveled with us that Thy name may be glorified!" John then sought divine guidance on which direction to take along the shore. He offered up supplication, saying, "O Lord Jesus Christ, my steps do Thou direct [Ps. 118:133]; for by the Lord are the steps of a man rightly directed [Ps. 36:23]. Be Thou my helper and lead me to do Thy will."

John then walked about for a short distance and found a monastery in those parts. He knocked at the door, which brought forth the doorkeeper. It was immediately observed that John was naked, at which sight the doorkeeper opened immediately and threw a cassock around him. The monk set a table of bread and vegetable broth before John. After John ate, the monk inquired, "From whence comest thou, brother?" John answered, "I am a foreigner and have recently suffered shipwreck. I was rescued by thy holy prayers." The monk wept a little, moved by compunction of heart, and gave glory to God. He then asked John, "And now, my child, where shouldest thou like to go?" He replied, "I should like, if the Lord wills, to become a monk. If it is possible, may I remain here?" The monk said, "In truth, my child, thou hast chosen a good work. I shall have a word with the hegumen. However God should move his heart, this do and thou shalt be saved." The hegumen was informed and had the young man brought to him. When he beheld John, he perceived in the Spirit that the youth would excel in virtue. He concurred that what had befallen him at sea was a calling to God, and then said, "Blessed be the God of thy father and mother; for He has plucked thee from out of the watery abyss and brought thee here!" The hegumen then instructed John in the order of the monastic conduct of life and then sealed him with the sign of the Cross. Shortly thereafter, he clothed John in the holy Schema of the monastics. Father John then took up the yoke of Christ in that monastery. He fasted, kept vigil, and prayed continually. He carried out diligently and cheerfully his monastic labors and obediences. In his heart, however, he was afflicted with the thought that his brother suffered death by drowning.

Meanwhile, Arkadios came forth from the sea. He fell on his face, prostrating himself before the Lord, saying, "I give thanks to Thee, O God of my father and mother, that Thou hast not left me to sink to the nethermost depths of that tempestuous sea. I beseech Thy compassion that, even as Thou didst rescue me, in like manner Thou wouldest preserve my brother. I also ask that I might be vouchsafed to gaze upon him before my end." Arkadios then wept bitterly. Upon collecting himself, he went to the nearby village, where they gave him food and clothing. When he ate, he received a little relief for his enfeebled body. He then went toward the church and entered. He prayed for his brother and wept. He then leaned against a pillar and fell asleep. He was vouchsafed a vision of his brother John, who said to him, "Brother Arkadios, why dost thou weep for me?" Straightway, Arkadios was awakened and was filled with joy. He gave thanks to the Lord and reasoned within himself, saying, "Should I now leave and pursue my studies? And what would be the benefit? Everything is transient and vain. I used to hear my father always expressing his high regard for the angelic life of the monastics. Well then, with the Lord helping me, let me become a monk." He then made a prayer and took up the path leading toward Jerusalem. He arrived at the holy places and offered veneration. He then went forth from the holy city into the desert, resolved to visit the monasteries and seek a place among one of them.

As he trod that wilderness path that day, he encountered a holy elder who had the gift of clairvoyance. Arkadios venerated the old ascetic and said to him, "For the Lord's sake, holy father, supplicate God to console my profound affliction." The elder then said, "Cease grieving, my child, for thy brother lives. All those who were with thee in the ship also survived. They became monastics, even as thy brother. Thou shalt see him, as well as thy father with thy mother, before thou diest." When Arkadios heard these unexpected predictions from that clairvoyant elder, he was stirred and fell to his knees, weeping and saying, "Since God revealed all these things to thee regarding me, I entreat thee, do thou make me a monk." The elder then declared, "Blessed be God, child, do thou follow me!" Arkadios was then led to the Monastery of Saint Savvas.[2] The elder gave Arkadios his own cell, a cell in which he had already passed fifty years. The elder then said, "Abide with me for one year," to which Arkadios consented. The elder then instructed him in the monastic rule of conduct. After that period, the elder departed for the wilderness. He bade Arkadios farewell, promising to return after three years to see how he was faring. Arkadios thereupon dwelt in that cell, eagerly and diligently observing all that the elder taught him.

Although two years had passed, the holy Xenophon still had not received news that his sons' ship had sunk to the bottom of the sea. Neither had he heard any word nor received any letter from either son. The parents were concerned at their sons' failure to communicate with them. Therefore, Xenophon sent his manservant to Beirut to investigate how the lads were faring and what progress was being made in their studies. The manservant was diligent in his search for his master's sons. He made inquiries in every quarter, until he determined that John and Arkadios had not returned to Beirut since their last departure to visit with their parents. The manservant then surmised that they probably went to continue their studies in Athens. He repaired to that city and continued his investigations. No one there had heard anything from either son. Heartsick and depressed at not being able to give some news to his master and mistress, he decided to return to Byzantium.

On the return road, he stayed at an inn. That same evening, a monk also rested at the same inn. The monk, on his way to make a pilgrimage to Jerusalem, recognized the manservant. A conversation ensued between the men. The manservant, while speaking with the monk, had the impression that he had met the monk elsewhere but could not place it in his mind. Then, after

---

[2] Some sources record that Arkadios was taken to the Lavra of Saint Chariton, called Souka.

they spoke at length and the monk said that he was on his way to make a pilgrimage to Jerusalem, the manservant inquired, "Wert thou not a former slave of Sir Xenophon of Constantinople? Wert thou not dispatched by our master to accompany the young masters, John and Arkadios, to their university in Beirut?" The monk did not deny that he had been recognized, but affirmed it saying that they had formerly been friends in Xenophon's household. "But thou art so altered," remarked the manservant, "and I see that thou hast been clothed in the monastic habit. What happened after thy party left Constantinople? I have diligently searched both Beirut and Athens to ascertain the whereabouts of the young masters, but have discovered nothing, other than that they did not return to Beirut after their last visit at home. What sayest thou regarding this whole odd affair? I implore thee that if thou hast any information regarding our young masters, tell me." The monk could not hold back his tears and began saying, "They drowned at sea, or so I think; for I believe I was the only one to have survived. For that cause I became a monk, not wishing to become the messenger of evil tidings to Sir Xenophon and Lady Mary."

The manservant, hearing of the youths' probable death by drowning at sea, wept and beat his breast, lamenting, "Woe is me, milords! How you must have suffered! How dreadful to have drowned in those deep cold waters! How shall I announce to your father such grievous tidings of your sudden and untimely deaths? And your mother, how shall she bear the pain and suffering? O kind masters, the hopes of the household rested in both of you. Who now shall inherit your parents' virtues and estate? Who shall be left to continue the work of welcoming strangers, providing a table for the poor, and visiting those in prison? Who shall give contributions to the churches and monasteries? Woe is me, the wretched one! How many poor have you helped who shall not bewail your loss? For their comfort and consolation have been snatched from them. You, their treasure and joy, have been seized from their midst. Alas! Has it devolved upon me to bring such tidings? What shall I do? Should I return to Sir Xenophon? How shall I deliver this most bitter and tragic of news, which assuredly shall draw sighs and tears from friends and neighbors, and laments and mourning among kinfolk, the nobility, and, yea, the emperor himself? How shall I face the parents and recount such an end, which grief might bring them to give up their own spirits? It is better that I should avoid the tumult and calamity that such intelligence would usher in. I shall not return to Byzantium, lest I should be responsible for the demise of such good masters." Now this conversation between the manservant and the monk proved so emotional that others staying at the inn could not help but see their evident distress and overhear their moving conversation. Some of them intervened and attempted to console the manservant, advising him in this manner and saying, "Cease, brother, lamenting to such a degree, lest even thou shouldest perish from thy worry and grief. But go and return to thy lord, disclosing all these events. What if thy master and mistress should learn of these woeful events from another quarter? Thou shalt be judged for this and thy name shall be blotted out of the book of the living." The manservant accepted their advice and returned to Constantinople. He entered into his master's house. He then went and sat in a corner, grieving and having a gloomy, lowering look.

When Mary learned that the manservant had returned from abroad, she summoned him and asked gravely, "How do my children fare?" He answered without much conviction, "They are well, milady." She continued probing and said, "Where are the letters which they have given thee?" He answered, "They were lost on the road, milady." The heart of his mistress was troubled by these words, so she said to him, "For the sake of the Lord, tell me the entire truth!" The manservant then let out a loud wailing sound and tearfully divulged, "Alas! The light of thine eyes, milady, has been lost at sea!" Beyond all expectation, mistress Mary revealed her inner strength and faith in God. She grew not

Saints Xenophon and Mary

fainthearted or fearful at these evil tidings. Her heart was fixed, trusting in the Lord. For a moment she fell silent and then said, "Blessed be the name of the Lord! The Lord gave, the Lord has taken away. As it seemed good to Him, so has it come to pass [Job. 1:21]." She then asked, "Hast thou told anyone else in the household of this?" "Nay, mistress." She then said, "Thou art not to disclose this news to anyone else."

When evening had come, Xenophon returned from the royal palace to his home, accompanied by many dignitaries. After he bade them farewell, he sat down to eat, according to his custom, once daily and after sunset. As Xenophon sat at table, Mary began speaking to him and said, "Milord, the manservant has returned whom thou hadst previously sent to Beirut." The holy man remarked, "Glory to Thee, O God! Let him come forward that I might have a word with him." She said, "He was thoroughly exhausted and took to his bed in order to rest." Xenophon then said, "Well then, have the letters of our children brought here that I might see them."

Then the woman, unable to hold back those maternal feelings which filled her womb, wept. Xenophon asked, "Why weepest thou? Have our children fallen ill?" She answered, "I should call that hour blessed if they had fallen ill, rather than to have lost our pearls in the sea." Xenophon then sighed deeply and gave thanks to God, saying, "Blessed be the name of the Lord! Cease grieving, milady. God has not permitted such grief as this to smite us in our old age. I have served Him and kept all His commands as best I could. Let us therefore keep a vigil this night, entreating God that He might reveal what has befallen our children." The parents then were on their knees all that night, shedding tears, till the morning light. They were exhausted from their labors, so they retired to their separate bedchambers. Both parents were vouchsafed to behold a vision in their sleep, wherein their children were standing before Christ. Both sons had splendid and costly crowns circling their brows. The crown of John appeared to be adorned with precious stones, and he had a throne also. The diadem of Arkadios was arrayed with the most brilliant of stars. John held a gold scepter in his hand, while Arkadios bore a gold cross in his right hand.[3] When Xenophon and Mary were awakened, they recounted to one another the same vision. The blessed Xenophon then exclaimed, "In truth, O wife, our sons have been accounted worthy of great honor. Moreover, I believe that they are in Jerusalem. Let us therefore not only go and find them, but also venerate the holy places."

Preparations were made. The steward was given instructions concerning their property. The saints took considerable wealth with them that they might dispense alms in the holy places. When they set out, they took some of their servants. When they entered the holy city of Jerusalem, they visited every place and abundantly distributed alms. They went around searching and inquiring after their sons, but they were unable to collect any intelligence of their whereabouts. They did, however, encounter one of their menservants who was part of that retinue that left to accompany their sons to Beirut. They observed that he was wearing monastic garb, so they made a prostration before him. He then made a prostration before them, saying, "Do not, milord and milady, do this before me; indeed, do not make a prostration before your servant." The holy Xenophon then remarked, "The holy Schema, with which thou art garbed, I honor. I beseech thee, do not be grieved, but tell us what has become of our children." His eyes welled up with tears as he said, "I do not know. As the ship was breaking apart, each man set about to

---

[3] *P.G.* 114:1032D-1033A.

preserve himself. Therefore, whether they are alive or dead, only God knows." Xenophon and Maria gave him generous alms and asked for his prayers, as they bade him farewell. It was then that Xenophon conceived the idea to go to those parts of the Jordan in order to venerate the monastics struggling in asceticism and provide them with alms.

The traveling party descended from Jerusalem toward the district around the Jordan. On the road, unbeknownst to them, they met the elder of their son Arkadios. The parents prostrated themselves at the feet of the elder and asked his blessing. He uttered a prayer on their behalf and then said, "What has compelled Sir Xenophon and Lady Mary to come to Jerusalem? Certainly it is the desire to see your children, is it not? Cease sorrowing. Your children live. God has vouchsafed to you a vision of the glory being prepared for them in the heavens. It is also the Lord's will that you behold them in this life. Go therefore, O good laborers of the vineyard of Christ God, to the river Jordan. Upon returning to the holy city, you shall see your children." He then bade them farewell and went his way.

That holy monk then walked to Jerusalem and venerated the shrines at the Church of the Resurrection. In that same complex, nearby Golgotha (Calvary),[4] he sat on the ground and rested. Then behold, by God's œconomy, John, the eldest son of Xenophon, also came from his monastery to venerate the holy places. He saw the elder and made a prostration. The elder blessed him and said, "Where hast thou been till now, master John? Thy parents have come. They are seeking thee. And for sure thou hast again come thither, seeking thy brother." Father John, astonished by the elder's gift of clairvoyance, made a prostration before him, saying, "I beseech thee, holy father, tell me, for the Lord's sake, where is my brother? For until this day the Lord has not revealed to me whether my brother lives. Only now, for the first time, have I heard a word regarding this matter from thy holy mouth." The elder then bade Father John to sit beside him.

After they had been sitting for a while, a monk approached. It was Father Arkadios, who had come to venerate the shrines. He appeared to be a man suffering bodily hardship and emaciation on account of abstinence, so that his eyes were deeply sunken. He then paid his respects to the elder and venerated him, saying, "Honorable father, thou hast left thy field for three years. Thou hast not paid one visit, so it is full of thorny and prickly plants. When thou wilt clear it, thou shalt need to put forth much labor." The elder commented, "Every day, my child, in the Holy Spirit, have I invisibly been

---

[4] Jn. 19:17, 18: "And bearing His Cross, He went out to the place called Place of a Skull, which is called in Hebrew, Golgotha, where they crucified Him." [Cf. Mt. 27:33; Mk. 15:22.]

visiting my field; and I trust in God that it is not thorns but rather a good crop from which Christ the King shall eat and drink and take pleasure." Father John was then invited by his elder to sit at his side, which he did. After remaining silent for some time, the elder then asked Father John, "Tell me, whence comest thou?" Father John answered, "I am a stranger and sinner, honorable father; nevertheless, I beseech God, by thy prayers, that He have mercy on me." The holy elder persisted and said, "But tell me of thy homeland and place of birth, thy parentage and rearing, that I might glorify God." Father John then began recounting his past, mentioning that he was born in the imperial capital. He said his father was a statesman and that he once had a brother named Arkadios, with whom he had been sent to university at Beirut. He then described the magnitude of the storm that destroyed his ship and how the passengers were lost, save himself. Father Arkadios, who was sitting on the elder's other side, also heard the account. He listened carefully to all that was being narrated and looked intently upon the narrator. Arkadios, at first taken aback, finally recognized the monk to be his very brother John. Arkadios could not restrain his tears. He rose up and said excitedly to the elder, "This man is my brother!" The holy elder remarked, "I knew this, child, but I did not wish to speak of it to either of you, until each alone should come to recognize the other." Father John, stunned at the unexpected discovery, then cast a searching glance at Arkadios' features and truly recognized him. The brothers, at the elder's command, embraced and kissed one another. They kept giving thanks to the Lord Who not only vouchsafed them to behold one another alive, but also consecrated and garbed them in the holy Angelic Schema of the monastics.

After two days, the parents returned from the Jordan. They were accompanied by a large retinue as they openly venerated the holy Sepulcher of the Lord Jesus and Golgotha, and they distributed many gold florins. When they came forth from the church, they noticed the holy elder. They hastened to him and made a prostration, saying to him, "For the sake of the Lord, fulfill thy pledge and show us our children." Now both sons were actually standing before them, but the holy elder had previously instructed them not to utter the least word, but to keep their heads down. Now the parents had not recognized the two monks, due to their sons' austerities and abstinence which had altered their features. As for the sons, only strict obedience to their elder provided the suppression needed to check their overflowing hearts at the sound of their parents' voices. The elder then said to the parents, "Return to your lodgings and prepare a table that you might treat us, including my two disciples, and then I shall show you your children." This made Xenophon exceedingly glad. He then left and prepared a table. In the meantime, the holy elder counseled Father John and Father Arkadios, saying, "Let us go, my children, to the supper and friendly society of thy father, for which you shall not be injured. I ask that you guard yourselves, only for a short time, from speaking at the table, until I should prompt you. You ought to know this: no matter how many toils you might engage in for the sake of virtue, you shall not arrive at the stature of your parents. Indeed, even entering into conversation with them brings one benefit."

The three fathers then went to where Xenophon was staying. He received the three monks as though they were angels of God. Then they all sat down together and ate. At length, after the elder spoke of edifying subjects with the parents, Xenophon asked, "How do our children fare, honorable father?" The elder answered, "They are well and struggling for their salvation." The par-

Saints Arkadios, Xenophon, and John

ents said, "May God raise them up and show them to be worthy laborers of His vineyard, that we too may be delivered from the everlasting fire of punishment!" Now Xenophon marvelled at the two monks, especially their orderly behavior, dutiful manner, and reverence. He then added this observation, remarking to the elder, "In truth, honorable father, thou hast excellent disciples. Both my wife and I indeed love them exceedingly. As soon as we saw them, we felt joy as if we had seen our own boys." The elder responded to this, saying, "Amen." Then he said to Father Arkadios, "Tell me from whence thou comest and who art thy parents." He answered, "I, holy father, was from Constantinople. I was the son of wealthy parents. My father was a senator. I had a brother, with whom my parents sent me to Beirut to complete our education. We set sail but suffered shipwreck. I was saved by the help of God with one wood plank." The parents heard the account to this point and could not bear to hear the rest. They rose up and wept copiously as they wrapped their arms around the two young monks, crying aloud, "These are our children, honorable father! And we entreat thee, rise up that we might give glory to God at the discovery of our children. May God be compassionate to us, the sinners! Let us supplicate Him that He might vouchsafe us His kingdom." The elder also wept and gave thanks to God, glorifying His wise and wonderful providence which works for the salvation of man.

Xenophon and Mary then besought the holy elder to clothe them with the holy Schema, to which he consented. He ordered them not to behold one another for the rest of their earthly lives. After these things had been done, the two brothers bade farewell to their parents and followed the elder into the desert, where they abided in the ascetic life to the end. They were vouchsafed by God to heal every infirmity of those who hastened to them. They also received the grace of clairvoyance. They struggled well in the Lord and received a blessed end, which was foreknown to them.

Saint Xenophon

The father, Xenophon, sent his plenipotentiary to the capital in order to sell all his goods and belongings, both movable and stationary. As his proxy was in the capital, he was empowered to distribute the monies from these sales to the poor. He also freed all his slaves, giving them costly gifts. Xenophon then arranged for his wife to enter a convent, where she struggled in a God-pleasing manner before God. She came to the stature of the saints, God granting her the gift of healing the blind and demon-possessed. She then reposed in the Lord. Regarding Saint Xenophon, he dressed himself in a hair shirt and went into the desert, where he lived out the remaining years of his life. God vouchsafed him to behold great mysteries and receive the gift of clairvoyance. He reposed in the Lord during the early 600s. Thus, the godly family of Xenophon, Mary, and their holy children, John and Arkadios, came to a deeper love of God through suffering and a greater reward in the heavens, where they behold the divine countenance of the Master Christ, to Whom be glory, honor, and worship with the Father and Holy Spirit, now and ever and unto the ages of the ages. Amen.

On the 26th of January, the holy Church remembers the great earthquake which struck Constantinople.

During the final years of Emperor Theodosios II (408-450), on a Sunday, at the second hour, there occurred such a great earthquake in Constantinople, that it destroyed the city walls, together with many homes and neighborhoods of the city. Extensive damage was particularly suffered from Troadision to the copper Tetrapylon. Earthquakes and aftershocks rumbled throughout the city for three months. The emperor then called for a procession to be formed with all the people participating. Theodosios then prayed to God, saying, "Redeem us, O Lord, and grant forgiveness of our sins. In Thy righteous judgment and indignation these punishments have justly come upon us, since our sins have shaken and sundered the earth. But do Thou forgive us that we might glorify Thee, our only good God and the lover of man; for 'if Thou shouldest mark iniquities, O Lord, O Lord, who shall stand [Ps. 129:3]?'"

On the 26th of January, the holy Church commemorates our venerable Father SYMEON the Ancient.[5]

Symeon, our holy father, had a great love for the eremitical life from his very early childhood. He first lived as a hermit in the desert to the east of Kyros. He then dwelt in a cave in the Amanos Mountains,[6] north of Antioch. He never partook of any prepared food; for he ate neither bread, nor anything else, but only the plants of the field.

On one occasion, certain Jews were passing by who had lost their way and could not find their bearings, due to the severe rains and wind. Hence, they wandered about until they ended up at the cave of the saint. Seeing him, they asked him to show them the way. He promised them that he would give them two guides. Behold, as they waited for the guides, two lions arrived, which licked his hands as though he were their master. He ordered these two lions to accompany the Jews, until they had found the path from which they had strayed; and thus it was accomplished.

It was during a harvest season when a certain farmer, dishonest in his ways, harvested his land and stole several stacks of wheat from the neighboring field, placing them on his threshing floor. Immediately, however, the power of divine grace censured him, for lightning came down from heaven and set afire his threshing floor. When he saw this, he ran to the saint in tears, relating to him what had happened, but not disclosing his misdemeanor. Then the holy one said to him that if he returned what he had stolen, the fire would be put out. He complied and hastened to return what he had stolen, and the fire was extinguished without water.

---

[5] The Life of Saint Symeon was recorded by Theodoretos of Kyros (Cyrrhus), in Number Six of his *Religious History*.

[6] The Amanos is a mountain that separates Syria from Cilicia; it forms part of the cedar-covered Taurus mountain range.

Saint Symeon the Ancient

Since the saint had a great desire to see Mount Sinai, and to worship at the holy places there, the saint traveled there once. When he arrived at the cave where Moses beheld God (as far as is possible for human nature to see Him), he entered within, fell to his knees, and remained there fasting for several days, awaiting God's grace with tears and praying. He did not stir from that place until he heard a divine voice order him to arise and to eat the three apples that, miraculously, had been placed before him.

When blessed Symeon left Mount Sinai, he departed with a few traveling companions. When they reached the desert, near the city of Sodom, he descried the hands of a man coming out of the ground. He drew nigh to that place and saw a pit like a fox's lair. The one who was in the ditch heard our saint approaching, and withdrew farther in. But the Elder Symeon leaned forward, entreating the anchorite to reveal himself. After many supplications, he finally yielded. His overall appearance was that of a wild man. His hair was filled with dirt and unkempt, his face was wrinkled, and every part of his body was parched. He wore tattered garments of palm leaves stitched together. The elder inquired of the anchorite how he happened to dwell in such a place. Though modest and meek, the anchorite answered, as he was courteous, saying, "I also had a deep desire to go to Mount Sinai, as thou didst. So I found a companion in a certain brother. We vowed not to separate from each other till death. Therefore, since he died on the way, I kept my vow, and I buried him. I dug this ditch, and I await here the end of my life. My food consists only of a few dates that a certain brother brings me from time to time."

After he said this, behold, a lion appeared, holding in his mouth a sheaf of dates. Those who were with Symeon became frightened when they saw the lion. The anchorite, however, arose and made a sign to the lion, and the creature departed from them. Later, however, it returned; but, again, it was ordered to withdraw. The beast went apart from them and went to sleep, obeying the orders given to him as though he were a logical being. Thus did that contestant in virtue subdue even wild beasts.

After Abba Symeon the Ancient returned from Sinai, he founded two monasteries, one on the ridge of Amanos, and one on the edge of the foot of the mountain. As teacher and instructor, he exhorted each monastic there to be modest and humble toward his fellow man, but urged them also to show confidence and courage against the enemy. The holy elder wrought wondrous miracles of every kind, to the glory of God, to the very end of his toilsome life (ca. 390).

**On the 26th of January, the holy Church commemorates
the holy Martyrs ANANIOS the Presbyter,
PETER the prison warden, and the SEVEN soldiers with them.**

Ananios (Ananias) and Peter, the holy martyrs, lived during the time of Emperor Diocletian, when Maximianos[7] was governor of Phoenicia. The year was 295 when the holy Ananios was brought before the governor. As a result of the holy presbyter's confession of the Christ as God and his scorn of the idols, he was thrashed with rods. The executioners also burned his sides with red-hot spits. Next, they applied vinegar and salt to the holy man's burnt members. Then, by the holy presbyter's prayers, the temple of the idols was shaken, causing the idols to fall to the ground and break into pieces. Consequently, the authorities cast him into prison, where he was nourished by God. This miraculous and divine sustenance was a cause of great wonder to the jailer Peter, who was drawn to the Faith of Jesus and also came to confess Christ. There were also seven soldiers, brought to the Christian Faith by the saint, who also witnessed the fact that Ananios was preserved from all the tortures he underwent. Thus, the blessed ones, all together, received crowns of the martyric contest from Christ when, at the governor's command, they were cast into the sea and drowned.

**On the 26th of January, the holy Church commemorates
the venerable AMMONAS, who reposed in peace.**

Ammonas the bishop, according to some, was the very youth whom Saint Anthony prophesied would progress in the fear of God. The great

---

[7] The *Synaxarion* of the *Menaion* (Athenian Publishers Zoe, Phos, and Apostolike Diakonia) identifies the governor as Maximos. Variants of the spelling of the saint's name are given therein as Ananios or Ananias.

Anthony showed him a rock and said to him, "Strike the rock and rebuke it." Ammonas did as he was ordered, and then Saint Anthony said to him, "Thou shalt also reach such a state that thou wilt not regard people's insults and reproaches." And thus it came to pass, for the all-praised Ammonas attained such a high state of goodness and meekness that he judged no one. He attained to such impassibility, as though he were ignorant of evil.

When he became a bishop, there was an occasion when a young damsel was brought before him. She had been corrupted and conceived a child. They also brought to Ammonas the man who had defiled her, and asked that he censure them both. The holy one, however, not only did not reprove or condemn them, but rather he made the sign of the Cross over the womb of the woman. He gave her six sheets of linen, lest she or her child should die in childbirth and not have any sheets for burial. Then the ones who had brought them said to the saint, "Wherefore didst thou so? Reprimand both of them!" But the holy one answered them, "You see, brethren, that she is near death, so what can I do?" After saying this, he dismissed them and did not venture to pass judgment on her at all.

At another time, the saint went to a certain place to obtain food. A monk was living there who was reputed to have committed many adulterous sins with one particular woman, who at the time was in his cell. When the local people heard that the holy Ammonas was there, they went to him, and asked him to go to the monk's cell, so that the fornicator might be exposed to public scorn. In this way, before Ammonas, they could cast him out from thence. The wayward monk was aware of their plan, and hid the woman in an earthen jar. Now our saint, in the Spirit, perceived this maneuver; so when he entered the cell he went directly and sat on the mouth of the jar. The blessed one then ordered them to search the cell for the woman. They searched, but could not find her. Then he said to them, "May God forgive all of you for the accusation you have made against this monk!" And after Saint Ammonas had prayed, he made everyone depart. Then he took the monk by the hand, and with a penetrating look said to him, "Brother, watch thyself!" After he had spoken thus, he departed.

The saint used to say that when he was in Sketis, he besought God night and day for fourteen years to grant him victory against the passion of anger.

Now there are others who say that this Ammonas, commemorated today, was the priest whose Life is recorded in the *Lausiac History*. This Father Ammonas, at one time, beheld an angel on the right side of the sacred bema. The angel was writing down the names of all those brethren who were present at the divine Liturgy, but the names of all those who were not present he crossed out. After three days those who were absent reposed. "I am," comments Nikodemos the Hagiorite, "with the former, and believe that this Ammonas was a bishop."

On the 26th of January, the holy Church commemorates
the venerable GABRIEL, who reposed in peace.

On the 26th of January, the holy Church commemorates
the holy TWO MARTYRS in Phrygia,
who were cudgeled to death.

On the 26th of January, the holy Church commemorates
our venerable and God-bearing Father CLEMENT,
who struggled on Mount Sagmation, near Thebes.

Through the intercessions of Thy Saints,
O Christ God, have mercy on us. Amen.

On the 27th of January, the holy Church commemorates
the translation of the relics of our
holy father among the saints,
JOHN CHRYSOSTOM, Archbishop of Constantinople.[1]

The Translation of the Relics of Saint John Chrysostom

John Chrysostom (ca. 347-407), the great pillar of the Church and
unshakeable tower of piety, was Patriarch of Constantinople during the reign
of Emperor Arkadios (395-408). This great father and teacher, an inextinguishable lamp, was persecuted, maligned, and banished for the sake of
Christ. He was not one to overlook wrongs and injustices before the faces of
the mighty, though it meant rebuking them openly.

---

[1] Several encomia have been written honoring the memory of the translation of the
relics of Saint John Chrysostom. The text of Kosmas the Vestitor is extant at the
Athonite monasteries of the Great Lavra, Dionysiou, and Iveron. The Great Lavra is
also in possession of two other encomia. Nikodemos the Hagiorite also penned an
encomium to the divine Chrysostom, as well as a Supplicatory Canon. A service,
consisting of twenty-four stanzas, was composed by the hymnographer of the Great
Church, Father Gerasimos Mikrayiannanites. The chief feast day of the saint is the 13th
of November, which entry contains the full account of his Life. A significant portion
of the English version presented herein was taken from our publication, "The
Translation of the Relics of Saint John," in *The Lives of the Three Hierarchs*, 2nd
edition, pp. 296-302, which is based on *The Great Synaxaristes* (in Greek) and other
sources.

Now there was a wealthy and distinguished Constantinopolitan, named Theognostos. He had been slandered by his enemies before Emperor Arkadios and Empress Evdoxia. They contended that he cursed and insulted the imperial couple. Arkadios was moved to wrath and sentenced Theognostos to Thessalonike for imprisonment. Theognostos' property was confiscated, except for one vineyard, lest his wife Kallitrope and his children should have no means of support. On the way to Thessalonike, Theognostos took ill and reposed. Kallitrope sought counsel and consolation from the spiritual fountain of the then Archbishop of Constantinople, John Chrysostom. Saint John invited Kallitrope and her children to come daily and eat at the table in the Church's hostels for the indigent. Saint John in the meantime was biding his time for the appropriate occasion when he might bring up the widow's case before the emperor. It was his hope that her property might be restored.

Now we all remember that Jezebel, for the sake of a neighbor's vineyard, which King Ahab coveted, had its owner, Nabouthai, stoned and slain.[2] In like manner, Augusta Evdoxia—a Frankish general's daughter who grew up in Constantinople—laid hold of the vineyard of the widow Kallitrope. Evdoxia not only craved it for her own selfish reasons, but also was more vexed with the widow for having taken recourse in Saint John. One day, the empress had plucked a cluster of grapes in this vineyard, without knowing that it was the vineyard of another. Evdoxia then used an imperial law claiming that since she trod the land and picked and ate the grapes with her own hands, it could no longer remain in the hands of commoners. She claimed that ownership must be transferred, making it an imperial possession. Thus, the empress dispossessed the widow. Troubled by this seizure, Kallitrope went again before Saint John Chrysostom, and poured out her heart to him. The only property left to feed herself and her children was now forcibly taken from her. Saint John was inspired to take up her cause, much as had Prophet Elias the Thesbite before Ahab. His well-meant defense of the widow was not received with good humor by the empress. Offended and vexed at his interference which she found officious, she could not keep her composure. A quarrel resulted between the state and Church. Now Evdoxia was seeking an accusation against John to have him removed from his see.

Saint John wrote the augusta and even visited with her. She refused to tolerate his entreaties and admonitions. "Let the widow select another vineyard, or receive money in compensation for it," said she. Saint John answered, "She does not ask for another vineyard, nor does she seek restitution for her own vineyard; only return her own vineyard to her." Saint John reminded Evdoxia that the old imperial law that she was citing was

---

[2] 3 Kgs. 20 LXX; 1 Kgs. 3:21 KJV.

promulgated by pagans. He asked her to annul the unjust law, and return the vineyard, lest a curse similar to what befell Jezebel should fall upon her. When the glaring similarity of her case and that of Jezebel was represented to the augusta, the augusta could no longer bear Saint John's presence. Unable to restrain her tongue, she vented screaming threats of revenge upon the caring hierarch. She refused to return the vineyard. Neither would she give another vineyard, nor compensate the widow. The augusta then commanded the palace doorkeepers that, in the event Patriarch John should return, the doors were to be closed to him. Thereupon, Saint John charged the cathedral doorkeeper that, if the empress should wish to enter, he was to close the door, and say, "John has also commanded me."

Saint John is Exiled

Later, in a sermon, Saint John was giving examples from sacred Scriptures of the cruelty of a number of women. The enemies of Saint John lost no time in conveying this to the empress, believing he was speaking of the augusta herself. The augusta complained to her husband, beseeching him to convene a council that John might be sent into exile. Evdoxia then wrote Archbishop Theophilos of Alexandria, inviting him to Constantinople. She asked him to summon bishops to drive out her enemy John. Theophilos and other bishops, whom Theophilos had disposed to his way of thinking, came to Constantinople. In the meantime, Arkadios wrote Pope Innocent of Rome (401-417) to send bishops. Rome willingly complied, but was waiting for a second letter with details. The letter never was sent, so Rome was not represented. Theophilos and Evdoxia then cooperated unimpeded. False accusations were drawn up against Saint John Chrysostom, who was predictably condemned by them. Emperor Arkadios did not even read the accusations made against Saint John. He approved the words of the unjust council that deposed him. This was to be the first exile of the patriarch. Then, when a riot ensued, followed by an earthquake, terror seized the imperial couple, so that Saint John was returned to his see.

Saint John's return, however, was not of any great duration. Within a couple of months, a column with the augusta's image was erected. At its unveiling, the shouts of revelers, and the noise of the games and shouts that accompanied it, interrupted the chanting of the divine service in progress where Saint John was celebrating. Saint John remarked, "Again Herodias rageth....Again she seeks the head of John [Mk. 6:16-28]!" The archbishop's enemies made haste to report this intelligence to the augusta. Angry and crying, she went to her husband and begged that another council be convened against John. Saint John was exiled again in 404, on the basis that, after he had been deposed, he dared to reoccupy the episcopal throne before a new synod could be convened.

Saint John was then placed under house arrest at the patriarchal residence, until the imperial decree regarding his exile and imprisonment was prepared. After he was banished, a fire broke out in the cathedral church. Saint John's supporters were charged with arson. Arsakios (ca. 325-405), at eighty years of age, was elevated to the position of archbishop of the capital city. Since he lasted only fourteen months until his death, the Priest Attikos, a chief opponent of Chrysostom, was chosen to succeed Arsakios. On account of questionable proceedings, most of the eastern bishops and laity were not in communion with him. As a result of threats, bribes, and ignorance, some were compelled by circumstances and their own weaknesses to be in communion, however unwillingly, with him. Later that year, Evdoxia suffered a miscarriage, which was interpreted as a punishment for her opposition to Saint John.

Our blessed and divine father, John Chrysostom, chose not to overlook justice for the sake of currying the favor of the imperial authorities. Instead he censured every injustice, including that of the augusta Evdoxia who transgressed by tyrannically seizing the vineyard of a widow. When the saint was banished to Koukousos (Cucusus) in Armenia, he was received by Bishop Adelphios. Koukousos was a little remote border town, with a garrison, in the area of the Isaurian mountains. It had no marketplace and not even one little shop. Exiles were not allowed to travel by the state post, even though Saint John was suffering from poor health with his constant stomach problems. It was to this place that our great father and angel in the flesh was dispatched. In Koukousos many people from neighboring parts came to hear his teachings. He had been in Koukousos for a year when some of the adherents of Severianos and Porphyrios, together with some bishops of Syria, schemed to have Chrysostom transferred to some other place, since he was proving troublesome to them. They surely did not want to see the pleasing philosophy that Chrysostom sowed in the Church of Antioch transplanted now to the Church of Armenia. He was therefore transferred to Arabissos.

During the time that Saint John was made to sojourn in Koukousos and Arabissos, some of his friends in the west were attempting to vindicate him. Pope Innocent felt his only option against the emperor of the east and the eastern bishops against Chrysostom was to seek help from Arkadios' brother, Emperor Honorius of the west, who was co-regent with his brother. In 405, the pope wrote to Honorius at Ravenna and sent him copies of pertinent documents in the Chrysostom affair. Although Honorius initially thought that the Italian bishops should investigate the matter, he then decided to write to his brother. His opening letter contained the following: "Brother Arkadios, I do not know what rebellious power incited thee to listen to one woman that caused thee to do what no other Christian emperor has enacted. Justifiably, the bishops here have condemned thee, because thou didst exile the great hierarch of God, which thy soldiers are slowly slaying by punishment and torture."

Honorius did not receive an answer to either his first or second letter. In the meantime, a synod of Latin bishops convened in Rome, under the presidency of the pope, at Honorius' request. They concluded that Emperor Honorius was to write his brother and co-Emperor Arkadios, and ask him to convene a general synod of both Greeks and Latins in Thessalonike. Chrysostom was also to appear before this synod, but only under the condition that his diocese and ecclesiastical fellowship be returned to him. He was to appear at spiritual court in possession of his rights and dignities. Honorius cooperated, provided the pope would be the chief negotiator. Honorius then wrote his brother: "For the third time, I am writing your clemency requesting that the matter of John, Archbishop of Constantinople, be corrected. I am dispatching this letter with five bishops, two priests, and a deacon of the great Roman Church, who are all honorable men. Show them all honor, and permit them to call upon the bishops of the east that they may meet in Thessalonike. If the Latin bishops believe that John was lawfully deposed, they shall inform me, that I too may sever communion with him. On the other hand, if an injustice has been done, they will have thee announce the fellowship.

"Also, I am enclosing some letters in regard to this affair. In addition, I particularly implore thee to see that Theophilos of Alexandria is in attendance, even if it should be against his will. He seems to be the chief cause of all this trouble, brother. Thus, the synod shall be able to secure peace without obstacle."

The Latin bishops, hopeful and optimistic, left for Thessalonike. Regrettably, the journey of the assembly was met with harassments all along the Greek coasts. They were forbidden entry in Thessalonike. They were forcibly detained and lodged in different locations around Constantinople. They were mistreated, threatened, and even offered bribes. Though the Latins rejected all their threats and bribes, they were allowed to return home safely to their dioceses. It is not clear what political personage dared such an insult and outrage to the political and ecclesiastic sensibilities of the west, which only came to seek the restoration of peace in the Church as a whole. As a result of the shocking treatment of his delegates, Pope Innocent broke off all communion with Theophilos, Attikos, Porphyrios, and all of the other chief opponents of the holy John Chrysostom.

Even in this place of exile in Arabissos, Chrysostom was eyed as an enemy of the state. Evdoxia decided to send him further away to Pityos, a deserted place in Tzane lying on the shore of the Black Sea. After a torturous portage by uncouth soldiers, he reached Comana. At the Church of Saint Basiliskos (who was from Comana and had been martyred by the pagans under Maximianos in Nikomedia), he partook of the Mysteries. Saint Basiliskos appeared to him in a vision and said, "Have courage, brother, tomorrow we shall be together." Chrysostom asked for white clothes and received them. He gave his own garments, except his shoes, to those around him. Then, after receiving holy Communion the following day, the victorious athlete lay down and surrendered his soul to God and said, "Glory be to God for all things!" At the last "Amen," he signed himself with the Cross and reposed. This took place in 407, on the 14th of September, when the Church commemorates the Exaltation of the Precious Cross. Saint John, at sixty-three years of age, was then laid to rest in that same church.

News quickly spread that the former Bishop of Constantinople had died in exile near Comana. From all parts of Syria, Cilicia, Pontos, and Armenia, faithful followers came to his tomb. His burial had been celebrated in the place where he reposed, in the Chapel of the Martyr Basiliskos. It appeared that political decadence and ecclesiastical corruption and envy had prevailed, but this situation was not to last.

Now while Saint John was in exile, he was accompanied by two priests and a deacon who followed him until his repose. After the holy hierarch's interment, they set out for the city of Rome and Pope Innocent I. It was reported to the pope that men were paid to slay Saint John when he went into exile, but an angel of the Lord protected him to the end, since it was not God's will that His holy one should be murdered. The pope was informed how the holy Apostles Peter and John appeared to Saint John just before he reached Comana. The apostles encouraged and strengthened the hierarch, and prophesied how Evdoxia would be riddled with worms and die in terrible agony. The two priests and the deacon also beheld with their own eyes the visitation of the apostles with Saint John. They also related to the pope that upon Saint John's departure from Constantinople, the city suffered a great earthquake and a fearful hailstorm. The entire city sustained terrible damage. The column with the image of Evdoxia was smashed. A divinely-sent fire issued from the archbishop's throne and burned much of the church's interior. The flames advanced toward the palace, which, inside of three hours, was destroyed. When the pope and the people of Rome heard these accounts they both rejoiced and sorrowed: they sorrowed over the torments the holy one was made to suffer on account of evil persons; but they rejoiced that the hierarch remained steadfast to the end. Filled with divine zeal, Pope Innocent and Emperor Honorius each wrote an epistle to Arkadios reproving his lawlessness and injustice.

From Rome, the pope sent the emperor a notice of excommunication, which said the following: "The blood of my brother John cries out to God against thee, O Emperor Arkadios! For thou hast brought about a time of persecution when the Church was in a time of peace, by exiling her true shepherd, and with him—alas!—Christ. Thou hast banished and delivered up this shepherd to false shepherds and hirelings. I am not sorrowing for Chrysostom, that blessed one, on account of his great accomplishments and the innumerable torments which he endured, through which he received the lot of inheritance in the kingdom of God with the apostles and martyrs. I do, however, grieve for thine own destruction; because thou, in order to do the will of one mindless woman, hast deprived all the world of his mellifluous teachings. On this account, I, the least one, who have been entrusted with the throne of him who was the summit of the apostles, have settled that both thee and she are to be separated from communing the divine Mysteries of Christ. And whosoever shall dare to communicate the Mysteries to you, shall be deposed and excommunicated. Moreover, if you should compel anyone—may it not be!—to communicate the Mysteries to you, disdaining this apostolic command, you shall be as publicans and those of the nations that know not God; and your sin shall abide even to the day of judgment, when you shall receive fitting punishment. Furthermore, Arsakios, whom you have put on the throne of Chrysostom, is deposed along with those in communion with him, because in a fraudulent manner the unworthy one laid hold of this dignity. And as for Theophilos, he is not only deposed and excommunicated, but he also is alien to Christ. These things which are bound here on earth are bound in heaven, even as it is written in the Gospel [Mt. 16:18]."

Arkadios finally came to his senses, and was exceedingly sorrowed, and shook with wrath. He first set about punishing those responsible for ill-treating the pope's legates. Indeed, some were scourged, and others were sentenced to death by hanging. All of the relatives of Evdoxia who collaborated in the deposition of the holy man had their property confiscated. Arkadios even chastened his own wife when he struck her and severely punished her. Unable to bear the distress and embarrassment, Evdoxia became very ill. Though she possessed outstanding beauty, it waned quickly. In the nine years from her marriage (395), she bore the emperor five children; in fact, she was pregnant during much of her short reign (400-404).

Arkadios then bound Menas, Theoteknos, and Ischyrion, who were the nephews of Theophilos. He also disciplined the Bishops Severian of Gabala and Akakios of Verea. Arkadios also ordered the seizure and imprisonment of those bishops in Constantinople who had participated in the unlawful condemnation of Chrysostom. He sent an epistle to Theophilos of Alexandria, demanding his appearance in Thessalonike for questioning. Then with utter humility, he took up his pen and wrote to Pope Innocent, saying, among other things, "I did not know of all those things perpetrated against thine ambassadors. When I was apprised of the incidents, the unjust were sentenced to death. Also, the deposition of John was not my doing, but certain wretched bishops pointed out to me ecclesiastical canons and the sin which they believe was committed by John, and thus I cast my ill-considered vote. Consequently, I am sending to thy holiness, Akakios, Severian, and the relations of the evil Theophilos. I have written the latter demanding him to come here.

"We ask forgiveness of thy fatherly philanthropy, and we beseech thee not to deprive us of the immaculate Mysteries. I have punished and severely scourged thy child Evdoxia. Thereupon, she has become gravely ill, and has taken to her bed. Therefore, do not punish us any further, honorable father, since we have repented with all our hearts; and, in accordance with the command of the boundless compassion of the all-good God, we pray that thy holiness might forgive us." Arkadios then wrote his brother Honorius, imploring him to act as mediator, that the pope might send his forgiveness and lift the excommunication.

Archbishop Attikos of Constantinople, urged on by Theophilos of Alexandria, considered the time favorable for reconciling with the followers of John, the Johannites. Theophilos himself also sought union with Rome. Nonetheless, several Greek bishops refused to be in communion with Attikos, Theophilos, and Porphyrios of Antioch. Pope Innocent also would not resume fellowship with the guilty patriarchs and bishops, without restitution for past misdeeds. With the death of Porphyrios, the new Patriarch of Antioch, Alexander, placed Chrysostom's name in the diptychs and renewed relations with Rome. Constantinople's Attikos also placed the name of the holy John in the diptychs. Thus peace was brought about between Rome and the patriarchates of the east, but not with Alexandria. As a result, some of the Johannites reconciled with Attikos. Saint Kyril of Alexandria (378-444), the nephew of Theophilos, refrained from entering Saint John's name in the diptychs until 418. Both George Kedrenos and Nikephoros Kallistos in their histories record that Saint Kyril received a vision, wherein Chrysostom appeared to him. Chrysostom was surrounded by the heavenly army, and threatened to expel Kyril from the episcopal palace. When the Theotokos interceded with John for Kyril, who had intrepidly defended her honor at the Ephesian Synod, Kyril made up his mind to seek peace with his uncle's nemesis.

When the pope received Arkadios' epistle, he rejoiced exceedingly at the emperor's humility. Therefore, he wrote to Proklos, Bishop of Kyzikos, who had been a faithful disciple of Chrysostom, bidding him to go to

Constantinople, in order to loose the imperial couple from the excommunication and to commune the divine Mysteries to them. He then charged Proklos to assume the guardianship of the patriarchal throne, until there should be a diligent examination of Attikos. The pope also wrote especially to Arkadios that he received his repentance, and loosed him from the excommunication. However, he also commanded that the name of Chrysostom should be written in the sacred diptychs, and that he was to order Theophilos of Alexandria to appear in Thessalonike. The pope himself declared that due to the gravity of the situation, he himself would be in attendance. Both cheered and satisfied upon receiving these commands, the emperor was in favor of performing them.

Arkadios sent a communication to Theophilos, as follows: "Thou hast shaken the entire inhabited world and in a satanic manner hast made thyself master of the place, without revering ecclesiastical laws or imperial authority. Therefore, depart straightway, without making even one pretext, and go to Thessalonike to be judged by the Archbishop of Rome." When Theophilos received the imperial communication, he trembled at the threats of the emperor. Nonetheless, he neither made haste nor found time at all to go to Thessalonike. The reason for his absence was that God permitted an incurable disease to befall him. Painful stony concretions began forming in his body (lithiasis). This disease usually affects the urinary tract or the gall bladder. He understood this visitation from God, and boldly confessed his wrongdoings which he carried out against Chrysostom. Theophilos died in 412. Saint John of Damascus (ca. 675-ca. 749) quotes a passage from the chronography of Deacon Isidore, in which it is related that when Theophilos lay on his deathbed, he was unable to die on account of his participation in the Chrysostom deposition. At last, someone brought an icon of Chrysostom, which Theophilos venerated, and then gave up his spirit.

The Saint's Enemies and Friends

Among the chief enemies of Saint John Chrysostom, the young Evdoxia was the first to die, after having been sorely afflicted with hemorrhaging. Her flesh began to rot, emitting a foul odor, and was infested with worms. She understood that these infirmities were a result of her unjust punishment of the holy hierarch. Thereupon, she mournfully called upon his name with plaintive cries. She returned the vineyard to the widow and made amends for her other injustices. After much pain and distress, she finally gave up the spirit. However, not even after death was she left unpunished, for her tomb quaked, to the astonishment of every beholder of the phenomenon. In fact, her tomb shook for thirty-three years, until the translation of the relics of Saint John Chrysostom to Constantinople. After her death, Evdoxia left four daughters: Flaccilla (d. 403), Pulcheria, Arkadia, and Marina. She also had one son, the heir Theodosios. In 408, eight months after Chrysostom's repose, Emperor Arkadios, who reigned fourteen years, died, leaving his heir and successor, the then fourteen-year-old Theodosios, and four unmarried daughters. Therefore, the pious nineteen-year-old Pulcheria reigned until her brother was of legal age.

Regarding the end of Saint John's persecutors, hearken: The foot of Bishop Kyrinos of Chalcedon was amputated, but later gangrene set in, and he died in 406. Another bishop who signed the decree of banishment died of dropsy; yet another rotted away while still living; a third became crippled and lay speechless for eight months on a bed of pain. Still another fell from his horse, broke his leg, and died as a result of it. Another developed an ulcer of the tongue. He lost the power of speech and at last wrote a confession of his guilt and remorse. Akakios of Verea outlived Saint John some thirty years. He partly atoned for his injustice. Severian of Gabala and Antiochos of Ptolemais returned to their dioceses and were never heard from again. The Armenian Attikos, who was the second successor of Chrysostom, died in 425.

Patriarch Proklos

After Theodosios II (408-450) reigned some thirty years, Saint Proklos, the disciple and deacon of the divine John Chrysostom, by a general vote, became the Patriarch of Constantinople. In 435, the fourth year for Proklos as patriarch, he persuaded the emperor to translate to Constantinople the relics of that holy father. The faithful also were zealous for the return of his relics from Comana to Constantinople. Patriarch Proklos reminded Emperor Theodosios that it was Saint John who had ministered at his Baptism, and that it was through envy that he was deposed and exiled. Proklos encouraged Theodosios, saying he would have Saint John as an intercessor if he were to translate his honorable relics. The emperor acquiesced and dispatched distinguished men of rank to Comana bearing a silver coffer to translate the holy relics.

Attempts at the Removal of the Relics

Upon entering Comana, the emperor's ambassadors inquired as to the whereabouts of the holy man's tomb in order that they might remove the relics. The townspeople were exceedingly embittered at the prospect of the deprivation of their precious treasure, but no one would dare gainsay the imperial command. Thus, the emperor's men were escorted to the tomb of the blessed one. The stone was removed so that they might take up the relics. When they attempted to lift the relics, they remained immovable. Behold the wonder! So many strong men were powerless to budge the relics from their resting-place. Thereupon, the envoys were constrained to return unsuccessful to the emperor. News of this occurrence went abroad. It was heralded throughout the city that the saint would not give himself over for the transfer, but held fast in his present spot. The reason for the saint's relics remaining fixed was on account of the emperor's audacity and pride in his desire to acquire them. It was the saint's desire to teach humble-mindedness and moderation to the monarch.

Theodosios acknowledged his attitude, and sent the hierarch an epistle: "To the Œcumenical Patriarch, teacher and spiritual Father John Chrysostom, I, Emperor Theodosios, offer to thee my prostration and veneration. We, honorable father, thinking that thy body happened to be dead, as other bodies of the departed, simply wished to transfer the relics to ourselves. Thereupon, deservedly, we were deprived of our wish. But do thou, most honorable father, forgive us who repent, for thou didst teach repentance to all. And, as a father who loves his children, give thyself to us, thy sons who love their father, and gladden those who desire thee by thy presence. Put me not to shame, honorable father. Come back to us in peace, and take up what is thine own with love!"

Envoys were again dispatched bearing the emperor's heartfelt and hopeful epistle. They arrived at the site ready to fulfill the emperor's command. Again, they beheld another wonder. An ineffable light leaped forth from the tomb, shining brilliantly, and an inexpressible fragrance emitted therefrom. The saint did not look as one dead, but appeared with a joyful countenance. The epistle was placed upon the saint's breast. An all-night vigil was then celebrated. At the end of the divine service, the emissaries, demonstrating a proper feeling of respect and veneration, merely touched his relics. Our holy father then rendered up his relics easily and without hindrance. The emperor's representatives were filled with holy joy and transferred the relics into the reliquary specially crafted at the emperor's behest.

Then there took place many miracles among those who came with faith to venerate the saint's relics. One noteworthy miracle took place upon a lame pauper. He had a history of a withered leg as a result of a serpent bite. He sustained himself by continuing to visit the sacred precincts of the churches, begging alms from the faithful who entered therein. Since such a large crowd flocked around the sacred relics, it was only with great exertion that he was able to draw near. As he inched up closer, he took hold of the saint's clothing and removed a patch of material. He was inspired to place that sacred cloth on his diseased limb; and straightway he received healing! The formerly shriveled limb was vivified and became as strong as the other leg. He walked up and down, and all about, giving glory to God and His mighty saint.

Soon it was time to secure the reliquary and translate the relics back to Constantinople. The sacred relics were escorted by the envoys and the faithful. While many hymns were offered, lamps were burning brightly, and incense filled the air. Every city and village that the saint passed through on the journey back to Constantinople received the blessing of his presence.

When the traveling party approached Chalcedon, scouts and messengers brought word to the imperial city. News of the report made both young and old hasten to the harbor, as was meet, that they might meet the sacred reliquary before it entered the city. The harbor was tightly filled with so many sailing vessels that the sea appeared as an extension of the dry land. In anticipation of this event, boats and barques were afloat in a calm sea, even as far as to the Propontis. Without exaggeration, thousands of brilliant lamps dotted the harbor like twinkling stars in the evening twilight. It was the 27th day of January, in the year 438, when the city surrendered joyfully to the solemnity of the occasion, and put aside all mundane affairs. Half the city was on its knees in prayer. So many multitudes streamed towards the shore as were never seen before—not even such numbers attended the circus, or theater, or the triumphal return of the emperor himself from the wars.

Saint John Chrysostom entered his episcopal city as a victorious conqueror over his enemies: Evdoxia, Arkadios, Severian, Theophilos, Antiochos, Kyrinos, Arsakios, and Attikos. The son of Arkadios and Evdoxia, Emperor Theodosios II, cooperated with Patriarch Proklos; but it was his sister, Pulcheria, who urged having the relics translated from Pontos to the capital city. The emperor, senate, and court desired to participate in the procession. Thus, the emperor and his retinue, together with the patriarch and the clergy, went to the dock at Chalcedon. At the wharf, they embarked into an imperial ship to meet the holy relics and escort them to their new resting-place. An imperial galley ship was made ready to take the precious cargo and return to the city. All preparations went along smoothly, and the weather was fine. Then, unexpectedly, as they were returning, a tempest arose. This, too, was in accordance with divine providence. As all the sailing vessels were being tossed about, the ship with Saint John's reliquary sailed of itself. It had no rudder, but it was guided by the power of God to the very shore where the widow Kallitrope's vineyard was located! Then the sea calmed, and the ships resumed their places again. There were no injuries or property damage as a result of the storm.

The Translation of the Relics to the Churches

When they put into the port, as some bore aloft the reliquary, it was evident that the reliquary was inclined to move in a certain direction. Now the emperor, before he met with the relics, had been planning to bring the relics to the palace, but the saint disposed otherwise. This is why the sea rose in the Hellespont so mightily. Therefore the relics were first brought to the Church of the Apostle Thomas of the Amantion. When the emperor first came face to face with the reliquary, he knelt down, gazed upon the bier, and prayed to Saint John, asking forgiveness for the sins of his parents. At the Church of Saint Thomas he draped the imperial purple cloak over the sacred depository of the relics. He then besought the saint on his mother's behalf, for her tomb, even after thirty-three years from her interment, kept on quaking. With tears he humbly supplicated Saint John, saying aloud, "Forgive the sins committed against thee. Allow me not to suffer punishment on account of the sins of my parents. Though I am verily the son of her who drove thee away, yet I did not bring this affliction upon thee. Pardon my mother, that I too may be delivered from the reproach that lies heavily upon her. I bow my office and my authority down to thy feet. She did repent of her foolishness. She speaks to thee through me, saying, 'Father, remember the homily thou gavest against remembrance of wrongs. As then, do now put away remembrance of my ill will and offenses. I desire to rise from my fallen condition. Stretch out thy hand to me, O thou who once said, "If anyone should fall, let him stand up, and be saved." O father, thy displeasure cannot be borne by me. See, even my tomb trembles, affording no rest to my bones. I am afraid of the everlasting punishment, that I may not be sent from a place at the right hand of Christ at the fearful judgment. Thou hast saved others through thy teachings, so do not let me be deprived of salvation. Avenge not thyself on me, but on the devil, who moved me to afflict thee. Thou didst not remember wrongs done to thee whilst thou wast alive; do not remember them in thy heavenly life. Aid my soul, and help me, O father. My glory has vanished, but do thou help me in the glory which thou hast received from God.'"

Throughout his petition for his mother's soul, the emperor could not suppress his violent weeping. With reverent fear, he planted many kisses on the precious relics, which were moistened by hot tears falling from his eyes. The relics were then moved to the Church of Saint Irene. The relics were placed upon the holy throne, and all in full voice, exclaimed, "Take up thy throne, O saint!" Afterwards, the relics were brought to the Church of the Holy Apostles. The relics were placed upon the bishop's throne and—O the wonder!—Patriarch Proklos and other distinguished dignitaries then observed that Saint John Chrysostom moved his lips. He then uttered aloud to the faithful, "Peace be to thee, and forgiveness to Evdoxia." Thus, the emperor, who loved his mother very much, received an answer to his entreaty; and his mother's tomb ceased shaking. The relics of Saint John were then placed in the sanctuary under the table of oblation.

When the divine Liturgy was celebrated, many miracles took place. We shall recount one of a man who suffered from chronic and crippling arthritis. Together with the great pain he suffered in his joints, he was rendered nearly paralyzed. Slowly, he made his way to the saint's relics, and—O the wonder!—immediately, he was completely freed from the disease. He glorified God and His saint.

Near to Saint John, in the Church of the Holy Apostles, were the tombs of Constantine the Great, Constantios, Theodosios I, Arkadios and Evdoxia, who were in the imperial mausoleum. Gradually, through Patriarch Proklos' efforts, the Johannites were reconciled and entered into fellowship with Saint John's successors. Later, the relics of Saint John began to flow myrrh. The scent was widely reputed to surpass that of any perfume. As attested to by many, the myrrh burst forth from his sacred relics, as a fast-flowing fountain. At the divine behest, it penetrates through the silver encasement made in his image, which lies above his relics. The rapid flow may be seen descending from his head or his hand. Ofttimes, it is seen streaming forth from his knee, or beard, or the border of his episcopal vestment. But it does overflow the whole reliquary.

For some eight hundred years Saint John's relics rested in the Church of the Apostles in Constantinople. When the Venetians sacked and looted the city in 1204, it is reputed that they took his relics to Rome, where they were laid in the shadow of Saint Peter. Now the Monastery of Vatopedi on Mount Athos has the sacred head of Saint John, intact and whole. The right ear into which Saint Paul spoke to him has remained incorrupt with the skin. The rest of the skull is a beautiful golden color. The Monastery of Saint Athanasios on Mount Athos possesses a hand of the saint. The monastery on Patmos also claims to have the relics of Saint John among its treasures. It is also reported that, in the year 1284, Emperor Andronikos II sent the Monastery of Philotheos on Thasos the right hand of Saint John.

On the 27th of January, the holy Church commemorates
the holy Empress MARKIANE, renowned for her charitable works,
who reposed in peace and was laid to rest in the
Church of the Holy Apostles.

On the 27th of January, the holy Church commemorates
the venerable KLAVDINOS (Claudinus), who reposed in peace.

On the 27th of January, the holy Church commemorates
the venerable PETER the Egyptian, who reposed in peace
after reaching deep old age.

Peter, our venerable father, an ascetic in the desert of the Cells of Egypt, was a disciple of Abba Lot, who is commemorated by the holy Church on the 22nd of October. A fellow monk came to visit him and complained, "When I am alone in my cell, my soul finds peace. Whensoever any of the brethren should come and speak of men in the world, my soul becomes agitated." Abba Peter said, "Abba Lot used to say that the key opens the door." The visiting brother, perplexed, said, "I do not understand properly that expression, my abba. What does it mean?" Abba Peter answered, "If any of the brethren should visit and thou art asked, 'How is it with thee?' or 'From whence comest thou?' or 'How are the brethren faring?' shouldest thou give a response and attend to him or not? Because know this: with the response to such questions, thou wilt be the first to open the door to what follows. Even if one does not wish to hear such a conversation from his guest, his soul is bound to be filled with agitation." That monk then said,

Saint Peter

"What thou sayest is true. Well then, what is one to do whenever one of the brethren comes visiting?" Abba Peter replied, "Whenever one is possessed of compunction and mourning, then those sentiments teach a man what he ought to do. Whenever they are not within a man, then it is not possible for him to guard himself." The monk said, "Whenever I am in my cell, I also find compunction and mourning. But whenever I exit my cell, then those sentiments depart from me." The old man Peter then said, "Even as a legitimate son does not desert his father; in like manner, compunction and mourning, when they abide in us, whensoever we should call upon them, they are within. Thus, though visitors should come, they would not disturb our quiet."

On another occasion, Abba Peter was asked, "What is the slave of God?" The old man answered, "As long as one is mastered by a passion, he cannot be accounted a slave of God. This is because he is already lorded over by a passion and is enslaved. Such a one, as long as he is dominated by a passion, cannot teach others who are dominated by the same passion; for it is shameful that he should instruct others regarding deliverance from a passion to which he is held captive."

**On the 27th of January, the holy Church commemorates
the holy New-martyr DEMETRIOS of Galata,
who was beheaded in Constantinople (1784).[3]**

Demetrios, the new-martyr of Christ, was a native of Galata in Constantinople and resided in the precinct of Karakoy, where he was a counterman at a tavern owned by a certain Batzi-Panayiotes. He was only

---

[3] The martyrdom of New-martyr Demetrios was taken from the *Neon Martyrologion*, 3rd ed. (pp. 211, 212), and incorporated into *The Great Synaxaristes* (in Greek).

twenty-five years old, handsome in appearance, and sober in conduct. For these virtues, he was always hated by the Laz Moslems,[4] who frequented the tavern. In various ways, they attempted to divert him from the Faith and make him a Moslem, but they strived in vain.

One day, according to their habit, they went to the tavern and indulged in heavy drinking to the point of intoxication. A brawl ensued, and one of them was stabbed. Seeing them, the blessed Demetrios went with his friends to pacify and disperse the quarrelers, according to the authority vested in him by the state—which all tavern operators possessed—to reconcile those who brawled on their premises. Demetrios and his friends succeeded in quelling the fracas and sent everyone home. However, the following day those sinister patrons, who nursed intense hatred for the Christian Demetrios, took the wounded Turk and brought him to the vizier. They falsely testified that Demetrios had knifed him. Therefore, according to their law, Demetrios had to either become a Moslem or face death. The vizier then ordered that Demetrios be brought to court, where he said to the saint, "Behold of what magnitude of crime thou art accused! What hast thou to answer regarding this charge?" Without fear, the young man recounted the entire matter to the judge as it had occurred. The vizier interposed, "Thou must do one of two things. Either thou shalt become a Moslem, or thou shalt die." Christ's confessor answered courageously, "Neither did I strike a Turk, nor will I become one. May God forbid it! For I was born a Christian and will die a Christian."

Perceiving his resoluteness, the vizier issued the order to behead Demetrios. When the executioners took the saint near the place of execution, the vizier decided to issue another order that he was to return to the court. When the martyr was brought before him, the vizier began to flatter him with promises of honors and financial rewards, if only he would become a Moslem and deny Christ. The valiant martyr, however, was not swayed by these words; much rather, he boldly and eloquently censured their religion. Consequently, the vizier turned him over to his accusers, who took Demetrios back to a coffeehouse where a large crowd of Turks had gathered. They plied him with compliments, urging him to become a Moslem. Nevertheless, Demetrios stood firm and continued to oppose them and their religion. Thereafter, the vizier commanded them to bring Demetrios before him again.

---

[4] The Laz tribes came to be identified with the southeast shore of the Black Sea as far as Trebizond, though it was first ancient Colchis lying along the east shore of the Black Sea, including the mouth of the Phasis River. The previously Christian Lazes suffered Arab invasion early in the 8th C., the capture of their capital Archaiopolis, and the islamization of their people. *The Oxford Dictionary of Byzantium*, s.v. "Lazika."

They varied their pressure upon him: at times they offered compliments, and at other times they pronounced threats if he did not adopt their beliefs. In spite of their wrangling, they failed to convert him; so the vizier withheld his ruling until a third hearing.

After they brought forth the martyr for the third examination, the vizier again offered privileges and gifts. He then resorted to threats; yet he was unable to change Demetrios' mind. Therefore, he sentenced Demetrios to be beheaded outside the tavern. In this manner the ever-memorable and thrice-renowned man of Christ received the unfading crown of martyrdom in the year 1784. During the entire night, a heavenly light shone about his martyred relics. Under cover of night, the Christians went to recover his relics. However, the guards snatched Demetrios away, and consequently had to be bribed with a considerable sum. After the passage of three months, one morning, the Laz Moslems also slew the blessed tavern keeper, Panayiotes, when he was leaving his home, because of the intense hatred they still harbored for the Martyr Demetrios. Through the intercessions of Saint Demetrios, may we all be made worthy to attain to the kingdom of the heavens. Amen.

Through the intercessions of Thy Saints,
O Christ God, have mercy on us. Amen.

**On the 28th of January, the holy Church commemorates
our venerable Father EPHRAIM the Syrian.[1]**

Ephraim, our wondrous
father among the saints, was a Syrian by parentage on both sides,
born in the city of Nisibis of Mesopotamia, around 305, at the end of
the reign of Diocletian or during
the earliest days of Constantine the
Great (306-307). His parents confessed the Faith of Christ valiantly
during the years of persecution. In
his own words, he later acknowledged that "I was born in the way
of truth, though in my boyhood I
understood not the greatness of the
benefit, but I knew it when trial
came."[2] And, "I had been taught
early about Christ by my parents.
They who begat me after the flesh
had trained me in the fear of the
Lord. I had seen my neighbors
living piously. I had heard of many
suffering for Christ. My own parents were confessors before the
judge. Yea, I am the kindred of
martyrs."[3]

Saint Ephraim the Syrian

Later in life, Saint Ephraim revealed that he had a vision in his
childhood, foretelling his gift of teaching. This was revealed by Saint Ephraim

---

[1] The Life of this saint was recorded in Greek by Saint Symeon the Metaphrastes,
whose manuscript begins, "Ephraim the wondrous..." [*P. G.* 114:1253-1268]. The text
is extant in the Athonite Monastery of Iveron and in other places. The text was
rendered in simpler Greek by Agapios the Cretan, who published it in his *Neon
Paradeison*. Saint Gregory of Nyssa wrote an encomium in which he names Ephraim
a "great father and teacher of the universe." Saint Ephraim was also praised by many
other Church fathers. The English version of his Life herein was taken from *The Great
Synaxaristes* (in Greek); Ephraim the Syrian, Nicene and Post-Nicene Fathers, 2nd
Ser., XIII:119-152; Sozomen, *Ecclesiastical History*, III, Chap. XVI; and Palladios,
The Lausiac History, 40.

[2] *Opera Syriaca*, Tom. ii, p. 499.

[3] *Confession Opp. Gr.*, 1. 129; cf. *Adv. Haereses*, XXVI.

himself to a virtuous monk and spiritual father. Ephraim said, "When my mother carried me on her bosom, I beheld a vine which bore innumerable grapes. Its roots were in my tongue and sprang forth out of my mouth. The branches laden with clusters grew high and to the heavens. They spread out all over the earth, so that the fowls of the air nested and fed in the branches. The more they ate of the fruit, the more was it multiplied. Indeed, God was the Giver. Glory to Him for His grace, for He gave to me of His good pleasure, from the storehouse of His treasures." This the saint consented to reveal about his early life, but little else than this was made known.

At an early age Ephraim was received by Iakovos (Jacob), the bishop of that city, who brought him up carefully and educated him, discerning the goodly nature of the lad. From his youth, the venerable Ephraim evinced virtue, avoiding injurious conversations of associates. He never dissipated his time with vain pastimes, but spent every moment reading the sacred books of the Scriptures, meditating on and studying them. In this activity he perceived such sweetness as to coincide with the words of the prophet, "How sweet to my throat *are* Thy sayings, beyond honey to my mouth [Ps. 118:103]!" On account of this, the blessed man accomplished all the virtues, including fasting, vigils, lying on the ground, goodness, kindness, poverty, meekness, and other practises that followed closely upon these deeds of faith. But especially did he keep inviolate humility, which slays the demons. He learned letters and went on to become a wise teacher, even as his marvellously written compositions make manifest, which every hour, even up to the present day, teach, admonish, console, and counsel us. Consequently, by these means, as an approved workman, he cut "in a straight line the word of the truth [2 Tim. 2:15]." He spurs us to eagerly attain the virtues, especially love toward God and neighbor, which is highly honored and in imitation of Christ. For the sake of Jesus, our godly Ephraim exerted himself with much dispatch and attention, which he attained to such a degree to the wonder of all.

The saint always wept, so that all his life he shed a river of salutary tears. This gift, which followed upon sighs from the depths of his heart, emerged as fire from his inward parts. Its effects may be confirmed by anyone who reads his writings filled with compunction, which texts often recount the second coming of Christ and the impartial judgment of that fearful trial. His writings concerning that day make such an impression on our mind that we anticipate it with trembling.

To these meditations, our venerable father assiduously devoted himself. He relinquished and fled from all the clamor of life, and withdrew into the wilderness, taking up his abode as he walked about from place to place, both receiving and bestowing benefit. In 337, when Emperor Constantine the Great reposed, Shāpūr, king of Persia, seized the opportunity to invade Mesopotamia. He besieged Nisibis (338), and brought her to the threshold of defeat. Yet the elderly Bishop Iakovos and the honorable Ephraim offered up unceasing prayer, and encouraged the defenders to repair the breaches in the city wall. Swarms of mosquitoes, gnats, and horseflies descended upon the Persian host. The horses, driven to distraction, flung their riders, and the elephants began a stampede and killed many soldiers. Shāpūr withdrew before anything worse should overtake him, but he would return to try again at a later date. Before the end of 338, Bishop Iakovos reposed; it was Ephraim who conducted the funeral.

The third siege (ca. 350) of the city also involved Saint Ephraim and Bishop Valgesh. Shāpūr and his Persian engineers attempted to employ the diverted waters of the Mygdonios to wash away the city walls. Saint Ephraim in five of his *Nisibene Hymns* describes the onslaught. The poetic sermon, written in lines of five, seven, or twelve syllables, included prayers for deliverance, forgiveness, and then thanksgiving. He makes mention of the bishops who helped to defend the city, namely, Iakovos, Babu, Valgesh, and Abraham. The newly-constructed embankments caused the Mygdonios to form a lake which completely encircled Nisibis, rendering it an island. Shāpūr launched his arms, men, and war engines on floats. However, the pressure of the waters burst the embankments and part of the city wall. The cavalry was ordered to attack. The intervening ground where an old moat previously surrounded the city delayed the progress of the advance, enabling the Nisibenes to ready their defenses by a shower of missiles. The elephants then became unruly and created a panic. Saint Ephraim and the bishop prayed all night, and exhorted the people to rebuild the smashed one hundred cubits of the city wall. The following morning Shāpūr withdrew, unwilling to suffer further discomfiting losses. In 363, the Nisibenes were finally expelled when a peace treaty relinquished the city to Shāpūr.

Having been moved by the divine Spirit, Ephraim departed Nisibis and went to Edessa of Mesopotamia. He desired to venerate the city's holy relics and to find a virtuous and learned man that he might receive spiritual benefit. For this cause he entreated God, saying, "Master, Lord Jesus Christ, vouchsafe me to meet in Edessa a man who shall speak to me beneficial words for my soul." After uttering this petition outside the city, he walked toward the entrance, watching closely for the petition's anticipated fulfillment. Thus he walked about, deep in thought, until he came upon a harlot decked out in a manner to ensnare youths. Now even in this meeting was God operating, Who, ofttimes, in a secret and ineffable manner, dispenses His will through things opposite and contrary. The holy man, looking at her, was both amazed and saddened. He wondered how it happened that the very opposite of what he had hoped should take place. The woman also stood there and fixed her gaze upon him for a considerable time. The saint, in order to instill a sense of shame in her, said, "How dost thou dare to gaze upon me, woman, with such

shamelessness and without turning thine eyes away?" She answered, "I am not so unjustified to watch thee, since I came into existence from thy rib when the Lord made us. Thou, however, shouldest watch the ground from where thou camest forth. More so rather, because thou art a monk and deem thyself dead to the body, thou shouldest not gaze intently into the face of anyone." When the saint heard these unexpected words, he thanked her for confessing the truth, and glorified God, Who hearkened to his entreaty and thus favored him. He left pondering, "If the women of this city are so wise, how much more exceeding wise must be the men!"

He therefore entered into the city, where he remained a few days in a certain house. Nearby that place there was a shameless and impudent woman who espied the holy man through a side-window. One day, while the saint was boiling some cooked food, she opened the window saying, "Abba, bless!" He responded with a humble voice, "May the Lord bless thee!" She then laughed indecently, saying, "Art thou missing any food that I might give thee?" The holy man answered, "Three

Saint Ephraim the Syrian

stones are missing and a little clay that I may close this window, so that thou mightest no longer trouble me." She said, "I sent to thee my heartfelt greetings, because I desire to lie with thee, but dost thou straightway behave in an arrogant manner and tell me that thou shalt fence off the entrance?" That woman, lacking all restraint, said this and many other like things, because the demon incited her to tempt the sober-minded and modest in this manner. Nevertheless, as much as she attempted with satanic words to urge him to unseemly desire, so much more did he again answer her with soul-benefitting and wholesome advice. Finally, seeing her shameless demeanor persist, he said to her, "If thou dost yearn that we lie together, let us go to a place of my choosing." She—thinking that he had a cell hidden someplace where he desired to commit the sin, lest any should see him—rejoiced and said, "Let us go wherever thou dost wish." He said to her, "In the midst of the city I wish to go." She asked, "And art thou not embarrassed before the people who shall mock us?" Then Ephraim, since he brought her skillfully to where he wanted—indeed, and by the very same weapons by which she warred—answered, "Before the people thou dost feel shame, but in the sight of God thou dost not fear, O hapless one? He it is Who beholds all our deeds, whether they be manifest or if they take place in secret, and metes out our deserved chastisement and everlasting punishment for our choice of a moment's unlawful pleasure." This and many other profitable correctives were applied by the all-wise one. God helping him, he fished and caught the harlot with a hook and line.

By reason of his words, such fear took hold of her soul that she repented from the bottom of her heart for all her iniquities. Weeping, she fell before Ephraim's feet and sought his forgiveness for her indiscreet desire and licentious judgment which she formerly held. She aspired now to have him guide her to salvation and to teach her how she ought to proceed with her life. The saint eagerly approved her repentance and advised that she never return to the former things, but to carry on her life soberly, and to continually labor to master every unbecoming thought and foul doing. He then conducted her to a convent, where she spent the rest of her life in a God-pleasing manner to the salvation of her soul. It is evident that the saint was the cause of leading her to amendment and piety, though she would have wrought his destruction with the snares of the dragon. Thus, the divine Ephraim, on the one hand, was greatly edified by the first harlot he encountered in the road, but, on the other hand, he greatly edified and benefitted the second harlot with the help of God.

The saint withdrew as a solitary to the rocky Mount of Edessa, outside the city, where he struggled in asceticism and studied the Scriptures for a considerable time. After this retreat he again entered Edessa. Ephraim earned his living when he entered the service of a bath-keeper. Outside of his employment, the saint spent his time teaching and preaching to the large pagan population thereabout. A fellow anchorite on the mount declared in the city that "Ephraim is the fan in the Lord's hand, with whom He will both thoroughly purge His floor and the tares of heresy. This is the fire whereof our Lord said, 'I came to cast fire upon the earth [Lk. 12:49; Mt. 3:12].'" The chief men of the city, heretics, pagans, and Jews, laid hold of the saint and brought him outside the city gates. They cast stones at him, leaving him nearly dead. The following morning Ephraim returned to the mount.

At length, he left the Edessenes and went away to Caesarea. He desired to meet the great Basil, the fountain of Orthodox dogmas and the champion of piety. Saint Ephraim, who was a clairvoyant, greatly commended the Archbishop of Caesarea, whom he beheld with the eyes of his soul. In his vision he beheld the great Basil. A dove, flashing forth light as brilliant as the sun, was to the hierarch's right and speaking in his ear. Ephraim then observed Saint Basil teaching the people whatever he heard being uttered by the divine dove. This same dove also illumined the mind of the venerable Ephraim that what was taking place was through the grace of the All-Holy Spirit, and he rejoiced in spirit.

Saint Ephraim's vision was also confirmed by the good report of the wonders of Saint Basil. Thereupon, Ephraim supplicated God to reveal to him of what sort was the saint. Then Ephraim was vouchsafed to behold a pillar of fire, which rose up unto the heaven; and he heard a voice saying, "Ephraim, Ephraim, even as this pillar of fire, so is the great Basil!" Then, without the least anxiety, Ephraim took along with him an interpreter who knew both the Greek and Syriac tongues, and went to Caesarea. It was then the Feast of the Theophany. He entered the church and observed Saint Basil clothed in splendid and costly vestments, celebrating the sacred Liturgy with great boldness. Ephraim then reproached himself and said to his interpreter, "In vain have we labored, brother, because this man, though he is found in such glory, is not as I saw."

The holy hierarch, having been informed in the Spirit of these words which were uttered by Saint Ephraim, called one of his deacons to him, and instructed him, "Go to the western door of the church, and thou shalt see two monks standing there: the one is beardless, tall, and thin; and the other has a black beard. Address the beardless monk, saying, 'Thou art to come to the holy bema, for thy father, the archbishop, calls thee.'" Thereupon, the deacon went; and with force he managed to make his way through the multitude. He announced the words of Saint Basil to the righteous Ephraim who, through the interpreter, answered, "Thou art in error, brother, because we are strangers and unknown. How then doth the archbishop know us?" Unable to answer, the deacon retreated to the archbishop. He related the words of Saint Ephraim to the sacred hierarch, who again sent him forth, instructing him, "Go and say, 'Lord Ephraim, come into the holy bema, because the archbishop calls thee.'" Therefore, the deacon went a second time. Greeting Ephraim with a prostration, he reported the message of the hierarch to the venerable monk. In turn, the righteous Ephraim made a prostration to the deacon, declaring, "Truly, the great Basil is a pillar of fire, but I beseech him that I may speak alone with him in the sacristy." When Saint Basil finished celebrating the divine Liturgy, he summoned Saint Ephraim. After he greeted him with a holy kiss, he conversed with the desert father on spiritual matters and divine purposes and design. He then encouraged Ephraim that if there were any hidden matter in his heart to tell him of it.

The righteous Ephraim spoke through the interpreter, saying, "I ask one favor of thy prelacy, slave of God." The saint interjected, "Whatever thou desirest, ask; for I am greatly obliged to thee on account of thy labor which thou didst endeavor for the sake of my lowliness." Saint Ephraim continued, "I know, holy master, that if thou shouldest make supplication for something to God, He would bestow it. Well, I desire that thou wouldest supplicate God that I might speak Greek, for I do not at all know this language of yours." The saint confessed, "Thy request, holy father and leader of the desert, is beyond my power. But inasmuch as thou hast asked this with faith, let us both entreat God, even as that One is able to make thy desire a reality; for even the Prophet David uttered, '*The* will of those fearing Him will He do, and their entreaty will He hear, and He will save them [Ps. 144:20].'" After Saint Basil recited this, he stood together with Saint Ephraim for a long while in entreaty. And when they fin-

Saint Ephraim the Syrian

ished their prayer, the saint cried with a loud voice, "The grace of the Holy Spirit be with thee, and speak Greek!" Straightway, as the saint uttered this command—O the wonder!—Saint Ephraim opened his mouth and was speaking Greek, even as Saint Basil and the Christians of that place. Afterward, they say that the holy hierarch ordained the venerable Ephraim to the diaconate and his translator to the priesthood. Now Saint Ephraim remained with the saint for three days and greatly profited by his teaching. Afterward, he departed again for the wilderness, glorifying and blessing God.[4]

---

[4] This account was taken from the Life of Saint Basil, who is commemorated by the holy Church on the 1st of January. It is the belief of the Greek compiler of Saint Ephraim's life that he probably only agreed to be ordained a deacon, lest a higher rank should prevent undistracted dedication to contemplation of the divine Scriptures and

(continued...)

After Caesarea, he went to Edessa upon hearing that the city was being contaminated by heretical notions. Now he had become very proficient in the learning and language of the Syrians, so when he learned that the heretic and Gnostic Bardesanes and his son Harmonios had set their philosophy to meter and musical laws—and that their songs attained great popularity among layfolk and even children—he countered the errors by setting godly words to their own music. He composed poems filled with sound doctrine, and used the same melodies. His compositions described the life of our Lord, His Passion, resurrection, and ascension. He also wrote on death, repentance, and the martyrs. He first taught his heptasyllabic-lined hymns to a choir of nuns who sang in the churches every morning and evening. The people gathered together to hear the hymns, and Bardesanes lost popularity. Henceforth, the Syrians sang Ephraim's odes according to the law of the ode established by Harmonios.

Teaching the souls of the people was a talent Saint Ephraim received from God, and which he diligently endeavored to increase in manifold ways, as a prudent slave [Mt. 25:14-23]. Now those who were vouchsafed to behold divine mysteries, beheld many revelations concerning Ephraim. One such holy spiritual father revealed that he beheld a multitude of angels who descended from on high bearing a book with writing. One angel asked another, "Who is worthy to take the book in his hands?" One angel was saying one name, another that of some other wise and godly individual. Finally the angels agreed that the venerable Ephraim was worthy to hold the book, and they gave it into his hands. The vision then came to an end. That pious man rose up terrified and went into the church. Finding the blessed Ephraim teaching the people with his mellifluous words, he made known the vision. From that very hour the grace of God gushed forth upon Ephraim, so that the flow of his thoughts rose like waves to his tongue. With such ease and quickness did he speak that it seemed as if he were reading what he was saying. At that time he wrote his extraordinary and edifying commentaries on Genesis and Exodus.

The saint, who had the gift of tears, also kept vigil at night, and partook of very little sleep, just enough so as not to injure his body from deprivation, toils, pains, lying on the ground, hardships, sufferings, and distress. He was conspicuous for indigence and voluntary poverty, in which no one surpassed him. At the translation of his relics, he bore witness to himself, saying "Ephraim acquired nothing, neither silver, nor gold, nor purse, nor provision bag, nor staff, nor any other earthly article, but he had

---

[4](...continued)
to his writings.

only the desire of the heavenly things from the hour that he heard the holy Gospel, wherein the Master commanded the apostles to take no earthly provision for themselves [cf. Mk. 6:8; Lk. 10:4]." These words are more to be trusted than if they were uttered by another. Behold, therefore, with how much desire the ever-memorable one kept the words of the holy Gospel, and with how much zeal he imitated our Teacher and Savior and His disciples!

The saint possessed humility and moderation. His bread was mingled with ashes and his water with tears. Anyone who lauded or praised him, he not only drove out, but also considered an enemy, even as do those who hate whoever derides or mocks them. When anyone acclaimed him, he blushed and perspired from the discomfort which he sensed in his soul. This virtue he preserved till his last hour when he prepared for his departure from life. When some Edessenes sought him out to admire him on account of his biblical commentaries, he fled out of modesty. An angel met him, and said, "Ephraim, why fleest thou?" He answered, "Milord, that I may sit in silence and flee the clamor of this age." The angel replied, "Take heed, lest the word be spoken of thee, 'Ephraim fled from Me as a heifer whose shoulder drew back from the yoke [cf. Hos. 4:16; 10:11].'" With tears, Ephraim said, "I am weak and unworthy." The angel said, "No man lights a lamp and puts it under a bushel, but upon the lampstand that all may see the light [cf. Mt. 5:15; Lk. 11:33]." Ephraim was obedient and returned. This time his admirers met him with reproach, as one returning looking for praise as a result of his feigned reluctance. Ephraim said, "Pardon me, my brethren, for I am a lowly man." They said, "Come, see the madman." He answered nothing, and continued teaching.

Before his repose he commanded, attaching an excommunication for any who disobeyed, that no one was to chant any troparia written in his honor, nor give an encomium, nor bury him with a good rason (cassock), nor in a separate tomb. He wished to be buried in old and worn-out garments in the tomb of the strangers. This is because, even as he used to say, he had a covenant with God to be buried with strangers, as a stranger and sojourner. Saint Ephraim was hospitable and compassionate to the poor, and when he had alms to give, he gave as much as possible. When he was in need (because he was utterly poor and most of the times could find nothing to give), he would take the strangers and poor and treat them with his saving teachings, which are far more essential than bodily food. His eloquence was such that his words were able to soften every soul, console the afflicted, and render meek the angry. His countenance, orderly behavior, good discipline, manners, character, and disposition moved many to feel compunction in their hearts. He was exceedingly zealous for Orthodoxy and an unvanquished champion of the blameless Faith. Hearken now to an excellent contrivance of that most wise man, in order that the faithful might not suffer harm.

The following account is also confirmed by Saint Gregory of Nyssa. At that time the impious Apollinarios, an innovator of novel ideas, attempted to pervert the correct dogma and teachings of the Church with his nonsensical talk. He put together two books with much labor and trouble. He prepared them that he might contend against the faithful when he found the opportune time. He had in his company a woman, beloved by him and of the same mind, not only as regarding the heresy but carnal pleasures also, according to the neighbors. Apollinarios put the two volumes in her care, lest they should be stolen by the Orthodox. Ephraim learned of this and feigned that he was a disciple of Apollinarian dogma. The elderly monk went to the house of this woman and secured her trust. He went many times, but only when Apollinarios was absent from the house. When Ephraim was sure that the woman suspected nothing of him, he requested the books that he might read them, so that he might know how to fight those "heretics" (thus the all-wise one named the Orthodox with the name given by the unorthodox), so that they might not defeat him as one unlearned and uninstructed. Thus the blessed man baited the woman with this plausible device. She handed over the books, making him promise to return them the next day.

Taking up the volumes, the venerable one began reading through them in various places. Since he did not have time to write a defense that he might destroy the heresies therein, what did the prudent one contrive? He prepared some fish glue and carefully pasted each of the leaves together so well that it was impossible to unglue them without tearing them. He then returned the books, which appeared unaltered from the outside. She did not open them, but returned them to their place. After a number of days, the saint urged the Orthodox to convene a synod, that he might discourse with Apollinarios concerning the truth. This was arranged and Apollinarios came to the synod meeting. Now he was very advanced in years and was unable to speak many words. He addressed the Orthodox, saying, "I, holy Fathers, am not able any longer to engage in contentions with a lot of shouting. I have, however, two very valuable books, which I wrote with immeasurable diligence. Let us read them here. Now whatever is written in these books, I confess those very things even with my own mouth." He then attempted to open one of the books, but was unable. He could find neither a beginning, nor an end, nor a middle, because the pages had become as one mass. In fact he could not even tear them. He took the companion volume into his hands and found that the pages were equally fixed to one another. No section would yield to his probing fingers. He experienced such sadness and despondency from his shame that he left the synod meeting. Unable to endure the mishap, in an evil manner the evil one expired. Thus were the pious delivered from his vile heresy, and the deceiver received the reward of his labors—an evil death as he deserved, as an earnest of everlasting punishment.

Now Saint Basil had been a great admirer of the holy Ephraim and was amazed at his erudition, though Ephraim had received no formal instruction. About this time Saint Basil desired for the holy hymnographer to return to Caesarea with the intention of elevating him in clerical rank, but Ephraim was resolved not to accept such a dignity, and decided to feign madness. He went about the streets indecorously, dragging multicolored clothes, chewing on bread, and drooling. Saint Basil's messengers were appalled at such conduct, and reported to him that they found his candidate a madman. Saint Basil exclaimed, "O hidden pearl of price, whom the world knows not! You are the madmen, and he the sane one!"

There was in the see of Saint Basil a certain widow, who had surpassed the other women of Caesarea with regard to her wealth and nobility, but then had come to enslave herself in gluttony and in profligacy, being enthralled in defiling carnal passions and squandering her fortune. At length, unsettled and shaking when she brought to mind everlasting torments, she resolved to go before the saint in order to confess the morass of her sins. But the enemy of the salvation of man, the devil, suggested to her thoughts of how intolerable her shame would be in confessing her deeds. Thus, in this manner, he hindered her from coming to repentance by means of a thorough confession. Though the devil may have postponed her good intention, by the grace and mercy of God she did not abandon her decision to change her life. What then did she think to do? She wrote down upon a paper her every sin. At the end of her listing, she recorded one deadly sin; and then she sealed the letter appropriately. Then, while Saint Basil was on his way to church, she intercepted him and cast the sealed letter before his feet. With tears, she cried aloud, "Have mercy on me, O saint of God, who am the most sinful of all the people!" Standing still, the saint asked her the cause for such a flow of tears. She replied, "Holy master, I have written all my sins in this letter. I beseech thy holiness not to open it, but only through thy prayer thou mayest blot out my sins." The saint took the letter and looked up to heaven, praying thus, "It is Thy work, O Master and Lord, to forgive the sins of this Thy handmaid; for Thou, the only sinless One, art good and the lover of man, and didst bear the sins of the people." After making this entreaty, the saint then entered the church and began to celebrate the divine Liturgy while holding the letter. After the dismissal, he summoned that woman who gave him the letter. "Hearken, woman, for no one is able to forgive sins, save God alone," the archbishop told her. "I did hear, holy master, and for this reason I besought thee to intercede with God for the forgiveness of my sins," said she. Then the woman broke the seal and unrolled the paper. And—O the wonder!—she found it unwritten upon, except for that last grievous sin she had penned. Seeing this one had remained, she became fainthearted and beat her breast with her hands. Falling at the feet of the saint, she held the letter and implored him, "Have mercy on me, O saint of the Most High God, even as my other sins were blotted out through thy holy prayers, in like manner entreat God to wipe out this lawless deed of mine." The saint, weeping, advised, "Arise, O woman, because I also am a sinful man, and I too have need of forgiveness. Go into the desert, and seek a certain great ascetic named Ephraim. When he offers up entreaty to God, He will blot out thy sin."

The woman, therefore, having received the blessing of the saint as a good fellow traveler, arrived in the desert and found the righteous Ephraim. Falling at his feet, she cast forth the paper and said, "The Archbishop of Caesarea, Basil the Great, sent me to thee, in order that after thou shouldest offer prayer to God that He might blot out my deadly sin. Therefore, do not esteem my request lightly, O holy father. Do thou entreat God to forgive also this lawless deed of mine." After he had given her a patient hearing, he counseled, "No, child, because that same one who besought God from Whom thou didst receive forgiveness of many sins is able to supplicate on thy behalf for even this one. Go, therefore, my child, and do not stop, to the end that thou mightest overtake him while he lives; otherwise by the time thou returnest, thou shouldest find him dead." As soon as she heard these words, she took her leave from him and sped off. But as she entered Caesarea, she met the precious relics of the saint being escorted by a multitude proceeding to the place of burial.

Straightway, the woman began to shout and cry out mournfully, "Woe is me, O slave of God! Didst thou send me out into the wilderness on this account, that thou mightest repose without annoyance from me? Thou didst send me forth to the righteous Ephraim; and behold, I returned unsuccessful. May God see this, and judge between me and thee; for even though thou wast able to have wrought the forgiveness of my transgression, thou didst send me off to another." After disclosing this, she cast the letter upon the bier of the saint and recounted her story before all the crowd. Now one of the clergy took up the letter, because he desired to know what was that great lawless deed, but he found the paper to be utterly blank. Then he cried out with a loud voice to the woman, announcing, "O woman, there is nothing written anywhere on the paper! Why art thou troubled? Dost thou not recognize the loving-kindness of God?" The woman laid hold of the letter. And acknowledging the compassion of God upon her, and the great help of the servant of God, she thanked Saint Basil and Saint Ephraim. Henceforth, she conducted the rest of her life in a prudent, chaste, and God-pleasing manner, until her repose in the Lord.[5]

Saint Ephraim never exhibited anger toward anyone after he took up the monastic call. Once, according to his custom of fasting several days, his disciple offered some food to him, but the dish with the food fell out of his hand as he was presenting it. The holy elder, perceiving his disciple's shame and fear, said, "Take courage, we will go to the food, since the food doth not come to us." Ephraim then sat down beside the broken dish and ate his dinner.

Toward the end of Saint Ephraim's life, a severe famine occurred in Edessa. The wealthy landowners were hoarding grain, while the poor went hungry. The saint reproved the landowners' lack of compassion, but they excused themselves, claiming that there was no one trustworthy to distribute their stores fairly. The holy man volunteered, "What do you think of me?" And straightway he was appointed. As did Patriarch Joseph of old, he distributed their vast bounty. One of the first things he did was to purchase three hundred beds for the sick who were brought to public stations, which were fitted up as clinics, that they might receive medical attention. All received help, whether they were natives or foreigners. The dead received proper burial. The holy man had deputies under his charge who helped administer relief not only in Edessa, but also in the surrounding hamlets and villages. The famine lasted one year and was followed by a year of plenty. The aged Ephraim then put down his stewardship and retired to his cell. He reposed one month later, and thus he won the crown of asceticism and love of neighbor.

Let us now come to the repose of the venerable one that we may conclude the narration. He knew his days were spent and his repose was imminent. At the approach of his translation from this life to the desired One, he himself confessed, not out of vainglory but for our edification: "Never in all my life did I act negligently before the Lord, nor did I revile anyone, nor did a senseless word come from my mouth, not did I curse anyone, nor did I tear asunder the faithful." All of these are certainly great accomplishments and extraordinary. Yet, in his humility, he considered himself a sinner and unworthy that his disciples should take any trouble on his account. He bade that they bury him in his own rason and cowl, and charged that no one was to bury him in expensive clothes. He repeated this injunction at the last hour of his repose. In case anyone had prepared such a garment, he instructed him to give it to someone who had need of it.

---

[5] This account was taken from the Life of Saint Basil.

Now one of the most renowned and beloved of his disciples had already prepared a splendid burial garment for his elder. It was his intention of clothing the holy man with it after his repose. But when he heard the bidding of the holy man, and how this was against his wishes, he sorrowed. He then had the notion not to give the garment to some poor man, as commanded, because he thought it more preferable to distribute its worth in money to the poor. "Surely," he thought, "the venerable one would be far more pleased with this." Yet the moment that he reckoned to do this, he received punishment for his disobedience. Straightway, in front of all, he was lorded over by a demon, and fell before the bier of the blessed one, convulsing and with his fingers twisted and his eyes turned in different directions. He foamed at the mouth and suffered in many other terrible ways. The divine Ephraim knew in the Spirit that what happened to this man was the fruit of disobedience. He prayed for the redemption of his disciple, and gave him a penance on account of the disciple's lapse of obedience. He then laid his hands upon the sick man and healed him, enjoining him to carry out his first command to the letter.

The saint also adjured them not to place him beneath an altar, and laid a penalty on whomsoever should so dare. He asked that they bear him on their shoulders for burial. He forbade them to carry tapers before him or apply sweet spices to his body. He asked that they conduct him to the grave with prayer, and offer incense and hymns to God alone. He did not want a sepulcher, for he said, "I have a covenant with God: that I shall be buried with strangers. I am a stranger as they were." Saint Ephraim then blessed his true disciples, Zenovios, Symeon, Isaac, Asuna, Julian, Abraham, Abbas, and Maras. Two other disciples, Paulanas and Aranad, though eloquent in speech, later strayed from sound doctrine. He then pronounced anathemas against the Arians, Anomoeans, Marcionites, Kathari, Manichaeans, Bardesanites, and others of unseemly doctrines and superstitions. Then, after he had sufficiently counseled the others in the spiritual life and the virtues, he surrendered his holy soul into the hands of his Master Christ in the year 379. The saint's precious relics were followed to the grave by a procession of bishops, priests, deacons, monks, anchorites, stylites, coenobites, city folk and others in the neighborhood. As he requested, he was laid in the strangers' cemetery. Thus, bearing the crowns of his labors, he entered into the everlasting abodes, which await such as Saint Ephraim. Later, the Edessenes made a grave for him among their bishops, since he was a clergyman. Through the prayers of Saint Ephraim, Lord Jesus Christ have mercy on us. Amen.

The Gathering Together (Synaxis) for Saint Ephraim the Syrian

The Writings of Saint Ephraim

There are six volumes of Saint Ephraim's writings: three in Greek and Latin, and three in Syriac and Latin. Saint Ephraim's commentaries on the sacred Scriptures include expositions of the Pentateuch, the prophets (including Lamentations), and Job, which have been printed. He commented on almost all the books of the Old Testament, except Ruth, Ezra, Nehemias, and Esther. In commenting upon the New Testament, he treated the Gospels not in their separate form, but in the continuous narrative known as the *Diatessaron*, compiled from them by Tatian in the second century. Both the latter and his *Commentary on the Epistles of Saint Paul* have been preserved for us in Armenian.

The saint's homilies vary in theme. Those that appear in English are entitled *On Our Lord*, *On Reproof and Repentance*, and *The Sinful Woman*. While one homily is directed against the Jews, another is opposed to paganism in the person of Julian the Apostate, or the heresies of Manes, Marcian, Bardesanes, or the Anomean followers of Arius. Other homilies reflect the Faith, as he writes upon the creation, the fall, redemption by the Passion and crucifixion, the Lord's descent into Hades, His resurrection, the mission of the Holy Spirit, the everlasting rest in Paradise, the second coming, and the completion of the ages and the end of the world. There are also expository homilies, treating accounts from both Testaments, such as the life of Joseph, the repentance at Nineveh, or the sinful woman, spoken of by the Evangelist Luke [Ch. 7]. Other homilies are hortatory, calling us to repentance or warning us against sin and speaking of the future retribution. He also extolls virginity.

Another class of his writings come under the title of hymns, which include such works as *Hymns for the Theophany*, *Funeral Hymns*, *Nisibene Hymns*, and *Hymns of the Nativity*.[6]

Saint Palladios

On the 28th of January, the holy Church commemorates our venerable Father PALLADIOS.

Palladios,[7] our blessed father, built a cell on a certain mountain, which was in the vicinity of a village called Immai[8] (according to Theodoretos who recorded his life). The saint enclosed himself in that cell, and he perfected himself in vigilance, fasting, and ceaseless prayer, and was counted worthy by God to perform miracles. Once, a certain merchant, who possessed a great deal of money, was walking along a road by night. Another man, seeing him, perceived that he had money, and accosted him and committed homicide. Afterward, he took up the victim's body and cast him at the door of the saint's cell. When daylight broke

---

[6] For further readings in English, see Ephraim Syrus, *Hymns and Homilies*, Nicene, 2nd Series, Vol. XIII; Ephrem the Syrian, *Hymns*, The Classics of Western Spirituality, translated by K. E. McVey, Paulist Press; Saint Ephrem the Syrian, *Hymns on Paradise*, translated by S. Brock, Saint Vladimir's Seminary Press; Saint Ephrem the Syrian, *Selected Prose Works*, The Fathers of the Church, Volume 91, translated by E. Matthews and J. Amar; *Saint Ephrem's Commentary on Tatian's Diatessaron*, Journal of Semitic Studies Supplement 2, translated by C. McCarthy, Oxford University Press.

[7] The Life of Saint Palladios was recorded by Theodoretos of Kyros (Cyrrhus), in Number Seven of his *Religious History*. See also *A History of the Monks of Syria, Cistercian Studies Series: Number Ninety-Eight*, pp. 58-62.

[8] Immai or Imma (present-day Yemi Shekin) is a large village twenty-five miles to the east of Antioch.

and the body became visible, everyone ran to the cell. Breaking in the door, they accused the holy one of slaying the man. While they all surrounded him, the righteous one prayed and resurrected the deceased. And when he arose, he revealed the true murderer, and that Saint Palladios was not guilty of the crime.[9] Not only was this miracle performed by the saint, but many others as well. He is most to be admired, however, for his works of virtue. Thus, in a God-pleasing manner, he finished the course of his life and left memorable writings to the Church of God for the benefit of those who read them,[10] and in peace was he translated to the Lord.

On the 28th of January, the holy Church commemorates our venerable Father IAKOVOS the Ascetic.[11]

Iakovos (James), our venerable father, hailed from a certain city called Porphyriane. According to the Lord's commands, true humility and meekness of spirit, which are very beneficial to pious Christian souls, bring

---

[9] Theodoretos adds that after the resurrected man pointed at the murderer with his finger, they seized him and stripped him of his clothes. They found the murder weapon on him, still bloodied. They also found the money of the victim, which was the cause of the murder.

[10] Some say that this Saint Palladios is the one who became Bishop of Helenopolis, and who lived at the time of Theodosius the Great (ca. 380). Others believe that he is also called Herakleides and became Bishop of Cappadocia, and that he is the one who wrote the lives of the saints that appear in the *Lausiac History*. They conclude this because Palladios wrote letters to Lausus Praepositus (royal chamberlain), to whom Herakleides also wrote. According to others, though, this Palladios is not the same as the one here; for Theodoretos who left us his hagiographic account does not mention that he became a bishop. A certain other Palladios also appears in the *Paradise of the Fathers*; to him are attributed many apothegms or sayings.

Some details of Bishop Palladios' life may be gleaned from his writings: *Lausiac History* and *Dialogue on the Life of Saint John Chrysostom*. He was born in 363/364 in Galatia and was the pupil of Evagrios of Pontos, and then became a disciple of Innocent on the Mount of Olives. He then went to Jericho and Alexandria. In 400, he went to Bithynia and was consecrated Bishop of Helenopolis, possibly by Saint John Chrysostom. He was with Saint John during the famous Synod of the Oak, but then fled the capital in 405 and went to Rome to plead Chrysostom's cause. He returned to Constantinople, where Emperor Arkadios had him arrested and exiled to Egypt. Therefore, the Palladios of this description does not fit the one of the anchorite outside of Antioch whom we commemorate today.

[11] The Life of Saint Iakovos was recorded in Greek by Saint Symeon the Metaphrastes, whose manuscript begins, "Many good and soul-benefitting things..." [*P.G.* 114:1213-1224], but concludes after the homicide. The parallel Latin text of this Life continues to *P.G.* 114:1230, giving details on the saint's life in the sepulcher and his miracles.

about many good things. Therefore, he who obtains these virtues has no fear of falling into any sin of the flesh or the spirit. However, those who are not  diligent, and do not zealously keep these salutary virtues, but instead fall into arrogance, become recipients of extreme harm and danger. We have learned this from many examples and reports, and in particular from the life of Saint Iakovos. For the edification and safeguarding of others, we recount the following history that all may be vigilant and not suffer a similar lot, resulting from indolence and vainglory. Therefore, take heed after hearing the following story, and let no one judge us for the way we have written it; for we perceive that the layman will read it and be scandalized that a saint fell into such a grave sin. But God wishes that His works should be made known, so that sinners might learn of

Saint Iakovos

His compassion and turn to repentance. This is why the holy fathers have recorded the lives of many who were formerly sinners, but afterward, through repentance, became saints. Behold how fervent tears and a contrite heart cleanse a man of iniquity and sanctify him! Attend therefore, and do not resent the fall of this saint; but rather, emulate the wonderful repentance that he made which vouchsafed him his previous state.

At first, for fifteen years, Saint Iakovos dwelt in a cave far from the city of Porphyriane. He progressed so rapidly in virtue and asceticism that he was accounted worthy by God to perform miracles. He cast out demons, healed incurable illnesses, and wrought many other similar wonders, so that he became famous in every quarter. Many people thereupon gathered at his cell for advice, among whom were not only the pious but also the impious Samaritans. He admonished them with teachings from the Scriptures and brought them back to piety. However, the sinister devil, observing what a great benefit the saint was to the people, raved and was intent on driving the holy one away from that place. Therefore, he found an instrument for his wickedness: a Samaritan, whom he entered and possessed. This man, after assembling together all his friends and relatives, sought ways and means to drive the saint from his cell. After conniving at length, they gave twenty golden dinars to a harlot, promising her even more if she could undermine Saint Iakovos. Thus by means of fornication, they would have cause to expel him from their borders.

Then, by night, that sinful and indecent woman went to the cell of the saint. She knocked on his door, begging him to let her inside. But he would not open the door. She nevertheless tarried there a long time, weeping and shamelessly imploring and pleading with him to open the door. Finally, the righteous one, exasperated at her unceasing clamor, opened the door. On seeing her, he thought she was a phantom. Iakovos closed the door and, praying, fell prostrate on his face. He entreated God with much ardor to preserve him from this temptation. But the woman kept making so much noise as she plaintively said, "O servant of God, have mercy upon me, for the wild beasts shall surely devour me!" Thus, she kept crying out until midnight. And the saint, hearing her, had pity upon her. He opened the door and asked her, "From whence comest thou? What art thou doing in this place?" She answered, "I am come from a convent. The mother superior has sent me to bring a blessing to this village, but I was overtaken by nightfall. Therefore, I beg thee to keep me here until morning. Then I shall travel safely on my way during daylight." He relented and gave her bread and water. He then retired to the inner room of his cell, while she remained in the outer.

She ate the bread given her and remained quiet—for a time. Then suddenly, she began screaming, as if she were being given a thrashing. When Iakovos called out and inquired what was wrong, she replied that she had a severe pain in her heart and was about to die. The woman begged him to place his hand on her breast and make the sign of the Cross upon it, so that the pain might cease. The saint believed her, so he emerged from his chamber and lit a great fire. As he held his left hand over the fire, with his right he anointed her chest with oil from the lamp which was placed before the saints. In the meanwhile, she tried to entrap him and said, "Please, for the Lord's sake, keep rubbing me over the heart for a long time until my pain should cease!" However, the righteous one knew the craftiness of the devil and dared not take his hand away from the fire for as long as he applied the oil. Thus, three hours elapsed, and the tendons of his fingers were burnt through. He drove away all evil thought with the unbearable pain. Now when the woman observed that his hand was totally burnt, she was moved to contrition. She fell at his feet crying and beating her chest, saying, "Woe is me, the depraved wretch! For I am a vessel of the demons and worthy of everlasting fire!"

Thus, she confessed the entire scheme before the saint and repented of her sin from the bottom of her heart. She promised to do penance and live prudently thereafter. The holy one gave the woman his blessing, catechized her, and sent her to the holy Bishop Alexander, who perceived that she truly had repented. He baptized the former harlot, sent her to a convent, and drove the Samaritans out from that area. Later, he went to Saint Iakovos and encouraged him. Everyone had great respect for Iakovos because of his temperance and discretion. As for this woman, she progressed to such a degree in the monastic life that she was vouchsafed to cast demons out of people. Consequently, the formerly indecent woman lived in a way pleasing to God and attained everlasting life.

On another occasion, some time later, a young girl, the daughter of a nobleman, became possessed by a demon. Now the demon would call out the saint by name. Her parents brought her to Saint Iakovos, begging him to drive out the foul demon. The blessed one then made a prayer. After he placed his hand on their daughter, the demon left at once, and she was restored to health. The parents were so grateful for this that they sent him three hundred gold pieces. But he did not even wish to look at money; instead, he said, "One cannot buy or sell the grace of God!" But those who were sent to him said, "Keep them, O servant of God, lest thou shouldest displease the nobleman. As for thyself, afterward, distribute the gold among the poor, and thou wilt receive a greater reward." But the saint said to them, "Let those who have the money distribute it to the poor."

At another time, they brought to him a certain young man who was paralyzed in both legs by demonic activity. After the holy one had fasted and prayed for three days, the paralytic rose up, thanked him, and returned to his house on his own. Many people who had various illnesses came to Saint Iakovos for succor and healing. They were all cured and returned to their homes happy and giving thanks to the Lord.

With all this activity taking place, Saint Iakovos became concerned when he observed how the people conferred great honor upon him. He was afraid, lest he should fall into vainglory and lose all that for which he had striven. Therefore, he decided to depart from that place. It was some forty miles away that he discovered a large cave by the bank of the river, where he would remain for the next thirty years. During that time, he took no care concerning food. He only consumed wild herbs. After a while, he planted a small garden. By his own labor, he cultivated it, and subsisted on the vegetables he grew. At length, he became so renowned for his sublime way of life that clergymen and monks from fifty monasteries, together with laymen, were coming to receive his blessing.

Even though the holy one arrived at such great virtue and was vouchsafed divine grace, he was ultimately corrected by God. He fell into a great sin through demonic complicity, probably because he fell into pride. God permitted him to fall that he might be humbled and not altogether lose his soul; for the sinner is saved when he recognizes the gravity of his sin and weeps. But the just man who is proud is condemned. Consequently, seeing the virtuous life of Saint Iakovos, the devil was full of envy.

The adversary therefore entered into the young daughter of a wealthy man, and would cry out, saying, "I will not leave this damsel, unless Iakovos the ascetic should order me!" Therefore, the parents of the damsel inquired after the whereabouts of the saint. They could learn nothing, because he lived far from their city. Finally, after great effort, they found his habitation. They took their daughter and servants and went to the great Iakovos, and fell at his feet saying, "O saint, have mercy on our daughter, for she is tormented greatly by an evil spirit. Moreover, she has not taken any food for twenty days, but only cries and calls upon thee!" Thereupon, the holy one prayed for a long time, and later he blew upon her, saying, "In the name of our Lord Jesus, come forth, O foul spirit!" And at once, the demon came out of their daughter, as if driven by fire. She fell to the ground and lay there for a long time speechless, until the saint raised her up. He returned her safely to her parents, who glorified God upon witnessing such a miracle. But, being afraid that the demon might enter into her again, they bade the saint to keep her with him for a few days, until they should come back for her. Then, the parents and their company went to their home.

But the crafty enemy of the servant of God disquieted him with a severe conflict in the flesh. The thrice-accursed one tormented Iakovos to such an extent that he brought him into a great sin. And—alas!—he fell into fornication, even in his old age. When he was younger, he defeated temptation with great courage, as is known. Indeed, this lapse happened after he wrought so many miracles and won significant victories and trophies against the demons. Also bring to mind that this took place after so many fasts, vigils, and other God-pleasing acts. He who was formerly an equal to the angels, spurned his many years of asceticism and became a prisoner of the demons. As if the sin of fornication were not enough, he did much worse. The malice of the demon instigated him to murder. The enemy placed in his mind that unless he slew the young woman, she could expose him. The enemy taunted him with the thought that if she were to reveal this, which was more than likely, he would be made a public spectacle. Therefore, with his mind blinded and dismal, he killed the young woman and cast her body into the river, so that his evildoing would not be revealed. But this happened to him due to pride and vainglory; for if this passion had not already been lodged in his soul, God would not have allowed him to fall into such a sin, as happened to many others, and is shown in other books of our Church.

However, God, in His love for mankind, Who desires the salvation of all sinners and wishes the perdition of none, would stretch forth a helping hand and raise him up with the herb of repentance. He would vouchsafe to Iakovos, despite the demons' malice, his former sainthood and grace. We have written these things, not in order to criticize the saint, but that everyone might guard his virtues and not trust in his own deeds, but in the man-befriending God, Who bestows upon us grace and power, and Who aids us in our needs, so long as we are humble.

Let us now return to the present narrative. After the wretched Iakovos had committed these two shameful and grave deeds, and the darkness was lifted from his mind, he awakened from the deep sleep of iniquity and came to himself. He entered his cell, fell prostrate to the ground, and began smiting his chest and his face. He kept sighing from the bottom of his heart and fervently shedding a torrent of tears. But the ravenous devil, seeing him repent in this manner, was afraid that he himself might be harmed; and so he planted in Iakovos' mind thoughts of despair. He whispered to him that he could not be saved and should not toil in vain. Iakovos arose therefore from the ground and left the desert and returned to the world extremely dejected. But the God Who loves mankind and thirsts for our salvation, remembered Iakovos' virtues, his arduous hardships, and his struggle of many years. Therefore, He sent help to him in the following manner.

As Iakovos walked along a road, he came upon a monastery. He observed that it was late in the day, so he decided to stop there and rest. The brothers washed his feet and set a table before him in order to show kindness. But he sighed within himself and did not wish to eat at all. Now the hegumen, a learned and virtuous man, perceived Iakovos' disheartened state. He understood that his guest had fallen into some great sin. For this reason, the hegumen brought him to his cell and asked him to relate why he was so downcast. Then, with many tears, Iakovos confessed the entire matter. The hegumen, an experienced and prudent spiritual father, discerned the snare of the devil. He embraced Iakovos and said to him, "O my beloved brother, do not grieve and fall into senseless despair. As long as thou knowest that there is repentance, come before God, the Lover of mankind, with a contrite heart. Weep before God, in imitation of the Prophet David with whom thou hast the same sins in common. The all-merciful God will receive and forgive thee that thou mightest return to thy former state. As He accepted David mercifully when he repented, so shall He receive thee. Remember that He not only forgave David of his sins, but He also made him famous with these words: 'I have found David, the son of Jesse, a man after Mine own heart [cf. 1 Kgs. (1 Sam.) 13:14; Acts 13:22].' If there were no repentance, how could blessed Peter, having the preeminence among the apostles, receive from Christ the keys to Paradise, although he had denied Him thrice? But later, he wept bitterly and received forgiveness of his sins, and also his previous eminent dignity."

With these and other similar examples, the most wise hegumen strengthened the heart of Iakovos. The hegumen besought him to continue with him at the monastery, for he was fearful lest perchance the cunning evil one should impede Iakovos' salvation. Therefore, after the entire night, it was in the morning when Iakovos obtained permission to leave. But the hegumen then knelt before Iakovos, entreating and admonishing him to remain there in the community of the brethren that they might guide him. But Iakovos would not consent to this. Therefore, against his judgment, the hegumen dismissed Iakovos, but he accompanied him along the road for a distance of fifteen miles, the better to correct him with words of repentance, and cited edifying examples. Then the hegumen kissed him, wishing him salvation. Thereupon, the holy abbot turned around and retraced his steps to the monastery. Meanwhile, Iakovos continued on his way.

By and by, he came upon an ancient and enormous sepulcher, which was as huge as a cave. Entering therein, he gathered together all the bones and stacked them in a pile in a recess within the sepulcher. Then the blessed one enclosed himself in the tomb, sealing the entrance. He then fell to his knees and began beating his breast and the earth violently. He shed torrents of hot tears and, sighing from the bottom of his heart, cried out to God, "How can I presume to gaze

Saint Iakovos

upon Thy holy icon, O Master, with my polluted eyes? How can I begin to confess my sins? With what heart and conscience can I approach? How will I move my impious tongue and soiled lips toward praise of Thee? For what sins shall I ask forgiveness first? How will I open my foul mouth to ask Thy forgiveness for my wickedness? O Lord, Lover of mankind, have pity on me and bestow Thy mercy upon me, unworthy as I am. Cast me not into perdition, though I am ungodly and iniquitous. I, the thrice-wretched, have committed fornication and murder, thereby defiling my soul in twofold measure! I am not worthy to walk Thine earth! I dare not lift these profane and indecent eyes of mine to Thee in the heavens; but I take refuge in Thine infinite compassion. Have mercy on me, though I am irreverent and undeserving. Have pity and compassion on me, who am filled with passions, and leave me not to the noetic dragon who will devour me greedily with his charming delights. But, with Thine almighty hand, raise me up from this unclean and insatiable abyss!"

This and a great many other similarly heartfelt utterances were spoken by the saint. Every day and hour, he lamented his misery and bitterness. He shut himself in that dark and gloomy tomb, which was lacking in all bodily comfort. He spoke with no one. Moreover, no one brought him food and drink, for the people of the city were not aware that he was within their

borders. Furthermore, the place was far removed from the main thorough-
fare. Iakovos, therefore, only came out at night and secretly twice a week to
eat. Even as the horses and cattle, he partook only of the grasses which grew
in the vicinity of the sepulcher; and in everything he thanked the Lord. He
was as one already dead and consigned to the grave, before his actual repose
and entombment. He was unknown to all and could not be helped or
strengthened by human means. Thus, he wept and lamented for ten years,
waiting and hoping for help from on high. Since God Who loves mankind
does not wish the death of the sinner, but instead that he turn and be restored,
He observed Iakovos' pure repentance and forgave his sins, in that He is
compassionate. Not only did our Savior forgive his transgressions, but He
also glorified Iakovos before men. This took place so that other sinners might
learn the great power of repentance.

In those years, there occurred in the area of that city an intense
drought, which afflicted the people. For this reason, they made a repeated
number of entreaties before the Lord with fasting and almsgiving. The
beneficent Lord revealed to that city's bishop, who indeed was a God-fearing
and saintly man, Iakovos' state. The Lord sent an angel who carried the
heavenly command and said, "O bishop, in that place of the ancient and huge
sepulcher, thou shalt find a humble ascetic, who is holy in both appearance
and soul. If he should consent to make entreaty before the Lord, there would
be so much rain that you could depend upon considerable advantage and
abundance at harvest time." The bishop assembled the clergy and the laity of
the city and told them of his vision. They all ascended to this place, forming
a holy procession with much piety. There they found the holy one and fell
before his feet with tears, praying and begging him to intercede before the
Lord that He would issue rain, lest they should perish from lack of water. The
saint made no answer to them at all, but he beat his breast. He then looked
about on the ground and said, "O Lord Jesus Christ, have compassion on me,
the ungodly, and forgive mine iniquities." In this manner did he pray, not
daring to lift his eyes heavenward. When they saw that he did not answer
them at all, they continued to beg him. Their tears, however, were in vain.
Therefore, the people left Iakovos and returned to their homes sorrowing. But
when they arrived at the church, they again fell to the ground, entreating the
Lord with tears to send them assistance from on high. Thus, they prayed and
wailed for many days. Once again, a divine voice came to the bishop and
said, "Go to My servant Iakovos, as I told thee previously, and entreat him
to make petitions on your behalf; and I will bestow what you wish." Then
they went again and told him that God had sent them a second time. They
besought him in a twofold manner: that he ought not to show himself
disobedient to God, and that he should do the proper thing by rescuing his

fellow man from impending danger. With difficulty then, they persuaded the blessed one. He raised his eyes and hands toward the heavens, giving utterance to a prayer of deep humility and meekness. Straightway, the merciful God hearkened to the prayer of His servant. There came a great abundance of rain upon the earth, as much as they could want. For this reason, they glorified God and thanked the saint. Not only that day, but also every year thereafter, they conducted a memorial in honor of the saint who had rescued them from that perilous situation. Not only did the holy one perform this miracle, but also he healed all the sick of that city. For when the people beheld the miracle of the rain, they recognized that the blessed Iakovos was a true servant of God. If anyone had a relative who was possessed by a demon or suffering from sickness, they brought such a one to the saint, who healed every ailment. Through these wonders, he came to understand that the Lord had forgiven him; and therefore, he labored with greater eagerness and joy.

A year after the miracle of the rain, the holy one knew his departure was imminent. He besought the bishop to carry out his instructions regarding his burial in the very sepulcher where he performed his supernatural struggles and divine achievements. The bishop promised to carry out joyfully Iakovos' final wishes. In a few days, on the 28th day of January, the saint reposed, at the age of seventy-five.

Then the holy bishop with his clergy, and all the people of the city, with fragrant incense and precious spices, buried the holy Iakovos' precious and cherished relics with reverence and esteem. They laid him to rest in the place where he had given them express orders. They returned to the city, glorifying and blessing the Lord. In time, the holy bishop erected a church in honor of the saint near the sepulcher, and thither they transferred his holy remains. Every year they hold a magnificent celebration, which is attended by the entire city. The surrounding villages also join the celebration, to the glory of God, to Whom glory, honor, and veneration are always due, now and ever, and to the ages of ages. Amen.

**On the 28th of January, the holy Church commemorates
TWO FEMALE MARTYRS,
a mother and daughter,
who were slain by the sword.**

**On the 28th of January, the holy Church commemorates
the holy Martyr CHARIS,
who suffered martyrdom when her two feet were cut off.**

On the 28ᵗʰ of January, the holy Church commemorates
our holy Father ISAAC the Syrian.

Saint Isaac the Syrian

Isaac, our holy father among the saints, was born in a region known as Beit Qatraye,[12] the Syriac name of Qatar. He flourished in the 7ᵗʰ C. Syriac sources state that the area contained monasteries at least from the mid-4ᵗʰ C. The Christians were tolerated and remained active after the conversion of the region's leaders to Islam (ca. 629). The bishops ceased attending synods after 676, but texts show that some Christian practise persisted until at least the late 9ᵗʰ C.[13]

The precise dates of Isaac's birth and death are unknown. No information about his parents is extant. We are led to believe, by two autobiographical comments found in the saint's homily on saintly men known to him in his youth, that early on he led a monastic life far from his home. He recounts that once he had fallen ill and went to the cell of a certain brother. Isaac remembers laying himself down in a corner of that cell, receiving care and being counseled by the kindly ascetic. Again, while still young, both he and his brother entered the lavra of Saint Matthew, where they received the monastic tonsure. Upon attaining a sufficient degree of ascetic discipline and virtue, Isaac desired greater silence. He departed the community life at the lavra and dwelt in an isolated cell. He led a solitary life, communing with no one but God. At length, his brother became abbot at the lavra. He implored Isaac to return to the monastery, but the latter would not leave the quietude of his beloved wilderness. Although Isaac did not hearken to his brother, yet divine revelation moved him to administer to the Church

---

[12] This included the Qatar peninsula, northeastern Arabia, and the Bahrain archipelago.

[13] R.A. Carter, "Christianity in the Gulf During the First Centuries of Islam," *Arabian Archaeology and Epigraphy,* 2008, 19:71-108.

of Nineveh.[14] He left his desert retreat and was consecrated bishop of the great city of Nineveh by the catholicos (katholikos), or patriarch, Giwargis (George I, 661-680). The holy Isaac was not long in this office. He departed his see for a reason known to God. For us, it continues as a subject of speculation, which shall be discussed further below.

Saint Isaac is absent from *The Great Synaxaristes* (in Greek), though he is commemorated in the Slavonic *Synaxaria*. As a Syrian mystical theologian, who flourished circa 680, it was probably not until the ninth century that some of his works were translated into Greek by the Monks Patrikios and Abramios of the Lavra of Saint Savvas in the Judaean Desert. Isaac's works were used by some Byzantine writers, as Peter Damaskenos, Symeon the Theologian, and Gregory Sinaites. Some of his writings were included in the *Philokalia* and *Evergetinos*.

Little has been left us about the saint's life. There exist two brief but detailed narratives. One account is given in the *Book of Chastity* of Isho dnah, Bishop of Basra, dating from the early ninth century.[15] The text contains short stories of famous monks of the Persian Church who lived prior to him. The other account is that of Rahmani, taken from a fifteenth century manuscript in Mardin.[16]

The first source, that of Isho'dnah, opens at Chapter 124, entitled "On the holy Mar Ishaq (Saint Isaac), the Bishop of Nineveh, who abdicated from his episcopacy and composed books on the discipline of solitude." It begins: "Isaac was ordained Bishop of Nineveh by Mar Giwargis the catholicos of the monastery of Beit'Abhe. But after he held the office of the shepherd of Nineveh for five months (in succession to Moses, the bishop before him), he abdicated his episcopacy for a reason known to God. He then departed and dwelt in the mountains. After that, the throne was vacant for a time; and then the blessed Sabrisho was ordained after him. He likewise abandoned his episcopacy and became an anchorite. This took place in the days of Henanisho the catholicos. He then fell asleep in the monastery of Mar Shehin in the region of Qardu.

"Now after Isaac abandoned the throne of Nineveh, he ascended the mountain of Matout, which is encircled by the region of Beit Huzaye. He thereafter dwelt in stillness, together with the anchorites who lived thereabouts. Afterward, he went to the monastery of Rabban Shabur. He was exceedingly well versed in the divine writings, even to the point that he lost

---

[14] E. Kadloubovsky and G. E. H. Palmer, *Early Fathers from the Philokalia*, p. 181.
[15] J. B. Chabot, "Le Livre de la Chasteté, compose part Jésusdenah Evêque de Basrah," in *Mélanges d'Archéologie et d'Histoire* 16 (1896), pp. 63, 64(277, 278).
[16] I. E. Rahmani, *Studia Syriaca* (Lebanon: Charfet Seminary, 1904), p. 33(32-33).

his eyesight by reason of his reading and asceticism. He entered deeply into the divine mysteries and composed books on the divine discipline of solitude.

"It was said, however, that he made three points which were not accepted by many. Daniel Bar Tubanitha, the Bishop of Beit Garmai, was scandalized at Abba Isaac on account of these three propositions. Howbeit, when Isaac reached deep old age, he departed from temporal life, and his body was placed in the monastery of Shabur. He had been born in Beit Qatraye. Now I think that envy was stirred up against him by those who dwelt in the interior, even as was the case with Jausep (Joseph) Hazzaya, Johannan (John) of Apamea, and Johannan (John) of Dalyatha."

With regard to the account of the three propositions, since Abba Isaac was not inclined to argue on dogmatic subjects, he retired. The subjects of the three points or propositions expounded upon by the holy man and Daniel's opposition remain an enigma.

The second source, preserved by the West-Syrians, has an unknown author and date. Similar information is provided in this account. "Further, we record the history, or indeed the triumph, of the blessed Father Mar Ishaq (Isaac), which declares his homeland, his way of life, and how he was Bishop of Nineveh; but afterward, he forsook this office and went to a monastery where he composed five volumes of instruction for monks. This Mar Isaac of Nineveh was born in the region of Beit Qatraye beneath India. When he had become versed in the writings of the Church and the commentaries, he became a monk and a teacher in his own region. But when Mar Giwargis the catholicos came to Saint Isaac's region in 676, he took him to Beit Aramaya, because one of Saint Isaac's relatives was Mar Gabriel of Qatar, the scriptural interpreter of the Church. Mar Isaac was ordained Bishop of Nineveh in the monastery of Beit'Abhe. But because of the acuteness of his intellect and his zeal, he could only endure the pastoral care of his city for five months; then he returned to his stillness. He persuaded the papa (catholicos) to dismiss him, and the papa gave him the command to depart.

"Then Isaac left and dwelt in stillness in the mountain of Beit Huzaye, together with the monks who lived thereabouts. Ultimately, he became blind which required that the brethren write down his teachings. They called him the second Didymos, for indeed, he was quiet, kind, and humble, and his word was gentle. He ate only three loaves a week with some vegetables; he did not taste any food that was cooked. He composed five volumes, that are known even until this day, filled with sweet teaching....Thereafter, when he had grown old and advanced in years, he departed unto our Lord, and he was placed in the monastery of Mar Shabur. May the prayer of the Theotokos Mary and his prayer and that of all the saints be with us! Amen."

In 648 or perhaps a little later, the bishops of Qatar, Isaac's homeland, separated themselves from the catholicos, Isho'yahb III, and the bishops of the Tigris-Euphrates region. Instead, they held communion with rebel bishops of eastern Persia. The cause for this schism is unknown. Five letters were sent by the catholicos.[17] He did not accuse them of heresy, but he does accuse them of rebellion. After 649, the catholicos convened a synod to depose the bishops who created the schism. He then bade the faithful of Qatar, monastics and layfolk, to shun the schismatics. These efforts failed. Some of the Qatari monks left the area or took refuge in remote spots, while others suffered persecution or were cast out because they refused to support the schismatical bishops.

Due to the disorder in the Church at Qatar, Isaac left his homeland and dwelt with monks in another region, in Persia. The place and duration is unknown to us. In 676, during the time when Giwargis was catholicos, the Church of Qatar was reunited with the mother Church of Persia. In that same year the catholicos went to Qatar to heal the schism. Abba Isaac at that time had returned to Qatar, conducting his life as a recluse. Giwargis learned of Abba Isaac and sought him for the episcopacy. Given Abba Isaac's love of stillness, it could not have been easy to persuade him to accept an office fraught with the tribulations of administering to and governing people. Abba Isaac, however, considered the good of the flock and the help he might render in reuniting Qatar with her mother Church. The Ninevites, however, were displeased to have a foreigner as bishop. As we mentioned earlier, he lasted but a short time in his see. Though it is accepted that he quickly retired from the see of Nineveh, the exact cause is unclear. Again, Isho'dnah suggests the root cause: "I believe that jealousy awakened against Abba Isaac."[18]

An Arabic manuscript has preserved the following narrative, derived from a West-Syrian source: "As Abba Isaac was sitting in the episcopal residence on the first day after his ordination, lo, there entered into the bishop's chamber two men who had a dispute with one another. The one man was demanding the return of a loan, while the other acknowledged to be the debtor. The debtor loudly begged for a short grace period, but his creditor refused him any extension. Then the wretched lender, a rich man, said, 'If this man refuses to give back what is mine, I shall be forced to summon him to court.' The holy Mar Isaac answered him, 'If according to the Gospel commandment thou shouldest by no means ask back thy goods that another

---

[17] *Isho'yahb Patriarchae III, Liber Epistularum*, ed. and trans. R. Duval, Corpus Scriptorum Christianorum Orientalium 11(12) (Louvain, 1904), pp. 260-283(188-204), Letters 17-21.

[18] Saint Isaac of Nineveh, "Introduction," *On Ascetical Life*, p. 11.

has taken away, how much more shouldest thou show magnanimity to a man who promises soon to repay his debt?' The impious lender replied, 'Put aside for now the teachings of the Gospel!' Then Saint Isaac said, 'If they do not obey the Gospel commandments of the Lord, what is there that remains for me to do here?' Seeing, therefore, that the office of Bishop was disturbing his solitary life with the unavoidable business of administration, the holy man abdicated from his episcopacy. He then fled to the desert."[19]

It is believed that the saint went to the mountainous region of Beit Huzaye, south of Nineveh. In his wilderness retreat, he was far from the controversies of the Persian Church. He dwelt for many years as a solitary on Mount Matout. While in utter solitude, he also spent time writing his homilies. Due to old age and the loss of his eyesight from weeping, he retired to the nearest monastery, that of Rabban Shabur. He spent the last years of his life among brethren who wrote down many of his teachings. The saint's writings were composed toward his more advanced years, after having lived both the life of a coenobite and anchorite. The writings of Saint Isaac have come down to us in the Syriac and Arabic tongues. Many of his works have been translated into Greek, and from Greek into Russian.

Amid the turmoil of the Persian Church, it is not difficult to determine Saint Isaac's position. The effects are evident of his thorough study of Saint Dionysios the Areopagite, the *Paradise of the Fathers*, certain writings of the great Cappadocians, Evagrios, Saint Makarios of Egypt, along with the works of Theodore of Mopsuestia. Abba Isaac modified and even supplanted some of Theodore's views. He is most certainly a Dyophysite, believing unequivocally that the Lord Jesus Christ is the "Mediator between God and man [1 Tim. 2:5]" and the One Who unites in His two natures. His confession of Faith is entirely Orthodox.

He affirms that the Word became Man and spoke to us in our body. In His humility He hid His glory lest creation should be utterly consumed by the contemplation of the Creator. Creation could not behold Him or converse with Him unless He condescended to take part of it to Himself. Although the angelic hierarchies could not approach the glory that surrounds His throne of His majesty, yet He has appeared to us and "we beheld Him, that He had neither form nor beauty [Is. 53:2]."

From a Christological point of view, it is safe to assume that Saint Isaac was with the party of moderates in the Persian Church. He disliked the

---

[19] This narration was translated into Latin by Assemani. See *Biblioteca Orientalis* I (Rome, 1719), p. 445; thereafter it was placed in the introduction to the Greek Edition of 1770 by Nikephoros Theotokis. See also Kadloubovsky and Palmer, *Early Fathers from the Philokalia*, pp. 181, 182.

practises of the extremists. He understood full well that there are many who do not understand the intent of the sacred writings. Thus, on account of their erroneous presuppositions or obtuseness, many do not comprehend the meaning of the passages in Scriptures and have been tripped up or have taken offense.

Brief History of the Church of Persia

At this point we insert a concise history of the Persian Church up to the seventh century. In 489, Emperor Zeno (474-491), a pro-Monophysite, closed the Persian School, which then transferred itself to Nisibis, where it became the main theological and spiritual center of the Church of Persia. In 572, Henana became the head of the school. He desired to replace the commentaries of Theodore of Mopsuestia (ca. 350-428) with those of his own making, which were based on the allegorical method of Origen. A local council (585) forbade anyone from removing the works of Theodore, whose authority the council did not question. In 596 (Synod of Sabrisho) and 605 (Synod of Gregor), Henana's interpretations were condemned in two other local councils. It was at the end of the sixth and the beginning of the seventh centuries when Babai the Great became leader of the conservative party, which also adhered to Theodore's teachings.[20]

For nineteen years (609-628) the Church of Persia was without a catholicos. After the death of Gregor the catholicos, the Church remained widowed, in accordance with the wish of the Persian King Chosroes II Parvez (591-628, second reign). Consequently, heretical Henanians and the Messalians gained ground roundabout. They took hold of churches and perverted the faith of many.

At present, the Assyrian Church of the East venerates Babai the Great who was born in Beth Aynata in Beth Zabday, on the west bank of the Tigris, near Nisibis. He received a primary education in the Persian (Pahlavi) books. He continued his studies at the Christian School of Nisibis under the directorship of Abraham of Beth Rabban. Sometime around the year 571, when the Origenist Henana of Adiabene became the new headmaster, Babai's teacher, Abraham the Great of Kashkar, founded a new monastery on Mount Izla above Nisibis. Babai taught for a while at the Xenodocheio of Nisibis. After that he joined the newly founded monastery of Abraham on Mount Izla. When Abraham died in 588, Babai left and founded a new monastery and school in his home country Beth Zabday. In 604 Babai became the third abbot of Abraham's monastery on Mount Izla. He expelled those monks that lived with women on the fringes of the monastery, and enforced strict discipline, emphasizing prayer and solitude. Though the result of this purge was a mass

---

[20] H. Alfeyev, *The Spiritual World of Isaac the Syrian*, p. 19.

exodus of married and unmarried monastics, yet the Church of the East was with Babai.

From 610 to 628 the last and most devastating wars between Byzantium and Persia took place. First Persia conquered parts of Byzantium, which were populated mostly by Monophysite and Chalcedonian Christians. To be popular in the newly gained provinces, King Khosrau II did not want to favor the Nestorians any longer. During the successful Byzantine counterattack 622-628, Chalcedonians and especially Monophysites were on the advance in Persia and several sees and villages were lost by the Church of the East.[21]

During the decades of this vacancy, the Nestorian Church required some authority figure. Two regents were selected: Archdeacon Aba, who handled matters in the south. In the north, Abbot Babai was chosen to lead. He was nominated Inspector-General or Visitor of the Monasteries of the three northern provinces by the Metropolitans of Nisibis, B. Garmai, and Adiabene. Therefore, Babai, even though not yet a bishop, acted as patriarch in all ecclesiastical matters, though he could not ordain or consecrate. However, this new position allowed Babai to investigate the orthodoxy of the monasteries and monks of northern Mesopotamia, and to enforce discipline throughout the monasteries, even against occasional resistance.

Babai and Aba administered the flock for seventeen years. Attempts were made during that time to ask the king to change his mind and allow an election, but influences in the court did not allow it. Thus, the situation, and vacancy, endured until Khosrau II was murdered in 628. After this, Babai was promptly, and unanimously, elected catholicos, but he declined. Soon afterward, he died in his seventies in the cell of his monastery on Mount Izla. His voluminous writings attempted to defend and clarify the Nestorian tradition against Henana's Origenism and the advancing ideas of the Monophysites. He developed a systematic Christology, the only one in Nestorian Mesopotamia. There is no evidence that he could read Greek, and so he probably relied on translations. While he viewed the Monophysites and the Origenist Henana as inner enemies, he also wrote against Mani, Marcion, Bar Daisan, the Messalians and the general loss of discipline since Beth Lapat. The *Book of Union* is his most systematic surviving Christological treatise. An important source on the position of Babai against Messalianism, Origen, and his follower Henana of Adiabene is his commentary on Evagrios

---

[21] Robert A. Kitchen, "Babai the Great," *The Orthodox Christian World*, Augustine Casiday, ed. (Routledge, 2012), chap. 21. See also David Bundy and Frederick Norris, "Babai the Great," *Encyclopedia of Early Christianity*, Volume 1, Everett Ferguson, Michael P. McHugh, Frederick W. Norris, ed. (Taylor & Francis, 1998).

Pontikos (b. ca. 345-d. 399). It also shows his opposition to Messalianism. The writings of Evagrios were important to the current mystical revival among Greek and Syrian monks. For the monks of Mount Izla, Evagrios was the pillar of mystical theology. The Greek text was condemned already in 553 for its Origenist heresies. But unlike the Greek, the Common Syriac Version, a translation of the Gnostic chapters of Evagrios by the Monophysite Philoxenus, was void of the specific Origenist-Evagrian Christology. Babai tried to eliminate the Origenist ideas even further and presented Evagrios as opposed to Origen and his follower Henana by pointing out apparent contradictions between them.

Thus, the normative Christology of the Assyrian Church was written by Babai the Great (551–628) and is clearly distinct from the accusations directed toward Nestorios. The main theological authorities of Babai were Theodore of Mopsuestia and Diodoros (Diodore) of Tarsus. He also relied on Saint John Chrysostom, the Cappadocian fathers, and Saint Ephraim the Syrian. In his exegetical methods he synthesized between the rational Theodore and mystical writers like Evagrios. Instead of breaking with Theodore of Mopsuestia, because of some extreme interpretations of his teachings, like others did, Babai clarified his position to the point that differences with western Christology became superficial and mostly an issue of terminology. His Christology is far less dualistic than the one Nestorios seems to have presented.

Babai wrote the Teshbokhta or *Hymn of Praise* explaining the theology of his Church: "One is Christ the Son of God, worshiped by all in two natures; in His Godhead begotten of the Father, without beginning before all time; in His humanity born of Mary, in the fullness of time, in a body united; neither His Godhead is of the nature of the mother, nor His humanity of the nature of the Father; the natures are preserved in their Qnumas (substance), in one person of one Sonship. And as the Godhead is three substances in one nature, likewise the Sonship of the Son is in two natures, one person. So the Holy Church has taught."[22]

Babai and his party pursued a radically conservative course that vehemently opposed the Monophysites and the Henanians, and the doctrine of a composite hypostasis. However, even among Babai's party of conservative zealots, the Chalcedonian Synod was rejected. This position was not shared by all.

In 628, when Kavad II Shiruya ascended the throne, he permitted the bishops of Persia to elect a catholicos. This election was realized in the person of Isho'yahb II of Gdala (628-646). The king died and Queen Boran bade the

---

[22] Http://www.nestorian.org/index.html.

new catholicos to visit Aleppo where the Byzantine Emperor Herakleios (610-641)[23] was then found. The catholicos and his party of clergy went and were received graciously by the emperor. The catholicos engaged in a discussion of the Faith with the emperor, to demonstrate that the Persian Church had not deviated from the Faith and that their Dyophysitism was not heretical. The term Dyophysites, "two natures," was a title by the Monophysites for the Orthodox. It had been a distinguishing mark of the Antiochene school of theologians. Dyophysites were those who accepted the definition given at the Chalcedon Synod (451), which states that Jesus Christ had two distinct natures, one divine and one human, in one person (hypostasis).

However, the catholicos and emperor could not reach an agreement over one point. On the one hand, the Persians would not have Saint Kyril of Alexandria (378-444) commemorated in the diptychs; but on the other hand, Herakleios refused commemoration of Diodoros of Tarsus (d. ca. 390), Theodore of Mopsuestia, and Nestorios (d. ca. 451).[24] As a result, all the names arousing distaste to either party were omitted. Two Liturgies were celebrated, whereupon the emperor communed with the Persians. The catholicos, upon returning home, was criticized by extreme conservatives.

Not much time passed before the Moslem Arabs conquered the Sasanid (Iranian) dynasty of the Zoroastrians; so that by the end of the seventh century, the Sasanian Empire, after five hundred years, came to an end during the reign of Yazdgird III (651). Political troubles, plague, famine, and the spoiling of the irrigation system caused Sasanian Persia to fall to the Arab armies. There was no longer any controversy over one or two hypostases. Let no one forget, however, that the first six centuries of Syrian Christianity were times of persecution. It was a Church which, due to political and ecclesial reasons, remained insular. She had her own liturgical life, hierarchy, dogmas, and discipline. During those years when the Roman Empire was pagan, the Persian king had little reason to persecute his Christian subjects. When the Roman Empire became Orthodox, Shāpūr

---

[23] Herakleios fought the Persian generals Shahrbarāz and Shāhīn. He broke the Sasanian state, and, in 628, Kavad Shiruya was forced to conclude a truce.

[24] The controversy over the relationship between the divine and human natures in Christ was rooted in the differing views of the schools of Alexandria and Antioch. The theologians of Antioch, the most notable of whom in this controversy was Nestorios, who had views which followed after Diodoros of Tarsus and Theodore of Mopsuestia. The Alexandrians were represented by Kyril of Alexandria, who managed to have Nestorios removed from the see of Constantinople as a heretic. The Synod of Chalcedon was convoked in 451 to settle the issue of the natures of Christ.

deemed the Christians in his borders as traitors.[25] Despite horrifying persecutions, missionary expansion would reach as far as central China in 638.

In the year 629, the Persians renounced all Byzantine territory. The Moslem Arabs then conquered Syria and Babylonia in 636. In 638, Iso'yaw III of Adiabene began his ecclesiastical career as Bishop of Nineveh. The letters of this bishop reflect the tension of that period. He writes of going down to Tabrit, "the great city of the heretics, to do battle with the Monophysites."[26] Prior to his death in 661, he chose as his successor a monk at Beit'Abhe, named Giwargis of Kaphra. He loved Giwargis for his wisdom, learning, and humility. When Iso'yaw reposed at eighty years of age, the patriarchate passed on to Giwargis, who had been named bishop of the Arabs at Akoula in 636. Giwargis was also a translator of Greek works into Syriac. It was this same Giwargis who would consecrate the holy Isaac to the bishopric of Nineveh.

Theodore, Diodoros, and Nestorios

Since the biblical commentary of Saint Ephraim the Syrian (ca. 306-383) was not complete, Syriac Christianity made the decision to translate from the Greek the entire body of exegetical works of Theodore of Mopsuestia, whom Saint Isaac referred to as "the blessed interpreter." As a result, Theodore's methods and views, including his Christological opinions, were incorporated into East-Syrian tradition.[27] These very opinions became a subject of heated discussions in the Greek-speaking east after the Synod of Ephesus (431), which condemned Nestorios. At that time, writers of extreme Dyophysite leanings were reckoned to be Nestorians. Theodore of Mopsuestia, pupil of Diodoros of Tarsus, at Antioch, had been accused of Nestorianism and Pelagianism by the Byzantines. His writings were among those condemned by the Second Synod of Constantinople or Fifth Œcumenical Synod (553). Saint Photios the Great (d. 897), however, commended

---

[25] Under Shāpūr II (309-379), Persia had more martyrs than any other part of the Christian world. The Roman Martyrology lists nine thousand martyrs, and Sozomen sixteen thousand. Ardashir II (379-383), Shāpūr's brother, perpetuated the carnage, as did Yazdgird I (399-420), until the edict of toleration in 409. See Saint Isaac of Nineveh, "Introduction," *On Ascetical Life* (NY: Saint Vladimir's Seminary Press, 1989), p. 8.

[26] The patriarchal letters of Iso'yaw, edited and translated by R. Duval, from *Liber epistularum*, Corpus Scriptorum Christianorum Orientalium 64, Ser. 2 (Louvain, 1905).

[27] East-Syrian is a term frequently used to describe the Persian Church rather than "Nestorian." The Christology of Nestorios was not really at issue in East-Syrian theology.

Theodore's refutation of Evnomios. The biblical commentaries of Theodore, so sought after by the Syriac Church, are historical and philological in approach, with minimal allegorization. His most important theological work was entitled *On the Incarnation*. It was aimed chiefly at Apollinarios with his definition of Christ as a union of two natures. Despite his posthumous condemnation at the Fifth Synod, the East-Syrian Christians remained loyal to him. This explains how the Church of Persia and the whole East-Syrian theological tradition came to be called "Nestorian," though the name was neither used by this Church nor was there any historical link to Nestorios.[28]

The Alexandrian tradition, represented in the person of Saint Kyril of Alexandria, came into conflict with Nestorios. Though the Ephesian Synod (431) confirmed Saint Kyril, yet the East-Syrian theological tradition rejected his terminology in favor of that of Theodore and Diodoros. Later, the Chalcedonian Synod (451) returned to the Antiochene school's strict distinction between the two natures of Christ. Why did the East-Syrian tradition not accept the Ephesian Synod? The name of Nestorios was barely known in Persia until the sixth century. The main reason for their refusal was that the synod had been conducted by Saint Kyril of Alexandria and his adherents in the absence of John of Antioch, who, upon his arrival at Ephesus, anathematized Kyril. The Church of Persia was displeased that the synod was "Alexandrian," taking no account of their Antiochene position, which was the Christology of the Church of the East, not Nestorian.[29]

The Meaning of Terms: Substance (*Qnoma*) and Hypostasis

It is more difficult to respond to the question of why the East-Syrians refused the Chalcedonian Council. The Greek word *hypostasis* meant a specific person, Jesus Christ, the Logos, whereas the word *physis* (nature) referred to His humanity and divinity. When these words were translated into Syriac, the terminological expression could not be adequately expressed. The Syriac word *qnoma* (used to translate hypostasis) carried the meaning of the individual expression of *kyana* (nature). Syriac writers normally spoke of natures and their *qnome*. Whereas Severus of Antioch thought that one hypostasis implies one nature, yet some Dyophysite writers claimed that two natures imply two hypostases.[30]

Catholicos Isho'yahb II explained why the Church of the East would not and could not accept the Chalcedonian definition of the Faith: "Although those who gathered at the Synod of Chalcedon were clothed with the intention of restoring the Faith, yet they too slid away from the true Faith: owing to

---

[28] H. Alfeyev, *The Spiritual World of Isaac the Syrian*, p. 18.

[29] Ibid., pp. 21, 22.

[30] Ibid., p. 22.

their feeble phraseology, wrapped in an obscure meaning, they provided a stumbling block to many. Although, in accordance with the opinion of their own minds, they preserved the true Faith with the confession of 'two natures (divine and human),' yet by their formula of 'one *qnoma* (substance),' it seems, they tempted weak minds. As an outcome of the affair, a contradiction occurred, for with the formula of 'one *qnoma*' they corrupted the confession of 'two natures,' while with the 'two natures' they rebuked and refuted the 'one *qnoma*.' So they found themselves standing at the crossroads: and they wavered and turned aside from the blessed ranks of the Orthodox, yet they did not join the assemblies of the heretics....On what side we should number them, I do not know; for their terminology cannot stand up, even as Nature and Scripture testify. For in these, many *qnoma* (substances) can be found in a single 'nature,' but that there should be various 'natures' in a single *qnoma* has never been the case and has not been heard of."[31] These words show very clearly why the Chalcedonian definition of Faith was unacceptable to the Syrian ear: it sounded illogical. Moreover, the catholicos' reluctance to reckon with the issue indicates that the Synod of Chalcedon was irrelevant to the east. It was not even a synod in which his own Church would have participated. It was a synod which took place within the Roman Empire. The Church of the East, located within the Persian Empire, had no direct links with that synod of the Byzantine world. If it happened that synods were recognized in the non-Byzantine east, it took place later than the date at which the synods convened. The First Œcumenical Synod (325) had not been recognized by the Persian Church until eighty-five years after the synod met.[32] The Second Œcumenical Synod (381) was not accepted until the fifth century.

Babai defined two terms: hypostasis (*qnoma*) and person (*parsopa*). However, the *qnoma* in Babai's explanation is not the Chalcedonian meaning of hypostasis. Although originally *qnoma* was the Syriac translation of the Greek hypostasis, it cannot be identified with it. *Qnoma* may be translated, "this or that substance," "substratum," "subsistence," "reality" opposed to the unreal or illusion. It is primarily referring to concrete reality or actuality rather than person (*prosopon* or *persona*). So to translate *qnoma* as "hypostasis" or as "person" is incorrect and highly misleading....*Parsopa* (person) is the property which distinguishes one *qnoma* (substance) from another *qnoma* of the same species. It is the sum total of the accidents, and properties, giving the particular characteristic to the *qnoma*. The indivisible

[31] Ibid., p. 23. Quoted from S. Brock, *The Nestorian Church: A Lamentable Misnomer*, in J. F. Coakley and K. and K. Parry, edd., *The Church of the East: Life and Thought*, Bulletin of the John Ryland's Library, vol. 78/3, Manchester 1997.
[32] H. Alfeyev, *The Spiritual World of Isaac the Syrian*, pp. 23, 24.

and singular property of the *qnoma* is given by the *parsopa* (person). Hence, according to G. Chediath's analysis, they are defined as follows: '*Qnoma* (substance) is the concretization of the abstract *kyana* (nature) such as this or that. *Kyana* never exists except as *qnoma*.'" [33]

Babai had insisted on the doctrine of "two *qnome*" in the incarnate Christ, employing the Syriac term meaning "being, substance," which was used to translate the Greek word hypostasis, which for Babai meant something different. Thereupon, Babai's reference to two *qnome* came into conflict with the Chalcedonian definition "one hypostasis, two natures." [34]

In his Fourth *Memra* (seventeenth chapter) Babai defines his terms for us. First let us consider his definition of *qnoma* (hypostasis, substance, essence): "A singular essence is called a *qnoma*. It stands alone, one in number, that is, one as distinct from the many. A *qnoma* is invariable in its natural state and is bound to a species and nature, being one numerically among a number of like *qnome*. It is distinctive among its fellow *qnome* only by reason of any unique property or characteristic which it possesses in its *parsopa*. With rational creatures this uniqueness may consist of various external and internal accidents, such as excellent or evil character, or knowledge or ignorance, and with irrational creatures, as also with the rational, the combination of various contrasting features. Through the *parsopa* we distinguish that Gabriel is not Michael, and Paul is not Peter. However, in each *qnoma* of any given nature the entire common nature is known, and intellectually one recognizes of what that nature consists, which encompasses all of its *qnome*." [35]

For Saint Basil the Great (ca. 330-379), hypostasis included the distinguishing property; for Babai *parsopa* (person) is the distinguishing property. Thus, because the hypostatic characteristic of the Son and Word of God is Sonship (begottenness), Babai can call this His *parsopa*,[36] 'the *parsopa* of Sonship' (or 'Sonness' υἱότης). On the subject of *parsopa*, Babai has this to say: "Again, *parsopa* is the collective characteristics of a *qnoma* which distinguish it from other *qnome* of the same species. The *qnoma* of Paul is not that of Peter, even though the nature and *qnoma* of both men are the same. Each possesses a body and a living soul,...yet through their *parsopa* they are distinguished from one another by that which is unique to each man, that is,

---

[33] G. Chediath, *The Christology of Mar Babai the Great* (Kottayam, India, 1982), pp. 89, 90.

[34] H. Alfeyev, *The Spiritual World of Isaac the Syrian*, p. 19.

[35] *The Book of Union, Liber de unione, and Against one qnoma*, Corpus Scriptorum Christianorum Orientalium, A. Vaschalde, ed. (Paris, 1915), pp. 159, 160.

[36] Ibid., pp. 160, 161(130).

stature, form, temperament, authority, fatherhood, sonship, masculinity, femininity, etc. Because of the unique property (*parsopa*) which a certain *qnoma* possesses, one *qnoma* is not the other one."[37] The *qnoma* of Paul does not otherwise differ from Peter except in numerical distinction. Paul's appearance and conduct are characteristics of his *parsopa*. The integrity of identity is bound up in the fact that Paul's *parsopa* is uniquely his and not another's, whereas the integrity of his *qnoma* lies in its faithful reflection, in exemplary form, of the exact nature of any other ordinary man.

The East-Syrian Tradition

This necessary and brief excursus from the biography of Saint Isaac was done that we might examine the history of the Christological controversies of the fifth century, especially the question regarding the "Nestorianism" of the Church of the East. If by this term we understand the teaching against which Saint Kyril of Alexandria fought—that is, the teaching about the two different persons in the Son of God which led to the recognition of "two Sons," then this doctrine was alien to the East-Syrian tradition. Yet East-Syrian theologians did speak of two *qnome* (substances)-hypostases in connection with the incarnate Son of God. The Church of Persia, therefore, having not recognized the Chalcedonian doctrine of 'one hypostasis, two natures,' found itself in verbal opposition to the Byzantine Church. From the fifth to the eighth centuries, writers of the Church of the East continued to use the Christological terminology of Theodore of Mopsuestia and Diodoros; but in the Greek-speaking east, this usage was generally identified as Nestorian."[38] By the end of the seventh century, political circumstances cut the Church of the East off from the Byzantine world.

An important letter was written in 680 to Mina the *chorepiscopos*, in the province of Fars. Originally written in Persian, it is the letter of Giwargis the catholicos.[39] Mina could not defend his beliefs before Monophysite missionaries. Giwargis' letter, following Babai's lead, wrote: "God the Word came willingly...and fashioned marvellously a body in which there was an intelligent soul and dwelt in it, uniting it with Himself in one union of His own Sonship. For although in His perceptibility and imperceptibility He was consubstantial with us in body and soul, yet in the union with God the Word His Taker, Who united Him with Himself, that through Him He might reveal His hiddenness, and in Him might show forth the greatness of the power of His divinity for our salvation and for the renewal of all, we confess and say that He is one Son in His divinity and in His manhood. Although He is two

---

[37] Ibid., p. 160.

[38] H. Alfeyev, *The Spiritual World of Isaac the Syrian*, p. 24.

[39] *Synodikon Orientale*, pp. 227-244(490-514).

natures—God in nature and *qnoma*, and man in nature and *qnoma*—yet we confess and glorify one Son of God, now and at His coming again and forever.

"When we say 'Anointed'—Man Who was anointed by divinity, and divinity which anointed manhood, according to the prediction of the prophecy of the blessed David, 'Therefore God, Thy God, anointed Thee with the oil of gladness beyond Thy companions [Ps. 44:7]'—it is not as those who were anointed with the blessed oil, for the manhood of Christ was anointed with the Holy Spirit and with power, as it is well written, and although we also confess and believe that Christ is God, yet indeed, when we say 'God,' it is not, by any means, 'Christ' we are defining, for the Father is God but is not 'Christ and the Holy Spirit is God but is not 'Christ,' and although we see and know the Man Christ, yet we also believe in and confess that He is God because of the Word of God Who took Him to Himself and joined Him with Himself in an inseparable union, and made Him His dwelling place forever."[40]

The catholicos also says: "Jesus' divinity was neither altered nor confined, nor did it cause His humanity to vanish. His humanity was not swallowed up in His divinity, but rather the assumed portion of our humanity retained its existence in the union with His divinity, that His divinity might be revealed in our humanity, that our salvation be accomplished by His divinity, and that the lowliness into which we slipped might be raised up to the lofty rank of His divinity, according to His grace from all ages. Who, then, would have been able to work such great goodness for corporeal and spiritual beings, except only God our Creator Who became Man, in the nature that is of us, and revealed in us our salvation?"[41]

The Dyophysite belief, which is held by the Orthodox Churches, was also declared by the Persian Church: "This Faith, which we hold to the capacity of our knowledge, is that of great Rome and all Italy, of Constantinople as well, of Jerusalem, and of all the renowned cities and catholic churches of the cities of the Rūm (that is, the Byzantines or Rhomaioi) which have not been defiled by the foetid mire that the heretics spill forth from the wellsprings of their hearts and the speech of their lips; for they hold fast to the truth of the confession of two natures with their properties and their operations (energies) in the single unity of Christ. But with especial clarity,

---

[40] *Is the Theology of the Church of the East Nestorian?* Assyrian Church of the East, 2002. Commission on Inter-Church Relations and Education Development. See web site at http://www.nestorian.org. Taken from the Pro Oriente Consultation (Vienna, 24-29 June, 1994), Subheading "Giwargis, Letter to Mina," p. 27. See also *Synodikon Orientale*, p. 241(508).

[41] *Synodikon Orientale*, pp. 236, 237(503).

exactitude, and lucidity, according to apostolic tradition and without any stain, this Faith is held by the catholic Church which is in this dominion of the Orient, that is, the land of Persia and the regions surrounding it."[42]

Why was the seventh-century Persian Church imputed by historians to be Nestorian? Theologically, they were supporters of the Chalcedonian Synod, but they did not accept that synod's condemnation of Nestorios. When Nestorios introduced the term "Christotokos," as an appellation for the Theotokos,[43] the Constantinopolitans accused Nestorios of reckoning Christ as a mere man (Psilanthropism) and deification by the action of the Holy Spirit (Adoptionism).

Saint Kyril wrote: "One must not, therefore, divide into two Sons the one Lord Jesus Christ; nor will it in any wise avail the right expression of the Faith to do so, though some should claim a union of persons (Gk. *prosopa*)."[44] Nestorios mistakenly taught that the Logos and His complete human nature were two separate beings with their own independent identities (*prosopa*) and existences. Thereupon, Saint Kyril presented the expression "union according to hypostasis" (ἕνωσις καθ᾽ ὑπόστασιν), by which he meant that "the Logos, in truth, is united to a human nature without undergoing any change or confusion; and He is conceived to be, and really is, one Christ, the same, both God and Man."[45] In 433, the bishops of Antioch stated to Saint Kyril that they also believed our Lord Jesus Christ to

---

[42] *Synodikon Orientale*, p. 244(514).

[43] The Persian Church is silent regarding the term "Theotokos" (God's birthgiver). She believed that the Logos was born of the Virgin, but could not accept any implication that His immaterial, uncircumscribable divinity became, in some way, corporeal and proceeded physically from the Virgin's womb. Babai acknowledged that the infinite dwelt in the finite, but it was the idea of ascribing change to divinity that the Persians loathed. Even though both Theodore and Diodoros accepted the term "Theotokos," its use by the Monophysites came to be associated in the Persian mind with the doctrine of Monophysitism of blending and Theopaschism. Thus, the Persian Church avoided the term. Saint John of Damascus explains Orthodox usage of the appellation, writing: "We do not say that God was born of her in the sense that the divinity of the Logos took its beginning of being from her, but in the sense that God the Logos Himself, Who was timelessly begotten of the Father before all ages,...did, in the last days, come for our salvation to dwell in her womb, and of her was made flesh and born without undergoing change." See *Precise Exposition of the Orthodox Faith* 3:12, *P.G.* 94:1028.

[44] Second Epistle to Nestorios. See E. Schwartz, Acta Conciliorum Œcumenicorum I, 1, 1, p. 28. This letter was produced at the Synod of Ephesus. It was voted upon and acknowledged as expressing the Faith of the entire Church.

[45] E. Schwartz, Acta Conciliorum Œcumenicorum I, 1, 6, p. 115; *The Ascetic Homilies*, pp. 513, 538(277).

be "perfect God and perfect Man, consisting of a rational soul and body, begotten of the Father before the ages according to His divinity, and in the last days the same, for us and our salvation, of Mary the Virgin, according to His humanity; the same essence (*homoousios*) with the Father according to His divinity, and the same essence with us according to His humanity, for there has been a union of two natures. Therefore, we confess one Christ, one Son, one Lord."[46] As a result, Saint Kyril accepted them into communion.

From the foregoing, it is evident that, through the sixth century, the Church of Persia never espoused a Nestorian doctrine, but rather maintained an Antiochene Dyophysite belief. In the early seventh century, when Babai flourished, the Persian Church appeared to be heretical on account of the extremism of the radical conservatives who rejected every other form of Dyophysite Christianity as heretical. Nevertheless, by the time of Giwargis and his successors, the moderates were at the helm of the Persian Church.

Although the Persian Church was not Nestorian in a strict doctrinal sense, her evolved Christological expression no longer resembled that of the Synod of Chalcedon, on account of her lack of information regarding the term hypostasis as understood in the Churches to the west of Persia. The philosophical terms employed by Nestorios to describe the incarnate Christ—two natures (*physis*), and two hypostases (*hypostases*), in one person (*prosopon*)—are also employed by the theologians of the Church of the East. There was also the misunderstanding regarding the commemorations of Saint Kyril, Nestorios, and Theodore of Mopsuestia. Due to the ancient autonomy and continual isolation from the rest of Christendom, the Church of Persia did not feel herself enjoined to accept the decrees of the western Churches. Two factors therefore brought about the application of the term Nestorian to the Church of Persia: the confession of two hypostases and the commemorations of Theodore and Nestorios. The rise of the number of Monophysites in Persia also gave rise to extremism. The more numerous party of moderates, however, were less vocal.

The legacy of Babai and his companions abides to this day. Nestorios is venerated by the Church of the East and his vocabulary is used, though the Assyrian Church rejects the epithet "Nestorian." According to the 2000 Commission of Inter-Church Relations and Education Development of the Assyrian Church of the East they confess "two natures in Christ, inseparable and unconfused, subsisting in one personal object, God the Word, God over all, Who is consubstantial with His Begetter in His own essential nature, and consubstantial with us in the nature which He took from the Virgin and made

---

[46] *The Formulary of Reunion*, Acta Conciliorum Œcumenicorum I, 1, 4, p. 17; *The Ascetic Homilies*, pp. 513, 539(278).

His own. Whether the formulae employed by this confession are adequate to express a true metaphysical union of the two disparate natures we are unable to say with any degree of certainty, for we are well aware that the 'mystery' of the incarnation has eluded the powers of human thought and tongue to express to the satisfaction of all....The Church of the East confesses, as do people of good will everywhere, that her tongue is too stammering, her mind too limited, and her vocabulary too inadequate to do justice to a concept so sublime."[47]

Through the intercessions of Thy Saints,
O Christ God, have mercy on us. Amen.

---

[47] *Is the Theology of the Church of the East Nestorian?* See http://www.nestorian.org. Taken from the Pro Oriente Consultation (Vienna, 24-29 June 1994), Subheadings "IV. Conclusion" and "A. A Confession of Inadequacy," pp. 17, 18.

**On the 29th of January, the holy Church commemorates
the translation of the relics of the holy Hieromartyr
IGNATIOS the God-bearer.**[1]

Saint Ignatios the God-bearer

Ignatios, the God-bearer, became a successor of the apostles. He was second Bishop of Antioch (A.D. 53), after Evodos, who is commemorated by the holy Church on the 7th of September. Ignatios became a disciple of the divine Evangelist John, together with the sacred Polycarp, Bishop of Smyrna, who is commemorated by the holy Church on the 23rd of February. Ignatios was ordained to the priesthood by the holy apostles. He suffered martyrdom in Rome. There is unanimous agreement that Saint Ignatios suffered martyrdom during the reign of Trajan (98-117), but to fix the precise year of his repose is difficult. Most accept the date of the second half of Trajan's reign (ca. 110-117). At Trajan's command, the holy Ignatios was to be fed to the lions. But even this death was desired by the saint. After the saint addressed the crowd, the executioners released the lions. When the lions caught sight of him, they sprang upon him and devoured him. The creatures left only his large bones; therefore the bellies of the wild animals became his tomb. After the crowds dispersed from the theater and departed, the Christians remained behind that they might take up and bury the holy man's relics with honor and reverence. The relics were interred in a distinguished place on the 20th day of December, the date when the holy Church commemorates his martyrdom. With the passage of time, the relics were returned to Antioch. The august translation of the sacred relics of Saint Ignatios is commemorated by the holy Church on the 29th of January. He was buried in Daphne; and later, after his relics had been wrapped in

---

[1] An encomium was composed by Saint John Chrysostom regarding the translation of the relics of Saint Ignatios [*P.G.* 50:587].

linen, they were removed to Antioch by Emperor Theodosios II (408-450). Thus, an inestimable treasure was left to the holy Church. When the Moslems captured the city of Antioch in 637, the relics of Saint Ignatios were moved to several places for safekeeping.

**On the 29th of January, the holy Church commemorates
the holy SEVEN MARTYRS of Samosata:
PHILOTHEOS, HYPERECHIOS, HABIB,
JULIAN, ROMANOS, IAKOVOS, and PAREGORIOS.**

Philotheos, and those holy martyrs with him who became soldiers of the heavenly King and Christ, censured and held up to public scorn the deceit and error of idolatry. They were living in the city of Samosata[2] during the time of Galerius.[3] In 296, the Persians seized control of Armenia from Tiridates and were heading toward Antioch. Galerius advanced but was worsted, suffering a heavy defeat on the plains of Northern Mesopotamia between Carrhae and Callinicum. Within months, Galerius launched a surprise attack on the Persians in Armenia, in'which he succeeded. Before his battle, Galerius summoned the populace to offer worship at the Temple of Fortune at Samosata where he was encamped. Philotheos and Hyperechios refused to attend. Instead, they went to offer up true worship in the chapel within Hyperechios' home, where they were joined by five fellow Samosatans, Habib, Julian, Romanos, Iakovos, and Paregorios. As they prayed together, an imperial officer with soldiers arrived. They came to arrest the well-known confessors of Jesus, Philotheos and Hyperechios. The other five Christians were also taken into custody. The idolaters inflicted many heinous tortures upon the seven martyrs. Thick rods were used to break their arms and thighs. Afterward, they were pitilessly flayed. They were bound at their necks with heavy chains and cast into prison. They were removed a second time and subjected to further flaying and scraping of their flesh. Next the torturers suspended on wood the blessed confessors and fixed their heads to the wood with nails. Thus, they surrendered their souls into the hands of God.

---

[2] Samosata (now Samsat in Turkey, 37°30'N 38°32'E) lies on the north bank of the Euphrates. During the Persian wars it was used as a campsite for the Byzantine army.
[3] Galerius (Gaius Galerius Valerius Maximianus), Roman emperor from 305-311, was born near Serdica (now Sofia) in Thrace, of humble parentage. He was nominated Caesar in 293 by Diocletian, to help in governing the east. He was a fanatical idolater and ruthless ruler. While in power, he persecuted the Christians until the winter of 310-311. At that time, he fell victim to a painful and disgusting disease, which he believed to be a retribution from the Christian God. Therefore, in 311, he issued an edict in which he grudgingly granted toleration of the Christians. He died shortly thereafter.

The ever-memorable martyrs then received the amaranthine crowns of the contest.

On the 29th of January, the holy Church commemorates
the holy Martyrs SILOUANOS the Bishop,
LUKE the Deacon,
and MOKIOS the Reader.

Silouanos, the holy hieromartyr, and those sacred athletes who contested with him, Deacon Luke and Reader Mokios, flourished during the reign of Emperor Numerianus (r. 283-284), who incited a persecution against the Christians. In 284, the elderly Silouanos, Bishop of Emesa for forty years,[4] together with Luke and Mokios, was denounced before the ruler. All three were arrested, bound, and made to stand before him. They underwent careful examination at the inquiry, where the pagan ruler learned that the three undoubtedly confessed Jesus Christ as true God and that they anathematized the idols. For this reason, he was angered by their responses and had them undergo a harsh beating. Afterward, they were cast into prison, where they were left to languish and die of hunger. Then, after the passage of a considerable number of days, the pagans, seeing that the prisoners had not perished, brought them out for another examination. Since the martyrs maintained the same confession of their Faith, they were subjected to another mighty thrashing and returned to prison. Again they were left to become enfeebled, and suffer hunger and thirst in prison. Though their bodies were greatly withered thereby, yet their resolve was undiminished. After this trial, they were transferred to the stadium for an encounter with wild beasts. A number of fierce creatures were set loose against them. The martyrs remained constant in prayer to Christ that they might complete their martyrdom in this contest. God hearkened to His slaves and received their souls, even as they had requested. The wild animals then came forward and reverenced the relics of the saints. Then, without touching them in the least, they scampered away. When night fell, certain Christians went and gathered the relics. They bestowed upon them an honorable interment, glorifying and giving thanks to God.

---

[4] Emesa (Homs in Syria, 34°44′N 36°43′E) was a city of the province of Phoenicia Libanensis, located at the crossing of routes from Palmyra to the sea and from Damascus to the north. It became an autocephalous metropolitan see under the Patriarch of Antioch, after the finding of the head of Saint John the Baptist in February of 453. *The Oxford Dictionary of Byzantium*, s.v. "Emesa."

**On the 29th of January, the holy Church commemorates
the holy siblings and Martyrs SARVELOS and VEVAIA.**

Sarvelos and Vevaia, the holy martyrs, hailed from Edessa[5] during the reign of Emperor Trajan (98-117). The handsome and notable Sarvelos was a priest who ministered at the odious sacrifices of the demonic idols. He would wear gorgeous and splendid apparel, topped with a gold miter upon his head. Many of the Greek pagans considered him a lesser king, while others honored him as a god. He would ofttimes order the people to worship and sacrifice to the idols. On many occasions, the holy Bishop Barsimaios of Edessa would both censure and exhort him. Nevertheless, Sarvelos would not turn from his deception. One day, at a festival of the demons, where Sarvelos was the master of ceremonies at the sacrifices, again the saintly bishop rebuked him, naming him the agent of destruction for many souls.

By the grace of Christ, this time, Sarvelos hearkened to the bishop. Persuaded by his words, Sarvelos and his sister Vevaia believed in Christ. They both received holy Baptism and catechism from the bishop. Thereupon, Sarvelos distributed all his goods among the poor and himself became needy. He then went to live with Saint Barsimaios.

The Martyrdoms of Saints Vevaia and Sarvelos

News of the conversion of the former pagan priest was learned by Lysias, the governor. Lysias ordered that Sarvelos be made to stand before him. It was then that the governor heard him openly confess Christ. Therefore, he ordered that Sarvelos receive stripes from rods. Christ's martyr vehemently condemned Lysias and his idols, together with the emperor who

---

[5] Edessa (modern Urfa in Turkey, 37°08'N 38°45'E), situated in the Mesopotamian plain, is dominated by a high rock and crossed by the Daisan River.

elevated him as governor. Consequently, the governor, mastered by excessive anger, commanded that the saint be flogged with bullwhips. Those that wielded the whip carried this out not only once, but seven times. Then, with iron hand tools, they lacerated his body and burned him with torches. As the martyr underwent all these punishments, he only looked upon God and prayed to Him. The Lord hearkened unto him and lightened His athlete's pains. Lysias, beholding the bravery and patience of the holy man, ordered that they drive nails into his head. When this had taken place, they laid him inside a mechanical contraption where they attempted to saw him in pieces. The holy man, however, was preserved unscathed by all these heinous torments, to the astonishment of all.

All these punishments were also witnessed by his sister, Vevaia. Alone, she approached the governor and announced herself to be a Christian. Lysias also had her thrashed and cast into prison. Further buffeting of Sarvelos with wooden swords was then ordered. This castigation tore open his face. His hands were then tied behind him, and the torturers proceeded to deliver blows to his abdomen. Afterward, they hung him up by one hand and burned divers members of his body. Lysias, on observing that his prisoner was still breathing, ordered that both Sarvelos and Vevaia be executed by decapitation. Thus, together, brother and sister received the crowns of martyrdom. Their august relics were then taken up secretly by certain Christians and honorably interred, to the glory of God.

On the 29th of January, the holy Church commemorates our holy father among the saints, BARSIMAIOS the Confessor, Bishop of Edessa.

Barsimaios, the holy Bishop of Edessa, whom we mentioned above in the account of the Martyrs Sarvelos and Vevaia, was the agent who brought salvation to Sarvelos. This conversion also led Sarvelos' sister Vevaia to holy Baptism. On account of the loss of the pagan priest Sarvelos to Christian piety, Bishop Barsimaios was denounced before the governor of Edessa, Lysias. The bishop, for his confession of Christ before Lysias, received a thrashing and was consigned to a dungeon. Afterward, an edict of toleration was issued by the emperor. This in effect put an end to the persecutions against the Christians. For this cause only was the holy Barsimaios released from prison. He thereupon entered his diocese and resumed his duties. He passed the remainder of his life in a God-pleasing manner and at last was translated to the Lord.

**On the 29ᵗʰ of January, the holy Church commemorates
our venerable Father APHRAATES.[6]**

Aphraates (Aphrahat), our holy father, lived at the time of Emperor
Valens (370). Born and raised in Persia, he was reared in the ways of the
Persians. However, he considered their religion an abomination. In imitation
of his forebears, the Magi who came to the Child Jesus, Aphraates left Persia.
He settled in Edessa, a Christian stronghold. There, he was baptized and
became a Christian. Later, he came upon a hut, outside the city walls, and
confined himself therein. He attracted attention with his God-given gift to
counter the arguments of heretics. Though he was considered an uneducated
barbarian, yet he knew just enough Greek vocabulary to draw crowds of
people. He shredded the arguments of the impious without leaving his hovel,
by holding conversations at the outer door. He did not accept anything from
those who came to see him. They offered bread, prepared food, and
garments, but he accepted none of their offerings. He had one friend who
supplied him with bread. Only after reaching a great age did Aphraates
partake of greens after sunset.

From there, he went on to Antioch and dwelt in a monastery near the
city, where he strived for the salvation of his soul. He never received another
into his cell, monk or layman, nor would he partake of bread or cooked food.
Only once, he accepted a garment from a friend. On a certain occasion, the
imperial general, Anthemios, was sent as an ambassador to Persia by the
emperor. On his return, he passed by Antioch and brought a Persian garment
to the saint. The holy Aphraates declined the gift. The blessed man then
explained politely to the general, saying, "I am already living with a single
companion. My rule is not to live with two. The one who has been with me
for sixteen years until now is agreeable. How can I expel my earlier
companion for another? It would not be just." The general agreed that it
would not be fair. Aphraates then said, "In that case, my excellent friend, I
shall not accept thy tunic. I cannot dwell with two, since the one that has
served me is the more pleasant, or at least in my opinion." The general knew
he was outwitted, and no longer pressed the holy man.

Saint Aphraates, observing that the hierarchs and bishops of the
Church of Christ were exiled by the Arian-minded Emperor Valens, thereby
leaving the rational flock untended and without spiritual guidance, took pity
and left his quietude. He entered Antioch and taught the Christians, strengthening them in Orthodoxy. It happened one day that the emperor met the

---

[6] The Life of Saint Aphraates was recorded by Theodoretos of Kyros (Cyrrhus), in
Number Eight of his *Religious History*. See also *A History of the Monks of Syria,
Cistercian Studies Series: Number Ninety-Eight*, pp. 72-80.

blessed one in the marketplace and questioned him: "Why didst thou abandon thy silence? Why dost thou now travel about the cities?" The saint replied, "Tell me, O emperor, if I were a virgin and hid in a room, and I saw someone setting fire to my father's house, what wouldest thou advise me to do? Indeed, thou shouldest expect me to extinguish the fire. Do thou thus advise me now, because I see that the house of my Father, the Lord, is ablaze, and this is the reason that I hasten about trying to extinguish the flames. If thou meanest to reproach me for leaving my silence, accuse thyself, thou who hast set fire to the house of God, and do not condemn one who is attempting to extinguish it!" One of the emperor's eunuchs heard this rebuke and threatened to put the blessed one to death. However, not long after, this eunuch was visited by the wrath of God for his audacity toward the saint; for while he was about to bathe, he fell into a pool that contained hot water and met an evil death by boiling. A hubbub arose and people were screaming as the water was being drained. When the emperor was informed of his eunuch's sorry end, he too became frightened. He understood that his eunuch paid for his impudence in his person. Valens, holding Aphraates in awe, therefore did not dare to either exile or punish him.

On another occasion, the holy man cured one of Valens' horses, which had caught a caught a disease that resulted in blocked urination. The horse had a fine pedigree, and it was trained to be an excellent mount. Therefore, the creature was very dear to the emperor; but none could treat the horse. At midnight, one of the men attached to Valens' stable and the care of the horses, took the sick horse and went to see Aphraates. He declared his faith and besought the holy man to remedy the ailment by the antidote of his prayer. Abba Aphraates straightway ordered water to be drawn from the well. He made the sign of the Cross over the water, which was to be given to the ailing horse. The abba then took some consecrated oil and anointed the horse's belly. At the touch of the holy man's hand, the disease departed, and natural secretion took place. Then the following day at evening, when Valens was wont to visit the stable, he asked the condition of the ailing horse. He was told that the horse had recovered during the previous night. When Valens inquired how this was achieved, his question was evaded several times. The caretaker who had taken the horse to Aphraates feared to reveal the physician's name, knowing the malice of Valens. When he was forced to divulge who brought about the cure and how it was done, he revealed what had taken place. Although Valens was astonished, he still railed against Jesus. Not much time passed before Valens fell victim to a death by fire during the defeat of the Roman army at the hands of the Goths in 378 near Adrianople.

On another occasion, the saint also made it possible for a certain man to love his wife whom he detested. The husband lived a dissipated life and had taken a concubine with whom he had illicit relations. On account of some magical spell, he loathed his wife and was hostile toward her and was resentful of their marital bonds. The wife bewailed her trouble to the saint. Since he did not receive women, she spoke loudly, imploring him while standing by the outer door. He took pity on her distress and put to nought the magic spell, by prayer and by invoking Christ's name over a flask of oil which she had brought. She was instructed to anoint herself with the oil. As a result, her husband forsook the concubine and her unlawful bed, and brought all his affection to his wife.

In another instance, by sprinkling with water which had been blessed by the saint, the fields and crops of a certain small freeholder were preserved from destruction by locusts. The farmer, a godly man, had come to the saint and implored his help. He had only the one farm to support an entire household and pay the imperial taxes. Abba Aphraates commanded the farmer to fetch a gallon of water. The holy man placed his hand over the water and supplicated God to endue it with power from on high. After he uttered a prayer to God, Abba Aphraates instructed the farmer to sprinkle the water around the boundaries of his farm. He obeyed, and that water served as an inviolable defense for his farm. No locusts ventured upon his property. They came up to the boundary and then retreated before the blessing that barred their entry. At last, after such divine acts and labors, Saint Aphraates, the Persian hermit, surrendered his soul into the hands of God ca. 407-413.

**On the 29ᵗʰ of January, the holy Church commemorates
our venerable Father AKEPSIMAS.**

**On the 29ᵗʰ of January, the holy Church commemorates
the glorious New-Martyr DEMETRIOS of Chios,
who suffered martyrdom in Constantinople (1802).[7]**

Demetrios, the gloriously triumphant new-martyr of the Christ, was born and raised on the famous island of Chios, in the city generally known as Palaiokastron. His parents were not distinguished or notable in this world's sense, but they were rich in their reverence toward God, which piety they transmitted to their children. Demetrios' father was Apostolos, and his mother was Maroulou. Demetrios had at least one older brother, named Zannes. The brothers sought their economic fortune in Constantinople, as did many young men of that day. The brothers, as businessmen, secured employment as

---

[7] The martyrdom of New-martyr Demetrios was borrowed and incorporated into *The Great Synaxaristes* (in Greek) from Athanasios of Parios, teacher of sacred things, in the *Neon Leimonarion*.

merchants with a firm. It was there that Zannes found a wife. After a little time, Demetrios also formed an attachment with a maiden from Stavro-dromion on the European side of the capital. Neither Zannes nor the brothers' employer was aware of Demetrios' engagement. Demetrios chose first to write to his father of his plans, which he had kept private from start to finish.

When Zannes and the employer learned of Demetrios' betrothal, they became indignant and expelled Demetrios from their establishment. Deprived of a livelihood and place to dwell, after a few days, Demetrios was destitute. Then Demetrios, as the younger son mentioned in the Gospel [Lk. 15:11-32], wished to have his share of what was due him. Demetrios then thought to visit a Muslim grandee, a customer of their firm, and collect the past due amount which was owed them. Poor Demetrios! He did not know that his intention to take his portion was a trick of the devil, in order to ensnare him. May God avert from us a pitfall such as that which entrapped Demetrios. Now we should comment here that Demetrios was not only young, that is, between twenty and twenty-two years of age, but he was also exceedingly handsome of countenance. Unknowingly and without any suspicion, due to a moment's inattention, he became his own betrayer in the loss of his soul. Now he had been to this Muslim's house many times in the past, purveying goods. Though he never paid any attention to the grandee's daughter, yet she would always gaze intently and longingly upon him. As another Egyptian temptress [Gen. 39:7] who tried to entice a latter-day Joseph the all-comely, so did this smitten Moslem woman allow the accursed yearnings of her heart to consume her with satanic lust. She, however, kept biding her time, until an opportunity arose to exhibit her shamelessness.

As we were saying, Demetrios went to that house, not having the tiniest notion of her wicked designs and mad deliberations. When she saw him at the threshold of her house, she was filled with unholy joy. She addressed him and said, "Be patient, but do come in and sit until the steward should come." She left the room for a short time, and returned. She was like a demon before him (so he later commented in writing). She had a tray with a cup of coffee and one *tsibouki* or tobacco-pipe. She then said firmly, "Now thou shalt not be able to escape from my hands. Either thou must become a Turk, that is, embrace my religion, or suffer the loss of thy head and thy life." The wretched one replied, "What will I have to do to leave without making a confession?" Though he did not wish to accept their filthy religion, he would sin by inclining to her wish for his conversion. Now when he uttered "What will I have to do to leave without making a confession?" he said these words with much simplicity and artlessness. But then he quickly reckoned the ramifications of yielding. Since he had no wish to suffer everlasting punishment as a sinner, he therefore imagined about being crowned as a martyr. However, he also thought that though he should slay his conscience, he thereafter would speedily correct the situation by giving a profound repentance and good confession. Thus the evil came to realization. He denied—alas!—his most sweet Master Jesus Christ, though his renunciation of his Faith was done with extreme sorrow. When he was alone in that great house, night or day, he shed hot tears. He acknowledged that his affliction was burning his heart. Gloominess, melancholy, and a sad countenance were his constant companions. This did not go unnoticed by the Moslems of that household, who kept a close watch on him. Demetrios perceived that he could not leave unscathed that vile house and that odious woman, without exercising extreme caution, so he bided his time.

He was actually a prisoner in that splendid household. He was kept under close surveillance for fifty-nine days. Then divine grace found the appropriate opportunity, while the Muslims were celebrating Ramadan. When all the Muslims were in a deep sleep, Demetrios made the sign of the Cross over himself. He very quietly then threw himself outside. He did this with great agility and speed. He repaired straight for Stavrodromion, where he hid inside the house of a Christian friend. He poured forth a river of tears and clawed at his face with his fingernails. With bitter wailing and lamentation, he sighed heavily for the evil he suffered. Afterward, he invited Father Agathangelos to that house. He made his confession with fervent tears, and incomparable compunction and contrition of heart. Demetrios' brother Zannes was also invited to that house, where Demetrios received forgiveness from him for past things. Demetrios, however, concealed from his brother his goal of martyrdom. Next Demetrios took up a pen and wrote to his parents. He explained everything from the beginning. He explained how and where the great fall of his denial took place, which we have described earlier. He sought their forgiveness also, since he had grieved them exceedingly. He did reveal to his parents that he was resolved to present himself before the tyrants, in order to confess from the beginning the sweetest Christ Jesus, Whom he had senselessly and mindlessly denied. He told them he was not writing these things to grieve them further; but rather, that they might rejoice and give him their blessing, so he should complete that most-desired contest that his thirsting heart might be quenched. He wrote thus far and then added that "for safekeeping, I have left the letter opened in the hands of my spiritual father, that he might write what shall follow hereafter until my end."

That spiritual father thereafter wrote that Demetrios straightway directed all his energies to the fulfillment of his aim. He wished to leave hurriedly and sacrifice his life, by spilling his blood that he might wash away the previous denial. The thought of death did not in the least diminish his resolve. Others perhaps would have continued with their lives, especially young persons. They would resume seeking after pleasure, wealth, fame, costly attire, and expensive things. Demetrios could have had these worldly attainments, but the blessed one was completely altered. His mind was filled with God and godly things. He now deemed the pleasing and attractive things of this life as abominations. He held them in contempt as dust and dung. He now judged such attachments as injurious to the soul and brokers of destruction. Demetrios wept unceasingly; and from the depths of his heart he called upon the Lord to have mercy and pity him. He did not wish to perish in the end and have his portion with the house of unbelievers. He thereupon implored Christ that he might be vouchsafed to confess Him as true God and to lay down his life for the love of Him.

Thus, Demetrios spent his time in ardent prayer, fervently and ofttimes reciting the stanzas to the most holy Virgin and Theotokos, and as many other prayers as he knew. Then one night, while he was alone, since the women of the household in which he was lodging had gone out visiting, as it was the eve of the Feast of Saint Nicholas, he remained constant in prayer. He then fell asleep and beheld a majestic Woman with an Infant in her arms. She was in the midst of a most beautiful plain. Now in the distance, he espied an executioner standing by. The Woman then spoke to Demetrios and said, "If thou wilt not fall into the hands of this executioner, thou shalt not inherit this most delightful plain." The young man was then awakened from his sleep. He understood that it was the will of God that he should undergo martyrdom, which disclosure gladdened his soul. Henceforth, he was filled with greater desire. He confessed and made known this visitation to his spiritual father. Nevertheless, Demetrios was unable to receive his blessing to go forth, since his spiritual father feared that perhaps all this was just the result of human reasoning and thoughts. He recited to Demetrios those words in Gethsemane of the Master to His sleeping disciples and Peter: "The spirit indeed is willing, but the flesh is weak [Mt. 26:41]." Father Agathangelos therefore recommended that Demetrios join a monastic brotherhood. He advised Demetrios to have fellowship there with, and struggle alongside, other Christians. In such a place, he could also make a good confession and be saved. This and other similar suggestions were proffered by the spiritual father. Despite these other proposals, Demetrios persisted in seeking a blessing. The spiritual father gave place, but not entirely. He wished to put Demetrios to the test. In order to prove his resolve, he gave him a rule, with fasts, prayers, prostrations, and the reading of a number of spiritual books. Either this rule would make trial of him, or it would contribute and help him in the contest that lay ahead.

The good athlete began to train. He utterly cut off everything and subsisted only on bread and water, partaking once every twenty-four hours.

During the day he spent his time studying spiritual books, which brought him to shed copious tears. He confessed daily. His nights were passed in prayer. He smote his breast and his head, saying, "Woe is me! How did I do such an evil thing?" On two occasions he tore at his face with his nails, as he bewailed falling into such impiety. His spiritual father consoled him, telling him that the compassion of God is boundless. He urged him to beseech God to reveal in what manner, if it were the divine will, Demetrios could achieve his goal. After the passage of fifteen days, Father Agathangelos thought it prudent to extend Demetrios' rule and struggles that he might further beg God's mercy. The young man hearkened and carried out his rule with joy. He increased the fasts, vigils, prayers, and tears. He made prostrations, going to his bare knees on wooden boards during a very cold season. He then passed five days in all-night vigils of prayer with extreme hardship to his undressed body.

During the fifth night, at the eleventh hour, as Sunday morning was drawing near, Demetrios was praying in the dark, because he had extinguished the candle. He then beheld a superabundance of light and heard a voice most sweet coming from that light which said to him, "Rejoice, martyr of Christ, Demetrios, and take courage! By the intercessions of our Lady the Theotokos, her Son, our Lord Jesus Christ, is with thee and shall empower thee, that thou mightest complete the course of martyrdom courageously and briefly." The valiant man, upon hearing these words, fell to the floor prostrate. With tears was he glorifying and thanking God and the Virgin Theotokos. As the new day dawned, he quickly sent for his spiritual father. When Father Agathangelos arrived, he observed that Demetrios was soaked from the torrents of tears he had shed. Demetrios, still weeping, began recounting the vision. Both the spiritual father and Demetrios then gave glory to the all-good God. By this vision, the spiritual father knew the counsel of God. He then made use of all that our holy Church prescribes. He recited the expiatory prayers, anointed Demetrios with holy Chrism, and communicated to him the immaculate Mysteries of the all-holy body and blood of Christ. Then, on Tuesday morning, with tears welling up in his eyes, he dismissed Demetrios. He offered up prayer that Demetrios might have as his guide and helper the Lady Theotokos, even as it was revealed to him in that divine revelation that Christ would be with him until his last breath.

Demetrios then left that place and went boldly to the *kaymakam*, the head official of the district, and addressed him: "Effendi (sir), it is generally known that I was a Christian and that with force and tyrannical methods they brought me to your profane and contemptible religion. For I not only was but, even now, am a Christian; and a Christian I shall die. On account of this have I come hither that I might confess before thee that though I previously stumbled, yet now I proclaim the truth of my holy Faith. I therefore concede that I erred greatly, and now acknowledge that there is only one true Faith. The Faith of which I speak is that of the pious Orthodox Christians." After he had spoken such words, Demetrios then cast to the ground his head-covering. He then stood upright and silent. The *kaymakam*, witnessing such daring words and the display of contempt, gave the order to bring the head-covering to him. The official began speaking to Demetrios in a gentle and soft tone of voice. He could not help but observe that Demetrios was not giving the least consideration to what he was saying, but instead boldly scorned his every word. The official then commanded that Demetrios be cast into the prison, until a second examination could be scheduled. He also ordered two sets of chains for Demetrios, one for his feet and the other for his neck. Thereupon, that evening, they kept him chained and lying prone on the ground, which position the Turks called *toumbrouki*. The ever-memorable Demetrios not only refused to lose heart or become downcast, but even rejoiced in very truth. It was as if he were found taking his ease in some royal chamber, with every comfort and convenience. Therefore, that entire night he offered up prayer, glorifying and beseeching God with tears that he might be accounted worthy not only of a good beginning but also of a blessed end.

A number of days passed until the judgment hall was opened. Once again, Demetrios was commanded to stand for a second appearance. During the examination, they plied him with blandishments and promises. They offered him both position and rank, a customary ploy of the tyrants before the divine martyrs. The Muslims observed the young man's immovable resolve from the start. He was determined to loathe and spurn all their promises as opposing God and injurious to the soul. Consequently, the Muslims began to threaten him in an attempt to strike terror, but his response to them was "do your worst." He then said, "I am prepared to endure every kind of wound and torture for the love of my most sweet Jesus Christ. I therefore say to you not to lose any time. But do whatever you have to do, for I came for this very reason." One of the officials, the *kaymakam*, answered angrily, "So sayest thou how thou wilt endure all, so that the old women might venerate thee. But I should much prefer to sever thy head suddenly, that thou mightest be condemned." The martyr of Christ then answered, "Before thou shouldest cut off my head, God would cut off thine own life; and thou, as one ungodly, shalt go to everlasting condemnation." Thus spoke the martyr, to which the official responded with a command to his men that Demetrios be returned to the prison until the following day, when the sentence of beheading would be carried out. The following day, another command was issued that the martyr be brought to the judgment hall. At that same time, news was received that Capetan Pasha, that is, the Turkish admiral of the fleet, had arrived. As the *kaymakam* went to receive him, divine wrath overtook that official, and he suddenly fell and gave up his spirit, thus fulfilling the prophecy pronounced by the martyr. A new *kaymakam* was installed. There was not a day that he was absent at the judgment hall. At times he employed flatteries upon Demetrios, and at other times he made threats. The brave athlete in both instances remained adamant in the course he set for himself. As Demetrios was unyielding, he was sent back to prison. Demetrios spent seven days in that prison, during which time the ungodly still attempted to mislead him with their fallacious reasoning. While he was immured, he was again vouchsafed that same vision, the one which he beheld in the house where he had been hiding. On the eighth day, once more was he brought before the *kaymakam*. Demetrios began insulting their religion in order to enrage them that they might end his case sooner. The tyrant then ordered that his servants take Demetrios to the city judge, whom the Turks called Stabul effendi. He also bade his men to deliver blows to the prisoner and drag him through the streets. Predictably, the judge, in accordance with their custom, offered the usual blandishments. The judge even went so far as to feign that he grieved for Demetrios' youth. If Demetrios would recant, the judge promised, they would do whatever they could to bestow favors upon him. When they saw that he disdained their lofty positions and ranks, they became wild and hostile in order to terrorize him. They were saying such things as: "Since thou dost despise whatever is offered thee and dost not wish to hear, I shall be compelled to hand down a judicial decree (*ilam*), ordering a death without mercy." Straightway, the martyr, with a great voice, cried out, "To God do I surrender my soul. I am ready!"

After making this declaration, Demetrios was sent back to prison. There, they stretched him out on the wood and administered a pitiless and mighty thrashing, so that he received more than seven hundred blows with rods. Afterward, Demetrios was placed in the stocks, where he was left utterly without any care or attention. His punishment was made the more bitter since it was excessively cold. The executioners therefore poured water underneath him, which congealed to ice, thereby ushering in tremendous pain and suffering to his flesh. The courageous contestant of Christ endured with great patience the affliction brought by the painful wounds, the frozen water, and the wooden stocks. All the while, he kept giving glory to God. He also prayed and entreated God to vouchsafe him the blessed end of martyrdom. Christ's goodly martyr therefore remained in that terrible place, being followed by two sets of observers. The temptations they alone engendered would have made Demetrios worthy of all the crowns of heaven.

The first of these onlookers was that loose and brazen woman who from the beginning laid a trap with cords. When she learned that Demetrios was in the imperial prison, that mad woman went alone to see the *kaymakam*.

She claimed that she had an outstanding account with Demetrios and requested permission that she might visit the prisoner and make an exchange with him. That senseless woman was hoping that she would be able to win him over. She received permission and went to the prison, where she met with Demetrios. Let each one guess how such a woman kindled all the flames to incite love. In general, she was nothing other than a living instrument of the satanic powers. What did not come out of her mouth? What did she not try? What allurements did she not use, so that she might have leverage and relax and make flaccid the brave athlete's soul? But by the grace of the victory-bestowing Savior and Christ, that dreadful trial of Belial (Beliar) was in vain and came to nought. Instead, the gloriously triumphant Martyr Demetrios was shown to be firm and steadfast in Christ. That shameless and bad woman then departed, saying, "I received my account, and so now do whatever you will."

The other observers were Christians, and, being from Chios, Demetrios' compatriots. Though unseen, they dreaded the contests that Demetrios would undergo. They feared that he might give way and decide for impiety, not being able to hold out during the tortures. They therefore endeavored to pay off those in power with a sufficient sum of money, in order to secure Demetrios' release, reasoning that the Muslims could always throw out the case by declaring the prisoner insane. Those holding Demetrios nodded their consent to the exchange. Their zeal for Islam was extinguished when they were inundated by their avarice. But what happened? The guileless and sincere athlete learned of the Christians' attempt to have him released. He thought they were trying to confound him, so he deemed them his great enemies, for they would deprive him of the martyric crown. It is for this crown that he disdained everything and patiently endured every machination used against him. He therefore sent them a message that, for their part, they should rather offer up prayer and supplication in the churches that he might be strengthened by Christ, so as to finish the course before him in a God-pleasing manner. Bravo! Well done! Hear, hear! O gloriously triumphant Martyr of Christ Demetrios! He showed himself truly and incomparably a martyr in mind and in heart and in disposition to the end! Although those good Christians bowed to his wishes, they still were opposed to the martyr's counsel, their only reason being their fear that he would suffer and that the outcome was uncertain. For they had already been apprised of some of the atrocities that the executioners had carried out against Demetrios. Later on, at the burial of the martyr, an executioner disclosed that a red-hot brick was placed on Demetrios' head and face at burial. This barbarous treatment and many other cruel acts were inflicted upon Demetrios. The people, however, came to praise Demetrios, because he persevered and remained vigilant to the end. But let us now return to the proper sequence of events of the blessed one's contest.

Now it was nine o'clock in the morning when the final round of the contest took place. The martyr was made to stand for the last time before the tribunal. His unshaken resolve was evident to all. Consequently, the decision to put him to death was meted out; that is, he was sentenced to decapitation at a place called Baloum Bazaar. They then quickly fettered his hands. They left him barefooted and his head uncovered. Next they made ready to bring him to the appointed place of execution. During the whole time that he was conveyed to the site, he kept crying out to the Christians to pardon him and asking that they beseech God on his account. They finally arrived at the execution site. The executioner asked Demetrios, "Where wilt thou kneel down?" Straightway, Demetrios fell to his knees. The executioner, according to the usual procedure, endeavored to tie a blindfold on the condemned prisoner. However, the stout-hearted athlete of Christ did not wish it. Then, as he was kneeling, he cried out with a great voice, "Remember me, O Lord, in Thy kingdom!" Now he pronounced this thrice, and then bowed his head before the executioner's sword. He surrendered his blessed soul into the hands of God on the 29th of January, at about twenty-two years of age, in the flower of young manhood and at that time of life which is most beautiful, pleasant, and promising. He disregarded all the things of this world and gladly gave it all away in one swoop. This was done with all the right powers and judgment of his mind. He preferred death to this most sweet life that he might gain the everlasting life.

Thus, by his words and actions, many martyr-loving Christians, both clergy and laity, were persuaded of the divine will in the blessed slaughter of New-martyr Demetrios. They hastened eagerly to follow the events surrounding him. The Hagarenes raised their hands and weapons against the Christians who sought to take a portion of the sacred relics. They beat the Christians and pushed them back, but they were unable to oppose the press of people. Some managed to dip their handkerchiefs or swabs of cotton in the holy Demetrios' martyric blood. Others seized the hairs from his sacred head. Still others attempted to take a portion from his neck or a swatch from his garments. Many suffered blows at the hands of the Muslims, but those Christians remarked, "The martyr died for the love of the Christ. And we, that we might receive some gift of grace from him, what great evil is it if we should receive two or three stripes from rods?"

Much zeal was in the camp of the Christians, so that one reverent clergyman made an agreement with the executioner. In exchange for the towel that would be used at the beheading of the martyr, that is, in the wiping of the blood from the executioner's blade, a payment of twenty-five *grosia* (piasters) was agreed upon. The exchange was made for the white towel, which held no design. Then—behold the miracle!—as the plain towel was unfolded, it was as if an invisible hand inscribed many a cross with the martyr's blood. Now not only one or two persons observed the studied design of crosses, but many folk with one mind and voice acclaimed and wrote about this extraordinary wonder.

The third day after the beheading of the martyr, an order was published. The remains were not to be given to the Christians, but instead were to be cast into the sea. The holy God, however, dispensed otherwise when, in a mysterious manner, the executioner was well disposed to convey the relics to the isle of Prote, the largest of the Princes' Islands in the Sea of Marmara. The saint was buried in the monastery located there. The executioner was present among those who had plucked up courage and attended. Despite the fear of trespassing the imperial order, a multitude of Christians was in attendance. They came in their own vessels. The hegumen of the monastery descended the following day into the city. He announced all that had taken place and verified that the towel used at the execution was adorned with crosses from the martyr's blood. He also testified to the ineffable fragrance which wafted from the towel. None of the Christians doubted that God accepted the shedding of the martyr's blood. Also, many miracles were wrought through God's saint for all those who invoked Saint Demetrios with faith. One such account is spoken of by the spiritual father of the martyr, the Priest Agathangelos, in a letter to a certain priest, his spiritual father, named Philotheos, the superior at the Church of Saint Phokas. Father Agathangelos speaks of a fire that took place in the district of Maktze Sarai shortly after the saint's martyrdom.

At that time, there was a Christian who had a pharmaceutical factory. During one night, he heard a voice say "Fire!" He rose up quickly and sped off to protect his factory. In the commotion, he roused his children from sleep, but his wife put them to bed. She too then fell asleep. It then seemed to her that she heard a knock at the door. She then observed two youths, clad in white, enter her home, each bearing a lamp in his right hand. The youths inquired of her, "Where is thy husband?" She answered, "He went off to see about the fire." Then one of the youths said to her, "And we also, on account of the fire, have come down and toiled greatly, until we should find a ship. We came that we might assist the Christians and thy husband, since these last few days he has kept company with them." The wife then asked, "And from whence are you?" They answered, "We are from the island." The one of them said, "I am Demetrios, and this is Araitzopoulos, who suffered martyrdom for Christ many years ago. Up until now, your factory has suffered no evil. However, thou art to tell thy husband to come to repentance, lest from a bondwoman he should lose his body and soul. If he, however, repents, God, Who is compassionate, shall deliver him from every evil thing. Let him go to Stavrodromion, where there is a spiritual father. Let him make his confession before him and do what is imposed upon him." When her husband returned, she disclosed all that she had seen. He wasted no time visiting the aforementioned spiritual father, and made a tear-filled confession. He also spoke of those things which occurred to the martyr, as he and others heard the executioner's descriptions when they were together at Prote.

This too is a beautiful and paradoxical phenomenon. We hear that the saints took up a great labor to find a ship. They did this that they might help the Christians. These were the very Christians who had piously followed Saint Demetrios' martyrdom and had come together, at no small peril, to accompany the martyr to burial. The Martyr Demetrios was aware of their pains and felt obliged to requite them. The martyr therefore also repaid the favor to the factory owner who also had participated in the ceremony. The martyr did not allow the factory to suffer any loss from the fire. The martyr not only rescued his factory, but also brought the owner to repentance. Let us therefore not criticize those martyr-loving Christians who follow the martyrs closely and subscribe to them; for such persons and their devotions are well-pleasing to God and the divine martyrs.

We have no doubt that the gloriously victorious Martyr Demetrios received great grace from God, and that he has wrought many extraordinary wonders. Most of these miracles are unknown to us, but let the one we have recounted suffice to describe the grace bestowed upon martyrs. Thus we have heard: "As I live," saith the Lord, "I will only glorify those who glorify Me; and he who despises Me shall be dishonored [cf. 1 Kgs. (1 Sam.) 2:30]." To our only God in Trinity, be glory, dominion, and veneration, to the endless ages of the ages. Amen.

Through the intercessions of Thy Saints,
O Christ God, have mercy on us. Amen.

On the 30th of January, the holy Church commemorates our œcumenical teachers and holy Fathers BASIL the Great, GREGORY the Theologian, and JOHN Chrysostom.[1]

The three holy hierarchs, Saints Basil the Great, Gregory the Theologian, and John of the Golden-mouth are commemorated today by reason of the following event. In 1081, Emperor Alexios I Komnenos of Constantinople (1057-1118) came to the throne with the support of the military aristocracy, after Nikephoros III Botaneiates. At that time there came to pass in Constantinople a contention among men of high repute and virtue. This vigorous controversy came about in regard to the three great teachers and hierarchs, and which of them should be the greatest. Some preferred the great Basil on account of his treatises, which vividly and articulately examined the nature of things in existence. This group also lauded Saint Basil's virtues, not only likening him to the angels, but even believing that he rivaled them. They also approved of his practise of not absolving sinners in an easy or offhand manner. They applauded his serious disposition, and his freedom from being possessed of anything earthly. Now this same group also would have placed the divine Chrysostom in a lower place than Basil, since they believed that he readily absolved sinners.

Yet another faction elevated the holy Chrysostom over both Basil and Gregory, maintaining that his teachings, filled with wise and agile expressions, guided all and drew sinners to repentance. This group mostly favored Saint John on account of the multitude of his mellifluous writings, and the loftiness and breadth of his thoughts.

Others, however, favored the writings of Saint Gregory the Theologian and gave him the preeminent position. They enjoyed his elegant and diversified manner of writing. His elevated and flowery style surpassed that of both the philosophers of Greek wisdom and Church writers to that date.

---

[1] See the individual dates of their chief commemorations, as follows: Saint Basil on the 1st of January; Saint Gregory on the 25th of January; and, Saint John on the 13th of November. To these three great hierarchs, Metropolitan John of Efchaita penned two encomia and one divine office. His two encomia are extant at Vatopedi, and one text is found at Iveron. Saint John of Damascus also composed an encomium, which text is extant in the Athonite monasteries of the Great Lavra and Dionysiou. The accounts of these three hierarchs were also authored by Agapios the Cretan, and is found in the *Neon Paradeison*. A sermon by Hierodeacon Makarios Patmios is found in *Evangelike Salpingi*. Twenty-four stanzas commemorating the three hierarchs were composed by Father Gerasimos Mikrayiannanites.

The Three Hierarchs:
Saints Basil the Great, John Chrysostom, and Gregory the Theologian

Thus the Christians were split into three rival groups, which named themselves Johannites, or Basilians, or Gregorians. Consequently, since the Christians could not settle the issue, a visitation, not a vision, was vouchsafed to Metropolitan John Mavropous (ca. 1050-1075) of Efchaita,[2] a holy hierarch

---

[2] Efchaita (now Avkat) was a small city of Pontos, west of Amaseia, between the rivers Alyos and Iris in Asia Minor. It had been a city of the Armeniakon theme. From the works of Metropolitan John, we known that Saint Theodore the recruit was greatly revered in that city. The city was originally a suffragan bishopric of Amaseia, but it became an autocephalous archbishopric by the 7th C. It had been a metropolis under Leo VI (r. 886-912), but no remains have survived. *The Oxford Dictionary of Byzantium*, s.v. "Euchaita."

who attained to the summit of virtue. He was a notable and erudite man, well acquainted with Hellenic wisdom, of which his writings bear witness to his learning. He was also acclaimed for his writing of hymnographic canons and the lives of the saints.[3]

Metropolitan John affirmed that the three holy hierarchs appeared to him first individually and then together. He says that they spoke to him as with one mouth, saying, "We are as one before God. Even as thou dost see, we neither have any opposition to one another nor have any quarrel among ourselves; but in accordance with the times in which we happened to live, each of us, moved by the divine Spirit, taught and wrote about various themes. Now as much as we learned by the Holy Spirit, these same teachings were also published for the salvation of the people. There exists among us no first or second place; for if the one should speak, straightway the other two also are in agreement. For this reason, command the rivaling factions not to remain divided on account of us; for even after our translation, as when we were among the living, we are concerned and eager to bring peace, unity and oneness of mind among the faithful, and not to be the cause of division. Therefore, when it seems fitting to thee, unite our commemorations on one day, and compose a troparion for the feast; for we are as one before God. And be certain that we shall cooperate toward the salvation of those who celebrate our general commemoration, since we have boldness before God."

After the saints uttered these things, they appeared to ascend again into the heavens, illumined with brilliant light and calling one another by name. Therefore, John of Efchaita was stirred in his heart and set about doing as the divine hierarchs gave him charge. Indeed, he calmed the multitude of people and brought peace among the contending factions, because he was known by all as a virtuous man. Therefore, his words were mighty and persuasive. He delivered to the Church of God the common celebration of these saints. And behold, thou reader, the understanding and discernment of this divine man. When he found that the month of January already dedicated three days toward the commemoration of these very saints (the great Basil on the 1st, the theologian Gregory on the 25th, and the divine Chrysostom on the 27th), he united their celebration on the 30th of January. The namesake of grace, Metropolitan John, was enlightened and directed by the holy hierarchs

---

[3] The Paphlagonian-born writer, Metropolitan John, had been a teacher in Constantinople, a court rhetorician under Constantine IX, and later a monk in the Monastery of Prodromos in Petra at Constantinople. He reposed in the capital. *Oxford*, s.v. "Mauropous, John."

when he composed a service, adorning it with superior canons and troparia, and an encomium, which was meet for such great fathers of the Church.

The three hierarchs, according to their physical appearance and facial characteristics, are described as follows. The divine Chrysostom was short in stature, lean, and slightly built. He was both pale and fair-skinned. He had a large head, long nose, and broad nostrils. His eyes, large and deep set, shone forth with beauty and grace, though his other bodily members seemed afflicted. He had a towering forehead, etched with many wrinkles, and with no hair on top. He wore a small but comely beard, which was putting forth a few white hairs. His cheeks were sunken from fasting. He was acclaimed for his accurate, florid, and eloquent words and expressions, and the breadth of his understanding, teachings, and wisdom, which surpassed those of all the wise men and rhetoricians of the Greeks. He not only became great in both practical and theoretical philosophy, but also surpassed all others by his virtues. He was a fount springing forth love, charity, and philanthropy. He reposed at the age of sixty-three.

Saint Basil the Great was a tall and slender man, but he looked emaciated. His complexion was swarthy and yellowish (on account of his liver ailment). His nose was long, and his eyebrows were rounded. A few wrinkles marked his face, and his cheeks were large. He had bushy hair at his temples which twisted up, encircling his head. Yet it gave the appearance of being slightly cropped. His beard, sufficiently long, was black, sprinkled with grey. Now he succeeded in attaining to every kind of learning. In anything that was taught in art or science, this saint surpassed all his distinguished contemporaries and those from times past. Saint Basil not only pursued secular studies, but also struggled and practised that true philosophy; and through activity he ascended to contemplation. He reposed at the age of forty-nine.

Saint Gregory the Theologian was of average height and build. Though somewhat pale, his countenance appeared grace-filled and his features elegant. His eyebrows were even and his nose broad. His right eye appeared somewhat inflamed when compared to his left, for in his boyhood he suffered an injury to the surface of that eye. His thick beard was substantial, but not very long. He was almost bald, except for the tuft of white hair that went round to meet his full turning beard. His easy-to-approach manner was mild and mellow. It is worthy of remark that if it were possible for one to become a living and breathing pillar made up of the virtues, this pillar certainly would be the great Gregory. This is because he was more than conqueror in both the active and contemplative life, and completely prevailed over all others with his wisdom, words, and dogmatic teachings. Thereupon, he deservedly received the title of theologian. He reposed at the age of sixty-two.

Since these three hierarchs labored for our salvation, we ought to commemorate their feast and please them as much as possible. These thrice-blessed saints have no other concern or thought, other than to make steadfast Orthodox piety with the pure confession of the Faith in God the unoriginate Father, God the only-begotten Son, and God the Holy Spirit Who proceeds from the Father.

Through the intercessions of this sacred triad of hierarchs, may the Church be granted peace, and may we be vouchsafed to glorify together the Father, Son and Holy Spirit, the one God, to Whom is due all glory, honor, and veneration, now and ever and unto the ages of ages. Amen.

On the 30th of January, the holy Church commemorates the holy Hieromartyr HIPPOLYTUS, Bishop of Rome, and those with him: CENSORINUS, SABAINUS, CHRYSE, AURAS, FELIX, MAXIMUS, HERCULES, VENERIUS, STYRACIUS, MENAS, COMMODUS, HERMES, MAURUS, EUSEBIUS, RUSTICUS, MONAGRIUS, AMANDINUS, OLYMPIUS, CYPRUS, THEODORE, TRIBUNUS, MAXIMUS the Priest, ARCHELAUS the Deacon, and CYRIACUS the Bishop. [4]

Hippolytus, the hieromartyr, and the holy martyrs with him, lived at the time of Emperor Claudius II, surnamed Gothicus (268-270), and Vicarius the governor, who was also called Vulpius Romulus, in the year 269. Among the Roman Christians whom we commemorate today, Censorinus, a leading statesman and magistrate, was first denounced as a Christian. When he was questioned, he confessed Christ with forthrightness. On account of the many miracles which he wrought, including resurrecting a dead man, all the soldiers present at his trial came to believe in Christ. They numbered twenty men, and all of them were beheaded.

The blessed Chryse was distinguished for her family background, piety, and being a Christian. Therefore, she was suspended from a great height and lashed with strips of rawhide, until her flesh was rent asunder. This was followed by a further thrashing, when she was stretched out on the ground and beaten with heavy rods. Next, the executioners took torches and

---

[4] Variants of the martyrs' names are given elsewhere, such as Sabinus for Sabainus and Herculianus for Hercules. Although the name of Auras (Latin *aureus* for "golden") in some lists is associated with that of Chryse (Greek for "gold"), yet it may be the name of another martyr, as some have interpreted Auras as Ares. The names of Theodore and Tribunus have in some *Synaxaristae* been recorded as one, that is, Theodore the tribune.

burned her sides. She was then cast into prison. Thus, Christ's handmaiden was tried like gold in a crucible. Afterward, they took her from the prison and crushed her cheeks with rocks and her spine with lead spheres. Following this, they tied a boulder to her neck and cast her into the sea. Thus, blessed Chryse, after passing through the tempest of temptation without foundering, received the indissoluble laurel of mar-

tyrdom.

Saint Sabainus confessed Christ, and so they tied heavy rocks around his neck. Later they suspended him from a post and flogged him with whips, and with torches burned his sides. During these tortures, he gave thanks to the Lord and surrendered his soul into His hands.

Upon learning of all these brave confessions of the Faith, Saint Hippolytus, Bishop of Rome, was stirred by divine zeal. He therefore appeared before the governor and rebuked him. The governor, driven by rage, ordered his men to strike the holy man on the face. The blessed one withstood many additional pains along with his presbyters and deacons. Finally, they tied the hands

Saint Hippolytus

and feet of these courageous Christians and cast them into the deep waters of the sea. Thus, the ever-memorable ones received the undying laurels of martyrdom.[5]

---

[5] Saint Hippolytus was a man of great learning and the most important theological writer in the early days of the Roman Church. He wrote in Greek and may have been a disciple of Saint Irenaeos (ca. 130-ca. 200). In Blessed Jerome's work *On Illustrious Men* (LXI), he comments upon Hippolytus the bishop, writing: "He was bishop of a church in some city. When he wrote the *Date of the Pasch and the Determination of Times* (the *Chronicon*, Clavis Patrum Graecorum or CPG 1896, Turnhout), he had used as the first year that of Emperor Alexander (Severus 222-235). He established a canon of a cycle of sixteen years, which gave the opportunity to Eusebius for the composition of a cycle of nineteen years. He wrote various commentaries on the Scriptures, of which I have found the following: *On the Hexaemeron, On Exodus, On the Canticle of Canticles, On Genesis, On Zechariah, On the Psalms, On Isaiah, On*

(continued...)

On the 30th of January, the holy Church commemorates the holy Martyr THEOPHILOS the New.

Theophilos, the holy martyr, lived at the time of the Orthodox rulers, Emperor Constantine VI and Empress-regent Irene (ca. 785), and was born and reared in Constantinople. He held the rank of military governor (*strategos*)[6] in the Kibyrrhaiotai theme.[7] At that time, the Romans launched a campaign against the Saracens, or rather the Hagarenes. He embarked on this campaign with two subordinate admirals,[8] but they were envious of him. At the commencement of hostilities, he attacked the Saracens with his forces. He was followed by his two admirals. With the employment of diverse

---

[5](...continued)

Daniel, On the Apocalypse, On Proverbs, On Ecclesiastes, On Saul and the Pythoness, On Antichrist, On the Resurrection, Against Marcion, On the Pascha, and *Against All Heresies."*

Butler writes that the Roman martyrology (13th of August) has proposed various identities for Saint Hippolytus the martyr. One is mentioned in the *Acta* of Saint Laurence. Another account speaks of him being a priest who censured Pope Zephyrinus (199-217) for not quickly denouncing heresy. On the election of his successor, Callistus I (217-222), he severed communion with the Roman Church. With Pope Pontianus (230-235), he was banished to Sardinia during the persecution of Maximinus (235), and was reconciled to the Church. He died a martyr's death on Sardinia. Afterward, his relics were translated to the cemetery on the Via Tiburtina. *Butler's Lives of the Saints,* Volume III:315, 316.

"There are not many authentic materials for a biography of Saint Hippolytus," according to the "Introductory Notice" to Hippolytus' works in English, arranged by A. Roberts, J. Donaldson and A. C. Coxe. They, however, note: "There can be no reasonable doubt but that he was a bishop, and passed the greater portion of his life in Rome and its vicinity....It is generally maintained that he was Bishop of Portus, a harbor of Rome, at the northern mouth of the Tiber, opposite Ostia." See Ante-Nicene Fathers, V:6. "Not less interesting, and vastly more important, was the discovery, at Mount Athos, in 1842, of the long-lost *Philosophumena* of Hippolytus....It is now sufficiently established as the work of Hippolytus." Ibid., pp. 3, 4.

[6] The *strategos* of Kibyrrhaiotai was a naval commander. He commanded seventy ships and about three thousand men from his headquarters, apparently at Attaleia. *Oxford*, s.v. "Kibyrrhaiotai."

[7] Kibyrrhaiotai was first among the naval themes (a military division and territorial unit), comprising the coasts of Asia Minor from Miletos to Cilicia, together with the interior of Caria, Lycia, Pamphylia, and parts of Isauria. Ibid.

[8] The naval commander's main subordinates were the *katepano* of the Mardaites (a people for hire, inhabiting the Amanus mountains and the Taurus region), the *ek prosopou* of Syllaion, and the *droungarios* of Cos. *Oxford*, s.v. "Mardaites" and "Kibyrrhaiotai."

military tactics and war engines, he overpowered the enemy. But only for a short while was he victorious. The two admirals, who hated the blessed one, abandoned him. Since the Saracens had a larger fleet, they surrounded Theophilos, won the advantage, and captured him alive.

They then brought him to their country and confined him to prison for four years. At length, they removed him from his cell. As they sacrificed to their gods, they insisted that he also offer sacrifice and deny Christ. But he would not yield to their flatteries or threats. Since they could not persuade the saint, they beheaded him, and the blessed one received the unfading crown of martyrdom.

On the 30th of January, the holy Church commemorates the holy New-martyr HATZI THEODORE of Mytilene (1784).[9]

Theodore, the blessed new-martyr, was from Mytilene (Lesbos).[10] He was a family man with a wife and children. One day, he became angry over a turn of events, denied Christ, and became a Moslem. Alas for his rashness! Not long after, the darkness lifted, and Theodore came to his senses and repented. He left his home and sailed to Mount Athos, where he remained for a long time. Theodore confessed his sin and performed the prescribed penance. After he was anointed with the holy Chrism, received the immaculate Mysteries, and was cleansed, Theodore returned to his country.

Some time later, with the blessing and advice of his spiritual father, he was encouraged to appear before the judge, asking him the following: "If one were the victim of injustice, is it possible to receive justice again?" The judge replied, "Yes, it is possible." The holy man continued, "I had my Faith, which was pure gold; then I was deceived and misled by the devil and denied it, accepting your religion as a better one. But now I have come to my senses and recognize that my Faith truly is pure gold, while yours is not even lead." With these words, he took off his turban and tossed it at the feet of the judge. He then proceeded to put on a black *skouphos* (monastic cap), which he carried under his arm. The judge retorted, "O man, what art thou doing? Hast thou taken leave of thy senses?" Theodore replied, "No, I am in my

---

[9] The martyrdom of New-martyr Hatzi Theodore was taken from the *Neon Martyrologion*, 3rd ed. (pp. 213, 214), and incorporated into *The Great Synaxaristes* (in Greek).

[10] Mytilene or Lesbos is the third largest of the Greek islands, and lies at the very edge of the northeast Aegean. In 1344, Emperor John Palaiologos ceded the island to the Genoese. From 1462 until the 1821 War of Independence, it was occupied by the Turks, but did not achieve liberation until 1912.

right senses and have all my wits about me." The judge repeated himself many times, but the martyr declared, "I am in control of my mind; I know what I am saying." As a result, the judge ordered his men to put him in jail. Later they brought him out, and the judge attempted in every way to make Theodore return to Islam.

The judge, perceiving that the martyr was steadfast and adamant in Orthodoxy, decided to put him to death. So he sent him to the *nazir* (minister) named Omer agha, who employed all forms of flattery and promises to make him yield. But the martyr would give no answer except the following: "I was deceived and gave away my Faith, which is pure gold, and I received yours, which is nothing but lead. Now I have come to my senses and perceive my folly, and that is why I confess that I am a Christian named Theodore." Those who were assigned to execute him, took Theodore and lashed him brutally. They also smote him on the thighs with a sword, which blows hurled him over the balcony railing of the *saray* (palace or government house). Seeing he survived the fall, they then led him to the place of execution. Theodore offered no resistance whatsoever; instead, his face was radiant and bright as he spoke to those who were about to execute him. It seemed that death was not death for him, but life. Then they said to him, "Behold, we are about to hang you." And he answered them joyfully, "Where is the rope?" The executioners handed it to him. He kissed it, put it around his neck, and remarked, "Now take me wheresoever you wish."

The executioners seized the martyr and brought him to the place of execution called Parmak Kapi. Before them paraded the herald, proclaiming: "Whosoever denies his faith shall suffer in this manner." The saint was saying his prayers. He also asked forgiveness of all the Christians that were present. Next, of his own accord, he ascended a high rock and surrendered himself to the executioners who hanged him. Thus, the blessed one received the crown of martyrdom in 1784. The Turks cast his sacred body into the sea, but within a few days it was washed ashore. Thereupon, the Christians received the judge's permission and buried the martyr's relics with honor in the Church of Saint John the Forerunner, at a site called Mothona. But later, a search failed to reveal the relics, and no one knows their whereabouts to this day.

Through the intercessions of Thy Saints,
O Christ God, have mercy on us. Amen.

On the 31ˢᵗ of January, the holy Church commemorates
the holy Wonder-workers, unmercenary Healers,
and Martyrs KYROS (Cyrus) and JOHN,
together with the holy Martyr ATHANASIA
and her three daughters, Virgin-martyrs
THEOKTISTE, THEODOTE, and EVDOXIA.[1]

Kyros (Cyrus) and John, the holy wonder-workers and unmercenary physicians, lived during the reign of the impious Emperor Diocletian in 292. The renowned and brilliant Kyros was born in the illustrious city of Alexandria of Egypt, the city built by Alexander the Great (d. B.C. 323) and named in his honor. John hailed from Edessa of Mesopotamia, which is commonly known today as Urfa. Kyros was brought up a faithful Christian by his parents and was virtuous in conduct. He was a most competent physician by occupation. His infirmary can be seen to this day, as everyone there well knows, for a church was later built on the site and dedicated to the holy Three Children; there, miracles are wrought daily. Infirmities are cured by the power of God, rather than medical means, which are accomplished with herbs and the various drugs of the healing art. This came about in the following manner.

At that time, the Patriarch of Alexandria was the remarkable Apollinarios the Great[2] (not the thrice-wretched heretic who disrupted Laodikeia with his shameful heresy, but another), who was most pious and a champion of the Truth. He had a nephew, whom he reared and taught the Orthodox Faith and a godly way of life, in order to make him his successor. Therefore, the young man was trained well and progressed accordingly.

---

[1] Their martyrdom is recorded in Greek by Saint Symeon the Metaphrastes, whose manuscript begins, "Kyros, the distinguished star among the martyrs..." [*P.G.* 114:1231-1250]. The text is extant in the Athonite monasteries of the Great Lavra and Iveron. The text was rendered in simpler Greek and incorporated into the *Neon Paradeison*. The miracles of the holy unmercenaries were recorded by Sophronios I of Jerusalem (634-638), who is commemorated by the holy Church on the 11ᵗʰ of March, as the saints themselves demanded of him in a vision in return for the cure they wrought to his eyes. Saint Sophronios describes their cures and informs us that the local cult of Isis disappeared, and that her temple sank into the sand. He also wrote an encomium to them, which begins "Let others honor the saints in other ways...." The text is extant at the Great Lavra and Iveron. In the Lavra, there is another sermon written in honor of the holy unmercenaries, together with those martyrs who suffered with them: Saints Athanasia, Theoktiste, Theodote, and Evdoxia, the beginning of which is, "The salutary word of the Gospel preaching...."

[2] According to B. Stephanides' index, Apollinarios was Patriarch of Alexandria from 551 to 568.

When he attained his majority, he spoke to his uncle about having him marry. Now the uncle found an excuse, saying, "My child, I wish to build a church to the holy Three Children, and it is necessary that thou shouldest take charge of this project; then I will have thee marry."

Thereafter, they began the work with great haste. The famous church was built in a very short period above an infirmary, that is, the clinic of Kyros which was in the courtyard. Afterward, Apollinarios sent a certain virtuous hegumen to Babylon, giving him a letter in which the patriarch petitioned and entreated the holy Three Children to consent to his taking a portion of their sacred relics and depositing them in the church he had erected in Alexandria. He held these saints in great veneration; having faith in them, he wrote the letter as if they were still physically alive and would read it themselves.

The pious hegumen departed with all dispatch for Babylon. Once there, he knelt down before the holy relics. With faith and tears, he besought the three holy youths to accept the epistle and grant the request written by the devout patriarch. Then the saint in the middle arose—O frightful event of divine œconomy!—and extended his hand to take the letter. Thereupon the saint, without speaking a word, lay down again. The hegumen marvelled at this wondrous sight, but he also was sad; for he failed to achieve that which he requested. He remained in the church, praying throughout the entire week. After seeing that the saints offered no further response, he returned to the patriarch sorrowing and bringing back tears instead of relics. But the latter sent him back again, saying, "Go thou a second time and entreat the saints with yet greater fervor. Do thou trust in God that thou wilt not return disappointed. If again, they do not give thee anything, bring back the letter which was sanctified by them; and I will keep it as a consolation." The good hegumen, humble and obedient, then traveled to Babylon with great difficulty and effort. He made supplication before the saints with tears, imploring them to have pity upon his exertion and condescend to the patriarch's pious request.

He prayed thus for many days, though he did not see any result at all. Therefore, despairing of achieving his desire, he leaned over in order to take the letter, even as he had been ordered. Now as he withdrew it—O the wonder!—the saint's hand holding the letter detached from the body. The hegumen took the sacred relic in his hand, rejoicing; for his former grief had been transformed into joy. Upon his arrival in Alexandria, a great celebration was held by the faithful. There was great jubilation as the archbishop consecrated the holy church, placing the letter to the right of the sacred hand and giving thanks to the Lord. Later, he ordained his nephew a priest, instead of marrying him as he had promised, and said, "To this church I wed thee, my child; and just as thou wouldest have loved thy wife, thou shouldest love the Church to obtain thy salvation." Enough concerning the building of the church and Kyros' quarters. Let us now return to the subject.

The pious Kyros, sympathetic and compassionate, was so diligent and eagerly intent on curing souls and bodies that he became the cause for the salvation of many; for under the pretext of medical science, he taught the Truth, saying, "Whosoever would not become ill, let him abstain from committing sin; as ofttimes sickness is the result of sin." He cured the sick neither with regard to the medical books of Galen and Hippocrates, nor by means of herbs or weeds; but rather, cures were wrought by the name of Christ the Savior, the almighty One and salvation of all. Kyros also gave instructions from the holy books of the Old and New Testaments. In this manner, he converted the pagans to the knowledge of God, and further strengthened the faithful. However, the hater of man, the devil, could not endure the sight of this goodness. He therefore incited certain individuals to betray

Saint Kyros

Kyros to the magistrate of the city, by denouncing him as a Christian. The magistrate was a very cruel and inhuman man, just like his master Diocletian, the godless and iniquitous one.

The governor then summoned Kyros before the court. Consequently, Kyros took flight into Arabia, neither out of timidity nor cowardice, but that the words might be fulfilled spoken by the Lord: "Whenever they persecute you in this city, flee ye to another [Mt. 10:23]." We can also say that it was by divine œconomy that he fled into Arabia, where he converted many Greek pagans. When he arrived on foreign soil, Kyros changed his attire, life, and vocation. He shaved his head and became a monk, and ascended to a more lofty contemplation. He cured the sick of every illness, by making only the sign of the precious Cross. Hence, the reputation of the wonder-worker Kyros spread. Word went into every quarter that Father Kyros healed the sick with but a word, and without herbs.

The pious soldier John, from Edessa, heard this good report. John was resolved to become a soldier of the heavenly King, instead of the earthly one, the better to combat the enemies of Christ. Therefore, he spurned wealth, glory, prosperity, and all bodily pleasures, and went to Jerusalem. In the holy city he learned about Kyros, whose fame had spread everywhere. John then decided to go to Egypt where the healing monk was last seen. He went to Alexandria, but Kyros had already departed. After much diligent inquiry, he discovered that the man of God was in Arabia. Upon finding Kyros, John remained in his company and emulated all his deeds and godly struggles.

Saint John

The persecutions increased. In Syria, there was a brutal ruler named Syrianos. He ordered three maidens to be imprisoned along with their mother, Athanasia. This was done because they proclaimed Christ to be the true God and berated the idols. Upon learning this, the holy Kyros and John were fearful that the tender maidens might quail before the torments and betray the Faith. Thereupon, they hastened to the prison and exhorted the maidens to be courageous in order to vanquish the adversary. The eldest daughter was Theoktiste, aged fifteen; then Theodote, aged thirteen; and then, Evdoxia who was eleven. Kyros feared for them, lest perhaps they should be terrified by the tortures and lose their crown on account of weakness and the infirmity of nature. Therefore, the all-wise ones went to support the women and to receive martyrdom themselves, which also came to pass through the cooperation of divine grace. This took place when Kyros and John were observed by some infidels, as they were advising and urging the women not to fear death but to valiantly despise the commands of Caesar.

Syrianos was infuriated by their intervention. He ordered that those Christian men be brought before him. When this was done, he said to them, "Are you the enemies of the blessed gods, O wretched ones, who revile Caesar and praise the Christ? Make haste at once to deny your Faith and offer sacrifice to the supreme gods. Only then shall you escape all the agonies of torture and be honored as my friends. Otherwise, I will see to it that you learn not only who I am and the Emperor Diocletian, but also the gods whom you revile." But the holy ones answered him, saying, "Know this, O governor: we have no need of your honor. We do not fear torture. We will not reverence stones and wood, but confess only Christ as the true God!" When the tyrant heard this, he became so enraged that he gnashed his teeth and said, "If you had any knowledge, O arrogant and proud ones, you would have shown remorse. But because you prefer torture and punishment, and spurn our friendship, I will render to you all that you deserve." He then commanded that the women be brought to observe the torments that would be inflicted upon the martyrs.

Syrianos had the saints flogged and beaten without mercy. He also bade the executioners to crush and burn all the bodily members of Kyros and John. Then he had them covered with vinegar and salt, that they should feel the pain more bitterly. He had their flesh abraded with coarse sacking and their legs daubed with molten tar. In short, he did not refrain from any form of torture against the prudent ones, for it was his intention that the women should become frightened and succumb to his iniquitous decree. Those who were present suffered by merely observing the diverse torments; but the holy ones endured all courageously. They rejoiced as they bore in mind the everlasting rewards that await Christ's martyrs. Then the villainous tyrant ordered the flogging of the women. He specified that the executioners were to use all their might in administering the lash. They were not to restrain themselves before the mother and the maidens. The women withstood the punishment with great courage and valor. As Syrianos observed their perseverance, he gave up all hope and ordered that their heads be cut off. The soldiers therefore brought Athanasia and her daughters to the place of execution. Once again, those blessed ones showed no sign of weakness, but gladly laid down their heads and received a most blessed end.

Thereafter, the villainous tyrant again tested the Martyrs Kyros and John in diverse ways. First Syrianos employed blandishments and subtlety, and then he resorted to threats. But seeing that all his attempts were in vain, he ordered that they be put to death by the sword. They were led as criminals to the above mentioned place of execution, where they were beheaded on the 31st of January. Hence, their holy and blessed souls departed for the heavens, while their sacred relics were recovered by certain pious Christians. The relics were buried with honor in the Church of Saint Mark the Evangelist.

Many years elapsed, and idolatry disappeared completely from the region. In the early fifth century, their relics were revealed in a miraculous way and were finally recovered. The translation of the relics of Saints Kyros and John is commemorated by the holy Church on the 28th of June. Saint Symeon Metaphrastes adds that Saint Kyril of Alexandria (378-444) transferred the relics from Alexandria to Menuthis.[3] Many miracles were performed then and are performed now to the glory of God and the honor of the saints, through whose intercessions may we be delivered from all manner of sickness, and be counted worthy of the kingdom of the heavens. Amen.

On the 31st of January, the holy Church commemorates the holy Martyrs VICTORINOS, VICTOR, NIKEPHOROS, CLAUDIUS, DIODOROS, SARAPINOS, and PAPPIAS.

Victorinos, also known as Wiktorinos, and his fellow athletes who contested in martyrdom, hailed from Corinth. They lived during the reign of Decius (249-251). In the year 251, on account of their confession and belief in Jesus Christ, they were arrested. Victorinos, Victor (also known as Wiktor), Nikephoros, Claudius, Diodoros, Sarapinos, and Pappias were led forth to stand before Tertius the proconsul, who had jurisdiction over Morea (an alternative name for the Peloponnesos). Tertius had these faithful Christians subjected to diverse tortures, by which some suffered together and some suffered individually. Victorinos, Victor, and Nikephoros were cast inside a stone mortar of great size, where their bodies were pounded and broken until they reposed. The holy Martyr Claudius suffered the amputation of his hands and feet. The Martyr Diodoros was cast into a fiery furnace and received his end in martyrdom. As for the holy Sarapinos, he underwent the severing of his head. Saint Pappias endured a bitter drowning when he was cast into the depths of the sea. Thus, they received from the Lord the crowns of martyrdom.

On the 31st of January, the holy Church commemorates the holy Martyr TRYPHAINA of Kyzikos.

Tryphaina, the holy martyr, was a native of Kyzikos on the Hellespont.[4] She was the daughter of the nobleman Anastasios. Her mother, a Christian, was named Socratia. Tryphaina was reported to the idolaters, but she came forward of her own accord and mocked their idols. She also denounced the pagans' shameful acts, by which the foolish ones honored their

---

[3] *P.G.* 114:1249C.

[4] Kyzikos (Cyzicus), now Balkiz near Erdek, is a city on the southern coast of the Sea of Marmara, at the head of routes leading into Asia Minor (Turkey). Emperor Diocletian made Kyzikos metropolis of the province of Hellespont, headquarters of a legion, and site of an imperial mint. *The Oxford Dictionary of Byzantium*, s.v. "Kyzikos."

falsely-named deities. Not only did she do this, but she also instructed them to forsake their religion of vain idols, so they might turn to the Faith of Christ.

The Martyrdom of Saint Tryphaina

Thereupon, by order of Governor Caesarios, the holy woman was cast into a fiery furnace. Since she was preserved unharmed by the grace of Christ, they suspended her from a high post. When the executioners cut the rope that bound her, she fell and was pierced by iron spikes jutting upwards. The cruel pagans then cast her to wild beasts to be devoured. At first, the beasts neither harmed nor touched her. However, a bull rushed toward her and gored the saint's body with its horns. Thus, Christ's victorious contestant in piety, Tryphaina, crowned with the chaplet of true Faith, received the undying laurel wreath of martyrdom.

It is said that, at the site where the martyr shed her blood, clear water gushed forth. When the water was consumed by women whose breasts did not give milk after childbirth, immediately their milk flowed. Moreover, it is reported that not only women, but even female animals lacking milk receive the same benefit when they drink of that water.

On the 31st of January, the holy Church commemorates the venerable and holy New-martyr ELIAS ARDOUNES (1686).[5]

Elias, the blessed new-martyr, came from Kalamata (ancient Kalamai) of Messenia, a region in the southwestern Peloponnesos. Elias was a barber

---

[5] The martyrdom of New-martyr Elias Ardounes was taken from the *Neon Martyrologion*, 3rd ed. (pp. 105, 106) and incorporated into *The Great Synaxaristes* (in Greek). A festal service was composed by the hymnographer Father Gerasimos Mikrayiannanites, which divine office was published by Metropolitan Chrysostom of Messenia (Athens, 1956).

by profession. Since he was sensible by nature and experienced in political affairs, the elders of the city held him in high esteem and always associated with him and received his advice. At times when they discussed various matters, they also spoke of the unbearable and numerous taxes, among the many other hardships, that the Christians of the Peloponnesos had to bear during the period of the first captivity.[6] The blessed Elias, with much pain and sorrow in his heart, cautioned the elders, saying that they should attempt to relieve the Christians of the heavy burden of taxation, for many of them were in danger of denying the Faith and becoming Moslems. But the elders did not share his opinion, assuring him that the Christians were not endangered at all. In the heat of the discussion, Elias blurted out a reckless challenge. Without properly considering the consequences, in order to prove his point, he said to them, "If someone should give me a fez, I would change my religion." One of the elders, wishing to humor Elias, sent someone to bring him a fez. Elias went straight to the local judge and changed his religion. Consequently, the Christian community was terribly grieved over this rash action.

After the passage of some time, he realized the gravity of what he had done, and repented. At once he left for Mount Athos, where he confessed his sin with great compunction and kept the appropriate canon of penance. After he was chrismated, Elias became a monk and spent eight years on Athos in virtue and piety. Even so, his conscience always chastised him, reminding him of the Lord's saying, "Whosoever shall deny Me before men, him will I also deny before My Father Who is in the heavens [Mt. 10:33]." He confessed these thoughts to a virtuous spiritual father, who advised him to go back to Kalamata and boldly confess Christ.

After receiving the blessing of his spiritual father, and being steadfast in his decision, Elias departed and returned to Kalamata. There he revealed his intentions to the spiritual fathers. However, fearing that he might weaken, they tried to dissuade him from martyrdom. Nonetheless, he was strong and inflexible and, fearing nothing, never wavered. He then received the holy Mysteries. Straightway, he went and appeared in the marketplace, walking up and down by the coffee houses until he should be recognized. At first, the Moslems did not recognize him, but after he passed twice and three times in front of their shops, the Turks finally identified him and said to him, "Art

---

[6] The first captivity of the Peloponnesos was the period of Turkish domination which lasted from 1460 to 1687, when the Venetians under Francisco Morozini captured the Peloponnesos and dissolved the Turkish yoke, thus becoming the new overlords. The second and last period of Turkish domination in the Peloponnesos was the period from 1715, when the Turks defeated the Venetians and recaptured it. They ruled up to the Greek Revolution, when at length the Peloponnesos was finally liberated.

thou not Moustafa Ardounes?" He answered, "Yes, it is I, but I am not Moustafa. Much rather, I am Elias, the Orthodox Christian." Immediately and without wavering, he began to mock and ridicule Islam. He declared Jesus Christ to be true God. When they heard this confession, they set upon him, striking and pushing him. Thus, they dragged him to the judge, crying out, "This fellow, of his own accord, accepted our religion; but now he dishonors it." When the judge questioned him as to the truth of the accusations, Elias admitted to everything. Therefore, the judge ordered Elias to be shackled in chains and confined to prison, until the judge should decide what to do with him.

The saint spent many days in prison, in the midst of much suffering. Then the Turks brought him to a second examination, where the judge inquired, "What hast thou decided? Hast thou made up thy mind?" Father Elias replied, "Why do you ask me? Even if you should put me through ten thousand tortures, I would not deny my Lord Jesus Christ. Do, therefore, as thou wilt with me." The judge saw that Elias was unbending, so he decided to have him burned with new wood. The executioners seized Elias and led him to the site of execution. As they were on the way, one of them struck the saint in the shoulder with a sword, cutting him deeply. But Elias was very courageous and, instead of weakening, chanted the psalms of David, from whence he drew courage and joy. When they reached their destination, they cast him into the fire. Behold the miracle! Neither his robes, nor his hair, nor his beard were singed, but rather the fire was extinguished, without harming his martyric body in the least. But the Martyr Elias surrendered his soul and received from our Lord, the all-seeing God and Prize-bestower, the imperishable crown of martyrdom. These events took place in 1686.

In the evening, those who guarded his body beheld a heavenly light descend and encompass the relics. When the Turks saw this, they declared, "Because the fire did not burn him, God has sent fire from heaven in order to consume him." The Christians ransomed the holy relics with money. The martyr was interred, with honor and respect, in Kalamata, where they erected a church in his honor. Out of their fear of the Turks, the Christians dedicated it to the holy Forty Martyrs. At the time of the uncovering of the relics, an unspeakable fragrance came forth. Therefore, they donated the saint's holy skull to a nearby monastery called Vourkanou, where the relic pours forth miracles to this day.

At Kalamata, the mother of a certain teacher, named Dionysios Podaros, who recorded this martyrdom, took part of the saint's relics and kept them in her home. There, one night, she saw a great light which shone to the glory of the martyr and our Lord Jesus Christ, to Whom is due glory, honor, and veneration, together with the Father and the Holy Spirit, now and ever and to the ages of ages. Amen.

Through the intercessions of Thy Saints,
O Christ God, have mercy on us. Amen.

Saints Gregory the Theologian and John Chrysostom

January Bibliography

Non-English or Greek Sources

Ο ΜΕΓΑΣ ΣΥΝΑΞΑΡΙΣΤΗΣ ΤΗΣ ΟΡΘΟΔΟΞΟΥ ΕΚΚΛΗΣΙΑΣ (THE GREAT SYNAXARISTES OF THE ORTHODOX CHURCH). 6th ed. Volume 1. Athens, GR: Archimandrite Matthew Langes, Publisher, 1978.

ΑΓΙΑ ΝΙΝΑ Η ΙΣΑΠΟΣΤΟΛΟΣ (SAINT NINA, EQUAL-TO-THE-APOSTLES). Published by the Holy Monastery of the Paraclete. Oropos, Attike, GR 1999.

Basileiade, Nicholas P. *Saint Mark of Ephesus and the Union of the Churches*. 3rd ed. Athens, GR: The Brotherhood of Theologians of Sotir, 1983.

ΒΙΟΣ ΑΓΙΑΣ ΚΑΙ ΙΣΑΠΟΣΟΛΟΥ ΝΙΝΑΣ ΦΩΤΙΣΤΡΙΑΣ ΤΗΣ ΙΒΕΡΙΑΣ-ΓΕΩΡΓΙΑΣ (LIFE OF THE HOLY AND EQUAL-TO-THE-APOSTLES NINA, ENLIGHTENER OF IBERIA-GEORGIA). Hieromonk Efthymios, Publisher. Kerasia, Holy Mountain, Athos: Kellion of Saint George, 1987. Originally from the publication of the Holy Monastery of Panteleimon, Holy Mountain, printed in Moscow 1900.

Kontoglu, Photios. *Ekphrasis*. 2 Volumes. Athens, GR: Astir Publishing, Al. & E. Papademetriou, 1979.

Koukey, Constantine. *Saint Theodosios the Coenobiarch*. Kymis: Transfiguration Monastery, 1983.

ΜΑΞΙΜΟΥ ΤΟΥ ΟΜΟΛΟΓΗΤΟΥ (MAXIMOS THE CONFESSOR). Hieromonk Efthymios and his synodia, Compilers. Kerasia, Holy Mount Athos: Kellion of Saint George, 1997.

Migne, J. P. *Patrologia Graeca*. Athens, GR: Kentron Paterikon Ekdoseon. Facsimile of the 1859 Paris edition.
——Volume 57. *Saint John Chrysostom*. Athens, 1996.
——Volume 59. *Saint John Chrysostom*. Athens, 1996.
——Volume 123. *Blessed Theophylact*. Athens, 1990.
——Volume 116. *Saint Symeon the Metaphrastes*. Athens, 1995.

ΜΗΝΑΙΟΝ ΤΟΥ ΙΑΝΟΥΑΡΙΟΣ (MENAION OF JANUARY). S. Michael Saliveros A.E. Amarousion, GR.

NEON MARTYROLOGION. 3rd ed. Athens, GR: Aster Publishing, Al. & E. Papademetriou, 1961.

+ + +

ΠΗΔΑΛΙΟΝ (The Rudder). Athens, GR: Astir Publishing, Al. & E. Papademetriou, 1982.

English Sources

A Greek-English Lexicon. Henry George Liddell and Robert Scott, Compilers. 9th ed. Oxford at the Clarendon Press, 1977.

A Patristic Greek Lexicon. 12th ed. Edited by G. W. H. Lampe. Oxford at the Clarendon Press, 1995.

Alfeyev, Hilarion. *The Spiritual World of Isaac the Syrian*. Cistercian Publications, Number 175. Kalamazoo, MI: Cistercian Publications, 2000.

Andrew Simonopetritis (Haralampos Theophilopoulos), Hagiorite. *Holy Mountain: Bulwark of Orthodoxy and of the Greek Nation*. Translated by John-Electros Boumis. Athens, GR: Eptalofos Co., Ltd., 1967.

Bundy, David and Frederick Norris. "Babai the Great." *Encyclopedia of Early Christianity*. Volume 1. Everett Ferguson, Michael P. McHugh, Frederick W. Norris, ed. Taylor & Francis, 1998.

Butler's Lives of the Saints. 4 Volumes. Edited, rev.and supplemented by Herbert J. Thurston, S.J. and Donald Attwater. Westminster, MD: Christian Classics, 1981, repr.

Callinicos, Constantine. *Our Lady the Theotokos*. Translated and revised by Rev. George Dimopoulos. Upper Darby, PA: Christian Orthodox Ed., 1987.

Carter, R. A. "Christianity in the Gulf During the First Centuries of Islam." *Arabian Archaeology and Epigraphy,* 2008, 19:71-108.

Chediath, G. *The Christology of Mar Babai the Great*. Kottayam, India, 1982.

Chitty, Derwas J. *The Desert A City*. Crestwood, NY: Saint Vladimir's Seminary Press, 1966.

Christodoulides, Charalambos G. *Saint Neophytos Monastery*. Nicosia, Cyprus: Zavallis Press, Ltd., 1980.

Christou, Panagiotis C. *Athos, The Holy Mountain: History, Life, Treasures*. Translated by W. J. Lillie. Thessalonike, GR: Kyromanos Publishers, 1990.

Christou, Pan. C. and Tom. M. Provatakis. *Athos*. Thessalonike, GR: Patriarchal Institute for Patristic Studies, 1970.

Corpus Scriptorum Christianorum Orientalium. A. Vaschalde, ed. Paris, 1915. See: *Liber de unione*; Mar Babai Rabba's *The Book of Union*, ACEYA Books, 2012.

de Voragine, Jacobus. *The Golden Legend*. 4th ed. Two Volumes. Translated by William Granger Ryan. Princeton, NJ: Princeton University Press, 1995.

Dionysius of Fourna. *The Painter's Manual*. Translated by Paul Hetherington. Redondo Beach, CA: Oakwood Publications, 1981, repr.

Durkit, Priestmonk Leonty. *The Lives of the Seventy Apostles*. Elkhorn, WV: The Orthodox Brotherhood of the Virgin Mary, 1997.

Early Fathers from the Philokalia. 5th ed. Translated by E. Kadloubovsky and G.E.H. Palmer. London, UK: Faber and Faber, 1973.

Encyclopedia of the Early Christianity. Everett Ferguson, editor. Garland Reference Library of the Humanities, Volume 846. NY/London: Garland Publishing, Inc., 1990.

Encyclopedia of the Early Church. Translated from the Italian. Institutum Patristicum Augustinianum. Edited by Angelo DiBerardino. NY: Oxford University Press, 1992.

Eusebius. *Church History* and *Martyrs of Palestine* and *The Life of Constantine*. The Nicene and Post-Nicene Fathers of the Christian Church. Second Series. Volume I. Second printing. Translated by the Rev. Arthur Cushman McGiffert, Ph.D. Grand Rapids, MI: Wm. B. Eerdmans Pub., February 1961, repr.

Freeman-Grenville, G. S. P. *The Beauty of Rome*. New York, NY: The Continuum Publishing Co., 1987.

Geanakoplos, Deno. J. *Byzantine East and Latin West: Two Worlds of Christendom in Middle Ages and Renaissance*. NY: Barnes & Noble, 1966.

Kadas, Sotiris. *Mount Athos*. Translated by Louise Turner. Athens, GR: Ekdotike Athenon S.A., 1980.

Kitchen, Robert A. "Babai the Great." *The Orthodox Christian World*, Augustine Casiday, ed. Routledge, 2012.

Lambertsen, Isaac. "Our Father Among the Saints Maximus the Greek." *Living Orthodoxy*. Volume XIII, Number 1, January-February 1991.

Lang, David Marshall. *Lives and Legends of the Georgian Saints*. 2nd ed. Crestwood, NY: Saint Vladimir's Seminary Press, 1976.
——*The Georgians*. Volume 51 of Ancient Peoples and Places Series. Bristol, UK: Thames and Hudson, 1966.

Levi, Peter. *Atlas of the Greek World*. New York: Facts on File. Oxford: An Equinox Book, 1989 repr.

Lloyds, Seton. *Ancient Turkey*. Berkeley and Los Angeles, CA: University of California Press, 1989.

Logos Electronic Edition of The Writings of the Early Church Fathers, extracted from the 38-volumes of the Eerdman's Reprint of the Edinburgh edition. Bellingham, WA: Logos Research Systems, Inc., 1997.

Matejic, Mateja. *The Holy Mount and Hilandar Monastery*. Columbus, OH: Ohio State University, 1983.

Obolensky, Dimitri. *Six Byzantine Portraits*. NY: Oxford University Press, 1988.
Ostrogorsky, George. *History of the Byzantine State*. New Brunswick, NJ: Rutgers University Press, 1957.

Ostroumoff, Ivan N. *The History of the Council of Florence*. Trans. from the Russian by Basil Popoff & Alek. Vasil. Gorskii. Ed. by Rev. John Mason Neale, D.D. London: Joseph Masters, 1861. See https://archive.org/details/historycouncilf00nealgoog.

Palladius. *The Lausiac History*. Ancient Christian Writers. Number 34. Translated and annotated by Robert T. Meyer. NY/NJ: Newman Press, n.d.

Rogerson, John. *Chronicle of the Old Testament Kings*. London: Thames and Hudson, 1999.

Rogich, Father Daniel. *Serbian Patericon*. CA: Saint Herman of Alaska Brotherhood and Saint Paisius Abbey Press, 1994.

Rousseau, Philip. *Basil of Caesarea*. Los Angeles, CA: University of California Press, 1994.

Runciman, Sir Steven. *The Fall of Constantinople 1453*. London: Cambridge at the University Press, 1965.
——*The Great Church in Captivity*. NY: Cambridge University Press, 1968.

"Saint Genevieve of Paris." *Orthodox Life*. Volume 22, Number 6, November-December 1972. Published by Holy Trinity Monastery, Jordanville, NY.

"Saint Mark of Ephesus and the False Union of Florence." Archimandrite Amvrossy Pogodin, M.Sc Eccl., D.D. *Orthodox Word*. Volume 3, Number 1(12), January-February 1967:9. Published by Holy Trinity Monastery, Jordanville, NY.
——"Saint Mark of Ephesus and the False Union of Florence." *Orthodox Word*. Volume 3, Number 2(13), March-May, 1967.

Scarre, Chris. *Chronicle of the Roman Emperors*. NY and London: Thames & Hudson, 2001, repr.

Schaff, Philip. *History of the Christian Church*. Volume III. Grand Rapids, MI: Wm. B. Eerdmans Publishing Co.

Socrates Scholasticus. *The Ecclesiastical History*. The Nicene and Post-Nicene Fathers. Volume II. Edited by Philip Schaff, D.D., LL.D., and Henry Wace, D.D. Grand Rapids, MI: Wm. B. Eerdmans Publishing Co., November 1983, repr.

Sozomen, Salaminus Hermias. *Ecclesiastical History*. The Nicene and Post-Nicene Fathers of the Christian Church, Second Series. Volume II. Revised by Chester D. Hartranft. Edited by Philip Schaff, D.D., LL.D. and Henry Wace, D.D. Grand Rapids, MI: Wm. B. Eerdmans Pub. Co., November 1983, repr.

Stories, Sermons, and Prayers of Saint Nephon: An Ascetic Bishop. Translated by Jeannie E. Gentithes and Archimandrite Ignatios Apostolopoulos. Minneapolis, MN: Light and Life Publishing, 1989.

Sulpitius Severus. *The Sacred History*. The Nicene and Post-Nicene Fathers of the Christian Church, Second Series. Volume XI. Translated by Rev. Alexander Roberts, D.D. Grand Rapids, MI: Wm. B. Eerdmans Pub. Co., June 1978, repr.

The Chronicle of Theophanes Confessor. Cyril Mango and Roger Scott, Editors. New York: Oxford University Press, Inc., 1997.

The Epistle of Barnabas. The Apostolic Fathers, The Ante-Nicene Fathers. Volume I. Edited by the Rev. Alexander Roberts, D.D. and James Donaldson, LL.D. Grand Rapids, MI: Eerdmans Pub. Co., May 1987, repr.

The Lives of the Pillars of Orthodoxy. 3rd ed. Compilation and translation by Holy Apostles Convent. Buena Vista, CO: Holy Apostles Convent, November 2000.

The Lives of the Three Hierarchs. 2nd ed. Compilation and translation by Holy Apostles Convent. Buena Vista, CO: Holy Apostles Convent, July 2001.

Theodoret of Cyrrhyus. *A History of the Monks of Syria*. Translated by R. M. Price. Kalamazoo, MI: Cistercian Pub., 1985.

Theodoret. *The Ecclesiastical History*. The Nicene and Post-Nicene Fathers. Second Series. Volume III. Edited by Philip Schaff, D.D., LL.D., and Henry Wace, D.D. Grand Rapids, MI: Wm. B. Eerdmans Publishing Co., February 1979, repr.

The Orthodox New Testament. 3rd ed. Buena Vista, CO: Holy Apostles Convent and Dormition Skete, 2003.

The Orthodox Psalter. Translated by Holy Apostles Convent from the Greek of *The Psalterion of the Prophet and King David*, of Apostolike Diakonia of the Church of Greece (1st ed., 1968; 3rd ed., 1981; and 11th ed., 2009). Buena Vista, CO, 2nd ed., 2012.

The Oxford Classical Dictionary. Second edition. Edited by N. G. L. Hammond and H. H. Scullard. New York: Oxford University Press, 1970.

The Oxford Dictionary of Byzantium. Alexander P. Kazhdan, Editor in Chief. NY and Oxford: Oxford University Press, 1991.

The Oxford Dictionary of Popes. J. N. D. Kelly, compiler. New York: Oxford University Press, 1989, repr.

The Oxford Dictionary of the Christian Church. F. L. Cross and E. A. Livingstone, Editors. NY: Oxford University Press, 1989, repr.

The Paradise of the Fathers. Translated by Ernest A. Wallis Budge. Two Volumes. Seattle, WA: Saint Nectarios Press, 1978, repr.

The Rudder (Pedalion). D. Cummings. Chicago, IL: The Orthodox Christian Educational Society, 1957.

The Septuagint Version. Greek and English. London, Gt. Britain: Samuel Bagster and Sons Limited.

"The Translation of the Precious Relics of the Holy Martyr Anastasius the Persian," *Orthodox Life*. Volume 35, Number 1, January-February 1985:5.

Smith, M.A. *The Church Under Siege*. Downers Grove: Intervarsity Press, 1976.

Titus (Sylligardakis), Metropolitan of Rethymnon. *Cretan Saints*. Translated by Rev. Dean Timothy Andrews. Saint Smaragdos Group. West Brookfield, MA: The Orthodox Christian Center, n.d.

Toal, M. D., D.D. *The Sunday Sermons of the Great Fathers*. 3rd edition. Volume I. Chicago: Henry Regnery Co., 1964.

Tsatsos, Jeanne. *Empress Athenais-Eudocia*. Brookline: Holy Cross Orthodox Press, 1977.

Velimirović, Bishop Nikolai. *The Prologue from Ochrid*. Translated by Mother Maria. Birmingham, UK: Lazarica Press, 1986.

Velimirovich, Bishop Nikolai. *The Life of Saint Sava*. Introduction by Veselin Kesich. Crestwood, NY: Saint Vladimir's Seminary Press, 1989.

Waddell, Helen. *The Desert Fathers*. 7th edition. Translated from the Latin. Ann Arbor Paperback. The University of Michigan Press, 1977.

Ward, Benedicta, SLR. *The Sayings of the Desert Fathers*. Kalamazoo: Cistercian Publications, 1975.

Webster's Third New International Dictionary Unabridged. Springfield, MA: G. & C. Merriam Co., 1967.

White, Carolinne. *Early Christian Lives*. NY: Penguin Classics, 1998.

Writings of the Holy Fathers in English

Blessed Jerome. *Letters and Select Works*. The Nicene and Post-Nicene Fathers.

Saint Athanasios the Great

Second Series. Volume VI. Translated by the Hon. W. H. Fremantle, M.A., Rev. G. Lewis, M.A., and Rev. W.G. Martley, M.A. Grand Rapids. MI: Eerdmans, October 1983, repr.
——*1-59 On The Psalms, Volume 1*. The Fathers of the Church. 2nd ed. Volume 48. Translated by Sister Marie Liguori Ewald, I.H.M. Washington, D.C.: CUA, 1981, repr.
——*60-96 On The Psalms, Volume 2*. The Fathers of the Church. 2nd ed. Volume 57. Translated by Sister Marie Liguori Ewald, I.H.M. Washington, D.C.:CUA Press, n.d.
——*On Illustrious Men*. Translated by Thomas P. Halton. Volume 100. Washington, D.C.: CUA Press, 1999, repr.

Saint Ambrose. *Exposition of the Holy Gospel According to Saint Luke*. Taken from *Expositio Evangelii Secundum Lucam*, Part IV of *Sancti Anbrosii Mediolanesis Opera*, Volume XIV of *Corpus Christianorum, Series Latina*. Turnhut, Belgium: Typographi Brepols Editores Pontificii, 1957. Translated by Theodosia Tomkinson. Etna, CA: C.T.O.S., 1998.
——*Letters and Select Works*. The Nicene and Post-Nicene Fathers. Second Series. Volume X. Translated by Rev. H. DeRomestin, M.A. Edited by Philip Schaff D.D., LL.D. and Henry Wace, D.D. Grand Rapids, MI: Wm. B. Eerdmans Pub. Co., August 1979, repr.).
——*Theological and Dogmatic Works*. The Fathers of the Church. Volume 44. Translated by Roy J. Deferrari, Ph.D. Washington, D.C.: CUA Press, 1987, repr.

Saint Aphrahat. *Select Demonstrations*. The Nicene and Post-Nicene Fathers of the Christian Church. Second Series. Volume XIII. Translated by Rev. A. Edward John-

ston, B.D. Edited by Philip Schaff, D.D., LL.D., and Henry Wace, D.D. Grand
Rapids, MI: Wm. B. Eerdmans Pub., May 1976, repr.

Saint Athanasios. *Select Works and Letters*. The Nicene and Post-Nicene Fathers.
Second Series. Volume IV. Edited by Philip Schaff D.D., LL.D. and Henry Wace.
Grand Rapids, MI: Eerdmans, August 1975, repr.
——"Life of Saint Anthony by Saint Athanasius." *Early Christian Biographies*. The
Fathers of the Church. 3rd ed. Volume 15. Translated by Sister Mary Emily Keenan,
S.C.N. Washington, D.C.: The Catholic University of America Press, 1981.
——*The Life of Saint Anthony*. Ancient Christian Writers. Number 10. Translated by
Robert T. Meyer, Ph.D. NY/NJ: Newman Press; and NJ: Paulist Press.

Saint Basil. *Letters and Select Works*. The Nicene and Post-Nicene Fathers. Second
Series. Volume VIII. Translated by Rev. Blomfield Jackson, M.A. Grand Rapids, MI:
Eerdmans, June 1975, repr.
——*Ascetical Works*. The Fathers of the Church. 3rd ed. Volume 9. Translated by
Sister S. Monica Wagner, C.S.C. Washington, D.C.: CUA Press, 1970.

Saint Bede the Venerable. *Homilies on the Gospels*. Book One: Advent to Lent.
Translated by Lawrence T. Martin & David Hurst OSB. Cistercian Studies Series: No.
110. Kalamazoo, MI: Cistercian Publications, 1991. Translated from *Corpus
Christianorum*, 122. Turnhout: Brepols, 1955.
——*Homilies on the Gospels*. Book Two: Lent to the Dedication of the Church.
Translated by Lawrence T. Martin & David Hurst OSB. Cistercian Studies Series: No.
111. Kalamazoo, MI: Cistercian Publications, 1991. Translated from *Corpus
Christianorum*, 122. Turnhout: Brepols, 1955.

Saint Cyprian. *The Treatises of Cyprian*. The Ante-Nicene Fathers, Fathers of the
Third Century. Volume V. Translated by Rev. Ernest Wallis, PH.D., and Rev.
Alexander Roberts, D.D. and James Donaldson, LL.D., Editors. Grand Rapids, MI:
Wm. B. Eerdmans Pub. Co., December 1986, repr.
——*Letters 1-81*. The Fathers of the Church. 2nd ed. Volume 51. Translated by Sister
Rose Bernard Donna, C.S.J. Washington, D.C.: CUA Press, 1981.

Saint Cyril (Kyril) of Alexandria. *Commentary on the Gospel of Saint Luke*. Translated
by R. Payne Smith. New York: Studion Publishers, 1983.

Saint Cyril (Kyril) of Jerusalem. *Catechetical Lectures*. The Nicene and Post-Nicene
Fathers. Second Series. Volume VII. Revised translation by Edwin Hamilton Gifford,
D.D., and edited by Philip Schaff D.D., LL.D. and Henry Wace, D.D. Grand Rapids,
MI: Eerdmans, August 1974, repr.
——*The Works of Saint Cyril of Jerusalem: Catechesis, Volume 1*. The Fathers of the
Church. Volume 61. Translated by Leo P. McCauley, S.J. and Anthony A.
Stephenson. Washington, D.C.: CUA, n.d.

Saint Ephraim Syrus. *Hymns on the Nativity*. The Nicene and Post-Nicene Fathers of the Christian Church. Second Series. Volume XIII. Translated by Rev. J. B. Morris, M.A. Grand Rapids, MI: Wm. B. Eerdmans Pub. Co., May 1976, repr.
——*Commentary on Tatian's Diatessaron*. Journal of Semitic Studies Supplement 2, an English translation of Chester Beatty Syriac MS 709 with introduction and notes by Carmel McCarthy. Cary, NC: Oxford University Press, 1993.

Saint Gregory Nazianzen (the Theologian). *Epistles*, and *Orations*, and *Prolegomena*. The Nicene and Post-Nicene Fathers of the Christian Church. Second Series. Volume VII. Translated by Charles Gordon Browne, M.A., and James Edward Swallow, M.A. Edited by Philip Schaff, D.D., LL.D., and Henry Wace, D.D. Grand Rapids, MI: Wm. B. Eerdmans Pub. Co., August 1974, repr.
——*Funeral Orations*. The Fathers of the Church. Volume 22. Translated by L. P. McCauley, J. J. Sullivan, M.R.P. McGuire, and R. J. Deferrari. Washington, D.C.: CUA Press, 1953.
——*Three Poems: Concerning His Own Affairs, Concerning Himself and the Bishops, Concerning His Own Life*. The Fathers of the Church. Volume 75. Translated by D. M. Meehan. Washington, D.C.: CUA Press, 1986.

Saint Gregory of Nyssa. *Selected Works*. The Nicene and Post-Nicene Fathers. Second Series. Volume V. Translated by Wm. Moore, M.A. and H. A. Wilson, M.A. Edited by Philip Schaff, D.D., LL.D and Henry Wace, D.D. Grand Rapids, MI: Wm. B. Eerdmans Pub., n.d.
——*The Life of Moses*. Translated by Abraham J. Malherbe and Everett Ferguson. NY: Paulist Press, 1978
——Song of Songs. Translated by Casimir McCambley. The Archbishop Iakovos Library of Ecclesiastical and Historical Sources No. 12. Brookline, MA: Hellenic College Press, 1987.

Saint Gregory Palamas. *The Triads*. The Classics of Western Spirituality. Translated by Nicholas Gendle. New York, NY: Paulist Press, 1983.

Saint Gregory the Great. *Dialogues*. The Fathers of the Church. Volume 39. Translated by Odo John Zimmerman, O.S.B. Washington, D.C.: CUA Press, n.d.
——Saint Gregory the Dialogist. Parables of the Gospel. 1st edition. Chicago: Scepter Press, 1960.

Saint Hilary of Poitiers. *On the Trinity*. The Nicene and Post-Nicene Fathers of the Christian Church. Second Series. Volume IX. Translated by Rev. E. W. Watson, M.A., Rev. L. Pullan, M.A. Edited by Rev. W. Sanday, D.D., LL.D. Grand Rapids, MI: Eerdmans, August 1976, repr.
——*The Trinity*. The Fathers of the Church. Volume 25. Translated by Stephen McKenna, C.SS.R. Washington, D.C.: CUA Press, 1968, reprinted with revisions.

Saint Hippolytus. *The Extant Works and Fragments of Hippolytus: Fragments From Commentaries*. Fathers of the Third Century, The Ante-Nicene Fathers. Volume V. Translated by the Rev. S.D.F. Salmond. Edited by the Rev. Alexander Roberts, D.D. and James Donaldson, LL.D. Notes and Prefaces by A. Cleveland Coxe, D.D. Grand Rapids, MI: Eerdmans Pub. Co., December 1986, repr.

Saint Irenaeos. *Against Heresies*. The Ante-Nicene Fathers, The Apostolic Fathers. Volume I. Rev. Alexander Roberts, D.D. and James Donaldson, LL.D., Editors, and notes in American edition by A. Cleveland Coxe, D.D. Grand Rapids, MI: Wm. B. Eerdmans Publishing Co., May 1987, repr.

Saint Isaac the Syrian

Saint Isaac of Nineveh, *On Ascetical Life*. Crestwood, NY: Saint Vladimir's Seminary Press, 1989.

Saint John Cassian. *The Seven Books of John Cassian*. The Nicene and Post-Nicene Fathers. Second Series. Volume XI. Translated by Edgar C. S. Gibson, M.A. Grand Rapids, MI: Eerdmans Pub. Co., June 1978, repr.

Saint John Chrysostom. *On The Priesthood*. The Nicene and Post-Nicene Fathers. First Series. Volume IX. Translated by Stephens & Brandram. Grand Rapids: William B. Eerdmans Pub. Co., 1975.
——*Homilies on the Gospel of Matthew*. The Nicene and Post-Nicene Fathers of the Christian Church. First Series. Volume X. Translated by Rev. Sir George Prevost, Baronet, M.A., Philip Schaff, D.D., LL.D. Edited and revised, with notes by Rev. M. B. Riddle D.D. Grand Rapids, MI: Wm. Eerdmans Pub., Co., 1975.
——*Homilies on the Acts*. The Nicene and Post-Nicene Fathers of the Christian Church. First Series. Volume XI. Edited by Philip Schaff, D.D., LL.D. Grand Rapids, MI: Wm. B. Eerdmans Pub. Co. June 1975, repr.

——*Homilies on Galatians, Ephesians, Philippians, Colossians, Thessalonians, Timothy, Titus, and Philemon*. The Nicene and Post-Nicene Fathers. First Series. Volume XIII. Edited by Philip Schaff, D.D., LL.D. Grand Rapids, MI: Wm. B. Eerdmans, May 1976, repr.

——*Homilies on the Gospel of Saint John and the Epistle to the Hebrews*. Nicene and Post-Nicene Fathers of the Christian Church. First Series. Volume XIV. Edited by Philip Schaff, D.D., LL.D. Grand Rapids, MI: Wm. B. Eerdmans Pub. Co., August 1975, repr.

——*Baptismal Instructions*. Ancient Christian Writers. Number 31. Translated by Paul W. Harkins, Ph.D., LL.D. NY/NJ: Newman Press, n.d.

——*Discourses Against Judaizing Christians*. The Fathers of the Church. Volume 68. Translated by Paul W. Harkins. Washington, D.C.: CUA Press, 1979.

——*Apologist: Demonstration Against the Pagans*. The Fathers of the Church. Volume 73. Translated by Margaret A. Schatkin and Paul W. Harkins. Washington, D.C.: CUA Press, 1985.

Saint John Klimakos (Climacus). *The Ladder of Divine Ascent*. Translated by Archimandrite Lazarus Moore. Willits, CA: Eastern Orthodox Books, 1959.

Saint John of Damascus. *Exposition of the Orthodox Faith*. Nicene and Post-Nicene Fathers of the Christian Church, Second Series. Vol. IX. Translated S.D.F. Salmond, D.D., F.E.I.S. Grand Rapids, MI: Wm. B. Eerdmans Pub. Co., August 1976, repr.

Saint Justin. *Dialogue with Trypho*. The Ante-Nicene Fathers, The Apostolic Fathers. Volume I. Rev. Alexander Roberts, D.D. and James Donaldson, LL.D., Editors, and notes in American edition by A. Cleveland Coxe, D.D. Grand Rapids, MI: Wm. B. Eerdmans Publishing Co., May 1987, repr.

Saint Leo the Great. *Select Letters and Sermons*. The Nicene and Post-Nicene Fathers. Second Series. Volume XII. Translated by Rev. Charles Lett Feltoe, M.A. Edited by Philip Schaff, D.D., LL.D and Henry Wace, D.D. Grand Rapids, MI: Eerdmans, September 1979, repr.

Saint Makarios (Macarius) the Great. *Fifty Spiritual Homilies*. Translated by A. J. Mason. Willits, CA: Eastern Orthodox Books, 1974.

——*The Fifty Spiritual Homilies and the Great Letter*. The Classics of Western Spirituality. Translated by George A. Maloney, S.J. NY/NJ: Paulist Press, 1992.

Saint Maximos the Confessor. *Ambigua*. *P.G.* 91:1032-1417.

——*Commentary on Our Father*. Selected Writings. The Classics of Western Spirituality. Translated by George C. Berthold. Mahwah, NJ: Paulist Press, 1985.

——*First Century on Various Texts*. The Philokalia, the Complete Text. Volume Two. Translated from the Greek and edited by G.E.H. Palmer, Philip Sherrard, and Kallistos Ware. London-Boston: Faber and Faber, 1984 repr.

——*Free Choice in Saint Maximus the Confessor.* Joseph P. Farrell, D. Phil. (Oxon)., compiler. South Canaan, PA: Saint Tikhon's Seminary Press, 1989.

——*Maximus Confessor: Selected Writings: The Four Hundred Chapters on Love.* The Classics of Western Spirituality. Translated by George C. Berthold. New York/Mahwah/Toronto: Paulist Press, 1985.

——"Opuscules."*The Theological and Polemical Works of Our Father Among the Saints, Maximus the Confessor.* Trans. by Bp. Photios Farrell. Catoosa, OK: Seven Councils Press, 2000.

——*The Ascetic Life, The Four Centuries on Charity.* Ancient Christian Writers. Number 21. Translated by Polycarp Sherwood, O.S.B., S.T.D. NY/Mahwah, NJ: The Newman Press, n.d.

——*The Disputation with Pyrrhus.* Translated by Joseph P. Farrell. South Canaan, PA: Saint Tikhon's Seminary Press, n.d. (*P.G.* 90:288-353).

Saint Paulinus. *The Poems of Saint Paulinus of Nola.* Ancient Christian Writers. Number 40. Translated by P. G. Walsh. NY, NY: Newman Press, n.d.

——*Letters of Saint Paulinus of Nola: Letters 1-22, Volume 1.* Ancient Christian Writers. Number 35. Translated and annotated by P. G. Walsh. NY, NY: Newman Press, n.d.

——*Letters of Saint Paulinus of Nola: Letters 23-51, Volume 2.* Ancient Christian Writers. Number 36. Translated and annotated by P. G. Walsh. NY, NY: Newman Press, n.d.

Saint Symeon the New Theologian. *The Practical and Theological Chapters and The Three Theological Discourses.* Translated by Paul McGuckin. Kalamazoo, MI: Cistercian Publications, repr. 1994.

——*On the Mystical Life: The Ethical Discourses.* Volume 1. Translated by Alexander Golitzin. Crestwood, NY: Saint Vladimir's Seminary Press, 1995.

Saint Paul of Thebes

Saint Theodore Stoudite. "Encomium on the Dormition of Our Holy Lady, the Mother of God." *On the Dormition of Mary.* Translated by Brian E. Daley, S.J. Crestwood, NY: Saint Vladimir's Seminary Press, 1988.

ALPHABETICAL INDEX OF JANUARY SYNAXARISTES

January Date: Page

ACHILLAS (ACHILLES) OF SKETIS, ASCETIC 17:566

AFXENTIOS, NEW-MARTYR 25:1058

AGATHON OF SKETIS, VENERABLE FATHER 8:240

Agnes, Martyr 14:404

AGNES OF ROME, MARTYR 21:879

Akepsimas, Venerable Father 29:1147

AMMONAS, VENERABLE FATHER 26:1077

AMMONIOS, VENERABLE FATHER 10:283

ANANIOS, PETER, AND SEVEN OTHER MARTYRS 26:1077

ANASTASIOS THE PERSIAN, MARTYR 22:900

ANASTASIOS THE PERSIAN, TRANSLATION OF RELICS 24:1003

Angels, Synaxis of Myriads of 11:320

Anna of Rome, Martyr 20:814

ANTHONY THE GREAT, VENERABLE FATHER 17:502

ANTHONY THE NEW, ASCETIC, WONDER-WORKER 17:562

APHRAATES, ASCETIC 29:1145

APOLLINARIA, VENERABLE MOTHER 4:133

APOLLOS OF HERMOPOLIS IN THE THEBAID, ASCETIC 25:1049

ARSENIOS, ARCHBISHOP OF KERKYRA, WONDER-WORKER . . . 19:661

ATHANASIA, THEOKTISTE, THEODOTE, EVDOXIA, MARTYRS . 31:1167

ATHANASIOS AND KYRIL, SYNAXIS 18:576

Athanasios, Martyr 13:334

ATHANASIOS, NEW-MARTYR 7:227

ATHANASIOS THE GREAT, ARCHBISHOP OF ALEXANDRIA 18:577

ATTIKOS, PATRIARCH OF CONSTANTINOPLE 8:244

BABYLAS OF SICILY, AND AGAPIOS AND TIMOTHY, MARTYRS . 24:999

BARSIMAIOS, BISHOP OF EDESSA, CONFESSOR 29:1144

Barsimas and His Two Brothers, Martyrs 24:1005

BASIL OF ANKYRA, MARTYR 2:88

BASIL THE GREAT, ARCHBISHOP OF CAESAREA 1:9

Basil the Great, Miracle of 19:661

BASSUS, EUSEBIUS, EUTYCHIUS, AND BASILIDES, MARTYRS . . . 20:809

CARTERIOS OF CAESAREA, HIEROMARTYR 8:239

Charis, Martyr 28:1121

Chrysanthos and Ephemia, Martyrs 4:135

CIRCUMCISION OF JESUS CHRIST 1:1

CLEMENT, HIEROMARTYR, AND AGATHANGELOS, MARTYR . . 23:920

Clement of Mount Sagmation, Venerable Father 26:1079

Consecration of the Monastery of Prophet Elias 13:334

DAMASKENOS OF BULGARIA, HIEROMARTYR 16:500

DANAKTOS (DANAX), READER, MARTYR 16:500

DEMETRIOS, NEW-MARTYR 29:1147

January Date: Page

DEMETRIOS OF GALATA, NEW-MARTYR. 27:1094
Demetrios, Skevophylax. 25:1058
DIONYSIOS OF OLYMPOS, VENERABLE FATHER 23:967
DOMETIANOS, BISHOP OF MELITENE 10:282
DOMNICA OF CARTHAGE, VENERABLE MOTHER 8:229
Domnina, reposed in peace. 5:193
EARTHQUAKE AT CONSTANTINOPLE 26:1074
EFSTRATIOS, WONDER-WORKER 9:255
Efthasia, Martyr. 12:325
EFTHYMIOS, HEGUMEN OF VATOPEDI, AND 12 MONK-MARTYRS . 4:135
EFTHYMIOS THE GREAT, VENERABLE FATHER 20:779
Efthymios the New, Ascetic 4:135
ELIAS ARDOUNES, NEW-MARTYR 31:1173
Elias, Wonder-worker 12:325
EPHRAIM THE SYRIAN, HYMNOGRAPHER. 28:1097
EPHRASIA OF NIKOMEDIA, MARTYR. 19:660
Evagrios, Makarios, Elladios, and Voëthos, Martyrs 18:638
EVGENIOS, VALERIAN, KANDIDOS, AND AQUILAS, MARTYRS . . 21:876
EVSEVIOS OF TELEDA, ASCETIC. 23:948
Gabriel, Venerable Father 26:1079
GENEVIEVE OF PARIS, VENERABLE MOTHER 3:107
GEORGE OF IOANNINA, NEW-MARTYR. 17:567
GEORGE THE CHOZEVITE, VENERABLE FATHER 8:230
GEORGE (ZORZEES) OF GEORGIA, NEW-MARTYR 2:90
GORDIOS, MARTYR. 3:104
GREGORY AT AKRITAS, VENERABLE FATHER. 5:190
GREGORY, BISHOP OF NAZIANZOS 1:58
GREGORY, BISHOP OF NYSSA 10:259
GREGORY THE THEOLOGIAN 25:1014
Gregory the Theologian, Translation of Relics 19:661
HATZI THEODORE, NEW-MARTYR 30:1165
Hermogenes and Mamas, Martyrs 24:1005
HERMYLOS AND STRATONIKOS, MARTYRS. 13:326
HILARY, BISHOP OF POITIERS. 13:358
HIPPOLYTUS, HIEROMARTYR, AND OTHER MARTYRS 30:1162
IAKOVOS, ASCETIC. 28:1113
IAKOVOS OF NISIBIS, ASCETIC 13:333
IGNATIOS THE GOD-BEARER, TRANSLATION OF RELICS 29:1140
INNAS, PINNAS, AND RIMMAS, MARTYRS. 20:811
Irene, Church of Saint, Synaxis 21:879
ISAAC THE SYRIAN, BISHOP OF NINEVEH, ASCETIC WRITER. . . 28:1122
JOHN CHRYSOSTOM, TRANSLATION OF RELICS 27:1080
John, Forerunner, nearby the Taurus 24:1007
JOHN, FORERUNNER, MIRACLE AT CHIOS 7:224

January Date: Page

JOHN, FORERUNNER, TRANSLATION OF THE RELIC OF HIS HAND 7:223
JOHN, PROPHET, FORERUNNER, AND BAPTIST, SYNAXIS OF 7:212
JOHN THE KALYVITE (HUT-DWELLER) 15:469
JOSEPH THE SANCTIFIED OF CRETE, HIEROMONK 22:914
JULIAN, VASILISSA, KELSIOS, AND OTHER MARTYRS 8:236
KASTINOS, BISHOP OF BYZANTION 25:1056
Klavdinos (Claudinus), Venerable Father 27:1093
KOSMAS, PATRIARCH OF CONSTANTINOPLE, WONDER-WORKER   2:89
KYROS (CYRUS) AND JOHN, UNMERCENARY HEALERS 31:1167
KYROS (CYRUS), ARCHBISHOP OF CONSTANTINOPLE 8:242
LEO THE GREAT, EMPEROR 20:812
Maïros, Martyr 11:320
MAKARIOS, CITIZEN OF ALEXANDRIA, PRIEST 19:648
MAKARIOS THE GREAT OF EGYPT, ASCETIC WRITER 19:639
MAKEDONIOS, ASCETIC 24:1000
MALACHIAS (MALACHI), PROPHET 3:92
MANUEL, HIEROMARTYR, AND OTHER MARTYRS 22:912
MARCIAN, PRESBYTER AND OIKONOMOS 10:285
MARIS THE CHANTER, ASCETIC 25:1048
MARK EVGENIKOS, METROPOLITAN OF EPHESUS 19:679
Mark, Venerable Father 2:88
Markiane, Empress, Philanthropist 27:1093
Markianos of Cyprus, Venerable Father 18:638
MAUSIMAS THE SYRIAN, ASCETIC 23:950
MAXIMOS THE CONFESSOR, VENERABLE FATHER 21:819
MAXIMOS THE GREEK 21:882
MAXIMOS, THE KAFSOKALYVES (HUT-BURNER) 13:335
Medoule, Martyr, and Other Martyrs 25:1056
MELETIOS OF MOUNT GALESIOS, CONFESSOR 19:664
MERTIOS, SOLDIER, MARTYR 12:324
NEOPHYTOS, MARTYR 21:866
NEOPHYTOS OF CYPRUS, THE ENCLOSED 24:1007
Neophytos of Vatopedi, Venerable Father 21:882
NINA, EQUAL-TO-THE APOSTLES, ENLIGHTENER OF GEORGIA . 14:433
ONOUPHRIOS, HIERODEACON, NEW-MARTYR 4:136
Pachomios and Papyrinos, Martyrs 13:334
PALLADIOS, ASCETIC 28:1112
PANSOPHIOS, MARTYR 15:485
PAUL OF THEBES, VENERABLE FATHER 15:461
PAUL, PAFSIRIOS, AND THEODOTION, MARTYRS 24:998
PAULINUS, BISHOP OF NOLA 23:953
Peter, Blessed 20:812
PETER, CHAINS OF THE APOSTLE 16:486
Peter of Tripoli, New-martyr 1:67

January Date: Page

PETER THE AVESALAMITE, MARTYR 12:322
PETER THE EGYPTIAN, ASCETIC 27:1093
Peter, Wonder-worker 3:107
PEVSIPPOS, ELASIPPOS, MESIPPOS, AND NEONILLA, MARTYRS . 16:499
Philippikos, Presbyter 24:1005
PHOSTERIOS, VENERABLE FATHER 5:191
PHYLON, BISHOP OF KALPASIOS 24:1005
POLYEFKTOS AT MELITENE, MARTYR 9:250
PUPLIOS OF ZEUGMA, ASCETIC 25:1046
RAITHU ABBAS, MARTYRS 14:378
Romanos, Hieromonk, New-martyr 6:211
ROMANOS OF KARPENESION, NEW-MARTYR 5:193
Saïs, Martyr 5:193
SALAMANES THE HESYCHAST, ASCETIC 23:952
SAMAIAS (SHEMAIAH) THE ELAMITE, PROPHET 8:248
SARVELOS AND VEVAIA, MARTYRS 29:1143
SAVA, ARCHBISHOP OF SERBIA, BUILDER OF HILANDAR 14:404
Sergios, Martyr 2:89
SEVEN MARTYRS OF SAMOSATA: PHILOTHEOS AND OTHERS . 29:1141
SEVENTY, APOSTLES 4:113
SILOUANOS, LUKE, MOKIOS, HIEROMARTYRS 29:1142
SILVESTER, POPE OF ROME 2:68
SINAI ABBAS, MARTYRS 14:376
SINAI AND RAITHU, NARRATIVE BY ABBA AMMONIOS 14:380
STEPHEN, BUILDER OF THE MONASTERY OF CHENOLAKKOS . . 14:403
Stephen, Theodore, Agapios, Venerable Fathers 11:320
SYMEON THE ANCIENT, ASCETIC 26:1075
SYNCLETIKE OF ALEXANDRIA, VENERABLE MOTHER 5:155
TATIANE OF ROME, DEACONESS, MARTYR 12:321
THEAGENES, BISHOP OF PARIUM, HIEROMARTYR 2:87
Theodosios, Hegumen of Trigleia in Bithynia 1:67
THEODOSIOS OF PHILOTHEOU, BISHOP OF TREBIZOND 11:318
THEODOSIOS THE COENOBIARCH 11:295
THEODOSIOS THE GREAT, EMPEROR 17:564
Theodote, Mother of Unmercenaries 2:88
Theodotos, Martyr 1:58
THEODOULE OF ANAZARBOS, MARTYR 18:636
THEODOULOS, NARRATIVE BY SAINT NEILOS THE SINAITE 14:396
THEODOULOS OF SINAI, VENERABLE FATHER 14:394
Theoëidos, Martyr 5:193
Theoktistos at Cucomo, Hegumen 4:133
THEOPEMPTOS AND THEONAS, MARTYRS 5:151
Theopemptos, reposed in peace 2:88
THEOPHANY, HOLY 6:197

                                                    January Date: Page
THEOPHILOS AND ELLADIOS, MARTYRS 8:240
THEOPHILOS THE NEW, MARTYR 30:1164
Theopistos, Martyr 2:89
THREE HIERARCHS: SAINTS BASIL, GREGORY, AND JOHN 30:1158
Thyrsos and Agnes, Martyrs 20:812
TIMOTHY, APOSTLE 22:897
TRYPHAINA, MARTYR 31:1172
VICTORINOS, VICTOR, NIKEPHOROS, AND OTHER MARTYRS . . 31:1172
VITALIOS, VENERABLE FATHER 11:320
XENE, DEACONESS, AND THOSE WITH HER 24:991
Xene, Martyr 18:638
XENOPHON, MARY, AND SONS, VENERABLE FAMILY 26:1062
ZACHARIAS, NEW-MARTYR 20:814
ZOSIMAS OF TYRE, ASCETIC 24:1006
ZOSIMOS AND ATHANASIOS OF CILICIA, MARTYRS 4:133
ZOSIMUS, BISHOP OF SYRACUSE 21:874

1 Female Martyr 8:239
2 Female Martyrs 28:1121
2 Male Martyrs 8:239
2 Martyrs of Parion 23:953
2 Martyrs in Phrygia 26:1079
3 HIERARCHS: SAINTS BASIL, GREGORY, AND JOHN 30:1158
3 Martyrs, a Mother and 2 Children 3:107
4 Martyrs of Tyre 21:881
6 Fathers, reposed in peace 15:485
6 Martyrs 4:135
7 MARTYRS OF SAMOSATA: PHILOTHEOS AND OTHERS 29:1141
8 Martyrs of Nicaea 12:325
70, APOSTLES 4:113